construction law HANDBOOK

2009 edition

Incorporating the *Construction Law Handbook Newsletters*
Issues 42 to 47 (November 2007 to September 2008)

Edited by
Sir Vivian Ramsey
Ann Minogue
Jenny Baster
Michael O'Reilly
and
Hamish Lal

ice
Institution of Civil Engineers

The Construction Law Handbook is online at constructionlawhandbook.com

Published by Thomas Telford Publishing, Thomas Telford Ltd, 1 Heron Quay, London E14 4JD, UK.
www.thomastelford.com

Distributors for Thomas Telford books are
USA: ASCE Press, 1801 Alexander Bell Drive, Reston, VA 20191-4400
Australia: DA Books and Journals, 648 Whitehorse Road, Mitcham 3132, Victoria

First published 2009

For subscriptions queries, contact
Customer services officer
Thomas Telford Publishing
Tel: +44 (0)20 7665 2460
Email: clh@thomastelford.com

The Construction Law Handbook 2009 edition comprises an annual update plus six editions of the newsletter throughout 2009, in print and online at www.constructionlawhandbook.com

A catalogue record for this book is available from the British Library

ISBN: 978-0-7277-3601-7
ISSN: 1752 6841 (Print)

Typeset by Academic + Technical, Bristol
Printed and bound in Great Britain by Antony Rowe, Chippenham

Preface

Many texts on the market focus on the purely legal aspects of construction law; they are books on law for lawyers. The *Construction Law Handbook* is different: our focus is to consider the practical and commercial implications of the case law and legislation. This handbook is designed for the construction industry and the professionals that work in it and with it. It covers the range of topics most commonly required, and is written for non-lawyers without, we hope, sacrificing accuracy or being patronising. The authors are acknowledged experts and hence the text is both authoritative and reliable, and, as a result of being an annual publication, will remain up to date.

This edition also contains the *Construction Law Handbook Newsletter*, the bimonthly digest, edited by Hamish Lal of Dundas & Wilson, and which includes the most recent relevant developments in legislation and case law and applies them to the appropriate chapter of the handbook. Newsletters up to and including September 2008 are included in this volume. Those publishing during 2009 will be available separately in print, and on the website, and will also be bound into the 2010 edition.

The editors and the publisher would like to thank the authors of the individual chapters for their unstinting commitment, hard work and adherence to deadlines.

Finally, we hope that you, the reader, will find this handbook valuable in your work. We are always keen to receive feedback and to consider changes for future editions. Please address any comments to the publisher, who will forward them onto us.

Contents

PART 1

Legal issues arising during the course of the construction project

Section editor: Ann Minogue

PART 2

Organizing an engineer's practice

Section editor: Jenny Baster

PART 3
General law

Section editor: Sir Vivian Ramsey QC

PART 4
Construction disputes

Section editor: Mike O'Reilly

Table of cases

Table of UK statutes and statutory instruments

1994	Conservation (Natural Habitats) Regulations 1994	650
	Construction (Design and Management) Regulations 1994	185, 312, 342, 473, 474, 507, 509, 513, 536
	Criminal Justice and Public Order Act 1994	487
	Electrical Equipment (Safety) Regulations 1994	526
	Insolvency Partnership Order 1994	
	Supply of Machinery (Safety) (Amendment) Regulations 1994	534
	Unfair Terms in Consumer Contracts Regulations 1994	315
	Value Added Tax Act 1994	251
	Waste Management Licensing Regulations 1994	632
1995	Civil Evidence Act 1995	834
	Disability Discrimination Act 1995	390
	Environmental Protection Act 1995	30, 638
	Public Supply Contracts Regulations 1995	54
	Reporting of Injuries, Diseases and Dangerous Occurrences Regulations 1995	511
1996	Arbitration Act 1996	785, 827, 829, 838, 864, 874, 879, 889, 894, 895, 899, 906, 916
	Carriage of Dangerous Goods (Driver Training) Regulations 1996	530
	Construction (Health, Safety and Welfare) Regulations 1996	514
	Employment Rights Act 1996	379
	Equipment and Protective Systems Intended for Use in Potentially Explosive Atmospheres Regulations 1996	535
	Finance Act 1996	633, 634
	Health and Safety (Consultation with Employees) Regulations 1996	509
	Housing Grants, Construction and Regeneration Act 1996	116, 312, 333, 341, 366, 470, 556, 673, 678, 776, 777, 833, 843, 907, 908
	Landfill Tax (Contaminated Land) Order 1996	633
	Law Reform (Year and a Day Rule) Act 1996	483
	Utilities Contracts Regulations 1996	54, 174
	Work in Compressed Air Regulations 1996	506
1997	Confined Spaces Regulations 1997	519
	Construction (Design and Management) Regulations 1997	185
	Diving at Work Regulations 1997	520
	Fire Precautions (Workplace) Regulations 1997	540
	Hedgerows Regulations 1997	30
	Lifts Regulations 1997	534
	Protection from Harassment Act 1997	606
1998	Civil Procedure Rules 1998	174, 893
	Commercial Debts (Interest) Act 1998	325
	Competition Act 1998	174, 275, 276
	Control of Lead at Work Regulations 1998	528
	Data Protection Act 1998	415, 441, 445, 447
	Electricity Supply Regulations 1998	522
	Employers Liability (Compulsory Insurance) Regulations 1998	513
	Groundwater Regulations 1998	637
	Health and Safety (Enforcing Authority) Regulations 1998	483

Table of European legislation

Section editors

Ann Minogue

Ann Minogue is a Partner and head of Linklater's real estate construction and engineering team, having originally been a Partner in McKenna & Co from June 1985. She read law at Clare College, Cambridge and qualified as a solicitor in 1980.

She specialises in non-contentious construction work and has drafted amendments to various of the standard forms as well as drafting new forms of contract to cater for more diverse procurement methods. In particular, she drafted the British Property Federation's standard forms, the new edition of DOM/1 and the new GC/Works/ Sub-Contract. She was involved in drafting the construction documentation for the major 1980s projects – Canary Wharf, Broadgate, Ludgate and the Channel Tunnel Project – and has since been involved in some of today's bigger projects – the Royal Opera House, Tate Modern, the Hungerford Bridges Project, Stockley Park, the British Museum Great Court Project.

In the Central London office market, she has also been involved in the construction documentation (including the construction aspects of development agreements and agreements for lease) on the recent developments at Garrard House, Gresham Street, 59 Gresham Street, the Paternoster re-development, 33 Holborn (the old Mirror building) and Atlantic House, Holborn.

She also sits on the BPF Construction Committee and advises the BPF on construction matters as well as representing the Construction Client's Forum on the JCT Drafting Sub-Committee.

She is a contributor on construction matters to *Freeman's Guide to the Property Industry* and the *Architect's Legal Handbook*. She had a monthly column in *Building Magazine* on construction law issues.

Jenny Baster

Jenny Baster qualified as a solicitor in 1978. Having worked first at a law centre and subsequently in a City practice, in 1985 she joined Arup where she is Legal Director. She has extensive practical experience advising on the legal aspects of the firm's day to day operations, with a particular involvement in contractual and insurance matters. She has experience of litigation, arbitration and other forms of dispute resolution in the UK and internationally. Jenny's role extends to in-house training on a variety of commercial and legal issues and she has, in addition, contributed to external training courses. She has worked closely with the construction industry professional institutions and has participated in a number of professional review bodies including committees of the Association of Consulting Engineers and the Construction Industry Council. Jenny's experience has centred on the practical application of the law to engineers in a commercial environment.

Sir Vivian Ramsey
Sir Vivian Ramsey studied Engineering Science and Economics at Oxford University before working as a civil engineer in the UK and overseas. During this time he became a Chartered Engineer and a Member of the Institution of Civil Engineers. After studying law in London he was called to the Bar in 1979 and was a practising barrister from 1981 to 2005. He became a Queen's Counsel in 1992 and from 2003 to 2005 he was Head of Keating Chambers, the largest London set of barristers' Chambers specialising in building, technology, IT and associated commercial disputes.

He practised around the world as an advocate, arbitrator, adjudicator and mediator in technical disputes, particularly related to construction and engineering projects. He acted for governments, public authorities, utilities, international contracting companies, consultancies, architects, engineers and other construction professionals. He continues to lecture at home and overseas and is a Special Professor in the Department of Civil Engineering at the University of Nottingham and a Visiting Professor at King's College, London. In November 2005 he was appointed as a High Court Judge in the Queen's Bench Division and in September 2007 became the Judge in Charge of the Technology and Construction Court. He received a knighthood on his appointment.

Michael O'Reilly
Mike O'Reilly is a chartered engineer, having worked on a number of prestigious projects with Arup including geotechnical designs for the Canary Wharf project. On passing his Bar Finals, he trained at Keating and Atkin Chambers before returning to academia, where he taught at the Universities of Nottingham and Sheffield and was then appointed Head of Civil Engineering at Kingston University. In 2000 he returned to independent practice at the Bar and appeared in a number of high profile cases reported in the Building Law Reports, the Competition Appeal Reports and the European Law Reports. In January 2006, he transferred to the Solicitor's branch of the profession in order to establish Adie O'Reilly LLP, a specialist property and construction law firm based in Lincoln, but with a national and international client list.

Hamish Lal (Newsletter Editor)
Hamish Lal is a Partner in the London Construction & Engineering Group at Dundas & Wilson LLP. Hamish has degree in civil engineering, a degree in law, and a PhD in civil engineering, and is a specialist in construction, engineering and project finance law. He has significant experience of and expertise in many forms of construction procurement (including PFI, project finance, construction management, partnering alliancing and target cost contracting) and has practised in the oil, nuclear, commercial property and PFI sectors. He has particular expertise in the legal analysis of delay and is the author of Quantifying and Managing Disruption Claims published by Thomas Telford Ltd. Hamish was awarded the inaugural Norman Royce Prize by The Society of Construction Arbitrators. In 2008 he received the Parkman Medal awarded by the Institution of Civil Engineers.

PART 1

Legal issues arising during the course of the construction project

Section editor: Ann Minogue
Partner, Linklaters

CHAPTER 1.1

The planning system

Michael O'Reilly
Adie O'Reilly LLP Visiting Professor at Kingston University

1 INTRODUCTION

1.1 The scope of this chapter

This chapter contains an overview of the planning system. It deals with those topics most likely to affect construction professionals. Due to constraints on space, there is no discussion of green belts, compulsory purchase or the development powers of local planning authorities. For information on these areas, please refer to specialist publications.

1.2 The nature of planning law

Prior to the 19th century, landowners were entitled to use their land as they wished. Many of the developments of that century caused disquiet and attempts were made to impose some order on poor and unsanitary living conditions and unrestrained development.

In 1909, the UK saw the first attempt at a unified system of planning control in the form of the Housing, Town Planning etc. Act 1909. This enabled local authorities to prepare schemes for the laying out of their towns in an well-ordered manner. But it was not until 1947 that an effective regulatory system was put in place, designed to give some democratic control over development proposals and to prescribe suitable locations for certain types of development. Since 1947, development control has burgeoned and we now have a system of great complexity which applies to all, including, now, the Crown.

In more recent years, it has been recognised that the planning system can be used to promote economic, environmental and heritage sustainability. It can be a vehicle for seeking to ensure security of energy and water supply/distribution and transportation capacity for a growing population. This means integrating policies, such as energy supply and transportation into planning. To that end the Government has, following reports by Barker and Eddington on housing and sustainability in respect of major projects, introduced the Planning Bill 2007. At the time of writing (30 September 2008) the Bill is completing its passage through Parliament. It is designed to provide more streamlined and coherent procedures for major infrastructure projects and any readers who are concerned with such projects will need to be familiar with that impending legislation.

Those involved with major schemes will necessarily be working within a team, including lawyers and hence this chapter is principally concerned with more routine planning matters, such as those which may be faced by engineers and architects on a daily basis.

In order to appreciate the law that applies to the modern planning system, a number of its facets must be understood first:

(1) The system of planning control is entirely statutory. The principal statute is the Town and Country Planning Act 1990 ('TCPA 1990'), which has been amended by various subsequent statutes including most significantly the Planning and Compulsory Purchase Act 2004 ('PCPA 2004'). Whilst judicial decisions play a role in planning law, large swathes of the law remain untouched by reported cases.

(2) It is 'plan-led'; that is to say that a series of hierarchical plans are drawn up, together constituting the Development Plan and decisions about e.g. the grant of planning permission are made in accordance with the plan.

(3) The process is democratically-driven: the drawing up of plans is managed by the central, regional and local government authorities and decisions e.g. about planning permission are usually taken by elected representatives. Their discretion

1.1 The planning system
1.2 Financing the project
1.3 Public sector projects
1.4 Public/private partnerships
1.5 Tender process
1.6 Construction contracts
1.7 Construction insurance

to grant planning permission is largely unimpeachable, provided they approach their decision making in accordance with their statutory powers, although their discretion to refuse planning permission is subject to appeal to the Secretary of State, acting usually through an appointed Inspector.

1.3 National and local government and oversight of the planning system

Since May 2006, the primary national government department overseeing the planning system is the Department for Communities and Local Government. (DCLG) Prior to that it was the Office of Deputy Prime Minister (ODPM) and before that the Department for Environment, Transport and Regions (DETR). Many relevant documents were originally issued by the DETR or the ODPM. In relation to some matters, other government departments may be involved in planning: for example, the Department of Culture, Media and Sport is involved in listing buildings.

At the local level, the situation is somewhat confusing. 'Local planning authorities' (being the bodies to whom an application for planning permission is made, or who enforce planning control) are:

(1) in the metropolitan areas: the London boroughs and the metropolitan districts;
(2) in the country: either unitary authorities (where they exist) or (where they do not) district councils for all matters except those specifically reserved for the county council, such as waste management.

When dealing with local authorities, it is always advisable to call up the planning department to check in the first instance that one is dealing with the right authority. In some cases, more than one authority may have jurisdiction: e.g. in relation to a waste transfer station, the county council and local district council may each have a role to play in relation to different aspects of any development.

1.4 Development plans

Because the planning system is plan-led, it is important to have some understanding of the creation and adoption of the Development Plan.

Prior to 2004, the Development Plan typically involved a Structure Plan and Local Plan. The former gave broad policy direction at a county level; the latter gave more detail and, in some cases, individual sites or areas could be identified for development.

In 2004, the Planning and Compulsory Purchase Act 2004 (PCPA 2004) introduced a new system designed to place more emphasis on the concept of 'sustainable development' and on the coordination of central, regional and local planning.

National planning: Central government determines national policies on different aspects of planning. These policies are set out in Planning Policy Statements (PPS) and Planning Policy Guidance notes (PPG) and Circulars (published on the DCLG website).

Regional planning: Regional Planning Bodies (in London, the Mayor) prepare and produce a Regional Spatial Strategy (RSS) (in London, the Spatial Development Strategy) which reflects and builds on policies set out at the national level. It is designed to accommodate a period lasting 10–15 years and can include policies relating to a geographical area that crosses local planning authority boundaries.

Local planning: LPAs (other than county councils) must then prepare a Local Development Framework (LDF). This will comprise a folder of documents for delivering the spatial or minerals planning strategy for the area. An LDF will include a Local

Development Scheme, Local Development Documents and a Statement of Community Involvement.

The acronyms created by the legislation are bewildering, even for lawyers. In the summary offered by the DCLG on its website:

> 'Local planning authorities (except county councils) must prepare a Local Development Scheme (LDS) which sets out a programme for the production of Local Development Documents (LDDs); what documents are to be prepared as LDDs; the timetables for producing them; and whether they are to be prepared jointly with other local authorities. LDDs, which can either be Development Plan Documents (DPDs) or Supplementary Planning Documents (SPDs), should reflect and build upon national and regional policies, taking into account local needs and variations. The PCPA 2004 requires LDDs to have regard to national policies and guidance issued by the Secretary of State, the local authority's Community Strategy, and also to be in general conformity with the RSS or, for London Boroughs, the Spatial Development Strategy.'

The statutory Development Plan is the critical document. It is the document by which, for example, planning applications will be assessed. It thus plays a central role in the planning system. Under the new legislation, the Development Plane will consist of: (1) Regional Spatial Strategies (or, in the case of London, the Spatial Development Strategy prepared by the Mayor); and (2) Development Plan Documents prepared by district councils and unitary authorities and Minerals and Waste Development Plan Documents prepared by county councils.

1.5 Sustainable development

Section 39 of the PCPA 2004 requires those responsible for preparing the RSS and LDDs in England, to undertake these functions with a view to contributing to the achievement of sustainable development.

2 DEVELOPMENT

2.1 Development and the need for planning permission

Section 57(1) of the TCPA 1990 provides subject to the following provisions of that section: 'planning permission is required for the carrying out of any development of land'. The definition of the term 'development' is central to the application of this part of the planning system.

Section 55(1) contains the primary definition of development: 'the carrying out of building, engineering, mining or other operations in, on, over or under land' or the 'making of any material change in the use of any buildings or other land'. Thus, planning permission is required whenever there is 'development'. Development may take one of two forms:

(1) operational development and/or
(2) change of use.

The legislation attempts to keep the two forms of development separate. The main form of development with which readers of this Handbook will be concerned is operational development.

Some developments, however, need no specific permission because they are subject to a blanket permission in a development order – this is known as 'permitted development'.

1.1 The planning system
1.2 Financing the project
1.3 Public sector projects
1.4 Public/private partnerships
1.5 Tender process
1.6 Construction contracts
1.7 Construction insurance

It is, generally speaking, not directly a criminal offence to develop without permission (in the case of carrying out unauthorised work e.g. in Areas of Archaeological Importance or to a listed building and other particular cases, carrying out work can involve criminal liability), but the financial penalties can be severe, particularly if the local planning authority ('LPA') takes action to have the works stopped. It is therefore prudent to ensure that any necessary planning permission is obtained before starting work.

2.2 What operations constitute development?

We shall divide operational development into the four elements set out in section 55(1): (1) building operations, (2) engineering operations (3) mining and (4) other operations.

Building

Section 55(1A) of the TCPA 1990 provides that the term 'building operations' includes: '(a) the demolition of buildings; (b) rebuilding; (c) structural alterations of or addition to buildings; and (d) other operations normally undertaken by a person carrying on business as a builder'. The definition of a building in the statute is wider than the everyday use of the word suggests: section 336(1) provides that it includes 'any structure or erection, or any part of a building, as so defined, but does not include plant or machinery comprised in a building'. So, for example, a mast may well be a building in this sense.

Conversely, there are works which would normally be undertaken by a builder but which are not development within the statute: section 55(2) provides that internal works which do not materially affect the external appearance are not development requiring permission, providing there is no enlargement of underground space or addition of mezzanine floors exceeding 200 m^2 in retail buildings. This latter provision has recently been introduced using powers under section 49 of the PCPA 2004 enabling the SSCLG to issue a development order to restrict the operation of section 55(2).

Prior to the Planning and Compensation 1991 Act ('PCA 1991'), the definition of building did not include demolition, as it does now. Accordingly, there was significant confusion as to whether or not demolition required planning permission. There was a potential paradox in that structural alteration might require permission, but that total removal might not. In 1991 it was decided to extend the definition of building to include demolition; but the SSCLG has power to exclude certain demolitions from this provision and this has created yet further confusion because the exceptions created by the Town and Country Planning (Demolition – Description of Buildings) Direction 1995 involve almost all buildings. In the case of a dwelling house, the General Permitted Development Order Schedule 2, Part 31 provides that before demolition, an application must normally be made to the LPA for approval of the method of demolition.

Engineering operations

The legislation does not contain any definition of engineering operations. The matter has been raised in a decided case where the judge said that the term should be given its natural everyday meaning, being an operation upon which an engineer might be engaged. There are some excluded activities, including road and sewer/pipe/cable maintenance.

Mining

The removal of material for their economic value from a site is development: see also the Town and Country Planning (Minerals) Act 1981.

Other operations

The scope of this provision is very uncertain. It can, however, be said that it must mean an operation of the same scope and scale as the other operations which fall within the definition.

2.3 Permitted development

Many kinds of relatively minor works or changes of use enjoy deemed planning permission and form the category of what is known as 'permitted development'.

At the national level, there is the Town and Country (General Permitted Development) Order 1995 ('GPDO') which has been amended on a variety of occasions. Amendments include the much-heralded (Amendment) (No. 2) (England) Order 2008 which extends permitted developments in the case of dwellings, e.g. making it easier to construct extensions without the need for permission; this comes into force on 1 October 2008 and is expected dramatically to reduce the number of minor planning applications. At the local level, there is a new power which came into force in May 2006 enabling LPAs to issue equivalent provisions affecting the locality.

In relation to changes of use, reference should be made to the Use Classes Order (UCO) which establishes a series of use classes and provides for where a change in use is not considered to be development. These rights can be constrained by agreement between the LPA and the developer. The UCO has recently been updated: see the amendment in SI 2005 No. 85 and explained in Circular 03/2005.

GDPO

Paragraph 3 of GPDO provides: 'Subject to the provisions of this Order . . . planning permission is hereby granted for the classes of development described as permitted development in Schedule 2'. There are exceptions and the SSCLG or LPA has power to constrain the development in individual cases.

Schedule 1 sets out the geographical areas to which the GPDO does not extend. This essentially includes National Parks, areas of outstanding natural beauty (and from October 2008 sites on UNESCO's World Heritage List ('World Heritage Sites') etc.)

Schedule 2 sets out a wide range of relatively minor developments in 33 parts. Part 1 relates to development within the cartilage of a dwellinghouse and Part 33 relates to the installation of closed circuit cameras. The intervening parts deal with minor developments, changes of use, temporary buildings, agricultural buildings and operations, forestry operations, industrial and warehouse development, repairs to unadopted streets, repairs to services, development by local authorities, highway authorities, drainage bodies, Environment Agency, sewerage undertakers, statutory undertakers, aviation-related developments, developments ancillary to mining (including waste tipping), electronic communications-related development, development at amusement parks, driver information, toll road facilities, demolition and development by schools, colleges, universities and hospitals.

Local development orders

Sections 61A–61D, inserted by the PCPA 2004 provide LPAs with a power to issue a Local Development Order ('LDO'). By this means, certain developments may be granted planning permission without the need to make an application. There are restrictions as to what may be permitted by way of LDO. For example, there must be no blanket permission in the case of listed buildings or for development that requires an environmental impact assessment. LDOs will not avoid the need for a conservation area consent for development in those areas.

1.1 The planning system
1.2 Financing the project
1.3 Public sector projects
1.4 Public/private partnerships
1.5 Tender process
1.6 Construction contracts
1.7 Construction insurance

It is anticipated that LDOs will be used for (1) small domestic development to avoid the resources spent on routine applications and (2) encouraging types of local development, such as regeneration development in specified areas of the LPA's area.

2.4 Certificate of lawfulness

Often the dividing line between permitted development and that which requires express permission is unclear. In order to determine whether planning permission is required, the developer can apply for a certificate of lawful use or development, including clarifying the status of existing development.

The application must provide sufficient information to allow the land to be clearly identified and give such details of its planning history as are available. Usually, a local conveyancing search or inspection of the public planning register will provide much useful background information.

Unless the LPA respond within the specified time with a certificate of lawfulness, the applicant may appeal to the SSCLG whose Inspector will review the issues and decide accordingly.

The one drawback to this procedure is that it does draw the LPA's attention to a possible unlawful use in respect of which they might decide to take enforcement action.

3 APPLICATIONS FOR PLANNING PERMISSION

The legal requirements and procedure for making a planning application are set out in the Town and Country Planning General Development Procedure Order 1995 ('GDPO 1995') as amended from time to time (and not to be confused with 'GPDO', which is the General Permitted Development Order, discussed above). This is a document which should be close to hand at all times when making applications for planning permission.

Applicants must ensure that they are using the latest amended version.

3.1 Preliminary matters

Checking that you have the right LPA

Anyone not familiar with the area should check which is the LPA for the area where the development is to take place. This will normally be the District or Borough Council. If the development relates to mining or waste disposal, then the local County or Unitary authority will deal with the planning application. In Wales, planning authorities are either the County or County Borough Councils. In London and other metropolitan areas, the London Borough or Metropolitan Council is responsible for all planning matters. The planning department of most councils will usually be pleased to guide applicants to the right place.

Planning history

It is frequently worthwhile finding out about the planning history of the site. Earlier applications for planning permission can be checked (e.g. to see whether a similar development proposal has previously been refused, or if any agreements exist that regulate how the site or buildings can be developed) by visiting the LPA and ask to see the Planning Register for the site, which is open for inspection to the public.

Consistency with the development plan

It is worth bearing in mind that the Development Plan is the key document against which the application will be judged.

Application for full or outline planning permission?

Outline applications can only be made for the construction of buildings, not any other kind of development.

An outline planning permission gives 'in principle' approval, reserving details such as: layout, scale, appearance, access and landscaping. LPAs do have the power to request detailed information on an aspect of the scheme that the applicant hoped to reserve for later, if the LPA considers that it is necessary to have that information when determining the outline.

For larger building proposals, it is often useful to seek outline approval before committing resources to preparing all the material needed to support a full application. In addition, an outline permission will have the effect of establishing the development value for the land (i.e. it assumes that a development of the type approved in principle is capable of being carried out on the land concerned). It will often be necessary to have reached this stage before finance can be raised to acquire the land and undertake the scheme. Development approved by an outline planning permission cannot be implemented until the reserved matters have been approved by the LPA.

Non-building development can only be the subject of an application for full or detailed planning permission. A full application must include details of access, siting, layout, design, external appearance and landscaping, so far as any of these are relevant to the scheme.

Discussions with the LPA

Potential applicants are encouraged (e.g. by Planning Policy Statement 1) to discuss their proposals with planning officers to enable the applicant to align his proposal with the Development Plan and understand how best to present his application and to ensure that issues of design and of planning can be resolved before the application is submitted. It goes without saying that the LPA does not guarantee any enthusiasm its officers may express; the final decision always resides with the democratically elected members, who have a wide range of discretion. Indeed, it seems that the LPA owes no duty of care at all; although it may form the subject of a complaint to the Ombudsman.

As a result of recent legislation (Local Government Act 2003, section 98), LPAs are empowered to charge for the time spent.

3.2 Making the application

Since April 2008 all applications must be made on the standard form prescribed by an amendment which can be located on the Planning Portal (www.planning portal.gov.uk) and must include the information prescribed by Article 4E of GPDO 1995 as amended.

The application form will require information on the nature and extent of the development proposal, and the existing planning status of the site or building. There is also a requirement for a 'design and access statement'. LPAs will issue policies in relation to design and access. In respect of design, the statement will set out the design principles and concepts applied. The access statement will deal with access to the development site and ensure that proper thought is given to safe and convenient access to roads etc. The statements will demonstrate the design and access thinking to ensure its quality and consistency with the requirements. This statement will be required both for full and outline planning applications.

For major schemes professional advice and assistance will usually be needed to complete the forms and provide the bundle of supporting documentation. A site location plan and description of the development is always required, but many LPAs will insist on appropriate detail being submitted, such as technical drawings of how the scheme will look (where the application is for outline planning permission this may not be appropriate).

The correct fee must be paid with each application that requires a fee. Section 303 of the TCPA 1990 provides the power for the SSCLG to make regulations: see Town and Country Planning (Fees for Applications and Deemed Applications) (England) Regulations amended in 2008 and also DCLG Circular Planning-Related Fees 04/08 isued in April 2008.

3.3 Applications by non-owners

It is not necessary to own land to make an application for planning permission. However, an application will not be valid unless it is accompanied by written confirmation that all owners of the land have been formally notified of the application. If the applicant is also the owner (which, in this context, means not just the freeholder, but anyone who is entitled to receive a market rent for the land and a tenant with at least seven years left to run on his lease), then he must sign a certificate that no-one else has an owner's interest in the land. If he is not the 'owner' then he must certify that he has given notice in writing of the application to every person who, on the date 21 days preceding the date of the application, had an 'owner's' interest in the land. Details of the minimum requirements are set out in the GDPO 1995, article 6 and schedule 2 although it is frequently appropriate to advertise more widely to avoid later challenges.

As we shall see later in this chapter, the use of obligations is becoming more widespread; only a person with an appropriate interest in the land may take on such an obligation and this is one area where a non-owner may be at a disadvantage.

3.4 The validity of the application

The LPA must acknowledge receipt of the application, and will then decide if it is valid or not. Since April 2008 amended Article 5 of GDPO sets out the requirements for a valid application. CLG Circular 02/2008 entitled 'Standard Application Form and Validation' states that validation should be notified within 3–5 working days for minor applications and 10 working days for major applications. The date of validation is 'day zero' in terms of the timescale available for determining the application. An application that is arguably invalid, and therefore not determined within the statutory period, may apparently still be the subject of an appeal to the Secretary of State (for non-determination). The Secretary of State is entitled to form his own view of the validity of the application.

3.5 Consultation

Depending on the nature and size of the development applied for, the LPA is obliged to consult with a wide range of organisations before determining the application. Everyone so consulted may object to, or make representations about, the development proposal. All such comment is a material consideration to which the LPA must have regard when determining the application.

Normally, letters of objection or comment are available to the applicant who may often be able to change elements of the scheme to overcome particular concerns.

4 DETERMINATION OF THE PLANNING APPLICATION

4.1 Who determines: calling-in

Ordinarily the planning application will be determined by the LPA. However, section 77 of the TCPA 1990 gives the SSCLG a power to call-in a planning application for his or her own decision, rather than leave it for the LPA to make the decision. The power is not frequently used, generally being limited to cases of much more than local interest. The SSCLG normally becomes aware of such cases by means of the requirement for LPAs to notify the DCLG of cases involving a departure from the development plan or exceeding specified thresholds for different categories of development. Alternatively, other contentious proposals may be brought to the attention of the SSCLG by Regional Offices, pressure groups or amenity societies.

In called-in cases, the LPA and the applicant are given the option of an inquiry, in which case, the procedure would be similar to that for a planning appeal, being governed by the same Inquiries Procedure Rules, and the inquiry held before an Inspector appointed by the SSCLG.

Below, we shall assume that the LPA retains the application.

4.2 The primacy of the development plan

Section 37(6) of the Planning and Compulsory Purchase Act 2004 ('PCPA 2004') provides: 'If regard is to be had to the development plan for the purpose of any determination to be made under the planning Acts the determination must be made in accordance with the plan unless material considerations indicate otherwise.'

The phrase 'unless material indications dictate otherwise' means that it may be possible to get permission to carry out a development which does not conform to the Development Plan, provided there is justification for doing so which is based on valid planning reasoning.

Regard must also be had to government policy in interpreting the Development Plan. The relevant publication can be viewed on line on the DCLG website or on the government's planning portal.

4.3 Planning committees

The democratic input into planning is seen most vividly in the planning committee system. The planning committee will usually consist of a group of the LPA's democratically elected councillors, although in the case of some very significant or controversial applications, the final decision may be made by the full council. There will, however, be rules made by each LPA allowing minor matters to be 'delegated' to planning officers to make 'delegated powers decisions'.

When taking decisions, the planning committee will have access to a report prepared by a planning officer and so will be assisted by professional opinion. The committee is not bound by the officer's recommendation; in some cases, the issues are determined on party political lines. Most planning committee are held in public, and many LPAs allow applicants or objectors to make a brief presentation (a few minutes) of their cases or to participate in the debate.

Where the recommendation is to grant a planning permission but subject to a legal agreement under section 106 of the TCPA 1990 (see below) the Committee will make a resolution to grant planning permission, but the planning permission will not be issued until the legal agreement has been settled. It is important to note that it is only the issue of a signed decision notice that constitutes a planning permission. The resolution of a Committee to grant does not constitute the grant of planning permission itself.

4.4 The application process and timescale

On receipt of an application, the Administrative Section of the LPA will do the initial processing for validity. A Planning Officer will undertake a preliminary review of the submission to assess the adequacy of the information submitted in support of the application. He will also give instructions to the administrative section as to whom should be consulted on the application. This process usually takes between one and two weeks to be completed, and is usually referred to as the validation or registration process.

Since August 2005, LPAs have had a discretion to decline to determine an application if it appears to the LPA to be substantially the same as a previous application. Guidance (Circular 08/2005) has clarified that the intention of the legislation is not to frustrate the submission of improved applications but to avoid the situation where it appears that the applicant is seeking to wear down the LPA.

As a result of recent amendments to the GDPO 1995 there are a variety of time-periods for determining planning applications – see the Town and Country Development (General Development Procedure)(Amendment)(England) Order 2006.

Normal applications: 8 weeks
Major projects: 13 weeks
Projects requiring an Environmental Impact Assessment: 16 weeks

There is no obligation upon a LPA to make their decision within the time; they may do so at any time. However, a right of appeal exists once the time has expired. LPAs are required to make statistical returns to the DCLG setting out details of the time they have taken to deal with their applications, and many achieve the target for up to 80% of applications received. However, a significant proportion of applications involve complex or contentious proposals. The amount of negotiation, revision and re-consultation can lead to some applications taking many months or even years to be concluded.

What an applicant always has to weigh up after the statutory period has expired, is whether there is a good prospect of obtaining planning permission in due course, and whether this is likely to be quicker overall than treating non-determination as a deemed refusal, and submitting an appeal.

Following the validation and acknowledgement of the application, the process of substantive consideration begins. Site notices will be put up, and consultation letters sent out. These will state that interested parties should make any representations about the application to the LPA within 21 days of the date of the notice; there is now a statutory duty upon consultees to respond within 21 days (see s. 54 PCPA 2004).

The application will then be allocated to a planning officer to be dealt with. The internal organisation and operating procedures of individual authorities vary, but the following would be a typical process. The officer is usually a qualified Town Planner working in the 'Development Control' section of the planning department. He or she will then review the application and decide which other specialist officers in the department need to be consulted, as well as other departments in the LPA. For example, the Highway Authority would be consulted if there are any traffic or transport implications, and a Conservation or Urban Design Officer if the proposals involve a site with a conservation area. Most large redevelopment schemes usually involve consultation with a number of specialist sections or other departments of the Council.

Site inspections will be carried out, and the Case Officer will assess whether the proposals conform to relevant development policies. These assessments and internal consultations should usually be complete by the time the 21 day public consultation period has expired (usually about 5 weeks after submission). At this point, the Case Officer will decide how the application should be dealt with; or whether in more marginal cases, the applicant should be requested to amend the proposals in order to make then more acceptable.

Assuming the proposals are considered acceptable without amendment, but are too important to be dealt with under 'delegated powers', the Officer will then prepare a report on the application for consideration by the Planning Committee. The report should contain a description of the site and its location, and the application proposals. It should state the relevant planning history of the site, and detail the consultations carried out and responses received. It should then include an appraisal of the proposals in relation to relevant development plan policies, and any other relevant planning considerations. Finally, it should contain a recommendation as to the decision that should be taken, and any conditions that should be imposed on the permission.

In more complex cases, the Officer may recommend that the applicant should be required to enter into a legal agreement with the LPA so that in order to make the planning application 'acceptable' the applicant gives undertakings in return, as provided for in Section 106 – 106B of the TCPA 1990.

5 CONDITIONS AND OBLIGATIONS

The grant of planning permission will rarely be unconditional. There may be two types of restriction:

(1) conditions on the planning permission
(2) the requirement for a contribution back to the community, known as an obligation pursuant to a Section 106 Agreement.

Where there is a choice between imposing conditions and entering into a planning obligation, the imposition of a condition is to be preferred – see Circular 05/2005, paragraph B2.

5.1 Conditions

Section 70(1) of the TCPA 1990 provides statutory authority for the LPA to grant planning permission subject to conditions.

Whilst stated in wide terms, the courts have insisted that for validity, a condition must fairly and reasonably relate to the development and not have an ulterior motive beyond the development. Lord Denning put the point like this as early as 1958 in the Pyx Granite case: 'Although the planning authorities are given very wide powers to impose "such conditions as they think fit", nevertheless the law says that those conditions, to be valid, must fairly and reasonably relate to the permitted development. The planning authority are not at liberty to use their powers for an ulterior motive, however desirable that object may seem to them to be in the public interest.'

It is generally recognised that conditions must be: (a) imposed for a planning purpose, (b) must fairly relate to the development permitted and (c) must not be so unreasonable that no reasonable authority could have imposed them. Circular 11/95 provides further guidance.

In some cases, conditions might apply to other land. Section 72(1)(a) provides a general power where it is in connection with the development – e.g. there may be a condition in relation to connection off-site to a main sewer. The 'Grampian principle', after the name of the leading case, is that it is possible to insist on a negative condition off the site, provided that it is properly connected to the development – in that case, the condition was the closure of a road to ensure that access did not harm other development objectives. For example, most larger developments will require the construction of new roads or the upgrading of existing roads which is often achieved using Grampian conditions (although PPG 13, 'Highway Considerations in Development Control', has cautioned against the use of Grampian conditions where this may delay the commencement and jeopardise the permission).

5.2 Planning agreements/obligations

There are limitations upon the types and scope of conditions that may be imposed. Where the LPA requires more from a developer than can be achieved by condition, it will insist that planning permission will be granted only in return for some obligation undertaken by the developer in the form of a legally binding agreement. The theory is that an application which would otherwise be unacceptable is made acceptable when combined with the agreement. Developers often see the use of obligations as little short of extortion, with LPAs requiring what developers perceive as unrelated obligations, such the obligation to provide social housing as part of the scheme.

An obligation in this sense is a formal legal instrument executed as a deed, registrable as a Local Land charge, and enforceable against the person entering the obligation, and any person deriving title to the land from that person. A standard form section 106 agreement is available on the DCLG website.

The legal framework in which such agreements are made has been frequently amended. The original legislation dates from 1932 but has been enacted subsequently in various guises in s. 52 of the TCPA 1971 and s. 106 of the TCPA 1990 (which was again replaced in 1991 by new sections 106, 106A and 106B). Existing agreements under s. 52 and the first s. 106 regime may continue to play a part in regulating development. The PCPA 2004, envisaged a yet further regime enabling developers to make contributions, including cash payments or benefits in kind ('planning charge') but this was not introduced. At the time of writing (30 September 2008), the legislation for a Comminity Infrastructure Charge (CIL) forms part of the Planning Bill currently before Parliament and a ministerial policy update on the proposed CIL was published in August 2008 (available on the DCLG website). Given present uncertainty over the implementation of the CIL, the existing system must be explained.

In Circular 05/2005 the Secretary of State set out guidance in relation to obligations. This gives strong government approval of the practice of requiring obligations in the interest of sustainable development. It is said in the circular that a planning obligation must meet each of the following tests. It must be:

(i) relevant to planning
(ii) necessary to make the proposed development acceptable in planning terms
(iii) directly related to the proposed development
(iv) fairly and reasonable related in scale to the proposed development and
(v) reasonable in all other respects.

Examples are given which indicate the type of agreement that is acceptable in policy terms. 'For example, developers may reasonably be expected to pay for or contribute to the cost of all, or that part of, additional infrastructure which would not have been necessary but for their development . . . [but] planning obligations should not be used solely to resolve existing deficiencies in infrastructure provision . . .' 'where not possible through a planning condition, planning obligations can be used to secure the inclusion of an element of affordable housing in a residential or mixed-use development where there is a residential component . . . in line with the Local Development Framework policies on the creation of mixed communities.' '. . . if a proposed development would give rise to the need for additional or expanded community infrastructure, for example, a new school classroom, which is necessary in planning terms and not provided in an application, it might be acceptable for contributions to be sought towards this additional provision through a planning obligation.' '. . . pooled contributions towards major infrastructure in growth areas . . .'

This guidance represents a strong endorsement of the concept of LPA requiring a contribution as part and parcel of the grant of permission for major projects. In order to enable developers to predict what will be required (and hence what they should build into their budgets when assessing the viability of a scheme) the government has indicated that LPAs should express their policies on planning obligations in the Local Development Framework which forms part of the Development Plan.

6 THE DURATION OF PLANNING PERMISSION

Prior to 1969, planning permissions had indefinite duration. LPAs were granted powers to limit the period by condition. Under section 91 of the TCPA 1990 the normal period was established as 5 years. By section 51 of PCPA 2004, which amends section 91, however, the normal period is reduced to 3 years which requires those with planning permission benefit to ensure that commencement is not delayed – whilst it is possible to make a re-application, development plans may readily change meaning that grant will be by no means assured. By amended section 91(1)(b) of the TCPA 1990, LPAs have a discretion to substitute a longer or indeed shorter period where warranted.

It is a question of some difficulty to determine whether or not the development has commenced on time. In one case, it was held that digging a trench for the footings constituted commencement despite the fact that they were immediately backfilled with the soil (in order, apparently, to stop children falling in). In another case, trenches had been dug, but they did not correspond to the development layout, so there was no commencement. It is now established that the developer's intention is not material to the question whether or not development has commenced and what must be shown is that there has been a substantial commencement of the scheme for which planning permission has been granted.

A more intractable and often significant facet of the problem is the so-called 'Whitley principle', named after the leading case in 1990. Planning permission was granted subject to a condition that a number of matters in relation to the scheme be agreed with the LPA in advance. There was difficulty reaching agreement but in order to avoid the expiration of the time period, the developer commenced on site anyway. The Court of Appeal stated that commencement meant commencement in accordance with the conditions. Commencement in breach of condition was not commencement at all and the planning permission was lost. This principle has been applied consistently, but with a modicum of common sense. For example, where the LPA had been aware of the scheme proposed and had not objected, the development was lawful despite the LPA not having formally approved the scheme.

In relation to outline planning permission, the provisions are somewhat different. Under section 92(2) of the TCPA 1990, application for approval of reserved matters must be made within 3 years of grant of outline permission; and the commencement must take place within 5 years of grant of outline permission or if later 2 years of the last approval received. Section 51 of PCPA 2004 modifies the period; it is now 3 years and within 2 years after last approval received but the LPA may vary the time allowed for an application for approval of reserved matters.

Whilst under the pre-2004 legislation, time limits might be extended, that is no longer possible and this adds to the purpose of these changes that once planning permission is granted it must be implemented quickly or be lost. A further piece of legislation that supports this is the completion notice provision in section 94 of TCPA 1990 which provides that the LPA may serve a notice requiring completion within 5 years (for pre-2004 matters) or 3 years (post-2004 matters).

7 PLANNING APPEALS

If the LPA (1) fails to determine the application within the statutory time limit or (2) refuses to grant planning permission or (3) makes a grant subject to conditions which the applicant considers unreasonable, the applicant may appeal under the provision in section 78 of the TCPA 1990. Appeals may also be made in respect of a listed building or conservation area consent application, an application for a Certificate of Lawfulness of an Existing Use or Development or an application for consent to display an advertisement.

Although the appeal is technically to the SSCLG, in practice the appeal is usually handled by an executive agency known as the Planning Inspectorate. Only a very small proportion of appeals are actually decided by the SSCLG.

7.1 Procedure

Appeals are made on a form produced by the Planning Inspectorate, with whom the appeal documentation is initially lodged. There are varying time limits for the submission of appeals after the date of the decision; for planning appeals the time limit is six months, for enforcement appeals the date will be the date set for compliance with the enforcement notice.

The appeal forms require details of the applicant, the decision being appealed against, the site and the proposal, and a summary of the grounds of appeal. Copies of the original application particulars must be provided together with the contested decision, if any. Finally, an indication must be given of the type of appeal procedure to be adopted.

There are three options for the method of pursuing the appeal:

(1) written representations only
(2) informal hearing
(3) public inquiry.

The applicant selects his or her preferred method, although the LPA may insist on a public inquiry.

Written representations

The written representations procedure is the most popular option. It is quicker, less costly, and generally considered quite adequate for most minor or non-complex cases. The procedural rules are dealt with under the Town & Country Planning (Appeals) (Written Representations Procedure) (England) Rules 2000.

The procedure is set out in diagrammatic form in Annex 1 of Circular 05/2000. In brief, the procedure following the lodging of the standard appeal form is that the LPA should respond within 14 days with a completed appeals 'questionnaire' and submit its full case in writing within a further 28 days. The appellant then has the opportunity to provide comments on the LPA's statement within a further 14 days. Third parties may also submit their written statements during this period. An Inspector from the Planning Inspectorate arranges to inspect the site. He may be accompanied by the parties, but no discussion of the merits of the case is allowed at the site visit. In most cases, the Inspector will then issue his or her decision letter within a few weeks of the site inspection. Overall, the timescale for such appeals is typically between 16 and 20 weeks.

Informal hearings

The procedure for informal hearings is set out in the Town and Country Planning (Hearings Procedure) (England) Rules 2000. The procedure is set out in diagrammatic form in Annex 2 of Circular 05/2000. A hearing is usually arranged within 12 weeks of the parties' agreement to use the procedure. Details are notified to the appellant and to any third party who made representations during the original application process. The hearing arrangements are also publicised locally.

The general aim of the process is to allow cases to be presented orally, in the format of an Inspector-led round table discussion. Written statements of case are required to be submitted to the Inspectorate and copied to the other side at least three weeks prior to the date of the hearing.

At the hearing, the Inspector leads a discussion on the main points at issue. Following this, an accompanied site visit is usually held. The Inspector's decision letter will then usually follow within a few weeks of the hearing. Overall, the timescale for such appeals is typically between 20 and 25 weeks.

Public inquiry

An inspector is appointed by the Planning Inspectorate to preside over an inquiry, which is held in public, at which the appellant, the Council and other interested parties are given the opportunity to present their cases, and to cross-examine the other participants on their cases. (Note that for Major Infrastructure Schemes the forthcoming Planning Act will establish streamlining procedures for the consideration and inquiries into such schemes.)

It is usual for the main parties to be legally represented and technical arguments being presented as 'proofs of evidence' by expert witnesses. In the case of major developments, it is not uncommon for public inquiries to last several days, with whole teams of expert witnesses presenting evidence on a range of technical issues.

Detailed procedural requirements for public inquiries are provided in the Town and Country Planning (Inquiries Procedures) (England) Rules 2000, and the Town and Country Planning (Determination by Inspectors) (Inquiries Procedure) (England) Rules 2000. The former apply where the SSCLG is to make a decision after considering a recommendation of the inspector ('recovered cases') whilst the latter deal with the case where the inspector will make the decision on behalf of the SSCLG ('transferred cases'). These Rules set out the procedures and requirements for submission of preliminary statements of case, inquiry arrangements and publicity, exchange of proofs of evidence, timetabling and handling of the inquiry itself. It is important to note that the Rules are designed to avoid a party being 'surprised' by the submission of evidence not previously signalled, so the procedure obliges the appellant and LPA to exchange copies of their witnesses' evidence three weeks before the inquiry starts.

The decision is usually made by the inspector a few weeks after the inquiry, and issued in the form of a letter. This letter will summarise the cases presented by each party at the inquiry, the inspector's findings and conclusions. If the appeal is allowed, the letter will

1.1 The planning system
1.2 Financing the project
1.3 Public sector projects
1.4 Public/private partnerships
1.5 Tender process
1.6 Construction contracts
1.7 Construction insurance

also provide details of any conditions to be imposed. In the few cases where the decision is to be made by the SSCLG, the inquiry inspector prepares a report of the inquiry for the SSCLG in a similar format to an inspector's decision letter, but with a recommendation for a decision instead of an actual decision. The SSCLG's letter of decision is then issued subsequently, together with the inspector's report. This process can in some instances take many months after the inquiry to be concluded. Other than in the case of public inquiry appeals to be determined by the SSCLG, the overall timescale for concluding such appeals is typically between 24 and 32 weeks.

The current provisions for dealing with major infrastructure projects are in the Town and Country Planning (Major Infrastructure Project Inquiries Procedure) (England) Rules 2002. Reference should be had to DCLG Circulars 07/2005 Planning Inquiries into Major Infrastructure Projects: Procedures and 04/2006 'Planning Inquiries into Major Infrastructure Projects: Economic Impacts Reports'. As indicated above, the forthcoming Planning Act is expected to provide for significant changes to streamline the system in respect of major infrastructure projects.

7.2 Appeal costs

The SSCLG has the power to award costs against one or other of the parties in any planning appeal where there has been a public inquiry, or an informal hearing. Costs awards are not available in the case of written representations. This power is given by the Local Government Act 1972 as amended by s. 320(2)/s. 322 of the TCPA 1990.

It is important to remember that although this power exists, Government advice (in DoE Circular 8/93) is that the basic principle for planning appeals is that each party is expected to bear its own costs, and that an award for costs will only be made where there has been unreasonable behaviour.

Application for an award of costs must be made at the inquiry or hearing, and the inspector will hear representations on the relevant issues from both parties. The decision on the application for costs is contained in a separate decision letter from the main appeal, although both decisions are usually issued together.

7.3 Challenging appeal decisions

Section 288 of the TCPA 1990 provides the power for an appeal decision to be challenged in the courts. Normally, this can only be done by one of the two principal parties, but in a few cases, it is possible for a third party to demonstrate a sufficiently material interest in order to obtain judicial review.

The time limit for challenges using Section 288 is six weeks from the date of the decision. The grounds on which a challenge may be made are principally legal or procedural. In the event that a successful challenge is made, the important point is that this does not mean that the SSCLG's decision is reversed, but that the decision is quashed, and the matter remitted to the SSCLG for reconsideration. It is not, therefore, uncommon for a successful legal challenge to be made, only then for the SSCLG to reconsider the case and come up with the same conclusion as before, having corrected the legal or procedural flaws of the initial decision.

7.4 Judicial review

A person who is not the applicant may feel aggrieved by the decision to grant planning permission. It may, in some cases, be possible to seek to have that decision reviewed by judicial review. Speed is required as there is an obligation to make a prompt application.

8 ENFORCEMENT

Development without permission is, ordinarily, not a criminal offence. The sanctions available are largely civil in nature. However, failing to act in accordance with notices to desist or to reinstate may bring the criminal law into play.

8.1 Lapse of time

Sometimes development takes place and no enforcement is carried out, either because the LPA does not get to know or because it is not considered a serious matter.

Time limits are set by the legislation. If development takes place and subsequently the time passes without enforcement action, then the LPA may not subsequently enforce. For operational development the time period is 4 years and for changes of use the period is 10 years. The exception is the case of a change of use to a single dwellinghouse, where the limit is 4 years.

8.2 Planning contravention notices

Where the LPA suspects that there may have been a contravention, it may serve (pursuant to ss. 171C–171D of the TCPA 1990) a notice, described as a planning contravention notice, requiring the occupier to give information so that the LPA can establish whether there has been a breach. A refusal by the occupier to cooperate may cause the next level of process – an enforcement notice – to be initiated and may adversely affect the recipient's ability to seek compensation in the event that a 'stop notice' is served. Failure to comply with any requirement of a planning contravention notice within a period of 21 days, or the giving of misleading information, is a criminal offence.

8.3 Enforcement notices

Powers and procedures

By section 172 of the TCPA 1990, a LPA may issue an enforcement notice where it appears to it: '(a) that there has been a breach of planning control; and (b) that it is expedient to issue the notice, having regard to the provisions of the development plan and to any other material consideration'.

The notice may be in respect of:

(1) any development for which there is no planning permission
(2) the breach of a condition attaching to the planning permission (there is also a separate power under s. 187A to issue a 'breach of condition notice').

The notice is to be served on the owner, occupier and any other person who has an interest which, in the LPA's opinion, is materially affected. The notice must state the date upon which it is to take effect; that is, the LPA must give time for compliance.

Strict time limits apply. The notice must be served within 28 days of its issue, i.e. from the date when it is made by the LPA. It must also be served 28 days or longer before it is specified to take effect. Different dates may be given for different steps or activities.

The notice must contain a number of prescribed matters, including identifying the breach and what the recipient must do to rectify the breach. This may include '(a) the alteration or removal of any building or works, (b) the carrying out of any building operation, (c) any activity on the land not to be carried out, (d) the contour of a deposit of refuse or waste materials on land to be modified...' (s. 173(5) of the TCPA 1990).

Under-enforcement and the deemed grant of planning permission

By section 173(11), if the notice could have required any buildings to be removed or activity to cease and it does not do so, planning permission is deemed to be granted.

The duration of an enforcement notice

Once the notice is served, it continues to have effect and is not discharged by compliance; thus later contraventions are caught by the notice even though the original contravention was remedied.

Failure to comply with an enforcement notice

By section 179 of the PCA 1991, a person who does not comply with the enforcement notice commits a criminal offence and may be charged and tried. Although the practice developed in some areas whereby the person charged would seek planning permission for the development and an adjournment of the criminal proceedings, the courts are now unwilling to adjourn the matter – the offence is the failure to comply and the merits of the planning application are irrelevant.

Appealing an enforcement notice

Section 174(1) of the TCPA 1990 provides a right of appeal to the SSCLG. Speed is essential as the appeal must be by notice in writing before the date specified in the notice upon which it is to take effect – there is no power to extend the date. The appeal may be made on a number of grounds set on out in s. 174(2): planning permission ought to be granted or the condition ought to be discharged; the matters complained of have not in fact occurred or do not amount to a breach of planning control; the LPA did not have power to enforce (e.g. because the development was sufficiently long-standing); the steps specified exceed what is necessary to remedy the breach; the period allowed for compliance is insufficient. Those grounds can only be raised on an appeal pursuant to s. 174 – however, other grounds, such as the alleged nullity of a notice may in some cases be raised e.g. as a defence in criminal proceedings.

An appeal is also deemed to amount to an application for planning permission – s. 177(5) of the TCPA 1990.

The applicable procedures are set out in the Town and Country Planning (Enforcement Notices and Appeals) Regulations 2002 to which reference should be made. This sets out a clear and rapid timetable within which the appeal will proceed.

By way of decision, the SSCLG may: '(a) grant planning permission . . . (b) discharge any condition . . . (c) determine whether . . . any existing use of the land was lawful . . .' (s. 177 TCPA 1990). The SSCLG may also vary the enforcement notice and this is frequently done.

A further appeal to the High Court is available to either party on a point of law, but requires permission of the court. Again, speed is essential: the appeal must be made within 28 days.

8.4 Breach of condition notice

Section 187A provides an alternative route for enforcement in the case of breaches of condition. Although there is no mechanism in the legislation for challenging the validity of a breach of condition notice, its invalidity may be raised as a defence in some cases upon prosecution for failure to comply with it.

8.5 Stop notices

Enforcement proceedings may take some time. It is useful, therefore, for LPAs to have a power to stop the development from proceeding any further. Section 183(1) of the TCPA 1990 provides: 'Where the local planning authority considers it expedient that any relevant activity should cease before the period of compliance with an enforcement notice, they may, when they serve a copy of the enforcement notice or otherwise, serve a notice (in this Act referred to as a "stop notice") prohibiting the carrying out of that activity on the land to which the enforcement notice relates.' Section 187(1) of the TCPA 1990 provides that it is a criminal offence to fail to comply with a stop notice.

If the stop notice is quashed on the grounds that planning ought to be granted, the LPA may have to provide compensation to the person adversely affected.

A new power to enable LPAs to issue a 'temporary stop notice' was enacted in the PCPA 2004 – which inserts sections 171E to 171H into the TCPA 1990.

8.6 Injunctions

Injunctions issued by the court may sometimes be successfully sought as an aid to planning control.

9 ENVIRONMENTAL ISSUES IN RELATION TO PLANNING

9.1 Introduction

Environmental issues generally are dealt with in chapter 3.5, but in this section we discuss specifically the application of Environmental Impact Assessment ('EIA') to planning applications.

Environmental assessment has been a feature of UK planning law since the 1985 EEC Directive was implemented in 1988. The Environmental Impact Assessment (England and Wales) Regulations 1999 provide the basic regime. Schemes authorised under other legislation than the TCPA 1990 (e.g. Highways) are subject to different environmental controls. Regard must also be had to the Strategic Environmental Assessment directive 2001/42/EC 'on the assessment of the effects of certain plans and programmes on the environment' transposed into UK law by the Environmental Assessment of Plans and Programmes Regulations 2004. This requires a formal environmental assessment of certain plans and programmes which are likely to have significant effects on the environment.

Even though only a small number of all applications will need to be supported by an environmental statement, there is a general obligation to have regard to biodiversity and geological conservation: see Circular 06/2005 which provides administrative guidance on the application of the law relating to planning and nature conservation and Planning Policy Statement 9: Biodiversity and Geological Conservation and the accompanying Good Practice Guide.

The terminology is as follows: an Environmental Impact Assessment (EIA) is the entire process by which decisions are reached as to whether or not a project is environmentally acceptable. The Environmental Statement (ES) is the documentation submitted by the developer in relation to his application for planning permission; the required content of an ES is set out in Schedule 4 of the Regulations, including measures to mitigate or offset adverse impacts.

9.2 The Environmental Impact Assessment (England and Wales) Regulations 1999

The Regulations distinguish three categories of development project: those in Schedule 1, those in Schedule 2 generally and those specifically in paragraph 13 of Schedule 2.

Those in Schedule 1 always require an ES to accompany the application for planning permission. The list comprises what may be described as traditional 'bad neighbour' projects, such as oil refineries, nuclear power stations, iron and steel smelters, asbestos factories, chemical processing plants, long-distance railways and airports, motorways and express roads and other major roads (more than 10 kilometres long), new inland waterways, ports and trading piers, waste incinerators, ground water extraction, gas, oil, chemical and water pipelines, sewage treatment plants above a specified capacity, dams, intensive poultry or pig farms above a certain size, pulp and paper plants, quarries and opencast mines and petrol and chemical stores above a certain capacity.

These types of development always require an ES, and planning permission for them will not be granted unless they have been subject to a full EIA of which the applicant's ES forms part.

Schedule 2 lists 12 kinds of project, including developments relating to agriculture, the extractive industry, the energy, chemical and mineral industries, metal processing, food and rubber industries, textile, leather and paper industries, infrastructure and tourism and leisure projects. Schedule 2 is designed to include smaller or lower-scale versions. These projects are generally less environmentally damaging or are of smaller scale. For these projects, an ES may or may not be required depending on whether it meets the criteria set out in terms of thresholds and its proximity to sensitive areas.

The third category is set out in paragraph 13 of Schedule 2 and comprises any development involving a change to or extension of a Schedule 1 project, or to a Schedule 2 project (whether or not the original project was itself subject to EIA), where that extension or change would bring the base scheme within Schedule 1 or 2.

9.3 Assessment procedure

When it is clear that the project falls within Schedule 1, or meets the thresholds/criteria for a Schedule 2 project and is to be located in a sensitive area, then an ES must be provided with the application. The LPA and the SSCLG can insist on an ES being submitted for such projects and can request further environmental material if they consider the ES is inadequate.

For Schedule 2 projects it is often unclear whether an ES is required. The developer may request a 'screening opinion' by the LPA to decide the matter. Some proposed developments within Schedule 2 could be carried out as permitted development; but if the LPA issues a screening opinion that an EIA is needed, then permitted development rights are withdrawn and a formal planning application, supported by an ES, must be made.

The developer may appeal against a positive screening opinion to the SSCLG, who, after considering the available material, will issue a screening direction, either upholding or dismissing the opinion of the LPA.

If the project does require an EIA, what should the developer's ES contain? For larger schemes it is likely that the developer will already have instructed environmental consultants to advise, and to prepare the initial submission of material where a screening opinion has been sought. However, the Regulations helpfully allow the developer to request a formal statement from the LPA on what the ES should contain. That is called a scoping opinion, and as with the screening opinion, an appeal can be made to the SSCLG, who can issue a scoping direction.

Every planning application that falls within the Regulations is called an 'EIA application'. The LPA has up to 16 weeks to determine such an application. That is largely due to the need to assess the environmental implications of the scheme, and to determine whether the ES addresses them all appropriately. In addition, wider consultation on the scheme is necessary, and any body that is believed to hold environmental information relevant to the environmental effects of the project may be requested (by either the developer or the LPA) to release that information.

Note that an ES is a publicly available document, so should not therefore contain information which the developer wishes to keep confidential.

9.4 Other types of scheme

There are types of development which either do not require planning permission or can be permitted under powers other than the TCPA 1990. Examples include: afforestation schemes, land drainage, railways and tramways, harbours and highways. These may require separate environmental assessment, and the Regulations relating to such projects should be studied carefully. In particular, some highway schemes that do not require an EIA for planning purposes (i.e. are not Schedule 2 projects) may require an environmental assessment under specific regulations.

10 PROTECTING HERITAGE

10.1 Introduction

Through various pieces of legislation, statutory protection exists for a wide variety of buildings and structures, ranging from archaeological sites, ancient monuments, historic buildings and gardens, and historic areas of cities, towns and villages.

10.2 Archaeology and ancient monuments

The principal legislation governing archaeology and ancient monuments is contained within the Ancient Monuments and Archaeological Areas Act 1979 ('AMAAA 1979'). Government advice on the subject is given in PPG16 – Archaeology and Planning. Nationally important sites are scheduled and are described as a 'scheduled monument'. In these cases, the consent of the SSCLG is required before any works are carried out which would affect the monument. However, government policy is that irrespective of whether remains are 'scheduled' or not, there is a presumption in favour of their physical preservation, and the preservation of their settings, when threatened by development.

The AMAAA 1979 also provides for the designation of 'Areas of Archaeological Importance' (AAIs). In such locations, developers are required to give six weeks' notice to the relevant LPA of any proposals to disturb the ground. The relevant authority then has the power to excavate the site for up to four and a half months before development may proceed – i.e. there may be a delay of up to 6 months.

Local Planning Authorities have a responsibility to include policies for archaeology in their development plans. These usually include policies for designating areas considered likely to be of archaeological potential, and for the protection of sites from the adverse effects of development. Where areas have been defined as likely to have archaeological potential, it is now common practice for LPAs to require an archaeological evaluation to be carried out prior to submission of development proposals which involve excavation.

In some case, it is not practically possible to undertake a physical archaeological investigation at the time of submission of a planning application. In these circumstances, the LPA (or its archaeological adviser) may agree to a 'desktop study' by an experienced archaeologist at the planning application stage. If this study indicates that the site has real potential for archaeological remains, which are likely to be disturbed or uncovered by the development, then a condition will normally be imposed preventing the development from proceeding until a full field evaluation has been carried out to confirm the potential or otherwise.

English Heritage is the principal consultee in respect of applications affecting sites or areas of archaeological interest. Developers may seek archaeological advice from any one of a number of archaeological consultants and, in some areas, County museums offer an archaeological consultancy service, such as the Museum of London.

In the event that archaeological remains are discovered, the consequences will be dependent on the quality and importance of the find. If the find is not significant, often all that is necessary is for an archaeologist to carry out a detailed survey and record of the find. Finds of more significance might lead to a requirement for preservation in situ, and in some cases, the scheduling of the remains as an ancient monument.

Occasionally, remains are discovered during the course of development. If the remains are of significance, the SSCLG has the power to schedule the remains. This means that development will at the very least be delayed until Scheduled Monument Consent is granted. At worst, it could lead to the revocation of the planning permission, in which case, there is provision for compensation.

10.3 Listed buildings

The principal legislation governing listed buildings and conservation areas is the Planning (Listed Buildings and Conservation Areas) Act 1990 ('P(LBCA)A Act 1990'). Government policy guidance on the subject is currently given in PPG15 – Planning and the Historic Environment.

The term building is broadly defined; Jodrell Bank telescope is listed which demonstrates the scope for listing.

The expression 'listed' derives from the fact that a list of Buildings of Special Architectural or Historic Interest is maintained by the Secretary of State for Culture, Media and Sport (SSCMS). Once a building is listed, any development – inside or out – requires listed building consent.

The building may be classified either as Grade I (of exceptional interest and importance to the nation's heritage) or Grade II (which constitute the majority of listed buildings). A Grade II* listing is also kept to identify the most important Grade II buildings. The grading system is important only in terms of the difficulty which a developer will have in obtaining consent or in obtaining a grant for work on the building.

The main criteria for listing are architectural and historic interest, including associations with nationally important figures or events. Listing may be applied to groups of building, such a squares, terraces etc.

The listing process

Anyone may request the SSCMS to consider listing any building. More commonly though, it is local planning authorities and English Heritage who request listings following surveys of their areas, or special interest groups, such as the Georgian Group, or the Victorian Society, for example.

Although listing normally involves consultation, there is no obligation on the SSCMS to do so. On occasion it may be believed that a building is in urgent need of protection and in such a case, the SSCMS may 'spot list'. Alternatively, by section 3 of the P(LBCA)A 1990 LPAs have the power to serve such notices on buildings considered to be of special architectural or historic interest which are in danger of demolition or unsatisfactory alteration and which provide a six month window in which the SSCMS must decided whether or not to list. An important factor of this particular process is that if the decision is taken not to list the building, the LPA may be liable to pay compensation to the building owner for any loss or damage caused by service of the notice. There are no compensation provisions in respect of the spot listing process.

There is no right of appeal against listing, but it is open to owners or other interested parties to make a case to the SSCMS that a building should not be listed. The decision of the SSCMS on such a request is final and there is no right of appeal against this decision.

If owners are concerned about the risk to a development of their building being listed, they may make an application under section 6 of the P(LBCA)A 1990 to the SCMS for a 'Certificate of Immunity' to avoid the expense of making applications which will falter because of subsequent listing. The certificate prevents listing for 5 years.

The protection

Section 7 of the P(LBCA)A 1990 provides that no 'no person shall execute or cause to be executed any works for the demolition of a listed building or for its alteration or extension in any manner which would affect its character as a building of special architectural or historic interest, unless the works are authorised'. Section 9 provides that a contravention is a criminal offence. A defence requires proof that: (a) the works were urgently necessary, (b) that no other reasonable alternative was available, (c) that he works were the minimum required and (d) that notice was given in writing to the LPA as soon as reasonably practicable.

Note, however, that whilst many of the listing buildings are churches, many of the provisions of the statute do not apply to them.

Applications for listed building consent

When considering work to a listed building a number of factors should be clearly in mind:

(1) if a building is listed, it is listed in its entirety, including everything within its curtilage
(2) any work on the building (whether or not that work would fall within the scope of development under the TCPA 1990 regime) which affects its character requires consent
(3) work to the building which also constitutes development requires planning permission as well as listed building consent.

Applications for listed building consent are submitted to the LPA for the area in which the building is situated. The procedure is set out in s. 10 P(LBCA)A 1990 and the Planning (Listed Building and Conservation Areas) Regulations 1990. The process is not dissimilar to an application for planning permission. It includes a requirement for a design and access statement.

The grant of consent

There is, obviously, a basic policy presumption in favour of preservation of the building, and all applications must be fully justified against strict criteria set out in PPG15. In summary this means: the presumption becomes stronger the more important the building; the facets of the building which justify its listing are most strongly to be retained. But consent will be granted if the criteria are established; indeed consent to demolish listed buildings is sometimes granted.

Conditions may be made on listed building consent and the LPA must give short reasons.

Although outline consent is not available, the LPA may grant consent subject to a condition reserving to itself a right of approval of subsequent details to be supplied.

Appeals

An appeal process is available which closely mirrors the section 78 process.

Enforcement

As well as prosecuting for contravention of the regime, LPAs may under section 38 P(LBCA)A 1990 issue a 'listed building enforcement notice'. There is generally no need for a stop notice because an offence is already by that stage being committed.

The notice will specify what is required, including restoring a building to its former state. A notice may be served at any time, even after the sale of the building to a new owner; in that case it will be the new owner who will be required to comply.

Repairs notices and compulsory acquisition

Under sections 54–55 of the P(LBCA)A 1990, LPAs have power to carry out urgent works of repair to unoccupied listed buildings, after giving notice to owners, and to recover their costs.

Alternatively, in the case of occupied buildings or non-urgent works, they can serve a 'repairs notice' on the owner in accordance with s. 48 of the P(LBCA)A 1990. In the event that the notice is not complied with, the LPA may then begin compulsory purchase proceedings.

10.4 Conservation areas

The principle of a conservation area designation is that not just isolated building but the character of the entire area is to be protected. The legislation covering conservation areas is also the Town and Country Planning (Listed Buildings and Conservation Areas) Act 1990. Likewise, government policy advice for conservation areas is also found in PPG15 – Planning and the Historic Environment.

Section 69 of the P(LBC)A 1990 imposes a duty on LPAs to designate areas of special architectural or historic interest, the character or appearance of which it is desirable to preserve or enhance, as conservation areas.

Conservation area controls

One of the main effects of conservation area legislation is to establish control over the demolition of unlisted buildings in designated conservation areas. The legislation establishes the requirement to obtain conservation area consent for the demolition of any building (other than a listed building) in a conservation area. Government policy (in PPG15) then takes this further. Although the intention of conservation areas is primarily to protect the character and appearance of areas rather than individual buildings, unlisted buildings which make a positive contribution are subject to a presumption in favour of retention. Furthermore, PPG15 indicates that proposals to demolish such buildings should be considered against the same broad criteria as proposals to demolish listed buildings.

The inference of this is that in conservation areas, all buildings other than those few which detract from the area's quality, or at least make no contribution to its character, are to be treated as though they were listed buildings in the event of demolition being proposed.

This policy statement has given rise to a degree of controversy and debate in planning circles, but has largely been supported by LPAs, many of whom contain conservation policies in their development plans which strengthen and reinforce the Government line.

Conservation area controls do not extend to alterations and additions to buildings, nor to internal alterations. To this extent, they fall short of applying the equivalent of listed building controls to all buildings in conservation areas. Where, however, an alteration proposed to a building is so extensive that it would result in the demolition of a substantial part of it, conservation area consent may be required.

Designation of conservation areas

Proposals to designate conservation areas are subject to public consultation and local publicity, but there is no legal obligation to notify owners of proposals for designation. Nor is there any right of appeal against designation.

Section 72 of the P(LBC)A 1990 imposes a duty upon Local Planning Authorities to pay special attention to the desirability of preserving or enhancing the character or appearance of conservation areas. This requirement is to be applied in the exercise of all the Local Planning Authorities' planning functions in its area.

Effect of designation on permitted development rights

Some permitted development rights are either removed or altered by conservation area status. Examples are stone-cladding of dwellings, insertion of dormer windows into roof slopes and erection of satellite dishes. Also, the size of automatically permitted extensions to dwellings and industrial buildings is reduced.

Other permitted development rights in conservation areas may be removed or reduced by the LPA through the use of directions under Article 4 of the GPDO 1995, subject to approval by the SSCLG.

Trees in conservation areas

All trees in conservation areas (subject to certain specified exemptions) are subject to a requirement to give six weeks' notice to the LPA prior to being cut down, lopped or topped. This is because trees are often considered to be important features in the townscape, and the notice period gives the LPA an opportunity to consider serving a Tree Preservation Order. Penalties for failure to comply are similar to those for tree preservation order contraventions, namely a fine or imprisonment.

Application procedures

All applications for conservation area consent are made to the relevant LPA, on the Authority's prescribed form. Applications for conservation area consents would rarely be entertained unless accompanied by a planning application for a replacement building. Outline planning applications for replacement buildings are unlikely to be accepted, as a detailed proposal is usually essential in order for the LPA to assess whether the proposal will result in the enhancement or preservation of the character or appearance of the area.

The procedure is similar to that for a listed building consent application, with the exception that there are no statutory obligations for notification of the applications to central government agencies. Many LPAs, however, have established conservation area advisory committees, whose views and advice are sought on applications in conservation areas.

Rights of appeal to the SSCLG exist in respect of non-determination, refusal, or the imposition of unreasonable conditions, adopting procedures almost identical to those for planning and listed building consent applications.

11 TREES AND HEDGES

Construction frequently involves cutting down trees or hedgerows. Due to constraints of space, this will be dealt with only in the briefest outline.

11.1 Trees

Cutting down trees does not appear to be within the definition of development and hence not subject to development control. However, there are two forms of protection:

(1) by s. 198 of the TCPA 1990 the LPA may make a tree preservation order which specifies the trees affected
(2) trees in a conservation area are protected.

The term tree is not defined and there has been some debate as to what is and is not caught by the definition. Lord Denning once remarked that a tree ought to be something over seven or eight inches in diameter, but other judges have said that the term should bear its natural meaning and judged on a case by case basis.

It is a criminal offence to destroy (or to lop it so that it is likely to be destroyed) a tree which enjoys the protection of a preservation order. The offence is one of strict liability; it is important therefore to check that a tree is not protected before destroying it.

In September 2008 the Government published updated guidance (available on the DCLG website) on tree preservation orders and tree protection within the existing legal framework.

11.2 Hedgerows

Some hedgerows are also protected. The primary legislation is to be found in s. 97 of the Environmental Protection Act 1995 and the Hedgerows Regulations 1997 came into force in June 1997. The scope of the protection extends to hedgerows 'growing in or adjacent to any common land, protected land or land used for agriculture, forestry or the breeding or keeping of horses, ponies and donkey, if the hedgerow has a continuous length of 20 m or more or meets another hedgerow at each end.' Before removing a protected hedgerow, a person must serve a 'hedgerow removal notice' on the LPA. The LPA will issue a 'hedgerow retention notice' if it is satisfied that the hedgerow is an important hedgerow.

Contravention of a number of the regulations constitute criminal offences.

Acknowledgement

The author gratefully acknowledges the use of some of the text prepared by the previous authors Richard Sherlock and Keith Hills. All responsibility remains with the author.

CHAPTER 1.2

Financing the project

John Scriven and Mark O'Neill
Allen & Overy LLP

1 TYPES OF PROJECT FINANCE

1.1 Introduction

A large proportion of major projects rely on external financing to fund the construction of the works. The type of financing can vary: it may be bank lending or a project bond issue arranged on similar terms. Financing can also be provided to a developer of commercial property by an investing institution entering into a development agreement under which it funds the development and would usually share with the developer the commercial risks and rewards of the project. In limited recourse project financings, the security of lenders for the repayment of the debt is dependent on the project revenues which are available from the time of completion of construction. On the other hand, in property financings, the sponsors of the project will often look to the sale of the assets to repay the loans and there may be substantial security in the value of the assets at any given stage of completion.

1.2 BOT and PFI schemes

A build, operate and transfer (BOT) scheme is a typical form of project financing which is used for projects where limited recourse financing is provided and the economic viability of the project depends on the revenue stream available from the completion of the project. There are numerous names and acronyms for this type of scheme, but the basic structure is similar. BOT schemes are used for a variety of projects including oil refineries, power and energy facilities, roads, bridges and water treatment plants and, in the UK and some other European countries, prisons, hospitals and schools.

In a typical BOT project, a government entity enters into a project or concession agreement with a special purpose project company under which the project company has the right to build and operate a facility, or provide services to the public sector, usually for a fixed period of time. The project company raises equity share capital and borrows from lenders in order to finance the construction of the facility. The intention is that the revenues which the company receives from operating the facility are sufficient to meet both interest and principal due with respect to the debt incurred by the project company in designing and building the facility, to cover its working capital and operation and maintenance costs and to provide a return for its equity investors. At the end of the concession period the facility is usually, but not necessarily, transferred back to the government entity.

Crucial to the viability of the project is the revenue stream generated by the commercial operation of the facility once it is built. Where the project company is supplying a service such as a road, hospital, schools or water treatment services to a government entity under a project agreement (as in projects under the UK Private Finance Initiative (PFI)), the offtake and payment arrangements will be contained within the main project agreement between the project company and the government entity. However, in some projects, such as electricity projects, there may also be separate offtake agreements with other entities which may be private or government entities. In other projects, for instance, an LNG (liquified natural gas) project, there may be a long-term offtake agreement with the commercial purchaser or, as in the refinery sector, there may be no long-term agreements but a reliance on the 'spot' market. Finally, in some projects the project company generates its revenue stream by charging members of the public a tariff, for instance for the use of a road or bridge or for water services, on the basis that the tariffs are regulated by a concession agreement or a legal regulatory framework. Whatever the nature of the offtake arrangements, the overriding purpose of the construction arrangements will be to construct a facility which, under the relevant project agreement, offtake agreements or tariff regime, will generate the necessary income to cover operational costs, repay the lenders and provide a return to the sponsors.

The project agreement is likely to contain detailed provisions in relation to the design and construction standards and the timing of the completion. In some projects the government may give the project company a relatively free hand in relation to design and construction, but in others the government may regard the concession agreement as being similar in some ways to a construction contract and will seek to include very detailed controls in relation to design and construction standards. Detailed government requirements will involve increased risks for the project company and its lenders will seek to ensure that these risks are passed on from the project company to the contractor. In UK PFI project agreements, the construction provisions resemble those in a design and build contract with design criteria and other requirements in an Authority Requirements document and detailed design in a Project Company Proposals document for which the project company takes responsibility. In any event, the project agreement is likely to include a requirement that the construction be completed by a specified date with a termination right on the part of the government entity for prolonged delay. Where the services are being provided to a government entity, there may also be liquidated damages for delay payable to that government entity. The way in which the obligations of the project company under the concession agreement are passed down to the contractor is discussed in Section 3.5, in *Back-to-back construction contracts,* below. (Further discussion of BOT and PFI schemes is included in Chapter 1.4.)

1.3 Property development

Having identified a site, a developer sponsoring a commercial property development project may arrange that the project company enter into an agreement or agreements for lease with one or more long-term tenants. This is known as pre-letting. The agreements for lease will specify the development obligations of the project company in terms of the specification of the building and timing of completion and will remove the letting risk so long as completion is achieved by the agreed longstop date and other obligations of the developer to the tenant are satisfied. Alternatively, the developer may build on a more speculative basis and will be responsible for letting the project after the financial close of the project. The letting risk will need to be accepted by the funder, whether this is a bank or an institutional investor which will eventually own the property. A bank in this situation will invariably seek the professional advice of valuers and letting agents as to the level of letting risk it is taking. Whether the development is fully pre-let, partially pre-let or entirely speculative, a lender funding the development will obtain a valuation of the development on a completed basis with a view to ensuring that it is comfortable with the anticipated level of bank debt as against the completed value.

2 RANGE OF FINANCING OPTIONS

2.1 Equity and mezzanine funding

A proportion of the funding for any project is normally provided by the equity sponsors or investors in the project. The level of this funding, which would typically range from 10–15% (but higher for property developments), will depend on the nature of the project and its associated risks and will usually be determined by the level of senior funding that is available. Part or all of this funding will take the form of equity share capital which confers on the holders rights of control in relation to the project company. In addition, some of the funds may be provided by the sponsors or other investors in the form of subordinated loans (often referred to as sub-debt on 'mezzanine' financing). The mezzanine financing normally carries a relatively high rate of interest and may be treated for tax purposes in some jurisdictions as equity share capital. The mezzanine financing will, in any event, be 'subordinated', that is, will rank behind the senior lenders in relation to payment of interest and principal and on a winding-up. The finance may not be required until the end of the construction period but would be secured by a letter of credit given to the project company at financial close.

2.2 Institutional funding for property development

The equity sponsor in a property development project is usually referred to as a developer. A developer, as the word implies, seeks to apply its skill in identifying suitable development sites and letting opportunities and ultimately selling the completed developments in the market. The developer is likely to require funding for the acquisition of the site and the construction of the development. Some developers may have the option of bank funding, but this funding may have limitations. The loan to value ratio required by the bank may mean that the developer has to provide substantial equity or subordinated loans itself in order to obtain the bank funding. Even where this is possible, a developer will need to find an ultimate purchaser of the property to repay the bank loan and realize the property's investment value. An institutional investor may be an alternative to bank funding. A development funding/sale arrangement, or forward funding arrangement, between an institutional investor and a developer, provides the developer with funding and the institutional investor with a long-term investment. The institutional investor is likely to acquire the land but two types of development arrangement are possible, one where the developer enters into the various contracts with the construction parties, and the other where the institutional investor enters into those contracts itself as principal and the developer acts as a project manager. These arrangements are discussed in more detail in Section 4 below.

2.3 Bank finance

Particularly in relation to BOT type schemes, bank finance remains the most common type of financing. Bank financing is available for both large and small projects, the smaller loan facilities being provided by a single bank and larger ones being provided by a syndicate of banks, with one or more banks acting as arrangers and leaders of the syndicate. The arranger may also underwrite the loan by committing to provide all the finance required for financial close, while aiming to sell a portion of the loan to other banks by syndicating the transaction following financial close. Since the credit crunch in July 2007, banks have been reluctant to underwrite finance and syndicate following financial close and so, where a number of banks are required, lead arrangers will endeavour to organise a 'club' of banks to take up loans on financial close.

In PFI projects there are likely to be an increasing number of funding competitions. In these cases the consortia bidding for a project do not include financing in their bids but the funders are selected following the appointment of the preferred bidder under a process monitored by the government authority. Legal and technical advisers appointed by the authority to act for funders will report on the project documentation and prepare funding terms. Prospective funders will bid competitively on the finance terms, thus enabling the authority to obtain the most advantageous finance (which will be reflected in the authority payments under the project agreement) available at the relevant time.

2.4 Bond finance

Bonds are transferable securities issued to a number of investors who would typically hold a portfolio of investment assets. The interest rate on the bonds will often be priced at a margin over the yield of government securities for a similar term and this can result in a more attractive rate of interest (which may be index linked) than bank financing. However, the commercial and legal arrangements for a bond issue are more complex than for a bank loan and a bond issue will therefore be appropriate only for larger projects. The market for project bonds developed until 2007 and most of the larger UK PFI hospital and accommodation projects have been financed by bond issues. Since the credit crunch the capacity of the monoline guarantors which guarantee bond issues (see Section 6.1 below), the perception of their creditworthiness and the expenses involved have limited the availability of monocline guarantees for bond issues. To date there have been very few 'unwrapped' bond issues (i.e. not guaranteed).

3 THE FUNDERS' REQUIREMENTS

3.1 Introduction

In their risk analysis of the project documents, the lenders or other funders will seek to ensure that each risk has been clearly accepted by one of the other parties involved in the project. They will expect the risks to be borne by the project company to be minimized by passing risks to others. This might involve increased costs, for example, of insurance or a higher construction price than might otherwise be the case and which the project company and the sponsors may consider to be uneconomic. Where a risk is to be borne by another party, such as the construction contractor, the funders will want to be satisfied that the party concerned has resources to bear the additional costs which could arise if that risk is realized.

3.2 The project company

The project company is at the centre of the project and, in very general terms, will bear all the risks associated with the project which cannot be covered by insurance or passed on to the other parties in the project under the terms of the various project contracts.

Most projects financed by lending are financed on a limited recourse basis. This means that the lenders' recourse is limited to the project company and its assets. In other words, lenders will not be able to claim repayment of their loans from the sponsors (who will normally be the shareholders of the project company). A risk borne by the project company is therefore, to some extent at least, a risk borne by the lenders. However, the risk borne by the lenders will be reduced to the extent that the shareholders inject equity or subordinated loans into the project company and by any direct guarantees which they give to the lenders.

Guarantees by shareholders in relation to particular risks or undertakings to inject further funds into the project company in specified circumstances, often referred to as 'sponsor support', are unusual in the projects market but reasonably common in the property development market. In the projects market they are normally only given in relation to particular risks and circumstances, such as the completion risk. In the property development market they can cover completion but also overruns and interest. For example, one or more of the shareholders may agree to additional equity or subordinated loans, up to a defined limit, equal to the amount of any cost overruns borne by the project company in achieving completion. Whether or not lenders require this type of sponsor support will depend on the current financing market and on the lenders' assessment of the risks taken by the project during its various stages.

3.3 Security, step-in rights, direct agreements and collateral warranties

A key issue for lenders will be the nature of the security given by the project company. Where a project company defaults on its repayment obligations, the lenders will wish to be able to take over the project and dispose of it to a third party. This will involve having appropriate security interests in all the assets and contracts of a project company necessary to carry out the project, and also usually over the shares of the project company. In the UK, the lenders will be able to take a fixed and floating charge over the shares in, and the assets and undertaking of, the project company. A floating charge will, for a number of larger projects within specified categories, entitle them to appoint an administrative receiver of the company and block an appointment of an administrator. Whether the lenders will have an entitlement to appoint an administrative receiver and block the appointment of an administrator will depend, among other things, on the nature of the project. Property developments do not normally benefit from these arrangements.

Where the security of the lenders is dependent on the project revenues available from completion, the lenders will seek to ensure that, when they enforce their security, they can maintain the integrity of the contract structure so that the project is completed and can produce the revenue necessary for the repayment of the lenders' debt. Direct agreements conferring step-in rights are an important method of ensuring that this is achieved. The step-in rights permit the lenders to take over the contract in two circumstances. The first is where the contractor would otherwise have been entitled to terminate the contract and the second is where there is an event of default under the loan agreements which entitles the lenders to enforce their security.

In the case of a termination right, the contractor will be required to give a period of notice before exercising that right, allowing the lenders the opportunity to step into the contract. Where the step-in right is contained in a collateral warranty given for a property transaction, lenders will normally be required to assume all the obligations of the project company, past, present and future; this will not necessarily be the case in relation to a project financing. Collateral warranties will usually provide for a permanent novation of the liabilities to a bank. A direct agreement in a project finance transaction will do this, but will also allow for the possibility of a temporary step-in by a company controlled by the lenders as an additional obligor, with (subject to insolvency law generally) a permanent novation to a third party at a later stage. The notice periods given by contractors to the lenders in collateral warranties tend to be fairly short (typically 21 days) but those in project financing direct agreements can extend for much longer periods.

The step-in and novation arrangements in relation to a collateral warranty will be much less complex than those in a direct agreement in project financing. However, collateral warranties in a property development project will also contain duties of care and obligations in favour of lenders in relation to the performance of the underlying contract as well as other provisions, for instance, in relation to a copyright licence. These provisions will allow lenders to assign the benefit of a collateral warranty to a purchaser of the property following an insolvency. This may be particularly relevant where the relevant contracting parties are under an obligation to provide warranties to purchasers and tenants but do not do so because they have outstanding claims against the project company. The extent to which the lenders can assign the warranties will therefore be an important issue both for lenders and the contracting parties.

It should, however, be borne in mind that where the insolvency occurs before the completion of construction and the contractor is not permitted to complete the work, the duty of care or direct obligation on the part of the construction contractor in favour of the lenders may be of limited value. The same considerations may not apply to a duty of care given by the consultants whose obligations are not principally to supply a completed project but to provide advice over a period of time.

3.4 The funders' technical adviser

The funders will usually engage a technical adviser to check the technical content of the project contracts and to advise generally on commercial and technical issues in relation to the project. This may be an in-house adviser employed by the lending bank or an institutional investor or may be an external consultant. In some project financings (for instance, energy financings), where the project company employs a separate technical adviser in addition to the consultants providing services in relation to the project, this technical adviser may report to the funders separately, usually after it has completed its work for the project company. In property financings the funders will normally appoint a project monitor to overview the development and attend site meetings. The technical advisers will often have a role after financial close monitoring compliance with the project undertakings by the project company in the financing documentation (see Section 5.3 below).

3.5 Construction contract issues

General

Like the project company, the funders will want to minimize the risks to them arising from the three principal construction issues of money, time and quality. In relation to money and time, they will therefore focus on the risks assumed by the project company, and in relation to quality they will wish to ensure that the project fulfils its commercial requirements. These requirements may be contained in a concession or offtake agreement or, in the case of a property development, in an agreement for lease.

Contract structures allocate the risk between the project company and the construction contractor in ways which define the scope of responsibility for performance and the bearing of additional costs should the unexpected occur. The more control the project company has over the construction process, the more risk it will assume, and vice versa. In a project financing, it is likely that the contract structure will be some kind of design and build contract, but the degree of the project company's control over design, and its responsibility for it, design will vary from project to project.

In commercial property development, the structure may be a traditional JCT contract under which the employer supplies design to the contractor or a design and build contract, although in this case the nature of the design obligations in relation to design are likely to be less absolute than in a project financing. Construction management or management contracting structures may also be used in commercial property development and exceptionally in project financings. Under these structures the project company bears the risk of non-performance of the individual sub-contractors (called 'trade' or 'works' contractors) and the risk of the coordination of design and of construction. These structures will therefore be less attractive to funders than traditional or design and build structures but the advantages to the project company in terms of flexibility in the timing of design and construction in using these structures may make it worthwhile for the sponsors to provide additional sponsor support to the lenders to cover the increased risks.

Where construction management or management contracting structures are used in project financings, for instance power projects, the sponsors will often be required to enter into documentation designed to achieve a 'virtual' turnkey under which the sponsors undertake to put the project company in the same position it would have been had there been a turnkey contract. Virtual turnkey structures may also be used where a turnkey contract is split for tax reasons, but in this case the relevant undertakings are given by one or more of the contractors who will, therefore, seek to manage the risks involved.

For a more detailed discussion of different types of construction contracts, see Chapter 1.6.

Key issues in the construction contract

Key issues for the funders in the construction contract will include the following.

Design Responsibility for design will be a key issue in the choice of the contract structure discussed above. Even where there is a design and build contract there is likely to be some reliance by the contractor on information or concept design provided by the project company. The funders will wish to identify those design elements for which the project company is responsible under the construction contract and to examine the recourse which the project company has to third parties in respect of them. The responsibility of the project company for design may effectively be reduced to the extent the design requirements reflect requirements set out in a project agreement with a public authority.

Performance tests and completion In many project financings there will be performance or completion tests under the construction contract which will test the ability of the project to fulfil the performance criteria required for generating the income necessary to repay the loans or other funding. These will need to be appropriately defined and it is likely that the funders' technical adviser will have a role in certifying or reporting on the carrying out of these tests.

Defects liability The liability of the contractor for defects and the responsibility of the contractor for latent defects after the expiry of the defects liability period will be important to the funders. In particular, unless this is clearly agreed between the parties, they will want to avoid any implication that the final certificate is conclusive that the works have been performed in accordance with the contract, thereby excluding any claims for defects after its issue. Similarly, they are likely to resist an 'exclusive remedies' clause having the same effect.

Payment systems The funders will want to ensure that payments to the contractor are consistent with the value of work performed at any time. The payment system will need to be looked at together with the provisions for retention or retention bonds. The loan agreement or institutional development agreement may contain provisions requiring the satisfaction of the funders' technical adviser that the amounts are properly due. Alternatively, the funders may be content with a collateral warranty from the certifying consultant.

Time and money events The funders will want to reduce to a minimum the circumstances entitling the contractor to additional time for completion or additional payment under the contract. In relation to those risks retained by the project company, they will want to ensure that the project company has adequate funding to meet liabilities arising as a result of these risks. They will also want to ensure that the rights of the project company to liquidated damages are safeguarded in the case of a breach of contract or acts of 'prevention' by the project company.

Delay Where the contractor is responsible for delays, lenders will wish to ensure that the liquidated damages cover at least the debt service obligations of the project company which, but for the delay, would have been covered by the project's revenues. Institutional investors will similarly want their loss of investment return to be covered. Particularly where a project agreement could be terminated for prolonged delay in completion, the lenders may also expect there to be a right on the part of the project company to terminate the construction contract long before that time, allowing it to employ a replacement contractor to complete the works within the longstop time allowed under the project agreement. In property transactions, where an agreement for lease could be terminated for prolonged delay, the funders will commonly seek the right to step into the shoes of the project company, by perhaps appointing a receiver, with a view to taking control of the development to achieve the deadline set by the agreement for lease.

Back-to-back construction contracts In certain BOT projects where the scope of the project company obligations and its entitlement to payment for services provided are defined in a project agreement, such as a PFI transaction in the UK, the funders will wish to ensure that the obligations and liability of the project company in relation to the construction of the facility are passed down to the construction contractor on a 'back-to-back' basis. The obligations will include design responsibilities and the requirement to achieve completion by a specified date on the basis that the definition of completion and the determination as to whether it is achieved is the same under the construction contract as under the concession agreement. The entitlement to extensions of time for completion may be dependent upon time granted by the authority under the project agreement. However, entitlement to additional money cannot be dependent upon certification or payment, since these 'pay when paid' provisions will be ineffective under the provisions of the Housing Grants, Construction and Regeneration Act 1996 (the Act) (see *Midland Expressway* v. *Carillion Construction and others* [2005] 2963 TCC). Although the PFI project agreement may be excluded from the operation of the Act, the exclusion will not apply to the construction contract. There should be scope for the payment to be dependant upon the entitlement of the project company under the project agreement, provided the construction contractor can establish this independently of any determination under the project agreement.

Since the pay when paid provisions are ineffective under the Act, contractor parent company loans may be requested to cover any mismatch of funding resulting from a claim for money being paid to a contractor before the project company recovers from the government authority under the project agreement. This may be resisted by the contractor and may not be appropriate unless the contractor is also a sponsor.

The provisions of the contract in relation to a wide variety of provisions such as the scope of the construction obligations, indemnities, defects, subcontracting, changes and force majeure will reflect, usually on a word-for-word basis, those of the project agreement. It may be important that not only are the words the same but that their interpretation and the determination of issues are the same. This may entail consistent dispute mechanisms, including adjudication, in accordance with the provisions of the Act. To the extent this is not practicable or not permitted by the relevant authority, the contractor will seek provisions ensuring that the project company represents its position in any dispute in which it has an interest.

In some respects, however, those provisions of the construction contract which are equivalent to those in the project agreement may need to be more onerous than the concession agreement for instance to reflect project company risks inherent in the concession arrangements (e.g. life-cycle risks). Similarly, time extensions may not necessarily be back to back. This is because, although the government entity grants a time extension to the project company in certain circumstances, thus relieving the project company of any liability for delay damages payable to the government entity and termination for default, it will generally not cover the loss of revenue which would otherwise be covered by liquidated damages payable by the contractor. While in some cases these losses will be covered by business interruption insurance for insured risks, there may be categories of uninsured events where the contractor may be asked to share risks.

As mentioned above, where the concession grantor has the right to terminate the concession agreement for prolonged delay in completion of construction, the funders will wish the project company to have the right to terminate the construction contract long before that time so as to enable it to appoint a replacement contractor to complete the works before the longstop date arrives.

Bonds and guarantees The funders will not wish to take any credit risk in relation to the contractor, so will assess the nature and terms of any advance payment, performance, retention or other bonds or guarantees given by banks or other institutions on behalf of the contractor to support its obligations. Where the contractor is a subsidiary, funders will usually require a parent company guarantee. Funders will also wish to satisfy themselves as to the creditworthiness of all parties giving bonds and guarantees.

In international projects, there may be a requirement for an on-demand bond which would give the project company access to immediate funds on the default or insolvency of the contractor. In the UK, on-demand bonds may be required for energy projects, but would be unusual in PFI or property development projects. A proven default bond can only be enforced when the quantum of the claim, for instance, in relation to additional completion costs, has been agreed or determined under the disputes resolution provisions of the contract. The bond may therefore be enforceable following an adjudication award or the bond may expressly provide that it may be called 'on demand' following an adjudication award for the amount of the award. However, the prohibition in the Insolvency Act 1986 on proceedings against a company in administration without the leave of the court may prevent the decision of an adjudicator being made, and this can prevent, the payment obligation under a bond arising in these circumstances. To deal with this it will be necessary to have alternative mechanisms to ensure that liability under the bond arises, such as expert determination under the construction contract, adjudication under the bond or the bond could be on-demand upon the insolvency of the contract.

Limits on the liability of the contractor Funders will wish to analyse any limits on the liability of the contractor, for instance in relation to the type of loss recoverable – it is normal for contracts for process plants to exclude recovery of consequential loss – or any monetary limits on liability. This will be particularly relevant in the context of UK PFI where the project company may be exposed to losses resulting from the 'liquid market' retender provisions on a default by the project company under the project agreement with the public sector entity.

Consultants' agreements The funders and their advisers will wish to ensure that the duties of the consultants are adequate, particularly in relation to the definition of the services provided by each of them and the coordination and interface between them. They would expect there to be an appropriate degree of skill, care and diligence, defined by reference to the type of project, and that the consultants will be wholly responsible for the default of sub-consultants. They will also wish to ensure that the level of professional indemnity insurance is adequate and in line with market practice.

In property development projects, consultants giving collateral warranties will frequently seek to limit their liability to funders and others by use of mechanisms such as 'net contribution' clauses – which require the contribution made by other consultants to the relevant loss to be taken into account – and by taking into account set-offs and counterclaims that the consultant may have against the employer. These are standard requirements of the insurance market in relation to collateral warranties and 'net contribution clauses' may also be requested in relation to consultants' appointments.

4 INSTITUTIONAL FUNDING STRUCTURES

Institutions investing in property may enter into agreements with developers under which the developer is the principal party involved in making the arrangements for the construction of a development. The funds for construction would be provided by the institutional investor who will usually be the owner of the land during the development phase.

The developer may be the contracting party in employing consultants and entering into the construction contract. Alternatively, the developer may be the facilitator or manager of the contractual arrangements entered into by the institutional investor as principal directly with the contractor and consultants. Where the developer acts as principal, it has primary liability to the contractor, and its risk *vis-à-vis* the institutional investor may involve taking responsibility for some cost overruns. In this structure, the developer will seek reimbursement of direct expenditure (which may include the price of the site), together with a share in the profits as and when this is achieved. Where the developer is a manager on behalf of the institutional investor which enters into the contractual arrangements, the developer is likely to receive a fee on an ongoing basis but with a smaller profit share.

In either case, the developer's profit share will be calculated by reference to the value of the property when completed and let, which in turn will be calculated by reference to the yield. The multiple of the yield which results in the price will depend on the nature of the property. This will reflect the risks inherent in the market for that type of property at the time. Usually, the profit share of the developer will increase proportionately as the target return of the institutional investor is exceeded.

Even though the developer may be acting as principal in employing the contractor and consultants, the institutional investor will retain the ability closely to control the activities of the developer in the course of carrying out development through an extensive approval and monitoring regime. This will include approval of the forms of contract and selection of contractors. The developer will be responsible to the institutional investor for ensuring that the development is carried out in accordance with the relevant design plans and specifications. The institutional investor and its advisers will closely control the payment of development costs and will wish to ensure that they are all in accordance with the relevant contracts; there may also be arrangements for the institutional investor to make payments directly to the contractor and consultants.

Where a developer acts as principal, the institutional investor will require collateral warranties with the contractor and consultants containing step-in rights. These would be triggered under the development agreement between the institution and the developer in the event of default or insolvency of a developer. Unlike banks, an institutional investor may not be reticent in exercising step-in rights since it will often have, or can usually acquire, the expertise to carry out and complete the development following the termination of the development agreement.

5 BANK FINANCING

5.1 Term, interest rate, prepayment and drawdown

Interest will commonly be rolled up or capitalized during the construction phase, reflecting the fact that the property will not be revenue generating. The principal may be repaid in one lump sum or in instalments over the period of a loan. A lump sum repayment may be appropriate in the case of a property development where the principal is repaid on the sale of the property or a refinancing. The interest rate is usually a margin over base rate or LIBOR (the London Interbank Offered Rate), the size of the margin reflecting the market for that type of lending. LIBOR is effectively a floating rate basis for the payment of interest, so lenders will frequently require that the risk of changes in interest rate is hedged, perhaps with an interest rate swap or, alternatively, that a fixed interest rate is used. Whether interest is charged at a fixed rate or a floating rate is combined with a hedge, prepayments will, depending on interest rate movements, cause a cost to the project company reflecting the costs of termination of the funders' fixed rate arrangements or the hedge. While there will be fees payable to the bank for making the loan facilities available, there may also be fees on prepayments. These will be greater if the prepayments are made earlier in the term of the loan.

The loan will be drawn down over the period of construction and, as referred to above, the lenders are likely to require that drawdown can only be made to pay the costs of construction as and when these are incurred under the relevant agreements.

Lenders may also require the proceeds of drawings to be paid directly to contractors and consultants to ensure that the proceeds are used for the purposes for which they were drawn.

There will be conditions precedent to the first and subsequent drawdown. These will include, in relation to the initial drawdown, completion of all necessary documentation and receipt by the lenders of satisfactory reports in relation to the technical aspects of the project. Subsequent drawdowns will frequently require the provision of invoices etc. to verify costs and a confirmation from the lenders' project monitor or technical adviser that the payment is appropriate.

5.2 Financial covenants and accounts

There is likely to be an ongoing requirement for the project company to have income which is greater by a specified ratio than the requirements of debt service (the debt service cover ratio). The projected revenue of the project during the life of the loan will also need to be greater by a specified ratio than the total amounts to be repaid under the loan agreement (the loan life cover ratio). There may also be a requirement to maintain specific funds in reserve accounts to cover the inability of the project company to meet expenditure should the revenue be insufcient. These might include a debt service reserve for payment of amounts due under the loan agreement, a maintenance reserve for periodic maintenance, replacement and refurbishment, a capital expenditure

1.1 The planning system
1.2 Financing the project
1.3 Public sector projects
1.4 Public/private partnerships
1.5 Tender process
1.6 Construction contracts
1.7 Construction insurance

reserve where capital expenditure is forecast, tax reserves and other contingency reserves. In property development financings there may be a loan to value covenant. For these purposes, the value during the construction phase which will be calculated on the basis of an assumption as to completion of works and, possibly, lettings. This is commonly tested only at the start of the development on the assumption that the loan facility is fully drawn.

5.3 Project undertakings

The loan agreement is likely to contain a large number of detailed undertakings on the part of the project company in relation to the way in which the project is carried out. These undertakings typically include an obligation not to alter the project contracts without the consent of lenders, an obligation to enforce those contracts and also rights for the lenders' technical adviser to inspect the progress of the project, to be provided with a wide variety of information and to monitor progress payments and the state of completion of the project. More specifically, there is also likely to be a list of 'reserved discretions' where the project company is obliged to act in accordance with the instructions of lenders in relation to the exercise by it of specified rights provided for under the construction contract. These can include matters such as variations, the settlement of claims and the rights of suspension or termination available to the project company.

For the project company, it may be important whether the consent in relation to the various reserved discretions can be given by an agent bank on behalf of a syndicate of banks or whether a majority consent of the syndicate of banks is required, since the process of obtaining consents can be time consuming.

Breach of the undertakings is likely to give rise to an event of default which, after appropriate cure periods, will entitle the lenders to accelerate repayment, call a default and enforce a security and take over the project from the project company and its shareholders.

6 BOND FINANCING

6.1 Types of project bond issue

As mentioned in Section 1, *Bond finance,* above, financing by means of a bond issue is confined to large projects, particularly in the PFI sector, although since the 'credit crunch' in 2007 bond financings may be less viable. Although there are examples of bond issues in the property sector, they are not at all common. The costs of the additional arrangements required for a bond issue mean that it is unlikely to be economic where the project cost is significantly less than £100,000,000. However, since the interest rate applicable to bond financing is usually a margin over the relevant government securities for an equivalent term, the interest rate was for many years more competitive than bank financing. In the first years of project finance, bank financing tended to be for under 20 years, typically 15 years (although much shorter for property development financing), and long-term financing was more easily available at that time from bond issues to make the annual payments more economic. Longer term bank financing has in the past few years been available particularly in PFI transactions, although an effect of the 'credit crunch' may be to shorten the periods.

Most bond issues have been 'wrapped', that is, guaranteed by a 'monoline' insurer with the efect that the purchasers of the bonds rely largely on the credit risk of the insurer rather than the commercial viability of the project. The credit risk of the insurers, reflected in their credit rating by rating agencies, has come under increasing scrutiny since the 'credit crunch' of 2007 and a number of insurers have ceased to operate. The offering circular sent to prospective bond holders will contain not only extensive details in relation to the guarantor but also much of the information in relation to the project which would be required in the case of a bond issue which is not guaranteed (an 'unwrapped' bond issue). To date, there have been very few unwrapped project bond issues.

6.2 Offering circular and listing

Whether or not the bond issue is wrapped, a financial institution, called the arranger, will be required to issue an offering circular to prospective bondholders, although it is likely to disclaim responsibility in relation to the project details supplied to it. The bonds are likely to be listed on the London Stock Exchange or another international stock exchange and the offering circular issued to prospective bond holders will need to fulfil the applicable statutory and regulatory requirements as to its contents and manner of issue. The offering circular will need to contain full details of the terms and conditions of the bonds which will cover most of the terms included in a loan agreement.

6.3 Role of the guarantor, arranger and bond trustee

Where the issue is unwrapped, the institution issuing the offering circular will also underwrite the subscription for the bonds. In this case, the underwriting institution will also take the lead in negotiating the terms and conditions of the bonds and, together with its professional advisers, commenting on the project contracts. Where the issue is guaranteed, this role will be undertaken by the guarantor.

In addition to the financial institution issuing the information memorandum, which may be the underwriter or arranger and/or the guarantor, there will also be a requirement for a trustee to exercise rights on behalf of the bond holders and to hold the security rights on their behalf.

Where there is a guarantor, the collateral deed between the project company and the guarantor will address similar matters to those covered in a loan agreement, in addition to the terms of the bond conditions. The degree of control over the carrying out of the project exercised by a guarantor will therefore be greater than that exercised by a trustee on behalf of the bond holders in relation to an unwrapped bond and will be more similar to that in a loan agreement. In the case of an unwrapped bond, the arranger and underwriter will negotiate the terms and conditions of the bond, which will reflect the principal terms to be found in a credit agreement, but the ability on the part of the bond trustee to intervene in the carrying out of the project, for instance in relation to reserved discretions, will be somewhat less than that of a bank lender or the insurer of a wrapped bond.

6.4 Verification

The offering circular will need to be verified by the project company's directors, although where the issue is characterised as one of international securities under the Financial Services Act, the personal liability of the directors in relation to the contents of the offering circular may be reduced, with the project company being the party primarily liable.

6.5 Rating

The bond issue will need to be rated by a rating agency in order to be marketable and the rating agency will need to review the technical aspects of the project together with the contract documentation. The rating agency is likely to pay particular attention to credit risk issues; for instance, the credit risk in relation to the contractor and the bonds and guarantees given by third parties on its behalf as security for any claims against it. In the case of a wrapped bond issue, the rating of the bonds issued will reflect the credit risk of the guarantor. However there will also need to be a 'shadow' rating which assesses the project as if the bond issue were not guaranteed. The ability of the monocline to guarantee the project, and its guarantee fee, will be dependent on this 'shadow' rating.

6.6 Timing

The timetable for a bond issue will reflect the requirements of the additional parties referred to above. The project contracts and the terms and conditions of the bonds will need to be largely agreed before a preliminary information memorandum is issued to prospective bond holders. As mentioned above, the information memorandum will need to be carefully verified. There should be very few changes between this version and the final preliminary offering circular issued prior to the launch of the bonds. On the day of the launch of the bond issue, the bonds are priced by reference to an interest rate and/or a sale discount on the nominal value. Where the price of services under other project contracts reflects the pricing of the bonds, these contracts will need to be simultaneously entered into to reflect this pricing on the basis that they are conditional only upon financial close. Financial close will typically take place a week or more later, when the moneys are subscribed by the bond holders. A feature of a bond issue compared with a bank financing is that the total proceeds to the bond issue will be available on financial close and will be held by the project company in secured accounts or lent under guaranteed investment contracts (GICs) to be drawn down as and when required for construction. Compared with a bank financing, funding for expected variations will be more complicated and provision for funding variations will need to be specifically made at the outset for instance by the provision for variation bonds.

CHAPTER 1.3

Public sector projects

David Marks
CMS Cameron McKenna LLP

Adrian Smith
College of Estate Management, Reading

1 INTRODUCTION

This chapter explores the procurement of construction projects in the public sector since these are subject to a form of regulated procurement. Here the 'public' sector means work carried out wholly or partly with public funds and should not be confused with the activities of public limited companies (plcs), who by and large must only satisfy their own shareholders and are part of the 'private' sector. Public–private partnerships using a combination of public and private sector funds, such as those developed under the Private Finance Initiative (PFI) are discussed separately in Chapter 1.4.

For completeness, reference is also made in this chapter to procurement by utilities. Certain procurements by utilities are also regulated, depending on the activity performed by the procuring entity, and irrespective of whether the utility is state or privately owned.

This chapter will consider a range of issues:

- why should the approach to public sector projects be different? (Section 2)
- what constitutes the public sector for these purposes? (Section 3)
- the substantive procurement law rules, principally deriving from EC Directives (Section 4)
- some problem areas in the application of procurement law (Section 5).

2 WHY SHOULD PUBLIC SECTOR PROJECTS BE DIFFERENT?

In substance there should be no difference between public and private sector projects. The underlying principles of contract law are the same and so too are the client's motivations. The difference is that the public sector must be seen to be accountable to the taxpayer. This arises in a number of ways as detailed below.

The way in which projects and services are procured Public sector contracts must be seen to be awarded fairly and without discrimination. The award process must be both transparent and accountable.

The expenditure of the public funds involved Public accountability is of paramount importance. Taxpayers, in a democracy, are entitled to know that their money is being spent in accordance with approved policies and that adequate safeguards are in place to prevent the misappropriation of funds. The need for good audit control and the provision of a clear audit trail are therefore central themes in a project procurement strategy.

Maximizing value for money Value for money does not necessarily mean lowest price. General principles of good practice are supported by the Treasury and mean seeking the optimum combination of price and quality for each specific project or service. In addition the Local Government Act 1999 imposes a legal duty to achieve 'best value' on local government.

The public sector is therefore subject to a rigorous accountability discipline which is a proxy for the profit or self-interest motive of the private sector. A substantial body of legislation and regulation has developed to ensure that these objectives are met.

Those working with the public sector for the first time are frequently confused by (if not contemptuous of) the apparent bureaucracy involved as a result. However, it does need to be understood that the obligations imposed on the public sector involve employees and consultants in a different level of responsibility, transparency and accountability than is conventionally the case in the private sector. Failure to comply with the letter of the law may render individuals or the client body as a whole liable to actions at civil law, or to possible criminal prosecution. In the local government context, central government would have powers to step in.

Much of the legislation, particularly in relation to larger projects, has derived from the European Community's (EC) aim to achieve a common market in goods and services. Breaches of the law may result in the European Commission taking infringement action against the responsible member state. Breaches of EC procurement rules also create rights of action by interested parties in national courts. The EC rules are the foundation of most of the substantive law on procurement in the UK. A further gloss to this set of rules derives from the World Trade Organisation's Government Procurement Agreement (GPA).

3 WHAT CONSTITUTES THE PUBLIC SECTOR?

Outside the utility sectors, contracting authorities which are subject to regulated procurement are defined in the EC rules as:

> 'the State, regional or local authorities, bodies governed by public law, associations formed by one or several of such authorities or bodies governed by public law'.[1]

The entities in the UK affected by EC procedures on regulated procurement include a wide range of organizations including:

- central government
- local authorities (including police and fire authorities)
- utilities (many of which have now been privatized but most of which are still subject to a regulated procurement regime specific to certain utility activities)
- a range of entities, corporations and other bodies which are in effect controlled by the public sector.

These categories will be considered briefly in turn.

3.1 Central government

There is a persistent drive for government to become a 'best practice' client quite independently of the policy drivers behind the EC rules. This has given rise to a considerable volume of procurement guidance and administrative advice, generally from the Office of Government Commerce[2] but also echoed by the various spending ministries,[3] aimed at providing a modern framework to guide those involved in commissioning construction work and placing contracts. These documents consolidate and build on other literature such as the *Guide to the Appointment of Consultants and Contractors* (GACC). The construction industry has also been the subject of a recent study designed

[1] For example, Directive 2004/18/EC on the coordination of procedures for the award of public works contracts, public supply contracts and public service contracts OJ L134/114 30.04.2004 Article 1(9). The GPA is much narrower in scope, being confined to named central government agencies and sub-central government agencies.

[2] Documents comprising procurement guidance include the Achieving Excellence in Construction suite of procurement guides, for example, *Initiative in Action* (PG01), *Project Organisation – rules and responsibilities* (PG02) and *Procurement and Contract Strategies* (PG06). See website of Office of Government Commerce: www.ogc.gov.uk.

[3] For example, Department of Health – see website: www.dh.gov.uk/ProcurementAndProposals/Procurement/fs/en.

to identify ways of increasing competition. The industry was the first to be subject to analysis under the Kelly Programme. This resulted in a set of proposals for the strategic management of public sector procurement in the construction market (for example in relation to embedding early supplier engagement and sharing market intelligence).[4]

3.2 Local government

Local authorities, like other public bodies, are subject to the procurement rules. The Local Government Act 1972 requires local authorities to draw up standing orders relating to the making of contracts for the supply of goods and materials or the execution of works. The detail of these regulations and the thresholds above which they will apply is for the individual authority to decide.

The thresholds for the application of the EC procurement rules are quite high (as detailed in section 4.5 below), but it is usually appropriate for local authority standing orders to require competition at a lower threshold since the use of competitive and transparent procedures is essential for realising the local authorities' objectives.

One particular objective is the duty imposed on local authorities by the Local Government Act 1999 to secure 'best value' in carrying out their functions.[5] An authority must 'make arrangements to secure continuous improvement in the way in which its functions are exercised, having regard to a combination of economy, efficiency and effectiveness'. Best value requirements therefore apply across the whole range of a local authority's activities and competitive processes are a necessary tool for demonstrating compliance.

3.3 Utilities

Utilities in the water, energy and transport sectors can also be subject to regulated procurement obligations by virtue of the EC rules. This is the case irrespective of whether the utility is owned in the private or the public sector. For this purpose, utilities are defined not by reference to their ownership but to specific activities, and only procurements related to such activities are regulated.

The regulated procurement regime applicable to utilities is much more flexible than that applying to the general public sector. The rationale for regulating the procurement of utilities, irrespective of ownership, is that utilities perform functions in the general interest. They also do so under governmental or regulatory supervision through statutory or licensing regimes. The public hand is therefore much in evidence and might be in a position to influence expenditure policy.

Many of the utilities covered by this special regime used to be in public ownership. In the UK, many of these companies have been privatized and the sectors in which they operate are now subject to considerable competition. Where a previously regulated sector enters a truly competitive environment, the rationale for regulating procurement by participating entities is no longer present. These areas are progressively being taken outside the scope of the EC utilities procurement regime (for example, telecommunications activities which are now no longer subject to the EC utilities procurement rules). As a result of recent changes to the utilities rules there is now also a specific mechanism which allows for member states or individual companies to apply for particular sectors to be removed from the scope of the rules on the grounds that the market is sufficiently

[4] See 'First Kelly Market Proposals at www.ogc.gov.uk'
[5] The Local Government Act 1999 s. 3(1).

1.1 The planning system
1.2 Financing the project
1.3 Public sector projects
1.4 Public/private partnerships
1.5 Tender process
1.6 Construction contracts
1.7 Construction insurance

competitive. The position of utilities is referred to at times in this chapter for the sake of completeness.

3.4 Other bodies

A range of other bodies which are in effect controlled by the public sector will also be covered by government procurement policy or the EC procurement regime. Such activities will include, for example, many higher education establishments or cultural institutions. The detailed position will depend on whether the entity carries out a function in the general interest, not of a commercial nature, and whether it is primarily financed, or controlled, by the public sector.

A procurement compliance obligation can also be placed on certain purely private bodies where the public sector is subsidizing a project to the extent of more than half the project's value. The public sector funding body has an obligation to impose on the recipient a contractual obligation that the recipient will follow the EC procurement rules in procuring the project. By this contractual device, the procurement compliance obligation can be made to follow the public funds. This factor commonly arises in relation to Lottery-funded projects.

4 SUBSTANTIVE PROCUREMENT RULES

4.1 Introduction

This discussion of the substantive procurement rules is intended to provide the reader with an understanding of the broad framework of the rules. It is necessarily an overview of an increasingly complex subject.

This section will cover the following:

- the main legal sources
- the role of the EC
- EC directives
- scope: works, supplies or services and value thresholds
- special rules: concessions, subsidized contracts, design contests
- types of procedure
- notices and time limits
- prequalification and selection
- enforcement.

4.2 The main legal sources

The bulk of the substantive rules in the UK on regulated procurement derive from EC obligations and in particular from EC directives. The EC directives have been implemented by detailed national regulations in the form of statutory instruments. These rules do, however, coexist with a miscellany of domestic common law rules affecting procurement procedures. Such common law rules include the following:

- A tendering procedure can create an implied contract between contracting entity and bidders that the process will be run fairly. This rule applies both to public and private sector procedures.
- A public authority's actions can be challenged in the courts if it acts unreasonably when taking decisions, including decisions on the conduct of procurement procedures.
- A public authority can be responsible for a misfeasance in public office which is actionable by interested parties.

The common law rules can be particularly relevant in those situations where the EC-inspired rules do not apply.

However, it is the EC-inspired rules which have imposed some system on an otherwise disorderly patchwork of national law rules.

4.3 The role of the EC

A key objective of the EC Treaty is the facilitation of trade within the Community. Achievement of this objective required the creation of a single internal market in which the free movement of goods, persons, services and capital is ensured for all member state nationals. An associated objective was to combat national preference by opening up public sector procurement to all EC nationals.

A high priority was given to opening up public procurement because of the huge sums at issue. The European Commission estimates that EU public procurement markets are worth over €1500 billion, more than 16% of total EU Gross Domestic Product. In turn, public sector construction output has historically constituted a significant component of the total value of public sector procurement, and the economic significance of the construction industry ensured that it received considerable attention.

The EC's approach has been to establish a legal framework founded on the following key principles:

- non-discrimination on grounds of nationality; and
- transparency and fairness of process.

EC rules have therefore concentrated purely on the demand side of the market, by forcing purchasing authorities into a consistent procurement framework. The EC's policy is part of a market integration strategy and, while much of the EC procurement regime reflects the Treasury's concerns for best practice and value for money, this is not always the case, and there are a number of areas where there is a mismatch between EC and Treasury objectives. For example, post-tender negotiations with bidders are generally prohibited under the EC public sector rules for fear of unfairness between bidders, notwithstanding the possible value for money advantages of such negotiations to the purchaser.

4.4 EC directives

EC rules to regulate procurement issues have been introduced through EC legal instruments called 'directives'. These are highly flexible in terms of their implementation. Directives specify the objectives to be achieved and the time frame within which they must be brought into force, but allow individual member states considerable freedom to determine the precise form in which these objectives are imposed within their own legal system. The EC has therefore adopted directives to regulate a procurement by the general public sector and by utilities. Table 1 summarizes the current EC directives in the procurement area and the corresponding UK rules which came into force on 31 January 2006.

The texts for both the general public and utilities sectors have a number of common features to promote principles of non-discrimination and transparency, including:

- the reiteration of the basic principle in Article 12 of the EC Treaty prohibiting discrimination against other member state nationals
- a qualifying value threshold for contracts above which contracts are to be advertised by specific procedures

- a distinction between open, restricted, negotiated and competitive dialogue procedures
- the publication of tender notices in the *Official Journal of the European Union* in the prescribed form
- the promotion of EC as opposed to national standards
- minimum time limits for publication and response
- the publication of award notices
- selection on the basis of lowest price or the most economically advantageous tender, and
- the preservation of compliance records by the contracting authority.

A number of distinctions need to be understood when dealing with the procurement directives:

(a) the sector – does it concern the provision of certain utilities functions (i.e. water, energy or transport)?
(b) the nature of the contract – does it concern works, supplies (goods) or services?
(c) what kind of directive? – some directives lay down rules on how tendering procedures should operate, others deal with methods of enforcing their compliance.

It should be remembered that the EC directives are complemented by the general internal market provisions of the EC Treaty itself, for example, the free movement of goods, the free provision of services and the freedom of establishment. These general EC principles can be relied on even in situations where the EC directives themselves do not apply.

Table 1 EC directives affecting procurement

	General public sector	**Utilities (water, energy and transport)**[a]
	EC: Directive 2004/18/EC[b] (This consolidated and updated three earlier directives for works, services and supplies: Directive 93/37/EEC, Directive 93/36/EEC and Directive 92/50/EEC)	EC: Directive 2004/17/EC[c] (This updated an earlier utilities directive: Directive 93/38/EEC)
	UK: The Public Contracts Regulations 2006 SI 2006/5 (This consolidated and updated three separate regulations for works, supplies and services implementing the old EC directives: the Public Works Contracts Regulations 1991, the Public Services Contracts Regulations 1993 and the Public Supply Contracts Regulations 1995)	UK: The Utilities Contracts Regulations 2006 SI 2006/6 (This updated the utilities regulations implementing the old utilities directive: the Utilities Contracts Regulations 1996)
Enforcement	Directive 89/665[d]	Directive 92/13[e]

[a] Postal services will have to be switched from the public sector rules from January 2009.
[b] OJ L134/114, 30.04.2004
[c] OJ L134/1, 30.04.2004
[d] OJ L395/33, 30.12.89. UK implementation is integrated in the Public Contracts Regulations 2006.
[e] OJ L76/14, 23.3.92. UK implementation is integrated in the Utilities Contracts Regulations 2006.

4.5 Scope: works, supplies or services and value thresholds

The EC rules make a distinction between procurements of works, supplies and services. The distinction is important because each type of procurement is subject in some respects to a different set of rules. Notably, the value thresholds above which the rules apply vary with the type of procurement at issue.

The scheme of the EC directives is designed to define procurements as either works, supplies or services in a seamless way, thereby preventing certain types of contract from falling outside the regime. The definitions themselves are somewhat circular and there can be occasional difficulties in determining the true nature of a procurement.

In a project for the construction of a building, the procurement is likely to be a work. However, if one were to dissect the construction process it would involve the provision of building materials (supplies) which are processed (services) yet which give rise to a finished building (a work). The project will have involved the appointment of construction professionals such as the design team, a quantity surveyor and a project manager (services). It is important to have an understanding of where each discipline begins and ends.

A *work* is defined as:

> 'the outcome of any works which is sufficient of itself to fulfil an economic and technical function.'[6]

A work is therefore defined by reference to an end result rather than to an individual input. The nature of 'works' in turn refers to the construction of new buildings and works, restoring and common repairs,[7] including:

- site preparation
- building of complete constructions or parts thereof; civil engineering
- building installation
- building completion.

The rules apply if the procurement is a 'public works contract'. This has a very wide meaning and includes contracts:

> 'under which a contracting authority engages a person to procure *by any means* the carrying out for the contracting authority of a work corresponding to specified requirements'[8] [emphasis added].

This broad definition involving procurement of works 'by any means' was designed to cover increasingly complex project structures.

In relation to *supplies*, a 'public supply contract' is a purchase or hire of goods. In the case of hire, the contracting authority need not become the owner at the end of any hire period. Where installation services are also involved, the contract remains a supply procurement if the value attributable to the goods themselves is equal to or greater than the value attributable to the installation services. An issue of this kind could arise, for example, in relation to the procurement of a standard type of escalator and it will often be difficult to determine whether the procurement should be a supply or a service (or in some cases even a work).

In relation to *services*, a 'public services contract' is a contract for the provision of services but specifically excludes contracts covered by the rules on works and supplies.

[6] Public Contracts Regulations 2006, Regulation 2(1).
[7] Ibid, Schedule 2.
[8] Ibid, Regulation 2(1).

One peculiarity of the services rules is the distinction between Part A and Part B services. The full rigours of the rules apply to Part A services (which include the procurement of services from construction professionals such as architects, surveyors, engineers and project managers) whereas the procurement of Part B services is only subject to certain requirements on use of standards, record keeping and the publication of an award notice. Part B services include, for example, the provision of certain transport, legal, education and health services and any other service not explicitly listed in Part A.

Certain procurements are excluded from the rules altogether, for example, if secret or requiring special security measures.

Having identified the nature of the procurement, consideration can be given to whether the procurement is likely to exceed the *value thresholds* at which the procurement rules begin to apply. The thresholds as set in the UK are shown in Table 2.

Table 2 Procurement value thresholds*

	General public sector		
	Supplies	**Services**	**Works**
Entities subject to WTO GPA	£90 319 (€133 000)	£90 319[a] (€133 000)	£3 497 313[b] (€5 150 000)
Other public sector contracting authorities	£139 893 (€206 000)	£139 893 (€206 000)	£3 497 313[b] (€5 150 000)
	Utilities		
	Supplies	**Services**	**Works**
All sectors	£279 785 (€412 000)	£279 785 (€412 000)	£3 497 313 (€5 150 000)

* The conversion rates for non € currencies such as £ sterling are as set on 1 January 2008. The level of the thresholds is adjusted every two years by the European Commission.

[a] With the exception of the following services which have a threshold of £139 893 (€206 000): Part B (residual) services; research and development services; certain telecommunications services; and subsidized services contracts.

[b] Including subsidized services contracts.

The thresholds have to be considered before a procedure is launched and the exercise requires some informed speculation. If elements of the project are budgeted to exceed relevant value thresholds they should be advertised under the rules. On the other hand, contracts should not be split up artificially to bring each below the thresholds. There are some special rules on how the thresholds are applied to each of supplies, services and works.

The services and supplies rules require the cumulation of similar supplies or services over a twelve-month period for the application of the thresholds. If the contract is for supplies or services over a number of years, then the value over the duration of the contract is taken into account. In the case of a hire contract whose duration is indefinite, the monthly hire charge is normally multiplied by a factor of 48.

Since a 'work' is defined by reference to an outcome which is 'sufficient of itself to fulfil an economic and technical function' the cumulation for the purposes of the works threshold is of expenditure to achieve that outcome rather than of similar works.

There are important and highly practical provisions for dealing with small works, services or supplies packages within an overall project whereby these small packages (frequently 'small lots') do not need to be procured by call for competition. In the case of works, a small lot for these purposes is capped at €1m (£679 090) and where the small lots, taken together, do not exceed 20% of the expected value of the works. The corresponding value for services is €80 000 (£54 327) instead of €1m.

4.6 Special rules: concessions, subsidized contracts, design contests

The rules have particular regimes for a number of types of procurement including concessions, subsidized contracts and design contests.

Special rules on *concessions* only appear in the Public Contracts Regulations in relation to works contracts.[9] (The use of concessions under the Public Finance Initiative is discussed in greater detail in Chapter 1.4.) A 'public works contract concession' is a public works contract:

> 'under which the consideration given by the contracting authority consists of or includes the grant of a right to exploit the work or works to be carried out under the contract'.[10]

A concession therefore involves some form of revenue exploitation risk on the part of the contractor. Typical examples would be toll roads or bridges.

Under the special regime, the concession award is subject to a call for competition. Following award the successful concessionaire then itself becomes subject to obligations to adhere to the procurement rules when letting sub-contracts. There are however important exceptions which can allow the concessionaire to reserve sub-contracts for members of its own consortium.

The favourable treatment of consortium sub-contracts is of considerable practical importance in such projects and can affect the level of private sector interest. A construction contractor would have less incentive to join a consortium to bid for the concession if it had subsequently to bid for sub-contracts as well. There are no similar rules for services concessions or anywhere in the utilities regime.

There are also special rules on *subsidized contracts* in relation to public works and services procurements. Where a contracting authority provides one-half or more of the funding for a project to an entity which is not itself a contracting authority with procurement obligations, the contracting authority is bound to include in the funding arrangements a contractual requirement that the recipient adheres to the procurement rules when procuring the project and ensure that the recipient does so comply or recover the contribution. The subsidized contract rules apply to works and to services procurements.

By this method, the procurement obligation is made to follow the public funds. However, the obligations of the recipient are contractual and are owed to the contracting authority rather than generally. It is common for a failure to adhere to the rules to be an event of default in the funding documentation which would trigger repayment of the funding. This mechanism is particularly important in many Lottery-funded projects. This rule on subsidized contracts does not apply in all situations but is confined to certain civil engineering projects and building work for hospitals, sports, recreation and leisure facilities, school and university buildings and buildings for administrative purposes.

---

[9] The Commission has published an explanatory communication on concessions OJ C121/2 29.04.2000.

[10] Public Contracts Regulations 2006, Regulation 2(1).

There is also a special regime under the services rules for *design contests*, such as architectural competitions. The procedure is not commonly used in practice. It is more usual for contracting authorities to procure the appointment of an architect or a design team for a project and they may require design concepts as an important part of that appointment process rather than to procure a design.

4.7 Types of procedure

There is an important difference between the types of procedure available under the rules. A distinction is made between open, restricted, negotiated and competitive dialogue procedures.

Open procedures do not involve any form of prequalification exercise. Because bids are invited from all comers, adjudication can be very burdensome. As a procedure, it is probably best adapted for a standardized procurement need, such as for generic supplies. It is largely inappropriate for use with complex works projects or for the appointment of construction professionals.

Restricted procedures involve a prequalification and short-listing exercise. This keeps the number of bidders low and thereby helps to contain bid costs for both procurer and bidder. The rules specify that the minimum number of bidders that should be invited to tender is 5.

Negotiated procedures are perhaps best described by reference to open and restricted procedures. As a matter of principle, negotiation is not possible as part of open or restrictive procedures in general public sector procurement. General public sector procurement permits negotiation in only very narrowly defined circumstances, some with and some without a call for competition. Where the negotiated procedure involves a call for competition, at least three candidates, if suitable, should be invited to bid. In the utilities sector, a negotiated procedure can be used as of right, rather than as an exception. The utilities rules therefore offer much greater procedural flexibility than the general public sector rules.

In the general public sector rules the rare situations where a negotiated procedure is possible are set out in detail. Because negotiated procedures are very much the exception, the exceptions are interpreted strictly. They therefore have to be treated with some caution. The following is a summary of the exceptional circumstances where a negotiated procedure *without* a call for competition is possible:

- if an open or restricted procedure is discontinued as a result of irregular tenders or because no acceptable tenders were made, and all operators who submitted a tender in the discontinued process are invited to negotiate the contract
- in the absence of tenders, suitable tenders or applications in response to an open or restricted procedure
- for technical or artistic reasons or for reasons connected with the protection of exclusive rights, the contract can only be performed by one contractor
- in case of extreme urgency
- the products are manufactured purely for research, experiment, study or development (supplies only)
- provision of additional comparable supplies (generally not for a period of over three years) (supplies only)
- for the purchase or hire of goods quoted on a commodity market (supplies only)
- to take advantage of advantageous terms for the purchase of goods in a closing down sale or other type of sale (supplies only)

- when the rules of a design contest require the contract to be awarded to one of the successful contestants, provided all successful contestants are invited to negotiate the contract
- for additional works or services not included in the initial project but which have become necessary through unforeseen circumstances for the performance of that contract and
  - the additional works or services cannot be technically or economically separated from the main contract without great inconvenience to the contracting authority, or
  - although separable, are strictly necessary for the main contract's completion

  however, the value of the additional works or services cannot exceed 50% of the amount of the main contract (works and services only)
- repeat works or services but where this prospect was referred to in the contract notice for the original contract, the value of the consideration for the repeat works or services was taken into account in determining the estimated value of the original contract and within three years of the conclusion of the original contract (works and services only).

Situations where a negotiated procedure *with* a call for competition is possible include:

- if an open or restricted procedure is discontinued as a result of irregular tenders or because no acceptable tender were made
- for works contracts carried out solely for research or testing purposes and on a not-for-profit basis
- where the nature of the works, services, or supplies, or the risks attaching to them, do not permit prior overall pricing
- if specifications for a service contract cannot be established with sufficient precision to enable an open or restricted process to be run.

Negotiated procedures can be used as of right in the utilities sectors. The inability to engage in negotiations except in limited circumstances is a severe constraint in the general public sector rules. Indeed, compliance with this requirement is often difficult to achieve in practice. The reform of the procurement directives resulting in Directive 2004/18/EC therefore introduced a new award procedure called *competitive dialogue*. This is the procedure under which most PFI/PPP contracts are likely to be tendered (although its remit is wider). It represents a compromise to the European Commission's opposition to the routine use of the negotiated procedure for PFI/PPP contracts in the UK. PFI/PPP contracts must therefore normally comply with the competitive dialogue procedure under which there is less flexibility for negotiation with the contracting authority.

The competitive dialogue procedure is available for 'particularly complex contracts'. More specifically it is available where the contracting authority cannot in advance define the technical specification required or specify the 'legal or financial make-up of the project'.

The basic principle of the competitive dialogue procedure is that it allows the contracting authority to hold discussions with bidders in order to develop the desired technical solution before submission of final, priced bids. A minimum number of three candidates should be invited to participate in the procedure. The contracting authority conducts a dialogue with these candidates in order to identify potential solutions. During this dialogue the contracting authority must ensure that there is no discriminatory treatment between the candidates, e.g. in relation to availability of information. The contracting authority also must not divulge a proposed solution or other confidential information of one candidate to the others without that candidate's permission. During the dialogue phase the contracting authority can narrow down the field of tenderers by applying evaluation criteria (including on price).

The contracting authority compares the proposed solutions and identifies which are capable of meeting its needs. It then invites the candidates to submit tenders based on 'any' solution presented during the dialogue. There is no further negotiation with the tenderers on these bids. Tenders may however be 'clarified, specified and fine-tuned' at the request of the contracting authority but without changing the 'basic features of the tender'.

4.8 Frameworks, e-auctions and dynamic purchasing systems

Framework agreements are agreements with one or more contractors setting out the terms and conditions under which specific call-offs can be made throughout the term of the agreement. The public contracts rules require that framework agreements are advertised and awarded in compliance with the standard tendering procedures. The specification contained in the framework should also be detailed enough to cover all the works, services, or supplies to be awarded under it (for example, in the case of a construction project, the individual projects involved, when it is envisioned they will take place and the different categories of work being procured).

A framework agreement can be entered into with a single contractor or with a number of contractors. In relation to frameworks concluded with a single contractor, the contractor's tender can be supplemented before a call-off but the contract must be awarded within the limits of the original framework agreement. In general, frameworks should be limited to four years' duration.

In relation to frameworks concluded with a number of operators (at least three) there are essentially two options. The first option is to award call-offs simply by reapplying the original evaluation criteria. The second option is to run a mini-competition between all the framework contractors capable of meeting the particular need (i.e. not just those whom the contracting authority wants to invite). The public sector regulations contain basic rules for the operation of mini-competitions. A more flexible regime for framework agreements exists under the utilities rules.

E-auctions for the purposes of the procurement rules are on-line auctions where selected bidders submit offers electronically against the contracting authority's specification. E-auctions can be used at the conclusion of any of the available procurement procedures. In particular that means e-auctions can be used at the mini-competition stage of a framework or for call-offs under a dynamic purchasing system. There are however two important limits on the use of e-auctions. First, e-auctions cannot be used for the award of service contracts where the subject matter is a product of 'intellectual endeavour' such as a design contract. Second, e-auctions can only be used to evaluate elements which can be automatically evaluated by reference to figures or percentages.

Dynamic purchasing systems can be set up under an open procedure. This is essentially a form of on-line framework agreement – with the difference that suppliers must be able to enter and exit the framework on an ongoing basis. The system is available for the purchase of 'commonly used' goods, works or services.

4.9 Notices and time limits

The EC rules achieve equality of opportunity and transparency by requiring most calls for competition to be published in the *Official Journal of the European Union* (commonly *OJ* or *OJEU*). There are various types of call for competition envisaged by the rules and notices must be submitted in the set format as published by the European Commission.[11]

The main types are:

- *prior information notice* (PIN): a contracting authority is to send, at the beginning of the financial year, a PIN covering supplies or services contracts for which it expects to invite offers during its financial year where the anticipated value of similar supplies or services is €750 000 (£509 317) or more. For works, the obligation to publish a PIN provides for this to be done as soon as possible after the decision authorising the programme of the works;
- *contract notices*: the same format is used for notices for open, restricted, negotiated and competitive dialogue procedures. There are separate forms of design contest notice and simplified contract notice on a dynamic purchasing system;
- *qualification system notice*: these are envisaged only in the utilities rules. Qualification systems allow considerable flexibility and help to accelerate short-listing;
- *contract award notice*: there is a requirement for a contract award notice in the relevant format to be despatched to the OJEU within 48 days of the award.

The contract notice is an important step in the procurement process. Any national publication of the procurement opportunity cannot be earlier or more extensive than the contract notice. The despatch of this notice to the OJEU triggers the start of procedural time limits. However, the notice defines the scope of the procurement and needs to be prepared with care. Should the procurement as conducted not relate to the procurement as described in the notice, it is likely that the procedural rules will have been breached and it may be necessary to relaunch the process.

A contract notice should give sufficient information for potential contractors to identify the commercial opportunity. At the same time it is sensible for a contracting authority not to limit its freedom of action by describing the project too prescriptively, particularly if tender documentation is still being developed at that stage, as will often be the case.

The OJEU is required to publish the notice within five days of despatch if transmitted by electronic means and within twelve days of despatch in most other cases. Since the date of publication is outside the contracting authority's control, the minimum procedural time limits run from the date of despatch, not the date of publication.

The rules set out minimum *time limits* for most stages of the relevant procedure. The rules relating to the public sector are illustrated in Table 3. Special time limits apply when documents are notified electronically to the OJEU.

There are a number of situations where shorter time periods can be used. This is possible, for example, where adherence to the nominal minimum periods is made impractical for reasons of urgency. In such cases a restricted procedure can be 'accelerated' by substituting periods as low as 15 and 10 days for 37 and 40 days respectively. Where there has been a contract notice there is some visibility as to whether the time

[11] Commission Regulation (EC) No. 1564/2005 of 7 September 2005 establishing standard forms for the publication of notices in the framework of public procurement procedures pursuant to Directives 2004/17/EEC and 2004/18/EEC of the European Parliament and of the Council OJ L257/1 1.10.2005.

Table 3. Time limits for procurement procedures

Procedure		Normal limit (days)	Electronic notification to OJEU	Electronic access to contract documents
Open	Minimum time from sending notification until tender return date	52	–7	–5
	With PIN (usual)	36		
	With PIN (minimum)	22		
Restricted	Minimum time from despatch of notice to receipt of requests to be selected to tender	37	30	
	If urgent (minimum)	15	10	
	Minimum time from despatch of invitation to tender until tender return date	40	35	
	If urgent (minimum)	10		
	With PIN (usual)	36	31	
	With PIN (minimum)	22		
Negotiated procedure	Minimum time from despatch of notice until receipt of requests to be invited to negotiate	37	30	
	If urgent (minimum)	15	10	
Competitive dialogue	Minimum time from despatch of notice until receipt of requests to be selected to participate	37	30	

limits are being adhered to. Where an accelerated procedure is being used, the pro forma notices provide for the justification for the acceleration to be given on the face of the notice.

4.10 Prequalification and selection

The rules set out the framework as to how prequalification and selection processes are to be conducted.

Prequalification is addressed in considerable detail in the general public sector rules. The rules list reasons why contractors may be ineligible to tender, for example in the case of insolvency or arrears of taxes. A contracting authority can add to these reasons provided that they are objective, non-discriminatory and are set out in the contract notice. The rules contain an obligation to exclude candidates or tenderers who have been convicted for participation in a criminal organisation, corruption, fraud, or money laundering. Contracting authorities must exclude such persons where they have 'actual knowledge' of the relevant convictions.

The general public sector contracting authority is, however, limited as to the information it can otherwise request from candidates as part of a prequalification exercise. It can only request certain specific information on economic and financial standing and technical capacity. For economic and financial standing this is limited to statements from bankers, published accounts and statement of turnover of business in the previous three years. For technical capacity the prescribed areas include issues such as similar activities in the previous five years, quality control certification, technical facilities or staff qualifications. Utilities have greater flexibility in their choice of prequalification criteria.

The pro forma contract notices provide for the prequalification basis to be set out on the face of the notice.

As for *selection* of the successful bidder, the rules provide that only one of two possible criteria are possible: either the lowest price or the 'most economically advantageous' tender. If the most economically advantageous criterion is used, the contracting authority is required to indicate in the contract notice or contract documents the relative weighting given to each of the evaluation criteria. The weightings can be expressed as ranges. This requirement can only be avoided where weighting is not objectively possible. Relevant evaluation criteria could include a range of issues including (but not limited to) timing, quality, aesthetics, price and technical merit. The 'most economically advantageous' tender criterion provides the opportunity for considering broader value for money issues in addition to price. This more holistic approach is also more open to subjective judgments and thereby to abuse.

The contract notice pro forma provide for the selection criteria to be set out on the face of the notice, but this can be provided to bidders with the contract documents, i.e. as part of the invitation to tender.

4.11 Enforcement

Legal protest about the conduct of a procurement procedure is only one manifestation of how these rules are enforced. Rules relating to procedural transparency should be considered equally important in achieving compliance. Contracting authorities have obligations to maintain an audit trail and records can be called for by the European Commission. Furthermore, those participating in tender procedures and who are eliminated have the right to receive reasons in writing within 15 days of request. These are important incentives for contracting authorities to adhere to the procedure they have set for themselves and in particular to apply the stated selection criteria. It should also be borne in mind that most contracting authorities are subject to the disclosure requirements of the Freedom of Information Act 2000. Guidance from the Office of Government Commerce suggests that disclosure under requests pursuant to the Freedom of Information Act can extend beyond what is required under the procurement rules.

The rules also provide for formal legal remedies in case of breach.[12] The UK implementation provides for injunction and compensatory remedies. Under these rules it is not possible to have a contract set aside once it has been entered into. However, there is now a statutory minimum 10 day standstill period between the announcement of the successful bidder and the entry into contract. This provides for a two day window in which to request a formal debrief and greater scope for injunctions to be sought by the objecting parties.[13]

The objecting party can be any contractor who is potentially affected. The objector has to inform the contracting authority of the breach before commencing proceedings. The proceedings have to be brought promptly and in any event within three months of the grounds for bringing the proceedings first arising.

These remedies sit alongside remedies generally available under the common law.

Although these remedies have been in place for a number of years they have not given rise to a significant number of national court proceedings in the UK. Also, the interface between the EC-inspired rules and the procedures and remedies available at common

[12] For the general public sectors Directive 89/665, OJ L395/33 30.12.89. UK implementation is integrated in the Public Contracts Regulations 2006.

[13] See Regulation 32(3) of the Public Contracts Regulations 2006 and Regulation 33(3) of the Utilities Contracts Regulations 2006.

law is still being worked out by the courts. Certainly there has not been the explosion of litigation in this area seen in a number of other member states (for example, Sweden, Denmark, Austria and the Netherlands) which have established special tribunals or procurement complaints boards and where procedural access is relatively inexpensive.

However, the rules do occasionally throw up high profile cases. *Harmon CFEM Facades (UK) Ltd* v. *The Corporate Officer of the House of Commons* [1999] All ER(D) 1178 involved the procurement of Portcullis House in Westminster which provides office accommodation for MPs. There was evidence of national preference and a departure from the stated tender procedures. The selection criterion was based on 'best value for money' which the court interpreted to mean, in the absence of greater clarity, the lowest price. The lowest priced bidder did not win and protested. The objector successfully recovered damages for tender costs and loss of profit, albeit on a discounted basis, since it could show that it had a real chance of winning. Interestingly the claims were both statutory under the then prevailing procurement regulations, and under common law including for misfeasance in public office.

Recovery of damages will usually be difficult to achieve because in most cases the objector will not be able to demonstrate that it should have won or had a real chance of winning.[14] Overall, this will be more difficult to demonstrate if the selection criterion is the more complex 'most economically advantageous' tender. The UK enforcement rules are therefore at their most potent when they are used to threaten an injunction to halt or to rectify the procurement procedure at any time before contract award. The 10 day standstill provision improves the potential for seeking injunctions.

Other recourse of a more informal nature is also possible. It is possible to bring irregularities to the attention of the European Commission who can bring infringement proceedings against member states before the European Court. It is also possible for the European Commission to secure 'interim measures' i.e. an injunction against member states. There are also information gathering procedures which the European Commission can invoke against member states.

Pressure can also be put on national authorities who might prefer to resolve matters quickly rather than be subject to unwelcome oversight from outside. This sensitivity can be exploited between national authorities and the European Commission as well as between local and central government authorities.

The pattern of enforcement is, however, set to change. The enforcement directives for both the public and utilities sectors have been modified by Directive 2007/66/EC.[15] One principal change will be that contracts entered into in breach of procurement law may be challenged in their first six months. This directive needs to be transposed into UK legal systems by December 2009.

5 SOME PROBLEM AREAS IN THE APPLICATION OF PROCUREMENT LAW

5.1 Introduction

The purpose of this section is to highlight some additional themes which commonly occur in relation to construction projects and which are worth identifying and discussing in greater detail, although these are by no means the only problems which arise from this increasingly complex legal area:

[14] The burden of proof is slightly lower for the recovery of tender costs under the relevant utility enforcement rules in the Utilities Contracts Regulations 2006 (Regulation 45(8)).

[15] OJ L 335/20.12.2007.

- typical breaches of the rules
- negotiations
- construction management
- speculative work and the Lottery
- reopening a deal.

5.2 Typical breaches of the rules

The rules are complex and contracting authorities should not underestimate the possibility of making mistakes. Where the contracting authority does make mistakes, these become opportunities for objectors and threats to the contracting authority. Practical experience suggests that the following types of breach are not uncommon.

Mismatch between the project described in the contract notice and the project as let

In an ideal world, the full tender documentation is in place before the contract notice is issued. In reality this rarely happens. The problem does give rise to practical difficulties. Where the thinking moves on after the contract notice is issued, the contracting authority may want to approach the project in a manner materially different from the way in which it was previously described.

Often the problem can be avoided by drafting the notice in a less prescriptive manner. Alternatively, there may be time to reissue the contract notice, suitably amended. In any event, it is important to address the problem sooner rather than later.

Time limits

A disrespect for the limits will be a very public breach of the rules. All parties involved in the procurement will be aware of the time limits and the contract notice itself may betray a departure from the rules.

If there is to be a protest it is most likely to come from a party which needs time for a particular procedural step.

No contract notice – no competition

This would be a radical breach since not even a flawed competition would be run. The contracting authority will only be relatively safe from protest if it is able to maintain secrecy. Ironically, the legal remedies could be particularly ineffective if a contract is entered into secretly. By then it will be too late to secure an injunction. Also it would be more difficult for any objector to claim damages for loss of chance and the objector would have incurred no tender costs.

Post-tender negotiations

This theme will be considered in more detail in Section 5.3 below. However, it is one of the most common breaches of the general public sector procurement rules.

Losing the papers

It is not uncommon for the contracting authority to mislay a bid, particularly where an open procedure is used (most commonly in the procurement of generic supplies). Administrative error is all too frequent and can be particularly embarrassing for the contracting authority. In one anecdotal example the objector secured by way of apology a different (and better) contract but without competition.

1.1 The planning system
1.2 Financing the project
1.3 Public sector projects
1.4 Public/private partnerships
1.5 Tender process
1.6 Construction contracts
1.7 Construction insurance

Misapplication of the prequalification or selection criteria

Contracting authorities have strong incentives to adhere to their stated procedure and criteria. As already seen, those eliminated from a procedure can ask for written reasons. It is important that the reasons given by the contracting authority relate to criteria stated in the competition itself and reflect its own internal file. Discrepancies will be hard to explain away. Even so, the more holistic selection criterion of 'most economically advantageous' tender is more open to subjectivity and potential abuse.

Wrong procedure

The procedure might be wrong because a negotiated procedure or competitive dialogue procedure is used when it is not justified. This will also be a very public breach of the rules since the type of procedure will be clear from the contract notice.

The procedure might also incorrectly classify the procurement as a work, supply or service. It will be particularly serious if a procurement is deliberately misclassified in order to take advantage of a procedural advantage. An example might be where the procurement is erroneously and deliberately construed as a Part B service (to which the full rigours of the rules do not apply) rather than as a Part A service or another type of procurement altogether.

Extending a contract

There is frequently the temptation to relet a follow-on contract to an incumbent provider without further competition. While there is some scope for doing so under the rules, it will not generally be possible and much will be depend on the detailed circumstances. Follow-on contracts will be fresh procurements which will usually need to be advertised.

5.3 Negotiations

The general public sector rules, unlike the utilities rules, do not generally permit negotiations between the contracting authority and bidders. It has already been seen that the rules severely limit the use of negotiations with bidders. The public sector rules provide that negotiations with bidders are only permitted where the conditions are satisfied for use of either the competitive dialogue procedure or the negotiated procedure. Both the public and the utilities regimes limit the scope of negotiations with the winning bidder.

Under the public sector regime the European Courts have endorsed the following statement as an accurate reflection of the position in relation to the open and restricted procedures:

> 'The Council and the Commission state that in open and restricted procedures all negotiations with candidates or tenderers on fundamental aspects of contracts, variations in which are likely to distort competition, and in particular on prices, shall be ruled out; however, discussions with candidates or tenderers may be held but only for the purpose of clarifying or supplementing the content of their tenders of the requirements of the contracting authorities and provided this does not involve discrimination'.

Clarification is therefore acceptable even if negotiation is not. The borderline between the two will often be difficult to determine. As already noted, post-tender negotiation which goes beyond mere 'clarification' is probably one of the most frequent technical breaches of the procurement rules.

The concern about negotiation in procurement procedures relates to fairness and transparency. It is feared that negotiations lead to inequality of opportunity between bidders, notwithstanding the potential value for money opportunities which negotiations could offer. For this reason there is always a restriction on negotiation with the winning bidder. This limit is reflected in the provisions governing the use of the competitive dialogue procedure. After selecting the best tender the contracting authority may request the bidder:

> 'to clarify aspects of that tender or confirm commitments contained in the tender provided that this does not have the effect of modifying substantial aspects of the tender or of the call for tender and does not risk distorting competition or causing discrimination'.

5.4 Construction management

Although not so much a problem area it is important to understand the procurement implications of construction management compared with other forms of construction procurements.

The procurement route for construction management differs from more traditional procurement. In construction management the client will let individual contract packages and these are coordinated by the construction manager. The construction manager appointment is one for services. However, in contrast to more traditional construction procurement, no single works contractor takes overall responsibility for the works packages. The client therefore does not deal with one head contractor. Figure 1 illustrates the procurement differences.

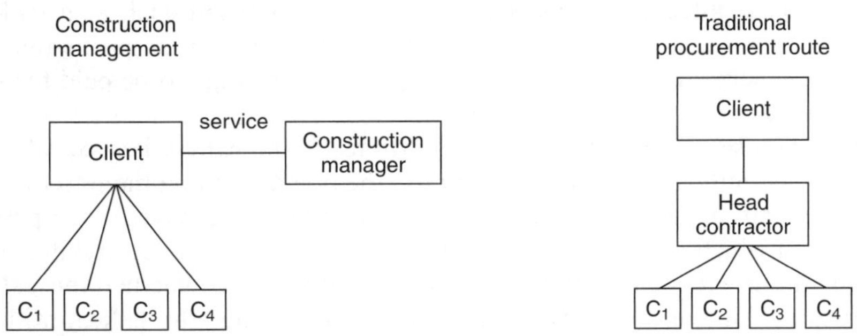

Figure 1. Construction management and traditional procurement

Under the traditional route the client lets one contract, which for a contracting authority would be subject to a regulated procurement procedure. The subcontracts will not be the client's procurement concern.

Under the construction management route the number of individual procurements proliferate. The contracting authority appoints a construction manager (a services procurement) who then coordinates the procurement of each package. The procurement of each package is in the name of the contracting authority. Under the cumulation rules all the packages would need to be taken together for the application of the works value threshold. Particularly helpful will be the small lots rules which dispense with the advertising requirements, i.e. where individual works packages are worth less than €1m (£679 090) and which in aggregate are worth less than 20% of the overall project value.

5.5 Speculative work and the Lottery

The advent of the Lottery has thrown up a number of procurement law difficulties. A particular problem is the position of a service provider who does speculative work to help an applicant develop its funding application.

In many situations the entity which is seeking Lottery funding is already a contracting authority for the purposes of the procurement rules. Such an entity will already be used to the compliance obligations which the rules place on it. This will be the case for many theatres, museums and galleries. Even if such a body has charitable status, it is often the case that a majority of the relevant governing body is appointed by central or local government. Outside this 'public' environment there is generally less familiarity with the rules.

Lottery funding is treated as public money. Thus, if it is used to fund a works or services project, that project can become a 'subsidized contract' for the purposes of the works or services rules. As already seen, where the subsidy runs to more than half the value of the procurement, the funding body must impose on the recipient the obligation to apply the procurement rules and makes the procurement obligation follow the public money. This principle is usually implemented through the funding agreement. Non-compliance with the procurement rules would usually be an event of default which could trigger the requirement to repay the funding received. This is a very strong compliance incentive. Where the Lottery fund applicant is already in the public sector it will be a contracting authority in its own right and will be subject to the procurement rules in any event, irrespective of the contractual obligation which might be imposed in the funding mechanism. Such a clause in the funding agreement is not necessary in this case.

A practical difficulty arises where early conceptual or design work is done, for example, by an architect for a private Lottery fund applicant such as a gallery or a theatre. The architect might be devoting considerable time on a speculative basis to help with the gallery's Lottery funding application and expects to be paid for past and future services if the application is successful.

This can give rise to a number of complications. If the gallery is successful with its application, the funding agreement will impose the obligation to adhere to the procurement rules on pain of repayment. The architect may therefore have to compete for the appointment in which he or she had already invested heavily. If the architect does not continue in the process there can be copyright issues as to whether the gallery can move forward with the architect's initial design or whether the gallery will have to start again. This could also cause difficulty for the continuing validity of the applicant's Lottery submission.

The gallery could have avoided this difficulty by advertising the architect's appointment in anticipation of receiving the Lottery funding and being subject to the procurement obligation. The appointment would have related to the entire design and supervision process and any payment to the architect would have been made conditional on the award of Lottery funding.

5.6 Reopening a deal

This is an area where there is little guidance other than the general principles behind the procurement rules and behind the EC Treaty.

One category of situations is readily dealt with. This is where, for example, a services contract is advertised to be for one year but with the option on the part of the contracting authority to extend for a further year. The option to extend was part of the original scope advertised and the exercise of that option is simply the implementation of the procurement in one of the forms in which it was originally conceived. Thus it does not involve reopening the deal at all. There can be many permutations of this example.

A more complex situation is where the parties to the procurement are in dispute and in settlement of their differences the scope of what the provider does is modified. A number of issues arise.

- Did the extension of the scope beyond the original contract fall within the scope of the original competition? If it did not, arguably the extension is a separate procurement. If it is a separate procurement, does one of the exceptions for running a negotiated procedure without a call for competition apply (for example, procuring from the same provider additional services or works not exceeding 50% of the value of the original contract, subject to certain detailed conditions)?
- Could it be argued that whatever the contracting authority is now procuring, it has the same economic value as the procurement originally entered into with the provider? Even if, materially, the new arrangement might involve a new procurement, financially it might not.

When approaching problems of this kind it is important to recognize that the revised deal is not a question of post-tender negotiation because once a contract has been entered into the competitive procurement is at an end. This is a post-contractual as opposed to a post-tendering situation. It is therefore important to draw a line under the initial procurement process which gave rise to the contract and to focus on how the rules apply to the new situation.

Because of all the uncertainties involved in this situation, it can be particularly important to make provision for some flexibility in the original contract. The case of a one-year extension to a one-year contract is a simple example. The more complex the contract, the more likely subsequent difficulties are to materialize. The drafting of the contract could devise a range of change mechanisms to deal with such problems. In such a situation the parties will be better placed to argue that the triggering of the mechanisms foreseen in the contract were part of the original procurement and that the restructuring of the arrangement is simply the natural outworking of that original procurement.

CHAPTER 1.4

Public–private sector partnerships

Nicholas Downing
Herbert Smith

assisted by

Tracy London
Herbert Smith

Marina Milner
Herbert Smith

and

Ray Wheeler
Campas Limited

Legal issues for Construction

1.1 The planning system

1.2 Financing the project

1.3 Public sector projects

1.4 Public/private partnerships

1.5 Tender process

1.6 Construction contracts

1.7 Construction insurance

1 INTRODUCTION

The procurement of capital projects by the public sector was transformed during the 1990s by the advent of the Private Finance Initiative (PFI). The PFI is one manifestation of what has come to be known as Public–Private Partnerships (PPP). PPP as a term of art has developed since the election of the Labour government in 1997. The notion of a partnership in this sense is not a legal one: it relates to the sharing of risk and reward between the public and private sectors in the delivery of public sector investment or exploitation of public sector assets. The Government has given strong backing to the PFI but has made it clear that it regards it as one of several methods of conducting successful public–private partnerships. The extent to which a particular project is a PFI project or some other form of PPP will ultimately depend on the nature of the project itself and the risk and reward allocation between the public and private sectors.

Underpinning all PPP transactions is the political desire to bring together the best of the private and public sectors to facilitate the delivery of badly needed capital investment or the achievement of other public sector objectives. This has led in turn to the construction industry being required to enter into radically different contractual relationships with the public sector for the delivery of construction-based projects.

This chapter will focus on the principles and aims of the PFI as it remains the dominant form of PPP currently being promoted by the public sector in the UK. The remainder of this introductory section sets out the basic principles of the PFI, the forms it can take and introduces the standardised contract documentation.

1.1 Basic structure of the Private Finance Initiative

The PFI seeks to involve the private sector in the provision of public services with the result that the role of the public sector moves from being an owner and provider to an enabler and purchaser. It is based on the belief that the public sector should focus on its core functions, leaving the private sector to perform those functions which it can perform more cost effectively and efficiently.

The traditional contractual arrangements between the public and private sectors for the procurement of public sector infrastructure and related services, where the public sector was the owner and operator with responsibility for securing design and construction, have been replaced by a contractual framework where the private sector has responsibility for design, construction, operation, management, maintenance and finance. The public sector (or in certain cases the public itself as the direct user) becomes the customer paying for the provision of a service.

In a PFI transaction, the key contract is a concession agreement between the public sector and the private sector (often called the project agreement). The private sector party will usually be a special purpose vehicle entity (the project company), typically including construction contractors and facility management providers as shareholders. These shareholders are usually the principal subcontractors of the project company, although equity-only investors may also be involved.

The project company will also secure finance for the project on a non-recourse basis. Its shareholders will usually only invest a limited proportion of equity into the project company. Given the non-recourse financing structure, the lenders will require a series of direct agreements with the public sector and the principal subcontractors of the project company which will enable them to take over the project if it is in jeopardy.

The focus on the provision of a service to the public sector rather than the purchase by it of a capital asset is at the heart of the PFI. The private sector has the responsibility for providing, maintaining and operating an asset, with the public sector defining a standard of service to be delivered, leaving the private sector to determine the means of delivery. The public sector will prescribe a set of outputs (the 'what'), which in turn drive the specification for the underlying asset, and the private sector will be responsible for devising the technical solutions (the 'how'). Since the private sector bears the responsibility and risk of determining how to deliver the required output, the public sector is able to transfer to the private sector risks which would otherwise have been borne by the public sector.

Once the asset is constructed and the services are being delivered, the public sector will pay a periodic payment ('unitary payment') to the private sector during the contract period, which in many PFI projects runs for 25 or 30 years. The private sector is generally responsible for the up-front financing of the project, although the Government has piloted a new form of financing – so-called Credit Guarantee Finance which involves the splitting of funding and risk-taking. In simplified terms, the Government acts as funder by raising the necessary finance through the issue of government bonds – thereby benefiting from the lower rates available to the public sector. Private financiers guarantee the payment of interest and principal by the project company to the Government. In this way the public sector is able to benefit from lower financing costs without having to take on project risk – its risk will be the credit-worthiness of the bank guarantor.

To date Credit Guarantee Finance appears to have had limited take-up in projects and indeed the Government has indicated that it does not see Credit Guarantee Finance being used in more than a limited proportion of its PFI programme. Other forms of financing public sector projects are also developing. One is so-called 'prudential borrowing', introduced in April 2004 and available to local government as an alternative to PFI. Under this framework, councils are free to borrow funds for capital investment without having to obtain 'credit approvals' from central government, provided that the level of debt is based on their resources and remains within 'prudent' limits (there is no bar on councils borrowing from commercial lenders). Because the borrowing must be backed by a revenue stream that will meet the repayments, prudential borrowing is suitable for fairly small-scale, self-financing projects such as car parks and leisure centres (up to approximately £20 million in value).

Interestingly, the market also seems now to be combining PFI with these other forms of finance. An example is where the awarding authority raises a proportion of the capital cost of the project by borrowing through the issue of a bond. The authority then makes capital payments for part of the construction works as they are carried out. The implications of this form of combined public and private finance need to be understood: as we explain in this chapter, under the PFI structure, compliance monitoring of the capital works is effectively (and in theory) self-policing in the sense that the public sector can to a large extent rely on the private sector financiers to deploy rigorous compliance monitoring functions. Put simply, financiers will protect their income stream from being disrupted by buildings becoming unavailable because of defects, by exerting pressure to ensure that the works cannot be signed off if there is any significant chance that they are defective. The rest of this chapter will explain these concepts further, focusing on traditional PFI, but it is worth noting that such combined funding can erode that 'self-policing' mechanism: the income stream normally comprises capital repayments plus interest, together with an amount for facilities management and other items, most notably profit. The financiers' concerns stem from protecting the capital repayment plus interest element; the smaller that is (and it would be reduced to varying degrees if this combined form of financing is used) the less they will be focused on compliance monitoring. The dynamics of compliance monitoring therefore shift: as capital payments are made, the incentive on the private sector to ensure compliance reduces, while the need for such mechanisms as certification, inspection, opening up of defective work (etc) grows. Many of these mechanisms of course apply in traditional forms of procurement. The PFI form may therefore need to be adapted to reflect such alternative payment regimes.

Some PFI projects, particularly smaller ones, are financed on a corporate finance basis where the private sector raises the required funds based on the strength of the balance sheet of the contractor or its parent company. Obviously the use of such corporate finance has an impact on various elements of the project documentation. The standard guidance is based on the typical project finance approach to PFI, although it does recognise the role that corporate finance may play and outlines the changes that will be required to the standard drafting.

Turning from these alternative forms of funding back to the main focus of this chapter, traditional PFI financing, the private sector will continue under the PFI to provide the financing; the public sector in its turn has to justify reimbursing the cost of capital incurred by the private sector which is inevitably higher than the public sector's cost of capital. The justification for this is made up of a number of elements.

The additional cost of capital may be offset by the ability of the private sector to construct and operate the asset more cheaply and efficiently than would be the case if there were to be a traditional procurement of the asset and a separate contract for its operation. For example, significant cost savings can be made by avoiding the mistake often made by the public sector of having assets over-engineered in an attempt to address every eventuality. Even if this results in the construction of an asset which will last (and experience has shown that this is not necessarily the case) the cost of such over-engineering can often outweigh the benefits. The world is now experiencing such a pace of technological change and rapid obsolescence that it no longer makes commercial sense to construct assets which will endure for generations.

The cost of private sector capital can also be mitigated if the private sector is free to generate revenue from the asset in addition to providing the service to the public sector. This additional third-party revenue can assist in minimizing the level of unitary payment which the public sector is required to pay.

Ultimately, however, the extra cost of private sector capital can only be justified if the private sector bears certain risks inherent in the project. The fundamental risk which is at the heart of the PFI is performance, namely delivery of the completed asset and related services to a requisite standard. The public sector, as the customer, is purchasing a service and will pay for that service provided it is delivered. In this way, the private sector is accepting the risk that it will only be able to repay the finance which it has raised to fund the project and make a profit, if the asset and services are delivered to the appropriate standard.

Under the PFI, the responsibility for the performance of the asset throughout the contract period is with the private sector, as is long-term maintenance and achieving the lowest overall life-cycle costs for the assets and related services. This is in marked contrast to assets procured on a traditional basis where a lack of public sector capital has often meant that assets have not been subject to sufficient periodic maintenance and have fallen into a state of disrepair.

1.2 Allocation of risk

The key aspect of risk allocation in a PFI transaction is that the risks should be borne by the party who is best able to manage them. The public sector is required to demonstrate that the price being paid for the private sector to bear a particular risk represents value for money. If the risk in question is one with which the private sector is unfamiliar or one which is outside its control (for example certain change of law risks) the price which the private sector requires for bearing that risk may be excessive. The private sector will assess the probability of a risk occurring and its likely impact and analyse its ability to manage and control that risk, and there may be certain risks which the private sector is unwilling to assume at any price.

The price charged by the private sector to assume a particular risk will reflect not only its assessment of the probability and impact of the risk occurring but also the consequences which this may have on the private sector's ability to perform its obligations. This is a critical issue as the public sector's obligation is to pay by reference to the level of performance achieved. The public sector is entitled to make deductions from the unitary payment for under-performance. In the final analysis the public sector must achieve a performance regime which genuinely reflects the concept of payment against performance and the private sector must have the incentive to bear the risks inherent in the project, in each case for a price which is value for money. The value for money test is critical as it must be applied wherever public money is involved in a PFI project.

The allocation of risks, or rather the allocation of those risks relating to property ownership, is of fundamental importance in a PFI project for an additional reason: it determines the accounting treatment of a PFI project, namely whether or not the resulting asset is reflected on the Government's balance sheet. If the asset is shown on the Government's balance sheet the capital expenditure for the asset has to count against public sector spending limits. As a result either there would be less public capital available for other purposes or the project in question might be unable to proceed because of the constraints of pre-set spending limits. The accounting treatment of PFI projects is covered by the Accounting Standards Board's Application Note F (*The Private Finance Initiative and similar contracts*) which was published in September 1998 and by the Treasury's publication *PFI Technical Note No. 1* (Revised) which was published in June 1999.

The Treasury has always stated that the key factor in deciding whether or not a project should go ahead is value for money and not accounting treatment. However, in the early days of PFI the preference was for projects to be off-balance sheet and at the very least sponsoring departments were conscious of the balance sheet implications when going through the risk allocation exercise. In addition, budgetary constraints restricted other procurement options. Inevitably this led to accusations that there was an inherent bias in favour of PFI as a procurement option and that projects were undertaken by PFI because they could be off-balance sheet and because there was no available budget to fund alternative procurement options.

The Treasury's 2003 report, *PFI: Meeting the Investment Challenge*, emphasized that the accounting treatment of a project is not material to the Government's decision about when to use PFI. PFI should only be used where it can be shown to offer value for money. The risk allocation in any particular project should not be distorted to try and give an off-balance sheet treatment; risk should be allocated to give the best value for money and that risk allocation should then form the basis of the decision as to how the project is treated from an accounting point of view.

1.3 Standardisation of contracts

The first PFI projects were negotiated on a case by case basis even though many of the issues were the same in all projects. This inevitably led to project teams wrangling over the same issues, often coming up with different conclusions and incurring significant costs in the process. To address these concerns the Treasury Taskforce, established by the Labour Government in 1997, carried out a widespread consultation process which resulted in the issue of guidance on the Standardisation of PFI Contracts in July 1999.

The second and third editions of the guidance were published in 2002 and 2004 respectively and an Addendum, dealing with various issues, was issued in December 2005. The fourth edition of the Standardisation of PFI Contracts (SoPC4) was published in March 2007. It incorporates the matters dealt with in the Addendum and updates the guidance where necessary to reflect new legislation and developments in the PFI market. It also includes new guidance on certain issues raised in the Treasury's 2006 report, *PFI: Strengthening Long Term Partnerships*. The objectives of the guidance remain the same as in 1999: to promote standardisation through achieving a common understanding of the risks, to allow consistency of approach and consistency of pricing across similar projects and to reduce the time and costs involved in getting a project to financial close.

The standard provisions in SoPC4 take three forms; first, standard drafting of a whole subject with guidance notes; secondly, standard drafting of parts of the subject with the rest of the subject being dealt with in explanatory notes and thirdly, a guidance note explaining how a subject should be dealt with in broad terms with a recommended approach to the issue. One of the interesting changes introduced in the third edition and retained in SoPC4 is the fact that significant parts of the drafting are now mandatory with no amendment allowed. The first two editions of the standardisation were generally used as guidance and as a starting point for negotiations. However, any project which does not now follow the standard wording will require express permission to deviate and derogations will only be allowed in exceptional circumstances.

Although SoPC4 does not contain drafting relating specifically to design and construction issues, it does cover a number of areas which have a major impact on design and construction. For example, it sets out the consequences of a delay in service commencement if that delay is caused by various types of event.

In addition to this generic guidance, sector specific guidance based on the Treasury's standardised documentation has also been produced for areas such as health, schools, housing, local government, waste management, leisure and culture, and street lighting. It is likely that new editions of such guidance will be issued in the coming months to reflect the changes introduced by SoPC4.

1.4 Types of PFI project

There are three basic types of PFI project currently in development or operation.

Projects in which services are sold to the public sector as purchaser and user

This comprises the largest group of projects which have been procured under the PFI. The private sector is responsible for financing the provision of a capital asset and providing services in relation to that asset (including asset maintenance). Examples would be the provision of prisons, hospitals and general government accommodation.

Financially free-standing projects in which services are sold direct to the end-user

The private sector is responsible for the design, construction, operation, maintenance and financing of an asset, recouping its costs through charges levied on the ultimate end user. Examples include the Second Severn Bridge and the Queen Elizabeth II Bridge at Dartford, both of which rely on tolls payable by the general public.

1.1 The planning system
1.2 Financing the project
1.3 Public sector projects
1.4 Public/private partnerships
1.5 Tender process
1.6 Construction contracts
1.7 Construction insurance

Projects in which services are sold direct to the end-user but which are not financially free-standing

These projects involve a mix of end-user charges and public subsidy or contribution. The public subsidy or contribution can take several forms including direct subsidy (for example capital grants) or the contribution of assets (for example surplus land or income generating assets) or a combination of both. Projects within this category include urban regeneration projects where land may be provided by the public sector in return for regeneration of a derelict site and light rail schemes which require direct public subsidy as part of the funding of the project as the end-user charges which can be recovered from passengers are not sufficient to fund the project on a free-standing basis.

The Government continues to be committed to exploring other forms of public–private partnership over and above these three types of PFI transaction. The term 'public–private partnerships' encompasses a wide range of different partnerships between the public and private sectors ranging from PFI transactions, asset sales and other commercial exploitation of public sector assets, partial or complete sales of state owned businesses, through to partnerships where the private sector is involved with the public sector in the development or implementation of policy.

1.5 Facilitating projects

Since the inception of the PFI in 1992, various bodies have been created to help facilitate PFI transactions. The first such body was the Private Finance Panel, which was created in 1993.

The PFI was reappraised by Sir Malcolm Bates, a founder member of the Private Finance Panel, following the election of a Labour government in 1997. This led to the creation of the Treasury Taskforce, which replaced the Private Finance Panel as a focal point for the PFI across government. The Treasury Taskforce was set-up with a limited life-span and was replaced by Partnerships UK (PUK) following its launch in June 2000. PUK is not an arm of HM Treasury. Instead, it is a PPP, with ownership in the hands of the private and public sectors.

Although it is part privately owned, PUK works solely for the public sector. Its stated mission is 'to support and accelerate the delivery of infrastructure renewal, high quality public services and the efficient use of public assets through better and stronger partnerships between the public and private sectors'.

PUK offers help-desk support to the public sector on all PFI/PPP projects. In addition, it offers more intensive support to individual projects which are particularly large, complex, innovative, politically sensitive and/or likely to prove a useful precedent. PUK also played a key role in the Partnerships for Health programme and is still involved in the Partnerships for Schools programmes. Where it is involved in an individual project it works in partnership with awarding authorities and shares responsibility for the procurement of the project. It does not usually act as an adviser, but rather as a PPP developer, for example, by assisting the awarding authority in the management of the project through helping with project evaluation and implementation, being represented on the project board and having an involvement in major decisions. PUK will share the costs of developing a PPP as agreed on a case by case basis. Its remuneration will relate to the successful procurement of the project in question. If the procurement of the PPP fails, PUK may lose some or all of its money and, if it is a success, PUK and the public body will share in its benefits. The return that PUK receives will reflect the risks that it is taking and the nature of the project and, generally, will be payable after the project has reached financial close either in the form of a lump sum or payments spread over the life of the project.

On occasions, PUK may provide finance for PPPs where better value for the public sector can be achieved. For example, it can provide development and bridging finance or other forms of capital where these are not readily available from established financial markets.

In the local authority sector, the Public–Private Partnership Programme (known as the 4Ps) has been in existence since 1996. It is an agency of local government and provides general assistance on local government PFI projects, for example by lobbying Government and supporting pathfinder projects to develop a course of dealing for future projects. One of the main aims of the 4Ps is to distribute detailed information about the processes involved in progressing PPP projects. For example, 4Ps has published guidance on topics such as *Achieving Quality in Local Authority PFI Building Projects* and in July 2004 published the *Local Government Supplement to Standardisation of PFI Contracts* which built on the standard guidance issued by the Treasury. It is also responsible for a range of sector specific guidance including schools, housing, leisure and culture, street lighting and waste management.

1.6 Stages of PFI project

There are numerous stages in a PFI transaction, but these fall broadly into three main phases, as follows.

Feasibility

The feasibility phase commences with the establishment of a business need and concludes with the preparation of the business case and the decision to proceed with the project. The aim of this phase is to establish the initial viability and scope of the procurement. The result of the feasibility phase will be the production of what is generally called the Outline Business Case (OBC). The objective of an OBC is to consider the specific characteristics of the project and determine whether the decision that the PFI procurement route offers the best value for money can be confirmed. At this stage in the process, it is accepted that firm costs for the PFI solution will not be provided, but rather reasoned argument and examples to show whether PFI is likely to offer the best value for money solutions.

New projects in Central Government have been subject to what is called 'Gateway Reviews' since February 2001. These involve a review of the project carried out by an independent panel at key decision points in its procurement and delivery. There are five gateways during the life of a project and at each gateway the project is analysed so as to provide assurance that it can progress successfully to the next stage. Therefore, if a business case has not been demonstrated, the project will not be permitted to continue unchecked with the risk of failure later.

Procurement

New procurement rules were introduced in the UK at the end of January 2006 in order to implement relevant European law. As part of the changes a new procedure has been introduced for use in particularly complex contracts such as PFI. The negotiated procedure which was generally used pre-January 2006 for PFI projects should now only be used for PFI projects in exceptional circumstances.

Under the new procedure a dialogue is carried on with pre-qualified bidders with the aim of refining the awarding authority's requirements. This dialogue may take place in various stages with a reducing number of bidders. However, by the end of the process and before selection of the preferred bidder all material points must be agreed; the scope for negotiations once a preferred bidder has been selected is extremely limited.

A competitive dialogue procurement is likely to include the following elements:

- issuing an OJEU notice and pre-qualification questionnaires to interested parties
- selecting participants
- commencing competitive dialogue procedure with prequalified bidders and inviting the submission of outline proposals
- evaluating of outline proposals and shortlisting to 3 or 4 successful bidders
- inviting the submission of detailed proposals
- evaluating and clarifying detailed proposals
- closing competitive dialogue and inviting final tenders
- selecting preferred bidder and notifying other tenderers
- gaining approvals
- limited fine tuning of the contract, and
- awarding contract/financial close.

Contract term

The third phase is the actual life of the project. Most projects comprise a construction phase, during which assets are created or upgraded and an operational phase when the assets are used to deliver the required service.

1.7 Aim of this chapter

The remainder of this chapter looks at the construction aspects of PFI transactions. It assumes that the project in question is a PFI project involving services sold to the public sector as purchaser and user with the private sector financing the initial design and construction with a mixture of project finance debt and sponsor equity and the awarding authority paying a unitary payment for a prescribed contract period from the date the asset is complete and the services to be delivered are operational.

In this chapter, the public sector body which enters into the PFI transaction is referred to as the awarding authority and the private sector contractor is referred to as the service provider. The building subcontractor is the construction contractor engaged by the service provider. References to SoPC4 means the Standardization of PFI Contracts Version 4 published by the Treasury in March 2007.

2 RISK TRANSFER

2.1 Risk transfer in PFI transactions

In a PFI transaction, the design and construction phase is relatively short when compared with the operational period but this is disproportionate to its importance. The design and construction of the facility has to be completed and the risks associated with the phase need to be overcome before the project can generate the income necessary to discharge the project debt and create a profit for the service provider.

The key risks which are applicable to the design and construction phase of a PFI transaction are considered below. These risks should be considered in the light of the considerations referred to on risk transfer in Section 1 of this chapter.

Design risk

As will be apparent from Section 4 of this chapter, the awarding authority will state in the output specification its requirements for the services to be provided under the project agreement. It is the responsibility of the service provider to propose a design solution which will enable it to deliver a service to the standards described in the output specification. After completion, the awarding authority will pay for the services rendered provided that they are compatible with the output specification. If there is non-compliance with the output specification, the awarding authority is entitled to reduce the amount payable to the service provider by making deductions from the unitary payment for poor performance as well as for what is commonly described as unavailability.

As a consequence of this principle of payment against performance, the service provider should be given the responsibility to determine the design solution for the facility. It will usually be inappropriate to allow the awarding authority to make deductions from payment when unavailability is attributable to design decisions made by the awarding authority. The responsibility given to the service provider on design matters also extends to the maintenance and operation of the facility. It will be to the service provider's advantage to design the facility in a way which ensures the efficient and economic operation of the facility and its planned maintenance (i.e. routine maintenance and minor repairs) and reduces life-cycle costs (i.e. major repairs and replacements of elements of the facility during the operational period).

Planning risk

The transfer of the risk of securing appropriate planning consents to the service provider can be difficult to achieve in practice. In particular, project financiers are not willing to advance funds until a detailed planning consent has been obtained. Accordingly, the project agreement is unlikely to be signed until, or will be made conditional upon, receipt of a satisfactory planning permission.

Because the planning application will be inextricably linked to the proposed design solution offered by the service provider, it is not uncommon for the detailed planning application to be made once a preferred bidder has been selected. The building subcontractor engaged by the service provider to design and construct the facility is unlikely to be prepared to finalize its fixed price for the construction works until planning issues have been resolved, since it would otherwise inherit the risk of having to absorb what may be significant design changes in order to comply with the finalized planning permission.

There may also be advantages in the awarding authority assisting in the planning application (e.g. support at a public enquiry or where local pressure groups may object). In effect, the planning process means that the planning risk is shared between the awarding authority and the service provider since the project will be delayed if satisfactory planning permission is not secured.

This should not be confused in any way with the discharge of detailed planning conditions or the obtaining of, and compliance with, building regulations and other similar approvals. The responsibility for securing such approvals and complying with all relevant conditions is a responsibility which is invariably placed on the service provider, who will in turn ensure that appropriate obligations are passed on to the building subcontractor. In particular, the building subcontract will probably impose an obligation on the building subcontractor to secure requisite approvals without delaying the programme and to ensure that the time and cost risk of any variations arising from the planning process is placed squarely with the building subcontractor.

Service commencement risk

In the context of PFI transactions, service commencement is the point at which service delivery is ready to commence. It is a key milestone in PFI because:

1.1 The planning system
1.2 Financing the project
1.3 Public sector projects
1.4 Public/private partnerships
1.5 Tender process
1.6 Construction contracts
1.7 Construction insurance

(a) the service provider will not receive any payment until it starts providing the services in accordance with the awarding authority's requirements (meaning that it must have completed the construction of the facility so that it is ready for operational use). SoPC4 does set out exceptions to this rule: for example, where the awarding authority wishes to make a capital contribution to the project or has some other form of co-financing proposal. The guidance is that any such contributions should be kept 'to a modest size' since they might alter the risk transfer balance and incentives of the project. Either way, the awarding authority should not make any payments towards advisers' fees or working capital; and
(b) the project agreement between the awarding authority and the service provider will usually provide for a date by which the services are to be available (liability for damages in the event of late service commencement is dealt with in Section 3 of this chapter) and/or a longstop date giving the awarding authority the ability to terminate if service commencement has not been achieved by that date.

The project agreement between the awarding authority and the service provider will address the time and cost consequences to the service provider of it failing to achieve service commencement by the originally programmed date, following certain types of event. In particular, provision will be made for:

- compensation events – SoPC4 defines a compensation event as a breach by the awarding authority of any of its obligations under the project agreement, although it recognises that it may be appropriate to add other events including those which are sector specific; the service provider will be entitled to an extension of time in order to avoid liability for damages for late service delivery (if applicable) and/or to the longstop date in order to prevent a right for the awarding authority to terminate from arising, and to recover from the awarding authority compensation for additional costs incurred as a result of consequential delays (including additional finance costs);
- relief events – these are events which are best managed by the service provider and the mandatory SoPC4 definition includes fire and other insured risks, riot, failures by statutory undertakers and strikes; the service provider will be given an extension of time but no compensation will be payable by the awarding authority and the period of the concession will not be extended; and
- force majeure events – the SoPC4 mandatory definition covers war, civil war, armed conflict, terrorism, nuclear, chemical or biological contamination and pressure waves caused by devices travelling at supersonic speeds; they are events which are beyond the control of either party and will give rise to an extension of time and eventually to a right of termination.

Cost risk

The awarding authority will need to give attention to the financial parameters applicable to a proposed project even before bids are requested and then to the various bids received in response to the Invitation to Negotiate and at the stage of Best and Final Offer (or any variants to the procurement process as described in Section 1 of this chapter). If it does not, there is a risk that time and costs will be wasted on bids which do not constitute value for money or are unbankable.

During the bid stages of the project, it is essential for the service provider to undertake a thorough appraisal of, and assess the risks inherent in, the various options it is considering before deciding on the basis of its bid. A rigorous view needs to be taken of whether the proposal is likely to be seen by the awarding authority as achieving value for money (see below). This exercise needs to be done both in relation to the initial capital spend and the subsequent maintenance and life-cycle costs. See Section 1.6 of this chapter for discussion on 'Gateway Reviews' and the Outline and Final Business Cases.

PFI transactions require the provision of a service in return for the payment of pre-agreed sums which are calculated, in part, by reference to the budgeted construction and associated finance costs. The payment for services will not be increased if the budgets are exceeded. In effect, therefore, the construction cost is fixed and the risk of cost overruns is placed with the service provider.

Quality risk

Issues of quality manifest themselves in similar ways to other risks mentioned in this section. In particular, the project agreement between the awarding authority and the service provider will ensure that commencement of the income stream is dependent on achieving service commencement to the requisite standards. 'Payment against performance' will be achieved thereafter through the implementation of detailed compliance monitoring procedures during the operational period and deductions for poor performance and unavailability.

Change of law risk

Changes in law occurring after financial close are outside the control of the service provider. However, the awarding authority will want the service provider to manage any additional costs associated with a change in law. The degree to which a change of law will affect the service provider's ability to provide the required service within the anticipated costs will vary from project to project. Accordingly, the precise allocation of risk between the awarding authority and the service provider will depend on where the risk can be managed most effectively.

The service provider usually bears the risk of a generally applicable change of law which affects construction costs, since such a change is regarded as foreseeable over a typical build period.

During the operational period, where changes of law are of a generally applicable nature, the service provider bears the revenue cost effect because it is protected through the combined effects of benchmarking or market testing of the service cost and indexation of the unitary payment, and usually shares (up to a cap) unforeseeable capital expenditure required.

Where the change of law is discriminatory or sector specific (as distinct from being generally applicable), the awarding authority bears the risk in both construction and operational periods.

Project obsolescence risk

The proposals of the service provider embodied in the contractual documentation may not represent the best technical solution for the awarding authority's needs. For example, if the awarding authority expresses its requirements for an IT system by reference to a specific technical specification such as a number of computers of a certain type configured in a specific way, rather than by way of a service provision requirement expressed in output terms (see Section 4 of this chapter), the solution offered by the service provider may have an element of obsolescence built into it at the outset.

The awarding authority may not be too concerned if this is the case provided that the standards of service are well defined and understood by the users of the building and have been delivered satisfactorily by the service provider. In these circumstances, the awarding authority may initially be indifferent as to how the service is provided, but ultimately the disadvantage of this approach is that the awarding authority will be unable to take advantage of the benefits offered by advances in technology which might in the longer term have provided the awarding authority with better value for money.

The awarding authority may approach its requirement for improving technological standards in different ways where this is a topic of importance to it (for example, in hospital projects where reliance is placed on specialized equipment). It may require technological standards to be enhanced in line with industry benchmarks or it may be able to create incentives for the service provider to ensure that the system is kept up to date by placing the residual value risk with the service provider.

2.2 Affordability

The proposals submitted by the bidder must be affordable by the awarding authority within the constraints laid down by its sponsoring government department.

2.3 Value for money

In its 2003 report, *PFI: Meeting the Investment Challenge*, the Government stressed that PFI should only be used where it was appropriate and where it offered value for money which is not at the cost of the terms and conditions of the relevant staff. The report states that PFI is unlikely to offer value for money where the costs of the transaction are disproportionate compared to the value of the project or in sectors where the pace of technological change makes it difficult to set out long-term requirements. The Government has therefore decided that PFI is not appropriate for IT projects or for individually procured projects with a capital value of less than £20 million.

The report recognizes that awarding authorities need to base their procurement decisions on an unbiased and rigorous assessment of which option presents best value for money and that to do so they need to have a robust means of assessing value for money. The Treasury therefore carried out a review of the value for money appraisal process and published new guidance in August 2004.

Historically value for money was assessed using the methodology set out in the Treasury's Green Book and by calculating a Public Sector Comparator or PSC (that is the cost of procuring the project under conventional means of procurement) which served as a benchmark against which private sector bids could be compared. The Treasury's *Technical Note No. 5 on How to Construct a Public Sector Comparator* advised that once the best PFI bid has been identified it must be compared to the PSC to determine which provides better value for money. The Technical Note has now been replaced by the Treasury's *Value for Money Assessment Guidance* published in August 2004 and the nature and use of the PSC has changed. Interestingly under the new guidance there is no comparison of the actual PFI bids received by the awarding authority against the PSC.

The new guidance requires awarding authorities to follow a three stage process in assessing value for money and the assessment now focuses on PFI as a procurement option rather than on particular PFI bids:

- The first stage should happen at the earliest stage of an investment programme and involves an assessment of the different procurement options and demonstration that PFI is the most appropriate route.

- The second stage is a comprehensive project appraisal carried out at OBC stage for a particular project; the quantitative comparison of the PFI procurement route and the conventional procurement route is now part of a much broader overall assessment of the project.
- The final stage in the appraisal of whether or not a project offers value for money comes just prior to the issue of the invitation to tender and continues throughout the procurement process. During this period awarding authorities are required to assess whether there is sufficient market interest and capacity for the project to generate the level of competitive tension needed to ensure maximum value for money.

The new guidance therefore has little impact on bidders in that it does not indicate how bids will be evaluated. It does state that the Treasury would publish additional guidance on bid evaluation, but at the time of writing no such guidance has appeared. Although there is no longer a comparison of bids against the PSC, bidders should still strive for maximum value for money to enhance their chances of winning the contract. In this sense, value for money involves more than allocating risk at the contractual level. It also demands a balancing act to be performed to achieve the best combination of whole life cost and quality to meet the requirements of the output specification (see also discussion set out in Section 1.6 of this chapter).

At a technical level, value for money is more likely to be achieved where the service provider's proposals presented to the awarding authority reflect the following factors:

- ensuring that the facilities are appropriate for the intended purpose so as to avoid over-design;
- maximizing overall efficiency by ensuring that the design life of the facility and its constituent parts is compatible with optimum maintenance and life-cycle costs;
- utilizing best practice for both initial design and construction and subsequent operational and maintenance activities; and
- requiring designers to consider the future use of the asset in order to enhance its residual value (if appropriate).

The process can be complex as the service provider tries to ascertain what exactly is required. For example, the awarding authority may need a high level of 'flexible workspace'. This could lead the service provider to over-design or -engineer the proposed design solution in order to deliver such a requirement. This in turn would not necessarily represent value for money. It is nevertheless the service provider's responsibility to ensure that these technical issues are managed effectively as this will increase the likelihood of achieving the best value for money solution and thereby enhance the chances of its bid being successful.

The awarding authority will encourage bidders to achieve best value for money if during the bidding process it emphasizes the delivery of services, rather than the provision of an asset, and strives to achieve the optimum transfer of risk. Issues associated with delivery of services are discussed in Section 4 of this chapter.

The Public Accounts Committee's report entitled *Managing the relationship to secure a successful partnership in PFI projects* (published 11 July 2002) stated that one of the key concerns of their review of some 400 project agreements was that value for money was not maintained over the life of the concession. Therefore, it recommended that it was essential for all project agreements to contain appropriate mechanisms such as benchmarking, market testing and open book accounting; in October 2006 the Treasury published guidance on benchmarking and market testing. Regardless of such mechanisms, however, awarding authorities will need to make a fundamental 'conceptual leap' from the beginning of the project, including directing the output specification of the project, rather than dictating the detail of the design required at an 'input' level.

It may be worth observing that, in our experience of public and private sectors, the value for money mechanism remains poorly understood. On the public sector side in particular, the belief can emerge that value for money equates to 'lowest price'; and another source of difficulty is the relationship between value for money and affordability; the one does not necessarily imply the other.

The approach required is explained in more detail below (Section 4.3).

3 CONTRACTUAL MATRIX

Construction contracts are well known for their complexity. In part, this is because the construction of buildings, facilities and infrastructure involves the bringing together of resources, skills and experience which are seldom found in one organization within the construction industry. The fragmentation of the industry into discrete sectors has had a direct impact on contractual arrangements and represents one of the principal reasons for the proliferation of interlinking contracts which need to reflect the interplay of the various parties involved in the design and construction process.

In the context of PFI transactions, the contractual arrangements are invariably more complex than would be found in traditional methods of procurement. This is due to the need to overlay traditional procurement techniques with contractual structures which are geared towards the delivery of services and the means by which PFI transactions are generally financed.

In the context of design and construction, the principal contracts are illustrated in Figure 1 of this chapter.

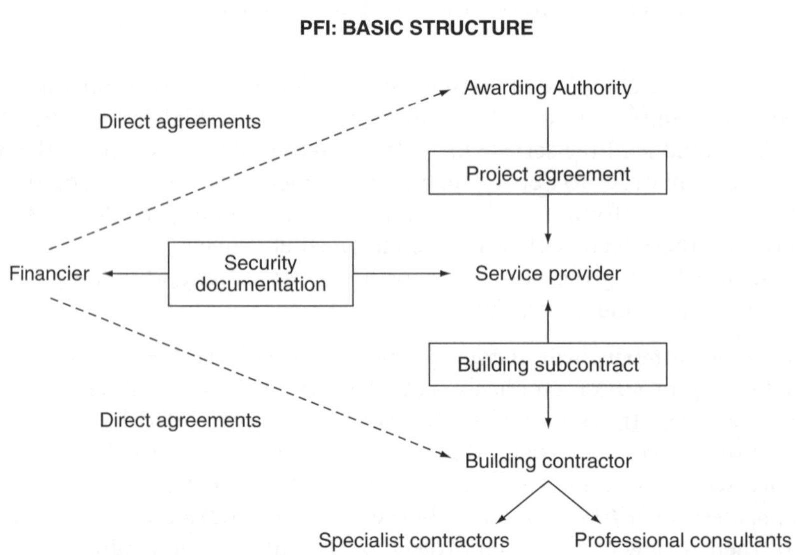

Figure 1. Principal contracts in PFI transactions

3.1 Project agreement

The project agreement is the principal agreement in a PFI transaction. It describes the rights and obligations of the awarding authority and the service provider throughout the life of the project.

The project agreement will make the service provider responsible for procuring the delivery of services (including by undertaking the design and construction of the facility in question). The project agreement will allocate responsibility between the awarding authority and the service provider for the key risks applicable to the design and construction phase described in Section 2 of this chapter as well as the ongoing risks applicable to the service delivery phase. It will also set out the service provider's obligation to deliver a facility that meets the requirements of the output specification.

Depending on how the payment mechanism responds to construction defects and the quality of the working environment of occupied areas, undertakings of a more general nature, concerning the overall standard and quality of the facility to be provided before the operational period can commence, may also be included in the documentation. These undertakings might extend to compliance with specified standards of design and quality of workmanship and materials. The quality of environmental clean-up works may also have to be addressed, whether in relation to the site of the project or land which may be sold when it becomes surplus to requirements once the new facility is operational.

Consideration will need to be given as to whether the project agreement needs to impose express design and construction obligations in relation to the execution of capital works during the operational period (particularly as a result of a service variation). It is sometimes argued that the standard and quality of any such capital works can be dealt with at the time they are to be procured (for example, in the service variation instruction), but the disadvantage of such an approach is a lack of certainty about the nature of these obligations going forward and certain problematic legal issues may also arise. For example, can a service variation instruction alter the terms of the project agreement?

The project agreement will also address a variety of commercial issues, such as force majeure, payment and performance, changes in law, termination, and compensation payable following termination.

3.2 Building subcontract

Sitting below the project agreement will be the building subcontract. This contract is likely to be awarded for a lump sum fixed price. It will be a design and build contract so as to impose single point responsibility on the building subcontractor covering all aspects of the design and construction of the facility.

The service provider and its financiers will want to ensure that the completion and pricing risks which have been assumed under the project agreement are passed through to the building subcontractor on terms which are no less onerous than those found in or assumed by the service provider under the project agreement. The key is to ensure as far as possible that the financial exposure of the service provider to the building subcontractor is as limited as possible. One example of how this is achieved is through equivalent project relief clauses, which seek to minimise the risk of inconsistent determinations of entitlements to payment/relief under the project agreement (arising from, say, compensation events) and the relevant subcontract. Such clauses have met with judicial resistance, however, when they deal with determinations under the Housing Grants, Construction and Regeneration Act 1996 (HGA). This aspect is dealt with more fully below, in section [10].

In any event, the contractual obligations placed on the building subcontractor may in some instances be more stringent than (or at least different to) the equivalent obligations found in the project agreement. Two examples are given below.

First, late completion of construction will give rise to delayed service commencement and a delay in the start of payments from the awarding authority to the service provider. Accordingly, SoPC4 makes the point that liquidated damages under the project agreement will be inappropriate in the absence of special circumstances which would make such damages represent value for money as the service provider will pass the risk of incurring such liquidated damages through to the awarding authority in the form of an increased unitary payment. The circumstances which justify liquidated damages will be confined to instances where the awarding authority suffers losses in excess of the unitary payment which the awarding authority would have paid if completion had been achieved on time after taking into account the cost of securing the services. Examples of this include the education sector, where it can be essential for completion to occur prior to the commencement of an academic year, and government office buildings, where vacant possession of the existing premises must be given by a specified date and this can only be achieved if the new facility is ready for occupation on the due date.

The approach under the project agreement should be contrasted with the position under the building subcontract which will invariably provide for the payment of liquidated damages for delayed completion. Such damages will often be secured to the financiers as they represent lost income needed to service the project debt. Most building subcontractors will accept liability for liquidated damages provided they are fixed at an appropriate rate. In agreeing the rate, the project company must not overlook the fact that liquidated damages operate as a cap on the building subcontractor's liability for late completion.

Secondly, the service provider and its financiers may require more stringent standards of quality from the building subcontractor than are contained in the warranties on design and construction set out in the project agreement. The principal justification for this is the fact that income generated during the operational period is, to a greater or lesser extent, dependent on performance, which in turn is dependent on quality and suitability of design and construction. For example, more stringent standards in the building subcontract are likely to be required if the payment mechanism in the project agreement provides for deduction from the unitary payment for unavailability due to defects, particularly if those deductions are not dependent on proving breach of the project agreement. In such circumstances, fitness for purpose obligations might be imposed on the building subcontractor.

The awarding authority will need to ensure that a proper balance is struck in the building subcontract on these kinds of issue. On the one hand, it should not think that it is getting something for nothing if the building subcontract is unduly onerous. A premium for any such stringent conditions will be included by the building subcontractor in its price which, as with liquidated damages, will feed through to the awarding authority in the form of increased unitary payment. On the other hand, the awarding authority should check that sufficient risk arising from the project agreement has been allocated to the principal subcontractors by the project company in order to deliver a robust project.

In addition to ensuring that the completion and pricing risks under the project agreement are passed through to the building subcontractor, SoPC4 provides some examples of reasons for the awarding authority to review the terms of the building subcontract.

First, if the project agreement requires the service provider to pay liquidated damages to the awarding authority for late completion, the awarding authority will need to ensure that the service provider is sufficiently robust so as to meet such obligation (taking account of the terms of the subcontract and the claims of the service provider's financiers). Secondly, if the awarding authority has the benefit of a collateral warranty it will need to ensure that the terms of the subcontract are satisfactory.

Other relevant issues for the building subcontract include the process of certification of completion and extensions of time (and how these processes and entitlements interrelate with those contained in the project agreement) and the integration of the building subcontractor with the service provider during the testing and commissioning phase of the project.

3.3 Security documentation

While it will be rare for parent company guarantees and performance bonds to be appropriate in a PFI transaction in order to support the design and construction obligations owed to the awarding authority by the service provider under the project agreement, it is not uncommon for the financiers to insist on the provision of a guarantee or a bond (or both) in respect of the building subcontractor's obligations under the building subcontract.

If the building subcontractor can offer a guarantor of substance, it is likely that a guarantee will be considered by the service provider and its financiers to be preferable to a performance bond. Most performance bonds are capped at or around 10% of the contract sum and will expire at practical completion or once the defects liability period obligations under the building subcontract have been discharged. In contrast, a parent company guarantee is likely to be entirely co-extensive with the building subcontractor's liability under the building subcontract and therefore will not be subject to a 10% cap and will be enforceable throughout a limitation period expiring twelve years after completion, assuming that the sub-contract is executed as a deed.

The financiers' views on security are dealt with in more detail in Section 1 of Chapter 1.2.

3.4 Professional consultants and specialist contractors

The awarding authority may already have technical expertise in-house which can be utilized for the purposes of preparing the output specification, reviewing the service provider's proposals in response to the output specification and compliance monitoring. However, these resources are often supplemented by professional consultants specifically engaged for the project in hand.

On the private sector side, the professional consultants responsible for the design of the facility will be instructed by the building subcontractor, rather than the service provider. This structure is driven by the requirement for the building subcontractor to offer single point responsibility for the whole design and construction process. However, in some instances the service provider may engage the professional consultants during the early stages of the procurement process when preparing the initial response to the invitation to submit outline proposals and for the purposes of briefing the building subcontractor. However, much depends on the nature of the consortium comprising the service provider.

As regards detailed design and construction, the building subcontractor will employ specialist subcontractors in a similar way to the manner in which they are engaged under design and build contracts awarded on traditionally procured projects.

3.5 Early Works Agreements

SoPC4 contains new guidance regarding early works agreements, providing that they should be avoided where possible. There are a variety of reasons for this, including the potential for breaches of EU procurement law and regulation and the principle that, in the ordinary course of events, the awarding authority should not be under any obligation to make payments prior either to financial close or to commencement of services.

SoPC4 acknowledges that early works agreements may sometimes be justifiable where particular programming issues apply: the example provided is where a school wishes to avoid facility handovers in term-time. In such circumstances, the guidance provides some ground rules for undertaking such early works, including that such works should be planned well in advance and as part of the overall procurement strategy. Consideration should be given to whether it is appropriate for the bidder to undertake such works or whether the awarding authority should independently commission a third party to undertake them. The works proposal should also offer demonstrable savings of a general nature (rather than specifically related to the bidder's preferred solution) so that they will be of value whether or not the project agreement is signed. The guidance states further that the works should only include items that the procuring authority wish to have done in any event (such as certain surveys, making safe, access roads etc.).

3.6 Ancillary construction contracts

The awarding authority's requirement for collateral warranties and direct agreements containing step-in rights are considered in more detail in Section 9 of this chapter.

4 DESIGN AND THE TECHNICAL DOCUMENTATION

Attached to the project agreement will be two sets of technical documents, the first being the output specification prepared on behalf of the awarding authority and the second being the detailed proposals which are prepared by the service provider to meet the requirements of the output specification.

Before considering the output specification and the service provider's proposals, it is important to consider the overall approach to design in the context of a PFI transaction.

4.1 Approach to design

The preparation of, and allocation of responsibility for, design in a PFI transaction is radically different from design production in a traditionally procured project even if it uses design and build procurement methods. The key conceptual difference is that in a PFI transaction the awarding authority requires the provision of services rather than the purchase of an asset from which it will operate its business. It is the service provider that maintains the asset rather than the awarding authority.

As mentioned above, PFI philosophy allows the service provider to choose between the provision of a facility which is expensive to build, but cheap to maintain, or cheap to build, but expensive to maintain. It reflects an intrinsic consequence of the transfer of design risk to the service provider and the payment mechanism found in PFI transactions. It also means that the awarding authority has no real interest in, and (if it wishes to maximize risk transfer) should not become involved with, design issues such as the type of structural frame for, or mechanical and electrical services to be used in, the facility. The awarding authority's interest is limited to securing the required outputs (for example, the specified ambient temperature subject to agreed tolerances).

It needs to be recognized that it will not be possible for this theoretical approach to be followed in all cases. As described below, there will be occasions when the awarding authority's requirement is so specific that certain elements of the output specification ought to be very similar to a traditional performance specification. In practice, therefore, the output specification may constitute a combination of pure output requirements coupled with specific performance requirements for certain elements. Some sector specific guidance recognises different approaches for different sectors.

The fact that there may be performance specifications included as part of the output specification does not mean that the awarding authority or its consultants should consider, for example, that it needs to approve the type of construction of the facility's car park because constant repairs would be disruptive to occupational use. Rather, the approach should be to ensure that the payment mechanism is sufficiently sensitive so that deductions for poor performance or unavailability can be made if the car park is constantly under repair and cannot be used.

This does not suggest that the awarding authority should not consider and specify its requirements as regards operational implications of design solutions. For example, it would be perfectly in order for minimum redecoration cycles to be included as an output requirement, particularly for areas where regular redecoration would be disruptive to operational use.

The awarding authority's involvement in design should therefore be restricted to what might be described generally as business or user requirements. These requirements will vary depending on the type of project. For example, in the case of an accommodation project, the interests of the awarding authority should centre around the architectural or aesthetic appearance of the building, visitor reception areas and other occupied areas, the location of fixed areas (for example, service risers) which directly affect occupation, the location of business units (including their adjacencies to one another), the location of partitions, quality of finishes, signage, room and workplace configuration and other operational issues.

4.2 Role of an output specification

In all PFI transactions, the awarding authority will provide an output specification which describes its requirements as comprehensively as possible. The 4Ps' glossary defines an output specification as 'a detailed description of the functions that the new accommodation must be capable of performing'. It provides further that an output specification should state only the outputs required of the services, and not the way in which the private sector will achieve them.

As the output specification represents the means by which the awarding authority describes its user requirements to the service provider, it is the awarding authority's responsibility to ensure that these requirements are adequately defined. If they are not, and alterations to the output specification become necessary, such alterations are likely to impact on the nature or scope of the project, and may give rise to variations which can only be implemented at extra cost to the awarding authority. However, the concept of variations should not be treated in exactly the same way as it is in conventional forms of procurement. For example, the awarding authority's requirements may change throughout the life of the project but if flexibility has been addressed properly in the output specification a variation may not necessarily arise even if it is subsequently discovered that the facility needs to be adapted. The *Waste Management Procurement Pack* for example highlights the point that key landfill diversion performance standards in the output specification will increase during the waste project's contract period to reflect the requirements of the documents such as the EU Landfill Directive, Waste Strategy 2000 (and so on). The output specification will therefore need to be drafted with sufficient flexibility to allow this, without use of the variation procedure.

A key point here is the difference between *design criteria*, which are the primary concern of the output specification (albeit translated into user requirements); and *ongoing performance requirements*. Specific wording, including a scheme for evaluating performance and the financial consequences of failure, is likely to be required where the latter are intended; such a scheme would normally be found in the payment mechanism and related clauses. Those familiar with PFI transactions may find this an obvious point to make but the parties in *London Bus Services Ltd* v. *Tramtrack Croydon Ltd* [2007] EWHC 107 did not. The case concerned a concession agreement to build and run the tram service in Croydon. The performance specification set out requirements in relation to 'Fleet Size and Tram capacity', which set out maximum numbers of passengers and seating requirements 'for the purposes of fleet size determination' (paragraph 3.11). In addition, under the rubric 'Design' the specification provided that the system should be 'capable ... of providing for a 33% increase in passengers carrying capacity above that initially required' elsewhere in the specification. The issue between the parties was who should pay for increased capacity to deal with overcrowding: if such increased capacity was within the specification then it was a 'Service Change' and the service provider paid; otherwise it was a 'Service Parameters Change' and London Buses (effectively, the awarding authority) paid.

The Court of Appeal found that the provisions dealing with capacity were design obligations not ongoing performance requirements: Longmore LJ said 'I cannot read paragraph 3.11 as intended to secure the result that if any time during service standing passengers exceed 5 per square meter then [the service provider] was in breach of contract. This is a paragraph dealing with the number of trams required to comply with the requirements as to frequency and journey times and with capacity, not with the conditions actually encountered in service.' Neither would increased density of standing passengers over that set out in paragraph 3.11 trigger an obligation to add capacity. 'The very absence of determinative criteria [as to how "over-crowding" was to be measured and when the service provider would be in breach] is at least an indication that this paragraph is dealing with the planning and design stage, not providing a trigger mechanism for the imposition of an obligation to provide enhanced capacity'. The court would have expected to see such criteria before translating a design obligation into a performance requirement. On the question of how the need for increased capacity should be categorised within the contractual framework (i.e. whether it was a Service Change or a Service Parameters Change), the court concluded that this would need to be re-pleaded at a future date.

The case serves as another reminder of the precision and care that needs to be taken when output specifications are drafted: the awarding authority needs not only to translate design into user requirements but also to consider those requirements in light of conditions likely to be encountered in service and specify the consequences of failing to provide them.

4.3 Nature of outputs

The preparation of a specification in output terms involves a huge conceptual leap for the authors of the document (as well, it might be noted, as for the building subcontractor, who may not be used to dealing with client specifications that are not specific and certain). In order to prepare such a specification, a thorough and detailed analysis of the user requirements will be needed and this can only be done effectively if a clear understanding of the awarding authority's business and operational needs has been acquired.

These needs have to be converted into outputs by concentrating on the use to which the facilities, equipment and services will be put rather than inputs, such as the physical specification of the facility. For example, a hospital for 1000 patients does not constitute an output whereas the delivery of a level of patient care *is* an output; the specification of a particular system of telephones and computer technology does not constitute an output whereas the delivery of an effective communication and information service *is* an output; and the specification of a certain type of heating system does not constitute an output requirement whereas specifying the temperature requirements for different areas of a facility *is* an output.

In preparing an output specification, just as much consideration should therefore be given to what information to omit as to what to include. Sufficient information to enable the service provider to understand the business or user requirements of the awarding authority will be essential. Requirements which are unnecessarily prescriptive or onerous will be detrimental to the objectives of PFI procurement, including best value for money and risk transfer.

If the output specification constitutes a clear and concise definition of user requirements, an opportunity will be created for the service provider to propose the most innovative, cost effective and flexible solutions. In particular, service providers will be given the freedom to consider how best to deliver the required service without being unnecessarily constrained by input requirements promulgated by the awarding authority which may not represent the most cost-and technically-effective solution. Care should be taken to ensure that any project constraints (e.g. operational policies of the awarding authority) do not unnecessarily restrict the opportunity for innovation.

To enhance the potential for maximizing flexibility, the output specification might also be prepared so as to identify core requirements which cannot be changed while allowing other, less essential, needs to be discussed and negotiated with the service provider prior to financial close with a view to maximizing efficiencies.

4.4 Typical content of an output specification

Typically, output specifications will address the facility to be delivered plus maintenance, furniture and equipment, energy and cleaning/waste management, and other 'soft services' (such as security, catering and caretaking).

Generalized across a broad range of sectors, the following list of items is typical of that which may be included as part of the output specification. The list is indicative and should not be considered to be exhaustive. Specific project types may require many more specific items to be included in the output specification.

For example, in August 2004 the Department of Health published *The Design Development Protocol for PFI Schemes – Revision 1* (first published in July 2001), which provides some guidance as to the contents of an output specification in a hospital PFI. It states that the information provided by the awarding authority at the Invitation to Negotiate stage should be sufficiently robust to enable bidders to provide a response which will in turn enable the awarding authority to evaluate and shortlist bids effectively. It lists a number of areas which should be covered by the output specification including:

- whole development statement
- clinical output specification

- architectural output specification
- engineering, structural and civil output specifications.

Overall project objectives

Some examples may include achieving corporate or departmental criteria such as:

- corporate strategy, including a description of the functions for which the facility will be used;
- rationalization and suitability, e.g. achieving greater efficiency by using less space and providing the right accommodation to operational and support areas;
- flexibility, e.g. to cater for increases or decreases in staff numbers or changes required for the working environment; and
- improving working conditions and modernization, e.g. by achieving specified BREEAM ratings.

In addition to the above, consideration should be given to providing high-level information regarding the structure of the organization, including the overall size of the various business departments and how they fit together.

If the awarding authority has a mission statement, consideration should be given to its incorporation into the output specification in order to provide an indication of the ethos of the organization.

The purpose of the required facility as a base requirement

The specification should include:

- a statement of the overall required outputs, including requirements for matters such as cellular accommodation and meeting rooms. This information may be supported by appropriate corporate or departmental guidelines and descriptions of current functions of individual occupants, together with how these roles and responsibilities may change over time;
- a statement of the services to be contained in, and provided by, the new facility, such as technical and security infrastructure, visitor reception areas and soft services varying from cleaning and catering to waste removal and internal postal or messenger services.

As much information as is possible should be provided about future plans and likely changes to the organization and the way in which work is undertaken. Information about requirements for location may be considered for inclusion. Information regarding the existing environment and working practices and how these may be subject to change in the future should be provided.

The scope of the project base requirements and the scope for alternative proposals to be considered

- Interfaces with other facilities or services which are not currently part of the project and the extent to which they may be incorporated into the wider project definitions should be considered. For example, in an education project the service provider will not provide teaching services but where it is providing library services there will be interfaces with the teaching staff, which should be defined.
- A description of the limitations placed on the project scope should be provided.
- A statement of the scope within which the project can accommodate programme slippage or alternative proposed programmes should be included.

Performance criteria for the facility and the services to be provided
Such criteria include:

- a statement of the environmental conditions to be provided; for example, in relation to energy efficiency in line with government policy;
- a statement of the physical conditions to be provided; for example, in relation to suitable access and facilities for disabled people and car parking requirements;
- a statement of the operating outputs which are required; for example, in relation to a fully integrated internal design taking into account occupational and functional issues to which the facility will be put;
- a statement of the frequency of the services to be provided; for example, for the delivery and collection of mail and likely usage (whether relating to internal circulation or signage or relating to heat levels arising from the use of IT equipment); and
- a statement of the standards to which a service must be provided, which will often be developed for the appropriate service level agreement; for example, for laboratory projects, how often cleaning has to be carried out and the standards of cleanliness which are to be achieved in laboratories, kitchens and other similar areas.

Compliance requirements
The criteria with which the service provider's proposals must comply will be spelt out in order to establish standards.

Such criteria include:

- government legislation;
- local authority legislation and bylaws;
- EC regulations;
- British Standards and Codes of Practice;
- specific technical design standards; and
- compatibility with existing systems and standards (e.g. IT systems).

Project constraints
Only essential project elements should be included as a constraint such as:

- overall project time-scale; for example, the date when the new facilities must be provided;
- phasing requirements for the commencement and completion of construction; for example, for early access to enable the awarding authority to prepare for decant into the new facility;
- budget constraints; for example, financial limits beyond which expenditure will not be authorized or constraints which stem from the availability of resources to meet unitary payments;
- client's working hours restrictions; for example, to minimize disruption caused by noisy or dirty work where the awarding authority remains in occupation of parts of the buildings which are to be refurbished by the service provider; and
- planning permission.

Consideration of alternative solutions
Scope must be given for the proposal by bidders of alternative solutions:

1.1 The planning system
1.2 Financing the project
1.3 Public sector projects
1.4 Public/private partnerships
1.5 Tender process
1.6 Construction contracts
1.7 Construction insurance

- the base requirements which must be provided before any variants will be considered must be defined. For example, the output specification may define minimum spatial requirements but for purposes of providing additional third party income the service provider may propose the provision of additional space;
- the extent to which alternative variant proposals will be considered must be defined. For example, any proposals to provide additional facilities above the base requirement must be self-financing and produce no additional increase in the unitary payment proposed for the base project; and
- ideas for alternative solutions with the bidders should be shared. For example, a bidder may consider that additional sporting facilities, over and above the stated requirement that a new school may have to satisfy its teaching needs, will provide additional income which can be shared with the school.

4.5 Development of the output specification and service provider's proposals

One of the key responsibilities of the service provider is to propose a design solution which enables the awarding authority to carry out its business to the standards and quality expected of it. In addition, the service provider will be required, as owner and manager of the facility, to provide support services to the awarding authority in a cost-effective fashion.

Because of its nature, the output specification is likely to be capable of a number of different interpretations. The scope for this will be much greater than would be the case with a conventional performance specification. During the pre-contract period, therefore, the awarding authority and the service provider will need to engage in discussions to ensure that the service provider's interpretation of the output specification accords with that of the awarding authority. This will continue while the service provider develops and finalizes its design proposals for incorporation into the project agreement.

The Design Development Protocol for PFI Schemes – Revision 1 was produced by a steering group comprising representatives of the major interest groups including the Major Contractors Group, the Royal Institute of British Architects and NHS Estates and a draft version was subject to extensive consultation. It is intended to represent an agreed approach to the design development process in a hospital PFI, starting at bidding stage, until financial close and the incorporation of the service provider's design into the project agreement.

The broad principle expressed, in respect of the scope and purpose of the awarding authority's review of design data between the selection of the service provider and financial close, is that the awarding authority has the right to review and object to certain design data so as to ensure that it can carry out its clinical functions in the facility.

It is important to emphasize that in agreeing the interpretation of the output specification, the awarding authority is not expected to accept responsibility for the technical competence or accuracy of the service provider's design proposals. To do so would transfer the design risk back to the awarding authority. However, it is not uncommon for the service provider to suggest a limited form of sign-off to provide it with the comfort of knowing that the design proposals have encapsulated the awarding authority's business or user requirements: awarding authorities should only be interested in details relating to 'occupied areas' and the sign-off itself should confirm solely that the business function can be carried out. Accordingly, the protocol makes it clear that this does not mean that there is a transfer of design risk back to the awarding authority. Therefore, the awarding authority is entitled to object and withhold 'approval' to the design data produced where:

- it believes that the design would not meet its requirements, as set out in the output specification, or
- the design does not achieve clinical functionality.

Although this protocol was produced by the Department of Health for particular application to hospital schemes, the principles expressed in it could equally be applied to other PFI/PPP schemes. The precise nature of this sign-off is dealt with in more detail in Section 5 of this chapter.

In return for the awarding authority agreeing to provide a limited form of sign-off in respect of the service provider's proposals, it is usually accepted by the service provider that it will carry out and complete the construction in accordance with the output specification, together with an obligation to deliver the service provider's proposals.

As part of the process for formulating design proposals, it may be necessary from time to time for the awarding authority to assist the interpretation process by clarifying its requirements. This may result in the output specification being developed or refined during the procurement process. In the course of this, however, the awarding authority may come under pressure from the service provider to be more specific in terms of the output requirements in order to give the service provider increased certainty. This would run counter to the principle of risk transfer inherent in the PFI approach, however, and the awarding authority needs to be aware of this tendency, in order to resist it. Either way, the interpretation process should be completed by financial close if at all possible but any issues left outstanding may have to be addressed as part of the design development procedure (see Section 5 of this chapter) or the compliance monitoring process (see Section 6 of this chapter) depending on their nature.

It is the responsibility of the service provider to translate the information contained in the output specification into a design brief which will then be issued to the building subcontractor and its design team for the preparation of detailed design proposals.

While these detailed proposals will assist the service provider in its discussions with the awarding authority on the output specification, the service provider will need to control the design process. In particular, it will be anxious to ensure that the design has been developed to a sufficient level of detail so as to minimize the risk of changes to design which could alter the interpretation of the output specification agreed with the awarding authority. In addition, changes in the detailed design which do not generate a change to the scope or nature of the project are unlikely to be treated as a variation under the project agreement but could nevertheless give rise to time and money claims under the building subcontract.

The finalized proposals of the service provider will typically contain the following:

- a statement and description of how the overall project objectives are to be achieved within the overall resources available to the awarding authority and from which it will make unitary payments;
- a number of other variant proposals may be offered to illustrate how the scope of the project may be altered and, possibly, extended to show their advantages to the project;
- the performance criteria for the facility and for the services to be provided will be contained in a series of room data sheets and service monitoring standards, and will show how the required compliance criteria will be met; for example, the temperature limits within which rooms are to be maintained and standards of air quality which are to be provided; and

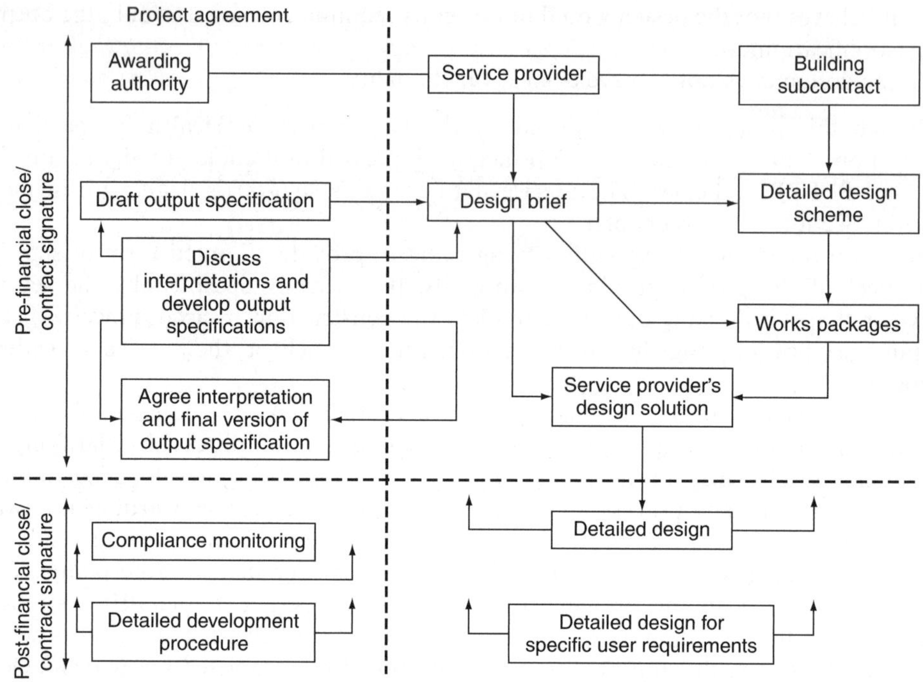

Figure 2. The design process in PFI transactions

- proposals to show how the allocation of risk is to be achieved within the matrix provided.

Consideration of alternative solutions is an important feature of successful proposals from service providers and is the foremost opportunity for them to show their innovative and commercial propositions; for example, the provision of additional hospital facilities to generate additional income and profit from private medical services such as sports injury clinics and patient hotels.

The process for establishing and finalizing the output specification and the service provider's proposals are shown in diagrammatic form in Figure 2 of this chapter.

5 DESIGN DEVELOPMENT

Although the parties to a PFI transaction will endeavour to settle as much of the design proposals as is possible prior to signature of the project agreement, it is unrealistic to expect all areas of design which impact on business or user requirements to be finalized at that stage. This may be due to the service provider's need to minimize design costs before financial close, but it may also be attributable to the needs of the awarding authority. For example, the awarding authority may not be in a position to confirm some aspects of its business or user requirements until much closer to service commencement, particularly where the awarding authority's requirements are technology driven, the design and construction period is lengthy or one of its key requirements is flexibility.

5.1 Design development procedures

The project agreement will therefore need to cater for the development and finalization after signature of the project agreement of the outstanding areas of design, but always limited to those aspects of the design in which the awarding authority has a legitimate interest (see Section 4 of this chapter). The procedures for this are often critical. For the awarding authority, they will represent the means by which its essential business or user requirements are to be crystallized and incorporated into the facility. For the service provider, there will be a concern to ensure that the process does not impact adversely on its ability to achieve completion within budget and on programme. For example, it will want to be assured that the business or user requirements do not result in redesign or reconstruction of any part of the facility, such as having to modify or relocate service cores in the facility. Time and cost implications would preclude this even if any reworking were technically feasible.

Accordingly, the design development procedure will address a number of issues:

- the nature and scope of design which is to be finalized;
- the level of detail of the design to be reviewed by the awarding authority;
- the mechanics for any briefings to be provided by the awarding authority and the production of design information by the service provider in a packaged and systematic format;
- any constraints on the awarding authority's briefings, which are then to be satisfied by the service provider in its design submissions;
- the period during which the procedures are to be implemented and completed;
- the circumstances in which the design submissions from the service provider can be rejected by the awarding authority;
- 'deemed sign-off' if the awarding authority fails to respond to a design submission within the appropriate time frame;
- maintaining records of submissions made by, and responses given to, the service provider; and
- a fast track procedure for resolving any disputes which might arise during the process.

5.2 Awarding authority's sign-off

From a legal perspective, one of the most important features of the design development procedure will be the contractual implication of the awarding authority's sign-off on the design submissions made by the service provider. The first version of the Treasury Taskforce Guidance published in 1999 suggested that there should be no formal sign-off as the design development procedure should not undermine risk transfer. The justification given by the Treasury Taskforce was that, in practice, the awarding authority would not allow the design to develop in a way that it knew would prevent it from delivering its public services. It followed from this approach that the awarding authority had the power to comment on, but not formally sanction, the design submissions presented to it.

In practice, the position described by the Treasury Taskforce did not provide a sufficient degree of certainty to the awarding authority through having the ability to ensure that its views on design submissions were reflected properly in the facility at service commencement. In addition, the service provider did not acquire a sufficient degree of certainty that its design proposals satisfied the awarding authority's business or user requirements, and that it could thereby avoid or minimize the risk of completion being delayed and hence the commencement of the income stream.

Subsequent versions of the guidance recognize this and that it may be acceptable for an awarding authority to accept a limited degree of design responsibility so far as it relates solely to the authority's ability to carry out its functions in the building. This is the approach, as to clinical function, reflected in the Department of Health's Standard Form Project Agreement.

Accordingly, the project agreement invariably provides for a formal sign-off by the awarding authority. The sign-off is limited in nature so that it does not extend to the technical competence of the design proposals. It simply confirms that the design proposals, once implemented, satisfy the business or user requirements. For example, the sign-off confirms the awarding authority's acceptance of the adjacencies of business units or departments for business use, but will not represent confirmation from the awarding authority that it is satisfied the facility will perform to other contractual standards.

1.1 The planning system
1.2 Financing the project
1.3 Public sector projects
1.4 Public/private partnerships
1.5 Tender process
1.6 Construction contracts
1.7 Construction insurance

5.3 Iterative process

The design development procedure is sometimes structured as an iterative process. This will allow for meetings and discussions on draft design submissions before they are presented formally to the awarding authority for sign-off. This is very different from the procedures for review and sanction found in traditionally procured design and build contracts where design proposals are presented for sign-off without much, if any, prior consultation and are simply checked for compatibility with a performance specification. Notwithstanding the benefits of iterative procedures, some sectors have adopted the traditional 'ABC' procedures. The NHS Executive has adopted such procedures as has the *School Standard Form PFI Agreement (non-BSF) August 2004*. Here, design data is submitted for review to the awarding authority and the service provider may only start construction works after the awarding authority has either returned the data within 10 days marked 'no comment' or allowed 10 days to elapse without making comment. There is also scope for the parties to agree that if the 10 day period lapses with no comment having been made in relation to certain specified classes of data, then the service provider is to assume that objection *has* been made to it. In either case, the grounds on which the awarding authority can object are carefully prescribed, and relate to the awarding authority's obligation to provide educational services at a certain level, or the rights and obligations of the awarding authority under the project agreement.

The attraction of an iterative process in a PFI transaction is that it reflects the fact that the service provider is not responding to a traditional performance specification, but to output based requirements. As explained in Section 4 of this chapter, the awarding authority's requirements may need to be clarified or amplified, or there may be more than one valid interpretation of them. The iterative process, involving the awarding authority and the service provider in a 'partnering' environment, is often regarded as the most likely means by which the parties can settle on an agreed solution as quickly and efficiently as possible and in a non-confrontational manner.

5.4 Design development and variations

A clear distinction needs to be made in the project agreement between matters properly falling within the ambit of design development and variations. The design development procedure should not be used by the awarding authority as a back-door method of securing variations to the output specification at no extra cost. By the same token, however, it is the service provider's responsibility to ensure that an appropriate allowance has been included within its budgets and programme for all work necessary to deliver a completed facility on a turnkey basis. A variation should only arise where the awarding authority changes its output specification as this will inevitably lead to a change in the nature or scope of the construction works.

The provisions in the project agreement governing variations are different from the provisions commonly found in traditional procurement methods and there will usually be restrictions on the types of variation which the awarding authority can request. SoPC4 suggests that a number of grounds on which it would be reasonable for the service provider to refuse to implement a change; for example, if the change is inconsistent with good industry practice, if it would materially and adversely affect the provider's ability to deliver the services or if it would materially and adversely affect the nature of the project including its risk profile. The project agreement may also contain provisions that limit the number or size of the variations which may be made during the construction period or the time at which any such variation can be requested by the authority.

In the light of these considerations, it is usually sensible to make provision for any variations that might arise during design development to be identified before they are implemented. In this way, the awarding authority and the service provider can determine in advance whether a variation has arisen and whether, and under what terms, it is to be carried out. The parties may agree that the most economic or practical way in which to implement a variation may be achieved by having it carried out on a 'retrofit' basis.

6 COMPLIANCE MONITORING

6.1 Need for compliance monitoring

HM Treasury has, in its publications on PFI, repeatedly stated that monitoring is the awarding authority's responsibility in a PFI transaction, even though service provision is delivered and performance monitored by the private sector provider.

It is often the case that the authority's role here is carried out by its contract manager and includes assuring the awarding authority and the taxpayer that all the obligations of both contracting parties are being met, overseeing service changes, carrying out negotiations for new services; and so on. The role will continue throughout both the construction and the operational phase.

Compliance monitoring also reflects a difficulty faced by the awarding authority in that, until the facility has been designed and constructed by the service provider, it is difficult for it to know precisely how the service provider will effect service delivery from the facility that is being provided. It is not surprising, therefore, that the awarding authority is interested in monitoring the activities of the service provider during design and construction just as it does during the operational phase.

Compliance monitoring during design and construction under a PFI transaction is nevertheless different from supervision carried out for a traditionally procured project. PFI requires the transfer of the completion risk to the service provider and payments are geared to performance after completion. In a traditional project, the client has paid the capital cost of the works to the contractor by completion and its remedies for defects are framed as claims for damages or (if the defects arise during the first year or so after handover) securing repairs (and in respect of which the client will hold a sum of money as retention or a bond until the obligations during the defects correction period have been discharged).

By contract in a PFI transaction, the awarding authority does not start making payments until the service provider has completed the facility and started providing services. It does not therefore need to have the contractual power to issue instructions to the service provider on the progress or quality of the work, including for the remedying of what may appear to be defective work. Indeed, there is a danger that such powers could undermine the payment mechanism because the service provider might not be prepared to put its income stream at risk if it is obliged to comply with such instructions. There is therefore a tension between the approach that an awarding authority might prefer to make, and that suggested by the legal framework.

1.1 The planning system
1.2 Financing the project
1.3 Public sector projects
1.4 Public/private partnerships
1.5 Tender process
1.6 Construction contracts
1.7 Construction insurance

6.2 Scope of compliance monitoring

Compliance monitoring ought, as a result, to be addressed in the project agreement at a much higher level than would be found in a design and build contract and in a less invasive manner. The project agreement may allow the awarding authority the right to inspect design information (as seen above) as well as manufacturing, fabrication and construction activities, whether carried out on or off site. The monitoring procedures may also provide for access to minutes of site and design team meetings, copies of significant instructions issued to the building subcontractor and, perhaps, any formal challenges to the validity of such instructions made by the building subcontractor.

Where it is possible that the service provider will require guidance from the awarding authority on its further interpretation of the output specification, the compliance monitoring procedures will need to establish the means by which those interpretations are settled and whether and to what extent they are to be contractually binding.

The awarding authority will also want to be kept informed of progress as this may have an impact on the design development procedure described in Section 5 and on its arrangements for decant to the new facilities following completion. The *Building Schools for the Future Standard Document (March 2005)* for example gives the awarding authority the right on reasonable notice to inspect the state and progress of the works (and to ascertain whether they are being properly executed) as well as the operation and maintenance of the project, and to monitor compliance by the service provider with its obligations under the project agreement. The awarding authority may also attend site meetings, training workshops, tests and inspections held by the service provider. Access to programmes will therefore be a matter of some importance to the awarding authority, but the service provider should not be expected to comply with programme or intermediary milestones (as distinct from the date for commencement of service delivery or the longstop date triggering liability for damages or rights of termination respectively, as mentioned in Section 3 of this chapter).

Similarly, the awarding authority should not have the right to approve generally the detailed design and construction programmes of the service provider. As discussed in Section 2 of this chapter completion to time is the service provider's risk.

It is unlikely that the awarding authority will have the resources to inspect construction works to any great degree, or consider that close supervision represents money well spent (by having to pay additional consultants' fees). Instead, the awarding authority will acquire comfort that the requisite standards are being achieved by the service provider through various activities. These will vary from project to project, but may include:

- having the power to comment on designs which are not subject to the design development procedure;
- being given the opportunity to witness tests throughout the construction phase and to inspect certain key aspects of the works before they are covered up;

- having the power to comment on matters of concern. Although the service provider is not obliged to comply with such comments, they could be taken into account at the time it is decided whether or not completion has been achieved; and
- setting up a compliance monitoring team that observes and offers clarification during both the design development and construction stages. This can prevent the need for changes, reduce cost for the service provider, and provide comfort to the awarding authority that the accommodation or services will be fit for purpose.

Some standard forms do nevertheless cater for opening up: the Building Schools for the Future document, for example, gives a right to the awarding authority to request the service provider to open up and inspect the works where it 'reasonably believes' that they are 'defective'. The form goes on to state expressly that the exercise of any such rights will not affect the obligations of the service provider under the project agreement (that is, effectively, that the risk profile of the project should not change as a result). A similar approach is taken in the standard form project agreement published by the NHS Executive.

6.3 Quality management systems

In most instances, the service provider will be required by the project agreement to establish and implement a quality management system. By way of example, in the standard form of project agreement published by the NHS Executive the service provider is required to have in place a design quality plan, a construction quality plan and a services quality plan for each service. The awarding authority or its representative (or perhaps the independent certifier – see Section 7 of this chapter) will be given the power to audit the management system and carry out inspections to determine whether the system is adequate and being implemented correctly. If it is, the awarding authority can more safely assume that the construction works are being undertaken in accordance with good industry practice.

6.4 Remedies for defects

It is sometimes suggested that more detailed compliance monitoring by awarding authorities is required in order to establish the existence of defects that manifest themselves prior to completion. However, this is not necessarily the case in PFI transactions. The tests to determine whether the criteria which trigger service commencement and the start of the unitary charge have been satisfied (see Section 7 of this chapter) should be sufficiently comprehensive to establish whether or not the requisite standards have been achieved.

Defects which are discovered after service commencement may be dealt with in different ways. In some project agreements, such as the standard form of project agreement published by the NHS Executive, there is no defects correction clause except for that relating to thermal and energy efficiency assessment post completion. This is because it is assumed that the rectification of defects will be addressed sufficiently in the performance monitoring regime. In addition, awarding the authority a right to step in for the purpose of remedying the breach if certain pre-conditions are satisfied (such as there being an immediate and a serious threat to the health or safety of any user, events that are prejudicial to the awarding authority performing its business function or where the service provider has accrued warning points for repeat defaults which exceed the threshold measured within the set timeframe).

However, in practice, availability regimes are sometimes and, some may say, often insufficiently sensitive to ensure the quality of the facility for the awarding authority. In addition, they may be designed specifically to allow the service provider flexibility during an initial period to gear up services. Accordingly, there is a good case for a defects correction clause being included in the project agreement, and there is usually an acceptance by the service provider of such a proposal as it will be capable of being fully backed up by appropriate obligations in the building subcontract.

It should be noted that the defects correction clause in the project agreement is unlikely to be linked to retention funds, as would be the case in a traditional building contract. The awarding authority under a PFI transaction has not paid the capital cost of the works and does not need to hold back a specified proportion of those costs as a means of incentivizing the service provider to return to site to repair defects.

The building subcontract will invariably contain defects liability provisions in the traditional way. The service provider's income could be at risk if defects manifest themselves and there needs to be a strong incentive placed on the building subcontractor to ensure that defects are remedied. In order to avoid arguments about whether the retention monies should be charged to the service provider's financiers, the use of retention bonds, which are assigned by way of security to the financiers, can be a useful device.

Where a defect gives rise to unavailability and, hence, a deduction from the unitary payment, the amount of the deduction will vary depending on the type of facility and the impact which the defect has on its use by the awarding authority. If a defect in a building prevents the operation of certain business units, it may be appropriate for other areas of the building to be treated as unavailable if they are occupied by related business units which are dependent on the operation of the unit directly affected by the defect in question. For example, a defect in the ITU of a hospital may render unavailable both the ITU and the operating theatres. It may also be appropriate for the amount of the deduction to vary from area to area (for example, storage areas may attract a lower rating than core business areas).

The question of whether deductions from the unitary payment for unavailability due to defects are the sole remedy for the awarding authority can represent an area of significant debate. In the absence of an exclusive remedies clause, the service provider can find that there is liability in damages for breach of the project agreement in addition to deductions being made from the income stream.

If the payment mechanism is not sufficiently sensitive to respond to the existence of defects, a claim for damages for breach of the project agreement may represent the principal remedy for the awarding authority. However, project agreements typically exclude the service provider's liability for consequential loss and/or contain a damages cap. As an alternative, the awarding authority may be able to require the service provider to repair the defect if necessary by specific performance or through the operation of 'self-help' procedures. The project agreement may permit such damages or the costs of 'self-help' to be deducted from the unitary payment.

The service provider will seek to ensure that any income which is lost as a result of defects can be recovered from the building subcontractor. However, the pass-through of liability may not, in all cases, be possible. For example, the ability to make deductions from unitary payments will last throughout the period of the concession, whereas the service provider's ability to sue the building subcontractor for damages may be subject to a limitation period which expires six or twelve years after completion, depending on the way in which the building subcontract has been executed.

7 SERVICE COMMENCEMENT

7.1 Significance

The provisions in the project agreement governing the certification of service commencement are of fundamental importance to both parties to the project agreement as well as the service provider's financiers. The issue of the requisite certificate will signify that the contracted services are ready for delivery, including confirmation that the asset from which the services will be provided is physically ready.

It will be of fundamental importance to the service provider and its financiers that there is an unbreakable link between the criteria which have to be met to achieve service commencement or availability and the issue of the certificate of practical completion under the building subcontract. In this way, the service provider is best placed to ensure that lost income for late service delivery can be recouped through the recovery of liquidated damages if the building subcontractor is in culpable delay.

The project agreement will describe what is meant by service commencement and the means by which the service provider is to demonstrate that the requirements for the same have been satisfied. In addition, the service provider's financiers may insist on high standards for completion as the building subcontractor will be released from any further liability for liquidated damages following completion and the financiers will be anxious to know that the income to be generated by the facility will be reliable and consistent.

7.2 Certification of service commencement

SoPC4 suggests that, although the method of demonstration that the requirements of the output specification have been achieved differs in each project, the pre-conditions to certification of service commencement may take the form of:

- a completion inspection of the facility and services;
- completion of acceptance trials for new services; and
- other performance tests or inspections.

In the majority of projects, the principal parties to a PFI transaction, including the financiers, will be keen to ensure that the criteria required to be achieved prior to certification are made as objective as possible. Complete objectivity may not be possible in all cases (for example, where the awarding authority is the best judge as to whether the requisite standards have been achieved), but even in these instances the parties are likely to insist on as much objectivity as is possible. However, it is worth noting that this approach is not followed in all respects in the Department of Health's Standard Form of Project Agreement, where it is suggested that, in addition to the satisfactory passing of specified tests, the construction works must be completed in all respects in accordance with the project agreement and this is required in order to permit certification.

While the matters which must be demonstrated by the service provider in order to trigger completion will vary depending on the type of project, these will usually involve the successful completion of specified tests to establish that the requisite standards of service or performance have been achieved. The *Waste Management Procurement Pack (July 2004)* for example advises awarding authorities to take technical advice as to the nature of the tests or inspections or demonstrations which are required to evidence acceptance, since they may need to be of an engineering rather than a construction nature. The project agreement will need to describe in detail these tests. Some of the tests may be described in a regime established at the time the project agreement is signed, but it may not always be practicable to describe a comprehensive regime at the outset of the project. In these circumstances, as in the case of the standard form of project agreement published by the NHS Executive, the broad parameters of the testing regime will be described in the project agreement, and the precise details will be developed after financial close but sufficiently in advance of commencement of the testing and commissioning procedures.

This sort of approach should not be treated as a justification for the output specification failing to represent a comprehensive description of the awarding authority's requirements – it is the methodology for testing that is fine-tuned, rather than the standards to be achieved.

As suggested by SoPC4, the project agreement should also address other procedural issues, such as the programme for the carrying out of the tests, the ability of the awarding authority to witness the tests and to review and retain copies of the test results, responsibility for providing facilities and resources for undertaking and witnessing the tests and the consequences arising if the tests are failed.

7.3 Who certifies?

There are differing views on who should be responsible for issuing the certificate under the project agreement to signify service commencement and trigger the income stream. SoPC4 suggests that in most cases there will be either a joint assessment by the awarding authority and the service provider or an assessment by an independent third party, although there will be cases where the awarding authority is the best judge. The service provider may wish the awarding authority to certify service commencement because it follows logically that, if the certificate is withheld improperly, commencement of unitary payment should be backdated to the date on which the certificate should have been issued. The awarding authority may not accept this because it could find that it has a liability for unitary payment even though it did not enjoy the benefit of the facility especially where, for good reason, it believed at the time that the criteria for service commencement had not been achieved.

7.4 Independent certifier

As in the case of the Department of Health's Standard Form of Project Agreement published by the NHS Executive, it may be agreed that the certificate should be issued by an independent certifier or tester who is appointed jointly by the awarding authority and the service provider. Similarly, the Building Schools for the Future standard PFI agreement provides for the independent certifier route. The attraction of appointing an independent certifier is that it gives both parties, and the financiers, confidence that the decision on whether to certify will be made impartially and promptly.

By acknowledging that the independent certifier is, in effect, an expert, owing an equal duty of care to the awarding authority and the service provider, the parties may consider it appropriate for the independent certifier's decision on whether the criteria for service commencement have been achieved to be treated as a final and binding decision of an expert which is not open to subsequent challenge under the dispute resolution procedure.

The role of the independent certifier can be perceived as being one attracting a high risk, particularly where the certifier has to make some sort of value judgment about the criteria triggering service commencement. Accordingly, it is likely that fees payable to the certifier will include a premium for this perceived risk unless the role is ring-fenced in an appropriate manner. For example, where the criteria are entirely objective, it may not be necessary for the certifier to be appointed throughout the entire length of the design and construction period or to review in detail the proposed design solutions or inspect quality of work on site. The certifier's role may be restricted to auditing the service provider's quality management system and carrying out periodic checks to see that it is being implemented properly, acquiring a sufficient understanding of the output specification and the service provider's proposals to understand the criteria and to establish whether the appropriate requirements have been achieved and the relevant tests have been passed.

Where service commencement is not to be judged by wholly objective criteria, it may be necessary for the role of the independent certifier to be expanded to enable the certifier to form an opinion about the general quality of work. However, it is unlikely that the role of the independent certifier should include extensive on-site inspection and the review of detailed design proposals or the provision of early warning regarding potential issues which may result in the completion certificate being withheld. This is, perhaps, inconsistent with the risk transfer embodied within PFI philosophy. There is a danger that the independence of the certifier might be compromised because, in practice, the independent certifier becomes inextricably linked with the service provider's design and construction and the independent certifier's review becomes something not dissimilar to progressive acceptance. In addition, the awarding authority may be paying twice for the transfer of the design and construction risk – i.e. to both the service provider and the independent certifier.

Where it is decided that the certificate under the project agreement is also to operate as the practical completion certificate under the building subcontract, the independent certifier's appointment may become tripartite with the building subcontractor added as an additional client, or the independent certifier may be asked to sign a collateral warranty in favour of the building subcontractor.

7.5 Risk transfer

The issue of the certificate triggering service commencement should not represent an acceptance of the means of service delivery as this may impair risk transfer. The certificate should, so far as possible, merely confirm the date on which the facility was ready.

7.6 Outstanding work

Flexibility is usually introduced into the project agreement by allowing the certificate to be issued notwithstanding the existence of minor outstanding works which need to be completed or minor defects which need to be repaired. Such snagging matters should not inconvenience the use of the facility by the awarding authority. The precise arrangements for rectification of snagging matters will vary from project to project, but the project agreement will usually have to establish the means by which the service provider is incentivized to complete the snagging exercise. The difficulty often faced is that the existence of snagging matters will not, by itself, give rise to payment deductions for unavailability, but can nevertheless cause annoyance to the occupants or users of the facility.

7.7 Post-occupation commissioning

The awarding authority and the service provider's financiers are likely to require as much as is possible of the commissioning process to be concluded by the time service commencement is certified.

1.1 The planning system
1.2 Financing the project
1.3 Public sector projects
1.4 Public/private partnerships
1.5 Tender process
1.6 Construction contracts
1.7 Construction insurance

It may not be technically or practically feasible for this preferred position to be achieved in all cases. For example, it may not be possible for the facility's mechanical and electrical services to be tested under full load or fine-tuned until the awarding authority has installed its equipment or has decanted its operations into the new facility; or where the awarding authority is to provide equipment for installation into the new facility, it may be necessary for the commissioning of this equipment and the new facility to be coordinated. In addition, it may be sensible to allow a period for the service provider to train and commission the 'soft' service provision.

In these circumstances, the project agreement needs to prescribe the procedures for post-occupation commissioning. Many of the issues mentioned above on testing procedures will apply on a similar basis. An extra layer of complexity will be added if a fully integrated commissioning programme is required for the commissioning of the awarding authority's equipment along with the new facility.

One of the key issues, however, to be addressed in the project agreement will be the consequences (if any) on payment if problems or delays are encountered during post-occupation commissioning. The precise consequences will, of course, vary from project to project, and the legal documentation will have to be adapted accordingly. For example, it may be appropriate for the commencement of payment to be postponed until the expiry of a fixed period after completion, during which it is anticipated that the commissioning process will be concluded and/or relaxed arrangements may be settled for payment deductions if there is interim unavailability as a result of prolonged commissioning. However, this should be considered with caution as the additional financing cost of effectively deferring the commencement of the income stream is likely to be factored into the cost of the project and will be reflected in the unitary payment.

From a practical perspective, one of the greatest difficulties arises where equipment is supplied by the awarding authority and the service provider and the performance of their respective equipment is dependent on the proper functioning of the equipment supplied by the other party. In this case, procedures allowing for accurate traceability of the source of any problems encountered are necessary so that the payment arrangements can operate fairly depending on the source of the problems encountered.

8 CONSTRUCTION (DESIGN AND MANAGEMENT) REGULATIONS 2007

The Construction (Design and Management) Regulations 2007 (CDM Regulations) are likely to apply to most, if not all, PFI projects. The Regulations operate whenever 'construction work' is undertaken, which is defined widely; additional obligations arise where the project is 'notifiable' and includes any project involving more than 30 days or 500 person days. The Regulations are still likely to capture many of the activities associated with PFI transactions, including the construction of buildings and other infrastructure and their maintenance and cleaning.

A more detailed analysis of the CDM Regulations is contained in [Section 6 of Chapter 3.2] and only those implications of the CDM Regulations in force since 6 April 2007 which are applicable to PFI transactions, are addressed below.

8.1 Client duties

The duties imposed on a client under the CDM Regulations are capable of applying to the awarding authority in a PFI transaction. A client is defined by the CDM Regulations as including a person who carries out a project himself or who seeks or accepts the services of another which may be used in the carrying out of a project for him. It is worth noting in this context that the previous Regulation 4 dealing with agency has now been deleted under the proposed Regulations. Clients can therefore no longer appoint an agent to act on their behalf as client.

It would be inconsistent with the principles of risk transfer in a PFI transaction for the client's duties under the Regulations to be retained by the awarding authority. Accordingly, the awarding authority is likely to insist that the service provider elects to act as the 'client' for the purposes of the Regulations under Regulation 8, and to consent to that election (there seems little doubt that the service provider falls within the definition of 'client' under the Regulations).

In practice, it may not be feasible for a total transfer of risk to be achieved even where the service provider agrees to fulfil the role of only client under the CDM Regulations. Firstly, the awarding authority (as a non-electing client) will retain residual duties under the CDM Regulations, including co-operation with those involved on the project so that the latter can comply with their obligations on site (Reg 5(1)(b)); giving necessary information about or affecting the site to anyone designing or building the project (Reg 10(1)) and to the CDM coordinator (Reg 15); and giving information to the CDM coordinator for the health and safety file (Reg 17). This means for example that both the service provider and the awarding authority will have duties to provide the CDM coordinator with all the health and safety information which is in their possession or reasonably obtainable relating to the project, for inclusion in the health and safety file. This has contractual implications: where the site for the project has been under the control or occupation of the awarding authority, the service provider will need to rely on the awarding authority to provide relevant information, if only in relation to previous use. The awarding authority may accordingly have to accept contractual (as well as statutory) responsibility under the project agreement for the delivery and accuracy of that information.

Secondly, a related and important issue is whether the awarding authority needs to comply with the client duties under the CDM Regulations before the project agreement is signed or financial close occurs. The position was unclear under the 1994 Regulations but it now seems that the awarding authority should appoint its CDM coordinator 'as soon as practicable after initial design work or other preparation for construction work has begun' (Regulation 14). It must be arguable that 'initial design work' includes the output specification. This point has been picked up by the HSE in its newly revised Approved Code of Practice and Guidance on the CDM Regulations entitled *Managing Health and Safety in Construction*. Unlike the previous edition, the HSE states clearly that 'project originators are legally the client at the start of the project, and should ensure that a CDM co-ordinator is appointed and HSE notified during the early design and specification phase. The project originator cannot wait until someone else, for example the Special Purpose Vehicle . . . takes over the client role.'

Unfortunately, the extent of the project originator's obligation is still not specified: an example is again design. If producing an output specification can be said to be a design activity (and practically speaking most specifications contain inputs, so that this is at least arguable) then the safest course for the project originator is to comply with the design obligations in addition to those of client. Designers are subject to the same general duties of cooperation, coordination and general principles of prevention, as clients (see below) and must not accept an appointment unless they are competent to do so. They must avoid in their designs foreseeable risks to the health and safety of not just those affected by the construction work but also anyone using the structure as a workplace; and provide information for the health and safety file.

Whilst there is a clear expectation therefore on the HSE's part that the awarding authority will have full health and safety responsibilities as client from project commencement as project originator, it may not be easy for the awarding authority to be sure exactly what this will entail, particularly when there are a number of bidders for a project, each of whom may have very different design or other proposals. However, the safe route would be for the project originator to assume that all obligations apply to it: these are set out briefly below.

If the awarding authority is undertaking its own direct works which are beyond the scope of the project so far as the service provider is concerned, the CDM Regulations may be applicable in the usual way to those works. There may be a need to coordinate the health and safety rules established separately by the awarding authority and the service provider for their respective projects in these circumstances.

The awarding authority may also retain other obligations under the Health and Safety at Work etc. Act 1974 or its subordinate legislation.

If the project agreement provides for the awarding authority to have early access prior to completion in order to carry out direct works in anticipation of occupation, it will be usual for the project agreement to regulate the means by which the early access is to be effected. This will include responsibilities on the awarding authority in relation to complying with the health and safety and site management rules of the service provider and its building subcontractor. Prior to completion, the facility continues to represent a construction site.

The project agreement should include an obligation on the part of the service provider to procure compliance with the respective duties under the CDM Regulations of designers, contractors, principal contractor and CDM coordinator. This obligation will apply not only in relation to the initial design and construction of the facility but also throughout the length of the concession since the CDM Regulations apply equally to some maintenance work and most capital replacement works carried out during the life of the project. Contractual obligations are necessary notwithstanding the statutory requirements in order to create the potential for civil liability, giving rise to claims for contractual remedies in the event of breach. Most of the obligations in the statutory code give rise to criminal liability only.

As for other duties, the client must seek the co-operation of, and co-operate with, any other person concerned in any project; co-ordinate its activities with all other duty-holders to ensure as far as reasonably practicable the health and safety of those carrying out or affected by the construction work; take account of the general principles of prevention in the performance of its duties; (the principles are those set out in Schedule 1 to the Management of Health and Safety at Work Regulations 1993) and take reasonable steps to ensure that arrangements are made, and maintained, for managing that project. These arrangements must be suitable to ensure that the construction work can be carried out without risk to heath and safety; that the facility (if it is to be a place of work) has been designed in accordance with relevant health and safety regulations; and that welfare facilities are provided for those carrying out the construction work. The Regulations specify that these arrangements include taking reasonable steps to ensure that sufficient time and other resources are allocated to the project; and that the arrangements themselves are suitable. The client must also appoint the relevant parties (Principal Contractor, CDM co-ordinator, designers) in a suitable sequence and in good time, and must not start the construction phase until satisfied that adequate welfare facilities will be provided and that the principal contractor has prepared a construction phase plan. The client also now has expanded duties relating to the provision and dissemination of 'pre-construction information'. This is widely defined as all information in the client's possession or which is reasonably obtainable, so setting a potentially onerous standard; it also includes any information about or affecting the site or the construction work, or concerning the use of the structure as a workplace, any information in any existing health and safety file and also information regarding how much time the contractors will have pre-construction for planning and preparation. The duties to check the competence and supervision of contractors, designers and co-ordinators remain.

8.2 Construction phase plan

The 2007 approach entails the 'management of risk by ... making [the] focus planning and management, rather than the plan and other paperwork – to emphasize active management and minimize bureaucracy ... ' (Consultative Document on the Revision of the CDM Regulations 1994). As a result, the client of a PFI project (whether awarding authority or service provider) must appoint a Principal Contractor, and must check (before construction work starts) that the Contractor has prepared a 'construction phase plan' (previously a health and safety plan) – that is, one that is developed before construction begins and is sufficient to enable the construction work to start without undue risk to health or safety (Regulations 16 and 23). A 'construction phase plan' is a document recording the health and safety arrangements, site rules and any special measures for the construction work for the project.

Given that the service provider ought to be in place before the construction phase begins, the awarding authority's involvement at this stage ought to be minimal. There is however the potential for overlap, depending on the timing of the project, so that the public sector will need to be aware of its duties in this regard.

8.3 Health and safety file

Under the project agreement, it will be the service provider's responsibility to establish and maintain the health and safety file in accordance with the requirements of the CDM Regulations. When the concession expires or is terminated, the service provider will be required to deliver an up-to-date health and safety file to the awarding authority. The project agreement will impose responsibilities on the service provider to provide the awarding authority with appropriate copyright licences to enable the information in the health and safety file to be copied and used for the remaining life of the facility.

During the period of the concession, the health and safety file will be used primarily by the service provider when fulfilling its maintenance and other obligations under the project agreement. Nevertheless, the awarding authority will need access to the health and safety file during this period (for example, whenever it is undertaking 'construction works' as defined in the CDM Regulations, such as where the awarding authority undertakes its own capital works or if it exercises 'self-help' or step-in remedies). The project agreement will therefore usually require a copy of each health and safety file prepared during the life of the project to be provided to the awarding authority.

9 DIRECT AGREEMENTS AND COLLATERAL WARRANTIES

9.1 Direct agreements

The purpose and effect of direct agreements in favour of the service provider's financiers is dealt with in Section 1 of Chapter 1.2. For current purposes, it is sufficient to appreciate that the financiers will require the ability to take over the building subcontract where the service provider defaults. It creates an opportunity for the financiers to complete the construction works and to minimize disruption to the income stream. The direct agreement will allow the financiers either to appoint a replacement company as the service provider or to assume itself the responsibilities of the service provider.

In parallel with the direct agreements for the financiers, it has become increasingly common for the awarding authority to be given an opportunity to take over the building subcontract or to appoint a replacement service provider if the project agreement is terminated for the service provider's default prior to completion. Similar arrangements may also exist in relation to the principal maintenance contracts.

Where such rights exist for the awarding authority, they are invariably subordinated to the step-in rights of the financiers. It is only if the financiers fail to exercise these rights in accordance with the terms of the relevant direct agreement that the awarding authority is given the opportunity to step in.

The value of direct agreements for the awarding authority needs to be questioned, however. They may be unnecessary for a variety of reasons.

First, in the majority of cases where there is a material default under the project agreement during the design and construction period, it is likely that the service provider's default is effectively a default by the building subcontractor of its obligations under the building subcontract. It may not make much sense for the awarding authority to take on the building subcontract in these circumstances.

Secondly, it is unlikely that it would be commercially sensible for the awarding authority to take over the building subcontract if the service provider's financiers have decided not to do so. The financiers will usually have every incentive to resolve the problems encountered by the service provider and the building subcontractor and to complete the construction of the project in order to trigger the income stream. It is unlikely that the awarding authority will be better placed to resolve problems which the financiers consider to be insoluble on commercially sensible terms (having regard to the potential level of compensation following a termination, which would be based on the price bid by a new service provider to take over the contract).

Thirdly, the service provider and its financiers may object to the awarding authority being given the opportunity to step in to the building subcontract where the building subcontractor has served a notice of its intention to terminate the building subcontract. If the awarding authority's entitlement to step in is triggered by the building subcontractor's notice, the service provider could be left with obligations to the awarding authority under the project agreement which it cannot fulfil because it does not have a building subcontractor.

The service provider's financiers may insist that the awarding authority cannot step in to the building subcontract until the financiers have been paid out in full. In other words, the benefit of the building subcontract has to stay with the service provider to enable the financiers to pursue the building subcontractor for any losses due to the latter's default. The awarding authority will need to ascertain the extent of these claims and losses as it would not wish to step in only to find that the building subcontractor is, or subsequently becomes, insolvent. SoPC4 does in fact note the incidence of projects closing with subordination provisions in place, stating that in general there should be no conflict between the interests of the Senior Lenders and those of the awarding authority. It goes on to warn however that blanket subordination provisions which prevent the authority from exercising its rights until the senior debt is fully paid out might preclude the awarding authority from stepping in where continuity of service will otherwise be disrupted. Treasury suggests that this situation be avoided and provides drafting to achieve this (please see Chapter 31.7 SoPC4 for further detail).

Where step-in rights are capable of being exercised, the direct agreement will contain procedures for the building subcontract to be transferred formally (usually by way of novation) from the service provider to a replacement selected by the awarding authority or to the authority itself. There will usually be an intermediary stage in the process under which the awarding authority can step in to the building subcontract on a temporary basis. This step-in period will end if the building subcontract has not been formally transferred before the end of a specified period or whenever the awarding authority decides to step out.

As a result of the decision of Court of Session in *Blyth & Blyth Limited* v. *Carillion Construction Limited*, the direct agreement will need to contain clear language to ensure that, following step-in, the awarding authority (or the replacement service provider appointed by the awarding authority) can rely on the works executed prior to the date on which the awarding authority exercised its step-in rights and recover from the building subcontractor compensation for the losses which it should have recovered had the building subcontract initially been entered into by the awarding authority (or the replacement service provider) in substitution for the service provider. In the absence of such language, the awarding authority (or the replacement service provider) may not be able to recover from the building subcontractor damages for its breach of contract in respect of losses which are of a different kind to the losses which would have been suffered by the original service provider as a result of the same breach. The service provider's financiers (or any replacement service provider appointed by the financiers) face similar concerns also in the case of novation to it (or to the replacement service provider) of the subcontracts or the project agreement.

It will be a condition of the awarding authority exercising its step-in rights that it undertakes to pay any amounts that are unpaid at the time the step-in rights are exercised (including as a result of a prior breach of the building subcontract by the service provider) and to discharge any future obligations owed to the building subcontractor which arise after that date during the step-in period or after the subcontract has been transferred formally.

A time limit will usually be imposed for the exercise by the awarding authority of its rights to step in. The building subcontractor is entitled to know within a reasonable period of time whether the building subcontract is going to be terminated or continued with a new employer.

In the meantime, it is likely that the building subcontract will allow the building subcontractor to suspend work and for claims to be made for extensions of time and additional costs as a consequence of the disruption caused.

Where the building subcontract is to be transferred formally to a replacement service provider, the direct agreement will usually specify the grounds on which the building subcontractor can object to the proposed replacement. The building subcontractor will need to know that the proposed replacement has sufficient capacity (including financial resources) to perform the obligations arising under the building subcontract, and other commercially sensitive issues may have to be addressed such as whether the proposed replacement consortium can include a direct competitor of the building subcontractor.

Figure 3 of this chapter shows in diagrammatic form the procedures typically found in a direct agreement for step-in.

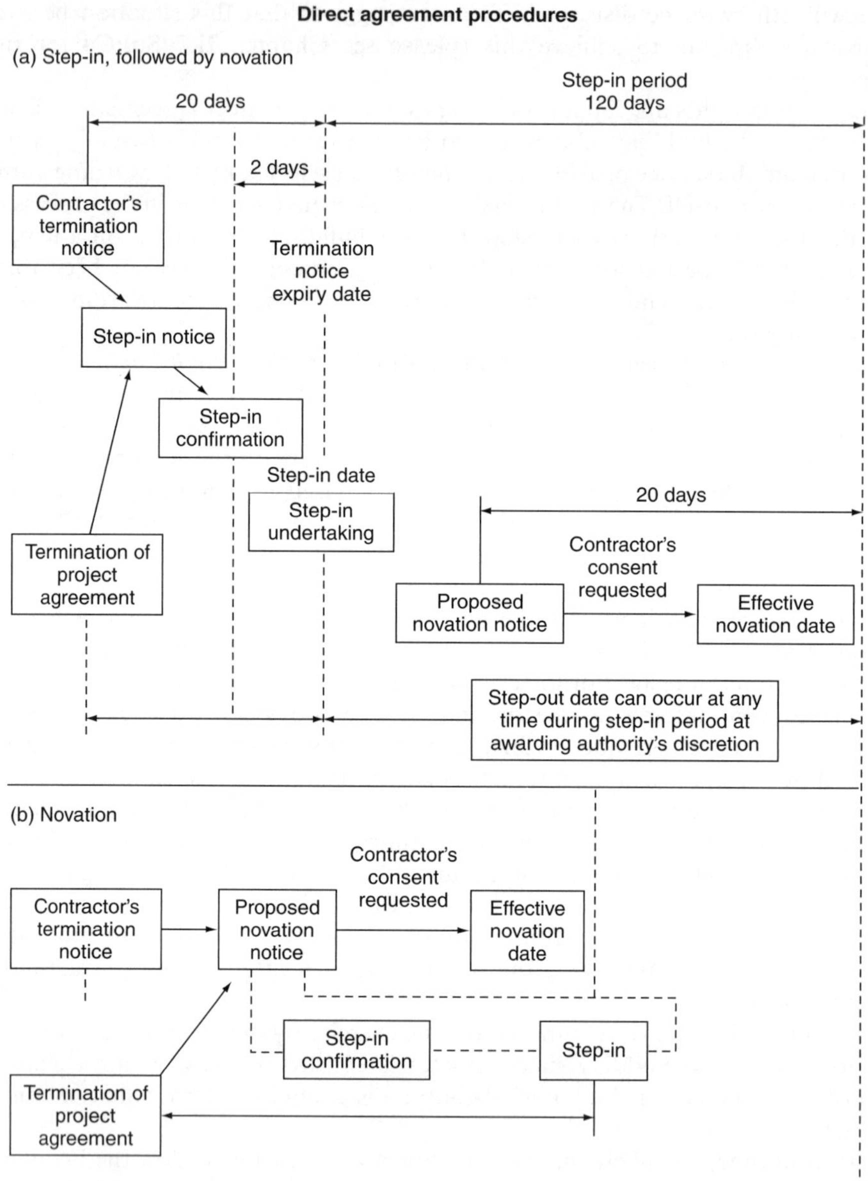

Figure 3. Direct agreement procedures

If the building subcontract is to be transferred formally, the financiers will have to release from the security package the building subcontract and any associated parent company guarantee or performance bond.

9.2 Collateral warranties

The practice of designers and contractors providing collateral warranties on traditionally procured projects has crept into PFI transactions. At first sight, it does appear unnecessary for the building subcontractor to provide a collateral warranty to the awarding authority since the latter's position as occupier or user in the PFI context is very different from an occupier who is a building owner or a tenant under a full repairing and insuring lease. Provision of such a collateral warranty may, however, be justified for the following reasons:

(a) The service provider will often be a special purpose vehicle entity with no track record and its assets will be limited to the project assets and income, all of which will be charged to secure the debt owed to the service provider's financiers.
(b) The payment mechanism may not be sufficiently sensitive to enable deductions from the unitary payment to be made regardless of the nature of, or reasons for, a construction defect or other inadequacy in the facility. While there may be contractual remedies available against the service provider under the project agreement, it may be more efficient for the awarding authority to claim directly against the building subcontractor rather than against the service provider.
(c) In the absence of any collateral warranty from the building subcontractor, the awarding authority may be left without a remedy for latent defects where the project agreement is terminated during the operational phase (the cost of repairing defects which are known to exist at the time of termination may be taken into account in calculating the compensation payable to the service provider on termination of the project agreement, but clearly this will not be possible in respect of defects that have yet to become apparent).

Despite the reasons provided in (a) and (b) above, it is generally accepted, as suggested by SoPC4, that collateral warranties in PFI projects should not grant rights to the awarding authority which are exercisable prior to termination.

Many of the issues usually associated with collateral warranties relating to traditionally procured projects apply equally to collateral warranties in the PFI context. However, some of these issues carry a different emphasis:

- it is unlikely that the building subcontractor will be able to justify the inclusion of a joint liability or net contribution clause in the collateral warranty which is applicable to other members of the design and construction team because, as a design and build contractor, it has already accepted the principle of single point responsibility; however, there may be cases where the building subcontractor's liability should be calculated after assessing the degree of blame attributable to other contractors (for example, where the awarding authority provides some of the installations or equipment to be incorporated into the facility),
- it might be arguable that joint liability provisions should capture default by the principal subcontractor responsible for hard services because substandard maintenance could exacerbate the consequences of construction defects, but in this case the awarding authority may insist upon a collateral warranty from other relevant subcontractors, and
- where the nature or use of the facility is unique, the awarding authority may agree to a restricted ability to assign the benefit of the collateral warranties to third parties.

Where the collateral warranty states that the building subcontractor's liability to the awarding authority is to be no greater than the liability owed under the building subcontract, the project agreement will need to allow the awarding authority some degree of influence over the service provider's ability to vary the terms of the building subcontract or to waive any claim it might have against the building subcontractor.

The rules embodied in the Contracts (Rights of Third Parties) Act 1999 apply to both the project agreement and the building subcontract. These rules may obviate the need for a collateral warranty to be given by the building subcontractor to the awarding authority. It is likely, however, that in practice the Act will be excluded.

10 APPLICATION OF THE HOUSING GRANTS, CONSTRUCTION AND REGENERATION ACT 1996 ('HGA'), PART II, TO PFI TRANSACTIONS

At the time of writing the HGA is under review: the Department of Business, Enterprise and Regulatory Reform ('BERR', formally the DTI) is carrying out a second consultation process, launched on 20 June and to be completed by 17 September ('*Improving Payment Practices in the Construction Industry*'). The amendments in this second consultation will 'seek to improve transparency and clarity in the exchange of information relating to payments, thereby enabling parties to construction contracts to manage cash flow better; and to encourage parties to resolve disputes by adjudication' according to BERR's website. Any relevant proposals to amend it are mentioned below.

10.1 Application to the project agreement

Although it applies to contracts which provide for the carrying out of construction operations, Part II of the HGA does not apply to the project agreement in a PFI transaction where the awarding authority has the characteristics described in Article 4 of the Construction Contracts (England and Wales) Exclusion Order 1998. For example, the Act does not apply to a project agreement where the awarding authority is a Minister of the Crown or a body whose accounts are subject to audit by the Audit Commission.

The status of the project agreement under the Exclusion Order has to be recited in order to confirm the applicability or otherwise of the 1996 Act to the project agreement (see paragraph 4(2)(a) of the Exclusion Order).

10.2 Application to the building subcontract

Although the legislation will not apply to the project agreement if the requirements of the Exclusion Order are met, the HGA will apply to the building subcontract and the building maintenance subcontract, and as explained elsewhere in this publication it is not possible for the parties to these subcontracts to override the operation of the statutory code. Accordingly, the service provider will need to ensure that the terms of the building subcontract governing payment and dispute resolution comply with the legislation.

10.3 Payment provisions

The implications of treating the project agreement and the building subcontract differently in relation to dispute resolution are touched on in Section 11 of this chapter. In relation to payment, however, a considerable amount of attention has been focused on the operation of section 113 of the HGA, which prohibits conditional payment provisions in the context of PFI transactions.

Section 113 currently renders 'ineffective' any provision in a construction contract which makes payment conditional on the payer receiving payment from a third party, unless that third party is insolvent. Such provisions are commonly known as 'pay when paid'.

It is generally accepted that section 113 does not cause any difficulty, in a PFI context, in relation to the payment to the building subcontractor of the instalments of the construction price itself. While these instalments will be dependent on draw-down of bank finance by the service provider, there is no need for the building subcontract to regard the building subcontractor's entitlement to such payment as being 'conditional' on release of funds by the banks. Instead, the payment timetable under the building subcontract can simply follow the timetable for draw-down by the service provider. This usually involves the passing down to the building subcontractor of any requirements as to progress milestones which the financiers place on the service provider. The service provider will, of course, be liable to the building subcontractor for payment of the relevant instalments if the financiers should default on their payment obligations, but the risk of this happening must be slight, to say the least.

The difficulty with section 113 arises from the fact that these arrangements do not deal with the position where the building subcontractor is entitled to additional payment as a consequence of the occurrence of compensation events. This will arise, for example, where the awarding authority wishes to implement a variation and it is agreed that it will pay the capital cost of the extra work.

Where the compensation event is an awarding authority's risk, the service provider and its financiers will be concerned to ensure that the building subcontract has what is, in effect, a pay when paid provision so that the service provider does not find itself in default under the finance documentation because it has mismatched its income from the awarding authority with its payment obligations under the building subcontract. However, any such arrangement conflicts with section 113 and runs the risk of being ineffective.

In order to resolve this difficulty, building subcontracts have attempted to circumvent Section 113 by, for example, providing that the building subcontractor's entitlement to compensation in relation to the awarding authority's risks is conditional on a corresponding entitlement of the service provider to payment being established under the project agreement: such provisions are known as 'equivalent project relief' (EPR) provisions. This structure (sometimes called 'pay when certified' or 'entitled when entitled') attempts to achieve compliance with the HGA by making it clear that the building subcontractor's underlying entitlement to payment does not arise until the service provider has established its own entitlement to payment from the awarding authority, as opposed to a provision which simply requires the building subcontractor to wait for payment of a sum already due until the service provider is put in funds by the awarding authority.

The courts have however now seriously undermined such arrangements. In *Midland Expressway* v. *Carillion Construction Ltd and Others* (2006) 106 Con LR 154, Jackson J applied a purposive interpretation to the HGA and held that the 'practical consequence' of the EPR clause considered in the case (which was fairly typical) was that the building subcontractor would not be paid for an awarding authority-instigated variation unless and until the service provider had received a corresponding sum from the awarding authority. The distinction between 'entitled-when-entitled' and 'pay-when-paid' was ignored, Jackson J stating that the 'contracting parties cannot escape the operation of s.113 by the use of circumlocution'.

The breadth of the court's approach to interpreting the HGA calls into question the enforceability of a variety of other provisions that might have been used to avoid the problem. Examples of alternative approaches include a provision in the building subcontract that if, for any reason, the 'pay when certified' provisions are rendered unenforceable, in circumstances where the service provider does not have available funds to meet the contractor's entitlement to additional compensation, then a 'parallel loan agreement' between the service provider and the subcontractor will take effect. Under such an arrangement, the building subcontractor is required to make a loan to the service provider of the amount necessary to place the service provider in sufficient funds to meet the building subcontractor's entitlement to compensation. In this way the risk of the service provider defaulting on its payment obligations under the building subcontract, and thereby being in breach of the finance documentation due to lack of funds, is avoided (or at least reduced). It seems doubtful that arrangements such as these would survive an approach such as that taken by Jackson J above.

The Treasury has not issued specific guidance on the point but has stated that SoPC4 was drafted against the *Midland Expressway* backdrop. SoPC4 does not however deal directly with the situation that arose in the case. It states that 'To the extent the Act applies to a PFI Sub-Contract ... the Authority should ... ensure that its position is commercially the same as it would be were the Act not to apply to the PFI Sub-Contract concerned.' In a footnote, it goes on to say that:

> 'a well-managed Contractor should ... be able to structure and run its Sub-Contracting arrangements so as to avoid payment mismatches occurring ... There are some areas however where equivalent payments may be made under the Contract as under the subcontracts; these may cover payments for Compensation Events, payments for variations, termination payments, and payments of Unitary Charge relating to hard services. For these matters the Contractor will need to ensure that its notice periods are such that it can give notices and receive relevant confirmations or certificates or payments under the Contract in sufficient time for it to give its own confirmations or certificates or payments under its Sub-Contracts. It may also agree with its Sub-Contractors to pursue, if required, the equivalent issues under its head contract or allow the Sub-Contractor to do so as its agent or, in the event of a common dispute, it may agree that ... written joinder provisions ... should apply.'

Meanwhile, BERR has proposed in its second consultation document to prohibit pay-when-certified clauses (adding to the current prohibition on pay-when-paid clauses). It makes no comment as to the effect of this on the PFI market. It is to be hoped that a full discussion of all aspects of this complicated problem will take place as part of BERR's second consultation.

BERR has also made recommendations regarding payment procedures but it seems unlikely that these will make a big impact on the market if they are brought into law.

In the meantime it is worth noting a further case on payment, decided by the House of Lords, regarding s.111 of the HGA. Under s.111 an employer cannot withhold any monies from the contractor unless a notice has been duly served explaining how much will be withheld and why. The case of *Melville Dundas Ltd* v. *George Wimpey UK Ltd* [2007] UKHL 18 has held that, where a contractor's employment has been terminated and there are certificates of payment outstanding, the employer can nevertheless withhold payment, even in the absence of a s.111 notice, if this is provided for in the termination clause (in this case a JCT standard clause). It was initially speculated that the case was relevant only to situations of insolvency but the subsequent case of *Pierce Design* v. *Johnston* [2007] EWHC 1691 has clarified that it is not. BERR's second consultation proposes a statutory solution, however, limiting the impact of *Melville Dundas* to insolvency situations.

10.4 Suspension

Section 112 of the 1996 Act will allow the building subcontractor to suspend performance of its obligations to the service provider if payment in full has not been received by the relevant final date for payment and no effective set-off notice has been issued. Where suspension is implemented validly, the building subcontractor will be entitled to an appropriate extension of time. The building subcontract will also usually allow the building subcontractor the right to recover from the service provider the extra costs arising from delay or disruption caused by such suspension.

The grant of an extension of time under the building subcontract could have significant implications to the service provider and its financiers. Service commencement under the project agreement may be delayed by the suspension thus creating a gap between the programmed date for commencement of the income stream and the building subcontractor's liability for liquidated damages. Further, if the project agreement imposes a liability in damages for late completion on the service provider then the service provider could find that it has to pay such damages without any recompense from the building subcontractor – the building subcontractor is entitled to any extension of time. It should be noted, however, that the right to suspend does not arise unless the date for payment has passed without all sums due having been discharged. Accordingly, the difficulties associated with this point should largely disappear if the concept of 'pay when certified' is incorporated into the building subcontract.

BERR's second consultation on the HGA makes proposals to improve compensation for a party suspending for non-payment. BERR's view is that the power to suspend in the case of non payment after the final date for payment has been only rarely exercised. The consultation sets out some proposals for making this option more attractive by providing for the costs of suspension. It is proposed that the party suspending should be able to recover their costs of suspension and remobilising performance. These may be substantial in particular as the present legislation appears to require the suspending party to recommence work immediately once payment is made. In order to mitigate difficulties arising from this requirement, it is proposed that the suspending party would be entitled to an extension of time for a suitable remobilisation period. In addition, he would be entitled to exercise the right of suspension in respect of part or all of his obligations under the contract. It may therefore be important for the building sub-contractor and the service provider to agree, for example, what constitutes a reasonable cost for re-mobilisation.

11 DISPUTE RESOLUTION

11.1 Procedures

The dispute resolution provisions for PFI transactions do not normally distinguish between disputes arising from the initial building works and disputes arising from the subsequent provision of services. This is because, for example, the defective execution of the initial building works could ultimately become manifest as a problem with the provision of services. Alternatively, questions could arise as to whether a dispute arose from the initial building works or the performance of ongoing building maintenance, so-called 'hard services'.

To accommodate the range of disputes which might arise over the life of a PFI project, the dispute resolution provisions included in project agreements normally provide for an 'escalating' procedure. There is commonly a liaison procedure, being a committee composed of operational managers from the awarding authority and the service provider

1.1 The planning system
1.2 Financing the project
1.3 Public sector projects
1.4 Public/private partnerships
1.5 Tender process
1.6 Construction contracts
1.7 Construction insurance

which meets regularly to discuss any issues that arise, with a view to avoiding these issues becoming fully fledged disputes. Any matters upon which the liaison committee cannot agree are passed to the respective chief executives of the awarding authority and the service provider. They may be able to settle disputes by taking a more strategic view of the issues than the operational managers involved.

Disputes which cannot be settled by the respective chief executives are then determined by an independent third party. Usually, this will be done by the appointment of an adjudicator, who may be selected from a standing panel or on an ad hoc basis, using an expedited procedure. The decision is normally binding on the parties and must be implemented. However, either party may normally challenge such a decision, provided they do so within a specified time from the decision. If the decision is challenged the dispute is reheard, either by the courts or by arbitration. However, the parties must normally comply with and implement the decision until it is altered, if at all, by the courts or an arbitrator. If the decision is not challenged in the time provided then it becomes permanent and cannot subsequently be reopened by either party.

Meanwhile, there are no current proposals in BERR's second consultation (see above) to extend the exclusion of Project Agreements from the HGA and so HGA adjudication is still available to parties to the construction sub-contracts.

11.2 Joinder

One contentious issue in the negotiation of most PFI transactions is that of the joinder and consolidation of disputes between the awarding authority and the service provider, on the one hand, with similar disputes between the service provider and its subcontractors, on the other.

As the service provider has normally negotiated its subcontracts back to back with the project agreement, there should be a corresponding default by one of its subcontractors for most defaults by it under the project agreement. Conversely, there should be a corresponding claim by the service provider against the awarding authority for many claims by a subcontractor against the service provider. It is these related disputes that service providers wish to have heard together to protect them from the consequences of inconsistent decisions concerning related disputes. These could be severe. For example, one arbitrator could find that the service provider has no right to additional payment, while another arbitrator determines that the same circumstances entitled the subcontractor to additional payment from the service provider. As this could affect the service provider's ability to repay its funding, this issue is also of concern to the financiers' advisers.

This is further complicated by the fact, as discussed above, that the exemption of PFI transactions from Part II of the Housing Grants, Construction and Regeneration Act 1996 only applies to the project agreement. As a result, the building subcontract between the service provider and its building subcontractor must include provision for the adjudication of disputes under the building subcontract. This also applies to disputes arising in relation to the building maintenance subcontract. As an adjudicator's decision normally relates to entitlement to payment, there is again a risk that the service provider may have to pay money to its subcontractor not provided for by its funding model, nor reimbursed by the awarding authority.

The structure of a PFI transaction is designed to enable the awarding authority to deal with one party only. This is lost if joinder and consolidation of disputes is allowed, as the awarding authority finds itself dealing with the subcontractors on any disputes as well as the service provider. As a result of the complication and additional expense resulting from the joinder of disputes, SoPC4 recommends that joinder be resisted wherever possible by awarding authorities, although the required drafting permits the service provider to include a subcontractor's submissions in its case to the body hearing the dispute. This has been followed in the dispute resolution procedure contained in the standard form of project agreement published by the NHS Executive where it is noted that joinder provisions have not been included so as to prevent the awarding authority from becoming embroiled in concurrent disputes running between the service provider and its subcontractors. However, in practice, many PFIs have allowed full joinder.

CHAPTER 1.5

Tender process

David Hudson
Guildhouse Group

Ann Minogue and Kirstin Warley
Linklaters

1 INTRODUCTION

1.1 The reasons for tendering in construction

The construction industry is almost unique in that the completed product has, with the exception of house building, little or no opportunity for repetition. It is one that is entirely project, rather than business, based; and it is one where a single product involves unusually large amounts of expenditure.

Construction projects often have a number of features which separate them from most industrial processes:

- in most projects, the design is very substantially separated from the production (even if in more recent times the design detailing is an integral part of the construction product);
- construction is subject to a high degree of regulation which is not only generic, such as Health and Safety and the Building Regulations, but is also specific to the individual site and project, such as planning and highways' permissions;
- a substantial part of any design depends upon and is related to individual site location, conditions, and circumstances: ground conditions influencing foundation design; street pattern influencing elevational treatment; economic environment influencing quality of materials; exposure influencing envelope design and internal services; and so on.

What all of this means is that there is a wide variety of potential prices for apparently similar products and, indeed, a significant spread of potential cost outcomes for an identified project, even where the client's brief establishes very clear outputs expected from the project. There has grown a belief, therefore, both within the industry and amongst its clients, that the only way satisfactorily to determine the right price for a construction project is by using a tender process to put it to the market place. To a client becoming involved in construction for the very first time, this may appear to be a straightforward way to proceed, but there are as many pitfalls along the way as there are alternative moves in a chess game.

Fragmentation

One of the biggest difficulties lies in the fragmentation of the industry. First of all there is the separation of design from construction, and within the design there are several main disciplines, usually carried out by entirely different organisations on the same project: architecture, structural engineering, mechanical engineering, electrical engineering, civil engineering, acoustic treatment and so on. Then there is the further contribution to design by specialist designers in certain parts of the building such as piling, structural steelwork, curtain walling, mechanical plant etc.

On the construction side, again there is invariably a plethora of organisations involved in a single project. Many component parts of a building are carried out by a specialist contractor or subcontractor, for example piling, cladding, services, roof, flooring, partitions and ceilings. Sometimes different trade skills, such as brickwork, joinery and glazing, exist within the same organisation, but more frequently nowadays these separate skills are represented by quite distinct organisations.

The construction client is, therefore, faced with a choice of just how many of these individual bodies he deals with. Historically, the client, advised by his right hand man, an engineer or a master builder (the architect), would contract separately with trade contractors and specialists. These various contractors were co-ordinated on behalf of the client to create the completed construction project. This, the original 'traditional' form of building procurement in England, has had a resurgence in recent years under the title 'construction management'. An alternative is for the client to access the industry via a single design and build contract, tendering all aspects of design and construction in a single price. Most commonly, however, clients let several contracts covering design and construction, and use competitive tendering to select some, or all, of the appointed organisations.

Transaction size

The commissioning of construction works by almost all clients represents a very significant commitment for the client which can dramatically affect his or her financial wellbeing. Paying 50% more than the best price for a batch of stationary is likely to prove little more than annoying but may be justified on the grounds of speed of delivery. Paying 25% more for a personal computer than an apparently identical product in the marketplace might be seen as an extravagant waste, but may also be justified by the supplier's reputation for quality and service. Paying 10% more for a construction project than a client could and should have paid may be financially ruinous, or at the very least damaging.

The fragmentation of the industry, diversification of potential suppliers, the uniqueness of the ultimate product and the relative importance of the total project price have all made the use of competitive tendering processes an inevitable and vital part of the procurement and management of construction. It is an unfortunate fact that the complexities and abuses that have developed alongside competitive tendering have meant that all too often the clients of the construction industry have been dissatisfied with the outcome. It is hoped that this chapter will assist practitioners in producing more satisfied clients.

1.2 The relationship between tendering and negotiation

Negotiation is both an alternative to competitive tendering and a common adjunct to it. Until recently, professional appointments were more commonly made following negotiation without any direct price competition, price being determined by reference to standard scales. In recent years, and especially in the public sector, professional appointments have been made following a competitive tender process, sometimes where price is the sole determining factor, and other times where there is an attempt to combine price and quality into a single determinant. It is a fact that the private sector much more commonly selects its professionals based upon perceived quality with little reference to price competition. With construction work, negotiated contracts are quite commonplace, although by far the majority of contracts are let following a competitive tender process.

The nature of competitive tendering, based upon a given set of parameters, is such that it is rarely possible to have absolute certainty on all issues. More commonly than not, tenders are not submitted as an inclusive single price, but are often accompanied by caveats qualifying that price. In such circumstances, and in circumstances where the design has developed further since the tender documentation was put together, it is necessary to follow the tendering process with negotiation to reduce uncertainty and achieve the client's objectives. Such negotiations also follow situations where the tendered prices are higher than expected and there is then a need to reduce the price by changing the design and/or omitting certain elements. Post tender negotiations are problematic for pubic sector clients – see Section 1.3.

Negotiations, if any are necessary, are best carried out at this stage before the contract is let as the client still has a strong negotiating position. Sometimes, however, it is necessary to conduct negotiations after the letting of the contract. This might be due to time constraints necessitating an early start on site before negotiations can be conducted or where things come to light after contracting, necessitating a change which has to be negotiated. Negotiations at this stage are invariably much more expensive than earlier because of the contractor's strong negotiating position. It is highly recommended, therefore, that negotiations should always be conducted whenever possible before the letting of the contract.

1.3 The significance of parity of tendering

One of the most difficult aspects of tendering construction and construction related contracts is making sure that the offers put forward are compatible and are based upon the same information. This is called parity of tendering. If contractors base their tenders on different levels of information then the lowest tender may arise as a result of a mistake and an under-allowance of costs. This could then put the contractor into difficulties once he is awarded the job, resulting, at best, in attempts to recoup lost monies, or, at worst, insolvency. In either case, it represents a significant potential problem for the client. There is also the need to eliminate any small print which might qualify a tender so that the product being offered is different from that offered by another tenderer. In such a case, the lower tender may not result from carrying out the works more efficiently but because he is merely providing less than that being offered by other tenderers. It is vital, therefore, to ensure that tenders are on the same basis, both to assist in selecting a contractor and also to ensure that the client accepts the best value offer.

1.4 The range of tendering elements

Traditionally, competitive tendering has been based substantially, if not exclusively on price. This particularly has occurred when the design has already been completed on behalf of the client, and the works have been specified and even quantified. Then, (in theory at least), the tendering contractors all having the financial and technical capabilities to carry out the project, the only differentiating factor between the tenders is the price. The length of the contract period is determined by the client so that this is not a differentiating factor, although it is common that alternative tenders are asked for with the contractor selecting his optimum contract period. There may be an equation to be calculated where a slightly higher price is offered for a shorter period as the saving achieved by earlier completion may more than offset the higher price. The analysis of tenders in such circumstances is, however, still quite straightforward.

Over the last 20–25 years there have been significant developments in procurement methodologies so that contractors are tendering on a much wider basis than merely price. Very often the whole selection process has become far more complex with price being only one of the selection criteria. Tenders are now very often submitted on the basis of provision of alternative designs, reflecting different levels of quality, based upon different programmes, using different construction methodologies and other construction variables. In addition, more intangible factors may also be taken into account in selection including the contractors' understanding of the client's objective, the general approach to the project and the degree to which the client and his team feel the contractor is compatible with them. Yet a further element that is sometimes part of the offer is the ability to finance the construction works. In this situation, the client pays only a single bullet payment at the end of the construction works rather than paying on account payments as the works progresses, so that the cost of financing the construction is part of the tendering price. Clearly when some, or all, of these variables are part of the tendering process, the analysis of the tender is far more complex and it is important to ensure that sufficient time is allowed properly to analyse the tenders. Very often it is necessary to hold meetings and negotiations and to receive presentations to clarify exactly what is on offer before a final decision is made.

1.5 Tendering and partnering

Partnering is a term that came into common usage in the 1990s, although interpretation of what exactly it means varies within the industry. In essence, partnering is about the establishment of a long-term relationship with the award of repeat business in return for high levels of service and commitment. It is acknowledged that prices may be higher than might be received by competitive tendering but, in the overall financial analysis, the expectation is that the project (or, more likely, series of projects) will produce better value by earlier finishes, higher degrees of co-operation between contractor and client, fewer disputes, less expenditure on adjudication, arbitration and litigation, and higher quality. Partnering pre-supposes a high level of trust being built up between the client and the contractor and this trust necessitates give and take on both sides.

It is clear that partnering does not sit completely comfortably with price competition as resources have to be allowed within a contractor's price for the resolution of problems which are not necessarily of his making. If selection is based upon lowest price, it becomes very difficult, if not impossible, adequately to build in such resources. However, the price for each project is still important and partnering cannot achieve its objectives if the price paid for achieving higher levels of co-operation and the elimination of disputes is so high that the project becomes unviable. There is, therefore, the need to have some basis for controlling price. This can be done by a tendering process where some prices are included in a competitive process, such as levels of overhead and profit, preliminary costs, labour constants or whatever else might be appropriate in the circumstances. Such prices would then be used as the basis for negotiating individual contracts.

An alternative to competitive tendering in a partnering relationship is to have some form of benchmarking where it is a condition of the ongoing relationship and the award of repeat business that prices are benchmarked against other similar projects. Using expert and experienced advisors, it is possible to ensure that the contract prices are sufficiently close to competitive pricing levels to be confident that in overall terms the client is receiving good value for money.

1.6 The law and tenders in England

Except in relation to government contracts which are examined in Chapter 1.4, there is no statutory intervention into tender procedures. The law relating to tenders in England sits within the general framework of common-law rules relating to contracts.

An invitation to tender given by a prospective client to contractors is not an offer to enter into a contract. It does not usually oblige the client to accept the lowest or any tender. It is merely an invitation to negotiate with those who respond. Usually, of course, invitations to submit competitive tenders for construction contracts contain a provision to the effect that the client does not undertake to accept the lowest or any tender. But this is probably unnecessary in law.

The contractor's tender to carry out the works is usually regarded as the 'offer'. The offer must be definitive, unqualified and unambiguous. Accordingly, it is usual practice to require conforming bids to be submitted even if tenderers also offer alternative bids as part of the tender process. If the offer is qualified in any way, then it cannot be accepted until the qualification has been removed by negotiation. So, for example, the practice of stating in tenderers that:

> '. . . if our tender is of interest, there are one of two matters which we would wish to discuss with you on the terms and conditions of contract'

prevents unequivocal acceptance of the tender without further negotiation.

1.7 Tendering cost

All tendering exercises carry with them a cost that has to be borne by the tendering companies. Such tendering costs form part, and sometimes a substantial part, of an organisation's overheads and are passed back to clients in the overhead additions made on successful contracts. In other words, clients generically pay the tendering costs. It is important, therefore, both from the perspective of the costs incurred by the industry generally, and those incurred specifically in relation to the project, that they are kept to a sensible level in all the circumstances. It should particularly be borne in mind that the cost of tendering is multiplied by the number of companies submitting tenders.

There is a direct relationship between on the one hand the cost of tendering, the likelihood of success and the potential returns; and on the other hand, the willingness of contractors to commit the necessary outlays required by any given tender in order to be competitive. Thus, if there are a very high number of tenderers, then it may well be that few or none are willing to commit the necessary resources to submit a competitive tender, so that a long tender list can have a counter-productive effect. If the cost of tendering is high, such as in a design and build contract where it is necessary to devote resources to producing designs as well as those necessary to price the project, then this inevitably means that there should be fewer tenderers. It also means that the returns expected on such projects are likely to be higher, as returns should be a reflection of risk. It is important, therefore, when tendering to ensure the documentation used as a basis for the tenders is accurate and concise and that it, and the number of pricing contractors, reflects the level of work required to prepare the tender.

The rules relating to acceptance and formation of contracts are covered in Section 9 of this chapter: Turning Tenders into Contracts.

In normal circumstances, the purpose of an invitation to tender is to obtain from tenderers a firm offer capable of acceptance and hence of immediate conversion into a binding contract. There is no obligation on the client to accept the lowest or any tender and the significant costs incurred by the contracting industry in submitting tenders are generally borne by it. Exceptionally, where work is carried out at the request of the client by a tenderer *beyond* that which is necessary in order to submit a tender, the tenderer may be entitled to be paid on a quantum meruit basis (see comments in Section 9 below).

In certain situations however, there may be an implied obligation on the client to consider a conforming tender in conjunction with other conforming tenders, and failure to do so will be a breach of contract. Though very much more developed in other Commonwealth jurisdictions, the English Court of Appeal has held in exceptional circumstances a tenderer is to be given some protection in law.

By way of example, in *Blackpool and Fylde Aero Club Limited* v. *Blackpool Borough Council*:

Facts The Council sent out tender invitations and stated on the form of tender:

> 'The Council do not bind themselves to accept all or any part of the tender. No tender which is received after the last date and time specified shall be admitted for consideration'.

The Club's tender was duly delivered well before the deadline but the Council staff did not empty the letter box on the deadline. The box was emptied the next day and consequently the Club's tender was date stamped and endorsed 'late' and not considered by the Council who accepted another tender. The events were reported to the Club who complained and, having established the true facts, the Council then re-tendered. But the successful tenderer from the first round argued that its tender had been accepted and a contract created. Accordingly, the Council then abandoned the second tender round. The Club argued that the Council had warranted that, if a tender was submitted by the tender deadline, it would be considered along with other tenders duly submitted and that the Council was in breach of this warranty by failing to consider the Club's tender. The Club claimed damages against the Council for breach of contract. The Council argued that no contract came into existence until the Council chose to accept any tender and there was no scope for implied warranties.

Judgment There had a been a clear intention to create a contractual obligation on the Council to consider the Club's tender in conjunction with other conforming tenders and that Council were, in principle, contractually liable to the Club. The Court clearly took into account the fact that tenderers are put to significant expense in preparing a tender usually without direct recompense and that that expense is borne by tenderers without any commitment from the client that the project will necessarily go ahead. But:

> 'The invitee is . . . protected at least to this extent: if he submits the conforming tender before the deadline he is entitled, not as a matter of mere expectation but of contractual right, to be sure that his tender will, after the deadline, be opened and considered in conjunction with all other conforming tenders or at least that his tender will be considered if others are'.

Just how widely can this decision be applied? The judgment is obviously limited to the circumstances of the case. The Court emphasised, in particular, the facts showed that the formal requirements imposed by the tender invitation were precise and the need for tenders to be returned in an official endorsed envelope was important. All of these factors indicated that the case was 'rare exception' to the general rule that an invitation to tender is no more than an invitation to negotiate. But in reality, just how special are the circumstances listed?

In a decision of the Privy Council in a New Zealand case, *Pratt Contractors Limited* v. *Transit New Zealand*, Lord Hoffmann acknowledged that this area of law concerns an important question for both tenderers and those who invite tenders:

> 'At the centre of the dispute lies the question of the extent to which the procedure for competitive tendering should be judicialised. Tenderers naturally want to be judged independently on their merits by an impartial selector and given the opportunity to rebut any suggestions of demerit which they regard as unfair. The parties who invite tenders . . . want to be able to choose in what they consider to be their best commercial interests and not be hobbled by quasi-judicial procedural rules.'

Facts Transit's request for tenders (RFT) for a major road contract made it clear that tenderers would be evaluated according to a 'weighted attributes method' whereby marks were to be given for certain qualitative attributes as well as for price. According to this procedure, the tender to be accepted would be the one that scored the best overall mark, although Transit reserved the right to reject all tenders. Transit appointed an independent tender evaluation team (TET) to advise upon the evaluation of tenders. While Pratt was the tenderer with the lowest price, it scored badly on technical skills and resources. Members of the TET had experience on another road project from which Pratt had been dismissed by the relevant council on grounds of delay. The TET report concluded with a statement saying that Transit would be unwise to consider the tender of Pratt. The first round of tenders were all rejected. On the second round of tenders, Pratt passed on all the non-price attributes but a different contractor got a higher – the highest – overall score and was awarded the contract. Pratt alleged that the RFT gave rise, upon submission of the tender, to a preliminary contract which contained express and implied terms as to the method by which Transit would select the successful tenderer. It argued that Transit was in breach of those terms by:

(i) considering a sub-attribute of technical skills and resources (namely, financial viability) contrary to Transit's internal tender evaluation manual in the first round; and
(ii) accepting the winning tender in the second round in one envelope instead of two, again in contradiction to advice in the internal manual.

Transit accepted that the RFT was not a mere invitation to treat and did give rise to a preliminary contract requiring it to comply with certain procedural obligations. It also accepted that the contract included an implied duty to act fairly and in good faith. Where the parties differed was over exactly what those procedural obligations were and what counted as acting fairly and in good faith.

Judgment The Privy Council, agreeing with the Court of Appeal of New Zealand, held that the RFT did not incorporate the terms of the internal manual. The RFT said only that tenders would be evaluated in accordance with the weighted attributes method. While the detailed procedures prescribed by the internal manuals were intended to guide Transit, they were not something on which an outsider could rely. Although the question of a duty to act fairly and in good faith was a somewhat controversial question, the parties had accepted that a duty existed. What this required, however, was quite limited:

> 'In their Lordships' opinion, the duty of good faith and fair dealing . . . required that the evaluation ought to express the views honestly held by the members of the TET. The duty to act fairly meant that all the tenderers had to be treated equally. One tenderer could not be given a higher mark than another if their attributes were the same. But Transit was not obliged to give tenderers the same mark if it honestly thought that their attributes were different. Nor did the duty of fairness mean that Transit were obliged to appoint people who came to the task without any views about the tenderers, whether favourable or adverse. It would have been impossible to have a TET competent to perform its function unless it consisted of people with enough experience to have already formed opinions about the merits and demerits of roading contractors. The obligation of good faith and fair dealing also did not mean that the TET had to act judicially. It did not have to accord Mr Pratt a hearing or enter into debate with him about the rights and wrongs of . . . [the other road contract]. It would no doubt have been bad faith for a member of the TET to take

steps to avoid receiving information because he strongly suspected that it might show that his opinion on some point was wrong. But that is all.'

While there is no general implied duty of good faith under English law contract, public sector clients tendering for contracts are subject to the provisions of the EC procurement rules. In certain circumstances, this may lead to an implied contract imposing various obligations on the client such as, that tenderers who respond to an invitation must be treated equally or fairly: *Harmon CFEM Facades (UK) Ltd* v. *The Corporate Officer of the House of Commons*. The implications of the EC procurement rules for public sector clients and projects is discussed in Chapter 1.3.

The limits on the doctrine of 'bid' or 'process' contracts are demonstrated by the case of *Fairclough Building Limited* v. *Port Talbot BC*.

Facts The Council advertised for builders to apply to be placed on a list of selected tenders. Fairclough applied and was placed on the list. Fairclough was subsequently invited to tender but, at the date of tender, the wife of a director of Fairclough had become a senior employee of the Council. The Council removed Fairclough from consideration. Fairclough argued that the Council (who had known of the potential conflict of interest) had warranted that its tender would be considered along with other tenders duly submitted and that the Council were in breach of this warranty.

Judgment The *Blackpool* case was distinguished on the basis that the process of evaluation in this case had begun and a situation had arisen which it was perfectly proper for the Council to consider. Clearly the situation was serious but the Council acted reasonably in removing Fairclough from the shortlist. The Court also referred to the issue of damages: even if there had been a breach of obligation by the Council, what damage would Fairclough have suffered? They had suffered the loss of the chance that they might have had if they had remained on the list but in the light of the situation and the decision to which the Council would have had to make, the chance would have been worth 'precious little'. Fairclough's prospects of winning were negligible due to the conflict of interest.

Furthermore, if an invitation to tender is issued and it can be shown that the client has no intention of letting the contract to the person invited to tender or to one of a number so invited, the invitation is clearly fraudulent and an action will lie in the tort of deceit enabling recovery of expenses by way of damages. Examples here are few and far between because of the difficulties of proving fraud/deceit.

2 TENDERING CONSTRUCTION CONTRACTS

This section deals with the processes involved in tendering contracts to carry out construction works, although much of what is included in this section also applies to subcontracts and to consultants' contracts. When dealing with these in Section 3 and in Section 6 of this chapter, we shall deal only with those elements which are different from the tendering of main construction contracts.

2.1 The process

The entire tendering process for main contract works starts with the identification of the need to approach the market place to obtain competitive prices to carry out the works and ends with the formal execution of the contract. The common steps in this process are as follows:

- Pre-qualification
- Selection of tender list
- Preparation of tenders
- Receipt of tenders
- Clarification and elimination of qualifications
- Selection of contractor
- Appointment of contractor
- Execution of contract.

Pre-qualification

In order to seek tenders from contractors, it is first necessary to determine which contractors are going to be able to submit bona fide tenders and are demonstrably likely to be able to complete the works satisfactorily. It is usually necessary to conduct a pre-qualification exercise in order to identify the tenderers.

At one extreme the pre-qualification may be no more than a response to an advertisement such as those placed in the *Official Journal of the European Union (OJEU)*. This would be the case where 'open tendering' is being used (i.e. where anybody meeting certain pre-set qualification criteria is entitled to submit a tender). In this case, it may merely be necessary for prospective tenderers to put forward credentials demonstrating their ability to meet the criteria and applying for the tender documentation. Such a system is, however, rarely followed since it may result in a very high number of tenders of variable quality giving rise to high reproduction costs for the tender documentation, difficult evaluation and the receipt of tenders from companies which, despite meeting the qualification criteria set out in the advertisement, are in fact unsuitable for the project for other reasons. In other words, this process tends to be very wasteful and is rarely, if ever nowadays, used.

More commonplace is 'selective tendering', a system whereby firms are invited either through placing advertisements (*OJEU*) or by invitation to companies known to the client and/or his professional advisors, to submit pre-qualification information. Table 1 sets out the sort of information that might be requested in a pre-qualification questionnaire. Based on the information received as a result of the pre-qualification enquiry, possibly in conjunction with interviews, from those contractors that submit information, a tender list is agreed. The pre-qualification process is increasingly common throughout the industry but on many occasions, particularly in the private sector, the client and its advisors will agree a tender list based on their own experience and knowledge without the need to conduct a formal pre-qualification exercise.

Tender lists

It is important that the length of the tender list agreed by the client and his advisors is appropriate to the type of contract being tendered – see Section 4 of this chapter for the recommendations on numbers of tenderers for the different types of contract.

Numbers of tenderers

In addition to the number of contractors properly identified for the type of contract, it is advisable that two reserves should be identified that can easily be slotted in should one of the chosen contractors withdraw. Once the list has been agreed it is advisable to contact those on the list, preferably in writing, informing them of their selection and providing sufficient information about the contract to enable them to decide whether they are interested (such information might include anticipated value, size of project, type of

1.1 The planning system
1.2 Financing the project
1.3 Public sector projects
1.4 Public/private partnerships
1.5 Tender process
1.6 Construction contracts
1.7 Construction insurance

Table 1 Typical pre-qualification information

Category of information	Details required	Purpose
General business information	Name, company registration information, names of directors, membership of professional bodies	Establish unequivocal identification of organization and its bona fides
Financial information	Company accounts for (usually) past 3 years: parent company accounts; recent management accounts	Establish financial strength and capability of the organization
Organization information	Company structure: staff and operative numbers and cost classifications; geographical areas of operation; sectors of operation	Establish organization type and operational capability
Project information	Information on recent projects undertaken similar (in size, type, complexity, location) to the one envisaged	Establish extents and depth of experience relevant to the project
Proposed personnel	Names of senior and intermediate personnel likely to be involved; CVs including qualifications and relevant experience	Establish relevant competence of personnel available for the project
References	Names and contact numbers of (usually) three clients	Establish a satisfactory track record
Project specific information	Comment on the specific project including, for example, method statement, programme, procurement	Establish project capability and approach

project, location of project, professional team, client, type of contract, site information and any other relevant information) and to confirm that they are able and willing within the envisaged timescale to submit a bona fide tender. Any declining contractor at this stage can be replaced by the reserves.

Tender preparation

Tender documentation should be sent to the selected list of tenderers providing exactly the same information to each and should be sent out to each at the same time. A set time should be allocated for the preparation of the tenders with tenders being submitted on the same day, at the same time. The tender period allocated should be sufficient to reflect the size, nature and complexity of the project and the type contract envisaged. Tender periods usually range from three weeks where tenders involve the pricing of a quantified document (such as bills of quantities) on a small project, up to three months on a design and build project where significant design development is necessary in order to submit a tender. If there are significant areas of risk transfer or there are significant amounts of design included in the tender, then it may be appropriate to conduct meetings with the tenderers to ensure that they have adequately understood the requirements and where questions can be asked of the client to assist contractors in progressing their tender. Where clarification is given to one tenderer which is not commercially sensitive

Table 2 Example tender record form

Project < Insert project name >
Tender for < Insert description of tender e.g. 'main contract' >
Tender for tender receipt < Insert date and time deadline for receipt of tenders >
Tenders received at < Insert tender delivery address >
Tenders open at < Insert where tenders being opened >
Tenders open on < Insert date and time of tender opening >
Tenders open by < Insert names of individuals, their companies and capacities on tender opening >
Form of contract < Insert brief description contract form >
Contract period < Insert contract period determined by client in weeks or months as appropriate >
Pre-tender estimate < Insert value of PTE >

	Name of tenderer	Tender value £	Alternative period		Comment
			Alternative no. of weeks/months	Tender value	
1					
2					
3					
4					
5					

Tenders received as above Signed Name
Signed Name
Date

to that particular tenderer, then that clarification information should also be provided to the other tenderers to ensure parity of tendering. Likewise and for the same reason, any other information given out during the course of the tender process should be distributed to all parties. It is essential that confidentiality of tendered information is retained and, for this reason, all tenders should be opened at the same time and it would be normal for any late tenders to be excluded and the tender envelopes returned unopened. Tenders should be submitted in unmarked envelopes identifying that they contain a tender for the particular project, but not identifying which contractor is the tenderer. The tender envelopes should be opened as a formal process preferably by more than one person and the key elements (such as the price and construction period offered) noted on a proforma and signed as being the tenders submitted by those opening the envelopes. A typical tender record form is reproduced in Table 2.

Tender receipt and evaluation

Once the tenders have been received and recorded it is necessary to check them for completeness and accuracy and to evaluate the bids submitted. Evaluation will depend entirely on the type of contract envisaged and may be as simple as ensuring that the financial offer is complete and unqualified or as complex as evaluating a variety of different elements such as price, design, programme and methodology using evaluation criteria, usually predetermined, enabling the client to weight all the relevant factors and determine a preferred contractor.

1.1 The planning system
1.2 Financing the project
1.3 Public sector projects
1.4 Public/private partnerships
1.5 Tender process
1.6 Construction contracts
1.7 Construction insurance

Clarification

Before it is possible to arrive at a preferred contractor is often necessary to seek clarification of certain issues raised as part of the tender and to negotiate the removal of qualifications attaching to the tender. It is also necessary to deal with any errors that have been found in the tenders and there are two established ways of dealing with any arithmetic errors found as follows:

(1) any arithmetic errors would be corrected and the tender adjusted with the tenderer asked whether he would like to stand by his original tender, or amend his tender to the adjusted figure; or
(2) any arithmetic errors should be notified to the tender who is then given the choice of standing by his original tender or withdrawing his tender.

It is usual that the method of dealing with arithmetic errors is notified to the tenderers prior to the submission of their tenders. In clarifying tenders, this may often lead to negotiations on the price. It is recommended that, if this is the case, then any changes brought about through negotiations should also be discussed with those contractors whose tender might be affected by similar adjustments making them more competitive once the adjustments have been made.

Selection

Once the client and all his advisors are satisfied that all the tender matters have been satisfactorily dealt with, it is necessary to select a successful tenderer. The basis for the selection will depend very much on the type of contract being used and may be based purely on price or on a combination of price and other relevant factors. In all cases, the basis should be the bid that, it is believed, represents the best value for money and not the bid that is merely the lowest price. It will, of course, be quite likely that the lowest price does represent best value for money, but it is very dangerous to assume that this is automatically the case. The client should be wary that a low price is not merely the result of substantial errors which will create future difficulties for both the contractors and the client; or that it is due to poor tender documentation in which the contractor has spotted weaknesses which it intends to manipulate to its benefit at a later stage; or that it contains qualitative deficiencies which are not clearly apparent based upon the documentation submitted; or that the contractor is cynically buying the project with the intention of using every available avenue, fair or foul, to manipulate a higher ultimate price or lower quality product at the end of the project.

Appointment

The appointment of contractors is included in Section 9 of this chapter.

It is then necessary to accept the successful tender, appoint a contractor and it is strongly preferable to do this in writing setting out the terms and conditions accepted. The appointment of a contractor can be made in one of several different ways:

(1) *Exchange of letters.* On the basis that the tender documentation and tender returns contain sufficient information, including the form of contract and any amendments to it (assuming a standard form has been used), then it is possible to effect a complete contract by writing an acceptance letter to the contractor identifying all of the tender and other documentation which govern the contract and identifying all of the information including price and start and ends dates giving certainty to the contract. This would be sufficient to create a complete and binding contract between the parties as a contract under hand.

(2) *Letter of intent*. The extent to which a contractually binding relationship is created by a letter of intent depends entirely upon the wording of the letter – see Section 9: Turning Tenders into Contracts for the effect of different wording. Such letters should be treated with caution as whilst they may start with the intention that the Client's obligations are limited in the first instance, it is possible that by the subsequent performance of both parties, the Courts may deem that a complete contract for the works has been effected but with some unclear elements. It is important, therefore, that such letters are unequivocal and that they become superseded by the execution of the formal contract at the earliest opportunity.

(3) *Execution of the main contract*. The complexities of most construction contracts make it extremely important and in the interests of both parties that the contract is created by the execution of formal contract documentation. This not only provides a high degree of certainty but also enables the contract to be entered into as a deed. Contract documentation with any amendments agreed should include not only the form of contract (with complete amendments) but also contract drawings, contract specifications, contract pricing document and all other relevant contract documentation such as collateral warranties, soil investigation reports, pre-contract health and safety plans and the like. All of the contract documents would then be signed by persons empowered to sign deeds on behalf of their organisations.

Tender variability

In the good old days, tenders were substantially won and lost on price alone. A fundamental problem with such tenders was, however, that they were only as good and as valid as the tender documentation provided by the client's team. Very often it was, and still is, the case that the final price paid by the client is very substantially different from the price tendered by the contractor. In truth there are a number of variable elements inherent in a tender which are beyond the bottom line price submitted but which may affect what the client gets, when he gets it, and how much he pays for it. In essence, these are the three things that concern the client and whilst the emphasis may vary from client to client, from project to project, no client is able to ignore any one of these factors completely. In order to illustrate the issues involved, it is helpful to look at examples of two projects where completely different procurement routes are being followed.

Example 1 A lump sum contract based upon priced bills of quantities submitted by six tenderers. In such circumstances tenderers should have been selected because of their ability to carry out a project of the type, size and complexity envisaged. It is difficult, therefore, to argue against a decision other than a selection of the lowest bidder. Nonetheless, there are a number of other factors which will make a significant contribution to the success of the project. All of the tenderers are tendering on the same design. It is rare, however, that the detail design is complete and the contractor's attitude towards design development drawings will make a significant difference to the ultimate outcome, both in terms of quality and price. Some will require every last nut and screw to be identified before proceeding and the contractor may claim, whatever detail is drawn, that it is different from that envisaged and, therefore, will necessitate both additional reimbursement and prolongation of the contract. This is in dramatic contrast to a contractor who will resolve many of the detailed issues which are best resolved three dimensionally on site, contributing expertise and specialist knowledge to producing a high quality and punctual output. The only realistic way of determining the likely attitude is track record. It is often said that a contractor is only as good as his last job and it is true that reputation is, or should be, a significant consideration when selecting a contractor. It is very often the case that a contractor would promise the earth before being awarded the contract and deliver nothing but the bare minimum that he can contractually get away with once he has been awarded it. Reputations for such attitudes should be heeded.

The length of the contract may be predetermined or may be the optimum length put forward by the contractor as part of his tender. However, the programme, and specifically the times and specific activities that are programmed to be carried out, has a knock-on effect on other aspects of the project and, in particular, design development. A shorter programme may appear attractive to the client because he gets his building operational much sooner, but it may give rise to undue difficulties for the designers who, by failing to achieve information by the dates required, give rise not only to delays (perhaps beyond a more realistic programme), but also to the additional prolongation costs that go with such delays.

The management put forward for a project, its attitude towards and its understanding of that project, are key to success. Whatever the merits and qualities of a contractor's head office staff, it is the site staff that run and build the project and the person nominated to run the site is of paramount importance. A contractor with a poor reputation but with a first class site manager, may produce a highly successful project from the client's perspective. Likewise, a contractor with a good reputation who puts on an inadequate site manager may contribute to a financially disastrous contract, both for the contractor and the client. It should be clear from the foregoing that when the contractor is selected purely on the basis of his price, this the client has not necessarily gone with the best option available to him.

Example 2 A design and build contract based upon a detailed set of employer's requirements. In these circumstances the contractors' tender is based upon a whole range of elements, none of which can be judged independently from the others. Particularly important is the design which may be significantly different in one case from another, even to the extent of the floor area being provided. The price cannot be judged without fully understanding what is being provided in design terms and how that design will affect the client's operational performance. A particular facet of design, namely the selection of materials, plant and the like, may not obviously affect the operational performance of the building, but may make a significant difference to the future maintenance and running costs of the building. At the time of the tender submission, the design will be at a relatively early stage. The ability of the contractor to understand the client's objectives and how decisions made in developing the project will affect his business might be key to the success in working the project up to fruition. The programme and the quality of the team all have a bearing on the bid that is likely to produce the best value for money.

From the above examples it can be seen that it is not necessarily a straightforward matter to select a contract once tenders have been received.

Price versus value

Too often price is judged ahead of value as it is much more visible. In selecting a contractor the focus should, therefore, be value rather than price, although the extent to which the value might change would depend upon the method of procurement. In Example 1 above the value is going to be much more substantially determined by the price than in Example 2 where there are a considerably greater number of variables which affect the best value.

Tender documentation

The essence of the documents prepared for tendering is to provide contractors with sufficient information fully and properly to tender on the correct basis. Thus, if a lump sum tender is required, the documentation must fully explain what it is that the client requires and the information can be drawn or written but it should always be unequivocal. Any difference between what the documentation calls for and what the client expects will lead either to additional costs to bring the project up to the client's expectations, or to a building which fails to meet those expectations. The level of detail required will depend upon what it is that the client does require. If he requires merely a 100 000 ft^2 shed with 9 m high eaves which keeps out the weather, the documentation can be very simple, but the client must expect a building with the cheapest possible materials and little or no aesthetic appeal beyond those required to meet planning and building regulations. If, however, the building has been substantially designed by the client's team and he is particular about every detail of the building, then the drawn and written information will be very extensive and the task of pricing that information will be complex. If the client wishes to keep tendering costs to a minimum, then he may procure that a document is produced identifying the quantities involved in that design. In these circumstances though, he must be careful that any inaccuracies in those quantities do not lead to additional costs and contractual claims. Table 3 sets out typical documentation for different types of contract.

The influence of procurement strategy

A wide variety of procurement strategies are available in the modern construction industry, ranging from design and build through develop and construct to lump sum contracts with bills of quantities to management and construction management contracts. All of these different procurement strategies will affect the way the works are designed, the documentation used in tendering and a number of different tenders required within the development process. Table 4 sets out the different tender processes required for some of the main procurement methodologies used in the industry. It must be borne in mind, however, that there are many bespoke and hybrid forms of procurement and it is always important to produce documentation that is appropriate to the particular circumstance rather than regurgitate standard or previously used documentation.

Marrying procurement and the tender process: client objectives

The greatest influence on the strategy adopted for the project is the division of risk between the client on the one hand and the construction industry on the other. Thus, the client looking to pass as much risk as possible is likely to select a strategy with as few separate contracts as are appropriate to the circumstances. Such a solution would be a form of design and build contract. At the other extreme, where the client believes that he can best control the risk and, by doing so, produce a better outcome whether it be financial, qualitative or in the programme, then it is more likely to go for a multi-contract strategy such as construction management. Secondary, but important influences on the strategy are:

Table 3 Tender documentation for contract types

Type of contract	A Essential tender documents	B Optional additional documents	C Comment
1. Drawings and specification – lump sum	1.A.1 Drawings 1.A.2 Detailed specifications 1.A.3 Form of tender 1.A.4 Form of contract and amendments 1.A.5 Tender instructions	1.B.1 Schedule of works 1.B.2 Pricing pro forma	1.B.1: should be provided in most cases. 1.B.2: useful to make tender comparison easier; often integrated with 1.B.1
2. Bills of quantities – lump sum	2.A.1 Details drawings 2.A.2 Bills of quantities (usually incorporating the specification) 2.A.3 Form of tender 2.A.4 Form of contract and amendments 2.A.5 Tender instructions	2.B.1 Detailed specification (as separate document)	
3. Design and build – lump sum	3.A.1 Client's requirements document 3.A.2 Form of tender 3.A.3 Form of contract and amendments 3.A.4 Tender instructions	3.B.1 Drawings illustrating operational requirements 3.B.2 Planning drawings (where planning permission already granted) 3.B.3 Detail drawings where client has specific requirements 3.B.4 Output specification 3.B.5 Detailed specification 3.B.6 Pricing analysis pro forma/schedule	The level of drawings to be provided (3.B.1 to 4) and specification information (3.B.4 and 5) will depend on nature and complexity of the project and the level of detail the client wishes to control. The pricing analysis/schedule can be in variety of forms ranging from a simple schedule to something akin to a bill of quantities.
4. Cost reimbursement – management contract	4.A.1 Drawings 4.A.2 Specifications 4.A.3 Estimated project value or estimated price cost (EPC) 4.A.4 Form of tender 4.A.5 Form of contract and amendments 4.A.6 Tender instructions	4.B.1 Schedule of works 4.B.2 Measured cost plan 4.B.3 Tender pricing pro forma	4.A.1 to 3: the level of detail provided will be dependent upon the level of design development at time of tender. 4.B.1 to 3: should normally be provided
5. Construction management – package contract	5.A.1 Project drawings 5.A.2 Package scope incorporating drawings, specifications and other descriptive information. 5.A.3 Interface information 5.A.4 Form of tender 5.A.5 Form of contract and amendments 5.A.6 Tender instructions	5.B.1 Schedule of works 5.B.2 Bills of approximate quantities 5.B.3 Bills of quantities 5.B.4 Other tender pricing pro forma	It is important to define: the project as a whole; the part(s) to be included in the package; the relationship between the contractor and construction manager/project co-ordinator and with other package contractors; how common services are to be provided; and a means for pricing/controlling change.

Table 4 Tendering under different procurement strategies

A Procurement Strategy	B Tender Options	C Pricing Document	D Comment
1. Cost reimbursement	1.1 Percentage fee on prime cost (PC) 1.2 Lump sum fee (LSF)	1.1 Estimated price cost (EPC) 1.2 Estimated price cost (EPC)	Contractor reimbursed all costs incurred (as defined) plus quoted fee. Not recommended except in very unusual circumstances.
2. Management contact	2.1 Percentage or LSF fee on PC 2.2 Fee on PC; priced preliminaries 2.3 Package tenders based on similar basis to 3, 4 and/or 6 below.	2.1 EPC 2.2 EPC and schedule of preliminaries 2.3 As 3, 4 and/or 6 below.	Management Contractor does not carry out works packages. All packages tendered on open-book basis. Major issue over whether management contractor is 'reimbursed' preliminaries or paid against quoted figures. Former can lead to uncontrolled expenditure; latter to abuses of costs passed down to package contractors (i.e. paid for twice by client).
3. Bills of approximate quantities (BAQ)	3.1 Priced, extended and totalled BAQ including preliminaries, measured work and subcontract work	3.1 BAQ	Rates inserted into BAQ should be extended and totalled to give 'approximate' contract value; care should be taken to avoid manipulative pricing designed to take advantage where quantities likely to change in final measure.
4. Single stage lump sum contract (not design)	4.1 Lump sum for work shown on drawings and described in specification 4.2 Bills of quantities (BQ)	4.1 Priced specification and/or schedule of works 4.2 BQ	4.1 should only be used for straightforward work where scope is clear and change unlikely 4.2 BQ gives advantage of clear basis for valuing works done and pricing change. Disadvantage that 'lump sum' really only relates to work described and measured in BQ and not necessarily work called for or implied from drawings/specifications. Accuracy depends upon quality of documentation prior to tender. Open to abuse and thought by many to be unduly expensive.
5. Two stage lump sum	*First Stage* 5.1.1 Overheads and profit (OH&P) 5.1.2 OH&P and priced preliminaries 5.1.3 OH&P, priced preliminaries and priced measured works (e.g. schedule of rates or BAQ)	*First Stage* Documentation written to suit level of design and project development, usually in some form of schedule	Two stage process is usually used to identify a preferred contractor at an early stage to assist in design development/financing/construction advice etc, particularly in circumstances where the lead in period is short. Care should be taken not to create unwittingly a substantial contractual commitment without completing the second stage negotiations at least to a sufficiently advanced stage.
	Second Stage 5.2.1 Tender by short-listed contractors with first stage tender information applied to and amplified on documents as 4.1 or 4.2 or hybrid documentation 5.2.2 Negotiation with preferred contractor based upon documents as 4.1 or 4.2 or hybrid documentation	*Second Stage* Ultimate documentation should vary little from single stage documents	
6. Single stage D&B	6.1 Statement of requirements – simple document setting out spatial and qualitative information 6.2 Statement of requirements – more complex document using drawn as well as written information including, for example, site information, operational parameters and relationships, planning constraints 6.3 Fixed brief for the building including detailed drawings as attached to and including planning permission 6.4 Substantially completed design contained in requirements document leaving only production design information to be provided by the contractor	6.1 Statement of price 6.2 Simple Price Schedule 6.3 Analysis of price in a variety of forms from elemental cost estimate to detail schedule of works to full or abbreviated bills of quantities 6.4 As for 6.3	Design and build procurement is used in a much broader context than where the entire design is provided by the contractor as part of a lump sum bid to meet a simply stated set of requirements. At the other extreme it can be successfully used where design is substantially complete but the issuance of final design details becomes a contractor responsibility, thereby avoiding the risk of such details being the centre piece of contractual claims.
7. Two stage D&B	Two stage D&B follows the principles of ordinary two-stage tendering but with design capability forming part of first stage and design proposals part of second	As 5 above	

- time constraint – a very short programme necessitating an early start on site before design is complete in which case the client should choose either to control the design development after the start of construction by letting the work in packages, or by passing the entire design development to a contractor, or
- financial constraints – where price certainty before the start of the construction is essential, leading to a need for a form of lump sum contract, or
- high quality – where it is essential that the design, right down to the last detail, is controlled by or on behalf of the client in order to ensure that the high standards required are, in fact, achieved, in which case, design and build is most likely to be excluded as an option.

Whatever the client's objectives and constraints that lie behind the procurement strategy, it is important that this is taken into account in the tendering process. If the client wishes to achieve a high level of risk transfer then the tender documentation must make it quite clear what risks the tenderers are expected to take on board, otherwise there will be a mismatch between the client's objectives and what is ultimately achieved. If the client's over-riding requirement is to start the works as soon as possible, then the documentation should make the task of tendering an easy one so that the time taken for the tendering process can be reduced to a minimum. If the works are being let in packages, then it is important to communicate how those packages are going to be co-ordinated, what interfaces with other contractors there will be, what the tenderers' responsibilities will be in relation to those interfaces and how the individual package fits into the overall scheme. This is essential in order to avoid disputes, claims and other disasters at a later stage.

Contractor selection and appointment

The first stage in the selection of the contractor is one that has now become common place in the industry and that is pre-qualification. This has already been mentioned but the objective of this stage is to assemble enough information about potential tenderers, and about how they would approach the individual project, in order to make an informed decision as to a list of contractors who are best able to tender for and carry out the project works. In order to elicit the best responses, the process should not be made unduly complex or onerous in relation to the size and type of project as this will discourage potential bona fide tenderers from participating in the exercise. Nor should it be so superficial that the client could end up with the lowest tender being a contractor who, in the final analysis, is unsuitable to carry out the works.

A significant problem in the industry is the wide diversity of formats in which pre-qualification information is requested, thereby imposing potential tenderers with increased overheads merely to responding to such pre-qualification questionnaires. General pre-qualification information can be obtained without the need to approach the individual contractor from Constructionline. Constructionline is a database, sponsored by the government, containing most contracting and consulting organisations that are active in the construction industry. Originally, the list of contractors and consultants on which Constructionline has been based was kept by the Department of Environment. Following Latham's recommendations, this was privatised and is now operated commercially with companies paying a fee for inclusion on the Constructionline database. The information contained on companies on Constructionline is shown below.

PART A Registered Name
Trading Name
Head Office Address/Contact Address/Contact
Registration Number
VAT Number
Date Formed
Date Incorporated
Registered Office
Taxation Construction Industry Scheme
Financial Information and Contact Details
Financial Document: Limited Companies: The Balance Sheet The Trading Account The Auditor's Report The Profit and Loss Account The Directors' Report Any notes to the accounts
Sole Traders and Partnership: Latest full audited accounts Or detailed loss and profit account, and Balance sheet with notes thereon
Directors, Partners, etc.
Branch Offices and Contact Details
Licences/Certificates
Licences/certificates for specific categories of work (e.g. asbestos licence)
Associated Companies

References three examples of contracts completed within the last three years for each category of work
Work categories for which you are seeking registration – contract limits, references and staffing details For each category Contract limits min. value £ max. value £ References Ref. No. Value
Staff details (No.) Directly employed Subcontractors Supervisors and Managers % Subcontracted
Additional staff information Total number of administrative staff Total number of professional staff Total number of staff in firm
Areas of Operation Please state preferred areas of work: The UK European Union Outside the EU
Professional Conduct Bankrupt Criminal offence Company Employment determined

PART B
Environmental Policy
Equal Opportunities
Health and Safety
Call Out: Do you operate a 24 hour call-out service?

Trades Associations/Federations and Professional Bodies
Other Qualification Lists
Insurance details
Quality Assurance
Access to your registration by third parties
Invoicing details

PART C
PFI interest and experience
Who is the person responsible for PFI projects? (if different from main detail)
Does your firm have previous PFI project experience?
Terms & Conditions
Payment of Subcontractors and Suppliers
Probity
Access to Information
Declaration
Please tick if you have enclosed the following: ☐ Account ☐ Environment Policy ☐ Tax Certificate ☐ Equal Opportunities Statement ☐ Quality Assurance ☐ Trade Association Membership Certificates ☐ Health and Safety Policy ☐ Constructionline Fee ☐ Insurance Policies

Once a tender list has been formulated, selection can proceed on a single stage tendering basis, or a two stage tendering basis. A single stage tender is one where prices and other information is submitted as a one off operation and a contractor is selected as a result of those tenders which represent a complete offer. Two-stage tendering is where less than complete information is used as a basis for tendering the first stage either to select a preferred contractor, or to eliminate all but, say, two contractors. The second stage would then be a negotiation of the complete contract, whether with one or both of the 'preferred' contractors. The complete contract is then signed following the second stage negotiation.

Special circumstances, such as a partnering relationship between a contractor and client, or where a contractor has particular expertise or where time simply does not allow a complete tendering process to be carried out, dictate the appointment of a contractor through a negotiation rather than tendering. In these circumstances, rather than selection of a contractor based to a large extent on price, the price and all the other contract conditions are negotiated with a single contractor.

3 TENDERING CONSULTANT CONTRACT

3.1 Similarities/differences with construction tenders

A substantial amount of the last section about tendering construction contracts also applies when tendering consultancy contracts. There is, however, one very real and important difference: construction tenders are geared to producing a product which has a clear definition, usually already expressed in terms of designs, specifications and other information, and what is on offer is a distinct product. Consultancy contracts are, however, purely for the provision of a service where, more often than not, whilst the nature of the service may be known, the full extent and implications inherent in the provision of the service are not. Thus, when appointing an architect or engineer, it might be clear at the time of appointment, what the ultimate objective is by way of building type and size, but the amount of work in going from a blank sheet of paper until completion of a construction project is far from clear. The workload will depend upon a number of issues such as planning permission, building control, site conditions, the client's decision making process, client change of mind, performance of other consultants, the performance of the contractor, difficulties created by the contractor and so on. It is, therefore, quite possible that the actual time and, therefore, the cost of providing the service may differ very dramatically from one building to an apparently identical one.

Furthermore, price should be only one of the factors taken into account as, more significant than price, is the quality of the service provided. After all, it is highly detrimental to the client's ultimate needs if a designer is appointed because he offers the lowest price, when in fact the construction project is poorly designed and is inefficient to operate and achieves much less than was potentially the case within the given time and budgetary constraints. Then, the saving in fees is dramatically outweighed by the detrimental effects of a poor service. It is imperative, therefore, that the quality of the service being provided is given a high level of importance and, in this regard, reputation is probably the most significant factor in assessing that quality.

3.2 Price versus value

A major issue when tendering consultants' services is, therefore, the need to devise a means whereby all of the relevant considerations can be properly evaluated. This is

Table 5 Consultant selection – example weighted assessments

PROJECT:

SERVICE:

COMPANY:

QUALITY CRITERIA

Project organization	**Weighting**	**Marks**	**Weighted marks**
Details of proposed team	10		
Previous experience of team	15		
Previous experience of practice	10		
Proximity of office from site	10		
Proposed resources to be applied	15		
Ability to cope with peak demands	10		
Quality of team leader	20		
Experience of interface with IT	10		
Current workload	10		
Project execution			
Method of approach to design coordination	15		
Means of ensuring programme compliance	10		
Process of collating user requirements	10		
Means of ensuring compliance with EMG	25		
Means of establishing design freeze	15		
Method of establishing and controlling design changes	20		
Method of dealing with on site quality monitoring	15		
Method of dealing with snagging and project handover	20		
Quality			
Quality assurance methods	20		
Approach to CDM	10		
Attitude to environmental and security issues	10		
	Total mark		
	Tti quality	Mark/100	

encapsulated in the Government's 'Best Value' policy which follows on from the recommendations made by Latham (see Section 4, paragraph A below). The usual way of balancing price and service to arrive at best value is by seeking a dual bid, with a financial offer and a qualitative proposal setting out the service, approach, experience and the like. These two are then assessed independently, weighted and a decision made based on the resultant weighted score. A typical set of weighted qualitative assessments is shown in Table 5.

There is, however, a fundamental problem with the qualitative assessments used, particularly in the public sector, as these ostensibly need to be objective, and as such they concentrate on the standard of the proposal documents submitted. In truth, however, this process does not really evaluate the quality of service but relies more on marking the firm's ability to submit a convincing proposal document. The true measure of quality of performance is best ascertained by assessing previous experience and, in particular, the views of previous clients and others who have had direct working experience with the particular consultant. The highest importance should be given to previous experience. As the performance of the consultant is to a significant extent a subjective matter it is, in the author's view, futile to attempt to evaluate suitability without incorporating subjective views of performance into the evaluation with a high level of weighting. This is commonly the case when the private sector client chooses its consultants but appears to find little favour in the public sector because of the inability to provide a satisfactory audit trail on subjective issues.

3.3 Deliverability

It is important to establish the ability of a consultant to deliver the required service within the price quoted. Budgets for all projects are limited and the amounts set have a direct correlation with the expected costs as estimated earlier in the project. It is totally counterproductive to base initial budgets on fee quotations if those quotations are inadequate and represent what has been described in a set of tender documents and cynically priced by a consultant, the objective being to win the price competition and then escalate the fees through loopholes in the documentation and through the inevitable process of change during the project development. It is an unsavoury fact that, since the advent of competition, there is often little correlation between final fees paid and the amount tendered.

It is also a fact that the range of prices received from consultant tenders usually vary much more dramatically than for construction works and often the range can be over one hundred percent or even several hundred percent. This reflects both the difficulty in truly assessing the extent of works required and the difficulty in describing the extent of services required in a fair and reasonable way which does not leave scope for discussion about additional fees due to changing circumstances.

The reality with price tendering of consultant contracts is that it is actually far more difficult to achieve satisfactory outcomes than in tenders for construction contracts. Prices received should be judged with extreme caution. Assessment of anticipated resources with reasonable normal hourly rates should be made against the prices received to determine sufficiency and it is in the client's best interest that any bids which are significantly inadequate in this respect should be rejected. Selection should be based largely upon the evaluation of the service and reputation, the price representing a very small element in the decision.

3.4 Good practice

Following the Latham Report, Working Group 4 published a Guidance Document *Selecting Consultants for the team: balancing quality and price*. This is described in Section 4, paragraph E.

4 TENDERING GUIDELINES

4.1 Introduction

Against the backdrop of the boom years of the 1980s and the major recession of the early 1990s, a number of reports were commissioned by various sectors of the construction industry to see how the industry could operate more efficiently. Re-examination of selection/tendering procedures formed a significant part of most of these reports. This section looks at each of the reports in chronological order and then examines some of the Codes of Practice which ensued.

A *Constructing the team* by Sir Michael Latham: July 1994. The final report of the Government/industry review of procurement and contractual arrangements in the UK construction industry

The seminal Latham Report looked at selection/tendering procedures for both consultants and contractors in Chapter 1.6. It contained the following key recommendations in relation to each sector.

Consultants The report notes the increase in selection of consultants by competitive fee bidding. It also reports survey information suggesting that this has resulted in a reduction in services provided: less consideration to reviewing alternatives, less checking, simpler design etc. It emphasises the need to select on the basis of a proper qualitative as well as price assessment of bids for creative professional services and recommends:

- A single register maintained by DETR of consultant firms with other local authorities and public bodies making use of this (Con Reg). Public sector works should be restricted to consultant firms who are on Con Reg.
- Firms on the register should be required to demonstrate appropriate professional and managerial skills, resources and professional indemnity insurance.
- DETR should lead a task force to endorse specific quality and price assessment mechanisms for the engagement of professional consultants.

The goal was to reduce tender costs for consultants and to ensure a basic quality threshold. These recommendations have been progressed: Working Group 4 examined the existing wording and made certain detailed recommendations about the improvement of the register. It also produced a report on Selection of Consultants (considered in more detail in paragraph E below). Following on from this ConReg has been incorporated into the renamed Constructionline (see Section 2 of this chapter) and is now privately maintained.

Main contractors and subcontractors Again the report notes the need for a single official register of contractors and subcontractors to avoid duplication of effort and the consequent wasteful burden for the construction industry. The registration system for public sector work must consider issues such as improvement of productivity and competitiveness, quality controls imposed, research and development, training arrangements and specialist skills. The following recommendations were made:

- A task force should prepare a single qualification document for contractors seeking to work in any public sector body. DETR will maintain the register. It must be consulted before any government department or agency commissions works.
- Other bodies should abandon their separate lists and forms.
- The national system should develop into a quality register with a 'star' system related to performance.
- Main contractors on public sector contracts should be required to employ only registered sub-contract firms on public sector works.

Again, steps have been taken to implement these proposals by the establishment of Constructionline by DETR (See Section 2 above).

1.1 The planning system
1.2 Financing the project
1.3 Public sector projects
1.4 Public/private partnerships
1.5 Tender process
1.6 Construction contracts
1.7 Construction insurance

The report also focused on the contentious matter of the length of tender lists. The cost of tendering both to clients and the industry needs to be kept at a sensible level. The report recommends that:

- Clients should adhere to the NJCC Code of Procedure for single-stage/two-stage selective tendering (which recommends that a maximum of six firms should be invited for single-stage tenders (with two names 'in reserve') and, for two-stage tenders, again a maximum of six firms or four if specialist engineering contractors are involved.
- On design and build contracts not more than three firms should be on the list (with one name in 'reserve') for single-stage tenders and for two-stage procedures a maximum of five firms (with one 'reserve') at first stage narrowing to two (or one if preferred) for the second stage.
- On large schemes a reasonable proportion of expenses should be paid to unsuccessful tenderers.
- Detailed advice should be given to public sector clients on the specific requirements for selective tendering under European Directives and departments should compaign for a change to EU Rules to allow two-stage tendering to be used by public sector clients.

There is evidence that since Latham, clients are more sensitive to the waste caused by long tender lists and, for the most part, it appears that the NJCC guidelines are followed. There has currently been no change to the EC Procurement Directives in relation to two-stage tendering: see further Section 1 of chapter 1.4 on Public Sector Projects although changes are in the offing.

The Latham Report also emphasised the need for clients particularly public sector clients to realise that value for money and cost in use must govern the selection of the successful tenderer and not just the lowest price. EU Directives permit acceptance of the most 'economically advantageous' tender provided set criteria for assessing this are stipulated in the tender documents.

Finally, the Latham Report recommended the production of a joint code of practice for the selection of contractors: these have since been produced and are considered in paragraphs D and E below.

The Latham Report (with remarkable prescience) also suggests that public authorities must be given guidance as to how they can experiment with partnering arrangements.

B Construction procurement by government: an efficiency unit scrutiny: **July 1995. Chaired by Sir Peter Levene**

This excellent and far reaching report was designed to consider how government could ensure that it become a best practice client. It was prepared against the backdrop of Sir Michael Latham's report. It concluded that:

> 'As key clients of the industry, government bodies are far from blameless for the way in which it behaves . . . to get the industry to change its way, government will have to change its own behaviour, practice and procedures.'

Among a large number of very far reaching recommendations, the specific recommendations and actions points in relation to tendering are relatively limited.

Recommendation 17 required that:

> 'Departments, working with CUP [Central Unit On Procurement based in HM Treasury] should develop more effective arrangements to build up and share

> knowledge about the performance of particular firms and the construction market generally so that their decisions about tender lists and tender evaluations and about the appointment of consultants and contractors are better informed . . .'.

The rationale for this is that a better informed client will be more likely to get the invitation to tender right and be in a much stronger position when going through the process. It is also much more focused in judging tenders especially in evaluating criteria like experience and past performance.

Recommendation 20 requires that:

> 'Departments should examine the scope for partnering, provided that "partners" are selected by a competitive process. Where for example they appoint consultants on term contracts, they should appoint at least two so that that have some basis for comparison and measuring performance on different jobs'.

While the Levene Report concluded that fully developed partnering (with open books and very long-term commitments by the client) is not appropriate for Departments because they must be demonstrably open to new entrants and to market testing. Departments must realize that there is scope for wider application of partnering procedures and they are not inhibited by accountability rules or by EU constraints. This is in fact wrong: EU constraints do limit the scope for partnering in the public sector.

Generally, the Levene Report demanded that Departments give a client lead to the industry by avoiding the conflict arising from the linked issues of the government's supposed tender price policy and the alleged claims conscious culture of many in the industry especially main contractors. If price is the dominant or deciding factor on bids the scene is set for confrontation from day one. The Departments should tender with the aim of getting those who offer 'the best service'. They should also spurn wasteful tendering methods and reduce absurdly long tender lists. Again, the Levene report required reduced lists: a maximum of three for design and build and six for others. It also urges better preparation of bids to cut-out re-tender costs. The Levene report too recognised the need to reimburse tenderers' cost particularly where Departments themselves increased the costs by making late changes.

C *Re-thinking construction: the report of the Construction Task Force to the Deputy Prime Minister, John Prescott, on the scope for improving the quality and efficiency of UK construction:* July 1998. Chaired by Sir John Egan

The Construction Task Force was set up against the backdrop of deep concern that the construction industry was under-achieving both in terms of meeting its own needs and those of its clients. It identified five key drivers of change to set the agenda for the construction industry at large: committed leadership, focus on the customer, integrated processes and teams, a quality driven agenda and commitment to people. It set ambitious targets for annual improvement including annual reductions of 10% in construction cost and construction time and 20% in defects in projects. In order to achieve integrated project processes the four key elements were identified as product development, project implementation, partnering the supply chain and production of components. These, it concluded, were incompatible with competitive tendering.

Accordingly, Egan insisted that the industry must replace competitive tendering with long term relationships based on clear measurement of performance and sustained improvement in quality and efficiency. Chapter 4: paragraphs 67 to 72 deal with the

1.1 The planning system
1.2 Financing the project
1.3 Public sector projects
1.4 Public/private partnerships
1.5 Tender process
1.6 Construction contracts
1.7 Construction insurance

establishment of long-term relationships. Specifically:

- An essential ingredient in the delivery of radical performance improvements in other industries has been the creation of long-term relationships or reliances through the supply chain of mutual interest. Alliances offer the co-operation and continuity needed to enable the team to learn and take a stake in improving the product.
- The industry must now go a stage beyond partnering and develop long-term alliances that include all those involved in the whole process.
- The criteria for the selection of partners is ultimately about best overall value for money not about lowest price. All players in the team share in success with proper incentive arrangements to enable cost savings.
- There must be an end to reliance on contracts.
- Discipline to relationships between clients and their suppliers must be based on the introduction of performance measurement and competition against clear targets in relation to quality, timelines and cost. Such relationships are much more demanding and regarding than those based on competitive tendering.
- Alliancing saves tendering costs. The task force believes that value for money can be adequately demonstrated and properly audited through rigorous measurement of performance as outlined above. The Treasury with DETR must consider the appropriate mechanisms further and give guidance to public bodies.

This debate continues.

D Code of Practice for the selection of subcontractors: April 1997, produced by Working Group 3 under the auspices of the Construction Industry Board

As noted above, this Code of Practice was recommended by the Latham Report. It was commissioned by the Construction Industry Board, and the Working Party comprised representatives from across the industry. The Code applies to the selection of subcontractors for work above £10 000 in value. It specifically applies to competitive tendering processes: both single-stage and two-stage.

It looks at each step in the tender process in turn.

Tender list The aim of the list should be to state a minimum number of comparable, competent suitable organisations willing and able to tender from whom compliant bids will be received. In-house tenderers may be included but other tenderers should know if they are. The criteria to be used in assessing tenders should be notified during the selection process and stated in the tender enquiry document.

The code notes the criteria for qualification:

- 'Quality of Work
- Performance Record
- Overall Competence
- Health and Safety Record
- Financial Stability
- Appropriate Insurance Cover
- Size and Resources
- Technical and Organizational Ability
- Ability to Innovate' (Paragraph 2.3).

Having devised the preliminary list, potential tenderers should be asked if they are willing to tender. This should establish anticipated available capacity and grasp an enthusiasm for the works. Details of the works, likely durations, number of tenderers to be invited to submit and details of the main contract client and relevant consultants should be given at this stage. The more information is given, the more likely compliant bids will be submitted. Briefing sessions may be appropriate.

Again, the Code prescribes maximum numbers of invitations to issue which are broadly consistent with the Latham Report. Reserves are discussed and may be needed if a tenderer wished to withdraw during the process. They obviously must be informed. If tender enquiry documents are not despatched within three months of the date of the confirmation of willingness to tender, those on the list should be asked to reconfirm.

Tender invitation and submission The best available information should be prepared and issued under identical conditions to all tenders. The procedures for submission of tenders and the criteria for assessment should be clear and should apply equally. Multiple rounds of tendering should be eliminated. All parties should respect confidentiality.

The Code sets out at Annex One a list of the information which *must* be included in tender enquiry documents. The better the information, the better the tender. Standard forms of tender should be used where possible.

The Code stresses the need for adequate time for tendering. The time required will vary from project to project and will be affected by size and complexity, the need for specialist design, the sourcing of unfamiliar or overseas products. It recommends suitable periods for tendering as follows:

Subcontract type	Minimum tender time: weeks
Design only	3
Construct only	6
Design and Construct	10

If alternatives are acceptable in addition to compliant tenderers, this should be stated.

If a tenderer raises a query, he should do so in writing and all responses should be circulated to all tenderers. If the contractor decides to amend the tender documents, all tenderers must be informed and if possible the time for submission of tenders extended where necessary. A deadline should be set after which queries will not be considered.

Extensions to the tender period should not be necessary if adequate time has been allowed for preparation of tenders but again if one is granted all tenderers must be notified.

Tenders should *not* be opened before the date and time stated for receipt. When opened, forms of tender should be signed and prices should be listed against the names of the tenderers. This list should be signed by the person opening the tenders. Late tenders should not be accepted.

Tender assessment The principles of balance in quality and price must be applied and references made by the Code to the CIB document *Selecting consultants for the team: balance in quality and price* (discussed in paragraph E below).

The tenders should be scored against the criteria stated in the invitations to tender. Tenderers cannot be assessed on an equal basis unless all submit compliant tenders. Any non-compliant tenders *not* accompanied by a compliant tender should be rejected. Further tenders may be necessary from the reserve list.

If unsolicited tenders are received at any time during the process they should be rejected. It undermines the willingness of tenderers to put forward their best price in their initial tender.

It may be necessary to interview tenderers in order to clarify or amplify their submissions but interviews must be carefully controlled to avoid the suggestion of supplementary rounds of tendering. Minutes should be taken.

Changes to tender prices post-tender may be appropriate but only in very exceptional circumstances, e.g. if programme or scope alter. Changes may also be appropriate in following up an alternative tender. Care should be taken to avoid practices such as second round tendering.

Tender acceptance If the main contract is in place, the subcontract tender should be accepted immediately. Otherwise, acceptance should occur after the main contract award.

Following placing of the subcontract, a list of compliant tender prices and tenderers should be available to tenderers on request. The names of the tenderers should *not* be matched to the prices. All unsuccessful tenderers should be informed and debriefed if appropriate.

Throughout the Code, great emphasis is placed on:

- the need to use unamended standard forms
- the need to avoid practices which encourage collusion
- the need to respect confidentiality.

E *Selecting consultants for the team: balancing quality and price* produced by Working Group 4 under the auspices of the Construction Industry Board

Again Working Group 4 – a larger group – also comprised representatives drawn from across the industry. The purpose of it was to pick up on Sir Michael Latham's recommendation that the task force produce specific quality and price assessment mechanisms for the engagement of professional consultants to ensure they are selected on the basis of quality as well as price (see paragraph 4 above). The Code notes that the mechanism set out can be used where selection is based on quality alone with price simply negotiated and also where both quality and price form the selection criteria. The advice is compatible with the Public Services Contracts Regulations 1993.

The Code identifies various steps in the selection and assessment processes:

Preparation of the brief The role of the brief as the fundamental basis of the project is emphasised, but the fact that the client might need assistance in developing the brief is acknowledged. *Briefing the Team*: published by the CIB is referred to as the source of guidance on matters to be included in the client's brief. The Code acknowledges that feasibility studies may need to be carried out by either the client in-house or using outside professional advice *before* the level of professional team involvement can be properly judged. Any such appointment should be made only for the feasibility studies after which it may terminate or may be expanded. At this stage it may also be possible to establish the likely form of contract which itself impacts on the professional team involvement. From the brief, it should be possible to establish:

- 'preliminary contract strategy (procurement route)
- the make-up of the consultant's team

- the need for stage appointment of consultants
- the level of their individual involvement
- the sequence and programme of appointment' (Section 3).

Establishing the quality/price mechanism The key steps are:

- appointment of Tender Board to set and apply the mechanism
- the Tender Board should then establish the quality/price ratio appropriate to the project. Complexity, the degree of innovation and flexibility required in its execution are influencing factors. Examples might be summarized as follows:

Type of project	Indicative quality/price ratio
Innovative projects	80/20
Straightforward projects	50/50
Repeat projects	20/80

- Weighting of quality criteria: once the quality/price ratios are established, the Board must establish project-specific quality requirements to assess tenderers. The Code draws on the suggested weighing and key aspects provided by CIC's *Guidelines for the value assessment of competitive tenderers*. (See also Table 5.)
- Marking and scoring: an objective rating system for assessment must be established using an absolute scoring system. The weighted mark is then calculated by multiplying the awarded mark by the project weighting for that criterion.
- Quality threshold: this is the absolute minimum quality score acceptable and must be determined by the client and established prior to the issue of tenders.
- Price scoring: the mechanism for evaluating the price is that the lowest price is given 100 points and 1 point is deducted from the other tenders for each one percentage point above the lowest.

Preparation of the tender list Usually a long list should be drawn up which is then subjected to a pre-selection to reach the short list. The consultants register that DETR should be consulted (see paragraph A above). A pre-qualification questionnaire is then usually used to gather information from the long list in order to establish a short list. Two weeks should be sufficient to respond to it. Again, an objective scoring system should be used, and excessively long short lists should be avoided.

Preparation of the enquiry/tender invitation This will usually comprise:

- Letter of invitation which should list other tender documents and note how many tenderers are on the list.
- Instructions to tenderers including date and time of submission.
- Project brief.
- Consultant's brief setting out the services required of the consultant.
- Principles of assessment giving the order of priority and weighting.
- Questionnaire to draw out issues such as methodology, management, personnel, etc.
- Conditions of appointment.
- Basis of fee required.
- Insurance requirements for professional indemnity.

Tender assessment and award Again, a series of steps is applied. These comprise:

- Assessment of each tenderer's quality by the Tender Board without prior knowledge of the commercial terms in accordance with the marking system previously established: application of quality threshold if appropriate so that tenders below it can be discarded.
- Interviews should then be arranged with preferred candidates with questions being asked on a common-structured basis so quality scoring can be reviewed afterwards.
- Price assessment on the basis outlined above. Extraordinarily low tenders should be reviewed and resource levels should be compared.
- Final quality/price assessment.
- Notification of award and debriefing.

The Code includes sample forms relating to each step of the process.

F Standard forms of tender

Various industry bodies produce standard forms of tender and/or invitations to tender. The model forms with the GC/Works Contracts include an Invitation to Tender and a Schedule of Drawings, together with a Tender and Tender Price Form. The 1999 editions of the FIDIC suite of contracts include letters of tender and the MF forms published for the Joint IMechE/IEE Committee by the Institution of Electrical Engineers include forms of tender. The JCT publishes a Practice Note (Practice Note 6) on Main Contract Tendering as well as various Invitations to Tender and Tenders as part of its Works Contracts forms and the documentation for named or nominated subcontractors.

5 PUBLIC SECTOR TENDERING

Special considerations govern the award of public sector contracts, which are also subject to review under administrative law procedures. These issues are dealt with comprehensively in Chapter 1.4 and are not referred to here.

6 SUBCONTRACT TENDERING

6.1 Traditional tendering

Traditionally, it is entirely within the remit of the main contractor to organise subcontract tenders and, very often, the process is carried out at least twice during a project duration. Firstly, when a main contractor in preparing his tender, he needs to organise subcontract tenders for all trades and work which he is unable to supply himself (nowadays, usually most). These tenders then form the basis of his own tender for the main contract. Some of these subcontract tenders are, however, for works considerably in the future and it is normal practice, therefore, to return to the market-place for updated tenders closer to the carrying out of the works. Very often subcontract tenders are less formal than the main contract tenders and they rely, to a considerable extent, on repeat business and a form of partnering. Generally speaking, however, the guidelines appropriate to main contract tenders are also appropriate to subcontract tenders and those comments previously made regarding construction management work apply equally to subcontract tenders.

Because of the time between the main contract tender and the carrying out of some subcontract works, significant risks are taken on board by the main contractor both in terms of inflation and perhaps more significantly in terms of changing market conditions. This is particularly the case on large construction contracts, which have a duration well in excess of a year.

6.2 Problems for the main contractors

Subcontract tenders are provided by organisations with a very wide variety of sophistication. It can sometimes be to the contractor's advantage that subcontractors are unsophisticated, but the reverse can be the case, particularly when the effect is that the enforceability of the subcontract is difficult due to the point blank refusal of a subcontractor to be bound by subcontract terms. In reality the substance of the organisation is such that resort to law is futile so that the ongoing working relationship between main contractor and subcontractor is of very high importance.

It is, nonetheless, important that subcontracts are on a back-to-back basis, as far as possible, with the main contract. For this reason, it is advisable to use a suite of contract forms which are compatible. This is obviously relevant in the area of contractual claims and it is contractor's objective to be able to pass all potential claims from subcontractors directly through to the client.

Contractors should also be conscious of the higher likelihood of subcontractor liquidation and receivership which in inherent in organisations with very little financial substance.

6.3 Problems for the subcontractors

Subcontractors have very often been the whipping boys of the construction industry. Practices such as pay-when-paid clauses were commonplace, the contractor having no contractual obligation to pay the subcontractor until he received the money from the client. This practice has now been outlawed by the Housing Grants, Construction and Regeneration Act 1996. Nonetheless, contractors make money out of positive cashflow and will usually attempt to manipulate cashflow so that payment is made only when received. Of course, a major threat to subcontractors is contractor liquidation, particularly when there is considerable unpaid work as there is little chance of receiving payment. It is illegal for clients to pay directly for works carried out before the liquidation as this would create a preferential creditor.

Design work is often carried out by specialist subcontractors but the cost of this design is recovered only once the works are underway and the subcontractor has, therefore, to fund these design works. There is obviously a significant risk where the design work is carried out without a firm subcontract order as the specialist subcontractor may not ultimately be awarded the subcontract.

There is invariably a high degree of negotiation around subcontracts but very often the balance of power in the negotiations lies within the contractor as size and legal know-how are on the contractor's side as well as the gift of this and future work. It is advisable and in the best interest of the ultimate client that as much as reasonably possible is done to protect the subcontractor in these circumstances, including the insistence on standard forms and by selecting contractors who have a reputation for fair dealings with their subcontractors.

7 THE RISKS IN TENDERING

Whatever the type of contract that is being tendered, there are a number of risks that must be identified, the costs ascertained and the risk evaluated if the tenderer is to be successful in the long term and have a prosperous business. It is a fact that all too often in the construction industry, risks are inadequately assessed and priced, leading to many loss making projects. The consequence is very low margin businesses which, in turn, gives rise to low levels of investment in future technologies and techniques. The result is poor performance and poor training and a tendency for continuing downwards spiral. The improved performance of the construction industry, as outlined in Section 4 of this chapter, has lead to some improvement in the situation and helped towards a less adversarial industry. As part of the improvement, however, there must be a continuing improvement in risk assessment and evaluation throughout the construction industry.

The main risks that have to be identified and priced as part of all tender processes are set out below.

7.1 Ascertaining costs

The ease with which it is possible to determine the basic cost of any given contract depends entirely on the type of contract that is envisaged. On the one hand, a contract based upon bills of quantities is easy to assess as the amount of resource required is easily identified. The risk relates only to pricing levels, or purchasing ability, for the various items of resource. At the other extreme, DBFO contracts need considerable work to determine how best to meet the client's outputs before levels of resources can be determined and then priced. However, the basic cost of providing the resources whether those resources be financial, personal or material based, will represent the substantial proportion of the total bid and it is vitally important that those skills exist to estimate both the levels of resources and the appropriate price.

7.2 Construction risk

Successful tendering relies on the ability to understand, assess and price all of the risks that are inherent in the construction works. These will of course vary very substantially, again depending on the type of contract, but all construction related contracts carry with them some level of risk. Too often in the past, risks have been ignored in the attempt to win business because of the high emphasis on pricing within the competition. The trends that have been described elsewhere in this chapter mean that in many instances the bottom line with price is becoming less important in the overall process. In order to deliver the project on time and to the satisfaction of the client, it is essential that risk evaluation is a major factor in the preparation of tender bids.

7.3 Overheads and profit recovery

This is an area that is relatively simple to determine. Over any reasonable period it is a matter of straightforward arithmetic to ascertain what the overhead and profit requirements are in relation to the value of contracts undertaken. It is, however, the area where, in the attempt to win a project, a project is deliberately under priced. The usual result of this is the inevitable attempt by the contractor to recover the short fall in overheads and profit by the manipulation of increases through disputes and by over-pricing of changes. In the long term this is detrimental to the image and performance of the construction industry. The proper pricing of overheads and profit is, therefore, important for the wellbeing of the industry.

Most contracting organisations have an overhead and profit requirement of at least 5% and up to 10% of contract value. It is impossible to obtain a credible and efficient head office facility and provide appropriate returns to shareholders and give comfort to bankers without a reasonable level of overhead and profit recovery. No substantial contracting business is sustainable with overhead and profit recovery of 1% or 2% or even 3% of the contract value. Nonetheless, this is the level of return, added to contract costs, that one finds in many tenders, particularly in times of recession. In evaluating companies' offers it is interesting to compare what is added for overheads and profit and what is achieved in the audited accounts. There is rarely very much correlation, so one must ask the question: 'What is making up the difference?'

7.4 Inflation and market conditions

A major risk, particularly in the periods of low inflation that we have had for the last several years, is the actual level of inflation within the construction market. Few, if any, contracts nowadays have an inflation mechanism built into them over the construction period. The risk of anticipating inflation during the one, two, or more years that the construction project takes place is, therefore, entirely the risk of the contractor and of the subcontractors. Of course, the main contractor tries to limit this risk by passing it down to his subcontractors. However, this strategy tends only to be successful for the earlier packages as sometimes, particularly with large projects, the subcontractor does not start work for several months or years after the tender is submitted and an unconditional fixed quote is not achievable. There is a considerable degree of exposure that rests with the main contractor. In the past this has been managed by contractors often abusing their powerful position *vis-à-vis* the subcontractor, and by recovering extra monies through the generation of contractual claims, not all of which is passed on to the party suffering the loss, namely the subcontractor.

7.5 Tendering costs

The risk of failing to win projects, combined with the risks of projects being aborted even if the tender is won, is a substantial concern. The cost of tendering is an overhead that must, over time, be recovered and becomes a higher burden as the number of tender failures increase. There needs, therefore, to be a correlation between the cost of preparing a tender, the likely overhead returns should it be won and the risk of failure.

7.6 The effect of change

Change can be derived from a number of sources; the client, force majeure, legislation, site conditions, planning conditions and so on. The degree to which the contractor is at risk for these changes depends upon the contract conditions entered into. In the main, however, changes are usually to the benefit of the contractor and to the dis-benefit of the client. Where change is at the contractor's risk, then it is important that the likelihood of change is properly evaluated. Most changes, however, are derived for reasons for which the contractor is not responsible and, in the main, the client's or designer's change of mind. In these circumstances, it has been common practice for contractors to abuse such change and to make enhanced profits from it. This has been the consequence of other unfortunate practices within the industry but it is to be hoped that with the increase in partnering and other long term arrangements will go a decrease in the bad practices and contractors would not need to take advantage of changes which the client requires.

8 PFI/PPP/DBFO CONTRACTS

Public/Private Sector Partnerships have been dealt with in detail in Chapter 1.4 and this section deals briefly with issues surrounding the tendering of such contracts.

1.1 The planning system
1.2 Financing the project
1.3 Public sector projects
1.4 Public/private partnerships
1.5 Tender process
1.6 Construction contracts
1.7 Construction insurance

8.1 Generic format

The generic format of PPP/PFI contracts, as described in Chapter 1.4, has become a significant method of procurement in the construction industry, almost entirely generated by deals between public and private sectors. These contracts incorporate a combination of a range of service provisions rarely experienced before the 1990s. Such contracts, however, need not be confined to those between public and private, but can also be used between private sector organisations and a trend is now beginning where major private sector organisations are procuring their property requirements through contracts very similar to PFI-type contracts. With this trend exactly what is included in such contracts will increasingly vary. The process is likely to become increasingly economic and advantageous.

The underlying ethos of all such contracts is the transfer of risk from one party to another, the level of risk transfer being fixed so that each risk is dealt with by the party best able to manage it. The minimum level of risk transfer is:

- the design of the asset
- the financing of the asset, both short and long term
- the construction of the asset
- some part of the operation of the asset, usually at least the building and engineering maintenance and life-cycle replacements.

Clearly, the nature of the contract entered into between the client (which in most cases has been the public sector body requiring use of a particular asset) and the supplier is considerably more than a construction contract. The tendering and the selection process is, therefore, more complex and more drawn out than any construction or consultancy contract.

8.2 Tendering process

There are a number of potential formats for a tender for the PFI/PPP/DBFO contract but the most common is in the form of an annual charge for a given concession period (commonly in the order of at least 25 years). This single price is invariably subject to some inflationary mechanism and to other price adjustments periodically following market testing or benchmarking exercises. The difficulty in analysing tenders is that the single annual price, described as an annual unitary charge or an annual rental, is made up of a large number of different prices which, in more traditional circumstances, would be tendered quite independently. The difficulty is, therefore, establishing what in overall terms represents best value for money and, once that is decided from the range of tenders received, how the pricing can be negotiated to improve value for money for the contracting parties. The range of prices included within the tender, which might otherwise be subject to separate tendering exercises, is as follows:

- Lead design fees (architect or engineer).
- Support design fees (e.g. structural engineers, services engineers, town planning, acoustic design etc.).
- Quantity Surveying fees.
- Land purchase costs (not always).
- Property advisor's and agent's fees.
- Construction cost.
- Specialist equipment.
- Fittings and furniture.

- Short-term funding based on the cost of funds, margin and MLA's.
- Long-term funding based on the cost of funds, margin and MLA's.
- Lender's legal fees.
- Lender's due diligence costs.
- Loan arrangement fees.
- Supplier's set-up costs.
- Facilities management fees.
- Facilities management set-up costs.
- Supplier's financial advisor costs.
- Supplier's financial modelling costs.
- Supplier's legal fees.
- Rolled up development interest.
- Development returns.
- Income from sale of land or other assets.
- Maintenance costs.
- Annualised costs of replacements over concession period (i.e. annual sinking fund for replacements).
- Cleaning costs.
- Security costs.
- Facilities management costs.
- Supplier's management costs.
- Costs for senior debt.
- Costs for subordinated debt.
- Returns on equity.

In addition, there are other costs which are common to all parties and which are also reflected in the annual charge such as:

- Planning fees.
- Building regulation fees.
- Corporation tax.
- Non-recoverable VAT.
- Insurance.
- Specified reimbursements to the client body.
- Planning Section 106 contributions.
- Other taxes and levies that are relevant.

Clearly, the number of variables included within a tender are enormous and it is extremely unlikely that for every single element the tender that represents overall best value for money is actually the cheapest in every case. Tendering evaluation and selection is consequently complex.

The normal tendering process employed is as follows:

(1) Ascertain the level of interest in the market-place through informal contact with perspective bidders.
(2) Ascertain formal expressions of interest through advertisements. In the case of public sector contracts over a contract value of £ must be tendered in the *Official Journal of the European Community (OJ)*.
(3) Send out pre-qualification questionnaire to be completed by those expressing interest.

(4) Select long list of six to twelve bidders (numbers depending on the size, nature and complexity of the project and the number of respondents to the advertisement).
(5) Seek further information from respondents to reduce to short list of no more than four and usually three.
(6) Sometimes an additional stage can be inserted between long list and short list referred to as an invitation to supply outline proposals (ISOP).
(7) Send out documents to be used as basis for preparing a priced proposal usually refers to as Invitation to Negotiation (ITN) documents.
(8) Based on ITN proposals, select short list of two (or sometimes three) as final short list.
(9) Send out refined documents for final short list to submit best and final offer (BAFO).
(10) Following receipt of BAFO submissions, carry out negotiations to identify best value proposal and to ensure that affordability and value for money criteria are capable of being met.
(11) Select a preferred contractor, usually referred to as preferred bidder or preferred partner.
(12) Negotiate detailed contract conditions and work up all details of the scheme including design, management and facilities proposals.
(13) Based on final proposals, submit full business case (FBC) for approval.
(14) Once FBC approval is given and negotiations are complete, enter into contractual commitment (contractual close) and the financial commitment (financial close).

8.3 Evaluation of tenders

It can be deduced from such a long and complex process, that there is a need for high level and in-depth evaluation of the proposals made at a variety of stages, along with negotiations that are in practice ongoing throughout the process. This is carried out on behalf of the client by a team drawn both from the client organisation and from outside advisors and consultants. The client's team would normally include legal advisors, financial advisors, technical advisors, construction and facilities advisors, a project sponsor and a project manager. The evaluation usually has two distinct threads.

Firstly, the submissions are evaluated against each other and against the pre-set minimal criteria relating to issues such as financial strength, technical competence, etc. In other words, all of the submissions are made competitively, one against the other, and the evaluation must end up with a single weighted score so that submissions can be ranked and ultimately a single bidder appointed.

Secondly, the submissions must be evaluated against the alternative of carrying out the project in more traditional ways, i.e. the project broken down into its traditional constituent parts which are let quite separately, with the project being funded by the client body. At that same time, the client body must always be able to proceed on the basis that the project is affordable within the funds available to it (notwithstanding that the bids received represent best value as a means of proceeding), as the costs of bidding the projects is very considerable indeed. A client proceeding with the tender process when it is aware or should be aware that the project is not affordable may be be open to claims (see section 1.6 'The law and tenders in England').

An evaluation of tenders is normally made against pre-set criteria which are published to the tenderers in advance of the tenders being submitted. An example of typical PFI tender evaluation criteria is given in Table 6.

Table 6 Example PFI tender evaluation criteria

A Tender requirements	B Main evaluation criteria	C Sub-criteria	D Weighting
Technical content	Service delivery	Satisfy output specification	
		Flexibility	
		Specialist provision	
		Maximize income	
	Project management	Project structure	
		Programme	
		Control procedures	
	Design	Aesthetics	
		Adjacencies	
		Environmental	
		Planning impact	
	Facilities management	Hard services	
		Soft services	
		Replacement reserve	
		Risk transfer	
Deliverability	Funding	Cost of funds and margins	
		Debt:equity ratios	
		Cover ratios	
		Senior debt support	
		Subordinated debt support	
		Equity support	
	Construction	Programme	
		Methodology	
		Phasing	
		Commissioning	
		Decanting strategy	
	Removals	Temporary arrangements	
		Organisation	
Quality	Overall	Comprehensiveness	
		Co-ordination	
		Compatibility	
		Added value	
	Quality assurance	Design	
		Construction	
		Operation	
	Management	SPV structure and management	
		Client liaison and co-ordination	
		Construction variation management	
		Change management	
		Dispute resolution	
Price	Annual charge	Comparative cost	
		Public sector comparator	
		Affordability	
		Value for money	
		Risk transfer	
		Land subsidy	
		Third party income generation	
	Price mechanism	Availability	
		Performance adjustments	
		Benchmarking/market testing	
	Inflation mechanism	Index	
		Risk	

8.4 The role of advisers

Given the complexity of this type of contract and the fact that to date few organisations have undertaken very many such contracts, it is clear that a large degree of expertise needed for these must be drawn from private sector's advisors. There are a limited number of lawyers, financial advisors, technical advisors and practitioners who have been involved in a significant number of projects and have developed the necessary expertise to advise on this type of project. The cost of tendering is very considerable indeed and much money in both the public and private sectors has been wasted in the past by inefficient tendering and, following poor evaluation of the project, aborted schemes. Furthermore, there has in the past been a lack of templates to follow, although this has been substantially remedied in recent years, particularly through the efforts of the Treasury Taskforce. The amount of expertise in putting together these tenders is also very considerable and compared to general construction contracting, there are relatively few organisations capable of putting in credible bids for these contracts. If the client is, therefore, to get the best out of the process then it is important that the documentation prepared on his behalf is well put together and that his own team is credible to the market-place. Without this, it may well be that there is insufficient interest from the market from credible bidders to ensure that best value bids are received.

The first rule of the advisors, therefore, is to put together the documentation that suits the needs. The documentation should be based on outputs required by the client and not the inputs to be made by the supplier. The inputs should be determined by the supplier as the best way to achieve the client's outputs.

Next, the advisors should have responsibility, as far as their brief enables them to, to ensure that unviable projects are not progressed or that the client is not progressing the project in such a way that its full business case will not be approved. This means that the advisors should ensure that there is the appropriate level of risk transfer to achieve such objectives that are necessary including the contract being off the client balance sheet. At the same time, the advisors should be able to ensure that there is no attempt to transfer risks to the supplier which are unduly expensive to transfer. To this end, the advisors should be able to advise the client as to what the private sector can realistically deliver and what it is unlikely to be able to deliver. For example, the impression sometimes created with potential clients for such contracts that the private sector suppliers can deliver almost anything asked of them result in the process being embarked upon when the most basic analysis would show the project objectives are demonstrably unachievable. If advisors are paid fees to advise on a process which ultimately and inevitably fails, then it seems only equitable that they should be responsible for the wasted cost both in the client and supplier organisations for encouraging such an unrealistic process. Whether the courts support such a view is still open to question.

Assuming that the project is viable, the key role of the advisors is to help the client prepare and obtain the necessary business case approvals. This requires the preparation of a large number of quite sophisticated financial models, demonstrating the affordability and value of the project on lifecycle basis, and quantifying the amount of risk that is transferred using discounted cashflow and a variety of risk modelling techniques.

A substantial problem that exists in the process is the imbalance in the teams working on the two sides of the bidding and evaluation process. On the one side, the client's team is invariably being paid and receiving substantial fees, often on a time basis. On the other side of the table, considerable costs are being incurred speculatively both by the principals and often by the consultants and advisors. It could be said that in some circumstances it is in the best interest of the client advisors to prolong the bidding and negotiations for as long as possible (their role substantially ending once the contract has been signed) and the consequence of a project aborting late on in the process being, financially at least, insignificant to them. On the other side of the table, very substantial costs are being incurred which are only reimbursed once the contract is signed. On some occasions the costs at risk have run into several million pounds and even on relatively small contracts run into not less than six figure numbers.

In conclusion, if this method of procurement is to continue and is to produce the benefit that it is clearly capable of doing, then it is necessary that the whole process is only embarked upon where there is a strong likelihood of the ultimate award of a contract and where tendering and negotiating costs are kept to realistic levels. In both of these areas there has been significant improvement in recent years, but this improvement must continue to become more standardised so that entry into the market-place becomes possible without unduly high levels of risk. Clearly those suppliers that have become expert in this particular field are capable of delivering significant improvements in long term value for money, but the investment necessary to achieve these improvements is considerable. If they are to continue, then it is essential that the returns are sure.

9 TURNING TENDERS INTO CONTRACTS

9.1 Introduction

This section looks at what happens after a tender has been submitted and evaluated. It examines when and how a contract arises and the effect of various commonly used terms and practices.

9.2 Letters of intent

The term is used to embrace a number of different contractual arrangements. Enormous care is needed in the formulation of a letter of intent to ensure that the correct relationship is created. The different forms of letters of intent are summarised below and in each case reference is made to a particular reported case to give an example of the wording used. A letter of intent ordinarily expresses an intention to enter into a contract in the future but creates no liability in regard to that future contract. In other words, it may have no binding effect. That is not however always the case and the following types of letter of intent arise in practice:

- The letter of intent constitutes an interim contract so that the contractor is entitled to interim costs for the work undertaken by the contractor after the date of the letter of intent. If the intended future contract is not made, it may also be construed as containing other obligations, e.g. in relation to the quality of work done. A good example of this type of letter of intent arose in the case of *Turriff Construction Limited* v. *Regalia Knitting Mills Limited.*

Facts Turriff submitted a tender to Regalia for a design and build project. Negotiations took place. The work was urgent. It was impossible to sign a formal contract because several matters and terms remained to be agreed. Regalia sent Turriff a letter which stated:

> 'As agreed at our meeting on 2nd June 1969 . . . it is the intention of Regalia to award a contract to Turriff to build a factory . . . phase 1 to be on a fixed price basis . . . the commencing date to be 1st August and the terms of payment to be negotiated . . .
> All this to be subject to obtaining agreement on the land and leases . . .
> The whole to be subject to agreement on an acceptable contract'.

Work could not start on the planned date but Turriff prepared a detailed design and negotiated with Regalia's architect over terms of contract. They discussed the issue of an 'indemnity' in respect of work to be done by Turriff before the contract could be signed. Turriff applied for an interim payment of £3500 for design work. The project was then cancelled and Regalia denied liability.

Judgment There was an ancillary contract for the preliminary costs claimed, albeit no contract for the project since this was still being negotiated. Regalia was obliged to pay Turriff for all of the services provided after the meeting of 2 June 1969. The Judge noted that normally letters merely expressed in writing a party's present intention to enter into a contract at a future date and that, save in exceptional circumstances, they would not have binding effect. However, what happened on the facts of this case was more than this: he looked at the background to the issue of the letter quoted and noted that minutes of meetings suggested that the letter was to provide, in Regalia's own words, 'indemnity' in respect of work done between 2 June and the execution of the contract. Clearly no design and build contract for the whole job had come into existence but Turriff had offered to proceed with urgency provided it had an 'indemnity' from Regalia. The letter issued amounted to acceptance of that offer.

- The letter of intent creates an entitlement to be paid on a quasi-contractual basis but without creating a formal contract for the project. Here, the case of *British Steel Corporation* v. *Cleveland Bridge Engineering Company Limited* provides a good example.

Facts CBE sent to BSC a letter of intent against the backdrop of incomplete negotiations and no formal contract stating:

> 'We are pleased to advise you that it is the intention of [CBE] to enter into a sub-contract with your company . . . the price will be as quoted in your telex . . . the form of sub-contract to be entered into will be our standard form of sub-contract . . . a copy of which is enclosed for your consideration . . . We understand that you are already in possession of a complete set of our detailed drawings and we request that you proceed immediately with the works pending the preparation and issuing to you of the official form of sub-contract'.

BSE were not in possession of a full set of drawings and did not reply expecting a formal offer shortly. They did not agree the conditions of subcontract or the price as noted. But they began preparation for manufacture so as not to delay deliveries. There were further discussions about specification and programme issues. Despite outstanding matters, it was agreed that BSE should proceed with the first casting. Further technical problems arose and there were further discussions about price and delivery, deliveries of steel nodes, however, continued despite the failure to agree contract terms. A steelworkers' strike caused further delays. CBE made no payment but submitted to BSE a claim for damages for late delivery. BSE in turn claimed payment for goods sold and delivered in quasi contract as a *quantum meruit* [i.e. reasonable costs plus profit].

Judgment The letter of intent was no more than a statement of intention: it created no contractual obligations. BSC was not contractually bound but was entitled to *a quantum meruit* as compensation for CBE's unjust enrichment. With no contract, CBE had no claim for damages against BSC. This case was different from the *Turriff* case because the request to proceed was qualified by the reference to the fact that it was 'pending the preparation and issuing... of the official form of sub-contract'. The parties were quite clearly still in negotiations and had not agreed primary obligations in relation to quality and time for performance. The parties had made no contract at all.

- Where the letter of intent sets out the basis of contract and provides for reimbursement of reasonable costs. This is perhaps a more common version of the letter of intent. It is illustrated by the case of *C.J. Sims* v. *Shaftesbury plc.*

Facts The builder submitted a tender. The owner responded with a letter of intent which advised that the builder would be awarded the contract on the terms of JCT 1980 but that works should start at once. The letter further stated that if the contract did not proceed the builder would be reimbursed reasonable costs 'such cost to include loss of profit and contributions to overheads, all to be substantiated by our quantity surveyor'. The dispute related to whether the builder had to substantiate all costs or merely the profit and overheads element.

Judgment The builder had to establish all costs. The letter of intent established a contract on a cost plus basis for work done under it.

- The letter of intent may be construed as creating an 'if' contract so that *if* the contractor carries out certain work he is entitled to be paid for it. Here a good example appears in the case of *Monk Construction Limited* v. *Norwich Union Life Assurance Society.*

Facts The project manager issued to the builder a 'letter of intent' which stated that 'our client instructs us to authorise you to proceed with preliminary work to a maximum expenditure of £100 000. In the event that no contract is concluded with you, your entitlement is limited to proven costs incurred by you in accordance with the authority granted by this letter'. Two months later the builder was asked to start main contract works. He wrote to the project manager confirming commencement 'for the client's benefit under the terms of the letter of intent without prejudice to the contract terms on which we are not yet agreed'. No formal contract was executed. The question was whether the letter of intent created an 'if' contract and, if it did, did that cover the main contract work?

Judgment The letter of intent authorized the builder to expend only up to £100 000 on preliminary work but did not mention main contract work. The 'proven costs' stipulation applied only to the situation where *no* contract was concluded and *no* main contract work was carried out: the term was not intended to apply to any work done under the main contract. Accordingly, the cap did not apply to further work carried out at the project manager's request, which work was to be paid for on a quasi-contractual basis (as in *British Steel* v. *Cleveland Bridge* above). There was no 'if' contract here in respect of the main work. An 'if' contract arises where a standing offer is held out that if the builder performs, the client will pay and the contract becomes binding when the builder, by its performance, accepts the offer.

- The letter of intent as pure 'letter of acceptance': here the letter of intent unequivocally accepts the tender offer. This type of letter of intent is looked at in more detail later.

There are obvious dangers for a client who allows a project to proceed (and in some cases to be completed) on the basis of a letter of intent which does not incorporate all the terms envisaged by the formal contractual documentation. A good example of this is provided by the case of *Tesco Stores Ltd* v. *Costain Construction Ltd.*

Facts Tesco issued a letter of intent to Costain stating that it was its intention to enter into a formal contract on Tesco's standard documentation under which Costain would be engaged to design and build a new supermarket. Costain signed and returned a copy of the letter and constructed the supermarket but no formal contract was entered into. In the course of later alteration works at the store, a fire broke out causing substantial damage. Tesco argued the spread of the fire was due to the absence of proper fire stopping measures. It brought claims against Costain. Under Tesco's standard documentation, Costain would have assumed liability for design as well as construction, notwithstanding that Tesco had separately engaged architects. Costain relied upon the fact that there was no formal contract to argue that it had not accepted contractual responsibility for the design. Tesco alleged that the terms of the standard documentation had been incorporated because the parties had conducted themselves in a manner that would have been appropriate if the contract had been completed and come into effect; it was Tesco's position that 'offer' and 'acceptance' were not relevant.

Judgment Tesco's argument was rejected. While there was a contract between the parties, it was a 'simple contract' in the terms of the letter of intent. The express terms of that contract was that Costain would commence construction in advance of making a formal contract and in return Tesco would pay Costain. While Costain accepted responsibility for its own works, it had not accepted responsibility for the work of the architects or other professionals retained by Tesco. There were implied terms in the contract that Costain would perform any construction work under the contract in a good and workmanlike manner and that any design element would be reasonably fit for its intended purpose. However, it had not accepted responsibility for the whole design of the project. It was also not a term of the contract that the limitation period in respect of breaches would be 12 years.

There are also dangers for a contractor who carries on working after the expiry of the letter of intent. This is highlighted by the decision in *Mowlem plc (T/A Mowlem Marine)* v. *Stena Line Ports Ltd*, a case where the parties accepted that the letters of intent entered into between them operated as 'if' contracts but differed as to their interpretation of those contracts.

Facts Mowlem carried out works for Stena in relation to the construction of a new ferry terminal. The works were carried out under a series of letters of intent issued by Stena. The last letter of intent confirmed Stena's commitment to expenditure up to a maximum of £10 million. This was stated to enable Mowlem to proceed with the works until 18 July 2003. Mowlem continued to carry out works after 18 July which it alleged were over a value of £10 million and claimed that it was entitled to be paid a reasonable sum for those works on the basis of an implied term in the letter of intent.

Judgment There was no such implied term and it would be contrary to commercial common sense if the financial limit could be avoided by Mowlem simply exceeding the limit and continuing work after 18 July. There was no evidence to suggest that

Stena had conducted itself in such a way as to lead Mowlem to believe that it would not seek to rely upon the terms of the last letter of intent; there was no request or instruction to Mowlem to complete the works; and there was no evidence of any waiver by Stena as to its rights to rely on the terms of the letter.

Where work proceeds after the expiry of the letter of intent with the consent of the client but without a contract in place, the question arises as to how the work is to be valued. This is illustrated by the case of *ERDC Group Ltd* v. *Brunel University*.

Facts ERDC submitted a tender for the construction of a new sports facility at Brunel's Uxbridge campus. The university did not want to enter into final contractual documentation until full planning permission had been granted. Instead, it issued a number of 'letters of appointment' instructing ERDC to carry out certain work. The letters stated that the work would be paid for in accordance with 'the normal evaluation and certification rules of the JCT standard form of building contract with contractor's design'. The last letter expired on 1 September 2002 but ERDC continued work on site until March 2003. In November 2002, the University issued contract documents for signature by ERDC. The latter refused to sign them and argued that it was entitled to be paid for all the work it had carried out on a *quantum meruit* basis. The basis for the *quantum meruit* valuation, argued ERDC, was its costs in carrying out the work, together with a reasonable amount for profit.

Judgment The letters of appointment were binding contracts. Under those letters, the work carried out was to be valued according to the JCT valuation rules. Once the letters of appointment expired, there was no contract between the parties. While the basis of recovery for work completed during the period when there was no contract was therefore *quantum meruit*, the same rates (i.e. the JCT rates referred to under the letters of appointment) were to be used: it was not appropriate to move from a rates-based assessment to one based upon ERDC's costs.

9.3 Acceptance

An unequivocal tender may be accepted at any time after it has been made unless before it is accepted it is expressly withdrawn or it is rejected (after which it cannot be revived except with the tenderer's agreement) or if it is revoked by a counter-offer.

It is common practice in the construction industry to stipulate that tenders remain open for acceptance for a certain period. Clearly, upon the expiry of this period the offer lapses and can no longer be accepted but, even within the period, the offer can be withdrawn at any time by the tenderer even though the period stipulated in the invitation has not expired. The use of bid deposits which are forfeited if tenders are withdrawn or bid bonds which can be called in the same circumstances are devices designed to protect clients from abortive costs which they may incur in these circumstances.

There is an acceptance of the offer bringing a binding contract into existence when the client unequivocally accepts the offer and communicates to the contractor that acceptance. The issue of qualified acceptances and the use of the phrase 'subject to contract' is discussed in the next section. If the acceptance contains new terms which were not contained in the original tender, then it amounts to a counter-offer which revokes the tender offer. The steps of offer and counter-offer are very frequent aspects of negotiations on construction contracts and the analysis required to ascertain the moment when agreement has been reached and the parties have genuinely concluded a contract is not always easy. It is for this reason that it is undeniably good practice to issue a formal letter of acceptance once final agreement has been reached in a long running negotiation and, ideally, to execute a formal written agreement (see also Section 9.6 below).

Once unequivocal acceptance has occurred and a contract has arisen, a party seeking to introduce a new term after that critical point will of course be seeking to renegotiate the terms of an existing contract and this can only be done with the express agreement of the other party. It is inevitably difficult to determine sometimes whether this sort of renegotiation is being contemplated or whether in fact this is an aspect of continuing negotiations about the original terms of the contract.

9.4 Effect of the phrase 'subject to contract' or 'subject to board approval'

The phrase 'subject to contract' means subject to and dependent upon a formal contract being prepared. It will usually be construed as meaning that no contract can arise until the formal contract is executed. It is important in commercial negotiations and plays a part in risk allocation. By use of the term, the parties guard against contractual force without more detailed discussion and agreement. Use of the term demonstrates lack of willingness to be bound. A good example appeared in the case of *Regalian Properties plc* v. *London Docklands Development Corporation.*

Facts LDDC accepted Regalian's offer 'subject to contract, valuation, quality of design and the obtaining of detailed planning consent'. Delays ensued while design and budget schemes were prepared at LDDC's request. Design costs increased. Further negotiations took place but no contract followed. Regalian sought a *quantum meruit* payment for expenses incurred. It argued that both parties had intended to bring about a contract and consequent to that understanding they had incurred expense to the benefit of LDDC.

Judgment LDDC was not liable. By the deliberate use of the words 'subject to contract' both parties accepted that if no contract was entered into any resultant loss would lie where it fell. Either party could have withdrawn without legal consequence from the negotiations at any time. Although LDDC encouraged Regalian to incur costs, it was in an attempt to satisfy LDDC's requirements before a contract could be entered into. It was not directly requested by LDDC so as to create any liability on their part to reimburse those costs. There was no ascertainable benefit accruing to LDDC and they obtained no copyright in the designs. The parties were in negotiation, subject to contract.

Apart from 'subject to contract', other conditions sometimes appear in invitations to tender/acceptances, e.g. 'subject to board approval', 'subject to loan sanction' or 'subject to satisfactory planning permission'. It is a question of construction whether the condition is a condition precedent to the contract coming into being or a condition of the contract itself: in other words, whether the parties are bound at all or whether they are bound but subject to the contract being cancelled if the condition does not occur. If work is carried out in anticipation of an approval not subsequently obtained then, of course, there may be an argument that the contractor is entitled to remuneration on a quasi-contractual basis. Alternatively, while the main contract may be 'subject to contract' and not binding, a more limited, interim contractual arrangement may have been created. A example of this situation is provided by the case of *Skanska Rasleigh Weatherfoil* v. *Somerfield Stores Limited.*

Facts An invitation to tender was sent to Skanska on behalf of Somerfield. Skanska sent in its tender with a list of 'salient points'. Following consideration of this, further tender documentation was sent to Skanska and further exchanges of correspondence followed. Somerfield then sent Skanska a letter headed 'subject to contract'. The letter expressed Somerfield's desire to appoint Skanska to provide maintenance services to Somerfield on the terms of a draft facilities management agreement (FMA). The letter made it clear that the appointment was 'strictly subject to contract, and to the approval of . . . [Somerfield's] board'. The letter went on to say that, while the parties were negotiating the terms of the FMA, Skanska should provide the services 'under the terms of' the draft of the FMA enclosed with the tender until 27 October 2000. Skanska carried out services and the 27 October date was extended twice expressly, first to 26 November 2000 and then to 21 January 2001. There was no further express extension but Skanska continued to carry out services. Meanwhile, the parties continued to negotiate the terms of the FMA, including 'timing-out' provisions to the effect that, if Skanska did not submit an invoice within a certain period, Somerfield would not be liable to pay it. Somerfield expressed dissatisfaction with Skanska's performance and a dispute arose between the parties as to the terms of the contractual relationship between them, particularly after 21 January 2001. Somerfield started to implement the timing-out provisions even though the FMA had not been signed by Skanska. The court had to consider whether the statement in the letter of that services were to be provided 'under the terms' of the draft FMA meant all of the terms of the draft FMA were incorporated or only some of them; whether the contract created by the letter continued in force after 21 January 2001; and whether or not Skanska was bound by the 'timing-out' provisions.

Judgment Only those terms of the draft FMA that were necessary to define 'the Services' to be carried out by Skanska were incorporated. After 21 January 2001, the parties continued to conduct themselves on the basis that an agreement between them was subsisting. On that basis, the contract continued until and unless they agreed on some other contractual basis. There was, however, no binding agreement between about the 'timing-out' provisions. The fact that this was an interim arrangement only, pending the negotiation of an acceptable FMA, was demonstrated by Somerfield's use of the phrase 'subject to contract' and its distinction between 'the Contract' (used to refer to the FMA) and 'the Agreement' (used to refer to the letter of intent).

Other difficulties can arise when, despite apparent acceptance, the employer lacks the necessary powers to contract, e.g. where a statutory corporation purports to enter into a contract which goes beyond its powers as set out in the act of parliament which created it, that purported contract is *ultra vires* and therefore void. Local authorities must make standing orders with regard to the making of contracts by them or on their behalf for the execution of works but usually a person entering into a contract with a local authority is not bound to enquire whether the standing orders have been complied with and non-compliance does not usually invalidate any contract entered into on its behalf. However, questions do arise as to the authority of persons purportedly acting on behalf of the local authority.

Where parties actually perform obligations under a document which is stated to be 'subject to contract', the agreement can no longer be considered executory. This is illustrated by the case of *The Rugby Group Ltd* v. *Proforce Recruit Ltd.*

Facts Proforce and Rugby signed a document which contained 'proposals' for a service cleaning contract and which stated that Proforce would supply workers to

Rugby and would also purchase from Rugby items of cleaning equipment. The document, which incorporated Proforce's standard terms and conditions, stated that it was 'subject to contract'. Proforce purchased the equipment and supplied the workers. Additional labour was then sought by Rugby from third parties and Proforce claimed that Rugby had breached part of the agreement which stated that Proforce was to hold 'preferred supplier status' during the term of the agreement. One of the arguments put forward by Rugby was that the document was not enforceable as a contract because it contained the words 'subject to contract'.

Judgment The agreement could not be considered as being executory because after it was signed the parties carried out their obligations under it. While generally, except in very strong and exceptional cases, the effect of the words 'subject to contract' prevented an executory contract from coming into existence, the parties to this agreement were taken to have entered into an implied and binding contract on the terms of the agreement.

9.5 Acceptance by conduct

Although it has limited application in the case of construction contracts, it is possible for acceptance of a tender to be evinced by conduct which shows an intention to accept the terms of the tender. It is a question in each case whether conduct shows such an intention. So, a client who, without any express acceptance, or counter-offer, permits a contractor to carry out work pursuant to a tender submitted by the contractor, can be bound by the terms of the tender.

9.6 The execution of documents

As noted above, no formal requirements are necessary to give rise to a contract. It may be written, oral or partly oral and partly in writing. It is this fact which causes the difficulties in relation to negotiation of construction contracts which are outlined above.

Contracts can be made subject to execution of a formal written contract in which case no contract necessarily arises until the formal contract is signed.

In any case, it is good practice to sign a binding contract. It clarifies the question of when a contract has arisen and avoids the offer/counter-offer debate. It clarifies precisely the terms of the contract and which documents are to form part of the contract. In the case of the client, it may have the additional advantage, if the contract is executed as a deed, of creating a twelve-year limitation period for claims for breach of contract rather than the period of six years which exists in the case of a simple contract (for discussion of limitation periods: see Chapter 3.4). There are also requirements for the contract to be in writing for the provisions of the Housing Grants, Construction and Regeneration Act 1996 to apply. It should be noted that it is no longer necessary to apply a seal to create a document which is effective as a deed.

Most standard forms of contract publish as part of the suite a formal agreement. So ICE Conditions of Contract contain a form of agreement comprising simple reciprocal obligations on the parties to carry out works and to pay for them respectively together with a list of documents incorporated into the agreement. Under clause 9 of the ICE Conditions the contractors are required to enter into the formal agreement even though the acceptance of contract may have been carried informally.

In the case of the JCT, it is assumed that the Articles of Agreement are executed when the contract is made.

Where a formal contract is subsequently concluded, not only will it usually be interpreted as superseding any previous agreement, but in the absence of indication to the contrary, it will be treated as applying retrospectively so as to validate actions or claims under the contract in respect of the period prior to execution of it.

10 TENDER ABUSES

10.1 Bribery and secret commissions

If a contractor obtains acceptance of his tender by offering of commission to the client or any of his employees or agents, the client can either repudiate the contract or treat it as subsisting. He can also recover the bribe and, in addition, damages both from the agent and the contractor.

10.2 Collusive tendering

The courts have over the years had to look at the enforceability of agreements between tenderers to the effect that they would not tender in competition with each other or that they put forward prices which are not genuine in the sense that, rather than refuse to tender altogether, they tender a price higher than that 'taken' from another contractor. In broad terms, the courts have enforced these agreements provided that their dominant purpose was to protect and extend the business of the parties rather than inflicting damage on the client. So, in the case of *Jones* v. *North* (1975) quarry owners agreed to sell stone to one of their group because that member was about to tender to Birmingham Corporation to supply its need for stone. By this agreement North agreed to sell stones to Jones and North agreed not to supply stones to the Corporation during the year in question. The Court enforced the agreement against North, and Jones' claims for breach of contract were allowed to proceed.

Similarly, in *Harrop* v. *Thompson and other* (1975) Harrop agreed to buy Thompson's farms at a public auction. Prior to the auction, Harrop entered into an agreement with another potential bidder to the effect that that person should stay away from the action and as a consequence Harrop acquired the farms at a cheap price. Thompson discovered the existence of the knock-out agreement and refused to complete the sale. Thompson argued that the agreement between Harrop and the other potential bidder was against public policy as being in restraint of trade and that Harrop should not succeed in an action for specific performance of the contract of sale in relation to the farm. 'No' said the court: an agreement not to bid is not contrary to public policy.

However, it is clear that on other facts an English court could find that a conspiracy amongst tenderers not to bid or to bid a price which was not arrived at independently when invited to tender by a client is a fraud against that client. The damages for such fraud seem likely to cover the client's costs of re-tendering and interest and other losses caused by the consequent delay. Increased construction costs and/or a drop in property values might also be consequences of the fraud. There are several forms which collusive tendering might take. A group of potential tenderers might make an agreement that only one or a limited number should submit a tender in response to a particular invitation. They might agree as to what price is to be submitted by each tenderer, or might even agree to submit the same price. Collusive tendering might arise as a result of premature disclosure of bids and the fault may lie with both the client and the tenderers. Collusive tendering can involve activities popularly referred to as 'cover pricing' and 'ring forming'. Cover pricing is described above and ring forming is where a group of tenderers arrange prices between them so that the 'chosen' firm wins. An even work load is achieved by each tenderer taking its turn to succeed.

Collusive tendering is now subject to the statutory regimes created by the Competition Act 1998 and the Enterprise Act 2002. Chapter 1 of the Competition Act prohibits agreements or practices which may affect trade within the UK and have as their object or effect the prevention, restriction or distortion of competition within the UK. Price-fixing is expressly prohibited by Chapter 1. On 16 March 2004, the Office of Fair Trading imposed fines of £330 000 in total on nine roofing contractors in the West Midlands for infringement of Chapter 1. The OFT found that companies bidding for certain local authority contracts agreed in advance the prices at which they would bid. The OFT concluded that the parties' collusion on setting tender prices was intended to restrict or distort competition and meant that buyers were unable to obtain competitive prices when tendering for these services. The OFT decision was upheld by the Competition Appeal Tribunal. Further fines were also imposed upon roofing contractors in Scotland and the north east of England for similar infringements in March 2005.

Under the Enterprise Act, it is a criminal offence for an individual to dishonestly agree with at least one other person that two or more undertakings will engage in prohibited cartel activities in the UK. These cover direct or indirect price-fixing, limitation of supply or production, market or customer sharing and bid rigging, that is, an agreement as to which party will bid or an agreement as to the terms of any bid submitted.

11 FREEDOM OF INFORMATION ACT 2000

Both public sector clients and contractors submitting tenders to public authorities need to be aware of the provisions of the Freedom of Information Act 2000 (FOIA) which places new legal duties of disclosure on 'public authorities' in the UK and grants the public a right of access to information held by public authorities subject to various exemptions. Depending on how it is used, the FOIA potentially enables private entities to gain information about public authorities' business relationships, as well as the chance to find out information concerning competitors. Therefore any private entity who submits sensitive information to a public authority will want to try and prevent such information being disclosed to competitors, the press and others. There is no guaranteed way of achieving this. The public sector client will need to be aware of its statutory duties and not restrict its ability to comply with those. However, under section 41 of the FOIA, if information is being provided in confidence and disclosure would amount to a breach of that confidence, the public authority does not have to disclose the information and, in some circumstances, does not even have to comply with the duty to confirm or deny the existence of that information. The decision in *Express Medicals Ltd* v. *Network Rail Infrastructure Ltd*, while relating to disclosure under the Civil Procedure Rules, may be of relevance to the question as to what will amount to confidential information in tenders.

Facts Express Medicals was an unsuccessful tenderer to Network Rail (formerly, Railtrack) for occupational corporate healthcare services. It brought a claim for damages against Network Rail alleging that the latter had failed to comply with the principles of transparency and equality of tenderers under the Utilities Contracts Regulations 1996. The judge had earlier made an order that disclosure was to be on the 'standard' basis save that Network Rail might obliterate the prices tendered. He also ordered that documents disclosed by Network Rail under the order were not to

1.1 The planning system
1.2 Financing the project
1.3 Public sector projects
1.4 Public/private partnerships
1.5 Tender process
1.6 Construction contracts
1.7 Construction insurance

be shown to any persons other than Express Medicals' legal advisors. The obliteration of the prices was not contested. However, Express Medicals contested the obliteration of the names and personal details (including contact details) of 'front line' medical staff, clients (who acted as referees) and a business plan by the successful tenderer with the support of Network Rail. The invitation to tender stated:

> 'The tenderer shall treat the contents of the documents enclosed with this invitation as private and confidential. Railtrack will treat your tender likewise.'

Judgment The court found that all the obliterated information was confidential. The continued confidentiality of the information was very important to the successful tenderer as it operated in a small, competitive industry where price, client lists, referees and business plans were closely guarded. Express Medicals was one of its major competitors. The latter did not need to see this information. The application amounted to a fishing expedition for information which should be rejected.

Legal issues for Construction

1.1 The planning system

1.2 Financing the project

1.3 Public sector projects

1.4 Public/private partnerships

1.5 Tender process

1.6 Construction contracts

1.7 Construction insurance

CHAPTER 1.6

The construction contract

Michael O'Reilly
Adie O'Reilly LLP Visiting Professor at Kingston University

1 INTRODUCTION

In this chapter, construction contracts are examined from a practical point of view. The legal rules associated with formation and interpretation of contracts are dealt with in Chapter 3.1.

Construction contracts are, by and large, made, interpreted and enforced in the same way as any other commercial contract. Contracts for construction work in Britain, however, must comply with requirements of Part II of the Housing Grants, Construction and Regeneration Act 1996. This includes the need for an adjudication clause, clauses dealing with stage payments and a prohibition on pay-when-paid clauses. Contracts in writing which do not comply with the Act become subject to the relevant provisions of the Scheme for Construction Contracts 1998.

Note that the Department of Business, Enterprise and Regulatory Reform published a draft of the Construction Contracts Bill in July 2008. Consultation on the draft has, at the date of writing (30 September 2008), just closed; it is expected that there will be changes to the currently proposed text. If enacted the new statute will e.g. extend the provisions to oral contracts; it is anticipated at the date of writing that the new legislation will come into force at a date to be specified in 2009 and will apply to all contracts made after the date of coming into force.

1.1 The use and importance of contracts in construction

The vast majority of construction work is performed under contract. A contract is simply an agreement which obliges the parties to do specified things. Most importantly, in the case of a construction contract, it requires the contractor to build the works and requires the employer to pay for them.

Contracts have a number of different functions. In the case of a construction contract, they include:

(a) specifying the work to be done by the contractor (or subcontractor, etc.), including the required quality and time for completion of various parts of the work
(b) defining what amount is to be paid, how any additional or reduced payments are to be computed and when payments are to be made
(c) defining which party is responsible for events occurring outside the parties' direct control which affect the work; such events may include bad weather, access difficulties, local authority restrictions, changes in the law, unexpectedly poor ground, etc.
(d) defining who has responsibility for undertaking the various administrative or dispute resolution functions which may be required, including giving instructions, making decisions about claims, appointing adjudicators, arbitrators, etc.

1.2 Construction contracts: variety and standardisation

Policy advisers call, from time to time, for the adoption of a single standard form of contract for the construction industry (e.g. Banwell, 1964; Latham, 1994). This suggestion is not inherently impractical. Nevertheless parties – and employers in particular – have always been keen to reserve the right to adopt forms of contract which suit their own approach. Public authorities, for example, have traditionally used contracts drawn up by professional institutions and which are seen as fair. Privatized public utilities, while often continuing to use the same standard forms as a basis of their contracts, frequently adjust the risk balance to one which they consider more commercially acceptable. Commercial employers may prefer the contractor to bear the majority of the risk in return for an enhanced price or risk premium.

Some might argue that a situation may now be developing where a standard, or something akin to it, may be adopted, particularly for larger projects. The NEC Contract, which is drawn up by a professional body representing all sectors of the industry, is being used for a significant proportion of major projects in the UK and elsewhere, including NHS ProCure21 Programme and the 2012 Olympic contracts. However, the number of contract forms issued by various institutions continues to grow and the adoption of a single contract used universally on construction projects is unlikely to be realised without statutory intervention (which is unlikely in the short term).

1.3 The main contract and the web of contracts that interlink with it

The main focus of this chapter is on the 'construction contract', that is the agreement made by the employer (who owns or commissions the project) and the principal contractor. However, as anyone who has been engaged to draw up the contracts on a construction scheme will confirm, a modern construction project often requires many contracts – sometimes more than 100 individual contracts. For example, there may be:

(a) a finance agreement between the employer and a bank – this will often have construction-related terms, including, for example, a right for the bank to step in if specified defaults occur
(b) a lease between the employer and a prospective tenant – again, the tenant may agree to full repairing and insuring terms so that the tenant will not be indifferent to the quality of the construction and may require assurances
(c) sub-contracts between the principal contractor and its subcontractors
(d) design and consultancy contracts – where the construction contract is made on a design and build basis; the design contract is frequently made with the employer and then transferred to the contractor
(e) warranties to establish contract links between parties who may not otherwise be in a contract – for example, the architect may issue a warranty in favour of the tenant undertaking to perform his design with reasonable care and skill; or the foundation sub-contractor may issue a warranty in favour of the employer, so that the latter can sue the sub-contractor director should the main contractor become insolvent.

In the sections which follow, the main focus will be on the construction contract. But towards the end of the chapter we shall return briefly to the question of the other surrounding agreements.

1.4 Risk and partnering in construction

Two features of modern contracts may be mentioned briefly:

(1) The use of risk as an analytical tool. When studying the various types of contract available, it is useful to consider what risks may eventuate, which parties may control those risks and how the responsibility for risk and opportunity is divided between the parties. For example one might contrast a cost-reimbursable contract or a lump-sum contract for a tunnelling project: subject as always to the detailed terms, the former places the risk of unforeseen ground conditions on the employer, whilst the latter places the risk on the contractor. In projects, such as tunnels, unforeseen conditions are often significant and, indeed, sometimes of overwhelming importance and risk allocation of this kind is an important factor. All construction contracts contain some degree of risk and it is important that there be well-defined allocation of the risks and opportunities.

(2) A facet of modern contract theory is the promotion of partnering by many organisations, including government departments. Partnering may be described as the arrangement between parties by which each shows a commitment to working with each other up to and beyond the project end and hence developing long-term cooperative modes of working. In some cases, this is given effect by parties sharing office accommodation etc. In some cases – particularly those affected by the European procurement regulations – the use of partnering requires a certain degree of delicacy as it can appear to be rather cosy and hence exclusive of other contractors who are entitled to compete fairly.

2 THE PRINCIPAL TYPES OF CONSTRUCTION CONTRACT

A number of contract types will be outlined in this section, in particular:

(a) traditional contracts, with Engineer/Architect's design and administration
(b) contracts with contractor's design, including international turnkey contracts
(c) contracts with specialist management
(d) term contracts
(e) concession (BOT) contracts.

2.1 Traditional contracts

The expression 'traditional contract' is widely used to describe an arrangement where the employer takes on a consulting engineer or architect to provide advice on all aspects of the scheme, to design the works and to administer the construction through to completion. The qualifier 'traditional' is somewhat misleading. These contracts originated in the eighteenth century and are a direct product of the separation of design and construction activities. The contracts were drawn up with the advice of these engineers or architects and reflect the supreme position occupied by 'the Engineer' or 'the Architect' who was wholly responsible for the design, approval of complete work and certification for payment of that work. The same pattern was seen for both private and public schemes. To begin with, contracts were highly individual; Brunel, for instance, liked to ensure that he had absolute say over every aspect of the work. By the end of the nineteenth century, many local authorities (who had, by this time, taken over responsibility for the majority of civil engineering works), began to adopt 'standard forms'. Later, in the late 1930s, these were taken as the basis for an industry-wide standard contract, described as the ICE Conditions of Contract. This contract form is now in its seventh edition. The concept has been exported and the general shape of the ICE Conditions of Contract is seen in many contracts used overseas, not least the FIDIC Red Book Contract. Similar evolution led to the RIBA standard form, the descendant of which is now published as the JCT 2005 Standard Form of Building Contract.

Outline features and procedure

An employer appoints an engineer/architect to be the lead consultant on the project. Other consultants may also be appointed directly by the employer, to work in consultation with and under the general coordination of the engineer. The project is developed, surveyed and designed by the engineer's/architect's staff, under the engineer's direction. When the design is complete, or nearly so, the engineer/architect (on the employer's behalf) invites tenders for the work. The engineer/architect appraises the tenders and selects a contractor. The employer then engages the contractor to do the work to the approval of the engineer/architect.

Design responsibility and construction responsibility

The key feature of a traditional contract is the almost complete separation of design and construction responsibility. The engineer/architect assumes a responsibility to the employer to exercise 'reasonable care and skill'. The contractor agrees to build what is shown on the drawings and described in the specifications. The contractor's design responsibility extends only to what is implied in the selection of good materials and in the provision of good workmanship.

The 'Engineer' and the 'Architect'

In the case of an engineering contract, the employer appoints an engineer (lower case 'e' to denote a general appointment) to carry out designs. When the contract is let, the engineer may become the Engineer (with upper case 'E' as described in the ICE and FIDIC Contracts) with a set of clear and distinct roles to perform under the contract. The Engineer is a defined person under the contract and the functions of the Engineer must be undertaken by him in that capacity. Under a traditional building contract, the Architect (capital 'A') refers to the defined appointment under the contract.

Computing the price

Traditional civil engineering contracts, such as the ICE Conditions of Contract, tend to use a measure and value scheme for computing the price. This is not essential to the traditional arrangement. In building work, the main traditional contract is based on a lump sum: and in the process industry, a common traditional form of contract uses cost reimbursement.

Perceived problems with the traditional arrangement

Four major concerns are expressed over contract types where the Engineer (or his Architect equivalent) is the administering professional. First, consulting engineers tend to be learned in technical matters, but their political and strategic management skills have been questioned: many employers ask whether it is appropriate for control of financially and politically sensitive projects to be handed over to an independent engineer. Secondly, Engineers/Architects under a traditional contract do not set out to 'manage and coordinate' the project; they assume a rather lofty detachment and many employers do not find this acceptable. Thirdly, the Engineers'/Architects' impartiality is often questioned, rightly or wrongly. It is said that they identify too closely with the employer's camp and are therefore unable to take impartial decisions as between employer and contractor. In any event, it is said that many important decisions which they must take (e.g. over the contractor's right to claim additional money) involve an indirect challenge to the Engineers'/Architects' own competence and that they cannot be trusted to be impartial in such a case. And fourthly, complete separation of design and construction means that opportunities for enhanced efficiency and buildability are lost. Many of these concerns are justified. Certainly, they are taken sufficiently seriously for many employers to experiment with new forms of contract.

2.2 Contracts with contractor's design

The separation of design and construction

The major projects of the industrial revolution demanded unprecedented innovation, requiring the application of skills possessed by a mere handful of engineers or architects. There was only one viable pattern of contract for these works, namely contractors working to designs produced by an engineer/architect, constructed under his direction.

The situation today is very different. Contracting companies employ graduate engineers and even architects and many have specialist design offices. There is, in short, far less need than hitherto to maintain the historical distinction between design and construction.

Benefits of contractor's design

The benefits of contractor's design depend to a large degree on the specific circumstances of the project and the design arrangements. They may include the following.

(a) Single point and clear cut liability. Defects of every character are the contractor's responsibility, unless it can show some special defence. Defects claims are more readily settled and, where resisted, it is easier and cheaper for the employer to succeed in litigation or arbitration. Beneficial side effects include less conflict on site and a reduction of defensive and uncooperative modes of behaviour.
(b) Enhanced design standard. Under a design appointment, the designer is obliged to do no more than exercise reasonable care and skill. This by no means guarantees that the works as designed will be suitable for their purpose. Under a design and construct arrangement, the completed construction must be, unless the parties agree otherwise, reasonably suitable for its purpose. In practice, many employers agree to a lower standard of design liability for commercial reasons, including the fact that many designers do not carry insurance for a fitness for purpose standard of care and this narrows the employer's market.
(c) Opportunity for the contractor to enhance the constructability of the project and enhance both time and cost efficiency. This advantage can be significant where the contractor is engaged as part of the team right at the outset, but may be very much diminished if the contractor is selected after the design is all but fixed.

Descriptions of contracts with contractor's design

Contracts with contractor's design are variously described as 'design and build', 'package deal' or 'turnkey'. The true meaning of a contract is not determined from its description, but from its terms, read as a whole.

Employer's control and contractor's responsibility

How can the employer retain sufficient control over the design, while at the same time passing full responsibility for it to a contractor? In many instances (e.g. in process plants), the employer's demand for control is answered by the stipulation of carefully defined performance criteria. In other cases, the employer wants a particular aesthetic look or structural arrangement (e.g. a cable-stayed structure). Here, the employer initiates the design itself and then passes it over to the contractor, who assumes responsibility for it *ab initio* (that is, from the start). While this procedure can be very effective, it is not without its difficulties. For example, the contract must deal with the possibility of fundamental design defects arising while the design was under the employer's control; for example, if the specified cable-stayed arrangement proves impracticable, how can the design be adjusted? Who must approve the new design? Will any necessary redesign be a breach by the contractor? If so, what damages flow? There are also practical shortcomings; indeed, many of the oft-cited benefits of the design-build arrangement may be lost because the project has, to all intents and purposes, been commenced on a traditional basis and the description 'design and build' is used to describe a legal rather than an engineering/architectural concept.

1.1 The planning system
1.2 Financing the project
1.3 Public sector projects
1.4 Public/private partnerships
1.5 Tender process
1.6 Construction contracts
1.7 Construction insurance

Contractor's design and contractor's responsibility for design

The essence of a contract 'with contractor's design' is not that the contractor necessarily does the design, but that the contractor is responsible for it. It may not design the works itself because it subcontracts the design to a specialist firm. But, very commonly, the reason why the contractor does not design most of the works is that the employer's own designer has largely completed the design before the contractor ever becomes involved; as part of its tender, the contractor checks the design before agreeing to take over responsibility for it. But its practical (as opposed to legal) involvement in the design is minimal. In principle, the contractor's liability for the design is not affected by whether or not the contractor actually carries out the design. What is important is whether or not the contractor has agreed to take responsibility for it.

The standard of design responsibility: general

Where a contractor agrees to design and construct works, its obligation is (in the absence of express terms) to provide works which are fit for their known purpose. In the House of Lords case *IBA* v. *EMI* (1980), Lord Scarman said:

> 'In the absence of a clear contractual indication to the contrary, I see no reason why one who in the course of his business contracts to design, supply and erect a television aerial mast is not under an obligation to ensure that it is reasonably fit for the purpose for which he knows it is intended to be used . . .'.

The design gap: express contract terms as to standard of liability

Many contractors are reluctant to assume a responsibility to provide works which are fit for their purpose, which leaves them exposed to the employer and deprives them of a similar cause of action against their own designers. Accordingly, many design and construct standard form contracts specifically limit the contractor's responsibility to the provision of a design which is done with reasonable skill and care.

Reasonable suitability for purpose

Where the obligation is to design the works to be suitable for their purposes, those purposes should be made clear in the contract. Where the works have only one proper purpose, then defects which render the works unsuitable for that purpose are clearly breaches. Where the works may have more than one purpose (e.g. a warehouse which can be used for storing a variety of items) it is thought that, unless the parties agree otherwise, the court will not burden the contractor with having to ensure suitability for unusual purposes.

Selection of materials

Where the contractor agrees only to exercise reasonable care and skill, it will nevertheless be responsible for selecting suitable materials, unless the contract expressly states otherwise. Where the employer specifies particular materials, the contractor will remain responsible for any lack of quality in them, even where there is only one source; in such a case the contractor will not, however, warrant (unless the contract states otherwise) that the materials are reasonably suitable for their purpose. Where the provision of materials requires a particular design input, the position is uncertain. For example, concrete is not merely selected, but designed; likewise, many new materials, including plastic composites, require advanced design.

Construction (Design and Management) Regulations 2007

Under the CDM Regulations, the designer must ensure that any design which it prepares pays proper regard to risks during and after construction and gives priority to measures which will protect people. Where the employer's requirements contain a provision that the design will accord with the Regulations and the works are not safe, e.g. for cleaning, as required by the Regulations, this may amount to a 'defect' entitling the employer to undertake 'remedial works', the cost of which may be claimed from the contractor.

Novation of designers

Employers frequently appoint designers to initiate the design. At tender stage, the employer may stipulate that the successful tenderer will be obliged to take over the appointment of the designers. This requires the prior approval of the designers, usually obtained at the time of their initial appointment. The legal device used is novation. This involves the dissolution of the contract between the designer and employer and the creation of a contract between the designer and contractor. This is usually achieved using deeds to avoid any question of lack of consideration and to ensure maximum duration of liability. Benefits of novation may include:

(a) the retention of the designer's experience of the scheme
(b) avoidance of a 'liability gap' where a new designer blames the first designer for not providing a good basic design and the first blames the new designer for failing to understand and/or implement the design properly
(c) added incentive for the designer, which knows that its involvement in the project will be a continuing one.

Contractor's concerns as to novation

As far as the contractor is concerned, the novation should preserve its reasonable rights against the designer. It will wish to ensure the following.

(a) That the duration of the designer's appointment is coterminous with the duration of design liability under the construction contract. For example, if the contractor is to be responsible for the design *ab initio*, the designer's appointment should also be novated to the contractor *ab initio*. Likewise, if the contractor's contract with the employer is under deed (with a twelve-year limitation period) then the agreement between the contractor and designer should also be by deed.
(b) That, insofar as it is commercially practicable, the designer's liability to the contractor is co-extensive with the contractor's liability to the employer. For example, if the designer's appointment is on a reasonable care and skill basis but the contractor's liability is on a fitness for purpose basis, the contractor has taken on an added exposure. This consideration is extremely important where key aspects of the design involve innovation; here the potential gulf between reasonable care and skill and suitability for purpose is greatest. In practice, it will normally be difficult to enhance the designer's standard of obligation at the time of novation.
(c) That the damages claimable by the contractor against the designer relate specifically to the losses which are suffered by the contractor, including the express likelihood of damages payable to the employer.
(d) That the designer's insurances are good and secure.

1.1 The planning system
1.2 Financing the project
1.3 Public sector projects
1.4 Public/private partnerships
1.5 Tender process
1.6 Construction contracts
1.7 Construction insurance

Employer's concerns as to novation

As far as the employer is concerned, the novation should not allow any uncovered risk. Considerations include the following points.

(a) Ensuring that there is a complete and absolute transfer of the designer's obligation to the contractor. It will not readily be presumed that there is any enlargement of the designer's obligation; any obligations retained may not be transferred as intended.
(b) Requiring a direct collateral warranty (supplementary to the novation) from the designer in the event of the contractor's inability to meet any claim.
(c) Ensuring that it is possible to assign the substantial benefit of the construction contract (including rights under the direct warranty).
(d) Ensuring that the designer's insurances are good and secure.

Novation and the designer's performance

The designer's performance may prove less than satisfactory for a variety of reasons, ranging from insolvency to incompetent work. The contractor's remedies, if any, will depend on an interpretation of the contract. Where the designer is unable to perform properly, it is thought that, in the absence of agreed terms, the contractor may appoint a substitute designer of its choice; the situation will normally differ from a nomination in which the employer is to appoint a replacement.

Tendering practice: general

Under a traditional contract, the employer (or its engineer/architect) will have completed (or virtually completed) the design at tender stage. The employer will be able to approve the final drawings and specifications prior to tender. The drawings and specifications are passed to the tenderers who price the works. Traditionally, a bill of quantities is provided, showing the quantities, or at least their approximate values. Under a design and build contract, the position can be very different. The tender process can be described in terms of the number and types of stages it involves. It is discussed more thoroughly in Chapter 1.5.

Single-stage tendering

This is where the contractor receives documents and submits its tender based on those documents. Although described as 'single stage' there is often a significant period of negotiation following the submission of tenders. A single-stage process is appropriate where the employer's requirements are purely functional (e.g. a temporary haul road) or the employer has already identified those features over which it wants strict control and has commissioned an outline design which fixes them. Tender documents for a single-stage design and construct project will include the 'employer's requirements'. In its submission, the contractor offers the 'contractor's proposals'. The former describes the criteria which the employer requires the design to meet and the latter sets out the ways in which the contractor proposes to meet them. Many design and construct contracts have a defined order of precedence in which the employer's requirements take priority over the contractor's proposals.

Multiple-stage tendering

Where the employer wishes the contractor to supply the conceptual as well as the detailed design, a multiple-stage approach is inevitable. Such cases include utility or process contracts, where the employer relies on the contractor's expertise, and design competition projects. Tendering contractors often compete through a number of distinct stages; competitive qualification for each subsequent round may be judged using aesthetic, environmental, safety, likely cost, risk and time criteria. In the final stage, where a significant element of detailed design is required, unsuccessful finalists may in some instances be partly compensated for their efforts during this final stage.

International turnkey contracts

Turnkey contracts are a sub-species of design and build contracts. There is no standard definition of a turnkey contract. In international civil engineering practice, it tends to mean a contract where the contractor 'engineers, procures and constructs' the facility in a state ready for operation and to a standard which meets pre-set performance specifications. A turnkey contract is, thus, a species of design and build contract; but in the international arena, the concept goes beyond a mere design and construct contract. It suggests a scheme in which there is significant utilization of intellectual property (e.g. patented technologies) and 'know-how' by the contractor. Turnkey projects usually combine major civil engineering works with mechanical and electrical installations. Frequently, there is also involvement by the contractor in the finance of the project (even if only by deferred payments) and in passing on skills to the employer's workforce during and after completion. Turnkey contracts are widely used for major utilities projects with an international dimension. They are coming to be used more and more for major infrastructural projects. Development agencies, such as the World Bank or the European Bank for Reconstruction and Development, prefer to minimize their risk exposure and, for that reason, prefer turnkey arrangements. But even where governments are able fully to finance major plant or infrastructural projects themselves, they prefer to adopt a turnkey arrangement because of the single-point liability and the opportunity to train local staff.

2.3 Contracts providing for a specialist management function

Traditional contracts assume a particular, and relatively simple, management and time structure. An engineer (or architect, as the case may be) considers, surveys and designs the scheme. A single contractor then takes on responsibility for the works, sub-contracting where necessary and always with the approval of the engineer. In the 1960s, employers became frustrated at the time taken by sequential design and construction and by the lack of control they appeared to have during the construction phase of the works. Employers in the oil and gas industries had, for many years, used contracts that explicitly enhanced the role of a project manager. These models led traditional construction employers to experiment with contract management arrangements. In the early 1980s, particularly in the building industry, a variety of new management-based contract arrangements was developed and used extensively.

Contracts with a specialist management function often hear names such as 'management contracting' and 'construction management'. These descriptions have, to some degree, acquired a recognized meaning. The effect of a contract at law, however, is derived from an analysis of its terms taken as a whole and this is nowhere more true than for a management contract. Descriptions such as 'management contract' are insufficiently fixed or certain to render any assistance whatsoever in interpreting the contract and can be misleading because they suggest that because two contracts are so described, then the same results and consequences follow. In fact, two documents, both described as 'management contracts' and both fitting the general descriptions of such contracts, can, in the most fundamental respects, produce quite different obligations.

The use of what are sometimes described as 'modern contracts', such as the NEC 3, which place management principles at the centre of the contract, have put management very much at the heart of the construction process. Indeed, there is a sense these days that a contract which is not based on management principles is somewhat archaic, at least for large projects where management input can be critical. It should be noted that the NEC suite of contracts includes a management contract option.

2.4 Term contracts

A term contract is an agreement between the parties that work of a specified description will be undertaken by the contractor for the employer at agreed rates for a stated period.

Payment

Payment is normally made in accordance with a schedule of agreed rates. Each class of work may have several associated rates, with the applicable rate depending on the quantity of work in that class to be undertaken in each location. In term contracts for a period exceeding two years, it is common for there to be a price adjustment formula. Where there is no express price adjustment, none will be implied.

The amount of work

Where a contractor maintains resources on standby, it will wish to ensure that there is a good and steady flow of orders. Unless it is expressly agreed, however, it will not readily be implied, either from historical figures or the resources which the contractor is obliged to have ready, that any minimum amount of work will be ordered.

Exclusive entitlement to the work

The parties may agree that all work of the specified type will be awarded to the contractor but the degree of exclusivity is a matter of interpreting the contract as a whole.

After the term has expired

Where the parties continue to operate the arrangement after the term has expired, it will normally be inferred that both parties agree to continue on the contract basis, unless some other intention is clear. The contractor will be entitled to the contract rates rather than a *quantum meruit*. Either party may discontinue the arrangement upon reasonable notice.

2.5 Concession (BOT) contracts

General

A concession (or Build–Operate–Transfer) contract is one where the concession-grantor (frequently, but not necessarily a government body) grants to the concessionaire a concession to develop a piece of infrastructure (often called an 'asset' or the 'facility') and to hold that facility for a defined period and in a defined way so as to recoup the initial cost of investment and also to make a profit. The facility is usually constructed using a turnkey contract and the concession-grantor usually takes the facility over at the end of the concession period. A concession contract is not primarily a construction contract. It is, in large part, a service contract in which the concessionaire provides to the concession-grantor (directly or indirectly) a service. In addition, it is a finance mechanism, enabling the concession-grantor to have the service (and, ultimately, the facility) without having to find the initial capital (although it may have to underwrite it, directly or indirectly). Concession agreements are discussed in detail in Chapter 1.4.

The service nature of concession contracts

Concession contracts usually entitle and/or oblige the concessionaire to render a service. Under power and water supply contracts, power/water is produced for supply either to a state or private distribution company; 'offtake' agreements – i.e. the agreement between the contractor and the party taking the power or water, etc. – may fix prices and quantities of power or water and may require the offtaker to guarantee the purchase of agreed quantities. Road, rail and bridge contracts require the concessionaire to make these facilities available for defined classes of user; direct or shadow tolls may be charged and a variable fee (depending on the quality of service provided) may also be payable. The service nature of the project becomes most obvious when the facility is a school, hospital or prison, with the concessionaire not only building the facility, but managing and providing support staff and upgrades to computing, communication and services during the concession period.

Concession contracts as a financing mechanism

A concession contract enables a party which desires the construction of a facility to have it done without having to find the initial capital. For example, private healthcare companies or school trusts may have facilities constructed for them, which are paid for over the term of the concession from recurrent funds. But the most significant promoters are government bodies. Concessions are used both in developing countries and in developed countries. In the former, governments may find it difficult to finance important but non-urgent infrastructural projects and private investment can assist them. Private finance is not a panacea here, of course, because while the money invested into the project is not sovereign debt, its repayment relies on the future availability of hard, rather than local, currency and concessionaires frequently look to the government to underwrite the availability of that money. In some ways, the major success of concession contracts is their use by the governments of developed countries (e.g. under the UK Private Finance Initiative) to produce an efficient private–public partnership for the development of the infrastructure.

Risk under concession contracts

Concession contracts often represent the ultimate risk assumption for a 'contractor' (concessionaire). Each contract involves its own unique risks because of:

(a) the nature of the product being constructed; for example, where a bridge is being constructed and the concessionaire is to recover its initial outlay by charging tolls, it takes the risk that there will in fact be demand at the rate of toll it proposes
(b) the nature of the construction process; projects such as tunnels often involve great cost uncertainty because of the uncertain nature of the ground conditions
(c) the risk division and safeguards in the contract; for example, where the project is a light rail system, the risks may be largely associated with the take-up by prospective passengers. Since the concession-grantor is likely to be an arm of government which can influence the attractiveness of the scheme through its transportation taxes and subsidies, the concessionaire may require some guarantees as to the base number of passengers.

1.1 The planning system
1.2 Financing the project
1.3 Public sector projects
1.4 Public/private partnerships
1.5 Tender process
1.6 Construction contracts
1.7 Construction insurance

The risks to banks (who usually take no equity stake in the project) and equity investors also need to be considered. Banks, in particular, are careful to carry out full risk assessments before lending money and may require 'step-in' rights, enabling them to take over the facility if there is a default by the contractor, with a view to letting the work to another contractor. The banks' approaches are considered in more detail in Chapter 1.2.

The contract description

A bewildering array of names and acronyms are used. These include:

(a) Design, Build, Own, Operate and Transfer (DBOOT) – this expression is frequently used for bridge and tunnel projects
(b) Design, Build, Finance and Operate (DBFO) – this expression is frequently used for school and hospital projects
(c) Design, Construct, Manage and Finance (DCMF) – this expression is frequently used for facilities such as prisons, where the project company not only constructs but also provides specialist management in the medium term
(d) Build, Lease, Transfer (BLT) – here the project company retains legal ownership, but the facility is leased back to the government. The government runs the facility, usually on a full repairing and insuring basis.

None of the above are terms of art. Each seeks to encapsulate what the concessionaire is required to achieve. In practice, there are so many variables and the contracts can be used in so many different contexts that such descriptions are of little value in themselves. The project company's obligations, as always, are determined by an interpretation of the contract terms taken as a whole.

Recouping the outlay

The concessionaire finances the project and must therefore recover its outlay plus profit when the works are complete. This may be achieved in a number of ways:

(a) *tolls*; for example, on a bridge project, the contractor will charge a crossing toll which will, over a number of years, pay back the initial outlay, cover maintenance and bring in a profit
(b) *shadow tolls*; for example on a road for public use, the government may pay the contractor for, say, the level of usage at a defined rate for each type of vehicle
(c) *rent-back or lease-back*; for example on a hospital or school project, the contractor may rent the completed facility back to the NHS or the education authority, thus enabling the authority to make accurate provision for its future expenditure from recurrent funds rather than using its capital which can be focused elsewhere.

The income may be generated from a combination of these; for example, a light railway project may generate income from a combination of passenger usage, attainment of various performance targets and for attracting custom from modes of transport which are less efficient in environmental terms.

3 DOCUMENTS FORMING PART OF THE CONSTRUCTION CONTRACT

A construction contract generally contains a standard form set of conditions (amended or unamended). In addition, there will be a variety of documents, some of which will be standard documents and some of which will be unique to the project, setting out the details of the scope of the work to be done, the standard which is to be achieved, ancillary (e.g. safety) requirements and mechanisms for computing the sums payable at any stage. Furthermore, method statements and programmes are frequently produced; these may either form part of the contract, or be produced as a management tool without direct contractual status.

While a construction contract is normally contained within and defined by a series of documents, it should be noted in passing that, in a number of situations, the parties are entitled to look beyond the written documents. This may be so where an agreed oral term has not been written down or where the law implies terms to supplement an incompletely defined agreement. These matters are dealt with in detail in Chapter 3.1.

3.1 Drawings and specifications

The scope of construction work is usually defined using drawings and specifications. The former set out the positional interrelationships between the items of work, while the latter set out the quality required. Where no specification is provided, it will be implied into the contract, for example, that work is to be done with proper skill and care, using good quality materials that are reasonably suitable for their purpose. The specification documents tend also to contain a variety of requirements and stipulations as to the manner of working. A number of standard forms of specifications are published which relate to specific sectors of the construction industry, including specifications for the water industry, tunnelling works, etc. It is common for large public and quasi-public sector bodies to have standard specification terms for use on their own projects.

It should be noted that parties frequently use the 'specification' to deal with all manner of sundry matters. In some cases, one finds some of the most important clauses in the specification. In contracts – such as the ICE Conditions of Contract 7th Edition – which do not specify an order of priority for documents, specification clauses can have important effects; where they are inconsistent with terms found in the main conditions of contract, the specification clauses may in some cases take precedence.

3.2 Bills of quantities, schedules of rates, etc.

Bills of quantities are lists of items with associated quantities. The effect of the bill of quantities within the contract is a matter of interpreting the contract as a whole in each case. The effect of the bill of quantities in one ICE 7th Edition contract may differ from its effect in another ICE 7th Edition contract because of amendments to the Conditions of Contract or even clauses introduced into the specification. As a result, caution is required and the following comments should be taken as indicative only.

In contracts for a lump sum price, items required to complete the works must generally be provided despite their being omitted from the bill; if there is no mechanism in the contract for recovering payment for these extra items, the contractor will have to pay for them.

For measure and value contracts, estimated quantities are set out for each class of work. When tendering, the contractor quotes a rate for each class. The bill total is the sum of all the products of rates and estimated quantities; but the sum payable is the product of the actual quantities and rates. The process by which the quantity of each item is determined is called 'measurement', which may be physical measurement on site or the computation of quantities using survey data. If an item of work is to be done for which there is no agreed rate, nor agreed mechanism for calculating its value, the contractor is entitled to be paid a reasonable rate/sum. In the ICE Conditions

1.1 The planning system
1.2 Financing the project
1.3 Public sector projects
1.4 Public/private partnerships
1.5 Tender process
1.6 Construction contracts
1.7 Construction insurance

of Contract 7th Edition, for example, the contract states that the bills are deemed to be prepared in accordance with the Civil Engineering Standard Method of Measurement, 3rd Edition. The quantities in the bill are expressed to be estimates; any errors or omissions are to be corrected by the Engineer and any items required to be added in will be paid for in accordance with the contract. Accordingly, where items have been accidentally omitted from the bill, the contractor is compensated.

In addition to documents described as bills of quantities, similar documents described as schedules of rates, schedules of prices, etc. are frequently used. None of these terms are terms of art and their effect is determined by interpreting the agreement in each case.

3.3 Programmes and method statements

Management tools such as programmes and method statements are frequently used in connection with construction contracts. The status of any programme or method statement is determined by interpreting the contract. The status of a programme or method statement may be one of the following.

Provided solely for information The contractor may be required to submit a programme solely for the purpose of demonstrating competence at tender stage. Such programmes or method statements normally have no contractual significance or effect.

Provided in accordance with the terms of the contract Some contracts – for example the ICE 7th Edition Contract – require the successful contractor to indicate how it proposes to execute the work using a programme; but such a programme occupies a rather passive role in the management of the project. In the NEC, 3 Contract, the programme assumes a more active role and is updated to enable positive management control.

Programmes etc. which rank as contractual (i.e. as terms of the contract) Here the programme or method statement is included within the contract at the time it is made. As a result, the contractor is required and entitled to perform the work in accordance with the programme and method statement; if it is prevented from so doing for reasons at the employer's risk, and thereby suffers a loss, it will be entitled to claim damages.

4 PART II OF THE HOUSING GRANTS, CONSTRUCTION AND REGENERATION ACT 1996

4.1 Application of the HGCRA 1996

The payment provisions of the Housing Grants, Construction and Regeneration Act 1996 apply to contracts in writing which relate to 'construction operations' in England, Wales or Scotland irrespective of whether or not the law of England and Wales or Scotland otherwise applies. Note that the Department of Business, Enterprise and Regulatory Reform has published a draft bill which it is anticipated at the time of writing (30 September 2008) will be enacted in 2009 extending the provisions of the Act to unwritten contracts. 'Construction operations' are given an extended meaning which includes not only contracts for the carrying out of construction operations, but also contracts for the arrangement and design of construction contracts. Accordingly, most construction management, design and construction contracts for work in Britain are included.

There are a number of specific exceptions. These include drilling or tunnelling for the purpose of extracting minerals, and access and machinery for works relating to the basic utilities and to the chemical, food and pharmaceutical industries. Where only part of the contract relates to construction operations, that part only is subject to the Act.

For other contracts, such as those relating to work abroad, the position is as it was prior to the coming into force of the Act.

4.2 The provisions of the Act

The Act deals with two principal matters.

Payment

The Act provides that the contract must allow for stage or periodic payments. It does not stipulate their frequency. Neither does it stipulate what proportion of the total amount which will eventually become due must be paid at any stage. Rather, the Act seeks to ensure that the time for payment and the amount of payment is clearly agreed and that the parties adhere to the agreement. The Act provides a framework for ensuring that the contractor (or subcontractor, etc. as the case may be) receives payment at the time stated in the agreement or, where the employer (or main contractor, etc. as the case may be) proposes to withhold payment, for ensuring that the contractor receives proper notice. Where an employer proposes to withhold payment, the contractor is then able to exercise a right to

(a) refer the matter to adjudication or
(b) in some situations, to suspend performance.

Dispute resolution Construction contracts must allow either party to refer any dispute or difference to adjudication 'at anytime'. Where there are no adjudication provisions in the contract or where the adjudication provisions do not comply with the list of requirements set out in Section 108 of the Act, the Scheme for Construction Contracts 1998 applies. This is dealt with in detail in Chapter 4.4.

5 THE APPLICABLE LAW OF THE CONTRACT

Two types of law can apply to a contract – procedural law and substantive law. Where a dispute arises, the dispute may be referred to the court or an arbitrator. The rules about procedure, evidence and enforcement of the decision are part of the 'procedural law' of the country where the case is being heard. But the law which the court or arbitrator will apply when interpreting the contract ('the substantive law') need not be the same as the procedural law. For example, where a Spanish contractor builds an office building in Moscow for a Hungarian bank and there is a provision in the contract (written in English) for arbitration in Stockholm or Paris, it is necessary for the parties to agree explicitly which substantive law is to apply. There is no such thing – as yet, at any rate – as general European law applicable to contracts, and the parties must decide which country's law is to govern such matters as interpretation of the contract. This is normally done in a single clause, using the wording: 'The law applicable to this contract is the law of England' (or Spain, Russia, etc.).

Note that the law chosen must be that of a 'legal country' rather than political state. If the parties chose the 'law of the UK' or the 'law of the USA' this would cause ambiguity because the UK contains three legal countries – England and Wales, Scotland and Northern Ireland and each state in the USA has its own law.

1.1 The planning system
1.2 Financing the project
1.3 Public sector projects
1.4 Public/private partnerships
1.5 Tender process
1.6 Construction contracts
1.7 Construction insurance

It is quite possible for parties to agree that a contract which concerns the nationals of one country only will be subject to the law of a different country. Most countries, however, have rules forbidding the use of this 'flag of convenience' device for avoiding safety and welfare obligations. In this regard, it is worth noting that the Housing Grants, Construction and Regeneration Act 1996 applies to construction within Britain, irrespective of the applicable law of the contract.

6 SELECTION OF CONDITIONS OF CONTRACT IN PRACTICE

6.1 Procurement and contracts

Construction professionals frequently talk about 'procurement systems'. By this, they mean the entire process of acquiring the finished construction. A major facet of this process is, of course, the choice of the principal construction contract. The contract may not define all aspects of the procurement process, but these are largely determined by the need for consistency with the principal construction contract. Examples of this include:

(1) If the employer wishes to establish a scheme whereby all the subcontractors will provide collateral warranties to the funder and to the prospective tenant, the route by which this is achieved is by including a term in the principal contract obliging the main contractor to procure these warranties, e.g. by refusing to subcontract with any person who is not prepared to enter into such a warranty when called upon to do so.

(2) If the employer wishes to pass all the risk for the construction – concept, design, materials and workmanship – to the contractor, it is inconsistent with this for the employer to retain his own designers without novating them to the principal contractor.

6.2 Standard form conditions of contract and bespoke contracts

A party letting construction work must decide what conditions of contract to use. There are a number of basic options:

(a) a bespoke set of contract conditions, designed specifically for the particular project
(b) a standard form contract, published by one of the major professional institutions, or
(c) a standard form contract with amendments to suit the particular circumstances.

In practice, these are not distinct options but really describe a spectrum of possibilities. Even a bespoke contract – or 'home-made' contract as it is sometimes called – will be based on experience expressed in existing standard forms. Home-made contracts often turn out to be revised versions of a standard form.

A bespoke form which fully addresses the likely problems, as well as the commercial concerns and risk attitudes of the parties may appear, at least superficially, to be the 'best' solution. Bespoke contracts are frequently drawn up for major projects with novel obligations. However, for more routine projects the disadvantages of bespoke contracts – relative to the use of a standard form – almost always outweigh the advantages. Standard form contracts are cheaper, are familiar to the parties and hence reduce the cost of tendering, enhance the parties' confidence in the arrangement and tend to contain fewer unforeseen anomalies.

One of the key benefits of using one of the main standard form contracts is that the contractor and the employer (or the professionals advising him) will be familiar with them. Where the standard form is drawn up by a body representing all sides of the industry – as are the NEC 3, ICE Conditions of Contract, the JCT Contract and the FIDIC Contracts – then the parties can have increased confidence in the balance of risk allocation. The parties know also that the contract is not designed to trap the unwary, although everyone accepts that unintended traps may remain. Thus, even where a standard form may appear to have disadvantages, it may nevertheless be the preferred contract for reasons solely of familiarity and confidence.

Nevertheless, parties frequently use the standard printed form as a basic 'template' and add, omit, substitute or revise particular clauses to suit their own requirements (and principally those of the employer). Indeed, the amendments can be so fundamental that the entire basis of a contract is altered. For example, a number of privatized UK water companies in the late 1990s used the ICE Conditions of Contract, 6th Edition as a template. Without amendment, this creates a build-only, measure and value arrangement. However, Clause 8 is amended to convert the obligation to design and build, Clause 60 is changed to convert the payment arrangements to a lump sum in accordance with a schedule of activities and there are a number of other necessary incidental amendments. This example demonstrates that the use of a few well-targeted alterations can change the very nature of a contract. On superficial examination it looks like a standard ICE 6th Edition, but it has a very different legal nature. The reason for the use of ICE 6th as a template is that the tendering contractors will be familiar with its wording, while they may be less familiar with the ICE Design and Construct Standard Form. This familiarity creates confidence and hence, it is hoped, a keener price and a fuller understanding by contractors as to what they must achieve. The tendering contractors need only examine the amendments (which are clearly highlighted) rather than read through an unfamiliar standard form. The intention of the water companies was, however, soundly based. A more appropriate method of attaining the same objective these days may be the use of a modular-based contract, such as the NEC 3.

6.3 A brief survey of standard form contracts

Standard form contracts are published by a variety of professional bodies or associations of professional bodies, too many to list. These include the following.

The Conditions of Contract Standing Joint Committee

This is a committee with representatives of the Institution of Civil Engineers, the Association of Consulting Engineers and the Civil Engineering Contractors Association. Although the publications are endorsed by all three bodies, the conditions are published under the title 'ICE'. They include:

- ICE Conditions of Contract, 7th Edition, 1999
- ICE Design and Construct Conditions of Contract, 2nd Edition, 2001
- ICE Conditions of Contract Term Version, 2002
- ICE Partnering Addendum, 2003

The Institution of Civil Engineers

The NEC contracts, 3rd Edition (2005)

The Civil Engineering Contractors Association

This body publishes a range of standard form of civil engineering subcontracts, including, e.g. a form for use with the ICE Conditions of Contract.

1.1 The planning system
1.2 Financing the project
1.3 Public sector projects
1.4 Public/private partnerships
1.5 Tender process
1.6 Construction contracts
1.7 Construction insurance

The Joint Contracts Tribunal

Originally, the Royal Institute of British Architects was the driving force behind the issue of the standard form of building contract. The form was commonly known as the 'RIBA Contract'. However, the committee which issues the contract has a wide membership, including the Association of Consulting Engineers, British Property Federation, Construction Confederation, Local Government Association, National Specialist Contractors Council, the Royal Institute of Chartered Surveyors and the Scottish Building Contract Committee as well as the RIBA.

Its many publications include:

- JCT Standard Form of Building Contract, 2005 (JCT 05)
- JCT Standard Form of Building Contract with Contractor's Design, 2005

The Institution of Chemical Engineers

The contracts include:

- IChemE Green Book Contract, cost reimbursable contract, 3rd edition 2002, with addendum
- IChemE Red Book Contract, lump sum contract, 4th edition 2001, with addendum 2004

The Institutions of Mechanical and Electrical Engineers

These two institutions jointly publish a form – the Model Form, MF/1 Revision 4 (2000) for use in connection with the installation of electrical and mechanical services in construction.

FIDIC

The Fédération Internationale des Ingénieurs-Conseils (FIDIC) is an umbrella body for associations of consulting engineers. It publishes a series of contracts, the most important of which are:

- **Conditions of Contract for Construction** for building and engineering works designed by the employer, 1995 (the *new Red Book*);
- **Conditions of Contract for Plant and Design-Build** for electrical and mechanical plant and for building and engineering works designed by the contractor, 1995 (the *new Yellow Book*);
- **Conditions of Contract for EPC Turnkey Projects** EPC being the abbreviation for engineer – procure – construct, 1995 (the *Silver Book*); and
- **Short Form of Contract** for projects of relatively small value, 1995 (the *Green Book*).

6.4 Selection of an appropriate contract: general considerations

Given the wide range of options available, choosing the appropriate contract is by no means a straightforward matter. There is no accepted 'rational' method of contract selection. The best that can be achieved is that a contract is chosen which – taking into account all considerations – will most strongly promote the interests and priorities of the party choosing the contract. This is normally the employer (or the employer's representatives) but the interests of the contractor cannot be ignored; indeed it is crucial to the success of the project that the employer pays keen attention to the interests of potential contractors. The employer must ensure that the contract will be attractive to contractors; they must be encouraged to submit competitive prices. Furthermore, the contract arrangement must enable the contractor to complete the work efficiently and supply incentives to the contractor to do so.

Ordinarily, the interests and priorities of the employer will include:

(a) minimizing the final cost
(b) reducing the uncertainty as to cost
(c) timely completion in accordance with a sensible programme
(d) appropriate quality, durability and serviceability
(e) maintaining good neighbourhood relations
(f) discharging environmental, welfare and safety responsibilities.

Many of these interests conflict and hence the 'optimal' form of contract is the one which balances them in the optimum way. For example, a local authority will pay high regard to its mix of social and economic interests and will, ordinarily, prefer a fair final price to a price which is unduly harsh on the contractor. On the other hand, there are limits to this because the local authority also has an obligation to safeguard the public purse. Even a private commercial company may – for reasons of pure self-interest – opt for a 'fair' price rather than an unduly harsh price; this creates a greater incentive for the contractor to complete the works properly and on time.

6.5 Practical considerations

In practice, the choice of contract will be influenced by many practical considerations, including the following.

The clarity of the contract

It is essential that the parties know what they have agreed. If they are unsure what the words mean, this may lead to misunderstandings and disputes. Some contracts are written using straightforward words in a sensible format. Others are not.

The type of work involved

While most construction contracts deal with the same generic issues and can be used across the full range of construction situations, one finds in practice that conditions of contract are developed with an eye to the terminology and traditions of a specific sector of construction. The ICE Conditions use terminology especially suitable for civil engineering works. The JCT and IChemE contracts use terminology suited to building and process plant projects respectively. This is not to say that, for example, a JCT contract cannot be used for civil engineering works. There may be some difficulties of terminology (e.g. the administering engineer may not be happy to be known as the Architect – although in many JCT Contracts the name is altered in practice to 'Contract Administrator') but the arrangement will, by and large, be workable. The NEC contract, which is specifically designed to be suitable across the range of construction activities, emphasizes the conceptual commonality between construction contracts.

The expertise of the employer and the amount of control effort it can dedicate to the project

Some employers – such as local authorities – have considerable skill and experience of construction. The situation is very different for one-off employers with no prior experience. Employers with expertise may prefer to carry out designs in house or to have them carried out by designers with whom they have worked well in the past; in such cases, a build-only contract (such the ICE Conditions of Contract or the FIDIC Red Book) may be most appropriate. Where, however, the employer has no special expertise, skill or resource base in construction, it may be sensible to adopt a contract type which enables it to outline its performance requirements and then to pass the responsibility for design and construction to a single entity. In such a case, a design and build contract may be most appropriate.

The degree of control which the employer wishes to exercise

Often, it is in the employer's interests to devolve responsibility for the construction, setting out clear performance criteria for the work and then leaving the contractor to carry it out with minimal supervision. In other cases, this is not acceptable; it could be that the construction work interacts closely with other crucial work, so that it is in the employer's interest to control the construction work, including reserving powers to suspend, rearrange, redefine and reschedule work. In the former case, it is possible to reach agreement on what amounts virtually to a fixed price (e.g. using a JCT 05 contract). The employer's right of interference in the latter case is incompatible with this and here a cost-reimbursable arrangement may be preferable (e.g. using the IChemE Green Book, or the NEC 3 cost-reimbursable option).

The importance of price certainty

Some commentators assert that what employers really want is price certainty, but this is not the overriding priority in every case. Some employers properly consider it in their best interests to seek the lowest price averaged over a number of contracts. Price certainty requires the contractor to assume additional risk and the contractor will increase prices to reflect this. On the other hand, a contractor who carries less risk will offer a lower price; the employer may have to pay more on some contracts, but may reckon to pay a lower average over a number of projects. Either strategy – and any intermediate strategy – can be justified. The employer's approach will depend on its:

(a) intrinsic risk attitude – does the employer prefer to offer the project at a lower price but with less price certainty; or would it prefer a higher price with greater risk certainty?
(b) budgetary constraints – some employers allocate money internally using a strict budget approach. Whatever their intrinsic risk attitude, the need to remain within closely ring-fenced budgets means that price certainty is the only real option;
(c) portfolio effects – where an employer takes on a series of projects, a risk retention approach often becomes very attractive. While one project may exceed budget, two others may come in below budget. This 'portfolio effect' is well understood by investment managers who invest in stocks whose performance is governed by different factors as a hedge against major losses which could result when investing in just one product.

Where a high degree of price certainty is important, an employer would be well advised to use a design and build arrangement with a lump sum, excluding extras for unforeseen conditions. Where price uncertainty is much less of a priority, then other forms down to a cost-reimbursable arrangement may be used.

The need for quick completion

The employer's priority is often quick completion. This may be so for a variety of reasons. For example, the construction may be a commercial property for a lease in a rising market. Or it may involve a flood relief scheme which must be completed before the risk materializes.

When quick completion is a priority, it is often necessary to consider new ways of approaching construction and these often affect the appropriate contract type. For example, a 'fast track' programme of building construction often involves building over-strength foundations. This avoids the need to wait for detailed ground strength investigations and detailed estimates of building loads. Foundations may be started within a day of receipt of instructions using a simple 'worse-case' analysis, whereas a conventional construction pattern would require several months between the receipt of instructions and the commencement of construction. Such an arrangement often requires a large degree of flexibility and hence a fully costed scheme is impossible; the early contractors may well be appointed on a cost-reimbursable basis. In order to manage this process, procurement methods such as 'management contracting' or 'construction management' may be considered.

The need for clear remedies

Under traditional forms of procurement in which the design and construction are separated, the responsibility for construction which failed to work could be unclear. In the first place, the employer had to determine whether the problem discovered was a design fault or a construction fault. If it was a construction fault, the employer took action against the contractor. If it was a design fault, the employer took action against the designer. Often it was necessary to sue both because they both blamed each other. But, even if it was shown to be a design fault, the employer could normally only succeed against the designer if the designer had failed to use 'reasonable care and skill' (see Chapter 2.4). Thus, the employer could end up an unsuccessful litigant against two defendants – with the consequent large costs bill – in possession of a faulty building. In order to provide less uncertainty and greater protection for the employer, a design and build approach can be adopted. This ordinarily has two effects:

(a) the design and build contractor is responsible for all faults whether they stem from design or construction; and
(b) there is no need to demonstrate that a party has failed to use 'reasonable care and skill' – the fact that the construction fails to work properly is sufficient. Note, however, that some standard form design and build contracts reintroduce the need to demonstrate a failure to exercise reasonable care and skill – see, for example, the JCT Conditions of Contract with Contractor's Design.

The factors described above are not unrelated. A contract form which promotes one interest often diminishes another and the selection in practice requires the use of judicious balance. Frequently, employers (or their advisers) will draw up a grid of objectives and score each possible contract scheme against its contribution towards promoting that objective and select a contract type which promotes most and undermines least objectives. This may readily be compared to a family selecting a summer holiday and assessing a number of proposals against the criteria they have identified as important: availability, cost, familiarity with the language/customs, convenience (e.g. a package or with elements purchased separately) etc. The 'right choice' involves a judicious balancing. As always, of course, inertia will play a part for some – many people continue to go to the same resort simply because they are used to it and see no reason to change; the same is true of contract selection.

7 SUBCONTRACTS AND COLLATERAL WARRANTIES

As indicated in Section 1.3 above, the construction contract is often just one of many contracts required on the construction project. In this section, a brief outline of the key issues in relation to subcontracts and collateral warranties is outlined.

7.1 Subcontracts

The prefix 'sub' in the word sub-contract does not imply any legal inferiority. It merely signifies that the sub-contract work is carved out of the main contract scope (in some cases it may be 100% of it) or is ancillary to it (e.g. in the case of a temporary works subcontractor). All the same requirements for a main contract are present in a sub-contract and the same considerations apply to the questions of selection of the payment mechanisms etc.

7.2 Collateral warranties

A collateral warranty is a contractual link, enabling person A (the warrantee) to sue person B (the warrantor) even though they do not have a direct service relationship. The word warranty is an old-fashioned word for contractual undertaking, which has been appropriated to express the essence of this device. The terms 'collateral' signifies that this obligation runs alongside and supplements the direct service relationship. Thus, for example, an architect's direct service relationship is with his client; but he may be required to issue a collateral warranty in favour of, say, a prospective tenant whose identity may not even be known at the date of completion.

Clearly, the architect cannot be compelled to give undertakings to a third party unless he has already agreed to do so. It is important, therefore, to consider the question of the need for collateral warranties at the outset and ensure that all parties who may be called upon to furnish them, have agreed to do so and have agreed the form of words.

Being a contract, a collateral warranty cannot be enforced if it is purely one-sided; English law requires consideration to support an agreement. There are two devices to overcome this. The first is the payment of a nominal sum, usually £1, by the warrantee to the warrantor to ensure that both sides are giving consideration. The second is to make the warranty by deed, which does not have to be supported by consideration. In many cases, both devices are used together in a belt and braces fashion. The use of a deed also extends the limitation period, which is frequently important.

The function of collateral warranties is to give assurance to the warrantee. Take, for example, an architect giving a warranty to a tenant. The tenant may agree a full repairing and insuring lease with the employer. This means that if, the day after signing the lease, he finds out that the brand new building has been constructed with defective materials, he must repair the building. He will be reluctant to enter into such a risky lease unless he has some comfort, e.g. the ability to sue the architect who specified the building. Hence the warranty, whilst on its face is for the benefit of the tenant, actually benefits the building owner because the owner can lease the building on safe and predictable terms.

It is not unusual for there to be in excess of 100 collateral warranties on a large project.

REFERENCES

1. Banwell, A., *The placing and management of contracts for building and civil engineering work*, HMSO, London, 1964.
2. Latham, M., *Constructing the team*, HMSO, London, 1994.

CHAPTER 1.7

Construction insurance

Marshall Levine
Marshall F. Levine & Associates

William Gloyn and Ray Robinson
Aon Limited

1 GENERAL INSURANCE

1.1 Insurance and risk management

It is to be hoped that properly arranged insurance programmes do not lead to disputes but rather to the speedy settlement of valid claims. Unfortunately, there is always considerable speculation about the attitude of insurers and therefore, before examining the main elements of construction insurance, it is worthwhile considering the background to this viewpoint.

Insurance does have a very important role to play in business life in general. If matters go smoothly it is rarely apparent. Unfortunately, things do go wrong and that is when it is needed. The cover provides the financial resources required for legal obligations to be met, damaged property to be replaced and a business to be maintained. This protection is especially important when undertaking a project in unfamiliar territory, one where business practices taken for granted in Western Europe may not always be encountered.

Insurance is the traditional way of transferring risk. As such it forms only a part of the risk management process. This consists of a three-part process:

- risk analysis and quantification
- elimination or reduction of risk
- transfer or retention strategies.

It is not appropriate to undertake a detailed examination of the whole risk management process. This can be dealt with very simply but effectively by experienced practitioners. On the other hand, far too much time can be spent over minute analysis which can often lead to overlooking major risks, not least because 'analysis paralysis' often sets in before the exercise is complete.

The minimization and reduction process should be an ongoing one. Insurers can quite rightly, and legally, expect that an insured will be taking all reasonable steps to avoid a claim. Insurance is there to protect against the unexpected and fortuitous. It is for that reason that the market in general imposed wide ranging exclusions in respect of the 'millennium bug'. Not only was this problem seen to be so internationally widespread as to be a potential source of insolvency for the world insurance market, but more importantly it was a matter substantially in the hands of those at risk. Insurance should never be considered as a licence for poor performance, although occasionally it is regarded as such. A valid method of risk reduction is by careful contract drafting. Insurers did just that by contractually excluding millennium problems from their contracts – otherwise known as insurance policies.

Many organizations, after adequate thought, are well able to absorb a certain amount of risk. This is often more cost effective than insurance which theoretically involves profit for a number of other parties. For many larger organizations this absorption is achieved by means of their own captive insurance company. For others the answer may lie in a mutual insurer, as many firms of major UK architects discovered when they set up the WREN to insure their professional indemnity risks. Yet another option is merely to expose the profit and loss account. It is, however, when a particular risk exposure threatens the stability of the balance sheet that some other form of risk transfer may be considered. Insurance may, of course, be imposed contractually; leases, funding agreements and building contracts are typical examples. Another possibility is the statutory imposition of an insurance requirement, as found under the Automobile or Workmans Compensation Regulations.

Finally, the importance of regular monitoring cannot be overemphasized. There is little value in carrying out an extensive analysis exercise only to let it gather dust on

1.1 The planning system
1.2 Financing the project
1.3 Public sector projects
1.4 Public/private partnerships
1.5 Tender process
1.6 Construction contracts
1.7 Construction insurance

the shelf. Ownership of the action plan must be clearly identified and performance of subsequent implementation kept under regular review. It is becoming rapidly established that this review is about allocation of responsibility.

Whether imposed or chosen, the insurance route is well trodden. The UK is fortunate in having London as the world centre of the insurance market. Western Europe also has one of the most mature markets in the world with a level of expertise which is unparalleled anywhere else. It is worth noting, however, that this international position is far from safe. Not least of all, the insurance companies, the traditional risk carriers, are threatened by other newcomers to the scene in the form of banks and capital markets. Many major commercial insurance contracts, especially those for international organizations, have substantial elements of risk transfer into the capital markets via a wide range of sophisticated financial instruments.

In common with most things, however, insurance repays careful preparation. Unfortunately, all too often this does not happen and the inevitable shortcomings are detected once a claim arises. Extreme diligence and caution should be exercised both professionally and personally in the handling of insurance affairs. There is a need, as never before, for specialist and expert advice – insurance today is not for amateurs. It demands careful consideration by the client, consultants and contractors to ensure that each one is adequately protected against their own risk exposures.

With this background in mind, the mystique of insurance law will be examined.

1.2 Insurance definition

Insurance in the construction context is generally a contract to indemnify; the insured will recover compensation for its actual loss and in order to recover will have to prove that loss. For claims relating to damage the basis of settlement will usually relate to repair or replacement costs. For liability claims this may occur where judgment has been given, or an award made against the insured, or where, with the insurer's consent, the insured has reached a settlement with the third party. The principle of indemnity will be implied in the contract. This type of contract should be distinguished from insurance contracts that promise to pay a specified sum upon the happening of an insured event (e.g. life insurance and contracts of guarantee, performance bonds, etc.).

An excellent general description of the nature of insurance was given by Channell J in *Prudential Insurance Co.* v. *IRC* [1904] 2 KB 658 where he stated:

> 'It must be a contract whereby for some consideration, usually but not necessarily in periodical payments called premiums, you secure to yourself some benefit, usually but not necessarily the payment of a sum of money, upon the happening of some event... the event should be one that involves some amount of uncertainty. There must be either uncertainty whether the event will happen or not, or if the event is one which must happen at some time there must be uncertainty as to the time at which it will happen. The remaining essential is ... that the insurance must be against something'.

Most insurance lawyers will break down this definition into five main requirements.

Contract

There must be a valid binding contract to indemnify the insured in certain circumstances (so the usual contractual principles of offer and acceptance, capacity, legality, etc., apply) that is, it should not be within the insurer's discretion as to whether or not it will pay out any claim. The insured is contracting for certainty that its claim will be properly considered, not that a discretion may be exercised in its favour. For a detailed discussion of these contractual principles see, for example, *Chitty on Contracts*, 29th edition.

The contract may be in any form, although a policy document is usually issued after the insurance is entered into (i.e. when the insured's proposal has been accepted by the insurer initialling a document known in the London market as a 'slip'). The slip sets out the main terms of the insurance. However, the slip is not the contract of insurance but merely evidence of its terms, and in fact the policy can be rectified if it does not accurately reflect the terms of the slip.

Consideration

Consideration is usually represented by a premium. Although Channell J refers to a payment of a premium, there is little authority on the significance of payment of premium. However, in *Hampton* v. *Toxteth Co-operative Provident Society Ltd* [1915] 1 Ch 721 a majority of the Court of Appeal held that the absence of a premium was not fatal to the existence of insurance. In addition, periodical payments for premium may be inappropriate; for example with contracts of indemnity insurance where only one payment of premium is made under each contract. In practice, many insurance contracts state that payment of the premium is a condition precedent to the insurer's liability under the contract.

In reality, due to the inefficiencies of the insurance markets administrative systems, sometimes no policy document exists until long after inception of the cover, in which case the parties to the insurance are required to refer to the slip or any relevant cover notes for evidence of the terms of the contract.

Benefit on the happening of some event

Although Channell J assumes that the benefit provided by an insurer will normally be money, benefits may be conferred which are 'money's worth'. Megarry V-C in *Medical Defence Union* v. *Department of Trade* [1979] 2 All ER 421 doubted that a fully satisfactory definition of insurance could ever be given and indicated that not every benefit can be the subject matter of a contract of insurance, but he was not prepared to go as far as holding that only a benefit in money or money's worth would suffice.

Megarry V-C stated that in most cases there were three elements to insurance and that in the absence of any of them, a contract was unlikely to be one of insurance. However, he stressed that the list was not necessarily definitive.

The three elements according to Megarry V-C are:

(a) the contract must give the insured an entitlement to a specified benefit on the occurrence of some event;
(b) the event must involve some element of uncertainty; and
(c) the insured must have an insurable interest in the subject matter of the contract.

Section 1 of the Life Assurance Act 1774 states that no insurance shall be made if there is no insurable interest and contracts contrary to the section shall be null and void. The Act, despite its title, applies to insurances on lives or 'any other event or events whatsoever' and therefore seems wide enough to include indemnity insurance, apart from those risks expressly excluded in s.4 (insurance on 'ships, goods and merchandises'). The Act also requires the policy to name all persons interested in the policy or on whose account the insurance is underwritten (s.2) and restricts the insured's recovery to an amount not exceeding its interest (s.3).

Megarry V-C also drew a distinction between indemnity contracts and contingency contracts. He described the former as giving an indemnity against some loss such as in a fire or marine policy. The latter is a payment contingent on an event such as death. However, he did not mention that indemnity policies can also be 'valued' (whereby the insured states in the proposal the specific value of the insured item for the purpose of any claim) so that a payment is made even if it does not reflect the true loss.

Uncertainty

The uncertainty to which Channell J refers relates to the occurrence of the event, for example, in relation to loss due to latent defects (i.e. physical damage resulting from defects in the design or construction of a building which is not discovered until after completion), theft or the possibility of an archaeological find that would delay the project and incur expense. The uncertainty is whether the event will occur at all, as contrasted with life assurance where the uncertainty relates to timing of death.

Against something

The insurance must be against something, which generally means that the insured must have an insurable interest in the subject matter of the insurance.

1.3 Insurable interest

Construction insurance contracts are examples of contracts of indemnity, whereby the insurer undertakes to indemnify the insured against pecuniary loss caused by or arising from particular risks. Therefore, an interest is required by reason of the nature of the contract itself. Unless the insured has such an interest at the time when the insured event occurs, he cannot claim under the contract because he has suffered no loss against which he can be indemnified. Furthermore, if the insured's interest is less than the full value of the subject matter, he can suffer no loss greater than the total value of his actual interest at the time of the loss.

It is common practice in the construction industry for the head contractor on a site to insure, in its name and on behalf of the subcontractors, the entire contract works against all risks. This is known as contractor's all risks insurance. The validity of such an insurance was challenged in *Petrofina (UK) Ltd* v. *Magnaload Ltd* [1983] 2 Lloyd's Rep 91 where the main issue was whether the lead contractor's name, as assured, could be used in subrogation proceedings against an allegedly negligent subcontractor, who had caused the loss on which the claim was based. The court held that the insurer could not recover on two grounds. First, on a true construction of the policy the defendants were technically sub-subcontractors for the purposes of the policy (therefore joint assureds) and rights of subrogation would be unavailable. Secondly, each insured was covered in respect of the whole contract works.

1.4 Utmost good faith

In addition, contracts of insurance are one of the few forms of contract subject to the principle of *uberrimae fidei*, or utmost good faith, which requires each party to make full disclosure of all material facts which may influence the other party in deciding to enter into the contract. To a limited extent, contracts for the sale of land, family settlements, the allotment of shares in companies and contracts of suretyship and partnership are also subject to this principle but in insurance utmost good faith remains fundamental to the contract.

The principle is generally understood to apply to the insured prior to entering into the insurance contract as the insured is in possession of all the facts concerning the risk so the insurer is entitled to trust the insured's representation. (See *Carter* v. *Boehm* (1766) 3 Burr 1905.)

1.5 Non-disclosure

The principle of utmost good faith applies to both parties to the insurance contract (see *Banque Financière de la Cité S.A.* v. *Westgate Insurance Co. Ltd* ('Westgate') [1988] 2 Lloyd's Rep 513. Where utmost good faith has not been shown by one party, the other party can avoid the contract. In such a case, the contract would be at an end and the insured would have no insurance cover. The House of Lords' decision in Westgate confirmed that the principle applies equally to the insurer. This may be relevant, if, for example, that insurer becomes aware of facts about a third party contractor involved in a joint venture with an employer which it does not pass on to the insured employer, who may be arranging a joint names policy, where knowledge of such facts would affect its decision to take out the insurance. The most important aspects of the principle relating to the duty imposed on the insured are:

(a) to disclose all facts known to the insured that are material; and
(b) not to make a statement that amounts to a misrepresentation of a material fact.

Such non-disclosure or misrepresentation would enable the insurer to avoid the contract. Claims already settled will therefore need to be repaid and a refund of the premium will be required. However, the insurer will not be entitled to damages.

The insured must disclose all material facts which lie within his knowledge, including those material facts which the insured ought in the ordinary course of its business to know or have known. The test as to whether a fact is material is whether it *might* (but not would) influence the judgement of a prudent insurer in deciding whether to accept the risk and at what level to fix the premium. Many facts are obviously material to the risk, for example, where the subject matter is exposed to a higher than normal degree of risk, as with the construction of the Channel Tunnel and/or Channel Tunnel Rail Link, where construction techniques are pushing engineering practices to their limits and where the nature of the project involves new hazards for the construction teams. Claims experience is also regarded as material.

Duration of the duty of disclosure

As a general rule, the proposer is not only under a duty to disclose material facts during the negotiations leading up to the formation of the insurance contract but also upon the renewal of such insurance, since the renewal is a new contract. The contract is concluded when offer and acceptance coincide, which depends on the formation procedure adopted. The relevant date for a Lloyd's policy is when the slip is initialled by the underwriter. A contract initiated by a proposal or other application will be concluded when the insurer accepts the proposal, although the parties may postpone commencement of the contract, for example, until the first premium is paid.

In the context of construction contracts, however, the common law position is often modified by an express provision for the insured to notify the insurers of any material change in the risk or any other material factors affecting the risk during the term of the contract. This is due to the enormous practical significance where any changes to the building risks are involved. A failure on the part of the insured to comply with this condition renders the contract voidable from the date of the breach at the insurer's option, so the insured will need to ensure that it has adequate systems in place, and exercises necessary supervision throughout the construction project, to enable compliance with the rule.

In this context, any material change in the risk would include, for example, an extension of activities or any other material factors affecting the risk during the currency of the contract, for example, any defects or change in working conditions on a construction project which arise to render the risk more than usually hazardous. Accordingly, this is a very onerous duty on those involved with the construction at least for the duration of the project, and in relation to a latent defects policy which may be taken out after completion, for up to ten or twelve years.

1.6 Misrepresentation

As part of their duty of good faith, the parties must not only make accurate statements, but must also ensure that accurate answers are provided to questions. The common law duty is enacted in s.20(1) of the Marine Insurance Act 1906:

> 'Every material misrepresentation made by the assured or his agent to the insurer during negotiations for the contract, and before the contract is concluded, must be true. If it be untrue the insurer may avoid the contract'.

Misrepresentation includes making statements which are true, but which by reason of their being incomplete are misleading (*Aaron's Reefs* v. *Twiss* [1896] AC 273). If a statement is untrue the insurer is still entitled to avoid the contract; it does not matter that the insured thought that the statement was true when it was made. However, where the insured qualifies the statement, adding that it is true to the best of the insured's knowledge and belief, then some protection may be afforded provided that the insured believed the statement to be true and the belief was reasonable (*Wheelton* v. *Hardisty* [1857] 8 ExB 232 (Exch Ch)).

If the contract provides that the truth of the statements is a condition precedent to the insurer's liability, then 'reasonable belief' will not assist and the insurer will not be liable under the contract. The truth of statements made by the insured in the proposal, and any other placing information, will often be made a condition precedent to liability under the insurance contract and incorporated as part of the contract. This means that the accuracy of such statements is effectively guaranteed so that even breach of a minor term will enable the insurer to avoid the contract.

1.7 Indemnity

It is a fundamental principle that the insured can only recover what it has lost, so it is an implied term of the insurance contract that it will provide no more than indemnity. There are three exceptions to this: first, relating to life policies (not discussed here), secondly, in relation to valued policies whereby the parties agree at the outset the value of the insured subject matter, and thirdly where a surplus is available following a subrogated claim.

1.8 Proximate cause

The principle of proximate cause implied in a contract of insurance requires an insured to show that the loss was caused by an insured peril. The proximate cause means the effective, dominant or real cause (*Symington & Co.* v. *Union Insurance of Canton Limited* [1928] 45 TLR 181) and will be a question of fact in each case. Application of the principle depends whether the question is

(a) was the loss caused by an insured peril?, or
(b) was loss caused by an excepted cause?

The principle may be modified or excluded by the contract.

1.9 Subrogation rights

Another fundamental principle of insurance is that under a contract of indemnity, and following payment of a claim to the insured, the insurers have the right to be placed in the position of the insured to pursue rights and remedies against third parties. This obviously puts them in an advantageous position compared with others who may suffer a consequential or economic loss as a result of a situation in which they had no direct contractual relationship. However, insurers have no subrogation rights against the insured, who is not a third party – one of the reasons why standard forms of contract require construction insurance to include all contracting parties as joint insured.

However, it may not be possible to obtain joint insured status. For instance, this frequently happens when a contractor is undertaking fit-out works in an existing building, insured by a party other than the client. It is possible that the insured, likely to be the landlord, may be prepared to request the insurers to waive subrogation rights but would certainly not be willing to allow a contractor to have joint insured status. This is an issue which is frequently causing problems as both insurers and insured become reluctant to waive subrogation rights, leaving the client in breach of contract unless the issue has been addressed at an early stage. Although a tenant reimbursing the landlord with the premium is likely to have some protection, either under the lease or as a result of the decision in *Mark Rowlands Ltd* v. *Berni Inns Ltd* [1986] 1 QB 211 (CA), the tenant's contractors will have no such protection. In those circumstances, it may be necessary to extend the public liability cover to include damage to the existing building, something that would not normally be required if the standard terms of the contract were complied with.

1.10 Insurer solvency

A number of substantial construction risk insurers have suffered financial problems in the past few years. Many well-known names, including the Municipal Mutual, The Builders Accident, Reliance and the Independent Insurance Company have entered into some form of insolvency proceedings. Internationally there have been many more examples, both of direct insurers and of reinsurers. More are anticipated in the current economical climate.

Although the insured will not have any relationship with reinsurers, failure of the reinsurance arrangements will have a substantial effect on the ability of the direct insurer to meet claims.

It is important to monitor the ongoing solvency of insurers. Public liability claims often emerge some years after the project has been completed and the subsequent failure of an insurer covering the risk during the contract period can expose the insured to an uninsured loss or, at best, considerable uncertainty as to whether any funds will be available from the insolvency to meet the claim. On the other hand, a court will not decide liability on the basis of the available insurance protection, although the provision in the Woolf Reforms allowing the court to demand details of insurance do indicate a worrying potential move in that direction. In the case of professional indemnity insurance, which has to be kept in force for the whole period of liability under the contract of

1.1 The planning system
1.2 Financing the project
1.3 Public sector projects
1.4 Public/private partnerships
1.5 Tender process
1.6 Construction contracts
1.7 Construction insurance

collateral warranty – being on a claims made basis, the situation is equally vulnerable. Only careful monitoring of the cover for the whole potential period of liability will allow the beneficiaries, who may well not be the direct insured, to attempt to make alternative arrangements prior to a claim situation arising.

1.11 Due diligence

The importance of thorough due diligence cannot be overstated. This is sometimes undertaken to satisfy a bank when a transaction is undertaken but is rarely followed up to check that any policy subject to renewal has indeed been maintained on at least the same terms as the original. Most parties involved in the construction process will have obligation to maintain insurance in a fairly detailed format, failure to do so will not only lead to a potential breach of contractual duties but, more importantly, may leave an uninsured exposure which could be disastrous to the long term financial viability of the project. The failure of an insurance company is only one area of concern. Others will be the reduction in the extent of cover or the increase in the underlying excess which could be imposed by insurers or chosen by the insured party in order to save costs. Not knowing what the cover is until a serious claim occurs could prove very expensive to the party at risk – often not the party arranging the actual cover.

2 TYPES OF INSURANCE

Construction insurance cover will be provided by either a single project policy, an annual policy or a combination of both. A single project policy provides cover for the whole or part of a specific construction project. An annual policy covers all relevant turnover during the period of insurance. There are various classes of policy that construction contracts normally require including liability policies (employers' liability and public liability), material damage policies, and consequential loss policies.

Care should be taken when analysing indemnity and insurance clauses under contracts to make sure they dovetail (see *Scottish Special Housing Association* v. *Wimpey Construction UK Limited* followed by *Scottish & Newcastle plc* v. *GD Construction (St Albans) Limited* [2003] EWCA Civ 16 which related to an IFC 84 Contract, and contractor's indemnity limited by insurance provisions.

Another recent case is *Tesco* v. *Constable & Others* which highlighted that indemnity clauses need to be agreed with insurers if the liability they impose extends beyond the normal scope of Public Liability insurance. In this case Tesco were undertaking the construction of a supermarket with part of the works being the construction of a tunnel for the railway passing through their site with subsequent building above. Part of the tunnel collapsed and the railway had to be closed for over seven weeks. Two indemnities were involved – one to Railtrack the owners of the nework and one to Chiltern Railways who were the train operator. The Public Liability insurers met the claim in respect of the indemnity to Railtrack but did not provide indemnity in respect of the contractual liability to Chiltern Railways as no damage had been incurred to their property; their losses were purely of a consequential or economic nature, not just for the period of closure but for the subsequent reduction in passenger revenue. This distinction between losses flowing from property damage and pure economic losses is one that affects the need for specific insurance in respect of latent defects (see section 5).

2.1 Liability policies

The principal types of liability policy are employers' liability, public liability and professional liability. These policies are designed to cover the insured's legal liability to third parties (i.e. liability to persons who are not a party to the insurance contract) subject to certain exceptions. The employer's liability policy covers the liability of an employer to its employees (i.e. those persons under a contract of service or apprenticeship to the employer) for personal injury or disease arising out of or in the course of their employment on the project. The public liability policy provides an indemnity against personal injury claims by the public (other than employees) and property damage claims by any third party, including employees. Professional liability insurance (PI) covers those professionals such as architects, engineers, surveyors and other design-related consultants involved with the construction project, against claims of professional negligence. Large contractors, particularly those engaged in design and build works, carry one annual policy which covers activities on several sites, and which covers several subsidiaries of works of varying types.

Strictly an insurer is not liable to pay under a liability policy until the loss has been incurred and ascertained although insurers take an interest earlier than this in establishing liability under the policy. The loss may be established as a result of a bona fide settlement with a third party or a result of an arbitrators award/judgment of the court (see *Pilkington UK Limited* v. *CGU Insurance plc* [2004] EWHC Civ 23).

In addition, it should be noted that a global settlement between a contractor and an employer, which brought into account issues that were not definitively evidenced was not sufficient for an insurer on its own to conclude that those issues led to a reasonable settlement, as extrinsic evidence would need to be deduced to prove liability of insurers under the policy. (See *Lumbermans Mutual Casualty Co.* v. *Bovis Lend Lease Ltd* [2004] AER 36).

Environmental impairment insurance

Following the introduction of new legislation regarding environmental impairment, property owners, contractors, tenants and funders may all find themselves liable for remediation costs even if they did not cause the contamination, did not have an interest in the land when it occurred and, indeed, have not been negligent.

The standard public liability policy will cover liability for personal injury or damage to property resulting from pollution or contamination provided it is caused by a sudden unintended and unexplained happening. In addition, the cost of removing or cleaning up such contamination will only be covered in the same circumstances.

The insurance market is willing to provide cover for gradual pollution in a variety of ways. However, all the options are likely to require detailed site investigation and, possibly, monitoring of the construction process. The cover is usually transferable to future owners and funders and will therefore give comfort to those involved on a long-term basis. It is also possible for funders to arrange contingency protection to protect their interest, provided that all available remedies against other parties have been exhausted.

Product liability insurance

The standard public liability cover is likely to exclude liability arising out of the failure of work undertaken or products and services provided by the insured party to perform as intended. It is therefore necessary to specifically extend the cover to include product liability insurance giving protection in respect of injury or death and damage to third party property arising from a defective product.

Legal Indemnity insurances

These are a group of policies with similar intent which may not be required for every development. However when they are, they are vital to insure that the insured event

1.1 The planning system
1.2 Financing the project
1.3 Public sector projects
1.4 Public/private partnerships
1.5 Tender process
1.6 Construction contracts
1.7 Construction insurance

does not effect the financial outcome of the project. Two of particular interest are Defective Title and Rights of Light policies.

Defective title insurance has been in existence for many years. It is called into play when there is some concern about the title of the site to be developed – often the case when this comprises of a number of separate parcels of land which often have either gaps or question marks over ownership. The insurers will provide indemnity in respect of any claim by a party alleging rights over land in question which can lead to the payment of damages, the increase in costs associated with change of plans needed to accommodate the challenge and the consequential losses that may flow from that or even the termination of the project entirely. The cover may also be purchased if there is a restrictive covenant on the site; for instance an old property, previously owned by a religious institution, may forbid the sale of alcohol but the planned new supermarket will certainly be doing that. The beneficiaries may be untraceable or no longer in existence, but the prudent developer will arrange cover to insure that at least the legal costs of defending the claim are met even if no damages can be justified.

Rights of light had a resurgence of interest with two recent cases – *Regan* v. *Paul Properties DPF No. 1 Limited* [2006] and *Tamares (Vincent Square) Limited* v. *Fairpoint Properties (Vincent Square) Limited* [2006]. In the former, the developer was instructed by the court to demolish part of the new project in order to restore the light to an acceptable level to his neighbour. In the second the building was allowed to remain but the developer had to pay a substantial part of his anticipated profit to the affected landowner. The rights of light policy would meet all the costs associated with these outcomes together with the legal costs incurred in reaching a settlement.

In both these types of insurance the underwriters play a very active role in analysing the legal documentation and often appointing their own professional consultants to advise on the risk exposure. They may demand that certain action is taken to either protect their position or to flush out potential beneficiaries. Only after they are satisfied that these steps have been taken will they be willing to issue a policy. In reality this is effective risk management and insurers cannot be expected to meet the costs of a claim which, given the circumstances, is a certainty.

2.2 Non-negligent damage – JCT Clause 21.2.1 (previously known as Clause 19.(2)a)

The cover required under this clause reflects the liability of the employer in tort for damage to third party property, when this does not flow as a result of the negligence of the contractor. This legal principle was established in 1958 following the case of *Gold* v. *Patman and Fotheringham*. The insurance required under the contract follows damage by certain specified risks: collapse, subsidence, heave, vibration, weakening or removal of support, or lowering of groundwater. Once again, the appendix to the contract states the limit of indemnity which is required. This must be considered separately to the public liability risk and indeed the cover may not be necessary at all, if working in a greenfield site.

Wherever possible, the cover should be arranged with the same insurers who cover the contractor's public liability risk. This will avoid any delay in settlement of a claim while different insurers dispute which has the effective policy.

2.3 Material damage policies

This type of policy covers loss or damage to property in which the insured has an insurable interest, either during the ownership or possession or contract to acquire that property. The material damage policy only covers loss or damage to the property specified. A contractor's all risks (CAR) policy is a material damage policy.

Damage to the contract works (i.e. the building, factory, road, bridge, etc.) may also include machinery and electrical plant while being installed.

Cover may be provided for:

(a) contract works including temporary works;
(b) construction plant – e.g. cranes, scaffolding, while in the course of construction or while in storage on site;
(c) plant erection – loss/damage to construction plant while being erected or dismantled on site;
(d) goods in transit – loss or damage to contract works materials during transit and incidental storage off site;
(e) damage to employees' property (other than contract works).

Cover is generally available for the period when the contractor is on site and stops at completion of works, i.e. extends to defects during the defects liability period. It does not embrace cover for completed works or structures.

2.4 Composite and combined policies

Contractors frequently have a combined policy, covering both the liability and material damage risks referred to above. This is more common for the smaller construction companies. The policy is divided into sections covering the usual types of liability, i.e. employers' liability, public liability and loss or damage to the contract works, construction, plant and equipment, machinery, etc., usually known as contractor's all risk or CAR.

Composite policies may include extra cover for consequential loss and possibly a degree of professional insurance indemnity cover for architects, engineers and professional advice given by a design and build contractor. However, these insurances may need to be arranged separately.

Composite policies have the following advantages over separate policies:

(a) they can be significantly less expensive in terms of premiums and discounts;
(b) only one proposal form is required;
(c) as only one policy is issued, a single renewal notice and renewal premium is required; and
(d) only one declaration of turnover for the purposes of adjusting the premium is required.

2.5 Difference in conditions method (DIC)

The DIC method is normally only effected by contractors in certain circumstances where the employer has arranged project insurance (see below) and involves extending the four main policies – CAR, PI, employers' liability and public liability by closing any gaps in cover. A shortfall in cover may exist where the policy arranged by the employer is limited in scope, a deductible or excess applies to any claim made under the policy, levels of indemnity are inadequate, etc., and where such limitations on cover are not acceptable to the contractor, perhaps because its usual cover is more extensive or the contract insurance requirements have not been met. A risk assessment will be required to determine what additional cover is needed.

The DIC method involves treatment of the conventional policies as a primary layer with the limits of indemnity they provide being used as an excess, and generally results in a variety of insurance arrangements, for example:

(a) public liability cover in excess of the contractual requirement
(b) additional cost of working; this would cover, for example, following a loss, additional plant, machinery, etc., required by the contractor to complete the project on time to meet contractual requirements
(c) marine and transport insurance
(d) products liability insurance
(e) non-negligent liability and damage insurance
(f) differences in excess limits.

DIC cover is not required where the employer has already arranged adequate insurance. There may be a false saving if the employer believes that the contractor should take out DIC cover for the additional risks, because the contractor could possibly pass the cost back as part of the overall project cost.

2.6 Project insurance

Comprehensive project insurance (sometimes referred to as 'wrap-up' or 'overall' insurance cover) provides an all-embracing insurance policy, as an alternative to requiring every participant in the project to arrange its own separate insurance policy for its part of the project and its own plant and equipment. Project insurance is a combined insurance policy arranged by the employer (although the contractor retains its contractual responsibilities and liabilities) frequently in the joint names of the employer and all contractors. Project insurance is usually limited to conventional risks covering CAR and public liability and does not generally include professional indemnity for the professional design teams, as this is a class of insurance written in a smaller, specialized insurance market, or employees' liability cover.

However, some insurance companies do provide a wider CAR project policy to include cover for architects, consulting engineers and quantity surveyors. The policy can then provide for design damage cover, so that the professionals referred to above are covered not only for their site activities but also for the office work involved in the design of the project. The policy only covers damage to the works caused by negligence (not defects without such damage) which arises during the construction period (not for any period thereafter). Although the cover is convenient, many underwriters load the premium rates and levels of excess of CAR insurance arranged by the employer because the employer's insurers do not know the identity of all the contractors from the inception of the project and therefore have no basis to rate that aspect of the risk.

If the CAR cover is insufficient, for example, certain risks are expressly excluded, the contractor will have to take out its own policy to cover these supplemental risks. The willingness of insurers to add a public liability section to the CAR policy varies. Some contractors have a long-standing relationship with their insurers and prefer to continue to arrange works insurance. However, significant advantages for such project insurance include:

(a) inclusion of defective design risk in the same policy, which overcomes settlement delay problems (due to the necessity of establishing the cause of loss or damage) and prevents the design team from being isolated from the employer
(b) in large contracts with many contractors, avoidance of consideration of various policies and consequential delay and possibly dispute between insurers, which would otherwise result in very complex settlement arrangements

(c) premium saving due to reduced administrative and other overheads of brokers, insurers and reinsurers. Premium is also saved due to the elimination of double insurance which necessarily involves payment of more than one premium. The cost can be assessed before the insurance is taken out
(d) the gap created by some insurers by separating the employer's and contractors' risks which they insure, can be eliminated without issuing a second CAR and public liability policy
(e) inconvenience caused by any dispute between the parties involved in a loss, damage or liability claim is avoided
(f) uninsured risks in large projects, where there are or could be many separate insurance policies are avoided, and
(g) special covers can be incorporated into the programme, for example:
    (i) the cost of completing outstanding works,
    (ii) loss of anticipated profit/income by employer, and
    (iii) end of term covers
(h) convenience.

The insurance market for construction projects changed dramatically after the New York tragedy of September 2001. This brought to an end the era of falling rates and intense competition and heralded a period when the emphasis is on a return to sensible rating in order to rebuild balance sheets. The reinsurers, who had been very concerned about underwriting trends prior to 2001, have exercised their muscle to encourage this. The construction industry has suffered worse than average claims experience. Insurers have reduced their capacity for what is often high-risk business and in many cases they have become risk averse and been unwilling to write construction business at all.

A shortage of underwriting skills in the market has not helped. All this means that the availability of cover cannot be assumed. Insurance clauses in contracts should reflect what is available now rather than what has been written in the past.

2.7 Annual policies

Annual policies (sometimes called floaters or declaration policies) enable the insured to maintain cover on an annual basis to provide cover for all projects undertaken during the term of the insurance. The insured is required to declare its annual turnover (together with details of any claims experience) at renewal.

Cover is provided for the contractor and usually also the employer and subcontractors, for losses in connection with the work described in the policy.

Cover is provided for all risks and within stated limits not usually more than £25–30 million per contract. The insurer effectively waives its right to specific information for each contract. Furthermore, the insurer has given up any right to decline a particular risk and has accordingly waived disclosure because the insurer has no decision to make regarding acceptance of the risk providing that it falls within the categories of work agreed at inception. The policy will usually exclude cover for construction of dams, bridges, tunnels, etc., i.e. the more hazardous risks.

Reliance by either the client or the bank on a contractors annual policy brings additional risks. Generally those policies do not specifically include the interest of any client or their bank and very often the insurers are not even aware of the identity of those parties. It therefore follows that, in the event of insolvency or termination of the cover – including just non renewal – insurers would not know who to advise even if there were some contractual obligation that they should do so. The ultimate beneficiary could therefore find themselves uninsured and it is unlikely that the insurers would have any duty to attempt to trace them in order to appraise them of the situation.

2.8 Consequential loss policies insurance for liquidated damages

If damage occurs to the works as a result of an insured peril the contractor generally has a right to the extension of time necessary to carry out the repairs without incurring liquidated damages. This right applies even if the contractor is negligent in causing the damage. Clause 22.D, which was introduced into the 1986 amendments to the JCT insurance clauses, attempts to provide some insurance protection against the consequences of this extension. Unfortunately, the one insurer who was generally willing to provide this cover ceased trading, although other insurers may be able to accept relatively small risks.

Anticipated loss of income or profits

There is a fundamental proviso under consequential loss insurances that a successful claim for material damage must precede one for consequential loss. This is to ensure that the funds are available to repair the physical damage that gives rise to the consequential loss, thereby minimising the period of that loss. It is therefore important to ensure that the material damage and consequential loss covers are on the same basis – if they are not provided under the same policy. This is unlikely to be the case if the contractor insures the construction risk because the employer's consequential losses will not be of interest to the contractor, and in any event he would have no insurable interest in them.

The cover suggested by clause 22.D is likely to be highly unsatisfactory to the employer, as it does not give protection for the full period of the effects of damage to the contract works and certainly not for the amount which could be at risk. The range of exposures really needs to be carefully analysed for each project. For a developer, there is loss of rental and other income which may be exceeded by the continuing burden of interest on development finance. Terrorism damage could cause loss of attraction, especially to residential or retail property. Denial of access may cause considerable delays without any real damage to the works. For the owner occupier there is an additional range of possible losses linked to the delayed occupation of the property. These all need detailed consideration before cover can be placed to provide realistic protection.

2.9 Terrorism insurance

As a result of the bombing activities of the IRA, leading up to and including the St Mary Axe incident in the City of London on 10 April 1992, almost all UK insurers included an exclusion clause relating to damage caused by terrorist activities in all commercial insurances covering material damage and any subsequent consequential losses.

Originally most UK insurers agreed to provide the insured with a small amount of cover at no extra cost and, so far as shopping centres and other commercial enterprises are concerned, this was limited to £100 000 for each of the main types of cover which they would be likely to take out.

In order to take care of the shortfall, the insurance industry and the Government set up a mutual insurance company – Pool Reinsurance Company Limited, generally known as 'Pool Re'.

This provided the additional cover over and above the £100 000 for the full insured values and involved payment of a separate premium to Pool Re which proved both a cumbersome and inefficient mechanism.

It is not within the remit of this handbook to go into detail about terrorism insurance. Basic policy wordings now exclude terrorism cover and if it is required the cover has to be purchased as an extension to the policy. Some insurers deal with this by amending the policy whilst others issue a separate certificate. Either way the loss is settled by insurers in the same way as other claims. Insurers then protect themselves against large individual claims or a series of claims in any one year by purchasing reinsurance protection from the Pool Re. This involves payment by them of substantial reinsurance premiums to Pool Re and they recover these by charging their own rates to insured. This has introduced an element of price competition between insurers. It is also the intention that insurers should bear a larger part of the terrorism risk themselves as time goes on so the level at which they buy reinsurance protection from Pool Re increases year by year.

2.10 Flood insurance

Following the serious flooding of summer 2007, when the insurance market paid claims of over £3 billion in respect of 180,000 claims, there has been considerable concern about the future of flood insurance, especially high risk areas. Most contracts will call for flood to be insured and therefore any failure to do that will create serious difficulties both contractually and in terms of the protection given to the parties concerned.

In July 2008 the Association of British Insurers announced that they had reached agreement on a revised Statement of Principles with the government. In that Statement insurers agree to continue to provide flood insurance subject to the government meeting undertakings to improve flood defences and evolve an effective strategy for the protection against flood in the future. The trigger point for insurers is where a property is subject to the risk of flooding in more than a once in 75 year period. In those circumstances they need to see that protections are planned and being implemented by government. The Statement does not contain any undertaking to maintain cover if such protections are not planned.

It should be noted that the agreement only applies to residential and small business policies; it has a 5-year life but is reviewable annually and is subject to there being no 'external shock' such as the withdrawal of reinsurance.

Of particular concern to the construction industry is the new inclusion in the Statement, which has been in place in different formats since 2002, that it will not apply to any property built after 2009. The ABI are planning to issue guidance to developers to outline their requirements for making a property insurable in future. Those requirements will certainly inform the attitude of underwriters for properties which do not fall within the residential and small business category.

Following the 2007 floods, the government established a review headed by Sir Michael Pitt into the circumstances which led to the damage and to deliver ideas on how the risk could be better managed in future. Although the outcome of that review and the action taken to follow up on its recommendations fall outside the scope of this book, it is salutary to note the response supplied by the Council of Mortgage Lenders which stated that 'There is a long standing link between the insurability and mortgageability of a property'. 'If insurance is not available then it is unlikely that a property will be mortgageable'. That comment, although applied only in this context to flood insurance, does resonate with the advise to be diligent about any insurance cover required under contract. The parties entering into the contract have often only done so on the understanding that its conditions will be complied with – one of them being undoubtedly insurance and the protection it provides.

2.11 Insurance premium tax (IPT)

On 4 November 1993 the then Chancellor of the Exchequer announced that he was imposing a tax on most insurance premiums effective from 1 October 1994.

This has resulted in a taxation on gross premiums (i.e. premiums inclusive of commission) and applies to all those insurances normally associated with shopping centres. Originally the tax stood at 2.5% but this was increased to 4% from 1 April 1997 and now (2005) stands at 5%. Further increases can be expected in the future as the UK rate is considerably lower than that in many other EC countries.

The tax is under the care of HM Customs and Excise, and the tax point is the date on which the 'premium is written'. In insurance terms, this is the renewal date or any other date that the risk attaches to the insurance company rather than the date that the premium is debited.

All invoices received from either insurance companies or brokers must show the gross premium due together with a separate figure representing the IPT. There are severe penalties for both evasion and any irregularities discovered by HM Customs and Excise. It should be noted that the inspection fees for plant and machinery no longer incur IPT but now attract VAT.

2.12 Good management

Insurance is no substitute for vigilance and good management; these should go hand in hand. Indeed, as we have seen, to rely too heavily on an insurance policy may excuse the insurer from honouring a claim or generate an increase in the premium.

Insurance is not for amateurs, and the passing of uneventful years without claims should not lull the insured into forwarding a routine cheque in response to a renewal notice. The policy needs an overhaul every twelve months in order to make sure that it functions properly and efficiently.

At each overhaul the questions to be asked are:

- what are the insurance requirements of the contract?
- what additional cover would be prudent?
- what risks are to be insured and in what sums?

This should be followed by an examination of the policy documents to check that the intended cover has been secured and that the premium is competitive.

The responsibility for arranging the insurance may not lay directly with the party most at risk. This is no excuse for not taking an active interest in the cover and any claims.

2.13 Loss prevention

In response to the continued high level of claims being incurred by construction insurers, the Association of British Insurers combined with a number of other parties to publish a Joint Code of Practice on the protection from fire on construction sites and buildings undergoing renovation. This joint code has been through a series of revisions, which have seen it become industry standard practice.

It is therefore unlikely that any construction policy, either project-based or annually-based, will not have a condition requiring compliance with the joint code. This condition will give the insurers the right to suspend or cancel all cover after a specified date, which must be a minimum of 60 days after issuing an appropriate notice, if the required remedial action has not been completed.

In order to ensure compliance, the insurers have the right to inspect the contract site at all reasonable times. In the event that they decide to issue a notice of breach they must do so to the employer and the contractor. In the case of a project policy they will obviously have the identities of the parties concerned readily available, but if the cover is under a contractor's annual policy the service of notices may not be so easily achieved. It should be noted that if the construction risk cover is suspended it is almost certain that the terrorism insurance will also be affected.

3 CONSTRUCTION INSURANCE PROVISIONS UNDER TRADITIONAL BUILDING CONTRACTS AND CIVIL ENGINEERING CONTRACTS

3.1 Traditional building contracts

Under a traditional building contract such as the JCT 98 family of contracts there are usually two important sections (apart from the definitions) that are relevant to insurance. The first relates to the indemnity provisions, and the second to the insurance provisions that follow it. In broad terms, the contractor is responsible for, and will usually indemnify, the client against liabilities (whether under the contract, statute or common law) in relation to personal injury or death caused by the works. In addition, the contractor will usually be similarly liable and responsible for loss or damage to property arising from the carrying out of the works.

There usually follows in the building contract an obligation in relation to insurance of the works either for the contractor to take out construction all risks insurance for the works itself in the joint names of the employer and the contractor, or for the client to take out such insurances in the joint names of the contractor and the client. How each option is decided will be based on the requirements of client or contractor, the cost of premiums offered to each, or the type of building that is being insured and the practicalities of allowing several insurances to apply to a single building. For example, if the employer carries out building insurance in relation to the shell and core, and the works which relate to the fitting out, it would be more practical for the employer to insure rather than the contractor, to avoid the danger of having too many policies in relation to one building.

The provisions would then go on to describe the basis of all risks insurance, the type of risks and the definition of loss or damage.

It is also common for the construction all risks insurance arrangements to lie alongside professional indemnity insurance carried by the professional consultants at the request of the client. Alternatively, a projects insurance policy can be procured (see Section 2.6 above) which wraps all the risks up together, including the risks associated with professional indemnity insurance.

Design and build contractors will be expected to carry professional indemnity insurance alongside CAR insurance in any event because of their designer's liability.

The JCT did publish the Major Project form of contract in 2003. This takes a radically different view about insurance and requires that the actual policy wordings are appended to the contract rather than some abbreviated description of what cover is required. This approach echoes the requirements of the Financial Services Authority in demanding 'contract certainty at exception' for insurance. Unfortunately, it does not appear that the form has been widely used and indeed there was considerable concern that the revised insurance regime, however laudable, could not be complied with in practice. Obviously that would be the case for any contract lasting more than a year where annual policies were involved – as would also be the case for a design and build contractors Professional Indemnity insurance.

1.1 The planning system
1.2 Financing the project
1.3 Public sector projects
1.4 Public/private partnerships
1.5 Tender process
1.6 Construction contracts
1.7 Construction insurance

3.2 Civil engineering contracts

The standard civil engineering contract is now the ICE 7th Edition being a measurement version issued in September 1999 by the Institution of Civil Engineers, Association of Consulting Engineers and the Civil Engineering Contractors Association.

The broad principles enunciated in relation to traditional building contracts are applicable under the ICE Terms and Conditions except that because the nature of the works are civil engineering biased, the choice of the employer or the contractor insuring does not exist.

The contractor is expected to take full responsibility for the care of the works and the materials, plant and equipment from the commencement of works until the works are completed. The contractor is obliged to rectify loss or damage to the works over which it has care.

The contractor is usually obliged to insure in the joint names of itself and the employer all the works other than in relation to the accepted risks as defined (this is similar to the accepted risks referred to in traditional contracts).

There is a similar provision in relation to indemnification by the contractor for death or injury to persons or loss or damage to property which is the contractor's responsibility under the ICE 7th with some suitable exceptions carved out.

4 PROFESSIONAL INDEMNITY INSURANCE (PI)

PI cover is usually taken out individually by the members of the project's design team to indemnify them against claims brought by the employer or by third parties for loss suffered as a result of professional negligence. PI cover includes a wide range of liabilities, therefore the negotiated insurance terms are central to the effective insurance of any construction project. Consequently, the insurance arrangements often represent a significant factor in the choice of consultants engaged and in the subsequent negotiations of their contracts of appointment.

It should be noted that this cover, unlike public and employers liability, is on a claims made basis. The policy in force when the claim is made against the consultant is the one which will respond, rather than the one in force when the negligent act is committed.

In the case of design and build contracts (e.g. JCT 98(WCD) and ICE Design and Construct), the contractor will also require PI to cover those aspects of the project normally undertaken by independent consultants (e.g. the architect or engineer).

4.1 The policy

The wording of the PI policy includes certain particular provisions.

(a) *Indemnity* In respect of any claim made against the insured during the period of the insurance as a direct result of any negligent act, error or omission in professional conduct of their business. Additional cover can be provided (for which additional premiums may be required) as follows:
  (i) fraud, dishonesty or infidelity of any past, present or future partner, director or employee of the firm;
  (ii) loss or damage or wrongful dealing with documents;
  (iii) libel and slander in respect of printed, typewritten and handwritten matters issued by the insured and oral utterances made or alleged to have been made by any partner, director or employee of the insured;
  (iv) costs incurred with the approval of insurers in connection with legal proceedings by the insured for the recovery of professional fees;

(v) costs, charges and expenses of legal representation of the insured at any proceedings for any duly constituted court or tribunal of enquiry or otherwise; and
(vi) compensation for court attendance.

(b) *Limits of liability* (which may include the insured's costs and expenses related to a claim incurred with the consent of the insurer).
(c) *Policy conditions* (see Section 4.3 below).
(d) *Exceptions* (see Section 4.4 below).

4.2 The cover

Cover provides indemnity against the consultant's legal liability for damages and costs in respect of claims for breach of professional duty by reason of any negligence, error or omission.

The usual policy wording will not provide indemnity in respect of breach of a 'fitness for purpose' obligation since its terms provide cover solely for 'negligent act, error or omission'. Thus, where the consultant has given an express or implied warranty that its design will be fit for the purpose required, there may be no cover for breach of that warranty. In the Court of Appeal case *Greaves & Co. (Contractors) Ltd* v. *Baynham Meikle* [1975] 3 All ER 99 if there had been a finding of liability for breach of warranty alone, a policy on the usual terms would not have covered the insured.

The usual legal and insurance interpretation of the words 'negligent act, error or omission' is that there has to be negligence and that the words 'error or omission' are to be interpreted only in the context of negligence. It can also be argued that not every loss caused by an omission or error is recoverable under a PI policy; it must be one which in principle could create liability and must not be a deliberate error or omission (*Wimpey Construction (UK) Ltd* v. *Poole* [1984] 2 Lloyd's Rep 499).

It is therefore important to ensure that the business and the work it carries out are properly described either in the policy or in the proposal. The precise terms of the liability covered will vary from policy to policy and the consultant will only be covered for liability falling within the description of the cover in the policy.

4.3 Policy conditions

There are a number of important conditions which commonly appear in professional indemnity insurance policies, for example, a Queen's Counsel Clause which provides that the insured should not be required to defend the claim unless a QC advises that this is likely to have a successful outcome. Usually the insurers exclude liability for penal, punitive, exemplary or aggravated damages, whenever identifiable as such.

4.4 Exceptions

The consultant, and indeed the client, should be aware of all the policy exclusions which will vary from policy to policy, but typical exceptions are:

- the excess
- a claim brought about by any dishonesty, fraud or criminal act on the part of the consultant
- debts incurred by the insured, failure to pay sums due and liabilities arising out of insolvency of the insured
- breach of obligations owed by the insured as employer to employees
- circumstances known to the insured on the effective date of the insurance

- claims against the insured as a result of dishonest, malicious or illegal acts of the insured or its employees
- any claim brought outside a specified geographical area (e.g. UK)
- libel and slander
- personal injuries caused to a third party, when they arise out of a breach of professional duty
- war and atomic radiation
- claims for consequential economic loss/loss of profit.

4.5 Choice of insurer

The consultant's choice of insurer may be of critical importance to an employer. Certain insurers have recently taken a more restrictive attitude towards the obligations permitted to be undertaken by their insured professionals, both in contracts of appointment and in the separate collateral warranties or duty of care deeds entered into for the benefit of third parties, and have attempted to reduce these obligations. This is usually done by the insurer requiring that its prior approval be given to any additional contractual obligations, outside an agreed standard contract undertaken by the insured, before they are covered by insurance.

4.6 The potential shortcomings of Professional Indemnity insurance

Most professional appointments will call for PI insurance to be maintained for a minimum period and a minimum limit of indemnity. That cover is often also required by collateral warranties to be passed to future owners funders or tenants. It backs up the indemnities given in respect of the professional duties of the consultant or design and build contractor.

However, insurance has limitations so far as those third parties are concerned; as identified above it is an annual policy, capable of change at any renewal, it is on a claims made basis and would cease should the party insured become insolvent as it is unlikely that any insolvency practitioner would maintain cover in force, despite contractual obligations to do so.

It should therefore be recognised by any third party intending to benefit from a PI policy that it is there to protect the party who caused their loss – the negligent consultant – rather than to give direct protection to the party who suffers the loss – the building owner, bank or tenant.

There have been a number of alternative PI insurance products available over the years most of them requiring the client to effect the cover and pay the premium. They all have the same fundamental flaw – they are still there to protect the negligent party and although it is of some comfort to know that the indemnity continues to have the backup of insurance it is nonetheless not cover upon which the aggrieved party can depend for direct protection, at least until negligence and quantum can be established.

It should also be noted that there have been problems with PI insurance required of contractors. Even if they have a design element to their work it is likely that they will only be able to obtain on an aggregate rather than each and every loss basis. Considerable care needs to be exercised to ensure that the aggregate amount is adequate and is maintained as such during the life of the indemnity. In addition, these D&B products are now likely to include the legal cost of defence within overall aggregate indemnity limit thereby reducing yet more of the amount available to pay damages.

4.7 Products Liability Insurance

Contractors and sub-contractors required to deliver PI insurance often counter that they cannot obtain it but offer Products Liability as an alternative. It is often stated that these provide the same protection but this is a fallacy. Products Liability is indeed another legal liability policy but it only covers death or injury to third parties or damage to third party property that arises from a defective product supplied by the insured party, the contractor or sub-contractor. It specifically excludes the costs of making good any defect and almost certainly will also exclude any inconsequential losses that arise from the defect so far as the client is concerned. As such it is therefore of no benefit to the client should you disregard it in considering what risk exposure there is to the design failure of any contractor or sub-contractor who is insured in this way.

5 LATENT DEFECTS INSURANCE

5.1 Type of policy

Latent defects insurance, sometimes referred to as building defects or inherent defects insurance has become increasingly popular since 1989 when several major UK insurers entered the market. More and more purchasers see it as a much better alternative to reliance on collateral warranties or the Contracts (Rights of Third Parties) Act 1999 and this is hardly surprising as it is a first party policy requiring insurers to pay valid claims without the need to prove negligence against a third party. The demand for the cover to be in place is often driven by lenders or tenants. For lenders it has the benefit of reducing risk because if the policy is in force there is much less likelihood of the borrower having to pay for expensive repairs and for tenants it reduces their potential liabilities under full repairing leases.

The basic cover indemnifies an insured against damage to the whole of a building caused by a latent defect in the structural parts (as defined) of the building. However it is most unusual and certainly unwise to buy just this basic cover. In practice most policies also automatically include indemnity against physical damage caused by water entering the building due to a defect in the weatherproofing envelope of the building at or above ground level or the waterproofing seal below the ground floor.

A more detailed explanation of the insurance protection is given in the paragraphs below but the basic cover available from the limited number of insurers prepared to issue policies does not vary much from one insurer to another. However, there are a number of pitfalls for the unwary that could result in the extent of cover being misunderstood or too much premium being paid so advice from an expert familiar with the class is advisable. The reluctance of many insurers to underwrite the cover is because of its long tail nature. The policy commences at practical completion of a new building and continues in force for up to 12 years. It cannot be cancelled and is assignable to new owners or lessees or anybody else acquiring an insurable interest.

Although latent defects cover may be taken out after the project is completed, this is inadvisable as it will cost a lot more, a higher deductible will usually apply and the market is limited. More importantly perhaps the benefits of the technical auditors referred to below will not be secured. It is far better if the decision to procure this insurance is taken before construction work commences. The insurer will appoint a firm of independent consulting surveyors or engineers to monitor the progress of construction and to liaise with the professional team. This independent firm are commonly referred to as the technical auditors. The insurance will be conditional on the technical auditor appointed being supplied with all necessary technical information. The insurers will require the employer to incorporate in the construction any of the auditor's recommendations as to its design, material or procedure, as these are likely to reduce the risk of post-completion problems. There is little evidence that the involvement of the auditors adds to the cost of the development and there are those who believe that a building is less likely to have latent defects if such a consultant has been involved. In fact this benefit does seem to be borne out by the loss experience of at least one insurer.

The technical auditors will ensure that not only is the structure designed to a reasonable standard but that it is constructed in accordance with the plans and good building practice. If the consultants refuse to pass any aspect of the work, damage arising from those aspects will be excluded from the policy. However, it is very rare for a policy to be issued with restrictions. Indeed, most consultants would see it as their role to try and make certain this does not happen.

5.2 The cost

The cost of latent defects insurance, with a standard excess, usually ranges from 0.65% to 1% of the total contract value, inclusive of the inspection service fee. However, cheaper terms, particularly when a high deductible is selected, have been known. If waivers of subrogation rights in favour of the contractors and professional team are required the premium element of the total cost will rise, usually by somewhere between 20% and 50%. It may be possible to recover either some or the entire additional premium from the beneficiaries.

5.3 Contents of the policy

The insured

The policy is often affected by the developer but is freely assignable to new owners, lessees or financiers and can be in one name or several names.

Policy cover

As mentioned above the basic policy covers physical damage to the property caused by a latent defect in the structural parts. The policy will also cover any remedial work essential to prevent actual collapse during the period of insurance, for example even if there is no physical damage to the premises but there is a latent defect in the structure which threatens its stability and strength.

A 'latent defect' is any defect in the structural works notified to the insurers during the period of insurance which is attributable to defective design or workmanship or materials and which was undiscovered at the date of issue of the certificate of practical completion.

The policy also provides cover against the cost of demolition and removal of debris, reasonable legal, professional or consultants' fees incurred in connection with such physical damage or threat of imminent instability (excluding fees solely incurred in preparing claims) and additional costs of repair or reinstatement following damage arising out of alterations in design, use or application of improved materials or improved or altered methods of working incurred solely in compliance with any building or other regulations.

It is important to appreciate that a latent defect alone will not constitute a claim. It has to cause actual physical damage, or there has to be the threat of imminent physical damage, before any claim can be made but the damage itself can be anywhere in the building. However, under the basic policy cover the damage to the building must arise from a latent defect in the structural works as defined in the policy. A typical definition reads as follows but they do vary and the variations are a factor to consider when comparing quotations:

> '(i) all internal and external load-bearing structures essential to the stability or strength of the Premises including but not limited to foundations, columns, walls, floors, beams; and
> (ii) all other works forming part of external walls and roofing but excluding moveable elements of external windows, doors, skylights and the like'.

The property insured includes all works forming part of the completed contract for which the certificate of practical completion and technical agent's certificate are issued. This includes, in addition to the above, all landlord's fixtures and fittings, permanent mechanical, electrical and other services necessary for the functioning of the building and external works immediately adjacent, for example drainage, road and car park surfaces, walls and landscaping.

Whilst the basic cover protects the whole building against damage caused by a latent defect in the structural works as defined it is possible to extend the policy to include other causes of damage.

Damage caused by a defect in the weatherproofing and waterproofing cover is usually but not always included as standard within the basic cover. As wall cladding and roofing is a major source of damage it is always best to include it. There is an exclusion of cover for the first twelve months after practical completion. Insurers take the view that the contractors should rectify defects in weatherproofing and waterproofing during that period.

The weatherproofing envelope will usually comprise roof coverings, skylights, external walls and cladding, external windows and doors (but excluding moveable elements) and the ground floor slab. The waterproofing envelope comprises those elements of the building below ground level that keep the damp out.

Some insurers now offer cover against damage to the building insured caused by a defect in the non-structural parts of the building. Non-structural parts are generally regarded as being all other parts of the building not included under the headings of structural, weatherproofing and waterproofing but excluding protective coatings, decorative finishes and floor coverings (but not permanent floor finishes).

Some insurers will also offer cover against damage caused by a defect in the mechanical and electrical services.

Mechanical and electrical services will usually comprise heating, ventilating and air conditioning systems and fresh and waste water systems, lifts and escalators, window cleaning equipment, electrical distribution systems (including fixed lighting), building management systems and building security equipment (including car park ticket machines and barriers and all types of electrical security doors). However, external services are excluded.

Period of cover

Cover used to be for ten years' duration but with more insurers prepared to offer twelve years this has become more common. Other policies may be arranged for only one year, for example, where a developer requires a short-term protection until transfer of the property to a long-term investor.

It may be possible for an interested party to buy an option for cover thereby allowing a long-term investor or tenant to take protection if required. This is done prior to the start of works, enabling the technical control to take place and avoiding the penal provisions which are charged for cover taken out after practical completion.

Obtaining cover

If an employer requires latent defects insurance it will contact its broker during the planning stage and provide details of site location, ground conditions, nature and design of the building and the contractors and professionals who will be engaged on the project. The insurer will require the employer to complete a proposal form.

Calculation of sums insured

Buildings

To begin with the insurers typically require the following values to be advised when the insurance is first proposed.

Structural works (including all types of cladding and floors)	£
Non-structural works not included in above (excluding M&E services)	£
M&E Services	£
External works & services	£
Total Contract Value	£
The approximate value of the waterproofing work	£
Amount to be included in the policy cover for site clearance and debris removal	£
Amount to be included in the policy cover for professional fees	£

These figures are then used to calculate an average rate for the basic cover (i.e. damage caused by defects in the structural works plus weatherproofing and waterproofing). The greater the proportion of the structural works to the total, the higher the average rate will be. The estimated premium payable for the basic cover is then calculated by applying the contract value, inclusive of site clearance, debris removal costs and fees, to this average rate.

If other cover is required, e.g. for non-structural works or M&E services, a separate and additional premium is added using the applicable rate and the appropriate value from above.

The value of the waterproofing works may not be required for premium calculation purposes. It will be entered in the policy as the maximum amount recoverable over the period of insurance in respect of waterproofing cover.

At the date of practical completion, insurers ask for the estimated cost of reinstatement of the property at that date inclusive of the cost of complying with European Union and Public Authorities Stipulations, site clearance, debris removal, professional fees and landscaping. This should be the same figure (i.e. the Declared Value) as is supplied for the annual fire and perils insurance The actual premium payable for the basic latent defects cover is then calculated using this figure and the above average rate.

If any of the costs incurred in the original construction, e.g. archaeological exploration, would not be repeated there would be no need to make allowances for them in the figure supplied at practical completion.

When comparing initial quotations for building defects insurance it is important to take account of how different insurers build into their policies adequate allowance for inflation during the ten or twelve year period of insurance.

Some insurers rely on index linking and/or regular reviews of sums insured and these may entail extra premium payments during the period of insurance.

Rent

The actual sum insured at practical completion should represent the annual rent receivable multiplied by the indemnity period selected. The premium will be based on this and the cover will be for the duration of the policy, usually ten or twelve years.

Again, care is needed because different insurers allow for rent inflation in different ways.

Other consequential losses

The basic cover offered by some insurers includes the cost of removing contents from the building whilst repairs of any defects are carried out. This is usually limited to a maximum £250 000 or 10% of the sum insured but may be increased on payment of additional premium.

Most insurers now offer a separate annual policy covering occupiers' business interruption and the sums insured would need to be assessed for each individual risk in the same way as they are for the tenants' usual all risks business covers.

Exceptions

The latent defects policy contains a number of reasonable exclusions, none of which appears unfair to the insured although the insured may require deletion or amendment in particular cases. Common examples include:

(a) faults, defects and errors of omission in the design, workmanship or materials of non-structural works;
(b) structural alterations, repairs, modification materially affecting the stability of the property (unless insurers have been informed, the policy endorsed and any additional premium paid);
(c) inadequate maintenance of structural works or abnormal use of the property;
(d) inadequate maintenance or abnormal use of the weatherproofing materials or any structural alterations, repairs, etc. which materially affect the weatherproofing;
(e) wilful acts, omissions or negligence of the insured;
(f) changing colour, texture, etc. or other ageing processes;
(g) nuclear exclusions;
(h) war, invasion, act of foreign enemy, hostilities, etc.;
(i) failure to carry out finishing operations after issue of the certificate of practical completion;
(j) substandard, unsatisfactory, etc. workmanship, design and materials notified to the insurers by the technical control referred to in the certificate of approval or the certificate of practical completion and not subsequently rectified and approved by the insurers;
(k) subsidence, heave or landslip from any cause unrelated to a latent defect (these risks will usually be covered under the building insurance);
(l) defects for which the insured's architect or engineers or building contractor are responsible and which are notified to the insured before the issue of the certificate of practical completion, unless subsequently rectified and accepted by the insurers;
(m) the insured's failure to repair damage or reinstate for which an indemnity is recoverable under the insurance unless the delay is due to reasons beyond the insured's control; and
(n) consequential or economic loss of any kind (although loss of rent and other consequential loss cover is available).

PART 2

Organizing an engineer's practice

Section editor: Jenny Baster
Group Legal Director, Arup

CHAPTER 2.1

Ways of operating

Richard Linsell and William Wastie
Addleshaw Goddard LLP

Louis Baker and Nigel Glover
Horwath Clark Whitehill LLP

1 SOLE PRACTICES

1.1 Nature

Where an individual carries on a business, other than through a limited company, on their own, they are called sole traders or sole principals. Given the absence of any other participator there are few formalities that need to be observed in setting up such a business (but it must comply with the Business Names Act 1985 and register with the appropriate taxation authorities, i.e. personal tax, NIC and VAT).

A sole principal is liable for all the obligations of a firm without limit of liability. While such firms are usually small, in some construction industry practices sole practitioners have sizeable businesses created by employing many professional staff. A problem often encountered with sole practices is succession. Selling such practices is not easy unless the principal is willing to commit to ensuring that the goodwill, which is usually very personal, is secured through the principal's continuing commitment to the successor practice.

1.2 Taxation

A sole practitioner may make two types of profit: income and capital. Both of these are taxable. Where the profits are recurrent on a periodical basis (e.g. trading, rent, interest), the sole practitioner will face a possible charge to income tax. Where profit derives from the disposal of an asset owned by the sole practitioner (e.g. the premises) a possible charge to capital gains tax may arise.

The profits of a business usually derive from the carrying on of a trade and will therefore be assessed to income tax under the Income Tax (Trading and Other Income) Act 2005 (ITTOIA). The net profit or net loss (the chargeable receipts of the trade less its deductible expenditure) is used by HM Revenue & Customs as a starting point for ascertaining the figure, which is taxable. If these profits have not been calculated in accordance with generally accepted accounting policies (GAAP), then the profits have to be recomputed onto a GAAP basis as a first step.

Receipts of the trade derive from the trading activity rather than from circumstances not directly connected with the trade. Receipts of the trade are only chargeable to income tax if they are of an income as opposed to capital nature. If something is purchased for the purpose of resale at a profit then the proceeds of sale will be of an income nature. Receipts of a capital nature will generally derive from the sale of an asset, which was purchased for the benefit, or use of the business on a more or less permanent basis rather than for resale.

In calculating taxable profit there must be deducted from income receipts of the trade any expenditure, which is of an income nature, which has been incurred wholly and exclusively for the purposes of the trade, and deduction of which, is not prohibited by statute (e.g. ITTOIA 2005, s.34). Capital expenditure is not deductible. For expenditure to qualify as income expenditure it must also have a quality of recurrence (e.g. electricity, rents, staff salaries, interest on borrowings, etc.) rather than being once and for all (e.g. the purchase of assets such as premises, vehicles or furniture). To be deductible, the expenditure must also have been incurred wholly and exclusively for the purposes of the trade, thus the expenditure cannot have a dual purpose, although some expenses are allowed to be apportioned for the purposes of income tax deduction.

Expenditure, which is not deductible in calculating profits because it is of a capital nature, may, nevertheless, qualify for income tax relief under a separate system. Under the Capital Allowances Act 2001 where expenditure is incurred on certain assets, notably the purchase of machinery and plant and (currently) the construction

Table 1 Assessment of profits for new businesses

Year of assessment	Accounting period ending in year of assessment	Basis of assessment
1st year	Irrelevant	Actual profits arising from date of commencement to 5 April following
2nd year	Less than twelve months	Pro rata profits for the first twelve months of trading
	Twelve months or more	Pro rata profits of the twelve-month period ending with the accounting date
	No relevant period	Actual profits of the tax year (pro rata)
3rd year	Twelve months or more	Pro rata profits of the twelve-month period ending with the accounting date

or acquisition of industrial buildings, an annual percentage of the capital expenditure will be allowed as a deduction from trading profits. However, the allowances for industrial buildings are to be phased out over the period 2008–2011.

For an established and ongoing business, income tax is assessed on the profits of the twelve-month accounting period, which ends in the tax year. There are, however, special rules for determining the assessable profits in the opening or closing years of a trade.

1.3 Opening years

When a business commences, the assessable profits in the first three years of trade will depend not only on the chosen accounting date, but also on the length of the opening years' accounting periods. Largely, profits will be assessable as shown in Table 1.

The only way to ensure a true matching of taxable profits with years of assessment is to employ a fiscal year accounting period, i.e. either a 5 April or 31 March year end. (Note that the HM Revenue & Customs will usually treat a 31 March year-end as coterminous with the tax year.) Such a year-end is also likely to simplify calculations, for example for loss claims in the opening years.

If a fiscal year accounting period is not used, some profits earned in the early years will be assessed to tax in more than one tax year. Therefore, in order to ensure that over the whole life of the business the profits earned equal the profits taxed, it is necessary to identify the 'overlap profits', i.e. the profits that are taxed twice. This overlap profit is then carried forward, and only relieved either when the business ceases to trade, on incorporation or the accounting period end is changed to a later date in the same fiscal year.

1.4 Closing years

Unless the final period of assessment is only the second year of assessment (in which case all profits are assessed on an actual pro rata basis), the basis period for the final year of assessment will be the profits arising in the period commencing with the day immediately following the end of the last assessed basis period and ending with the day of cessation. Should the final accounting period exceed twelve months straddling a complete tax year, the last two years of assessment are as follows:

- *penultimate year*: twelve months beginning immediately after the end of the basis period for the previous year, and

- *final year*: period beginning immediately after the basis period for the penultimate year, and ending with the date of cessation.

1.5 Payment of income tax

Under self-assessment, tax on income is payable in three instalments, being

(a) a payment on account due on 31 January in the year of assessment (based on 50% of the prior year total income tax liability)
(b) a second payment on account due on 31 July following the year of assessment (again based on 50% of the prior year total income tax liability)
(c) a balancing payment/repayment due 31 January following the year of assessment.

Interest will be charged on any amounts not paid by the normal due dates.

If the total income tax liability for a year is expected to be less than the total income tax liability of the previous year, an appropriate claim may be made to reduce the payments on account accordingly.

Once the income tax liability is established on the submission of the tax return the reduced payments on account are recomputed to 50% of the tax liability (unless the liability now proves to exceed that of the previous fiscal year). To the extent that the reduced payments on account subsequently prove inadequate interest is charged on the underpayments.

1.6 Trading loss relief

The calculation of receipts of the trade less expenditure (including capital allowances) may produce a loss. Various provisions in Income Tax Act 2007 (ITA) allow the taxpayer to deduct a trading loss from other income in order to provide relief from tax on that other income. There are restrictions if the trade has not been carried out on a commercial basis. Where the circumstances are such that relief could be claimed under more than one provision, the taxpayer may choose under which to claim. It may be that the taxpayer's loss is greater than can be relieved under just one of these provisions; if so, the taxpayer may claim as much relief as is available under one provision and then claim relief for the balance of the loss under any other available provision. Generally, the taxpayer will want to claim relief under whichever provision is best for cash flow; some allow a repayment of tax previously paid, while others allow avoidance of payment of tax which will become due in the future.

Start-up loss relief (s.72 ITA 2007)

If the taxpayer suffers a loss in any of the first four tax years of a new business, the loss can be carried back or deducted from any other income of the taxpayer in the three tax years prior to the tax year of the loss. This provision might be particularly useful to a person who starts a new business after being made redundant. While the new business becomes established, it may make losses, but the practitioner may be cushioned by claiming back from the HM Revenue & Customs some income tax paid during the previous years' employment. This would be especially beneficial if the income tax, which was paid, and can now be claimed back, was at the higher rate of 40%.

Carry-across relief for trading losses generally (s.64 ICTA 2007)

A trading loss which arises in an accounting period, which does not match a tax year, is treated as a loss of the tax year in which the accounting period ends. The loss can be carried across to be deducted from any income or chargeable capital gains of that tax

2.1 Ways of operating
2.2 Working with others
2.3 Working internationally
2.4 The engineer's appointment
2.5 Collateral warranties
2.6 Indemnity insurance
2.7 Employment law
2.8 Information technology

year and/or of the preceding tax year. If the taxpayer claims to set the loss against income or chargeable capital gains of that tax year and they are not sufficient fully to absorb the loss, the balance of the loss can be set against income or chargeable capital gains of the preceding tax year.

If the taxpayer claims this relief, the loss must be set against all available income, which may result in the taxpayer having no income left against which to set the taxpayer's personal relief(s); this would mean that the taxpayer's personal relief(s) for that year were wasted, since there is no provision for personal reliefs to be carried to another tax year.

Carry-forward relief for trading losses generally (s.83 ITA 2007)

If a taxpayer suffers a trading loss in any year of a trade, the loss can be carried forward indefinitely to be deducted from subsequent profits of the same trade, taking earlier years first. This has the disadvantage for the taxpayer, compared with relief under s.64, that he or she must wait until future profits of the trade would become taxable before the taxpayer benefits from the loss relief. Also, this section is more restrictive than s.64 in that it only provides for the loss to be set against profits, which the trade produces – it does not provide for relief against other sources of income or against capital gains.

Carry-back of terminal trading loss (s.89 ITA 2007)

If a taxpayer suffers a trading loss in the final twelve months in which he or she carries on the trade, this loss can be carried back to be deducted from trading profit in the three tax years prior to the final tax year. The taxpayer may thus reclaim from the HM Revenue & Customs tax, which he or she has paid. Note that s.89 does not allow relief against non-trading income or against capital gains.

Carry-forward relief on incorporation of business (s.86 ITA 2007)

If the taxpayer has suffered trading losses which have not been relieved, and transfers the business to a company wholly or mainly in return for the issue to himself or herself of shares in the company, the losses can be carried forward and deducted from income received from the company, such as a salary as a director or dividends as a shareholder. In order to be 'wholly or mainly in return for the issue of shares', at least 80% of the consideration for the transfer must consist of shares in the company.

1.7 National Insurance Contributions

A sole practitioner will pay two types of National Insurance Contributions (NICs), i.e. Class 2 and Class 4. Class 2 NIC is a weekly contribution (£2.20 for 2007/08), and Class 4 NIC is calculated as a percentage of profits between certain levels (8% on annual profits between £5225 and £34 840 for 2007/08 and 1% on profits in excess of £34 840).

On becoming a sole practitioner, a professional should contact their local HM Revenue & Customs office to make arrangements for payment of the Class 2 NIC. The Class 4 NIC, on the other hand, will form part of the total income tax liability for the year, and will be collected under the normal payment arrangements detailed above.

1.8 Summary of sole practice

A sole practice is a very simple means of operation. Accounts are very straightforward, and these are not subject to audit or other statutory requirement. Administration and administration costs should, therefore, be minimal, and the business results are not available for public inspection. Subject to tax adjustments to profits, the professional will be taxed on the profits the business earns, whether amounts are drawn and used personally by the professional or not. National insurance costs are relatively low, and the proprietor can withdraw funds from the business without accounting for PAYE or becoming involved in any other employee administration (assuming that no one else is employed in the business). This means of operating is also fairly flexible, in as much as when the business grows, the proprietor can take on partners to work as a partnership, or incorporate into a company or limited liability partnership at a later date.

However, a sole practitioner may encounter difficulty in raising finance, find that professional indemnity insurance is more expensive than may otherwise be the case or, indeed, find that some businesses are unwilling to contract with him or her, simply because the business appears to the outside world to be small scale, or because the practitioner is not incorporated. The biggest disadvantage of all though is, of course, unlimited liability. If the business fails, the professional will be liable for the business' debts, to the full extent of his or her personal wealth.

2 PARTNERSHIP

2.1 Nature

There are three types of business structure referred to as partnerships:

(a) general partnerships in which the partners have unlimited liability and are jointly and severally liable for the debts of the firm. These are governed by the Partnership Act 1890 but it is advisable to have a partnership agreement, which overrides much of this Act and regulates fully the relationship between partners
(b) limited partnerships in which limited partners have limited liability up to the amount of their capital contribution but which must have at least one general partner carrying on the business who cannot have limited liability. Limited partnerships are governed by the Limited Partnerships Act 1907
(c) limited liability partnerships (LLPs), where all the members (other than those who could personally be liable for negligence or breach of contract) enjoy limited liability and can participate in the business. These are a new form of business vehicle created by the Limited Liability Partnerships Act 2000, which came into force, together with the Limited Liability Partnerships Regulations 2001, on 6 April 2001. Although retaining some of the characteristics of a partnership, an LLP is a new body corporate, having its own separate legal personality. Its members are technically identified as 'members' rather than 'partners' and it is only for taxation purposes that, despite its legal title, an LLP is treated as a partnership.

With effect from December 2002 the rule that partnerships may not consist of more than 20 partners unless they were given a specific exemption under company law or were exempt by virtue of their profession has been repealed.

There is no set procedure for the formation of a partnership. A partnership may be established orally or in writing. If two people come together and carry on a business with a view to making profits they will create a partnership governed by the Partnership Act 1890. Because that Act is structured to govern smaller partnerships based on equality which have to be dissolved when any member leaves, it is most unwise for a professional practice not to draw up a formal partnership agreement and there are many modern cases on the difficulties which arise on the final distribution of the assets of a business which operates as a 'partnership at will' (i.e. without a partnership agreement).

A partnership agreement is often evidenced by:

- a partnership deed
- an agreement signed by the partners
- an unsigned document drafted by one partner and adopted and acted on by the others
- an informal document initialled by the partners and intended only to form instructions for a formal document.

A partnership agreement should at the least cover:

- the commencement date
- the firm name including its protection
- place and nature of business
- the capital required, whether it is provided in terms of assets or cash, how much each partner is contributing and whether interest is payable on each contribution (and possibly the question of future increases in contributions if such increases are anticipated)
- the division of income profit and losses if such are not to be shared between all of the partners equally. Profits may be split in a variety of ways. For example, many partnerships have fixed percentage shares that have to be renegotiated from time to time; other practices may operate a strict 'lockstep' system, whereby a partner obtains an escalating number of shares in the firm over, for example, a 5–10 year period. Alternatively, the parties may pay themselves a notional salary, with the balance being split in a way which reflects merit and/or seniority
- details of the firm's banking account and the drawing of cheques, particularly the amount that each partner can withdraw from the business from time to time in respect of their shares of the profits. An agreement may state a monthly limit and stipulate the consequences of exceeding the stated limit
- the procedures for drawing up and adopting accounts including whether all partners must sign them
- particulars of ownership of assets and increases or decreases in asset values and the shares each of the partner has in these with particular attention to goodwill and any freehold premises that may be used in the business
- work input of each partner and their role in the business
- the provision of insurance and in particular purchasing any minimum professional indemnity cover required by a regulator and the provision of cover to retired partners – this being of particular concern to construction professionals
- the decision-making processes of the firm, which for larger firms may be along corporate lines but with regular partners' meetings
- loans by a partner to the firm
- provisions for holidays and illness
- provisions for admitting new partners
- provisions for the expulsion and retirement of a partner and the financial entitlements of departing partners
- the circumstances which would lead to the dissolution of the partnership (either by effluxion of time or the death, bankruptcy or retirement of a partner). The continuing partners may be required, or given an option, to purchase the share of a

deceased or retiring partner, in which case the partnership agreement may provide for an indemnity against partnership liabilities
- provisions restricting competition after a partner has left the practice. These may include 'non-competition' or 'non-solicitation' clauses and will be enforceable only if they are reasonable and designed to protect the on-going business. They are governed by a different body of law than restraints in employment contracts and depend substantially on their being freely arrived at between the partners as a fair bargain
- means of resolving disputes between partners. Often partnership agreements contain arbitration clauses, as arbitration is seen as being a more private means of resolving disputes than litigation. But with the strong growth in mediation, many professional firms are committing themselves to mediate disputes before incurring the costs of arbitration proceedings
- whether any provision will be made in the accounts for the partners' tax on the profits of the business, and if so, how this will be dealt with. (Although partners' tax liabilities on partnership profits are their own responsibility, many partnerships provide for tax in the accounts, and withhold tax liabilities from drawings, to ensure that the individual partners are able to meet their responsibilities.)

In the absence of any express agreement to the contrary, partners of a firm have the following rights and obligations under the Partnership Act 1890

- to take full part in its management
- to have an equal share in profits and capital
- to contribute equally to any losses sustained by the firm
- to object to the admission of a new partner
- to object to a change in the nature of partnership business (although the majority vote will prevail)
- to an indemnity from a fellow partner(s) in respect of liabilities incurred by that partner in carrying out necessary acts in the ordinary and proper course of partnership business
- to inspect the partnership books
- not to be expelled
- to dissolve the practice on immediate notice to the other partners.

The Limited Liability Partnerships Regulations 2001 provide for a similar set of default rules, which, like those for general partnerships, will normally be unsuitable in practice. Such issues should always be addressed in the LLP members' or partnership agreement.

2.2 General partnerships

Section 1 of the Partnership Act 1890 defines a partnership simply as 'the relation, which subsists between persons carrying on a business in common with a view of profit'.

Sharing facilities is not normally seen as evidence of partnership; sharing profits is. It is therefore strongly advisable to put the terms of any partnership into writing.

Every partner is an agent of their firm and their other partners for the purpose of the business of the partnership. Any act by a partner within the scope of the usual business is within the implied authority of the partners, so long as that act is the usual way that it would be done in businesses of that kind. These acts will bind the other partners and the firm.

Every partner in a firm is liable jointly with the other partners for all debts and obligations of the firm incurred while they are partners. Partners are jointly and severally liable for the wrongful acts or omissions of any of them which cause loss or damage to third persons, if such acts are either done by a partner in the ordinary course of the business or with the authority of the co-partners. They are also jointly and severally liable where a partner receives and misapplies the money or property of a third person while acting within the scope of his or her apparent authority and where the firm receives in the ordinary course of its business, money or property which is misapplied by one or more of the partners while in the firm's custody.

Consent of all existing partners is required to change the nature of the partnership business. A majority of partners cannot expel any partner unless the power to do so has been conferred by express agreement between the partners.

Larger partnerships are often managed by a single partner (known as the managing partner) or a group of partners (who are selected by the managing partner or elected by their peers).

A managing partner, like any other partner, is not entitled to remuneration for acting on partnership business unless there is an express or implied agreement to that effect.

General partnerships often consist of partners who are known as equity, fixed equity, salaried and associate partners.

The difference between an equity partner and a fixed equity partner is that the latter has a first charge over the profits of the firm, whereas an equity partner participates only in any remaining profits.

The terms 'salaried' and 'associate' partners are misleading as the persons concerned are not, in truth, partners at all but employees of the practice (and are often given an indemnity by the equity and fixed equity partners against any claims). However, if it is shown that a salaried partner has been held out as a partner in the firm, that person is jointly and severally liable to the party to whom they are held out. Putting a partner's name on letterhead is not definitively holding out, because each case has been shown to depend on its facts, but no one should let their name go forward without being aware of this risk. There is a pattern of cases, usually involving smaller firms which show the danger of being held out when the firm or its insurance cover fail or are exhausted.

2.3 Limited partnerships

A limited partnership is governed by the Limited Partnerships Act 1907. Such partnerships are rare although they are encountered quite often in property and other areas of finance. It is a partnership where some of the members have liability limited to the amount of capital or property they have advanced to the firm. The purpose of such partnerships is to encourage investment in firms by sleeping partners who take no part in day-to-day management. However, because limited partnerships are not usually an appropriate vehicle for a professional practice this section is deliberately brief.

2.4 Limited liability partnerships (LLPs)

Limited liability partnerships first emerged in the USA and, since the State of Delaware passed its law in August 1993, have become commonplace. The Limited Liability Partnerships Act 2000 (LLP Act) and the Limited Liability Partnerships Regulations 2001 (LLP Regulations) came into force on the 6 April 2001. The law now applies to Great Britain and Northern Ireland and by the summer of 2008 over 35 000 LLPs, mostly in England and Wales, had been registered showing how popular these business vehicles are becoming not just for professional firms. We believe most major practices that are still partnerships will be LLPs by 2008. The fundamental characteristics of a UK LLP are:

- that it is a body corporate with limited liability incorporated under statute with filings of its registration details at Companies House
- the LLP has the capacity to contract in its own name with the members and staff acting as its agents when making contracts
- that, internally, it may be governed by a members' agreement, which will be a private document, and not articles of association
- members have limited liability except where, under common law principles, a litigant can prove them liable for tort or breach of contract
- that it is 'tax transparent' meaning that the profits of the LLP are taxed in the hands of its members, as if they were partners in a general partnership.

Given the absence of joint and several liability, the flexibility of organization and the tax transparency, LLPs are proving particularly attractive to construction industry professionals who are exposed to ever-increasing risk in a market where professional indemnity insurance is often not available to underwrite the larger projects. Although there is an obligation to file audited accounts, this is unlikely to be an issue in the construction industry because many rival firms will already be incorporated and therefore under the same duties of financial disclosure. Because of the rise of the LLP there are few major general partnerships left in the construction industry.

A non-negligent member will not be directly liable to third parties dealing with the LLP even where the LLP's assets have been exhausted. LLPs are not a reason to reduce PI cover, because the business will still be liable to the full extent of its assets, and clients dealing with the practice may require disclosure of the PI cover before commissioning work, but for new members there will be the added comfort of knowing they are not potentially 'liable to the grave' for the actions of their fellow partners whilst they were in partnership. There is some uncertainty regarding the position of a member's (as opposed to the LLP's) liability for his or her own wrongful acts or defaults. It is hoped that the courts will apply the same rules applicable to company directors and only find a member personally liable where the member has accepted a close and personal responsibility, which has been relied upon by the claimant. Inevitably much will turn on the facts of each case. The Courts approach to the liability of professionals is a notoriously difficult area, with a mixture of public policy and causation interfering with the chain of legal precedent.

There are important consequences of the LLP being a body corporate. The most significant of these are that much of UK company and insolvency law is imposed upon the LLP, conferring upon it statutory power to grant fixed and floating charges in favour of its bankers, requiring it to appoint auditors and providing that the corporate insolvency regime govern its failure or dissolution.

The members' agreement will need to cover those issues dealt with in a general law partnership agreement such as profit share and retirement rights but, because of the substantial new law attaching to the LLP's external conduct, there will need to be a careful review of each company and insolvency law provision to decide how, if at all, it should be dealt with internally in the private arrangements between the members. The LLP Act specifically states that partnership law does not apply to LLPs and, as a result, established concepts such as duties of good faith need to be set out in the agreement. The regime set out in the LLP Regulations as the default in the absence of a members' agreement is unlikely to be suitable in practice and, just as with a partnership agreement, those issues should be addressed in the agreement.

Every LLP has to have at least two designated members who are primarily responsible for many of the statutory duties imposed on the LLP. If two members are not nominated for this purpose, all the members will be liable as designated members. Their responsibilities are akin to those of a company secretary, although rather more onerous in that they share some of the responsibilities borne by company directors.

Because the LLP is incorporated, it must file statutory accounts drawn up essentially in the same form as a private limited company. Those accounts will need to be audited by a registered auditor, except where the LLP qualifies as small under the Companies Act.

Partnerships seeking to convert to LLP status must seek advice from their accountants as to the effect that statutory accounts may have on partnership accounting policies and practices. After much consultation a statement of recommended accounting practice (SORP) was published in May 2002 (and revised with effect from 31 March, 2006) which seeks to assist LLPs in complying with Companies Act 1985 accounting requirements while allowing the accounts to show third parties what they want to know without creating some of the distortions that will otherwise arise. One issue, which has arisen, is when some or all of a member's profit share and capital contribution must be shown as a debt owed by the LLP to the member. The application of corporate accounting standards to LLPs is not always harmonious. Under the 2006 SORP what members perceive to be permanent capital of the LLP may not be reported as such. This may require explanation to institutions lending to LLP, or could even restrict some LLPs capacity to borrow without personal guarantees from members. However most informed readers of LLP accounts will understand the distinction which is drawn between 'debt' and 'equity' of the LLP.

In any winding-up of the LLP a member's interests in the LLP might rank alongside other ordinary creditors, particularly if that member has advanced a loan to the LLP. Those lending to an LLP may well wish to enter into agreements with members subordinating members' interests to those of other creditors. There is also a requirement that a provision should be recognised for annuities with the contingent cost being accrued and reported subject to actuarial calculations in each set of accounts.

To become an LLP it is necessary not only to incorporate a new business entity but also to transfer to the LLP all the business that is currently being carried on. This business transfer may be a time consuming project. Although it should be tax neutral it will involve looking at contracts, leases, insurances, employment terms and, provided the transfer is of an existing partnership business (there being severe risks in transferring a limited company to an LLP), a host of other issues (including entering into new banking arrangements). Carefully planning this process to effect the transfer is vital. The process will be similar to that involved in the incorporation of a general partnership. The forms necessary for registration of LLPs are very similar to those used for incorporating companies.

The DTI has identified 60 000 businesses which it expects to see adopt LLP status. With its stricter legal and accounting regime and full financial disclosure, it must not be assumed that all general partnerships will become LLPs. But the LLP format has proved to be particularly attractive to larger and multi-disciplinary partnerships where it is very difficult for each partner to be aware of the skills and risks his or her fellow partners are exhibiting or assuming.

2.5 Taxation

Because a partnership does not have a separate legal identity it is the partners themselves who have a taxation liability rather than the partnership as an entity. The partnership income, however, is taxable, but each partner has sole responsibility for the tax owed in respect of their share of partnership profits. The profits (or losses) of a trade or profession are computed taking the partnership as a whole as if it were a single entity. Once these are determined the question is how the taxable profits are allocated to the individual partners. Each individual partner is assessable on their share of the taxable profits of the partnership as a whole.

Although an LLP is a body corporate, the income of the LLP is taxed in the hands of the members as if it were partnership income. Borrowings for subscribing partnership capital to the LLP will also attract tax relief in the same way as borrowings into a partnership. There is a stamp duty and stamp duty land tax exemption on the transfer of assets from the old partnership to the LLP. This is subject to certain conditions, the most important of which is that on transfer there must be no change in the constitution of the partnership and the LLP in terms of membership. National insurance contributions due from the members of the LLP are the same as for partners (who are assessed as being self employed – see the section on sole practitioners above), which will represent significant savings for those who would otherwise have incorporated. The LLP is the taxable entity for VAT registration.

For the purposes of assessing the taxable profits, each partner is treated as setting up business when they become a partner; they are then assessed on the current year basis of assessment (see under Section 1.2 of this chapter) while they continue to be partners. A partner is treated as discontinuing business either when he or she ceases to be a partner or when the firm itself ceases to be in business.

The partnership is required to submit a partnership return, to facilitate the taxation of the individual partner, not to tax the partnership as a whole. This return should contain a partnership statement which should show all the information necessary for the calculation of the trading profits of the partnership, including any capital allowances claims. It should show the total income, losses, tax credits and charges of the partnership for each period of account included in the return. It should also show the shares in which those sums are allocated to the particular partners.

The individual partners must replicate this information in their individual tax return, and both the partnership and partners' individual returns must be submitted to the Inspector of Taxes by 31 January following the year of assessment, if penalties are not to be charged.

Under self-assessment, all the partners are required to keep such records as may be required to enable correct and complete returns to be made. All the records required for the individual or corporate partners' tax returns and the records required for the partnership statement must be kept until five years after the 31 January following the end of the relevant year of assessment.

The records required to be kept include records of all amounts received and expended in the course of the business and what each receipt or item of expenditure is for. If the business deals with goods, records of all sales and purchases of goods must also be kept.

A partner is able to obtain tax relief on the interest on a loan to subscribe capital to the partnership (s.398 ITA 2007) provided the partnership employs the funds in pursuing its trade.

A partner making a loss in a LLP conducting a trade is only able to obtain tax relief on his loss up to the level of his capital in the LLP (s.107 ITA 2007). This restriction to loss relief does not apply to a loss in a LLP conducting a profession.

New legislation in the 2007 Finance Act restricts the s.64 ITA 2007 loss relief for 2007/08 losses onwards of non-active partners, or limited partners, to £25 000.

Non-active partners are those who spend less than 10 hours a week involved in partnership activity.

Corporation tax rules apply to the share of profits attributable to a partner who is a company rather than an individual.

Otherwise, the loss reliefs, payment of tax and NIC liabilities are as for sole practices as mentioned above.

2.6 Name of practice

The Business Names Act 1985 regulates those firms where the business name differs from that of the partners of it. It requires them to display prominently on the business premises the names and addresses of the partners. Non-compliance with this provision is a criminal offence or may render void contracts into which the firm enters.

The Business Names Act 1985 provides that business documentation of the firm must set out the names of each of the partners. However, if there are more than 20 partners, the names of the partners need not be set out if the documentation in question discloses the name and address of the principal place of business and states that a full list of partners' names and relevant addresses may be inspected there. These rules also apply to LLPs where the LLP carries on business under a name which does not consist either solely of the name under which it was incorporated or of its corporate name with an addition which simply states that it carries on business in succession to the previous business. This means that many professional LLPs still need to comply with this legislation.

2.7 Service companies

Service companies are formed to provide services to a partnership. They may employ staff and own premises and provide professional services and equipment to the practice. Service companies were initially established because of the inability of partnerships to retain untaxed profits and the differing marginal rates of tax between a company and a partnership.

2.8 The reform of partnership law

The consultation document gathered some very positive and other negative comments, particularly around the proposal that partnerships should have continuity (to avoid the damage caused by dissolution) and separate legal personality. Given the controversy it would appear that the 1890 Act still has much life in it. It remains however the authors' concern that there are still partnership cases, involving usually small firms, but no written agreement, that have unfavourable outcomes, especially at first trial in local courts, and which have to be 'remedied' at considerable cost and inconvenience by the Court of Appeal. In some instances the reforms would have prevented costly litigation. The Government has, despite 'shelving' the reform of partnership law, committed itself to a new limited partnership Act.

2.9 Summary of partnerships

The advantages and disadvantages of partnerships are much the same as for a sole trader, except on a larger scale. With more than one professional, the business will seem much more substantial to the outside world, and so finding finance and cheaper indemnity insurance may be easier. There are, however, other particular advantages of partnership as a means of operating, over an incorporated business:

- they are ideal for professional firms where personal energies can be channelled into the goal of achieving partnership with its apparent equality of status
- each partner has a personal stake in the business, providing a further strong motivational force for its success
- the affairs of the business are private, not public; for example, there is no obligation on partnerships, other than LLPs, to publish accounts
- partnerships are characterized by flexibility, by the freedom of contract and by the absence of registered shares.

There are, however, disadvantages:

- each of the partners has unlimited liability for the debts of the business other than in a LLP
- there are fewer sources of finance for the business (there being no shareholders from whom to raise more funds) and lending is often guaranteed by all partners
- partnerships are potentially less easy to manage if each partner considers that they have a say in the business. This requires different leadership skills from those which a corporate chief executive might display.

3 COMPANIES

A company is owned by its members (the shareholders) and managed by its directors under supervision of its shareholders. However, it is an entity which is a distinct and separate legal entity to its members and directors.

A company may be limited by shares or by its shareholders' promise to pay up to a fixed sum on insolvency (known as limited by guarantee) or unlimited. If it is unlimited, the shareholders are liable to pay the liquidator whatever is needed to pay all of its debts and obligations in the event of it being wound up. To that extent, an unlimited company differs little practically from a partnership and now that partnerships of more than 20 persons are widely permitted, unlimited companies are very rare.

The Companies Act 2006 (2006 Act) is a substantial consolidation and revision of UK Company Law and will largely replace the Companies Act 1985 (1985 Act) and related legislation. The intention of the Government is to introduce the 2006 Act in stages, with the final provisions coming into force on 1 October 2009. The Law below reflects the transitional position in force as at 1 October 2008 and is therefore a mixture of the provisions of both Acts.

3.1 Private company limited by shares

Limited companies may be private or public. Public companies can apply to be listed on the Stock Exchange or other public markets and offer their shares to the public, thereby raising capital in the public arena. Private companies cannot be listed or offer their shares to the public. It is possible to convert a private company into public and vice versa.

3.2 Procedure for incorporation

Incorporation of a new company

A company is incorporated by sending to the Registrar of Companies the constitutional documents (see below), signed by the initial shareholders and first officers, and certain

2.1 Ways of operating
2.2 Working with others
2.3 Working internationally
2.4 The engineer's appointment
2.5 Collateral warranties
2.6 Indemnity insurance
2.7 Employment law
2.8 Information technology

other forms detailing the registered office (the formal address, which need not be the principal place of business), first director(s) and secretary, and a declaration of compliance with the 1985 Act and the fee. (The company may also need to appoint auditors once it is operational, who must be members of a 'recognized supervisory body'.) In order to qualify for audit exemption as a small company the company must qualify as a small company for accounts and reports for financial years beginning before 5 April 2008 by meeting two of the following three criteria:

- have a turnover of not more than £5.6 million
- have a balance sheet total of not more than £1.4 million
- have an aggregate number of employees, not more than 50.

For accounts and reports for financial years beginning on or after 6 April 2008 two of the three criteria:

- have a turnover of not more than £6.5 million
- have a balance sheet total of not more than £3.26 million
- have an aggregate number of employees, not more than 50.

The actual incorporation takes place when the Registrar issues the certificate of incorporation and this normally takes approximately two weeks from the papers being filed. For a small increase in fee, incorporation can be done on a same-day basis.

Shelf company

An alternative is to purchase a 'shelf company', that is, one, which has already been incorporated but has never commenced business. The shelf company will usually have nominees as its directors, secretary and subscribers. New directors can then be appointed, the subscriber shares transferred, the name of the shelf company changed and, if necessary, the Memorandum and Articles of Association altered to meet any special requirements. Clients usually opt for purchasing a shelf company because it is a quicker method.

Names

The name of the company must include the word 'Limited' if a private company, or 'public limited company' or 'plc' if a public company. However, a private company limited by guarantee may be exempt from the need to include the word limited in its name if it satisfies certain criteria. The choice of name is restricted such that a name cannot be used if there is already a company with that name on the index of names at Companies Registry. The Registrar may refuse the use of a proposed name in certain circumstances; where, for instance, the name may suggest a connection with the royal family or the government. Certain other words can only be used if certain conditions are met. The most common of these are 'Group', 'Holdings' and 'International'.

A company may carry on business under a name other than its corporate name, subject to compliance with various requirements relating to disclosure of the corporate name and address.

Correspondence and business documents

The company letterhead and email or other electronic communications, its business letters, its websites and all order forms must set out the company's name, registered office, the registered number, the country of registration. If it is exempt from having 'limited' as part of its name it must disclose it is a limited company. If it is a private community interest company or an investment company it must disclose this fact. Also, if it makes reference to share capital in such documents this must be reference to paid up share capital. Further, the registered name must appear, amongst other things on invoices, cheques, notices, demands for payment and other forms of business correspondence and documentation (which could include compliment slips and business cards). The company must also display its name outside its registered office, any location where company records are kept for inspection and other business locations and every place where it carries on business.

Registered office

Every UK company must have a registered office, which must be located in the country of registration (England, Scotland etc.).

Constitutional documents

Every limited liability company must have a constitution consisting of a Memorandum of Association and Articles of Association. These two documents form the basis of the company's capacity, the corporate management, and the rights of members and directors. They can generally be amended at any time but the resolution to amend them requires a 75% majority.

Memorandum of association

The memorandum governs a company's relationship with the outside world, or more particularly the persons with whom a company will transact either directly or indirectly in the course of its business. Contained within the memorandum are the objects clauses which set out a company's objectives, being the businesses it proposes to carry on and any incidental or ancillary powers, which it may require to allow it to conduct its business. A company should not act outside the objects, which are set out expressly or by implication in the memorandum. If it does so, the action may be invalid depending on the circumstances and the directors face a personal liability.

Articles of association

This document sets out a company's regulations for its internal management, and will cover such matters as the rights of shareholders, procedure on an issue or transfer of shares, rights attaching to shares, the appointment, removal and powers of directors and the conduct of Board and general meetings. Many of the rules for meetings etc. are set out in the 2006 Act but companies have a wide scope to adapt this to suit their particular requirements. The 1985 Act provides for a model set of articles for a company known as Table A. A company may adopt all or any of the regulations contained in Table A as its articles of association. Companies are generally free to amend the application of Table A and to choose whatever form of articles of association they choose to adopt.

3.3 Structure, management and administration

Funding and profit distribution

The company must have an 'authorized' and an 'issued' share capital. There are no limitations on the amounts of authorized or issued share capital and the share capital may be in a currency other than pounds sterling, though a plc must have at least £50 000 sterling of issued share capital (€65 000 being the euro equivalent) (of which not less than 25% must be paid up) and obtain the related trading certificate under section 762 of the 2006 Act before it can trade or borrow money.

A company may distribute its profits by means of payments to employees including its directors (provided they are not at uncommercial and excessive rates) or by distribution of dividends. Dividends must not exceed its 'distributable profits'.

Shareholders and directors

A private company must have at least one registered shareholder but this may be a nominee for a third party whose name need not appear on official documents. A private limited company must also have a board of directors (consisting of at least one director) in whose hands the management of the business is usually placed. A plc must have a minimum of two directors. There are no restrictions on the nationality or residence of shareholders or directors and meetings may be held in or outside the UK although care must be taken to not unwittingly make a company liable under more than one tax regime. There are also no requirements for a director to be a shareholder in the company. However, a public company (but not a private company when it wishes to or is required by its articles to) is required to have a company secretary (who as a matter of convenience should be present in the UK), and is responsible for the maintainance of certain registers in the UK.

Board meetings

Proceedings at board meetings are governed by the company's articles. Regulation 88 of Table A gives authority to the directors to meet from time to time as they think fit, but good corporate governance requires a company to hold sufficient board meetings to ensure the company's business is properly conducted.

The frequency of meetings will depend on the nature of the company's business and the composition of its board. Where there are both executive and non-executive directors, board meetings will normally be held at monthly intervals, with intervening committee meetings of the executive directors, usually on fixed days or dates. Notice of board meetings should be given to all the directors unless the articles provide otherwise. Proceedings at board meetings are usually informal, but if there is no unanimity on any item of business, the chairperson should put the matter formally to a vote. Many companies have a board meeting each month to renew the previous month's financial and general performance.

Modern communication techniques now enable directors to hold meetings without being physically present in the same room, e.g. by video conferencing, though care should be taken to make sure the articles allow this (Table A does not). If urgent business arises and it is inconvenient to summon a board meeting at short notice, it is useful to take advantage of the provisions of Table A Regulation 93 by sending one or more copies of the resolution by post to each director for their signature. Such signed resolutions are equivalent to a resolution passed at a board meeting and should be inserted in the minute book.

General meetings

Shareholder general meetings may be either general, annual or class (the last only being held in the case of business when shareholders hold different classes of shares). A general meeting (GM) may, subject to the articles, be convened at any time.

The only business, which may validly be transacted at a GM, is the business specified in the notice convening the meeting. Business that would be undertaken at GM by means of resolutions (voting) would include the following.

(a) *Ordinary resolutions*: (these require over 50% of the votes cast to be in favour)
- alteration to share capital

2.1 Ways of operating
2.2 Working with others
2.3 Working internationally
2.4 The engineer's appointment
2.5 Collateral warranties
2.6 Indemnity insurance
2.7 Employment law
2.8 Information technology

- the giving of authority for the allotment of securities
- removal of directors.

(b) *Special resolutions*: (these require a 75% of the votes cast to be in favour)
- alterations to memorandum and articles of association
- change of name
- reduction of capital (which for public companies also require a court order and for private companies require either a court order or solvency statement)
- disapplication of allotment pre-emption rights
- various alterations to the company's status by re-registration
- purchase of own shares.

Shareholder written resolutions

Anything which may be effected by resolution of a private company in general meeting (other than removing a director or auditor) may, instead of a meeting being held, be done by a written resolution. The 2006 Act lays out the procedure for written resolutions. Generally these must be issued by the board and to be valid must be signed and returned to the Company within 28 days. Who needs to sign them depends on the class or resolution. An ordinary resolution being passed by written resolution needs to be signed by (at least) those members who in a general meeting would have been able to cast over half the total votes on the resolution. A special resolution being passed as a written resolution must be specified as such on the face of the written resolution and needs to be signed by (at least) those members who in a general meeting would have been able to cast 75% of the total votes on the resolution.

Annual general meetings (plcs only)

Every plc must hold a general meeting in each calendar year as its annual general meeting (AGM). These must be held within six months of the company's accounting reference date.

The usual business at AGMs includes consideration of the reports and accounts laid before the meeting, the declaration of a dividend (if any), the election of directors, the reappointment of the auditors and fixing of their remuneration, renewal of directors' authority to allot shares and disapplication of pre-emption rights.

A private company is not required by the 2006 Act to have an AGM, though this may be required by the articles if that is desired.

Powers of directors and officers of a company

A director of a UK company owes certain duties to the company (which in most cases, means to its members as a whole, but can, in some cases, extend to its creditors as a whole) including a duty to act in a manner he believes is most likely to promote the success of the company and a duty to carry out his or her responsibilities with reasonable care and skill. Breach of some of these duties can result in the director incurring personal or criminal liability. It has become increasingly common to take out insurance at the expense of the company to protect directors against civil claims for breach of duty and other director's risks.

Statutory books

A company is obliged to maintain certain statutory books: the register of members (listing details of shareholders), the register of directors and secretaries, the register of charges, the register of directors' interests in shares, and minute books of the shareholders' and board meetings. The statutory books are in certain cases open to public inspection and copies must be provided on request. Each year, the company is obliged to file an annual return with the Registrar of Companies, giving details of share capital, shareholders, directors, its activities and the location of its registered office and statutory books.

Accounting requirements

A company must maintain accounting records showing cash flow and the assets and liabilities of the company. The directors are required to produce a profit and loss account and balance sheet in respect of each accounting reference period of the company, which (in the case of a plc) may be laid before a general meeting, in practice for a plc, at the AGM (see above). They must also produce a directors' report (annual report) on the development of the company's business. If subject to an audit, the company's auditors must produce a report on the accounts (the Auditors' Report), confirming that they give a 'true and fair view' of the company's affairs. The exact content of the accounts and annual report is determined by the Companies Acts. Small and medium-sized companies (defined by reference to turnover and balance sheet) are exempted from certain accounting requirements, and dormant companies are exempt from the requirement to appoint an auditor (but may appoint one if they wish).

Taxation

There are two taxes which will affect a company registered in the UK, whether or not it is a subsidiary of a non-UK based company. These are corporation tax and value added tax (VAT).

Corporation tax

An incorporated business will pay corporation tax on both income profits and chargeable gains. The main corporation tax rate has been 30% since 1 April 1999 but will fall to 28% from April 2008. This applies if the combined income profits and chargeable gains of a single company, unconnected with any other, are £1.5m or more. The rate at which small single companies unconnected with each other, with profits and gains of up to £300 000, paid corporation tax rose from 19% to 20% on 1 April 2007. Further increases are planned of 21% on 1 April 2008 and 22% on 1 April 2009. Between the two thresholds of £300 000 and £1.5m, a marginal rate applies. Where a number of companies are connected with each other, or 'associated', these limits, for each company, are divided by the number of companies that are associated with each other.

Companies that pay tax at the small company rate or marginal rates are generally required to pay corporation tax nine months after the end of the financial year. However, companies that pay tax at the full rate are required to make quarterly payments on account of the estimated tax due for a year in the middle of the 7th, 10th, 13th and 16th months following the *beginning* of the financial year. Any balance of tax will then be due nine months after the end of the financial year. Interest will be charged and paid on any payments on account that do not equal those which should have been paid, once the final tax liability has been determined.

Capital allowances are generally available in respect of capital expenditure on plant, machinery and industrial buildings. Such allowances can then be set off against taxable profits in the relevant period.

In relation to plant and machinery, the annual allowance is 25% of the original cost less any allowances already given. Small and medium sized companies are entitled to a higher rate of allowance (50% and 40% accordingly) for the year of acquisition of machinery and plant. Industrial buildings have an allowance of 4% of the original cost per year.

Changes in the 2007 Finance Act will extensively alter the rates of capital allowances available. Among these changes, industrial buildings allowance will be abolished, with a phased withdrawal planned for between April 2008 and April 2011. The annual allowance for plant and machinery will reduce from 25% to 20% in April 2008.

Losses

A trading company can only utilize trading losses in a limited number of ways. They can be set off against other income and capital gains of the current financial year or the previous year, or carried forward indefinitely against future *trading profits* from the *same trade*. (Note that the losses may not be carried forward and set off against other income or capital gains arising in the future.)

Alternatively, where a trade ceases, terminal losses of the last twelve months' trade may be carried back up to three years against other income and capital gains.

VAT

VAT law is harmonized across Europe and UK VAT law is mainly contained in the Value Added Tax Act 1994 (VATA 1994). VAT is chargeable on each stage of the supply of goods and/or services process. There is a credit mechanism for VAT registered businesses which provides that the amount of VAT payable to Customs and Excise (C&E) is calculated by deducting the amount of VAT a taxable person charges his or her customers (i.e. the output tax), from the VAT charged to the taxpayer on business purchases (i.e. the input tax). The resulting balance is the amount of VAT due to C&E. Normally, VAT cannot be reclaimed if it relates to non-business activities or 'exempt' supplies. In principle, VAT is neutral for businesses, as taxpayers are collecting tax from their customers on behalf of the Government and reclaiming from the Government tax which they have had to pay out to their suppliers.

VATA 1994, Schedule 9 details specific businesses that can make 'exempt supplies' (in which case no VAT is chargeable), these include the granting of an interest in land and buildings – although there are exceptions, and it is also possible to waive the exemption by 'opting to tax' thereby creating a supply subject to VAT.

The supply of services by construction industry professionals is likely to be a taxable supply, providing the taxable limits have been reached.

The UK standard rate of VAT is currently 17.5%.

All new businesses will need to register with Customs and Excise for VAT purposes if taxable supplies of goods and services are in excess of £64 000 (for 2007/08) per annum.

National Insurance Contributions

A company is not required to pay National Insurance Contributions (NICs) in respect of its own profits. However, it must pay employer's NIC, at variable rates up to a maximum of 12.8% (for 2007/08) of any amounts paid to its employees. As 'employees' includes any shareholder/directors, this constitutes an additional charge on amounts drawn by way of salary by the owners of the business. This charge is in addition to the NIC payable by the employees themselves, at rates of up to 11% (for 2007/08).

The employer's NIC charges mentioned above may be avoided if income is taken by shareholder/directors by way of dividend, rather than salary. However, taking a reduced salary in preference for dividends can have other repercussions, for example in terms of

2.1 Ways of operating
2.2 Working with others
2.3 Working internationally
2.4 The engineer's appointment
2.5 Collateral warranties
2.6 Indemnity insurance
2.7 Employment law
2.8 Information technology

the maximum amount of pension contributions that may be made. The amount of income taken by way of salary versus dividend must, therefore, be weighed carefully in each individual case.

3.4 Public limited company

Nature

A public company is a company, limited by shares or limited by guarantee and having a share capital (the latter type are very rare and can no longer be formed), whose memorandum of association states that it is a public company, and which has registered or re-registered as such. Any other company is a private company.

A public company must include the words 'public limited company' (or the abbreviation 'plc') at the end of the company's name and (before trading etc.) satisfy requirements as to the minimum amount of its issued share capital (presently £50 000 or €65 000).

A public company may (but need not) apply to have its shares listed on the Stock Exchange or on the Alternative Investment Market or other public market. In each case, this means that a price will be quoted at which dealings in the company's shares will take place. All companies which are listed on the Official List of the Stock Exchange are public, however not all public companies are listed. The majority are not.

The Listed Market

Except in exceptional cases, only a large public company, which has traded for at least three years, can apply for its shares to be listed on the Official List maintained by the UK Listing Authority (UKLA) (a branch of the Financial Services Authority) and admitted to trading on the main market of the London Stock Exchange, the Stock Exchange's market for 'blue chip' securities (and, as such, a 'regulated market'). To do so, the company must comply with the initial and ongoing requirements of the UKLA and the Stock Exchange as to publication of information about the company's affairs. Listing on the Official List/main market means that the company's shares are among the most marketable of all shares; only around 2000 of the UK's companies are listed on the Stock Exchange, compared with a total of over 1 000 000 companies registered in the UK.

The Alternative Investment Market (AIM)

AIM, which was set up in June 1995, is less stringently regulated than the main market of the Stock Exchange. AIM deals in the shares of smaller and growing companies and provides a market place with lower costs and less regulation than the main market. There is no minimum capital requirement, no minimum number of shares required to be in public hands and no requirement for a minimum trading record.

Differences between public and private companies

The 1985 Act and the 2006 Act apply to both public and private companies but there are many differences of detail that (in the case of a plc) apply to all plcs, not just listed companies.

- A public company must have at least two directors and at least two shareholders while a private company can have just one director who may also be the only shareholder – though the sole director cannot also be the secretary.
- A private company is no longer required to have a company secretary subject to express requirements in the articles, but if it does have a secretary, the secretary need not be specially qualified or experienced. The company secretary of a

public company must have certain professional qualifications, the requisite knowledge and experience for the position.
- A private company can buy back the shares of a member who wishes to leave the company even if the company's accumulated profits are not sufficient so that it is necessary to use capital for the purchase.
- A private company is prohibited from offering to issue its shares to the public.
- There are more onerous provisions regulating directors' dealings with their company if the company is a public company.
- Private companies up to a certain size may be permitted to file abbreviated accounts with the registrar of companies.
- Only a private company can dispense with the statutory obligation to have its year-end accounts audited.
- Private companies have no statutory obligation to hold an annual general meeting.
- Only private companies can dispense with the formality of holding general meetings by having shareholders sign resolutions in writing.

Differences in practice

- In a private company, the directors and shareholders are often substantially the same persons. In a public company (especially if it is listed), there will usually be significant differences in personnel between the shareholders (who are likely to include institutional investors) and the directors (whose position is more like that of employees who are paid to manage the business).
- In a private company, the shareholders cannot easily sell their shares because the articles of association usually contain restrictions on transfer (often in the form of directors' power of veto on the registration of the transfer) and because of difficulties of valuation, given that there is no ready 'market' for the shares. In a public company, there is less likely to be any restriction on transfer and, if the shares are listed on a public market, such as the main market of the Stock Exchange or AIM, there can generally be no restriction.
- A private company may, or may not, choose to pay dividends to its shareholders; many private companies pay no dividend at all. In practice, a public company, which is listed, must have a record of paying dividends every year in order to encourage investment in that company by share ownership.
- An indefinite authority to issue shares may be conferred on the directors of a private company but not of a public company.

3.5 Procedure for incorporation

A company can either be incorporated as a public company, or an existing private company can be re-registered as public.

The process of incorporating as a plc is similar to the incorporation of a private company in that certain documents must be lodged with the Registrar of Companies, namely the memorandum and articles of association, Form 10 (statement of first directors and secretary and address of the registered office), Form 12 (statutory declaration of compliance) and a fee. A plc, incorporated as such, cannot trade until its issued share capital statutes certain requirements and it has applied for and obtained a trading certificate. Alternatively, it can be registered as private, so that a trading certificate is not longer required.

The memorandum and articles of association must be in a form suitable for a plc. The name must end with the words 'public limited company' or 'p.l.c.' (The Registrar will accept 'plc') or, for companies registered in Wales, if the promoters wish, the Welsh equivalent. The share capital shown in the memorandum must be not less than the 'authorized minimum', currently £50 000 or €65 000.

A private company may be re-registered as a public company by passing a special resolution to that effect. The 1985 Act provides that as well as approving the re-registration, the special resolution must also make such alterations to the memorandum and articles of association as are necessary to conform with the requirements of the Act relating to the constitution of a plc (e.g. the memorandum must state that the company is to be a plc and the name must be changed to reflect that status). An auditor's report and balance sheet are also required.

At the time when the resolution is passed, the nominal value of the company's allotted share capital must be not less than the authorized minimum. This reflects the requirement (in the case of a new plc incorporated as such) on applying for a trading certificate. Further, each of the allotted shares must be paid up at least as to one-quarter of the nominal value of that share and the whole of any premium on it. Certain shares, such as shares allotted under an employees' share scheme, are disregarded both when considering whether the allotted shares are adequately paid up and when determining whether sufficient capital has been allotted.

After the passing of the special resolution, the company then applies for re-registration in the prescribed form. The form must be signed by a director or secretary and be accompanied by the following documents:

- a printed copy of the revised memorandum and articles of association
- a copy of the relevant balance sheet (prepared not more than seven months before the application) and of the auditors' unqualified report on it including confirmation about the level of the company's net assets as revealed in the balance sheet
- a 'valuation report' must be provided, subject to certain exceptions, where shares have been allotted by the company otherwise than for cash between the date of the relevant balance sheet and the date on which the special resolution was passed
- a statutory declaration in the prescribed form made by a director or secretary.

When a company registers as a plc there is no separate need to apply for or have a trading certificate. This is because the share capital criteria needed for a trading certificate are already met because a private company share capital must already satisfy these criteria in order to register.

Once the company is incorporated as a plc, the company name must appear in a conspicuous position outside every place in which it carries on business and on business letters, invoices, cheques and other items of stationery. The company and any officer in default are liable to a fine and an officer in default may also be personally liable. If the company has a common seal it should also be changed.

Memorandum of association
The memorandum is the same as that for private companies except for the extra statement that the Company is to be a public company.

Articles of association
These are as for private companies. If the plc is listed, the rules applicable to listed companies also specify certain additional requirements for inclusion in the articles.

3.6 Structure, management and administration

Board of directors

English companies do not (as is the case in many European jurisdictions) have separate supervisory and executive boards. Rather, the articles typically vest management in a single board of directors. There is no company law reason why there should be more than two directors for a public company. Commonly, however, particularly in the case of substantial companies, the board often contains a number of directors, both executive and non-executive. Whereas the executive directors perform executive functions (for which they are separately paid) over and above their duties as directors, the non-executive directors play a less active role, which may extend simply to regular attendance at board meetings and meetings of committees of the board.

The Combined Code applicable to Officially Listed companies admitted to the main market of the Stock Exchange suggests that all directors, whether executive or non-executive, should be subject to election by shareholders at the first opportunity after their appointment and thereafter every three years.

The board of directors includes a balance of executive and non-executive directors so that no one individual or small group of individuals can dominate board decisions.

In addition, the UKLA, when deciding whether a company is suitable for the admission of its securities to Official Listing, places great emphasis on whether the composition of the board displays the range of skills and experience appropriate for a quoted company.

In order for a company to be efficiently run, the Institute of Directors states that the members of the board

> 'must possess sufficient breadth of experience and knowledge in the wide range of subjects, situations and disciplines which may impinge upon the company's affairs and its business environment... the executive directors must provide specialist knowledge and a close understanding of the workings of the company and the practical implications of executing policies and strategies... complementary skills [of] worldly wisdom, objectivity, independent judgement and broad experience of the non-executive directors provide the necessary additional ingredient to ensure that the board can adequately address all the complex issues which are required of it.'

The board is overseen by the chairperson who may or may not also be the chief executive (managing director). The chairperson is primarily responsible for the working of the board and its balance of membership subject to board and shareholders' approval. He or she should retain sufficient distance from the day-to-day running of the business to ensure that the boards are in full control of the company's affairs. The Chief Executive is, however, in day-to-day operative control of the company. Generally, it is recommended that the two roles are *not* combined.

Executive directors

The executive directors provide the top level of day-to-day management and often within particular spheres of specialism which may be reflected in their titles such as finance director, marketing director, etc. Usually the executive directors have service contracts with notice or contract periods generally of one year and, frequently, their remuneration includes not only a basic salary but other benefits over and above, such as performance-related earnings and/or share options in order to align their interests closely with the interest of the company's shareholders.

Non-executive directors

The non-executive director's role varies depending on the circumstances. In some cases the director may be a nominee of a major shareholder appointed for the purpose of monitoring that shareholder's investment but it is recommended that the majority of non-executive directors should be independent of the company, its management and any business or other relationship, which could interfere with their independence.

A non-executive director has equal status and legal responsibility with the executive directors. They are equal board members and participate fully in board decisions. Their role is:

- to provide a balancing influence between those who have an interest in the company and the public
- to give the board independent advice and provide a greater depth of skill and experience
- to monitor the activities of top management and the board itself and report any deficiencies to the shareholders
- to help ensure that adequate financial information about the company is disseminated to shareholders and the public.

Non-executive directors are usually appointed for an initial period of three years with a review at the end of that period to consider a further limited extension.

Audit committee

The audit committee is primarily concerned with the copious amounts of financial information which statutory and Stock Exchange regulations require to be revealed to the shareholders and the public. Usually it will select accounting policies, review draft accounts and discuss various matters with the auditors, such as the nature and extent of the audit and any problems arising from it. It is recommended that such a committee comprises at least two members all of whom should be non-executive directors.

Duties of directors

Prior to October 2007, directors' general duties were to be found in the common law, therefore in the judgements of a large number of cases. In an attempt to make them more accessible, the 2006 Act has taken the Government's perception of the most important of them and put them into statute for the first time. Among other duties, the 2006 Act requires directors to act within their powers, not to accept benefits from third parties, to avoid conflicts of interest and to exercise reasonable skill, care and diligence. Above all, the Act requires directors to promote the success of the company while taking into consideration a non-exhaustive list of factors (including shareholders, employees and the wider community) and the likely consequences of a decision in the long term and its impact on the environment).

Directors still have a number of general duties remaining in the common law, such as the duty to consider the interests of creditors in circumstances of potential insolvency. In addition, they have numerous specific statutory and regulatory duties including the duty to have certain transaction between themselves (or their family etc) and their companies first approved by shareholders.

Directors owe their duties to the company and not to individual shareholders. Until October 2007, if directors breached their duties (subject to certain exceptions) only the company, acting through its board, could bring a claim. The exceptions broadly require an element of personal benefit and wrongdoing by the directors, generally tainted by fraud. The 2006 Act gives individual shareholders the right to bring an action in the name of the company for breach of duty and negligence against directors and, while there are safeguards against vexatious litigation built into the legislation, it remains to be seen the degree to which the Act involves the Courts in second-guessing the commercial decisions of directors.

Where a public company obtains a listing, the directors must steer the company through the flotation process and are also responsible for the accuracy of the prospectus. Errors or omissions in the prospectus may give rise to personal liability on the part of the directors. Following the flotation, the directors must ensure that the company complies with the requirements of the 'continuing obligations' imposed by the Listing Rules. Some of these obligations directly impinge upon the director's personal freedom of action.

One of the key advantages of a public company is that it can offer its shares or debentures to the public. Although there are considerable advantages in being able to raise finance from the public, a company upon becoming public is subject to a much more exacting statutory regime.

Share capital

- The authorized minimum capital of a public company must be in issue and allotted shares must be paid up as to at least one-quarter of their nominal amount plus the whole of any premium.
- A public company is obliged to obtain a valuer's report on the allotment of shares for a non-cash consideration (with certain exceptions).
- The statutory rights of pre-emption on an issue of securities may only be disapplied in respect of shares, which the directors already have authority to allot, and must be done by means of a special resolution or a provision in the articles.
- Where the net assets of a public company have fallen to half or less of its called-up share capital, the directors must convene a GM to decide what to do.
- A public company may not purchase or redeem its own shares out of capital without first re-registering as a private company which, as we have said, has such powers.

Directors

- Public companies need at least two directors.

Shareholders

- The minimum number of shareholders for a public company is two. A public company will lose its limited liability if it carries on business for more than six months without having at least two shareholders. The second can be a nominee, if desired.
- The shareholders of a public company must notify the company of certain interests in the company's shares.

Administration

- A resolution of the company in general meeting or a resolution of a meeting of a class of members will usually be required to perform certain actions, especially if the public company is listed.

2.1 Ways of operating
2.2 Working with others
2.3 Working internationally
2.4 The engineer's appointment
2.5 Collateral warranties
2.6 Indemnity insurance
2.7 Employment law
2.8 Information technology

Financial assistance

- A public company is generally prohibited against the giving of financial assistance for the acquisition of its own shares. Limited exceptions apply, for example for employee share schemes.

Accounts

- The period for laying and delivering accounts is generally six months after the end of the relevant accounting period (for accountancy periods commencing on or after 6 April 2008) in the case of a public company.

Listed companies

- Once a company seeks a listing it becomes subject to more regulation, especially as a result of the Listing Rules and the Disclosure and Transparency Rules, the application of which is overseen by the UKLA. The rules (in addition to other, more procedural, requirements contained in the Stock Exchange's Admission and Disclosure Standards) lay down the procedures for obtaining a listing of securities and the obligations to which a company and its directors will be subject once the securities are listed.
- A company whose shares or debentures are listed on 'prescribed markets' (these include the main market, AIM and PLUS markets – formerly OFEX) must notify the Exchange of information about its listed securities disclosed to it by a director complying with his or her obligations (i.e. duty to disclose the shareholdings of the director, the director's spouse and children).

Marketing

The marketing of a public company's securities is strictly regulated in order to afford as much protection as practicable to potential investors. On the issue of securities to the public, a company must generally issue a formal document known as a 'prospectus' containing detailed information about the company and its business. The purpose of this document is to ensure that potential investors have sufficient information to be able to make an informed decision as to whether or not to invest.

The Alternative Investment Market

As an alternative to obtaining a quotation or listing on the Official List, companies can join the Alternative Investment market (AIM), which opened in June 1995. This is less strictly regulated than the Official List and its intention is to minimize costs for companies wishing to have their shares traded on an identifiable market. It is a distinctly separate market from which companies may choose never to move to the Official List, although they may do so if they wish (assuming that they meet the suitability criteria). Features of the market in comparison with the Official List are that:

- there are no minimum limits on capitalization or on the amount of shares in public hands. It is a basic condition of listing on the Official List that the expected market value of the shares for which listing is sought be at least £700 000 and that at least 25% of the shares be in the hands of the public by the time of admission to listing
- there is no minimum trading record requirement (an Official Listing requires a three-year trading record
- there are only limited continuing obligations imposed on the company and its directors following admission to AIM.

Certain basic conditions must still be satisfied, however, before a company will be admitted to the AIM:

- the issuer must be a public company
- the securities must be freely transferable
- the issuer must have a code for directors' share dealings.

Taxation, VAT and NIC
All these are as for private companies.

Summary of companies (public or private)
In summary, the advantages of limited companies are:

- the limited liability of the members – shareholders are not liable for the torts and obligations of a limited company other than to the amount (if any) unpaid on their shares
- the ability to raise capital from outside the existing membership
- the ability to borrow money in the company's name
- a company is taxed in its own right as distinct from its members
- the continuance of existence of the business notwithstanding the debt or bankruptcy of all or any of its existing members;

The disadvantages of limited companies are:

- the requirements of the Companies Acts to disclose information about the company
- a greater formality is involved in setting up, running and winding up a company
- various tax considerations may prove a disincentive
- the requirement to undergo a formal audit of the accounts of larger companies each year.

4 EEIGS

4.1 Nature

An EEIG (or European Economic Interest Grouping) is a special form of business organization set up by the European Community in 1989 with a view to making the single market more accessible. The purpose of an EEIG is to enable cooperation between individuals and organizations in different member states. It may operate in any part of the EU and enter into arrangements with organizations outside the EU.

4.2 Advantages

- An EEIG is a flexible structure and no fixed capital contribution required.
- It is a legal structure recognized in all member states.
- It enables cooperation without loss of independence.
- It has legal capacity and tax transparency.

4.3 Disadvantages

- There is no public investment.
- It cannot buy shares in its members or other EEIGs or employ more than 500 people.

- It has unlimited joint and several liability.
- It must carry on the same or similar business to its members, with the aim of enabling its members to improve their own results, not making profits for itself in isolation.

4.4 Procedure for setting up an EEIG

An EEIG is formed by virtue of the drawing up of a contract which is registered either in the member state where it has its centre of administration or where one of its members has its registered office. In the UK, EEIGs are registered at Companies Registry. There must be at least two members based in different member states. The contract must include at least the name, address, objects and duration (may be indefinite) of the EEIG and details of its members.

The establishment of an EEIG must be announced in the *Official Journal of the European Communities* and the *London Gazette*.

The name of the EEIG must include either 'European Economic Interest Grouping' or the abbreviation 'EEIG' – otherwise substantially the same restrictions apply as do to UK companies.

Table 2 Tax and NI obligations

Limited company	Unincorporated business
Profits subject to corporation tax at max. 30% for the financial year 1999 where profits exceed £1 500 000. Profits taxed at 19% for the financial year 2006 if below £300 000	Profits subject to income tax at max. 40% where individual's taxable income exceeds £33 000 (for 2006/07)
Owner/manager subject to income tax on amounts withdrawn as dividend or remuneration	Owner/manager subject to income tax on net profits irrespective of amounts withdrawn. No tax on drawings themselves
Owner/manager and family member employees must be paid the national minimum wage (NMW). Dividends do not count as pay for NMW purposes	The NMW does not apply to the genuinely self-employed. Furthermore, guidance on NMW indicates that it does not need to be paid to family members who live at home and participate in the family business
Owner/manager's salary an allowable deduction from company's profits	Owner's salary not allowable
Income tax charge on company car and other benefits provided to owner/manager	Private mileage and expenses disallowed in business accounts
Start-up losses can only be set against company profits	Start-up losses in first four years can be carried back three years against other income prior to start of trading
National Insurance Contributions payable by both employer (max. 12.8%) and employee (max. 11%) on remuneration paid to employees and directors. Contributions are levied at a reduced rate of 1% on earnings above £33 540 p.a. (for 2006/07) for employees	Two types of National Insurance Contributions payable by self-employed: flat rate of £2.10 (for 2006/07) per week (£109 p.a.); *plus* 8% on annual profits between £5035 and £33 540 (for 2006/07) and 1% on profits above £33 540
National Insurance also payable by company in respect of company cars and private fuel	No National Insurance on proprietor's car

4.5 Constitutional documents

The EEIG is formed by a contract between the members, which in the UK is registered with the Registrar of Companies.

4.6 Structure, management and administration

The members decide (usually in the contract of formation) how the EEIG will be run. There is no requirement for regular meetings or for decisions of the members to be taken only at meetings. Each member has one vote, but this can be overridden by the contract of formation. Unanimous decisions are required on issues concerning the existence and operation of the EEIG (see Article 17 of the EC Regulation).

The members appoint managers (individuals or companies represented by individuals) who run the EEIG and make routine decisions, according to the powers conferred on them by the members. However, the EEIG will only be bound by the joint action of two or more managers. This is called the 'double signature'.

The EEIG has legal personality as a 'body corporate' in the UK from the moment of registration, and is subject to EC and UK competition rules.

An EEIG can be financed by capital invested by the members or by loans or donations from outside. Members may make contributions in terms of skills and services but are not obliged to subscribe any capital. No public investment is allowed.

Taxation

For tax purposes, an EEIG is regarded as acting as the agent of its members, rather than as a taxable entity in its own right. The members are treated as owning shares of the EEIG and its property in the proportions specified in the contract of formation, or if nothing is said, then in equal shares. Hence, the EEIG is tax transparent, as each member is taxable on its own share of the results. The EEIG is VAT registrable.

5 SUMMARY

When starting a new business, a decision that needs to be made, and reviewed on a regular basis, is whether or not the trade is carried on via a limited company. The main alternatives to a company are to carry out the business as a sole trader or possibly in partnership with others.

There are numerous tax, accounting and commercial factors that need to be considered before the decision is made. The tax and NI table (Table 2) summarizes some of the more important factors to be considered. From a tax point of view, the decision will depend primarily on the level of profits and the amount that the proprietors wish to withdraw from the business.

CHAPTER 2.2

Working with others

Caroline Cree
Carillion plc

Paul Henty, Associate
Shadbolt LLP

1 INTRODUCTION

A joint venture is a contractual arrangement in which resources are combined – be they equipment, expertise or finance – by two or more participants with a view to carrying out a common purpose.

A more basic definition could be 'a combination of resources (assets and expertise) by two or more participants with a view of achieving a particular objective'. Often the key objectives of entering into a joint venture are to secure particular expertise that complements those of the other joint venture partners, to provide suitable financial backing and to develop a long-term relationship.

In reviewing these two expressions of what a joint venture is, it should be recognized that the term is not precise. It is frequently used in the context of two or more businesses working together without consideration of the actual contractual relationship. Typically, such relationships might be:

- a consortium agreement
- a limited liability company
- a partnership
- a limited partnership.

While the sharing of liabilities and profit is regulated under a legal arrangement, to which only the joint venturers are the parties, there will generally, in addition, be a separate contract with a client. This will regulate the joint venturers' obligations and rights *vis-à-vis* that client, once the tender is successful. The risk and opportunity sharing in these two relationships, that is the joint venture and the client contract has to be matched such that delivery objectives for the joint venture partners are harmonized. For example, delays within the design process should not ultimately be left to lie with the joint venture partner who is responsible for the construction on site or the operator.

As indicated above, all joint ventures need to be considered on an individual basis to establish precisely the obligations and contractual risks being taken on by the parties to the joint venture. For example, a client is often looking for joint and several obligations with the joint venture to spread risk. This would leave one joint venture partner accountable to the client for the entirety of the joint venture should the other joint venture partner fall away. In looking at joint ventures, it is issues like joint and several liability that require careful assessment of the strengths of your potential joint venture partner.

2 REASONS FOR ESTABLISHING A JOINT VENTURE

The particular advantages or disadvantages for establishing a joint venture will depend on the type of project or work for which the parties are tendering. Joint venturing can provide a flexible vehicle to achieve a variety of objectives, including the following.

2.1 Limitation of risk

Responsibilities and liabilities can be shared between the participants and the risks spread among the parties, thereby limiting each party's potential exposure.

The limitation of risk will often be undermined by the fact that the participants are generally jointly and severally liable to the client or third parties (e.g. lenders) for the failures of the other joint venturers. However, the joint venture agreement may be drafted to distribute the liabilities between the parties according to the services carried out by each of the parties or in either proportionate or disproportionate shares. It is quite common to have segregated joint ventures where the risks and opportunities are defined for each party to the joint venture, i.e. there is a clear division of the services and, consequently, liabilities between the joint venture parties.

In contrast with these apparent advantages there are practical issues which need to be considered by the joint venture partners.

(a) When the services are integrated or segregated, the implications of joint and several liability to the client need to be addressed. Many clients perceive that they have a greater degree of security through a joint and several arrangement because each joint venture partner would be available to be pursued in the event of default and the adverse affects of insolvency of one partner could be mitigated.
(b) The drafting of a joint venture agreement that genuinely reflects the intention of the joint venture partners is complex both in the drafting and in the operation should anything go wrong during the project.
(c) As a generality, professional indemnity insurers like joint ventures to be clear and unambiguous, they can therefore be reticent about accepting proportionate sharing of liabilities, particularly where one partner is providing a fundamental expertise about which the other has limited knowledge.

2.2 Pooling of resources

The skills, expertise and equipment offered by each tendering party in isolation may be inadequate to meet a client's needs in the case of complex projects. Equally, some small and medium-sized companies may offer very specialized skills but, because of their size, they can only operate in collaboration with other tenderers. By combining their strengths they will multiply their potential, thus increasing the likelihood of being successful in tendering. Each participant will be in a position to benefit from the strengths afforded by the other participants, e.g. local knowledge, specialized expertise.

The corollary of this creates a downside when considering the merits of entering into a joint venture.

(a) While the different cultures of each participant may establish clear boundaries between them, equally those cultures can cause management problems. Thus, it is essential that each participant's role and responsibilities are clearly defined in a joint venture agreement. Matching cultures and ways of working are unfortunately not readily handled in the legal drafting of a joint venture agreement and in practice a mismatch or misunderstanding in cultural terms can produce a significant hurdle to be overcome in a joint venture.
(b) It is often a requirement to include a local partner within a joint venture and the merits of this for the host country are readily recognized. The reverse of that has historically been a requirement to manage an inexperienced team. This can create significant pressures if the roles and responsibilities have not been approximately allocated and structured.

2.3 Exploitation of opportunities

If the parties come from different jurisdictions, it is essential on occasions to join forces with a local partner in the area where the project will be carried out. While one party may provide special skills or expertise which are scarce in the area, the local partner may contribute local knowledge and contacts. This can be particularly relevant in relation to local practices in connection with importation of goods and materials as well as understanding and managing tax and foreign exchange issues.

Furthermore, a joint venture may be the only way of obtaining access to certain markets, particularly in developing countries. The reason is two-fold: since the parties interested in tendering in less developed regions often come from different countries, a joint venture will normally be an adequate means of representing the parties' interests *vis-à-vis* the client. In addition, projects in such areas often involve high costs, which derive from the shortage of materials, ability to attract suitably skilled manpower and basic infrastructure facilities. These costs may be such as to prohibit or discourage potential parties, unless they can proceed under the umbrella of a joint venture.

2.4 The whole operation is more harmonized

The joint venturers will often be represented in the preparation of the tender by a management team (usually comprised of representatives from each joint venture participant) or body that will represent the joint venture. When negotiations take place, the client can benefit not only from dealing with one body, but may enjoy closer or greater cooperation between the joint venture participants.

There is also greater coordination and communication among the participants as the links provided by the joint venture give them the incentive to work more closely than they would otherwise.

A major drawback when working closely together and taking decisions collectively is that the joint venturers may not be readily prepared to lose the element of total control over the operation which they would have had when operating in isolation.

In addition, the commercial and managerial approach of the parties may be very different, particularly where different interests are being represented. For example, a party with a pure design responsibility for a major piece of equipment may not be attuned to the operational issues affecting a civil engineering contractor's requirement to import plant to a remote and unsophisticated location.

3 PRINCIPAL CONSIDERATIONS IN ESTABLISHING A JOINT VENTURE TO TENDER

The different considerations to be examined when setting up a joint venture are numerous, but the main practical and legal issues are as outlined below.

3.1 Choice of partner

The client may decide from the outset that a joint venture is the most suitable vehicle to carry out the project. Therefore, groups of companies may be invited to tender for the contract. Alternatively, a number of companies may decide to tender together as a joint venture and put themselves forward to the client for a particular project. This latter situation is more common as it allows the joint venturers to choose their partners. In addition, the local law of the country where the work is to be carried out may impose on the participants an obligation to involve a local partner as a party to the joint venture.

It is important that the financial resources, creditworthiness, expertise and reputation of each of the participants are carefully examined before forming the joint venture. The principal reasons for exercising caution being:

- the potential liability that each of the participants may incur as a result of, for example, the insolvency of another participant
- the scope for potential conflicts of interest, management, clashes of personalities and cultures.

If these considerations outweigh the advantages of a joint venture, the parties should perhaps reconsider the merits of proceeding individually. The ability to work together effectively may be very difficult to achieve in practice. It is perhaps worth recognizing that some forms of client contract do provide a better environment in which to try to create a harmonious working relationship at joint venture level. However, the frequent legal 'sting in the tail' in terms of placing all significant risk with the joint venture, regardless of which party is best placed to manage it, can undermine the apparently supportive nature of the head contract.

3.2 Suitability of a joint venture for small and medium-sized companies

In principle, joint ventures can be formed for all sizes of project. The main reason for establishing a joint venture should be the complexity of the works and not the financial size. The National Joint Consultative Committee (NJCC) does not recommend joint ventures for projects with a construction value of less than £5m. In practical terms, this value-based recommendation may be less relevant to joint ventures between professional parties where complexity may be better viewed in the light of design innovation and specialization.

Notwithstanding the size, complexity and international profile of some projects, medium and small-sized companies may be key partners, as they can offer highly specialized skills and local knowledge. These companies should not, therefore, be put off by size or complexity factors when considering whether to tender with other companies in a joint venture. A further incentive for the small and medium-sized company will be the spreading of risk and costs among the participants. Despite these advantages, the small and medium-sized company should not lose sight of the implications of joint and several liability.

3.3 Status of the client

In order to ensure that the client is fit to comply with the obligations under its contract with the joint venture, the joint venturers should satisfy themselves of the identity, resources and strength of the client and also that the project is well defined.

3.4 Split of work and costs

Once the decision has been taken, the parties should agree on the terms of the joint venture before the tendering process starts, including the roles and responsibilities of each party and the way in which the joint venture is to proceed. It is good practice to put in place confidentiality agreements at the outset so that parties to the joint venture can be open in their discussions.

The distribution of the work should also be established. This can be a difficult area where the work is not specialized but influential in relation to the management and control of the joint venture. The price and the ratio of sharing the expenses incurred in the preparation of the tender can also be a sensitive subject which needs to be dealt with clearly at the outset; as does the split of fees. How the risks are to be shared and the insurances that each party to the joint venture may put in place should also be addressed.

3.5 Main provisions

Each joint venture agreement will differ, but there are some fundamental provisions that should be considered whatever contractual arrangement is adopted, including the following.

- Management of the project and procedure for decision making – it is generally necessary to have a board or management forum through which decisions are taken. This forum will need rules as to quorum and decision making, and also access to information on which decisions can be based. A critical area is deadlock, therefore the possibility of having a chairperson with a casting vote, or having to refer the deadlock to senior management, for example the chief executives of the respective parties, a professional body in the industry or mediation or even arbitration. However, to be truly effective there does need to be a mechanism for resolving everyday differences at site level without escalation.

- If the parties are not equal, it may be appropriate to specify that, on certain issues, there is weighted voting by reference to contributions to the joint venture. However, agreement of all the parties is normally required for key issues as such as:
  - setting a budget
  - appointment and removal of key personnel and approval of their remuneration
  - incurring of debt and the provision of security over assets
  - third party guarantees
  - profit distribution
  - material changes in the joint ventures objectives.
- Management of the project, particularly in its form, procedure for its appointment, and powers and liabilities *vis-à-vis* the joint venturers.
- Scope of services to be provided by each participant, particular arrangements for the use of equipment or personnel.
- Financial arrangements, including split of fee, maintaining accounts, procedures in submitting and payment of invoices.
- When the parties are jointly and severally liable, the procedure to be followed in the event of default by one of the parties should be set up, including prior risk allocation and indemnity.
- Cross-indemnification is likely to be necessary so that each party is held responsible for the work it performs for the joint venture or for that portion of the project that is commensurate with the profit/loss sharing arrangements in the joint venture agreement.
- Duration and termination – this may be linked to the scope of services provision or to the date of the success or otherwise of the tender. Reasons for early termination should be stipulated: for example, on default of a party and provision made (if desired) for the joint venture to continue following default or insolvency of a participant.
- Procedure for the settlement of disputes which may include procedure for the continued operation of the joint venture in spite of the dispute and a provision to arbitrate, and for termination in the event of the parties falling out without prospects of reconciliation. Frequently, an escalation process to handle disputes between the parties is included in the joint venture agreement. More sophisticated ways of dealing with disputes include reference to determination by an independent third party expert or by the inclusion of deadlock provisions, so that where there is an inability to agree on operational matters, a call option or sealed bids clause could enable one of the parties to buy out the others' interests or be bought out by the other parties.
- One way of redistributing risk and minimizing loss is by way of insurance. Which parties are covered will depend on the type of joint venture arrangement and will be of far greater relevance if the tender is successful. However, consideration should be given to such issues as minimum umbrella coverage, termination of liability and extent, type and duration of cover.

- Insurers will have views in relation to subrogation rights which have to be reflected in the way in which the joint venture operates. In essence, insurers will need to understand where risk lies and how it is to be controlled and managed.
- Letters of credit or bonds may be required as security for any indemnities. On larger projects, bid bonds and (if the tender is successful) performance bonds are likely to be required. These can be in the name of the joint venturers, with provision for the costs of procurement to be divided on the same basis as each party's interest in the joint venture or they may be supplied to the client by each joint venturer on a pro rata basis.
- The relevant law which is to govern the joint venture agreement should be established from the outset, together with the procedure and forum for the settlement of disputes. The choice of law will depend on whether the project has a national or international dimension, where the work is to be carried out, who are the main parties, and the presence of any requirements on the part of any financiers/lenders involved. Local law may impose certain legal constraints on the joint venture, such as part-ownership by a local company or use of local materials and labour. The client may, of course, seek to influence the choice of law applicable to the joint venture.

Further, in certain jurisdictions, notably the European Union, there are laws governing actual and potential anti-competitive practices that prohibit certain forms of joint venturing (see part 5 of this chapter).

3.6 Relationship with client

The joint venturers should consider carefully the terms of the main contract with the client and its potential interrelationship with the joint venture agreement.

Full consideration of the client's perspective should always take place whether there is an express requirement for a joint venture or not. Inevitably, the business drivers for the joint venture partners should take priority while complying with the client's requirements.

4 TYPES OF LEGAL STRUCTURE

The choice of legal vehicle with which to tender will depend on the particular characteristics of the project for which the participants are tendering. If the project requires a variety of different skills, a corporate structure may be appropriate. If, on the other hand, the project is carried out by two or three partners in the same field, a consortium agreement may be more suitable.

The joint venture entity can be structured either vertically or horizontally. Vertical integration involves joining two or more parties who are upstream and downstream of each other, possessing different capabilities and resources. This structure may be used by a main contractor and equipment supplier, or by the main contractor and a design professional. On the other hand, where two or more undertakings are engaged in similar or the same type of business and possess similar capabilities and expertise they may integrate horizontally to pool these resources. This may occur when the project to be constructed is large, complex and carries great risk and two or more similar businesses join forces to produce a body of expertise and experience whose value is far in excess of that of each of the individual firms.

Where the work is performed by the joint venture parties as if by a single entity, the relationship can be said to be integrated – profits and losses are shared in accordance with an agreed ratio. A non-integrated arrangement may be preferred where one or more of the parties has specialized areas of expertise and for the most part will undertake its respective portion of the work separately. In this arrangement, profit and losses will not be split up, but each party will deal separately with its own financial arrangements. Equally, a hybrid of the two may be appropriate.

Consideration should also be given to the way in which personnel will be employed if the tender is successful. They may be employed directly by the joint venture, furnished by the participants pursuant to a subcontract or other seconding type arrangements. While a straightforward arrangement such that personnel remain employed by the individual participants of the joint venture has its benefits, it has to be decided on merit. In particular, consideration should be given to the impact on an individual's personal motivation if this course is followed.

While liability for the other parties to the joint venture can be apportioned accordingly, if any gaps appear, the residual liability will have to be shared by all the parties. Some smaller organizations may not wish to see this happen. For example, design consultants or other professionals are unlikely to be prepared to assume the risks of construction by entering a joint venture arrangement with a contractor. Indeed, they are unlikely to have available capital to share in the funding. Therefore, in these circumstances separate terms of engagement may be more appropriate. A principal contractor may also prefer to enter the necessary subcontracts to procure certain specialist work or equipment in order to enjoy the advantages of retaining total (or certainly greater) control of a project and of reaping the rewards.

The main structures which joint ventures usually adopt are:

- consortium agreement
- limited liability company
- societas europaea (european company)
- partnership
- limited liability partnership.

4.1 Consortium agreement

This is a structure widely used in construction single-project joint ventures, and which provides the joint venturers with a more flexible way of catering for their particular needs than a partnership, but without having to create a new legal entity.

It differs from a partnership mainly in that there is no distribution of profits on a joint basis and the principle of agency does not apply. In addition, the parties' contributions are regulated by the agreement, to which contract law primarily applies.

Joint venturers should be careful in respect of the extent of their cooperation, otherwise they may in effect establish a partnership. The partnership rules for partnership matters including liability for each partners acts and omissions, termination and ownership of the property will apply if the partners' behaviour fulfils the definition contained in the Partnership Act 1890.

Consortium agreements are quite common, particularly in a start up situation (new service offered to the market-place) or an initiative to develop business in a new geographical region. These are frequently loose arrangements and it is only when an individual opportunity is identified that the arrangement is formalized on a project-specific basis.

Joint and several liability is generally an essential feature of a consortium agreement and one of the reasons why such a structure is used in joint venture tendering. The client will normally insist that the consortium agreement caters for this type of liability before the project is awarded to the tenderers and this arrangement can act as a deterrent for some companies who would otherwise enter joint venture arrangements.

Each of the participants is responsible for the completion of the project, notwithstanding that one or more participants have abandoned the project or otherwise breached the contract. Under the principle of agency, each participant can also bind the others when acting on their behalf. This, undoubtedly, represents a clear benefit to the client and participants entering into this type of joint venture should be aware of the full implications of this type of liability.

As regards the consortium's management, the day-to-day decisions are taken by one of the participants who will, in addition, be in charge of harmonizing the operation of the whole project. The important decisions are taken by the management committee, which is formed by representatives of the joint venture participants.

4.2 Limited liability company

This involves the creation of a new legal entity for the purposes of tendering. Its main features include the following.

(a) A separate legal existence from that of its shareholders – thus, the company can sue and be sued and own property in its own right. The liability of the shareholders is, however, in principle, limited to the amount contributed by way of their shares. However, this limited liability is normally qualified by the requirement for guarantees. The parties, for instance, may decide to set up a subsidiary with very small capital for a specific project. The subsidiary's liability will be limited in principle to its capital. However, the employer or the financier will often insist on the parent company giving direct guarantees. The provision of a parent company guarantee gives rise to some drafting issues, particularly in relation to ensuring that there is no greater liability passed on to the parent company than there is in the main contract.

(b) The incorporation of a limited company as a joint venture follows the same pattern as any other limited corporate structure. Therefore, articles of association are necessary and a shareholders' agreement may well be desirable.

(c) A management team will be normally appointed for the day-to-day running of the company's operations and negotiations with the client. Due to the high costs involved in recruiting new staff, the normal practice is for the joint venturers to provide the management team from their own employees, thus cutting expenses, which may not be recoverable if the tender fails.

(d) Directors of the company will be appointed. They are responsible to the company as a whole and have ostensible authority to bind the company. They could also be personally liable in the event of an insolvent liquidation if they are found guilty of fraudulent or wrongful trading. In addition, the Companies Act 2006 codifies duties of directors. Most of these new duties came into force on 1st October 2007 apart from the duty relating to conflicts of interests which came into force on 1st October 2008. The main new statutory duty is that of 'enlightened shareholder value'. This duty requires the Directors to act in such a way in which they consider is most likely to promote the success of the company for the benefit of its members while having regard to matters which a responsible business should such as the long term consequences of their decision and the effect of their actions on the company's employees, the community and the environment. The duties on directors set out in the new Act are not exhaustive and duties in other statutes will continue to apply such as duties on directors pursuant to environmental law, health and safety law and competition law. Directors can be pursued legally by the shareholders in the event of a breach of their duties. The Companies Act 2006 makes it easier for minority shareholders to bring a claim in the company's name against directors.

This legal structure has proved valuable where some of the participants contribute more work and resources to the project than others. This will be reflected in an unequal allocation of shares and voting rights, which will give some shareholders more benefits and control than others.

Other circumstances when a limited company may be a suitable legal structure include where the participants are large companies, a mixture of partnerships and companies, or when the participants wish to create a long-standing relationship.

The incorporation of a limited company must comply with certain statutory requirements set out in the relevant Companies Acts. These Acts contain restrictions as to shareholders consent being required for certain transactions with directors, the decrease and withdrawal of capital and the winding-up procedure that must be followed.

Some disadvantages can be perceived with this particular structure, which include the following:

- The parties have to go to considerable expense (drafting articles of association and possibly a shareholders' agreement) at an early stage in the preparation of the tender.
- If the client requires the parties to be jointly and severally liable in respect of their obligations to the client and third parties, this legal structure becomes a less favourable vehicle than other options, where liability can be dealt with more easily.
- The majority shareholders must respect the rights of the minority. These rights can be contained in the shareholders' agreement or, in its absence, there are certain statutory minority rights, such as the right to block certain decisions and to call meetings which will apply. These rights cannot, however, be ignored by the majority shareholders. Pursuant to the Companies Act 2006, minority shareholders will also have 'derivative rights' which are enforceable through the courts.
- If the parties have equal shares in the company, or where unanimity is required by the shareholders' agreement to take certain decisions, a deadlock can take place. The shareholders' agreement should cater for these and other disputes. Possible solutions are arbitration, sale of one party's shares to the others, or termination when the parties cannot find a solution.

4.3 European Company

On 8 October 2001 the European Union's Council of Ministers adopted a regulation to establish a European Company Statute (ECS) and the related Directive concerning worker involvement in European Companies. The ECS came into force in October 2004.

Basically, a European Company will operate on a European-wide basis meaning that companies operating in more than one member state will have the option to establish as a single company under EU law. This will mean that the company will be able to operate throughout the EU using one set of rules and a unified reporting and management system, rather than all the different laws of each member state.

The main benefits include:

- By using a single set of rules and unified management and reporting system, companies will be able to avoid setting up a network of subsidiaries in various member states, which can be time consuming, administration-heavy and therefore expensive in terms of legal and administration costs.
- If costs are cheaper, companies may attract more business overall, in particular European companies may find it easier to attract venture capital than if they are operating in several member states.
- European Companies will be able to avoid the burden of winding up and re-registering in a new EU state every time they want to move into another country to do business.
- A business will be able to restructure easily and quickly enabling it to take advantage of the opportunities in the market place and move across borders according to the needs of the business.

A European Company may be set up by one of four ways:

(1) By the merger of two or more existing public limited companies from at least two EU member states;
(2) By the formation of a holding company promoted by public or private limited companies from at least two EU member states;
(3) By the formation of a subsidiary of companies from at least two different EU member states; or
(4) By the transformation of a public limited company which has, for at least two years, had a subsidiary in another EU member state.

The European Company is a new entity and therefore may change as it develops. Administration of the European Company is currently as follows:

- Registration – Each European Company will be registered in the member state where it has its administrative head office on the same register as companies established under the national law of that state.
- Taxation – The European Company will be taxed at national levels according to national fiscal legislation within each member state. It will pay tax in each member state where it has a permanent establishment.

4.4 Partnership

Whether a partnership is in existence or not is a matter of fact.

The Partnership Act 1890 stipulates that a partnership exists between persons who carry out a business or occupation in common with the view to profit. The preparation and negotiations carried out for the purpose of tendering for a specific project will normally fit this definition. If the arrangement falls within the Act, stricter rules will apply to its termination and the issue of joint and several liability of all the parties to the partnership will arise.

This legal structure is suitable for small and medium-sized participants or where the parties are sharing benefits and contributing to the project on an equal basis, and where the parties are unlikely to subcontract the work. However, the partners can establish in a partnership agreement an unequal ratio of contributions and benefits among the partners.

Many of the matters considered in relation to a consortium agreement apply equally to a partnership.

Many venturers will avoid an unincorporated partnership due to the existence of unlimited joint and several liability of all the partners to it.

4.5 Limited Liability Partnerships

As from 6 April 2001, limited liability partnerships (LLPs) became available in the UK as the newest form of business medium. LLPs are incorporated at Companies House and are required to file at Companies House annual accounts and an annual return. Therefore, there is more transparency and information available to the general public than with an unincorporated partnership.

As with limited companies, LLPs have a separate legal existence and accordingly will enter into contracts in its own name. Members of an LLP will enjoy the benefit of limited liability subject to similar instances when that limited liability could be eroded, as set out in part 4.2.

Despite LLPs having the structure of a company, the LLP is taxed on the whole as a partnership.

It should be noted that the Government has now taken steps to extend certain provisions of the Companies Act 2006 to LLPs. The first set of regulations, which will extend the rules on audit and accounting to LLPs came into force on 1 October 2008. The remaining regulations, which have not yet been published, are to come into force on 1 October 2009.

LLPs are not required to have a memorandum or articles of association and accordingly the LLP will enjoy a great deal of flexibility to organize its own internal affairs. Matters usually contained in the articles of association of a company or in a shareholders' agreement should be drawn up in a 'members agreement'. The members Agreement does not have to be filed at Companies House.

It is essential to carefully consider with the venturers' legal and financial advisers whether a limited liability partnership is the most suitable structure to form the basis of a joint venture.

5 COMPETITION ASPECTS

Potential joint venturers should always bear in mind the effect, at both national and European (EU) level, of the rules regulating anti-competitive practices. Ensuring compliance with these rules is important, as failure to do so can result in full or impartial invalidity of the arrangements, as well as a fine of up to 10% of turnover of the participants and/or the joint venture. Where the joint venture has an effect only on national trade, parties must consider UK competition law, principally set out in the Competition Act 1998 and the Enterprise Act 2002. For joint ventures with a European dimension, the applicable provisions of EU competition law are found primarily in Article 81 of the EC Treaty, Regulation No. 139/2004/EC (the 'Merger Regulation') and various other EC regulations and guideline notices. Article 81 does not generally apply to cooperation agreements if they relate to a project that the individual parties could not deliver by themselves.

It is normal practice for joint venture agreements to contain covenants restricting competition. For example, the parties may agree that they will not compete with the venture to allow it breathing space to take off. Any restrictions must be proportionate and not unduly restrictive of competition. Problems become more likely to arise where participants in the arrangements have a high market share or the restrictions go beyond what is reasonably necessary for the venture to succeed. Where the joint venture has an effect only on national trade, such covenants must be drafted in the context of UK competition law and avoid breaching the Chapter I prohibition of the Competition Act 1998. Article 81 of the EC Treaty applies to arrangements for working together which may affect trade to an appreciable extent between member states of the European Union. The parties to such an agreement should follow the Commission's notices on permissible forms of co-operation in order to avoid infringing Article 81. Much of the Commission's advice will also assist parties in avoiding an infringement of Chapter I of the Competition Act 1998.

The Merger Regulation applies to joint ventures with a 'community dimension'[1] which are largely autonomous and intended to be long lasting. It is unlikely, therefore, that it would apply to a single project construction joint venture or a specific single private finance project.

If the joint venture agreement is subject to the Merger Regulation then the European Commission must be notified prior to the signing of a binding agreement. Once notified, the Commission then has a maximum of 115 days to make a decision as to whether to clear, clear subject to conditions or prohibit the joint venture. If a joint venture is subject to the Merger Regulation controls but is not notified for clearance, the parties may be subject to a fine of up to 1 per cent of turnover. Where a domestic joint venture is created it may be advisable to notify the Office of Fair Trading ('OFT') under the merger provisions of the Enterprise Act 2002. The creation of a new joint venture or a shift in control or influence, over an existing joint venture, may give rise to a relevant merger situation, if the joint venture will result in the creation or enhancement of a 25% share of a particular type of product or service in the UK (or a substantial part of it), or if the turnover of the largest participant in the joint venture is greater than £70 million. Although notification is not mandatory, the OFT can initiate an after the event inquiry into a completed joint venture which causes a substantial lessening of competition and the Competition Commission, in such circumstances, is empowered to order an unscrambling of a joint venture of a compulsory divestiture of parts of its assets or business.

6 CONCLUSIONS

Joint ventures offer a flexible approach to business operations – agreements can be structured in a legal format and content to suit the parties' needs; differing tax considerations can be accommodated. Furthermore, a joint venture agreement can be tailored to

[1] A merger or creation of a joint venture has a community dimension where the combined aggregate worldwide turnover of all the undertakings concerned is more than EUR 5 billion and the aggregate EC-wide turnover of each of at least two of the undertakings concerned is more than EUR 250 million. A concentration that does not meet the thresholds laid down above has a community dimension of the combined aggregate world wide turnover of all the undertakings concerned is more than EUR 2.5 billion; in each of at least three member states, the combined aggregate turnover of all undertakings concerned is more than EUR 100 million; in each of at least three EC member states included for the purpose of point; (b) the aggregate turnover of each of at least two of the undertakings concerned is more than EUR 25 million; and the aggregate EC-wide turnover of each of at least two of the undertakings concerned is more than EUR 100 million unless each of the undertakings concerned achieves more than two thirds of its aggregate EC-wide turnover within one and the same EC member state.

complement the business environment, whether an emerging market is being developed or the objective is to spread risk and combine differing spheres of expertise.

However, regard must be had to national and European Union laws when entering into arrangements, as well as exercising caution when deciding on the parties to these arrangements. It is wise to specify at the outset provisions covering dispute resolution for misunderstandings which may arise during the period of the association.

CHAPTER 2.3

Working internationally

Steve Priddy
Arup Group Limited

Chris Morgan, Dominika Litak and Karen McGrory
KPMG

1 INTRODUCTION

This chapter falls into four main sections. The first provides a strategic overview of some of the issues that the engineer must consider when working internationally. The next two sections look in greater detail, and with examples, at the practical issues of being an international worker. The final section concentrates on tax issues, both with regard to the business and also regarding personnel. Additionally, a short taxation check-list is included.

This chapter is not intended to be exhaustive, but gives a general view of the range of issues and risks which the consultant faces when working internationally. A good professional adviser is essential if these issues and risks are to be dealt with properly.

2 STRATEGIC CONSIDERATIONS

2.1 Reasons for working internationally

It is, of course, possible to work on projects in non-UK locations without shifting the centre of gravity from home base. Because of the nature of engineering consultancy and the service bias of its product a presence outside the UK may simply be limited to strategic studies carried out from home base. This can be done without attracting any of the regulatory restrictions outlined later in this chapter.

So, at the outset, the engineer must be clear about why he or she wants to go 'on shore' in the first place. Simple reasons may be expansion in a certain geographic sector; having the right person to lead the venture; diversifying the business by penetrating economies in different phases of the construction cycle; obvious engineering opportunities. One thing is certain – the time for entering a new location is not when the financial press, investor or real estate journals, or politicians are saying 'now is a good time'. It is already too late!

One very good reason for the engineer to work internationally is the edge that can be brought to the market-place. This edge will need to be refined and guarded. It is likely to be either at the forefront of existing technology, i.e. the engineer is doing something that no one else can currently do; or an innovation that produces a leap in the quantity of what can be produced; or, perhaps more likely, it has come about via multidisciplinary working, i.e. the solution was arrived at by solving a problem in another field. Wherever the edge is, and no matter how well it is protected, it is likely to be common property in the profession within eighteen months unless backed by economies of scale to deliver a broad range of skills such as Building, Engineering, Infrastructure, Acoustics, IT, Fire, Facades, Sustainability etc. from the same organisation.

2.2 Fieldwork

There will be extensive fieldwork to do, once the reasons for wanting to work internationally are clear. Social anthropologists, as part of their training, spend up to two years living within the culture which they are studying. For the consulting engineer, living for two years without producing won't work. Recruiting locally can help to speed up the process. Success, however, can take several years – at least two successful projects are needed, so that collaborators see some kind of track record. A period of acclimatization is essential for the international business. Many of the factors to be considered are listed later in this chapter. The approach should be from the macroeconomic down to street level where the engineer intends to fix their name-plate. In reality it is the very local market that will result in success. Macro issues are important, but it is the local clients that make the difference. This voyage of discovery will be a challenge but also exciting. In today's increasingly globalized environment, issues in the built environment can sweep rapidly around the world. It is the way in which they are interpreted nationally and locally which is of most relevance. Sustainability in design, for example, is felt and reacted to and legislated for in very different ways in the UK, Denmark, China or the USA (and within States of the USA).

A business plan is an essential step. While the plan may not really yield the answers required, it will provide a good focus and also a source of motivation for those who will lead the business.

The plan must have clear short, medium and long-term measurables and should contain, among other things:

- target turnover year on year
- turnover analysed by sector and project size
- target clients and a marketing strategy
- a cash flow forecast indicating best, likely and worst cases
- a staffing plan, including staff mix between expatriate and nationals, skill base, seniority, non-technical support
- a statement about what the consulting engineer can bring to the market-place that is different
- a profit forecast
- an appraisal of the investment
- a clear understanding of the cost basis – start up costs, accommodation, salary basis, local licensing, tax issues etc.

The next question is how the engineers will organize themselves in the new territory. Will they aim to continue with a reconnaissance office? Will the project office become independent and look for further work locally and in its own right? Will it be necessary to establish a locally registered branch or company? Or is it intended to work in joint venture? Or even to acquire a local well established practice whose founder is retiring but wants the business to continue?

Each of these scenarios demands different questions and leads to different solutions in different time frames.

2.3 Understanding the culture

No matter how well the engineer understands the official version of the territory in which they intend to work, the reality will be different. They will need to understand the power brokers and the patrons of the built environment as well as the local professional cliques. They will have to learn to navigate the bureaucracy. In many countries they will have to recognize and handle corruption within both the legal and the customary framework.

Lastly, the engineer must totally understand the regime of fee calculation and duties and scope of service. They must understand the extent to which different countries value design, reward design and integrate cost into design. The variations between even two very similar Western cultures – the UK and the USA – are astonishing . They become even more significant in other cases.

2.4 Identifying leader and staff

A leader for the venture

For most countries this position cannot be filled by a young enthusiast who is technically excellent. Increasingly, clients are looking for 'grey-hairs' who bring many years of experience and reassurance. It is necessary to have the technical and design flair behind the wisdom, but this alone is not sufficient. The leader, by definition, will be wholly exceptional. Nationality, linguistic skill and cultural awareness and a good commercial head may be more important than technical skill. Expertise in business development will need to be combined with controlling cash flow, all aspects of facilities management, staff recruitment, HR, legal/contractual matters as well as project delivery. Nationality is an important marker. In most of the sophisticated mainland European economies there can be no substitute for the native speaker as leader. In some of the most regionalized European economies the right accent or dialect can be critical. In many of the emerging markets expatriate leadership is accepted, but a rapid transfer of know-how and power will be expected.

With the right leader must come the right human resources (HR) strategy. Because the centre of any technical consultancy is its people, the HR policy is critical to financial success. The policy has to be firm, fair and realistic, while dovetailing with the legal and customary framework of the specific territory. The remuneration and benefits package has to be a balance between motivating staff while not becoming prohibitively expensive in the market-place. Also critical here will be skill sets and achieving the right mix between technical and business orientated people.

This short section gives an overview of just some of the strategic issues facing the engineer wishing to work internationally. What follows is a more detailed check-list of the practical issues that have to be addressed.

3 PRACTICAL ISSUES – LOGISTICS

3.1 International project management

Bringing the international aspect to project management will be a key ingredient in the commercial success of any venture outside home territory. In the early stages of being in another country this aspect is likely to be glossed over. Collaborators will be keen to have an international engineer on the team, and will go to great efforts in those early days to help with the administrative set-up. Much of the early technical work will be at the level of a concept and scheme design as understood in the UK. This may itself lead to failure – the delivery should be to the client's needs, not necessarily UK standards. There will be comparatively few drawings. Reports will be written and accepted at a fairly abstract level. This early warmth and the attractiveness of the abstracted level of service, coupled with an apparent low risk atmosphere can easily lead to a sense of false security.

Effective international project management will depend on crystal clear lines of communication and responsibility, agreed inter-office trading protocols and scopes of service, and a programme and critical path which all parts of the consulting firm have agreed to. For the international client, it is also necessary to demonstrate constantly that the entire resources of the international engineer's network are available and able to deliver the product. And that there is a key contact at senior level to deal with major issues.

The engineer planning an international venture must therefore identify at the outset not only who will lead the operation on the ground, but also who will be the key leaders in the home base. Often there will be a need to parallel the client's organization. A mode of accountability has to be established which ensures that such staff are as committed to the international workload as they are to their own domestic commitments. It is most unlikely that the virtual office can in itself be sufficient for effective international project management. Face to face contact, the experience of working with someone in the past, knowing and respecting each others' strengths and weaknesses will all be vital ingredients for success.

3.2 Internal working and subconsultancy

A robust system of working for internationally resourced projects will need to be in place. Such a system will have to be multi-currency in nature and therefore have a clear management accounting policy for dealing with foreign exchange differences. Therefore early involvement of the organisation's accounting function is fundamental.

Procedures will be needed in relation to internal subconsultancy arrangements. How are internal scopes of service to be defined? What are the profit and loss sharing arrangements? Do the management accounting arrangements have the blessing of the UK and local taxation authorities?

External subconsultancy can be an effective method of delivering the international project. To work well, the subconsultant must be well known to the engineer and they must mutually respect each other in the delivery of their respective tasks. In some countries subconsulting can be viewed adversely by clients as an abdication of responsibility. Conversely this may be required in other places. The use of high skill/low cost locations may also be an option to consider in subconsulting arrangements.

3.3 Business systems and the centre of management

The centre of management of the engineer may be critical in the treatment of tax losses. It can also be a factor in establishing whether a taxable presence exists in a country other than that in which the parent company is established. All new international ventures, unless they are simple acquisitions of existing businesses, are likely to incur opening years' trading losses. The utilization of those tax losses in an effective manner then becomes a key consideration. This is discussed in detail below. A series of 'badges' or attributes will be considered by the UK tax authorities to establish where the centre of management of a locally registered subsidiary is, for example:

- where are the named leaders of the local venture actually resident
- who has the ultimate authority for hiring and dismissal of staff
- where does the Board of the subsidiary meet
- what powers are given to local leaders in terms of limits to their authority to sign contracts on behalf of the venture.

In some countries, notably the USA, there are also the layers of tax law that go from Federal to State to City, plus corporate and individual registrations to be able to practise etc.

The business systems of the local venture must be carefully selected both to be appropriate and adequate for local requirements but also provide sufficient information to the centre to meet the organization's statutory and management accounting requirements. Typically, for example, in the early days of operation in a new territory, local leadership will operate an *Imprest* system of petty cash and bank accounts, recording transactions as and when they occur, and then making monthly returns to the central accounting function in order that statutory and project accounting records can be kept up to date and local funds topped up to agreed levels. Maintaining such a system is another drain on a local leader's time and entails at least a rudimentary knowledge of double entry bookkeeping, coupled with the confidence to handle comparatively large sums of money.

2.1 Ways of operating
2.2 Working with others
2.3 Working internationally
2.4 The engineer's appointment
2.5 Collateral warranties
2.6 Indemnity insurance
2.7 Employment law
2.8 Information technology

Even in this early stage of business development it is obvious that an additional overhead attaches to the engineer working internationally in the double reporting requirement, both to local regulatory frameworks, but also back to the centre. As the business develops, the systems required become more complex. A bookkeeper will have to be found at some point. The decision then is whether to use an agency or permanent employee, and whether full or part time. Very often the role will be filled by a 'Person Friday' who doubles as office manager and administrator. The recruitment should probably be done earlier rather than later in the process.

Once any mode of formal presence is established, an *Imprest* system is unlikely to be acceptable to the local tax and regulatory authorities. A complete set of accounting records will have to be put in place including nominal ledger, bank and cash books, fee and purchase ledgers and a fixed assets register. These records are called different things in different places, so language needs to be clear. In some countries audit of overhead costs for government contracts is commonplace. In many countries these books will have to be maintained in the language and currency of the territory. Also, the local nominal ledger package should be compatible with that used in head office.

Other systems will often have to be developed from scratch. For example, the database of business contacts, new leads, probable and possible projects, target clients and corporations will only be relatively poorly developed in the centre. Similarly, technical software may need to be purchased locally to meet local requirements. In order to transmit and translate drawings over borders and time zones, high-level decisions will have to be taken about software purchase and system development.

3.4 Banks

Establishing a strong relationship with a reputable bank at the outset of the international venture is also very important. The bank must understand international business and have its own strong links to the home country bank. Building up trust quickly means that the bank will act swiftly on your instruction. In a new location, for someone a long way from home, being able to act promptly to send money, to pay a salary or place a flat deposit with a landlord is critical for the efficient running of the business and for motivating staff. The larger banks frequently have their own economists providing useful up-to-date assessments on key industrial sectors, as well as their own project identification departments.

3.5 IT

It will be necessary to establish the constraints on software, communications and IT generally. For example, does the financial reporting application in the engineer's head office, which imports data from the project database into, say, a Microsoft spreadsheet, work when the locally available version of the spreadsheet is used with the same database? How long does it take to process bank transfers internationally or even intra-nationally? What costs are associated with such transactions? How quickly can telephones, fax or email be installed?

The effectiveness of the system's architecture will be a function of PC capability, application requirements, area networks and communication links. And it is vital to be able to communicate effectively and seamlessly with local clients and collaborators. Diagnosing where an IT fault lies can be a complex and time consuming affair.

3.6 Accommodation and location

The type of office that the client walks into provides a critical first impression and needs serious design consideration. If first contact in a new location is via architects for example, a modicum of chaos, preliminary sketches pinned to the wall, and a bright 'atelier' feel may be fine. But if this collaborative, fairly informal mode of working is unsuitable, then consideration needs to be given to the ordering and neatness of space and also its size. Prospective clients are going to be very watchful of whether you are capable of actually delivering their project on time and in budget. What means is the engineer using to maximize the international flavour brought to projects? How is this conveyed on that first visit?

Equally important is the location of the office. This again depends on a clear focus and target sectors following on from a well thought through and hotly debated business plan. For example, in the Netherlands different cultural perceptions attach to an international engineer being established in Amsterdam or Rotterdam or The Hague or Utrecht. The architectural community has one centre, the multinational inward investment another, the industrial community another. Such perceptions may be no more than banter which is easily corrected (although usually in the language of the country). In other territories, to get above a certain critical size it may be essential to be established as a network of offices spread throughout the country. This is certainly the case for working in Germany, Poland or the USA for example. It need not be the case in Spain or in the UK. But this relates to the business objectives in the first place, e.g. a focused boutique or an all-encompassing engineering machine delivering major infrastructure projects.

Within the city itself, location can be an important means of communicating an intention. For example, setting up shop in the financial sector might endear you to large banking and other financial institutions, but it might alienate one-off building clients, industrialists, heavy civils work or local architects. Great sensitivity is needed and clear thinking about the message which the engineer wants to convey about their presence in the territory.

3.7 Infrastructures

An in-depth understanding of the physical and fiscal infrastructure is essential. Physical infrastructure will involve considerations such as getting from A to B and the relative merits of road, rail and air transport. The mode of travel feeds through to relative costs and, ultimately, how such costs are built into local fee proposals to clients. The client looking for an international perspective will expect a clear and non-parochial approach to incidentals such as travel, translations, hotel and subsistence costs. Equally, for travel and communications not directly related to the job, establishment in the wrong location with a poor understanding of the local, national and international infrastructure can lead to unacceptably high overhead costs.

The fiscal infrastructure entails an understanding of the relative freedom of movement of financial assets. For example, do exchange controls exist in your chosen territory? Some countries which claim no such controls can often impose significant bureaucratic hurdles which then may lead to months of delays in repatriating funds deposited in a local bank. Sometimes blocked deposits may be required in order to secure rented accommodation. Some countries can restrict the free international flow of funds by demanding strict inter-company invoicing arrangements and subconsultancy agreements. Cash dividends may only be declared and paid once a year and be the sole means of transferring funds between affiliated companies and across national boundaries. Without sufficient understanding of the fiscal infrastructure, the engineer's cash flow could be seriously adversely affected.

3.8 English as a global language

Assuming that English is a global language cannot be the basis of working internationally!

While English may be suitable in some situations as the written and spoken medium, there are many situations when the local language must be used and even English words may carry different meanings in different countries, e.g. 'schedule' or 'programme'; 'program' or 'brief'. In the early days of arrival in a new territory there will be a natural tendency for local design collaborators to shield the would-be international engineer from those contexts where either being a native speaker, or being totally fluent, are essential. However, even in these days it is easy to transgress cultural boundaries unwittingly. Simple examples are the inappropriate use of the 'tu' rather than 'vous' form in France, or addressing both the senior German engineer and a more junior employee by their christian names when both are in the same room.

While the language of many engineering contracts may be specified as English, design development, design arguments, defending the client's budget against change from architects or others in the design team, handing over a design at a pre-agreed stage to a local engineer, all these instances will be conducted vigorously in the local language. The importance of this cannot be overestimated.

3.9 Cost and income

Another feature of working internationally that cannot be overestimated is understanding thoroughly the cost structure of the local consultancy profession, their profitability and productivity, how that relates to the service they provide and how the international engineer differentiates himself.

The engineer will bring to the local situation a higher cost base – they are likely to have a leader on an attractive remuneration package (because he or she will be in great demand). Overheads are likely to be higher as they will be carrying a central overhead cost. Productivity is likely to be lower, particularly in the opening years of the venture and this will also push up overheads. Incidental job expenses such as travel, translations, hotel bills, subsistence in particular, are likely to be higher than competitors'.

Because of these factors the engineer must be clear about the limiting factors on their venture's financial performance and where competitive edge resides. There may be a simple efficiency gain. In less developed engineering cultures the engineer may be able to produce the deliverables far more quickly than a local firm. This would need to be matched against the lower salary and overhead costs of such firms. The engineer may be providing a service that no local consultant can provide. For example, many American multinational clients looking to establish in mainland Europe are seeking above all someone whom they can trust and who will guide them through the entire local procurement process, someone who understands how to deliver an American job in a foreign context.

The engineer should conduct serious analysis of the financial position of competitors while recognising that this can only be indicative, but not an accurate comparison as the business model is likely to be different. Find out especially:

- what is the optimal size of consulting organization in the territory
- what is the optimal mix of staff by age and grade and salary level
- how do local organizations account for salary and overhead costs
- what is the typical profit margin
- what is an acceptable level of credit control (say debtor weeks)

2.1 Ways of operating
2.2 Working with others
2.3 Working internationally
2.4 The engineer's appointment
2.5 Collateral warranties
2.6 Indemnity insurance
2.7 Employment law
2.8 Information technology

- what is the typical cash flow profile of a local consultancy.

Obtaining this kind of information will not be easy but will repay dividends in understanding, and beating, local competition.

3.10 Local advice

Building relationships with local professional advisers will be critical. Increasingly, the old professional barriers between law, accounting, tax, HR and company secretarial functions are breaking down. Business consultancy is able to provide a 'one stop' shop to setting up a sustainable presence in new territory. In addition, there are State bodies, investment agencies, commercial attachés and the like, who will be keen to encourage UK investment in their country. Banks may also be able to provide advice or key contacts.

Building the relationships is a process of asking the same question from as many perspectives as possible to as many listeners as possible and testing independently wherever possible. For example, a question such as 'Will establishing a locally registered subsidiary affect my existing work?' has implications for corporate, sales and personal taxes and national insurances, existing local registrations, publicity for existing and future clients, possible separation of staff and projects between offshore and onshore activities and so on.

4 REGULATORY FRAMEWORKS

4.1 Insurances

Different territories can have different insurance regimes. For example, projects for construction in France have a requirement for decennial insurance which runs for ten years from the date of completion of a building and covers major latent defects. Such a policy can be requested on a stand alone basis from all members of the constructing team and premiums can be significant. Other policies in the US include commercial liability and automobile insurance.

The client may opt for specific project insurance cover. How the premiums are to be borne then becomes a subject for negotiation.

The engineer's professional indemnity (PI) insurer will be able to give advice on the cover provided in specific territories of operation. It is unwise to assume that PI automatically gives global cover.

Similarly, other forms of insurance may not be extended to specific territories and are often unavailable in those territories themselves.

There will be certain risks, especially in new or emerging markets where the engineer will have to take the decision either to seek appropriate cover or choose to self-insure. For example, the simplest commercial risk an engineer can face is that a client is unable to pay the fee because of insolvency. Establishing the client's commitment to the project, where the engineer has never worked with the client before, involves shrewd commercial judgement. The credit rating agencies can provide limited information about the financial strength or otherwise of the potential client, but agencies rely on limited sources of hard financial information (e.g. the filing of financial statements) as well as unofficial sources. In certain territories the latter becomes the predominant source of information.

Where the engineer is not familiar with the client or has concerns about payment, the following is a guide, although what is customary in different territories may vary.

(a) Make the agreement conditional on a mobilization payment before commencement of work.
(b) Try to match a monthly invoicing schedule to the s-curve of cost associated with the performance of the project.
(c) If possible, build in a 'right to stop work' should fees not be paid within the payment terms of the agreement. Include interest payments on outstanding invoices.
(d) Try to ensure that payment of fees is not linked to 'approval' of deliverables; ensure that any link between technical progress and fee invoicing is via neutral terms such as 'receipt' or 'delivery' of drawings, reports or calculations, not via their 'final approval'.
(e) Recognize that relatively long payment terms can be the cultural norm in many countries.
(f) Don't invoice fees and incidental expenses together – why hold up hundreds of thousands for a missing taxi receipt.

4.2 Rights and responsibilities for design

The engineer needs to understand what rights they have over their design. This will vary across territories. For example, in Italy it is possible to qualify and practise as both architect and engineer. It is possible to work in joint venture with an architect sharing the design fees in almost equal proportion. Conversely, if something happens to the architect which means that the parties cannot perform, then notwithstanding what might be stated in the internal jv agreement, both parties are jointly and severally liable for the performance of the scope of services specified in the head agreement.

In certain of the much poorer countries of the world plagiarism of design is a commonplace.

4.3 Corporate reporting

In connection with professional advisers, the engineer will have to establish at an earlier stage what the corporate reporting framework requires. The kind of questions which will have to be answered include:

- When do annual statements have to be prepared by?
- Must they be to the calendar year end or can they be to the holding company's year end?
- Who approves the financial statements?
- By what date must they be approved?
- What are the necessary meetings that a company must hold?
- How many shareholders/directors must there be?
- By what date does the tax return have to be filed?
- Is an external audit required?
- Do accounting policies in the territory depart from generally accepted accounting principles (GAAP) or International Financial Reporting Standards (IFRS)?
- How is Work in Progress accounted for on long-term contracts?
- Is there any constraint on the level of dividend that can be declared?

4.4 Technical registrations

The key question here is: is the engineer legally competent to conduct engineering consultancy in the territory? Two separate issues are commonly encountered. The first is whether the engineer's locally registered branch or company is properly structured to work legally. In many territories as diverse as, for example, New York or Singapore, there is a requirement that local nationals must make up a significant part of the leadership of the entity. The second issue is a local prohibition against 'foreigners' being on site or directing site operations; or drawings being issued unless they have first been approved by a local qualified engineer. This latter is not uncommon in the Middle East.

Being ignorant of such registrations and procedures can at worst lead to court actions against the engineer and at best to significant delays, reworking and consequent eroding of profit margins.

This can apply individually and corporately.

4.5 Contracts for services, fee scales, stages and deliverables

Some territories have standard contract forms and fee scales which may vary considerably from UK standards. In Germany for example, the HOAI Conditions of Engagement, set out over nine phases with clearly defined duties attached to each, are far more codified than other territories' Conditions of Engagement.

However, HOAI only provides design fee levels for buildings with a maximum cost of works budget of €25m. Above that level fees are negotiable. Complexity factors can be applied to the published scales. Most German clients will expect the engineer's service to cover HOAI Phases 1 to 8, although there will always be a break at HOAI 4 while various planning approvals are obtained. HOAI contains no remedy for prolongation of a contract for engineers and imposes a cost engineering duty on the engineer. Quantity surveying as a separate discipline does not exist in Germany (as in many other mainland European territories).

Above all, HOAI is significantly skewed when one compares effort involved over each stage with the rewards for each stage – earlier stages are significantly more profitable than later site involvement.

Each territory may have its own more or less well developed fee scale book. Reading what the book says is one thing; understanding what it means in terms of resourcing and delivering a project is altogether a much harder task.

Fédération Internationale des Ingénieurs-Conseils (FIDIC) *Client/Consultant Model Service Agreement* is a standard form of agreement that has been developed for international use by consulting engineers. It represents the highest level of consensus between various national engineering institutions and provides a useful basis on which a proposal or contract can be made.

In the US, the defined project stages are fairly commonplace. Programming (DPP), Schematic Design, Design Development, Construction Documents, Bid and Construction Administration. In some circumstances there are agency approvals that can take months. Some organizations have very defined deliverables for each stage, others less so. The key thing is to understand fully the local requirements at the outset and get documents from other projects to see what is the standard.

4.6 Guarantees, bonds, powers of attorney

Bonds and guarantees are a common requirement in some parts of the international construction industry. The following are the most typical.

- *Tender (Bid in the USA)*: to guarantee that the tenderer will not renege on his or her commitment – normally valid for the period between the submission of tender and the date of announcement of tender award.
- *Advance payment*: to guarantee that the consultant will not disappear having received a payment in advance of work being performed.

- *Performance*: to guarantee that the consultant will perform his or her duties properly.
- *Retention*: to allow early release of retained portions of fees.

Most guarantees are issued 'without recourse', i.e. no conditions are attached to the guarantee being called. Most guarantees also contain no expiry date. Their effective expiry is therefore only when they are returned by the client and can be cancelled and destroyed.

A guarantee represents a cost, both in the annual banking charges but also because guarantee commitments are set against any engineer's bank borrowing facility. A parent company guarantee will generally be a better option for the engineer, while still providing security to the client.

Powers of attorney will be required in almost all new locations since legal proof will be required to demonstrate that the named individual can act on behalf of the engineer. Powers will normally need to be written in the language of the territory and will often require notarization and legalization.

4.7 Notarization

Working internationally, the engineer will often be required to provide notarized documents which have also often to have a formal stamp from the relevant territory's Embassy. Notarization can be required, for example:

- in connection with the appointment of a fiscal representative for VAT
- in the setting up of a branch or subsidiary
- in connection with major public sector bids.

Additionally, European Journal (OJEC) bids are increasingly requesting references from the bidders' home country and/or certificates from the tax authorities and self-declarations showing the good financial health and probity of the bidder. If these are not provided on time or in the right format the bid can be delayed or disqualified.

4.8 Professional bodies

In some territories, there may be certain local professional rules which preclude engineers from being able to be considered in competitive tender for certain kinds of work. For example, in Spain there exists a process of 'clasificacion' which entails presenting a portfolio of work and references together with background material on the engineer's staff and organization to the local college of engineers. Only after approval is the engineer able to bid in his or her own right for public sector contracts in clearly defined building types. Without the qualification they must always link up with others to prepare a consortium bid.

Such networks are becoming rarer on mainland Europe although they are still very important in the newly emerging central and eastern European states.

In California (and other States), registration is required by the State Department of Consumer Affairs or similar for company and individuals. For Federal work there are complex security requirements that have, of course, got stricter. Professional bodies have less impact in the USA, at least for engineers. However, drawings have to be stamped and signed by the Professional Engineer (PE) in each major discipline.

4.9 Understanding bureaucracy

An inevitable, but often new, experience for the internationally based engineer will be recognition of, and navigating through, bureaucratic regimes. On our home territory we already do this, albeit unconsciously. It is well known, for example, that the English are masters of the ability to queue, whereas in many of the Latin American countries queuing is non-existent.

We become frustrated with procedures and regulations which we take for granted at home. Bureaucracy is often identified with the public sector but it is rarely confined to that sector.

The engineer needs to be able to recognize that in certain countries a realistic maxim to observe is that a written, signed fee agreement is a good basis for negotiation.

In certain countries there is a fine distinction between bureaucracy and corruption. This is obviously a very sensitive area. Guidance as to how to conduct oneself and what constitutes corruption must be gleaned carefully from as many sources as possible including the Foreign Office and DTI, established local competitors, professional advisers and the country's legal framework.

4.10 Exchange rate risk

This non-technical risk category is perhaps the most volatile and the hardest to predict. Hedging instruments are in the main wholly inappropriate for the international engineer – certain 'American' style currency options come closest to meeting their needs. However, since the currency markets are dominated by transactions which are fuelled by currency speculation they are of limited relevance. The engineer should therefore seek to maximize currency of income to currency of expenditure and acknowledge that the fiscal world order is moving inexorably towards two world currency zones.

5 SOME TAX ISSUES

5.1 Introduction

An engineering firm may be involved in international projects in various ways. It may undertake one-off projects in various non-UK territories, it may 'set up shop' in a non-UK jurisdiction where it will undertake several projects, it may provide designs from its UK base and only send personnel abroad on a very temporary basis – say for a site visit – or it may simply second an employee to a company overseas to assist it with its own business without undertaking any specific project. Although commercial considerations should be the most important factor, each excursion to an overseas jurisdiction has its own tax consequences and these need to be considered well in advance of undertaking the project. Tax is often the last thing on the engineer's mind, but it is an operating cost and, like any other overhead, needs to be factored into the investment plan.

From a practical point of view, dealing with non-UK tax authorities, many of whom do not speak English, can be frustrating for even the most diligent taxpayer. With careful tax planning in advance, it should be possible to mitigate the effect that overseas taxes will have on the project. A thorough analysis of the legal and tax systems of the country where the engineering firm proposes to do business will prevent bitter and often expensive problems.

These notes are an aide-mémoire and check-list of the tax issues that should be raised with the overseas adviser. The starting point is to ascertain whether or not domestic law imposes tax on the profits or payments made in connection with the project. It is then necessary to check if there is a double taxation treaty between the UK and the overseas country which either reduces or eliminates the tax payable.

5.2 What taxes may be payable in the non-UK territory?

(a) *Corporation tax or corporate income tax* (federal and state, where applicable): this is a tax on profits. With tax planning it may be possible to keep income to a minimum and maximize deductions, keeping taxable profits low. Remember that fees and charges from related entities must be determined at arm's length to comply with transfer pricing requirements.

(b) *Withholding tax*: this is a tax which is deducted at source from various payments – e.g. interest or royalties. It may be reduced or eliminated under a tax treaty between the country of residence of the paying and recipient entities. Withholding taxes create a cash flow cost. In the UK it is possible to credit foreign tax withheld against UK tax on the same income but it will be an absolute cost to the extent it cannot be relieved in the UK. The withholding applies to the gross payment, so that if the profit margin on, say, fees or royalties is low, the withholding may actually exceed the profit.

(c) *Local and municipal taxes*: many local authorities have taxing rights and may levy charges by reference to different criteria, such as the amount of corporation tax paid, turnover, profits, number of employees, location, type of industry.

(d) *Value added tax/sales tax* (VAT): branches and companies will probably need to register for VAT. To the extent that the VAT is recoverable, it should only be a cash flow issue. Where fees are received from overseas, the branch or subsidiary may have to reverse charge itself. Early registration and fulfilment of all legal requirements are important to ensure full recovery. Some countries require a minimum turnover to be able to register for VAT. In other countries, registration may be required irrespective of turnover and before the entity is entitled to carry on economic activities.

(e) *Payroll and income taxes*: resident employees will have to pay local income tax on their wages. When seconding employees abroad it is also important to understand if and at what point they become liable to pay local income tax. Often the company or branch is liable for deducting income tax from wages but it may also be necessary for individuals to file their own tax returns.

(f) *National Insurance Contributions/social security charges*: these are normally payable by reference to the employee's salary, but in many countries it is difficult to know in advance what the charges will amount to. Different criteria may apply, such as the amount of the salary, risk of the employment, category (skilled/unskilled), age, number of employees working for the entity. In countries where unemployment is high, tax breaks (such as reduced contributions) may be available, but this will be more likely to apply to the unskilled local workforce rather than highly qualified architects or engineers who have arrived from the UK or other countries.

5.3 Is there a double taxation treaty between the UK and the overseas country?

The first question is always whether or not the non-UK country imposes tax on the activity envisaged. The second question is whether the local rules are modified by the existence of a double tax treaty between the UK and the other country.

The existence of a double taxation agreement between the UK and the non-UK territory will help to determine (and, generally, narrow down) the circumstances in which the UK entity has a taxable presence in the non-UK territory and the tax on any income it derives. Fortunately, the UK has a very large treaty network (with over one hundred countries).

Depending on what specific corporate vehicle the UK firm has adopted (see Section 5.5 of this chapter) the most relevant articles of the treaty are likely to be those relating to permanent establishments, business profits, royalties, avoidance of double taxation and non-discrimination. Many, but not all of the treaties signed by the UK, are based on the OECD Model Convention and the Commentary is a useful aide. Some countries have made reservations on how they interpret specific treaty provisions and this may be especially relevant in determing if a particular payment is subject to withholding tax. These are noted in the Commentary, which should always be checked.

5.4 Foreign taxes and the existence of a taxable presence overseas?

It is not necessary to carry on business *in* the non-UK territory to be subject to tax there and the local tax legislation of the non-UK territory will, in the first instance, determine when a non-resident entity will be subject to tax. Depending on the commercial requirements and the local law, the UK entity may establish (have to establish) a local company, have a taxable presence (referred to as permanent establishment – see below) or simply be subject to local withholding taxes on the fees it receives.

Local company

The most obvious form of taxable presence overseas is a subsidiary. The basic position is that where an overseas subsidiary is set up to carry out a project, it will be considered 'resident' for tax purposes in that country and all its profits will be taxed locally. If a subsidiary is not set up, the business profits arising from the project will normally only be taxed in the non-UK territory if the UK parent has a permanent establishment (see below) in that country.

Permanent establishments

A permanent establishment is defined as a *fixed place of business*. It exists where a foreign enterprise carries out business in another country through a *fixed place* which is of more than a temporary nature. It amounts to a projection of the foreign enterprise of one country into the soil of another country.

Most treaties have an illustrative list of what type of presence does or does not constitute a permanent establishment in the signatory countries. A place of management, a branch, an office, a factory and a workshop will normally constitute a permanent establishment. However, the maintenance of a fixed place of business solely for the purpose of carrying on, for the enterprise (i.e. head office) any activity which is of a preparatory or auxiliary character is unlikely to constitute a permanent establishment. Carrying out initial site visits may fall within the preparatory category. Short-term non-recurring visits to an overseas location – e.g. for the purposes for information gathering – should not generally be enough to constitute a permanent establishment, though the position for the country concerned should be checked before any such visits are undertaken. Whether or not a presence abroad is sufficient to constitute a permanent establishment can be affected by the length of time the employees concerned stay in the country as well as type of activity they carry on. Again the rules applicable in the particular case should be investigated.

A permanent establishment will also be deemed to exist where a person has authority to, and habitually does, enter into contracts on behalf of the foreign entity. In order to avoid unnecessarily establishing a permanent establishment in case of travelling employees, employees visiting the overseas country should not enter into legally binding obligations on behalf of their employing company or substantially conclude their negotiations.

Many treaties provide that 'a building site or construction or installation project' constitutes a permanent establishment where it lasts for a period exceeding twelve months (six months in some treaties, such as with Greece and Turkey), whereas other treaties are silent. Some countries have made reservations as to the length of the project and the type of activities included within the definition of 'a building site or construction or installation project'. The Commentary to the Model Convention should be checked to confirm whether the country in which the firm intends to operate has made any such reservations. In the absence of a treaty between the UK and the non-UK territory, what amounts to a taxable presence in a non-UK territory is determined solely by that country's domestic law. In the case of construction work, the taxable presence is most likely to result from having a physical presence in the non-UK territory. The implications of trading through a company or a permanent establishment are considered below.

Where a permanent establishment exists the non-UK jurisdiction will subject the profits to local corporation or other business profits tax. The treatment of business profits under any double taxation treaty will then be relevant as it will determine how the taxable profits should be calculated. Most treaties state that the taxable profits of a permanent establishment are only those profits which it might be expected to make if it were a distinct and separate enterprise engaged in the same or similar activities under the same or similar conditions.

It is not unusual for some of the preparatory work for a specific project to be done in the UK before even touching base in the non-UK territory and later to send one or more engineers on site to supervise the construction. In some cases it is possible to claim that fees for such work are not part of the business profits of the permanent establishment and so not subject to tax in the non-UK jurisdiction. However, although the work may have been carried out in the UK, some non-UK jurisdictions will seek to tax the profits attributable to it on the basis that such fees are connected with the permanent establishment in their territory even if paid directly by the client to the head office. This is known as the 'force of attraction' rule. It may be possible to mitigate the force of attraction rule by ensuring that preparatory work in the UK is carried out by a company in the group different from that which will carry out the construction work overseas through a permanent establishment.

The force of attraction rule may also result in having attributed to the permanent establishment other income arising in the overseas jurisdiction which is not related to the construction project, such as interest on loans or fees from unrelated assignments in that jurisdiction carried out in the UK by the head office.

Withholding taxes on royalties and other payments

Most countries charge withholding tax on payments of royalties outside their jurisdiction. Usually, the definition of royalties in double taxation treaties includes fees for information concerning industrial, commercial or scientific know-how. It is important to check with the overseas tax adviser whether, under the relevant treaty, fees charged for designs produced by engineers will be treated as royalties. Some countries also apply a withholding tax to any service fees paid abroad.

A tax treaty will often reduce or even eliminate a withholding tax. It may be necessary to make sure that the wording in the contract is properly drafted to support the argument that the fees are not subject to a withholding – or that only part of the fees are so taxed.

Such withholding taxes can arise – where applicable – irrespective of whether or not the UK entity has a taxable presence in the local jurisdiction. It is necessary to consider the impact of such withholding tax:

- if the payment is made directly by the client to the UK head office;
- by a local permanent establishment to the head office or another group company;
- by a local subsidiary to another group company.

In some cases the UK company may be able to choose – either under local law or in the way it structures the operation – to have a local taxable presence (permanent establishment or company) to be paid fees in the UK subject to a withholding tax.

Because withholding taxes are charged on gross fees not profits, if the withholding tax is high in comparison with the commercial profits generated by the activity (it could even be higher in some cases), it may be worth while choosing to establish a local taxable presence so as to be able to offset the costs and only bear foreign tax on the actual profit. This will also depend upon the extent to which the UK entity can use the credit for foreign taxes against UK tax on its other profits.

5.5 Choosing the form of investment: branch or subsidiary? joint venture, consortium, alliance?

Some countries impose restrictions on ownership by non-nationals or non-residents either by limiting the value or size of their shareholding in a local company or simply forbidding it altogether. Although not imposing such restrictions, other countries require that directors be either nationals or residents in the country. These conditions by themselves are likely to have a significant impact on the choice of corporate vehicle. Where no limitations apply, or these are not insurmountable, tax considerations come next.

Where a significant amount of work will be carried out in a non-UK jurisdiction, it is important to determine in advance whether to trade through a branch of the UK company (no separate legal identity) or through a subsidiary incorporated in the non-UK territory (a separate legal entity).

In the case of one-off projects, a branch may be simpler, as the legal requirements are usually simpler than those involved in incorporating a company. However, some countries tax branches at a higher rate than companies and, in addition, some apply withholding taxes on remittances back to the head office, increasing the tax burden. For one-off projects, a branch may nevertheless be advisable where the complications of liquidating a company are too cumbersome and leaving a dormant company in place is expensive (e.g. because dormant companies need to file certain documents on an annual basis) or, very simply, because setting up a company for each and every project is likely to result in a very complicated group structure.

Where the UK consulting engineering company has longer term projects outside the UK, it may also be advantageous to start trading with a branch if it is expected that losses will be incurred in the first years of trading. These losses will normally be deductible from other profits arising in the UK. Once the non-UK operation becomes profitable, the branch can be incorporated without incurring UK tax. It is crucial to know how the non-UK territory will tax the incorporation. Some jurisdictions may tax the transfer of goodwill from the branch to the company or claw back deductions granted for losses where the parent company (UK head office) has used them to reduce its profits at home (the UK).

It may still be possible to use non-UK tax losses in the UK where a subsidiary is incorporated in the non-UK territory. Subject to treaty provisions, a company incorporated outside the UK but managed and controlled in this country is tax resident in the UK. The place of central management and control broadly means the ultimate place where control is exercised. This is a matter of fact and the UK HMRC considers several factors, such as the place where the Board meets, place of residence of the directors, powers given to local managers. Thus, the losses of the overseas company could be set against the profits of its UK parent company (or other UK company in the group) under the 'group relief' provisions. When it is anticipated that the non-UK operation will start making profits, the company may be able to leave the UK tax net by migrating, although this may not be necessary if the local rate of tax is higher than the UK rate. The tax implications of migrating need to be considered.

It is possible that the company may be tax resident in two jurisdictions at the same time for example because the other country treats a locally incorporated subsidiary as being tax resident. Some countries (e.g. the USA) limit the use of losses against their local tax charge where a dual resident company can use losses in another jurisdiction.

Another consideration in determining whether to operate through a branch or subsidiary is the taxable base. Even if the rate of corporation tax is the same and there is a treaty according to which a permanent establishment will be taxed as if it were an independent company, it will not necessarily be so. Different items may be taken into account when computing income and deductions (for instance, many countries refuse the permanent establishment's deductions for payments to the head office on the basis that the company is paying itself). Also, double taxation treaties apply to persons (including companies) resident in the territory of one of the signatory parties. Permanent establishments are part of the same entity as the head office and are treated as resident for tax purposes where the head office is located. This results in certain treaty benefits being denied to permanent establishments which would normally be available to resident companies.

Frequently, the UK engineer will work on international projects jointly with other firms (UK and non-UK) of technical engineers. The use of the joint venture, consortium or other forms of alliance may be an attractive organizational option. The format of this joint venture work is very important for tax purposes and needs to be considered in advance of teaming up. The format could include setting up a jointly owned local subsidiary, operating through a local partnership, or simply a contractually arrangement which does not have any presence in the overseas country. However, often the best result is to ensure that the affairs of the joint venture will be tax transparent so that each joint venture partner is treated independently and according to its own particular circumstances for tax purposes.

However informal the arrangement, there should always be a written agreement reflecting the rights and responsibilities of each participant towards the common client and towards each other, as this will impact on the tax treatment. It is also necessary to consider the legal and accounting issues arising from a joint venture. The rules may differ depending upon the type of arrangement and the location of the venture. For example, in Germany any sizeable project must be registered as an 'Arbeitsgemeinschaft' (or Arge) for VAT and corporate tax purposes. The Arge must be led by a named 'Federführer' who handles the business affairs of the Arge. Even where the Arge's affairs are totally transparent, periodic returns are required for both VAT and corporate tax purposes.

5.6 Mitigating the non-UK tax burden

To minimize the taxable profits of a non-UK entity, it is important both to reduce the items of income arising to it and to maximize deductions. The following should be considered.

(a) Can part of the work be done outside the non-UK jurisdiction, and so outside its tax net?
(b) Can the non-UK entity claim a deduction for fees paid? Some jurisdictions will not allow branches to claim a deduction for fees or interest paid to the head office (on the basis that the entity cannot do business with itself). In such cases, it should be considered whether an entity other than the head office (e.g. another group company) could provide the service and charge the fee. In all cases, when fees are paid between connected entities, fees should be at arm's length to comply with transfer pricing regulations.

5.7 Repatriation of funds: withholding tax

Withholding tax is an absolute cost of the overseas operation if the UK parent cannot get full relief for the withholding tax suffered. Double taxation treaties generally reduce or even abolish withholding taxes. Where no treaty is in place, the domestic rate of withholding tax will apply. Whether withholding applies needs to be considered by reference to payments of fees, interest, royalties and dividends:

- from a non-UK branch or subsidiary to the UK parent company
- from a third party in the non-UK territory to a branch of the UK company in that non-UK territory
- from a third party in the non-UK territory to the subsidiary of the UK company in that non-UK territory, and
- from a third party in the non-UK territory directly to the UK company.

Where a fee for, say, design services is subject to withholding tax, it is important to bear in mind that the withholding will be calculated by reference to the gross fee, not just the profit element. It is important to calculate the impact of the withholding in the UK as all or part of it will be wasted if the tax payable in the UK on that fee etc., is lower than the tax withheld overseas.

As a practical point, and where trading through a branch, some non-UK tax authorities agree to limit the level of withholding tax to the actual amount of tax payable in their country. This possibility should be explored, as it may do away with the need to prepare tax returns and claim a refund for overpaid tax which, in many countries may take years or simply not happen.

5.8 Employee issues

A UK company which has decided to engage in projects overseas, whether on a long or short-term basis, would normally employ one or more local employees for administrative tasks. Engineers and other skilled personnel are likely to be seconded from the UK.

Many countries impose restrictions on non-residents and may refuse to recognize the qualifications of technical staff qualified outside their jurisdiction. This normally results in having to employ local architects and/or engineers. In some countries there has to be a certain ratio of local to expatriate employees.

Income tax for employees

The tax treatment of those posted to a non-UK jurisdiction (host country) will usually depend on whether the employee is or is not tax resident in the host country and the UK.

Generally speaking, a person is treated as resident for tax purposes if he is physically present in a country for a period of at least 183 days in the relevant fiscal year. Residence can be also determined by a person's intentions. The rules vary from country to country so advice should be sought.

Where an employee is seconded abroad from the UK, but remains resident in the UK, the employee may be taxed in both the UK and the host location. He should usually receive a credit in the UK for overseas tax paid; ensuring double taxation does not arise.

In some countries non-residents are subject to a lower flat rate of tax, but may be disadvantaged by not being able to claim deductions. Tax residents are normally subject to the local rates of income tax on their worldwide income (few countries have the UK concept of 'domicile', according to which for those who are not 'domiciled' in the UK but are tax resident here, non-UK income may not be taxable unless remitted to the UK). This can lead to seconded employees being subject to tax on all their income – even if it is not related to their employment in that country.

Income tax is normally chargeable on all emoluments, including benefits in kind. In some countries benefits in kind allow scope for tax planning, especially if these are akin to travel and subsistence costs such as accommodation, utilities and in certain cases, per diem allowances.

Tax breaks

Some jurisdictions offer special tax breaks for individuals who bring particular skills to their economy. Some territories will specify a maximum period for which the allowance can last and if the maximum period is exceeded the tax benefits already granted may be clawed back. Employers should ensure that any conditions for obtaining these allowances are, or will be met, before agreeing terms with employees.

Delivery of salary and multiple employment arrangements

It is not unusual for an employee posted overseas for two or three years to want to receive part of his or her income in the UK. This could be due to financial commitments (family, mortgage) or simply because the overseas currency is unstable, payment in foreign currency may not be possible, or exchange control regulations make it impossible or very expensive to take money out of the host country.

As a result employers may wish to consider splitting the delivery of the salary between the home and host country where this is practicable. This can result in tax savings, as some locations will provide relief for amounts paid and retained offshore. Structuring of this kind is common but such arrangements must be checked on case by case basis, and must, obviously, involve full transparency for the local tax authority. Advice should be sought.

Alternatively, a few countries will permit multiple employment arrangements i.e. dual contracts. In this case, the employee has two contracts. One contract will be for services rendered in the host country with the remuneration under that contract being subject to tax in that country. Under a second contract of employment, the employee is paid outside the host country for services rendered outside that country. Even where dual contracts are accepted, there must be commercial substance and it is usually necessary to prove that the employee does indeed render services in other jurisdictions. Having two roles which are kept completely separate with no cross over of where the duties are performed can also be a requirement in certain jurisdictions.

Where split contracts are not possible there may be alternatives which ensure that the employee can receive amounts which are outside the local tax net. Such arrangements must be checked on a case by case basis and must, obviously, involve full transparency for the local tax authority.

Exchange control

Usually an employee will need to bring back funds to the UK, either during the overseas posting or at the end of it (bank charges could be incurred and the employee may suffer as a result of an adverse movement in exchange rates, etc.). In a limited number of countries exchange control restrictions exist; however, it is not given that the secondee will fall within these rules. The employer will need to address these issues at the very beginning to determine how the secondee will be paid and the employee should be made aware of these issues also so that he may plan his affairs and to ensure no case for claiming compensation for loss from the employer will arise (unless this is part of the intended policy).

Pensions

Most UK employers contribute to the employee's UK pension fund. The following questions arise: first, is it possible to continue to contribute to that fund in the UK especially where the person sent overseas may cease to be an employee of the UK company? Secondly, if a contribution is made, what are the tax implications in the UK and in the non-UK jurisdiction? Is it a taxable benefit of the employee? Thirdly, if the pension contribution is recharged to the non-UK branch or subsidiary, is it a deductible expense for the latter and does it become taxable locally? Local tax rules need to be checked in each case to ensure that local laws have been complied with.

In addition, many countries require employers and/or employees to contribute towards a pension in that country. In some cases, this will be money lost as entitlement to draw the pension may never arise. But some jurisdictions will refund contributions made where the employee remains in the country for a short period. It is always worth inquiring.

It should be also borne in mind that there are implications where a worker is seconded to a country within the European Union for a period of 5 years or more and remains in the UK plan. This could trigger cross-border status for the UK plan and may lead to funding implications.

Tax equalization

Employees sent overseas will expect not to pay more tax as a result of working in the host location than they are paying in the UK, unless this is already compensated for in the salary being offered. Employers often institute 'tax equalization' or 'tax protection' policies to deal with this. Under a tax equalization policy the employer will reduce the salary by an amount equivalent to the tax which the employee would have paid if he had remained in the UK. In return for this, the employer agrees to pay any UK or host country tax arising on employment income. Under tax protection, the employee initially bears all taxes but has the right to ask the employer to reimburse any amount in excess of the UK tax which would have been due.

Often employees will be provided with benefits abroad to which they would not have been entitled had they remained in the UK, such as accommodation. These benefits might attract a tax liability. It will be appreciated that most or all of the tax so arising is in excess of the tax which the employees would have suffered in the UK.

Both tax equalization and tax protection policies can prove expensive. Not only is there a potentially high cost in terms of tax if an employee works in a high tax country, but also the administration involved can prove costly. Furthermore, the employee will usually be taxed on the tax equalisation element meaning that it has to be grossed up. However, these policies will aid the mobility of workers especially if the employer needs to move its workforce to a high tax country and can also encourage consistency. The employer will need to consider the location of the secondment and the number of workers involved.

Often social security contributions will be regarded in the same way as tax and incorporated into a tax policy.

Social Security

To determine where social security should be paid the world is split into 3 groups which are the European Economic Area (EEA), Reciprocal Agreement Countries and the 'rest of the world'.

Most employees seconded overseas who remain employed by the UK company will continue to pay UK Class 1 contributions for a given number of years if they are seconded to a country within the EEA or a Reciprocal Agreement Country.

For 'rest of the world' countries, the UK contributions will cease after the first 52 weeks of the assignment and the employer will need to consider whether a liability arises in the host location. The individual could elect to pay voluntary Class 2 or 3 contributions to maintain their UK social security record and may wish to obtain a Pension Forecast to establish any shortfall in their record. They may also be subject to host country social security contributions.

If the employment contract moves to a non-UK entity then Class 1 contributions will cease.

5.9 Regulatory matters

It is worth knowing in advance of setting up shop whether a fiscal representative needs to be appointed and how the local tax authorities operate: are they flexible and willing to negotiate? Do they give tax rulings? What are the penalties for failing to comply with what seems to be mere regulatory requirements? With respect to fiscal representatives, in some jurisdictions they are jointly liable for the tax due by the entity and finding one willing to assume such responsibility may be difficult and/or expensive.

6 TAX CHECK-LIST

Is there a double taxation treaty between the UK and the overseas country?

- Permanent establishments.
- Business profits.
- Royalties.
- Rates of withholding tax.

Tax presence overseas; branch or subsidiary?

- What rate of tax applies to a branch and to a subsidiary?
- Cost of repatriating profits in each case.

- Determination of the taxable base.
- Availability of deductions.

Repatriation of funds; withholding tax.
What taxes are payable in the foreign country?

- Corporation tax.
- Withholding tax.
- Local and municipal taxes.
- Value added taxes/sales tax.
- National Insurance Contributions/social security charges.
- Payable and income taxes.

Employee issues:

- Income tax.
- Tax breaks.
- Dual contracts.
- Exchange control.
- Pensions.
- Tax equalization.
- Social Security.

Regulatory matters:

- Registering for CT, VAT, social security/national insurance.
- Need for fiscal representation.

CHAPTER 2.4

The consulting engineer's appointment

Clive Marsden
Royal Haskoning

Rachel Barnes
Beale & Company

1 FORM OF APPOINTMENT

The general principles relating to the formation of a contract with a contractor have been set out in Chapter 1.6. Exactly the same principles apply to the contract between a client (including a contractor client) and a consulting engineer. This chapter deals with some aspects of the formation of the contract that affect consulting engineers.

1.1 Exchange of letters

Again, as with a contractor's contract, the appointment of the consulting engineer can be contained in an exchange of letters. At its simplest, this could be a letter from the consulting engineer to carry out certain services for a specified fee that is then accepted by the client. There is nothing to prevent such letters being complex, containing lengthy provisions concerning the rights and obligations of the parties, after going through offers and counter-offers until agreement is reached and the contract concluded. Whether there is indeed a concluded contract will depend on the general principles of contract law – see Chapter 3.1.

1.2 Incorporating standard terms

Consulting engineers' appointments can be made by letters or agreements that incorporate standard terms. A consulting engineer could offer, for example, to undertake a commission on the terms of a particular edition of an ACE Agreement or in accordance with its own firm's standard terms of business. If accepted by the client, those terms then become incorporated into and form part of the contract between the consulting engineer and the client. Care needs to be taken to match the conditions of appointment to the project in question. There should also be no inconsistency between the letter or agreement incorporating the conditions of appointment and the conditions themselves. Further, an ACE Agreement, for example, has a memorandum that needs to be completed. If it is not completed, or the requisite information is not in an accompanying letter or document, there is a danger that some important terms of the appointment are not considered completed and agreed. It is always prudent to attach a copy of the standard terms referred to so that there is no doubt as to the identity of the document or indeed, the edition being used.

1.3 Bespoke forms

Many clients have their own form of appointment that the consulting engineer is asked to agree. Negotiations on these can be lengthy and if the appointment document is not fully agreed, the general principles of contract law will determine whether there is a concluded contract. If the draft appointment document is incomplete or contains several documents of which not all have been provided, the consulting engineer should insist on having all the missing information before agreeing to the appointment. Something may be contained in a later document that could significantly affect the fee or substantially alter the risks that the consulting engineer is being asked to undertake.

1.4 Standard forms

There are at present only four institutions that produce standard forms of appointment for consulting engineers – the Association for Consultancy and Engineering (ACE), the Institution of Civil Engineers (ICE), the Construction Industry Council (CIC) and the International Federation of Consulting Engineers (FIDIC). Some large client bodies, such as Network Rail, and government bodies, such as the MoD and NHS Trusts, have their own standard forms, but these should be treated as 'bespoke forms'.

The Association for Consultancy and Engineering has produced a series of standard conditions for the appointment of consulting engineers. The latest editions are the Agreements 2002, many of which were revised in 2004. At the time of writing, new editions of the ACE Agreements are due to be published in 2008/2009 The Institution of Civil Engineers has produced the Professional Services Contract as part of the NEC contract documents. The third edition of this contract (NEC3) was issued in June 2005. More recently, in 2007, the Construction Industry Council has published The CIC Consultants' Contract Conditions together with a comprehensive CIC Scope of Services. FIDIC has produced a Client-Consultant Model Services Agreement known as 'The White Book' that is now its fourth edition (2006). A brief description of each of these standard forms is contained in Section 4 of this chapter.

1.5 Signing under hand or as a deed

The effect of signing a professional appointment under hand or as a deed has been set out in Section 3 of Chapter 3.1. If an agreement or a collateral warranty is being signed as a deed after the services have been started, or even after their completion, consideration should be given to incorporating a term that reduces the number of years for bringing any claims under that agreement or collateral warranty. If this is not done, the client may have a longer time for bringing claims than would otherwise have been permitted by law.

It is also important that all the agreements relating to a particular project are signed in the same manner. For example, where the consulting engineer employs subconsultants, each of the subconsultants' appointments must be signed as a deed if the consulting engineer's appointment is so signed. If not signed in this way and if the consulting engineer were sued in respect of something that a subconsultant had done, then the consulting engineer could find that it is unable to sue the subconsultant under the subconsultant's appointment because the claim was time barred.

2 KEY ISSUES THAT ARISE IN APPOINTMENT DOCUMENTS

This section looks at some of the key issues that arise in appointment documents and their implications for the consulting engineer and compares clauses that can be found in bespoke appointments with the equivalent clauses in the ACE Agreements.

2.1 Duty of care

As has been stated elsewhere, the standard of care imposed on consulting engineers at common law is to carry out their services with 'reasonable skill and care'. The test is that of the ordinary skilled and competent practitioner in the relevant profession. The ACE Agreements incorporate this duty expressly: 'The Consultant shall exercise reasonable skill, care and diligence in the performance of the Services'.

The differences between construction design and construction itself are many, but those differences may be summarized in the following two propositions:

(a) The designer creates an idea, whereas the contractor brings that idea to physical reality. Both are processes, but it is only the latter that results in something tangible that fulfils the client's (stated) functional needs.
(b) The idea resulting from a design process may not be imaginable at the start, but the result of a construction process is clearly identifiable from the moment the contractor's tender is accepted.

Thus, a design has a more uncertain outcome than that of construction itself. The difference is reflected in the law of implied terms (see preceding and next chapters) and in the insurance arrangements for designers that often cover reasonable skill and care but not any higher duty.

Bespoke appointments can, however, impose a higher duty of care, for example

> 'The consulting engineer shall exercise the skill, care and diligence to be expected of a properly qualified consulting structural engineer experienced in carrying out work of a similar size, scope and complexity to the project'.

Such a higher duty may be acceptable if the consulting engineer has the requisite experience, but other factors may also be relevant, such as the nature of the project, any professional indemnity restrictions and whether all other professionals, any subconsultants and any contractors or subcontractors (or others with design or other responsibilities that may affect the services) have undertaken an equivalent duty of care.

2.2 Warranties for fitness for purpose

'Fitness for purpose' requirements sometimes arise in bespoke appointments and in collateral warranties. A detailed description of warranties for fitness for purpose is contained in Chapter 2.5. The important distinction in law is that a consulting engineer provides professional services and is obliged by law to exercise reasonable skill and care, and a contractor carries out construction and is obliged by law to warrant that the completed works will be fit for their intended purpose. In practice, too, the consulting engineer designs the works but does not physically construct them, nor does the consulting engineer have any of the same control over workmanship or choice of materials as does the contractor.

A contractor under a design and construct contract may take on a 'fitness for purpose' obligation in relation to design and seek to pass this on to the consulting engineer it engages. Both ICE and Joint Contracts Tribunal (JCT) standard forms of design and construct contracts do not, however, impose fitness for purpose obligations in relation to design. Warranties for fitness for purpose as to design should be resisted.

If a consulting engineer gives a warranty for fitness for purpose, for example that the completed works will be fit for their purpose, and they are not, the consulting engineer will be liable even if it has used reasonable skill and care and therefore has not been negligent. The damages flowing from a breach of warranty (which, very briefly, represent the cost of making the works fit for their purpose) are different from and can be higher than those for negligence (that, again briefly, are the reasonably foreseeable losses caused by the negligence). Further, a 'state-of-the-art' defence would not be available. A consulting engineer could not therefore argue that a particular piece of knowledge was not available at the time the design was prepared.

The professional indemnity insurance arrangements of consulting engineers reflect the obligation imposed on them by law – that is, to exercise reasonable skill and care. Thus, a professional indemnity insurance policy that is on a negligence-only basis would not cover warranties for fitness for purpose. There are, however, some professional indemnity insurance policies that can be taken out on a legal liability basis that cover warranties for fitness for purpose, but even these policies can specifically exclude such warranties if the risk is considered too high.

The ACE, NEC, CIC and FIDIC Agreements contain no warranties for fitness for purpose.

2.3 Absolute or strict obligations

Bespoke appointments often contain absolute or strict obligations, for example 'The consulting engineer shall ensure the most efficient and cost effective solution' or 'The consulting engineer shall comply with the Employer's Requirements' or 'The consulting engineer shall procure that the construction is in accordance with the consulting engineer's design'.

The effect of undertaking an absolute or strict obligation is exactly the same in law as if the consulting engineer had given a warranty for fitness for purpose – see above. The performance of such obligations is also often dependent on factors outside the consulting engineer's direct control or is dependent on other parties, such as the contractor, doing certain things. It would therefore not be possible for the consulting engineer alone to fulfil such an obligation.

'Ensure' means to guarantee and is an absolute performance obligation. 'Comply' and 'procure' are also absolute performance obligations. If the obligation is 'to comply' with the employer's requirements, it could also amount to the consulting engineer undertaking a warranty for fitness for purpose because the employer's requirements often contain such warranties. Where the consulting engineer is employed directly by the client for the project, it is only the contractor that is in a position to comply with the employer's requirements, not the consulting engineer. Even where the consulting engineer is employed by the contractor, the consulting engineer does not have the power to stop construction work or compel the contractor to make changes to the construction.

None of this means that the consulting engineer can disregard the client's brief or requirements or budgets. A consulting engineer must have regard to them as part of its professional duties. The ACE Agreements do not include such duties expressly, but some bespoke appointments do include obligations to have 'due regard' to such matters.

2.4 Time-scale for professional services

If nothing is said in a consulting engineer's appointment about the time for performing services, the law implies a term that they will be carried out within a reasonable time. In the ACE Agreements the obligation is expressed as

> 'Subject always to conditions beyond his reasonable control (including acts or omissions of the Client or third parties), the Consultant shall use reasonable endeavours to perform the Services in accordance with any programme agreed with the Consultant from time to time'.

The qualification is necessary because there are many factors that can cause delay or non-compliance with a programme over which the consulting engineer has no control, for example late information from the client or other consultants or late approvals from statutory undertakers or other third parties.

Bespoke appointments may include a specific requirement that the services are completed within a certain time-scale with no qualification at all. (The difficulties inherent in undertaking strict or absolute obligations have been considered above.) 'Time is of the essence' is an example. This should only be agreed to where the programme is absolutely achievable. A failure to comply can lead to a client (that may be a contractor) incurring losses that are claimable from the consulting engineer. When considering and agreeing a programme to be incorporated in an appointment, the consulting engineer should also make sure that its services have been fully defined, that resources can be relied upon and that there is no liability for the actions of either the client itself or third parties that may not be under the direct control of the consulting engineer. If these cannot be achieved, the obligation should be qualified.

A client's late delivery of information (whether this is to be supplied by the client or its other professionals or contractors), instructions, or approvals to a consulting engineer can result in delays to the consulting engineer's timetable. Generally, if nothing is said expressly, there will be implied into a contract an obligation that such matters will be provided in a reasonable time and so as not to delay the consulting engineer. The ACE Agreements include such an obligation expressly and it is better that it is so included, particularly where the programme is very tight and/or where it is helpful to the client to spell out what has to be provided to the consulting engineer and when.

2.5 Certificates and statements

This section is not concerned with the certificates that have to be given by consulting engineers under construction contracts (for example, as to the value of the work carried out by the contractor). These are outside the scope of this section. This section deals with certificates or statements required by clients, often to be given to third parties, for example as to what the consulting engineer's services may or may not have achieved or in respect of matters concerning the construction works. Government departments often require such certificates. They are generally in a fixed *pro forma* form and may contain statements describing a level of performance different from or beyond what can reasonably be expected from the consulting engineer.

Any claims arising out of such certificates (and this does not include any other claims that the client might be able to bring in contract or a third party might be able to bring in tort) would arise under the Hedley Byrne principle (see Chapter 3.4).

The problem for the consulting engineer arises if the statement made, for example about what the works will achieve, turns out to be untrue. The consulting engineer will be liable despite having used reasonable skill and care in relation to its own services.

The consulting engineer should seek to include in its appointment wording that:

(a) does not compel the giving of a certificate in a certain form to a certain person, regardless of the actual circumstances at the time. The consulting engineer will then not be in breach of contract if it then refuses to give or qualifies the certificate;
(b) the certificate should be such that it accurately records only what the consulting engineer has or has not done and does not amount to a statement as to what others have done or what they or the works will or ought to achieve.

These principles apply equally to any other statement that the consulting engineer may be required to give to a third party, for example to a funder in a letter concerning the works or in a collateral warranty to a third party or in a report to a prospective purchaser. If the statement made is not true, the consulting engineer can become liable under the Hedley Byrne principle to that third party as if a contract had been made with that third party, regardless of whether or not any fee was paid for the production of the statement.

The services in the ACE Agreements contain no duty to give certificates to the client or third parties, nor to make any statements.

2.6 Terms 'for the benefit of third parties' and the Contracts (Rights of Third Parties) Act 1999

Clients may have very complex and close arrangements with funders and other third parties, such as future purchasers or tenants, none of whom will have a contract with the consulting engineer as they are not parties to the appointment. In these circumstances, clients may seek a guarantee that interested third parties can recover from the consulting engineer the more extensive damages that would have been available had those third parties been a party to the original contract and there had been a breach of contract. This can only be achieved by including provisions in the appointment that would bring the third parties within the circumstances required by law. For example, there could be a clause requiring the consulting engineer to acknowledge that if it is in breach of contract specified third parties will suffer loss and damage and that this is foreseeable as a result of the breach. Alternatively, the contract could state that the contract has been entered into on behalf of, or for the benefit of, identified third parties as well as the client.

The Contracts (Rights of Third Parties) Act 1999 confers rights on third parties to enforce any term of a contract that is for their benefit. Detailed consideration of the effect of this Act is contained in Chapter 2.5.

In the writers' view, it is better to deal expressly in the appointment (for example, by agreeing to the provision of collateral warranties in an agreed form) in a way that sets out the extent of the obligations and liabilities the consulting engineer is prepared to assume to any third parties and, at the same time, exclude the Contracts (Rights of Third Parties) Act. Excluding the Act would also remove any uncertainties as to whether any obligations in the appointment, such as an obligation to give information to the contractor for passing to the subcontractor, gave that subcontractor a right to enforce the term directly. The ACE Agreements exclude the Act by providing that 'nothing in this Agreement confers or purports to confer on any third party any benefit or any right to enforce any term of this Agreement pursuant to the Contracts (Rights of Third Parties) Act 1999'.

2.7 Deleterious materials

Deleterious material clauses are now sometimes included in bespoke appointments and often in collateral warranties. The consulting engineer is usually required to state that it has not and will not specify certain listed deleterious materials.

A consulting engineer already has a duty 'to exercise reasonable skill and care', and this extends to the specifying of materials, so such a clause is not necessary. It is not included in the ACE Agreements. The consulting engineer may be prepared to agree to such an obligation expressly, provided the list is acceptable and not too widely drawn. For example, an obligation not to specify materials 'generally known to be deleterious' is unspecific and could be open to argument. Words such as 'materials used will comply with all applicable codes' or 'British Standards' are often inappropriate because not every building material is covered by a British Standard and different national standards might conflict.

The obligation should also be limited to the time that materials are specified, and not to the time of their use, unless the consulting engineer has agreed to check the specifications again at the time of use.

The obligation is also often extended so that it extends to 'ensuring' or 'seeing that' such materials are not used in the construction of the project. Even if such an obligation is limited to those parts of the project where the consulting engineer is carrying out site inspection, it is not acceptable because a consulting engineer will not and cannot know all the materials that the contractor and subcontractors have used. It may be acceptable, in these circumstances, to agree to notify the client if the consulting engineer becomes aware that any deleterious materials are being used.

2.8 Commencement, termination and suspension of appointment

Commencement

The time at which the terms of any appointment are agreed will depend on the circumstances of each case. Sometimes the formal appointment is not agreed and signed until well into a project, or even after it has been completed. In such circumstances, it is usual to include in the appointment document that the effective date of the commencement of the appointment is the earlier of the date of signature or the commencement of the services. It is important to check, however, that the terms and the services described in the appointment correctly reflect what has actually been done – there could have been variations since the consulting engineer first started to perform the services. The ACE Agreements have such a provision.

Termination

Historically, the right of a client to terminate a consulting engineer's appointment was usually limited to breaches of contract or insolvency. Clients were prepared to employ their consulting engineers on the basis of a 'whole appointment' – that is for the whole project. The consulting engineer, as a result, could plan both work and fee accordingly. The ACE Conditions prior to the 1995 Edition were written on the basis of a whole appointment with limited rights to terminate. This meant that if a client terminated the appointment for any reason not stipulated in the appointment, the consulting engineer would be entitled to the losses that flowed from that repudiatory breach. These could include unavoidable expenses such as redundancy costs and loss of profit.

Present-day appointment documents (including the present ACE Agreements) almost invariably contain an express right for the client to terminate at any time. The entitlement to payment is also often restricted to the amount due up to the date of termination and any claim for any damages against the client for loss of profit or other losses arising out of termination is excluded altogether.

There is also usually an express right for the client to terminate if the consulting engineer is in breach of its obligations or is insolvent. The consulting engineer should also have such an express right, particularly where the breach is non-payment In such an instance the consulting engineer has to decide how long the work should continue or whether it can be suspended or whether the non-payment amounts to a repudiatory breach.

Some bespoke appointments seek to deal with the consequences of a breach of contract (for example by saying that any breach will be deemed to be a 'repudiatory breach') or by stipulating what the client may or may not be entitled to claim as damages in those circumstances. The common law has sophisticated rules for assessing the damages payable and any such express provisions will usually be intended to improve the client's position.

Suspension

The client's right to suspend is usually tied in with the right to terminate and generally the client reserves the right to suspend at any time. This may be essential because of the nature of the project. However, the consulting engineer needs to consider how many times the client can do this and how long the periods of suspension should be before the fee and/or the services fall to be reassessed. Bespoke appointments often do not recognize the disruption that can be caused to a consulting engineer's work by many or lengthy suspensions. The ACE Agreements give a right to the client to suspend at any time for periods of up to twelve months in aggregate, following which the consulting engineer has the option to give notice of termination. The ACE Agreements also give a right to the consulting engineer to suspend for up to 26 weeks if it is being prevented or impeded from carrying out the services as a result of circumstances outside the consulting engineer's control.

There is a right under most standard appointments to stop work if a payee has not been paid, but in these circumstances the payee takes the risk that it may eventually be held by the courts or in arbitration that the payer was justified in not paying. In those circumstances the payee would be liable for the costs incurred by the payer as a result of the suspension of its work.

The Housing Grants, Construction and Regeneration Act 1996 (the 'Construction Act') also gives a statutory right to suspend performance if there is non-payment of any sum due under a 'construction contract' and an effective notice of withholding has not been given within the proper time limits.

2.9 Key personnel

Although professional firms, be they solicitors, accountants, surveyors, architects or consulting engineers, are appointed by reputation or competition, it is well known that the client may want the services of particular individuals or at least a say in the choice of those individuals who are to work on the project for which the client is paying.

Clauses dealing with particular personnel are therefore proper but need to balance the client's demands, the demands of the job and the demands of other clients for other jobs. Some of the matters that should be covered are detailed below.

- The demarcation between full and part-time involvement – the more senior the employee, the more likely a part-time involvement will suffice, but it has to be balanced by a commitment to be involved, say, at important meetings when required, and on reasonable notice.
- The more senior the employee, the more likely it is that the person may be specifically asked for by name and curriculum vitae.
- Substitution of committed employees – this could cover
  - an employee leaving and going to work for another firm;
  - illness, resignation, retirement or death;
  - unsuitability for the role;
  - client's preference.

  For the first three of the above reasons the costs of replacement should be borne by the consulting engineer and for the last reason, by the client.
- Promotion – this could lead to a higher charge rate for an individual. The client could be made aware at the outset that many firms' staff are not static entities and that, within reason, the client should expect to pay for increases in rates resulting from promotion.
- Mutual non-poaching provisions – these may be appropriate, but for no longer than, say, two years after the individual concerned has finished work on the project.

The provision of site staff for supervisory purposes requires separate treatment. The first step is to agree on the number, if any, of full-time or part-time supervisory staff. Considerations such as housing, cars, travel, overtime, subsistence and other allowances are generally relevant.

The ACE Agreements provide for representatives of the client and the consulting engineer to be appointed but there are no commitments concerning key personnel.

2.1 Ways of operating
2.2 Working with others
2.3 Working internationally
2.4 The engineer's appointment
2.5 Collateral warranties
2.6 Indemnity insurance
2.7 Employment law
2.8 Information technology

2.10 Client obligations

Bespoke appointments usually place no obligations on the client except the obligation to pay. Although common law will generally imply a term into such appointments that the client will provide the information and decisions that the consulting engineer will need, it is better that the appointment sets out the client's obligations in relation to information, decisions, approvals and assistance so that it is clear to the client what it has to provide or do. A timetable for the release of crucial information or decisions should also be included in a bespoke appointment, and, in particular, there should be a set period within which the client has to signal its approval, or otherwise, of any draft reports submitted by the consulting engineer.

The ACE Agreements place an obligation on the client that it will supply the information needed, including that in the possession of other consultants or contractors. The client also undertakes that it will give, and procure that other consultants and contractors give, such assistance as the consulting engineer needs and that all the client's decisions, instructions, consents or approvals will be given in reasonable time.

2.11 Indemnities

Indemnity clauses are often included in bespoke appointments. Indemnities have particular characteristics of which consulting engineers should be aware.

A contract of indemnity can be defined in several ways. In this section 'indemnity' is being used in its narrow sense, i.e. to cover only the specific forms of indemnity that consulting engineers can be required to give to clients under their appointments.

Unless indemnities are very carefully worded there is a danger that the amount that the consulting engineer will have to pay under the indemnity in respect of some default on the consulting engineer's part will not properly reflect the damages that would have been due if the claim had been decided in the absence of an indemnity. The indemnity often extends not only to the amount the client has suffered but also to the amounts that the client has to pay to third parties because of the consulting engineer's default.

An indemnity could allow the client to recover the following types of damages:

(a) those that would not normally be recoverable because they are too remote
(b) those that would otherwise be reduced by the client's duty to mitigate its loss or by reason of the client's contributory negligence
(c) those that would not be recoverable because they may not have been properly or reasonably incurred.

They could also include the liquidated damages that a contractor client has to pay to its employer.

It is also possible that an indemnity will allow legal costs and expenses to be recovered that would otherwise be disallowed on an assessment of costs conducted by the court.

A consulting engineer may not have to have been negligent before becoming liable to pay under an indemnity if it is not based on negligence. If a client has suffered a loss for which the consulting engineer is providing an indemnity, the consulting engineer has to pay regardless of whether or not the loss can be recovered from the consulting engineer's professional indemnity insurer.

Settlements of claims can also give rise to difficulties. A client may decide for commercial reasons to settle a claim with a third party for, say, half a million pounds when the damages properly payable by the consulting engineer if decided by the court would be £350 000. If the indemnity is drafted in such terms, the consulting engineer will have to pay the £500 000.

The client has from six to twelve years from the time the indemnified loss is suffered to make a claim under the indemnity, depending on whether the indemnity is contained in a contract under hand or in a deed unless the indemnity is against 'liability' in which case time will start to run from the breach. It is therefore possible that a claim can be made under an indemnity after the limitation period in respect of the main contract has expired. Indemnities are not needed. If a consulting engineer is in breach of the terms of appointment, a client will be entitled to the damages prescribed by law, and it may also be able to sue the consulting engineer in negligence. If third parties sue the client because of something the consulting engineer has done, the consulting engineer can be joined in those proceedings or damages can be claimed from the consulting engineer afterwards in contribution proceedings. An indemnity therefore only makes it easier for a client to collect money from a consulting engineer and can increase the damages it can recover.

As a general rule, indemnities should only be given where it is absolutely necessary, such as for commercial reasons. It is important to consider the extent and nature of the indemnity that is being requested and what type of losses are being covered, for example personal injury or death, property damage or even all losses arising out of the contract. A widely drafted indemnity clause can create onerous liabilities and it may be called upon in situations that the parties had not originally envisaged.

2.12 Limitation and exclusion of liability

Many standard forms of appointment for construction professionals now include clauses limiting liability. An increasing number of bespoke appointments also do so. This can be vital where the project carries unusual risk or where the risk is out of all proportion to the fee, as can happen, for example, in environmental assessments. Such attempts to limit liability have happened in response to the development of several factors, including the following.

(a) Consulting engineers are being sued with increasing frequency, although there is no evidence of declining professional standards of engineering work.
(b) An increasing number of groundless claims are made; something has gone wrong on a project or certain expectations of the client have not been met and statements of claim are served on all suppliers without regard to apparent blame. Irrecoverable legal costs can exceed the full quantum of an established, substantial claim and heavy costs can be incurred in defending a claim that should not have been brought.
(c) Where more than one supplier is responsible for the same damage on a construction project, each is fully liable but able to seek a contribution from the other or others on a just and equitable basis under the Civil Liability (Contribution) Act 1978. For the consulting engineer, a typical case will involve poor workmanship attributable to the contractor directly and to the consulting engineer indirectly for poor supervision. The problem is not an inability to claim contribution – it being assumed for this purpose that the client has fully recovered from the consulting engineer's professional indemnity insurer – but that no such contribution, for which a legal claim is established, is in fact available due to the contractor having insufficient funds or no funds with which to meet the claim for contribution, for example because the contractor is insolvent. Also, contractors do not, or possibly cannot, cover by insurance their own poor work and thus no insurance cover is available to meet the claim. Thus, the

consulting engineer picks up more than a fair share of the damage restitution costs.

(d) Insurance cover itself has its own limitations and is no substitute for sensible calculation of risk. Professional indemnity insurance generally only covers negligence and does not cover design guarantees as such. There are imposed excesses, beneath which the insured takes the risk and, of course, a maximum limit to the cover provided. Sometimes these maxima include legal costs, thereby reducing the quality of the cover and as a result of major claims for pollution damage, cover is also reduced from a figure for each and every claim to a figure for all such claims in aggregate. More recently, further limitations and exclusions have been added for asbestos claims and terrorism claims respectively. Finally, the cover does not last for a project but is annually renewable. All these insurance restrictions have entirely proper commercial weight from the point of view of the insurer but it is important that consulting engineers do not assume risk that cannot be sensibly insured.

(e) Since the early 1970s, there has been seen the creation of a new legal specialism – construction law. Before that, few construction projects were litigated. However, construction law is not by any means a settled, sophisticated and clear body of law. This may be due to over-litigation. There is the difficulty of developing precedent in the face of too many cases, but the upshot is that, without a reasonable degree of certainty, such litigation favours the holder of the deepest purse.

(f) One of the particular reasons for major doubt on the outcome of construction litigation is the great scrutiny that occurs of one or several of a large number of forms of contract for construction work. With little standardization, interpretation of these contracts by the courts is unpredictable.

(g) Following the retreat of tort after the D&F Estates case in 1989, third parties (typically, purchasers of the completed project or users thereof) began to insist on the various suppliers to the project (contractors, consulting engineers, architects, subcontractors of various sorts) supplying warranties to them in place of their weakened right under the general law in tort. The problem with this development was not only that consulting engineers found themselves becoming liable to third parties other than their client (the client being aware of the details of the consulting engineer's appointment, the third parties not) but also opportunities arose to impose further and onerous terms in the warranties, which were in many cases taken.

The law relating to clauses limiting or excluding liability and the details about the Unfair Contract Terms Act 1977 are set out in Chapter 3.1. Where the appointment is with a consumer, as defined by the Unfair Terms in Consumer Contracts Regulations 1994, those Regulations may also apply to limitation and exclusion clauses. The same principles apply to professional appointments.

Parties to an appointment can never agree to limit or exclude liability for damages for personal injury or death because this is expressly prohibited by law. They are, however, able to agree to limit or exclude any other liability they may incur to each other. It is not possible to exclude or restrict liability in relation to third party claims because there is no contract with that third party. Thus, if, for example, a claim is made against a consulting engineer by a tenant of a building designed by the consulting engineer under a contract with the building owner, the consulting engineer will not be able to rely on any limitation agreed with the building owner because that limitation was not contained in a contract with the tenant and agreed with the tenant. The only way in which a consulting engineer can be protected against such third party claims is if the client will agree to give the consulting engineer an indemnity against them (see the preceding section).

However, if the consulting engineer were to enter into an agreement directly with the third party, for example in a collateral warranty, a clause limiting or excluding the liability of the consulting engineer could be included and could be effective.

A party in breach of contract cannot rely on a clause excluding or limiting liability for that breach unless that clause is 'reasonable'. What is reasonable is determined having regard to the circumstances known to the parties at the time the contract was made. It is therefore important that these clauses are considered at the time the appointment is being negotiated.

Such clauses have to be clear, because they are construed strictly against the party relying on them. The clause is more likely to be considered reasonable if it restricts liability rather than excludes it (although exclusion may be reasonable in some circumstances).

In deciding the maximum liability that it is prepared to accept, the consulting engineer should assess the nature of the risks for the particular project and also the damages that could be payable if the consulting engineer is in breach of contract or is negligent. These will include not only the costs of putting things right but could also include other losses that could be caused to the client, because, for example, it is unable to use or rent its building. An assessment would also need to be made of the damages that could flow from any particular matters, such as contamination if the consulting engineer has advised on this.

If the limitation is by reference to a monetary amount, the court is required by the Unfair Contract Terms Act to have regard to:

(i) the resources the consulting engineer could be expected to have available to meet the liability, for example the assets of the company or partnership; and
(ii) how far it is open to the consulting engineer to cover itself by insurance.

This does not mean that if the consulting engineer has £5 million insurance cover, the limit of liability for every appointment should be £5 million. The monetary amount included in the limitation clause should be appropriate for the type of commission being undertaken.

An obligation in an appointment to maintain professional indemnity insurance does not limit a consulting engineer's liability to the amount of cover provided by that insurance. A separate, express clause is needed, agreeing that liability should be limited.

In *Moores* v. *Yakeley Associates* (Court of Appeal 1999) the Court of Appeal considered the effect of a monetary limitation in the RIBA's standard form of appointment SFA/92. The Court of Appeal upheld the judgment of the judge at first instance. The judge had held that a limit of £250 000 was reasonable because it was not an arbitrary figure but was based on the architect's assessment of the likely cost of the works; the fees were in the order of £20 000 and the ceiling was ten times that amount; the client was in a stronger bargaining position than the architect – he could have instructed any architect; the client and its solicitor had both been aware of the clause and had had an opportunity to object, and a comparison of their respective resources showed that the architect had none and the client was very wealthy. The fact that the architect had insurance cover of twice the amount of the ceiling did not make the amount unreasonable.

Liability can also be limited by reference to other matters. For example, liability could be limited to the costs of repair or of cleaning up a site, or to the amount recoverable under a consulting engineer's professional indemnity insurance. Certain types of damages can be excluded or limited, such as relocation costs, loss of profits or consequential losses.

If liability is to be limited by reference to the sort of damages payable, this needs to be approached very carefully with appropriate advice. A discussion of all the damages that may flow from any breach of a consulting engineer's appointment is outside the scope of this section.

There is no reason why a clause limiting liability cannot use the amount of the engineer's 'net contribution' as a means of establishing a maximum that should be paid in relation to a claim. Such a clause may be necessary where the engineer has to review, check or supervise others' work as described in Section 2.17 of this chapter and thus becomes jointly liable with others. The objective of the clause is to limit the consulting engineer's liability to its part of the overall damages where the other parties with whom it is jointly liable have no or insufficient assets to pay their part. In a case involving monitoring a contractor's work, for example where both the consulting engineer and the contractor have been negligent, such a clause could limit the consulting engineer's liability to 20% or 30% of the total damages suffered by the client. It needs to be remembered, however, that such clauses have not been tested by the courts either as to their efficacy or their 'reasonableness' and that they can only apply where the claim is such that two or more parties are 'liable for the same damage'. If the consulting engineer is found to be solely responsible for the damage arising out of that claim, such a clause will not be effective in limiting liability at all.

As has been said, in exceptional cases it can be 'reasonable' to exclude liability in respect of some particular claims or matters. For example, if a consulting engineer has not been asked to consider pollution or contamination in relation to a particular project because the client is taking separate specialist advice about this, it could be reasonable to state in the appointment that the client is doing this and any liability of the consulting engineer for any claim arising out of or in connection with pollution and contamination is excluded. It might also be 'reasonable' to exclude liability or limit liability to a relatively small amount for pollution and contamination claims where the client asks a consulting engineer to carry out a preliminary site investigation for a small fee but where the clean-up costs could run into millions of pounds if the consulting engineer negligently failed to discover that the site was contaminated. In such a case, the risks to the consulting engineer would be out of all proportion to the fee paid.

Limiting the time within which claims can be brought must also satisfy the requirement of 'reasonableness'. This may prove difficult because there are different time periods for bringing claims in contract and in negligence.

Time limits that relate only to claims in contract will more readily satisfy the test of reasonableness – six to ten years might be reasonable, depending on whether the contract is under hand or signed as a deed (see Section 1.5 of this chapter) because such claims can only be brought within six or twelve years from the date of the cause of action. Claims in negligence, however, can be brought long after any claim in contract would be time barred. A limitation that excluded claims in negligence after, say, six years from completion of the services might not be considered 'reasonable' as it could be a sizeable reduction in the position under the law at present.

Examples of tailored limitation of liability clauses are to be found in the ACE Agreements 2002 and in the revised versions published in 2004.

2.13 The obligation to maintain professional indemnity insurance

A discussion of professional indemnity insurance is contained in Chapter 2.6.

Most professional appointments contain specific obligations to maintain professional indemnity insurance. (This is positively desirable where there is also a limitation or

2.1 Ways of operating
2.2 Working with others
2.3 Working internationally
2.4 The engineer's appointment
2.5 Collateral warranties
2.6 Indemnity insurance
2.7 Employment law
2.8 Information technology

exclusion of liability to help with the test of 'reasonableness' under the Unfair Contract Terms Act 1977 – see Section 2.12 of this chapter.)

The consulting engineer should check that the obligation matches its present professional indemnity insurance arrangements, including any particular restrictions or exclusions such as those that can attach to pollution and contamination claims, asbestos or terrorist claims. The consulting engineer also needs to bear in mind that the nature of professional indemnity insurance can change and that professional indemnity insurance could become prohibitively expensive or even be unavailable for some or all claims. It is the policy in existence at the time the claim is made that is the relevant policy.

As a result, any obligation to maintain professional indemnity insurance should be qualified. First, the consulting engineer should be relieved of the obligation to insure if insurance is not available at commercially reasonable rates. Secondly, the length of time for which the consulting engineer undertakes to maintain insurance should be reasonable. For example, if the appointment has been signed under hand, the obligation should only last six years.

The amount of the insurance cover also needs to be considered. The amount should be appropriate for the risks associated with the particular project, not the amount of the cover presently maintained by the consulting engineer. Agreeing to maintain professional indemnity insurance in a certain amount is not the same as limiting liability to that amount – see Section 2.12 of this chapter.

Some clauses concerning the maintenance of professional indemnity insurance in bespoke appointments seek to stipulate the terms of that insurance, for example that it is in joint names of the consulting engineer and the client, or the amount of the excess, or that the insurers should be UK insurers. These sorts of provision could severely restrict the consulting engineer's ability to obtain professional indemnity insurance and should be considered carefully before being accepted. An obligation not to settle or compromise any claim that the consulting engineer may have against its insurer in respect of the client's claim without the client's consent may be expressly prohibited by the consulting engineer's professional indemnity insurance.

The ACE Agreements include an obligation to maintain professional indemnity insurance in an amount to be agreed and set out in the memorandum, for a period to be agreed and stated in the memorandum. There is an annual aggregate for claims for pollution and contamination, which is to be an amount not less than the amount stated for this in the memorandum. There is also a proviso that such insurance has to be available at commercially reasonable rates and subject to all exceptions, exclusions and limitations to the scope of cover that are commonly included in such insurance at the time it is taken out. This is to reflect the fact that in recent years, further limitations and exclusions to the scope of cover have been introduced by insurers.

2.14 The Construction (Design and Management) Regulations 2007 (CDM)

CDM Regulations are dealt with in Chapter 3.2. As far as the consulting engineer is concerned, it is necessary in this section only to reiterate that any obligations as 'designer' are imposed by statute and last only while acting as designer and while the construction work lasts.

Because the designer's obligations under CDM Regulations are imposed by statute, there is no need for an appointment to set out the designer's obligations under CDM. The Regulations have specific provisions concerning civil liability but do not impose civil liability generally in respect of breach of the Regulations. Some bespoke appointments include: 'The Designer shall comply with all its obligations under the Construction

(Design and Management) Regulations 2007'. This is a strict obligation – see Section 2.3 of this chapter – but the obligations in the Regulations concerning designs are qualified, for example by 'so far as is reasonably practical to do so'.

If the obligations are set out in full, the wording should be identical to that in the Regulations. If other wording is used, the consulting engineer will have to comply both with the Regulations and with the obligations set out in the appointment. The first, because of the consulting engineer's requirement under statute and the second because of its contractual requirement.

Paraphrases or extensions of the consulting engineer's duties can be dangerous because they can be misleading and/or they can increase the consulting engineer's risk by extending the duties beyond those in the Regulations.

The ACE Agreements contain no specific CDM services, except a reminder to discuss with the client the role of the consultant and its relationship with (and in the case of the lead consultant the need for) other consultants and contractors, sub-contractors and planning supervisors in accordance with the Regulations.

A consulting engineer should not warrant or undertake to a client that it has the requisite competence to act as 'designer' as required by the Regulations even though it is now an express duty not to accept an appointment unless it is competent. It is for the client or other person arranging for the design to be carried out to check the designer's competence before making the appointment. If such a warranty is given and if, for example, a designer's appointment is terminated due to a deficiency of resources to devote to the health and safety requirements concerning the design, the client may be able to recover from the designer all its costs of delay while a new designer is appointed and any difference in the fee payable.

2.15 Subconsultancies

A consulting engineer may sometimes subcontract (or sublet) to another consulting engineer part of a project or may be asked by the client to act as lead consultant for a project and employ all the other professionals, regardless of their disciplines.

The important thing to remember is that in both cases the original consulting engineer is the person who is responsible to the client for fulfilling all the obligations under the appointment. Therefore, that consulting engineer will remain responsible for all the services that it has undertaken, notwithstanding that some were carried out by a subconsultant and if that subconsultant is negligent the consulting engineer will be liable to the client for all the resulting losses. Because the consulting engineer will in turn have (or should have) a 'back to back' contract with the subconsultant, it should be able to pass those losses on to the subconsultant and recover them from the subconsultant. If, however, the subconsultant has gone into liquidation, or has insufficient professional indemnity insurance cover, the consulting engineer will still have to pay the client in full. The consulting engineer should therefore make a careful selection of subconsultants and make sure that its insurance arrangements cover the acts or omissions of subconsultants. The consulting engineer also needs to check that its appointment does not prohibit any subcontracting of any of its obligations.

The consulting engineer should also ensure that the subcontract with the subconsultant is 'back to back' with its own, so that the subconsultant's obligations are identical to the consulting engineer's.

The consulting engineer will also have independent obligations to the subconsultant, for example in relation to payment, information and decisions, and these too should be in the subcontract. Historically, payment to subconsultants has been on a 'pay when paid' basis.

This is no longer permitted where the contract is a 'construction contract' (under the 'Construction Act'). Thus, in these cases, the consulting engineer will be responsible for payment of the subconsultant regardless of whether payment has been received from the client. The exception is where the consulting engineer's client becomes 'insolvent'.

The ACE Agreements provide that the consulting engineer may recommend to the client that some of the services are sublet to a specialist subconsultant and that the client may not unreasonably withhold consent to such a recommendation.

2.16 Remuneration

In deciding upon remuneration for a consulting engineer's appointment, the first distinctions to be made are between the nature (and amount) of the fee, its terms of payment and then any other remuneration conditions.

Fee

Experienced clients will tailor a consulting engineer's fee to the concept of certainty. A fully-defined series of tasks may well allow a fixed fee to be negotiated to the benefit of both parties. In instances where the client has not yet made up its mind, or where several options are to be investigated by the consulting engineer, a more flexible approach to fees has to be more appropriate. The consulting engineer should exercise caution in instances where the extent of the work is flexible and the fee is fixed – from a commercial viewpoint the two concepts may well be incompatible. The more common fee structures are discussed below.

Lump sum fees These include both a fixed lump sum and adjustable lump sums. One important aspect is the need to provide fully for circumstances in which a fixed lump sum may vary, for example, by the lapse of time, by performance of additional work beyond that contracted for or by accelerated or delayed completion of parts of the contracted services before or after stated dates. Adjustable lump sums generally require a 'shopping list' of tasks from which the client chooses what it wants doing and in what order. Since many construction projects take place over an extended period, it is important that even lump sums include a mechanism for variation, e.g. linking them to a price or cost index. Lump-sum fees are not suitable for consulting engineers' commissions where the amount of work cannot be accurately measured at the outset. At first glance, lump-sum fees give certainty, but given the nature of the construction industry, such certainty often evaporates should the scope of the consulting engineer's work change. Unless the consulting engineer's scope of work is clearly defined, lump-sum fees also stifle innovation and thus work against clients achieving value for money. Consulting engineers run the risk of miscalculating the amount of work involved in achieving the client's objectives.

Ad valorem *fees* Such a method of payment is often regarded as the 'traditional' means whereby a consulting engineer is remunerated. The fees are calculated as a percentage of the capital cost or construction out-turn cost. However, the method of payment is not as popular as it once was due to the apparently arbitrary nature of its final value. The method relies on the consulting engineer's professionalism in producing an economical design for the minimum effort. It would appear all-too-tempting to conceive an expensive concept, and thus increase the fee. On the plus side, *ad valorem* fees invariably include a full client service – a client can expect to be able to call on its consulting engineer frequently without being bothered by the *minutiæ* of additional invoices, time sheets or complicated fee calculations. Clearly, a percentage figure based on experience and adequate definitions of capital cost or construction out-turn cost are essential to the proper assessment of an *ad valorem* fee. *Ad valorem* fees are useful on large, high-capital-value projects where the design and construction processes are clearly understood at the outset, e.g. construction of a power station. Clients will see an opportunity to encourage competition through comparison of the percentage multipliers with the added advantage of being able to manage their cash flow as construction advances. Consulting engineers see the risks that they may calculate their percentage figure incorrectly.

Time based fees Typically, these cover salary multiplier rates and all-inclusive rates. Generally, each is given as a range of rates according to seniority, experience and speciality of the person concerned. Such rates are charged on an hourly, weekly or monthly basis. Salary multiplier rates have a built-in protection against inflation and promotion and should include benefits in kind and annualised costs of pension, life insurance and national insurance, as well as overheads, amongst others. All-inclusive rates are generally regarded as including all elements of salary multiplier rates plus, possibly, printing costs, travel costs and any other costs necessary to bring the consulting engineer's commission to a conclusion. All-inclusive rates are usually effective for a pre-determined period but should have an escalating factor should the period be exceeded. Non-productive time must be dealt with – for example, does time spent travelling, sickness, public holidays or overtime come within or without chargeable time? To the extent that they do not, they must be covered within the rate. Time-based fees have advantages in that innovation allows construction costs to be reduced (a skilled designer has considerable leverage on construction costs) whilst at the same time moving away from a claims culture. However, clients perceive a lack of certainty in their expenditures, though this should be viewed in the light of total project costs.

Expenses Sums necessarily expended in the course of providing the services, other than the time of the staff involved, for example printing of documents and travelling, have to be covered in one way or another. They may simply be costed into the fee, charged separately on, for example, an at-cost reimbursable basis or, perhaps, subject to a percentage handling-charge.

Committed work/additional work/supervision work The agreed fee (including treatment of expenses) will generally only apply to the services described in the contract between client and consulting engineer. Additional work occurs if requested by the client or rendered necessary for reasons beyond the consulting engineer's control. For example, additional work on a lump-sum contract could be paid for by reference to similar work already in the contract or by reference to a schedule of time-charges especially designed to cater for such an eventuality. Whatever method is chosen, it would be wise for the consulting engineer to give its client an approximate estimate of the additional fee in advance so as to allow the client the opportunity of arranging any additional funding. Generally speaking, the more accurately the extent of the additional work can be estimated in advance, the more appropriate a lump sum fee would be; the less accurately it can be estimated, the more sensible time-based fees become. Such 'change control' ought to be an intrinsic element of the consulting engineer creating a design efficiently – there are benefits to both parties. Supervision work is probably best paid for on a time basis to accommodate construction period over-runs.

Terms of payment

This section deals with the Construction Act provisions concerning payment. It will be recalled that the Construction Act only applies to 'construction contracts' – see Chapter 1.6.

Intervals for payment of fees and amounts payable

Except where the work lasts less than 45 days (or where the parties agree that it is to last less than 45 days) the payee is entitled to payment by instalments. If the construction contract fails to provide the instalment intervals, the Scheme for Construction Contracts (England and Wales) Regulations 1998 (the Scheme) will stipulate that this is 28 days. However, the Construction Act itself does not prescribe any minimum or maximum periods for the intervals – the parties are free to agree what these should be. The parties could agree, for example, that there are only two instalment intervals over a fairly lengthy contract period with a small initial payment and the balance on completion. Milestone payment intervals or payment by reference to completion of particular stages of work are therefore within the Construction Act.

The parties are also free to agree the amounts of the payments due at each interval or the method of calculating the amount. If they do not do so, again the relevant parts of the Scheme will apply. It is not advisable, however, to adopt this part of the Scheme or indeed to have it incorporated in a consulting engineer's appointment. This is because the Scheme has been drawn up with contractors', not consulting engineers', contracts in mind. The basis of calculation of the amount due at any interval under the Scheme is done by reference to aggregate amounts over periods and is stated to be the 'value of any work performed' plus 'an amount equal to the value of any materials manufactured on site or brought on to site' plus 'any other amount or sum that the contract specifies'.

Lump sum fee instalments Amounts of each instalment may be varied, as may periods between instalments. There could be a down payment, receipt of which being a condition precedent to the commencing of the services. This is unlikely to be negotiated unless there are significant start up costs, which there are on any relatively large job. Frequency of payment of instalments can be by dates, periods (for example weekly, four weekly) or by events. In the last case, the consulting engineer must take into account while pricing, if practicable, the control it will be able to exercise over the events in question.

Ad valorem *fee instalments* Much of the information given about the terms of payment of lump sum fees applies in this case, save that the final out-turn capital cost or construction cost will not be known at the time of payment of any instalment, save the last. This can be dealt with by payments on account, by reference to the latest estimate of capital cost, adjusted as necessary when the final capital cost is known.

Time-based fee instalments The most convenient method for dealing with these fees is to provide for monthly or quarterly instalments in arrears.

Expenses If separately reimbursed, it is recommended that similar arrangements to those entered into for time-based fees are adopted for the reimbursement of expenses.

The ACE Agreements provide for payment in instalments with the payment intervals being set out in the Memorandum. The amounts due at each interval depend on the method of payment, and again the details, for example whether this is to be on an hourly basis, a lump sum basis or a percentage fee basis with instalments at the completion of various stages, set out in the Memorandum.

When payment becomes due and the final date for payment

Each construction contract has to contain an adequate mechanism for determining when payments become due and a final date for payment of any sum that becomes due.

Again, the parties are free to stipulate the 'due' date and to agree the period between the date on which a sum is due and the final date for payment.

It is a moot point as to whether providing for intervals for payment, such as the first of each month, also means that the payment is 'due' on that first day of the month. It is more usual, and probably better practice, for the appointment to state when an amount is due. The ACE Agreements state that 'payments . . . shall become due for payment on submission of the Consultant's invoice . . .'. They also provide that the final date for payment is 28 days thereafter.

If nothing is said, the Scheme provides that the 'due date' is the later of 'the expiry of seven days following the relevant period or the making of a claim by the payee'. The 'relevant period' is the 28-day period prescribed by the Scheme for instalment periods (if the construction contract fails to provide for this) or the instalment period fixed by the appointment itself. 'Making a claim' is

> 'a written notice given by the party carrying out the work under a construction contract to the other party specifying the amount of any payment or payments that he considers to be due and the basis on which it is, or they are, calculated'.

An invoice or an application for payment would qualify as 'making a claim', provided that it contains the information prescribed by the Scheme.

The 'final date for payment' under the Scheme is 17 days after the due date. This makes a total time of 24 days in which payment should be made following receipt of the invoice. It was the intention of the Construction Act to encourage regular and fair payments. However, as the parties are allowed to agree the due date and the final date, payment periods in appointments can be very much longer than the 24 days under the Scheme. It is important, therefore, to check the due date and the final date for payment.

If the contract is so short that there are no instalments, or where it is the last payment, the Scheme provides that payment becomes due on the expiry of 30 days following completion of the work or the making of a claim by the payee, whichever is the later, and the final date for payment is again 17 days thereafter.

Notice of payment and of withholding payment

The Construction Act requires formal notices to be given both in relation to payment and the withholding of payment. The payer has to give notice

> 'not later than five days after the date on which payment becomes due from him under the contract, or would have become due if:
>
> (a) the other party has carried out his obligations under the contract and
> (b) no set off or abatement was permitted by reference to any sum claimed to be due under one or more other contracts
>
> specifying the amount (if any) of the payment made or proposed to be made and the basis on which that amount was calculated'.

If the construction contract does not contain such a provision, the relevant provisions of the Scheme apply. The Scheme simply repeats the provisions set out above.

The notice of payment must be given, even if payment is to be made in full or if no payment will be made.

Failure to give the notice of paying is a breach of contract (although it is difficult to see what loss a payee suffers in the absence of such a notice if it receives the amount asked for by the final date for payment).

The five-day notice period for the notice of paying is the only mandatory period in the payment provisions of the Construction Act. The parties cannot alter it, but they can arrange the due date (by reference to which the notice is fixed) so that it minimizes administrative inconvenience.

It is not necessary to set out in an appointment document the payer's obligation to give a notice of paying in respect of each payment, because this will be implied into every construction contract. The ACE Agreements have set out the requirement expressly, however, as a reminder to payers and they will apply even there the appointment is not a construction contract.

As to notice of withholding, the Construction Act provides:

> '(1) A party to a construction contract may not withhold payment after the final date for payment of a sum due under the contract unless he has given an effective notice of intention to withhold payment.
> (2) To be effective such a notice must specify:
> (a) the amount proposed to be withheld and the ground for withholding payment, or
> (b) if there is more than one ground, each ground and the amount attributable to it,
> and must be given not later than the prescribed period before the final date for payment.
> (3) The parties are free to agree what that prescribed period is to be'.

As usual, if the appointment does not set out what the prescribed period is to be, the Scheme will apply. That stipulates that the prescribed period is not later than

> 'seven days before the final date for payment determined either in accordance with the construction contract or, if there is no such provision, in accordance with the provisions of the Scheme'.

The notice of payment can be used as the notice of withholding (although it would have to be given earlier) provided that it contains the information prescribed by this section.

Most bespoke appointments provide that the notice of withholding has to be given not later than one day before the final date for payment to give the client the maximum time to decide whether it is going to withhold any monies and to calculate the amount. The ACE Agreements again expressly incorporate the notice of withholding provisions with the notice to be given not later than seven days before the final date for payment – as in the Scheme.

The Construction Act also includes a right to suspend performance if there is non-payment if no effective notice of withholding has been given in the correct time before the final date for payment. This is considered in Section 2.8 of this chapter.

Conditional payment/pay when paid

The Construction Act severely restricts the rights of parties to 'construction contracts' to make any payment conditional on the receipt of monies from a third party. For non-construction contracts, of course, such provisions are not outlawed.

The only time that a pay when paid provision is allowed is when the third person on whom the pay when paid provision relies is 'insolvent'. This is defined in the Construction Act and the definition should be checked by anyone seeking to take advantage of this section, because some commentators suggest that the definition is incomplete.

Other remuneration conditions

Ancillary to basic provisions on fee and terms of payment The Late Payment of Commercial Debts (Interest) Act 1998 now applies to all contracts for professional services. The Act stipulates that there is now a statutory right of interest on late payment. The late payment interest rate is the 'reference rate' plus the statutory rate of interest (currently 8%). Alternatively, the parties are free to agree an interest rate that will apply provided it is 'substantial'. The ACE Agreements now apply the Late Payment Act provisions to late payment.

It is vital that a VAT clause is added to the effect that VAT is payable in addition. Otherwise, the recipient will have to account to Customs and Excise for 17.5% of receipts (as from 31 July 1999).

Adjustment of fees to account for inflation is best done by reference to standard indices, but these are only necessary for fees that do not have inherent inflation protection, for example a fixed lump sum.

A right to the client to audit some of the consulting engineer's records could be inserted where appropriate, so as to verify for example the number of chargeable hours worked. This would not be appropriate in the case of lump sum fees.

Disputed invoices should be provided for, so that interest charges on late payments do not apply in the case of legitimately challenged parts of an invoice, save to the extent subsequently shown to be valid.

2.17 The services

A clear description of the tasks involved in a professional appointment is essential in order to clarify the respective responsibilities of all parties to the project. If a consulting engineer has agreed to carry out something specifically, but has in fact done something else, that will be a breach of the consulting engineer's obligations under the appointment.

It cannot be emphasised strongly enough that the more attention is paid to the sections in a contract dealing with what will be done and delivered, and what and when the consulting engineer is to be paid, the less effective will be any clauses that are disadvantageous to the consulting engineer. Of equal importance are the services that the consulting engineer will *not* provide – if only to concentrate the minds of the parties at the outset. The trouble is that too much time in pre-contract negotiations between a client and a consulting engineer is spent on contingent risk distribution and not enough on what the client is to get for what it is prepared to pay.

Initially, the draftsperson should describe in outline a chronological set of duties or tasks required of the consulting engineer by the client, tailored to the eventual outcome, namely the achievement of a design brief, which brief should be obtained from the client in the client's own terms. It is possible that the brief will have been provided in the bidding documents, if any, for the job in question.

Next, each duty should be considered to see whether or not its performance requires any contribution from others. This could involve any one or more of the following:

(a) consent to move to the next stage from the client and/or the client's client and/or an external party, for example the local planning authority
(b) design or information supplied by the client and/or others working on the project, for example, contractors, subcontractors, other consultants and/or statutory undertakers
(c) the results of work by others on the project, for example geotechnical investigations
(d) assistance by the client, for example licences, permits, customs clearances, access to sites
(e) facilities provided by the client, for example site offices, etc.

The draftsperson should then describe, in as much detail as possible, using advice from those who will carry out the work, the series of tasks, but this time qualifying such tasks by reference to the contribution from others over which the consulting engineer has, or will have, no control.

Finally, consideration might be given to events that are not only beyond the control of the consulting engineer but also of anyone else, including the client: strikes, civil insurrection, Acts of God, are examples – a *force majeure* clause will deal with such eventualities. *Force majeure* clauses are more common in overseas forms of appointment than they are in forms of appointment appropriate to work in the United Kingdom.

Clearly, all words should be used in their ordinary meaning. If technical terms have to be used they should be defined with the lay person in mind.

Many purchasers of consulting engineering services, even on major projects, have limited technical background but are, as it were, general buyers where detailed knowledge of what is being bought is not considered essential provided that the buyer can construct an adequate brief. It is not only important to describe the services in the detail suggested above, in a sequence and subject to qualifications and explanations, but so as to avoid any doubt in the mind of the lay person, also to state

(i) what is not being provided by the consulting engineer within the fee, and
(ii) further, if a service is not being provided (presumably because it was not asked for within the client's brief and has been identified by the consulting engineer as an essential missing service), what it would cost if the consulting engineer were able to provide that missing service.

Having produced a full description of the services to be provided, in sequence, subject to various consents, provision of assistance, information, data and facilities, together with a section on what is not included, it is recommended that the whole sequence is subdivided so that each section requires the consent and/or approval of the client before it is begun.

It can be most helpful to set up a contractual organization with regular meetings and a reporting system. This should include named representatives on both sides, fixed meetings at regular intervals, with decisions recorded (and signed off) by both sides.

It is important to realise that if a consulting engineer undertakes to approve, review, comment on, examine or otherwise check someone else's work it will incur some responsibility for that work jointly with others. However, the law provides that each person who is jointly liable with another is 100% liable to the person to whom they owe the duty – usually the employer. The employer can choose whom to sue and from whom to collect the damages he has suffered. A contribution can then be sought from the other parties who are jointly liable with the payer. If that person has insufficient or no assets, insufficient or no contribution may be recovered.

The extent of the responsibility to approve, review, comment, examine or check will depend on what was required to be undertaken as well as what was actually undertaken. It is always prudent to state the exact nature and extent of the review and its purpose and the purpose of any approval.

The Construction Industry Council produced in November 2007 a Consultant's Contract with a comprehensive scope of services for a whole range of consultants for use by members of the project team employed for major building projects which is now being used on some projects.

Supervision of construction The contractor is responsible for supervising the work being constructed. Whatever the level of 'supervision', i.e. monitoring of construction, by the consulting engineer, the contractor remains responsible for the standard of the materials and workmanship. 'Supervision' by the consulting engineer can be nothing more than selective monitoring by means of random inspection and testing. It is vital that the actual job of the monitoring team is specified in detail or covered by adequate generic wording, for example

> '... to monitor (on a sampling basis) the works for general compliance with the drawings and specification of the contract between the contractor and the client'.

'Supervising' or monitoring a contractor's work has peculiar difficulties and this is described in Section 3 of this chapter. In order to avoid the misunderstanding that the word 'supervision' can cause, the words 'supervise' and 'supervision' were excluded from the ACE Agreements, the more correct description of 'monitor' or 'monitoring' being used instead, combined with a statement as to the purpose of such monitoring: 'to monitor that the Works are being executed generally in accordance with the contract documents'.

The question of site staff is, of course, linked to 'supervision' or 'monitoring'. The ACE Agreements for non-contractor clients include provisions whereby the consulting engineer recommends the appointment of site staff if appropriate and agrees details, scope, payment and so forth, as well as the number of site visits, with the client. The Agreements also deal with the responsibilities of the contractor (or any subcontractors), notwithstanding the provision of the consulting engineer's site staff so that the respective responsibilities are made clear, as follows.

> '... Neither the provision of Site Staff nor periodic visits by the Consultant or its staff to the site shall in any way affect the responsibilities of the Contractors or any Sub-Contractors for constructing the Project and the Works in compliance with the relevant contract documents and any instructions issued by the Consultant'.

A client will sometimes attempt to alter a consulting engineer's site staffing establishment. However, it is the consulting engineer's duty to recommend to a client the resources necessary to administer the contract. If the client insists on employing an insufficient number of site staff, it is most important to specify what will be monitored and what will not.

As implied above, particular attention needs to be paid where the consulting engineer is specifically asked by the client to 'supervise' or inspect a contractor's work without the randomness of such 'supervision' or inspection being agreed. Since a contractor's own supervisory activities are assumed to be those necessary to enable the contractor to meet its 'fitness for purpose' obligation, the purpose of the consulting engineer's 'supervision', therefore, needs to be made clear. Failing clarity, an agreement to 'supervise' or inspect could cause the consulting engineer to become involved in any claim that is made relating to the contractor's work on the basis that the consulting engineer failed to pick up defective work by the contractor. If the consulting engineer is found to be jointly liable with the contractor, and the contractor has gone out of business, the consulting engineer could be liable for 100% of the damages (see above in this Section and Section 2.12 of this chapter concerning net contribution clauses).

A particular case in point is where the consulting engineer is employed by a contractor on a design-and-construct contract. The contractor is thus the consulting engineer's client. It often happens that the consulting engineer is asked by the employer to inspect, 'supervise' or comment upon the contractor's workmanship. The consulting engineer should avoid being placed in this position and should decline if asked. It is the consulting engineer's duty to design the works and it is the contractor's to construct them. To repeat what is stated above: the former is prepared with reasonable skill and care and the latter to achieve fitness for purpose. If the consulting engineer was not careful, it may find itself saddled with an uninsurable obligation. The converse also presents problems; if the contractor attempts during the design process to impose on the consulting engineer measures that the consulting engineer considers unwise, or, especially, a risk to health and safety, then the consulting engineer has an obligation to the contractor and, perhaps, to the public at large, to resist such measures. Thus, many design-and-construct contracts produce tensions between designer and contractor that can only be overcome by understanding and experience on both sides.

'As-built' or 'as-constructed' drawings Bespoke appointments sometimes require the preparation and issue of 'as-built' drawings and documents. However, 'as-built' drawings and documents may not fully represent the as-built condition, as a consulting engineer's site staff cannot be expected to measure and record the actual detail of everything that the contractor constructed or supplied. It is arguable that on a large project not even the contractor will be able to complete such a task accurately but, almost certainly, will be better placed than the consulting engineer. There is a risk that, if the consulting engineer undertakes production of 'as-built' drawings, the client could find itself relying on substantially incomplete or inaccurate information and will incur unexpected costs, which the client then attempts to recover from the consulting engineer. 'As-built' drawings are therefore best left to the contractor to prepare, though the consulting engineer may well undertake the task of vetting the completeness, relevance, clarity and subsequent delivery to the client of the drawing and document sets, but not the accuracy of individual drawings and documents.

2.18 Bonds, parent company guarantees, liquidated damages, set-off and retention

Bonds, parent company guarantees, liquidated damages, set-off and retention are all measures introduced by clients into bespoke consulting engineering appointments in an attempt to secure performance by financial control. It is arguable whether any of them are necessary. If something has gone seriously wrong with a design that by due legal process has been shown to be down to the consulting engineer's negligence, insurance is there to cover that contingency. For less serious matters, withholding of fees, like any commercial deal, has proved an adequate means of putting matters right. With the possible exception of parent company guarantees, all the remaining measures are simply punitive and often do not lead to solution of the difficulty that caused them to be applied in the first place.

Bonds – types and uses

Despite the label of bond – an insurance instrument – the typical bond imposed on a consulting engineer is a contract guarantee issued by a bank. Such a bond guarantees, in certain circumstances, to pay the beneficiary of the bond, the client, a sum of money. The bank will require the consulting engineer to back the guarantee by promising to reimburse the bank should the client call the bond.

There are three types of bond in common use: tender bonds (also known as bid bonds), advance payment bonds and performance bonds. Usually,

- tender bonds are asked for to provide comfort to the client of the commitment of the bidding consulting engineer to sign a contract for the work if that consulting engineer's bid is accepted. Tender bonds are also used as a disincentive to the consulting engineer withdrawing its tender before the bidding period is over. As a rule-of-thumb, tender bonds run at a level of anything up to 5% of the estimated value of the proposed consulting engineer's contract though this percentage should be treated with a degree of caution,
- advance payment bonds act as a surety for fees paid by the client as a loan in advance of work being completed by the consulting engineer, e.g. to cover the cost of commissioning a specialist survey or hiring a particular subconsultant in advance of any invoice being submitted by the consulting engineer. The values of such bonds reduce in value as the loan is repaid bit by bit by the consulting engineer over a pre-determined period. Thus, the value of the bond should equal the amount not repaid at any one time; at the outset, this will be the full value of the advance payment, and
- performance bonds hold the consulting engineers to continue with their contracts until all services have been completed. The justification for the existence of such bonds is that they enable the client to appoint a substitute consulting engineer should the first consulting engineer not perform as envisaged. The value of the bond is set at a percentage (often 10%) of the consulting engineer's fee and remains at that level throughout the contract.

All the three types of bond above constitute a separate contract between the client and the bondsman. Since no money changes hands, they are invariably written as deeds. Nowadays, such bonds are unconditional, i.e. they can be called 'on-demand, by the client, and therein lies the problem. All the beneficiary has to do in the case of an on-demand bond is to make the demand and the bank will pay. There is no examination of whether or not the demand is justified. The demand of the beneficiary is sufficient. Thus, on-demand bonds are extremely risky instruments for the consulting engineer to furnish.

In all cases, there is one vital provision that must be present. There needs to be a validity period, preferably a date after which the bond becomes invalid, so that the financial exposure is limited by time. Applying such dates to:

- a bid bond: the bond should cease to have value on a date at the end of the client's stated tender review period or on award of contract to one of the tenderers, if earlier. If the client has not stated a tender review period in its invitation to tender or it is not possible to calculate a date when the tender review period ends then the consulting engineer should state a date in its offer and make sure that the wording of the bid bond reflects that date;

- an advance payment bond: in the unlikely event that the client has not stated in its invitation to tender the period over which the advance payment bond has to be repaid then the consulting engineer should give a mechanism in its offer whereby a date when the advance payment will be repaid can be calculated. Of course, setting such a date works both ways. It imposes an obligation on the consulting engineer to repay the loan, but at the same time prevents the client calling the bond earlier than anticipated;
- a performance bond: the date of completion of the consulting engineering services as set by the design programme upon which the client and consulting engineer agreed at the time they entered into contract. Setting a date in this instance is particularly important. Often clients ask for the performance bond to be valid until a final certificate is issued to the contractor. Since the issuing of such a certificate may well be outside the consulting engineer's control, there is a very real risk that the validity period, and thus the risk to the consulting engineer, may well become extended.

Bonds – use of banking facilities

Providing the bonds above will cost the consulting engineer money. Banks charge for providing such bonds and their continuing existence will often affect the consulting engineers' overdraft limits. Consulting engineers thus have a good commercial reason for reducing the value of such bonds to a minimum and agreeing exactly the date after which such bonds cease to have any value. Should the client have need for the bonds to remain in place longer than anticipated then the consulting engineer should be well placed to negotiate reimbursement of the cost of providing any such extension in time.

A particular problem of bonding is that the consulting engineer's bank will generally only allow so much aggregate bonding at any one time. Further, despite the presence in the bond of an effective end date, many banks insist on the return of the signed bond itself before treating the bond as having no call on the consulting engineer's overdraft facility.

Parent company guarantees

In lieu of, and sometimes in addition to, clients frequently ask for parent company guarantees in addition to the three types of bond mentioned above.

Parent company guarantees can only be provided by a parent company if the consulting engineer is not just trading corporately, as opposed to individually or in partnership, but also as a subsidiary, as defined by section 736 of Part XXVI of the Companies Act 1985. This situation is not unusual, as a group company may have a subsidiary company acting as a consulting engineer to the remainder of the group or, indeed, providing professional consulting engineering services independently outside the group. Another instance is where a large multi-national consulting engineer has subsidiary companies operating in various countries around the globe. The main point, though, is that the parent company must have a controlling ownership of the subsidiary company that is being asked to provide a parent company guarantee.

There is a reasonable case to be made that parent company guarantees are better than bonds: they do not cost money and do not restrict the consulting engineer's capacity to trade (by exhaustion of overdraft facilities). Parent company guarantees, in effect, provide the client with a much greater level of confidence that its project will be completed, as opposed to simply receiving a 10% cash payment normally available from a performance bond. Having said that, a parent company guarantee does not necessarily embody the certainty of outcome of a performance bond and it must be recognised that the strength of a parent company guarantee is only as strong as that of the parent company and provided its resources are independent of those of the subsidiary. The parent company guarantee may expose the parent company to any combination of the following:

- if the parent company is trading in the same discipline as the subsidiary, to finish the project at no cost to the client
- to simply indemnify the client against all the client's costs in completing the project
- to ensure that another consulting engineer replaces the subsidiary at no cost to the client.

There is government support for the use of parent company guarantees but as an alternative to, not in addition to, bonds.

There are opportunities available to clients for drafting parent company guarantees that are more onerous in their content than the contracts with the subsidiary companies. Clearly, this is a matter to be resisted, but a few examples might be helpful:

(a) *Conversion of a guarantee to an indemnity*. In these cases, the whole character of the instrument is changed so that there is no longer a duty on the part of the beneficiary (the client) to mitigate its loss and the type of loss recoverable is broader in that the normal rules on proximate causation do not apply. There is also the practical consequence that exposure is longer as the amount of the loss covered by the indemnity has first to be ascertained before the time to collect the money under an indemnity starts to run.

(b) *Recoverable loss extended to third party claims*. A third party claim may be admitted in full without any regard to liability or quantum, and the full amount would be recoverable.

(c) *Use of subjective criteria*. There have been examples of this approach by the public sector where the question of whether there has been any breach and the amount to be paid are to be determined by an employee of the employer, often in the form of a certificate.

There are a number of important drafting points that should be taken to render the parent company guarantee acceptable. First, there should be a provision that the exposure of the guarantor i.e., the parent company, is no greater and is for no longer than that of the guaranteed subsidiary consulting engineer under the subsidiary consulting engineer's appointment with the client. Secondly, a qualification could be made limiting the scope of the guarantee to that which is insurable and available under the subsidiary consulting engineer's professional indemnity insurance policy. Thirdly, and specifically to deal with third party claims, it could be provided that the guarantor takes over the conduct of a defence of a third party claim. Finally, if the guarantee extends to 'losses, damages, costs and expenses' (which should be resisted), it could be inserted that the guarantee covers those to the extent that they are properly recoverable in law.

Given that parent company guarantees could involve the parent company in costs that far exceed the value of a 'standard' performance bond, and are often more onerous than the contract that the subsidiary company entered into in the first instance, parent companies may well be reluctant to support their subsidiaries in this way.

Liquidated damages

Such provisions have been common in construction contracts for many years in order to provide an automatic mechanism for claiming for the effects of culpable delay in the completion of such contracts. Providing that the figure inserted in the contract, usually an amount per week, is a genuine pre-estimate of the expected loss due to delay, it stands, and there is no need, upon culpable delay occurring, to assess the actual losses incurred.

Not until recently have such provisions found their way into consulting engineers' bespoke appointments. However, unlike the contractor, the consulting engineer is often in the hands of others with regard to the timing of its design work and it may find itself unable to control events as it struggles to complete on time and thus avoid the application of liquidated damages. A consulting engineer that finds itself with a bespoke contract that includes an obligation to pay liquidated damages might well be wise in taking every opportunity to have the completion date extended should the client's requirements change or unexpected events occur that are not within the consulting engineer's control.

In the case of failure to complete the construction, the loss of use of the constructed works can be costed at the outset and an appropriate figure for liquidated damages included in the contractor's contract. However, in the case of design delay there are opportunities open to the client, but not the consulting engineer, to make up any lost time, since other parties and other activities are invariably involved after the design work has been completed. It is thus far more problematical to calculate a sensible pre-estimate of the client's expected loss at the time that the consulting engineer's services have been completed – a time often long before the client takes possession of the completed works. Hence, any such liquidated damages clause in the consulting engineer's contract must run the risk of being unenforceable. The other major problem with liquidated damages clauses for the consulting engineer is that they are uninsurable. Firstly, delay may not be due to negligence and secondly, even if delay is due to negligence, liquidated damages are, by definition, not equivalent to the losses under such insurance due to negligent delay. Therefore, consulting engineers should resist such clauses. If accepted, they should be viewed as commercial risk and treated as such.

Set-off

Clauses in consulting engineers' contracts providing rights to set-off claims by a client under one contract against that or another contract are common, but are they necessary? Until the relevant part of the 'Construction Act' came into force on 1 May 1998, all a client had to do was to withhold payment of fees and fight the matter out in court, if the consulting engineer was so minded, where the competing claims would be decided and a balancing award made. The Construction Act does not ban this practice; it merely interposes certain procedural requirements to the right of set-off. These procedural requirements amount to a period within which a notice must be given specifying the amount being withheld and the reasons for withholding. Thus, set-off remains the traditional mode of financially controlling the relationship between the consulting engineer and client. However, in order to isolate commercial risk a consulting engineer might have very good reasons for resisting set-off between separate contracts and may well wish to negotiate on the matter before signing the design appointment with the client.

Retentions

Retentions are commonly used in construction contracts and sometimes appear in consulting engineer's bespoke appointments. In recent years the use of retentions in construction contracts has received a great deal of adverse comment. Retentions add nothing to the quality of construction, do not result in shorter construction periods and simply add to the price. The use of retentions in both construction and consulting engineers' contracts is contrary to the principles of partnering and the sharing of risk as set out in Sir John Egan's *Rethinking Construction*. Many central government departments and local authorities have abandoned retentions as a means of achieving their required standards of quality.

The argument in favour of retention under a construction contract goes thus: a construction contract has been handed over to the client, most of the work is satisfactory and the client has released half of the sum of 5% that it had hitherto retained in an attempt to secure the contractor's performance during the construction period. The remaining 2½% is retained so as to make sure that the contractor deals with a number of minor problems during the maintenance period. It is generally assumed that the release of the final element of retention is wholly within the contractor's hands and that the contract is finalised on time to the satisfaction of both client and contractor. In effect, the retained sum is acting as a form of performance bond (see above).

In the case of a designer, the argument does not hold. Errors are generally not known at the end of the design, nor, often, at the end of the construction period. Any errors in design appear much later – long after the contractor has left the site and long after the client has been using the constructed works for the purposes, and sometimes not for such purposes, for which they were designed. A retention provides nothing of benefit to the client and merely retards the consulting engineer's cash flow, the cost of which the consulting engineer may well include in its fee.

2.19 Dispute resolution

This section deals only with adjudication under the Housing Grants, Construction and Regeneration Act 1996, 'the Construction Act', and not with other methods of dispute resolution, such as mediation, which might be included in consulting engineers' appointments. The Construction Act provides a right to either party to a 'construction contract' at any time to refer a dispute arising under that contract to adjudication under a procedure that complies with the Construction Act, regardless of whether such a right is expressly incorporated in the contract.

If there is no adjudication provision, or if the adjudication procedure in the contract does not comply with the Construction Act, the Scheme for Construction Contracts (England and Wales) Regulations 1998, 'the Scheme', will apply. The Scheme governs both the appointment of the adjudicator and the conduct of the adjudication.

The Scheme is suitable for consulting engineers' appointments. The Scheme does not, however, deal with the right to challenge the adjudicator appointed by a third party/nominating body. It may be best, therefore, to agree the identity of the adjudicator beforehand (or the body to nominate the adjudicator). Because a consulting engineer will not know the nature of the dispute until it arises, it will usually be best for a large organisation to be appointed, such as the Construction Industry Council (CIC) or the Institution of Civil Engineers (ICE), which can then select an adjudicator of the right discipline for the dispute in question. If the Scheme is incorporated expressly, consulting engineers should check to see that no amendments have been made to it. Such amendments in bespoke appointments sometimes favour the client or are not entirely even-handed.

Under the Construction Act and Scheme, there is no express power to award either of the parties' costs, so each must bear their own. However, sometimes there are clauses

2.1 Ways of operating
2.2 Working with others
2.3 Working internationally
2.4 The engineer's appointment
2.5 Collateral warranties
2.6 Indemnity insurance
2.7 Employment law
2.8 Information technology

within a bespoke contract that introduce other 'schemes' that may amend this. Examples of such private schemes are ICE, Technology and Construction Solicitors Association (TeCSA) and CIC schemes. Some major clients have also produced their own. Each scheme should be considered individually and checked with insurers who sometimes impose conditions or limitations, for example that the adjudicator's decision should not be final and binding, or that the adjudicator can only base his or her decision on legal grounds, not commercial grounds or fair and reasonable grounds. Many insurers also prefer that adjudicators should give the reasons for their decisions.

It would also be prudent if the appointment stated that a specific person in the consulting engineer's firm has to be served with any notice of adjudication and that service is not effective until the notice has been received by that person. This is because of the very short timetable for dealing with the dispute and within which the adjudicator has to give a decision. It could prejudice a consulting engineer's ability to deal properly with any referral if a notice was sent by post, for example, and the recipient failed to realize its importance or was on holiday and did not return until most of the 28 days had expired.

The following matters should be noted in relation to some of the published schemes.

(a) The CIC Scheme (Fourth Edition March 2007) provides that the adjudicator must apply the law of the contract. He has to give reasons for his decision unless the parties agree otherwise.
(b) Under the ICE Scheme (1997), the adjudicator is not required to give reasons for a decision and nothing is said about the adjudicator having to make a decision in accordance with the applicable law. Therefore, the adjudicator could make a decision on, say, commercial or fair and reasonable grounds.
(c) Under the TeCSA Adjudication Rules 2002 Version 2.0, reasons are to be given for any decision if the parties so request within seven days of the referral, the adjudicator's decision can be made on a fair and reasonable basis (and therefore not in accordance with the law), the parties are not entitled to make any application to the court in relation to the conduct of the adjudicator or his decision until that decision has been complied with and neither party is entitled to raise any set-of/counterclaim or abatement in connection with any enforcement proceedings.
(d) The Joint Contracts Tribunal (JCT) contracts issued in 2005 now incorporate the statutory Scheme provisions for adjudication.

2.20 Copyright

This section deals with copyright issues as they affect consulting engineers.

Broadly speaking, the purpose of intellectual property rights is to confer on their owner the exclusive right to use the particular intellectual property concerned. These rights can then be commercially exploited by the owner, by licensing them on appropriate terms to others.

Copyright protects literary and artistic works (among others). These do not have to be works of any specified quality – any document is a literary work and any drawing is an artistic work. A software program is a literary work.

In the absence of any special agreement, copyright in a literary or artistic work belongs to the author or artist of that work. However, if the author or artist is an employee producing the work in the course of his or her employment, copyright belongs to the employer in the absence of any agreement to the contrary.

Infringement of copyright in a work by another party includes copying it (i.e., reproducing it or a substantial part of it in any material form) or making an adaptation of the work or selling an infringing copy. Copying includes storing the work in any medium by electronic means. The transient reproduction of any work on a computer screen will amount to copying. In the case of a drawing, copying can include constructing the subject matter of the drawings, i.e. reproducing the drawing in three-dimensional form.

Protecting copyright is, therefore, straightforward, as long as it is clear who the copyright owner is and that no licence (express or implied) has been granted to the infringer.

Having established in which documents the consulting engineer has copyright, the provisions concerning copyright in the appointment need to be checked. Is copyright to remain with the consulting engineer or is it to pass to or be vested in the client? The latter should be resisted if at all possible (although the Crown and other statutory bodies will insist on having copyright in all the consulting engineer's materials). If copyright is vested in another party, all the rights belonging to the author also pass to that party who can then copy and use the documents for any purpose and not necessarily for the project for which they were prepared. Further, the consulting engineer will be infringing the client's copyright by copying its own documents. It is essential, therefore, in these circumstances that a licence back to the consulting engineer is included in the appointment and that this extends, if necessary, beyond the particular project.

The ACE Agreements provide inter alia that copyright in drawings and/or documents and other intellectual property rights remains vested in or becomes vested in the consulting engineer.

Each appointment should set out in full the documents in which the consulting engineer has copyright.

Copyright belonging to a third party, for example to a subconsultant, can only be vested in the client by that third party. Therefore, if it is a condition of the consulting engineer's appointment that all copyright, including that belonging to third parties, be vested in the client, the consulting engineer must ensure that the third parties agree to do this in their contract with the consulting engineer.

For reports and documents produced in circumstances where there is no formal agreement about copyright, it is helpful to include a statement in such reports and documents concerning copyright and the extent, if any, of the licence given.

The licence in copyright works sets out the terms on which someone other than the copyright owner (the licensee) can copy or use the copyright works. The licence agreement will, for example, deal with the right to copy, which includes building the subject matter of a drawing, adapting documents and, perhaps most importantly, state the purpose for which the documents can be used. Care needs to be taken to identify the purpose correctly and that the purpose does not, except in appropriate circumstances, extend beyond the particular project or purpose for which the information was provided.

If nothing is agreed in writing, a licence may well be implied when the copyright owner releases its copyright work to the other party to the contract or to a third party, such as the contractor and other consultants. The terms of that licence may, however, be unclear. It is better, therefore, to have express licence terms included in the appointment.

The licence in the ACE Agreements gives the client the right to use the consulting engineer's drawings and other documents and the consulting engineer's other intellectual property rights for any purpose related to the project. It also expressly reminds the client that it cannot make copies, nor make use of any of the other rights in connection with any other works without the prior written approval of the consulting engineer and that the consulting engineer will not be liable for the use by any person of any such drawings or documents or other rights for any purpose other than that for which the same were prepared by or on behalf of the consulting engineer.

The licence to the client in the ACE Agreements is also dependent on the payment of fees. If the client is in default, the consulting engineer is given the express right to revoke the licence.

An 'irrevocable' licence would mean that whatever the circumstances, such as a breach of its obligations by the client, the licence will not cease.

Some bespoke appointments include more onerous licences, for example that they should be 'exclusive'. This is tantamount to handing over copyright because it would confer on the licensee sole rights to copy and use the documents etc. and generally the other consultants, contractor, subcontractor, etc. will also need this facility. It will also prohibit the consulting engineer from exploiting its copyright work freely. If a licence is 'freely assignable' or the licensee is permitted to grant further sub-licences, the consulting engineer could lose control of the number of people who have the right to copy the documents and the uses to which they can be put, and so again such a right needs to be considered carefully.

The documents in respect of which the licence is given also need to be considered carefully. These are often different from those for which copyright is claimed. It is best if the licence is limited to those drawings and documents that the client or other members of the team need.

The Copyright, Designs and Patents Act 1988 created several 'moral rights', including the right to be identified as the author of (or person who created) a copyright work (s.77). For a consulting engineer, this would mean the right to be identified as the author of the drawings for a building, for example. Such a right has formally to be positively asserted either on the copyright work or by an instrument in writing, for example the appointment document, before it can be enforced (s.78). Though it was constructed over one hundred years before the above Copyright Act, 'Brunel's Clifton suspension bridge' is an example of an engineer being identified with a particular work; 'Stephenson's "Rocket"' is another.

The right is infringed if certain acts are done without the author's consent, for example if the work is published commercially.

There is also a right to object to a derogatory treatment, which includes the adaptation of copyright work (s.80).

These rights can cause administrative problems for a client and many bespoke appointments include a provision that the consulting engineer agrees not to assert the right to be identified as the author by expressly waiving this right or by agreeing not to assert the right and this is usually done by reference to the relevant sections (ss.77 and 80) of the Copyright Act.

Whether such a waiver is acceptable will depend on the nature of each particular appointment.

3 WORKING FOR DESIGN AND CONSTRUCT CONTRACTOR

Consulting engineers are often engaged by contractors for a design and construct project. The main difficulties here relate to the obligations taken on by the contractor, which it will seek to pass on to the consulting engineer, and the question of inspection or supervision during construction.

Design obligations

In the absence of an express provision in the construction contract, the contractor will have undertaken an obligation to ensure that the construction will be fit for its intended purpose. This is a different and more onerous obligation from that imposed on designers under common law, which is to use reasonable skill and care in carrying out their designs. However, commonly used standard conditions of contract, such as the ICE Design and Construct Conditions of Contract, for use on design and construct projects do provide that a contractor's design liability shall be the same as the consulting engineer's, i.e. one of reasonable skill and care (or a close variation of those words). Thus, difficulties are avoided as long as the level of duty of care in the consulting engineer's appointment is no more onerous than that in the contractor's contract with the employer.

Serious risks, though, are run by consulting engineers that sign up to contractors' bespoke forms of engagement that simply seek to pass on the contractor's obligations to its employer in their entirety. It is a fact of life that many such bespoke forms treat the supplier of a design as if it were the supplier of materials or a constructor of the works, i.e. the obligations in the contractor's contract with the employer are simply passed down to the consulting engineer with no amendment, or, perhaps even worse, confusing, ambiguous and onerous amendments. Such bespoke contracts pass a level of risk down to the consulting engineer, which is invariably the party least able to accommodate such risks. Bespoke forms of contract that do not reflect the inability of the consulting engineer to influence events once construction has commenced often lead to tension between contractor and consulting engineer. Such tension can be avoided by separating the contractor's obligations to its employer from the consulting engineer's obligations to the contractor – the ACE has produced forms of Agreement (Agreement C(1) and C(2)) for just this situation.

Supervision

As to supervision, a consulting engineer may sometimes be asked by a design-and-construct contractor to undertake supervision of the works that the consulting engineer has designed and that the contractor is in the process of building. With the sole exception described in the following paragraph, the consulting engineer would be well advised to avoid any such supervision of the contractor's work. Quality of workmanship and supervision are the contractor's responsibility, and there is no good reason why the consulting engineer should share that responsibility.

The services described in ACE Agreements C(1) and C(2) (for consulting engineers employed by a design-and-construct contractor) do not include any such obligation to supervise unless the consulting engineer is to perform 'Performance Services'. These are, however, restricted to satisfying itself generally as to the execution of the works 'insofar as it reflects upon the design intent', but even then what the consulting engineer actually does on site could easily be misinterpreted.

A consulting engineer engaged by a contractor undertaking a design-and-construct project should normally visit the site only to obtain confirmation/information (for example, ground conditions) related directly to the consulting engineer's design services.

However, it is recognised that a contractor may well expect its consulting engineer to attend regular meetings on site, especially if those meetings involve the contractor's employer. In such instances the consulting engineer should exercise discretion when invited to inspect a particular part of the construction or to accompany both contractor and employer for a general tour of the works.

If the services include the production of a specification (or the supply of a standard specification) that is to relate to any portion of the contractor's work, the specification should be checked to see that it does not place an obligation on the consulting engineer to 'supervise' or 'approve' work on site.

3.1 Assignment and novation

The general legal principles concerning assignment and novation have been set out in Chapter 3.3. This section deals with the particular implications for a consulting engineer where its appointment by the client is assigned or novated to a design-and-construct contractor.

Some bespoke appointments expressly prohibit the assignment of any rights of action in respect of accrued breaches (i.e. 'benefits') without consent. More usually, a client will not want any restrictions on its freedom to assign the benefits of its contract to third parties, such as funders or tenants.

The ACE Agreements permit assignments by both parties of the benefits and obligations with consent, but that consent may not be unreasonably withheld.

Where contractual obligations or burdens are to be assigned with the consent of the other contracting party, this is achieved by the parties to the original contract and the third party, to whom the obligations are being assigned, entering into a new agreement (a novation agreement) whereby it is agreed that the obligations will now be undertaken by the third party.

Such a novation agreement replaces the original contract, so the usual requirements for the validity of contracts will apply on the making of the novation agreement.

A consulting engineer does not have to agree to a third party taking over the client's obligations under the appointment. This would include the obligation to pay. There could be real objections to this. For example, the consulting engineer may not wish to work for that particular client, who might be close to insolvency or there may be a conflict of interest. Some bespoke appointments, however, may provide for the assignment of the burdens and benefits of the contract without consent, or may oblige the consulting engineer to agree in advance to a novation in a certain form to a third party. This arises most often where there is to be a design-and-construct contractor and the client wishes to novate its professionals to that contractor.

Where the novation is to be from one client to another client (not a contractor), the following matters should be considered:

(i) The novation agreement should be checked for any unusual or onerous terms in the same way that any other contract would be checked. A novation agreement should not be used as an opportunity to change the terms of the original contract.

(ii) The novation agreement should also be drafted so that the retiring party is discharged from any further liability and thus steps out of the contract completely, and the new party assumes responsibility for all the contractual obligations, including past obligations.

(iii) Some clients want to split responsibility between the old and new client, and, for example, make it a term that the original client is responsible for any past defaults, including non-payment of fees. This is not satisfactory. The new client is going to want to sue the consulting engineer for any breaches that may have occurred before it took over and this should work both ways. The consulting engineer will not want to sue the old client for some things (and particularly not for non-payment when the reason why the appointment is being novated could well be that the client is in financial difficulties) and the new client for others.

(iv) There should also be no variation to the time within which claims can be brought. The time limits to apply should be those that would have applied if the original client had remained the consulting engineer's client throughout. Some novation agreements try to give new clients extra time for bringing claims in respect of pre-existing breaches. Also, if the original appointment was under hand, the novation agreement should not be signed as a deed.

Some additional considerations apply where an consulting engineer is to be novated to a design-and-construct contractor. The consulting engineer will, in these circumstances, have performed some services for the original client and after novation will perform different services for the design-and-construct contractor. The consulting engineer does not re-perform the services it carried out for its original client. It is not, therefore, a true novation and this distinction ought to be preserved in any 'novation' agreement.

As a result of the decision in *Blyth & Blyth* v. *Carillion*, additional provisions are now appearing in novation agreements novating consulting engineers to design-and-construct contractors. In this case, the contractor sought to recover from the consulting engineer the losses associated with an underestimate of steel reinforcement upon which the contractor relied when preparing its tender. This was before the consulting engineer took on any duties directly to the contractor. It was held that these were not losses that the employer would have suffered and were therefore not recoverable under the novation agreement signed by the consulting engineer. Particular care therefore needs to be taken in considering the effect of any clauses in novation agreements designed to address this point. These are mainly included in '*ab initio*' novation agreements that seek to impose liability on the consulting engineer on the fictitious basis that it has been employed by the contractor (as well as by the original client) from the beginning of the project. Thus the clauses in such agreements seek to recast the consulting engineer's duties retrospectively. Others seek to state the sort of losses for which the consulting engineer is to be responsible. All such clauses need to be considered very carefully if the consulting engineer is not to be made liable for matters for which it was not responsible and in respect of which it did not advise. In the writers' view, the correct basis for the novation in this context is that set out in the CIC Novation Agreement published in 2004. The CIC Novation Agreement is on the basis that the contractor 'steps in' as the client under the appointment only from the date of novation, which is usually when the construction contract is let and the consulting engineer performs its services for the contractor only from that date.

There is no difficulty, in the context of a CIC-type novation only, in a consulting engineer giving a warranty to the contractor in respect of the services provided to the employer up to the date of novation, but this should only be that the consulting engineer has exercised reasonable skill and care in the performance of those services for the client.

Whatever the basis, the consulting engineer should check the extent and description of the duties and obligations that it has agreed to carry out for the original client to ensure that they are correct in the first instance for the original client and that post-novation they correctly state what services the consulting engineer will provide for a design-and-construct contractor. The way supervision is described is particularly important – see above. The CIC Novation Agreement makes provision for this.

Further, in such bespoke agreements the original client may try to ensure that some of the obligations of the consulting engineer continue to be owed to the client, even though the consulting engineer has been novated. For example, the client could either, through the novation agreement or by a direct warranty, ask the consulting engineer to supervise the works or report to it on various matters during construction. Quite apart from the potential conflict of interest, the contractor is now the consulting engineer's client. If, however, the consulting engineer has taken on an obligation to report, the consulting engineer should notify only the contractor of matters that the consulting engineer thinks the contractor is doing incorrectly (but see cautionary text above with respect to supervision). Of course, the contractor does not have to act on the consulting engineer's report but the original client may not understand this.

4 STANDARD FORMS

4.1 The ACE Conditions

In 2002, the ACE produced the following forms of agreement:

- Agreement A, where a consulting engineer is engaged as a lead consultant
- Agreement B, where a consulting engineer is engaged directly by the client, but not as a lead consultant
- Agreement C, where a consulting engineer is engaged to provide design services for a design and construct contractor
- Short Form Agreement, for use with a concise brief.

These Agreements were revised in 2004, either by republication as the revised 2004 version or by way of amendment sheets. These amendments were mainly directed at incorporating new limitations of liability to cover not only an overall limit per claim and aggregate limits or exclusions of liability for pollution and contamination claims as before, but also limits or exclusions of liability for terrorism and asbestos claims following the restrictions on such cover that had been introduced into consulting engineers' professional indemnity insurance since the 2002 Agreements. The net contribution clause remains.

- Agreement for Planning Supervisors jointly badged with the Association of Planning Supervisors
- Sub-Consultancy Agreement for use with the other ACE Agreements.

These two Agreements were not revised in 2004.
There are also two earlier Agreements produced in 1995 and updated in 1998.

- Agreement D, where a consulting engineer is engaged to provide report and advisory services now replaced by the Short Form
- Agreement E, where a consulting engineer is engaged as a project manager.

Agreements A, B and C are each published in two variants for different consulting engineering disciplines as follows:

- civil and structural engineering
- engineering of electrical and mechanical services in buildings.

Each Agreement comprised a memorandum of agreement, conditions of engagement and a schedule of services. In the case of Agreement B(2) and C(2) there are alternative services schedules – one for detailed design services and one for performance services.

Although not all appointments under the ACE Agreements will be 'construction contracts', the ACE decided to include the payment provisions of the Construction Act in all ACE appointments. As to dispute resolution, the ACE Agreements provide that 'the parties shall attempt in good faith to settle any dispute by mediation'. Adjudication is provided for in accordance with the CIC's Model Adjudication Procedure but only if the agreement is a construction contract. The arbitration clause has been deleted.

A new, revised suite of ACE Agreements is due to be published in 2008/2009.

4.2 The Professional Services Contract

The series of standard form contracts produced by the New Engineering Contract (NEC) Panel have been described in Chapter 1.6.

The NEC Professional Services Contract (PSC) was first published in 1994. The 2nd Edition was published in June 1998 and a 3rd Edition (PSC3) was published in June 2005.

As with the other contracts in this family, the contract contains core clauses dealing with the parties' main responsibilities, time, quality payment, compensation events, rights to material, indemnity insurance and liability and disputes and termination.

There are then four main option clauses: for priced contracts with activity schedule, target contracts, time-based contracts and term contracts.

Finally, there are secondary option clauses dealing with such things as price adjustment for inflation, changes in the law, parent company guarantees, sectional completion, delay damages, collateral warranty agreements and the Housing Grants, Construction and Regeneration Act 1996 and the Contracts (Rights of Third Parties) Act 1999.

PSC3 is now substantially different from the ACE Agreements discussed in Section 2 of this chapter. Some of the main differences are as follows.

Duty of care

Under clause 21.2 of the PSC, the Consultant's obligation is 'to use the skill and care normally used by professionals providing services similar to the services [as defined]'. This is different from 'reasonable skill and care', which is the duty in the ACE Agreements and under the common law. The fact that this latter wording has not been used could be construed as incorporating a different and possibly higher standard – see Section 2.1 of this chapter.

Defects

Under clause 41.2 of the PSC, the Consultant is obliged to 'correct Defects within a time that minimises the adverse effect on the Employer or Others'. If the Consultant does not correct 'Defects' within the time required by the contract, the employer assesses the cost of having Defects corrected by other people and the Consultant pays this amount.

A Defect is defined (in clause 11) as a part of the services (as defined) that is not in accordance with the Scope or the applicable law. The Scope is defined as 'information which specifies and describes the services or states any constraints on how the Consultant provides the services'. This information is set out in a document identified in the Contract Data, provided by the employer or in an instruction given in accordance with the contract.

There is no indication that a Defect can only result from a failure to exercise reasonable skill and care. Thus, the Consultant could be liable to pay for the costs of rectifying a Defect even if the Defect is not the result of a failure to exercise reasonable skill and care, or in cases where the employer may have suffered no loss, where nominal damages only might be payable. This is fundamentally objectionable and insurers may refuse to indemnify consulting engineers.

The Consultant also has to notify the employer of Defects at completion and until the Defects Date. This may go beyond the duty imposed on a consulting engineer under common law in certain circumstances.

The ACE Agreements contain no similar provisions, leaving the matter of damages arising from any defect and the question of notification to be dealt with under the common law.

Limitation on liability

In the PSC Second Edition the 'Consultant's liability' to the employer 'resulting from a failure to Provide the Services' was limited to the amount stated in the Contract Data.

This has been replaced by a new clause 82.1 in PSC3 giving a total liability in an amount to be agreed for all matters other than excluded matters and this is to apply 'in contract, tort or delict and otherwise to the extent allowed under the law of the contract'.

The excluded matters include delay damages, loss or damage to third party property and death of or bodily injury to a person other than an employee of the Consultant.

A new Option X18 has been added that allows the parties to agree other limitations, i.e. for indirect or consequential losses and for defects not found until after the defects date. It is not clear how this fits in with clause 82.1. The parties can also fix a time limit for claims.

Clause 82.2 is meant to be a net contribution clause. This is clear from the guidance. However, what clause 82.2 says is that 'the Consultant's liability to the Employer is limited to that proportion of the Employer's losses for which the Consultant is responsible under this contract'. Since the proportion for which the Consultant 'is responsible' would be 100% in such circumstances, this clause could be ineffective.

Time obligations

PSC3 has strict obligations on the consulting engineer to comply with Key Dates and it is relieved of that obligation only if the event preventing the achievement of the Key Date is a compensation event.

This is again a very different basis to that in the ACE Agreements – see Section 2.4.

4.3 FIDIC Client/Consultant Model Services Agreement

The Client/Consultant Model Services Agreement entered its fourth edition in 2006. It is familiarly known as 'The White Book' and is published by FIDIC (Fédération Internationale des Ingéneurs-Conseils). Its primary use is for international consultancy contracts where the parties are free to choose a number of aspects that would normally be taken 'as read' in any other standard form of contract used in the United Kingdom. Examples of the choices available are those of language, governing law and currency of payment.

The fourth edition of the FIDIC Client/Consultant Model Services Agreement, much like the ACE Agreements, imposes, through clause 3.3.1, a duty on the consulting engineer 'to exercise reasonable skill, care and diligence in the performance of his obligations'. The contract also allows the consulting engineer to agree a total limit of liability, rather than a recurring 'each and every' limit of liability. This is in marked contrast to the principle behind the ACE Agreements. Additionally, and unlike the other standard forms discussed in this chapter, clause 6.4.1 introduces an indemnity clause, which should be treated with a great deal of caution as highlighted in paragraph 2.11 above.

Generally speaking, the FIDIC White Book is a form of agreement that transmits itself across frontiers without too much difficulty. In the writers' view any attempts to amend the wording so as to make them overly-sophisticated or more suited to a particular legal jurisdiction may be wasted effort. Consulting engineers run significant commercial risks in working internationally and one of those risks is the interpretation of the wording of the contract by clients and legislators whose first language may not be English. Relying on elaborate legal argument in some cases might not prove effective.

4.4 The CIC Consultants' Contract Conditions

The Construction Industry Council published the first edition of its Consultants' Contract Conditions in November 2007 together with a comprehensive scope of services, which is now available on-line using DefinIT software. This standard form is specifically tailored for use by experienced clients and consultants of all disciplines undertaking large commercial building developments.

One of the primary intentions of the CIC Consultants' Contract is that it is used to engage all members of the professional team. The attitude of the client is, therefore, of paramount importance in achieving this objective. The result will be that the project manager, architect, civil and structural consulting engineers, building services consulting engineer, landscape architect, cost consultant, CDM co-ordinator, quantity surveyor and any other consultants are all on an equal contractual footing and all working within a scope of services, the elements of which have been clearly allocated to individual members of the design team.

The layout of the CIC Consultants' Contract is not dissimilar to that of the ACE Agreements, in that the first part of the contract (the Form of Agreement and Schedule) identifies the parties, and sets out what is intended to be achieved and the amount to be paid. One difference in the layout is that the definitions of the various terms used is included at the end of the document rather than towards the front.

The CIC Consultants' Contract imposes a higher duty of care on the Consultant than does an ACE Agreement. Such duty of care is one of 'reasonable skill, care and diligence to be expected of a competent consultant of the relevant discipline undertaking the relevant role who is experienced in providing similar services in connection with projects of similar size, scope and complexity to the Project'. As stated earlier in this section, a consulting engineer entering into an ACE Agreement is simply committing itself to acting with 'reasonable skill care and diligence in the performance of the Services'. However, in order to sweeten the pill, the Consultant's limit of liability under the CIC form of contract is one of total liability, as opposed to 'each and every' liability as currently used in the ACE Agreements.

Attempts to settle disputes are via a mediation and adjudication route, with a final decision resting on legal proceedings through the courts.

CHAPTER 2.5

Collateral Warranties

Hamish Lal
Dundas & Wilson LLP

1 WHAT IS A COLLATERAL WARRANTY?

A Collateral Warranty is entered into between two parties that would not normally have a direct primary contractual relationship. Before, during and after the completion of the project there will be many parties who are interested in a successful project outcome: essentially there are many stakeholders in the project – stakeholders who do not all have direct contractual relationships. The so-called '*privity of contract*' doctrine holds that, generally, a contract cannot confer rights or impose obligations on any person save those who are party to the contract. The point was established in 1861 in *Tweddle* v. *Atkinson* and in 1915 the then Lord Chancellor, Viscount Haldane, delivering his judgement in *Dunlop Pneumatic Tyre Company Limited* v. *Selfridge & Co. Limited* said:

> '. . . in the law of England certain principles are fundamental. One is that only a person who is a party to a contract can sue on it.'

In practical terms this means that although a Funder will have issued funds its involvement will not stop there because it will want safeguards to ensure that its investment is suitably protected. Another example would be a purchaser/tenant of a new property – as the property has not stood for very long it is not tried and tested (there may be snagging problems) and they will want assurances that the building will not collapse! More realistically they will want assurances that if a roof is leaking or a window is not closing properly then it will be fixed. Indeed, it is often the case that developers are making use of contaminated land. Before this can be sold the developer will want it cleaned up and will also want assurances that this has been done properly and to the appropriate environmental standards.

In all these examples the Funder and the purchaser/tenant could try to rely on the tort of negligence but establishing the duty of care is both time consuming, costly and not guaranteed. Indeed in recent years the courts have condensed the use of negligence. Therefore a direct agreement, the collateral warranty is a tangible way of formalising this duty of care in a binding contractual document and avoids the time and costs in establishing a duty of care under negligence. With a collateral warranty in place if a problem arises (for example after the sale, the land is discovered to still be contaminated) then the purchaser has a range of options. It may still choose to take action against the seller – however if that seller is fiscally weak then there will be little point in taking action against them. This is where the collateral warranty becomes vital because the purchaser can instead choose to take action against one or all of those who actually carried out the work and/or professional services.

Collateral warranties usually run for a period of twelve years from the date of practical completion of the works or the completion of services. Collateral warranties issued under English Law are normally given by way of a deed and therefore have a limitation period of twelve years.

There are many parties involved in giving and receiving collateral warranties. As shown in Figure 1, below these include:

- between Building Contractor and Funder;
- between Building Contractor and Authority (especially in PFI arrangements);
- between Design Consultant and Funder;
- between Sub Contractor and Funder; and
- between Sub Contractor and Project Co

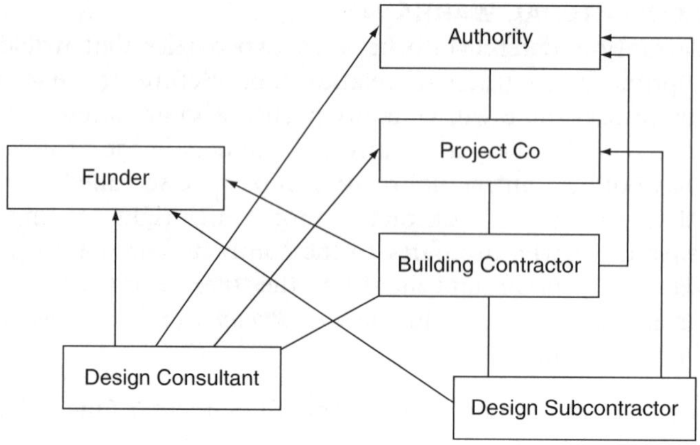

Figure 1. Collateral Warranties in a PFI Structure

2 COMMONLY USED WARRANTIES

There are two main types of building agreement, the JCT Building Contract (Private with Quantities) and the JCT Building Contract (with Contractor's Design).

In the first the Contractor agrees to follow the design, drawings and plans prepared by the Developer's architect, mechanical and electrical engineers, structural engineer and other consultants. The Contractor will enter into the JCT Building Contract directly with the Developer who will appoint the architect, mechanical and electrical engineers, structural engineer and other consultants. The Developer will, therefore, be able to raise an action against any or all of these people for breach of contract(s) on the basis that there is a direct contract relationship. As discussed above, the problems occur for Tenants and Funders and indeed any one who has interest in the end-product but who does not have a direct contractual with the Contractor, the architect, mechanical and electrical engineers, structural engineer and other consultants. The problem can be remedied by collateral warranties.

In the JCT Building Contract (with Contractor's Design), the Contractor is effectively given an outline or employer's requirement and agrees to undertake the design using his own professional team or by appointing external architect, mechanical and electrical engineers, structural engineer and other consultants. It is important to understand that the only direct agreement in respect of the development is between the Contractor and the Developer. Neither the Developer, the Tenants and Funder have any form of contract with any member of the professional team. The Tenants and Funder will have direct form of contract with the Contractor. Again, collateral warranties, therefore, provide for the Tenant and/or Funder to be able to claim against either the Contractor and/or any of the professional team or, in the case of the JCT with contractor's design, for the Developer to have a claim against the professional team used by the Contractor.

It is commonly a requirement of the JCT contracts that the professional consultants agree to enter into collateral warranties with the Developer and Tenants and Funder of the new building. Clearly, this then allows the Developer, Tenants and Funder to bring an action against the Contractor and any member of the professional team for any breaches and defects that may occur in the property caused through the fault or negligence of that particular person. Collateral warranties are in addition to the defects liability period set out in the JCT Contracts. As discussed elsewhere in the

Construction Law Handbook it is now common practice for Contractors to provide a twelve-month defects liability period from the date of issue of the certificate of practical completion.

Members of the professional team will often seek to restrict their liability under a collateral warranty. It is common for members of the professional team to try to limit any liability for consequential and economic loss and, preferably, to exclude it from the warranty. A Tenant may not be able to use premises because of defects arising through the negligence or breach of contract of one of the professional team. If the Tenant has agreed to limit liability for consequential and economic loss then that professional is only liable for the costs involved in remedying the physical defect. Loss of income of the Tenant is usually excluded under this type of collateral warranty. Naturally, there will be a requirement in the collateral warranty that the professional maintain indemnity insurance.

The collateral warranty will usually specify that there can only be a specified number of assignments of the warranty to another third party. It is important that the Developer and Tenant and Funder be able to assign the benefit of the warranty to any purchaser of the property. An assignee of the lease in that period would be advised to have the benefit of the warranty legally assigned to him so that he in turn could have recourse against the original Contractor and professional team.

The Construction Industry Council published (in August 2007) a liability briefing for use in the Industry. It compares the following collateral warranties:

(i) CIC/ConsWa/F for use where a warranty is to be given by a consultant to a funder (first edition 2003); and
(ii) CIC/ConsWa/P&T to be given to a purchaser/tenant of the whole or part of a commercial or industrial development (first edition 2003);

and the equivalent BPF forms are:

(i) CoWa/F for use where a warranty is to be given to a company providing finance for a proposed development (4th edition 2005) and
(ii) CoWa/P&T for use where a warranty is to be given to a purchaser or tenant of a proposed development (3rd edition 2005).

And makes the following recommendations:

The CIC warranties

The balance of risk between consultants and funders or purchasers/tenants is, in general terms, the same as under the old BPF forms. Points to note are:

Cost of repairs – The damages recoverable by a purchaser/tenant are limited to the reasonable cost of repairs.

Net contribution – The others whom it is assumed have also provided contractual undertakings (warranties) are described generically and the list is very wide, being 'all other consultants and advisers, contractors and subcontractors involved in the [project]'. The wording of the clause has also been amended to take into account the decision in the *Co-operative Retail Services* case.

No greater liability – The consultant is entitled to rely on any exclusion of liability in the appointment, in addition to any limitation of liability. This takes account of the fact that, for example, the consultant's appointment may exclude liability for claims arising out of terrorism or asbestos, due to limitations on insurance cover available.

The consultant is also expressly entitled to raise the equivalent rights in defence of liability as it would have against the client under the appointment.

Deleterious materials – The clause refers to the publication *Good Practice in Selection of Construction Materials* (Ove Arup & Partners). The obligation is confined to the specification of materials and is subject to other instructions that may have been received from the client under the appointment.

Licence – The licence is subject to the fees being paid (or tendered), save that the licence in respect of the documents needed for the health and safety file is not subject to the payment of fees.

Insurance – The obligation to maintain professional indemnity insurance refers to aggregate cover available for pollution and contamination, asbestos and date recognition.

Assignment – Assignment of the purchaser/tenant warranty is limited to twice only and the funder's warranty to one other funder only.

Limitation – The time for bringing claims is not to be greater than a specific number of years (which is to be inserted) from practical completion or, if that is not achieved, from the date the consultant finishes its services. The warranties can be signed under hand as well as executed as a deed.

Third party rights – The rights given to third parties by the Contracts (Rights of Third Parties) Act are excluded, as is usual in collateral warranties.

The BPF warranties

These are similar in many ways, but differ in a number of important respects:

Cost of repairs – The purchaser/tenant warranty provides that the damages recoverable are limited to the cost of repairs, as did the old BPF warranties, but also provides for an additional sum to be stipulated for other losses. Liability for such further losses is not made expressly subject to the net contribution and equivalent 3 rights clauses; it could therefore be argued that it is not intended to be, resulting in a serious qualification to those clauses.

Net contribution – The net contribution clause has been revised from that in the old BPF warranties. Those whom it is assumed have provided warranties are described as the *Project Team*. What this term means will depend upon the definition (if any) in the underlying appointment (Clause 1). It is used in the BPF Consultants' Appointment, but the definition covers consultants only (in contrast with that in the CIC warranties). It may not therefore be wide enough to cover all those who are liable with the consultant. Moreover, if any other form of appointment is used, there is a danger that the term will not be used at all. The net contribution clause is not stated to be without prejudice to other limitations (e.g. limitations in the appointment incorporated into the warranty by clause 2(c)).

No greater liability – The equivalent rights clause is very similar to that in the CIC warranty, save that it refers to limitation only, which might not include outright exclusion.

Deleterious materials – The clause also refers to the Ove Arup publication in the context of specification. There is a further provision which requires the consultant to use skill and care to see that materials as used in the construction are in accordance with the Ove Arup guidelines.

Licence – The licence is also subject to the fees being paid (or tendered), though there is no exception for documents for the health and safety file. There are references to *Intellectual Property* and *Design Documents,* terms which are used in the BPF Consultancy Appointment, but might not be used in any other form of underlying appointment.

Insurance – The consultant is not free to agree in relation to each warranty the amount of insurance and the length of time he maintains it, but is bound to the funder or purchaser/tenant in the same terms as in the appointment. There is a reference to clause 8 of the appointment, which will only apply if the BPF Consultancy Agreement is used. The test is *reasonable premium rates* rather than the more usual *commercially reasonable rates.*

Assignment – Assignment is limited (as in the CIC warranties) to twice only without consent (in earlier editions the parties could agree the number of assignments).

Limitation – The time for bringing claims is a fixed 12 years from practical completion or completion, or abandonment of the services if earlier.

Third party rights – The Contracts (Rights of Third Parties) Act is excluded.

3 COLLATERAL AGREEMENTS/CONTRACTS?

The Courts may find a collateral contract or agreement where they seek to construe the parties' relationship. An example of a collateral contract is found in *Shanklin Pier Ltd* v. *Detel Products Ltd* 1 [1951] 2 KB 854.

In *Shankljn Pier Ltd,* Shanklin who were owners of a pier entered into a contract with C.M. Carter (Erectors) Ltd for the repair and repainting of the pier, the repainting to be carried out with two coats of bitumastic or bituminous paint. Under the terms of their contract with Carter, S reserved the right to vary the specification, Detel were paint manufacturers who produced a product known as DMU which they represented to Shanklin as being suitable for the repainting of the pier in that its surface was impervious to dampness and could prevent corrosion and creeping of rust with a life of 7–10 years. In consideration of this representation Shanklin specified to Carter that Carter should only use Detel's paint. The paint failed and Shanklin sought to recover its loss. Shanklin claimed against (not Carter as main contractor), but against Detel as supplier of the paint.

Detel sought to argue that they had not given any warranty to Shanklin and even if they had it did not give rise to a cause of action because they were not parties to the contract for repainting the pier. The Court rejected Detel's argument and held that on the facts there was a warranty and that the consideration for the collateral warranty was that Shanklin required C.M. Carter (Erectors) Ltd to enter into a contract with Detel for the supply of their paint for repainting the pier. Further that the representations given by Detel to Shanklin were contractually binding in the form of a collateral contract. In *Greater London Council* v. *Ryarsh Brick Co Ltd* 1 [1985] 4 Con LR 85, in similar circumstances to *Shanklin,* Judge Newey QC accepted that even without express representations there may be a collateral contract containing implied terms as to fitness or suitability of the goods.

In *Shanklin*, Detel was aware that their product was to have a specific use by a third party. This was not the situation in *Wells (Merstham) Ltd* v. *Buckland Sand and Silica Co Ltd* [1965] 2 QB 170. Buckland Sand were sand merchants who warranted to Wells (who were chrysanthemum growers) that their sand conformed to a certain analysis that would be suitable for the propagation of chrysanthemum cuttings. Wells ordered sand direct from Buckland and a further two loads via a third party who were builders merchants and not horticultural suppliers. The third party purchased two loads of sand from Buckland for onward sale and delivery to Wells and gave no indication to Buckland that the sand was required for Wells or for horticultural purposes. The sand did not conform with the analysis and as a result Wells suffered a loss in the propagation of chrysanthemums. The court held that Buckland was liable on the basis of a collateral contract and that it was irrelevant that the purchase of the sand had been made through a third party; as between a potential seller and a potential buyer only two ingredients were required to bring about a collateral contract:

(1) a promise or assertion by the seller as to the nature, quality or quantity of the goods which the buyer might regard as being made with a contractual intention; and
(2) the acquisition by the buyer of the goods in reliance on that promise or assertion.

More recently in *Ing Lease (UK) Ltd* v. *Harwood* [2007] ALL ER (0) 131 the Court considered the scope of statements alleged to constitute collateral agreements. It concluded that the relevant principles regarding pre-contract promises or assurances as collateral warranties may be stated as follows:

(1) a pre-contractual statement will only be treated as having contractual effect if the evidence shows that parties intended this to be the case. Intention is a question of fact to be decided by looking at the totality of the evidence;
(2) the test is the ordinary objective test for the formation of a contract; what is relevant is not the subjective thought of one party but what a reasonable outside observer would infer from all the circumstances;
(3) in deciding the question of intention, one important consideration will be whether the statement is followed by further negotiations and a written contract not containing any term corresponding to the statement. In such a case it will be harder to infer that the statement was intended to have contractual effect because the prima facie assumption will be that the written contract includes all the terms the parties wanted to be binding between them;
(4) a further important factor will be the lapse of time between the statement and the making of the formal contract. The longer the interval, the greater the presumption must be that the parties did not intend the statement to have contractual effect in relation to a subsequent deal;
(5) a representation of fact is much more likely intended to have contractual effect than a statement of future fact or a future forecast.

4 THE CONTRACTS (RIGHTS OF THIRD PARTIES) ACT 1999

The Contracts (Rights of Third Parties) Act came into force on 11 November 1999 and applies to contracts entered into on or after 11 May 2000, unless the contract excludes the operation of the Act. The Act gives a person who is not a party to a contract (a third party) a right to enforce a term of the contract if the contract

2.1 Ways of operating
2.2 Working with others
2.3 Working internationally
2.4 The engineer's appointment
2.5 Collateral warranties
2.6 Indemnity insurance
2.7 Employment law
2.8 Information technology

expressly provides that he may, or the term purports to confer a benefit on him. Section 1(1) of the Act provides:

> 'Subject to the provisions of this Act, a person who is not a party to a contract (a "third party") may in his own right enforce a term of the contract if –
> (a) the contract expressly provides that he may, or
> (b) subject to subsection (2), the term purports to confer a benefit on him.'

The first point to note is that the right created is to enforce a *term* of a contract, not the *whole contract* itself. For example, if a building contract contains a term that the contractor is required to use materials of good quality, then that term might be the subject of a third party enforcement right. For example, the Contract Data section of the NEC3 standard form of contract requires the Parties to expressly state which terms are to be the subject the Act. Option Y(UK)3 is the option dealing with the Act.

The Act does not apply if on proper construction of the contract it appears that the parties did not intend the term to be enforceable by the third party. The Act therefore facilitates third party rights, but these rights may be specifically excluded or excluded by implication on construction of the contract. Section 1(2) of the Act provides:

> 'Subsection 1(b) does not apply if on a proper construction of the contract it appears that the parties did not intend the term to be enforceable by the third party.'

The statute does not confer any right on a party to the contract to recover loss suffered by a non-party, an issue which remains a matter for the common law. For example, the beneficiary of a warranty cannot enforce a term of the Building Contract as he has his own warranty to rely on. The Act removed the need for warranties although the construction industry has been slow to embrace the idea. The industry's immediate reaction was to maintain the status quo and the effect of the Act was expressly excluded in all standard forms. The JCT 2005 and NEC3 standard forms are two notable exceptions.

A third party will only be able to enforce a contractual term if: the contract expressly provides for this to happen; or the term confers a benefit on the third party, unless it is clear that this was not intended. The provisions of the Act can be used to give rights to third parties without having to procure the execution of individual collateral warranties.

In practical terms, Sections 1 and 2 of the Act provide that:

- A person who is not a party to a contract (i.e. a 'third party') may, in his own right, enforce a term of that contract if either the contract expressly provides that he may do so or the relevant term purports to confer a benefit on that party.
- The third party must be expressly identified either by name, as a member of a class or by a particular description.
- The party need not be in existence when the contract is entered into.
- The Act only confers a right to enforce contractual terms in accordance with the other relevant terms of contract.
- The third party has available to it any remedies that would have been available to it in an action for breach of contract as if it had been party to the contract (including all equitable remedies such as injunctions for specific performance).
- Finally, the parties to the contract cannot vary the contract or alter the rights of third party once a third party has communicated acceptance of rights or the

party offering the rights is aware that the third party has not relied on them or it could have been foreseen that the third party would rely and had relied on such rights.

In order to give effect to this arrangement and remove the need for time-consuming and costly individual collateral warranties in favour of third parties, some small amendments are required to be made to a building contract and the consultants' appointments and there needs to be a memorandum or schedule setting out the rights enforceable by each third party. It should be noted that different third parties will require different terms of the underlying contract to enforceable.

Advantages to Consultants & Contractors of the Act

Clearly drafted enforceable third party rights have the same effect and application as the rights contained in a collateral warranty. The advantage to the contractor/consultant of using the Act is that it reduces the administrative burden and the commercial tension that can arise when obtaining collateral warranties. In addition, the fact that these rights are crystallised once the Appointment/Building Contract is entered into protects the consultant/contractor from further amendments that can arise during the Developer's negotiations with beneficiaries.

Although the clause and the rights to be given to third parties would still require negotiation, there would be a cost and time saving in the avoidance of needing separate documents executed in favour of future tenants, purchasers, funders and other third parties when identified.

The third parties gaining rights need to be clearly identifiable in the same way that beneficiaries under collateral warranties are. For example, if the third party was identifiable at the outset then the identity of that third party would be set out in the clause bestowing the third party rights in the appointment/building contract. If the identity of the third party was not yet identified, such as a first tenant that had yet to sign up to its agreement for lease, then the clause would, for example, describe this interest 'a first tenant of the development'.

In practical terms the clearest and safest means of drafting third party rights is to create a schedule in the appointment/building contract which sets out the full extent of third party rights granted. This schedule would look almost exactly like a collateral warranty but without the parties and the recitals provisions at the beginning and without the formal execution provisions at the end.

The application of the Act would be restricted to the provisions contained within this schedule. The application of the Act would then be excluded throughout the rest of the appointment/building contract. This protects the consultant/contractor from entering into any obligations that are greater than they would have entered had they been obliged to provide collateral warranties.

Advantages to Funder/Purchaser/Tenant of the Act

The rights granted in favour of these beneficiaries are the same whether granted by express collateral warranties or by a declaration that they are enforceable third party rights pursuant to the Act.

By setting out the full extent of the third party rights in a separate schedule, in a format similar to a collateral warranty, the relevant party is to have a clearly identifiable set of rights which are easily accessed in a separate section. A further benefit is that collateral warranties are often required after practical completion, when

2.1 Ways of operating
2.2 Working with others
2.3 Working internationally
2.4 The engineer's appointment
2.5 Collateral warranties
2.6 Indemnity insurance
2.7 Employment law
2.8 Information technology

the parties providing them might either no longer be in existence or are may be, in practical terms, reluctant to execute the documents. Reliance on the Act removes such problems.

Furthermore, rights contained in a collateral warranty are generally stated to be subject to the terms of the appointment/building contract. In practical terms, attempting to enforce the terms of a collateral warranty without reference to the express terms of an appointment or building contract is difficult. Therefore, with each beneficiary having a copy of the appointment/building contract containing their respective rights, enforcement would, in theory, be a relatively straightforward process.

By using the Act, the need for a power of attorney in the appointment or building contract, allowing the employer to grant a warranty in the name of the consultant or contractor (where they have failed to do so of their own accord), is also removed. Ultimately, the process of 'chasing' consultants and contractors for collateral warranties long after the underlying agreements have been concluded (both a costly and time consuming exercise) is thereby avoided.

Disadvantages of The Act to be considered by all parties

- Limitations of Loss and Net Contribution Clauses
  Arguments over limitations are commonplace when collateral warranties are negotiated. The removal of collateral warranties (and use of the Act) will not make these issues go away. They will remain as important to the parties and therefore as contentious as they are now.
- Step-in Rights
  It is very important to realise that the provisions of the Act can only provide the beneficiary with rights and not obligations. One of the provisions required to exercise in a right of step-in is an obligation upon the party seeking to exercise the right to commit to pay all sums due under the building contract and/or appointment as a condition of stepping into it.

  This is commonly seen as a disadvantage but it can be dealt with by the Act. For example, the schedule containing third party rights would confer the right of step-in. Then, in common with all the step-in provisions, the exercise of the right to step-in requires the beneficiary to issue a notice to the contractor/consultant stating that it is stepping in. The third party rights schedule would therefore state if, and only if, the third party beneficiary exercised its rights to step-in, then it would be a requirement upon stepping-in that the notice it served contain a commitment to pay the sums due. This is not inconsistent with the Act as the schedule grants the rights and then it is the exercise of the right and the serving of the notice that establishes the obligation on the beneficiary.
- Assignment
  The Act does not specifically cover the issue of whether a third party is able to assign its rights under the Act to another third party. The law Commission has said that this was because the ordinary contractual rules of assignment would apply, but the issue has not yet been resolved by the courts. In practical terms, rights given under the Act can be assigned in the same way as any other right under an appointment/contract and it is therefore up to the parties to place any commercial limitation on assignment.
- Variation to Contracts
  Another argument sometimes used against the use of third party rights is that any variation to a contract can only be made with the consent of all of the recipients of

the third party rights. It has been suggested that this would apply to a variation under the building contract.

Although this is seen as a disadvantage it can easily be overcome. When conferring third party rights, the extent to which the parties to the contract (the employer and the consultant/contractor), can amend or vary the contract needs to be expressly set out. The legitimate interest to protect is that the contract parties cannot vary a third party right once vested, without the consent of the third party. Otherwise agreed third party rights could be eroded. The drafting would also make it clear that the contract parties were able to vary the remaining contract terms. This puts the parties and third party beneficiaries in the same position that they would have been in if a collateral warranty had been in place.

The Growing Acceptance of the Act

Given the points outlined above, there is no reason why a well-drafted third party rights schedule cannot replace the need for collateral warranties. The disadvantages simply place the parties in a similar position to that which would be experienced when using collateral warranties. Given this, a beneficiary seeking to rely upon the Act for its rights against the contractor and professional team should experience no difference in enforcing those rights than it would have done relying upon a collateral warranty, provided the memorandum and appointment/contract are properly drafted.

The new JCT Major Projects Form of Contract relies exclusively on third party rights as opposed to collateral warranties, and this should give all parties comfort that third party rights are a safe and sensible method of protecting the rights of groups that have to date relied upon collateral warranties.

5 STANDARD TERMS OF COLLATERAL WARRANTIES

The main provisions one would expect to see in a collateral warranty are:

- A clause confirming that the contractor or consultant (the warrantor) owes a duty of care to the beneficiary in carrying out the works or performing design services. The standard of care will usually be 'bench-marked' with reference to the standards expected of a competent and experienced professional person of the relevant discipline to carry out and complete the works using all reasonable skill and care or to ensure that the works will be fit for their intended purpose.
- The warrantor confirming that he has not used, specified nor permitted the use of materials that are known in the industry to be harmful or 'deleterious'. This provision normally only applies to building projects.
- A clause granting the beneficiary an irrevocable, royalty-free licence to use drawings and other documents prepared in connection with the contract, copyright in which is owned by the warrantor.
- The warrantor confirming that he will hold professional indemnity insurance covering risks arising from their work. Given that a warrantor's potential liability may far exceed the level of his assets, it is important that warrantors are required to hold and maintain such sufficient insurance cover or the warranty may be of little practical value.
- A clause allowing the beneficiary to assign the benefit of the warranty to a person taking an interest in the development. Any assignment by the warrantor of the warranty is usually prohibited. Assignment by the beneficiary of the rights and obligations under the warranty is usually permitted, without the warrantor's

consent, to any person taking an assignment of the beneficiary's interest (subject to a maximum number of assignments).

- The warranty should be executed as a deed because this means that the warrantor remains liable for a longer period than if it is executed underhand (12 years rather than 6 years).
- In funder warranties, the warrantor should undertake that before exercising any right to terminate its employment or suspend its performance, it will give the funder notice of its intention to do so.
- Again, a funder specific provision is that the warrantor undertakes, on the insolvency of the employer, to novate the contract to the funder on request or allow the funder to 'step in' and assume the employer's rights for a certain period.

Limitations

There are 3 main limitations which may have a significant impact on the enforceability of the warranty and/or recovery of loss under the warranty:

- The net contribution clause under which if there is more than one party at fault the warrantor will only be liable for any damage that he has caused and therefore a percentage of the total damage. In practical terms, therefore, it is necessary to consider carefully who else is providing warranties.
- The original contract limitation clause under which the original contract limitation clause, the warrantor owes the same liability to the beneficiary as he does to the party instructing him (making it important for the beneficiary to check the terms of the original appointment or contract to find out how the warrantor's liability is limited).
- The direct loss limitation clause the warrantor will only be liable for the costs of repair, renewal and/or reinstatement of the building, especially excluding consequential losses such as the loss of trading profits. Beneficiaries do not always agree to these limitations.

6 FITNESS FOR PURPOSE

A fundamental issue is the duty of care imposed on contractors that carry out design. Is it the same as the professional man, that is to say reasonable skill and care? Should their work be fit for purpose? A useful starting point is *Greaves & Co (Contractors) Limited* v. *Baynham Meikle & Partners* [1974] 1 WLR 1261 where Lord Denning stated:

> '... now, as between the building owners and the contractors, it is plain that the owners made known to the contractors the purpose for which the building was required, so as to show that they relied on the contractors' skill and judgment. It was, therefore, the duty of the contractors to see that the finished work was reasonably fit for the purpose for which they knew it was required. It was not merely an obligation to use reasonable care. The contractors were obliged to ensure that the finished work was reasonably fit for the purpose.'

In *Viking Grain Storage Limited* v. *T. H. White Installations Limited* (1985) 33 BLR 103 White Installations were contractors for the design and construction of a grain drying and storage installation. The installation was not fit for its purpose and the employer argued that there were implied terms of the contract that White Installations would use materials of good quality and reasonably fit for their purpose and that the completed works would be reasonably fit for their purpose, namely that of a grain drying and storage installation. The court held that there were no terms of the contract or any other relevant circumstances which were inconsistent with the implied terms of quality and fitness for purpose and further that there was no reason to differentiate between White's obligation in relation to the quality of materials and their obligation as to design. The Employer had relied upon White in all aspects, including design, and on the skill and judgment of White, and in the circumstances, the terms contended for should be implied.

The position is not so clear cut for Employers if an Employer is deemed not to have relied on the Contractor. For example, in *Norta Wallpapers (Ireland)* v. *Sisk & Sons (Dublin)* (1978) IR 114 where a roof structure, which had been supplied and erected by a specialist sub contractor, subsequently leaked and was unsuitable for its purpose, the fact that the main contractor was given no choice but to use the specialist sub-contractor, his design and price constituted circumstances which meant that there was no reliance by the employer on the main contractor and, accordingly, there was no fitness for purpose obligation on the main contractor in respect of the specialist sub-contractor's failure.

In the (unreported) case of *Trolex Products Limited* v. *Merrol Fire Protection Engineers Limited* there was a question as to whether a design obligation was created by the bringing together of what otherwise would have been standard components. Trolex were the sub-contractors for the supply of an electronic control system which was incorporated into Merrol's own works comprising the installation of a fire protection system. In response to the submission by Trolex that there was minimal design obligation in the sub-contract, Potter J stated:

> 'I should perhaps add that at one stage I had evidence from Trolex which minimised the work of design carried out, suggesting that it was no more than, in effect, a matching of pieces of standard equipment to make up a package to do the job; or as Mr B put it 'logic design work created from standard equipment'. Even if that was so in fact, I am satisfied from the answers of Mr B that there was a conscious realisation that design work was involved and that Trolex were consulted as experts in their field. Further, it is clear that substantial time was spent on this work. Again, whether or not that was so, it is not suggested that anything was said by Trolex to delimit or belittle the design work involved and the construction of the written contract is clear in my view, namely as one for work of design as well as the supply of goods.'

Similarly, in *Gloucestershire County Council* v. *Richardson* [1969] 1 AC 480 the House of Lords found that the particular circumstances of the case excluded both the implied warranty of suitability and the implied warranty of merchantable quality. In that case Richardson entered into a contract with the employer for the construction of an extension to a technical college. The contract included bills of quantities provided for a PC sum for concrete columns to be supplied by a nominated supplier. Richardson contracted to erect the columns. Clause 22 of the conditions of contract dealing with nominated suppliers did not entitle Richardson to make reasonable objection to a proposed supplier, nor to object on the ground that the supplier would not indemnify him in respect of his main contractor's obligation. The Employer's architect instructed Richardson to accept a quotation given by the third party supplier for the supply of the concrete columns. The supplier's standard conditions of trade restricted their liability in respect of good supply by them. The columns supplied had latent defects because of faulty manufacture and after erection cracks appeared in them; the columns were unsuitable for use as structural members of the extension.

The House of Lords considered that the facts set out above indicated an intention on the part of the Employer and Richardson to exclude from the main contract any implied terms that the concrete columns should be of good quality and fit for their required purpose.

7 ASSIGNMENT

The first point to note is that if there is no provision for assignment, then the benefit of a warranty is freely assignable without the consent of the other party. Such an assignment can be legal or equitable. Where there is in a contract an express prohibition on assignment, then such prohibition is likely to be effective in law.

In practice problems arise where a contractual provision seeks to impose a limit on the number of assignments that can be made. If that provision is simply incorporated into the warranty, then every time there is an assignment the assignee steps into the shoes of the assignor and he has the right to make two assignments – in simple terms the counting may never start. A practical legal solution to this difficulty is to include an express provision in the warranty that assignment is prohibited save where the express consent in writing of the original giver of the warranty has been obtained – the provision could continue to recite that the giver of the warranty shall not withhold his consent where the assignment is a first or second assignment. The approach used in the JCT warranty, MCWa/F, is that there can be two assignments by way of a legal assignment, provided written notice is given to the contractor.

If a contract is a personal contract then the benefits of that contract cannot be assigned either by a legal assignment or by an equitable assignment. In any event it may be preferable, therefore, to prohibit assignment by an express term rather than seeking to do it by this indirect method.

8 NET CONTRIBUTION CLAUSES

Contractors and Consultants of all tiers and specialists and perhaps more importantly their insurers are concerned that if they provide collateral warranties and the other members of the professional teams do not, then they will be (solely) liable to the third party for the full amount of the loss. The problem for the sole provider is exasperated because he would be unable to claim contribution from those other parties who did not give collateral warranties and since those other parties cannot be liable in respect of the same damage, there will be no relevant remedy available under the Civil Liability (Contribution) Act 1978. The sole-provider therefore seeks to ensure that they are not liable for the full amount of the loss in circumstances where other parties ought properly to be liable at the same time – this is the so-called 'net contribution' clause.

This provides that the liability under the collateral warranty be limited to such losses as is just and equitable having regard to the extent of the warrantor's responsibility and on the further basis that certain named parties (other contractors and consultants) are deemed to have given a warranty in similar form. This is the approach in the BPF warranties (CoWa/F and CoWa/P&T). A similar approach is adopted in the 2001 Editions of the JCT Collateral Warranties (MCWa/F, MCWa/P&T, SCWa/F and SCWa/P&T).

The Institution of Civil Engineers (ICE) has produced guidance to its Members on how best to resist giving of collateral warranties:

'• Everyone else is signing them: This may be true, but should not override the engineers' judgment as to whether in the particular circumstances the risk of providing a warranty outweighs the benefit of the fee being offered by the client. The client may pursue alternative solutions, such as commissioning a review of the design or a survey of the building, or by procuring latent defects insurance cover.
• If you are confident in your work, you should not hesitate to provide such a warranty: The loss which may be claimed by a third party may be far greater than loss which could be suffered by the original client. This constitutes an increase in risk which the warrantor would need to factor into the fee.
• This warranty is in the same terms as the normal obligations: The wording of the warranty can be misinterpreted. Legal opinion should be sought and obtained. However, there is no guarantee that a judge or arbitrator would agree with those opinions.
• This warranty only reflects the current state of the law: The warranty only reflects current market practices. It is, however, fixed in form once signed, so would preclude any possible benefit accruing to the warrantor from favourable changes in the law which may occur in the future.
• You are insured in any case: The insurer must be informed and must give its approval of the warranty. It is to be borne in mind that the insurers may not accept the terms of the warranty and that generally insurers do not cover liability assumed under an agreement which would not have existed in the absence of that agreement. In any case, the availability and the cost of insurance may change and may be totally different in the future.'

Glasgow Airport Ltd v. *Kirkman and Bradford* [2007] CSIH 47 provides excellent warning on how net contribution clauses needed to be drafted more restrictively if they are to exclude certain types of damage.

In this case the Airport engaged a building contractor, Kensteel Structures Limited, to build a cargo handling building. The contractor appointed the Defendant to design the works. The Airport argued that the floor slab was defective and sought to recover damages in the sum of £2 million directly from the Defendant designer by using the collateral warranty. The contractor had entered insolvency and therefore was not a viable Defendant. The Defendant's liability was limited to £2 million under the Appointment. The Defendant also sought to rely on the wording of the net contribution to exclude liability for costs claimed by the Airport in respect of losses sustained by Tenants of the Cargo Handling Building caused by the remedial works. In fact the Tenants had sought to recover £2.15 million from the Airport – this was expenses in relation to the replacement of the floor slab (£775 000) and losses in respect of disruption to their business and loss of profits.

The net contribution clause stated:

'(a) the Sub-Consultant's liability for costs under this Agreement shall be limited to that proportion of such costs which it would be just and equitable to require the Sub-Consultant to pay having regard to the extent of the Sub-Consultant's responsibility for the same and on the basis that the Contractor and its sub-consultants and sub-contractors shall be deemed to have provided contractual undertakings on terms no less onerous than this Clause 1 to the Employer in respect of the performance of their obligations in connection with the Works (other than those obligations which relate to the Services) and shall be deemed to have paid to the Employer such proportion which it would be just and equitable for them to pay having regard to the extent of their responsibility.'

The Defendant argued that 'costs' were limited to the costs of repair, renewal and/or reinstatement of any part of the Works. The Court ruled that the Defendant, by giving a collateral warranty, undertook liability only for losses which would comply with the first rule of *Hadley* v. *Baxendale* [1854] (such as may fairly and reasonably be considered . . . arising naturally) but not for losses which could only, in ordinary course, be claimed if they complied with the second rule ('such as may reasonably be supported to have been in the contemplation of both parties, at the time they made the contract, as the probable result of the breach of it'). The Court held that the reference to 'costs' was not restricted to the cost of reinstating the defective work but allowed recovery of all losses directly caused by the breach.

It is very clear that warrantors seeking to limit liability in respect of certain costs/losses/damages should do so very clearly in the body of the collateral warranty. The net contrbution clause in this case was a common version and re-drafting/negotiation is contemplated.

9 NO GREATER LIABILITY

Safeway Stores Ltd v. *Interserve Project Services Ltd* [2005] EWHC 3085 (TCC) (01 December 2005) provides a fundamental reminder of the problems, for beneficiaries, of so-called 'no greater liability' clauses.

Safeway was the Employer for the construction of a new supermarket and 2-storey car park. Safeway employed Chelverton Properties as the developer who in turn employed a Contractor, Tilbury Douglas, (later known as Interserve) who in turn employed a specialist sub-contractor to install the waterproof surface to the car park. Problems occurred with and between the waterproof membrane and the concrete surface. The facts are further complicated because the Developer was in liquidation.

Safeway raised an action against the Contractor relying on a collateral warranty. Clause 3.3 of the collateral warranty stated:

> 'The Contractor shall owe no duty or have any liability under this deed which are greater or of longer duration than that which it owes to the Developer under the Building Contract.'

Safeway had carried out remedial works in the sum of £413 048.82 and sought to recover this sum from the Contractor. However, the Contractor relied upon Clause 3.3 and argued that it could rely upon the defence of equitable set-off. This was because the Developer owed the Contractor £1 million when it entered liquidation. The Contractor argued that had the Developer raised the claim for £413 048.82 then it could have relied on its larger claim of £1 million by way of set-off. The Court agreed and held that the Contractor had a complete defence to Safeway's claim.

Following this case, Employers have sought to resist the inclusion of such clauses as clause 3.3. Ultimately, the success of such an approach will depend on the commercial framework.

CHAPTER 2.6

Professional indemnity insurance

Stephen Bamforth
Griffiths & Armour

John Moore
Wren Managers Limited

1 INTRODUCTION

Professional indemnity insurance has, in common with other categories of insurance, developed from three main sources: statute, principally the Marine Insurance Act 1906, the common law, and practice in the insurance industry. However, the general principles of contract law apply in respect of the creation of professional indemnity insurance policies as elsewhere. Insurance law is, of course, an additional strand of legal development which is touched upon where relevant. Any such references made are intended to be of general assistance only and are not in any sense a review of the relevant principles.

Frequently, differences arise between the insurer and insured as to the interpretation of certain clauses, terms and conditions of the professional indemnity policy. Where any dispute or ambiguity arises, the court may be asked to interpret the meaning of the policy. In most cases the policy should be read as a whole, the principle being that effect should be given to the intention of the parties where such appears from the words used.

The courts have developed a set of criteria or standards against which the terms in issue are considered. These include: the ordinary meaning of the words used; the business interpretation of them; the commercial objective of the policy; the technical meaning where terms of art are employed; the express definition of any terms used (if such is set out in the policy) and the previous interpretation adopted by the courts where the words or phrases used have been held in earlier cases to have a particular meaning.

This application of precedent may, of course, be displaced if the words used are not precisely similar, or if the context or situation can be distinguished.

The general principles referred to above are of equal application to professional indemnity (PI) insurance. However, this particular form of cover does have its own individual character.

PI is a third party cover. Its intention is to protect the professional against liabilities owed to third parties, *including his client*. The policy will only respond to the extent that a liability attaches to the insured consultant.

There is a common misconception within the construction industry that PI policies are in force primarily to protect the client. This simply is not true. In order to access the policy proceeds, the client will need to establish liability against the consultant. Recourse to legal action is lengthy, uncertain and costly. Clients would be better advised to retain, manage and insure more risk rather than to seek to pass that risk out to others by way of contract. It is difficult to see what constructive part liability-based contracts play in the post-Egan environment.

2 PROFESSIONAL INDEMNITY INSURANCE

The prime intention and purpose of professional indemnity insurance is to provide protection to the insured against liability to pay damages for breach of professional duty. However, it is now common for these policies to extend into other areas, as referred to below.

2.1 The policy form

Professional indemnity insurance policy wordings vary according to the nature of the work or profession to whom cover is being provided and the identity of the insurers underwriting the policy. Certain professional bodies, such as The Royal Institution of

Chartered Surveyors and The Royal Institute of British Architects, require members to carry cover in accordance with certain requirements which underwriters have to meet in order to be included within an 'Approved List of Insurers'.

2.2 Requirements of professional bodies

The Architect's Registration Board, set up under the terms of The Housing Grants, Construction and Regeneration Act 1996 has issued a Code of Practice which makes professional indemnity insurance for architects mandatory as from 1 April 1998.

The Architect's Registration Board also issues Guidelines for Professional Indemnity Insurance which contain provisions that the policy should be written on a civil liability wording, and 'any one claim' limit of indemnity; should cover 'standard' collateral warranty documents with extensions for loss of documents and criminal prosecution defence costs.

The minimum limits of indemnity should be £250 000 when the fee income is between less than £100 000 per annum, and £500 000 when the fee income is between £100 000 and £200 000 per annum and £1 000 000 where fees exceed £200 000, all figures excluding legal costs.

The Architect's Registration Board review and amend their Code of Practice and Guidelines, so it is important for all architects to ensure that they are aware of the current requirements of the Board, Code and Guidelines.

Figures produced by other bodies show that the Institution of Structural Engineers have no requirement to insure, but a Council recommendation to consider taking cover has been issued: The Chartered Institution of Building Services Engineers has no specific requirements as to professional indemnity insurance. The Association of Consultancy and Engineering has a Code of Conduct requiring members to maintain appropriate professional indemnity insurance arrangements. The Institution of Civil Engineers has no requirement, but a strong recommendation to insure with a minimum cover of £100 000. The British Institute of Architectural Technologists makes professional indemnity insurance mandatory for its members, but does not recommend a minimum level of indemnity, and the Royal Institution of Chartered Surveyors requires that its private practice members have professional indemnity insurance, the minimum levels being based on fee turnover – practices earning up to £50 000 needing a minimum of £100 000 cover.

Since the insurance market-place and the liabilities of professionals practising in the construction industry are dynamic in nature, each of the representative bodies referred to should be contacted to ensure that the appropriate code or guidelines as to professional indemnity insurance are adhered to.

2.3 Common features

There are a number of features which are common to almost all professional indemnity insurance policies within the construction industry and these are discussed below. Most commonly, the policy can be divided into five principal areas:

- the recital clause
- the operative clause
- exclusions
- exceptions
- conditions.

2.4 The recital clause

The recital clause is usually found in policies issued by Lloyd's Underwriters, and is now always a component of company policies. The recital clause may be used to establish a description of the insured, record the significance of the payment of the premium and it may also expressly incorporate the proposal form as the basis of the contract, thereby making every fact within it material.

If any material fact is later found to be inaccurate, the underwriter may be entitled to avoid the policy for non-disclosure or misrepresentation, without the requirement to prove that such would have been a significant element in a reasonably prudent underwriter forming a judgement as to the risk.

2.5 The operative clause

The operative clause sets out the basic cover that is provided by the policy. It is restricted and further defined by way of policy exclusions and conditions.

Not all operative clauses work in the same way. One common form seeks to limit the scope of the cover to liabilities which arise directly from the negligent performance by the insured of his or her professional services. A variation on this theme is to base cover on liability for breach of professional duty. Examples of policy wording commonly in use for these two variations are quoted below.

(a) 'The Insurers will indemnify the Insured in respect of any claim which may be made upon the Insured and which is notified to the Insurer during the Period of Insurance in respect of liability arising from any neglect, error or omission by the Insured in the provision of Professional Services'.

(b) 'The Insurers will indemnify the Insured in respect of any claim which may be made upon the Insured and which is notified to the Insurer during the Period of Insurance in respect of liability arising from any negligent breach of professional duty by the Insured'.

Policies with operative clauses limited to negligence or breach of professional duty are, in fact, quite restrictive. With the increasing proliferation of non-standard conditions of appointment and collateral warranties within the construction industry, it is not uncommon for consultants to accept contractual liabilities over and above simple negligence.

A wider basis of cover may be necessary in certain circumstances and most professional indemnity insurers are prepared to provide what is known as a 'civil liability' or 'full legal liability' cover. Reference to 'civil liability' is perhaps a misnomer in that the UK is not a civil code country. However, that is a matter of semantics as the 'civil liability' and 'full legal liability' bases of cover are essentially the same.

The operative clause of a full legal liability policy wording might read as follows.

> 'The Insurer will indemnify the Insured in respect of loss arising from any claim which may be made against the Insured and which is notified to the Insurer during the Period of Insurance in respect of any legal liability or alleged legal liability arising in connection with the conduct of the Business carried on by or on behalf of the Insured.'

The distinction between the negligence and liability based covers is an important one. Subject to the policy exclusions, a full legal liability policy will respond to all liabilities that the insured may incur, including extended contractual liabilities. By contrast, the narrower form will only respond to the extent that the insured has been negligent.

More frequently these days, the insured may be a group of architects or engineers practising as a limited liability company or a limited liability partnership. Historically, the insured would be a group of individuals practising as a firm, in either case it is important to ensure that the practice is properly and fully described within the term 'insured'. Changes in the partnership, especially when new partners join the practice, should be immediately and fully disclosed to the underwriter or insurer.

2.6 Legal liability

This expression embraces all forms of legal liability that may result in an award of damages. It may include all potential liabilities for negligence, therefore it is usual for the legal liability to be qualified or restricted by words in the operative clause, exclusions or the recital clause itself.

Certainly, cover will be restricted to liability for breach of professional duty arising out of the work of an architect or engineer, there will be specific exclusions relating to public or general liabilities, e.g. road traffic accidents.

Insurers will almost invariably require to take over and manage the handling and settlement of any claim. Therefore, the original intention of the policy – that the insured must be found 'legally liable' to pay a claim before being entitled to an indemnity by insurers – is in practice rarely followed.

2.7 'Negligence only' wording

These policies do not usually provide protection in relation to claims arising out of additional voluntary liabilities, such as may arise out of collateral warranties.

Architects and engineers should ensure that their professional indemnity insurance policy gives them cover for as wide a class of claims or potential claimants as they require. The 'negligence only' wording may not provide such cover in all circumstances. If the architect or engineer has given, or is likely to be asked to give, collateral warranties, or may take on duties which may be considered to be outside the standard within his or her profession, it is advisable to consider the policy wording carefully, as even the legal liability based policy may exclude the more onerous terms.

2.8 'Claims made' policy

All professional indemnity insurance policies operate on what is known as a 'claims made' basis and the relevant section from a typical operative clause is quoted below:

> '. . . any claim which may be made upon the Insured and which is notified to the Insurer during the Period of Insurance'.

This distinction is important. It is the policy in force when a potential claim is first *notified* that dictates the extent of cover available and not the policy in force when the work in question was carried out or when the alleged act of negligence took place.

If a consultant cancels his or her professional indemnity insurance cover or allows it to lapse, the consultant is effectively uninsured for any work previously undertaken. It is for this reason that almost all professional appointments include requirements for consultants to maintain cover into the future provided, of course, that it continues to be available at reasonably economic rates.

The 'claims made' nature of cover can give rise to difficulties on retirement for sole traders. Most PI policies provide automatic indemnity to former partners, directors and employees. With sole traders, the problem is that there is no ongoing entity to maintain cover and yet the liabilities continue to exist. One potential solution is for sole traders to effect six or twelve year run-off policies, the premium for which can be off-set against tax during the final year of trading.

Although professional indemnity policies are written on a 'claims made' basis, they should more properly be described as 'claims made and circumstances likely to give rise to a claim' basis, or similar wording.

Almost all policies permit, and some even require, the notification of matters, situations or events which are likely to, or potentially may, give rise to a claim. If, subsequently, a claim is made, the effective date of notification is that on which the circumstance or event was reported, not when the claim itself was formulated.

Wordings or terms of professional indemnity policies vary between policies or insurers – some permit the notification of circumstances likely to give rise to a claim, others permit circumstances which may reasonably be expected to give rise to a claim.

Difficulties can arise when the insured changes insurer and the notification requirements of the old policy and proposal form requirements of the new are not compatible. In such a situation the insured can suffer the problem of not being in a position to notify a claim to the outgoing insurer (as none exists before the expiry of the policy) allied to a non-disclosure of a circumstance likely to give rise to a claim as required in the proposal form of the new insurer. If a potential claim or circumstance is identified in the proposal form to the new insurer it may well be specifically excluded. If there is no entitlement to notify a circumstance to the old insurer (before the expiry of the outgoing policy) the two policies create for the insured a potential black hole into which the claim falls without cover.

2.9 Limit of indemnity

The limit of indemnity is the maximum liability of insurers under the policy. It is a monetary amount selected by the insured based on a combination of:

(a) the requirements of its clients; and
(b) an assessment of the maximum liability that might be incurred.

The limit of indemnity can operate on either an 'each and every' or an 'aggregate' basis.

Where cover operates on an 'each and every' basis, the limit of indemnity applies separately to each claim notified during the period of insurance. For example, if a consultant carries £5m of cover on an each and every claim basis, that £5m limit will apply in full to each separate claim that is notified during the policy period.

By contrast, where cover operates on an 'aggregate' basis, the limit of indemnity applies to all claims notified during the period of insurance. While most PI policies operate on an each and every claim basis, it is common practice for certain types of claim to be subject to an aggregate limit, most notably claims which involve pollution/contamination, date recognition issues or which arise out of the activities of design and construct contractors.

Selecting an adequate limit of indemnity is an important consideration for consultants. The limit should be set at a level which reflects the maximum likely damages which could flow as a consequence of any negligent act – both in relation to past and current work. The limit should be set so as to include awards made in relation to the claimant's legal costs in addition to damages.

It is also important to bear in mind that an agreement to maintain PI at a certain level is not a limitation of liability – a common misconception within the construction industry. Any contractual limitation of liability must be expressly stated as such and comply with the requirements of the Unfair Contract Terms Act 1977.

Other costs and expenses

Insurers will usually also pay for other costs and expenses incurred in defending claims. Such defence costs can either form part of the limit of indemnity (a 'cost inclusive' limit) or in addition thereto ('costs in addition').

2.10 Exceptions

A number of exceptions are common to most construction professional indemnity insurance policies, as follows:

(a) claims involving bodily injury to or death of employees (these claims should be covered under an employer's liability policy)
(b) claims for third party property damage or third party personal injury (such claims are covered by a public liability policy)
(c) claims arising from circumstances already notified under previous policies (to avoid duplication of cover) or which were known prior to the inception of the new policy
(d) claims arising from any agreement to pay fines, penalties or liquidated damages
(e) any loss, destruction, damage, etc. caused by ionizing radiations or contamination by radioactivity
(f) supersonic bangs
(g) war, invasion, etc.
(h) most construction PI policies now routinely exclude claims involving asbestos-related liabilities; where cover for such claims is provided it is on an 'aggregate', 'cost inclusive' basis and does not apply to claims for personal injury or economic loss.

A number of the exclusions referred to above are worthy of further comment. Employer's liability insurance is a compulsory requirement in the UK. With some limited exceptions this form of cover is mandatory and is best dealt with by way of a separate, more appropriate policy. To avoid any duplication of cover, PI policies routinely exclude liabilities arising out of employment including, more recently, employment malpractice issues such as unfair dismissal and discrimination.

There is still much confusion between public liability claims and claims which fall to be dealt with by PI policies. The distinction is perhaps best seen by describing PL claims as being those which arise from 'physical mistakes' whereas PI claims relate to 'intellectual mistakes'. If an engineer on site were to negligently injure a third party by way of a physical act, that would give rise to a public liability claim. If the same injury were caused by spalling concrete, which arose as a consequence of defective structural design, that would be a matter for PI insurers. While the effect might be the same, the cause differs and it is the cause which dictates which policy will respond.

In addition to the generic exceptions listed above, which are common to most construction professional indemnity policies, there are also a number of exceptions peculiar to particular professions. Examples of these are set out below.

Consulting engineers/architects

It is usual, if not standard, for professional indemnity insurance policies issued to consulting engineers to exclude liability arising out of fitness for purpose and any other express guarantees. An example of the exclusory language often used in this regard is shown below.

'The Insurers will not be liable in respect of any claim arising from

(a) an agreement by the Insured warranting or guaranteeing that any installations, structures or other works constructed in accordance with his advice or design or proposals will be suitable for any specified purpose,
(b) any other express guarantee insofar as his liability under such an agreement or express guarantee exceeds the amount of his liability in the absence of such agreement or express guarantee'.

The exclusion of fitness for purpose guarantees is an important consideration. Fitness for purpose obligations represent strict liabilities – it is no defence for a party to claim that it had not been negligent or had acted in accordance with best industry practice at the time. PI insurers are not in the business of guaranteeing the work of their insureds. Despite the wide policy wordings that are currently available, PI insurers still operate against an expectation that their insureds contract on no wider a basis than the exercise of reasonable skill and care.

Liquidated damages present a similar problem. PI insurers provide cover in relation to proven losses which flow as a consequence of negligence on the behalf of their insured. Liquidated damages only serve to cloud the issue – they may not be linked to negligence and may be set at a level in excess of any level of damages that might have been awarded. It is for this reason that an exclusion of liquidated or ascertained damages is incorporated into policies.

Surveyors
Due to the exposure of insurers in respect of survey, inspection and valuation reports, as evidenced by large numbers of significant claims in the late 1980s and early 1990s in particular, insurers are keen that only suitable individuals undertake such work.

It is standard for policies to restrict cover to claims where the survey, inspection or valuation report was undertaken by a Fellow or Associate of a recognized professional body such as the RICS or ISVA, or where the individual has at least five years' experience of this specific type of work.

2.11 Conditions
Conditions may be divided into three types. It is the consequence of each which makes them important.

(a) Conditions precedent to the policy, the breach of which will void the policy from inception.
(b) Conditions subsequent to the policy, a failure to observe these by the insured rendering the policy voidable from the date of the breach.
(c) Conditions precedent to liability, breach of which relieves the insurer from liability to make a payment under the policy.

3 CLAIMS
Accepting that professional indemnity insurance policies are written on a 'claims made' basis, two points should immediately be clarified. First, what is a claim? Secondly, when, and perhaps how, is it made?

The Oxford English Dictionary defines a claim as an assertion of a right to something. In the case of an architect or engineer, the claim is likely to be a demand for money.

Occasionally, the claim may be for the performance of a duty, but that is quite a rare situation.

The claim is likely to be against the professional individual for money, the demand being based on an alleged breach of duty or an act of negligence, whether by deed or omission.

The claim need not be made in writing to require notification to insurers, neither does it require to be justified. The unfounded or unattractive claim must be notified with the same promptness as one which clearly has merit.

3.1 Notification of claim

This is a very important policy condition which deals with the insured's obligations in relation to claims notification and the provision of information and assistance in relation to the defence of any claim. The condition usually also includes a deeming provision dealing with the question as to when a 'potential circumstance' becomes a 'claim'.

An example of a wording in common use is shown below:

> 'The Insured shall give written notice to the Insurer as soon as reasonably practicable of any claim or intimation to the Insured of possible claim made against the Insured or upon the Insured becoming aware of circumstances which might give rise to a claim under this Policy regardless of any excess and the Insured shall upon request give to the Insurer all such information and assistance as the Insurer may reasonably require and as may be in the Insured's power to provide and will in all such matters do and concur in doing all such things as the Insurer may require. Any claim arising from such intimation to the Insured of possible claim or such circumstances which might give rise to a claim shall be deemed to have been made during the Period of Insurance in which such notice has been given'.

An alternative wording requires the insured to give notice 'immediately' rather than 'as soon as reasonably practicable' which can give rise to practical difficulties. The looser wording is potentially of significant benefit to the insured. It is important that the insurers are informed of any potential claim circumstances as soon as practicable in order that legal opinion can be obtained and experts appointed, where this is necessary. Equally, however, the claims notification condition should be couched in terms that allow the insured to comply in practice.

If the condition requiring notification of the claim is expressed to be a condition precedent to the insurers' liability, any breach may permit the insurer to decline to indemnify in respect of any particular claim. It is unnecessary for the insurer to show prejudice.

If the clause is not expressed to be a condition precedent, then the insurers' remedy will be in damages, if any loss can be shown. If any delay in notification can be shown to have had no effect on the insurers' position, then a claim for damages is unlikely to be successful.

3.2 Late notification

In connection with late notifications, it has been held in relation to commercial cases at least that it is difficult to conceive of circumstances where it would be reasonable for an insured to delay notification of an occurrence by as long as a month.

3.3 Admission of liability

The insured is prohibited from admitting liability for or settling any claims without the written consent of insurers.

3.4 Circumstances likely or event

Almost all professional indemnity insurance policies require immediate, or at the very least prompt, notification of certain events. These may include:

(a) claims made against the insured
(b) circumstances or occurrences that are likely to, or may, give rise to a claim under the policy
(c) any indication given verbally or in writing that a claim may be made against the insured
(d) the realization, fear or concern that any party or person covered by the professional indemnity insurance policy may have, by act or omission, committed a breach which may give rise to a claim.

Notice of a claim may be required to be 'immediate', 'as soon as possible' or 'as soon as practicable'. In some policies a period is specified, e.g. within 14 days. If no period for notification is expressly set out in the policy it will be implied that notification must be given within a reasonable period of time.

Clearly, the insurer is concerned that there should be no unreasonable or prejudicial delay in notification of the claim in order that such steps or measures as are appropriate to investigate, defend or settle the claim may be taken within good time.

3.5 Blanket notifications

Whether 'blanket' or 'laundry list' notifications of circumstances may be acceptable or valid depends on the wording of the particular provision of the professional indemnity insurance policy and the facts of each case.

Generally, the architect or engineer must identify the relevant circumstance and there must be reasonable grounds for anticipating that a claim may arise out of the circumstance, as it appears at the date of notification.

It is likely that the court will be inclined towards the view and opinion of the architect or engineer in the matter, not least because the subject matter of any dispute between them and their insurer will be (what has become) a claim against them.

Blanket notifications cannot be rejected, however, as a matter of course. It is necessary to look at the whole position and particularly the wording of the professional indemnity policy.

3.6 The QC clause

The QC clause states that the insured shall not be required to contest legal proceedings unless a Queen's Counsel advises that the action has a reasonable prospect of success. The intent behind the clause is to deal with situations where there is a dispute or disagreement between insurer and insured as to whether or not to defend a particular claim. The insured may, for example, have a strong commercial relationship with a client which it would prefer not to prejudice. At the same time, and quite understandably, the insurer would be equally reluctant to pay out in relation to a claim against which a reasonable defence existed. In such circumstances an independent QC would be called upon to decide whether or not a defence had a reasonable prospect of being successful.

3.7 Fraudulent claims

If an insured deliberately submits a claim which he or she knows to be false or fraudulent, then the professional indemnity policy becomes void. All claims notified under that policy are negated as a consequence. What is the position under policies with multiple insureds where only one insured has been negligent? Court cases on this point have indicated that it is only the position of the fraudulent insured that is prejudiced and not that of the innocent insureds.

3.8 Innocent non-disclosure

Innocent non-disclosure provisions are becoming increasingly common. The intention behind such a provision is to prevent insurers from declining claims on the basis of, for example, late notification. Provided that the late notification is not deliberate or fraudulent then insurers will accept the claims notification. Where late notification occurs, although the claim is accepted it will be on the basis of the cover in force when the claim should have been notified. This prevents selection against insurers in circumstances where an insured delays notification until after renewal, by which time either the limit of indemnity has been increased or the excess decreased.

In the absence of an innocent non-disclosure provision, the only options available to insurers are to pay the claim regardless or seek to avoid the entire policy on the basis of material non-disclosure or misrepresentation. In order to do this, insurers need to satisfy two tests:

(a) that disclosure would have caused a prudent insurer to reject the risk or at least to have imposed more onerous terms, and
(b) that the non-disclosure or misrepresentation induced the insurer to enter into the policy.

3.9 Discharge of liability

This condition enables the insurer to discharge its liability under the policy by making a payment to the insured equal to the amount for which a claim could be settled.

The intention behind this condition is clear – it enables insurers to discharge their liability to the insured in circumstances where the insured is being either difficult or obstructive in reaching settlement with the plaintiff. The condition is rarely invoked but provides a useful protection to insurers. The condition can be invoked in circumstances where the limit of indemnity is clearly insufficient given the quantum and merits of the claim that is being brought by the claimant. Insurers have the option of paying to the insured the full indemnity limit, leaving the insured then to negotiate the best possible settlement with the claimant. The ability of insurers to discharge their liability under the policy in this way is a useful reminder of the importance of an adequate limit of indemnity.

3.10 Prejudiced claims

In circumstances where the actions of the insured result in prejudice to the handling or settlement of any claim, insurers are entitled to reduce the extent of indemnity in relation to that particular claim in proportion to the prejudice that has been caused.

3.11 Differences

Any differences which arise out of the policy are to be referred to arbitration. In the first instance, insurer and insured should seek to reach agreement as to the identity of the arbitrator. If they cannot, then either side appoints their own arbitrator who will endeavour to reach agreement on the points at issue. An umpire is then appointed by the two arbitrators to decide the issue(s) in the event that they cannot agree.

4 EXTENSIONS

Almost all construction professional indemnity insurance policies include extensions to cover by way of 'bolt-on' extras. A number of these such extensions do provide important elements of additional cover and these are discussed below.

Extensions to cover vary from profession to profession and between policies. Extensions for architects and engineers include damage resulting from the loss of documents and the cost of replacing, recreating or restoring such documents.

4.1 Libel and slander

This is a very common policy extension and provides indemnity against the consequences of libel or slander, provided that such libel or slander was committed in good faith.

4.2 Joint ventures

Where consultants participate in joint ventures they may attract joint and several liability, that is to say they can be held liable for the consequences of any neglect, error or omission by the co-venturers with whom they are working.

Whether a particular professional indemnity insurance policy would respond to such a liability will depend very much on the policy wording under consideration.

If the operative clause provides cover in relation to 'any legal liability' then it is sufficient for the policy to remain silent on the issue of joint ventures in order for cover to be provided. Assuming that a liability attaches to the insured and is not the subject of an exclusion, the policy will respond accordingly.

However, a number of insurers who issue 'legal liability' wordings feel that joint ventures are of sufficient sensitivity to warrant closer scrutiny and require that details of any proposed joint venture be provided in advance prior to cover being granted. This is normally achieved by way of a limitation to the effect that any claim arising from a joint venture is not covered unless the existence of the joint venture has been disclosed to insurers. It is always prudent for consultants to check with either their broker or insurer the operation of cover in relation to joint ventures. It is also an important risk management tool to check that any co-venturers carry adequate insurance.

4.3 Indemnity to employees

A majority of PI policies extend to include an indemnity to any employees who might be held personally liable. The extension either applies automatically or at the request of the principal insured – normally the employer.

Indemnity to employee extensions have become increasingly topical given the decision in *Merrett* v. *Babb*.

4.4 Loss of or damage to documents

Again, this is a standard extension applying to most professional indemnity insurance policies, it is intended to respond by paying the costs incurred by the insured in replacing or restoring lost or damaged documents.

However, this element of cover is, in itself, subject to conditions and limitations, mainly that:

(a) any loss or damage is sustained while the documents are either in transit or in the custody of the insured
(b) the amount of any claim for costs and expenses is supported by proper documentary evidence.

4.5 Infringement of copyright

There is often a policy extension which covers legal costs incurred by the insured in seeking damages or an injunction following an alleged infringement of the insured's copyright. Usually this policy extension is subject to a rather modest inner limit of indemnity – a figure of £25 000 in the aggregate is not unusual.

4.6 Health and safety at work (prosecution defence costs)

Construction consultants are faced with increasing obligations in relation to health and safety issues, particularly following the implementation of the CDM Regulations. A failure to comply with those Regulations could give rise to either a criminal prosecution or a civil action for damages, or both. In either event, as a matter of law it is the criminal prosecution that is heard first. It is important that the criminal prosecution be properly defended, if it is not, then the defence of any subsequent claim for damages could be prejudiced.

In order to ensure proper representation at any health and safety prosecutions it is now normal practice for construction professional indemnity insurers to include criminal defence costs within cover. However, the extent of cover is carefully controlled – insurers are particularly keen to ensure that any claims notified do relate to health and safety issues arising from professional services and not employment-related risks. Furthermore, no cover is provided in relation to any fines or penalties.

While some insurers seek to impose an inner aggregate limit of indemnity for prosecution defence costs cover, say £300 000, others prefer to allow the full limit of indemnity to apply to such claims, albeit on an aggregate basis.

5 DISCLOSURE REQUIREMENTS

Most, if not all, appointments in the UK require consultants to carry PI at a set level for an agreed number of years, provided that cover continues to be available at reasonable economic rates. It is also a common requirement for the consultant to produce on request documentary evidence that cover has been renewed and continues in force.

The format of documentary evidence varies. A number of clients insist on formal certification signed by either the broker or insurer, confirming details such as the period of insurance, policy number, identity of insurer and the applicable limit of indemnity and excess. By contrast, others are happy to rely on a broker's letter which simply confirms that cover is in place.

CHAPTER 2.7

Employment law

Jonathan Exten-Wright
DLA Piper UK LLP

1 CONTRACT OF EMPLOYMENT OR CONTRACT FOR SERVICES?

1.1 Who is an employee?

When interpreting employment legislation, it is critical to distinguish an employee from a self-employed person. Legal rights enjoyed by each differ, although in areas such as anti-discrimination law, working time legislation and the national minimum wage, the trend has been towards extending rights to those with a wider working relationship with an employer.

Section 230(1) of the Employment Rights Act 1996 ('ERA') defines an employee as 'an individual who has entered into or works under . . . a contract of employment'. Section 230(2) ERA states that 'contract of employment' means 'a contract of service or apprenticeship . . . whether express or implied'. The contract between the parties determines the status of the worker: is it a contract of service (employment) or a contract for services (self-employment)? Labels will not necessarily decide the issue. A Court will look at the exact nature of the relationship between the parties and all the facts in determining employment status.

Under a contract of apprenticeship, an apprentice is bound to his or her employer in order to learn a trade and the employer agrees to provide training in that trade. Normally an apprenticeship will be for a fixed term or until a set qualification is achieved, terminable only if gross misconduct occurs, a business shuts completely, or if the apprentice refuses to perform his or her duties.

1.2 Distinguishing between an employee and a self-employed person

The distinction between employed and self-employed status decides liability for income tax and national insurance contributions ('NICs'), entitlement to statutory sick pay and entitlement to employment protection. An employer is responsible for operating PAYE and Class 1 NICs where the worker is an employee. Where the worker is self-employed, however, the payer does not have such obligations. HM Revenue and Customs ('HMRC') has always sought to apply employment tax rules to individuals who are, in reality, employees, even where they are described as self-employed. On 6 April 2000, legislation known as 'IR35' was introduced to enable HMRC to deal with situations where individuals supply services through personal service companies ('PSCs') in circumstances where they would otherwise have been employees, in order to avoid liability for income tax and NICs. The effect of IR35 is that most of the fees received by the PSC are deemed to be paid to the worker as salary. Income tax and NICs are collected from the PSC accordingly.

Deciding whether an individual is self-employed or an employee involves a three stage inquiry:

- Did the parties enter a legally binding contract?
- If so, what were its terms?
- Was it a contract of employment?

The Courts will imply terms to reflect the parties' true intention when making the contract, to give it 'business efficacy', i.e. to make it work. The Courts will investigate whether the apparent contractual status is a device to deprive employees of their employment protection rights or avoid any tax.

Employment indicators

The presence of the following non-exhaustive factors indicates that an individual is an employee. The first factor is critical as a bare minimum.

- Is there mutuality of obligation, i.e. must the employer provide regular work and must the employee make him or herself available to do the work?
- Does the individual work under the company's direction and control?
- Must the work be done regularly, within a certain time?
- Does the employee have to provide personal service or can they nominate someone as a substitute?
- Are tools, equipment and/or clothing for doing the work provided by the company?
- Does the individual attend the company premises to work, or at places decided by the company?
- If, and when, the individual is at work, does he or she have similar terms and conditions to other staff?
- Is the individual paid by the hour, week or month? Is overtime payable?
- Are payments wholly or partially attributable to a regular basic wage, paid at regular intervals?
- Does the company deduct PAYE and social security contributions from payments?
- Is the individual required to work set hours or a given number of hours a week or month? Is attendance required at certain times on certain days? Are there any regular or assured working hours?
- Is permission required for time off?
- Is holiday pay, commission, bonus or similar payments made by the company?
- Is the 'engagement' subject to termination by notice from either side?

Self-employment indicators

The following factors indicate self-employment:

- Is the employer a professional client of the individual?
- Does the individual work for more than one client company or organisation?
- Is payment on a fee basis?
- Are services invoiced?
- Does the individual provide the main items of equipment needed to do the job?
- Is the individual free to hire other people on his or her own terms to do work that has been commissioned? Does he or she pay such additional workers directly?
- Has the individual invested his or her own capital in the business, gaining or losing from its commercial success?
- Is the individual recognizably in business on his or her own account, as a person, a partnership or a limited company?
- Has HMRC accepted that the individual is self-employed?
- Is the individual registered for VAT?

1.3 The legal consequences of the distinction

The legal consequences of distinguishing between the employed and the self-employed are outlined below. For certain purposes, self-employment is divided between those doing work personally and those doing business on their own account, as a provider to a customer or client.

ERA

Employees have rights under the ERA, including the right not to be unfairly dismissed. Generally speaking, workers do not have rights under the ERA. One exception is the

2.1 Ways of operating
2.2 Working with others
2.3 Working internationally
2.4 The engineer's appointment
2.5 Collateral warranties
2.6 Indemnity insurance
2.7 Employment law
2.8 Information technology

right for workers (other than those in business on their own account), like employees, not to have unauthorised deductions made from wages.

Discrimination legislation

For equal pay, sex, sexual orientation, gender reassignment, race, age, religion or belief and disability discrimination legislation, 'employment' means employment under a contract of service or apprenticeship, or a contract personally to perform any work, i.e. self-employed persons who carry out the work themselves.

The Health and Safety at Work etc. Act 1974

This is not limited to the health and safety of employees: in addition, it covers the public who visit the employer's premises or who may be affected by the work carried out for the employer, or self-employed persons, or another employer's employees working alongside. The Health and Safety at Work Act 1974 covers work activities at a place of work and the risks created by the people working there, both for themselves and for those affected by them.

The Transfer of Undertakings (Protection of Employment) Regulations 2006 ('TUPE 2006')

For business transfers covered by TUPE 2006 (see Section 5 below), only employees' rights are protected (not those of the self-employed), with employment being transferred automatically to the new employer.

The Working Time Regulations 1998 ('WTR')

The WTR (see Section 6 below) protects 'workers', meaning all those individuals employed under a contract of employment or any other contract to provide personal work or services to the other party to the contract, where the other party is not a client or customer of any profession or business undertaking carried on by the individual. The definition of 'workers' includes employees, agency workers, temporary workers, freelancers and the self-employed but not those self-employed individuals who are genuinely pursuing a business activity on their own account. The term 'worker' also includes non-employed trainees, i.e. those undertaking work experience or training on a course run by an educational institution or establishment whose main business is to provide training.

National Minimum Wage Act 1998 and National Minimum Wage Regulations 1999

The National Minimum Wage Act 1998 applies to workers who are over the school leaving age and who are working in the UK. The term 'worker' means an individual who either works under a contract of employment or a contract for services to provide work or services personally. The latter type of contract includes self-employed freelancers, who are not in business on their own account, and who work exclusively for an employer. Agency workers must be paid the national minimum wage by the entity which is responsible for paying them.

The Public Interest Disclosure Act 1998 ('PIDA')

PIDA, through its implementation in the ERA, protects 'workers' against dismissal or detriment for making a 'protected disclosure' about an employer's malpractice. The definition of 'worker' includes not just employees, but also those who are genuinely self-employed, such as freelancers and third party contractors whose work is controlled by the employer. The definition also includes homeworkers, trainees and agency workers.

Workers who make 'protected disclosures' are protected from dismissal, selection for redundancy or from being subject to a detriment, such as the refusal of a pay increase or promotion. A worker may bring a claim in the employment tribunal if they are subjected to any detriment by any act, or any deliberate failure to act, by their employer on the ground that they have made a protected disclosure. The claim may be for unfair dismissal, unfair selection for redundancy, dismissal for participating in unofficial industrial action or victimisation or detriment where these are alleged to be the consequence of having made a protected disclosure.

In bringing a claim for unfair dismissal, a successful claimant would be entitled to the remedies of reinstatement, reengagement or compensation. There is, however, no limit on the compensation which may be awarded in a claim for unfair dismissal which is related to whistleblowing.

Part-time Workers (Prevention of Less Favourable Treatment) Regulations 2000 ('Part-Time Workers Regulations')

The Part-Time Workers Regulations came into force on 1 July 2000 and entitle part-time workers to terms and conditions which are *pro rata* to comparable full-time workers. Employers are required to ensure that their terms and conditions do not discriminate against part-time workers.

Fixed-term Employees (Prevention of Less Favourable Treatment) Regulations 2002 ('Fixed-Term Regulations')

The Fixed-Term Regulations came into force on 1 October 2002 and apply to employees (and not workers). The following individuals are specifically excluded from this legislation: apprentices, certain agency workers, employees undertaking work experience or temporary work schemes, students on work experience as part of a higher education course and members of the armed forces. Under the Fixed-Term Regulations, employees on fixed-term contracts have the right not to be treated less favourably than comparable permanent employees. If a fixed-term employee believes that his or her rights under the Fixed-Term Regulations have been infringed, he or she will be entitled to request a written statement giving particulars of the reasons for the treatment. Fixed-term employees are entitled to be informed by their employer of any suitable available vacancy which arises during their employment. In addition, an employee is entitled to claim automatic unfair dismissal where he or she is dismissed because he or she sought to enforce his or her rights under the Fixed-Term Regulations.

PAYE and NIC – Income Tax (Earnings and Pensions) Act 2003 ('ITEPA') and Social Security Contributions and Benefits Act 1992 and regulations made thereunder

The main statutory provisions governing the taxation of employment income are to be found in ITEPA, which came into force on 6 April 2003. The main national insurance legislation can be found in the Social Security Contributions & Benefits Act 1992.

The PAYE regulations require all employers with employees in the UK to deduct tax and NICs from their earnings under PAYE and to report details of their non-cash benefits and expenses to HMRC. If an individual is deemed to be self-employed, there is no obligation to deduct tax or NICs at source. As previously mentioned, special rules also apply if a person provides his services through a PSC and IR35 applies. The recipient of those services will not be under an obligation to withhold any income tax or NICs or pay NICs in that instance. VAT may, however, be payable.

1.4 Summary of differences

An employee enjoys (subject, in certain circumstances, to qualifying conditions) the following key rights:

- unfair dismissal protection;
- redundancy payment entitlement;
- written particulars of terms of employment;
- statutory minimum notice period;
- guarantee payments (when work is not provided in certain circumstances);
- medical suspension payment;
- protection from discrimination on grounds of race, sex, sexual orientation, gender reassignment, disability, religion, belief or age;
- equal pay;
- maternity rights;
- time off for trade union activities/public duties, etc.;
- not to be refused employment because of trade union membership or non-membership;
- to be employed for the agreed period or be given the agreed length of notice;
- to work in a healthy and safe working environment;
- to be paid statutory sick pay;
- to be paid wages without unauthorised deductions;
- for shop workers or betting workers, the right not to work on Sundays;
- automatic transfer of contract and protection of terms and conditions in business transfers;
- to benefit from the limits on working time under WTR;
- to receive the national minimum wage;
- protection against dismissal or detriment for making a protected disclosure under ERA; and
- not to be discriminated against because they are a part-timer.

A worker enjoys the following key rights:

- to benefit from all entitlements under his or her contract for service;
- not to be discriminated against on grounds of race, sex, sexual orientation, gender reassignment, disability, religion, belief or age and to receive equal pay (if they must do the work personally);
- to be paid wages without unauthorised deductions;
- to benefit from the limit on the maximum working week/night shift working, rest periods, rest breaks and the right to paid annual holidays, under WTR;
- to receive the national minimum wage;
- not to suffer a detriment under WTR, the National Minimum Wage Act 1998/ National Minimum Wage Regulations 1999; or for making a protected disclosure;
- to work in a healthy and safe working environment; and
- not to be discriminated against because they are a part-timer.

Note that the third, fourth and fifth bullet points above only apply to self-employed individuals who are not in business on their own account; i.e. who work exclusively for the employer, and who cannot select another employer to whom to provide a service.

Case study 1 – Self-employed consultant

Mr Adams has taken early retirement in order to set up his own business which offers specialist services in the design of steel structures. His former employer wishes to engage him on a regular part-time basis (two days per week) to use his expertise on various projects. A contract is drawn up, with payment based on an hourly fee plus reimbursement of all travel and other out-of-pocket expenses. Mr Adams wishes to be paid gross without deduction of income tax or NICs. However, Mr Adams has no other clients and has not established himself with HMRC as self-employed. The employer, therefore, has to treat Mr Adams as an employee, subject to PAYE and NIC. If Mr Adams later finds similar work with other clients and HMRC confirms that he is self-employed for tax purposes, he may then be paid gross.

1.5 The IR35 Rules for PSCs

What is IR35?

In March 1999, the Government announced measures aimed at preventing perceived income tax and NIC avoidance from the use of PSCs. The proposals were contained in press release IR35 in the Chancellor's 1999 budget and provisions are now within ITEPA 2003. Under the typical PSC structure, an individual forms a company, with himself or herself as the sole director, shareholder and main employee and the PSC contracts with other organisations (the 'client') to provide services. The individual carries out the work and the PSC invoices the client and receives payment. Monies may be retained inside the company, used to defer expenses, or paid as salary or dividend to the employee/shareholder. This arrangement carries significant fiscal advantages compared with the taxation of employment income through PAYE: dividends do not attract NICs; companies enjoy more generous rules for expenses and borrowings; family members may be paid a salary; and pension provisions are advantageous. There are also commercial benefits such as status, limitation of liability and enhanced flexibility.

When does IR35 apply?

The main conditions for IR35 to apply are, *inter alia*:

- an individual has an obligation to provide services **in person**;
- the services are provided through an 'intermediary' (such as a PSC); and
- if instead the services had been provided directly between the individual and client, the individual would have been regarded as employed by the clients 'in employed earner's employment' for NIC purposes.

How does IR35 work?

If the conditions set out above are satisfied, the PSC (and not the ultimate client) is responsible for applying the legislation. It is required to account to HMRC for an amount equivalent to PAYE and NICs on the excess of deemed employment income over actual employment income. Payments for the previous tax year are due by 19 April.

The relevant income constitutes, broadly, the amounts received by the intermediary plus any benefits received directly by the individual, less any actual salary paid by the PSC. The allowable deductions include a statutory 5% deduction from income received by the intermediary (to cover the company's overheads), plus expenses equivalent to those which would have been allowable if the individual had been an employee. The remainder is deemed to be the notional salary of the individual and the PSC is responsible for paying the tax that would have been payable under the PAYE and NIC regulations. If a PSC fails to pay over the correct amount of tax it may be subject to interest and/or penalties.

Interaction between IR35 and the Construction Industry Scheme ('CIS')

A PSC falling within IR35 may also be a subcontractor for the purposes of the CIS (further details of which are explained in Section 1.6 below). In this situation, the PSC suffers a tax deduction on income received and is itself required to operate deemed PAYE and NICs under IR35. The IR35 payment is due on 19 April, so in many cases the company will have overpaid tax until its corporation tax return has been agreed. This problem has been addressed by legislation introduced by the Finance Act 2004. This allows a PSC to defer paying the tax due under the IR35 rules, so it will be able to set off the amounts deducted under the CIS scheme against the PAYE and NIC it owes.

1.6 CIS

Overview of the CIS

The CIS sets out the rules regarding the handling by contractors of payments to subcontractors for their construction work. Under the CIS, a contractor may be required to make a deduction from payments made to subcontractors, and pay this to HMRC. This deduction would only be in respect of that part of the payment which does not represent the cost of materials incurred by the subcontractor.

On 6 April 2007, a new CIS was introduced with the aims of:

- reducing the regulatory burden on construction business;
- improving the level of compliance by construction businesses with their tax obligations; and
- helping construction businesses to correctly interpret the employment status of their workers.

Under the new CIS, contractors who make payments to subcontractors registered with HMRC are required to make deductions, where appropriate, at the rate of 20%, whereas if the payments are made to subcontractors who are not registered with HMRC contracts are required to make deductions at a rate of 30%.

Interaction between the CIS and employment status

The CIS applies only to self-employed workers operating as 'contractors' or 'subcontractors' in the construction industry. It does not apply to employees subject to PAYE. The test for employment status must be considered for each engagement. A subcontractor may hold a tax certificate but if he or she is deemed to be an 'employee' in relation to a particular job, the employer must operate PAYE for that work. This is because construction industry employers continue to be responsible for the deduction of PAYE and NIC for all employees under normal HMRC procedures. As with other industries, the hirer/employer is responsible for determining whether an individual is an employee. If an organisation incorrectly fails to operate PAYE, it will generally be liable to account to HMRC for the tax which should have been deducted (plus interest and possibly penalties). This is the case notwithstanding that the organisation acted in good faith. Conversely, if the organisation contracts with a PSC, it is the responsibility of the PSC to determine whether IR35 applies.

The terms 'contractor' and 'sub-contractor' are broadly defined by HMRC. 'Contractor' means a business or other concern that pays subcontractors for construction work. Contractors may be construction companies and building firms but may also be Government departments and local authorities. Non-construction businesses which spend on average £1 million per year on construction work (averaged over the previous three years) are counted as contractors. Consequently, any business authorising substantial amounts of building works will be caught by the CIS, irrespective of its industry sector. Businesses which spend less than an average of £1 million per annum or construction work and private householders are not contractors and will not be covered by the CIS.

A 'subcontractor' is a business engaged by the contractor to carry out construction work. 'Construction work' is restricted to work carried out in the UK and its territorial waters. Where a contract includes both construction and non-construction work, the labour element of the entire contract will fall within the CIS.

'Construction work' includes the following:

- construction, alteration, repair, extension or demolition of buildings/structures (including temporary structures);
- installation of heating, lighting, air conditioning/ventilation, water or power supply;
- installation of fire protection; and
- preparatory works, such as earth moving, site clearance or excavation.

It does not include:

- extraction of oil, natural gas or minerals;
- manufacture or building or delivery of engineering components, equipment, plant or machinery;
- manufacture or delivery of components for heating, lighting, air conditioning/ventilation, sanitation/water supply, draining or fire protection;
- artistic works;
- professional fees; and
- installation of security systems.

Note that some businesses may act both as contractor and subcontractor and will need to apply the appropriate set of rules for each transaction.

Mechanics of the CIS

All contractors must register for the CIS with HMRC. Subcontractors who do not wish to have deductions made from their payments at the higher rate (i.e. 30%) should also register with HMRC.

Before making a payment to a subcontractor for construction work, a contractor should verify with HMRC that the subcontractor is registered. HMRC will then check whether the subcontractor is registered and will inform the contractor of the rate of deduction to be applied to the payment, or whether the payment may be made without deductions. If no deduction is required, the contractor may make the payment to the subcontractor in full.

If a deduction is required, the contractor must calculate the value of the deduction; deduct it from payment; record details of the payment, materials and deduction; make the net payment to the subcontractor; and complete and give a statement of deduction to the subcontractor.

Each month, contractors should send HMRC a complete return of all payments made under the CIS or report that they have made no payments. The return must reach HMRC by the 19th day of each month. Contractors who miss this deadline will be charged an automatic penalty of at least £100. The penalty will be charged for each month that a return is late. Contractors must also make a 'statutory declaration' on the return that none of their workers listed are employees.

2 DEFINING A CONTRACT OF EMPLOYMENT

There is no legal requirement for a written contract of employment, but the ERA requires employees with at least one month's service to be given a written statement of their main terms and conditions of employment, for example, pay, hours, holidays, etc. (see Section 2.4 below). Such a statement is not, however, a contract of employment. Many other terms can be part of the contractual relationship, for example, a staff handbook, works' rules, disciplinary rules and procedures, terms in collective agreements and verbal agreements. Contracts may incorporate various types of terms which establish the rights and obligations of the parties, including:

- express terms – clearly agreed, whether written or verbal;
- implied terms – necessary to give the contract effect or where deemed included for example, by custom and practice;
- incorporated terms – included from another source, for example, staff handbooks, collective agreements;
- statutory terms – required by law, for example, minimum notice periods.

2.1 Employees' implied obligations

Some employees' obligations are implied. Breaching these terms could, if sufficiently serious, provide grounds for summary dismissal. Examples of such implied obligations include:

2.1.1 Duty of fidelity and good faith. The employer/employee relationship is based on mutual trust and confidence. It is implied that an employee will serve an employer with fidelity and in good faith. An employee must not compete with or act against his or her employer's business interests during employment. Employees must deal with their employer honestly, account for all property entrusted to them, and disclose all information relevant to the employer obtained during employment;

2.1.2 Duty of confidentiality. While in employment, an employee must not disclose to third parties confidential information or trade secrets about an employer or an employer's clients which was gained during employment. This restriction continues after employment ends;

2.1.3 Duty to exercise reasonable care and skill. An employee implicitly undertakes that he or she has and will exercise reasonable skill and care in performing his or her duties; and

2.1.4 Duty to obey lawful and reasonable orders. An employee implicitly consents to obey the lawful and reasonable orders of his or her employer under the contract. This duty provides a legal basis for compliance with company policies, for example those contained in an employer's staff handbook.

2.2 Employer's implied obligations

Employers are subject to a number of implied terms. If breached, an employee may claim a breach of contract and, in some circumstances, may resign and claim constructive dismissal. Such terms include those listed below.

2.2.1 Duty to pay wages. A duty to provide work (and thus wages to follow) will be implied for piecework; where wages consist entirely or in part of commission; and where the nature of the work means that the employee must work to maintain or develop skills;

2.2.2 Duty to ensure employee's safety. Employers must take reasonable care and reasonable steps to ensure employees' safety at work. Statute and various European directives implemented in the UK by health and safety regulations impose detailed obligations. Non-compliance constitutes a breach of this implied term and risks civil claims and statutory or regulatory penalties. This duty cannot be delegated and exists even when an employee works abroad on a site owned and controlled by another company;

2.2.3 Duty to monitor the environment. Employers must provide and monitor, to the extent that it is reasonably practicable, a working environment which is reasonably suitable for its employees to perform their contractual duties; and

2.2.4 Duty to allow redress of grievances. Employers must reasonably and promptly give employees a reasonable opportunity to redress grievances.

In certain circumstances employers may be under a duty to inform employees of a contractual benefit. While generally not under a duty to give a reference, employers are under a duty to exercise reasonable skill and care in giving a reference, which must be fair. A third party may sue an employer if it relied on a misleading reference and suffered loss as a result.

2.3 Obligations on the employer and the employee

The employer-employee relationship is based on mutual trust and confidence. There will be a breach of this implied term where one party behaves in a manner calculated or likely to destroy that trust and confidence, for example:

- unjustly operating a disciplinary procedure;
- abusing an express contractual right;
- making unwarranted suggestions that the employee is incapable; and
- not supporting an employee over harassment or bullying by fellow employees or the public.

2.4 Written particulars of employment

As previously mentioned, employees must be given a written statement of the main particulars of their employment.

Written details must be supplied to all new employees within two months of the start of their employment. It is prudent, however, to give this information to employees at the outset of employment. Existing employees not supplied with written details may request them and must receive them within two months of making such a request.

The details that must be included are:

- names of the employer and the employee;
- date on which employment began;
- date on which continuous employment began;
- the scale or rate of pay or the method of pay calculation;
- the intervals at which remuneration is paid;
- terms and conditions relating to working hours, including any overtime provisions;
- job title or, if this inadequately describes the duties involved, a description of the work;
- the place of work;

- for temporary employment, either the period for which it is expected to continue, or for a fixed term employment, the date it ends;
- terms and conditions for holidays, including public holidays, and holiday pay, enabling calculation of entitlement, including accrued holiday when leaving employment;
- any collective agreements affecting terms and conditions;
- any requirement to work outside the UK and, if so, the terms applicable;
- terms relating to sickness or injury including any sick pay provision;
- terms relating to pensions and pension schemes;
- whether a contracting-out certificate is in force, i.e. contracting out of SERPS;
- any disciplinary rules;
- the person (specified by description) to whom to appeal in the first instance if dissatisfied with any disciplinary decision, together with the appeal's method;
- any further steps available after the first stage of an appeal;
- the person (specified by description or otherwise) with whom to raise a grievance in the first instance and the method;
- any further steps available after the first stage of a grievance; and
- the length of notice to be given and receive.

If there are no relevant details in respect of the above, that fact must be stated.

The employer must inform the employee in writing of changes to the above particulars as soon as possible and no later than one month after the change.

The key difference between a contract and a written statement is that a contract requires an agreement to be reached between two parties. A written statement does not as it simply constitutes information which must be given to employees.

To ensure that a written statement or notification of change is part of a contract, employers should:

- ensure that a letter offering employment to a prospective employee is accompanied by a statement of written particulars, stating that these form part of the contract;
- ensure that the written statement expressly states that it is part of the contract; and
- ensure that the employee signs off words such as *'I have read the above [terms and conditions of employment] [change/s to my terms and conditions of employment]. I fully understand the terms as detailed and accept that they form part of my contract of employment'*.

Employers wishing to change an employee's terms of employment should seek agreement from that individual. Non-consensual change could go beyond mere variation and could constitute a breach of contract. This could in turn form the basis of a constructive dismissal claim.

2.5 Types of employment contract

There are two types of employment contract:

(a) Permanent: the most common form for an indefinite, open-ended period which ends either when terminated by the employer, when the employee resigns, or when he or she retires.
(b) Temporary: for either a fixed term or for the duration of a specific task or project for example, where the contract is for a defined period and ends at a pre-determined fixed date or ends when a project or task is completed, or a specific event occurs. Expiry will be treated as a dismissal at law.

2.1 Ways of operating
2.2 Working with others
2.3 Working internationally
2.4 The engineer's appointment
2.5 Collateral warranties
2.6 Indemnity insurance
2.7 Employment law
2.8 Information technology

Forming a contract

Forming a valid contract requires:

- an offer: the employer offers to be bound by a clear and enforceable contract;
- consideration: value being exchanged between the parties such as wages for work;
- acceptance: the offer must be accepted completely and unconditionally; and
- intention to create legal relations: the parties must intend the agreement and its terms to be legally binding.

Conditions in an offer

Offers of employment can be subject to conditions, such as satisfactory references, evidence of qualifications, or a valid driving licence (where driving is essential). Such a contract is not complete unless or until the condition is satisfied and this should be made clear before the parties sign.

Illegal contracts

In general, no Court will enforce a contract which is forbidden by legislation or by common law, for example, one designed to defraud HMRC of tax. However, if a contract is illegal, an employee can still bring a sex, sexual orientation, gender reassignment, race, disability, age or religion or belief claim which is not based on that contract, for example, as to an act of discrimination in the workplace, but not discrimination in a contract term.

An employer and an employee cannot contract out of the rights conferred by any of the following legislation and attempts to do so renders the contractual provision void.

- Sex Discrimination Act 1975, Race Relations Act 1976 or the Disability Discrimination Act 1995;
- Equal Pay Act 1970;
- Trade Union and Labour Relations (Consolidation) Act 1992 ('TULRCA');
- ERA;
- Transfer of Undertakings (Protection of Employment) Regulations 1981;
- WTR;
- The National Minimum Wage Act 1998;
- The Public Interest Disclosure Act 1998;
- The Part-time Workers (Prevention of Less Favourable Treatment) Regulations 2000;
- The Fixed-Term Employees (Prevention of Less Favourable Treatment) Regulations 2002;
- The Employment Equality (Sexual Orientation) Regulations 2003;
- The Employment Equality (Religion or Belief) Regulations 2003; and
- The Employment Equality (Age) Regulations 2006 ('Age Regulations').

Restrictive covenants

Contracts may also specify certain post-termination restraints, i.e. restrictive covenants, limiting the ex-employee's activities after employment. The overriding rule is that such terms are unenforceable unless they: protect a legitimate interest, are clear, specific and precise; and are otherwise reasonable. Only a well drafted covenant will, therefore, be enforceable. Typical restraints include:

- non-disclosure of trade secrets and confidential information;
- non-competition against the employer;

- non-solicitation (poaching) of customers;
- non-dealing with customers; and
- non-solicitation (poaching) of staff.

At common law, the remedy for breach of a restrictive covenant is an award of damages. However, in most cases, an employer would prefer to have the breach stopped by an injunction, i.e. a court order preventing further breaches by the employee, as set out in the order. An employer cannot rely on a restrictive covenant in a contract of employment where it has itself breached the contract.

2.6 International agreements

General principles governing jurisdiction

Any international service agreement will need to address the following:

- the applicable law to the agreement;
- the country of jurisdiction for resolving disputes;
- the mandatory local laws which will prevail over any agreed terms in the agreement; and
- if appropriate whether the agreement complies with the Posting of Workers' Directive ('POWD').

There are three broad categories of employment contracts to be considered when working outside the UK:

- staff (of any nationality) who are already permanently employed in the UK or in another country and who are being assigned to work in another country as expatriates, on a short or long-term basis;
- staff (of any nationality) who are employed as expatriates just for the specific project and have no ongoing employment expectations after the expiry of their contract; and
- nationals of the country where the project is being undertaken.

Some considerations concerning the first category are given below.

Lawson v. Serco

Under Section 94(1) ERA, employees have a right not to be unfairly dismissed by their employer. Before being repealed on 25 October 1999, the territorial scope of Section 94(1) was clarified by Section 196(2) ERA, which excluded an employee 'who ordinarily works outside Great Britain'. Since repeal of Section 196(2), however, four conflicting decisions on the territorial scope of Section 94(1) ERA emerged before the issue went to the Court of Appeal in 2004 and the House of Lords in 2005.

In 2004, the Court of Appeal held, in the case of *Lawson* v. *Serco*, that:

- the test of territorial scope is whether the employment in question is in Great Britain;
- employees who ordinarily work outside Great Britain cannot claim unfair dismissal under Section 94(1) ERA;
- dismissal during a 'single, short absence from Great Britain' would not normally exclude the protection of ERA; and
- 'borderline' cases will depend on an assessment of all the circumstances of the employment in that particular case.

The Court of Appeal's judgement in *Lawson* v. *Serco* was applied by the EAT in *Botham* v. *Ministry of Defence* and *SSAFA Forces Help* v. *McClymont* and four conjoined appeals.

The House of Lords heard the *Lawson, Crofts* (one of the conjoined appeals) and *Botham* cases together in November 2005. It held that the application of Section 94(1) ERA should depend on whether the employee was working in Great Britain at the time of his or her dismissal, rather than what was contemplated at the time his or her employment contract was made.

Lord Hoffman identified three categories of employees who would be able to bring a claim under Section 94(1) ERA:

- employees who are working in Great Britain at the time they are dismissed;
- peripatetic employees, whose base should be treated as their place of employment; and
- expatriate employees. Section 94(1) ERA only applies to expatriates in exceptional circumstances however, such as where an employee works abroad as the representative of a British employer for the purposes of a business carried on in Great Britain.

The decision in *Lawson* v. *Serco* has been followed by the EAT in the conjoined cases of *Burke* v. *The British Council*, *ADT Fire & Security plc* v. *Speyer* and *Camerson* v. *NAAFI*.

In 2007 the EAT found that the decision in *Lawson* v. *Serco* was limited to domestic legislation. In the case of *Bleuse* v. *MBT Transport Limited and Tiefenbacker* it said that different principles applied to directly effective rights conferred by EU law whether or not the UK courts had exclusive jurisdiction to hear the claim. The EAT accepted that the Working Time Regulations give domestic effect to an EU right. Therefore where English law was the proper law of the contract or where it provided the mandatory rules applicable to the employment relationship by virtue of the Rome convention an English court properly exercising jurisdiction had to construe the English statute in a way which was compatible with the EU right. Mr Bleuse who was a German national, living in Germany but employed by a company registered in the UK (although never working in the UK) was therefore able to bring a claim under the WTR in the English courts.

The Posting of Workers Directive ('POWD')

The POWD requires that, where a Member State has certain minimum terms and conditions of employment, these must also apply to workers posted temporarily by their employer to work in that State. A 'posted worker' is someone who, for a limited period, carries out his work in the territory of a European Community Member State other than the State in which he or she normally works. The POWD only applies to specified terms and conditions, such as minimum rates of pay, holiday entitlement, non-discrimination, etc. Existing UK legislation was amended as from the end of 1999 to guarantee minimum employment rights to workers posted temporarily to the UK. Employers posting workers throughout Europe will need to check that their contracts include local minimum provisions.

Existing employees transferred to another country

Staff employed in their home country, whether in the UK or elsewhere, may be asked to make short visits or to take up a longer-term assignment in another country. For short visits (for example, up to three months, although this varies between companies), it is usual for an employer to pay all of an employee's travel expenses, subject to company guidelines regarding mode and class of travel. Other considerations for short visits include:

- daily allowances to cover accommodation, food, laundry and other personal expenses;
- alternatively reimbursement of actual out-of-pocket expenses;
- daily allowances or salary mark-up to compensate for additional and unsocial hours, hardship and separation from family and normal social life; and
- additional insurance cover for medical expenses and emergency repatriation.

For longer visits, it is usual for an expatriate to be offered an international service agreement, which provides for matters such as:

- start and end dates of the international employment (and provisions for any extension);
- role, terms of reference or job description;
- status with respect to dependants, e.g., accompanied by spouse and children, accompanied by spouse without children, unaccompanied, single;
- salary based either on home country salary plus a mark-up to reflect extra and unsocial hours, relative hardship, relative cost of living, etc. (a build-up system) or on local market salaries for similar staff (a host country package);
- working hours (normally in accordance with local custom and practice);
- leave – amount and timing;
- passages – beginning and end of tour, leave passages for self and family;
- accommodation standards and rent and utility allowances (and who finds and provides);
- assistance with school fees for any children in the home or host country;
- taxation – employees must remain responsible for home and host country income tax liabilities, but the employer should build in appropriate provision in;
- the salary – sometimes salaries are quoted 'after host country tax', with the employer negotiating the amount due with the host country tax authorities. The employer may also agree to meet the cost of local professional advice taken by the employee in respect of this;
- medical costs – usually reimbursed under an international private medical insurance scheme. It is normal to require staff and accompanying family to undertake a medical before travelling. The agreement should clarify whether the costs of routine dental treatment, spectacles and cosmetic treatment are included and who bears the costs associated with any pregnancy;
- insurances – accident and property;
- pension scheme arrangements;
- termination and preparation provisions;
- rules requiring respect for local customs and other specific requirements; and
- rules for deduction of local tax and/or social security contributions.

Case study 2 – Deriving the international salary

Paula Bates is permanently employed in the UK and is going to Hong Kong on a 36-month assignment. The company use a build-up system based on the home country salary. She will not be liable to pay UK income tax on her salary from the date of departure, as the assignment extends over a complete tax year. She will, however, be liable to pay Hong Kong income tax at the applicable rate on that income. Elements of mark up for cost of living, hardship and tax equalisation are added to the standard salary and paid gross.

Expatriates recruited for the project

A service agreement similar to that for existing employees is often used, but with changes to exclude certain benefits available to established employees, such as pension. Alternatively, in countries with developed economies and freely convertible currencies, it is often simpler to employ expatriates on the same terms as local staff, paying them the market salary.

Local staff

Local staff are often nationals of the country where the project is being undertaken and will be employed in accordance with local employment laws and standards. It may be necessary to work through an established, locally-registered company, for example, a subsidiary, joint venture partner, or similar entity.

3 TAXATION OF SUBSISTENCE AND TRAVEL ALLOWANCES IN THE UK

Generally, employees are taxed on all income they receive from their employment including pay, benefits in kind (such as company cars) and any expenses payments (including payments relating to business travel). However, employees are entitled to tax relief on expenses incurred wholly exclusively and necessarily in the course of their duties of the employment. Where tax relief is available for travel expenses, relief will also be available for 'reasonable' subsistence. Tax relief is available in two ways.

(a) By *exemption* – certain payments or benefits in kind that an employee receives are technically subject to tax, but the employee is entitled to claim relief for such amounts. In such cases, the employer can claim a dispensation, which effectively renders the payments in question exempt from tax; and
(b) By *deduction* – certain amounts can be deducted from an employee's total income before arriving at the amount on which he or she will be taxed. Where relief is available by deduction, the employer must report expenses payments or benefits in kind to HMRC, and employees need to make a claim for further relief to their Tax Office.

The tax rules determine the amount on which relief is due. They do not determine the level of payment or provision an employer can or should make. So the amount paid by the employer may be more or less than the amount on which tax relief is available. If the employer pays the employee more than the tax allowable amount, the surplus will be chargeable to income tax and NICs.

Cost of travel to work

There is no tax relief for 'ordinary commuting' costs: that is, travel from home to a permanent workplace. Provision of free workplace parking is not currently a taxable benefit. Most travel from home to a temporary workplace will be allowable by exemption, for example travel to a temporary site. In addition, travel between workplace locations, for example different offices of the employing organisation, will also be similarly allowable. For most employees who have one normal workplace, the rules are fairly straightforward.

Private travel

There is no tax relief for travel undertaken for private reasons: that is, a journey between

- an employee's home and any other place they do not have to be for work purposes, or
- any two places where an employee does not have to be for work purposes.

Site-based employees and Working Rule Agreements ('WRA')

Employees who are site-based may receive travel and subsistence allowances at a flat rate set out in a WRA negotiated between the relevant trade union and employers organisations. HMRC is not a party to such agreements, but will often have agreed the tax treatment of payments within the WRA. For many agreements, payments for travelling time will be taxable, but agreed travel and/or subsistence allowances after an initial threshold distance will often be non-taxable. This provides a measure of clarity for both employer and employee. This treatment only applies to travel and subsistence; if the individual receives other benefits (for example, use of a van) normal taxation rules will apply.

General rules for site-based employees

Some individuals may have more than one 'normal' workplace; for example, someone who works in branch A on Mondays and Tuesdays, and branch B on Wednesdays to Fridays. As a general rule, HMRC applies a '40% test' so that where an employee attends a workplace for 40% or more of their time, that workplace will be considered 'permanent'. Below this threshold, HMRC will consider other factors, including frequency or pattern of attendance or the presence of 'permanent' office or support facilities. Where an individual has more than one permanent workplace, travel from home to *either* workplace will be considered as 'normal commuting' and any expenses reimbursed will be taxable. Travel between the workplaces will be allowable.

Conversely, where an employment is defined by a geographical area, (for example a sales area), and there is no permanent office or base, travel to the boundary of the area will be treated as 'commuting' but all travel within the defined area will be eligible for tax relief.

Site-based workers may spend short periods at each site before being relocated. In these circumstances, provided the assignment is not expected to (and does not in fact) exceed 24 months, the travel costs will qualify for relief.

Case study 3 – Travelling expenses and time

Fred Campbell is an engineer who is normally based in offices in London. He is assigned to a site for a period of twelve months and is reimbursed for the costs of local accommodation and travelling from home to site. This is paid tax free. However, the assignment is extended after nine months so that the total assignment will be more than 24 months. From the time of the extension, both income tax and NICs are payable on any travel and subsistence costs paid.

The amount of relief

Tax relief can be claimed on the full costs incurred, provided these are reasonable. As a general rule, where travel costs are eligible for relief, reasonable subsistence can also be claimed. What is 'reasonable' will depend on the timing and duration of the journey and the seniority of the worker. In most instances there are no standard allowances. HMRC may require receipts or other evidence that expenses have been incurred. If the costs are borne or reimbursed in full by the employer, no further relief can be claimed. However, to the extent that costs are not reimbursed, the employee can claim tax relief on the outstanding amount through the self-assessment tax return.

Where travel involves an overnight stay, costs of personal incidental expenses (such as private telephone calls or newspapers) which would not otherwise be allowable, they can be reimbursed by the employer without incurring a tax charge. This relief avoids a charge to income tax, but cannot be used to claim tax relief on such expenses borne by the employee. The employer can claim the exemption treatment by obtaining a dispensation from the local office of HMRC as set out above.

If an employer pays 'round sum allowances' to cover expenses, the allowance will generally be taxable, but the employee will be able to claim relief for expenses incurred. Exceptionally, it may be possible to agree an acceptable level of expense allowance with HMRC, but this is generally only available for overseas travel in locations where it may not be practical to obtain full receipts.

Cash advances in a foreign currency to cover business expenses are treated in the same way as advances in sterling; expenses incurred must be documented and the balance of any currency returned. Many organisations offer a company credit card to avoid the need for cash advances, however, HMRC still require expenditure to be supported by receipts.

Small allowances for clothing and tools

HMRC does allow standard levels of expenses for specific industries. These are small in amount and generally cover such items as tools and clothing. A list of these allowances can be obtained from any HMRC office.

HMRC requirements

The tax implications of expenses will be of concern to employers, not least because HMRC can require an employer to account for under-deductions of PAYE and NICs (with interest and/or penalties). This could arise, for example, where round sum allowances have been paid. Employers can also be fined for late or incorrect submission of tax returns, including returns of employee benefits in kind and expenses (forms P9D/P11D). Inspection of expenses records and receipts form a standard part of HMRC payroll audits.

HMRC will only take action against an employee if collusion is suspected in the avoidance of PAYE/NICs or where the employee has made a fraudulent claim for tax relief.

4 WRONGFUL AND UNFAIR DISMISSAL

4.1 Wrongful dismissal

There will be a wrongful dismissal if an employer breaches an employee's contract of employment in a way which terminates it, for example using shorter notice than the entitlement specified or in a way contrary to the terms set out. The normal remedy is for damages, which are limited to the loss of earnings during the notice period required to terminate the contract, if it had been performed on the basis that the employer would have given proper notice. Common law rarely requires an employer to reinstate a wrongly dismissed employee. Moreover, there is no requirement of fairness in any such dismissal.

Generally, dismissal on due notice will not be a breach of contract. If there is a breach of contract, the employee is also under a duty to mitigate his loss in most circumstances, i.e. take reasonable steps to find alternative employment.

Given the limited remedies available for wrongful dismissal, the statutory regime has created the separate concept of unfair dismissal.

4.2 Unfair dismissal

As previously mentioned in Section 2.6 of this chapter, an employee has the right not to be unfairly dismissed by his or her employer under Section 94(1) ERA. In determining whether an employee's dismissal is fair or unfair, the employer must show the reason for the dismissal and that it is either one of the potentially fair reasons prescribed by Section 98(2) ERA. The statutory provisions relating to unfair dismissal apply to all employees with continuous employment of one year or more. The six potentially fair reasons are:

- the capability or qualifications of the employee for performing work of the kind which he was employed by the employer to do;
- the conduct of the employee;
- retirement of the employee;
- redundancy of the employee;
- breach of some other legal requirement; or
- 'some other substantial reason' which justifies dismissal.

Capability

In most circumstances it will not be enough simply to assert that the individual is incapable of performing his or her job. In order for an employer to ensure that a dismissal is fair, it needs to demonstrate that it acted reasonably in the circumstances. In relying on capability as the reason for dismissal, the employee will need to be given a fair opportunity to improve, having been warned of the consequences of the failure to do so.

Conduct

General misconduct will not justify summary termination. Only gross misconduct of a nature which goes to the root of the relationship will do so. However, there must be a proper investigation of any allegations as to the individual's conduct, and he or she must be given a chance to make his or her case known. Again, dismissal must be a reasonable sanction. It must be made known that such conduct will constitute gross misconduct.

Retirement

Retirement will be the reason for dismissal where:

- the employee has no normal retirement age ('NRA') and the operative date of termination falls on or after the date on which the employee reaches 65;
- the employee has an NRA of 65 or older and the operative date of termination falls on or after the date the employee reaches that age;
- the employee has an NRA below 65 and that retirement age has been objectively justified.

Redundancy

A redundancy situation arises where the employer ceases to carry on business for the purposes for which or in the place in which the employee is employed, or where the requirements of the business for employees to carry out work of a particular kind have ceased or diminished or are expected to cease or diminish. Before selecting an individual for redundancy, it is essential to establish the appropriate pool of workers from whom to select, using objective criteria to do so. The criteria must be explained and considered in the process of individual consultation with the individual. The individual must be consulted as to ways of avoiding redundancies. There is also a requirement to look for suitable alternative employment, if it exists. An individual has the right of a trial period of up to four weeks in suitable alternative employment. For those with over two years' continuous employment, there is a right to a statutory redundancy payment on a tax free basis, calculated by reference to gross weekly wage (which is currently capped at £330), length of service and with a multiplier factor for age.

Breach of another enactment

This applies where the continued employment of an individual would be in contravention of another statute. An example of this would be where an individual had lost his or her driving licence, which was key to his or her employment, or where a work permit was required but not held by the individual. An employer must, however, consider whether there were alternative roles to which the individual could be deployed before resorting to dismissal.

Some other substantial reason

This is a general catch-all, but does not justify dismissal on any reason whatsoever. It must be material to the business, and be for a very real need. Mere convenience will not suffice. For example, in a business reorganisation leading to change in working practices or where the relationship has completely broken down for reasons other than conduct, dismissal must still be a reasonable response.

4.3 Automatically unfair dismissals

There are some instances where the law states that there will be an automatically unfair dismissal, irrespective of length of service. Examples include those dismissed because of health and safety responsibilities, for trade union activities or pregnancy.

4.4 Reasonableness

While the law will not substitute its own judgment for that of a reasonable employer, an employer must demonstrate that it has behaved reasonably throughout. It will need to demonstrate that it has acted in accordance with the spirit of the ACAS Code of Practice on disciplinary practice and procedures in respect of such matters as communication of the procedures, incremental stages, warnings, the right of representation at hearings, and the right to respond to any case. In addition, an employer must show that the rules of natural justice have been satisfied.

4.5 Disciplinary and grievance process

In October 2004 the Employment Act 2002 made it a legal requirement for all organisations to have disciplinary and grievance procedures in place. The statutory procedures amount to a minimum standard required of employers. Failure to follow the statutory procedures will render the dismissal automatically unfair for those employees with one year's service or more.

The statutory disciplinary procedure must be followed in virtually all dismissal situations (not just misconduct dismissals), for example, on the grounds of:

- redundancy;
- competency;

- ill-health; and
- expiry of a fixed term contract.

There are two procedures – the standard procedure (which will be used in most situations) and the modified procedure (used only in limited circumstances). The standard procedure involves three steps:

1. Sending the employee a written statement setting out in writing the employee's alleged conduct, capability or other circumstances which could lead to dismissal or taking disciplinary action against the employee (except for oral or written warnings or suspension on full pay) and inviting the employee to attend a meeting to discuss the matter;
2. Meeting between employer and employee, at a reasonable time and place, to discuss the issues set out in the statement. The meeting must take place before action is taken and the employee must be given a full opportunity to respond at the meeting; and
3. If the decision is taken to dismiss, the employer must provide the employee with written confirmation of this together with details of his or her right of appeal. It is for the employee to advise the employer of his or her wish to appeal and an appeal hearing must be arranged in the event that the employee wishes to appeal. After the appeal hearing, the employer must inform the employee of its final decision.

As previously mentioned, there is also a modified procedure which can be used if an employer has decided to dismiss an employee summarily. An employer will only be able to justify proceeding on this basis in limited circumstances, such as an instance of gross misconduct where an employer dismisses an employee immediately and without notice, where it is reasonable to dismiss the employee without making any enquiries.

An employer's failure to follow either of the procedures set out above (as appropriate) will make a dismissal automatically unfair. Where an employee fails to comply with the statutory dismissal procedure, a tribunal must decrease the amount of any award by 10% and may make a further reduction of up to 50% in total, if it deems it just and equitable to do so.

Where an employer fails to comply with the statutory dismissal procedure, a tribunal must increase the amount of any award by 10% and may make a further increase of up to 50% in total, if it deems it just and equitable to do so. Employers should, however, bear in mind that following the statutory procedure does not guarantee a finding of a fair dismissal at tribunal, if the dismissal was unfair for other reasons.

The statutory discipline and grievance procedures are expected to be repealed in April 2009. Instead, employers and employees will be expected to follow a revised ACAS Code of Practice on Discipline and Grievance. An unreasonable failure to follow the Code of Practice will potentially make employers liable for increased compensation (by up to 25%) in unfair dismissal cases. The Code of Practice will not be legally binding and a breach of it will not automatically lead to a finding of unfair dismissal.

4.6 Remedies

An employee who successfully claims unfair dismissal may seek the following remedies: compensation; reinstatement to his or her old job; or re-engagement to a different job but with the same employer or an associate employer. Compensation is the most popular remedy. A tribunal is entitled to make an award of compensation in two parts. Firstly, it may make a 'basic award', which is calculated on the basis of age, length of service and gross weekly wage (currently capped at £330) to a maximum of £9 900. In addition, the tribunal may make a compensatory award which is designed to compensate the employee for loss of salary and benefits to the date of the hearing, future loss of earnings and expenses incurred as a result of dismissal. The compensatory award is currently capped at £63 000.

Where a tribunal makes an order for reinstatement, but the employer fails to comply with it, the employee will be entitled to apply at a second hearing for further compensation, i.e. an 'Additional Award', unless the employer can show that it was not reasonably practicable to comply with the order. An Additional Award will be valued at between 26 and 52 weeks' pay, subject to the current statutory limits.

Case study 4 – Capability?

A member of staff has, over a period of two years, not been performing at the level expected for the job. The employer conducts annual career development reviews with all staff. Each employee meets with a manager to discuss performance, future plans and training and career development. At the last two annual reviews for this individual, the employer has discussed the employee's underperformance with him and has recorded the issues on the relevant review forms. The employee has, however, never been warned that he may be dismissed or demoted if he does not improve his performance and the company's capability procedure has not been followed. After the second review, the employee is dismissed without any further meetings regarding his performance. The employee takes the case to tribunal and wins compensation on grounds of unfair dismissal.

4.7 Taxation of termination payments

The taxation of payments to former employees in connection with termination of employment falls into two categories: contractual payments, which will be subject to income tax and NICs in the normal way; and other payments, which will be taxable only to the extent that they exceed £30 000. The rules apply to benefits as well as cash payments, for example the continuation of medical insurance or the use of a company car. If an employee has worked abroad, some tax relief may be available in relation to time spent outside the UK.

Payments arising out of the contract of employment

These will be subject to income tax and national insurance contributions as employment earnings. This category will include pay during a notice period, accrued holiday pay or any other contractual entitlements. In practice, most difficulties tend to arise where the notice period is not fulfilled and a payment is made *in lieu* of notice (PILON); the question arises whether the employer has paid damages for breach of contract (the first £30 000 of which is tax free) or has made a payment within the terms of the employment contract (which is taxable as set out above). PILONs will be considered to be contractual if the employer:

- is required to pay *in lieu* of notice if the contractual notice period is not honoured or
- has discretion to pay *in lieu* of notice and the employer exercised this right to make the payment (as opposed to paying damages for breach of contract).

In determining the content of the contract, it may be necessary to consider documents such as staff handbooks, where these form part of the employment contract. HMRC may seek to impute a contractual term by reference to past practice where an employer habitually makes payments in lieu of tax on termination of employment.

Whether an employer has exercised discretion or whether the payment represents damages for breach of contract, is strictly speaking a matter of fact. Where the amount is equivalent to pay for the notice period, HMRC is likely to tax it in full as a contractual reward. In contrast, where an employer can state that it has decided NOT to exercise its right, the payment may be viewed as damages (with the exemption for the first £30 000 compensation paid).

Other payments

Other payments in connection with the termination of employment which are not otherwise taxable, such as compensation for breach of contract or damages for wrongful dismissal, will be taxable under a separate charging provision, the first £30 000 of which will be tax-free. Such payments will often be made under a statutory compromise agreement.

Redundancy payments are derived from an employee's employment law rights, rather than from the terms of the employment contract. Therefore the first £30 000 of any payment is tax free.

Payments to an employee for entering into restrictive covenants are taxable in full. HMRC may examine a compromise agreement to check whether some or all of the payment made under the terms of the agreement is attributable to a restrictive covenant. Payments to a departing employee approaching retirement age will be taxable in full if they are paid as 'retirement benefits', rather than on a genuine redundancy. It is the employer's responsibility to determine whether a payment is taxable and HMRC will generally seek to recover any under-deduction of tax from the employer. In cases of uncertainty, HMRC may provide an advance ruling, which will only be binding if all relevant information is disclosed to it in that application.

4.8 Discrimination

4.8.1 Discrimination Law

In the UK, it is unlawful for an employer to discriminate against employees and applicants for employment on the grounds of sex, marital or civil partnership status, gender reassignment, age, race, colour, nationality, ethnic origin, religion or belief, sexual orientation and disability. The law relating to discrimination has developed in a piecemeal fashion and different pieces of legislation govern different types of discrimination. A new Equality Act is expected in 2009. It will bring all the different strands of discrimination law together in one place. The government has not yet released a draft bill but it is expected in late 2008.

A claim for discrimination may be brought before a tribunal if the claimant has suffered direct discrimination, indirect discrimination, victimisation or harassment. Briefly, an employer directly discriminates against an employee if it treats him or her less favourably on the basis of a personal feature, such as the employee's ethnic origin or sex. An employer discriminates indirectly against an employee where it makes that employee subject to a provision, criteria or practice (or, in some instances, a requirement or condition) which it applies equally to other employees but which puts that employee at a disadvantage. An employer may defend a claim for indirect discrimination (but not direct discrimination except in the case of direct discrimination on the grounds of age) if it can show that the discrimination was objectively justifiable. In *Bilka–Kaufhaus GmbH* v. *Weber von Hartz*, the ECJ held that, in order to satisfy the test of justification, the measures taken by the employer:

2.1 Ways of operating
2.2 Working with others
2.3 Working internationally
2.4 The engineer's appointment
2.5 Collateral warranties
2.6 Indemnity insurance
2.7 Employment law
2.8 Information technology

- must correspond to a real need on the part of the employer;
- must be appropriate with a view to achieving the objectives pursued; and
- must be necessary to that end.

It is for the tribunal to decide whether the employer's actions were objectively justifiable.

Note, however, that the law relating to age discrimination differs as both direct and indirect age discrimination may be objectively justifiable.

Victimisation occurs when an individual treats another individual (the 'victim') less favourably because the victim has done a 'protected act' or the individual knows or suspects that the victim has done or intends to do a 'protected act'. An example of a protected act is the victim bringing discrimination or equal pay proceedings, or alleging that a person has committed an act which would amount to a contravention of the discrimination legislation.

Harassment occurs where, on a prohibited ground, an individual engages in unwanted conduct which has the purpose or effect of violating another individual's dignity or creating an intimidating, hostile, degrading, humiliating or offensive environment for that individual. 'Prohibited grounds' include grounds relating to sex, race or ethnic origin, sexual orientation, disability, gender reassignment or age.

If a claimant can show a prima facie case of any form of discrimination, the burden of proof will shift to the employer, who will be required to demonstrate that discrimination has not taken place. If an employer cannot provide a non-discriminatory explanation for its conduct, a court may draw an adverse inference and make a finding of discrimination. Compensation awards for claims of discrimination are unlimited in amount.

4.9 Collective consultation

Under TULRCA, an employer must consult with trade unions or employee representatives when proposing to dismiss 20 or more employees at one establishment within a period of 90 days for a reason which is not individual e.g. redundancy. If the employer proposes to make between 20 and 99 employees redundant, it must start the consultation at least 30 days before the first proposed redundancy. If it proposes to make 100 or more employees redundant, the consultation must start at least 90 days before the first proposed redundancy. A failure to do so before any notices of dismissal are issued will almost certainly render dismissals unfair, and more particularly involves an additional penalty, namely a protective award of up to 90 days' uncapped pay for each affected employee. Consultation should take place with trade union representatives if there is an independent recognized trade union, failing which the employer should invite the workforce to elect representatives. If the workforce fails to elect representatives, then the employer should nonetheless communicate on the issue of dismissal to all the employees on an individual basis.

Collective consultation is not the same as collective bargaining, but it is still necessary to consult with a view to seeking agreement, disclosing reasons for the dismissals, how they will take effect and considering ways of avoiding them.

Since April 2005, the duty to consult collectively must also be considered in light of any obligations the employer may have under the information and consultation of Employees Regulations 2004 ('ICE Regulations'). If those obligations arise, then the ICE Regulations allow employees in organisations with at least 50 employees to be:

- informed about the business' economic situation;
- informed and consulted about employment prospects; and

- informed and consulted about decisions likely to lead to substantial changes in work organization or contractual relations, including redundancies and transfers.

In order to satisfy the requirements of the ICE Regulations, employers should set up information and consultation operations, such as staff forums and national works council, which enable the employer to consult the workforce. ACAS recommends that employers keep employees informed both face to face with one-to-one and team meetings or at arm's length using company handbooks, newsletters, notices and electronic methods such as emails and intranets. Managers should not rely on 'the grapevine' to pass on news and information accurately.

5 TUPE TRANSFERS

The Transfer of Undertakings (Protection of Employment) Regulations 1981 ('TUPE 1981') implemented Directive 77/187/EC ('Acquired Rights Directive') in the UK and was introduced to protect the rights of employees on the transfer of an undertaking. On 6 April 2006, TUPE 1981 was repealed and replaced by TUPE 2006, which implemented EC Directive 2001/23 in the UK.

Amongst other things, TUPE 2006 widened the scope of TUPE 1981 to cover more clearly outsourced and insourced services, as well as the assignment of services by a client to a new contractor. English courts and employment tribunals are required to give TUPE 2006 a purposive construction, i.e. to give effect to the purpose of the underlying Directive, which is to safeguard employees' rights on the transfer of a business. Courts and tribunals are bound by decisions of the ECJ in applying TUPE 2006.

5.1 When does TUPE apply?

TUPE 2006 applies whenever there is a 'relevant transfer', which is defined in the legislation as:

- a transfer of a business, undertaking or part of a business or undertaking where there is a transfer of an economic entity that retains its identity ('business transfer'). A part of a business can include just one employee as there is no specified threshold in terms of employee numbers; or
- a client engaging a contractor to do work on its behalf, reassigning such a contract or bringing the work in-house ('service provision change').

Relevant transfers may, however, be both a business transfer *and* a service provision change.

Business transfers

In order to establish whether a business transfer has taken place, it is necessary to consider whether

- an economic entity is being transferred; and
- the economic entity retains its identity following the transfer.

TUPE 2006 defines an 'economic entity' as 'an organised grouping of resources that has the objective of pursuing an economic activity, whether or not that activity is central or ancillary'.

The definition is not, therefore, limited to a going concern. To establish whether there is an 'economic entity', the Courts will consider a number of non-exhaustive factors to see if TUPE applies, such as whether:

- physical assets are transferred;
- intangible assets, such as goodwill, are transferred and their value;
- staff are transferred;
- the customer circle remains the same;
- the business remains similar before and after transfer; and
- there was any interruption to the business, and, if so, its duration.

None of these factors will be independently conclusive.

In identifying whether an economic entity has been transferred, it is necessary to consider whether the economic entity still exists post-transfer. The case of *Spijkers* v. *Gebroeders Benedik Abbatoir* established the 'going concern' test, i.e. an economic entity is transferred whether the operation is being continued, or has been taken over, by the transferee carrying on with the same or similar economic activities. Consideration should be given to the following factors:

- has goodwill been transferred?
- who is servicing the seller's intangible assets?
- what activities were carried on before and after the transfer?

Note, however, that the importance of each factor will vary according to the nature of the transaction. A change in the way that the business of an economic enterprise is carried out does not necessarily prevent TUPE 2006 applying.

A transfer can happen in one stage, or involve a series of transfers.

Service provision changes

Where there is a change in service provider, there will be a transfer directly from the outgoing contractor to the subsequent contractor. TUPE 2006 sets out a detailed definition of a service provision change. It is necessary for one person to cease to provide the activities and for another to take them over. TUPE 2006 also specifies the situations in which there will *not* be a service provision charge, for example, when the client intends that the activities will be carried out in connection with a single specific event or task of a short-term duration.

Note, however, that employment tribunals will focus on the intention of the parties. It is unlikely that the effects of the legislation could be avoided by entering into a series of short-term contracts or deliberately rotating the employees who provide the service.

5.2 What are the consequences of TUPE 2006 applying?

All of the transferor's rights, powers, duties and liabilities under or in connection with the contract are transferred to the transferee, including any claims and liabilities arising before the transfer. All those employed by the transferor transfer to the transferee on their existing terms of employment.

All terms and conditions involving benefits such as company cars, private health assurance, loans and life assurance will transfer. Where benefits cannot be identically matched, for example, where a profit share is calculated by reference to the transferor's profits, a similar benefit will have to be provided by the transferee. Failure to match existing terms risks claims by the employees concerned for breach of contract on the ground of unilateral variation of the contract without consent.

All collective agreements relating to the transferring employees automatically transfer, binding the transferee. Union recognition also transfers to the transferee, provided that the organised grouping retains a distinct identity after the transfer. The transferee may, however, de-recognize the union if it so wishes, and bring the collective agreement to an end. Those terms which have been incorporated into the employee's contract will, however, continue to be effective.

5.3 Who transfers?

Where there is a TUPE 2006 transfer, those employees employed by the transferor and 'assigned to the organised grouping of resources or employees that is subject to the relevant transfer' will transfer to the transferee under their existing terms of employment and with their continuity of employment unbroken. Whether or not an employee is 'assigned to an organised grouping' is a question of fact. If an employee is multi-skilled and has a range of functions, the law will consider to which undertaking, as a matter of fact, he or she can be said to be assigned.

TUPE 2006 does not specify a percentage of time which an employee must spend working for an organised grouping before it is regarded as being 'assigned' to it. TUPE 2006 does not transfer any employees who are only temporarily assigned. When determining whether or not an assignment is 'temporary', regard should be given to the length of the assignment and whether a date has been set for the employee's return.

The transferor must provide the transferee with certain 'employee liability information', on an accurate basis, before the transfer. If the transferor fails to do so it risks being liable to pay significant compensation to the transferee.

5.4 How does TUPE apply to rights under pension schemes?

Old age, invalidity and survivors' benefits under occupational pension schemes do not transfer under TUPE 2006 because they are expressly excluded by Regulation 10. An obligation for an employer to pay a percentage of salary into an employee's pension scheme will not fall within the above exemption and will therefore be covered by the automatic transfer principle.

The exclusion does not, however, apply to other benefits under an occupational pension scheme, i.e. those which are not old age, invalidity or survivors' benefit.

Thus, if the transferor had an obligation to provide pension benefits to its employees, that obligation does not pass to the transferee following the relevant transfer, but remains with the transferor. However, because the employees now employed by the transferee cannot continue to accrue benefit under the transferor's pension scheme, it is usual for the transferor to require the transferee to offer comparable pension benefits for the employees who are transferred to it.

For this reason, business transfers on outsourcings will invariably involve the parties setting up pension arrangements for the transferring employees which are broadly equivalent to those they enjoyed with the transferor. This is done either by granting the employees the right to enter an existing pension scheme of the transferee or by the transferee creating a new scheme for the purpose. This is expected as standard practice by the Government in transfers involving the public sector.

Employees who accept an invitation to join the pension arrangements of the transferee will usually also be given the opportunity to choose whether to have their rights earned in the transferor's pension scheme transferred to the transferee's scheme. If the employees choose to leave the rights with the transferor's scheme, they will on their ultimate retirement receive separate pensions from the transferor's scheme and the transferee's scheme in relation to their different service periods. If the employees do agree to the transfer of rights they will receive a single pension from the transferee's scheme which incorporates the entitlements earned in the transferor's scheme.

In the case of *Beckmann* v. *Dynamco Whicheloe MacFarlane Ltd* the ECJ ruled that early retirement benefits on the basis of redundancy do not fall within the exemption granted to occupational pension schemes by the Acquired Rights Directive. As indicated above, new contractors do not have to give employees who transfer to them equal pension rights to those they enjoyed under their previous employer but this means that a significant unfunded liability in an occupational pension scheme in the event of redundancy (or on retirement other than on the ground of reaching the relevant normal retirement age) could transfer (as to which see below).

Since 6 April 2005, transferees have been obliged to provide pension benefits for transferring employees where:

- there is a TUPE transfer;
- the employee in question becomes employed by the transferee rather than the transferor;
- immediately before the transfer there is an occupational pension scheme in relation to which the transferor is the employer and the employee is either an active member of the scheme; or eligible to be such a member; or in a probationary period to become eligible to be a member.

Where the transferor's scheme is a defined benefit scheme, the transferring employee automatically qualifies for protection. Where the transferor's scheme provides money purchase benefits, the transferring employee only qualifies for protection if the transferor was required to make employer contributions. If the transferor was not required to make employer contributions, the transferring employee will qualify for protection if the transferor made at least one such contribution.

Where an employee qualifies for protection, it becomes a term of their contract with the transferee that the employee will be offered access to a money purchase scheme or a defined benefit scheme. The transferee may decide which arrangement to offer the new employees and is not obliged to match the type of scheme offered by the transferor. Where the transferee offers its new employees a money purchase scheme, it is required to match the employee's contributions up to a maximum of 6% of earnings per annum.

5.5 Varying terms and conditions

Under TUPE 1981, attempts to vary terms and conditions for a reason connected with a transfer were void. Under TUPE 2006, however, changes are only void if the sole or principal reason for the change is the transfer itself or a reason connected with a transfer which is not an economic technical or organisational ('ETO') reason entailing changes in the workforce.

Changes may be made to employment terms before or after a transfer where the sole or principal reason is unconnected with the transfer or is connected with the transfer but is an ETO reason. This change to the law remains controversial and it remains to be seen how the Courts will interpret it.

5.6 How are reorganisations and dismissals affected?

Dismissals of employees with continuous employment of a year or more will automatically be unfair where the sole or principal reason for dismissal is the transfer itself or a reason connected with the transfer which is not an ETO reason entailing changes in the workforce. The protection against dismissal applies to both those employees who transfer and any other employees who are dismissed as a result of the transfer. The rule can apply to dismissals by both transferor and transferee.

This defence is unavailable where there is a bare attempt to harmonise the terms and conditions of the transferring staff with those of the transferee's existing staff. It would, however, include a redundancy scenario after transfer. In such cases, [the transferee or transferor] would still have to follow a redundancy procedure and make the necessary payments, dealing with any enhanced severance terms that had transferred. In addition, recent case law has thrown doubt on the ability of transferors to make employees redundant for a reason that only arises after the transfer.

5.7 What consultations have to take place?

Both the transferor and the transferee must consult with employee representatives prior to the transfer. TUPE 2006 also requires the transferor to provide certain information about the transferring employees, for example, the identity and age of the employees who will transfer and information on any collective agreements affecting those employees which will still have effect after the transfer. If there are recognized trade unions present, they must be used for the purposes of consultation with staff in the scope of recognition. Otherwise, elected representatives can be consulted. In the absence of such representatives, the affected employees must be invited to elect representatives. If they do not, the employer has a defence if it gives out information on the transfer on an individual basis.

No specific timetable is laid down for the provision of information to the relevant trade union or employee, but particular terms and information must be provided, to the trade union or employee representatives namely:

- the fact of the transfer, the reason for it being proposed, and when it is proposed that it will take place;
- the legal, economic and social consequences of the transfer;
- any measures proposed by the employer in respect of affected employees; and
- the transferor must state the measures which the transferee envisages it will take in relation to the transferring employees in connection with the transfer. If the transferee envisages taking no measures that fact should be stated or, if none, the fact that there are none.

In relation to the last bullet point, a transferee is obliged to provide the information to the transferor in sufficient time to allow the transferor to perform its obligation to give the information to the trade union or employee representatives (as appropriate).

The obligation to consult with the recognized trade union and/or employee representatives is triggered if the employer envisages that, in connection with the transfer, it will be taking measures in relation to any affected employees. In practice, however, the provision of information is likely to trigger the consultation process.

Failure to comply with the obligations to inform and/or consult may result in the trade union or employee representatives bringing a claim in the employment tribunal. If successful, the tribunal will make a declaration that the claim was well founded and will award compensation to the relevant affected employees of up to 13 weeks' uncapped pay each.

Under TUPE 2006, both the transferor and the transferee are jointly and severally liable for:

- any compensation awarded by a tribunal against the transferor for failure to inform and consult; and
- any failure by the transferor or transferee to pay compensation that has been ordered by the tribunal for a failure to inform or consult.

The representatives of the transferring employees will be able to bring a claim against either or both of the parties and the Tribunal will then apportion liability. Where the transferor establishes that it failed to inform or consult because the transferee failed to give it the relevant information, the tribunal *may* order the transferee to pay the compensation.

It is the employer's responsibility to ensure that the elections of employee representatives are fair. The employer must make sure that there are sufficient representatives. Before the election, while the employer can decide the length of time that the employee representative's term of office will last, it must be sufficiently long to enable the proper provision of information and full consultation to take place.

No affected employee can be unreasonably excluded from standing for election and all employees affected by the proposals at the date of election will be entitled to vote for an employee representative. The election must be conducted in secret and votes counted accurately. Where, after the election, one of the elected representatives ceases to act as an employee representative, another representative will have to be elected in accordance with the relevant rules outlined above. Employees who have been elected as representatives, acted as such, stood for election or taken part in an election of employee representatives have the right not to be dismissed or to suffer any detriment as a result.

5.8 Commercial context

As an indication only, commercial negotiations and agreements should consider:

- as a condition of any agreement, identifying which employees are transferring, and their terms and conditions, by way of due diligence and disclosure;
- warranties as to the accuracy of such information;
- indemnification for liabilities before and after transfer, in other words the transferor indemnifying the transferee for liabilities before transfer when the transferor is in control and the transferee indemnifying the transferor for liabilities arising after transfer when the transferee is in control;
- treatment of occupational pensions and benefits will require detailed consideration and implementation of similar schemes;
- consultation with the staff by both transferor and transferee;
- if it is an outsourcing or joint venture, since these will not last forever; and
- what happens on exit, i.e. whether staff retransfer.

5.9 Right to object

Transferring staff have a right to object to their transfer to a new employer. If an employee informs either the transferor or the transferee of their wish to object, his or her employment with the transferee is treated as terminating with effect from the transfer date. Since there will have been no dismissal or resignation, the employee would not be entitled to any statutory or contractual compensation on termination. An individual is not, however, prevented from maintaining that he or she has been constructively dismissed, as such a claim is not precluded by exercising the right to object.

Case study 5 – Post-transfer integration of terms and conditions after a TUPE transfer

Staff working for a public sector organisation are transferred to a private company under TUPE. Under their terms and conditions they have a right to a limited free physiotherapy treatment under a policy taken out by their previous employer. The new employer does not have such a policy but replaces this with the right to free private medical insurance for the employees and their families under a company scheme. The employees also had a right to more days' annual leave with the previous employer than the private sector employer normally allows. The new employer reduces the annual leave entitlement and increases the salary by a day's pay for each day of leave lost. The company has a policy of allowing staff to take unpaid leave by prior arrangement. Staff who wish to take the same amount of leave as before may take the extra as unpaid leave. The benefits after the transfer are at least as good as the benefits before the transfer so it would be difficult for employees to demonstrate any true loss even if there is a technical breach.

6 WTR

What follows is a brief summary of the WTR, which came into force on 1 October 1998, to implement the EC Working Time Directive. The WTR take advantage of a number of 'derogations', i.e. permitted exceptions to the Directive's application. Employers should consider which exceptions, if any, are available to them.

6.1 Coverage

The WTR apply to workers over the minimum school leaving age. 'Worker' covers those with a contract of employment plus a wider group undertaking work under various forms of contract (for example agency workers, temporary workers and freelancers), but not the genuinely self-employed operating a business on their own account. The WTR do not apply equally to all workers and some types of worker are excluded, for example sea and air transport workers (to whom specific legislation applies) and independent service providers.

Certain special provisions relate to adolescent workers; i.e. those over the minimum school leaving age but under 18.

6.2 Meaning of 'working time' and record keeping

'Working time' is defined as any period during which the worker is working, carrying out his duties or is at the employer's disposal; any period during which the worker is receiving 'relevant training'; or any additional period which is agreed in an agreement (such as an employment contract or workforce agreement) to be 'working time'. Sensible employers will define 'working time' by agreement from the outset. Records must be kept of time worked. Failure to do so will be a criminal offence, as well as depriving an employer of evidence in disputes with employees. Records need not be kept in relation to those 'opting out' (see Section 6.3 below) but it is prudent to keep such records in case of any health and safety challenges from such individuals. Certain days are excluded from the calculation of working time, such as annual leave, sick leave, and maternity leave.

6.3 Weekly working hours limits

The WTR set a limit of an average 48 hours per week over a standard averaging period of 17 weeks. That can be extended to 26 weeks if the workers are covered by derogations, or up to 12 months by collective or workforce agreement.

Individuals may voluntarily agree to disapply the weekly working hours limit by 'opting out'. They must do so in writing, and the opt-out can last for a fixed period or indefinitely. Any opted-out worker can cancel his or her opt-out by giving at least

2.1 Ways of operating
2.2 Working with others
2.3 Working internationally
2.4 The engineer's appointment
2.5 Collateral warranties
2.6 Indemnity insurance
2.7 Employment law
2.8 Information technology

seven days' notice, unless the opt-out agreement provides for longer notice, which cannot exceed three months.

6.4 Measures relating to night time working

The WTR make particular provisions for 'night workers', which limit their shifts and require employers to offer them regular health assessments. These limits are in addition to the limit on average weekly working time.

'Night work' is 11 p.m. to 6 a.m., unless defined by an employment contract, collective agreement or workforce agreement, then being at least seven hours between 12 a.m. and 5 a.m. Night workers are subject to a limit of an average of eight hours in each 24-hour period, again over 17 weeks, but this can be extended. Night workers whose work involves special hazards or heavy physical or mental strain are subject to an eight-hour limit for each 24-hour period (without averaging).

Adult night workers must be offered a health assessment (an adolescent worker a 'health and capacities assessment') before being required to perform night work, and periodically thereafter. Those with illnesses relating to night work may have to be moved.

In the case of *SIMAP*, the ECJ held that, if there is a business and operational need for a worker to be present on-call at the premises and available for the purpose of providing continuity of service, this should be viewed as working time.

6.5 Rest periods and breaks

Under the WTR, adult workers are entitled to one day off each week. Adolescent workers are entitled to two days off. Both are subject to derogations in certain circumstances.

Adult workers are entitled to 11 hours' consecutive rest per day. Adolescent workers are entitled to 12 hours' consecutive rest per day. Both are subject to derogations in certain circumstances.

Adult workers are entitled to a minimum 20 minute rest break if their working day is longer than six hours. Adolescent workers are entitled to a minimum 30 minute rest break if they work for longer than four and a half hours. Both are subject to derogations in certain circumstances. There is also a requirement to alleviate 'monotonous' work.

6.6 Paid annual leave

All workers (including temps) are entitled to 4.8 weeks' paid annual leave (this was increased from 4 weeks in October 2007). This is equivalent to 24 days for a full-time worker who works a five day week. The minimum annual leave entitlement will increase to 5.6 weeks in April 2009 (28 days for a worker who works a five day week). A leave year will run from 1 October unless otherwise agreed. Where a worker's employment commences after the beginning of the annual leave period, the worker is entitled after one month to annual leave in proportion to the length of the annual leave year which is outstanding at the commencement of employment. If pay is not agreed, it will be averaged over the last 12 weeks. There cannot be payment in lieu except on termination or, until April 2009, in respect of the additional 0.8 weeks introduced in October 2007. Employers can require employees to take or postpone leave in certain circumstances, and there are notice provisions for both sides. Where there are part-time workers, it is sensible to make clear how any payment entitlement will be pro rata.

Employers have made a number of attempts to 'roll up' holiday pay. In the case of *Marshalls Clay* v. *Caulfield and Ors*, the EAT held that it was lawful to roll up holiday pay provided that:

(1) it was clearly incorporated into the contract and expressly agreed by the worker;
(2) the allocation of pay to holiday was clearly identified in the contract and preferably also in the worker's pay slip;
(3) reasonably practicable steps were taken to require workers to take their holiday;
(4) records of holiday were kept.

The Marshall Clay decision was appealed to the Court of Appeal which decided to refer the issue of rolled up holiday pay to the ECJ. The ECJ held that rolled up holiday pay is unlawful but that any sums already paid to the worker under a rolled up holiday pay scheme could be set off against the holiday pay due to the worker, provided the arrangements are sufficiently transparent and comprehensive and the sums represent an addition to pay for work done. The UK government has not amended the WTR to reflect this decision. However, DBERR's guidance does state that rolled up holiday pay is considered unlawful and payment for statutory holiday should be made at the time when leave is taken. Despite this, a recent EAT case of *Lyddon* v. *Englefield Brickwork Limited* found that an employer could offset rolled up holiday pay against a worker's entitlement to annual leave under the WTR. However, in light of the ECJ judgment and DBERR's guidance employers should still be cautious about rolling up holiday pay and adopt alternative arrangements for paying holiday pay.

6.7 Derogations

There are certain derogations (i.e. exceptions) to the requirements set out above which are summarised below.

(a) *Unmeasured working time:* exceptions from breaks, rest periods, the length of night shifts and the maximum working week. This covers workers whose working time is not measured and/or predetermined or can be determined themselves. Examples include managing executives and family workers. Effectively these workers will only be subject to the paid annual leave provisions. Also, part of a worker's time (even if other time is fixed) can in certain circumstances be unmeasured where they undertake it voluntarily and not at the employer's direction; obviously, however, this would not include overtime.
(b) *Specified circumstances:* exceptions from breaks, rest periods, and the length of night shifts, as long as the workers receive compensatory rest. The specified circumstances include security and surveillance activities, activities involving the need for continuity of service of production (such as dock work, hospital services, the provision of utilities, civil protection services and agriculture) and where there is a foreseeable surge of activity such as in tourism. Other specified circumstances include the situation where the worker must travel long distances between a temporary place of work (for example a site) and home, and it is better to work longer hours for a shorter period to complete the work.
(c) *Force majeure:* where there are unexpected and unpredictable occurrences beyond an employer's control such as imminent danger. Compensatory rest must still be given.
(d) *Shift workers:* exceptions from daily and weekly rest periods exist for workers with a shift pattern where employees succeed each other, but compensatory rest must still be given.
(e) *Collective or workforce agreements:* exceptions from daily and weekly rest periods. Collective agreements can be made with an independent trade union. Workforce agreements can be made with workers where there is no recognised

trade union. In the case of workforce agreements, the workforce can either sign the agreement individually (for small firms with under 21 employees) or the workforce can elect representatives to negotiate on their behalf. The WTR provide a mechanism for representatives to be chosen and detail how an agreement is to be reached.

6.8 Enforcement

The limits (for example which relate to weekly working time and night work) and the obligations to keep detailed records will be enforced by the health and safety enforcing authorities, for example the Health and Safety Executive and local authorities.

7 COLLECTIVE CONSULTATION

7.1 When is consultation required?

Collective consultation when there is a transfer of an undertaking or mass dismissals has already been described at Sections 4.7 and 5.7 of this chapter respectively. Where the employer proposes mass dismissals; for example because of a tactic of dismissal and re-engagement on new terms to force through a variation of contract, aside from other consequences, the employer will need to consult collectively as if it were a redundancy approach, before any notices of dismissal can be issued. This is because the original European Collective Redundancies Directive, which was implemented in the UK by TULRCA, refers to mass dismissals unrelated to the individual workers, which is wider than the UK perspective of a 'redundancy'.

The ICE Regulations, as referred to at Section 4.8 above, may also be applicable here.

Many employers nowadays embrace the notion of a staff council with elected representatives of the workforce. The aim is to provide a forum for consultation over changes, health and safety issues, proposed redundancies, etc. A staff council does not, however, have a legal standing apart from where it is part of a European Works Council arrangement. It would not prevent claims for compulsory trade union recognition, as discussed below.

7.2 Trade union recognition

The Employment Relations Act 1999 allows employees to have a trade union recognised by their employer where the majority of the relevant workforce wishes it, i.e. where a majority of those voting and at least 40% of those eligible to vote are in favour of recognition. A trade union or union seeking recognition to be entitled to conduct collective bargaining for a bargaining unit of workers may make a request to the Central Arbitration Committee ('CAC'). The scope of collective bargaining is limited to pay, hours, conditions of work and holidays. The request must be preceded by a request to the employer. The employer must employ at least 21 workers when the request is made, or as an average over the last 13 weeks. In the first 10 working days, the employer can end the proceedings by agreeing to a bargaining unit and recognition. Failing that, the employer can indicate a willingness to negotiate for 20 working days after this first period, or longer if both sides agree. If the employer fails to respond or rejects the request in the first 10 working days, the application goes to the CAC. If the negotiations in the 20 working day period fail, the application goes to the CAC, unless the employer proposes that ACAS assist negotiations within 10 working days of stating a willingness to negotiate. In the latter case, the union is barred from proceeding if it rejected the proposal to use ACAS or failed to accept it.

7.3 Deciding the bargaining unit

Once an application is before the CAC, it must assist the parties to reach an agreement within 20 working days, or on an extended period which it sets. If there is no agreement, then within the following 10 days the CAC itself must decide the appropriate bargaining unit. It will take into account the following factors:

- the need for the unit to be compatible with the effective management; the views of the employer and the union(s);
- existing national and local bargaining arrangements;
- the desirability of avoiding fragmented bargaining within the undertaking;
- the characteristics of workers within the proposed unit and other employees whom the CAC considers relevant; and
- the location of workers.

7.4 Sufficient support

Once the bargaining unit is agreed or decided, the CAC must then decide whether the union is likely to have the support of the majority of the workers in the bargaining unit. If the union shows that the majority are members of the unions, the CAC must automatically award recognition. However, if the CAC believes it is in the interests of good industrial relations, or

(a) 'significant' number of the union members inform the CAC that they do not want collective bargaining; or
(b) evidence leads to the CAC doubting that a sufficient number of members want collective bargaining (such as the circumstances of becoming union members or the duration of membership), then the CAC must hold a ballot.

Other than in cases of majority membership, the CAC can only proceed with an application by way of a ballot, and then only if at least 10 % of the workers are members of the union and there is evidence that a majority would be likely to favour recognition for collective bargaining.

7.5 The ballot

The ballot will be conducted independently, with gross costs shared 50–50 between employer and the union. It may be by post or at the workplace(s). The union must be given 'reasonable' access to the workers to inform them of the ballot's object and seek support. The employer must also give the CAC the workers' home addresses for forwarding union information. Provided that a majority of the workers voting and 40% or more of the bargaining unit are in favour, recognition will then be granted.

7.6 The consequences of recognition

Once recognition is granted, the parties will negotiate for 42 days to agree a method by which they are to conduct collective bargaining. Failing agreement, the CAC must specify a method. No model formula is set out. An agreement reached or specified will have legal effect, and the only remedy available will be specific performance, i.e. a court order can compel either side to comply with the prescribed method of collective bargaining.

7.7 Derecognition

There is a similar procedure for derecognition. This largely mirrors the recognition procedure, for example, if the employer has less than 21 workers, or at least 10% of the workers favour an end to recognition and there is evidence that a majority would support derecognition. New recognition/derecognition applications to the CAC will only be allowed after three years.

Last, but not least, an employee campaigning for recognition will be protected against detrimental treatment. Also, if the employee were dismissed for campaigning, that would automatically be an unfair dismissal, irrespective of length of service, and any selection for redundancy on such a ground would also be unfair.

7.8 Existing voluntary trade union recognition

Training will not be automatically covered by an award of trade union recognition. Instead, employers must inform and consult about training with recognised trade unions. In other words, this will embrace a situation where trade unions are voluntarily recognised. This should be at least every six months, with the employer providing the union with enough information two weeks beforehand, without which the unions would be impeded in negotiations. An employer must respond to written representations at the meeting within four weeks. If an employer fails to comply, an employment tribunal can award up to two weeks' pay for each employee affected.

8 LEGISLATION UPDATE: RECENT AND FORTHCOMING LEGISLATION

This section gives brief details of recent and forthcoming UK legislation that affects employment.

8.1 Recent legislation

Health Act 2006 ('Health Act')

Under the provisions of the Health Act and five new sets of related regulations, smoking in enclosed or substantially enclosed public places and workplaces in England was banned with effect from 1 July 2007. The Smoke-free Premises etc (Wales) Regulations 2007 brought the smoking ban into force in Wales on 2 April 2007. In Scotland a similar ban came into force on 26 March 2006 and in Northern Ireland on 30 April 2007.

Working Time (Amendment) Regulations 2007

Introduced on 1 October 2007, this legislation increased paid employees' annual leave entitlement from 4.4 to 4.8 weeks per annum. On 1 April 2009, statutory annual leave entitlement will increase from 4.8 weeks to 5.6 weeks per annum.

Companies Act 2006 ('CA 2006')

The CA 2006 introduced a statutory statement of duties which replaced many existing common law and equitable rules. The provision on the general duties of directors came into force on 1 October 2007, other than the duty to avoid conflicts of interest, duty to accept benefits from third parties and duty to declare an interest in proposed transaction or arrangement, which came into force on 1 October 2008.

Equality Act 2006 ('EA')

This piece of legislation, which came into effect on 1 October 2007, established a Commission for Equality and Human Rights ('CEHR') to replace the existing equality commissions. The CEHR has been given powers to promote human rights and strives to prevent discrimination on the grounds of race, sex, disability, age, religion and beliefs, and sexual orientation. The EA contains a number of other provisions, such as a prohibition on discrimination on the ground of religion or belief in the provision of goods and services and the introduction of a duty on public bodies to promote gender equality.

Data Protection Act 1998 ('DPA')
On 24 October 2007, the remaining provisions of the DPA came into force. Any manual filing systems in existence before 24 October 1998 is required to comply with the DPA.

Sex Discrimination Act 1975 (Amendment) Regulations 2008
Women with an expected week of childbirth on or after 5 October 2008 can bring a claim of sex discrimination if they do not continue to receive all the benefits of their terms and conditions of employment (except remuneration) throughout both ordinary and additional maternity leave.

National Minimum Wage Act 1998 (NMWA)
Increases in the national minimum wage took effect on 1 October 2008 and rose to: standard (adult) rate (workers over 22 years of age) £5.73 (up from £5.52); development rate (workers between 18 and 21 years of age) £4.77 (up from £4.60), young workers rate (workers under 18) £3.53 (up from £3.40).

Maternity & Parental Leave etc and the Paternity & Adoption Leave (Amendment) Regulations 2008
Employees giving birth or adopting on or after 5 October 2008 have the right to the same terms and conditions during additional maternity and adoption leave (an extra 26 weeks) as enjoyed by employees during the ordinary maternity and adoption leave period.

8.2 Forthcoming legislation

Work and Families Act 2006 ('WFA')
This legislation provides the Government with the power to extend and modify certain employment rights. The Government is expected to use this legislation to give employed fathers, or the partner of the mother, regardless of sex, a new right of up to 26 weeks' Additional Paternity Leave, some of which may be paid if the mother returns to work before the end of her maternity leave period. This will be introduced alongside the extension of maternity pay to 12 months. The relevant regulations have not yet been published but are expected to come into force in April 2010.

Employment Bill 2008 ('EB 2008')
The Bill proposes a number of changes to employment law, including repealing the need for statutory dismissal and grievance procedures, extending ACAS's powers of conciliation and reviewing fixed conciliation periods. The Bill is currently progressing through Parliament with an anticipated implementation date of April 2009.

The Equality Bill
The government published detailed information about a proposed Equality Act in June 2008. Current proposals include: positive workplace discrimination towards under represented groups in the workplace; a single equality duty for public bodies, to cover gender, race, disability, gender reassignment, age, sexual orientation and religion/belief; and an extension of the prohibition of age discrimination to the provision of

goods, facilities, services and the carrying out of public functions. It is intended to introduce the Bill in the next parliamentary session in late 2008.

Temporary Agency Workers' Directive

Political agreement on the Temporary Agency Workers' Directive was reached in June 2008. The proposed directive will give temporary agency workers the right to be treated in the same way as the client's workers from the start of their assignment with the client. In the UK agreement has already been reached to derogate from this and temporary workers will only be entitled to equal treatment after a 12 week qualifying period. Further, in the UK equal treatment will not extend to statutory sick pay and pension payments. The directive must now go back to the European parliament for a further reading.

Working Time Directive

Political agreement to amend the Working Time Directive was reached in June 2008. The directive will introduce a new definition of 'on-call time'. It will include time spent on-call at the workplace and 'inactive on-call time' during which the worker is not required to 'effectively carry out his activity or duties'. Inactive time will not be regarded as either working time or a rest period. Workers will also retain the right to opt-out of the 48 hour week. However, an opt-out signed at the same time as an employment contract or within 4 working weeks of starting work will be void. Each worker will have to renew their opt-out after a year (unless national law provides otherwise). Workers will not be permitted to work more than 60 hours per week averaged over 3 months unless permitted in a collective agreement or otherwise agreed.

CHAPTER 2.8

Information technology in the construction industry

Clive Seddon
Pinsent Masons

Derek Blundell
Derek Blundell Consulting

1 INTRODUCTION

Although IT remains a hard sell in the construction industry, there are a number of factors which are leading and will in the future lead to greater investment in and development of IT within the construction industry. Perhaps the most significant is the move by the industry into services. A number of contractors see themselves, and wish to be seen by their customers and the markets, as services providers supplying a range of services including in some cases IT and telecommunications infrastructure services. This marks a significant strategic shift by the industry. If it wishes to compete in the public and private sectors in this area, it knows that it has to invest in more sophisticated IT systems and applications.

Secondly the industry is to a degree being dragged along by the tide. If one speaks to any IT director in the industry they will tell you that their company's graduate recruits, who will in time become their most able and successful project and commercial managers demand IT applications to support their activities. The industry has struggled to recruit good graduates and will not do so if graduates perceive the industry to be traditional and isolationist when compared to other sectors. Further the ubiquity of email, the home use of PC applications and text messaging is exerting its influence. The growth in email usage itself is making significant demands on IT infrastructure in terms of bandwidth. This is adding to the costs and investment required, even where antipathy exists towards such expenditure.

Thirdly, alongside increased user demand to facilitate operational processes comes management's wish for improved financial information, which enables it to respond more quickly to the demands of its customers and to adjust its business activities to meet more general market trends. Although many contractors have operated a decentralized business model leaving subsidiaries to support themselves, it is noticeable that the need for competitive advantage, better quality financial information demanded by management and auditors, and the structural move into services has led to a more centralized approach and a desire to ensure that each operating subsidiary operates from a common platform or series of platforms. The reality in the recent past has been of operating subsidiaries within the same group using different applications in various operating environments which have been unable to communicate with each other.

Fourthly, although the e-commerce hype has evaporated, there is no doubt that project collaboration applications and electronic ordering and invoicing applications are here to stay. Although their use is relatively limited no one in the industry can seriously believe that these are a passing fad. Substantial developers and customers in both the private and public sectors consider, rightly, that the use of these applications will lead to greater transparency and visibility in terms of project progress and cost. This has led to something of a battleground which we consider below, with significant legal implications.

1.1 Scope and structure of this chapter

Against this background, we seek to highlight a number of the legal risks and issues, of which construction managers or those working with contractors in a project environment need to be aware. Knowledge of these issues should assist the reader to gain an informed understanding of some of the contractual structures, the different forms of agreement and detailed legal terms which are commonly used within the IT industry. It is recognized that these are often unfamiliar to those working in the construction industry, even if they have a legal background or practice as legal counsel. In doing so, we concentrate on certain high-level issues, often where experience has taught us that misunderstanding and conflict can arise. The objective in this respect is to educate and inform a construction professional who has a working knowledge of basic contractual principles but is relatively inexperienced in IT legal terms. The scope of the chapter is therefore limited and does not give a detailed explanation of particular types of agreement or clause. As every IT project has its unique aspects and no IT contract is ever the same, except those shrink wrapped licences used for off-the-shelf applications, we are comfortable with this general approach.

We have attempted to provide practical guidance based upon experience and we therefore offer a subjective view. As is readily apparent from the text, the issues are approached predominantly from the perspective of a customer, user or buyer, rather than from that of an IT supplier selling into the industry. We have also tended to view matters from the perspective of a contractor which is where our respective experience has been gathered. We have however sought to retain some balance in the views expressed. The delivery of IT and telecoms applications remains a technically complex and increasingly costly activity. The construction environment is not straightforward. Contrast in this respect an IT supplier working in the financial services arena where the expertise, training, finance, resourcing and stable environmental conditions have existed until recently in abundance, with that of an industry, criticized for its fragmentation and lack of investment in IT, where business is driven by projects with tight timescales and budgets, and where IT is delivered and operates in a relatively hostile environment with a largely untrained and in many cases unskilled workforce. It is perhaps not surprising that IT suppliers frequently struggle.

The structure of the chapter has been simplified by the current authors. The last edition was written at the height of the e-commerce boom, November 2000, and this led to the identification by the previous authors of e-commerce as a significant facilitator of change. We do not necessarily dissent from this view but consider that the emphasis has undoubtedly changed over the succeeding years as suppliers in this area have refocused their offerings upon delivering a narrower range of applications and related services. As every builder will tell you Rome was not built in a day: the e-commerce revolution will take time to deliver.

In terms of content we look first at a high level at the broad types of system and application in use or supplied by the construction industry. We highlight a number of legal risks in this context. We then consider the legal issues arising under two broad headings: technology which is both procured and supplied by construction companies as product and secondly, technology which is both procured and supplied by construction companies as services. The distinction is useful because the legal issues and contracts adopted in each case are very different although in a number of cases common legal issues arise.

Finally there are an increasing number of either common legal issues or regulatory and compliance matters which are iterative. Health and safety compliance is covered in detail in a separate chapter. We concentrate solely here on the legal issues which impact upon the use of IT by the construction industry.

1.2 Systems and applications

In order to give practical context to the legal and contractual environment described later in this chapter, it is worth summarizing the type of systems, applications and services which are in use and which are supplied by and to the industry. These are considered from a lawyer's rather than an IT professional's basis. In doing so, we highlight some of the areas of legal risk which arise in each case. A common thread which links each of these systems and applications is that they are now being looked at and judged as services. As such, attempts are being made to define the nature of service, ascertain an acceptable or desired level of service and agree a form of applicable service level against which the delivery of the service by the supplier can be monitored and improvements effected. Although such service level agreements are often associated with outsourcing, many companies look at their internal services on the same basis. In some cases these services are being grouped together and managed by a separate corporate entity responsible for delivering services internally and sometimes externally.

Financial and management systems

Financial and management applications are core systems which sit at the centre of any business. A number of specialist applications dominate the current construction marketplace. Substantial contractors are increasingly considering more expensive Enterprise Resource Planning ('ERP') applications which are general financial database applications, rich in functionality and performance but with significantly higher costs in terms of implementation and ownership.

As business critical applications, the implementation of financial and management systems carries significant risk and it is therefore surprising that in some instances, contractors appear content to procure and implement such applications on the basis of a suite of standard terms and conditions, comprising:

- a software licence which can be annual or for a term of years;
- a contract for services which sets out the implementation services including project management which the supplier and/or a third party consultant or firm of consultants is contracted to deliver; and
- a support and maintenance contract: another form of contract for services which describes the services which the supplier will deliver after going live. Again these contracts can be annual or for a term of years.

The significance of the standard nature of these seemingly separate contracts is considered further below.

The difficulties, cost and time necessary to procure and implement such complex systems are invariably underestimated by both the customer, for budgetary and management approval reasons, and by the supplier due to the nature of competitive tendering; all of which should be very familiar territory for the industry. Where the projects can and have come unstuck in the past is in the degree of work and resource commitment, often including considerable process change which is required of the customer in order to implement the application. On the supplier side, the integrated nature and ease of use of the functionality and applications is sometimes over sold, leading ultimately to disappointment in the management team and user communities.

Frequently the terms of the licence, particularly the copyright provisions and payment mechanisms are not properly understood at the outset by the customer. We have also experienced a disconnect in terms of the support service which the supplier contracts to deliver for its annual support fee and the nature of the service the supplier is able and willing to deliver.

Payroll, personnel and HR systems

Contractors will often carry legacy systems or will outsource this service. Ideally these applications should be integrated with the financial and management systems referred to above. The ERP applications will also have appropriate modules.

The legal issues arising from the implementation and the support of such systems are similar to those in any substantial IT project and subsequent live operation. As such systems by their nature process substantial quantities of personal data, data protection compliance is necessary.

IT infrastructure services

This is the backbone or network upon which the software applications sit. This typically will comprise print and file servers, database servers and application servers connected together and to the end user via a LAN and/or a WAN.

The watchwords in this area are network reliability and performance, and increasingly network security. As any IT director will tell you, these are the critical issues which he or she faces on a daily basis and which are of little or no interest to the user community until the network goes down or the system is unable to support a business critical application. With the rise in email usage and use of down-loaded applications from the internet, IT security has caused increasing problems.

Telecommunications infrastructure

In terms of applications and processes this is an area which is technically complex and is frequently neglected. Telecommunications is becoming increasingly important with the widespread use of mobile telephones, voicemail, text messaging, video conferencing and remote working. These are becoming standard business requirements. The main legal risk is downtime during normal business hours. A particular risk for the construction industry which applies equally to IT systems, is connecting to remote sites which are environmentally hazardous for such applications. In order to achieve efficiencies, companies are seeking to use the same infrastructure for all of their voice and data traffic by forming a virtual private network. Concerns often expressed in this are the dominance of the telecommunications operations ('telcos') and the time it takes to implement any change to telecommunications systems. The telcos operate on the basis of standard terms which are product rather than service based and are effectively non-negotiable.

Project management, document management and project collaboration applications

Bespoke document management applications have been employed within major projects for some time with varying degrees of success. The future lies with standard applications with a web-based front end to permit use by partners and third parties, or applications accessible via the web. These have developed significantly but are still in the early stages of usage. Further, on-line document management processes remain undeveloped leading to document mixes of hard copy, email and project documents stored on a shared file.

In this area there has been a significant shift by the suppliers away from e-commerce business models based on the establishment of user communities to a more traditional IT model based upon service revenue linked to value added services such as training and support.

Not unnaturally in this environment the parties have been reluctant to define their obligations to each other in the form of a negotiated and developed form of contract. In many instances, a written contract has not been used. In other cases, the supplier trades from standard terms and conditions developed for a web-based environment.

2.1 Ways of operating
2.2 Working with others
2.3 Working internationally
2.4 The engineer's appointment
2.5 Collateral warranties
2.6 Indemnity insurance
2.7 Employment law
2.8 Information technology

Electronic ordering and invoicing applications

Although the concept of an internet exchange or portal where goods can be bought and sold has not found favour in the industry, most of the financial systems either permit or will in the future allow the processing of electronic ordering and invoicing, on a point to point basis, between customer and supplier. This is similar to Electronic Data Interchange ('EDI') but is more flexible and less costly as it relies upon a common form of programming language (XML) and is a web-based application. Its use is generally confined to major supplies of the particular customer. This is however true e-commerce which will spread as applications improve and its use spreads.

Other desktop applications

For many years the industry has employed a range of applications to support its design, such as CAD/CAM packages and its estimating and programming processes. Suppliers have sought with a mixed degree of success to integrate such applications around a particular financial and management platform. Their use will depend upon the terms of the standard form software licence.

Information and knowledge management systems

Knowledge management have been buzz words in the construction industry for a number of years. Directors and managers dream of the day when they can learn from the successful projects and ditch processes or incidents that have led to project problems; and that this information can be easily accessible to everyone within the company. The company wide intranet is seen as a solution to both the process and system issues which exist in all knowledge-based organizations.

In terms of legal risk, managers often assume they can capture and move data around at will. There are significant intellectual property issues in doing so and where personal data is concerned, data protection regulation prevents such movement.

Intranets have very obvious attractions particularly in an industry which relies heavily upon its most recent project experiences and at the same time is seeking continuous improvement to meet customer requirements and demands. While excellent in concept the implementation of an intranet needs to be treated as an IT project in its own right which often requires considerable process and possibly culture change in order for the site to be launched as a valuable information source. Further an intranet requires considerable on-going investment and support. This often involves those individuals within the organization who are on the front line and who consequently have the valuable experience and know how which can enhance a company's development and operational activities.

Supplied systems and applications

In major infrastructure projects, along with substantial builds, the industry has for many years supplied to its customers a variety of systems and applications ranging from forms of instrumentation and telemetry to sophisticated central control systems and telecommunications systems.

These items have been supplied under the umbrella of a standard form construction contract and have been often poorly specified. There is a need to procure and develop these applications on a long lead. Where design instability exists due to project problems, this presents a significant commercial opportunity for a specialist M&E subcontractor or sub-supplier due to the poor specification of the project and services required.

Legally, standard form construction contracts do not adapt well for use in relation to, for example, the design, build and supply of IT systems and applications. Although such standard forms have the advantage of familiarity, in commercial and projects terms, it is suggested they can be unsuitable.

This is likely to become an increasingly significant issue as the industry assumes long-term responsibility for IT assets over the term of a facilities management or PFI contract.

Outsourcing

Although neither a system nor an application, the use of outsourcing has been a significant development in the industry in the recent past and we anticipate that this trend will continue. This is of interest from the perspective of a contractor as customer and of a contractor as a supplier of services. There is a significant temptation, sometimes encouraged by management strategists advising at board level, to regard IT as an expensive problem in management terms, which is non-core to the activities of the business or businesses and which is therefore ripe for outsourcing to a third party service provider.

With the initial demand for new applications and the legacy problems which exist in some parts of the industry resulting from a lack of investment in the past, the desire to catch up quickly is a further attraction for outsourcing services to a third party.

In an industry which is moving towards a more service-based provision, the antipathy towards outsourcing is disappearing and a number of contractors have recently concluded outsourcing agreements with mid-range IT suppliers.

Many companies are considering outsourcing on a more limited basis, for example, the outsourcing of their hardware support or their network support.

2 PROCURING AND SUPPLYING TECHNOLOGY AS PRODUCT

2.1 Introduction

In this section we look at technology as product; typically the supply of some form of system comprising hardware which is purchased and software which is licensed for use by the licensee.

Almost all supplies of technology will involve the licensing of software – whether off-the-shelf or bespoke. Such licensing raises various questions, primarily as regards the manner in which the software can be used. This section therefore begins by looking at software licensing and intellectual property. Where the user has commissioned software, or a system including software, more complex issues arise and these are considered in Section 2.4 of this chapter under the heading of systems development and implementation. We then look at the implementation of complex financial systems, a particular form of systems integration project. Finally we comment upon telecommunications infrastructure.

2.2 Software licensing

Any construction company seeking to exploit software (particularly high-value software) for financial gain must have standard terms of licence for its end-users. Good practice requires that the licence is in place before the software is supplied to the user.

A software licence will include a number of provisions. Some of these provisions will be standard and found in most commercial contracts – for example, confidentiality, limitation of liability and so-called 'boiler plate' provisions. Other provisions will be peculiar to a software contract. These are largely provisions imposing restrictions on the use of the software. While a detailed discussion of software licences is beyond the scope of this chapter, some of the characteristics of these 'peculiar' clauses will be discussed here.

Depending on the type of software that is being licensed, licences can be broadly categorized as named user licences, concurrent user licences, machine licences, site/location licences or business licences. A named user licence, as the title suggests, will limit the use of the software to a number of identified people in the user organization. These are generally regarded as being expensive particularly if the use of the system is intermittent. These are often contrasted with concurrent user licences which specify a limited number of users, although the users are not named. A machine licence will limit the user to loading and running the software application on a designated machine. A site or location licence will limit use of the software to a specific location, normally allowing use by any number of users provided that they are based at the licensed site. Lastly, a business licence will restrict use to a particular business. There are, of course, many other variations of licence (including hybrids of the above) but these are the major types.

The extent of permitted use is a key issue for both the supplier and user of software. While back office applications may exist in a comparatively stable environment, front office applications will often be used in an environment which is subject to continual change. This can have an impact on the desirable extent of permitted use. For example, a customer might well express concern at a business licence which limits use to the existing business of a named company in its group. What if the company changes its business? What if there is a reorganization and the same business is carried on by a different group company? What if the business is sold to a third party? The supplier will respond that it has fixed the proposed licence fee on the basis of the current usage and that to allow a provision under which, for example, a small business could be backed into a huge one, with the huge business then being entitled to a licence on the same terms as the small business, or in which the customer could set itself up as a bureau supplying the software as a commercial enterprise, would be commercial suicide. Finding a fair balance between the two competing interests will depend on a variety of commercial factors, such as the availability of alternative software and the respective bargaining powers of the parties.

As a general guide in relation to licence fees, change is likely to have some impact upon revenue. Another example of this is where there is a change of platform. Suppliers will often use this as a reason to consider revision of their licence fees, and this can sometimes become a source of contention.

As well as the definition of permitted usage, common provisions in a software licence include the following:

(a) a restriction on making copies of the software (except copies for back-up and security purposes);
(b) a restriction on making the software available to a third party or allowing a third party service provider to run the software on behalf of the user – a restriction which will have to be removed, by agreement, if the software is to be managed or maintained by a third party under an outsourcing contract. Particular problems arise where the service provider is based offshore;
(c) a restriction on any modification of the software or decompilation of source code without the licensor's consent – particularly relevant if the licensor is providing

on-going support and maintenance for the software, as an obligation to support numerous different copies of the software is unlikely to be commercially viable;

(d) a right for the licensor to terminate the licence – for example, in the event of any default by the user, including non-payment of charges, breach of the restrictions, insolvency, etc.; and

(e) charges and payment terms – licence charges will normally take account of the mode of use so that a named user licence will be based on the number of agreed users and an additional fee will be charged for each individual or group of users. Similarly, the fee for a machine licence will be based on a designated processor with an additional charge for another machine with increased processing power. Payment terms can vary between a recurring or annual licence fee (with or without the ability to make occasional increases) and a one-off licence fee, or in some cases a hybrid of the two.

Most importantly, the terms of the software licence should clarify the intellectual property rights in the software which is being licensed. We now consider intellectual property rights in this context.

2.3 Intellectual property

'Intellectual property' is property of an intangible nature which exists as a result of an activity involving some creative effort, for example music and literary work. The term 'intellectual property' is usually defined to include patents, trademarks, design and database rights and know-how as well as copyright.

Under the Copyright, Designs and Patents Act 1988 software or computer programs are treated as a literary work and protected by copyright. By virtue of the Act, and in the absence of any specific contractual provision to the contrary, the copyright in a software program will vest in the 'author' or the 'creator' of the software program or lines of code. Where an employee writes the code, the default position is that the copyright vests in his or her employer: where an independent contractor writes the code, the default position is that copyright vests in the contractor.

Ownership of copyright in software programs can be a contentious issue – particularly in large software development projects. A customer will often ask for ownership of the copyright in the software to be assigned to it by the contractor. The customer's view has traditionally been that it has commissioned and funded the development and should therefore be entitled to ownership of the copyright. This has particularly been the case where the software constitutes a strategic application which gives the customer competitive advantage. However, the modular nature of much modern software often makes an assignment impractical: if the contractor is re-using modules of software which have already been used for other customers, and which it intends to use again in the future, it is not in a position commercially to assign copyright – it can only grant a software licence. It is for this reason that it is assumed, in this section, that a construction company will normally licence software to its customers and obtain a licence of software from its suppliers. (The difference between a licence and an assignment of copyright will, of course, be taken into account in setting the consideration – as will the extent of the usage permitted by the licence (see Section 2.2 of this chapter).)

The fact that the supplier retains ownership does not, of course, necessarily mean that the customer cannot agree restrictions on the manner in which the supplier exercises its ownership rights. For example, where a customer has funded the development of a product which is capable of commercial exploitation elsewhere, it might require the supplier

2.1 Ways of operating
2.2 Working with others
2.3 Working internationally
2.4 The engineer's appointment
2.5 Collateral warranties
2.6 Indemnity insurance
2.7 Employment law
2.8 Information technology

to agree (subject to competition law concerns) not to licence the software to a competitor for an agreed period so that the benefit of any lead time is still realized and/or to pay royalties to the customer in respect of any future exploitation.

It is important that parties do not, however, seek to rely solely upon the general law of copyright or the law of confidence, which arises under the common law in regulating their activities in this area. The issues should be expressly covered in the parties' contract. It is particularly important to remember in this respect that confidential information may be passed prior to the conclusion of a more formal contract. If significant commercial concepts are to be disclosed, this should be protected by a form of confidentiality agreement.

Patents have traditionally not been available for software. There is a move (starting in the USA but now being adopted in Europe) to make patent protection available for certain types of software but further discussion lies outside the scope of this chapter.

2.4 Systems development and implementation

Introduction

Software can be loosely categorized by its method of sale or purchase into:

(a) software that is shrink-wrapped and purchased 'off the shelf';
(b) software that is in standard or packaged form but which requires a degree of configuration to adapt it to a particular customer's requirements; and
(c) software that is especially written and developed to meet a particular customer's requirements.

There is little to say about the first category of shrink-wrapped software, such as Microsoft Office, except that it can be purchased off the shelf from large computer retailers, generally at a low cost, and almost entirely at the customer's risk. It will be subject to a licence but the terms of the licence will be the supplier's standard published terms and they will not be subject to negotiation. Large enterprises buy such licences in bulk on terms which are different from those available to the general public, and while those terms are themselves largely standard, some negotiation may take place. Negotiated differences normally go to price (for example, an increased discount) and usage (for example, use by a FM company may be allowed if for the purpose of the user's business).

Contracts for packaged applications requiring development services to configure or adapt the core software and full bespoke software development projects deserve much greater attention. At the core of both lies the goal of matching the particular customer's requirements with the capability of the developed software.

In a construction context where a substantial system is being supplied by a main contractor as part of a substantial infrastructure project or under PFI, the complexities of systems development and implementation and the risks which frequently arise are often not identified properly and the project is subject to standard construction contract documentation. Where problems arise and costs escalate this lack of foresight can cause difficult contractual disputes. In our experience there is a particular problem where the subcontractor has made some attempt to protect itself from variations to the programme and these matters are not recognized and backed off in the main contract. This can be an area of great risk in major infrastructure projects. In the public sector arena, contractors need to be aware of recent Office of Government Commerce guidance and model contracts published on its website: www.orc.gov.uk/. This has been developed due to the many high-profile public sector IT projects which have failed to deliver the value for money required by Government. Some of the core areas of risk are now addressed.

User requirements

If bespoke software is to be developed (or packaged software to be adapted) to meet a customer's requirements, it is essential that those requirements are stated clearly and (as near as may be) exhaustively. This proposition appears self-evident but failure to properly document business and user requirements is one of the most common reasons for the failure of software projects. Clarity is important for both parties. The customer will not be happy if the developed software does not meet its requirements and the supplier will not be happy if an ambiguous statement in the customer's requirements requires it to incur development costs which are significantly in excess of the contract charges which have been estimated or fixed. To minimize disputes at a later stage in the development, time spent on agreeing detailed and thorough requirements (using external consultants if necessary) is time well spent. (However, see the warning under 'Charges' below against over-ambitious contracts.)

In the case of bespoke software, the user requirements will normally form the basis of a design or functional specification – usually prepared by the supplier. Whether the user requirements or the specification (or both) should be the document which prescribes the form of the software (against which the supplier is required to deliver and against which the acceptance testing strategy will be carried out) is often a source of much debate. The customer may prefer the former; the supplier will definitely prefer the latter. If both are used, care should be taken to ensure that they are consistent.

A related issue is whether either or both documents should be incorporated in the contract. Suppliers may resist this but we consider that substantial procurement contracts should expressly incorporate, essentially, what the customer is buying.

Acceptance testing

Acceptance testing is required in order to determine if the software written by the supplier meets the agreed requirements or specification. Acceptance testing should cover both functionality – whether the software does what it is intended to do; and performance – whether the software can operate under the required loads without the occurrence of an unacceptable level of bugs or faults. Acceptance testing is a technical process which usually includes many different types of test (for example, factory testing, unit testing, stress testing and integration testing) and agreement is required as to the acceptance test strategy (broadly how the customer is going to accept the software), the acceptance criteria (the detailed standards which have to be met), the test plans (the types of test which are to be performed, when they will be performed and by whom), the test data and the test scripts. Ideally, the acceptance procedures should be agreed as part of the contract but it is often not feasible to do so (particularly where the development proceeds by incremental stages). In these circumstances, the contract should at least provide a mechanism for agreeing the procedures during the development stage of the project. Too often, discussions concerning acceptance testing are left to the last minute and when these discussions coincide with project delay and cost overrun, the goodwill necessary to read agreement can be missing. As the conclusion of acceptance testing and the signature of an acceptance certificate will be linked to the release of monies to the supplier the contract will often contain deemed acceptance provisions which provide that acceptance will take place upon or soon after go live. Customers need to consider carefully whether they are prepared to agree such provisions as it will impact any termination rights the customer might wish to exercise.

Integration risk

A key issue in many development contracts is apportionment of the risk of integration. Where the contract relates only to the supply of software, the customer will wish to ensure that the software operates as anticipated on the customer's chosen hardware platform. In such circumstances it might appear self-evident that the entire risk should be on the supplier – if it is told the customer's chosen platform (even more if it suggests or supplies the chosen platform), it should surely be responsible for ensuring that the software performs on that platform in the manner which the customer reasonably expects? Unfortunately, it is rarely as simple as that. First, the software supplier, even if it supplies the hardware platform, often knows no more of its workings than its manufacturer chooses to put into the public domain (a point which was forcefully illustrated by the Year 2000 problem). Secondly, the supplied software is rarely intended to operate alone. At the least, it will have to operate in conjunction with an operating system and with data which may originate with the customer or may be supplied by third parties. The activities of the customer may be restricted in this respect by the terms of the supplier's licence. It will also have to operate with other applications, either on the same machine or over a network. These other applications will rarely be within the supplier's control and may even have been designed specifically for the customer by another supplier. For all these reasons, it is important to determine, at an early stage, who will be responsible for ensuring that the software works with each of the elements which make up the environment in which it will operate – a subject which is clearly linked to the question of acceptance testing referred to above.

Project timetable

Where a software development is to last for any length of time, a project plan should be included within the contract, specifying any important milestones and dates for delivery. A project plan serves the interest of both parties. If payments are linked to milestones and/or deliverables, the supplier will know what it has to do in order to be paid the next instalment of the price and the customer will be able to determine the remedies which should apply if the milestone is not achieved. Where performance of the supplier's obligations is dependent in part on the customer taking certain steps (for example, obtaining third party software licences or making a computer room available), the project plan also gives the supplier an opportunity to specify the remedies which will apply if those steps are delayed. In each case, the remedies will probably include an extension of time, but may also include (at least in the case of delay by the supplier) liquidated damages. Extended delay may give rise to a right of termination.

Charges

Charges for the development of software are usually on a fixed-price or a time and materials basis. Typically, where the contract for development services is on a fixed-price basis, the supplier will seek to include a margin to cover risks associated with accepting fixed-price contracts, such as the risk of project overrun.

From the customer's point of view, the argument for a fixed-price development is that it gives assurance as to the project costs. However, a supplier who is faced with a fixed-price contract will clearly be concerned to ensure that any work which lies outside the scope of the contract is treated as a change and priced accordingly, and where the contract is sufficiently large, the chance that a specification drawn up some months (or even years) before will turn out to be a comprehensive description of all the customer's requirements is comparatively slight. The cost of changes may therefore turn out to be a large proportion of the overall cost of the project. It is mainly for this reason that the Office of Government Commerce has warned against over-ambitious development contracts, whether or not on a fixed-price basis, and have stressed the desirability of using packaged software and undertaking incremental development.

In development contracts where services are provided on a time and materials basis, the customer will wish to include certain mechanisms to allow management of the project costs: for example, initial estimates linked to milestones; regular time sheets (in sufficient detail to allow activities to be mapped); regular comparisons of actual against budgeted cost (with explanations of any deviations); a joint risk register which is maintained by both parties' project managers and, where appropriate and particularly under a partnering type of arrangement, a risk sharing scheme which rewards the supplier for coming in under budget but shares the downside if cost overruns occur. Expenses are normally treated in a similar manner.

Where there is an agreed list of milestones, payment of some or all of the instalments of price is often linked to the achievement of key milestones. Milestones which are commonly used are agreement of specification (if the first phase of the contract includes design); delivery of software to initial testing; acceptance; and expiry of the warranty period. Where the software is developed in phases, payment may be linked to delivery and testing of the phases. The extent to which payment is loaded towards the front or back of the contract is a fertile subject for discussion between customer and supplier. It is in neither party's interest that the supplier is starved of funds throughout most of the contract, but neither is there likely to be much value in an 80%-developed piece of software, so the customer will wish there to be strong incentives for successful completion.

Maintenance and escrow

Intellectual property rights have already been touched on earlier in this section and the conclusion drawn that in most (although not all) cases, the supplier will own the copyright in the software program with the customer being granted a licence.

Aside from the terms of the licence, discussed above, the customer who has paid a substantial amount for packaged or bespoke software will have an interest in ensuring that it remains usable in the future. Most software suppliers offer maintenance terms covering both the delivery of certain upgrades and the repair of identified faults. For certain products, maintenance can also be obtained from third party suppliers. However, effective maintenance of software requires access not only to the code running on the machine (the object code – which is only readable by a machine) but also to the source code from which the object code was developed (a version of the software which is readable by a human). In addition, efficient alteration of the source code will often require consideration of design documentation.

A customer may be able to negotiate the delivery of software in both source and object code forms. More commonly, a supplier will agree to deposit the source code and design documentation with an independent third party, for example the National Computing Centre (an escrow agent) who will agree to release them to the customer only in certain extreme events: normally when the supplier is no longer capable of maintaining, or willing to maintain, the software itself. We question in these circumstances how useful the source code will be, however, particularly if it is an unsupported version of the software.

2.5 Financial systems and multi-functional applications

Introduction

ERP systems, multi-function implementations, are a form of systems integration project. Multi-function systems are notoriously difficult to implement and in our experience they demand significant board commitment and involvement. Such an involvement can prove a mixed blessing if management decides to raise users' expectations in order to secure investment and buy-in. Extravagant claims made internally and externally, often encouraged by the supplier, are too often made which come to haunt the management and the project team at a later date. This is particularly the case when users find the system difficult to use and management discovers information difficult to find, without the production of reports which involves further development work using specialist report writing tools.

Multi-function implementations have certain features which have a significant impact upon the contractual position which is likely to exist between customer and supplier. All of the issues raised in relation to systems development and implementation are relevant here. In this section we highlight some of the special features particularly as a number of major contractors and many companies outside the sector have struggled with this type of project.

Due diligence

First and foremost a multi-function system will support the finance and accounts functions and its processes within a business or group of businesses. It is therefore critical that in terms of project sponsorship, project management and resource allocation, there is complete buy-in from the finance function at every level. There needs to be a thorough understanding of the way in which the finance function currently works in its own right and in relation to the business it supports. Secondly, there needs to be an appreciation as to how the finance function and the businesses it serves wish to improve or change. Thirdly the existing and proposed future processes and structure need to map well with the solution under consideration. Multi-function systems are sold by their suppliers as flexible packages which can be adapted to suit any specific industry's requirements. Customers need to undertake thorough investigation and due diligence to ascertain the degree to which the modules comprising the system are truly integrated and/or require adaptation or development to meet the particular needs of the customer. Such systems and process analysis often called a gap analysis, or mapping exercise is often undertaken with the assistance of IT consultants with domain expertise in the application and the particular industry or sector. Again the reality of this expertise needs to be determined by the customer prior to the engagement.

This due diligence phase, which is often undertaken in haste against an unrealistic programme, is a mini project in its own right. Consultants will advise under their standard form of engagement. These terms and conditions need to be considered carefully by the customer to ascertain the scope of the advice which the consultants have contracted to supply and the deliverables from the assignment.

On a longer term basis, the customer needs to ensure that the results of its due diligence exercise and the critical factors in its decision-making process to proceed with the project and with particular suppliers are, so far as possible, given contractual effect. This can be in the form of detailed recitals in the contract or repetition of statements made by the supplier in the form of specific warranties or statements in the appropriate schedules. Although the customer may not have seen the supplier's standard terms and conditions at this stage in the process, it can be certain that those terms will contain a wide ranging entire agreement or whole agreement clause which will seek to exclude any representations and most importantly reliance upon any representations made by the supplier in the due diligence process.

Project planning

If the customer wishes to proceed having undertaken its due diligence exercise, the next step is to plan the project going forward and identify the roles and responsibilities of each of the parties during the project implementation. It is perhaps trite to state that without such a planning process it is impossible to determine with any certainty the resources required, the budget and the programme. A lack of planning frequently occurs however due to normal business pressures combined with the supplier's enthusiasm to commence work. For an industry which lives by its projects, it must be appreciated from the outset that a multi-function project or indeed any other substantial IT procurement demands a full time project manager and full time resource.

The planning process is key to a determination of the project risks, the dependencies, project costs and milestones. It is worth repeating here that one would expect all of the main features of the planning process to appear in schedules to the contract.

Contract structure

The reality however is in many cases very different. This is due in part to the way in which multi-function applications are sold and to the strong bargaining position which the major IT suppliers have enjoyed for historic reasons. Although the supplier may sell a complete solution during the tender and procurement process, generally they will wish to contract on the basis of a suite of standard terms and conditions referred to above which do not contain any form of commitment that a solution or the requirement will be implemented. Instead the supplier will licence the use of the software to the customer and will supply certain implementation services typically on a time and materials basis. The scope of these implementation services requires careful consideration and comparison with the dependencies and resource allocation identified in the project plan. The major suppliers are specific in the standard form contracts about the responsibilities of the customer; particularly customer dependencies and therefore the allocation of risk which the customer will bear. The customer needs to consider whether this reflects its understanding of the position and is consistent with the project plan.

In broad terms the major suppliers of multi-function systems will not act as systems integrators which therefore leaves the customer with a requirement to contract with a separate supplier such as a systems integrator or consultancy under a contract for services for them to assist with the project implementation. The systems integrator may be prepared to prime the contract, subcontracting the development of the multi-function system to the supplier. This gives the customer the considerable advantages of a single point of contact and makes risk allocation more straightforward. This is an area of significant risk which needs to be properly covered off in the contracts with the supplier or the consultancy.

The risk is significantly enhanced where the customer is unable to properly resource the project management function within the project and looks to the consultancy or systems integrator to do so. Although having obvious attractions, there is a significant danger that the consultancy will be pursuing different objectives from those of the customer who is seeking to satisfy a number of user communities. The consultancy will seek to drive the project forward to a 'go live' date, and will take steps where possible to facilitate this objective. Without close control and supervision at project and project board level, requirements may be re-phased or dropped without a proper understanding of the implications. It is strongly recommended that the customer does not divest itself of its project management function. In an industry where such skills abound, good project managers need to be identified and allocated responsibility for delivery of the customer's dependencies and obligations.

Standard terms

If the customer undertakes a thorough due diligence and planning process, there is no reason in principle or in practice why it should not contract on negotiated terms and conditions with its supplier or suppliers. The construction industry has some of the most developed forms of contract of any industry with a thorough understanding of the risk and liability which exists in construction projects and how these are borne and covered off in the forms of contract. It is therefore something of a surprise to us that more effort is not made to prepare a bespoke contract suitable for a project, which will in many cases involve expenditure of several millions and is business critical. In our view better definition during the planning process can be achieved through such a negotiation.

The contract also needs to be viewed as an agreement which will potentially cover a long-term relationship rather than being a snapshot in time during a tortuous tender process. Tying the supplier down might result in short-term gain but in time the supplier may take a more rigorous approach to change control.

Project methodology

There is one further area which requires consideration as part of the planning process, carries significant risk and should therefore be adequately specified in the contract or contracts with the suppliers of the multi-function system and related services. This is the form of project methodology to be used by the parties which should underpin the implementation.

The major suppliers and consultancies will often have their own unique project methodologies. These are held out as a form of quality standard or assurance: a guarantee, in a non-legal sense that the supplier's team knows how best to successfully deliver the project with the assistance of the customer.

The public sector has traditionally used the Prince 2 methodology which places a great deal of emphasis upon rigorous planning and control of activities by the customer by reference to the project plan; full and proper documentation of all meetings; and perhaps most importantly control of change. The Office of Government Commerce has undertaken a great deal of work in this area recently due to the high profile IT project problems in the public sector; much of which lends itself to use in the commercial world.

There are three significant points to follow when discussing or considering the use of a project methodology. The methodology itself may be set out in a document called the Project Initiation Document or 'PID'. The first is to have a thorough understanding of what the methodology entails. With a supplier's methodology, the customer should ensure that there is an element of transparency concerning the supplier's methodology. The customer should also have a reasonable understanding of the interfaces or dependencies and whether those meet the project plan.

Secondly, the parties should ensure that the project methodology is consistent with or incorporated within the contract. It is regrettably common for a PID to set out timescales, deliverables and dependencies which are inconsistent with the terms of the contract. Such inconsistency can only lead to expensive legal argument should the project run into difficulties.

Thirdly, if the parties agree to follow a specific methodology, it should be rigorously followed. Furthermore, where changes occur formally or informally, the PID should be varied accordingly.

2.6 Telecommunications infrastructure

The legal landscape in this area is a mixture of contract law and regulation. From a construction industry perspective it is appropriate to look at telecoms infrastructure and regulation separately. Telecommunications services are covered in Section 3.4.

Infrastructure

It has been difficult to escape from the specialist M&E contractors which have undertaken considerable works installing cabling networks and routes throughout the UK over the past 5 years. Such works are undertaken under standard form contracts prepared by the telecommunications operators ('telcos'). There has been little room for negotiation of these contracts.

Regulation

Telecommunications regulation has undergone significant change due to the Communications Act 2003. It is rare in our experience that contractors' activities are subject to regulation as this is principally directed towards the regulation of the telcos.

3 PROCURING AND SUPPLYING TECHNOLOGY AS SERVICES

3.1 Introduction

Construction companies are increasingly buyers and sellers of services. This chapter looks at three broad categories of services. First, outsourcing is considered in some detail. We then consider e-commerce in this context concentrating upon project collaboration applications and the services which they deliver. Finally we mention telecommunications services.

3.2 Outsourcing

The terms 'outsourcing' and 'facilities management' have long been common terms in the IT and construction industries – often used interchangeably. As indicated above, 'facilities management' is used here to mean an arrangement whereby the third party service provider operates and manages the customer's internal non-core function without necessarily taking over the staff and assets. Services which are commonly provided on a facilities management basis include building maintenance, cleaning, security and catering, as well as IT.

Outsourcing, on the other hand, is usually a more complex transaction involving the transfer by the customer of an internal function (including staff, assets and contracts) as a going concern to the service provider. The staff are then employed by the service provider who supplies services back to the customer to pre-agreed service levels.

Benefits of outsourcing

For many customers one of the drivers of outsourcing is cutting costs. It is envisaged that the service provider will be able to deliver IT services more cheaply than the customer can do itself, for example, because it can use the resources more efficiently by using them to provide similar services to other customers and thereby reducing any unused capacity. Outsourcing can also provide customers with flexibility as it allows for the customer to purchase back services on a more flexible basis, according to need.

A customer organization needing to upgrade its technology might use the flexibility and skills available from its outsourcing partner to implement a technology upgrade. Most customers want to keep abreast of new technology during the outsourcing contract. This can be achieved by having benchmarking and technology refresh mechanisms.

The benefits of outsourcing for service providers include a medium- or long-term revenue stream; the development of a long-term relationship with a customer which will provide further sales opportunities; and profit (although this is not always the case, for instance when there is an economic downturn).

Phases of an outsourcing

A conventional outsourcing arrangement typically falls into three phases: transition phase, run phase and exit phase. The 'transition phase' covers the period when the relationship between the customer and the service provider is established; the preparatory work is undertaken to effect the transfer of the services from the customer to the service provider; and the services begin to be supplied by the service provider. The 'run phase' covers the period when the services are performed to the agreed standards in accordance with the outsourcing contract. The final phase, the 'exit phase', covers the period when the outsourcing relationship comes to an end. The contractual documentation that is required to give effect to the outsourcing arrangement needs to address each of the phases. The output from the preparatory work will form the basis of the information to be included in the request for proposal issued to the service providers during the tendering stage, which will also ultimately form many of the details required to be included in the contractual documentation. Independent studies indicate that the success or failure of outsourcing arrangements is dependent in large part on the time and attention which the customer gives to the preparatory stages, contract negotiation and management of the contract post-completion.

Planning and structuring an outsourcing

One of the key elements to a successful outsourcing is detailed and strategic planning throughout the process. The level of commitment and the resources required to put in place a significant outsourcing are often underestimated. The main reason for the resource requirement is the knowledge gap which often exists between the customer and the service provider. While the customer may well be encountering the outsourcing process for the first time, outsourcing is the service provider's business. The service provider therefore starts with an immediate advantage and the knowledge gap between the parties will increase – creating the possibility of misunderstanding and disagreement – if the customer is ill-informed about its existing IT environment and the services (and service levels) which it requires in the future.

The preparatory activities of an outsourcing should therefore include the internal steps of forming the project team (using external advisers where necessary); defining the scope of the services; identifying assets and staff to be transferred; measuring and recording existing services and service levels; considering the services and service levels which will be required in the future; and preparing draft legal agreements – as well as the external steps of examining the market and information gathering as to potential service providers.

Financial considerations

As stated above, as outsourcing is often seen by organizations as a means of reducing costs, the financial aspects of an outsourcing can dominate negotiations. If cost savings are to be realized, the customer must have a thorough understanding of its own IT operations and its current cost base. Only with this understanding can the customer put together a financial case for outsourcing which will justify the outsourcing internally, serve as a basis for comparison with the service provider's proposal, and allow the customer to measure actual against anticipated cost savings over the term of the outsourcing arrangement.

In an outsourcing which is to last for more than two or three years, the customer must also, so far as is possible, take account of any potential future change of direction of the business in putting together the financial model and agreeing a charging structure. An inflexible pricing structure will prevent the customer from gaining the benefit of business and technological changes during the life of the outsourcing agreement (although the customer's desire for flexibility often has to be balanced against the service provider's need to obtain a return on its investment in the initial staff and asset transfer). Benchmarking and other forms of market testing can be used to verify the continued competitiveness of the contract pricing.

Benchmarking is the process whereby an independent third party reports on the extent to which the service provider's services (including any agreed service levels) and charges match the market norms for the relevant market sector. It is an expensive process but can be worthwhile if it ensures that the customer is receiving good value for money through the term of the outsourcing and the service provider compares well with its competitors. The contract should specify the consequences of the service provider not achieving the improvements identified by the benchmarking process in a specified time. These may include an appropriate increase in service levels or reduction in the charges where the supplier's services are found to be uncompetitive.

Service scope and description

One would expect the exercise of defining and agreeing the services to be relatively simple. However, it can prove both time consuming and contentious. As a general rule, the customer desires improvement in the existing services and flexibility to adopt new services – but flexibility within a price which is fixed or, at any rate, predictable. The service provider, however, wants the required services to be exhaustively defined so that it can scope its contractual service commitments and produce a predictable return. There is a balance to be struck between unnecessarily tight and inflexible service descriptions (with the threat of increased pricing whenever a change is introduced) and a contract which is so flexible that it lacks certainty, but that balance is not always easy to achieve.

Service levels

Detailed work is also required in documenting and agreeing service levels. The customer's objective is to purchase cost-effective services which are reliable and delivered to measurable standards. To achieve the requisite standards it is essential to define service levels in the contract. The service levels must be agreed by both parties as achievable and measurable. The process is made easier if service levels have previously been measured internally by the IT department as the more information that is available as to previous service history, the easier it is to reach agreement as to future targets. Conversely, agreeing service levels for areas of services which have not previously been measured can prove difficult. The service provider will be reluctant to commit to service levels which the customer's IT department has no record of achieving.

Service levels will be categorized according to their business criticality which will be determined by the customer. Some service levels will be absolutely critical while others are not so important. The contract should set out the different service levels for each service being provided.

Service credits and liquidated damages

Outsourcing contracts should contain provisions which address the consequences of failure on the part of the service provider to deliver services to the agreed service levels. In the context of a long-term relationship between the supplier and customer, termination of the contract will not be a practical remedy except in the most extreme cases. Instead, outsourcing contracts commonly provide for escalating remedies, normally in the form of service credits and liquidated damages.

Service credits and liquidated damages are pre-agreed sums of money which can be recovered by the customer as a form of compensation from the supplier for non-achievement of service delivery. Service credits are generally smaller sums of money which the supplier will credit against the next invoice. Liquidated damages are often larger sums which are calculated to reflect the criticality of the service that has not been delivered. Some failures to achieve service levels will have no penalty attached as the service has been identified by the customer as being less critical. The contract should ensure that the service provider is obliged to provide regular reports on service performance (including attainment of service levels) and whether service credits have accrued in the previous measurement period.

Employee arrangements

As part of an outsourcing, employees may be transferred from the customer to the service provider (whether under the TUPE Regulations or by agreement of the parties – for further information refer to Chapter 2.7 on Employment law). Adequate arrangements need to be put in place for those employees. By its very nature, the transfer of employees in an outsourcing is a sensitive issue. The affected employees, particularly those with many years' service with the company, may feel threatened by the pending change, resulting in poor morale and the threat of potential service degradation. If a climate of uncertainty is created, skilled staff may seek alternative employment creating difficulties for both parties. This problem can be addressed by implementing a policy of clear and regular communications to ensure that the affected employees (and indeed the employees who are not affected) are kept abreast of events, but such a policy is not always consistent with the need to maintain the parties' respective bargaining positions.

Third party consents

In a conventional outsourcing, the customer will either transfer relevant contracts with its third party suppliers to the service provider or otherwise permit the benefit of the contracts to be enjoyed by the service provider (at least in the transitional phase). Relevant contracts (that is, contracts relating to the transferred business function) can include software licences, leasing agreements, and hardware and software maintenance agreements. The third party contracts may not contain appropriate rights for the customer to permit the service provider to use the software or hardware, nor rights to transfer the contract to the service provider without the third party's consent. The customer will therefore need to approach the third party supplier to obtain the necessary consents

– a time-consuming and costly exercise if the supplier seeks to recover payment in return for granting consent. An alternative is to place the burden and cost of obtaining consents on the service provider, although the customer, as the party with the contractual relationship, will usually need to maintain sufficient involvement to protect its position.

Exit arrangements

On expiry or earlier termination of the outsourcing, as well as the option of renewing the service contract, the customer must have the ability to take the services back in-house or transfer them to a new service provider. Typical transfer activities include the migration of the services; the transfer or licensing back of software used by the service provider in its provision of services; assistance with the transfer of employees affected by the retransfer (who may be caught by TUPE); and dealing with bidders enquiries (where the customer has retendered the services). The outsourcing contract should require the service provider to provide the necessary assistance with minimal disruption to service delivery and the cost of providing that transfer assistance should preferably be factored into the overall pricing proposal to prevent future arguments.

3.3 E-commerce in the construction industry

True e-commerce is buying and selling goods and services using the web. In its traditional incarnation this was and is the electronic data interchange (EDI) which gained favour particularly in the retail, automotive and aerospace sectors. The e-commerce model was the internet exchange or hub, which is a website which functions as a large procurement engine, bringing suppliers and purchasers together in one virtual marketplace and automating substantial parts of the procurement process. Neither the traditional nor the e-commerce procurement models have gained significant favour or use in the industry. It may be that the next edition of this chapter needs to revisit the legal issues which arise with on-line procurement. Currently we do not see the need to do so here. We do however look at ordering and invoicing applications in the context of certain EU directives which are commonly mentioned in the context of e-commerce and can therefore cause some confusion.

Project collaboration applications

Project collaboration applications replicate the traditional project office but they offer the possibility of expanding the opportunity for collaboration between the various contractual parties by:

(a) enabling some or all of the project participants to communicate with each other using the same system; and
(b) offering all of them access to the same materials and the use of the same tools.

The benefits are a reduction in cost through the elimination of duplication (all parties use the same set of tools) and a reduction in errors through enhanced version control or use of a single set of documents.

Certain common elements can be identified. A feature of most forms of project collaboration applications is the provision of an on-line document management system – a website on which all the documents relating to the project can be filed and stored under a strict regime of version control designed to prevent the creation of inconsistent versions of the primary documents (for example, plans and specifications).

More advanced forms of project collaboration application provide not only a storage space for documents but also the tools for creating and amending those documents –

CAD/CAM software, spreadsheets, word processors and project management software – either in a form in which they can be downloaded and used off-line or for on-line use only.

There is a significant process change occurring to the way in which documents are stored and managed on-line. Many project participants communicate by email rather than hard copy. We have not as yet reached the nirvana of the paperless office.

If a project problem arises and some form of investigation is required, it is no longer possible (if it ever was) to go to one source of information. Instead one has a mixture of hard copy documentation; email stored in individual's in-boxes and perhaps documentation held on a shared drive. This situation is made worse by email storage policies which dictate that any email over 3 months old will be deleted from systems unless archived and, equally damaging in terms of evidence, email being deleted from an employee's in-box when he or she has left the project without any form of copy being taken. It is of course the case that, with good housekeeping, every communication will be backed-up. Retrieval of backed-up data however is expensive, time consuming and does not necessarily lead to a successful search as information is not backed-up to facilitate ease of retrieval in relation to a particular issue, for example. Peoples' working processes are rapidly changing and many of the processes upon which the construction industry has relied to manage projects will have to change to meet this challenge.

A further challenge for managers is the nature in which people communicate by email. In the 'old days' if an employee was dissatisfied with an aspect of management, for instance, he or she might mention it to a colleague standing at the coffee machine. These days the individual is just as likely to email it round a group of colleagues. When projects or businesses suffer problems, potentially damaging email traffic is likely to arise, all of which will be disclosable in the event of legal proceedings. Further it is not just that this damaging type of documentation is created at critical periods, the tone used in email communication is more conversational in form and differs from the more formal language much loved of quantity surveyors.

It remains to be seen what evidential value or weight Judges will attach to such email communication. It is difficult to see how a company can prevent such traffic arising. The only way, it is suggested, is for employees to be aware that their email communication using the company's network will be disclosable in legal proceedings and may end up being reviewed by a Judge or Arbitrator!

Legal questions to be answered

The legal considerations which apply to the project collaboration application have mostly been encountered elsewhere in this chapter. However, one or two new problems are raised.

First, there is the position of the company which supplies the project collaboration application. This may be a third service provider or it may be one of the participants to the construction process, having developed its own application. The role of supplier of the site is analogous to the position of an internet service provider (or ISP) which provides an internet connection and web space to its subscribers. As with an ISP, the supplier will undertake to make the site available at certain hours (probably 24 × 7 less any periods of scheduled maintenance) but will be concerned to limit its liability for interruptions beyond its control (for example, faults in the telephone network) and to avoid any responsibility for the contents of the site (to the extent provided by the participants). In its role as provider of software tools, the supplier is analogous either to a licensor of software or to an applications service provider (or ASP). Where management of a complex project is dependent on these applications, as they will be, the extent of liability to be borne by the supplier as ASP if the site or the tools become unavailable, or fail to function as they should, is likely to be a subject for debate.

What of the position of the participants in the project? Clearly, they will enter into contracts with the supplier for the provision of the applications. Such contracts will oblige the participants to pay the relevant fees and may contain other terms such as an obligation to use the software in accordance with specified licence terms and a restriction on using the site for any purpose other than a named project. As mentioned above, the contracts will also apportion liability between the provider of the site and the participants. Who, for example, is to be responsible if the document management software contains an error which allows certain amendments to appear without revision marks?

However, they may also have to enter into contracts with each other (or amend existing contracts) to recognize the legal consequences which might flow from the change in working methods. For example, version control should not be an automatic process. There may be legal significance in saying that a draft has been approved or has moved from version 1 to version 2, but the designers of software cannot be expected to think of such matters. It will therefore often be necessary to put a legal gloss on the technical processes in order to align them with the desired contractual position: to agree, for example, at what point in the technical process a draft becomes approved; the means which are to be employed to signal that approval; how one establishes that the person nominally accepting the draft on behalf of a participant has the necessary authority to do so; and the consequences of approval (e.g. does it waive any future right of objection).

These matters require the agreement of a protocol. The standard terms of such a protocol or contract could be devised by the IT supplier, and apply to all subscribers to the site, or the subscribers could agree their own protocol or adapt one produced by an industry body.

It is because of these legal challenges that the e-legal project was commenced, with EU funding led by Loughborough University. The project's objective is to develop a legal framework to allow project participants to understand the legal risk and by way of model contracts cater for the risk in a fair way, which is in the interests of the project rather than one individual party. Information concerning the project can be obtained from http://cic.vtt.fi/projects/elegal/public.html.

3.4 Telecommunications services

Telecommunications services can be usefully sub-divided.

First there is the standard telephone services provided by the telecommunications operators ('the telcos') in the form of a connection to their network. The telcos trade from standard terms and conditions, and are generally unwilling to negotiate their terms. The customer's only choice is to line switch between different networks in order to secure preferential telephone rates.

Secondly, there are the telephone operating systems and applications such as voicemail which are installed and supported locally by the company in its various premises. These will be subject to installation contracts, and support agreements following installation. Again these tend to be in standard form, although there is an increasing wish on the part of customers to negotiate service level agreements providing, for example for 99.9% availability. Suppliers will be reluctant to do this. In our experience when telephone systems fail, the fault can be attributed to a number of different causes and a situation quickly develops with each supplier blaming the other. The only firm piece of practical advice in this area is to ensure that a fault log is maintained which can be used as evidence in any discussions with the supplier.

In the newer installations, such as 'intelligent buildings' the use of wireless LAN networks is causing increased security concerns due to the ability of hackers to access the network.

As the range of telecoms services increases and commensurately the cost of those services and the management costs, larger companies outside the construction sector have sought to bundle those services and outsource them to a third party. This is often part of a wider IT outsourcing deal.

4 GENERAL LEGAL ISSUES AND COMPUTERS

4.1 Introduction

As businesses become more reliant on the use of technology it is inevitable that their exposure to the risks involved with such use will grow. Risk areas include health and safety, data protection, freedom of information, internet and email usage and security. Finally we look at certain EU e-commerce directives which can cause misunderstanding in the context of ordering and invoicing applications. The following section provides a brief overview of each of these areas. Further free information upon the issues referred to here can be obtained from out-law.com which contains 5000 pages of legal news and guidance, mostly on IT and e-commerce issues.

4.2 Health and safety

Health and safety issues are dealt with in detail in Chapter 3.4 on health and safety law. However, the use of computers, in particular the use of display screen equipment and keyboards, requires specific preventive and protective measures.

Under the Health and Safety (Display Screen Equipment) Regulations 1992 an employer must carry out an analysis of the work stations used by its employees in order to assess the risks to health and take appropriate measures to deal with them. The principal risks are those relating to mental stress, physical problems and visual fatigue. The Regulations require an employer:

(a) to plan a worker's activities in such a way that work on a display screen is periodically interrupted by breaks or changes of activity not involving the screen;
(b) to ensure that workers who use display screens have appropriate eye and eyesight tests at regular intervals or at any point when they experience visual difficulties;
(c) to pay the basic cost of glasses which are purely for VDU work; and
(d) to provide employees who use work stations with adequate health and safety training and information about all aspects of health and safety relating to the work stations.

4.3 Data Protection

Introduction

Data Protection law is concerned with the protection of personal data and the management of standards for the processing of personal data. Personal data are those data which identify a living individual and an individual who is the subject of personal data is termed a data subject by the law. The current law is contained in the Data Protection Act 1998 (the 1998 Act) which came into force on 1 March 2000.

The law is designed to safeguard the interests of data subjects whose data are processed by companies or organizations, or even on occasions individuals, who determine the purpose and manner in which those data are used. These organizations are termed data controllers. The 1998 Act imposes a range of obligations on data controllers and gives certain rights to data subjects.

Data protection issues arise across a wide range of areas and it is important that a company or organization has processes and procedures in place to ensure compliance with the law. Personal data are also valuable assets and data controllers will be keen to ensure that data sets are managed for the long term. E-commerce transactions involve collecting and handling large quantities of data, some of which (particularly if collected for marketing) will be personal data. Outsourced facilities often include systems, such as personnel and customer relationship systems, which include personal data and indeed Human Resources departments collect and use large volumes of personal data.

Even where it is not immediately apparent that personal data might be involved – for example, when all transactions are business to business – a company needs to audit its procedures in order to ensure either that it is not processing any personal data at all (a very unlikely scenario) or that it is complying with the terms of the legislation. Guidance on how to carry out audits and assess compliance can be found at the website of the Office of the Information Commissioner (the OIC), www.dataprotection.gov.uk.

The definition of processing is very wide and covers almost any operation on data including obtaining, recording, storage, use, disclosure archiving and destruction. Most organizations will process personal data relating to their employees, customers, contacts and suppliers and will therefore be data controllers.

Data controllers are subject to higher standards in relation to a category of personal data termed sensitive personal data. These comprise data that relate to political opinions, religious beliefs, ethnic origin, health information, sexual life, criminal convictions or membership of a trade union.

Data Processors

A data processor is any person, organization or company appointed by a data controller to process personal data on the data controller's behalf. For example, a company that delivers IT services under an outsourcing agreement and has access to personal data to deliver these services will be a data processor. Data controllers are required by the 1998 Act to ensure that they put in place a contract in writing with each data processor setting out the terms on which personal data are to be processed. The contract should include restrictions on use of the personal data by the data processor and set out the security standards the data processor should adopt.

What obligations are placed on data controllers by the 1998 Act?

In broad terms a data controller is required by the 1998 Act to notify its processing to the Information Commissioner, observe the eight data protection principles set out below and comply with the obligations arising out of the rights given to data subjects under the 1998 Act.

Notification

Notifications can be made online or on a standard form which can be obtained from the OIC.

The uses notified must accurately reflect the purpose for which the personal data will be used. For example, it is necessary to know what databases are used to operate the business, the types of personal data held on them, how personal data are processed, if personal data are disclosed to a third party (and, if so, to whom), if personal data are transferred to a third party (and, if so, where) and what security arrangements are in place to prevent unauthorized access to personal data.

There are circumstances when a data controller will not be required to register its use of personal data. These include personal data or information which are held by an individual for domestic or recreational purposes.

Compliance with the eight data protection principles (DPPs)

On notification, a company must comply with the eight data protection principles of good practice which require:

- personal data to be processed fairly and lawfully (Principle 1);
- personal data to be obtained only for one or more specified and lawful purpose or purposes and not to be further processed in any manner incompatible with the purpose(s) notified (Principle 2);
- personal data to be adequate, relevant and not excessive in relation to the purpose or purposes for which they are processed (Principle 3);
- personal data to be accurate and, where necessary, kept up to date (Principle 4);
- personal data to be kept for no longer than is necessary for the purpose(s) for which the data are notified (Principle 5);
- personal data to be processed in accordance with the rights of the data subject under the 1998 Act (Principle 6);
- personal data to be subject to appropriate technical and organizational measures to protect against unauthorized or unlawful processing of personal data and against accidental loss or destruction of, or damage to, personal data (Principle 7) (see Section 4.6 for further guidance on how to comply with this principle); and
- that personal data should not be transferred to a country or territory outside the European Economic Area unless that country or territory ensures an adequate level of protection for the rights and freedoms of data subjects in relation to the processing of personal data (Principle 8).

The application of each Principle requires the consideration of a whole range of issues. As a rule of thumb, a company's processing of personal data should be restricted to the core purpose for which it was originally obtained. Complications normally arise when personal data are obtained and used for wider purposes than that which was originally intended, without first informing and getting consent from the data subject.

Data subjects' rights

The 1998 Act sets out a range of rights for data subjects:

- the right of access to personal data (including archived and back-up data), and information about sources and disclosures of data (Subject Access right);
- the right to know any logic behind any decision taken using solely automated means;
- the right to prevent processing which is likely to cause damage or distress;
- the right to prevent processing for the purposes of direct marketing; and
- the right of any person (not only the data subject) affected to claim compensation for damage or distress in respect of any breach of the 1998 Act.

Subject access requests pursued by disgruntled or former employees are becoming increasingly common. It is important that companies have an established process for dealing with such requests.

Non-compliance

The Information Commissioner has extensive enforcement powers. If, following the service of an 'information notice', the data controller fails to provide the requested information within the prescribed time limits, the Commissioner may serve an 'enforcement notice' if he or she considers that there has been a breach of the 1998 Act. The effect of such notice would require the data controller to cease processing data. Sanctions can be imposed for failure to comply with an enforcement notice.

4.4 Freedom of Information Act 2005

The Freedom of Information Act 2000 ('FOIA') requires public bodies to publish and maintain a publication scheme which sets out categories of information which they undertake to publish. In addition, FOIA gives a right to request access to information held by the public sector not already published as part of a publication scheme. This means that any information held by a public body potentially publicly available.

This does not just affect the public sector. Although private sector organizations do not have to provide information directly to enquirers, information that an organization has provided to a public sector body may be disclosable by that body. This may include information on the organization's goods, services and performance. Furthermore, there is no legal obligation on the public body to advise the private organization that the information will be disclosed although a Code of Practice issued by the Lord Chancellor's Department under FOIA (the 'Code') does suggest that a public body should consider consulting the private organization.

There are exemptions in FOIA for information provided in confidence and trade secrets but as FOIA is retrospective much of the information provided by the private sector in the past will not have distinguished what is confidential from what is not and this will now fall to the public body to determine.

Businesses should consider the information that they provide to the public sector and how to protect confidential information. Simply writing 'Confidential' on all information will not guarantee protection as public bodies are advised in the Code not to agree to hold information 'in confidence' which is not in fact confidential in nature. A systematic approach to evaluate and mark commercially confidential information is more likely to succeed. Public authorities are also advised in the Code to reject confidentiality clauses in contracts restricting the disclosure of the terms of the contract, its value and performance and that acceptance of such clauses must be for good reasons which are capable of being justified to the Information Commissioner, the regulator responsible for FOIA.

When providing information, private organizations should consider requesting public authorities to consult them before disclosing this further. Retrospective requests can also be lodged if information has already been provided which may cause difficulties if disclosed.

On the positive side, businesses can use FOIA to request information from public authorities which may not previously have been available to them and this may provide a competitive edge for example when tendering.

4.5 Internet and email usage policy

Introduction

Email is now an accepted form of communication in most businesses. Email systems used appropriately improve communication within a construction practice and between companies within the construction industry as a whole. However, inappropriate use can cause problems ranging from employee time wasting to legal claims. As an employer, a company will be vicariously liable for the acts and omissions of its employees if they are committed in the course of their employment, so it is important that employers can control employees' use of their business equipment. There are a number of laws, however, which govern the extent to which employers can monitor their employees' communications, such as faxes, telephone calls and email, and their use of the Internet.

The legal position

The Regulation of Investigatory Powers Act 2000 (RIPA) covers the interception of communications and surveillance. It draws a distinction between monitoring business communications and personal communications. It provides that an employer who controls a private telecommunications network will be open to a civil action for unlawful interception from either party to the communications if it intercepts personal communications without the consent of both parties to the communication or if it intercepts business communications without lawful authority to do so.

Personal communications Personal emails cannot be monitored without the consent of both the sender and receiver, which in effect means that external personal emails cannot be monitored at all. Personal emails between employees can be monitored if both employees have consented to the interception.

Business communications Lawful authority for intercepting business emails is provided in the Lawful Business Practice Regulations 2000 (LBPR). The LBPR state that provided reasonable steps are taken to inform both the sender and receiver, business emails may be monitored: to ascertain whether the organization's standards and procedures are being complied with; to establish the existence of facts; for national security; to prevent or detect crime; to detect unauthorized use; and to secure the effective operation of the system. The interception must always be in connection with the employer's business and on a telecommunications system which is provided wholly or partly in connection with its operations. The correspondents can be notified by including a header in all emails which alerts them to the company's monitoring practices.

Under the Human Rights Act 1998, employers also have a general duty to respect the privacy of their employees and any measures which interfere with this right must be a proportionate response to a legitimate concern. Therefore, if there is a less intrusive means of achieving the company's aim, such as by using purely automated monitoring systems or monitoring traffic data alone, it must be used.

The monitoring of communications is likely to involve the processing of personal data about employees and as such it is also covered by the Data Protection Act 1998. The Information Commissioner advises that a minimalist approach should be taken to any such monitoring. Monitoring personal emails and collecting a record of internet sites visited by employees could easily reveal sensitive personal data about them (see Section 4.3 on Data Protection) and the explicit consent of employees to such monitoring will therefore be required. In addition to seeking explicit consent, employers could employ devices which block certain sites, thereby reducing the risk that employees will be able to access inappropriate sites in the first place.

The difficulty for businesses interpreting this legislation is determining what is a business and personal email. The best solution is for businesses to provide employees with two email accounts. One would be for work-related emails, it would contain the company's standard email notice and disclaimer and could be monitored in accordance with the LBPR. The other account would be entirely separate. Its address would not identify the company in any way, its notice and disclaimer would make clear that it was a personal email, it would not be capable of attaching documents from the company's network and it would not be subject to the company's monitoring devices and procedures.

If this is not possible, the company should completely ban personal use of business equipment, enshrining that ban in a policy and enforcing it in practice. This would then allow businesses to argue that all emails were work-related and could be monitored in accordance with the LBPR. If a personal email is sent despite a complete prohibition, any potential claims for breach of privacy under the Human Rights Act would be less persuasive to a court if the employer had provided alternative means of communicating privately, such as a non-networked PC which bypasses the monitoring systems.

A further advantage for a company of having personal emails clearly identified as such, is that should it receive a subject access request (see Section 4.3 on Data Protection) it will not have to supply personal emails, since the writer of those emails will be the data controller of them.

In practice, however, the reality is that if companies do not consider that the establishment of separate accounts or a complete prohibition is practicable, they often take the risk of their monitoring being in breach of the legislation.

Internet and email usage policy

Any prudent employer should therefore put in place a corporate policy for internet and email use. The policy should explain whether there is a complete ban on personal emails or whether there is a separate account which should be used for any personal emails. If the business permits employees to use business equipment for personal communications (whether or not its policy states that there is a complete ban), any monitoring of those communications without consent of both parties will be unlawful.

The policy should explain what constitutes authorized use of the business equipment and what sanctions will apply in the event of inappropriate or unauthorized use. Consent to the policy should be obtained by including it in the company's employment contracts or staff manual for all new employees and by asking all existing employees to sign it. The following section lists some of the issues that should be covered in such a policy.

Employees' use of Internet for personal reasons Restrictions on an employee's surfing the Internet (unless for reasons connected with his or her work) are generally easier to impose than restrictions on personal emails. In addition to blocking certain sites, employees should be told that a record of the websites they visit will be compiled to ensure that they are not abusing their right to use the equipment and, for example, downloading material which may not be illegal but may offend their colleagues. The policy should state that inappropriate use is subject to appropriate sanctions, including the ultimate sanction of dismissal.

Defamation and discrimination The informal nature of email encourages casual comment. Emails that have been sent without thought and with no intention of reliance by the author have led to companies incurring legal liability due to defamatory statements. For example, Norwich Union had to pay Western Provident substantial damages due to defamatory statements relating to the financial standing of Western Provident circulated by an employee. Emails and postings on the company's Intranet can also lead to similar claims. The policy should make clear that business emails should be treated like letters on company letterhead and should not contain informal personal opinions of employees which may be defamatory or could give rise to vicarious liability under other laws, such as for racial and sexual discrimination.

Copyright infringement anti-viruses Much of the material available on the Internet is subject to copyright protection. The company policy should therefore include a statement about the dangers of possible copyright infringement when downloading from the Internet. Copying should be expressly forbidden without careful authorization and clarification that all necessary intellectual property rights have been acquired. As viruses are normally attached to executable code, the policy will also wish to ensure that proper virus-protection procedures are followed.

Personal data Employees should be made aware that any information in emails which is capable of identifying individuals is personal data and the individuals so identified will be entitled to a copy of such emails should they request them from the company (see Section 4.3 on Data Protection). Employees should therefore be advised to be cautious in including any personal data in emails.

4.6 Security

Introduction

Security breaches are common both from inside and outside an organization and they can be both intentional and accidental. Examples of external threats to security are computer viruses and Trojan programs. Viruses are often easily recognized and can be combated with anti-virus software products. Trojan software often appears to be legitimate software, but has a second program hidden within it. This second program is run when the main program is run, without the user knowing about it and can install itself on the computer in order to carry out tasks in the future. The impact of external breaches can be devastating. A single virus or Trojan program on a file server can destroy all the data on it or, more worryingly, copy the data and send it back to the hacker.

An organization also needs to think about internal security breaches, both intentional and accidental. For example, a departing employee may copy files and take confidential business information on to their next job or an employee may accidentally delete database records which have not been backed up because they had access which they should not have had. The impact of such breaches can also be tremendous, often with access to key business information being obtained or lost.

Security is becoming more important to businesses for a number of reasons, not least the incidence of previous breaches and the increasing recognition of the importance and value of business information.

There are also security obligations in various pieces of legislation, an important one being the Data Protection Act 1998 which is covered under Section 4.3. Under the seventh principle organizations have an obligation to protect personal data against unauthorized or unlawful processing and against accidental loss, destruction or damage by implementing appropriate security measures.

Information security policy

In order to minimize the risk of security breaches happening in the first instance, an information security policy should be integrated into business processes. The information security policy should cover personnel, physical and environmental security. The existence and content of this policy should then be communicated to all customers/users as well as employees of the organization. It is important that all people in the organization are aware of the need for and feel responsibility for security for the policy to be effective. In this regard, training should be provided.

Examples of overall good information security practice include limiting access to certain information to authorized personnel and securing access, for example, through password protection; good document management so that confidential information is ordered and is secure; and preventing unauthorized access to information by locking away confidential documents/computers.

There are various levels of security. For example, it is commonplace for a user to have password access to their email account. However, a much higher level of security would be to encrypt email messages containing confidential information. The level of security required will depend on the sensitivity of the data.

The International Standard code of practice on how to secure information systems is ISO/IEC 17799. This should be referred to as a starting point for drafting a company's information security policy as it sets out the kind of issues that an information security policy should cover. It characterizes information security as the preservation of:

(a) confidentiality: ensuring that information is accessible only to those authorized to have access;
(b) integrity: safeguarding the accuracy and completeness of information and processing methods; and
(c) availability: ensuring that authorized users have access to information and associated assets when required.

It outlines the following critical success factors for any information security policy to be effective:

- security policy, objectives and activities that reflect business objectives;
- an approach to implementing security that is consistent with the organizational culture;
- visible support and commitment from management;
- a good understanding of the security requirements, risk assessment and risk management;
- effective marketing of security to all managers and employees;
- distribution of guidance on information security policy and standards to all employees and contractors;
- providing appropriate training and education; and
- a comprehensive and balanced system of measurement which is used to evaluate performance in information security management and feedback suggestions for improvement.

Web security policy

The organization should also have a web security policy.

The *AEB web security guidelines (Alliance for Electronic Business 2002)* set out guidelines for businesses running websites for either information or transactional purposes, but especially for organizations that are just getting into eBusiness. They state that web security encompasses safeguarding the accuracy and completeness of information used in website and eBusiness processes; ensuring that only authorized users can access website and eBusiness services and that they can access such services when they need them; and ensuring that the availability, confidentiality and integrity of information of those visiting the website, or transacting business through it, is maintained.

When thinking about security an organization needs to do identify what software, hardware and information business assets need to be protected and the risk of exposure of these assets. The organization then needs to develop a web security policy which will set out the procedures and policies for dealing with information as well as future objectives. The policy should be a written document, which is regularly reviewed and updated, available to all employees responsible for information security and should cover all business assets and systems.

As well as trying to improve web security, measures can also be taken to protect the organization in the event of a breach. For instance, taking regular back-ups of information and retaining a copy of information in a secure place will minimize the effect of loss of data.

The detailed AEB guidelines can be found at http://www.cssa.co.uk/home/reports/websecfinal.pdf.

Criminal offences

Under the Computer Misuse Act 1990 unauthorized access to computer material (i.e. program or data); unauthorized access to a computer system with intent to commit or facilitate the commission of a serious crime; and unauthorized modification of computer material are all criminal offences.

4.7 EU e-commerce directives

Introduction

In terms of e-commerce, we have looked at on-line project collaboration applications upon the basis that these applications have gained currency in the industry. We anticipate that there will be a place for the use of on-line procurement applications, perhaps even internet exchanges for certain parties in the construction supply chain in the future. This is likely to be driven by the builder's merchants rather than contractors. Currently more discrete ordering and invoicing applications are being used which are web-based but *are* point to point as with EDI transactions. These are used to undertake paperless back office processing of orders and invoices.

This area has been the subject of a number of EU directives which have been implemented in UK national law. The broad objective of these directives is to protect consumers and achieve uniformity and fairness of dealing across member states. As consumers have only a peripheral involvement in the construction process, sitting at one end of the long supply chain, it remains to be seen how relevant and significant the terms of the directives and UK legislation will be for the industry. As the conclusion of on-line contracts may occur in a different context, for example, the conclusion of an on-line variation to a contract, it is appropriate to consider the contractual issues and relevant legislation here.

Contracting on the web

A contract will only be created when, in common law terms, there is an offer and acceptance to purchase identified (or identifiable) goods and services at an identified (or identifiable) price. This is where the main difficulties begin. The common law concept of offer and acceptance, although attractive in its simplicity, was developed when most contracts were made face to face and has come under considerable strain in the modern world.

The Internet adds a further degree of complexity with on-line procurement: is the supplier's tender an acceptance of the purchaser's offer or is it an offer? If it is an offer, then the buyer's communication accepting the tender is presumably an acceptance, but when is that acceptance given? When the buyer clicks on the 'send' button? When the message crosses the buyer's gateway and hits the Internet? When the message is received by the supplier's ISP? When the message crosses the gateway onto the supplier's system? When the supplier is capable of reading the message? When the supplier actually reads the message?

English law currently provides no answer and European law, in the form of the Electronic Commerce Directive, provides an answer which, while eliminating certain of the options, leaves the matter completely undecided. The only remedy is for the purchaser or the internet exchange to specify – in terms and conditions which are communicated clearly before any acceptance is transmitted – what will constitute acceptance and when a contractual obligation will come into effect. (The second stipulation is advisable because, under certain systems of law, reflected in the Electronic Commerce Directive, a contractual obligation does not come into effect until after acceptance – it arises only when the acceptance is acknowledged.)

Where the parties are trading partners and they wish to undertake their ordering and invoicing on-line, they should conclude an agreement to cover this type of issue. EDI model forms can be used and the legal issues which arise are very similar. The JCT Forms of Contract include supplementary provisions, although these are for use in projects which rarely occurs. Other forms are readily available on the web. Whatever the form of the agreement, it will include references to the following issues.

Security and authenticity of messages

Both parties will need to agree to take certain security measures to protect the message. Depending on the nature and value of the transaction and the data that is being exchanged, different security measures will be required – for example, encryption may or may not be desirable.

To provide a degree of security the parties should also agree that all messages received need to be acknowledged and the content confirmed. Alternatively, the sender can request the recipient to acknowledge the message. Similarly, where a message has been received by the recipient by mistake it should be required to inform the sender and to delete the message in question. As mentioned above, the effect of all these practical steps has to be mapped onto the legal process. If a contract is created by a message sent by mistake, does it still stand or is it rescinded?

Maintaining a data log

For evidential and audit purposes the agreement should require both parties to maintain a trade or data log so that there is a full record of all messages sent and received (including unauthorized or misdirected messages). The parties should also agree the content of such records and whether the data log can be maintained in electronic form. If an electronic log is kept, a further procedure must be agreed for recovering the data without any modification to that data. In particular, the Civil Evidence Act requires that for computer evidence to be admissible there must be a certificate stating that the system was functioning when the evidential record was produced.

2.1 Ways of operating
2.2 Working with others
2.3 Working internationally
2.4 The engineer's appointment
2.5 Collateral warranties
2.6 Indemnity insurance
2.7 Employment law
2.8 Information technology

Trust

Trust can be characterized as follows.

(a) Identity – how do you know the identity of the party you are dealing with over the Internet?
(b) Authenticity – how do you know that a message you receive over the Internet is the same message that left the sender's machine (in other words, how do you know it has not been tampered with)?
(c) Evidence – how can you associate a sender with a message (in other words, how can you prevent a sender from disclaiming any knowledge of a message which he or she has sent but then regretted)?

The most common solution, which is propounded to all three problems, is the use of digital signatures – a solution sanctioned in the UK by the Electronic Communications Act 2000 and in the EU generally by the Electronic Signatures Directive.

Electronic signatures

Electronic signatures are technological methods of reproducing the same identifying function which is performed by a written signature. Digital signatures are a particular form of electronic signature which make use of public/private key encryption in order to combat all three problems identified above. The essential components are that each contracting entity should have a unique pair of public and private keys. The private key is used to 'lock' (i.e. encrypt) messages which the contracting entity sends. The messages can only be unlocked with the contracting entity's public key, which is freely available to all other contracting parties from a key registry. Because the private/public key combination is unique, a message which can be opened with the individual's public key must have been locked with his or her private key, thus providing proof of identity. (It does not, of course, prove that the person with the private/public key is who he or she says they are – only that he or she is the person with that particular private/public key. The evidence linking the key with the holder of the key has to come from the key registry or from a certification authority which will probably require evidence of a more mundane and familiar sort – e.g. a passport or certificate of incorporation – before certifying that the holder of the key in question is 'X'.)

The public key can also be used by the sender to send a compacted replica of the original message with the message itself. The recipient, by applying the public key a second time, can check that this replica is identical with the original message, thus providing proof that the message has not been tampered with.

Finally, by transmitting the message through a certification authority, the sender and recipient can obtain proof that the message was sent at a certain time, in a certain form, by a certain sender – thus removing the risk of repudiation.

As can be seen, digital signatures require a considerable degree of administrative and technical coordination which has hampered its adoption and use in industry generally. It is likely that other forms of electronic signature (for example, biometric identification) will find readier acceptance in time. Currently there is little evidence of take up in this area and therefore the issues underlying trust are being largely ignored by those seeking to bind themselves contractually using the Internet.

The problem of paper

None of these solutions to the problem of making a contract electronically are of any effect if the country under whose law the contract is purportedly made does not recognize contracts of the type in question unless they are made in a certain (normally paper-based) form. Even in the UK, which has traditionally recognized most contracts without the need for writing or a particular form, there have always been certain types of document – for example, contracts concerning land which require particular formalities to be complied with if they are to be enforceable. The requirement for formality is greater in most other jurisdictions and while the Electronic Commerce Directive requires member states of the EU to phase out most such restrictions, and the UK Government has taken power, under the Electronic Communications Act 2000, to remove any remaining obstacles to electronic commerce from the UK statute book, it will still be several years before all contracts can be concluded electronically. It is therefore important, when making contracts on the web, to ensure that the governing law of the contract is the law of a jurisdiction which recognizes contracts of the type in question that are made in electronic form.

PART 3

General law

Section editor: Sir Vivian Ramsey QC
Keating Chambers

CHAPTER 3.1

The law of contract

Martin Bowdery QC
Atkin Chambers, Gray's Inn

Guy Cottam
Consulting Engineer

Patrick Clarke
Atkin Chambers, Gray's Inn

1 WHY BOTHER?

Many engineers and engineering contractors have an attitude to contracts which can best be described as indifferent if not hostile. They remark 'contracts are a waste of time', 'we've never had any trouble because we know our customers and our contractors', 'if we needed to rely on a contract with a client we wouldn't deal with them', 'Lawyers just get in the way'. This attitude is confusing and misleading. It mixes up a contractual frame of reference with the use of the law in order to enforce rights. The legal system should be used, at best, as a last resort, to enforce self-regulation by contract. However, that does not mean that the self-regulation contained within the contractual agreement is unimportant in guiding or influencing contractual behaviour. The contract will still be used or misused as a point of reference during negotiations towards a compromise of disputes even though for good and sufficient reasons neither party has any intention of resorting to law.

To understand how the law of contract can govern commercial behaviour it is important to identify not just the requirements for a valid contract but also why contracts are usually always incomplete. The four basic requirements for a valid contract are tediously well known:

- an agreement between the parties (which is usually but not invariably established by the fact that one has made an offer and the other has accepted it)
- an intention or commitment to be legally bound by that agreement (often called an intention to create legal relations)
- certainty as to the terms of the agreement
- consideration provided by each of the parties.

In addition, the parties must be legally capable of forming a contract and, in some cases, certain formalities must be complied with. It is not necessary for a contract to be in writing – a contract is an agreement not a piece of paper. A 'gentleman's agreement' is invariably neither an agreement nor an arrangement entered into by gentlemen.

Before considering in greater detail each requirement for a valid or complete contract it is appropriate to consider what an agreement does not necessarily usually include or why it is sometimes more important to review what a contract does not encompass rather than consider what it does.

Agreements are almost always incomplete; contract lawyers are employed ostensibly for two different tasks:

- to plan or to record a transaction
- to participate in dispute resolution.

Cynics may say that weaknesses in fulfilling the first function are more than amply compensated by taking part in the second function. However, when contract lawyers seek to translate the economic deal into a legally enforceable written agreement, they must acknowledge that, although they can plan or draft for various contingencies or risks through the terms of the contract, such planning can never be complete. The risk can never be fully identified or offloaded. Recognizing this inevitable incompleteness and uncertainty in tying down contractual risks is as important as the tedious drafting of clauses to regulate the parties rights and obligations.

Contractual documents often attempt to allocate all risks, no matter how unexpected the contingency, by general phrases such as 'the contractor will be responsible for all disruption howsoever caused'. However, general words may often fail to cover specific risks if such unexpected risks only occur outside the contemplation of the contractual documents.

In an uncertain world, with a complex and challenging construction or engineering project, the parties may acknowledge and accept that they will want to modify their arrangements over time in the light of changing market conditions, changing requirements or changing technologies. In these circumstances the contract lawyer in drafting the contract, should avoid tight or rigid commitments but emphasize the need for flexibility, discretion or the intervention of an outsider to regulate the parties' rights and obligations in the face of changing circumstances. The parties can then achieve flexibility in their contractual agreements albeit at the cost of contractual certainty.

Contract documents do frequently provide for dispute resolution procedures, such as arbitration and adjudication considered elsewhere in this handbook. However, these procedures are generally only enforced by the courts to the extent that they provide for or result in a binding resolution. Agreements to enter into negotiations about disputes are generally not enforceable (as confirmed in the case of *Halifax Financial Services Limited* v. *Intuitive Systems Limited* (1999) CILL 1467), however the courts will enforce agreements to participate in a defined dispute resolution procedure properly construed as a condition precedent to litigation (*Cable & Wireless Plc* v. *IBM United Kingdom Ltd* (2002) CILL 1930).

The gaps or holes in the contractual arrangements will pose difficulties when disputes or differences arise. The parties to the contract may quite sensibly refrain from addressing detailed problems of remote or unforeseen risks in their business deals. However, when their risks become eventualities, the parties must either negotiate a compromise to deal with such an event or the courts must intervene.

Traditionally, the courts have been biased towards a literal interpretation of the express obligations of the parties and have been biased against any argument that these obligations or risks can be reallocated or allocated afresh in the light of the parties' expectations once that risk has become an eventuality. The critical question is how the parties, and, if necessary, the courts should resolve issues which arise during engineering projects where the contract has not precisely or clearly allocated these risks. Should these issues be resolved on the basis of:

(a) the contract documents, and/or
(b) the business deal and the context in which it was made.

Judicial intervention which leads to the judicial reallocation of risk is almost, but not wholly, foreign to the English courts. Under the relief offered by doctrines such as *force majeure*, frustration or commercial impracticability, the allocation of risk can sometimes be re-allocated by the courts so as to do justice between the parties.

Some might say that the courts should generally try to do justice between the parties rather than adjudicate as to which set of contract lawyers has been luckier in allocating risks within the thousands of pages of contract documents assembled within an imposed or unrealistic tendering timetable. Judges should attach less weight to the paperwork but concentrate their minds on a study of the background, context, market circumstances, assumptions and expectations of the parties to the contract. Such investigations might lead to more judicial decisions that the contract documents so expensively and comprehensively prepared by the parties contract lawyers fail to begin to grasp how risks arising from improbable contingencies should be allocated. Having grasped that the contract documentation is a servant and not the master of the parties commercial expectations, the courts might become more enthusiastic in engaging in a judicial review of these documents.

Lord Diplock, in *Pioneer Shipping Limited* v. *BTP Tioxide Ltd 'The Nema'* [1982] AC 724 suggested that the Court should, in that case, defer to:

> 'A commercial arbitrator's findings as to mercantile usage and the understanding of mercantile men about the significance of the commercial differences between what was promised and what in the changed circumstances would now fall to be performed'.

However, the English courts generally remain biased against allocating the consequences of unidentified risks other than by interpreting what the contract says even if, as a matter of logic, the contract has nothing to say about such risks. The courts should recognize that for good and sufficient reasons contracts are often left incomplete because the allocation of unforeseen risks can only be dealt with as they arise and, having arisen, can only be allocated on the basis of the circumstances within which they arose.

In seeking to regulate contractual agreements the legal system overemphasizes the significance of the formal contractual documentation at the expense of the parties legitimate commercial objectives and at the expense of the parties own priorities which are often their long-term business relationships and the commercial success of the particular transaction they have worked together on. When enforcing the contractual agreement the courts will tend to ignore the parties' own view that the contractual documentation only provides a partial reflection of the parties' commercial expectations.

This refusal to acknowledge that we live and operate and endeavour to cooperate in an uncertain world is typified by the English courts' general refusal to acknowledge any obligation by a contracting party to act in good faith. As Bingham LJ stated in *Interfoto* v. *Stilletto Visual Programmes* [1989] 1 QB 433:

> 'In many civil law systems, and perhaps in most legal systems outside the common law world, the law of obligations recognises and enforces an overriding principle that in making and carrying out contracts parties should act in good faith. This does not simply mean that they should not deceive each other, a principle which any legal system must recognise, its effect is perhaps most aptly conveyed by such metaphorical colloquialisms as "playing fair", "coming clean" or "putting ones cards face upwards on the table". It is in essence a principle of fair open dealing... English law has, characteristically, committed itself to no such overriding principle but has developed piecemeal solutions in response to demonstrated problems of unfairness.'

However, a specific (rather than general) duty to act fairly or in good faith has been held to apply by implication to certain contractual obligations such as those between an employer and employee and the exercise of a unilateral discretionary power where conferred on one party by the contract (*Paragon Finance* v. *Nash* [2002] 1 WLR 594 CA).

In endeavouring to summarize the law of contract in the remainder of this chapter, emphasis will be given to the formal requirements of a contract and to the formal rules adopted in construing contracts even though it is envisaged that a more flexible and purposive construction of complex and complicated contract will, one day, be adopted by the English courts.

2 MAKING A CONTRACT

There are four key elements to the making of a valid contract:

- an agreement between the parties
- an intention or a communication to be legally bound by that agreement

- certainty as to the terms of the agreement
- consideration provided by each of the parties.

The contract need not be in writing save for a few exceptions such as a contract for a guarantee. A contract is an agreement not a piece of paper. However, when considering what is required to form a valid contract concerted efforts should be made to ensure:

- that the contract is reduced to writing
- the parties do not stumble into an agreement without realizing that they have in fact concluded an agreement
- that the parties do not leave loose ends during these negotiations which can be exploited later when the disappointed party runs claims based on misrepresentation, collateral contracts or on the basis of contentions that the contract was, in fact, made partly in writing and partly orally.

To avoid or limit such opportunism, negotiations leading up to an agreement can be marked 'subject to contract' and/or subject to any written contract being signed by both parties. The written contract should also contain an 'entire contract clause' which provides that the parties' rights and obligations are defined and are contained by the four corners of the written contract.

2.1 Unilateral or bilateral contracts

The classification of contracts into unilateral or bilateral is not helpful. The distinction means only that with a unilateral contract, just one party undertakes an obligation. Bilateral contracts, or synallagmatic contracts, are those under which both parties undertake obligations. A unilateral contract would be the offer of a reward for the return of property or lost cat. A bilateral contract comprises the exchange of a promise for a promise such as 'I will find your cat if you promise to pay me £10'. A similar distinction rests between 'executory' consideration and 'executed' consideration. Consideration is called executory when a party's promise is made in return for a counter-promise from the other party. Executed consideration is when a party's promise is made in return for the performance of an act. So, a unilateral contract relies upon executed consideration. A mutual contract relies on executory consideration. Given that both types of contract are binding contracts, these distinctions identify differences of academic and limited interest.

2.2 Letters of intent

Documents described as letters of intent are often exchanged. Such a document usually expresses an intention to enter into a contract in the future. Each letter of intent must be construed in its own factual content. For example, it may be:

- just a letter of comfort intended to have no legal effect
- an intention to carry out work pending the formal agreement of a more complex contract for which one party will pay the other party a reasonable sum if the final agreement is not concluded
- an executory ancillary agreement entitling the recipient of the letter of intent to reasonable costs if the future complex contract is not concluded and imposing an obligation on the recipient of the letter regarding the quality and suitability of the work carried out pursuant to the terms of such a letter.

The uncertainty created by the wide use of such letters of intent in differing factual circumstances would be eliminated or at least reduced if the parties accepted that, pending the agreement of a formal executed contract, the parties entered into a separate contract, called a preliminary contract, which spelt out the rights and obligations of the parties pending the agreement of the formal contract and the rights and obligations of the parties if that formal contract cannot be agreed. The fact that the parties both anticipate that the letter of intent is to be superseded by a later, more complex formal contract does not of itself prevent the letter of intent being interpreted as a contract in itself. What is important is to achieve certainty in the terms of this preliminary or anticipatory simple contract and to agree what happens if the more complex contract cannot be agreed.

3 OFFER AND ACCEPTANCE

Generally, for a contract to come into existence one party must make an offer which the other must accept. Once acceptance takes effect a binding contract exists. Complex rules of offer and acceptance have been developed by the courts in order to identify the precise moment in time when a series of often complex negotiations have reached the point where a contract has been concluded. These rules are complex and sometimes archaic because there can be no halfway house: there is either a binding contract or there is not and the parties' negotiations can continue.

Before examining these rules in further detail, a third way should be considered. Steyn LJ in *G. Percy Trentham* v. *Architral Luxfer* [1993] 1 LR 25 stated that a contract may come into existence even if there is no coincidence of offer and acceptance during and as a result of performance. This third way of determining when parties during the course of long and complex negotiations, often while work is being carried out pursuant to the letter of intent, slip into a binding contract has not been endorsed by many judges or commentators. For example, the editors of the Building Law Reports take a conservative position on this case and state:

> 'The proposition that a contract may come into existence even if there is no coincidence of offer and acceptance (by whatever means), "during and as a result of performance", is one to be applied with care. The cases cited by Steyn LJ do not perhaps fully support all his propositions.'

An alternative interpretation of the 'third way' is that a contract may come into existence by a coincidence of an offer that arises out of the conduct of the offeror followed by acceptance by the conduct of the offeree. In any event, for present purposes the old rules of offer and acceptance need to be understood.

3.1 Invitations to treat

Most complex transactions require a preliminary stage in which one party, or a representative of one party, invites the other to make an offer. This stage in the dance which leads to a concluded contract is called an invitation to treat. The distinction between an invitation to treat and an offer is that an invitation to treat cannot be made with the intention that it becomes a binding agreement as soon as the person to whom it is sent communicates agreement to its terms. A statement is obviously not an offer where it expressly provides that the person who makes the statement is not to be bound by the other party's ratification of their consent, but only when the statement maker has actually signed the document containing the statement.

However, the courts have had difficulty in distinguishing between invitation to treat and offer, and in certain circumstances a statement has been held to be an invitation to treat even though it contained the word 'offer', and a statement has been held to

3.1 The law of contract
3.2 Construction health and safety
3.3 Insolvency in construction
3.4 Law of tort
3.5 Environmental issues

constitute an offer although it was expressed as an 'acceptance', or even where it required the person to whom it was sent to make an 'offer'.

As always, clarity and certainty should be created by the maker of the document. An invitation to treat or an invitation to tender for proposed works should not only state clearly that it is not an offer but that there will not be a binding contract until the person asking for the tenders accepts one of them and then, and only then, both parties sign the contract documentation.

3.2 Offer

An offer is an expression of being ready, willing and able to enter into a contract made with the intention, actual or apparent, that the terms of the offer will become binding on the person making it as soon as it is accepted unequivocally by the person to whom it is addressed. Under the objective test of construing agreements, an apparent intention is sufficient. A binding contract is made if a lawyer, having been instructed to settle a claim for £10 000, by mistake offered to sell it for the higher sum of £100 000, i.e. it is not what the parties do rather than what they may have intended to do that matters. An offer, to be effective, must be:

- clear and certain
- communicated before it is accepted.

However, an offer may be withdrawn at any time before it is accepted. An offer may expressly state the precise time within which it is open for acceptance. If that time expires without acceptance then the offer also expires. If no time is stated during which the offer must be accepted, the offer remains open for a reasonable time and on the expiry of that time the offer expires. What is a reasonable time depends on the facts of each case. To avoid uncertainty, each offer should contain a 'sell-by date' beyond which it cannot be accepted.

3.3 Acceptance

There can generally be an acceptance of an offer bringing a binding contract into existence only when the person to whom the offer is made responds with an unconditional acceptance. If any new terms are suggested or any proposed terms are revised in the letter of acceptance there cannot be an acceptance unless these new terms or revised terms are insignificant in the overall scheme of things. What the courts decide are insignificant terms or insignificant revisions of offered terms will depend on the facts of each case and are difficult to define.

If the parties wish to avoid including contracts by playing an elaborate form of the children's card game 'snap', it would be sensible to agree that no agreement is concluded unless some condition, such as both parties signing the written contract documents, is fulfilled. In the absence of such a precondition being fulfilled, the parties must abide by the rules of offer and acceptance, which include the following.

- Acceptance must be unconditional and correspond to the terms of the offer.
- Acceptance may be made by conduct.
- Acceptance must be communicated, although postal acceptance generally takes place when the letter of acceptance is posted not when it is received.

Problems of offer and acceptance

Most, if not all, legal systems with European origins play the elaborate game of offer and acceptance to determine when the parties conclude a contract. This game distinguishes an offer from a counter-offer and an invitation to treat and requires an acceptance in accordance with legal rules which demand an unequivocal communicated acceptance. These rules are not self-applying but are imposed by the courts on the basis of an objective investigation of what the court thinks that the parties agreed and not what the parties thought had been agreed. This formal, pedestrian enquiry is regimented by rules developed by commercial practices based on the nineteenth century not the twenty-first century. This pedantic approach to determining when parties reach a concluded agreement will fall out of use and be replaced by a more modern approach. It is already disintegrating, but before it is replaced by a more modern approach to contract formation based on modern communications, commercial sense and the parties expectations, these rules of offer and acceptance must be recognized and the parties must play this game by its rules to avoid drifting into agreement without realizing that the time for negotiation has ended.

4 CONSIDERATION

In English law an agreement is not usually binding unless it is supported by what is called 'consideration'. This means that each party must give something in return for whatever is provided by the other party. You get 'nowt for nowt'. Consideration is normally said to be something which represents either a benefit to the party making the promise or some sort of detriment to the person to whom the promise is made. This doctrine has been called upon in support of general proposition such as 'English law will enforce a bargain but not a gift (or a promise)'. This doctrine has also attracted a series of contractual or legal rules to assess the adequacy or sufficiency of considerations, such as:

- consideration must be real or sufficient
- consideration must be something additional to the parties' existing obligations
- consideration must not be past consideration
- consideration must be given in return for the promise or act of the other party – something given as promised beforehand will not count as consideration
- consideration must be of economic value
- consideration can be a promise not to sue
- consideration must be from the person who wants to enforce the promise.

4.1 Problems with consideration

The requirement for consideration can enable parties who make promises that ought to be morally binding to avoid legal culpability. This has been one reason for a long legal tradition of judicial hostility to this doctrine. Lord Mansfield, at the end of the eighteenth century, held that a moral obligation could amount to consideration and for some 60 years that view effectively demolished the doctrine of consideration. In 1937, the Law Revision Committee proposed that:

- a written promise should be binding with or without consideration
- part consideration should be valid
- consideration should no longer need to move from the promisee
- performance of an existing duty should always be good consideration for a promise.

These reforms have not yet been implemented. As the author of *Chitty on Contracts* states: 'The present position therefore is that English law limits the enforceability of agreements (and deeds) by reference to a complex and multifarious body of rules known as "the doctrine of consideration" '.

As the law of contract is modernized this will be one of the first doctrines to fall. However, at present, forming a binding agreement still requires consideration.

5 CONSTRUCTION OF A CONTRACT

The terms of an agreement will describe the duties and obligations that each party has assumed under their agreement. When endeavouring to discover the meaning of a contractual term, the court will approach the task of ascertaining the intention of the parties objectively. The courts are not interested in what the parties may have meant or understood by the words used, but in the meaning which the document could convey to the reasonable person having all the background information available to the parties when the contract was concluded.

5.1 Expressed intention

Lord Hoffman, since joining the House of Lords, has, in a succession of cases, been considering the weight to be attached to the meaning of the words 'expressed intention'. In *Mannai Investment Co. Ltd* v. *Eagle Star Life Assurance Co. Ltd* [1997] AC 749, Lord Hoffman stated:

> 'It is of course true that the law is not concerned with the speaker's subjective intentions. But the notion that the law's concern is therefore with the "meaning of the words" conceals an important ambiguity. The ambiguity lies in a failure to distinguish between the meanings of words and the question of what would be understood as the meaning of a person who uses words. The meaning of words, as they would appear in a dictionary, and the effect of their syntactical arrangement, as it would appear in grammar, is part of the material which we use to understand a speaker's utterance. But it is only a part: another part is our knowledge of the background against which the utterance was made. It is that background which enables us, not only to choose the intended meaning when a word has more than one dictionary meaning but also to understand a speaker's meaning, often without ambiguity, when he has used the wrong words.'

Lord Hoffman in *ICS Ltd* v. *West Bromwich BS* [1998] 1 WLR 912 gave perhaps a clearer and less convoluted structured analysis of how, over recent years, what he described as 'all the old intellectual baggage' of legal interpretation has been discarded. Lord Hoffman thus provided a summary of the principles to be applied when construing or interpreting contractual documents. These principles are as follows.

(a) Interpretation is the ascertainment of the meaning which a document would convey to a reasonable person having all the background knowledge which would reasonably have been available to the parties in the situation in which they were at the time of the contract.
(b) The background was famously referred to by Lord Wilberforce as the 'matrix of fact' but this phrase is, if anything, an understated description of what the background may include. Subject to the requirement that it should have been reasonably available to the parties and to the exception to be mentioned next, it includes absolutely anything which would have affected the way in which the language of the document would have been understood by a reasonable person.
(c) The law excludes from the admissible background the previous negotiations of the parties and their declarations of subjective intent. They are admissible only in an action for rectification. The law makes this distinction for reasons of

practical policy and, in this respect only, legal interpretation differs from the way in which utterances are generally interpreted in ordinary life. The boundaries of this exception are in some respects unclear, but this is not the occasion on which to explore them.

(d) The meaning which a document (or any other utterance) would convey to a reasonable man or woman is not the same thing as the meaning of its words. The meaning of words is a matter of dictionaries and grammars; the meaning of the document is what the parties using those words against the relevant background would reasonably have been understood to mean. The background may not merely enable the reasonable person to choose between the possible meanings of words which are ambiguous but even (as occasionally happens in ordinary life) to conclude that the parties must, for whatever reason, have used the wrong words or syntax; see *Mannai Investments Co. Ltd* v. *Eagle Star Life Assurance Co. Ltd* [1997] AC 749.

(e) The 'rule' that words should be given their 'natural and ordinary meaning' reflects the common sense proposition that we do not easily accept that people have made linguistic mistakes, particularly in formal documents. On the other hand, if one would nevertheless conclude from the background that something must have gone wrong with the language, the law does not require judges to attribute to the parties an intention which they plainly could not have had. Lord Diplock made this point more vigorously when be said in *Antaios Compania Naviera S.A.* v. *Salen Rederierna A.B.* [1985] AC 191, 201:

> 'If detailed semantic and syntactical analysis of words in a commercial contract is going to lead to a conclusion that flouts business commonsense, it must be made to yield to business commonsense.'

So-called rules of construction can now be used to provide what is called a purposive construction of a contract document to reflect the parties' intentions and what they meant to agree, not what the courts think they did in fact agree to.

5.2 Rules of construction

Rules of construction, like many if not most rules, are there to be broken. Rules of construction are not rites of law. They are no more than guidelines to the interpretation of the English language. As Megarry pointed out in the *Law Quarterly Review* as long ago as 1945:

> 'The great truth about interpretation in England seems to be that the Bench has been provided with some degree of "principles" from which a judicious selection can be made to achieve substantial justice in each individual case. From time to time all the relevant principles point in the same direction and leave the Court no choice but in most of the cases susceptible of any real dispute the function of counsel is merely to provide sufficient material for the Court to perform its task of selection.'

In these circumstances, if the tribunal adopts a pick-and-mix approach to the rules of construction it is necessary to be familiar with the more popular so-called 'rules'.

Constructing the document as a whole

To determine the true meaning of a contractual document, a clause must not be considered in isolation but must be construed in the context of the whole document.

Internal consistency

A draftsperson is assumed to aim at a uniform consistency and the same words will be presumed to have the same meaning in different parts of the contract and different words are perceived to refer to different things or matters.

Giving a role to all parts of the contract

In construing a contract, all parts will be interpreted so as to be effective where possible and no part should be regarded as inoperative or surplus to requirements. Where a clause or sentence is ambiguous, a construction which will make that clause or sentence valid will be preferred to a construction which would make that clause or sentence void.

Written words prevail

Where there is a contract contained in a printed form with additional clauses added which are inconsistent with the printed words the general rule is:

> 'The written words are entitled to have a much greater effect attributed to them than the printed words in as much as the written words were the immediate language and terms selected by the parties themselves for the expressions of their meaning' – Lord Ellenhorough in *Robertson* v. *French* (1803) 4 East 130.

Express terms prevent the implication of terms

An express term in a contract excludes the possibility of implying *any* term dealing with the same subject matter as the express term.

A party should not be able to take advantage of its own wrong

A contractual document should be interpreted where possible in such a way that one party cannot take advantage of its own wrongful behaviour. This analysis can result in the implication of a term that prevents that result (The Bonde [1991] Lloyds Rep 136).

Presumption of impossibility

Courts will generally expect a party not to agree to do what is impossible and there is a general presumption of contractual interpretation that a contractual document will not require the performance of the impossible. As Sir John Donaldson MR said in *The Epaphus* [1987] 2 UR 213:

> 'My starting point is that parties to a contract are free to agree upon any terms which they consider appropriate, including a term requiring one of the parties to do the impossible, although it would be highly unusual for the parties knowingly so to agree. If they do so agree and if, as is inevitable, he fails to perform, he will be liable in damages. That said, any court will hesitate for a long time before holding that, as a matter of construction, the parties have contracted for the impossible, particularly in a commercial contract. Parties to such contracts can be expected to contemplate performance, not breach.'

The reasonableness of the competing constructions

Where there is doubt as to two or more possible constructions of a contractual document the reasonableness of the result of any particular construction is a relevant if not decisive factor in determining which construction should prevail. As Lord Reid stated in *Schuler* v. *Wickham Machine Tool Sales* [1974] AC 235:

'The fact that a particular construction leads to a very unreasonable result must be a relevant consideration. The more unreasonable the result the more unlikely it is that the parties can have intended it, and if they do intend it the more necessary it is that they shall make that intention abundantly clear.'

Considerations to be taken into account in determining whether or not a particular construction is reasonable will include the factual circumstances and commercial common sense (*Somerfield Stores Ltd* v. *Skanska Rashleigh Weatherfoil Ltd* (2007) CILL 2449).

Clerical or typographical errors

Where the contractual documentation contains an obvious mistake or error the court will recognize the mistake or error and should correct the mistake or error or construe the construction discussed as if the error or mistake had been corrected or eliminated.

Recitals to a contract document used only in cases of doubt

Recitals to a contract document are part of the introductory part of a document which tend to set out what the parties intend to achieve by their contract. If there is any doubt or ambiguity regarding what the effective part of the agreement is trying to achieve, the recitals can be considered to resolve that doubt or that ambiguity. However, in the absence of any such doubt or any ambiguity, the meaning of the document can only be defined by the operative parts of the agreement and not the recitals to the agreement.

Irreconcilable clauses

Where a tribunal cannot resolve an apparent inconsistency between two points of the contractual documentation it will endeavour to give effect to the contentions of the parties. If it is still unable to ascertain which claim should prevail it will reject the latter claim and give effect to the earlier claim.

The ejusdem generis *rule*

This rule is that where there are words of a particular class followed by general words, the general words are construed as referring to matters of the same particular class. A simple example is that of a ship being exempted from liability for non-delivery of a cargo if the destination of the cargo is unsafe 'in consequences of war, disturbances or any other cause'. It was held that danger from ice was not within the meaning 'any other cause' which must be limited to causes similar to 'war or disturbance'.

Construction against the grantor

Before reference to Latin phrases was forbidden by the courts, this rule used to be known as the *contra proferentem* rule. This expression is intended to mean that where there is an ambiguity in the contract documentation, as there are two alternative meanings to certain sentences, the tribunal should construe the words against the party who drafted or put forward the document. However, where the contract documentation has been drafted by representative bodies or committees such as the Institution of Civil Engineers or the Joint Contracts Tribunal, the *contra proferentem* rules, as it used to be known, should not be applied. This seems particularly harsh if one has any sympathy with the views of the edition of *Hudson* which, at page 116, states:

> 'It has to be said that even modern standard forms, or modern amendments to earlier forms, are replete with obscure and unconsidered draftsmanship, often leaving, whether deliberately or not, immediately obvious questions unanswered. Examples might include the new ICE fifth edition provision for interest to be payable on certificates, a new right to extension of time in the RIBA/JCT forms for failure to give possession, apparently failing to deal with possession of the site itself, the long-standing provisions in both the ICE and RIBA/JCT forms prohibiting "assignment of the contract" without consent, a new and complicated redefinition, the purpose of which is left to speculation, of the provisions relating to the architect's satisfaction introduced into the RIBA/JCT contracts in 1977, and a new apparent finality accorded in that regard to the architect's final certificate, with an initial and, it is submitted, incorrect interpretation of the latter by the courts in 1992. These examples are quite apart from the well-known major gaps in RIBA/JCT standard form draftsmanship, such as the silence and unknown intentions of the RIBA/JCT pre 1980 contracts in regard to the consequences of nominated sub-contractor repudiations, or as to the allocation of responsibilities for nominated sub-contractor design or as to the availability of set-off to owners resisting payment of sums due under interim certificates, or as to extensions of time for variations ordered after the contractor is in delay. "In addition, there are the cases where, presumably under combined producer and professional influence, the scope of contractors' financial claims for additional payment have obviously been deliberately left quite undefined and subject to the widest possible discretion by, ultimately, a court or arbitrator." A further area where careless draftsmanship has gravely damaged the interest of owners lies in the failure to provide practical and necessary remedies where defects are discovered during construction.
>
> All these factors make construction contracts eminently suitable for a liberal "business commonsense" or "genesis and aim" interpretative approach; but it has to be said that whereas that approach was often a characteristic of the nineteenth and early twentieth century judges, modern judges, and in particular the higher judiciary, have in recent years, perhaps aware of the difficulties caused by lack of knowledge of the background and the excessive complication and difficulty of the draftsmanship of the contracts, and in some cases at least expressing an exaggerated respect for the quality of the draftsmanship, have tended to fall back on a policy of "literalist construction". This has produced, in a noticeable number of cases, results at serious odds with the aim or purpose of the transaction viewed as a whole.'

Whether the courts adopt a more purposive or 'business commonsense' construction to standard form contracts or whether standard form contracts are simplified and clarified so that the more arcane excrescences are removed may not much matter; however, a 'literal' construction of the present-day standard forms will continue to create unexpected and somewhat surprising judicial interpretations of how these contracts are intended to work.

Subsequent conduct of the parties

The conduct of the parties following the formation of it is not relevant to the construction of written contract terms but may be a relevant consideration in the construction of the terms of an oral or partly written/partly oral contract (*Brian Royle Maggs (T/A BM Builders)* v. *(1) Guy Anthony Stanyer Marsh (2) Mars Jewellery Co. Ltd* (2006) CILL 2369).

Implied or inferred terms

For a term to be implied the following conditions must be fulfilled according to Lord Simon in *BP Refinery (Westernpoint) Pty Ltd* v. *Shire of Hastings* (1978) 52 AUJR 20.

(a) It must be reasonable and equitable.
(b) It must be necessary to give business efficacy to the contract so that no term will be implied into an agreement if the contract is effective without it.
(c) It must be so obvious that it goes without saying.
(d) It must be capable of clear expression.
(e) It must not contradict any express term of the contract.

There is some dispute whether conditions (b) and (c) are alternative or cumulative. The stronger view may be that:

- implied terms are implied by reasons of business efficacy
- inferred terms are inferred by reason of obvious inference

so terms can be inferred and/or implied into a contract depending on the particular circumstances of each contract. However, implied terms can also arise by way of:

- the operation of law
- custom
- statute.

Each is dealt with in turn below.

Terms implied by law

The following terms are generally implied into any commercial agreement unless explicitly or implicitly excluded by the express terms of the agreement.

- Neither party to an agreement shall prevent the other from performing their obligations arising out of the contract.
- Where the performance of the contract cannot take place without the cooperation of the parties, it is implied that the parties will cooperate with each other.
- Where a contract provides for continuing performance and does not provide for the expiry or determination, the term will be implied that the agreement can be determined after a reasonable period of time after a party has given reasonable notice.
- Where there is no express time by which the parties should perform any contractual obligation the parties will perform their contractual obligations within a reasonable time.
- Where there is no express agreement for the price to be paid for any contractual benefit the price to be paid will be a reasonable price for any such benefit.

Eventually, the English courts will imply a term that parties to a commercial contract will act in good faith. Some might say this is the very least one would expect from a commercial contract. Sadly, at present the English courts cannot go that far and do not expect or require parties to a commercial contract to act in good faith!

Terms implied by custom or usage

Where a term or provision would automatically be part of an agreement made by the parties involved in a particular trade or enterprise, such a term will be implied by the courts provided that there is no conflict between the usage and the terms of the contract.

To be implied, such a usage must be notorious, certain and reasonable and not contrary to law. It must be something beyond a mere trade practice. These usages are incorporated on the basis that the courts are spelling out what both parties knew and would, if asked, unhesitatingly agree would be part of the bargain.

Terms implied by statute

Parliament, irrespective of which government is in power, increasingly seeks to interfere in the freedom of parties to agree the terms which govern their business relationships. The incorporation of compulsory payment provisions and adjudication into most engineering and construction contracts by the Housing Grants, Construction and Regeneration Act 1996 is a recent example of where Parliament predetermines what terms must be implied into commercial contracts. Further examples of terms implied by statute are to be found in the Supply of Goods and Services Act 1982. In a contract under which a person or party agrees to provide a service other than a contract of service or apprenticeship and certain other exempted types of agreements, the Supply of Goods and Services Act 1982 implies by statute, various terms. For example, by section 13 it is implied that the supplier will carry out the service contracted for with reasonable skill and care. By sections 14 and 15 under this 1982 Act where, under a contract for the supply of a service by a supplier acting in the course of the time for the service to be carried out or the price for the service being performed has not been fixed or agreed, there will be statutory implied terms that the supplier will carry out the service within a reasonable time and for a reasonable price. Furthermore, a term is implied into contracts for the supply of goods and services by the Late Payment of Commercial Debts (Interest) Act 1998 whereby any qualifying debt created by contract is to carry statutory interest subject to the terms of that Act.

Exemption clauses

Any commercial agreement would wish to cover what Americans might describe as the upside and the downside of any bargain. It is a common feature of most written standard contracts that the party offering the document will seek to limit its liabilities if the contract turns sour. The use of exemption clauses is an important tool in apportioning risk between the parties and determining which party should bear which risk and indeed which risks neither party should bear but which should be protected by insurance.

Exemption clauses fall into the following categories.

- Clauses which seek to exclude all liability for certain breaches are called exclusion clauses.
- Clauses which seek to limit or reduce what would otherwise be the defendant's duty: this would be done by expressly restricting a party's substantive obligations, for example, by excluding from the contract express or implied terms or by restricting liability to cover of wilful default.
- Clauses which seek to limit or reduce the obligations of the party in default to fully indemnify or compensate the other party by limiting the damages recoverable against it or by providing a time limit within which claims must be instigated.

The modern approach to exemption clauses, including exclusion clauses, is not to construe the contract as if the clause did not exist and then to consider whether the clause provides an effective defence to the claim, but to construe the whole contract together with the exemption clause to discover the presumed intention of the parties as to whether a particular risk has been included or excluded as a potential liability. A commercial agreement, particularly a standard form entered into by two significant parties, may contain relatively ferocious exemption clauses which the courts will tend to uphold. The Unfair Contract Terms Act 1977 was intended to control the use of clauses excluding or limiting liability by breach of contract, particularly where one of the parties is a consumer. Where the contract imposes a 'business' liability, exclusions or exemptions clauses may have to satisfy the statutory test of reasonableness but, between two organizations of reasonably comparable negotiating strengths and weaknesses, any agreed apportionment of risk should be held to be reasonable by most tribunals.

Unenforceable terms

As well as adding terms to a contract by the operation of law or statute that did not form part of the agreement between the parties as described above, the courts will also decline to enforce certain terms that the parties may have agreed thereby depriving them of any meaningful effect. The courts will not enforce:

(a) Agreements to agree or negotiate (but see the *Halifax and Cable & Wireless cases referred to above*). Such terms are also considered to be too uncertain to have binding force.
(b) 'Unreasonable terms' are not enforced in certain circumstances pursuant to the provisions of the Unfair Contract Terms Act 1977.
(c) Terms or contracts where the agreement or the performance of the same is or would be illegal by common law or statute.

6 TERMINATING OR DETERMINING A CONTRACT

Crucial differences between determining a contract and terminating a contract can be confused. 'Determination' means the exercise of an agreed contractual machinery to bring to an end the parties continuing contractual obligation. 'Termination' means that the innocent party has accepted the repudiatory breach of the guilty party and terminates the agreement. All primary obligations are then discharged, to be replaced by the secondary obligations to determine what damages should be paid as a result of the wrongful repudiation of the contract.

6.1 Discharge by agreement

The editors of *Chitty on Contracts* acknowledge that the law relating to the discharge of a contract by agreement is a subject of 'considerable artificiality and refinement'. This may be an understatement. The most obvious way in which a contract is discharged is if both parties fully perform their obligations under it. In most cases this should be quite simple. However, in a complex building or engineering project, parties may legitimately disagree as to whether each party has fully performed their obligations under the contract and as a result the law which the judges have to address is the question of what constitutes performance. In reality, agreements, particularly engineering or construction agreements, which require entire performance are the exception rather than the rule. The courts have adopted several methods to avoid the consequences of a rule that entire performance is required in all contracts. These methods include those presented below.

Substantial performance

This doctrine provides that a party who has substantially performed their contract with only minor defects or deficiencies can claim the price of the work carried out less any

3.1 The law of contract
3.2 Construction health and safety
3.3 Insolvency in construction
3.4 Law of tort
3.5 Environmental issues

sum the other party may have to spend to complete or remedy the minor defects or deficiencies which prevent entire performance.

Severable rather than entire contracts

An agreement is said to be severable rather than entire when payment becomes due and owing at various stages during performance of the works. Most engineering and construction contracts will be severable rather than entire since instalments of the price become due as each stage of the construction are completed. Where the contract is a severable and not an entire contract, the price for each instalment is due when each instalment of the works is complete.

Rescission by agreement

Where a contract is executory on both sides and where neither party has performed the whole of its obligations, the agreement can be rescinded by mutual agreement, express or implied.

An agreement which is partially executed can only be rescinded by agreement provided that there are unfulfilled obligations on both sides. An agreement, once rescinded by agreement, is completely discharged and not capable of being revived.

Abandonment

A court can infer that the parties to a contract have agreed to abandon the contract because of delay or maturity. To prove abandonment the court must be satisfied on the facts of each particular case that the parties conducted themselves in such a manner that neither party was entitled to assume that the parties will have agreed that the contract had been abandoned.

Variations

The parties may effect a variation of the contract by commanding, allowing or modifying its terms by mutual consent. However, any agreement which varies the terms of an existing contract must be supported by considerations.

Waiver or forbearance

Where one party decides to accede to a request from the other party that a contractual obligation need not be performed, a court may hold that that party has waived any right to require that contractual obligation to be performed. Such a waiver may be in writing, may be oral or, indeed, may be inferred from conduct. This doctrine of waiver can be compared and contrasted with a variation of the contract in that there is no need for any consideration for the forbearance moving from the party to whom it is given. For this reason it may be simpler if this type of waiver is regarded as a form of estoppel which requires a change of position in reliance on any such act of forbearance.

Provision for discharge in the contract itself

Most engineering or construction contracts will have an internal machinery for one or other party to determine (not to terminate) the contract exercisable usually on a breach of contract, sometimes just on notice and, somewhat more rarely, at the sole discretion of the other party. What causes confusion and uncertainty is the fact that, even though one party may be entitled to determine the agreement, say, in the event of a particular breach of contract, that in itself does not prevent the other party from electing to treat the contract as having been terminated by reason of the other party's repudiatory breaches. When a major project goes seriously wrong there is often an unseemly jockeying for position by each party, with ever increasing numbers of technical advisers, all instructed to determine whether it is more advantageous to determine or to terminate the agreement. Where a party decides to rely on the procedure laid down in the contract and to determine the contract, it is necessary to comply with the strict procedure laid down in the contract. The advantages and disadvantages of determination and termination are as follows:

- A contractual right to determine can be exercised even if the triggering event or breach of contract is not a repudiatory breach.
- The consequences of determining the contract pursuant to the contractual machinery will restrict the party determining the contract to the remedies specified by the contract which may not include its loss of profit on the outstanding work.
- A common law termination of the contract does not require notice or warning from the party wishing to accept the repudiatory breach or breaches of contract.
- A repudiatory breach of contract is a breach which is difficult to define definitively. The breach must go to the root of the contract. The guilty party must have evinced an intention no longer to be bound by the contract. However, the consequences of terminating a contract by accepting a breach which a court, years later, finds not to be a repudiatory breach of contract, can be catastrophic.

6.2 Discharge by frustration

A contract may be discharged by frustration only when something occurs after the contract is concluded which renders the contract physically or commercially impossible or an event occurs which transforms the obligation to perform into a radically different obligation from that originally envisaged. This doctrine is concerned with the allocation of the risks flowing from an unforeseen event occurring which makes the originally envisaged contractual performance much more onerous, impracticable or impossible. The judicial basis of this doctrine is unclear. Some say it is based on some sort of implied term. The contract is discharged because by implication the parties have agreed that they will no longer be bound by the original terms of the contract if a frustrating event occurs. This theory has been analysed on the basis of the legal difficulty in seeing how the parties could, even impliedly, have provided for something which *ex hypothesi* they neither expected nor foresaw. An alternative theory is based on the 'just solution' theory which considers that the court will adopt the doctrine of frustration to impose a fair solution when unforeseen circumstances arise which are wholly different from those originally envisaged. The second theory, which disregards the parties' intentions but is based on the intervening court's wish to do justice between the parties, is probably the more fashionable justification for this doctrine.

However, the doctrine of frustration is examined by the courts with enormous circumspection. The courts are reluctant to rewrite bad or imprudent commercial bargains. The intervention of a frustrating event has always been much easier to plead than to prove.

It is also the case that most standard form engineering and construction contracts make provision for the effect of various catastrophic frustrating events and, where express provision has been made in the contract itself for the otherwise frustrating event, then the contract cannot be discharged by frustration.

3.1 The law of contract
3.2 Construction health and safety
3.3 Insolvency in construction
3.4 Law of tort
3.5 Environmental issues

The Law Reform (Frustrated Contracts) Act 1943 provides for most of the legal consequences of frustration. The purpose of this Act is to prevent unjust enrichment of either party to the contract at the other party's expense. Its aim is not to apportion loss between the parties. Section 1(2) of the Act provides that:

> 'All sums paid or payable to any party in pursuance of the contract before the time when the parties were so discharged (in this Act referred to as "the time of discharge") shall, in the case of sums so paid, be recoverable from him as money received by him for the use of the party by whom the sums were paid, and, in the case of sums so payable, cease to be payable:
>
> Provided that, if the party to whom the sums were so paid or payable incurred expenses before the time of discharge in, or for the purpose of, the performance of the contract, the court may, if it considers it just to do so having regard to all the circumstances of the case, allow him to retain or, as the case may be recover the whole or any part of the sums so paid or payable, not being an amount in excess of the expenses so incurred.'

This subsection should entitle a party to the contract to recover monies paid to another party to the contract. This Act modifies the common law position which held that rights which had not yet arrived at the time of frustration were unenforceable. The Act also goes beyond the common law position by providing that monies paid are recoverable even where there is only a partial failure of consideration and the payee may be entitled to set-off against a claim by the payer 'the amount of any expenses incurred before the time of discharge in or for the purpose of the contract'.

6.3 Discharge by breach

Any breach of contract will give rise to a cause of action but not every breach of contract gives a discharge from liability. To be relieved from further performance of the contract by the other side's breach of contract, the failure of performance must go to the root of the contract. In the case of *Rice* v. *Great Yarmouth Borough Council* (2003) TCLR 1 the Court of Appeal confirmed that there are three categories of breach of contract that are considered so serious as to justify the innocent party bringing the contract to an end:

(a) those cases in which the parties have agreed either that the term is so important that any breach will justify termination or that the particular breach is so important that it will justify termination;
(b) those cases where the contractor simply walks away from his obligations thus clearly indicating an intention no longer to be bound; and
(c) those cases in which the cumulative effect of the breaches which have taken place is sufficiently serious to justify the innocent party in bringing the contract to a premature end.

Once a repudiatory breach occurs, the contract is not automatically discharged. The innocent party can elect whether to accept the repudiatory breach and terminate the contract or the innocent party can affirm the contract and insist that the contract should continue. Where the innocent party elects to terminate the contract by accepting the repudiatory breach, the contract is terminated in that all primary obligations of both parties which remain to be performed come to an end and there is then substituted by implication of law for those primary obligations of the party in default which remain unperformed, a secondary obligation to pay financial compensation to the innocent party for all losses sustained by it in consequence of the guilty party's non-performance in the future and, just as important in many cases, the unperformed primary obligations if the innocent party are discharged.

7 DISPUTES AND REMEDIES

Whereas litigation, arbitration or adjudication should not be used as an alternative to negotiation, the absence of efficient, economical and expeditious dispute resolution processes will turn any analysis of the appropriate remedies for breach of contract into an academic analysis. Without confidence in the dispute resolution process any analysis of the appropriate remedies for breach of contract will be an academic analysis. Without confidence in the dispute resolution process, parties can break or bend contracts believing that they are immune from any effective sanctions. In considering the appropriate remedies for any breach of contract it is just as important to consider that these remedies can or will be enforced. If the contract breaker believes that the innocent party does not have the time, resources or commercial incentive to enforce its contractual rights, then fair compensation for any inadvertent or deliberate breach of contract will not be negotiated or agreed.

7.1 Remedies for breach of contract

When considering how a party can be recompensed for any breach of contract the parties to the contract should focus on the following questions.

- What is the speediest, fairest and cheapest method of resolving disputes?
- Will proper or even punitive awards of interest be paid as a contractual right?
- Can the financial consequences of common breaches of contract be predetermined to avoid the consequences and cost of having to plead and to prove actual losses?

Two general principles underlie the law on loss and damage.

(a) 'The rule of common law is, that where a party sustains a loss by reason of a breach of contract, he is, so far as money can do it, to be placed in the same situation, with respect to damages, as if the contract had been performed' *per* Parke B, *Robinson* v. *Harman* [1848] 1 Exch 850, 855.

(b) As a general rule, damages for breach of contract should be assessed as at the date when the cause of action accrued (i.e. the date of the breach). This is not an absolute rule. The date for the assessment of damage can be varied if, in all the circumstances, it is appropriate to do so, so as to compensate the claimant for the damage suffered by reason of the defendant's wrong. See *Johnson* v. *Agnew* [1980] AC 367, 400(h)–401(b), summarized in *Smith New Court Ltd* v. *Scrimgcour Vickers* [1996] 3 WLR 1051, 1059 (g–h). Certainly, this general rule is the appropriate one in circumstances in which the plaintiff's loss is capable of quantification all at once. See dicta of Lord Hoffmann, *Banque Bruxelles S.A.* v. *Eagle Star* [1996] 3 WLR 87, 101 (d–g):

'On the contrary, except in cases in which all the loss caused by the breach can be quantified at once, calculation of damages is bound to be affected by the extent to which loss in the future still has to be estimated at the date of trial...

It is true that in some cases there is a prima facie rule that damages should be assessed at the date of breach... But the purpose of this prima facie rule is not to ensure that the damages will always be the same irrespective of the date of trial. It is because where there is an available market, any additional loss which the buyer suffers through not having immediately bought equivalent goods at the market price is prima facie caused by his own change of mind about wanting the goods which he ordered... The breach date rule is thus no more than a prima facie rule of causation. It is not concerned with the extent of the vendor's liability for loss which the breach has admittedly caused.'

7.2 Calculating loss

Once it has been established that a loss is one for which the defendant is liable, the tribunal will calculate the damages; what amounts will compensate the claimant for the loss? In an influential article published in 1936, American academics Fuller and Perdue pointed out that there are two main ways in which the losses of a claimant in a contract action can be calculated.

- *Loss of expectation (also called loss of bargain)*. This is the usual way in which contract damages are calculated, and it aims to put claimants in the position they would have been in if the contract had been performed. It means, for example, that a claimant who was buying goods with the intention of selling them can claim the profit that would have been made on that sale; and that a claimant who is forced to sell goods at a lower price when the original buyer pulls out, can claim the difference between the contract price and the price at which the goods were eventually sold.
- *Reliance loss*. There are some cases where it is difficult or even impossible to calculate precisely what position the claimant would have been in if a contract had been performed correctly, and in this case the courts may instead award damages calculated to compensate for any expenses or other loss incurred by the claimant when relying on the contract.

However, to recover any loss the claimant must have at all times acted reasonably and mitigated the loss.

7.3 Equitable remedies

Where damages would be an inadequate remedy to compensate the claimant, there is a range of equitable remedies provided only at the discretion of the contract taking into account the position of both claimant and defendant. The alternative remedies include the following.

Specific performance

Specific performance will not be applied to a contract which is uncertain as to the required performance and it will be subject to the principle of mutuality which means that it will not be ordered against one party where it could not be ordered against the other party. Furthermore, it should not be ordered in the case of a contract which contains a contractual right to determine the contract because once ordered the contract could be determined. However a claim for specific performance, if available, may not be the subject of the usual contractual limitation period, or any limitation period (*P&O Nedllyod BV* v. *Arab Metals Co & Others* [2006] EWCA Civ 1917).

Injunctions

Before ordering a party not to do something, or in rare cases to do something, the court will apply a balance of convenience test and may refuse the application if the defendant could lose a lot more by restoring the previous position than the claimant would gain. In deciding whether to grant an injunction, the contract should take into account the nature of the breach, the circumstances which gave rise to the breach and whether damages by themselves would be an adequate remedy.

Declarations

In granting the aforementioned remedies the court, or other tribunal, will almost invariably be required to make some determination as to the construction, interpretation and effect of the terms of the contract. However it is possible to make a claim limited to a declaration by the court of how the terms of the contract should be interpreted or how the contract should operate. The declaration may then assist the parties in the continuing operation of the contract or the resolution of further disputes concerning the consequence of the proper construction however determined. The prevalence of claims for declarations has increased with the introduction of adjudication provisions in contracts whereby the parties can seek a binding determination on the proper construction of the contract during the course of its performance. The obvious disadvantage of claims for declarations is that it remains possible that further proceedings would be required to secure one or more of the aforementioned remedies in any event.

CHAPTER 3.2

Construction health and safety

Donald Lamont
Health and Safety Executive

Mike Appleby
Housemans Solicitors

1 INTRODUCTION

Health and safety responsibilities stem primarily from the Health and Safety at Work etc. Act 1974 (HSWA), and are shared by various parties who may be connected with construction and engineering projects. This chapter explains the system of health and safety legislation in the UK and how it is enforced. The regulations which expand and elaborate on safety duties relating to projects and work on site are described and a range of other detailed regulations that are likely to be encountered are summarized.

2 THE REGULATORY AGENCIES

2.1 Health and Safety Executive

The Health and Safety Executive and the Health and Safety Commission existed as separate entities from their formation until 1st April 2008 when they amalgamated to form a single regulatory body the 'Health and Safety Executive' to discharge the functions which were formerly their individual responsibility. The Health and Safety Commission (HSC) was established under Section 10 of the Health and Safety at Work etc. Act 1974 with the Health and Safety Executive (HSE) as the executive arm of the HSC, responsible for implementing the Commission's policies as well as enforcing health and safety legislation. The decision for the merger was reached after consultation with stakeholders and through the process determined by the Legislative and Regulatory Reform Act 2006. The new HSE remains part of the Department for Work and Pensions.

The HSE's primary function is to promote the cause of better health and safety at work. The Chair of the HSC has become the Chair of the Board of the new Executive. The potential size of the Board of the HSE will be no more than eleven members plus the Chair. Members are appointed by the Secretary of State. They represent employers, the trades unions and the public interest (through local authority members).

The HSE has a duty to bring forward proposals for regulations, power to undertake research and to disseminate information, power to direct investigations and inquiries into accidents and similar events. The HSE is advised by a number of industry advisory committees (see Section 2.2 of this chapter). The HSE also retains a duty to enforce health and safety legislation.

Inspection of industrial premises and construction sites is achieved through a network of regional and area offices. Within that structure are specialist units providing engineering and scientific advice. Depending on the location of the construction work, other HSE inspectorates, including those for mines, explosives, nuclear installations, or offshore safety may also have enforcement responsibilities over the site on which the construction work is being carried out. In respect of construction work on the railways enforcement of health and safety legislation is the responsibility of Her Majesty's Railway Inspectorate which transferred from the HSC/HSE to the Office of Rail Regulation (ORR) on 1st April 2006.

In addition to its enforcement role, the HSE operates various licensing and approval schemes, one of which in the construction sector licenses asbestos removal contractors. The HSE is also the enforcing authority under legislation implementing European Community directives dealing with machinery and equipment safety.[1]

[1] Further information on the HSE can be obtained from its website – www.hse.gov.uk.

2.2 Construction Industry Advisory Committee

The Construction Industry Advisory Committee (CONIAC) till April 2008 advised the HSC on matters relating to the construction industry but now advises HSE. The Committee is representative of all sections of the industry. Members are appointed by the HSE normally for a period of three years. The CONIAC members principally represent employer organizations and employee organizations, however, in addition the CONIAC includes representatives of the construction professions, client organizations, materials suppliers, the plant hire industry and the public interest.

The CONIAC commissions and publishes guidance and advises the HSE on legislation and accompanying Approved Codes of Practice and guidance. The CONIAC is supported by a number of working parties dealing with specific topics including training and education, occupational health and the particular problems of small businesses within the construction industry.

2.3 Health and safety legislation in Scotland and Northern Ireland[2]

The HSWA applies only within Great Britain, i.e. Scotland, Wales and England. Separate but similar construction health and safety legislation, enforced by a separate inspectorate (HSENI), exists in Northern Ireland. In addition, the Isle of Man and the Channel Islands have their own health and safety authorities. Occupational health and safety is not a responsibility which has been devolved to the Scottish Parliament or the Welsh Assembly. Some EC directives in the construction sector affect Great Britain, some the UK as a whole.

2.4 Approved Codes of Practice and guidance

Much current health and safety legislation is supported by Approved Codes of Practice (ACoPs) and guidance. It is important to understand where Approved Codes of Practice and guidance come within the hierarchy of legislation which follows from the general framework of legal requirements in the HSWA. An Approved Code of Practice is a document which, following a period of consultation with all sides of industry, is 'approved' by the Health and Safety Commission under section 16 of the HSWA.

Apart from containing information amplifying and supporting the requirements of regulations, ACoPs have a unique legal status. When cited in support of a prosecution, the burden of proof passes to the defendant to show that what was done was at least as good in respect of health or safety as the work practices set out in the ACoP.

Guidance in documents such as HSE guidance notes come below ACoPs in terms of legal standing. The HSE guidance documents are statements of good practice and, as such documents are the subject of consultation with both sides of industry prior to publication, reflect a consensus view.

2.5 British and CEN standards

A number of safety-related British Standards and BS codes of practice on construction-related topics, are published by the British Standards Institution. Although, in law, most British Standards have only the standing of guidance documents, courts increasingly seem to be placing greater importance on them because of the consultative process under which they are drafted and the consensus within industry which they reflect.

[2] The text of Acts and Regulations coming into force after 1988 can be found on the website of the Office of Public Sector Information – www.opsi.gov.uk/legislation.

The CEN – the European Standards organization – had largely completed the harmonized standards required to support EC directives e.g. the Machinery Directive 98/37/EC; however the adoption of a revised EC Machinery Directive 2006/42/EC, has resulted in a large number of machinery standards having to be updated to reflect the requirements of the revised directive.

Harmonized standards, which are common to all EC member countries, are a way of removing barriers to trade within the Community. The CEN standards are drafted by committees of experts representing the national standards bodies of member states and draft standards are consulted and voted on by all EC member states.

Most construction-related CEN standards fall into two broad categories – machinery safety standards and product standards. Construction machinery must conform to the essential safety requirements of the EC Machinery Directive. Self-certification of conformity with the relevant CEN standards, by the supplier of the machinery into the European Community, is the most common way of demonstrating conformity with the essential safety requirements of the Directive. While CEN standards are not mandatory, conformity with the Machinery Directive is mandatory, so the role of standards in demonstrating has increasingly made them regarded as quasi-mandatory by industry. Construction product standards perform a similar role for materials used in construction work in respect of the requirements of the EC Construction Products Directive.

3 ENFORCEMENT

3.1 Jurisdiction over work

Although the HSE is the principal body for enforcement purposes, the HSWA provides for a specific authority to be designated for the purposes of particular health and safety regulations and, more importantly, for local authorities to be responsible for enforcing statutory provisions in certain lower risk situations.

The local authorities have designated areas of responsibility under the Health and Safety (Enforcing Authority) Regulations 1998, and have jurisdiction over, for example, retail or wholesale distribution activities (subject to certain exceptions such as for supply of dangerous substances), office activities, catering and the provision of residential accommodation. This jurisdiction is usually exercised by local Environmental Health Officers acting with the same powers as HSE inspectors. These jurisdiction rules are, however, altered in relation to construction work. The 1998 Regulations provide that the enforcing authority role of local authorities reverts to the HSE in relation to the following activities carried on at any premises by persons who do not normally work in the premises:

(a) construction work if:
  (i) Regulation 21 of the Construction (Design and Management) Regulations 2007 (which requires projects which include or are intended to include construction work to be notified to the Executive) applies to the project which includes the work, or
  (ii) the whole or part of the work contracted to be undertaken by the contractor at the premises is to the external fabric or other external part of a building or structure, or
  (iii) it is carried out in a physically segregated area of the premises, the activities normally carried out in that area have been suspended for the purpose of enabling the construction work to be carried out, the contractor has authority to exclude from that area persons who are not attending in connection

with the carrying out of the work and the work is not the maintenance of insulation on pipes, boilers or other parts of heating or water systems or its removal from them

(b) the installation, maintenance or repair of any gas system, or any work in relation to a gas fitting
(c) the installation, maintenance or repair of electricity systems
(d) work with ionizing radiations except work in one or more of the categories set out in Schedule 3 to the Ionising Radiations Regulations 1985.

The consequence of this is that Environmental Health Officers are responsible for enforcement of health and safety requirements in relation to minor internal works in shops, offices and other low risk premises.

3.2 Enforcement powers

Inspectors have available to them a wide range of statutory enforcement powers enabling them to undertake routine inspections and incident investigations, to stop contraventions of statutory requirements or positively require steps to be taken. The powers of inspectors are contained mainly in section 20 of the HSWA and relate to powers of entry, seizure of evidence (documentary evidence and physical objects) and questioning witnesses. In circumstances where there has been no death, the investigation will by HSE (or other appropriate authority such as a local authority).

However if a death occurs in the workplace then, under the *Work-related Deaths: A protocol for liaison* (which can be downloaded at www.hse.gov.uk/pubns/misc149.pdf) is implemented and the death is treated as a manslaughter investigation led by the police with the HSE providing technical assistance. If there is sufficient evidence to bring manslaughter charges the case will be prosecuted by the Crown Prosecution Service (CPS). If there is insufficient evidence for a manslaughter prosecution, the investigation is handed over to HSE to consider if there have been any breaches of health and safety legislation. If there is sufficient evidence the HSE will prosecute.

It is therefore necessary to look at the enforcement powers of both HSE and the police.

3.2.1 Powers of inspectors

Powers of entry

Inspectors are empowered to enter any premises where they believe it is necessary to do so to carry out their duties. These visits can be by appointment, but they are usually made spontaneously at any reasonable time (or at any time at all if the inspector has reason to believe there is a dangerous situation). It is an offence to obstruct an inspector attempting to exercise these powers (see below) but an inspector may be required to supply identification and establish credentials as a duly appointed person before gaining entry or exercising any powers. Once on the site or other premises an inspector has various powers to carry out examinations, or require that evidence on site is left undisturbed while investigations continue, and to make various records of what is found, including taking photographs.

Seizure of evidence, taking samples, etc.

Inspectors' powers in relation to the collection of physical evidence include the right to take samples, for example, of substances or items of equipment, or samples from the atmosphere to test for environmental hazards. They can also dismantle equipment, or take possession of it so that it can be preserved for use as evidence in proceedings. There are certain rules relating to the rights of persons under investigation to be present or to receive samples of their own when these powers are exercised.

Access to documentary evidence

The powers of inspectors to require production of documents are virtually unlimited. Save for material which is subject to legal privilege, they are entitled to access to any documents they deem necessary to see for the purposes of their investigations which may include not only formal records kept pursuant to statutory requirements (such as accident books) but also papers such as a company's correspondence and the internal memoranda of its staff, any reports on health and safety and minutes of board meetings. Confidentiality is not a ground for refusing to give an inspector such documents.

Interviews

There are three types of interview by an HSE inspector. These are:

(1) An interview under caution. In terms of a company this will be of a 'company representative'. This can be anyone who is specifically authorised by the company to talk on its behalf. This might be a director or senior manager.
(2) An interview by an HSE inspector using his powers under section 20(2)(j) HSWA (often referred to as a 'section 20 interview').
(3) An interview by an inspector of a potential witness where the witness will be asked to make a voluntary statement under section 9 of the Criminal Justice Act 1967 (often referred to as a 'section 9 statement').

An HSE inspector does not have the power of arrest. Thus the inspector cannot compel someone to attend an interview under caution. Any interview under caution is subject to the provisions of PACE. However section 34 CJPOA only applies where an interview under caution takes place. Thus no adverse inference can be drawn if a defendant (whether individual or a company) declines an invitation to attend an HSE interview under caution.

Under section 20(2)(j) HSWA an HSE inspector can require any person who he/she has reasonable cause to believe is able to give information relevant to the investigation to answer questions asked by the inspector that he/she reasonably believes are required as part of HSE's investigation. The person interviewed under this provision will be required to sign a declaration of truth of his/her answers.

It is an offence to refuse to answer the HSE inspector's relevant questions. However any answers given by the person cannot be used in evidence against that person.

Anyone who gives a statement as a witness for the HSE (or the police) will be asked to give a statement in 'section 9' of the Criminal Justice Act 1967 form. This means that there is a declaration at the start of the statement which must be signed and dated by the witness and then the foot of each page should also be signed and dated. In this form, if the statement is uncontested then it can be read out at trial and accepted in evidence.

The declaration for a section 9 statement is:

> 'This statement, consisting of [ ] page(s), each signed by me, is true to the best of my knowledge and belief and I make it knowing that, if it is tendered in evidence, I shall be liable to prosecution if I have wilfully stated in it anything which I know to be false or do not believe to be true.'

In a section 9 interview the HSE inspector cannot insist on his/her questions being answered. However this approach does not afford the interviewee the same protection as under section 20(2)(j) HSWA. If the inspector believes the person is incriminating him/herself then the interview should be terminated and the inspector must caution the interviewee.

Additional powers

The HSWA provides that inspectors can require any person 'to afford him such facilities and assistance . . . as are necessary to enable the Inspector to exercise any of the powers conferred on him . . . ' and also to exercise 'any other power which is necessary . . . '. Thus, provided the inspectors are in the course of an investigation (which will not usually be difficult for them to show), there is in principle no limit to the powers they can take in addition to those already described above. In practice this provision has not been used by inspectors to take draconian steps and, in fact, with their powers of entry, seizure and questioning there is little else they are likely to need in order to obtain all the evidence they require to satisfy themselves whether or not they need to take action.

There are further powers in Section 25 of the HSWA enabling an inspector to seize and render harmless articles or substances where there is reasonable cause to believe that the product in question is a cause of imminent danger of personal injury (this is separate from the powers to take samples and detain objects referred to earlier). If the circumstances warrant it, these powers may extend even to destroying products in order to render them harmless with certain rules enabling the person from whom they are being seized to be provided with samples and be given a report on the circumstances in which the seizure took place.

3.2.2 Powers of the police

The police's powers are set out in the Police and Criminal Evidence Act 1984 (PACE) and the Codes of Practice to the Act.

Power to search

Police have the power to enter and search any premises without a warrant in order to make an arrest or to search premises occupied or controlled by an arrested person providing the officer has reasonable grounds for suspecting there is evidence at the premises, other than legally privileged items, that relates to the suspected offence.

There is also power to search under a warrant. Searches can also be carried out with the consent of a person entitled to grant entry.

Power of seizure

The police have a general power in respect to the seizure of evidence. A police officer, who is lawfully on any premises has the power to seize anything he has reasonable grounds for believing is evidence in relation to an offence and it is necessary to seize it in order to prevent the evidence being concealed, lost, altered or destroyed. This extends to the seizure of computer records. Items seized can be retained for so long as it is necessary 'in all the circumstances'.

Interviews

The police have the power to arrest a person for any offence (providing the officer has reasonable grounds for doing so) and to interview them at the police station under caution. The caution given at the start of the interview is:

'You do not have to say anything. But it may harm your defence if you do not mention when questioned something which you later rely on in court. Anything you do say may be given in evidence.'

On being arrested the person will be taken to the custody suit where he/she will be presented to the custody sergeant and the arresting officer will explain why the person has been arrested. The custody sergeant will then authorise detention at the station and will open a custody record. The person will be informed of their rights to have a legal representative (if he/she does not have a solicitor they will be informed of the duty solicitor scheme), a person informed of their arrest and to be able to consult the Codes of Practice. The person will then have his/her photograph, fingerprints and DNA sample taken.

If the person declines to answer the police's questions then an adverse inference might be drawn if the matter later comes to trial. Section 34 of the Criminal Justice and Public Order Act 1994 (CJPOA) states that a court, in determining whether a defendant is guilty or not may draw such inferences as appear proper from the evidence of silence either when the defendant was interviewed under caution or on being charged or officially informed that they might be charged, the defendant failed to mention any fact that they later rely on in court in their defence which in the circumstances existing at the time they could reasonably have been expected to have mentioned. Note that a defendant cannot be convicted upon an adverse inference alone.

3.3 Powers of inspectors

Enforcement notices

Inspectors have a large measure of discretion over how they deal with non-compliance with health and safety requirements. Very often their response is to issue warnings to the employer or other person concerned, usually confirmed in writing, and requesting that action be taken within a set time. They may at the same time advise on the shortcomings that they have discovered and suggest that certain actions be taken or refer the person concerned to Approved Codes of Practice or relevant guidance. These actions do not involve the exercise of formal enforcement powers. However, where a situation is regarded as sufficiently serious, an inspector will issue one of two types of enforcement notice pursuant to powers under the HSWA.

Improvement Notices

An Improvement Notice can be issued where an inspector is of the opinion that a person is contravening the statutory requirements or has contravened the statutory requirements in circumstances that make it likely that the contravention will continue or be repeated. These contraventions may consist of the failure to comply with one of the general duties of the HSWA, or contravention of health and safety regulations. An Improvement Notice has to meet a number of requirements laid down by the Act. It must:

- specify the provision or provisions which the inspector believes are not being complied with
- give particulars of the reasons why the inspector is of that opinion
- specify the period of time within which the person is required to remedy the contravention, being a period of not less than 21 days.

In addition, an inspector may add to a Notice a Schedule containing information about the steps which the inspector would regard as necessary to remedy the contravention.

Prohibition Notices

Prohibition Notices differ from Improvement Notices in that they may take effect immediately, and they require the recipient to the Notice to cease the activity in question. There is no requirement for an inspector to demonstrate that statutory requirements have actually been contravened. The requirement for a Prohibition Notice to be served is that the inspector should be of the opinion that the activity in question involved, or will involve, a risk of serious personal injury. Such a Notice can be served in anticipation that activities carried out will pose such a risk. A Prohibition Notice can be served in any circumstances where an Improvement Notice could have been used. In circumstances where to cease activity immediately would present additional risks e.g. shutting down a refinery process, the coming into effect of the Prohibition Notice can be deferred for a period specified in the Notice. An inspector attaches a Schedule setting out the steps which should be taken to remedy the contraventions.

Appeal procedures

There are procedures whereby the recipient of an Improvement or Prohibition Notice can challenge the issue of the Notice, or may seek to have the terms (for example, the time limits allowed for improvements) varied. These appeals are dealt with by industrial tribunals. An application to a tribunal has to be made within 21 days from the date of service of the Notice (subject to any further time the tribunal may allow). The effect of this procedure pending the hearing varies depending on the type of Notice:

- the operation of an Improvement Notice will be suspended until the proceedings are finished (either with a ruling by the tribunal or with the proceedings being withdrawn)
- the operation of a Prohibition Notice may also be suspended in the same way, but this will only be the case if there was an interim application by the recipient of the Notice and the tribunal agrees that the Notice should be suspended. (Even then, the Prohibition Notice is only suspended from the time the tribunal so directs.)

On the hearing of an appeal (which may be a matter of weeks after an appeal is lodged), the tribunal has various options available including cancelling the Notice completely, affirming it unchanged or affirming with such modifications as it thinks fit. In such an appeal, the onus of proof lays with an inspector to demonstrate that the Notice has been validly served, which means that the inspector is required to show either the serious risk of personal injury or the contravention of statutory requirements as the case may be.

Two particular limitations on the service of enforcement notices should be noted. First, where an inspector is proposing to serve an Improvement Notice relating to a contravention of statutory requirements applying to a building, the Notice cannot correct any measures to be taken to remedy the position that are more onerous than those that are necessary to secure conformity with the requirements of any Building Regulations that apply at the time and to which the building would be required to conform if it were being newly erected (unless, that is, the health and safety requirements which the inspector has identified are themselves more onerous than the requirements of the Building Regulations). Secondly, before an inspector serves an enforcement notice affecting means of escape in case of fire, he or she must first consult the Fire Authority.

Details of an enforcement notice will be included in a public register (if not withdrawn or cancelled in consequence of an appeal) unless it relates solely to the protection of persons at work. (A notice covering risks to private citizens would be made public under the Environment and Safety Information Act 1988.) Details of the appeals procedure are usually given out by the inspector with the notice.

3.4 Prosecutions

If the police prosecute in relation to a work related death they will prosecute an individual for manslaughter based upon gross negligence and a company for manslaughter under the new Corporate Manslaughter and Corporate Homicide Act 2007 (CMCHA) which is applicable for all work related deaths that occur after 6th April 2008.

HSE increasingly prosecutes employers under the general duties of the HSWA (see section 4 below), often pursuant to section 2 HSWA, failing to ensure the health safety and welfare of an employee 'so far as is reasonably practicable' or section 3, failing to conduct his undertaking (i.e. business) so as to ensure, 'so far as is reasonably practicable' persons not in his employment are not exposed to risks to their health or safety as opposed to prosecuting for contravention of health and safety regulations reflecting the higher penalties available on conviction. Even if the failures of an employer are adequately covered by a specific regulation, this does not prevent HSE from prosecuting under the general duties (see *R.* v. *Bristol Magistrates' Court ex parte Juttan Oy* [2003] UKHL 53.

Individuals when prosecuted by HSE are usually prosecuted for a breach of section 7(a) HSWA (this covers employees and managers) or under section 37 HSWA (if a director or very senior manager).

Prosecution Codes

Prosecutions by the police and HSE must satisfy the Code for Crown Prosecutors which can be viewed at www.cps.gov.uk/publications/docs/code2004english.pdf. It sets out two fundamental steps in deciding whether to prosecute: the evidential test and the public interest test.

The evidential test requires the prosecutor to be satisfied that there is enough evidence to provide a 'realistic prospect of conviction' against the defendant on *each* charge. They must consider what the defence may be and how that is likely to affect the prosecution case.

A realistic prospect of conviction is an *objective test*. It means that a jury or bench or magistrates, properly directed in accordance with the law, *is more likely than not* to convict the defendant of the alleged charge.

In relation to public interest the Code quotes Lord Shawcross's statement of 1951 on public interest when he was Attorney General when he said: 'It has never been the rule in this country – I hope it never will be – that suspected criminal offences must automatically be the subject of prosecution.' (House of Commons Debates, volume 483, column 681, 29th January 1951.)

Prosecutors are required to balance factors for and against prosecution '*carefully and fairly*'. Public interest factors that can affect the decision to prosecute usually depend on the seriousness of the offence or the circumstances of the offender. Some factors may increase the need to prosecute but others may suggest that another course of action would be better.

HSE also have an *Enforcement Policy Statement* (2002) which can be downloaded at www.hse.gov.uk/pubns/hsc15.pdf. It sets out the general principles and approach. The Statement says:

3.1 The law of contract
3.2 Construction health and safety
3.3 Insolvency in construction
3.4 Law of tort
3.5 Environmental issues

> 'The appropriate use of enforcements powers, including prosecution, is important, both to secure compliance with the law and to ensure those who have duties under it may be held to account for failures to safeguard health, safety and welfare.'

Paragraph 39 of the statement says that prosecutions will normally follow where one or more of the following circumstances apply:

- Death was a result of a breach of the health and safety legislation;
- The gravity of an alleged offence, taken together with the seriousness of any actual or potential harm, or the general record and approach of the offender warrants it;
- There has been reckless disregard of health and safety requirements;
- There have been repeated breaches which give rise to significant risk, or persistent and significant poor compliance;
- Work has been carried out without or in serious non-compliance with an appropriate licence or safety case;
- A duty holder's standard of managing health and safety is found to be far below what is required by health and safety law and to be giving rise to significant risk;
- There has been a failure to comply with an improvement notice or prohibition notice served by the enforcing authority; or there has been a repetition of a breach that was subject to a formal caution;
- False information has been supplied wilfully, or there has been an intent to deceive, in relation to a matter which gives rise to serious risk;
- Inspectors have been intentionally obstructed in the lawful course of their duties.

Prosecution of Employers for breaches of their general duties under HSWA

The three general duties under the HSWA relevant to the construction industry are sections 2, 3 and 4 (see section 4 below). Each of these duties is qualified by the term 'so far as is reasonably practicable'.

An offence occurs under these general duties as soon as there is an exposure to health and safety risks. The exposure to risk can be over a period of time or can relate to a single incident. The prosecution must prove this exposure to the criminal standard i.e. so the court is sure ('beyond reasonable doubt').

The employer has a defence under section 40 HSWA if it can show it took all reasonably practicable steps to avoid the exposure to risk. Section 40 HSWA states:

> 'In any proceedings for an offence under any of the relevant statutory provisions consisting of a failure to comply with a duty or requirement to do something so far as is practicable or so far as is reasonably practicable, or to use the best practicable means to do something, it shall be for the accused to prove (as the case may be) that it was not practicable or not reasonably practicable to do more than was in fact done to satisfy the duty or requirement, or that there was no better practicable means than was in fact used to satisfy the duty or requirement.'

This defence has to be proved on a balance of probabilities i.e. not to the criminal standard.

The general duties impose 'strict liability' upon an employer, subject only to the defence reasonable practicability (see *R.* v. *British Steel plc* [1995] 1 WLR 1356, *R.* v. *Associated Octel Co Ltd* [1996] 4 All ER 846 and *R.* v. *Gateway Foodmarkets Ltd* [1997] 3 All ER 78). By strict liability this means that the prosecution does not have to prove any intent on the part of the defendant to commit an offence or any negligence.

In relation to section 2 HSWA it was said in *Lockhart* v. *Kevin Oliphant* [1992] SCCR 774 that once there is a 'prima facie' case against the employer that the health, safety and welfare of employees was not ensured, then the onus under section 40 was on the employer.

The term 'risk' is defined in the Approved Code of Practice to the Management of Health and Safety at Work Regulations 1999 as:

> 'the likelihood of potential harm from that hazard (which is defined . . . [as] . . . being something with the potential to cause harm) being realised. The extent of the risk will depend on:
> (i) the likelihood of that harm occurring;
> (ii) the potential severity of that harm i.e. of any resultant injury or adverse health effect; and
> (iii) the population which might be affected by the hazard, i.e. the number of people who might be exposed.' (Emphasis added)

'Risk' was widely interpreted in the Court of Appeal case *R.* v. *Board of Trustees of Science Museum* [1993] 3 All ER 853, a prosecution pursuant to Section 3 HSWA where the issue concerned whether there had been exposure to risk from legionella bacteria present in a cooling tower that was not in usc. It was held the possibility of danger was sufficient and there was no need for the prosecution to show that there was an actual danger.

The following passage from the judgement explains what is meant by the 'possibility of danger':

> 'The critical question of interpretation is as follows. Was it enough for the prosecution to prove that there was a risk that [the legionella bacteria] might emerge or did the prosecution have to go further and show that [the bacteria] did in fact emerge into the atmosphere and was available to be inhaled? Mr Carlisle, leading counsel for the prosecution, illustrated the problem with a simple example. Imagine, he said, a loose object on the roof near a pavement. In case A, the loose object is in a position in which it might fall off and hit a pedestrian. In that case there is a mere risk. In case B, the object in fact falls and exposes pedestrians to actual danger. In case C, the object falls and causes actual injury to a pedestrian. The prosecution submits that exposure to risk in case A constitutes a prima facie case under section 3(1). The defence submits that section 3(1) only covers cases B and C.'

The Court of Appeal found in favour of the prosecution.

Thus the possibility of danger is the risk. However in the recent case of *R.* v. *Porter* [2008] All ER (D) 249 (May) the Court of Appeal appear to have stepped back from such a wide definition saying the risk must be a 'real' risk as opposed to a 'fanciful or hypothetical' one. HSE were refused leave to appeal to the House of Lords in October 2008.

In the case of *R.* v. *Chargot Ltd and others* [2007] EWCA Crim 3032 the Court of Appeal has upheld the approach that the prosecution only has to prove an exposure to risk for the defendant to be required to prove it had taken all reasonably practicable steps to avoid the exposure to risk. However the matter was appealed to the House of Lords and heard in November 2008. Judgement is expected in early 2009.

In the case of *R.* v. *HTM* [2006] Crim 1156 it was held by the Court of Appeal that foreseeability was relevant to the issue of what is reasonably practicable. The court said:

> '. . . it seems to us that a defendant to a charge under section 2 or indeed sections 3 or 4 [HSWA], in asking a jury to consider whether it has established that it has done all

that is reasonably practicable, cannot be prevented from adducing evidence as to the likelihood of the incidence of the relevant risk eventuating in support of its case that it had taken all reasonable means to eliminate it.'

In the case of *R.* v. *Nelson Group Services (Maintenance) Ltd* [1998] 4 All ER 331 the Court of Appeal held an employer was not precluded from relying upon section 40 HSWA merely because an employee carrying out the work was careless or omitted to take precaution. The employer could show it had done all that was reasonably practicable by proving appropriate instruction and training had been given and that there was a safe system of work in place. It was held in the *HTM* case that the *Nelson* is still good law.

The Corporate Manslaughter and Corporate Homicide Act 2007

Prior to the CMCHA to convict an organisation of manslaughter following a work-related death, it had to be proved that someone senior in the organisation, often referred to as the *directing mind*, was also guilty of manslaughter. This made prosecuting large organisations difficult.

The new offence does away with the requirement for proving the guilt of a directing mind. In the future an organisation will be guilty of corporate manslaughter if death is *caused* by a *gross breach* of its relevant *duty of care* that is *substantially* due to *senior management* failure (see section 1 of the CMCHA). Now the failures of a number of senior managers can be added together.

The organisations that can commit the offence include:

1. A corporation
2. A partnership
3. A local authority

The relevant duty of care is that owed by an organisation to its employees and non-employees arising out of its business. Thus the CMCHA does not impose any additional duties to those that exist under the Health and Safety at Work Act 1974 (HSWA). All that it changes is the mechanics of prosecution.

Section 2 of the CMCHA sets out the meaning of the 'relevant duty of care' and specifically states it includes '*the carrying on by the organisation of any construction or maintenance operations*'.

The breach of duty does not have to be the only cause or indeed the major cause of death, only one of the causes.

These are persons who play a significant role in the decision-making or management of the organisation. Following the line of reasoning in *El Aljou* v. *Dollar Land Holdings plc* [1994] 2 All ER 685 (concerning the definition of a 'directing mind') it is possible a person may be deemed senior management for only part of their job function. The duties of various duty holders set out in the CDM Regulations may be relevant in a prosecution concerning a construction project to determining the relevant senior management for the purposes of the CMCHA.

A 'gross breach' is defined in section 1 CMCHA as conduct amounting to a breach of duty that '*falls far below what can reasonably be expected of the organisation in the circumstances*'.

A jury will be asked to consider how serious the organisation's failure was and how much of a risk of death it posed. The jury may also take into account (see section 8 CMCHA) the 'attitudes, policies, systems or accepted practices' of the organisation relevant to the failure (in other words 'safety culture') and relevant health and safety and industry guidance.

Mistakenly, people believe the new law means there will be no prosecutions of directors or senior managers. The CMCHA does not make provision for secondary liability (e.g. aiding and abetting) but it does not prevent a director or senior manager from being prosecuted either for gross negligence manslaughter and/or a breach of section 37 HSWA.

Prosection of Individuals for breaches of HSWA

Section 37 HSWA states:

> 'Where an offence under any of the relevant statutory provisions committed by a body corporate is proved to have been committed with the consent or connivance of, or attributable to and neglect on the part of, any director, manager, secretary or other similar officer of the body corporate or a person who was purporting to act in any such capacity, he as well as the body corporate shall be guilty of that offence and shall be liable to be proceeded against and punished accordingly.'

Section 37 is concerned with the secondary liability of an individual, in certain circumstances, for the offence committed by a corporate body which is primarily liable. It is only relevant where a corporate body has committed a health and safety offence.

In order to prove the case against the individual, the prosecution must first prove the corporate body committed a health and safety offence and then that this breach was due to the defendant's consent or connivance or was attributable to the defendant's neglect.

Consent is where the defendant had knowledge of the risk being run by the company but consented to it nonetheless. Connivance is where the defendant once again has knowledge of the risk but 'turns a blind eye' to what is happening.

In terms of the meaning of the word neglect in the Scottish case *Wotherspoon* v. *HM Advocate* [1978] JC 74 it was said 'in its natural meaning pre-supposes the existence of some obligation or duty on the person charged with neglect'. The case goes on to say:

> 'in considering in a given case whether there has been neglect within the meaning of HSWA 1974 s37(1) on the part of a particular director or other particular officer charged, the search must be to discover whether the accused has failed to take some steps to prevent the commission of an offence by the corporation to which he belongs if the taking of those steps either expressly falls within or should be held to fall within the scope of the functions of the office which he holds.'

In terms of what is 'attributable' it was said in the same case that any degree of attributability was sufficient.

As for knowledge in the case of 'neglect' it was held by the Court of Appeal in *R.* v. *P Ltd and G* [2007] All ER (D) 173 (Jul) (CA) that if a director:

> '... had no actual knowledge of the relevant state of facts, the question would always be whether, nonetheless, he should have been put on inquiry by reasons of the surrounding circumstances whether the relevant safety procedures were in place...
>
> The prosecution case might be such that in order to establish a case to go before the jury, it had to establish that the [director] did know of the unsafe practices; however, it did not have to prove that, if it could prove that the circumstances ought to have put him on inquiry to the extent that there was a duty on him to act.'

3.1 The law of contract
3.2 Construction health and safety
3.3 Insolvency in construction
3.4 Law of tort
3.5 Environmental issues

In relation to the definition of a 'manager' it was held In *R.* v. *Boal* [1992] 3 All ER 177, CA, a case on the almost identical wording of the Fire Precautions Act 1971, section 23(1), that only those responsible for deciding corporate policy and strategy were 'managers'. Thus a defendant will have to in practice be a very senior manager to come within this definition.

Section 36 HSWA, like section 37, concerns secondary liability. It is committed when the commission of a health and safety offence by another person is due to the act or default of some other person, and that other person is also liable to be prosecuted for the offence. An example of a prosecution under this section is of Christopher Hooper, a health and safety consultant. He prepared an inadequate risk assessment upon a machine for a client on which an employee of that client was later injured.

Individuals can also be prosecuted under section 7(a) HSWA. This covers a wide range of employees from front line workers to fairly senior managers. It states that:

> 'It shall be the duty of every employee while at work – to take reasonable care for the health and safety of himself and of other persons who may be affected by his acts or omissions at work.'

This is somewhat of a grey area of law since the vast majority of cases are dealt with in the magistrates' courts and as a consequence there are very few reported cases.

For a frontline employee to be prosecuted his or her actions normally have to be bordering on the reckless. An example is the prosecution of Mr Holland in 1998 who was an employee at a fertiliser company. As a practical joke he exposed a 17 year old colleague to hydrochloric acid which resulted in the teenager being injured.

For a manager to be prosecuted the negligence does not have to be so bad. A manager can be prosecuted if he or she has failed to carry out his/her job (or has violated procedures) so that health and safety standards are consequently significantly lowered.

Prosecution of Individuals for manslaughter

In a work related death incident the police will be considering manslaughter by gross negligence. The leading case on this area of law is *R.* v. *Adomako* [1995] 1 AC 171. To be guilty of gross negligence manslaughter the jury must be satisfied:

1. The defendant owed a duty of care to the deceased; and
2. He/she was in breach of that duty; and
3. The breach of duty was a substantial cause of death (i.e. something more than trivial); and
4. The breach was so grossly negligent that the defendant can be deemed to have had such disregard for life of the deceased that it should be seen as criminal and deserving of punishment by the State.

3.5 Sentencing

Penalties for Health and Safety Offences

Section 33 of the HSWA sets out the Offences and maximum penalties under health and safety legislation. The maximum sentence depends upon whether the defendant is being sentenced in the Magistrates' Court (the lower court) or in the Crown Court (the higher court). The various penalties are detailed below.

Failing to comply with an improvement/prohibition notice or a court remedy order

Magistrates' Court	£20 000 and/or 6 months imprisonment
Crown Court	Unlimited fine and/or 2 years imprisonment

Breach of sections 2–6 HSWA
Sections 2–6 of the HSWA are the general duties of employers, self-employed, manufacturers and supplies to ensure the health and safety of employees and non employees who may be affected by their work activities:

Magistrates' Court	£20 000
Crown Court	Unlimited fine

Other breaches of the HSWA and breaches of 'relevant statutory provisions'
This includes all health and safety regulations e.g. failure to carry out a risk assessment pursuant to Regulation 3 of the Management of Health and Safety at Work Regulations 1999:

Magistrates' Court	£5 000
Crown Court	Unlimited fine

The Health and Safety (offences) Act 2008
This Act was passed on 16 October 2008. It takes effect on 16 January 2009. The Act extends the £20 000 maximum fine in the Magistrates' Court to a wider range of offences and provides the courts with the power to imprison for most health and safety offences.

Disqualification of Directors and Managers
If a defendant is convicted under section 37 HSWA, the prosecution can apply for his/her disqualification from acting as a director (and in a management position of a company) pursuant to the Company Directors Disqualification Act 1986. The maximum period in the Magistrates Court is 5 years and in the Crown Court 15 years. In recent times applications for disqualification orders have become more common.

The Objects of Sentencing: Section 142 Criminal Justice Act 2003

The objects of sentencing in criminal cases are set out in section 142 of the Criminal Justice Act 2003. It says any court dealing with an offender in respect of his/her offence must have regard to the following purposes:

(a) the punishment of offenders,
(b) the reduction of crime (including its reduction by deterrence),
(c) the reform and rehabilitation of offenders,
(d) the protection of the public, and
(e) the making of reparation by offenders to persons affected by their actions.

The Court of Appeal in *R.* v. *Balfour Beatty Rail Infrastructure Services Ltd* [2006] EWCA Crim 1586 observed that most of these can be applied in the case of a company, although there are 'obvious difficulties' in applying (c).

Fixing a Fine: Section 164 Criminal Justice Act 2003

Section 164 of the Criminal Justice Act concerns the level of fine to be imposed for an offence. It applies equally to health and safety offences as well as to any other criminal conviction where the sanction includes a fine. It is particularly relevant to health and safety matters where an unlimited fine can be imposed. This section of the Act requires:

1. Before the amount of a fine is determined in relation to an offender who is an individual, then the court must enquire into the offender's financial circumstances.
2. The fine must reflect the court's view of the seriousness of the offence.

3. Where the offender is an individual or a company, when fixing a fine the court must take into account the circumstances of the case including, among other things, the financial circumstances of the offender 'so far as they are known, or appear, to the court'.
4. In taking into account the financial position of the offender this can have the effect of *increasing or reducing* the amount of the fine.

3.1 The law of contract
3.2 Construction health and safety
3.3 Insolvency in construction
3.4 Law of tort
3.5 Environmental issues

Sentencing an Employer/Company for Health and Safety Offences

The Court of Appeal in 1999 in the case *R.* v. *Howe & Son (Engineers) Ltd* [1999] 2 Cr App R(S) 37 said the purpose of health and safety prosecutions is to achieve a safe environment for employees and non employees who may be affected by the defendant's business activities. It said the fine should be large enough to bring that message home and where the defendant is a company not only to the managers but also the shareholders.

The brief facts were that a 20 year old employee of the defendant company was electrocuted and killed while cleaning his employer's factory which had shut down for this purpose.

An electric vacuum cleaner known as a 'Freddy' was being used to suck up water from the factory floor. The cable to the machine became trapped between the wheels and the floor. As a result the cable became damaged and 'live'. The deceased was holding the cable when he was killed.

For a number of technical reasons the company failed to ensure that the safety at work of its employees had been safeguarded 'so far as was reasonably practicable', and the lack of a system to check its electrical equipment fell far short of the appropriate standard. The court observed: '... the tragedy that befell [the deceased] was unfortunately an accident waiting to happen....'

A fine was imposed of £48 000 plus costs of £7 500. On appeal the fine was reduced to £15 000 but the order for costs remained unchanged.

The Court of Appeal said that it was:

> '...impossible to lay down any tariff or to say that the fine should bear specific relationship to the turn over or net profit of the defendant. Each case must be dealt with according to its own particular circumstances.'

The court also said that in its judgement magistrates should always think carefully before accepting jurisdiction in health and safety cases, where it is arguable that the fine may exceed the limit of their jurisdiction or where death or serious injury has occurred.

The court provided guidance as to the factors to be considered when sentencing employers for health and safety offences. These factors have been approved in a number of subsequent appeals against sentences imposed for health and safety breaches. Firstly the court pointed out the seriousness nature of breaches of Sections 2 and 3 HSWA which it said should be seen as 'the foundations for protecting health and safety'. Secondly it set out a number of general factors that should be considered as either aggravating or mitigating. These are:

Mitigating Factors

1. Guilty plea or prompt admission of responsibility.
2. Previous good safety record.
3. Steps to remedy deficiencies after they have been brought to the defendant's attention.

Aggravating Factors

1. How far the defendant has fallen below the standard of care to be expected.

2. Death or serious injury resulting from the breach (the penalty should reflect the public disquiet at unnecessary loss of life).
3. Where a deliberate breach has occurred with a view to cutting costs or maximising profits.
4. The degree of risk and the extent of the danger created by the offence.
5. Any failure to heed warnings.

In the case of *R.* v. *Jarvis Facilities Ltd* [2005] EWCA Crim 1409, which concerned health and safety failures of a company carrying out maintenance on the railways, the Court of Appeal said a more serious view of a defendant's breaches can be taken where there is a 'significant public element', particularly where the defendant has been entrusted to carry out work competently and efficiently which affects the public's safety. The company's fine was however reduced from £400 000 to £275 000.

In *R.* v. *Transco* [2006] EWCA Crim 838 the Court of Appeal made the distinction between health and cases involving systemic failure and those that did not. This case concerned an incident in November 2001. Transco engineers were called to an old flour mill in Ashton-under-Lyme that had been converted into flats after gas had entered the property from a fracture in the gas main. All the residents were evacuated and allowed back into the building once the gas main had been repaired and the flats ventilated. Unfortunately the engineers had failed to notice a 2 metre void between the ceiling of one of the flats and the one above. A resident lit a cigarette and was killed in the resultant explosion.

The Lord Chief Justice pointed out that the *Howe* case involved a serious systemic fault, as do most health and safety prosecutions. This case on the other hand involved no systemic fault but merely a mistake on the part of individuals managing an emergency situation on the ground. The fine of £1 million was reduced to £250 000.

Therefore where there is systemic failure on the part of an employer the guidelines in *Howe* apply. Where the failure is non-systemic and due to failings by frontline workers the *Howe* guidelines do not apply and the fine will be significantly lower.

In sentencing more than one defendant for health and safety breaches resulting from the same incident, it is not appropriate in the sentencing exercise to consider an overall figure for the incident and then divide it between those defendants. In criminal trials, fines should not be apportioned between defendants in the same way as damages in a civil claim, nor should a sentence be apportioned as if it was the apportionment of liability.

R. v. *Yorkshire Sheeting & Insulation Ltd* [2003] 2 Cr.App.R. (S) 93 concerned a company that had acted as subcontractor to the main contractor of a company involved in converting premises. The company successfully appealed on the basis that the sentencing judge had attributed a greater degree of responsibility to it than was justified. The Court of Appeal said:

> '. . . the approach adopted by the judge appeared somewhat to mask the true nature of the sentencing exercise. This was to assess the degree of culpability and criminality on the part of the appellant by reference to the offence charged and its failure to take steps to ensure, so far as is reasonably practicable, the safety of the roofers. The judge placed too much emphasis on seeking to apportion overall liability (by reference to the projected total figure) . . . on a percentage basis and not enough on assessing the appellant's own culpability in respect of the offence charged.'

The duties upon an employer under sections 2 and 3 of the HSWA are non-delegable duties (see the House of Lords decision in *R.* v. *Associated Octel* [1996] 4 All ER 846. This is relevant when it comes to sentencing a company who has contracted out part of its undertaking (i.e. business).

3.1 The law of contract
3.2 Construction health and safety
3.3 Insolvency in construction
3.4 Law of tort
3.5 Environmental issues

In *R.* v. *Mersey Docks and Harbour Company* [1995] 16 Cr App Rep (S) 806 a harbour company had failed to take adequate precautions to avoid an explosion, which killed two men, on a vessel which had previously carried a dangerous cargo. The Court of Appeal stressed that the duty under section 3 HSWA was non delegable and it was no mitigation for the company to say it had relied upon the master of the vessel to ascertain whether there were dangerous areas on the vessel. The Court of Appeal also said that where a company has this 'attitude' to discharging its duty then it is important that the courts impose a fine which leaves people like the harbour company '*in no doubt that it is their duty and they have to discharge it*'.

The largest fines to date, both in 2005, are £15m for Transco in Scotland relating to an explosion killing a family of four in their home, and a fine of £7.5m (reduced on appeal from £10m) of the maintenance arm of Balfour Beatty for its part in the Hatfield train derailment of 2000 which killed four passengers.

A recent briefing note in 'Civil Engineering' by Lamont noted that in 2006–07 fines for breaches of HSWA averaged around £25 000 but that fines of £100 000–£200 000 were becoming increasingly common.

The Sentencing Advisory Panel is currently considering its advice to the courts for sentencing companies in work related criminal matters. At the time of writing it is considering corporate manslaughter fines should be between 2.5% and 10% of turnover and for health and safety breaches between 1.5% and 7.5% of turnover.

Compensation Orders

Criminal courts have a general power to make a compensation order in favour of anyone who has been injured or suffered loss or damage as a consequence of the defendant's offence for which he/she has been convicted. The maximum that can be awarded in the Magistrates' Court is £5 000 and in the Crown Court there is no limit. Such orders are rare.

Name and Shame

The HSE website has a public record of health and safety convictions (www.hse-databases.co.uk/prosecutions/). The site gives details of all prosecution cases by the HSE which has resulted in convictions. This has become known as the 'name and shame' list. It seems that the list is becoming of interest to insurers when considering employers' liability insurance and public liability insurance.

Remedial Orders

Both the HSWA and the CMCHA have provision form remedial orders to be made. Under the HSWA in the past these orders have been rarely used.

Sentencing an Individual for Health and Safety Offences

Often fines for section 7 HSWA breaches are dealt with in the Magistrates' Court and are below £1 000, particularly if the Defendant is a frontline worker.

Fines for section 37 HSWA offences have been increasing in recent years and the average fine is now above £3 000. The average for section 36 offences is around £1 000.

However the case of Gillian Beckingham in 2006, acquitted of manslaughter but convicted of a breach of section 7 HSWA in relation to a legionella outbreak, may be an indication that fines for directors and managers convicted of health and safety offences are also on the increase in line with fines for employers. She was fined £15 000 representing 50% of her gross annual income.

In November 2006 at Preston Crown Court, George Ruttle, Managing Director of Ruttle Contracting Ltd was found guilty of breaching section 37 HSWA. He was fined £75 000 and ordered to pay £103 500 costs. The case concerned a worker who had died as a result of a truck overturning. On appeal the Court of Appeal said the fine was not excessive.

Manslaughter

If an individual is convicted of gross negligence manslaughter as a result of a work related death, then, based on past cases, he/she can expect a custodial sentence in the region of 18 months to 2 years.

However there are occasions when the sentence can be much greater than two years. Mark Connolly was convicted of gross negligence manslaughter at Newcastle Crown Court and imprisoned on 17th March 2006 for 9 years (later reduced to 7 years on appeal).

The case concerned an incident on the railways at Tebay in February 2004. A railway trailer heavily loaded with scrap steel freewheeled wholly uncontrolled at about 40 miles per hour for several miles until colliding with four workmen on the track killing them. Mr Connolly's business operated the trailers. He was convicted upon the basis that he had deliberately disabled the braking system of the trailers solely for profit.

It is very unlikely these days that the sentence will be suspended. This was confirmed in *A-G's Reference No. 89 or 2006* [2006] EWCA Crim 2570, a case concerning a defendant who had pleaded guilty to gross negligence manslaughter. Here the Court of Appeal held it was unduly lenient to suspend a custodial sentence where an employee of the defendant had died due to a faulty machine.

A company convicted of manslaughter is liable to an unlimited fine which is the same as for a breach of the HSWA.

3.6 Funding

There are a number of policies that may cover representation of a company or an individual charged with health and safety or related offences.

The usual insurance policies to consider are:

Employers' Liability

This insurance is arranged to protect employers in relation to claims involving injury to their employees. It should be noted this cover is required by law pursuant the Employer's Liability (Compulsory Insurance) Act 1969 and it is an offence not to have such cover.

Public Liability

This insurance is designed to protect against the risk of incurring legal liability, usually for negligence, to third parties. Cover can be offered as part of a general policy or alternatively it can be offered separately.

D&O Policy

Directors' and officers' liability and company reimbursement policies (often referred to as D&O policies) provide insurance for senior executives against legal bills arising from their corporate responsibilities. D&O policies are not compulsory.

Professional Indemnity

This insurance cover protects professional specialists such as physicians, architects, engineers and others against third party claims arising from activities in their professional field.

Insurance policies like public liability cover may cover not only the company itself but also named individuals and indeed even employees.

Legal defence costs insurance may be contained in a separate policy. Costs recoverable should include the costs of defending criminal proceedings and health and safety prosecutions. Legal expenses insurance, contractors' at risk and other specialised insurances may also be in a position to respond.

It is good advice to any company to check its insurance policies and when they respond before an incident occurs.

3.7 Inquests and Judicial Reviews

An inquest, which is held before a coroner, is an inquisitorial hearing not an adversarial one (like a criminal trial). The purpose of an inquest is to determine (a) who the deceased was and (b) how, when and where the deceased died. In work related death inquest the 'how' question has become extended to look into the circumstances of the deceased's death.

If the police prosecute for manslaughter there will be no inquest until the criminal proceedings have been concluded. However if the police decide not to prosecute and pass the matter over to HSE then it is usual for the HSE prosecution not to be commenced until after the inquest. Thus the inquest can be instrumental in ascertaining HSE's approach to the issues and is an opportunity to test the evidence. Further it is possible that after the inquest the matter could be transferred back to the police, if there is a finding of 'unlawful killing'.

A judicial review is a form of court proceedings in the Administrative Court in which a judge reviews the lawfulness of a decision or action made by a public body. It is a challenge to the way the decision has been made, not to the decision itself.

In the recent past there have been examples where the family of a deceased has challenged the police's or the HSE's decision not to prosecute and the court have ordered the decision be reconsidered.

On 6th May 2008 at Cardiff Crown Court, Roy Clark, owner of North Eastern Roofing was sentenced to 10 months imprisonment for gross negligence manslaughter. This followed the death of Daniel Dennis, a 17 year old worker, who fell through a fragile skylight in 2003.

The case is of note because of its route to trial.

The inquest did not take place until almost two years after the deceased's death. The inquest jury returned a unanimous verdict of unlawful killing.

In March 2006 the CPS concluded there was no realistic prospect that a criminal prosecution of Mr Clark (or any other person) would succeed stating '*the degree of negligence exhibited was not such as to amount to criminal negligence*'. The deceased's parents commenced proceedings to judicial review this decision.

Lord Justice Waller in December 2006 ruled the CPS should reconsider its decision not to prosecute concluding the CPS had failed to give sufficient consideration to the evidence that the deceased had been instructed to go on the roof as part of his duties, without any training or induction course, or any serious warning about roof lights, and had not been told not to do so prior to receiving such training. The judge observed that the file note of the CPS lawyer said the inquest verdict was perverse and contrary to the evidence.

Lord Justice Waller, whilst emphasising he did not wish to prejudge the issue, concluded it was '*. . . seriously arguable that a different decision might be made once account is taken of these issues*'.

On the eve of his trial, five years after the incident, Mr Clark pleaded guilty.

4 THE HEALTH AND SAFETY AT WORK ETC. ACT 1974

The HSWA imposes a number of all-embracing 'general duties', and three of these duties in particular combine to impose obligations on everyone involved in a project. When the Act was proposed it was intended that these general duties would reflect the common-law obligations of the parties, the difference being that under the HSWA regime these obligations could be enforced directly by inspectors, not just through the courts after an accident, but in anticipation of a danger that might arise from work being carried out. In the following paragraphs the main provisions of the relevant parts of the HSWA are outlined.

4.1 Section 2: general duties of employers to their employees

Section 2 of the Act provides as follows:

'(1) It shall be the duty of every employer to ensure, so far as is reasonably practicable, the health, safety and welfare at work of all his employees.
(2) Without prejudice to the generality of an employer's duty under the preceding subsection, the matters to which that duty extends include in particular:
(a) the provision and maintenance of plant and systems of work that are, so far as is reasonably practicable, safe and without risks to health;
(b) arrangements for ensuring, so far as is reasonably practicable, safety and absence of risks to health in connection with the use, handling, storage and transport of articles and substances;
(c) the provision of such information, instruction, training and supervision as is necessary to ensure, so far as is reasonably practicable, the health and safety at work of his employees;
(d) so far as is reasonably practicable as regards any place of work under the employer's control, the maintenance of it in a condition that is safe and without risks to health and the provision and maintenance of means of access to and egress from it that are safe and without such risks;
(e) the provision and maintenance of a working environment for his employees that is, so far as is reasonably practicable, safe, without risks to health, and adequate as regards facilities and arrangements for their welfare at work . . .'

These obligations need to be viewed in light of the remaining provisions of Section 2 dealing with requirements for written health and safety policies (see below), and also provisions which deal with the requirement for employers to consult with safety representatives and safety committees in certain circumstances. It is also important to note that each of the matters dealt with in sub-paragraphs (a)–(e) above are now expanded upon and subject to additional rules applicable to particular circumstances that are contained in numerous health and safety regulations.

Whatever the exact circumstances of a project, and whatever regulations apply, it needs to be borne in mind that the fundamental duty under Regulation 2(1) to ensure safety of employees will always exist and it is important to understand that compliance with a particular regulation (for example the CDM Regulations), does not necessarily discharge all an employer's responsibilities. There may be some residual area of risk or some interface with another employer on site which steps taken under such regulations do not adequately cover. In this case, the employer will remain potentially liable under the general duty of the Act.

There is no exact meaning or measure of what will be reasonably practicable in any given case. The test tends to be less strict than a requirement simply to do what is 'practicable', since the courts recognize that there may be practicable measures which are not reasonable to take. The classic definition of the phrase was given by Asquith LJ in the case of *Edwards* v. *National Coal Board* [1949] 1 KB 704 who said:

> 'Reasonably practicable is a narrower term than physically possible, and implies that a computation must be made in which the quantum of risk is placed in one scale, and the sacrifice, whether in money, time or trouble, involved in the measures necessary to avert the risk, is placed in the other; and that, if it be shown that there is a gross disproportion between them, the risk being insignificant in relation to the sacrifice, the person upon whom the duty is laid discharges the burden of proving that compliance was not reasonably practicable. This computation falls to be made at a point of time anterior to the happening of the incident complained of.'

The lack of definition for the term 'reasonably practicable' was criticised by the Work and Pensions Committee in its 3rd Report of Session 2007–2008: *The Role of the Health and Safety Commission and the Health and Safety Executive in regulating workplace health and safety*. It said:

> We are concerned that the test of 'reasonable practicability' introduces a lack of clarity that can increase the burden on employers in meeting their health and safety obligations. We recommend that the Law Commission reviews the test of 'reasonable practicability' and how it applies to the Health and Safety at Work Act 1974.

Although the reasonably practicable qualification is obviously of considerable importance in relation to Section 2 (and the other general duties described below) it should be contrasted with the standard of care that arises under other health and safety regulations which are often stricter and not qualified in this way.

The courts construe the wording of Section 2 as being of wide application to any works that it has undertaken. An employer will, for example, be subject to the duty where plant and equipment is not yet meant to be in use but it is nevertheless available. Section 2 also extends to situations where there are employees working in a situation where their safety may be dependent on the way in which activities of people working alongside them are conducted, for example, employees of a contractor who are on the premises. There may be a duty for the employer, in such circumstances, in ensuring a safe system of work for its own employees, to give information and instructions to the visiting workers or to coordinate their activities with the contractor (*R.* v. *Swan Hunter Shipbuilders Ltd* [1981] ICR 831).

4.2 Section 3: general duties of employers and self-employed to persons other than their employees

Section 3 states the following:

> '(1) It shall be the duty of every employer to conduct his undertaking in such a way as to ensure, so far as is reasonably practicable, that persons not in his employment who may be affected thereby are not thereby exposed to risks to their health or safety.
>
> (2) It shall be the duty of every self-employed person to conduct his undertaking in such a way as to ensure, so far as is reasonably practicable, that he and other persons (not being his employees) who may be affected thereby are not thereby exposed to risks to their health or safety.'

This section is treated as being of broad application to any 'undertaking', a word which means not just a business carrying out physical work, such as the construction process, but also the provision of services or trading. Even a business which is not operational, e.g. while maintenance is being carried out, is still likely to be viewed as an undertaking (although this is a question of fact for the magistrates or jury to decide). It had been held in one recent case that an employer who employs an independent contractor to do work is not himself 'conducting his undertaking' in circumstances where the employer is under no duty to control the work of the independent contractor and does not actually exercise control. It was said that the mere capacity or opportunity to exercise control over an activity was not sufficient to be within the scope of Section 3(1) of the HSWA. However, this has now been overruled by the House of Lords in *R.* v. *Associated Octel Co. Ltd* [1996] 4 All ER 846 which is considered further below.

Section 3 is of particular importance to health and safety in construction as those 'other than their employees' includes members of the public, a small number of whom are killed or injured by construction activity each year. Also, in principle, anyone involved with the project is charged with this general duty.

4.3 Section 4: general duties of person concerned with premises to persons other than their employees

In view of the expansive approach taken by the courts to the scope of Section 3 as described above, the rationale for a separate general duty dealing with control of premises is perhaps less clear now than it was to those drafting the legislation. As can be seen below there are in fact, over and above Section 3, additional obligations arising out of control of premises imposed by Section 4, and overall the effect of this section is to place liability primarily on the person directly controlling the premises, rather than those carrying on activities within them even if persons in the latter category have obligations of their own under Section 2 or 3. Section 4 provides:

'(1) This section has effect for imposing on persons duties in relation to those who:
  (a) are not their employees; but
  (b) use non-domestic premises made available to them as a place of work or as a place where they may use plant or substances provided for their use there and applies to premises so made available and other non-domestic premises used in connection with them.

(2) It shall be the duty of each person who has, to any extent, control of premises to which this section applies or of the means of access thereto or egress therefrom or of any plant or substance in such premises to take such measures as it is reasonable for a person in his position to take to ensure, so far as is reasonably practicable, that the premises, all means of access thereto or egress therefrom available for use by persons using the premises, and any plant or substance in the premises or, as the case may be, provided for use there, is or are safe and without risks to health.

(3) Where a person has, by virtue of any contract or tenancy, an obligation of any extent in relation to:
  (a) the maintenance or repair of any premises to which this section applies or any means of access thereto or egress therefrom; or
  (b) the safety of or the absence of risks to health arising from plant or substances in any such premises; that person shall be treated, for the purposes

3.1 The law of contract
3.2 Construction health and safety
3.3 Insolvency in construction
3.4 Law of tort
3.5 Environmental issues

of subsection (2) above, as being a person who has control of the matters to which his obligation extends.

(4) Any reference in this section to a person having control of any premises or matter is a reference to a person having control of the premises or matter in connection with the carrying on by him of a trade, business or other undertaking (whether for profit or not).'

As with the previous duties, Section 4 is capable of applying to more than one party, since it refers to control 'to any extent' and the courts may well find that, in the circumstances of works being carried out, control is shared. The only significant restriction on the application of this duty is in relation to domestic premises, but the duties nevertheless apply where work is being carried out in parts of premises which are not in private occupation (such as lifts and service areas). Section 4(3), by referring to any contract, extends shared responsibility within its duties to anyone managing or undertaking property maintenance, or installing or maintaining plant and equipment.

The leading case in this area is *Austin Rover Group Ltd* v. *HM Inspector of Factories* [1990] 1 AC 619 which concerned maintenance work being undertaken under contract by specialist industrial cleaners at a car assembly plant. The owners of the premises gave instructions as to precautions for work in a potentially flammable atmosphere, but the employees of the subcontractors did not follow these instructions and there was a flash fire. The House of Lords held that the occupiers of the premises had not contravened Section 4(2); the words 'such measures as it is reasonable ... to take ...' require consideration to be given not only to the extent to which the person in question has control of the premises, but also to that person's knowledge and *reasonable foresight* at all material times. In making premises available for use by another, the reasonableness of the measures which the individual is required to take to ensure safety of premises have to be determined in the light of this knowledge and of the *anticipated use* for which the premises have been made available and of the *extent of the individual's control* and *knowledge*, if any, of the actual use thereafter. The word 'reasonable' in the context of Section 4(2) relates to what is reasonable for the person concerned, and not the measures themselves. This latter question is something to be considered in the light of what is reasonably practicable which, as has been explained earlier, is a matter for the defendant to prove on the balance of probabilities. It now appears that the matter of foreseeability of risk is to be treated differently under Section 4 to the way it is treated under Section 3 (and, for that matter, Section 2 in relation to the duty to ensure that persons are 'safe').

R. v. Associated Octel Petroleum Ltd [1996] 4 All ER 846

This case is of particular significance to the construction industry.

R. v. *Associated Octel Petroleum Ltd* has certain similarities in the facts of this case with those of the Austin Rover case described earlier, but the difference was that this prosecution was brought under Section 3(1) of the HSWA. In the course of an annual shutdown for the cleaning and repair of the company's chemical plant by a specialist contractor there was a flash fire and explosion and the contractor's workman was badly burned. The investigating inspectors identified a number of aspects of the contractor's operations to clean a tank within the chlorine plant which were unsafe including the storage of acetone in an open container, failure to use a safety lamp, and inadequate ventilation arrangements. Octel argued that it was not liable on account of the work being carried out by an independent contractor whose operations it did not actually control. This argument was put in terms that Octel did not 'conduct its undertaking' for the purposes of Section 3(1) in relation to an operation which was essentially the conduct of the contractor's undertaking.

The Court of Appeal's view The Court of Appeal heard Octel's appeal in 1994 and disagreed, holding that the activities of the contractor necessary for carrying on the employer's business are part of the employer's conduct of *its* undertaking for these purposes, imposing the duty on Octel under the contract whether it is done by its own employees or the independent contractor. Given that this was a 'risk' (as broadly defined previously) it was not necessary to show that the employer had actual control over how the work was done.

The Court of Appeal held that the general principle of the law of tort, under which a person is not normally (subject to a number of exceptions) liable for the acts of independent contractors, was *not* mirrored in Section 3(1), which was to be given a wider interpretation. The notion that actual control had to be exercised over the works for liability to arise under the HSWA was rejected (the Court at the same time overruling the decision in an employer's favour in *RMC Roadstone Products Ltd* v. *Jester* [1994] ICR 456 which also concerned safety of contractors). The Court of Appeal said that the degree of control was relevant to the issue of whether or not the employer had done what was reasonably practicable, i.e. it was something for Octel to prove in its defence.

> 'The question of what is reasonably practicable is a matter of fact and degree in each case. It will depend on a number of factors so far as concerns operations carried out by independent contractors: what is reasonably practicable for a large organisation employing safety officers or engineers contracting for the services of a small contractor on routine operations may differ markedly from what is reasonably practicable for a small shopkeeper employing a local builder on activities on which he has no expertise. The nature and gravity of the risk, the competence and experience of the workmen, the nature of the precautions to be taken are all relevant considerations' (Stuart-Smith LJ in *R.* v. *Associated Octel* (Court of Appeal)).

The company had elected not to give its own evidence on this point and had been convicted at trial.

Decision of the House of Lords The decision of the House of Lords affirmed the Court of Appeal, and its strict interpretation of the law has to be followed by all other courts. The key points of its analyses were as follows.

(a) An employer is free to engage either employees or independent contractors for any task.
(b) The control over – or 'independence' of – the contractor is not decisive for determining liability under Section 3.
(c) The question is 'simply' [*sic*] whether the activity in question can be described as part of the *employer's undertaking*: in Octel's case its undertaking of running a chemical plant *included* 'having the factory cleaned' by contractors.

Lord Hoffman described the duty as regards risks that arise in such a situation in this way:

> 'If therefore the employer engages an independent contractor to do work which forms part of the conduct of the employer's undertaking he must stipulate for whatever

> conditions are needed to avoid those risks and are reasonably practicable. He cannot, having omitted to do so, say that he was not in a position to exercise any control.'

The House of Lords rejected the HSE's argument for a wider interpretation that any 'works of cleaning, repair and maintenance necessary for the conduct of the employer's business' would be covered by Section 3. They held that it is always a factual question to be considered in each case whether or not a contractor's work is on the one hand 'entirely separate' from the employer's undertaking, or 'an activity integrated with the general conduct of this business'.

In Octel's case, the integration of the contractor's work with its own was clear to the House of Lords. However, having equipment such as cars sent out for repair, or office curtains sent out for cleaning, was rejected as being within the scope of Section 3. Although these off-site activities were viewed as not generally creating a statutory duty, 'the place where the activity takes place' regarded by Lord Hoffman as being 'very important and possibly decisive' is unlikely in future to prove workable as a determining factor in whether or not a duty exists. In particular, the situation described in the judgment is not wholly analogous to construction projects where the employer under the contract to build a new building may be a more remote figure for whom the project is itself the undertaking. No attempt is made in the Octel case to analyse the implications for new build.

5 MANAGEMENT DUTIES

5.1 Written health and safety policies

The legislation contains a variety of obligations on employers to produce and operate a number of management tools to assist in meeting the wider statutory duties to minimize risks. In addition, a number of requirements of an administrative nature must be observed in day-to-day activities. Accidents, 'near-misses' and industrial diseases must be notified and records kept.

Every employer who carries on an undertaking employing five or more people must prepare a written statement of its safety policy to ensure that thought has been given to potential hazards and their management. These policies serve several purposes:

- to state the undertaking's health and safety aims
- to identify hazards and to avoid or reduce them and to control residual hazards
- to increase employees' awareness of the arrangements made
- to provide a vehicle for consultation and employees' involvement
- to define clearly the claim of responsibility for safety from the directors downwards
- to provide explicit statements which can be reviewed and brought up to date to respond to changing circumstances.

There are HSE guidance publications available on writing safety policy documents, and on devising effective management systems.

5.2 The Management of Health and Safety at Work Regulations 1999

These regulations which were most recently amended in 2006 supplement the existing requirements of the Health and Safety at Work etc. Act and specify a range of management exercises which must be carried out in all businesses. The aim is to map out the organization of precautionary measures in a systematic way, and to make sure that all staff are familiar with the measures and their own responsibilities.

Table 1

Hazard/Activity	Regulations
Manual handling and lifting	Manual Handling Operations Regulations 1992
Suitability of personal protective	Personal Protective Equipment at Work Regulations 1992
VDUs and associated work stations	Health and Safety (Display Screen Equipment) Regulations 1992
Noise	Control of Noise at Work Regulations 2005
Vibration	Control of Vibration at Work Regulations 2005
Chemicals	Control of Substances Hazardous to Health Regulations 2002, 2003 and 2004
Asbestos	Control of Asbestos at Work Regulations 2006
Lead	Control of Lead at Work Regulations 2002
Design work for construction and engineering	Construction (Design and Management) Regulations 2007
Pregnant and new mothers	Management of Health and Safety at Work Regulations 1999, 2003 and 2006
Young persons	Management of Health and Safety at Work Regulations 1999

Risk assessment (Regulation 3)

Every employer is required to make a 'suitable and sufficient' assessment of risks to employees, and to other people who might be affected by the business, such as visiting contractors and members of the public. A comprehensive investigation of risks involved in all areas and operations is required, together with identification of who is affected, and definition of appropriate precautions.

The assessment must be written down (or recorded by other means, such as on computer) when there are more than five employees. The assessment needs to be reviewed and kept up to date.

Various other regulations contain hazard-specific or activity-specific risk assessment requirements (see Table 1). These do not need to be duplicated for the purposes of Regulation 3 of the Management of Health and Safety at Work Regulations when they have already been done – so long as they remain valid.

Formal arrangements for health and safety (Regulations 4, 5, 6, 8 and 9)

It is very important to remember that producing a risk assessment is not in itself the purpose of these Regulations. The assessment is only a tool by which risks arising from work activity can be identified, quantified and prioritized. Thereafter formal arrangements must be worked through (and recorded) for effective planning, organization, control, monitoring and review of measures to reduce the risks identified through the assessment under Regulation 3. The implementation of these measures must be in accordance with the 'General Principles of Prevention' (in Schedule 1 of the Regulations):

(a) Avoiding risks.
(b) Evaluating the risks which cannot be avoided.
(c) Combating the risks at source.
(d) Adapting the work to the individual, especially as regards the design of workplaces, the choice of work equipment and the choice of working and production methods, with a view, in particular, to alleviating monotonous work and work at a predetermined work-rate and to reducing their effect on health.

(e) Adapting to technical progress.
(f) Replacing the dangerous by the non-dangerous or the less dangerous.
(g) Developing a coherent overall prevention policy which covers technology, organization of work, working conditions, social relationships and the influence of factors relating to the working environment.
(h) Giving collective protective measures priority over individual protective measures.
(i) Giving appropriate instructions to employees.

In appropriate circumstances, health surveillance of staff may be required – the Approved Code of Practice describes more fully when this duty will arise.

Procedures must be established for dealing with serious and imminent dangers, including fire evacuation plans and contacts with emergencies.

Access to dangerous areas should be restricted to authorized trained staff.

Competent assistance (Regulation 7)

Every employer is obliged to appoint one or more 'competent persons' to advise and assist in undertaking the necessary measures to comply with the statutory requirements. They may be employees or outside consultants, but the regulations specify that the 'preference' shall be for the appointments to be made internally.

The competence of the people appointed is to be judged in terms of their training, knowledge and experience of the work involved; it is not necessarily dependent on particular qualifications. These people have to be provided with adequate information, time and resources to do their jobs.

Information and training (Regulations 10, 13 and 15)

Information must be provided to staff on the risk assessment, emergency procedures, and the identity of the people appointed to assist on health and safety matters. Specific information requirements apply for temporary workers.

Adequate training should be provided to staff when they are recruited, and periodically afterwards, with more later if their work changes.

In entrusting work to an employee, account must be taken of the individual's capability to do the job safely.

Employees must be informed of certain standard information directly or by approved leaflets or posters under the Health and Safety Information for Employees Regulations 1989.

Shared workplaces and visiting workers (Regulations 11 and 12)

Shared workplaces When using shared workplaces:

(a) employers must cooperate so as to enable compliance with statutory requirements
(b) each employer's safety measures need to be coordinated with the others
(c) other employers concerned must be informed of risks to their employees' health and safety.

These rules apply whether the sharing is temporary or permanent. (See also Regulation 13 relating to giving safety information to temporary workers and their employers.)

Working in host undertakings Host employers and the self-employed are required to provide the outside employer, and its employees, and every self-employed person who is working in the host undertaking, with comprehensible information concerning risks to health and safety. The outside employer, and its employees and the self-employed, also have to be told how to identify the person nominated by the host employer under the regulations to implement evacuation procedures.

These requirements are, in effect, the principles underlying the CDM Regulations, the latter expanding them to deal with the complexity, scale and inherent danger of construction and engineering work being carried out on sites requiring careful management of the various participants.

5.3 Employee consultation

These are two main sets of regulations on consultation, reflecting the historical development of legislation in this area and changing work patterns. In addition, other hazard or activity specific regulations may have applicable provisions.

Safety Regulations and Safety Committees Regulations 1977 (as amended)

These regulations permit trade unions (where recognized by the employer) to appoint an unspecified number of safety representatives, who acquire rights of time off with pay to undertake their roles and to undergo training. Their functions include:

- consultations with the employer on the introduction of significant safety measures and appointments
- investigation of potential hazards, dangers, occurrences and causes
- carrying out inspections of the workplace and certain safety documentation
- investigation of complaints by employees
- making representations to employers about the above or safety matters generally
- representing employees in consultations with HSE/local authority inspectors and receiving certain information from them.

A safety committee may be required on the request of at least two representatives and this committee's functions are to be agreed between the employer, representatives and relevant trade unions.

Health and Safety (Consultation with Employees) Regulations 1996 (as amended)

Where there are employees who are not represented by trade union safety representatives under the 1977 Regulations, employers are required to consult with them on significant health and safety issues. The consultation may be directly with individual employees, or with elected employee representatives: if the latter, they are entitled to time off with pay for carrying out their functions and undergoing training.

Construction (Design and Management) Regulations 2007

The Construction (Design and Management) Regulations 2007 have replaced the Construction (Design and Management) Regulations 1994.

In the construction and engineering construction sector, the 2007 CDM Regulations placed an obligation on the principal contractor to ensure that workers (including the self-employed) were able to discuss and offer advice in safety-related issues and to ensure there are arrangements for coordination of the views of workers or their representatives.

5.4 The Working Time Directive

This measure, which the European Court of Justice has affirmed is a health and safety measure in spite of its essential characteristics being those of employment rights, is

3.1 The law of contract
3.2 Construction health and safety
3.3 Insolvency in construction
3.4 Law of tort
3.5 Environmental issues

implemented in the UK by the Working Time Regulations 1998 (as amended). Responsibility for enforcement lies with HSE/local authority inspectors. The rules apply to 'workers', so freelancers and agency workers as well as direct employees will be covered by it. The key provisions of the Regulations are as follows.

- Maximum working week of 48 hours, averaged over a reference period of 17 weeks subject to opting out provisions if employees agree.
- Minimum daily rest period of 11 hours.
- Minimum annual leave of four weeks.
- Minimum rest period of one day per week.
- Workers will qualify for annual paid leave after they have worked continuously for three months.
- A worker's daily break must last at least 20 minutes and be taken away from the workplace where possible.
- Provided that certain conditions are met, employers may enter into agreements with their employees on an individual or collective basis in order to be able to take advantage of some derogations from the provisions of the Working Time Regulations.
- There are special provisions relating to 16- and 17-year-old workers: they can only be assigned to work during the period between 10.00 p.m. and 6.00 a.m. after they have had a free assessment of their health and capacities; they are entitled to 12 consecutive hours' rest in each 24-hour period and to 2 days' rest in each 7-day period (which should be consecutive if possible); and they are entitled to a rest break of at least 30 minutes if they work more than 4½ hours a day.
- Employees will be entitled to claim compensation in the Employment Tribunal if their 'entitlements', principally the entitlement to paid annual leave, are not granted to them.

5.5 Notification of construction work

Quite separate from the notices that have to be given for the purposes of planning applications or any requirements relating to compliance with Building Regulations, construction work may be notifiable to the Health and Safety Executive.

Under the CDM Regulations 2007, the notification is required to be sent to the relevant local HSE Area Office, and it has to be in writing, submitted as soon as practicable after the appointment of the coordinator. When some of the required particulars cannot be notified at that time, the remaining information has to be given as soon as practicable after the appointment of the principal contractor for the project, and in any event before construction work begins. The information required in the notification is set out in Schedule 1 of the CDM Regulations 2007, as detailed below. Similar notification requirements are likely to be incorporated in the revised CDM Regulations.

(1) Date of forwarding.
(2) Exact address of the construction site.
(3) Contact details of the client.
(4) Contact details of the coordinator.
(5) Contact details of the principal contractor.
(6) Date planned for start of the construction phase, (j).
(7) Time allowed for the planning and preparation for construction work.
(8) Planned duration of the construction phase.
(9) Estimated maximum number of people at work on the construction site.

(10) Planned number of contractors on the construction site.
(11) Name and address of any contractors already appointed.
(12) Name and address of any designers already engaged.

There is no mandatory format for presenting this information but HSE Offices have available a standard form (Form 10(rev)). To be notifiable for these purposes a project is one where the construction phase will:

(a) be longer than 30 days, or
(b) will involve more than 500 person days of construction work for a client.

The construction phase for these purposes means the period of time starting when construction work starts and ending when the construction work in the project is completed. The task of giving the notification is that of the coordinator acting on behalf of the client who is appointed for the purposes of the CDM Regulations (see Section 6 of this chapter). Where works are being carried out for a domestic client (i.e. for private purposes), which do not require a coordinator, responsibility for the notification will lie with all the contractors. Notification will still be required under CDM 2007. The precise requirements will be set out in the Regulations.

5.6 Accident reporting and incident requirements

The Reporting of Injuries, Diseases and Dangerous Occurrences Regulations 1995 (RIDDOR) which are currently under revision require that certain events, accidents or illnesses that happen at work must be notified and/or also formally reported to the enforcing authority. Primarily, the duty to report lies with the employer of the employee injured or (if no employee is involved) the person having control over the premises. Reference should also be made to the Regulations for criteria determining who is the 'responsible person' for these purposes.

The incidents covered by RIDDOR include the following.

- The death of any person as a result of a work-related accident.
- Any fracture, other than to the fingers, thumbs or toes.
- Dislocation of the shoulder, hip, knee or spine.
- Any amputation.
- Loss of sight (whether temporary or permanent); a penetration injury to an eye or a chemical or hot metal burn to an eye.
- Any injury resulting from an electric shock or electrical burn leading to unconsciousness or requiring resuscitation or admittance to hospital for more than 24 hours.
- Acute illness requiring medical treatment, or loss of consciousness, resulting from absorption of any substance by inhalation, ingestion or through skin.
- Incapacitation for work of a member of staff for more than three consecutive days (including any days which would not have been working days but excluding the day of the accident).

In addition, the Regulations now contain a specific duty to report injuries to non-employees where the person injured is taken from the site of the accident to a hospital for treatment.

The notification and reporting requirements are illustrated in Fig. 1 of this chapter.

Diseases which have to be reported are listed in RIDDOR and are reportable if the person concerned has been involved with certain specified work. They include decompression illness, various skin and lung diseases as well as a number of forms of cancer.

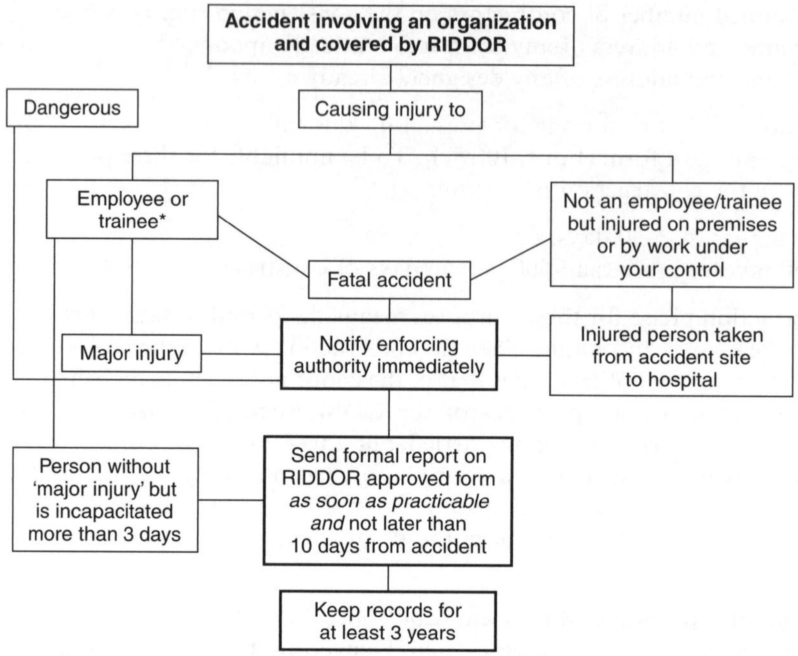
Accident involving an organization and covered by RIDDOR
Dangerous
Causing injury to
Employee or trainee*
Not an employee/trainee but injured on premises or by work under your control
Fatal accident
Major injury
Notify enforcing authority immediately
Injured person taken from accident site to hospital
Person without 'major injury' but is incapacitated more than 3 days
Send formal report on RIDDOR approved form *as soon as practicable and* not later than 10 days from accident
Keep records for at least 3 years

* Applies to employee/trainee incapacitated for more than three days.

Figure 1. Based on a chart in Tolley's Health and Safety at Work *Looseleaf and CD-ROM*

In addition, a fire or explosion, or the collapse of any lifting machinery, scaffolding, floor, wall or other structure may in some circumstances be reportable as dangerous occurrences. There are various other circumstances in which matters are reportable and reference should be made to the Regulations themselves.

The manner of making the report is governed by the Regulations, and involves the use of approved forms (F2508 or F2508A or approved equivalents). However, where notification of an accident is also required this must be by the quickest practicable means which, in practice, is treated as a telephone call to the local office of the relevant enforcing authority. When someone dies or suffers a specified major injury or condition, or there is a gas incident covered by the Regulations, there is a duty to notify the HSE by the quickest practicable means, which will usually require telephone notification followed up by the requisite form. The RIDDOR also contains record-keeping requirements for particulars of accidents, dangerous occurrences and diseases, and the records must be preserved for at least three years. These records are in addition to the Accident Book records which are required to be kept for the Social Security (Claims and Payments) Regulations 1967.

5.7 First-aid arrangements

The extent of obligations in this area will vary according to the circumstances of the workplace: the principal requirements of the Health and Safety (First Aid) Regulations 1981 (as amended) for employers are:

- to provide or ensure the provision of adequate and appropriate equipment and facilities

- to provide or ensure the provision of adequate and appropriate numbers of suitable persons as first-aiders (properly trained), unless the activities are so low-risk that an 'appointed person' (see below) will be sufficient
- to make provision for temporary absences of first-aiders to be covered by a person appointed to take charge of situations when people may require medical assistance including the use of first-aid equipment and facilities
- to inform employees of first-aid arrangements
- detailed guidelines on appropriate numbers and training of first-aiders and the provision of first-aid services are set out in the Approved Code of Practice (L 74).

The provisions must take into account shift and weekend working, remoteness of the worksite, special hazards etc.

The self-employed are under a lesser obligation to provide or ensure the provision of adequate and appropriate equipment to render first-aid to themselves while at work.

5.8 Employer's liability insurance

Except for certain government-related bodies, all employers are required to maintain cover in respect of their own employees by the Employers Liability (Compulsory Insurance) Act 1969. This must be an 'approved policy' which is not subject to conditions or exceptions prohibited by the Employers Liability (Compulsory Insurance) Regulations 1998 so that, for example, take notification of a claim under the policy would not invalidate the cover as it might under a normal policy. Under the 1998 Regulations the minimum cover requirement is for £5 million in respect of claims by one or more employees arising out of any one occurrence. (It is sufficient for a parent company to take out such cover on behalf of itself and its subsidiaries – see Regulation 3.)

6 MANAGEMENT OBLIGATIONS – CONSTRUCTION AND ENGINEERING PROJECTS

Employers and the self-employed have duties under Section 3 of the HSWA in respect of ensuring the health and safety of those not in their employment but affected by their undertaking. These duties are particularly relevant in the construction industry due to the amount of subcontracting which is carried out and also because of the effects which construction operations can have on the general public. Each year a number of members of the public are killed by construction operations from hazards including falling debris, construction plant, collapsing scaffolding, roadworks or inadequately guarded excavations.

Likewise, in the Management of Health and Safety at Work Regulations 1999, the requirement in Regulation 3 for risk assessment extends to risks to the health and safety of persons not in an employer's employment but affected by its undertaking. A similar duty is placed on the self-employed. By implication, the preventative measures required under Regulation 4 are similarly extended to non-employees.

6.1 Construction (Design and Management) Regulations (CDM) 2007

The Construction (Design and Management) Regulations 2007 (SI 2007 No. 320) came into effect on 6 April 2007. They replaced the 1994 Construction (Design and Management) Regulations 1994 (as amended in 2000).

The Regulations apply to construction projects and parties associated with them once a construction project exists. A project is deemed to exist as soon as a client has decided to proceed to design and construction.

3.1 The law of contract
3.2 Construction health and safety
3.3 Insolvency in construction
3.4 Law of tort
3.5 Environmental issues

As the EC directive which the CDM Regulations implemented (Temporary or Mobile Construction Sites Directive 92/57/EEC) has not been revised, the scope for change in the regulations is limited to a reworking of existing requirements. Another structural change in CDM 2007 is the incorporation of most of the requirements of the Construction (Health, Safety and Welfare) Regulations 1996 (CHSWR). The CHSWR requirements relating to work at height were revoked by and incorporated in the Work at Height Regulations 2005 (see below).

There are probably more books and articles written about the CDM regulations in construction than all other construction-related regulations put together. Readers seeking in-depth information should consult publication catalogues of respected industry publishers such as Thomas Telford Publishing or the Construction Industry Research and Information Association (CIRIA).

Traditionally, parties to construction work in the UK have included a client, an engineer/architect responsible for design, and contractor(s). Construction-related health and safety legislation prior to the coming into force of the 1994 CDM Regulations predominantly placed duties on contractors only. The 1994 CDM Regulations changed this. The change has been continued in the 2007 regulations also along with the removal of the planning supervisor and the introduction of the coordinator.

There are duties on five key parties to a contract:

- client
- designer
- coordinator
- principal contractor
- contractors.

The client

The client who is considered by HSE to have a key role in ensuring proper attention is paid to health and safety matters has duties under these regulations. Clients must select and appoint a coordinator and principal contractor for the project. In making such appointments the client should be satisfied that the appointees for these roles are competent and will devote adequate resources to health and safety.

Similar duties apply to the client in respect of the appointment of designers and other contractors. Again, clients should ensure, so far as is reasonably practicable, that sufficient resources, including time, have been or will be allocated to enable the project to be carried out safely. Client duties do not apply to domestic householders when they have construction work carried out on their homes.

Before starting work, both designers and contractors must ensure the client is aware of his duties.

A client can no longer appoint an agent to act on its behalf.

The coordinator

The introduction of the planning supervisor brought a new role to the UK construction industry. This role has been redefined with the replacement of the planning supervisor by the coordinator. The coordinator has overall responsibility for coordinating the health and safety aspects of the design and planning phase, and for ensuring preparation of the early stages of the health and safety plan and the health and safety file.

The coordinator has to ensure that designers undertake their duty in respect of risk avoidance and reduction as well as cooperate with other designers over health and safety matters. When required to do so by the client, the coordinator should advise the client on matters relating to the competence of designers and contractors and on the adequacy of their resource allocation for health and safety as well as on the health and safety plans prior to the start of construction.

Coordinators have duties under the CDM Regulations to ensure notification of the project to the HSE and that the health and safety file is prepared. They are responsible for ensuring that other parties discharge their duties under the regulations, although they have no statutory powers to force these parties to act.

The designer

The designer has a key role under these regulations in contributing to health and safety. Designers have a duty to consider health and safety matters during development of their designs. They should ensure, as much as they can, that structures are designed to avoid or, if this is not possible, to minimize risks to health and safety while they are being built and maintained. Under CDM 2007 these duties are extended to the health and safety of those who will be using the structure – in particular to the aspects of the structure covered by the Workplace (Health and Safety) Regulations 1992, see 10.1 below. The definition of 'structure' is very wide and includes tunnels, pipelines and earthworks in addition to more conventional structures. Where risks cannot be avoided, adequate information on residual risk has to be provided. The design should include adequate information on health and safety and this information should be passed to the coordinator for inclusion in the health and safety plan. Design is not limited to drawings but includes the preparation of specifications.

In addition, designers have a duty to ensure their design has with it, sufficient information about aspects of the design of the structure or its construction or maintenance to assist clients, other designers; and contractors to comply with their duties under these Regulations.

Where a project is notifiable, a designer shall not commence work on a project unless a CDM co-ordinator has been appointed for that project. The designer shall take all reasonable steps to provide the coordinator with sufficient information about the design of the structure, its construction or maintenance to assist the CDM co-ordinator to comply with his duties under CDM.

Designs prepared outside the UK but for UK structures must also comply with these regulations.

The principal contractor

The principal contractor should take account of the health and safety issues when preparing and assessing tenders or similar documents.

The main duties of the principal contractor under these regulations include the development, implementation and updating of the health and safety plan as well as the coordination of the activities of all contractors on site so that they comply with that plan. The principal contractor should also coordinate the activities of all contractors to ensure that they comply with health and safety legislation. Principal contractors have duties to ensure the provision of adequate information and training, including induction training, for employees and for consulting with employees and the self-employed on health and safety.

In particular the principal contractor should plan, manage and monitor the construction phase in a way which ensures that, so far as is reasonably practicable, it is carried out without risks to health or safety. He should facilitate co-operation and co-ordination between other parties to the contract and generally apply the principles of prevention to construction of the structure.

The principal contractor should liaise with the CDM co-ordinator during the construction phase in relation to any design or change to a design. He should ensure that adequate welfare facilities are provided throughout the construction phase. Where necessary for health and safety, the principal contractor should draw up rules which are appropriate to the construction site and the activities on it and give reasonable directions to any contractor as necessary.

The principal contractor should ensure that every contractor is informed of the minimum amount of time which will be allowed for planning and preparation before construction work begins and where necessary, consult a contractor before finalising the part of the construction phase plan relevant to the work to be performed by him.

Every contractor should be given relevant information and sufficient time to prepare properly before he begins construction work and be given access to those parts of the construction phase plan relevant to the work to be performed by him.

In turn each contractor should provide promptly that information relating to his activity which is likely to be required by the CDM co-ordinator for inclusion in the health and safety file.

The principal contractor should ensure that the particulars required to be in the notice given under Regulation 21 are displayed in a readable condition in a position where they can be read by any worker engaged in the construction work and should take reasonable steps to prevent access by unauthorised persons to the construction site.

Contractors

Contractors, other than the principal contractor, and self-employed workers should cooperate with the principal contractor to provide relevant information on the health and safety risks created by their work and how these risks will be controlled. In addition, contractors have duties for the provision of other information to the principal contractor and to employees. The self-employed have duties similar to contractors.

6.2 CDM documentation and information transfer

The CDM Regulations require the provision of relevant information and the production of certain key documentation relating to the project – the construction phase plan and health and safety file.

The client is required to provide designers and contractors with relevant pre-construction information. The information provided is that in the client's possession or which is reasonably obtainable by the client including any information relating to the site or the construction work, the proposed use of the structure as a workplace, the minimum amount of time before the construction phase which will be allowed to the contractors appointed by the client for planning and preparation for construction work and any information in any existing health and safety file. The purpose of this is to ensure so far as is reasonably practicable the health and safety of persons engaged in the construction work, of those liable to be affected by the way in which it is carried out, and who will use the structure as a workplace. This is to allow them to perform their duties under these Regulations and to determine the resources (see Regulation 9(1)) which they are to allocate for managing the project.

For notifiable projects, the client shall provide the CDM co-ordinator with the pre-construction information noted above along with any further information in his possession or which is reasonably obtainable, relevant to the CDM co-ordinator, including information on the minimum amount of time before the construction phase which will be allowed to the principal contractor for planning and preparation for construction work.

Also for notifiable projects, the client shall ensure that the construction phase does not start unless the principal contractor has prepared a construction phase plan which complies with the requirements of Regulation 23 and he is satisfied that the requirements for welfare facilities will be complied with during the construction phase.

A single health and safety file can relate to more than one project, site or structure but the client shall ensure that the information relating to each site or structure can be easily identified.

The client shall take reasonable steps to ensure that after the construction phase, information in the health and safety file is kept available for inspection by any person who may need it and it is revised as often as may be appropriate to incorporate any relevant new information.

A client who disposes of his entire interest in a structure should deliver the health and safety file to the person who acquires that interest and should ensure the purchaser is aware of the nature and purpose of the file.

The documents are to ensure the availability and transmission of key health and safety information between the parties to the project.

The construction phase health and safety plan is the foundation on which health and safety management of construction work should be based and should include arrangements for ensuring the health and safety of all who may be affected by the construction work, arrangements for the management of health and safety of the construction work, monitoring of compliance with health and safety law, and information about welfare arrangements.

The health and safety file is a record of relevant information for the client/end-user which tells those who might be responsible for the structure in the future of the risks that have to be managed during maintenance, repair or renovation. The planning supervisor has to ensure that it is prepared as the project progresses and given to the client when the project is complete. The client has to make it available to those who will work on any future design, building, maintenance or demolition of the structure.

To supplement the CDM legislation, there is an Approved Code of Practice as well as a suite of guidance documents on managing health and safety in construction and guidance for designers.

The requirements in respect of work at height which are now contained in the Work at Height Regulations 2005 CHSWR have been revoked in full.

The principal duty holders under these regulations are employers and the self-employed but Regulation 25 extends the duties to those who control construction work. Employees have duties under the regulations to carry out their individual task in a safe manner. Other organizational duties resulting from the regulations include one on those undertaking construction work to cooperate with others on health and safety matters.

The regulations are grouped into generally related topics as listed below.

Safe places of work

There is a general requirement in the regulations to provide a place of work which is safe and without risk to health, so far as is reasonably practicable, and with sufficient working space at that place to do the work safely. Access to and egress from that place of work should also be safe and without risk to health. These requirements apply equally to work places below ground, at ground level and above ground.

Good order and site security

There is a requirement that every part of a construction site should be kept in good order and workplaces kept clean. In addition the site perimeter should be identified and fenced off if the site poses a risk.

Unsafe structures or premature collapse

Employers must take steps to prevent the accidental collapse of structures under construction or of existing structures. Demolition and dismantling work should be carried out to a predetermined plan and in a safe manner under the supervision of a competent person.

Explosives

Explosive charges should only be fired if suitable and sufficient steps have been taken to prevent injury directly from the explosives or from flying material.

Excavations

Excavations, which include shafts and tunnels, should be supported as necessary and the support works carried out under the supervision of a competent person.

Cofferdams etc

Cofferdams and caissons should be of suitable and sound construction and of sufficient strength for their purpose.

Energy distribution installations

Energy distribution installations should be suitably located, checked and clearly indicated. Electric power cables should be directed away from the works area or cables should be isolated or earthed as necessary. Barriers or similar may be required to prevent vehicles striking overhead power lines.

Steps should also be taken to prevent risk from striking any burial service.

Avoidance of drowning

Employers must take steps to prevent people falling into water and drowning. In addition, the necessary personal protective equipment should be provided and rescue equipment should be immediately available for use in the event of a fall.

Water-borne transport should be under the control of a competent person.

Traffic routes

Traffic routes throughout a site should be arranged to allow pedestrians and vehicles to operate without risk to people. Pedestrian and vehicle routes should be segregated. Unintended vehicle movements should be prevented and warning given of hazardous movements such as reversing.

Prevention and control of emergencies

The employer should take steps to prevent or control the risk from fire, explosion, flooding and asphyxiation. Emergency routes and exits should be available and procedures should be in place for dealing with emergencies. All necessary fire fighting, fire alarm and detection systems should be provided.

Welfare facilities

Welfare facilities should be provided by the employer, including all necessary sanitary, washing and rest facilities and facilities for changing and storing clothing.

Workplace environment

The employer's duties in respect of the workplace environment extend to ensuring that there is sufficient fresh air or ventilation, adequate temperatures in indoor workplaces, or facilities for protection against the weather and the provision of lighting. Emergency lighting may also be required. The site perimeter should be adequately fenced.

Training, inspection, etc.

There are various obligations on employers to ensure that employees are adequately trained. Certain operations should either be carried out under the control of competent persons or be inspected prior to any work taking place by competent persons.

7.2 Confined Spaces Regulations 1997

These apply only to confined spaces as defined in the regulations. Confined spaces are defined as places which, by their enclosed nature, give rise to the risk of death or serious injury through lack of oxygen, the presence of toxic gas, fume or vapour, dust, drowning in liquid or free-flowing solid, fire or explosion, or hot conditions.

The regulations do not contain specific requirements for the assessment of risks from the confined space but rely on Regulations 3 and 4 of the Management of Health and Safety at Work Regulations 1999 for this.

Once such an assessment has identified the risk from the confined space, the Confined Spaces regulations require that work should only be carried out in the confined space if that work cannot reasonably be done from outside. In addition, if entry is unavoidable, the work should be done in accordance with a safe system of work. Before any work in the confined space begins, appropriate emergency arrangements should be put in place to deal with foreseeable emergencies and the risk to those responding to the emergency must also be taken into account.

7.3 Work in Compressed Air Regulations 1996

General

These regulations set out requirements for the engineering, management and medical aspects of work in compressed air. They are supported by an extensive guidance document (ref L96). In 2001 oxygen decompression became mandatory from exposure pressures of 1.0 bar and over. L96 is currently being revised.

The regulations apply to all work and all working in compressed air carried out in the course of construction work as defined in the Construction (Design and Management) Regulations 2007.

There should be a competent 'compressed air contractor' who is central to the safe execution of the works and most of the duties in subsequent regulations are placed on this contractor. Often the compressed air contractor is the 'principal contractor' as defined in the Construction (Design and Management) Regulations 2007.

The compressed air contractor must appoint a contract medical adviser, whose role is to advise on current best practice in all aspects of occupational health related to the work in compressed air.

Compressed air contractors are required to give 14 days' notification of work in compressed air to the HSE.

All work in compressed air should be carried out in accordance with a safe system of work. One aspect of the safe system of work is the involvement of a competent team to undertake the work and the guidance sets out the roles to be fulfilled. Another aspect is the provision of plant and equipment.

Medical surveillance

This is required for all people exposed to compressed air.

The regulations require that compression and decompression of persons be carried out in accordance with a regime approved by the HSE.

The regulations include extensive requirements for record keeping. 'Adequate facilities' for the medical treatment of decompression illness are also required.

Fire and flood are two of the major safety hazards associated with work in compressed air.

There are requirements for the provision of instruction and information about the specific hazards associated with work in compressed air.

Only persons fit for work in compressed air should be allowed through the airlocks.

7.4 Diving at Work Regulations 1997

These regulations apply to all diving projects in which at least one diver is at work either as an employee or as a self-employed person. The regulations place duties on all parties to the diving project from the client to the working diver. They should all ensure that the diving work is planned and executed safely. The regulations are supported by a series of ACoPs of which the one relating to commercial inshore diving is particularly relevant to construction.

The client has to appoint a competent diving contractor to carry out the work. In addition, the client should ensure that the diving site is safe and details of known hazards are identified to the contractor.

The diving contractor's duties include assessing the risks from the project and ensuring that a diving plan is prepared. In addition, the diving contractor should ensure that a diving team of sufficient size and competence is assembled and that the plan is known to the diving team. The diving contractor also has duties in ensuring that appropriate plant and equipment is available and in a suitable condition to be used.

Arrangements for first aid and medical treatment and the keeping of appropriate records are further duties of the diving contractor.

Within the diving team is a diving supervisor on whom extensive duties are placed in respect of ensuring the safe conduct of the diving work in accordance with the diving plan.

Duties on the working divers generally relate to their possession of a certificate of competence to dive, a certificate of medical fitness to dive, a first-aid certificate and the keeping of personal exposure records, normally in a logbook. In addition, the diver should be competent for the work in hand and follow the instructions of the supervisor.

Extensive duties are placed on the diving contractor to ensure the safety of the diving project. These relate to the planning of the project, the appointment of competent supervisor(s) and the provision of sufficient other competent personnel, the provision of sufficient plant and equipment, and the communication of information on the project to those involved.

Diving contractors are required to notify the HSE of their trading as such.

8 HAZARD-SPECIFIC REGULATIONS: USE OF EQUIPMENT

8.1 Provision and Use of Work Equipment Regulations 1998 (PUWER)

PUWER was most recently revised in 1998. They apply to any equipment which is supplied or controlled by the employer and used by employees at work. Duties on employers under PUWER also apply to equipment for use at work which is provided by the employees themselves. 'Equipment' covers all machines, plant and equipment, tools including hand tools, etc. for use at work. The 'use' of equipment includes starting or stopping, repairing, modifying, maintaining, servicing and cleaning the equipment as well as transporting it.

There are also duties under the regulations on the self-employed if they supply equipment for use at work or control the use of equipment at work.

Employers and the self-employed must ensure that the work equipment is suitable for use and for the purpose and conditions in which it is used. Work equipment must be maintained in a safe condition for use so that the equipment itself does not present a risk to the health and safety of those using it. The regulations also contain requirements for the inspection of certain types of equipment.

Employers and the self-employed must also ensure that the risks arising from the use of work equipment are, where possible, eliminated or, if that is not possible, that the risks are controlled. Construction involves the extensive use of powered equipment and mobile machinery so in most cases it will not be possible to eliminate the risk. Control of the risks may in some cases be achieved by the provision of guards or other protective devices, e.g. the provision of appropriate two-handed controls or emergency stop devices. With some equipment, risk control can be achieved by the use of a safe system of work accompanied by appropriate information, instruction and training with adequate supervision.

All employees must receive adequate information, instruction and training in the use of the equipment which they are using.

Mobile work equipment is used extensively in construction and there are additional duties in respect of such equipment arising from its mobility. Mobile work equipment which is used for carrying persons should be suitable for that purpose. There should be measures in place to ensure the safety of the operator and others on it from risks arising from the mobile nature of the machine. One such risk, particularly in construction, is overturning.

Plant hire companies may find it beneficial to seek expert advice on the application of these regulations to their business.

8.2 Lifting Operations and Lifting Equipment Regulations 1998 (LOLER)

These regulations consolidated the requirements in respect of lifting from legislation covering construction and other industries. They complement the requirements of the PUWER in that they cover requirements for equipment used for lifting at work.

The regulations apply to employers and the self-employed who provide lifting equipment for use, as well as to those who have control of lifting equipment.

The regulations require that lifting equipment provided for use at work is suitable, sufficiently strong and stable for the particular use. Lifting equipment includes any equipment used at work for lifting or lowering loads, including cranes, hoists and mobile elevating work platforms. Lifting accessories such as chains and slings are included. The load must also be suitable.

Lifting equipment provided by employees is also covered by the regulations.

The regulations require lifting equipment to be marked to indicate its safe working load. Lifting equipment should be positioned and installed to minimize risk. Lifting equipment should be used safely and, to achieve this, the lifting operation should be planned and carried out by people who are competent.

In addition, there are requirements for lifting equipment to be inspected and thoroughly examined. Where appropriate, lifting equipment should be thoroughly examined by a competent person before it is used for the first time and again at periodic intervals. The interval varies from six months for lifting accessories and equipment for lifting people, to annually for other lifting equipment. The precise interval should be set out in an examination scheme drawn up by a competent person. Reports of examinations and inspections should be submitted to the employer.

The duties in the regulations in respect of lifting operations require that lifting operations are carried out in a safe manner as a result of being planned and supervised by competent persons.

8.3 Electricity at Work Regulations 1989

These regulations set out the precautions to be taken against the risks to health and safety from the use of electricity at work. They place duties not only on employers and the self-employed but also on employees, including trainees. In quarry premises, duties are specifically placed on the quarry manager.

There is a fundamental requirement for all electrical equipment and systems to be constructed and maintained in a condition which prevents danger, and for associated systems of work to be safe.

Electrical equipment in use should be of sufficient strength and capability not to be exceeded in a dangerous way. Equipment should also be constructed or protected from foreseeable mechanical damage or hazardous environmental effects.

Among the technical requirements are those requiring live conductors to be either insulated or safe by position. Appropriate earthing should be provided. Joints and connections should be suitable for use and a means of protection from excess current should be incorporated in the system. In addition, there should be means of cutting off the supply and for isolating equipment.

The fundamental requirement for work on electrical equipment is for that equipment to be made dead prior to work being started, however, the regulations recognize that, in some circumstances, work on or near live conductors may be required. A further requirement for ensuring the safety of those working on electrical equipment is for there to be adequate access and working space around the equipment and for the equipment to be adequately lit.

Persons engaged in electrical work should be competent or, if trainees, under supervision.

The supply of electricity is regulated under the Electricity Supply Regulations 1998.

Although the Institution of Electrical Engineers produces so-called 'wiring regulations' (reproduced as a British Standard), these are non-statutory and have the status of guidance. Nevertheless, compliance with them should satisfy some technical aspects of the Electricity at Work Regulations in respect of electrical installations in the workplace.

8.4 Personal Protective Equipment at Work Regulations 1992

These regulations are linked with the regulations arising from the product directive relating to personal protective equipment. They place various requirements on employers in relation to the general provision, maintenance, storage and use of personal protective equipment.

They do not apply to the provision of personal protective equipment against certain specific hazards including lead, ionizing radiation, asbestos, noise and head protection in construction works in respect of which there are more specific statutory requirements for personal protective equipment.

The regulations place duties on employers to provide their employees with personal protective equipment which they have assessed as being suitable to protect them against residual risk to their health and safety. The self-employed are under similar duties in respect of their own health and safety.

The personal protective equipment supplied should be suitable for the risk against which it is intended to provide protection and under the conditions of expected use. It should take into account ergonomic requirements and be capable of fitting the wearer correctly. Personal protective equipment should be designed and manufactured in accordance with the requirements in the PPE (EC Directive) Regulations as amended.

Where people are exposed to more than one risk simultaneously, the various items of personal protective equipment required should be mutually compatible.

Employers are also required to maintain personal protective equipment and to make appropriate arrangements for its storage and maintenance, and for the provision of appropriate information, instruction and training for its safe use. Employers are further required to provide information instruction and training to ensure that employees properly fit and use the personal protective equipment issued to them. Employees are required to ensure that personal protective equipment issued to them is properly used, maintained, and any loss or defect is reported to the employer immediately.

8.5 Construction (Head Protection) Regulations 1989

These apply to all construction activity and deal only with the control of risk of head injuries. The regulations apply to building operations and works of engineering construction as previously defined in the Factories Act, but not to diving operations. All employees should be provided by their employers with suitable head protection which shall be maintained and replaced as necessary. The suitability of the head protection has to be determined by an assessment of its characteristics and the perceived risk of head injuries as well as those of the situation in which employees are working. Self-employed persons must provide their own head protection.

The main duties of employers are to ensure that employees wear suitable head protection and that duty is extended to employees who have control over other persons. Hence, all supervisory staff should be ensuring that others wear head protection. These duties extend to the self-employed. Head protection is not required where there is no risk of head injury other than by persons falling over.

A further duty is placed on 'the person for the time being in control of the site' to make rules for the wearing of head protection in writing, and to bring the rules to the attention of the employees.

Employees and the self-employed are required to wear the head protection provided in accordance with the site rules. Employees are further required to take reasonable care of their head protection and to report any defect in or loss of it to their employer without delay.

8.6 Control of Noise at Work Regulations 2005

The Control of Noise at Work Regulations 2005 (SI No. 1643) revoke and replace the Noise at Work Regulations 1989 (SI 1989/1790), and implement in Great Britain the requirements of EC Directive 2003/10/EC concerning minimum health and safety standards for workers exposed to noise. The Regulations impose duties on employers and on self-employed persons to protect both employees who may be exposed to risk from exposure to noise at work and other persons at work who might be affected by that work.

The 2005 Regulations impose more stringent limits on exposure. lower exposure action values, upper exposure action values, and exposure limit values for daily or weekly personal noise exposure and for peak sound pressure (Regulation 4).

The regulations apply to virtually all work activity including construction.

Regulation 4 defines a number of exposure limit values and action values. The lower exposure action values are a daily or weekly personal **noise** exposure of 80 dB (A-weighted); and a peak sound pressure of 135 dB (C-weighted).

The upper exposure action values are a daily or weekly personal **noise** exposure of 85 dB (A-weighted) and a peak sound pressure of 137 dB (C-weighted).

The exposure limit values are a daily or weekly personal **noise** exposure of 87 dB (A-weighted) and a peak sound pressure of 140 dB (C-weighted).

There is a caveat for situations in which the exposure of an employee to noise varies markedly from day to day. In these circumstances an employer may use weekly personal noise exposure in place of daily personal noise exposure for the purpose of compliance with these Regulations. (Previous limits were a first action level of 85 dB (A), a second action level of 90 dB (A) and a peak action level of 200 Pa).

The employer is required under Regulation 5 to make an assessment of the risk to health and safety created by exposure to noise at the workplace. That assessment is required when the employee is liable to be exposed to noise at or above a lower exposure action value. Additionally the employer shall use the assessment to identify the measures which need to be taken to meet the requirements of these Regulations. In undertaking the risk assessment, the employer shall assess the levels of noise to which workers are exposed through observation of working practices; making reference to relevant information on the probable noise levels arising from the use of equipment and specific working practices and if necessary by the measurement of actual noise levels to which employees are likely to be exposed.

As a result of this assessment the employer shall assess whether any employees are likely to be exposed to noise at or above a lower exposure action value, an upper exposure action value, or an exposure limit value. Regulation 5 outlines additional factors to be considered in making the assessment. It further requires the risk assessment to be reviewed regularly, or immediately there is reason to suspect that the assessment is no longer valid or there has been a significant change in the work to which the assessment relates. Any changes in mitigation measures shown to be necessary must be made.

The employer must consult the employees concerned or their representatives and the employer shall record the significant findings of the risk assessment as soon as is practicable after the risk assessment is made or changed along with details of the mitigation measures taken.

The employer is required by Regulation 6 to ensure that risk from the exposure of his or her employees to noise is either eliminated at source or, where this is not reasonably practicable, is reduced to as low a level as is reasonably practicable.

If any employee is likely to be exposed to noise at or above an upper exposure action value, the employer shall reduce exposure to as low a level as is reasonably practicable by changing the system of work or by introducing technical measures, in accordance with the general principles of prevention set out in the Management of Health and Safety Regulations 1999, excluding the provision of personal hearing protectors. Examples of appropriate means of reducing exposure are given in the Control of Noise at Work Regulations.

If any employee is exposed or likely to be exposed to noise above an exposure limit value, the employer must reduce exposure to noise to below the exposure limit value, identify the reason for that exposure limit value being exceeded and modify the mitigation measures taken to prevent it being exceeded again.

Personal hearing protectors should be made available upon request to any employee who is exposed above a lower exposure action value. They should also be made available to an employee who is likely to be exposed to above an upper exposure action value but only if an employer is unable to reduce the levels of noise to which an employee is exposed by other means.

Any area of the workplace in which an employee is likely to be exposed to noise at or above an upper exposure action value should be designated a Hearing Protection Zone, demarcated and identified by means of appropriate signs and access to the area restricted to those wearing personal hearing protectors.

The employer shall be responsible for maintenance of personal hearing protective equipment.

If the risk assessment indicates that there is a risk to the health of his or her employees from noise exposure, the employer must arrange for his or her employees to be placed under suitable health surveillance, including testing of their hearing and maintenance of appropriate health records. Where, as a result of health surveillance, an employee is found to have identifiable hearing damage the employer shall ensure that the employee is medically examined if the damage is likely to have been the result of exposure to noise. The employer shall ensure that the employee is informed accordingly and the risk assessment and mitigation measures are reviewed.

Employees exposed to noise, and their representatives, are entitled to suitable and sufficient information, instruction and training on the nature of the risks, the mitigation measures being taken and the general results of health surveillance.

8.7 Safety of Pressure Systems and Gas Cylinders

The Pressure Systems Safety Regulations 2000 re-enact with amendments the Pressure Systems and Transportable Gas Containers Regulations 1989 ('the 1989 Regulations') as amended. The 1989 Regulations imposed safety requirements with respect to pressure systems which are used or intended to be used at work. They also imposed safety requirements to prevent certain vessels from becoming pressurized. The Regulations specified a number of exceptions.

Any person who designs, manufactures, imports or supplies any pressure system or any article which is intended to be a component part of any pressure system must ensure that the pressure system or component is properly designed and properly constructed from suitable material; that all necessary examinations for preventing danger can be carried out; that where the pressure system has any means of access to its interior, access can be gained without danger and the pressure system is provided with such protective devices as may be necessary for preventing danger and such device, designed to release contents, shall do so safely (Regulation 4).

Any person who designs or supplies a pressure system or component, shall provide sufficient written information about its design, construction, examination, operation and maintenance to enable the provisions of the Regulations to be complied with.

3.1 The law of contract
3.2 Construction health and safety
3.3 Insolvency in construction
3.4 Law of tort
3.5 Environmental issues

Similar information is require following modification or repair. Guidance on the information required is given in the regulations.

The employer of a person who installs a pressure system at work must ensure that it is not installed in a dangerous manner or in a manner which impairs the operation of any protective device or inspection facility.

Pressure systems must be operated within safe limits established by the user of an installed system or the owner of a mobile system.

Pressure systems must not be operated unless the user has a written scheme for the periodic examination, drawn up by a competent person, of all protective devices; every pressure vessel and every pipeline in which a defect may give rise to danger and those parts of the pipework in which a defect may give rise to danger.

The user of an installed system and the owner of a mobile system shall ensure that those parts of the pressure system included in the scheme of examination are examined by a competent person within the intervals specified in the scheme and, where relevant, before the system is used for the first time.

The competent person doing the examination must subsequently submit a report of his or her findings, the contents of which are specified in Regulation 9.

If the competent person carrying out the examination is of the opinion that the pressure system or part of it will give rise to imminent danger unless certain repairs or modifications have been carried out or unless suitable changes to the operating conditions have been made, he must immediately report that in writing to the user, identifying the band, the repairs, modifications or changes to be made.

The person operating the pressure system shall be provided with adequate and suitable instructions covering the safe operation of the system and the action to be taken in the event of any emergency. It is the responsibility of the user of a pressure system to ensure that it is not operated except in accordance with the instructions provided.

The user should also ensure that the system is properly maintained in good repair, so as to prevent danger. The employer of a person who modifies or repairs a pressure system must ensure that nothing about the way in which it is modified or repaired gives rise to danger or otherwise impairs the operation of any protective device or inspection facility. The user of a pressure system must keep various records of its inspection.

The Carriage of Dangerous Goods and Use of Transportable Pressure Equipment Regulations 2004 (SI No. 568) amend the Pressure Systems Safety Regulations 2002 and impose requirements and prohibitions in relation to the carriage of goods by road or by rail and the use of transportable pressure equipment. They implement three EC Directives and also make other provisions in what are a complex and highly detailed set of regulations of only marginal interest in construction.

8.8 Manual Handling Operations Regulations 1992

These regulations as amended by the Health and Safety (Miscellaneous Amendments) Regulations 2002 (SI No. 2174), apply to manual handling operations in virtually all work activities, including construction. Manual handling includes all lifting, loading, pulling, pushing and carrying operations. The primary duty on an employer is to do what is reasonably practicable to avoid the need for its employees to carry out manual handling operations which give rise to a risk of injury to them, and, where that is not possible, the employer should assess the risk of injury to the employees and then take appropriate steps to reduce that risk to the lowest reasonably practical level. Although means of risk reduction are not specified in the regulations, it will normally be achieved by the use of mechanical handling equipment. In addition, where manual handling is undertaken, the employer should inform the employees of the weights of the loads being handled. Additional information has to be provided if the loads are of irregular shape.

Assessment made under these regulations should be reviewed as appropriate whenever any change in the operation is identified. Employees are under a duty to make use of any system of work provided to reduce the risk to them. Contrary to many people's belief, there are no minimum weights or loads specified in the regulations.

8.9 The Control of Substances Hazardous to Health Regulations 2002

The Control of Substances Hazardous to Health Regulations 2002 (SI No. 2677) as amended, are the most recent version of this set of regulations which implement the requirements of a number of EC Directives relating to hazardous substances. The Regulations impose duties on employers, employees and self-employed persons to protect their health from exposure to hazardous substances and prohibit the import of certain substances and materials.

These regulations apply to substances which are classified as 'very toxic, toxic, harmful, corrosive or irritant' under the Chemicals (Hazard Information and Packaging for Supply) Regulations 2002 along with certain biological agents and dusts above concentrations specified in the regulations as 'workplace exposure limits'. Lead, asbestos and radioactive substances are subject to separate regulation. Simple asphyxiants, flammable or explosive substances are not subject to COSHH. The control of exposure to a hazardous substance shall only be considered adequate if the principles of good practice for the control of exposure to substances hazardous to health are applied and any workplace exposure limit for that substance is not exceeded. For certain hazardous substances including those causing occupational asthma, exposure should be reduced to a level 'as low a level as is reasonably practicable'. There is extensive published guidance on compliance with these regulations – see for example http://www.hse.gov.uk/coshh/

Employers' duties under COSHH begin with the need to identify the hazardous substances present in the workplace and the nature of the hazard and then make an assessment of the risk from those substances to the health of those exposed. Factors to be considered in making that assessment are set out in the Regulations. The assessment should cover all means of exposure including ingestion, skin contact and inhalation. Having made the assessment and if there are risks to health, the employer should use the assessment to identify the measures needed to eliminate or control these risks. Principles of god control practice are set out below.

Employers should takes steps to ensure control measures are properly applied while employees must utilize the control measures provided. Employers must maintain and test control measures and undertake periodic monitoring of the workplace to demonstrate the ongoing adequacy of the measures.

Health surveillance should be carried out as appropriate and detailed requirements for that health surveillance are set out in Regulation 11. Employers should provide information, instruction, training and supervision. There are also requirements for employers to have in place arrangements to deal with accidents, incidents and emergencies involving the presence of the hazardous substance in the workplace.

The Principles of good practice referred to above are:

(a) Design and operate processes and activities to minimise emission, release and spread of substances hazardous to health.

(b) Take into account all relevant routes of exposure – inhalation, skin absorption and ingestion – when developing control measures.
(c) Control exposure by measures that are proportionate to the health risk
(d) Choose the most effective and reliable control options which minimise the escape and spread of substances hazardous to health.
(e) Where adequate control of exposure cannot be achieved by other means, provide, in combination with other control measures, suitable personal protective equipment.
(f) Check and review regularly all elements of control measures for their continuing effectiveness.
(g) Inform and train all employees on the hazards and risks from the substances with which they work and the use of control measures developed to minimise the risks.
(h) Ensure that the introduction of control measures does not increase the overall risk to health and safety.

8.10 Control of Lead at Work Regulations 2002

The Control of Lead at Work Regulations 2002 (SI No. 2676) re-enact, with modifications, the Control of Lead at Work Regulations 1998 (SI No. 543) which imposed requirements for the protection of employees who might be exposed to lead at work and of other persons who might be affected by such work and also imposed certain duties on employees concerning their own protection from such exposure.

Part of these Regulations implement in Great Britain, EC Directive 98/24/EC on the protection of the health and safety of workers from risks related to chemical agents at work insofar as it relates to risks to health from exposure to lead.

There is a complex series of prescribed limits set out in Regulation 2, depending on the nature of the exposure, the sex and age of the person exposed and whether a blood or urine sample is involved.

Under the Control of Lead at Work Regulations 2002, where there is a risk of exposure to lead, employers must carry out an assessment of the health risk to which employees or others affected by their work with lead (or certain lead compounds), are being exposed. Guidance of the factors to be covered in the assessment is given in the Regulations. Employers with five or more employees must record the findings of the assessment.

Every employer is required by Regulation 6 to ensure that the exposure of his or her employees to lead is either prevented or, where this is not reasonably practicable, adequately controlled. Possible control methods are set out in the regulations and the general principles of prevention are to be found in Schedule 1 of the Management of Health and Safety Regulations 1999. Employers should takes steps to ensure control measures are properly applied while employees must utilize the control measures provided.

Because of the range of routes by which exposure to lead can occur, employers must ensure, so far as is reasonably practicable, that employees do not eat, drink or smoke in any place which is, or is liable to be, contaminated by lead, and employees must not eat, drink or smoke in any place that may be contaminated by lead.

Employers must maintain and test control measures and where the control measures include the use of personal protective equipment, the employer must have in place an adequate scheme for maintaining and decontaminating such equipment. Periodic air monitoring in the workplace to demonstrate the ongoing adequacy of the measures is also required.

Employers shall ensure that all employees who are or are likely to be significantly exposed to lead are subject to appropriate health surveillance, in particular where their blood-lead concentration or urinary lead concentration is measured and equals or exceeds the action levels detailed in the Regulations.

Employers should provide information, instruction, training and supervision. There is also a duty to ensure that the contents of containers and pipes for lead used at work are clearly identifiable.

There are also requirements for employers to have in place arrangements to deal with accidents, incidents and emergencies involving the presence of lead in the workplace.

8.11 Control of Asbestos at Work Regulations 2006

These Regulations revoke and replace the Control of Asbestos at Work Regulations 2002 (SI 2002/2675) and make changes to the Asbestos (Licensing) Regulations 1983 (SI 1983/1649) as amended and the Asbestos (Prohibitions) Regulations 1992 (SI 1992/3067) as amended.

They implement in Great Britain a number of EC directives including 'the Marketing and Use Directive' 76/769/EEC as amended relating to restrictions on the marketing and use of certain dangerous substances including asbestos. They also implement Directive 83/477/EEC as amended on the protection of workers from the risks related to exposure to asbestos at work.

Other directives which they implement include Directive 90/394/EEC on the protection of workers from the risks related to exposure to carcinogens at work insofar as it relates to asbestos and Directive 98/24/EC which requires protection of the health and safety of workers from the risks related to exposure to chemical agents at work including asbestos.

Part 1 of the regulations covers application and definitions, Part 2 covers the practicalities of work with asbestos, Part 3 deals with prohibitions whilst Part 4 sets out miscellaneous provisions.

Changes to existing requirements include a restriction on licenses of three years. Transitional arrangements for existing licences are set out in Regulations 32(1) and 35(1).

Part 2 of the Regulations replaces the Control of Asbestos at Work Regulations 2002 (SI 2002/2675) and makes a number of changes including additional definitions and a new control limit common to all types of asbestos which is lower than that applying previously; adoption of the 1997 World Health Organisation ('WHO') procedure for the measurement of the control limit. It applies the duties in the regulations to all work with asbestos, apart from exceptions relating to licensing, notification, accident and emergency arrangements, asbestos areas and health surveillance in respect of sporadic and low intensity exposure which is deemed to include textured wall coverings. The 2006 Regulations are disapplied in respect of ships other than naval ships.

The 2006 Regulations extend the list of topics on which information, instruction and training must be given to employees (Regulation 10(1)). Part 2 requires the provision of respiratory protective equipment so far as is reasonably practicable to any employee who is exposed to asbestos and requires that the control limit shall not be exceeded sets out the actions to be taken if this should occur. It provides that only competent persons should enter respirator zones or supervise employees in respirator zones and also in respect of competence, under Regulation 20(4), it provides for accreditation of persons who are requested to assess premises for the issue of a site clearance certificate for reoccupation. Labelling requirements are set out in Part 3.

There is a duty to manage asbestos in non-domestic premises, along with requirements for the identification of the presence of asbestos are set out. Regulation 6 deals with the assessment of work which exposes employees to asbestos, the requirements for planning such work is set out in Regulation 7. Requirements for the licensing of work with asbestos are detailed in the Regulations. HSE must be notified of work with asbestos. Details of the information, instruction and training for those working with asbestos are set out in Regulation 10. In keeping with normal control principles, exposure to asbestos should be prevented if reasonably practicable or reduced if not. Reduction of exposure can be achieved by the use of control measures which once in place should be maintained. Employers have duties to provision and clean protective clothing and to make arrangements to deal with accidents, incidents and emergencies. Employers also have a duty to prevent or reduce the spread of asbestos. The cleanliness of premises and plant is covered under Regulation 17. Regulation 18 requires the employer to designate and enforce entry controls on areas where exposure to asbestos could occur along with respirator areas where exposure levels above the control limit could be experienced. Eating, drinking or smoking is not allowed in such areas. However washing facilities are required. Control of exposure to asbestos is to be monitored through a programme of air monitoring with standards for analysis set out in Regulation 21. Successful completion of the work should be proved by air testing and the issue of a site clearance certification. As with Regulations controlling similar occupations health hazards, health surveillance is required. Finally the Regulations cover the storage, distribution and labelling of raw asbestos and asbestos waste.

8.12 Ionising Radiations Regulations 1999

The main application of these regulations within the construction industry is to the use of radioactive sources for instrumentation and testing purposes. The regulations themselves are divided into a number of parts. These deal with general matters including the cooperation between employers whose employees are likely to be exposed to radiation from the one employer's activities and notification of work with IR to the HSE.

Other parts of the Regulations deal with dose limitation, the regulation of work with IR, dosimetry and medical surveillance, arrangements for the control of radioactive substances, monitoring of IR and equipment safety.

Work with IR is limited to specialized applications in construction and any employer who intends to use IR or suspects that its employees may be exposed to IR should see more detailed HSE guidance for an in-depth description of these regulations.

8.13 Explosives

Legislation governing explosives is extensive and somewhat complex. There is separate legislation for the manufacture, storage and transportation of explosives from that governing their use. The principal legislation governing the manufacture and storage was the Explosives Act 1875 and its subordinate legislation however significant changes came about with the coming into force of the Manufacture and Storage of Explosives Regulations 2005 (SI No. 1082). These Regulations set out requirements for licensing the manufacture and storage of explosives and for registration in respect of the storage of explosives. As such, they repeal a large number of provisions contained in the Explosives Act 1875 ('the 1875 Act') and its subordinate legislation.

Acquisition of explosives is governed by the Control of Explosives Regulations 1991 as amended by the Manufacture and Storage of explosives Regulations 2005 which require persons acquiring explosives to obtain a certificate from the local police authority. These regulations also apply to the keeping and storage of explosives. The transfer of explosives and associated record keeping is also regulated by these regulations as well as the Placing on the Market and Transfer of Explosives Regulations. Transportation of explosives is regulated by the Packaging of Explosives for Carriage Regulations 1991, the Carriage of Explosives by Road Regulations and the Carriage of Dangerous Goods (Driver Training) Regulations 1996. Explosives are normally stored for use on site in a licensed store under the control of the local authority.

The use of explosives in construction works is regulated by the Construction (Design and Management) Regulations 2007. Regulation 30 states

(1) So far as is reasonably practicable, explosives shall be stored, transported and used safely and securely.
(2) Without prejudice to paragraph (1), an explosive charge shall be used or fired only if suitable and sufficient steps have been taken to ensure that no person is exposed to risk of injury from the explosion or from projected or flying material caused thereby.

The use of explosives in quarries is separately covered by the Quarries (Explosives) Regulations 1988 with further requirements for shot firers being set out in the Quarries Regulations 1999 (SI No. 2024).

A contractor wishing to store **explosives** requires a licence to do so. Where only a certain amount of **explosives** is to be stored, a person can apply to a licensing authority for registration in respect of that **storage**, instead of seeking a licence for it. The Police or Local Authority should be approached in advance to licence or register the intended place of storage. The Police are likely to be the licensing authority for storage for explosives for which an Acquire and Keep Certificate is required under the Control of Explosives Regulations which would include blasting explosives, accessories and detonators. The Police and Local Authority have powers to licence storage of up to 2 tonnes of explosives, but can only do so where certain conditions are met. It is important therefore to seek the view of the licensing authority for the intended place of storage well in advance of the need so that whatever arrangements are specified can be made.

The Health and Safety Executive issues licences for magazines for explosives which allow the keeping of amounts greater than 2 tonnes. Such a licence is not likely to offer advantage to a short-duration construction contract but would be more suited to an operation such as significant harbour, road or tunnel construction works which might be expected to last for periods running into years.

Explosives might be delivered to site with the intention of using them straight away, or for placement ready for use, as would occur, for example, in the charging of many holes in a large structure to be demolished. Explosives loaded into holes are not regarded as being in storage, but there should be maintained sufficient and adequate security to prevent their unauthorized removal. There is no bar to explosives being stored on behalf of the construction or demolition contractor by some third party at that third party's existing licensed storage place. This third party might be the explosives manufacturer. There would then need to be put in place arrangements for daily deliveries or some sort of call-off system so that explosives would be delivered to the site of intended use only at appropriate times. This would obviate the need for the construction site to be licensed to store explosives. When siting an explosives store, a specified separation distance must be maintained between the store and buildings and other places not on the site where the storage takes place.

8.14 Work at Height Regulations 2005

The Work at Height Regulations 2005 (SI No. 735) (WAHR) amended in 2007 (but amendment not relevant to construction) impose health and safety requirements applicable to all work activity at height not just in the construction industry. Work at height can take place at any location either above or below ground level and includes temporary means of access to and egress from such work. The WAHR implement the requirements of EC Directive 2001/45/EC. The WAHR replaced the provisions in the Construction (Health, Safety and Welfare) Regulations relating to falls, fragile materials and falling objects, the latter set of regulations itself being replaced by CDM 2007.

The regulations impose duties on employers and the self employed relating to the organization and planning of work at height by employees, the self employed and to persons under their control to the extent of that control. The Regulations require that work at height is properly planned including the selection of the relevant equipment, appropriately supervised and carried out in a reasonably practicably safe manner. Planning must also cover emergency and rescue procedures. Avoidance of adverse weather conditions is a further matter to be covered at the planning stage.

Those working at height should be competent to do so. In accordance with the principles of prevention in Regulation 4 and Schedule 1 of the Management of Health and Safety at Work Regulations 1999, employers shall take cognizance of the risk assessment and shall seek only to carry out such work at height as cannot reasonably practicably be done otherwise provided also that they take measures to prevent falls likely to lead to injury of the employee. Work at height should preferably be done from an existing workplace but if not with the use of work equipment capable of preventing a fall that failing through the use of equipment to minimize the consequences of this fall.

When selecting equipment for work at height, an employer shall consider the circumstances in which it will be used and give priority to collective protection measures such as the provision of a scaffold working platform over personal protective measures such as rope access equipment, and similarly in minimizing the consequences of a fall shall favour collective measures such as a net or airbag over personal measures such as a harness. Detailed requirements for the respective types of equipment are given in Regulation 8 and in the schedules to the Regulations.

Employers are required to ensure that employees do not work on, near or pass close to fragile materials. When these conditions cannot be met, the employer must cover or guard the fragile material or failing that, provide a means of minimizing the consequence of any fall. Prominently placed notices must be posted at the approach to fragile materials or equivalent warnings given.

Employers must, in order of preference, take reasonably practicable steps to prevent objects or materials from falling and causing injury, or failing that to prevent injury from falling objects. Objects or materials should not be thrown from height where there is a risk of injury to a person below. Where by the nature of the work a person could still be injured by falling or from falling materials, access to that area should be prevented and the danger area clearly defined.

Safety critical work equipment and workplaces should be inspected once in position and before use and where degradation could occur, at periodic intervals thereafter. Appropriate records of inspections should be made and kept.

Those who work at height are required to report to their employer any activity or equipment which is defective.

8.15 Dangerous Substances and Explosive Atmospheres Regulations 2002

The Dangerous Substances and Explosive Atmospheres Regulations 2002 (SI No. 2776) implement in Great Britain, Council Directive 98/24/EC which sets out requirements for the protection of the health and safety of workers from the risks related to chemical agents at work and Council Directive 99/92/EC on minimum requirements for improving the safety and health of workers potentially at risk from explosive atmospheres.

These Regulations impose requirements for the purpose of eliminating or reducing risks to safety from fire, explosion or other events arising from the hazardous properties of a 'dangerous substance' in connection with work.

'Dangerous substance' is defined by Regulation 2(1) and includes a substance or preparation which is classified as explosive, oxidizing, extremely flammable, highly flammable or flammable under the criteria in the *Approved Guide to the Classification and Labelling of Dangerous Substances and Dangerous Preparations* (5th Edition) (ISBN 0717623696), also any substance which because of its physical and/or chemical properties behaves as if it were explosive, oxidizing, extremely flammable, highly flammable or flammable or any dust, whether in the form of solid particles or fibrous materials or otherwise, which can form an explosive mixture with air or an explosive atmosphere. Dangerous substances can be naturally occurring – e.g. methane in a tunnel or other excavation.

The duties under the Regulations also extend to self-employed persons.

An employer is required to extend the risk assessment under Regulation 3 of the Management of Health and Safety at Work Regulations 1999 to include a suitable and sufficient assessment of the risks to his or her employees where a dangerous substance is or may be present at the workplace (Regulation 5). 'Risk' in this instance implies fire, explosion or other events arising from the hazardous properties of a dangerous substance.

Employers are required by these Regulations to eliminate or reduce risk so far as is reasonably practicable. Where risk is not eliminated, employers are required, so far as is reasonably practicable and consistent with the risk assessment, to apply measures to control risks and mitigate any detrimental effects.

The parts of the workplace where explosive atmospheres may occur must be classified as hazardous or non-hazardous. Hazardous places must be classified into zones on the basis of the frequency and duration of the occurrence of an explosive atmosphere. The Regulations also require that equipment and protective systems in hazardous places must comply with the requirements of Schedule 3 and, where necessary, hazardous places must be marked with signs at their points of entry in accordance with Schedule 4. The use of mining equipment in a non-mining application such as tunnelling is acceptable provided the dangerous substance (in this case methane) is the same as that for which the equipment was originally designed.

Employers are required to make arrangements for dealing with accidents, incidents and emergencies.

Employers also need to provide employees with precautionary information, instruction and training where a dangerous substance is present at the workplace.

Containers and pipes used at work for dangerous substances must, where not already marked in accordance with the requirements of the legislation listed in Schedule 5, have their contents clearly identified.

Where two or more employers share a workplace in which an explosive atmosphere may occur, the employer responsible for the workplace is to coordinate the implementation of the measures required by these Regulations.

8.16 Control of Vibration at Work Regulations 2005

The Control of Vibration at Work Regulations 2005 (CoVAWR) (SI No. 1093) implement in UK legislation, the requirements of the EC Physical Agents (vibration)

Directive 2002/44/EC which sets minimum requirements for protecting worker health and safety against exposure to vibration. The Directive and CoVAWR cover exposure to both hand-arm vibration and whole body vibration.

Four 8-hour weighted (A(8)) exposure values are defined in Regulation 4 – for hand-arm vibration a daily exposure action value of $2.5\,m/s^2$ and a daily exposure limit value of $5\,m/s^2$ and for whole body vibration, a daily exposure action value of $0.5\,m/s^2$ and a daily exposure limit value of $1.15\,m/s^2$.

An employer whose employees are at risk from vibration must undertake a suitable and sufficient risk assessment to identify the extent of the risk and the protective measures which are required. Specific requirements for how the assessment is to be undertaken and what it should cover are also set out in this regulation. The assessment should be reviewed regularly and its findings recorded.

As with similar recent legislation, the action required of the employer is the elimination of exposure to the hazard (vibration) if reasonably practicable but if not, reduction of risk to as low a level as reasonably practicable. The latter should be achieved through a programme of organizational and technical measures in accordance with the principles of prevention. (Schedule 1 of the Management of Health and Safety at Work Regulations 1999). Methods of reducing exposure suggested in the Regulations include changing working method, shorter working shifts, task rotation, change of tool, better tool maintenance to reduce emission at source, additional rest periods and as a final resort the use of anti-vibration gloves.

The employer shall ensure employees are not exposed to vibration levels above the exposure limit value and, if they are that immediate steps are taken to reduce that exposure to below the exposure limit value, the reason for the limit being exceeded is identified and steps are taken to prevent a recurrence. There is a relaxation for otherwise low-risk activities where vibration levels fluctuate widely, which allows vibration exposure to be averaged over a week rather than over 8 hours, provided additional health surveillance is undertaken.

All employers are required to provide health surveillance for those likely to be exposed above the exposure action value to prevent or to diagnose any vibration related ill-health. Health surveillance records must be kept and when evidence of vibration related ill health is discovered, the employer should ensure the employee affected is appropriately advised of the situation, that he or she (the employer) reviews the risk assessment in conjunction with a source of occupational health advice, and he or she reassigns the employee affected to other, less hazardous tasks, where appropriate.

Regulation 8 covers the provision of information, instruction and training for those at risk from exposure to vibration.

9 SUPPLY OF WORK EQUIPMENT AND MATERIALS

9.1 Section 6 of HSWA – Other UK legislation relating to machinery

Section 6 of the HSWA has, from the time of its coming into effect, placed extensive duties on any person who designs, manufactures, imports or supplies any article for use at work to ensure that such articles are designed and constructed to be safe and without risks to health while they are being set, used or maintained. Articles for use at work include plant, machinery or similar equipment. That person must also carry out such testing as may be necessary to meet the requirements of this section of the Act, and must provide all necessary instructional information to accompany the machine to ensure its safe use.

9.2 Supply of Machinery (Safety) Regulations 1992

The Supply of Machinery (Safety) Regulations 1992 (SI No. 3073) which came into force on 1 January 1993 implemented the requirements of the Machinery Directive in UK law. The regulations were subsequently amended by the Supply of Machinery (Safety) (Amendment) Regulations 1994 (SI No. 2063) which came into effect variously between 1 September 1994 and 1 January 1995. A revised Machinery Directive has been adopted within the EC, however a corresponding revision of the regulations has yet to be published.

The regulations incorporate the essential safety requirements of the directive as a schedule accompanying the regulations. The enforcing authority under these regulations in respect of machinery used at work is the HSE.

The regulations apply only to the supply of 'relevant machinery' as defined. They place duties on the 'responsible person', defined as the manufacturer of that machinery or the manufacturer's authorized representative established in the EC or where the manufacturer is from outside the EC and has not appointed a representative within the EC, the person who first supplies the machinery within the EC (this could be a contractor).

The regulations contain measures relating to the design, construction, placing on the market and putting into service of machinery. They place general duties on suppliers of relevant machinery. These duties include requirements that the machinery satisfies the relevant essential health and safety requirements (normally of the Machinery Directive); that an appropriate conformity assessment procedure has been undertaken; that the responsible person has made a declaration of conformity; that the CE mark has been fixed to the machinery and that the relevant machinery is in fact safe.

The duties of the responsible person are set out in the regulations and include the need to comply with the 'conformity assessment procedure' with details of the technical file which must be drawn up. The technical file should contain certain prescribed details about the machine including its construction, and details of any harmonized or transposed harmonized European Standards which it meets.

There are a number of general exclusions in the regulations relating to machinery for export to countries outside the European Community and transitional exclusions for machinery already in service or in the market-place when the regulations came into effect. Other exclusions relate to specific machinery which is entirely the subject of separate directives such as electrical equipment and certain types of protective structure for construction plant.

Provision is also made in the regulations for enforcement procedures and forfeiture of dangerous machinery.

Requirements for mechanical and electrical equipment for use in potentially explosive atmospheres, such as in tunnels, can be found in the Equipment and Protective Systems Intended for Use in Potentially Explosive Atmospheres Regulations 1996.

9.3 Electromagnetic compatibility

Requirements in respect of electromagnetic compatibility (EMC) also arose from an EC product directive and have been incorporated into UK legislation. In the past, requirements in respect of electromagnetic compatibility were contained in regulations made under the Wireless Telegraphy Act, until it became a topic related to machinery (product) safety under EC directives.

Electromagnetic compatibility relates to the electromagnetic disturbance caused by one electrically powered device on another. In general, the effect manifests itself as a malfunction in a control system or as interference in an electromagnetic transmission. Control system malfunction has obvious safety implications. The EMC issues, therefore, relate both to the effects of external electromagnetic interference on a machine and the unwanted electromagnetic disturbances generated by that machine.

Electromagnetic compatibility is regulated through the EMC Regulations 2005. These are technically complex and it is not intended to cover them in detail in this text. In general, the regulations make it an offence to supply electrical or electronic apparatus which does not conform to the specified protection requirements – essential requirements requiring the apparatus not to generate excessive electromagnetic disturbance or fall below a prescribed level of immunity to electromagnetic disturbance from an external source.

Machines conforming to relevant CEN standards for machinery safety should already have been shown to conform to the electromagnetic compatibility standards by the manufacturer.

9.4 Lifts Directive

Lifts are frequently installed in buildings as part of construction work, in commercial premises such as offices, shops or healthcare premises, in an 'at work' situation or in private premises for domestic use. In both cases the supply of lifts (as defined in the regulations) is regulated under the Lifts Directive 95/16/EC which has been incorporated into UK legislation through the Lifts Regulations 1997. The Directive is a product directive so, again, the essential safety requirements relate to the safety of the product.

A lift is defined as an appliance serving specific levels and having a car moving along rigid guides or along a fixed course and inclined at an angle of at least 15° to the horizontal and intended for the transport of persons and/or goods. The definition distinguishes lifts from other equipment for lifting persons or goods which is subject to the Lifting Operations and Lifting Equipment Regulations 1998.

The enforcing authority for the regulations is the HSE and otherwise the Department for Business, Enterprise and Regulatory Reform (BERR). The regulations came into force in July 1999 and apply to all lifts and safety components for lifts placed on the market from that date. Earlier legislation on lifts is revoked. There are transitional provisions in the regulations relating to lifts supplied under that earlier legislation.

The general duties under the regulations apply to the company which places the lift or safety component on the market or puts it into service and require conformity with the essential safety requirements, either directly or through conformity with the relevant harmonized CEN standards. There is a duty for the transfer of information between the lift installer and those responsible for construction of works into which the lift is to be installed. The regulations also set out procedures for assessing conformity with the essential safety requirements. Because of the somewhat complex nature of these requirements, anyone concerned with supplying or installing lifts is advised to consult the text of the regulations. Any overlap with the requirements in the PUWER should also be considered.

9.5 Construction Products Regulations 1991

The Construction Products Regulations 1991 as amended in 1994, and other 'product' regulations were made for the purpose of ensuring the free movement of goods within the European Community and not for worker protection purposes. The regulations are not enforced by the HSE but by local authority Trading Standards officers.

The safety of construction products – materials for permanent incorporation in both building and civil engineering works – is covered by the Construction Products Regulations 1991 as amended in 1994. The regulations apply to construction products which are products for incorporation in a permanent manner in construction work. The regulations also include provisions in respect of 'minor part products' which are products which play a minor part only in respect of health and safety.

One of the main requirements of the regulations is that it is an offence to supply a construction product (other than a minor part product), unless that product has such characteristics that the construction work in which the material is to be included if properly designed and built, satisfies the relevant essential requirements where and to the extent that the works are subject to regulations containing such requirements, e.g. the Building Regulations. It is also an offence to supply minor part products which have not been manufactured in accordance with an 'acknowledged rule of technology' which essentially means in accordance with currently agreed good practice which is taken to be the appropriate British or CEN Standard.

The essential requirements are set out in a schedule to the regulations and relate to the finished structure rather than the product as such. Despite this indirect way of referencing the essential requirements, any structure cannot meet the essential requirements unless its constituent products do so. The essential requirements of the structure include its mechanical resistance and stability under both construction loads and, when in use, safety in case of fire which covers both fire resistance and durability. Further requirements include the need for the construction work not to present a risk to health or hygiene through the emission of toxic or otherwise hazardous material from the construction work. The construction work must not pose a risk of accidents during service such as slipping, falling or electrocution. The construction works must be designed and built in such a way that noise emissions are not a nuisance or risk to health and that energy requirements for heating and cooling are minimized.

Construction products intended for export outside the European Community and products which are not supplied new are excepted from the requirements.

All products bearing the CE mark are deemed to be supplied lawfully and there are extensive requirements for procedures to be gone through before this mark can be affixed by the manufacturer. These procedures include compliance with relevant national standards (BS) or European technical approval or an appropriate attestation procedure.

There are requirements in the regulations relating to the CE marking of construction products. Such marking is not compulsory. It is an offence to supply products which are CE marked but do not confirm to the requirements of the regulations.

The enforcing authorities have a range of powers in respect of non-conforming products. They can issue suspension notices prohibiting the supply to the market of products which do not satisfy the requirements of the regulations. Similarly, a supplier can be required to publish a public warning in respect of a product which does not satisfy the regulations.

9.6 Low Voltage Directive

This product directive applies to the safety of electrical equipment supplied for normal industrial and domestic use and which is designed for use between 50 and 1000 volts ac (75–1500 volts dc). It is implemented in the UK through the Electrical Equipment (Safety) Regulations 1994.

The regulations apply to anyone who supplies electrical equipment in the course of business. The fundamental requirement is for electrical equipment, when connected to the electricity supply system, to be safe through being constructed in accordance with good engineering practice and in accordance with the 'safety objectives' specified in the directive and regulations. In addition, equipment should be CE marked, which can only be done after the appropriate declaration of conformity and technical documentation have been compiled.

10 GENERAL WORKPLACE SAFETY REQUIREMENTS

10.1 Workplace (Health, Safety and Welfare) Regulations 1992

These regulations which, in addition to transposing an EC Directive, consolidate a considerable number of former parts of health and safety legislation, apply to all work premises *except* construction sites at which the Construction (Design and Management) Regulations 2007 apply, means of transport and sites where minerals extraction or exploration are carried out. (Agriculture and forestry are exempt from most requirements.) The regulations are concerned with good housekeeping and have many practical provisions. Whilst they do not apply to construction sites, the Construction (Design and Management) Regulations 2007 extend designers duties to the use of structures to the extent of the requirements in respect of workplaces set out in the Workplace Regulations.

The internal environment

The following provisions regulate the internal environment.

- Ventilation must be effective in enclosed areas, and any plant used for this purpose must incorporate warning devices to signal breakdowns which might endanger health or safety.
- Lighting must be suitable and sufficient.
- A reasonable temperature must be maintained.
- Room dimensions have to allow adequate space to work in and to move about freely.
- Suitable arrangements must be made, including adequate seating, in the places where employees carry out their work.

Accident prevention

The following provisions relate to the prevention of accidents.

- Safe passage of pedestrians and vehicles must be arranged.
- Windows and skylights must open and close safely, and be arranged so that people may not fall out of them. They must be capable of being cleaned safely. Windows and transport doors and partitions must be appropriately marked and protected against breakage.
- Doors, gates and escalators have to be of sound construction and fitted with appropriate safety devices.
- Measures must be taken to prevent people falling, and to guard against them being hit by falling objects.
- Floors and other surfaces need to be even, free of obstructions and not prone to slipping.

Provision of facilities
The regulations require the provision of various welfare facilities including:

- toilets and changing rooms
- washing, eating and drinking facilities
- rest facilities, with arrangements made for non-smokers and pregnant women or nursing mothers.

Maintenance
Maintenance is also covered by the Regulations.

- Workplaces, furniture and fittings have to be kept clean.
- Waste materials must not be allowed to accumulate.
- Premises, plant and equipment are to be subject to suitable maintenance regimes.

10.2 Health and Safety (Display Screen Equipment) Regulations 1992
The regulations apply wherever there is a 'user' who operates 'display screen equipment'. The statutory definitions of these terms are important.

- 'User' means an employee who habitually uses display screen equipment 'as a significant part of his normal work'. (Self-employed users are termed 'operators' for these purposes.)
- 'Display screen equipment' means equipment used for the display of text, numbers or graphics.

Employers therefore need to make an initial determination whether staff do carry out work which is covered by these terms. If so, the requirements summarized below will need to be met.

Analysis of workstation
The regulations use the term 'workstation' to mean the display equipment itself, any optional accessories that go with it, any keyboard, disc drive, telephone, modem, printer, document holder, work chair, desk, work surface or other peripheral item, and – in very general terms – the immediate working environment around the equipment.

Workstations must be analysed for any risks to health and safety they might present to users, or other operators, and the analysis must be reviewed and up-dated where appropriate. (The HSE Guidance Note discusses the possible risks, and concentrates on visual fatigue, stress and postural problems.) Risks identified are to be reduced to the lowest extent reasonably practicable.

Requirements for workstations
All workstations must meet the standards set out in a schedule to the regulations. Three main aspects are covered.

- 'Equipment': design and conditions of use of screens, keyboards, desks or work surface, and chairs.
- 'Environment': space requirements, lighting, reflections, glare, noise, heat, humidity and radiation.
- 'Interface between computer and operator/user': suitability of software and systems.

Welfare of users

Work routines of users are to be planned to provide periodic interruptions of display screen equipment work by breaks or changes to different activities.

Staff are entitled to have (at the employer' s expense) initial eye and eyesight tests, and subsequent tests at regular intervals or when experiencing visual difficulties associated with work on display screen equipment. Employees are entitled to receive special spectacles where these are needed to correct vision defects at the viewing distance used for the work involved and when their normal spectacles cannot be used.

Information and training

Appropriate health and safety training has to be given to existing users and to employees who are going to become users: modifications to a workstation may necessitate additional training.

Information on safety measures is to be given to users and operators, including information about entitlements to free testing and special spectacles.

10.3 Fire safety

Fire legislation was extensive and was located in numerous statutes and statutory instruments. Information on requirements could be found under the Buildings Regulations, fire certification requirements under the Fire Precautions Act 1971. Fire regulation was reviewed to simplify and consolidate the various requirements and the result of that review is the Regulatory Reform (Fire Safety) Order 2005 (SI No. 1541).

This reforms the law relating to fire safety in non-domestic premises in England and Wales only. It replaces fire certification under the Fire Precautions Act 1971 with a general duty to ensure, so far as is reasonably practicable, the safety of employees, a general duty, in relation to non-employees to take such fire precautions as may reasonably be required in the circumstances to ensure that premises are safe and a duty to carry out a risk assessment. The Order imposes a number of specific duties in relation to the fire precautions to be taken. The Order provides for the enforcement of the Order, appeals, offences and connected matters. It amends or repeals other primary legislation concerning fire safety to take account of the new system and provides for minor and other consequential amendments, repeals and revocations. The Order also gives effect in England and Wales to a number of EC Directives including Directive 89/391/EEC on the introduction of measures to encourage improvements in the safety and health of workers at work ('the Framework Directive'). The Order applies to most non-domestic premises. The main duty-holder is the 'responsible person' as defined in article 3. The duties on the responsible person are extended to any person who has, to any extent, control of the premises to the extent of their control (article 5).

Part 2 imposes duties on the responsible person in relation to fire safety in premises. Article 23 imposes various duties on employees.

Part 3 provides for enforcement. The enforcing authority is defined in article 25. Articles 27 and 28 set out the powers of inspectors. Articles 29 to 31 provide for the service of alterations, enforcement and prohibition notices in certain circumstances.

Part 4 (articles 32 to 36) provides for offences and appeals. Part 5 (articles 37 to 53) provides for miscellaneous matters including fire-fighters' switches for luminous tube signs (article 37), maintenance of measures provided to the ensure the safety of fire-fighters (article 38), civil liability for breach of statutory duty by an employer (article 39), special requirements for licensed premises (article 42) and consultation by other authorities (article 46).

Schedule 1 sets out the matters to be taken into account in carrying out a risk assessment (Parts 1 and 2), the general principles to be applied in implementing fire safety measures (Part 3) and the special measures to be taken in relation to dangerous substances (Part 4). Schedule 2 amends various enactments, including amendments to limit the scope for other public authorities to attach conditions to licences in respect of fire precautions to be taken in premises and amendments to local acts to remove reference to fire safety. The remaining amendments in Schedule 2 and those in 3 are minor or consequential. Schedules 4 and 5 contain repeals and revocations.

The Fire (Scotland) Act 2005 received Royal Assent on 1 April 2005. Parts 1, 2, 4 and 5 of the Act commenced in August 2005. Part 3 introduces a new fire safety regime for non-domestic premises and came into force on 1 October 2006. It replaced the Fire Precautions Act 1971 and the Fire Precautions (Workplace) Regulations 1997, as amended. Fire certificates are no longer required and the fire safety regime is based on the principle of risk assessment (similar to the Fire Precautions (Workplace) Regulations).

Construction sites may be subject to two, and in some cases, more, enforcing authorities. HSE will be responsible for the enforcement of the Regulatory Reform (Fire Safety) Order 2005 and the Fire (Scotland) Act 2005 in relation to general fire precautions within the curtilage of the site. Fire & Rescue Authorities will enforce the rules for accommodation (e.g. site offices and sleeping accommodation) not within the site curtilage. General fire precautions and fire risks that arise from the construction process are dealt with under the Construction Design and Management Regulations 2007. Duty holders are required to ensure suitable and sufficient steps (so far as is reasonably practicable) are taken to prevent the risk of injury to any person during construction work from fire and explosion. Measures must be taken to reduce the likelihood of fire due to work process, including storage. Duty holders are also required to have, in the event of danger:

- a means of raising the alarm
- means of fire fighting
- a means of escape that is clear from obstruction, have emergency lighting and protected where necessary
- and have emergency procedures and training.

The Regulatory Reform (Fire Safety) Order 2005 and the Fire (Scotland) Act 2005 have revoked the Fire Certificates (Special Premises) Regulations.

CHAPTER 3.3

Insolvency in construction

Richard Davis and Alison Cull
Pinsent Masons Solicitors

Neil Burton
Burton Marriott Limited

1 INFORMAL INSOLVENCY

Insolvency means the inability to pay debts. It can be formal or informal. Formal insolvency means the implementation of one of the recognized procedures, which are considered later. Informal insolvency occurs when a person fails one of the statutory tests. These vary depending whether the person is a company, an individual or a partnership.

There are two alternative tests of insolvency for limited companies. The first is known as the 'cash flow' test: 'A company is deemed unable to pay its debts... if it is proved to the satisfaction of the court that the company is unable to pay its debts as they fall due': Section 123(1)(e) of the Insolvency Act 1986. The second is called the 'balance sheet' test: 'A company is also unable to pay its debts if it is proved to the satisfaction of the court that the value of the company's assets is less than the amount of its liabilities, taking into account its contingent and prospective liabilities': Section 123(2) of the Insolvency Act 1986. The balance sheet test adopts different criteria from those used on a statutory audit because full account is taken of liabilities which are 'contingent and prospective'. An example of a contingent liability is a guarantee given by a parent company: unless and until the subsidiary is in breach of contract with the beneficiary, the parent's liability remains contingent. A prospective liability could be a claim for damages for defective work. The test requires that an estimate be made of both liabilities, however difficult this may be. The cash flow test is, therefore, much easier to apply than the balance sheet test.

Even if a company fails one of the tests, it may still be able to trade out of its difficulties and return to solvency. For example, a property developer may fail the balance sheet test if its portfolio is re-valued downwards but remain able to pay its debts as they fall due with the support of its bankers. It can then wait until the market improves and its properties can be re-valued upwards. Similarly, a company with temporary cash flow difficulties might be supported by its lender or by its creditors agreeing an informal moratorium to allow its cash flow to be restored. On the other hand, informal insolvency may simply be the prelude to a formal insolvency procedure. The key to avoiding formal insolvency is to continue to pay debts as they fall due.

A creditor can prove informal insolvency by a number of means under the Insolvency Act 1986, including the service of a statutory demand at the registered office of the company. Service of a statutory demand is the usual method of proving informal insolvency. If payment is not received within 21 days of service and the debt cannot be disputed on bona fide and substantial grounds, the debtor is deemed to be insolvent under Section 123(1)(a) of the Insolvency Act 1986. Even in the absence of a statutory demand, the mere fact of non-payment can give rise to the inference of inability to pay unless the debtor has a bona fide defence: *Re Taylor's Industrial Flooring* [1990] BCC 44. That case concerned a claim by a plant hire company for recovery of invoiced amounts from a subcontractor who argued that the money was not due as its credit period had yet to expire. This defence was rejected on a finding of fact and a winding-up order was made.

The test for insolvency of an individual is different. An individual is insolvent under Section 267 of the Insolvency Act 1986 where he or she owes a liquidated sum payable immediately or at some certain, future time and it is a debt which the individual appears either to be unable or to have no reasonable prospect of being able to pay. Inability to pay can be proved either after service of a statutory demand, (which takes a different form from that used in connection with a company), or where execution has been levied on a judgment and returned unsatisfied (Section 268 of the Insolvency Act 1986).

A partnership can be wound up as an unregistered company on the ground that the partnership is unable to pay its debts under Section 221(5) of the Insolvency Act 1986. It can also go into administration or enter a voluntary arrangement under the Insolvent Partnerships Order 1994. A partnership cannot, however, be placed in administrative receivership although individual partners can be made bankrupt or agree an individual voluntary arrangement with their creditors.

2 FORMAL INSOLVENCY

The most common procedures of formal insolvency for companies are administration, receivership, liquidation, and company voluntary arrangement; and for individuals, bankruptcy and individual voluntary arrangement.

2.1 Administration

Administration was introduced by the Insolvency Act 1986. Like liquidation, it is intended for the benefit of the creditors as a whole but its purpose is much wider and can extend to the survival of the company as a going concern. It provides a breathing space for the company and usually the objective is to rescue the business by keeping the company and its business intact wherever possible.

The Enterprise Act 2002 provided a radical review of both the procedure and aims of administration. As from 15 September 2003, when the corporate insolvency aspects of the Enterprise Act 2002 came into force, there are three methods of appointing an administrator:

- by the court;
- by the holder of a qualifying floating charge ('QFC'); and
- by the company or its directors.

A company, its directors or one or more creditors may apply to the court for the appointment of an administrator. The court may only appoint an administrator if it is satisfied that the company is, or is likely to become, unable to pay its debts and that the administration order is reasonably likely to achieve the statutory purpose of administration set out in paragraph 3 of Schedule B1 to the Insolvency Act 1986.

The applicant must notify any person who has appointed or is in a position to appoint an administrative receiver or any person who could appoint an administrator of his intention to appoint an administrator.

The holder of a QFC may now appoint an administrator without the need for a court order. However, the holder of a charge which is not a QFC is not entitled to appoint an administrator.

Under the Insolvency Act 1986, a QFC is defined as a floating charge over the whole or substantially the whole of the company's property which is created by a document which states that paragraph 14 of Schedule B1 to the Insolvency Act 1986 applies to the floating charge or which purports to empower the QFC holder to appoint an administrator or an administrative receiver of the company. The holder of a QFC must give two business days' prior written notice of its intention to appoint an administrator to the holder of any prior ranking QFC, unless the holder of that prior ranking QFC consents in writing.

A QFC holder may not appoint an administrator if the QFC is not enforceable or either a provisional liquidator or an administrative receiver has already been appointed to the company.

A company or its directors may now also appoint an administrator without the need for a court order. However, this out-of-court procedure cannot be used by the directors or the company if:

(1) within the previous 12 months:
   (a) an administration of the company at the instance of the company or its directors has come to an end;
   (b) a voluntary arrangement has ended prematurely (for example, because the company has defaulted in making payments due under the voluntary arrangement); or
   (c) a moratorium under schedule A1 of the Insolvency Act 1986 has ended without a voluntary arrangement having been approved; or
(2) a winding-up petition or administration application is pending; or
(3) an administrative receiver is in office.

The directors or the company must give five business days' prior written notice of their intention to appoint an administrator to any QFC holder and to other prescribed persons (such as a sheriff charged with execution or other legal process against the company, a person who is known to have distrained against the company or its property and the supervisor of a company voluntary arrangement). Although the holder of a QFC can no longer prevent the appointment of an administrator by the court, he can prevent the appointment of an administrator by the company or its directors, as after receiving their notice of intention to appoint out of court, he can pre-empt them by himself appointing an administrator (or, if he has a QFC which pre-dates the coming into force of the Enterprise Act 2002, an administrative receiver).

Schedule B1 of the Insolvency Act 1986 prescribes the formalities which must be followed in order to appoint an administrator without a court order, whether by the holder of a QFC or the company or its directors. These formalities relate largely to the giving of notice and to the filing, form and contents of the supporting documents required. If the company or its directors are proposing to appoint an administrator, the directors must swear a statutory declaration that the company is, or is likely to become, unable to pay its debts. This does not apply to an appointment by a QFC holder.

The Enterprise Act 2002 imposes a new test which must be satisfied before an administrator can be appointed (whether the appointment is to be made by court order or one of the out-of-court routes described above). This test can be conveniently sub-divided into three parts: the primary purpose, the secondary purpose and the fallback purpose.

The primary purpose is to rescue the company as a going concern and not to sell the company's business and assets to a third party. The secondary purpose is to achieve a better result for the company's creditors as a whole than would be likely to be achieved on a winding up (for example, by the administrator effecting a sale of the company's business and assets to a third party). The administrator can seek to achieve the secondary purpose if he believes that the primary purpose is not reasonably practicable or that the secondary purpose would achieve a better result for the creditors as a whole. The fallback purpose is to realise the company's property in order to make a distribution to one of more of the company's secured and/or preferential creditors. The fallback purpose will only apply if the administrator believes that neither the primary nor the secondary purpose is reasonably practicable and that no unnecessary harm will be caused to the interests of creditors as a whole. In practice, the secondary purpose is the most commonly used.

This is a new test which has greater emphasis on acting in the interests of creditors as a whole instead of, for example, acting for the benefit of a secured creditor.

The effect of an administration order is that, while it is in force:

- the company cannot be wound up;
- no legal proceedings can be taken against the company; and
- a receiver cannot be appointed by any charge holder and no other steps can be taken to enforce any security, without the permission of the court or the consent of the administrator.

Permission is unlikely to be granted in the absence of special circumstances (*Re Atlantic Computers* [1992] 1 All ER 476). It has been held that adjudication is a 'proceeding' under Section 11(3) of the Act: *A Straume (UK) Ltd* v. *Bradlor Developments Ltd* [2000] BCC 333. In that case, and two other reported cases, permission to bring an adjudication against a company in administration was refused: *Joinery Plus* v. *Laing* [2003] BLR 184, *Canary Riverside* v. *Timtec* (2003) 19 Const LJ 283.

Once an administrator has been appointed he will take over the day to day management of the company from the directors. It is not the usual role of an administrator to distribute assets to creditors, except where he is seeking to achieve the fallback purpose (having determined that the primary and secondary purposes are not achievable and creditors as a whole will not be unnecessarily harmed). The forum for distribution of assets will normally be a voluntary arrangement, a scheme of arrangement under Section 425 of the Companies Act 1985 or a liquidation. However, there is now provision for the company to move automatically from administration to creditors' voluntary liquidation in certain circumstances and an administrator may apply to the court for permission to distribute the assets to the creditors.

2.2 Receivership

Receivership is a remedy afforded to creditors who have obtained a charge over the whole or part of the company's property as security for payment. In the event of default of payment, the creditor can appoint a receiver to sell the charged property. Typically the company will be served with a demand for repayment of the monies due, which will be followed within hours by the appointment. Alternatively, the company may invite the charge-holder to appoint a receiver. Any surplus of the proceeds of sale over the debt plus interest has to be returned to the company which is then free to continue trading as before. In practice, receivership often leaves the company as a mere shell without assets and liquidation is bound to follow (see Fig. 1).

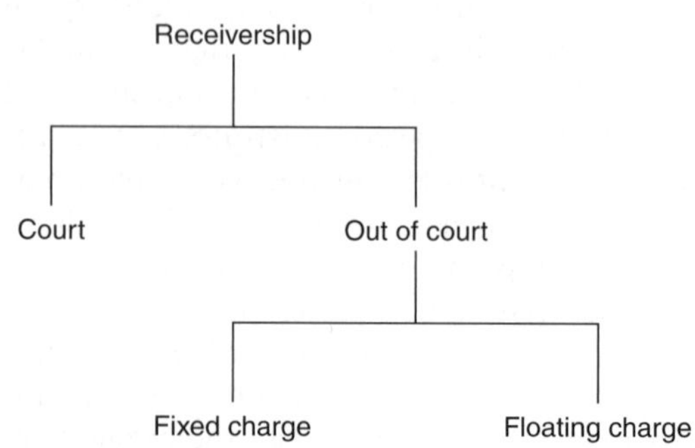

Figure 1. Forms of receivership

The court has jurisdiction to appoint a receiver, e.g. where a creditor has a charge but the document is defective in some way.[1] The vast majority of receivers are appointed out of court pursuant to a fixed or floating charge or a combined fixed and floating charge.

Only the holder of a fixed charge takes priority under the 'statutory scheme' over preferential creditors (see Section 2.6 below). As its name suggests, a fixed charge prevents any dealing with the charged property without the holder's consent: *National Westminster Bank* v. *Spectrum Plus Ltd* [2005] 2 AC 680. Such charges are usually taken over assets which the borrower does not need to deal with as part of its business such as land or fixed plant and equipment. A 'fixed charge receiver' has power under Section 109 of the Law of Property Act 1925 to receive rents and profits if appointed over land and other powers granted by the charge, e.g. to complete building work on the land. By contrast, an 'administrative receiver' (i.e. appointed under the terms of a floating charge over the whole or substantially the whole of the assets and undertaking of the business), has full power to carry on the company's business, including the right to bring or defend proceedings in the company's name and collect and get in the company's property (Schedule 1 to the Insolvency Act 1986). A floating charge has been defined as a security which charges assets present and future, allows the assets to change from time to time and allows the company to dispose of them in the ordinary course of business (*Re Yorkshire Woolcombers* [1903] 2 Ch 284).

A document containing fixed and floating charges will identify which assets are caught by which charge. There is no reason why a floating charge cannot be taken over land but this would usually be appropriate only for companies whose business consists in the buying and selling of land. A floating charge is often taken over stock, movable items and the company's undertaking as a whole.

As a result of changes made by the Enterprise Act 2002, a charge-holder is no longer entitled to appoint an administrative receiver unless the security which provides for such appointment was created prior to 15 September 2003. Such a charge-holder now has the ability to appoint an administrator if his security comprises a qualified floating charge ('QFC'). Holders of fixed and floating security created after 15 September 2003 (but not holders of fixed charges) will normally have the ability to appoint administrators as their security is in practice likely to be a QFC. There are certain other limited exceptions where the holder of a floating charge created after the introduction of the Enterprise Act is entitled to appoint an administrative receiver (for example in connection to an insurance undertaking).

The charge document will state that the receiver is the agent of the company rather than the chargeholder. This is an unusual use of agency designed to give protection to the chargeholder.

However, the agency of the administrative receiver ceases the moment the company enters liquidation (Section 44 of the Insolvency Act 1986). Administrative receivers owe a duty to the chargeholder, the company and its guarantors to obtain the best price but they do not owe any general duty to the company's creditors actionable directly by them: (*Downsview Nominees* v. *First City Corp* [1993] 3 All ER 626).

The holder of a floating charge has an inchoate interest in every class of asset described in the charge. This is perfected on the appointment of an administrative receiver by an equitable assignment to the chargeholder of all the assets falling within the charge at that moment which takes effect by operation of law. The administrative receiver has power to deal with the assets by asserting the chargeholder's title as assignee (*Biggerstaff* v. *Rowatt's Wharf* [1896] 2 Ch 93). It is important that the chargeholder gives notice of assignment as soon as possible to all those owing obligations to the company. This prevents third parties getting a good discharge by paying the company and also, broadly speaking, prevents debtors acquiring enforceable cross-claims against the charge-holder as assignee after receipt of the notice. If the contract prohibits assignment, there is Australian authority that a charge would not attach to it (*Re Turner Corporation* (1995) 17 ACSR 761). The position is different if there is a waiver of the bar on assignment or an estoppel precluding reliance on it (*Orion Finance* v. *Crown Financial Management* [1994] 2 BCLC 607).

Given their different functions, a receivership, whether under a fixed and/or floating charge, can exist at the same time as the company is in liquidation. For example, a company might have granted a floating charge to its lending bank and separate fixed charges to project financiers over sites being developed. An unsecured creditor might petition to have the company wound up, the holder of the floating charge may appoint an administrative receiver and the holders of the fixed charges may each appoint a different fixed charge receiver all at the same time. The exception is administration since there can be no receivership or liquidation of any kind when an administration is in force.

If an administrative receiver is appointed, the directors will be relieved of their power to manage the company's affairs, though they will remain subject to their statutory duties. An administrative receiver has powers to obtain information from officers of the company and can examine persons capable of giving information concerning the company or its property. It is usual for a company to be placed in liquidation at the end of administrative receivership.

2.3 Liquidation

Liquidation, also known as winding-up, is the corporate equivalent of dying. The directors are ousted and replaced by a liquidator who acts as agent for the company. Any receivers appointed before the liquidation remain in office but they can no longer act as the company's agent. Liquidation is of two kinds: voluntary and compulsory. Voluntary liquidation accounts for two-thirds of all liquidations. There are two kinds of voluntary liquidation: members' and creditors' (see Fig. 2).

A members' voluntary liquidation is not strictly an insolvency procedure. It is most often used on group reorganizations, often for tax reasons. The directors have to swear a statutory declaration that the company will be able to pay its debts in full with interest within a maximum of twelve months after the start of the liquidation. The shareholders, also known as members, can then pass a resolution to wind up the company and appoint a liquidator. If it turns out that the company cannot pay its

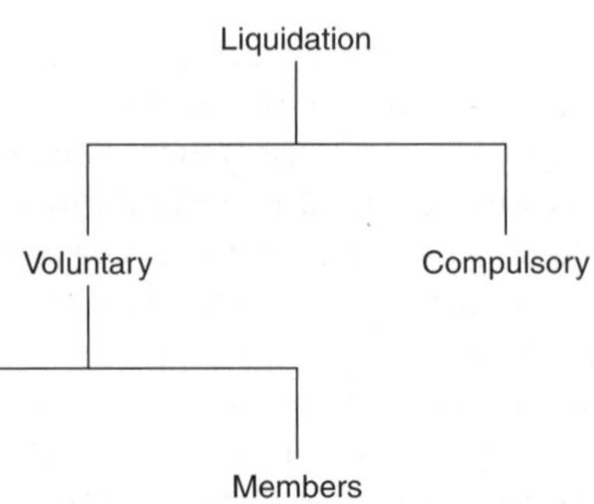

Figure 2. Forms of liquidation

debts in full within that time, the members' voluntary liquidation will be converted into a creditors' voluntary liquidation (e.g. *Re William Thorpe* (1989) 5 BCC 156), and the directors can be liable for a fine or even imprisonment if their original statutory declaration was not made on reasonable grounds (Section 89(4) of the Insolvency Act 1986). Members' voluntary liquidation is usually excluded from the list of insolvency events entitling the parties to terminate a construction contract.

Creditors' voluntary liquidation is the most common form of winding-up. It is initiated by the directors convening a board meeting at which they resolve that the company should cease trading and call separate meetings of shareholders and creditors under Section 98 of the Insolvency Act 1986. The shareholders then pass a resolution that the company be wound up and appoint an insolvency practitioner as liquidator. The directors prepare a Statement of Affairs for the creditors who may either confirm the shareholders' nominee or appoint another insolvency practitioner as the liquidator. Voting for this purpose is carried out by reference to the amount of the creditors' debts.

In construction cases, this is sometimes a contentious area since the directors may feel that a creditor's claim is invalid or that the company has a cross-claim which equals or exceeds it. Where the creditor's claim is unliquidated, it is the duty of the chairman of the creditors' meeting to place an estimated value on it for voting purposes. Not uncommonly, the estimated value is set at a nominal sum. but this is for voting purposes alone.

Once the liquidator has been confirmed in office, he or she will:

- identify the assets of the company and have them valued
- deal with property claims by third parties, e.g. where goods are supplied subject to retention of title or a creditor claims that a bank account or other property is held in trust
- invite creditors to submit details of their money claims (known as 'proofs of debt')
- sell the company's property
- distribute the net proceeds of sale to the creditors in accordance with an order of priority known as 'the statutory scheme'
- investigate the conduct of the directors and, if appropriate, file a report on their fitness to act as such in the future
- pursue claims to recover any property of the company misappropriated in the run up to the liquidation.

Compulsory liquidations are commenced by the issue of a winding-up petition against the company. A petition will usually be filed by a creditor, but it is also open to the company, certain shareholders or the directors to do so.

A petition can be presented on the ground (inter alia) that a company is unable to pay its debts. This can be shown by failure to comply with a statutory demand for payment of a debt exceeding £750 or by showing that a company's liabilities exceed its assets. Wilful failure to pay a debt has also been held to be sufficient evidence of inability to pay. The procedure is quite simple. The petition is listed for hearing on a date about six weeks after presentation at court and is served at the registered office of the company. The petitioning creditor must allow at least seven days to expire after service of the petition before arranging for it to be advertised in the *London Gazette*. The advertisement must be placed at least seven days before the hearing. The court is prepared to waive procedural defects in certain circumstances. Other creditors are entitled to serve notice on the petitioner indicating their intention to support or oppose the petition. Where the petition is opposed, it is usually adjourned so as to allow adequate time for submissions to be made.

3.1 The law of contract
3.2 Construction health and safety
3.3 Insolvency in construction
3.4 Law of tort
3.5 Environmental issues

The consequences of a winding-up petition being filed are that disposals of property will be invalid from the date of filing the petition if a winding-up order is ultimately made (see Section 4.7 below). Hence, the company's cheques will be dishonoured immediately.

On a winding-up order being made, the official receiver assumes office as liquidator. Where there are assets, a meeting of creditors will be convened to consider whether an insolvency practitioner should be appointed in the receiver's place. This also applies where there is cause for concern about the conduct of the directors or the possibility of claims against them and others. An insolvency practitioner can also be appointed where a creditor obtains an order that the company should be placed in provisional liquidation pending the hearing of the petition. (This occurs where the court is satisfied that the company's property would otherwise be seriously prejudiced.) A compulsory liquidation follows the same course as a creditors' voluntary liquidation.

When the liquidation process has been completed, the liquidator files a final account and return with the Registrar of Companies and the company is deemed to be dissolved three months later (Section 201 of the Insolvency Act 1986). Dissolution is the corporate equivalent of death. However, it is possible for the liquidator or an interested person to apply to the court under Section 651 of the Companies Act 1985 (with effect from 1 October 2009 re-enacted by Part 31 of the Companies Act 2006) for an order restoring the company to the register in certain situations, e.g. where an asset comes to light after the dissolution. On dissolution, any property which had not been distributed by the liquidator is forfeited to the Crown as *bona vacantia*. Such property automatically revests in the company if the dissolution is set aside and the company restored to the register.

2.4 Company voluntary arrangement

A company voluntary arrangement (CVA) is a court procedure enabling a company to propose a composition with its creditors whereby they accept a dividend in full settlement of their debts. The directors make the proposal to an insolvency practitioner who files a report at the court stating whether a creditors' meeting should be called to consider it. All creditors receiving notice of the proposal and entitled to vote on it are bound by the arrangement provided at least 75% in value of creditors attending the meeting vote in favour. A CVA does not prejudice the rights of secured or preferential creditors. It is fundamental that the creditors are realistic when considering the company's proposal (especially in relation to the percentage of their debt to be written off), and that the company is realistic when proposing the dates by which sums will become payable. The CVA will set out the means by which payments are to be funded, e.g. the disposal or refinancing of assets, a management buy out, other external finance or from future profits. Aside from these formal procedures, there are number of informal ways in which companies can be restructured while presenting a normal face to the world.[2] Section 1 of the Insolvency Act 2000 provides for a moratorium similar to that which applies on an application for an individual voluntary arrangement (IVA) but the section is only in force in respect of small companies (as defined in the Companies Act 1985). As a company proposing a CVA has no automatic protection from creditors, companies will apply for administration to obtain protection from creditors while a CVA is being proposed.

2.5 Bankruptcy and individual voluntary arrangements

Bankruptcy applies only to individuals not companies. A bankruptcy petition can be presented and issued by a debtor, a creditor or a supervisor under an individual voluntary arrangement. The minimum sum on which a petition can be based is £750. There are several different forms of statutory demand for debts owed by individuals (see Section 1 above). A statutory demand served on an individual as a means of enforcement of an adjudication award is liable to be set aside under r.6.5(4) Insolvency Rules 1986 if the individual asserts that he has a cross-claim, even though it would not be sufficient to prevent summary judgment being entered against him: *George Parke* v. *The Fenton Gretton Partnership* [2001] CILL 1712. The court has power to dismiss the petition if it can be shown that the individual can pay all his or her debts or has made an offer to secure or compound the debt on which the petition was brought, that the acceptance of that offer would have required the dismissal of the petition and the offer has been unreasonably refused (Section 273 of the Insolvency Act 1986). Until the bankruptcy order is discharged, a bankrupt cannot incur credit exceeding £250 without disclosing his or her status (Section 360 of the Insolvency Act 1986) or act as a company director (Section 11 of the Company Directors Disqualification Act 1986). A bankrupt is entitled to keep the 'tools of his trade' (which include items such as computers) and other property of a personal nature (Section 283(2) of the Insolvency Act 1986). As with liquidation, the creditors submit proofs of debt and, if there are sufficient assets, receive a dividend from the trustee.

The Enterprise Act 2002 introduced reforms relating to personal insolvency which came into force in April 2004. In most cases individuals will be discharged from bankruptcy no later than 12 months after commencement. The Official Receiver may file a notice at court, effecting earlier discharge once his investigations are completed or if thought unnecessary.

Whilst the aim of the Enterprise Act is to liberalise the existing bankruptcy regime, certain 'culpable' bankrupts whose conduct is such that some court sanction is thought appropriate, will be subjected to a new regime, namely the bankruptcy restriction order. The effect of such an order is to extend the bankruptcy period by a further two to 15 years. The procedure is similar to the Company Directors Disqualification Act proceedings and agreed undertakings may be given replacing the need for a hearing.

To counter perceived injustice the Enterprise Act has introduced a provision that the trustee in bankruptcy must take steps to realise the bankrupt's interest in the principal residence of the bankrupt, bankrupt's spouse or former spouse within three years (calculated from the date of the bankruptcy) otherwise it will cease to form part of the bankrupt's estate and automatically revert back to the bankrupt. However, if the trustee in bankruptcy's interest is below a certain prescribed value, proceedings will be dismissed.

The bankrupt will continue to make payments where his or her income exceeds that required for his and his family's reasonable needs after discharge for a period of up to three years in total from the commencement of the date of bankruptcy. An income payment agreement may be entered into which will avoid the need for a hearing. The restrictions on a bankrupt holding certain public offices have been liberalised, again in a further attempt to reduce the stigma of bankruptcy.

An individual voluntary arrangement (IVA) is an increasingly popular alternative to bankruptcy. It involves the individual making a formal proposal to his or her creditors and applying to the court for an interim order. The granting of an interim order prevents further proceedings being taken or judgments executed pending a report from an insolvency practitioner on whether the debtor's proposal is such as to make it worthwhile summoning a meeting of creditors. If a meeting is held and more than 75% in value of those voting are in favour, the IVA is approved and binds all creditors present at the meeting or who had received notice of it. An IVA is a practical way out for both debtor and creditors: the debtor avoids bankruptcy and the creditors stand to receive a higher dividend than they might have done on a bankruptcy.

2.6 Company insolvency priority of payments

It is a fundamental principle of insolvency law that creditors who have not taken security in respect of the sums due are treated *pari passu* (literally 'with the same step'). Such unsecured creditors should be treated equally and receive as a dividend the same percentage of their debts. Where a creditor proves that certain goods are subject to retention of title or a valid trust, they do not form part of the property of the company available for distribution to creditors (e.g. Section 283(3) of the Insolvency Act 1986 for individuals). Where property is subject to a fixed charge, provided that the charge has been properly registered under Section 395 of the Companies Act 1985 (with effect from 1 October 2009 re-enacted by Part 25 of the Companies Act 2006), (if the charge needs to be registered), that property will also fall outside the scheme.

The Insolvency Act 1986 dictates the priority in which creditors will be paid namely:

(a) Debts secured by fixed charges and the costs of realising such fixed charged assets. These are payable out of the proceeds of the specific fixed charge asset. Any surplus will go back into the general pot for creditors. Any shortfall will be unsecured debt; then
(b) The expenses of the winding up. The liquidator's own expenses are not payable in priority to floating charge debts; then
(c) Preferential debts. Certain limited employee claims and other debts (debts owed to HM Revenue & Customs are no longer preferential debts); then
(d) Debts secured by floating charges. A small proportion of the assets available to be applied towards floating charge debts calculated in accordance with the Insolvency Act 1986 (the 'prescribed part') is withheld for application towards the unsecured debts; then
(e) Unsecured debts; then
(f) Interest on preferential and unsecured debts; then
(g) Debts or other sums due from the company to its members (e.g. unpaid dividends); then
(h) Any surplus is to be distributed among the members generally, in accordance with their respective rights and interests.

Each of the above classes of debt (save for the 'prescribed part') must be satisfied in full before assets can be applied towards the next class of debts.

Debts secured by like security (fixed or floating) are prioritised with regard to the dates upon which the security was granted e.g. an earlier floating charge will take priority over a later floating charge, but not over a later fixed charge. To the extent that there are insufficient assets to satisfy a class in full, each creditor will receive such proportion of the remaining assets as is proportionate to claims.

3 INSOLVENCY SET-OFF

Set-off functions informally as a kind of security. For example, if A and B owe debts to each other, A can be said to have security for the debt owed by B to the extent that A can set off its cross-claim. Outside insolvency, the purpose of set-off is one of convenience, to prevent the need for A and B to issue proceedings against each other. Where insolvency intervenes, the purpose of set-off is different depending on the procedure concerned.

3.1 Liquidation

If A or B were to go into liquidation, the general law or the parties' own contractual set-off arrangements are replaced by a set-off pursuant to r.4.90 of the Insolvency Rules 1986. The key provisions are:

(1) This Rule applies where, before the company goes into liquidation there have been mutual credits, mutual debts or other mutual dealings between the company and any creditor of the company proving or claiming to prove for a debt in the liquidation.
(3) An account shall be taken of what is due from each party to the other in respect of the mutual dealings, and the sums due from one party shall be set off against the sums due from the other.
(8) Only the balance (if any) of the account is provable in the liquidation. Alternatively the balance (if any) owed to the company shall be paid to the liquidator as part of the assets except where all or part of the balance results from a contingent or prospective debt owed by the creditor and in such a case the balance (or that part of it which results from the contingent or prospective debt) shall be paid if and when that debt becomes due and payable.

The purpose behind liquidation set-off is to do justice between the parties: otherwise if A and B owed debts to each other and A went into liquidation, the liquidator could recover in full from B, but B would only have an unsecured claim for a dividend in A's liquidation. 'Debt' is defined very widely and includes a liability which is present or future, certain or contingent, liquidated or unliquidated: r.13.12 of the Insolvency Rules 1986. Set-off in liquidation is therefore much wider than the general law.

The requirement for mutual credits, debts and dealings is normally satisfied in a construction contract: *Willment* v. *North West Thames RHA* (1984) 26 BLR 51, 62.

The set-off is compulsory and cannot be excluded by agreement: *Halesowen Presswork* v. *National Westminster Bank* [1972] AC 785. The set-off is self-executing: *Stein* v. *Blake* [1996] AC 243. As it is rare for a liquidator to continue trading in the construction industry, the usual components of liquidation set-off where the contractor goes into liquidation are certified sums and the amount of uncertified work in progress and loss and expense owed to the contractor and the employer's claims arising out of the completion contract. The account is taken as at the commencement of the liquidation. Until the works have been completed and the balance ascertained, the employer remains a contingent creditor. The creditor's proof of debt will be valued by the liquidator under r.4.86 of the Insolvency Rules 1986 or, in the event of a dispute which could impact on the recovery of other creditors, by means of an arbitration or an appeal by the creditor against the liquidator's rejection of its proof.

Since only the balance is provable, it is not possible for the liquidator to assign the debt owing to the company without taking into account liabilities owed by the company: *Farley* v. *Housing and Commercial Developments* (1984) 26 BLR 66, *Stein* v. *Blake* [1996] AC 243.

Some changes were made to r.4.90 following the Enterprise act 2002 which may well be significant for a construction insolvency. Formerly, a contingent debt owed *by* the insolvent company could be included in the account for set-off purposes but, as there was no similar mechanism for valuing a contingent claim owed *to* the company, such a claim was not available for set-off . The position now is that contingent and future debts owing to and by the insolvent company are to be set-off provided they arise out of obligations incurred before the start of the liquidation.

Debts which have been acquired by way of assignment under an agreement entered into after the commencement of the liquidation cannot be taken into account for set-off purposes.

There is a tension between the insolvency legislation and the Housing Grants, Construction and Regeneration Act 1996. Where a claimant in an adjudication is in liquidation and the defendant asserts a cross-claim which might qualify for set-off under r.4.90, the court ought not to grant summary judgment to enforce an adjudicator's decision as the proper forum (assuming the liquidator does not admit the cross-claims) is the Companies Court where the matter would proceed as an appeal against the liquidator's rejection of the defendant's proof of debt: *Bouygues* v. *Dahl-Jensen* [2000] BLR 522, CA. In that case, the claimant went into liquidation the day before the adjudicator's decision was issued but liquidation set-off was not raised in argument by the defendant at the enforcement hearing. As a consequence, the Court of Appeal ordered summary judgment but granted a stay of execution until after the expiry of the time for lodging an appeal in the Companies Court or until after the outcome of any appeal. It is not thought that the changes made to r.4.90 following the Enterprise Act 2002 would have affected the outcome of this case.

3.2 Administration

By contrast, set-off against a claim made by a company in administration is governed by the ordinary rules of common law. This is because the administrator does not usually make any distributions to creditors or accept proofs of debt. Payment of dividends is left to a subsequently appointed liquidator or a supervisor under a voluntary arrangement. The appointment of an administrator is therefore a neutral event as far as rights of set-off are concerned.

The position changes, however, if the administrator gives notice that he proposes to make a distribution to creditors under r.2.85 of the Insolvency Rules 1986. This provision was added by the Insolvency (Amendment) Rules 2005. If the administrator serves such a notice, then rules in the same terms as liquidation set-off will apply to the distribution.

As a result of the changes to the administration regime brought about by the Enterprise Act 2002, a company can now move between liquidation and administration or between administration and liquidation. Amendments have been made to the rules for quantifying a proof of debt in administration or in liquidation so as to clarify that the relevant date in such situations for the conversion of foreign currency debts, payments of a periodical nature, interest on debts and debts payable at a future time is the date of the first insolvency procedure.

3.3 Administrative receivership

The position is different again with administrative receiverships. Set-off against a company in receivership depends on the rules which apply to set-off against claims by assignees. This can be illustrated by *Rother Iron* v. *Canterbury Precision Engineers* [1974] QB 1: see Fig. 3.

A granted a floating charge over all its assets to a bank. A became indebted to B for £124. A then agreed to sell goods worth £159 to B. The bank then appointed a receiver over A. A delivered the goods to B, who set off its cross-claim of £124 and tendered the difference of £35. The receiver failed in his claim for the £159. On his appointment, the floating charge crystallized and there was an immediate equitable assignment to the bank of the benefit of the contract to sell the goods to B. On the receiver performing the

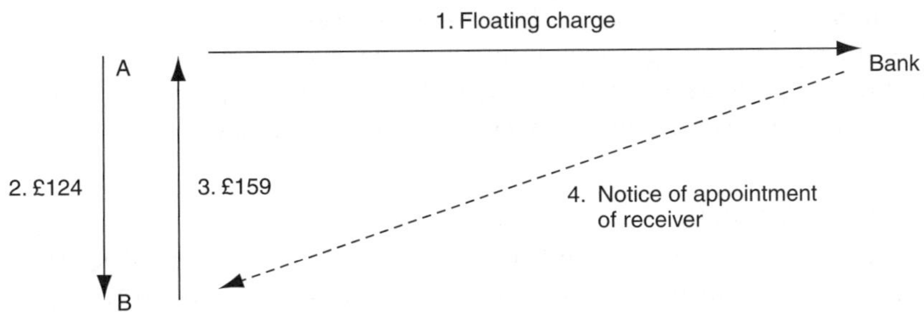

Figure 3. Administrative receivership

contract, the consideration was payable to the bank as assignee who could recover it by issuing proceedings in A's name. However, the assignment was subject to equities, which included B's existing claim for £124, and as assignee the bank could be in no better position than A as assignor. All that the bank acquired was the right to the balance of £35.

This was a case of legal set-off. In contrast, cross-claims for equitable set-off and contractual set-off can normally be made by way of defence to claims brought by receivers, even if technically they accrue after the notice of appointment was received.[3] The operation of legal, equitable, receivership and liquidation set-off is illustrated by *Hargreaves* v. *Action 2000* [1993] BCLC 1111. There were nine separate subcontracts between the same parties, signed on the same day and for the same employer but on nine different sites. Most of the work was completed before the subcontractor went into administrative receivership. The receiver issued proceedings to recover a liquidated sum owing to the subcontractor on one of the contracts. The contractor instructed a surveyor who found evidence of overvaluation on two of the others such as to give rise to a cross-claim for an amount exceeding the receiver's claim. By the time proceedings were issued, the subcontractor was also in liquidation. The contractor failed in its attempt to set off its cross-claim.

- The claim for legal set-off failed because the cross-claim for an overpayment was neither liquidated nor easily ascertainable with certainty since it depended on the judgment of the contractor's surveyor.
- The claim for equitable set-off also failed because the contracts were independent of one another and it could not be said that the claim and cross-claim were so closely connected as to make it inequitable not to allow the set-off.
- In the absence of any right to legal or equitable set-off, there was no equity in the contractor subject to which the charge holder took the benefit of the contracts on the receiver's appointment.
- The equitable assignment to the charge holder preceded the liquidation, and therefore the claim asserted by the receiver could not be taken into account by the liquidator under r.4.86 of the Insolvency Rules 1986. The contractor had to pay the claim in full and, if it so wished, to pursue its cross-claim by way of a proof of debt in the liquidation.

If the claimant in an adjudication is a company in administrative receivership, it will normally be entitled to summary judgment to enforce the adjudicator's decision as r.4.90 of the Insolvency Rules 1986 (discussed in Section 3.1 above) only applies to companies in liquidation: *Rainford House* v. *Cadogan* [2001] BLR 416. In that case, however, the receivership was regarded as 'special circumstances' within RSC Order 47 and a stay of execution was granted, conditional on the employer paying the disputed sum into court, with liberty to the receivers appointed to the contractor to apply to lift the stay on providing adequate security for repayment were the employer's counterclaim to succeed. See also *Baldwins Industrial Services* v. *Barr* [2003] BLR 176.

4 INSOLVENCY CLAIMS

The Insolvency Act 1986 contains wide powers for an insolvency practitioner appointed as either an administrator or liquidator to investigate the background to the insolvency and the conduct of the directors prior to the insolvency. The Insolvency Act provides such an insolvency practitioner with the ability to 'unravel' certain transactions and 'claw back' money into the company. Liability for an insolvency claim is also relevant when the court is asked to disqualify a director under the Company Directors Disqualification Act 1986. This section briefly summarizes the claims available and their potential impact on construction.

4.1 Fraudulent trading

Where any business of the company has been carried on with intent to defraud creditors of the company or creditors of any other person or for any fraudulent purpose, the court has power under Section 213 of the Insolvency Act 1986 to order anyone who is knowingly a party to the carrying on of the business to contribute to the company's assets. The Singaporean case of *Tong Tien See Construction* v. *Tong* [2002] 3 SLR 76 is a recent example of a successful claim in the industry. 'Fraudulent trading' is also a criminal offence under Section 458 of the Companies Act 1985 (with effect from 1 October 2007 re-enacted by Part 30 of the Companies Act 2006) whether or not the company is in liquidation.

4.2 Wrongful trading

In order to provide liquidators with a more effective remedy than fraudulent trading, Section 214 of the Insolvency Act 1986 introduced a cause of action known as 'wrongful trading'. This is a civil claim requiring proof on a balance of probabilities and can be made against a director or a shadow director (defined by Section 251 as 'a person in accordance with whose directions and instructions the directors of the company are accustomed to act'). The liquidator has to show that the director allowed the company to continue to incur liabilities to creditors after the point had been reached when it was known or should have been known that there was no real prospect of the company avoiding insolvent liquidation. The director can be made personally liable for the amount of credit incurred after the 'point of no return' is reached. The claim is unusual in applying both a subjective test of whether the director acted properly in the light of his or her own abilities and an objective test of whether the director acted as a person with his or her role in the company ought to have done. It is not necessary to prove dishonesty.

A higher standard is expected from a director of a large company with sophisticated accounting procedures than a small company in a modest way of business: see *Re Produce Marketing* (1989) 5 BCC 569. However, in *Re DKG Contractors* [1990] BCC 903, a husband and wife acting as directors of a groundworks subcontractor were both held liable for wrongful trading and ordered to contribute £400 000 to the company's assets representing credit incurred between April 1998, the 'point of no return', and December 1998, when the company actually went into liquidation. The company was set up in parallel to a business carried on by one of the directors personally. An important factor is that the directors took no independent advice, whether from an auditor, a lawyer or a specialist insolvency practitioner. Wrongful trading is particularly relevant where a company is informally insolvent and the directors are trying to persuade the creditors not to enforce their rights while a rescue package can be put together. It is always a question of judgment whether there is a 'reasonable prospect' of avoiding liquidation.

4.3 Preference

Under Section 239 of the Insolvency Act 1986, a preference occurs if a company does or allows anything to be done which has the effect of improving the position of a creditor or a guarantor over that which would have obtained on the company's liquidation. It has to be shown that the company was 'influenced in deciding to give it by a desire' to produce the preference. A claim can only be brought in respect of a preference made no more than six months before the start of the liquidation or two years where the creditor is a connected person. The most common situation arises where a director makes a personally guaranteed payment into the company's overdrawn bank account. The liquidator can make the preference claim against the bank and/or the director. The need to establish motivation is troublesome. For example, pressure applied by the creditor can negative a preference.[4] Hence, where a creditor is offered a settlement at a time when the company appears to be insolvent, it is important that the creditor asserts its rights (e.g. to petition to wind up the company) so that any payment can be viewed in the light of the creditor's pressure rather than simply the director's subjective desire to improve that creditor's position. Commercial considerations did not, however, save the director from liability for preference in *Re DKG Contractors* [1990] BCC 903.

Otherwise, preference arguments in construction have revolved around direct payments and construction trusts. It is important to identify the act which constitutes the preference. In the case of a direct payment, it could be the direct payment clause, the payment or the set-off following payment. This will depend in each case on the construction of the contract. Several Australian cases have rejected claims for preference in this situation on the ground that, properly construed, the direct payment clauses did not provide for payment out of sums due to the contractor: see, for example, *Gericevich* v. *Sabemo* [1984] 9 ACLR 452. In contrast, an Australian court has held a direct payment to be a preference where it was made pursuant to a collateral contract between a contractor, subcontractor and sub-subcontractor after the subcontractor went into liquidation: see *Analogy* v. *Bell Basic Industries* (1996) 12 BCL 291. The possibility that setting up a trust, even pursuant to a contract term, could be a preference was discussed in *MacJordan Construction* v. *Brookmount Erostin* (1992) 56 BLR 1 at 16. Once again, it is important to consider what the preference would be: entering into the contract, setting money aside on request, complying with a court order, or making payments from the trust account. A possible preference is where an employer has a number of contracts with different contractors using the same JCT standard form, has sufficient funds to set aside retention in respect of them all, is asked to do so by all of the contractors, but does so only for one of them. It is possible that the employer's action in excluding the others gives rise to an inference that it was influenced by a desire to place one of them in a better position on a liquidation.

4.4 Transactions at an undervalue

Under Section 238 of the Insolvency Act 1986 the court has power to set aside a transaction entered into at an undervalue, e.g. where the company receives no consideration or the value given is significantly more than that received. The company must have been insolvent at the time or have become so as a result but this is presumed where the transaction is with a connected person, such as a director, or a company controlled by that connected person. There is a defence that the transaction was entered into in good faith for the purpose of carrying on the company's business and there were reasonable grounds for believing that it would benefit the company. It must have taken place within two years before the start of the insolvency procedure and the court has power to make such order as it thinks fit to restore the status quo. Transactions which might fall within this head of claim are the transfer of assets from the company to a director for less than market value or the giving of a guarantee by a subsidiary on behalf of a parent company for no apparent benefit: *Phillips* v. *Brewin Dolphin* [2001] 1 WLR 143, HL. An industry example is *Buildspeed Construction* v. *Theme* [2000] 4 SLR 776 where the novation of a contract by an insolvent contractor to a new company owned and operated by its directors was held to be a transaction at an undervalue.

4.5 Transactions to defraud creditors

Where a person enters into a transaction at an undervalue, the court may make an order under Section 423 of the Insolvency Act 1986 to restore the position to what it would have been if the transaction had not been entered into, and to protect the interests of persons who are victims of the transaction. The court must be satisfied that the transaction was entered into for the purpose of putting assets beyond the reach of a person who is making, or may at some time make, a claim against him, or of otherwise prejudicing the interests of such a person in relation to a claim. See *Re Ayala Holdings* [1993] BCLC 256 for an industry example. There is no fixed period within which a transaction must have occurred nor is it necessary for the company to have begun any insolvency process for a transaction to be liable to be set aside under this section.

4.6 Misfeasance

Section 212 of the Insolvency Act 1986 provides for a remedy against directors and other officers and persons involved in the promotion, formation or management of a company who have been 'delinquent'. It creates no new liability against directors but provides a quicker procedure for enforcing certain rights which might have been enforced by an ordinary action before winding up.

If any of the directors or any of the other persons referred to in Section 212 has misapplied, retained, become liable or accountable for any money or property of the company, or has been guilty of misfeasance, breach of fiduciary duty or any other duty in relation to the company, the Official Receiver, liquidator, creditor or any contributory standing to benefit is allowed to recover money or damages for the benefit of the company in liquidation. The court may examine the conduct of such persons and compel them to repay or restore the money or the property with interest or to contribute money to the assets of the company by way of compensation.

Section 212 covers a variety of wrongs including the improper payment of dividends, the application of monies for ultra vires purposes, the application of monies contrary to the Companies Act 1985 and any unauthorised loans or payment of unauthorised remuneration to directors.

Construction examples include:

(a) misappropriating money and cheques belonging to the company (*Re DKG Contractors* [1990] BCC 903)

(b) diverting tender enquiries for personal use (*Schott Kem* v. *Bentley* [1990] 3 All ER 850)
(c) using company resources for building work to a director's home without paying for it (*Halls* v. *O'Dell* [1992] 2 WLR 308)
(d) a director registering a trademark belonging to the company in his own name (*Ball* v. *The Eden Project* [2002] 1 BCLC 313).

Section 727 of the Companies Act 1985 provides that a court may grant relief from liability for negligence, breach of duty or breach of trust on such terms as it thinks fit if the director has acted honestly and reasonably and if having regard to all of the circumstances of the case, including those connected with his appointment, he ought fairly to be excused. Relief from liability for misfeasance may be available under this section. This is a discretionary remedy. Whether the court will grant relief will depend on what view the court forms of the conduct of the director in the particular case. As a minimum, the director must show that he acted honestly and reasonably.

4.7 Post-petition disposition

Any disposition by a company after a winding-up petition has been presented is void unless validated by the court under Section 127 of the Insolvency Act 1986. An application for validation can be made before or after the disposition is made: e.g. *Re Tain Construction* [2003] 2 BCLC 374 (validation refused). In the industry, this could invalidate a direct payment made to a nominated subcontractor (*Re Right Time Construction* (1990) 52 BLR 117). It might also invalidate a retention trust whether set up voluntarily or pursuant to an injunction: compare *Re Flint* [1993] Ch 319.

4.8 Invalid floating charge

Where a floating charge is granted within twelve months before the start of liquidation, or two years if in favour of a connected person, and the company was insolvent at the time or became so as a result, and did not receive proper value in return, the charge is liable to be invalidated on an application by the liquidator under Section 245 of the Insolvency Act 1986.

4.9 Unregistered registrable charges

Certain charges granted by a limited company must be registered with the Registrar of Companies within 21 days of their creation otherwise they will be void against a liquidator, administrator or creditor of the company under Section 395 of the Companies Act 1985 (with effect from 1 October 2009 re-enacted by Part 25 of the Companies Act 2006). These are listed in Section 396 and include a charge on land or an interest in land, a charge on book debts, a floating charge, and a charge created or evidenced by an instrument which, if executed by an individual, would require registration as a bill of sale. A power of sale in respect of plant and equipment contained in the termination clause of the ICE Conditions (5th Edition) was held to be a floating charge and invalid for want of registration as against an administrator appointed over the contractor in *Smith* v. *Bridgend County Borough Council* [2002] BLR 160, HL. Other types of security used in the industry may not be registrable. For example, a trust of the contract sum operating by way of informal security was held not to be a floating charge or a charge on book debts in *Lovell Construction* v. *Independent Estates* [1994] 1 BCLC 31. The assignment by way of legal mortgage of a management contract considered in *L/M International* v. *The Circle* (1995) 48 Con LR 12 was a formal security but did not require registration under Section 396 of the Companies Act 1985.

4.10 Extortionate credit transaction

Under Section 244 of the Insolvency Act 1986, a liquidator or administrator can apply to set aside or vary a transaction if it can be shown that it was extortionate, in that the terms required grossly exorbitant payments to be made having regard to the risk accepted by the person providing the credit, or where it otherwise grossly contravened ordinary principles of fair dealing.

4.11 Contravention of the *pari passu* rule

There are a number of nineteenth century cases invalidating provisions in termination clauses in building contracts on the ground that they infringed the *pari passu* rule considered earlier under Section 2.6. The classic example is *Re Harrison, ex parte Jay* (1880) 14 Ch D 19 in which the court struck down a term which forfeited a builder's plant and materials in the event of his bankruptcy. In more modern times, the House of Lords invalidated an IATA clearing house arrangement on this ground in *British Eagle* v. *Air France* [1975] 2 All ER 390. The decision has caused great uncertainty as to the effect of the *pari passu* rule on commercial contracts.[5] The High Court of Northern Ireland regards it as invalidating direct payment provisions so far as they take effect on the contractor's liquidation (*Mullan* v. *Ross* (1996) 86 BLR 1). Many academic writers support this view.[6] The *pari passu* rule may also invalidate certain provisions in termination clauses found in joint venture and consortium agreements: *Money Markets* v. *Stock Exchange* [2002] 1 WLR 1150, *Fraser* v. *Oystertec* [2004] BCC 233.

5 TERMINATION OF CONTRACTS

Most of the value of a contractor consists in its receivables: debtors, retention, work in progress, claims. Where the contractor becomes insolvent before completion, its insolvency practitioner has to ensure that the contracts are completed in order to recover the receivables either by arranging for the works to be completed or by novating the contracts to another contractor with the employer's consent. The problem for insolvency practitioners is that their ability to achieve this goal is limited by the fact that construction contracts almost invariably provide for termination in the event of the contractor's insolvency. The reason why these clauses are included is that insolvency is not normally a breach of contract, whether informal, in the sense of failing either of the tests in Section 123 of the Insolvency Act 1986, or formal where the contractor enters one of the recognized insolvency procedures. The only exceptions are where the contract contains a covenant not to become insolvent or where the insolvency event or the surrounding circumstances amount to an 'anticipatory breach'.

'Anticipatory breach' is a term of art used in the law of contract. In construction, it could be an act by the contractor which, although not in itself a breach, is such as to entitle the employer to conclude that the contractor will be unable to perform its side of the contract when the time for performance arrives. Insolvency is not an anticipatory breach of contract in the absence of special circumstances (*Re Agra Bank, ex parte Tondeur* (1867) LR 5 Eq 160), nor is administrative receivership (*Laing and Morrison Knudson* v. *Aegon Insurance* (1997) 86 BLR 70 at 91). Even the possibility of treating administrative receivership as an anticipatory breach cannot arise where the contract has excluded the common law (*Perar* v. *General Surety* (1994) 66 BLR 72). It follows that any discussion of the options following the insolvency of a party to a project must involve a careful review of all the circumstances, including the terms of any termination clause and the relationship between that clause and the common law.

5.1 Termination under the contract

Against that background, it is not surprising that standard forms have developed express terms providing for termination on insolvency. Although the building and engineering forms adopt different approaches, they follow the same structure.

- They identify specific events which trigger the power to terminate on notice, normally by reference to the formal insolvency procedures discussed in Section 1 above, although informal insolvency may also be included.
- The termination clause provides for the contractor's exclusion from site to allow the employer to engage an alternative contractor to finish the work. This may be expressed in different ways: determining the contractor's employment, terminating the contract, taking the works out of the contractor's hands, etc.
- The employer's duty to make any further payment to the insolvent contractor, even if accrued due at the date of termination, is suspended and postponed until the works have been completed and a final account has been prepared (see *Melville Dundas* v. *George Wimpey* [2007] BLR 257).
- A contractual set-off is then made between what would have been due to the contractor had it performed the contract and the actual cost incurred by the employer in having the work completed, together with any loss resulting from the termination.
- Some forms entitle the employer to make direct payments to suppliers and subcontractors and to deduct the amount of such payments from sums due or to become due to the contractor. This right has been omitted from the 2005 Edition of the JCT forms.

Probably the most comprehensive insolvency termination clause in any standard form is contained in the JCT Standard Form of Building Contract, 1998 Edition. Clause 27 deals with termination by the employer. Unusually, it makes a distinction between two groups of insolvency event: bankruptcy and liquidation, which automatically terminate the contractor's employment, and administration, administrative receivership, composition, voluntary arrangement or scheme of arrangement, which give the employer a discretion to terminate by serving a notice. The appointment of a fixed charge receiver is not made a termination event.

Clause 27.5 introduces a special regime which applies where the insolvency event gives rise to a discretion to terminate. There are three elements to this regime.

(a) In the period between the insolvency event and the employer's decision to terminate, the employer's duty to pay and the contractor's duty to carry out work are suspended. This means that the employer could not treat the contractor's abandonment of the site during this period as a repudiation.
(b) The suspension continues until the employer either serves notice of termination or agrees to novate the contract. During the suspension, either party can agree an interim arrangement whereby work can continue. The employer agrees not to set-off any cross-claim against any sums due under the interim arrangement.
(c) During the suspension, the employer can take reasonable steps to protect the site and is entitled to set-off the cost of so doing against any monies due or to become due to the contractor whether under a novation or an interim arrangement. The intention behind this clause is to encourage the employer to pause for thought and negotiate with the insolvency practitioner rather than automatically exercising its discretion to terminate.

JCT Practice Note 24 (1992) gives some useful guidance to employers on how to weigh up the options. If the employer decides to terminate, the relief to which it is entitled is set out in Clause 27.6. This is broadly the same as under termination for default. Under this sub-clause, the employer acquires a bundle of valuable post-termination rights to:

- engage another contractor to complete the works
- take possession of the site
- use all temporary buildings, plant, tools, equipment and materials on site
- buy further goods and materials necessary to complete the works and make good any defects
- require the immediate assignment of the benefit of subcontracts and supply contracts (but only where the insolvency event is a proposal for a company voluntary arrangement or a scheme of arrangement)
- pay suppliers or subcontractors direct 'insofar as the price . . . has not already been discharged by the contractor' and deduct such payments from any sum due or to become due to the contractor (except in cases of bankruptcy or liquidation)
- require the contractor to remove temporary buildings, plant, tools, equipment, goods and materials or in default sell them and hold the net proceeds to the credit of the contractor
- suspend payment of all sums due or to become due to the contractor until the final account for the completion contract has been agreed (except in respect of sums 'properly due' and which have been outstanding for at least 28 days before the termination event)
- recover all expenses properly incurred by and any direct loss and/or damage caused to the employer as a result of the termination
- to set off such expense and loss against sums otherwise due to the contractor and treat the difference as a debt payable by the contractor (or the employer as the case may be).

Clause 27 is a long and complicated provision which seeks to protect the employer without unfairly penalizing the contractor. There are five aspects worth noting.

First, the employer has to act reasonably in selecting the completion contractor, otherwise it risks not being able to recover all its expenses on the grounds that they were not 'properly incurred', by analogy with principles of mitigation of loss for breach of contract. Broadly speaking, the employer is given the benefit of the doubt as the victim of the contractor's financial failure. There is some authority, however, for reducing the employer's claim after termination on the grounds that the employer ought to have sent the works out to competitive tender and that there had been a fall in the tender price index since the original contract was let: see *Bank of East Asia* v. *Scottish Enterprise* (unreported, 19 June 1992, Lexis).

Secondly, the direct payment provision has been challenged by administrative receivers on the ground not of the *pari passu* rule (as this does not apply to receiverships) but because it contravenes public policy by giving the subcontractor priority over preferential creditors. If the payment would otherwise have fallen within the ambit of the floating charge, or the floating element of a fixed and floating charge, it would, so the argument goes, have had to be made available to pay preferential creditors and only if they were paid in full would it become payable to the chargeholder. The argument has not yet been tested in the court.

Thirdly, the employer's duty to pay amounts which are 'properly due' at least 28 days before the termination event only applies where the employer has 'unreasonably not discharged' them. It seems to follow that suspension of payment would be total where the employer had a set-off in excess of such amounts before the termination event occurred. This would require the employer to establish set-off in accordance with the normal principles; it would not appear to justify non-payment on the ground that defects might emerge even though they were not apparent at that stage.

Fourthly, the employer has to inform the contractor within six months after termination if it decides not to have the works completed. Within a reasonable time after that, the employer has to send the contractor a financial statement indicating the financial position between them after setting off any expenses or losses following termination.

Finally, the express right to recover expenses and direct loss and/or damage ought to be sufficient to enable the employer to recover to the same extent as if it had been entitled to treat the insolvency event as a repudiation. In most cases, the employer will not need to rely on Clause 27.8 which makes it clear that the termination clause, including the post-termination rights, is 'without prejudice to any other rights and remedies which the employer may possess'. This brings us to the question of overlap between rights conferred by contractual termination clauses and rights generally available under the common law.

5.2 Termination at common law

It may be necessary sometimes to rely on the common law rather than (or in addition to) an express termination clause, for example:

(a) where the relief allowed by the termination clause will not enable the employer to recover its losses in full
(b) where the employer fails to comply with an essential requirement of the termination clause
(c) where some aspect of the clause is invalidated, e.g. as a penalty or through the operation of the *pari passu* rule, or
(d) it is unclear whether a contractual termination event has in fact occurred but there has been an anticipatory or repudiatory breach.

Provided common-law rights have not been excluded (or perhaps provided they have been expressly preserved), it is possible both to terminate under the contract and accept a repudiation at common law (*Laing and Morrison Knudson* v. *Aegon Insurance* (1997) 86 BLR 70).[7] In that case there was a contractual termination of 'the works'. This kept the contract alive, enabling the management contractor to have the remaining work completed and accept the works contractor's repudiation at a later date.

It remains a difficult question whether, and in what circumstances, a notice of termination under the contract can also serve as the acceptance of a repudiatory breach. In *Dalkia Utilities* v. *Celtech International* [2006] 1 Lloyd's Rep. 599, the contractor successfully invoked a clause allowing it to terminate for 'material breach' where the employer had failed to pay three outstanding invoices. It was held that the non-payment was not repudiatory conduct, and that even if it had been, the notice of termination did not amount to an acceptance of the repudiation. The court stated however that such a notice could constitute an acceptance if it merely exercised the right to terminate without stating the ground or, where a contractual termination clause was referred to, it was evident from the context that the party was not relying on it exclusively (paras. 143–4).

3.1 The law of contract
3.2 Construction health and safety
3.3 Insolvency in construction
3.4 Law of tort
3.5 Environmental issues

5.3 Novation

Novation is the procedure whereby an insolvency practitioner appointed over a contractor obtains value for the company's contracts by introducing a completion contractor to the employer. It differs from assignment in three important respects.

(a) Assignment is a transfer of rights under a contract which continues in being after the assignment whereas novation brings the existing contract to an end and creates a new one in its place (*Scarf* v. *Jardine* (1882) 7 App Cas 345 at 351).
(b) Assignment transfers the benefit but not the burden of a contract whereas a novation also transfers the burden with the consent of all parties: such a transfer is not an assignment of the burden but a novation of the contract.
(c) Consideration is not generally required for assignment but is necessary on a novation as a new contract is being formed; consideration is however normally implicit in a novation agreement.

Novation has been defined as 'the substitution of a new contract for an old by the agreement of all parties to the old and the new' (*Tito* v. *Waddell (No. 2)* [1977] Ch 106 at 287). This usually consists in the release of one party and the introduction of a new party in substitution. Most of the reported cases concern implied rather than express novation. In order to establish a novation 'what the plaintiff has to prove is conduct inconsistent with a continuance of his liability, from which conduct an agreement to release him may be inferred' (*Rouse* v. *Bradford Banking* [1894] 2 Ch 32 at 54).

The case usually cited as an example of novation in the construction industry is *Chatsworth* v. *Cussins* [1969] 1 All ER 143. After practical completion a contractor assigned the benefit of the contract to a purchaser who undertook direct to the contractor to discharge all its liabilities. The purchaser then changed its name to that of the contractor. The employer issued proceedings against the purchaser in respect of defects in the works in the mistaken belief that it was the original contractor. The Court of Appeal held the purchaser liable to the employer on the basis of an implied novation. On closer examination, however, it appears that two essential ingredients for a novation are missing:

(a) there was no release by the employer of the original contractor from its obligations, and
(b) there was no direct promise from the purchaser to the employer (compare *The Tychy (No. 2)* [2001] 2 Lloyd's Rep 403).

In a similar case in which the contractor became informally insolvent and hived down its assets to a purchaser, the employer *failed* in a claim based on implied novation: see *Westminster City Council* v. *Reema Construction (No. 2)* (1990) 24 Con LR 26. There was no evidence that the Council was aware that the original contractor had hived down its assets or that the purchaser had agreed with the contractor to fulfil any unperformed obligations. It will be difficult to infer a novation if it would mean the employer losing the benefit of security for performance such as a cash deposit (*Aktion Maritime* v. *Kasmas* [1987] 1 LR 283).

The law of novation has developed in cases involving the transfer of debts. In its simplest form, a novation of a debt owed by B to A occurs when, with the consent of A as creditor, B is replaced as debtor by C: see Fig. 4.

The release of B apparently comes before A's acceptance of C in its place (*Re United Railways* [1960] 1 Ch 52 at 85). The position is rather more complicated with a

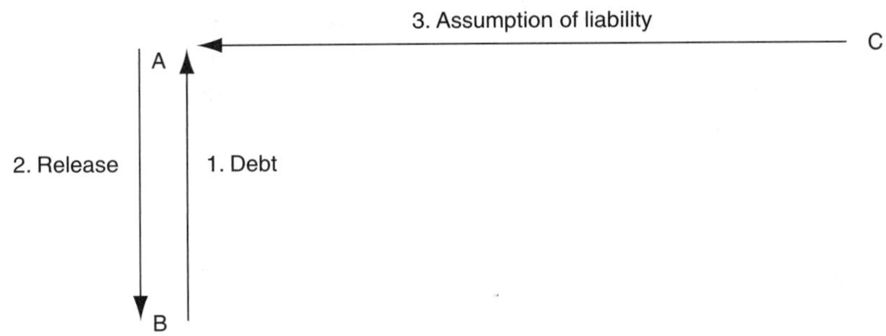

Figure 4. Novation: transfer of debts

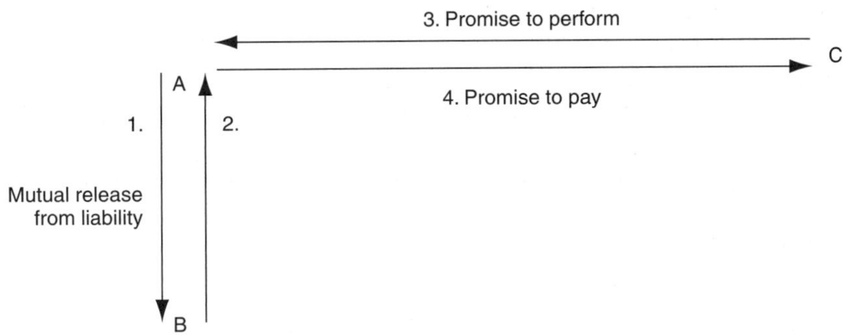

Figure 5. Novation: under a construction contract

construction contract under which each party owes obligations to the other. A novation in this context has to take account of the benefit and burden of both A and B: see Fig. 5.

Figure 5 assumes a straightforward novation whereby one contractor is substituted for another. There are four steps:

(1) the employer releases the contractor from liability
(2) the contractor releases the employer from liability
(3) the purchaser promises the employer to complete the contract, and
(4) the purchaser accepts the employer's promise to pay for the work.

The old contract is terminated by steps 1 and 2. The new contract is created by steps 3 and 4. The correct analysis is probably that the mutual releases come first followed by the mutual promises between A and C.

For forms of novation agreement see Newman[8] and JCT Practice Note 24.[9] Standard forms have recently been issued by the Construction Industry Council (2004), and the City of London Law Society (2004).

The agreement should deal with any changes necessary to the terms of the original contract. Such agreements normally expressly provide that the purchaser assumes liability to the employer as if it had been a party to the original contract from the inception. The intention is that the purchaser should become liable for any current breaches there may be as if it had signed a contract with retrospective effect. In *Blyth and Blyth* v. *Carillion Construction* [2002] 79 Con LR 142 the Court of Session held that a contractor was not entitled to recover its own losses arising from an engineer's breach of contract where the breach occurred before the novation of the engineer's appointment to the contractor. This finding appears to be contrary to English authority on novation (*W&J Leigh* v. *CBI Nederland*, 20 June 1985, Otton J) but may be correct on the facts. The Court of Session seems to have viewed the arrangements between the parties as a merger of contracts for which novation (at least in the form of this case) was an inappropriate vehicle.

Other areas which are usually addressed include:

- pricing provisions
- scope of works
- the completion date
- liability for delay following the insolvency
- liability for patent and latent defects
- liquidated and ascertained damages already incurred
- availability of plant and materials on and off site
- retention of title claimants
- subcontractors' claims
- willingness of subcontractors and suppliers to novate their contracts
- bonds and guarantees
- the effect of the Transfer of Undertakings (Protection of Employment) Regulations 1981
- the availability of the professional team for novations.

6 CASE STUDY

This case study is from the perspective of the insolvency practitioner and/or the lending bank. In an ideal world, the investigating team appointed to a contractor collates the relevant information on its contracts before insolvency occurs so that a strategy for each contract and an assessment of the collectability of debts can be made in advance. However, in practice the team often has limited access to the key staff (estimators, surveyors and contracts managers), and the details have to be taken from management accounts and debtor ledgers which can be very inaccurate or omit the essential information. Obtaining the right information and interpreting it correctly is critical if the course of an insolvency is to run smoothly and the recovery of assets maximized.

6.1 Base data

Management accounts are normally taken from a rolling series of figures, with profit and loss projections taken from tender estimates, adjusted for reserves and accruals. This does not give an appropriate view of a contract on which a decision can be made. For this purpose, a snapshot or 'freeze-frame' approach needs to be taken. If the company cannot or will not provide the basic information then this should sound double warning bells. Key information on a contract-by-contract basis is needed as set out below for both contracts in progress (CIP) and completed contracts (CC).

(a) *Estimated final account*. This should be a realistic assessment of the total amount that will be received on the contract net of any discounts and with amounts assessed for claims for loss and expense or damages for late completion clearly identified and allowed for within the figure.
(b) *Value of work done*. This should be assessed on the basis of the cumulative gross value certified or applied for, plus a reasonable assessment of work in progress (WIP) between the certificate and the snapshot date. It should be noted that

WIP can be negative, and often is on design and build contracts, if the stage payments are front-end loaded. An allocation between fixed and floating charge assets can be undertaken if the WIP figure is known.

(c) *Sums previously paid*. This should be the cumulative total paid as at the snapshot date. If a large sum will become due for payment in the near future, i.e. shortly after the snapshot date, this should be taken into account in considering when a decision should be taken on a particular contract.

(d) *Completion dates*. For CIPs a realistic anticipated completion date is required so that this can be looked at in comparison to the amount of work still to be done. It is also valuable in assessing the value of claims for loss and expense or the amount of damages for late completion. For CCs the actual completion date is needed to give a view of when the defects liability period might expire.

(e) *Retentions*. Although desirable it is not normally essential to identify retentions separately. The exception is for main contractors where nominated subcontractors are involved as their retention may be held by the client in trust. In these cases the amounts should be separately identified and deducted from any balances shown due.

(f) *Client name and contract*. Details of the client and the project enable a view to be taken as to the grouping of contracts and debts with a particular client and work type.

(g) *Other information*. If it is readily accessible other information should also be obtained such as:
- form of contract
- date and number of last certificate
- estimate of cost to complete
- warranties
- bonds and guarantees.

However, care must be taken not to spend too much time at the early stages obtaining information which is desirable rather than essential, otherwise the initial consideration of the key issues will be delayed.

6.2 Presentation of findings

The tabular presentation of key statistics enables a clear review of a portfolio of contracts to be undertaken. Typical figures for a small- to medium-sized main contractor are set out in Table 1.

6.3 Insolvency practitioner's options for contracts

From the basic statistics presented for the contracts, various possible options can be explored. It is important to remain mindful of common clients for both CIPs and CCs where there will be a risk of set-off between one and another. In the example given it will be important to ensure there is no linkage between the contracts in these three groups: (1) contracts 2, 3 and 6, (2) contracts 1 and 5, and (3) contracts 4 and 8.

Contracts in progress

Contract 1 – with a distant completion date, a large value to complete and a nominal amount outstanding, this contract will either be abandoned or novated as part of a package if there is sufficient profit in the value to complete.

Contract 2 – if detailed investigations and negotiations ensured that the £500 000 outstanding was definitely due, then with a close completion date and only £200 000

Table 1
A Contracts in progress (all figures in thousands)

A Client and contract	B Estimated final account	C Value of work done	D Previously paid	E Value to complete (B–C)	F Completion date
1. Local authority (school extension)	2000	100	0	1900	Aug. 2000
2. Housing association (20 units refurbishment)	1200	1000	500	200	Sept. 1999
3. Housing association (30 units new build)	1500	750	600	750	March 2000
4. Manufacturer (new warehouse)	1000	200	0	800	March 2000
		2050	1100		
		(1100)			
Balance due		950			

B Completed contracts as at 30 July 1999 (all figures in thousands)

A Client and contract	B Estimated final account	C Previously paid	D Balance B – C	E Completion date
5. Local authority (sports facility)	2000	1800	200	April 1999
6. Housing association (10 new build)	600	500	100	June 1999
7. Developer (office block)	1900	1400	500	Sept. 1988
8. Manufacturer (new workshop)	1300	1100	200	Jan. 1999
		Total balance	1000	

Notes:
(a) Assumes no nominated subcontractors involved.
(b) Figures are exclusive of VAT.
(c) Figures are rounded to thousands only for ease of presentation.

of work to do this may be a prospect for completion by the insolvent company or a novation to a third party for a sensible consideration.

Contracts 3 and 4 – with only nominal amounts outstanding and significant amounts of work to complete over an extended period, these contracts will either be abandoned or novated for nominal amounts as part of a package.

Completed contracts

Contracts 5, 6 and 8 look fairly straightforward in terms of reasonable balances of final account and retentions outstanding for a relatively short period of time. Debt collection for these, on the assumption there are no major defects, should be a relatively simple case of agreeing final accounts and reasonable client contra charges.

Contract 7 is more difficult in that a significant amount is shown as due and has been for some time since completion. A detailed investigation may reveal claims and counterclaims, defective work or a difficult client. Key company staff may need to be retained to assist with the collection of this debt.

Arrangements for debt collection can include incentivized deals with existing staff, sale of contract debts for a lump sum or a percentage of recovery, and the appointment of

Table 2 Case study – collectable debts (figures in thousands)

	Balance due	Recoverable
CCP	950	250–350 (assuming novation)
CC	1000	200–400
Totals	1950	450–750

third party agents on hourly rates or percentage-based fees. Care needs to be taken in structuring any arrangements for debt collection to allow for the long time-scale that the process takes when a company is no longer trading.

Realisable assets

Basic book values for contract debts are not recovered on a pound-for-pound basis in insolvency situations. Clients have a duty to mitigate loss and substantiate the amounts they are seeking to deduct from monies due to an insolvent company. However, there are many items which legitimately reduce the asset value. These include but are not limited to:

- excess completion costs
- additional professional fees
- absence of warranties
- inability to pursue claims
- inability to defend counterclaims
- enhanced costs of rectifying defects
- set-off between contracts
- negotiable settlements.

A statistical analysis of main and subcontractor's debts and collectability using data from insolvencies handled by GVA Grimley shows that over a ten-year period, recoverability in the range of 5–69% was achieved, with an average rate of 19%. In the case study, Table 2 sets out a good result representing a return of 23–38% (figures in thousands).

7 SECURITY FOR PERFORMANCE

Security for performance protects the paying party. It covers a very wide range of measures which can be taken:

(a) before deciding to enter into the contract
(b) by means of the contract terms
(c) by taking security outside the contract (see Table 3).

These are discussed in detail in Davis[10] and Newman.[11] Termination, insolvency set-off and some aspects of formal security were considered earlier in this chapter. This section looks at title to materials, vesting of plant, retention and bonds and guarantees.

7.1 Title to materials

Contractors often have few tangible assets on which a creditor can levy execution. Employers are therefore concerned to ensure that title to materials intended for their project passes to them as quickly as possible.

Table 3 Security for performance

Precontract	Prequalification Tender process Professional advice Financial modelling
Contract	Termination Set-off Vesting Indemnities Retention Conditions precedent
Security	Collateral contracts Suretyship Demand bonds Insurance Formal security

Where the materials are fixed, they cease to be chattels and become part of the land by operation of law. This can cause hardship in cases where, unknown to the contractor, the employer is not the owner of the land or has mortgaged it. As a consequence, the contractor may be contractually obliged to continue to add to the value of the land even where the employer is informally insolvent because no event has occurred entitling the contractor to terminate. The construction process is such as to make it uncertain sometimes whether a chattel has become fixed. Where the object simply rests on the land by its own weight, the burden of proof is on the person asserting that it has become part of the land. Where the item is fixed, even if only slightly, the burden of proof is on the person contending it is a chattel (*Holland* v. *Hodgson* (1872) LR 7 CP 328). The intention of the parties is relevant only insofar as it can be inferred from the degree and purpose of annexation (*Elitestone* v. *Morris* [1997] 2 All 513).

The second informal security arises from the linking of main and subcontracts. In the absence of any express provision, title to materials under a contract for goods and services will not pass until they are fixed to the land (*Tripp* v. *Armitage* (1839) 4 M&W 687). The mere fact that the value of materials is included in an interim certificate does not mean that title passes to the employer on payment. What is required is an express term that title to unfixed or off-site materials will become the property of the employer on payment to the contractor: see *Egan* v. *State Transport Authority* (1982) 31 SASR 481, not following *Banbury and Cheltenham Railway* v. *Daniel* (1854) LJ Ch 265. Such terms can be found, for example, in the JCT forms.

Where materials are provided to the contractor pursuant to a sale of goods contract, and the employer pays the contractor for them in good faith and without notice of any retention of title clause in the supplier's terms and conditions, the employer can claim ownership of the materials under Section 25 of the Sale of Goods Act 1979. The section only applies where the goods are transferred to the employer under a 'sale, pledge, or other disposition'. It was impliedly held in *Archivent* v. *Strathclyde General Council* (1984) 27 BLR 111 that payment of a certificate issued under JCT 63 which had specifically referred to the goods in question amounted to a 'disposition' within the section. Had the contract not specifically provided for title to pass on payment of a certificate, however, then the section could not have applied (see *P4 Ltd* v. *Unite Integrated Solutions* [2006] EWHC 2640). Section 25 is sometimes raised as a defence to applications by suppliers for delivery up of materials. If there is an argument that the section might apply and that the project would be unreasonably delayed if the materials could not be used, the balance of convenience may lie against the supplier: see *Modern Structural (Scotland) Plastics* v. *Tayloroof* (unreported, 3 December 1990). Where the contractor is in administrative receivership, and the receiver gives a personal undertaking to return the goods or pay their invoice value, the supplier may also be denied an injunction: see *Lipe* v. *Leyland DAF* [1993] BCC 385, *UCA France* v. *Fisher Foods* [2003] BPIR 299.

7.2 Plant and equipment

On some contracts, it is particularly important that plant and equipment is not removed from site by the contractor until after completion. This could be where it has had to be designed specifically for the contract, or specially imported, is in short supply or simply to prevent the contractor prejudicing the programme by diverting resources to another contract. These availability risks are met in part by terms which prevent the contractor removing plant from site without the engineer's consent and special provisions known as 'vesting clauses' that confer a proprietary right or a security interest in the plant in the employer until completion. There is considerable variety in these clauses and it is hard to generalize on their effect. The only recent English authority is *Re Cosslett Contractors* [1997] 4 All ER 117, CA, affirmed, sub. nom. *Smith* v. *Bridgend County Borough Council* [2002] BLR 160, HL, which is the starting point on any discussion of vesting clauses and their effect. Very broadly, the relevant principles are as follows.

(a) If the contract says the title passes on delivery of the plant to site, it will be treated as an absolute transfer to the employer (*Bennett & White* v. *Municipal District of Sugar City* [1951] AC 786).
(b) If, instead of a clear transfer, the contract 'deems' the plant to be the employer's property for the purposes of the contract, the contract will be treated as ambiguous and subject to rules of construction (*Re Cosslett Contractors* [1997] 4 All ER 117).
(c) If the court concludes that, notwithstanding the ambiguity, the parties did intend to create a proprietary right, it will so hold (*Brown* v. *Bateman* (1867) LR 2 CP 272).
(d) Otherwise, the provision will be treated as having no legal effect, leaving it to the employer to rely on any protection in the termination clause (*Re Keen & Keen, ex parte Collins* [1902] 1 KB 555).

In *Re Cosslett Contractors* itself, the court had to consider Clause 53 (vesting) and Clause 63 (termination) of the ICE Conditions (5th Edition). It held that the vesting clause was too uncertain to pass title and that the power of sale in the termination clause constituted a floating charge, which was not binding on the administrator of a contractor for want of registration under Section 395 of the Companies Act 1985. Nevertheless, the termination clause remained contractually binding on the contractor and the employer was entitled to use the plant to have the works completed. The employer sold the plant to the completion contractor and the administrator obtained substantial damages in conversion: *Smith* v. *Bridgend County Borough Council* [2002] BLR 160, HL. Other standard forms have subtly different provisions.[12] Vesting clauses are challenged in various situations, e.g. where termination is disputed, that they amount to a penalty, or infringe the *pari passu* rule, or where a claim is made in conversion, but not, it seems, on the ground that the clause is invalid as an unregistered bill of sale (see *Reeves* v. *Barlow* (1884) 12 QBD 436).

7.3 Retention

Retention is an informal security protecting the employer against the contractor's default. Some contracts restrict the cross-claims which the employer can make against retention while others preserve it as an asset of the contractor freely available for set-off by the employer on whatever ground. Retention accrues gradually as the contract proceeds until half is released at practical completion and the balance paid to the contractor on making good of defects. Where the employer agrees not to withhold retention in consideration of the contractor procuring a retention bond in the on demand form, the contractor obtains the benefit of improved cash flow but at some risk to itself. For example, the amount of the bond may not accrue gradually but be for the total amount of retention from the outset. Also, any contractual limitations on the employer's right of set-off against retention are not likely, in the absence of express provision, to restrict the employer's rights to make demands under the bond (*Costain International* v. *Davy McKee* (unreported, 25 November 1990)). Conversely, where retention is withheld but made subject to a trust in favour of the contractor, the court has, in some cases, construed the employer's rights of set-off as restricted in scope to such amount of the retention as represents money earned by the contractor as opposed to proportions attributable to work done by subcontractors. This is considered later.

7.4 Insolvency and bonds

As insolvency is not likely to be a breach of contract, the beneficiary of a conditional bond containing a secondary obligation has no claim against the bondsman until the contractor's insolvency results in a breach. In contracts providing for termination on the contractor's insolvency, the only breach which can occur is of the contractor's duty to pay such sum as may be found due to the employer after setting off the expenses incurred in having the works finished by another contractor (*Perar* v. *General Surety* (1994) 67 BLR 72).

If the beneficiary of a bond needs cash flow rather than certainty of payment at the end of the day, it needs an on demand form of bond, a hybrid bond entitling it to a payment on account or to insert an expedited form of dispute procedure. In *Balfour Beatty* v. *Technical & General Guarantee* (1999) 68 Con LR 180, CA, a contractor obtained an on demand bond in support of a subcontractor's performance under the FCEC conditions. The bondsman had to pay on receipt of the contractor's first written demand 'stating that the Sub-Contractor has failed to fulfil its obligations under the said Sub-Contract and that the sum demanded is due and payable and such demand shall be accepted by the Surety as conclusive evidence that the sum of demand is due hereunder'. The subcontractor went into liquidation and the contractor called the bond in full. The subcontractor failed in an attempt to prevent the bondsman from paying on the ground that the demand was fraudulent since liquidation of itself was not a breach (and presumably that the subcontractor had not failed to perform its obligations in some other way). The court commented:

> 'Whereas going into liquidation may not be a breach of contract in most cases, I am not sure . . . whether on the terms of this contract that is right. I am clear that [the subcontractor] could not succeed on this point unless he could show first that it was unarguably right that liquidation was not a default under the contract, and that the plaintiffs did not honestly believe that the breach of contract they described as a breach, was a breach. . . . It is only if the fraud exception applies that the surety could resist payment on this bond'.

Unfortunately, the Court of Appeal did not give any reasons why liquidation could have been a breach of contract in this case. The subcontractor's evidence did not even give rise to an arguable case of fraud.

8 SECURITY FOR PAYMENT

Virtually the whole focus of protection against insolvency concerns security for performance. Insolvency risk is perceived almost exclusively from the perspective of the paying party. A study carried out in 1998 found that only 6% of contracts had any form of security for payment. The authors concluded:

> '[Security for payment] would reduce risk and uncertainty in the industry and, consequently, lead to greater efficiency. It is likely that it would reduce the number of insolvencies or at least ensure that those who became insolvent did so from their own fault rather than the fault of those who employed them . . . Perhaps the industry should be less defensive about performance protection and more pro-active about security for payment'.[13]

Even where the contract obliges the employer to provide security on request, the contractor may not ask for it in order to avoid upsetting the employer. Another survey found, for example, that employers under JCT forms found requests to place retention into a separate account 'insulting'.[14]

Security for payment takes various forms depending on whether the mechanism is intended as the primary means of payment or as secondary protection against non-payment: see Table 4. Letters of credit are used in construction, especially on international projects. They entitle the beneficiary to payment on production of specified documents. Problems occur where the issuer of the document is the supervising officer under the contract and he or she has not been paid or where his or her duty to issue the document is not laid down in the contract: see, for example, *Lovell Construction* v. *Independent Estates* [1994] 1 BCLC 31. Other difficulties arise where the issuer is beyond the control of the employer.

Similar problems occur where the employer agrees to pay the contract sum into a bank account subject to specific terms for its release as the works proceed (escrow account) or to its being held in trust on specific terms (trust account). The difference between the two is that failure to operate an escrow account gives rise only to a claim for damages for breach of contract whereas as a beneficiary under a trust the contractor has additional protection in the equitable remedies of tracing and claims for breach of trust which can extend beyond the parties to the contract. Ideally, the precise terms of the arrangement will be carefully negotiated and properly drafted. They can either be contained in a separate agreement or included in the contract, but whichever approach is taken it is

Table 4 Security for payment

Means of payment	Letter of credit Escrow account Trust
Protection against non-payment	Third-party bond or guarantee Parent company guarantee Formal security Contractual term

essential that the operation of the account be fully integrated with the contract terms for payment. In *Lovell Construction* v. *Independent Estates* [1994] 1 BCLC 31 the employer's agreement to channel payment of the contract sum through a trust account was evidenced partly by a separate agreement and partly through amendments to the payment and termination clauses of JCT 81 and a letter from the employer and the contractor to their respective solicitors who were to act as trustees of the account. The employer went into liquidation and the contractor successfully claimed payment from the account. One of the difficulties stemmed from the fact that, after the contract had been terminated, the trust agreement required the contractor to produce a certificate from the architect of the amount it was entitled to claim, but the parties had failed to confer the power to issue such a certificate under the contract. The liquidator also argued that the arrangement amounted to a floating charge over the account which was invalid for want of registration under Section 395 of the Companies Act 1985 (with effect from 1 October 2009 re-enacted by Part 25 of the Companies Act 2006). The court held that the trust account was the means of payment rather than a security for payment and therefore did not require registration.

Using a trust as the means of payment can have a further advantage in addition to conferring the right to equitable tracing and personal remedies for breach of trust such as 'knowing receipt' and 'knowing assistance'. This appears from *Rafidain Bank* v. *Saipem* (unreported, 2 March 1994) which concerned a contract between an Italian consortium and the Iraqi Government which, in essence, was a barter of construction services in return for oil. The contractor built a pipeline for one agency of the Iraqi Government who then supplied oil to another state agency who sold it to an associated company of the contractor who paid for the oil in US dollars by remitting payment to an escrow account in London, from which the contractor was paid on production of documents to the trustees of the account. Among other things, these documents consisted of tax clearance certificates which the contractor had to obtain from yet another Iraqi state authority. After completion, the contractor sought payment of the second half of retention but, before the certificates could be issued, the Gulf war broke out and the pipeline was destroyed.

It appears that the employer did not dispute that the work had been properly done and local taxes paid, but the contractor could not obtain the relevant certificates. The court took a two-stage approach. First, it examined the position in contract. It found that the production of the certificates was a condition precedent for payment from the account and the contractor's claim would fail if that were its only ground. It then asked whether the imposition of a trust made any difference. The court held that, since the contractor had obtained an immediate equitable proprietary interest in the account, the production of the certificates was just an administrative detail. Payment from the account in London was ordered notwithstanding the absence of the certificates. The case shows how overlaying a trust over the contractual matrix can enlarge the court's jurisdiction to deal with what is essentially a contractual claim.

Whether the escrow or the trust approach is taken, problems can arise because the parties have failed to define with sufficient clarity the purpose for which the account has been set up. This is especially so where the arrangement is only agreed right at the end of the contract negotiations. In *Bouygues* v. *Shanghai Links* [1998] 2 HKLRD 479, the employer was a company formed under the law of the PRC for the sole purpose of the development. The contractor did not want to prejudice its prospects of winning the contract by raising the question of security for payment at tender stage. Instead, the issue was left until the end of the negotiations on the contract terms. It was finally agreed that the contractor's duty to start work would be conditional on acceptable terms for payment being reached. Owing to the delicacy of the situation, the contractor accepted letters from lawyers acting for the employer's parent company and investors to the parent confirming that they would comply with an agreement between the parent, investors and the employer that funds required to pay the contract sum of US$33.25 million would be deposited into an account at Standard Chartered Bank in Hong Kong. The letters continued: 'Payment of the contract price under the contract will be made from this account and funds can be paid out of this account by the signature of Barry Hansen and one other director of the [parent]'.

The contractor accepted the letters in lieu of a payment guarantee. Relations between contractor and employer later broke down and there were mutual allegations of termination and monetary cross-claims which were referred to arbitration. The contractor failed in a claim for a declaration that the parent held the account either on trust to pay whatever was found due to the contractor once all disputes with the employer had been resolved or on terms that it would not withdraw funds from the account other than to pay sums due under the construction contract. The parent argued that the letters were merely letters of comfort without any legal effect. The court concluded that the letters were contractually binding but the obligation undertaken by the parent and the investors was limited to ensuring payment from the account of sums due for performing the works but not of sums which might become due to the contractor after the contract had been terminated. The language was not sufficiently clear to amount to a trust and there was a danger that the project might not be completed unless the money in the account could be made available to finance a completion contract.

For a comparison between the trust agreement used in *Lovell Construction* v. *Independent Estates*, the optional trust clause in The Engineering and Construction Contract (omitted from the 3rd edition, 1995), the trust proposed by Sir Michael Latham,[15] and the SEACC standard form, see Davis (1996).[16] Where money is advanced to a contractor for the specific purpose of enabling it to pay its creditors and the contractor fails to do so, the money is held on resulting trust for the employer: see e.g. *Re Niagara Mechanical Services International* [2000] 2 BCLC 425, where the contractor went into administration and negotiated a payment with the employer intended for a specialist subcontractor in order to procure the commissioning of air conditioning equipment. The administrator kept the payment, applying it towards sums otherwise due to the contractor, but had to repay it to the employer.

Where the account is not intended as the means of payment, it will probably be regarded as a form of protection against non-payment. It is possible for the employer to offer formal security for payment using one of the recognized devices of mortgage, charge, lien or pledge. Of these, the most often encountered is the charge, often a second or third charge over the site being developed. A more practical alternative is for the employer to procure a bond or guarantee from a third party, such as a bank or a specialist insurance company, or a parent company guarantee. Otherwise the contractor has to rely on its normal contractual terms for protection, e.g. rights of set-off, suspension or termination.

8.1 Retention trusts

As a result of the intensive negotiations between industry bodies in the 1920s, a consensus emerged that it was reasonable for the contractor to receive security for payment of its retention. This was initially conferred by an optional clause in the RIBA 1931 form, a precursor to JCT 63. This obliged the employer, on the architect's certificate, to open a trust account in the joint names of itself and the contractor once the retention reached £1000. On completion, or if the employer became insolvent or repudiated the contract, the retention and accrued interest were to be paid to the contractor. Owing to the special status of nominated subcontractors, the Green Form of subcontract included a clause stating that the contractor's interest in the retention withheld by the employer was 'fiduciary as trustee for the subcontractor'. In *Re Tout and Finch* [1954] 1 All ER 127, these words were construed as creating a trust operating 'by way of an equitable assignment of assets described as the contractor's interest in the retention money' (at page 134). The nominated subcontractors in that case obtained a declaration that, on receipt of their proportion of retention from the employer, the liquidator appointed to the contractor was obliged to pass it immediately to them.

The introduction of the trust into an agreement as complex as a construction contract has not been easy. There have been five cases in the Court of Appeal on the JCT retention trust in the last 25 years. In practice, the problems come down to two questions.

(a) Is the trust created by the terms of the contract alone, or does a separate fund have to be set aside, and if so when?
(b) How do the employer's rights of recourse against retention under the contract square with its duties as trustee? Are they exercisable against the proportions attributable to subcontractors?

While the first of these issues has largely been resolved, the second is still in a somewhat confused state.

8.2 Constituting the trust

When preparing the 1963 edition, the JCT drafting committee abandoned the optional clause in the 1931 form and instead adapted wording taken from the Green Form. The JCT 63 trust Clause 30 stated that:

> 'The Employer's interest in any amount so retained shall be fiduciary as trustee for the Contractor (but without obligation to invest), and the Contractor's beneficial interest therein shall be subject only to the right of the Employer to have recourse thereto from time to time for payment of any amount which he is entitled under the provisions of this Contract to deduct from any sums due or to become due to the Contractor'.

When used in the Green Form, the trust property consisted in the contractor's rights against the employer to payment of retention. Under JCT 63, however, there is no apparent trust property because the 'amount so retained' is a conditional debt owed to the contractor; it is not the employer's property and cannot therefore be the subject of a trust created by the employer.[17] The clause was therefore construed as imposing 'an obligation on an employer to appropriate and set aside as a separate trust fund a sum equal to that part of the sum certified in any interim certificate as due in respect of work completed which the employer is entitled to retain during the defects liability period' (*Rayack Construction* v. *Lampeter Meat* (1979) 12 BLR 30 at 37). In that case the court granted an injunction ordering the employer to open a new account and pay into it an amount equivalent to the retention.

Unless a separate account is opened there is no trust, only a contract to create a trust for which specific performance will be ordered by way of injunction. The question arises whether the court will grant an injunction where the employer is insolvent. Different criteria apply depending on whether the insolvency is formal or informal, and which insolvency procedure is involved. It may well be impossible for the court to tell, on hearing an application for an injunction, whether the employer's insolvency is temporary or final. The court is sometimes nervous about issuing an injunction in this situation for fear of preferring the contractor over the general body of creditors, e.g. *MacJordan Construction* v. *Brookmount Erostin* (1992) 56 BLR 1 at 16. It is true that an action taken in pursuance of a court order can amount to a preference (Section 239(7) of the Insolvency Act 1986), but to refuse an injunction to constitute a trust simply because there are doubts about the employer's solvency goes against the court's normal policy of *laissez faire* in this situation. Provided liquidation has not intervened, the court is always ready to assist one creditor over another in perfecting its rights: see *Roberts Petroleum* v. *Kenny* [1983] 2 AC 192, discussed in Lightman and Moss.[18]

Where a company is informally insolvent but, at the time that the contractor applies to the court for an injunction, a winding-up petition has been issued, the position may be different. If it is by no means clear that the employer is insolvent, the court may grant the injunction leaving it to the court with jurisdiction over the winding-up to discharge it later as a post-petition disposition under Section 127 of the Insolvency Act 1986, by analogy with *Re Flint* [1993] Ch 319. Where the employer is already in liquidation, whether voluntary or compulsory, the court will refuse an application for an injunction: see *Re Jartay Developments* (1982) 22 BLR 134. This is because, on the commencement of a liquidation, a statutory trust is imposed on all the assets of the company in favour of the general body of creditors (*Re Ayerst* v. *C&K (Construction) Limited* [1976] AC 167). There is, therefore, no property from which the company could comply with an injunction. Where the company is in members' voluntary liquidation, the position ought to be different as this is intended as a means of dissolving a solvent company. However, it is not likely that an application would be made since the directors would normally have provided for the satisfactory conclusion of any long-term contractual liabilities when swearing the declaration of solvency.

The Court of Appeal has held that, in normal circumstances, an application for an injunction will be refused if made after the commencement of an administrative receivership: see *MacJordan Construction* v. *Brookmount Erostin* (1992) 56 BLR 1. In this case, MacJordan was carrying out work under JCT 81 terms. Before completion, the employer went into administrative receivership and the contractor's employment was automatically terminated. It transpired that the employer had £150 000 in a bank account with Barclays. The contractor was owed retention of £110 000 and claimed additional sums following the termination. The receivers had been appointed by Generale Bank pursuant to a floating charge granted by the employer in consideration of a loan to fund the development. Generale had made it a condition of the loan that it approve the terms of the building contract and receive a certified copy. MacJordan argued that, although receivers had been appointed, an injunction should still be granted because the floating charge had been taken subject to a prior equity, namely its right to have retention funded. In refusing MacJordan's application, the court had to compare the nature of a floating charge with MacJordan's contractual right.

It held that, at any time before the receivers were appointed, it would have been prepared to grant an injunction against Brookmount. This would have been entirely consistent with the floating charge which authorized the borrower to take any steps in regard to the charged assets which were in the ordinary course of business. Not only was the funding of retention under JCT contracts such a step, but Generale must be taken to have had express knowledge of it since it had approved the terms of the contract. The appointment of the receivers took effect as an equitable assignment to Generale of all the employer's property including the bank account at Barclays. After their appointment, therefore, the employer had no property from which to comply with its contractual obligation to set retention aside. Specific performance would not be ordered against the receivers personally in this situation. On the receivership, the employer was not even in breach of contract under JCT 81 since that form derogated from the absolute obligation to create a trust of retention (*Wates Construction* v. *Franthom* (1991) 53 BLR 23) by inserting the requirement to do so only on the contractor's request, which had not been made. It followed that, before the receivers were appointed, MacJordan had a contractual right to have a trust created and Generale had an inchoate security interest in the body of assets falling within the charge, but that on their appointment, MacJordan's contractual right became unenforceable and Generale's rights over Brookmount's property were perfected by an automatic equitable assignment by operation of law.

The position where the employer goes into administration has not yet been clarified by the court.

8.3 Rights of recourse

The distinction between a contractual right against another person and an equitable interest by way of trust in a person's property is also relevant when considering the extent of the employer's rights of set-off against retention once it has been set aside. At common law, the employer has wide rights of set-off against retention unless they have been excluded by the contract. In equity, the employer as trustee has no rights in the retention fund apart from those conferred by the contract. It must follow that the employer, by giving the contractor security for payment in this way, has agreed to limit its rights of recourse to those expressly or impliedly set out in the contract. If the employer's cross-claim has already arisen by the time the contractor asks for a fund to be set aside, the court is not likely to grant an injunction (*Henry Boot* v. *The Croydon Hotel* (1985) 36 BLR 41).

The question arises whether the imposition of a trust prevents the employer from setting off against those proportions of retention withheld in respect of subcontractors' work. The doctrine of privity of contract means that the employer can only ever owe a debt to the contractor rather than the subcontractors. Even though the contractor may withhold retention from the subcontractors which, when aggregated, is the same as the retention withheld by the employer, the two are entirely separate debts. It follows that, if the employer has a cross-claim which can be exercised against retention, it can do so against the whole retention withheld against the contractor which must of necessity include sums equating to retentions withheld by the contractor from subcontractors. A trust ought to make no difference to this as the employer's rights of recourse are an inherent restriction on the contractor's retention, i.e. on the property which the contractor offers as subject matter of the subcontract trusts. Retention is a conditional debt defeasible by the employer's rights of recourse. Making it trust property should not affect these intrinsic limitations.[19]

However, in *Re Arthur Sanders* (1981) 17 BLR 125, it was held that a proportion of retention withheld by the employer which was attributable to work by nominated subcontractors could not be said to be 'due' to the contractor at all. 'To hold otherwise would necessarily involve the consequences that the subcontractors were deprived of the security which this elaborate scheme of things was clearly intended to give them at the very moment when they most needed it, that is to say on the insolvency of the contractor' (at 140). However, the court did not have to reach this conclusion in order to dispose of the issue in the case since the employer was attempting to set-off a cross-claim on one contract which it had with the contractor against retention withheld on another. The contractor being in liquidation, the employer's cross-claim would normally have qualified for liquidation set-off, but not in this case because the imposition of a trust restricted the employer's rights of set-off to those exercisable against claims arising under the same contract (*Hsin Chong* v. *Yaton Realty* (1986) 40 BLR 119 at 129).

The notion that proportions of retention attributable to subcontractors are not 'due' to the contractor also found favour with the Court of Appeal in *Harrington* v. *Co Partnership* (1998) 88 BLR 44 in which retention of about £300 000 withheld against a management contractor's fee and works contract sums had been aside into a fund before the management contractor went into administrative receivership. The architect certified that the employer's additional loss in having the works completed amounted to £650 000 which the employer set off against the retention. It was agreed that the contractor had no cross-claim against that works contractor on its own account. The Court of Appeal held this to be wrongful and allowed a claim made by one of the works contractors for its retention of about £20 000. There are several unsatisfactory aspects to this decision,[20] the most puzzling being that the Court of Appeal interpreted the trust as limiting the employer's rights of recourse to the retention withheld against the management contractor's fee. This appears to negate the whole purpose of retention from the employer's point of view. The Scottish court seems to take a different view of the matter (see *Balfour Beatty* v. *Britannia Life* [1997] SLT (OH) 10), although there a trust had been constituted by the time the management contractor went into receivership.

REFERENCES

1. Lightman, G. and Moss, G. *The law of administrators and receivers of companies*. Sweet and Maxwell, London, 2007, 4th edn, ch. 29.
2. Totty, P. and Moss, G. *Insolvency*. Sweet & Maxwell, London, 1986, (looseleaf), ch. H19.
3. Davis, R. *Construction insolvency: security, risk and renewal in construction contracts*. Sweet & Maxwell, London, 2008, 3rd edn, para. 18-003.
4. Totty, P. and Moss, G. *Insolvency*. Sweet & Maxwell, London, 1986, (looseleaf), para H4.06.
5. Oditah, F. Assets and the treatment of claims in insolvency. *Law Quarterly Review*, 1992, **108**, 459.
6. McCormack, G. *Proprietary claims and insolvency*. Sweet and Maxwell, London, 1997.
7. Davis, R. *Construction insolvency: security, risk and renewal in construction contracts*. Sweet & Maxwell, London, 2008, 3rd edn, para. 14-09.
8. Newman, P. *Insolvency explained*. RIBA Publications, 1992.
9. Joint Contracts Tribunal/Society of Practitioners of Insolvency. *Practice Note 24: for use by Employers in the event of the insolvency of the Main Contractor*. RIBA Publications, 1992.
10. Davis, R. *Construction insolvency: security, risk and renewal in construction contracts*. Sweet & Maxwell, London, 2008, 3rd edn, chapters 2, 6, 7, 10 and 19.
11. Newman, P. *Bonds, guarantees and performance security in the construction industry*. Jordans, 1999.
12. Barber, P. (Palmer, N. and McKendrick, E. (eds)) 'Title to goods, materials and plant under construction contracts', in *Interests in goods*. LLP, 1998, 2nd edn.

13. Hughes, W. *et al. Financial protection in the UK building industry*. E&FN Spon, 1998.
14. Hopper, R. (Davis, R. and Odams, A. M. (eds)) 'Construction sector retention survey', in *Security for payment*. Construction Law Press, King's College London, 1996.
15. Latham, M. *Constructing the team*. HMSO, London, 1994.
16. Davis, R. (Davis, R. and Odams, A. M. (eds)) 'Payment Issues and Legislation', in *Security for payment*. Construction Law Press, King's College London, 1996. (See also the trust deed annexed as Appendix A (project bank account) to the *Guide to Best "Fair Payment" Practices* (2007), Office of Government Commerce. http://www.ogc.gov.uk
17. Hayton, D. J. 'The significance of equity in construction contracts'. *Construction Law Yearbook*, 1994, **2**, 19.
18. Lightman, G. and Moss, G. *The law of administrators and receivers of companies*. Sweet and Maxwell, London, 2007, 4th edn, ch. 25.
19. Hayton, D. J. 'The significance of equity in construction contracts'. *Construction Law Yearbook*, 1994, **2**.
20. Davis, R. *Construction insolvency: security, risk and renewal in construction contracts*. Sweet & Maxwell, London, 2008, 3rd edn, para. 10-007.

CHAPTER 3.4

Law of tort

Graham Chapman
Barrister, Four New Square

Emilie Jones
Barrister, Four New Square

The law of tort, much like the law of contract, imposes obligations on individuals towards other individuals giving rights to the latter against the former. These rights and obligations arise independently of any contract but instead are derived in the main from the common law (the product of decisions by the court) or alternatively from statute law enacted by Parliament.

The law of tort is broad in its compass and covers a wide spectrum of wrongs including trespass, assault, libel and statutory torts. Some civil torts are also criminal offences. A criminal offence will arise from obligations that are owed to the state at large and proceedings are usually brought by the state. The civil wrong, in contrast, arises from obligations owed by certain individuals to certain other individuals or groups of individuals. The wronged individual is usually the person who brings proceedings against the wrongdoer or 'tortfeasor' in respect of the 'tortious' duty or obligation that is said to have been breached. This chapter examines the various areas of tortious liability and types of tortious duty in so far as they impact on the construction industry.

1 NEGLIGENCE

The tort of negligence gives rise to the widest range of tortious duties. For a cause of action in negligence to arise:

(a) there must be a duty of care owed by the tortfeasor to the injured person,
(b) a breach of that duty of care must have taken place, and
(c) that breach must have caused the injured person to suffer loss.

The word 'injured' is used here to signify that the person has suffered some form of loss or damage and is not intended to suggest that tortious duties are in any way limited to the realm of personal injury. Indeed, the range of duties in tort is vast and, given this, it might be thought strange that until 1932 a single tort of negligence did not exist. Liability for negligent conduct was recognised only in discrete categories where particular circumstances were said to give rise to a 'duty of care'. Often these situations were readily identified as being akin to those where a contract would be said to arise. Today, identifying when a duty of care will arise can still be a difficult exercise.

1.1 Duty of care

The origin of the modern law of the tort of negligence is the decision of the House of Lords in *Donoghue* v. *Stevenson* [1932] AC 562. In this case, which famously concerned a snail in a bottle of ginger beer, the House of Lords sought to set out a single theory of negligence. This was based on what became known as the 'neighbourhood principle':

> 'The rule that you are to love your neighbour becomes in law, you must not injure your neighbour; and the lawyer's question, who is my neighbour? receives a restricted reply. You must take reasonable care to avoid acts or omissions which you can reasonably foresee would be likely to injure your neighbour. Who, then, in law is my neighbour? The answer seems to be – persons who are so closely and directly affected by my act that I ought reasonably to have them in contemplation as being so affected when I am directing my mind to the acts or omissions which are called in question' (Lord Atkin at 580).

In other words, a duty of care (on the facts of *Donoghue* not to cause personal injury to others) is owed by an individual to other persons whom that individual ought to foresee might be injured by a particular act or omission. Thus, the establishment of a duty of care was founded on the reasonably foreseeable consequences of an individual's acts and omissions and the test of 'reasonable foreseeability' became known as the touchstone of liability in negligence. However, the *Donoghue* case did not lead to an explosion of litigation or a rapid and extensive expansion in tortious liability. Rather, new areas or 'pockets' of liability were established by the courts on a case-by-case basis with each new area being relatively confined to specific factual scenarios.

Then, in *Anns* v. *Merton London Borough Council* [1978] AC 728, the House of Lords attempted to lay down a simple two-stage test for the existence of all liability in negligence. The leading judgment was given by Lord Wilberforce who set out the test as follows, at 751, 752:

> '... the question has to be approached in two stages. First one has to ask whether, as between the alleged wrongdoer and the person who has suffered damage, there is sufficient relationship of proximity or neighbourhood such that, in the reasonable contemplation of the former, carelessness on his part may be likely to cause damage to the latter – in which case a prima facie duty of care arises. Secondly, if the first question is answered affirmatively, it is necessary to consider whether there are any considerations which ought to negative, or to reduce or limit the scope of the duty or the class of person to whom it is owed or the damages to which a breach of it may give rise.'

Thus, the two elements for the establishment of a duty of care were:

(i) reasonable foreseeability of the type of loss suffered, and
(ii) the absence of any consideration of public policy to negative or limit the scope of the duty or to whom it was owed.

This test was criticised for essentially establishing a presumption of liability where the defendant ought to have foreseen injury to the claimant, unless public policy dictates otherwise. Not surprisingly, the scope of the tort of negligence widened as a result of the decision and new areas of liability were established. Still less surprising is that in the face of these developments the courts have retreated from the *Anns* approach.

In *Murphy* v. *Brentwood District Council* [1991] AC 398 the House of Lords effectively overturned *Anns*, particularly in so far as it applied to duties of care owed by local authorities. Lord Keith expressed the view that Lord Wilberforce's test should not be treated as being definitive, and emphasised the importance of finding a relationship of 'proximity'. In *Caparo Industries plc* v. *Dickman* [1990] 2 AC 605, a three-stage test was established.

What emerges from *Caparo* is that, in addition to the foreseeability of damage, necessary ingredients in any situation giving rise to a duty of care are that there should exist between the party owing the duty and the party to whom it is owed a relationship characterised by the law as one of 'proximity' or 'neighbourhood' and that the situation should be one in which the court considers it fair, just and reasonable that the law should impose a duty of a given scope on the one party for the benefit of the other (per Lord Bridge at 617, 618).

Therefore, the three elements for finding that a duty of care is owed were established as being:

- foreseeability
- proximity
- fair, just and reasonableness.

However, as Lord Bridge himself admitted, such concepts should not be treated as a rigid formula and are, in fact, no more than 'useful labels' employed by the courts when examining the policy considerations of whether or not to impose a duty of care in a given case. Such policy considerations are not limited to the effects of the imposition of the duty as between the two parties before the court, but include the effect of imposing a duty of care on all other members of society in the same position as the parties currently before the court.

Importantly for the construction industry, the courts have encountered less difficulty in imposing duties of care in situations where physical loss – be it to person or property – has been caused than where only financial or purely economic loss has been suffered. It is in this latter area that policy considerations have particularly exercised the courts, which have adopted a more cautious and restrictive approach so as to limit the boundaries of liability. This is based on the fear that a less restrictive approach would open the 'flood-gates' of liability such that tortfeasors would be flooded with substantial claims for pure economic loss (for example, loss of profits) by others which would be difficult to bear.

It is still arguable (despite a recent willingness by the courts to allow the recovery of economic loss) that the general rule is that pure economic loss is not recoverable in an action for negligence, or at least is not as readily recoverable as personal injury or property damage losses. The application of this rule is most readily seen in the situation where the defendant's alleged negligence causes damage to property which does not belong to the claimant, but which, because of an interest which the claimant has in that property, causes the claimant loss.

Thus, in *Spartan Steel and Alloys Ltd* v. *Martin & Co. Ltd* [1973] QB 27 the defendant negligently cut through an electric cable which did not belong to the claimant, but which supplied the claimant with electricity for his metal processing plant. The claimant was not able to claim for the lost profits caused by closing his business for the day while the electricity supply was disrupted, but was able to claim for damage caused to the metal being processed at the time the electricity was cut off, this being economic loss flowing directly from damage to the claimant's property.

In the construction industry a more difficult case is where defects arise in products and buildings. The courts have held that, where a product or building is defective, and the only loss occasioned is the cost of repairing or replacing that property when the defect is discovered, this is irrecoverable on the basis that it is pure economic loss. The manufacturer, builder or designer of the product or building will not be liable (because it owes no duty to take care so as not to cause purely economic loss) unless the defect causes damage to other property, or personal injury (in respect of which a duty is owed). The application of this rule can be seen in *Murphy* v. *Brentwood District Council* [1991] AC 398 in which the claimant suffered loss because the foundations of his house were defective which led to subsidence and cracking. The loss suffered on the subsequent sale of the house was not recoverable because the damage had been caused to the building itself ('the defective product') and not to other property. (However, now see the Defective Premises Act 1972 which is considered in Section 6 of this chapter.)

The 'other property' argument was argued in the recent case of *Baxall* v. *Sheard Walshaw* [2002] CILL 1837 but addressed general questions about duty of care and causation in negligence. In relation to duty of care, the Court of Appeal held that such a duty can be owed to future tenants of a building (See also *Turner* v. *Watkins* (TCC, 9 November 2001)). In this case, the claim was for damage to equipment inside a building due to two floods caused by leaking gutters and drains. Baxall, the current building tenant claimed that the original architect (Sheard Walshaw) owed all future owners a duty of care to design the drainage system so as to avoid damage to the contents of the building.

A possible exception to the general rule that pure economic loss is only recoverable where damage has been caused to other property might be found in what has become known as the 'complex structure' argument. From one point of view this is not in fact an exception to the rule laid down in *Murphy* at all but an application of it as it rests on how 'other property' is defined. In short, the complex structure argument demands that a building be treated as being the sum of its many parts with each part being regarded as distinct so that damage caused by one part of the building to another part of the same building can be classified as damage to 'other property'. The origin of this theory lies in *D & F Estates Ltd* v. *Church Commissioners* [1989] AC 177 but it has not been adopted and developed by the courts; indeed the Court of Appeal in *Warner* v. *Basildon* (1990) Constr LJ 46 has suggested that such a theory has no place in English law. However, this view was not expressed in *Murphy* v. *Brentwood* itself (which was decided the day after the Court of Appeal case) and four of their Lordships thought that such a theory might have some role to play in the future. At present, the theory seems unlikely to be allowed to develop as in *Tunnel Refineries* v. *Brya Donkin* (1998) CILL 1392 the Recorder held that he was bound by the Court of Appeal's decision in *Warner*, and in *Tesco* v. *The Norman Hitchcox Partnership* (1997) 56 ConLR 42 the judge refused to apply the theory. Nevertheless, it is as well for those in the construction industry to be aware that such an argument exists.

It has been argued that a further possible exception to the rule in *Murphy* can be found in *Junior Books* v. *Veitchi* [1983] AC 520. In this case, the defendants were found to have been negligent in laying a defective floor at the claimant's factory and were held liable in damages for the cost of re-laying the floor and also for consequential financial loss suffered by the claimant. However, it is difficult to reconcile this judgment with the reasoning in the later case of *Murphy* and the status of the decision is therefore uncertain. It is likely that *Junior Books* will be confined to its own facts and the decision justified on the basis that the relationship between the parties was so close as to be akin to contract.

The courts have exhibited a more relaxed approach to the recovery of economic loss outside the building sphere. In particular, the courts have been prepared to sanction the recovery of purely economic loss where it has been caused by a negligent statement.[1] It was thought that such a relaxed approach would not apply where the loss had been caused by negligent acts or the supply of negligent services. However, since *Henderson* v. *Merrett* [1994] 3 All ER 506 it now seems clear that liability for negligent statements and liability for the performance of negligent services is governed by the same test: that of 'assumption of responsibility'. The impact of this might be particularly felt by professionals working in the construction industry such as engineers and architects who supply services rather than labour or materials.

It is certainly arguable that the three-stage *Caparo* test has now been left behind and that, motivated by a need to incrementally extend the boundaries of liability (particularly in the area of pure economic loss) without opening the floodgates, the courts have adopted a pragmatic approach which entails simply deciding whether it is fair to impose a duty on the facts of a particular case. This simple process is then screened by result-pulled reasoning that may or may not employ some of Lord Bridge's 'labels' to mask what is essentially a policy decision taken by the court. The current label that is most fashionably used by the courts is 'assumption of responsibility'. This may be a

[1] See *Hedley Byrne & Co Ltd* v. *Heller & Partners Ltd* [1964] AC 465 and *White* v. *Jones* [1995] 2 AC 507.

facet of proximity or reasonable foreseeability or both. In practice it does not really matter much as the courts will decide on the facts and having weighed questions of policy whether or not one party has assumed responsibility toward another.

So in what situations will a duty of care be imposed to take care not to cause purely economic loss? It seems that there are three such situations.

(a) 'Quasi-contractual': that is where a direct contractual relationship exists between the claimant and defendant or where the relationship between the two of them is such that it is at least quasi-contractual.
(b) 'Negligent misstatement': where the defendant has made a negligent statement to (or for the benefit of) the claimant in circumstances where the defendant knows that the claimant may rely on that statement to his or her detriment and the claimant does in fact so rely on the statement and sustains loss.
(c) 'Provision of services': where the defendant is retained by another party to provide (usually professional) services and is or should be aware that those services are for the benefit of the claimant third party (i.e. not a party to the contract) who is likely to suffer economic loss if the service is performed negligently (see for example *White* v. *Jones* [1995] 2 AC 507).

It is in the last two of these three situations that the language of 'assumption of responsibility' is most often employed. In practice, whatever the language used, there is little to choose between the *Caparo* 'three-stage test' or the 'assumption of responsibility' test. However, the use of 'assumption of responsibility' in the last two situations serves to illustrate that for liability to arise in these circumstances there must be a readily identifiable assumption of responsibility on the part of the defendant. Put another way (or to use the *Caparo* test), there must be a very close relationship of proximity between defendant and claimant for a duty of care to be imposed. This will certainly be the case where the defendant undertakes to render a service or statement which is designed to confer on the claimant the economic benefit of which he or she has been deprived as a result of the defendant's negligence, or is designed to protect the claimant from the same kind of economic loss as has been suffered. In such circumstances, an assumption of responsibility on the part of the defendant will be readily identifiable. This type of assumption of responsibility now often provides the touchstone of liability at the frontiers of the law of tort where it is unclear whether a duty of care should be imposed.

In *Tesco Stores Ltd* v. *Costain Construction Ltd* [2003] EWHC 1487 (TCC); (2003) CILL 2062 the court found that a building contractor did owe a duty of care to his employer not to cause economic loss. *Tesco* clarifies what many have long suspected namely that:

(a) *Murphy* v. *Brentwood District Council* [1991] 1 AC 398 did *not* decide that a builder/contractor will *never* owe a duty of care not to cause economic loss to his employer/the building owner. To the extent that HHJ Humphrey Lloyd QC found to the contrary in *Samuel Payne* v. *John Setchell Ltd* [2002] BLR 489 then he was wrong to do so and his judgment ought not to be followed.
(b) Rather, *Murphy* decided that a duty not to cause economic loss will not be owed in the absence of a special relationship between builder and employer.
(c) Such a special relationship will exist where the builder consciously undertakes a responsibility for design under the terms of his contract: *Storey* v. *Charles Church Developments Ltd* (1996) 12 Const LJ 206.

(d) In fact, where a party undertakes by contract to perform a service for another upon terms, express or implied, that the service will be performed with reasonable skill and care, it will also owe a duty of care to like effect to the other contracting party which extends to not causing economic loss. There is no reason for the law not to apply this general principle to the case of a builder or a designer of a building.[2]

Thus Costain (the building contractor) was found to owe to Tesco a duty to take reasonable skill and care not to cause economic loss in respect of both physical works of construction and design work which Costain itself undertook pursuant to its contract with Tesco.

This decision was based squarely on the development of the law following *Henderson* v. *Merrett Syndicates Ltd* [1995] 2 AC 145 and *Stovin* v. *Wise* [1996] AC 923. It would seem to follow that, even where a builder's contract provides for him to build only and not to design but where the builder voluntarily undertakes works of design, he will owe a duty of care to his client[3] in respect of both the construction and the design work which he himself undertakes.

Importantly, Costain's duty of care was found not to extend to work which Costain did not undertake itself but which (to the knowledge of all parties) was performed by others.[4] This demonstrates the important effect of the contractual matrix that exists between the parties on the scope of any duty of care in tort that may be found to be owed.

What then, is the current approach for determining if a duty of care is owed in a novel situation? In such circumstances, the Court is effectively presented with a variety of analytical approaches from which it may choose in assessing whether or not a duty should be owed. The approaches are the 'assumption of responsibility', 'three-stage test' and 'the incremental approach'. Recent guidance on the interrelationship between these approaches was given in the *Barclays Bank* case by the House of Lords where Lord Mance said this:[5]

> [93] This review of authority confirms that there is no single common denominator, even in cases of economic loss, by which liability may be determined. The threefold test of foreseeability, proximity and fairness, justice and reasonableness provides a convenient general framework although it operates at so high a level of abstraction. Assumption of responsibility is particularly useful as a concept in the two core categories of case identified by Lord Browne-Wilkinson in *White* v. *Jones* (at p. 274B-C), when it may effectively subsume all aspects of the three-fold approach. But if all that is meant by voluntary assumption of responsibility is the voluntary assumption of responsibility for a task, rather than of liability towards the defendant, then questions of foreseeability, proximity and fairness, reasonableness and justice may be very relevant. In *White* v. *Jones* itself there was no doubt that the solicitor had voluntarily undertaken responsibility for a task, but it was the very fact that he

---

[2] The court also suggested obiter relying on *Bellefield Computer Services Ltd* v. *E. Turner & Sons Ltd* [2000] BLR 96 that the duty may also be owed to a subsequent building owner.

[3] And arguably, following *Bellefield*, to a subsequent purchaser too.

[4] The court distinguished the un-loved decision of HHJ Stabb QC to contrary effect in *Cynat Products Ltd* v. *Landbuild (Investment and Property) Ltd* [1984] 3 All ER 513.

[5] *Her Majesty's Commissioners of Customs and Excise* v. *Barclays Bank plc* [2006] UKHL 28; [2007] 1 AC 181.

> had done so for the testator, not the disappointed beneficiary, that gave rise to the stark division of opinion in the House. Incrementalism operates as an important cross-check on any other approach.

This tends to suggest that whichever approach is employed (or a combination of them) the same result ought to be reached.

The courts have recently had to grapple with a number of cases where it was alleged that a provider of information or the maker of a statement owed a duty of care to a recipient of that information or statement who had acted upon it. Thus, in *The Law Society* case,[6] in which Lord Woolf held that accountants retained by solicitors to prepare an annual report to the Law Society owed a duty of care to the Law Society:

> 12. [Sir Richard Scott V-C] applied the three criteria which must be met for there to be a duty of care identified by Lord Bridge of Harwich in *Caparo Industries plc* v. *Dickman* [1990] 1 All ER 568 at 573–574, [1990] 2 AC 605 at 617–619, namely: (a) reasonable foreseeability of damage; (b) a relationship of sufficient 'proximity' between the party owing the duty and the party to whom it is owed; and (c) the imposition of the duty of care contended for would be just and reasonable in all the circumstances.
>
> 13. Sir Richard Scott V-C also referred to the passage in the speech of Lord Oliver of Aylmerton in the Caparo Industries case. Based upon the decision of the House of Lords in *Hedley Byrne & Co Ltd* v. *Heller & Partners Ltd* [1963] 2 All ER 575, [1964] AC 465, Lord Oliver listed the circumstances which should exist in order to establish the necessary relationship of proximity between the person claiming to be owed the duty and the adviser: '. . . (1) the advice is required for a purpose, whether particularly specified or generally described, which is made known, either actually or inferentially, to the adviser at the time the advice is given, (2) the adviser knows, either actually or inferentially, that his advice will be communicated to the advisee, either specifically or as a member of an ascertainable class, in order that it should be used by the advisee for that purpose, (3) it is known, either actually or inferentially, that the advice so communicated is likely to be acted upon by the advisee for that purpose without independent inquiry and (4) it is so acted upon by the advisee to his detriment.' (See [1990] 1 All ER 568 at 589, [1990] 2 AC 605 at 638.)

In the Scottish case of *Bannerman*,[7] Lord MacFadyen, after a detailed review of the cases, concluded that there was:

> . . . a consistent line of authority that finds proximity in the act of making the information or advice available in the knowledge that it will be passed to the pursuer for a specific purpose and is likely to be relied on by him for that purpose.

While these dicta suggest that a duty of care may be imposed in favour of a third party recipient of information or advice in particular circumstances, it is right to acknowledge that these passages also indicate that in order for such a duty to be imposed there has to be a relatively close degree of proximity (to move from the incremental to the three-stage test) as between the information provider and the recipient of the information for a duty to be owed. The key to the imposition or otherwise of the duty is that the information provider should know (actually or inferentially) that the information it provides will

[6] *Law Society* v. *KPMG* [2001] Lloyds Rep PN 929 per Lord Woolf at paras [12]–[13].
[7] *RBS* v. *Bannerman* [2005] CSIH 39 at para. 41.

be provided to a class (one might add 'identifiable' here) of potential recipients to which the third party claimant belongs and should know also that the information so-provided and received is likely to be acted upon.

What the Courts have been concerned to do is to limit those who can bring claims against the maker of widely published statements for fear of opening the flood gates to claims from an indeterminate number of claimants and thus giving rise to indeterminate liabilities. Thus, while a duty has been found to be owed in cases such as *The Law Society*, no duty of care was found to be owed by auditors of company accounts to investors who purchased shares in reliance on those accounts[8] and no duty of care was found to be owed by a classification society which surveyed vessels for the purposes of maintaining class to a purchaser of the vessel who relied on the classification survey when completing the purchase.[9] These examples show the importance of the purpose for which the information or advice is provided in considering whether a duty of care should be owed (to a third party recipient of that information or advice).[10] Thus, the auditor producing audited accounts pursuant to statute owes no duty to the investor who purchases shares in the company whose accounts are being audited. Similarly, the classification survey is provided for the purposes of maintaining class and not for enabling a purchaser to decide whether or not to purchase the vessel.

While it is important to have these considerations and analytical approaches in mind, in the construction field the contractual matrix and relationships between the various parties will often prove to be determinative of whether a duty of care was owed.

1.2 Breach of duty

Once it has been established that a duty of care was owed by the defendant, the next question is whether the defendant has acted in breach of that duty. This requires an assessment of whether the defendant's conduct has fallen below the standard of care required by the duty. The standard of care is a question of law, but whether or not the defendant has failed to attain the requisite standard is a question of fact and so will depend on the circumstances of each case.

The standard of care is an objective standard which usually means that the defendant's conduct is measured against the conduct of the 'reasonable man'. In the past, this fictional reasonable man would take the form of the man on the Clapham omnibus, but it may be that the woman in the Ford Focus is a more appropriate test today.

If the defendant holds him or herself out as a person possessing a special skill he or she will not be judged against the 'reasonable man' but against the conduct of an ordinarily competent person possessing that special skill. Thus, an engineer will be judged against the conduct to be expected of the ordinarily competent engineer.

In addition to defendants possessing special skill, the standard required of the defendant may be modified by special circumstances in which the defendant acts (for example, the fact that the defendant is acting in an emergency situation and/or as a rescuer) and the legal capacity of the defendant (for example a child will be judged by the conduct to be expected of a child rather than an adult – see *McHale* v. *Watson* (1966) 115 CLR 866).

[8] *Caparo* (above).

[9] *The 'Morning Watch'* [1990] 1 Lloyd's Rep. 547 and see also *Marc Rich & Co AG* v. *Bishop Rock Marine Co Ltd* [1996] AC 211.

[10] See *Jackson & Powell* (above) at para. 2-116.

Further, the court may consider the following matters when assessing the standard of care.

(a) Foreseeability of loss: defendants should take steps to guard against causing loss that is a reasonably foreseeable consequence of not acting as they should.
(b) Degree of risk: in short, the greater the risk, the more care should be taken.[11]
(c) Degree of loss: the more dire the consequences of failing to take care, the higher the degree of care that should be taken to avoid causing it.

Against these three factors is weighed the expense and difficulty in taking care to avoid the risk. As Lord Reid put it:

> '... a reasonable man would only neglect a risk if he had some valid reason for doing so, e.g. that it would involve considerable expense to eliminate the risk. He would weigh the risk against the difficulty of eliminating it.'[12]

As far as evidence is concerned, in *Bolam* v. *Friern Hospital Management Committee* [1957] 1 WLR 582 McNair J drew the distinction between, on the one hand, 'the ordinary case which does not involve any special skill' and, on the other hand, the 'situation which involves the use of some special skill or competence'. In the former case, negligence is judged by 'the conduct of the man on the top of the Clapham omnibus' and in the later case 'the test is the standard of the ordinary skilled man exercising and professing to have that special skill'. Accordingly, in cases where the defendant has exercised a special skill then it will usually be sufficient for the defendant to show that he or she acted in accordance with the way that a recognised body of those in that particular field would regard as reasonable. This 'Bolam' test has been qualified, however. In *Bolitho* v. *City of Hackney Health Authority* [1998] AC 232, it was held that it is not always the case that an opinion held by a recognised body can withstand logical analysis and therefore be relied upon. Also, in *Nye Saunders & Partners* v. *Alan E Bristow* [1997] 37 BLR 92 it was held that expert evidence given to the court of other professional opinion was just the personal view of the expert rather than the view held by a recognised body.

1.3 Duties in the construction industry

Having reviewed these basic concepts in the tort of negligence it is worth considering a few examples of how these can operate in a construction environment.

Contractor

A contractor will owe a duty not to cause physical damage (be it to property or person) to those whom it can reasonably foresee might suffer loss as a result of negligence on the contractor's part. Following the decision in Tesco, a duty not to cause economic loss may well be imposed particularly where such a duty is concurrent, and co-extensive in scope, with contractual duties owed by the contractor. Further, where a contractor undertakes design functions under a design and build contract a claimant may well be able to show that there has been such an assumption of responsibility, at least in so far as design is concerned that a duty of care will be owed.

[11] See *Glasgow Corporation* v. *Muir* [1943] AC 448 at 456 and *Bolton* v. *Stone* [1951] AC 850 at 860.
[12] *Overseas Tankship (UK) Ltd* v. *The Miller Steamship Co. Pty (The Wagon Mound (No. 2))* [1967] 1 AC 617 at 642.

Construction professional[13]

A construction professional will owe a client a duty to employ a reasonable standard of skill and care in carrying out a retainer as would be expected of an ordinarily competent professional practising in the same discipline. The scope of this duty will often be determined by the contract between the professional and the client and, indeed, a term will usually be implied that the professional will exercise reasonable skill and care when performing the contract (Supply of Goods and Services Act 1982, s.13).

The existence of a contract will not prevent the existence of concurrent duties in tort (see *Henderson* v. *Merrett* [1994] 3 WLR 761 and the discussion above). The claimant is entitled to rely on whichever action is the more favourable.

A key advantage of having the option to sue in tort as well as in contract is that the action in tort will benefit from more advantageous limitation periods. In contract law, time begins to run from the date of breach whereas in tort, time will not run until damage has been sustained. In addition, the tortious action benefits from the alternative limitation period provided for latent defects.

A construction professional, just like the contractor, will owe duties to take reasonable care so as to avoid causing damage to property or persons that is reasonably foreseeable. However, it seems unlikely that a construction professional will owe a duty to someone other than his or her employer (who may be able to show the requisite assumption of responsibility) in respect of purely economic loss[14] (although a contractual relationship may exist between them). This will require exceptional circumstances and while there is no case where it has as yet been established, it is by no means impossible.

Causation

Once the claimant has been able to show that the defendant owed it a duty of care and has acted in breach of that duty, the claimant will then have to show that the breach caused the loss of which it complains.

The starting point for this inquiry is to ask 'but for' the defendant's negligence would the claimant have suffered the loss? (the so-called 'but for' test). A good example of this test in action is to be found in *Barnett* v. *Chelsea and Kensington Hospital Management* [1969] 1 QB 428. Here the claimant's husband went to casualty complaining of feeling ill after drinking some tea. The doctor refused to examine him and sent him home. The gentleman then died of arsenic poisoning. The court held that the doctor's negligence did not cause the death because it would have been too late to treat the poison even if the doctor had seen him in the casualty department. That is to say, but for the negligence, the same harm or loss would have been suffered.

The 'but for' test can be difficult to answer. It frequently involves hypothesising about what someone would have done had the defendant not acted in breach of duty. For example, in a case where it is alleged that a defendant construction professional provided negligent advice, the claimant must be able to show that he would have acted differently, thereby avoiding the loss which occurred, if given proper advice. Cases where there is more than one potential cause of the claimant's loss also give rise to particular problems. Take for example the situation where there are four different possible causes of the loss,

[13] For a much more detailed discussion see Jackson & Powell on *Professional Liability*, 6th Edn, Sweet & Maxwell, 2007.

[14] Although it is highly unlikely that a professional will be found to owe a general duty to the main contractor (who is not his or her employer) on a project.

of which only one is attributable to negligence on the part of the defendant, and it cannot be ascertained which of the possible causes was in fact the cause of the claimant's loss. Each might have a 25% chance of causing the loss, but as a general rule it does not follow that the claimant will succeed on 25% of the claim. On the contrary, given that the claimant must prove the case against the defendant on the balance of probabilities (more than 50%) the claim will fail – see *Wilsher* v. *Essex AHA* [1988] AC 1074. However, there are certain circumstances in which the court is prepared to bridge the 'evidential gap' as to which of the potential causes in fact caused the claimant's loss. The claimant does not have to prove that the defendant's breach of duty was the sole, or even the main, cause of his loss provided that he can demonstrate that it made a material contribution to the damage. Moreover in some cases the court has been prepared to say that causation is established provided that the negligent act complained of materially contributed to the risk of damage. In *Fairchild* v. *Glenhaven Funeral Services Ltd* [2003] 1 AC 32, the House of Lords considered the situation in which an employee has been negligently exposed to asbestos while in the employ of a number of different employers, and has contracted mesothelioma. The mesothelioma has been contracted due to exposure to asbestos, but it cannot be determined in the employ of which employer the causative exposure took place. It was held that the claimant could succeed against a particular former employer even though he could not prove on the balance of probabilities that the exposure which caused the mesothelioma occurred during the period of employment by that employer. This is a complex area and the limits of the so-called 'Fairchild exception' remain somewhat uncertain.

There is also a difficulty with subsequent causes of the claimant's loss. For example, in *Performance Cars* v. *Abraham* [1962] 1 QB 33 the defendant negligently drove into the claimant's car which had been damaged by another driver just a few days before. Both collisions caused damage that required the car to be resprayed and the court held that, as a result, the defendant had not caused the claimant's loss – the car would have had to have been resprayed in any event.

However, in *Baker* v. *Willoughby* [1970] AC 467 the unlucky claimant had his leg injured by the defendant in a car accident. Subsequently, but before the case came to court, the claimant was shot in the same leg by an armed robber and the leg had to be amputated. This was a different case from Performance Cars as, here, the second tortfeasor (the robber) had made the situation worse. However, the House of Lords rejected the argument that the defendant should only be liable for the loss caused by the original injury up to the date of the shooting. The first injury was still a cause of the claimant's unfortunate condition, it had not been subsumed by the second, and the defendant's responsibility was to be assessed as if the second incident had never occurred.

It is perhaps not surprising that this reasoning has been the subject of criticism. In *Jobling* v. *Associated Dairies* [1982] AC 794 the claimant suffered an injury at work and then from a natural disease. The House of Lords upheld the decision in *Baker* on its facts and suggested that the reasoning in that case may be appropriate where there are two successive torts. This was easy to justify on the basis that if the first tortfeasor were not to remain liable then the claimant would be left under-compensated because the second tortfeasor would be able to rely on *Performance Cars* to escape liability. However, where the claimant has suffered first a tort and then the onset of a natural disease, the latter falls to be treated as a vicissitude of life and the defendant will only be liable up until the intervention of the disease. The disease is treated as the cause of the claimant's continuing condition. How far the reasoning in *Baker* can be sustained is open to real doubt, particularly in circumstances where a second tortfeasor has made a condition worse or where two torts combine to achieve a result that each on their own would not have caused. This is of particular relevance in the construction industry where the possibility of multiple causes is high. For example, a defect in a building may have been caused by a combination of poor design and substandard workmanship; determining whether either or both of designer and builder should be liable will depend on the considerations discussed here.

Also important is the concept of a 'new intervening act' or 'new intervening cause' which may break the 'chain of causation' between a defendant's breach of duty and the claimant's loss. This concept is often referred to by its Latin name: a 'novus actus interveniens'. The basic principle is that, in some cases, even though a breach of duty on the part of the defendant sets in motion a sequence of events which leads to the claimant's loss, things may have happened in the interim which make it unjust that the defendant should be held legally responsible for that loss. The intervening cause can be an act of nature, an act or omission by a third party, or an act or omission by the claimant himself, but in order to break the chain of causation the new intervening cause will need to be of such impact that it effectively eclipses the wrongdoing of the defendant. A classic example is the case of *Knightley* v. *Johns* [1982] 1 WLR 349. The first defendant's negligence caused the blockage of a road tunnel. The second defendant, a police officer, took charge. He did not immediately close the tunnel, which should have been standard practice. He later instructed the claimant, a police motorcyclist, to ride the wrong way back through the tunnel, to ensure that the tunnel was closed. The claimant was hit and injured by the third defendant who was driving too fast into the tunnel. The Court of Appeal found that the sequence of events subsequent to the original negligence eclipsed the first defendant's wrongdoing and he should not be held liable.

What has also become clear in recent years is that a claimant must prove that his or her loss has been caused by the defendant in the sense that the type of loss caused was within the scope of the duty owed by the defendant to the claimant (see *South Australia Asset Management* v. *York Montague Limited* [1997] AC 191). A defendant may only 'assume responsibility' to the claimant for certain matters and so the defendant in breach of that duty will only be liable for loss that falls within the scope of the duty that he or she has assumed. This concept – called the SAAMCO principle (taking its name from one of the parties in the case) – influences considerations of duty, causation, remoteness and damages and so merits consideration in some detail.[15]

SAAMCO was actually a number of joined appeals considered by the House of Lords. The common feature of the cases was that in each the plaintiff had instructed the defendant valuers to value properties which were to provide security for mortgage advances to be made by the plaintiffs. In each case the defendants negligently overvalued the properties. The advances were made and, subsequently, the borrowers defaulted. The lenders were left with insufficient security to cover their losses. In the meantime, the property market had fallen sharply, thereby increasing the losses suffered by the lenders. The question that fell to be decided was to what extent could the plaintiffs recover the extensive losses that they had suffered?

The Court of Appeal ([1995] QB 375) held that in circumstances where the lender would not have entered into the transaction if the valuation had been accurate, the

[15] While SAAMCO impacts on each of these areas, Lord Hoffmann has taken the view that the principle is one of causation and so it is dealt with here. Nevertheless, SAAMCO should be borne in mind is considering remoteness and damages below.

lender was entitled to recover from the negligent valuer the net loss of having made the advance. The Court of Appeal considered that the starting point for determining the measure of damages was that the damages ought, insofar as it was possible, to put the plaintiff in the position in which it would have been had it not suffered the wrong committed by the defendant. Lord Hoffmann, who gave the only speech in the House of Lords, disagreed ([1997] AC 191 at 211A–B):

> 'I think that this was the wrong place to begin. Before one can consider the principle on which one should calculate the damages to which a Plaintiff is entitled as compensation for loss, it is necessary to decide for what kind of loss he is entitled to compensation. A correct description of the loss for which the valuer is liable must precede any consideration of the measure of damages. For this purpose it is better to begin at the beginning and consider the lender's cause of action.'

The starting point, then, must be the duty owed to the lender and its scope. Lord Hoffmann was at pains to suggest that such a duty does not exist in the abstract and that the lender must show that the duty owed was in respect of the kind of loss which it has suffered (see 211H). He then went on to set out the general principle (at 214C–F).

> 'It is that a person under a duty to take reasonable care to provide information on which someone else will decide upon a course of action is, if negligent, not generally regarded as responsible for all the consequences of that course of action. He is responsible only for the consequences of the information being wrong. A duty of care which imposes upon the informant responsibility for losses which would have occurred even if the information which he gave had been correct is not in my view fair and reasonable as between the parties. It is therefore inappropriate either as an implied term of a contract or as a tortious duty arising from the relationship between them.
>
> The principle thus stated distinguishes between a duty to *provide information* for the purpose of enabling someone else to decide upon a course of action and a duty to *advise* someone as to what course of action he should take. If the duty is to advise whether or not a course of action should be taken, the adviser must take reasonable care to consider all the potential consequences of that course of action. If he is negligent, he will therefore be responsible for all the foreseeable loss which is a consequence of that course of action having been taken. If his duty is only to supply information, he must take reasonable care to ensure that the information is correct and, if he is negligent, will be responsible for all the foreseeable consequences of the information being wrong.'

The valuer had a duty to provide information and not advice. The consequence of the information being wrong was that the lender's security was worth less than the valuation suggested it was. The limit of the loss recoverable from the valuer was thus the difference between the valuation given and the true value of the property at the date of the valuation. Only loss that fell within this sum was loss properly referable to the valuer's duty.

This principle is perhaps best understood by looking at how it was applied to the facts of the cases under appeal in SAAMCO. In SAAMCO itself, the negligent valuation was £15 million. In fact, the actual value of the property at the time of the valuation was £5 million. Accordingly, the maximum liability of the valuers was £10 million. The lender had advanced £11 million and the sale of the property realized only £2.5 million. The total loss incurred by the lender was some £9.7 million. As Lord Hoffmann put it, at 222B–C:

3.1 The law of contract
3.2 Construction health and safety
3.3 Insolvency in construction
3.4 Law of tort
3.5 Environmental issues

> 'The consequence of the valuation being wrong was that the Plaintiffs had £10 million less security than they thought. If they had had this margin, they would have suffered no loss. The whole loss was therefore within the scope of the Defendant's duty.'

In the other appeals, however, not all of the loss suffered by the lenders was within the scope of the valuer's duty. Thus, in *United Bank of Kuwait Plc* v. *Prudential Property Services Limited* the valuation was £2.5 million and the advance £1.75 million. The trial judge found that the correct value of the property had been between £1.8 million and £1.85 million. The lender's total loss as a result of the fall in the property market was quantified at £1.3 million and the trial judge awarded this sum in damages. Lord Hoffmann argued (at 222D) that this was wrong because:

> 'the damages should have been limited to the consequences of the valuation being wrong, which were that the lenders had £700 000 or £650 000 less security than they thought.'

The lender's argument that the overvaluation increased the risk of default by the borrower was also rejected, with Lord Hoffmann saying this on the matter (at 222E):

> 'The greater risk of default, if such there was, is only another reason why the lender, if he had known the true facts, would not have entered into the particular transaction. But that does not affect the scope of the valuer's duty.'

It is the scope of the duty of care that determines the extent of the valuer's liability and not whether the case is a 'no transaction' or a 'successful transaction'.

In the final appeal, *Nykredit Mortgage Bank Plc* v. *Edward Erdman Group Ltd*, the damages were again reduced to the difference between the negligent overvaluation and the true value of the property at the date of valuation. The lender in this appeal advanced one further argument which was that in this case the loan was made to a single asset company in order to finance the purchase and redevelopment of the property. The value of the property lay in its development value and the lender argued that if the valuation had been accurate, it would have appreciated that the development was not viable and that default was virtually inevitable. This argument was rejected by Lord Hoffmann, at 223F, as it was concerned with what the lender would have done if the valuation had been accurate, which was not the test of the valuer's liability.

Finally, it should be noted that Lord Hoffmann distinguished between the measure of damages in an action for breach of duty to take care to provide accurate information and that in an action for breach of a warranty that the information is accurate. In the former case, one must compare the loss which the claimant actually suffers with what its position would have been if it had not entered into the transaction and then ask what element of that loss is attributable to the inaccuracy of the information. In the latter case, the comparison is between the position in which the plaintiff finds itself and the position it would have been in if the information had been accurate (see 216D–F). Lord Hoffmann seems to have been moved by the idea that it would be strange, indeed unjust, if the measure in the former case were higher than in the latter; that liability for failing to take care could be more extensive than for giving an inaccurate warranty.

In general terms, the implications for the construction industry are likely to be that a greater emphasis will be placed on the extent and nature of the duty owed by the defendant to the claimant. It is therefore now even more important for those in the construction industry to be aware of the type and scope of the duties that they are assuming and to guard against 'assuming responsibility' for loss that they would rather avoid. The decision in SAAMCO is likely to be of most direct relevance to the industry in relation to the provision of information or advice (the distinction will be crucial) to a client which is used by him in deciding whether to proceed with a project. For example, in *HOK Sport Ltd* v. *Aintree Racecourse Co Ltd* [2002] EWHC 3094, it was held that the SAAMCO principle applied generally to claims against construction professionals and would be particularly important where (a) a professional is engaged to provide information for a specific project; (b) the client is to decide whether to proceed with the project; (c) the information to be provided by the professional is to be relied on by the client in the decision-making process; and (d) the decision is not participated in by the professional nor dependent upon his advice. In the HOK Sport case itself, the architect failed to warn the client racecourse owner that various design changes would result in fewer standing places than expected. The client therefore did not have an opportunity to redesign the project to remedy the loss of places. It was held that the architect's duty was to provide information as to the number of places which its design would provide; it was not to advise the client on whether it should postpone the project to allow for redesign. The loss which fell within the scope of the architect's duty was limited to the loss attributable to the racecourse owner's decision to proceed with the project on the incorrect assumption that a larger number of places would be provided.[16]

Issues of causation were considered in the case of *Baxall* v. *Sheard Walshaw* (see above), where the Court of Appeal considered whether the negligent designer can be liable for the losses caused by a defect after the owner should have known about the defect. The Court of Appeal answered this in the negative, reasoning that as soon as a defect becomes apparent ('patent') rather than hidden ('latent') then the owner must take steps to avoid the risk the defect presents. The Court of Appeal also said that where, as was the case in *Baxall*, the tenant did not know of the defect but *should have known*, then that defect becomes patent. The Court of Appeal also considered whether, where there are two defects in the design and one is hidden and one disclosed, the designer is liable for damage caused by the hidden defect if the damage in question would not have happened had the owner cured the disclosed defect. Again, and consistently, the Court of Appeal answered this in the negative. This would suggest that owners of new buildings should take care: it is not simply enough to say that you were not aware of a defect; if the defect was reasonably discoverable then you may fail on causation. However, note that Baxall was not applied in the recent case of *Pearson Education Ltd* v. *Charter Partnership Ltd* [2007] BLR 324. A firm of architects negligently designed a rainwater drainage system at a warehouse. This led to a flood which caused damage to property belonging to the claimant tenants. Eight years before this flood, when the warehouse was leased to a different company, there had been a previous flood. After that first flood, it had been discovered by loss adjusters that the capacity of the rainwater system was inadequate, but that information was not conveyed to the then tenants. The architects argued that the first flood brought their potential liability to an end in that it was not reasonably foreseeable that any further damage would flow from the defective design once it had led to a flood, as it was reasonable to expect that this would lead to the identification of the defect (see further below as to the concept of 'reasonable foreseeability'); that it was not fair, just

[16] But cf. *Hancock* v. *Tucker* [1999] Lloyd's Rep. P.N. 814.

or reasonable that their duty of care should extend beyond the occurrence of the first flood; and that the occurrence of the first flood broke the chain of causation between their negligence and the second flood. The Court of Appeal rejected this argument. There was no reason, when the architects specified the capacity of the drainage system, for them to expect that an inspection would be carried out that would reveal any error that it might make. The design shortcoming was truly latent: the claimants neither knew nor should have known of the first flood, so there was no reason why they should carry out any investigation into the adequacy of the drainage system.

Foreseeability and remoteness

The concept of foreseeability, as described above, plays an important role in determining whether a duty of care is owed, but it also has a role to play – once duty, breach and causation have been established – in determining whether the claimant can recover some or all of its loss. In short, the claimant must show that the loss which it has suffered was a reasonably foreseeable consequence of the defendant's negligence.[17] The test here is relatively easy to satisfy as even if the mere possibility of causing loss is contemplated by the defendant then this will be enough to fix the defendant with liability.[18] If the loss is not reasonably foreseeable it is too remote and will be irrecoverable even though, as a matter of fact (though not law), the defendant has 'caused' the loss.

The claimant need not show that the extent of loss or the manner in which it was suffered were foreseeable but simply that the type of loss suffered was a reasonably foreseeable consequence of the defendant's negligence.[19] Thus, if personal injury is foreseeable it will not matter that the claimant has suffered more severe injuries than would otherwise be expected as a result of being particularly susceptible to that type of harm: the defendant must take the claimant as he or she is. This is the so-called 'egg-shell skull' rule and, while this is sometimes considered separately from the usual rules as to foreseeability and remoteness, the relationship between the concepts is clear.

1.4 Damages and the measure of loss

Damages in the law of tort are compensatory in nature and are designed, insofar as is possible, to put the claimant in the position it would have been in had the tort not been committed. Very rarely the courts will award exemplary damages which go beyond this and do more than compensate the claimant, although this is unlikely to occur in the construction context. This will usually involve a deliberate breach of duty by the defendant designed to result in a greater profit than any award of damages that the defendant will have to pay to compensate the claimant.

Broadly speaking, a claimant may suffer two types of loss: pecuniary and non-pecuniary. Where property is damaged, the usual measure of damages will be the cost of repair or the diminution in value of the property. The cost of repair will not be awarded if this would be unreasonable, for example, by being disproportionate to the value of the property in its repaired state.[20]

[17] *Overseas Tankship (UK) Ltd* v. *Miller Steamship Co. Pty (The Wagon Mound No. 2)* [1967] 1 AC 617.

[18] *The Wagon Mound No. 2* [1967] 1 AC 617 and *The Heron II* [1969] 1 AC 350 at 385–389.

[19] *Hughes* v. *Lords Advocate* [1963] AC 837.

[20] *Ruxley Electronics and Construction Ltd* v. *Forsyth* [1995] 3 All ER 268 (a case in contract but illustrative of the principle nevertheless).

Non-pecuniary loss most commonly arises in personal injury cases where the court will award damages in respect of the pain, suffering and loss of amenity caused to the claimant by his or her injuries. It is important to note that damages for disappointment and distress are not normally recoverable in either contract or tort, but where the claimant suffers anxiety and mental distress as a direct result of physical inconvenience caused by repairs to property, damages will be recoverable.[21] This has particular relevance to the construction industry in the context of remedial works necessitated by faulty design or workmanship when the works were initially completed. Thus, the liability of the construction tortfeasor may not be limited merely to the costs of putting things right.

In recent years, an increasingly important remedy in terms of damages has been the development of the lost opportunity claim. In the ordinary course of events, in order to recover damages the claimant must prove on the balance of probabilities that it has suffered a loss. By way of contrast, in a lost opportunity claim, once the claimant has proved that it has lost an opportunity of some value the court may assess the value of the chance by making a series of deductions to reflect contingencies from the 'full' value of the chance had it materialized. This type of claim most often arises in the field of solicitors' negligence where, for example, by reason of the solicitor's negligence an otherwise good claim becomes statute-barred (see below). The claimant in such circumstances cannot prove on the balance of probabilities that his or her claim definitely would have succeeded but instead can show that he or she has lost the chance of pursuing the defendant in the original action. If his or her claim was a good one, then the discount to be made to reflect, for example, the inherent risks of litigation and the chance of an early settlement of the claim at a figure below the full amount claimed, may by small, say 10–20%. The type of claim has an increasing relevance in the construction sphere. Thus, for example, in *Royal Brompton NHS Trust* v. *Hammond* [2002] 1 WLR 1397 the employer settled arbitration proceedings with the contractor and then brought claims against the professional team. Whereas the claim against the contractor was for delay in the completion of the works, the claim against the professional team was for the impairment of the employer's rights against the contractor. As a result, contribution proceedings brought by the architects against the contractor were struck out.

Defences

There are several recognized defences to an action brought in negligence, the most common being voluntary assumption of risk, exclusions of liability and contributory negligence. The defence of limitation of actions is considered separately below.

Voluntary assumption of responsibility is a complete defence to an action brought in negligence – also known by the Latin maxim '*volenti non fit injuria*'. It will arise where the defendant can show that the claimant has freely assumed the risk of being harmed in the manner in which it has in fact been harmed by the defendant. The claimant must have acted freely and voluntarily in full knowledge of the risk it is agreeing to run and accept that it is the claimant and not the defendant who is assuming responsibility for that risk. (However, a claimant which exposes itself to risk in order to avert injury (be it to itself or others) is unlikely to be defeated by this defence.) In the construction industry it is more likely that parties will have agreed to apportion the risk in respect

[21] *Watts* v. *Morrow* [1991] 4 All ER 937. Any award is likely to be modest and less than £1000.

of various types of loss between them. This may have the effect of excluding liability (see below) or simply meaning that a duty will not be owed in respect of the type of loss that is claimed.

It should be noted that, in practice, the defence of voluntary assumption only rarely succeeds, it being more common for a claimant to be found to have been only contributory negligent and thus suffering a percentage reduction in damages rather than the claim failing altogether. This power is derived from the Law Reform (Contributory Negligence) Act 1945. Under Section 1(1) the court may reduce an award of damages to:

> 'such an extent as the court thinks just and equitable, having regard to the claimant's share in the responsibility for the damage'.

A claimant may not be 100% contributory negligent as this amounts to a finding that the claimant rather than the defendant has caused the claimant's loss, and so the action against the defendant will fail completely.

It is important to bear in mind that the claimant is not under a duty to the defendant but to itself to take due care and that contributory negligence may arise even where the occasion of the claimant's loss is entirely a result of the defendant's conduct (an example being where the claimant fails to wear a seat belt and is involved in a collision caused by the defendant).

Turning finally to exclusions of liability, at common law a defendant could employ various devices in order to exclude or limit liability for negligence. For example:

(a) by an express contract with the claimant to that effect
(b) by giving the claimant notice that it was not accepting responsibility for harm caused to the claimant
(c) by issuing a disclaimer disclaiming responsibility for information or advice proffered to the claimant.[22]

However, the power of the defendant to do this is severely limited by the Unfair Contract Terms Act 1977 (UCTA). Section 2(1) prevents a defendant from excluding liability for personal injury and death. Nor can a defendant simply give the claimant notice excluding or restricting liability as the Act provides that mere awareness of the risk of harm on the part of the claimant is not effective to exclude liability on the part of the defendant. In all cases, liability can only be excluded in so far as the exclusion is reasonable (UCTA 1977, s.2(2)). Reasonableness is defined in Section 11 and Schedule 1. Reference should be made to Chapter 3.1 for a more detailed discussion of the operation of the Act.

Limitation[23]

The defence of limitation is an important and useful tool for the defendant. A claimant must bring an action within a set period of time ('the limitation period') and failure to do so means that the action becomes 'statute barred'; that is barred by the Limitation Act 1980. The limitation periods for various different types of action are set out in the Act and the period for most torts, including negligence, is six years. It is important to note, however, that if the claim includes a claim in respect of personal injuries, then the period is three years.

---

22 As was the case in *Hedley Byrne* v. *Heller* [1964] AC 465.

23 Limitation is a substantial topic and further reference should be made to Clerk & Lindsell on *Torts*, Chapter 33 and Jackson & Powell on *Professional Negligence*, Chapter 5.

Time, for the purposes of the limitation period, will begin to run when the claimant's cause of action accrues. Because a cause of action in negligence does not accrue until damage has been suffered, time will begin to run when the damage complained of occurs.

In the construction industry it will not always be easy to identify when damage has first been suffered. For example, in *Pirelli General Cable Works* v. *Oscar Faber and Partners* [1983] 2 AC 1 the House of Lords held that the cause of action for negligent advice in relation to the design of a building accrued when cracks were first visible rather than when the damage was reasonably discoverable. However, doubts have been raised concerning this decision[24] and the position has in any event been altered by the Latent Damage Act 1986[25] which inserted Section 14A into the Limitation Act 1980. This section provides an alternative limitation period of three years from when the claimant had (or is deemed to have had) sufficient knowledge to enable the claim to be brought ('date of knowledge'). The relevant date of knowledge is when the claimant knew:

(a) that the relevant damage was sufficiently serious to justify proceedings,
(b) that the damage was attributable in whole or in part to an act or omission of the defendant, and
(c) the identity of the defendant.

These requirements mirror those of Section 14 which provides a similar alternative period for personal injury claims. In addition, for personal injury actions the court has discretion under Section 33 to, in effect, overlook the expiry of the limitation period if it considers it just and equitable to do so.

A further alternative limitation period is provided in Section 36 for cases involving fraud or deliberate concealment of facts relevant to the claimant's claim of six years from the date on which the fraud or concealment could, with reasonable diligence, have been discovered.

Finally, under Section 28, where the claimant is under a disability – that is an infant or of unsound mind – as at the date when the cause of action accrues, then time will not begin to run until such time as the disability ceases or when the claimant dies, whichever is the sooner.

2 NUISANCE

2.1 Introduction

Nuisance divides into two categories: private and public. Apart from this distinction, commentators have found nuisance difficult to define. Possibly the best description is:

> 'An act or omission which is an interference with, disturbance of or annoyance to, a person in the exercise or enjoyment of (a) a right belonging to him as a member of the public, when it is a public nuisance, or (b) his ownership or occupation of land or of some easement, profit, or other right used or enjoyed in connection with land, when it is a private nuisance.'[26]

Nuisance and negligence share some of the same qualities, but there is an important difference between the two, namely that negligence is concerned with the protection of

[24] Pirelli was not followed by the Privy Council in *Invercargill City Council* v. *Hamlin* [1996] AC 624.
[25] Discussed below. A significant problem remains in relation to economic loss, discussed in Section 2 of this chapter.
[26] Clerk & Lindsell on *Torts*, 19th Edn, Sweet & Maxwell, 2005, 20–01.

personal rights and nuisance is concerned with the protection of proprietary rights. However, both impose a similar standard of care on the potential tortfeasor and are subject to similar rules of causation and remoteness of damage. Damages for nuisance differ slightly to those for negligence because injunctive relief rather than damages is more often sought and gained.

Nuisance is an important factor in the construction industry because of the rules in relation to demolition and building and the effect they have on neighbouring land. It is also a factor to be aware of when planning new uses of land, for example a refinery or nuclear installation. In construction, knowing the restrictions in relation to nuisance may avoid unnecessary litigation at a later stage.

2.2 Public nuisance and statutory nuisance

Public nuisance has been described as 'an amorphous and unsatisfactory area of the law covering an ill-assorted collection of wrongs, some of which have little or no association with tort and only appear to fill a gap in the criminal law'.[27] While this view may be a little extreme, it is true to say that there are very few similarities between public and private nuisance.

Public nuisance is actionable in both criminal and civil law. A person can sue for public nuisance without the requirement of an interest in land, unlike private nuisance.

A person can sue for public nuisance in civil law if it can be shown that he or she suffers special damage beyond inconvenience suffered by others who have also been affected (per Laurence LJ in *Harper* v. *Haden & Sons* [1933] Ch. 298 at 308). In order for an action to exist, the claimant must also show that a 'class' of people has been affected by the defendant's activities. The definition of a class has been held to be a matter of fact and degree.

Traditionally, public nuisance has been seen to cover the majority of 'highway' cases involving actions due to obstruction of the highway. This is particularly relevant to construction cases as building works will often affect the passage along highways or cause obstruction. For example, scaffolding on a building adjoining a busy main road.

In *Hubbard* v. *Pitt* [1976] QB 142 at 1491, the judge said:

> 'The vital characteristic of a highway is that it is land dedicated for a purpose; that purpose is for use by the public for passage to and fro'.

At common law, the public have an implied easement of the right to access the highway. Any obstruction or prevention of access is actionable in tort as a public nuisance. Reasonableness of use will be taken into account in particular in access cases and courts will balance the competing interests of the ordinary member of the public and the user of the highway. So, for example, actions have failed where the court held that scaffolding erected for the construction of an additional storey to premises was a reasonable use (*Harper* v. *Haden & Sons*). In the recent case of *Hiscox Syndicates Ltd* v. *Pinnacle Ltd* [2008] EWHC 1386 (QB), when considering the variation of an injunction to enable, in effect, obstruction of the highway in connection with the construction of 'The Pinnacle' building in the City of London, Mr Justice Akenhead described it as 'eminently arguable that reasonable, temporary obstruction of the highway is or may be allowable before it becomes a public nuisance'; this will, however, be a matter of fact and degree.

[27] *Markesinis & Deakin's Tort Law*, 6th Edn, Oxford University Press, 2008, p. 550.

Distinguishable from, but similar to, public nuisance is statutory nuisance. Those working within the construction industry should be aware of the relevant legislation, in particular the Environmental Protection Act (EPA) 1990 which covers emission of noise and fumes among many other things. Statutory nuisances are often nuisances which would be actionable as public nuisance if not for the relevant statute.

Environmental protection legislation is discussed in Chapter 3.5. In essence, prior to the EPA 1990, a range of statutes covered the different nuisances actionable by statute. The EPA 1990 consolidated many of these, introducing streamlined procedures. Statutory nuisances under the EPA 1990 are actionable by local authorities and, in some cases, by individuals. Part III of the EPA 1990 defines statutory nuisance widely, including the state of any premises, smoke emitted from premises, emission of fumes, gas, dust, steam or other effluvia arising from an industrial trade or business premises and any other matter declared by enactment to be a statutory nuisance.

Moreover, Part IIA of the EPA 1990 creates a regime specifically aimed at the contamination of land, which will be relevant to any case where a nuisance is alleged to have been caused by an escaping contaminant. Any party that knowingly permits potential contaminants to come onto, or remain on, their land will be liable under Part IIA of the EPA 1990 if doing so leads to the contamination of land. Under s.78A(9) 'any natural or artificial substances, whether in solid or liquid form or in the form of a gas or vapour' are covered by the Part IIA of the EPA 1990 if they have caused contamination of land.

In practice, where a substance has escaped from a party's land and caused contamination of land, the relevant local authority is under a duty to serve a 'remediation' notice on him or her requiring the cleaning up of the contaminated land. The land must be restored so that it is again suitable for use. The polluter is generally required to pay for the cost of such remediation, even where it is arranged by the Local Authority.

2.3 Private nuisance: who can sue?

Lord Evershed MR in *Thompson-Schwab* v. *Costakis* [1956] 1 WLR 335 at 338 divided private nuisance into three categories:

(a) causing an encroachment on another's land,
(b) causing physical damage to another's land or building works or vegetation upon it, and
(c) unduly interfering with the comfort and convenient enjoyment of another's land.

In the case of *Hunter* v. *Canary Wharf* [1997] 2 WLR 684, the House of Lords took the opportunity to reaffirm this area of law. The Lords restated that the tort of nuisance is a tort directed against the plaintiff's enjoyment of rights over land and, accordingly, an action in private nuisance will only lie at the suit of a person who has a right in the land affected.

This is an example of a major difference between nuisance and negligence, nuisance being concerned with protection of rights over land and negligence being more concerned with the rights of the individual.

It was thought that the law was moving away from this stance in the case of *Khorasandjian* v. *Bush* [1993] QB 727. Here, the plaintiff was the daughter of the freeholder of the property and successfully sued the defendant for harassment in the form of telephone calls. The Court of Appeal held that it was sufficient that the property was her 'home' even though she had no formal proprietary interest. This decision was overruled by the House of Lords in *Hunter* v. *Canary Wharf*. The House upheld the traditional test of possession and occupation (see *Malone* v. *Laskey* [1907] 2 KB 141, CA) and refused to distinguish the right to sue in cases of direct physical damage to or encroachment on neighbouring land from situations involving interference with enjoyment. The reaffirmation appears perfectly logical when one works from the premise that the tort of nuisance is concerned with the rights of land. A possible reason for the departure from stated law in *Khorasandjian* is that, at that time, the law did not recognise a remedy for personal harassment not resulting in financial or other loss. This is no longer the case after the Protection from Harassment Act 1997.

When must the potential claimant's interest in the land have been acquired in order to give rise to an entitlement to sue? It might have been thought that the claimant must have had the relevant interest when the damage caused by the nuisance was suffered. However, this does not now appear to be the case. In *Delaware Mansions* v. *Westminster City Council* [2001] 3 WLR 1007 (HL) the successful claimant brought an action against the defendant local authority in respect of damage to a mansion block caused by tree roots. The claimant acquired its interest in the property at a time after the damage, or at least much of it, had already been suffered. The House of Lords held that nuisance was a continuing one and that the claimant had acted reasonably in carrying out the remedial works that it did. What seems to have been important was that the nuisance was a continuing one. The position may well have been different had the nuisance ceased and the damage been suffered prior to the claimant's acquisition of an interest in the property.

2.4 Public nuisance – who can sue?

In public nuisance, there is no qualification as to proprietary rights. A claimant must show that he or she has been affected by the nuisance caused. Public nuisance is generally constituted by acts which hinder the public from exercising their rights.

At common law, it is necessary to show that a class of person has been affected, although it is not necessary to prove that every member of that class has been injuriously affected and it is a matter of fact whether the number of persons affected is large enough to term the nuisance public.

Apart from the statutory remedies available, if public nuisance is governed by statute, the Attorney General may bring an action for an injunction on his or her own initiative or on the part of another person or a local authority, who will then be joined as co-claimant (see *A. G.* v. *Logan* [1891] 2 QB 100).

2.5 Who can be sued?

The general rule is that the actual wrongdoer is liable for the nuisance caused, whether or not he or she is in occupation of the land (see *Hall* v. *Beckenham Corp.* [1949] 1 KB 716). This means that, in construction, a contractor will be liable if it is employed to erect a building and that building becomes a nuisance.[28] Even if the contractor moves away from the nuisance, if the nuisance continues and even though the contractor is no longer in control to prevent it, it will be liable. A person taking over the land and continuing the nuisance will also be liable for carrying on that nuisance and therefore the claimant will have a choice of defendants. It will often be easier to pursue the current landowner who may be more readily available than the person or body originally

[28] *Thompson* v. *Gibson* (1841) 7 M&W 456; also *Wilcox* v. *Steel* [1904] 1 Ch. 212.

responsible, who may have moved away. Therefore, purchasers of new developments should be wary as they may face a claim from a party affected by nuisance which they did not create.

An individual may also be liable for nuisance created by servants and agents as well as personally. In the case of independent contractors, whether the employer is liable for nuisance depends on whether it could reasonably have foreseen that the work instructed was likely to result in a nuisance (see *Bower* v. *Peate* [1876] 1 QB 321). If the nuisance was reasonably foreseeable and the employer did not take steps to prevent it, then the employer is liable. Otherwise, the independent contractor will be considered liable.

A party may not be liable in nuisance if to impose such liability would be inconsistent with statute. This principle is demonstrated by the decision in *Marcic* v. *Thames Water Utilities* [2004] 2 AC 42 in which the House of Lords held that to render a statutory sewerage undertaker liable in nuisance for the discharge of sewage into the claimant's house caused by inadequate sewer pipes would be inconsistent with the statutory scheme imposed by the Water Industry Act 1991. The Act provided a comprehensive scheme governing the obligations of sewerage undertakers and it was not for the courts to add to these by imposing liability in nuisance. However, in the recent case of *Hanifa Dobson* v. *Thames Water Utilities Ltd* (2008) 2 All ER 362, it was held that the decision in Marcic did not prevent certain causes of action in nuisance based on negligence existing alongside the duties under the Act, where the exercise of adjudicating on that cause of action was not inconsistent with the statutory process under the 1991 Act. There is an obvious parallel here with the effect of the contractual matrix on the scope of any duty of care in tort that may be owed by a party discussed above.

2.6 Establishing liability and damages

In private nuisance, the claimant must be able to show that, as a result of the nuisance, damage has been caused. This can either be in the form of physical damage to land, encroachment on the claimant's land or inconvenience materially affecting the enjoyment of the land by the claimant.

The damage must be reasonably foreseeable for the claimant to have a successful claim. In *The Wagon Mound (No. 2)*,[29] Lord Reid set out the generally accepted statement as to reasonable foreseeability. The defendant discharged inflammable oil into Sydney Harbour. The trial judge held that the damage to the plaintiff's ships by fire from the ignited oil was not reasonably foreseeable and so damages were not recoverable for negligence, but that the defendants were liable in nuisance because nuisance liability did not depend on foreseeability. On the facts, the Privy Council decided that the damage was reasonably foreseeable and therefore the plaintiff was entitled to damages in negligence. On the question of nuisance, Lord Reid said that 'although negligence may not be necessary, fault of some kind is almost always necessary and fault generally involves foreseeability'. He went on to state that 'it is not sufficient that the injury suffered by the respondent's vessels was the direct result of nuisance if that injury was in the relevant sense unforeseeable'.

In the more recent case of *Cambridge Water* v. *Eastern Counties Leather* [1994] 2 AC 264, HL, the defendants were held not to be liable in nuisance for the pollution of an underground water supply on the ground that seepage was not reasonably foreseeable. Lord Goff stated that:

[29] *Overseas Tankship (UK) Ltd* v. *Miller Steamship Co Pty* [1967] 1 AC 617.

'by no means [should] the defendant be held liable for damage of a type which he could not reasonably foresee; the development of the law of negligence in the past sixty years points strongly towards a requirement that such foreseeability should be a prerequisite of liability in damages for nuisance'.[30]

Nuisance is a tort connected with land, therefore damage unconnected with land, for example, personal injury, is not recoverable.

Whether or not physical damage or encroachment has occurred is a matter of fact for the court to determine. Often, expert evidence will be required to show relevant causation in physical damage cases. In encroachment cases, the very fact of the encroachment, i.e. a cornice projecting over the claimant's garden, is sufficient.

In *St Helen's Smelting Co. Ltd* v. *Tipping* (1862) 11 HL Cas 642; 11 ER 1483, Lord Westbury drew a distinction between material damage to the claimant's premises and interference with the use and enjoyment of property.

In the case of interference with the use and occupation of land, there is no definite standard at which interference with enjoyment is considered a nuisance; it is very much a matter of the circumstances of the case. In deciding what constitutes interference the courts have had to strike a balance between the right of the defendant to use its property for its own lawful enjoyment and the right of the claimant to the undisturbed enjoyment of its property.

In *Bonford* v. *Turnley* 3 B & S 66; 122 ER 27, Bramwell B termed the courts' approach to the conflicting interests of the plaintiff and defendant as a 'rule of give and take, live and let live'. The court will look to the reasonableness of the plaintiff's enjoyment compared with the defendant's use of its land.

Various tests have been applied to determine whether the defendants' actions constitute a nuisance. In *St Helen's*, Lord Westbury referred to whether 'the thing alleged is productive of sensible personal discomfort'. The test is flexible and in *Thompson-Schwab* v. *Costakis* [1956] 1 WLR 325 the court stated that whether or not a nuisance had been committed would vary according to the 'usages of civilized society at the relevant date'. The nuisance has to be considered substantial, not trivial, in the eyes of the reasonable man. Therefore, the sensitive claimant will not succeed on the basis that the activity offends his or her particular sensitivity. In *Robinson* v. *Kilvert* [1889] 41 ChD 88, the plaintiff did not succeed in his claim for damage to paper kept on his premises as the court held his trade to be 'exceptionally delicate'. The activities of the defendant would not otherwise affect an ordinary business.

The courts will also consider locality and have stood firmly by the principle that 'what would be a nuisance in Belgrave Square would not necessarily be so in Bermondsey'.[31]

2.7 Planning permission

As set out above, the nature of the locality is relevant, and the nature of an area may change due to the grant of planning permission. In *Gillingham BC* v. *Medway (Chatham) Dock Ltd* [1993] QB 343, the court held that where planning permission has been given to change the use of an area, nuisance will 'fall to be decided by reference to a neighbourhood with that development and use and not as it was previously'.

---

30 See also *Arscott* v. *Coal Authority* [2004] EWCA Civ 892.

31 *Sturges* v. *Bridgeman* (1879) 11 ChD 852 per Thesiger LJ.

This appears to sit uncomfortably with the landowner's right to enjoyment of his or her land as the landowner may not have a choice in the development of the area. In *Hunter* v. *Canary Wharf* (1997) 2 WLR 684, the case concerned an action by a group of residents for damages due to, *inter alia*, interference to television reception between 1989 and 1991/2 caused by the building of the Canary Wharf tower.

While the issue of planning permission was considered, their Lordships ruled against the plaintiffs on the separate ground that the right to build on land is an immutable right in common law, only restricted by agreement. In other words, neighbouring landowners have no right to light or air unless otherwise agreed. In most situations this will be the case.

In *Hunter*, the House of Lords endorsed the concept that residents of an area have the opportunity to make representations at planning permission stage. In theory this should give residents the opportunity to ensure that the area use is not changed if they do not want it to be. However, on the facts in *Hunter*, the local residents in practice had very little choice but to accept the development as the Secretary of State had designated the area an enterprise zone with the effect that planning permission was deemed to have been granted for any form of development and no application for permission was necessary. Lord Hoffman, at 712, justified this situation on the ground that Parliament had authorised the ordinary protections to the local residents to be removed on the ground that national interest required the rapid regeneration of the Docklands area.

In *Gillingham* and *Hunter*, however, the courts did maintain the view that a planning authority 'has no jurisdiction to authorise a nuisance' (*Allen* v. *Gulf Oil Refining Ltd* [1980] QB 156). This is evidenced in the more recent case of *Wheeler* v. *Saunders* [1996] Ch. 19. There the plaintiffs sued the defendants on the basis that the smell from the defendant's pig farm constituted a nuisance. The defendant argued that as planning permission had been sought and gained and the plaintiff had had the opportunity to make representations at that stage, the plaintiff had no claim. The Court of Appeal stated that on the basis of *Gillingham* and *Allen*, notwithstanding the fact that planning permission had been granted, that permission did not license the nuisance. A distinction was drawn between a large-scale or strategic planning decision affected by considerations of public interest and permission to change the use of one small piece of land for the benefit of an individual.

2.8 Building and demolition

Building and demolition works will not generally be considered a nuisance as long as the builder ensures 'he uses all reasonable skill and care to avoid annoyance to his neighbour'.[32] The builder should be able to show that it has taken all reasonable steps necessary to avoid noise, dirt and dust. Examples of other factors which a builder could put forward to discharge the burden are that the hours during which the work was done were restricted, the limits placed on the amount of any particular types of work done simultaneously, or that a special arrangement has been entered into with the neighbour to suit the neighbour's particular needs.[33]

The court will attempt to reconcile the interests of local inhabitants and the desirability of developing sites. In *City of London Corporation* v. *Bovis Construction Ltd* [1992] 3 AER 697, Lord Bingham recognised that while unreasonable and excessive noise has been recognised as capable of being a nuisance for many years, a balance

32 Vaughan Williams J in *Harrison* v. *Southwark and Vauxhall Water Co.* [1892] 2 Ch 409.
33 For more detail see Wignall – *Nuisances*, Sweet & Maxwell, 1998, p. 16.

must be struck between local inhabitants' interests and the general desirability of re-developing sites of great economic value. In this case, Bovis were construction managers at the Beaufort House site in the City of London and subject to noise abatement notices which they contravened. The case concerns other principles[34] but Lord Bingham's comments are of interest and develop the principle that building operations carried out inconsiderately will be stopped by injunction.

2.9 Building and the right to light

When deciding to construct a building in and around other buildings, the potential constructor/developer should take account of rights of light. Rights of light may be acquired by grant or prescription (long usage). In *Colls* v. *Home and Colonial Stores* [1904] AC 179 at 208, Lord Lindley stated that the owner of such rights to light (termed 'ancient lights') is entitled to:

> 'sufficient light, according to the ordinary notions of mankind, for the comfortable use and enjoyment of his house as a dwelling-house, if it is a dwelling-house, or for the beneficial use and occupation of the house, if it is a warehouse, a shop, or other place of business'.

Sufficient light has been further defined as 'the amount of light left' and can vary depending on the nature of the occupation and in some circumstances, locality.

It should be noted that interference with rights of light of the owner of such rights on adjoining land will not necessarily prevent planning permission being granted, but if a constructor/developer were to construct a building that interfered with ancient lights then it may be faced with the prospect of an injunction by the owner of those ancient lights. However, there is authority that damages may be granted instead of an injunction, depending on the facts of the case.[35]

2.10 Defences

The general defences available in tort are available for an action in nuisance (see Section 1.4 of this chapter). In addition to these, there are some specific defences to an action in nuisance which should be considered, particularly in construction cases.

It is not a defence to an allegation of nuisance that an individual has taken all reasonable steps to prevent the activity becoming a nuisance.[36]

Generally, no liability is imposed on the owner of land for nuisance caused by a trespasser or natural causes unless it can be shown that the owner had knowledge or means of knowledge of the nuisance and should have corrected or obviated the effects of the nuisance (see *Sedleigh-Denfield* v. *O'Callaghan* [1940] AC 880). This principle has been recently considered in *Bybrook Barn Centre* v. *Kent County Council* 1 December 2000, CA. Here, Kent County Council (in its capacity as a highway authority) diverted a stream under a road through a circular section culvert in 1936. Sixty years later the culvert became overloaded, water backed up in the stream and it burst its banks, flooding a garden centre and causing substantial damage. At first instance Bybrook (the garden centre)'s claim was dismissed. However, the Court of Appeal firmly stated that if a person is able to regulate a nuisance emanating from his or her property then

[34] Principally the responsibility of management contractors and the terms of injunctions.

[35] See the recent cases of *Regan* v. *Paul Properties Ltd* [2007] Ch. 135 and *Tamares (Vincent Square) Ltd* v. *Fairpoint Properties (Vincent Square) Ltd* [2006] EWHC 3589.

[36] See Lindley LJ in *Rapier* v. *London Tramways* [1893] 2 Ch. 588.

they have an obligation to take reasonable steps to abate it, even it is caused by a third party or natural causes. The Court found that the Council knew the stream was overloaded and the expenditure to remedy the problem was not excessive. The Council was therefore ultimately held liable.

It is generally a defence to show ignorance of the facts constituting the nuisance. This defence will not work if the ignorance is due to the omission to use reasonable care to discover the facts. However, in *Wringe* v. *Cohen* [1940] 1 KB 229 the court stated that if premises become dangerous due to the owner's actions, the owner is liable even if he or she did not know of the danger and was not negligent in not knowing. If the premises become dangerous because of the act of a third party or a latent defect, the occupier is not liable without proof of knowledge or the means of knowledge and failure to abate it.

A fourth defence to nuisance is that of contributory negligence. It is a defence to an action in nuisance, except where the consequences of the act were intended by the defendant.

It is not generally a defence to lay the blame for the nuisance at the foot of an independent contractor (see *Bower* v. *Peate*, considered in more detail above). Further, it is no defence for the defendant to claim that the plaintiff 'came to' the nuisance. In *Sturges* v. *Bridgeman* (1879) 11 ChD 852, the doctor plaintiff built up a consulting room against a wall which adjoined his neighbour's kitchen in which mortars were pounded between 10 a.m. and 1 p.m. The plaintiff was successful, the courts upholding the principle that a person cannot be deprived of the right to land and comfortable enjoyment of that land.

It may also be possible to defend a claim on the basis that it was not reasonably practicable to abate the nuisance. This has had particular relevance for statutory undertakers such as utility companies – see *Glossop* v. *Heston & Isleworth Local Board* [1879] 12 ChD 102.

2.11 Statutory authority

A further defence to consider, particularly in relation to public nuisance, is that of statutory authority. Where a statute has authorised the doing of a particular act, or the use of land in a particular way, which inevitably causes nuisance, it is not actionable provided that every reasonable step consistent with the exercise of the statutory powers has been taken to prevent the nuisance occurring. This is relevant to construction operations which may normally constitute a nuisance but which are permitted by statute.

For example, in *Allen* v. *Gulf Oil Refining Ltd* [1980] QB 156 the House of Lords construed the Act in question, authorising the construction of a refinery, as conferring immunity from an action in nuisance upon the company involved.

Each Act must be interpreted separately and the burden of proving that the nuisance is inevitable falls on those with the statutory authority. They must show that all reasonable care and skill, according to the state of scientific knowledge at the time, has been taken (see *Allen* v. *Gulf Oil Refining Ltd*). Statutes sometimes provide compensation for those affected but this is not always the case.

This defence can be successfully defeated if the plaintiff can show that any nuisance caused by the activities granted by statute exceeded that for which immunity was conferred or that the acts authorised by statute had been carried out negligently.

In *Allen* v. *Gulf Oil*, the court stated the plaintiff had no action provided the defendant company could prove that it was inevitable that, using all due diligence, neighbours should sustain the harm complained of, even though no compensation for that harm was directly given by the Act. The only remedy the plaintiff then had was for the extent that the nuisance exceeded that for which immunity was conferred.

If reasonable care is not taken then liability will arise. In *Tate & Lyle* v. *Greater London Council* [1983] 2 AC 509, it was held that the GLC had not acted with due diligence in exercising its statutory powers in relation to the construction of various ferry terminals in the Thames and consequently should pay three-quarters of the costs which the plaintiff had incurred in dredging, the remaining quarter being the amount of cost that would have been incurred if it had acted diligently.

In the recent case of *Andrews* v. *Reading Borough Council (No. 2)* [2005] EWHC 256, the claimant was awarded compensation for interference with his right to Private and Family Life under Art. 8 of the Human Rights Convention, due to an increase in traffic noise experienced in his house as a result of the defendants' road improvement scheme. The defendants argued, unsuccessfully, that the award of compensation was precluded since the claimant's situation fell outside the criteria stipulated by the Noise Insulation Regulations 1975. The court held that there was no indication in the Regulations that immunity was to be conferred upon highway authorities from any action by those not included within them. Note that in the case of *Hanifa Dobson* v. *Thames Water* (see above) Mr Justice Ramsey considered that damages could be awarded under the Human Rights Act where such damages were necessary to afford just satisfaction.

It can be seen in these cases it might be said that Parliament and the courts are trying to balance the public and the private interest.

3 *RYLANDS* v. *FLETCHER*

3.1 Introduction

The rule in *Rylands* v. *Fletcher*[37] is an offshoot of the law relating to nuisance. It encompasses 'escaping liability'. In construction this is often seen in the form of flooding from, for example, drainage to buildings which causes substantial damage. A question that arises in those cases is whether the flooding is due to defective design and often, therefore, breach of contract. However, another option to consider is tort liability under *Rylands* v. *Fletcher*. The main difference between private and public nuisance and *Rylands* v. *Fletcher* liability is that it was considered that the rule in *Rylands* imposed liability on defendants regardless of foreseeability of damage. The law has now been substantially reviewed in *Cambridge Water* v. *Eastern Counties Leather* (1994) 2 AC 264.

3.2 The rule in *Rylands* v. *Fletcher*

In *Rylands* v. *Fletcher* the defendants built a reservoir on their land. Water collected and flowed into the plaintiffs' mine causing damage. The defendants were held liable on the ground that they kept the water on their land at their own peril. Blackburn J said:

> 'the person who for his own purposes brings on his land and collects and keeps there anything likely to do mischief if it escapes must keep it in at his peril, and, if he does not do so, is prima facie answerable for all the damage which is the natural consequence of its escape'.

In the House of Lords this was refined to bring in the concept of the 'non-natural user'. That is to say that the defendant must be using his or her land for a non-natural use. The

[37] (1866) LR 1 Ex 265 at 279; affirmed in HL (1886) LR 3 HL 330.

rule was interpreted to impose strict liability, that foreseeability of damage was not necessary to establish liability. This principle has now been very much eroded.

In *Cambridge Water* v. *Eastern Counties Leather*, the defendants were leather manufacturers whose tanning chemicals had seeped through a concrete floor into the soil and subsequently into the plaintiff's underground watercourse used to supply the local public. The water was deemed unfit for human consumption. The seepage was unforeseeable and the plaintiffs attempted to establish liability on the basis of the *Rylands* rule. The House of Lords took a narrow view of the extent of strict liability and held that the defendants were not liable on the ground that the rule in *Rylands* did not apply.

The reasoning behind the decision is clearer. Their Lordships denied the existence of a general principle of strict liability and stated that, in the absence of negligence, liability would only be imposed in certain defined situations. The view was taken that the rule in Rylands should be no more than an extension of the law of nuisance to cases of isolated escapes. Lord Goff stated that instances of strict liability should be imposed by Parliament rather than by the courts. Parliament has not responded to this invitation. The courts' view is to some extent similar to that of Australia where it is considered that the rule in Rylands is absorbed by the law of negligence generally (see *Burnie Port Authority* v. *General Jones Pty Ltd* (1994) 120 ALR 42), although it should be noted that in the later case of *Transco* v. *Stockport MBC* [2004] 2 AC 1, in which the House of Lords endorsed its view in Cambridge Water, their Lordships denied that the principle had been absorbed by the tort of negligence.[38]

After an analysis of the judgment of Lord Blackburn in Rylands, Lord Goff (in Cambridge Water) concluded, at 302D, that:

> 'the general tenor of his statement of principle is that knowledge, or at least foreseeability of the risk, is a prerequisite of the recovery of damages under the principle; but that the principle is one of strict liability in the sense that the defendant may be held liable notwithstanding he has exercised all due skill and care to prevent the escape occurring'.

This significantly waters down the original effect of the rule. Particularly as Lord Goff went on to hold, at 309E, that 'foreseeability of damage of the relevant type should be regarded as a prerequisite of liability in damages under the rule'.

It is worth noting that the courts are increasingly taking the view that the concepts of 'natural' and 'non-natural' use of land are unhelpful, and that an approach similar to the concept of 'reasonable user' in nuisance is more appropriate: see for example *Arscott* v. *Coal Authority* [2004] EWCA Civ 892, per Laws L.J. at 29.

3.3 Who can sue and who can be sued?

The person liable is the owner or controller of the dangerous thing. If he or she brings or collects it on land, he or she is liable even if that individual is not the owner or occupier of the land. Therefore, in construction a contractor bringing dangerous chemicals onto site may be liable for their escape and subsequent damage. The occupier will be liable as well in such a case if the dangerous thing is brought or collected on his or her land for the occupier's purpose or with his or her permission. The plaintiff need not have an interest in land affected to sue but must be affected by the escape. For example, in *Charing Cross Electricity Supply Co.* v. *Hydraulic Power Co.* [1914] 3 KB 772, a water company

[38] See also *LMS International Limited* v. *Styrene Packaging and Insulation Limited* [2008] EWHC 2065 (TCC).

authorised by statute to carry water under the surface of a highway was liable for the escape of water from a broken main which damaged the cables of an electricity supply company which also ran under the highway.

It is very doubtful whether a claimant can recover damages for personal injury under the rule (see *Read* v. *J. Lyons & Co. Ltd* [1947] AC 156 at 169 and 173 and the obiter comments of the House of Lords in *Transco* v. *Stockport MBC* at 9 and 35).

There is no liability unless the thing which does the damage escapes from a place where the defendant has occupation or control over land to a place outside the defendant's occupation or control. In *Read* v. *J. Lyons & Co.* a worker in a munitions factory failed to recover when injured by a shell exploding within the factory on the basis that there had been no 'escape'.

3.4 Special rules for water, gas, electricity, fire, explosives, poisonous waste and oil pollution, aircraft and nuclear installations

As mentioned above, the *Rylands* v. *Fletcher* rule allows for particular exceptions which now are exceptions mainly because they impose strict liability! The exceptions are too numerous to detail here, but it is worth noting that in many cases there are specific statutes in place governing liability on a *Rylands* basis.

4 BREACH OF STATUTORY DUTY

4.1 Introduction

Statute imposes numerous duties on many different organisations from local authorities and statutory undertakers to private companies. If any of these bodies breach their obligations under statute, then a claimant may have an action in tort against them for that breach.

4.2 Is the breach actionable?

In addition to showing that the obligations under the relevant statute have been breached and that the breach caused loss or harm to the claimant, the breach must be capable of being actioned. This area of law has been subject to much interpretation by the courts. The important point is that not all breaches of statutory duty can be actioned by a claimant in the civil courts. This is satisfactory if there are other remedies within the Act for a breach of obligations under the Act but much less satisfactory if there are no such provisions.

In addition to showing that the breach caused loss, the claimant must also show that the damage was of the type that the legislation in question was intended to prevent. Further a claimant must be within the category of persons that the statute was meant to protect. This area of law is governed by the common law.

In *Cutler* v. *Wandsworth Stadium Limited* [1946] AC 398 at 407, Lord Simonds stated that whether or not a breach was actionable 'must depend on a consideration of the whole Act and the circumstances, including the pre-existing law, in which it was enacted'.

In *Lonrho Limited* v. *Shell Petroleum Limited* [1981] 2 AER 456, Lord Diplock in the House of Lords approved the general rule that 'where an act creates an obligation, and enforces the performance in a specified manner. . . that performance cannot be enforced in any other manner'.

Lord Diplock recognized two exceptions to this rule. First, where the obligation or prohibition is imposed for the benefit of the protection of a particular class of individuals. Secondly, where the statute creates a public right and an individual member of the public suffers 'particular damage'.

Therefore, the general principles appear to be that if an Act provides for a penalty, that penalty is the only remedy, subject to the two exceptions. Sometimes if another common law remedy is available this may affect the decision of the court as to whether the breach is actionable in tort.

4.3 The two exceptions

The first question concerning the first exception is what is a class of individuals? The courts have made a distinction between a class and the public at large. For example, visitors to premises which are in breach of fire regulations due to the lack of an adequate fire escape are considered a class whereas the public using a highway are not,[39] although pedestrians using a pedestrian crossing are.[40]

However, in the recent case of *X (minors)* v. *Bedfordshire County Council* (1999) 3 WLR 1252, the House of Lords held that the social services authority was not liable for breach of statutory duty in respect of child care legislation despite the fact that such legislation had been put in place for a limited class, that is to say, children at risk.

Lord Diplock's second exception comes into play when a statute creates a public right and an individual member of the public suffers 'particular damage'. The damage must be direct and substantial and different from that which was common to the rest of the public.

In considering the two exceptions, the first is by far the most important. In determining whether or not the statute was designed to protect a limited class of individuals, a broad analysis of the statute is required – see *Phelps* v. *Hillingdon LBC* [2000] 3 WLR 776 at 789E-H per Lord Slynn. Recently the courts have appeared reluctant to hold that the local authorities owe a duty of care in respect of the exercise of their statutory duties and powers for fear of challenging decisions of policy. However, a route to liability may be found in holding that the employees of the statutory body owe duties of care in discharging their functions. The statutory body is then vicariously liable (as employer) for any breaches of these duties: see *Phelps* (above). On this basis, it might be argued that a significant new extension to the potential liability of statutory bodies has been fashioned.

4.4 Construction and breach of statutory duty

The courts are more likely to infer a breach in cases of industrial safety legislation. Therefore those in the construction industry must be aware of such legislation and enforce it or be at risk of multiple actions by contractors, employees or other parties that may be affected. Some statutes will state expressly whether it is intended to create a right of action in favour of someone who suffers loss.

5 OCCUPIERS' LIABILITY

5.1 Introduction

Occupiers' liability is governed by two statutes, the Occupiers' Liability Acts 1957 and 1984. The former is concerned with invitees coming onto the land and the 1984 Act is

[39] *Solomons* v. *Gertzenstein Ltd* [1994] 2 QB 243. Compare *Phillips* v. *Britannia Hygenic Laundry Ltd* [1923] 2 KB 832.

[40] *London Passenger Transport Board* v. *Upson* [1949] AC 155.

concerned, *inter alia*, with trespassers. In the context of construction, the 1957 Act is of more importance. For example, it governs the liability to and of independent contractors when carrying out work on another's land.

5.2 The Occupiers' Liability Act 1957

The main purpose of this Act was to replace the old common law duties with a standard duty of care. Prior to the Act, a fine distinction was placed on the law relating to 'invitees' and the law relating to 'licensees'. The Act went some way in trying to level the standard of care owed and is now more akin to the law of negligence.

Section 1(1) states:

> '[the Act] shall have effect in place of the rules of the common law, to regulate the duty which an occupier of premises owes to his visitors in respect of dangers due to the state of the premises or to things done or omitted to be done on them'.

5.3 The occupier

The Act does not define an 'occupier' and therefore one must look to the common law for a definition. 'Occupier' is a wide term encompassing anyone with a degree of control associated with and arising from his or her presence in and the use of the premises (*Wheat* v. *Lacon* [1966] AC 552). A contractor may be liable as an occupier (*Bunker* v. *Charles Brand & Son Ltd* [1969] 2 QB 480). For example, a builder may be considered an occupier if it is in control of part of the house even though it has no power to permit or prohibit the entry of other persons to the house. There may be multiple occupiers, in the case of the builder the householder may also be deemed to occupy. The owner is not always considered to be the occupier.

An interesting case in the context of building and the status of contractors and subcontractors is *Ferguson* v. *Welsh* [1987] 3 AER 777. Here, a local authority subcontracted building work to an independent contractor. An express condition of the tender was that the work should not be subcontracted without the local authority's express permission. Despite this, the contractor subcontracted the works to a firm of builders which employed an unsafe system of work. This led to the collapse of a wall, injuring the plaintiff. The plaintiff sued the builders, the contractor and the council. It was most likely that the only party able to pay damages was the council.

The House of Lords upheld the Court of Appeal judgment that the council was not an occupier in relation to the 1957 Act. Both the contractor and subcontractor were deemed to be occupiers but the council had not invited the plaintiff onto the premises and had not delegated that right to the contractor. The House of Lords went on to state that an occupier would not usually be liable to an employee of a contractor employed to carry out work on the occupier's premises if the employee was injured as a result of an unsafe system of work used by the employer as it would not be reasonable to expect the occupier to supervise the contractor to ensure that the duty owed to employees to use a safe system of work was being carried out.

5.4 Visitors

Visitors under the Act are the same people who under the common law would be treated as licensees or invitees. Visitors have implied or express permission to come onto the land. Permission may be implied, for example in the public part of a shop, or when the public habitually uses the premises with the knowledge of the occupier and no steps are taken to prevent this. If visitors stray from the usual access then they become trespassers (discussed in Section 7 of this chapter). Repeated trespass does not constitute a license to come onto the property (see *Edwards* v. *Railway Executive* [1952] AC 737).

The occupier's permission may be limited to only part of the property. A license may be implied to enter only the parts of the property where the visitor may reasonably be supposed to go in the belief that he or she is entitled or invited to be there. Similarly, visitors may be limited to the time when they visit the property – for example a public house. Special considerations apply to children, however. The presence of an attractive but dangerous object, on land may aid the inference of an implied licence (Cmd. 9305 (1955)). This is an important point for those with building sites which should be secured from children.

In the recent case of *Jolley* v. *Sutton LBC* [2000] 1 WLR 1082, the House of Lords upheld the plaintiff's appeal that liability under the 1957 Act can be very much a question of fact and circumstance, particularly in relation to children. In this case, the claimant was a 14-year-old boy who had been playing with an abandoned boat on the council's land when the boat fell on him and he suffered serious injury. The House concluded that the council was liable although on slightly differing grounds. Of interest is Lord Hoffmann's view in concluding that the accident had been reasonably foreseeable on the basis that the defendants had admitted they were negligent in failing to remove the boat and that, given these circumstances, the defendants were liable for 'the materialisation of even relatively small risks of a different kind'. Further, the judge stated that the ingenuity of children in finding different ways to do mischief should not be underestimated. Therefore builders who leave dangerous but attractive items on land should be careful if reasonable care demands that the item should be removed, otherwise the builder could be liable under the 1957 Act.

5.5 Duty of care

The duty of care imposed by Section 2 of the 1957 Act provides that:

> 'it is a duty to take such care as in all the circumstances of the case is reasonable to see that the visitor will be reasonably safe in using the premises for the purpose for which he is invited or permitted by the occupier to be there'.

The situation is one of fact to be determined with regard to all the circumstances of the case, for example, how obvious the danger is, warnings, lighting and fencing are all relevant. Also, occupiers must be prepared for children to be less careful than adults.[41]

Further, the 1957 Act imposes a duty on the occupier not just to take care of negligent acts but also negligent omissions.

If the visitor enters under a contract then Section 5 of the 1957 Act states that the occupier owes that person the statutory duty of care. It is implied into the contract.

5.6 Entering the premises to carry out works

Section 2(3)(b) of the 1957 Act states that an occupier 'may expect that a person, in the exercise of his calling, will appreciate and guard against any special risks ordinarily incident with it'. For example, a scaffolder's work is inherently dangerous and it would be wrong to expect an occupier to take responsibility for factors inherent in the scaffolder's job. On the other hand, if the scaffolder were to be caused injury by a

[41] Occupiers' Liability Act 1957, s. 2(3)(a), see also *Jolley* v. *Sutton LBC*, *supra.*

loose tile, then the duty of care owed by the occupier should bite. In *Clare* v. *Whittaker & Son Ltd* [1976] ICR 1, QBD the occupier of a building site was not liable to the experienced workmen of an independent roofing contractor for failing to urge them to use the crawling boards which had been provided for their protection.

5.7 Duty to warn

Whether or not the occupier has discharged his or her common duty of care to the visitor must be assessed in relation to all the circumstances of the case. Section 2(4) of the 1957 Act states that where damage is caused to a visitor by a danger about which he or she had been warned by the occupier, the warning ought not to be treated without more as absolving the occupier from liability unless in all the circumstances it was enough to enable the visitor to be reasonably safe. Therefore a warning is not an absolute bar to recovery. It should be borne in mind on building sites that warnings should be centrally placed and easily visible and specific as to the danger that may occur. It is not a defence that the visitor was merely aware of the risk.

5.8 Defences

The most common defence to a claim under the 1957 Act is *volenti non fit injuria* (that the risk was willingly accepted by the visitor). For example, in the case where a visiting rugby player injured himself it was held that he willingly accepted the risk of playing on a field which he knew had a concrete wall running at a distance of seven feet three inches from the touchline (*Simms* v. *Leigh Rugby Football Club* [1969] 2 AER 923). Willingly accepting the risk usually means having knowledge of the precise risk in advance. Therefore, the spectator to motor racing who was catapulted into the air by safety ropes was held not to have willingly accepted the risk. The fault lay with the organisers' failure on safety arrangements (*White* v. *Blackmore* [1972] 2 QB 651).

Another defence is that of contributory negligence. The apportionment provisions of the Law Reform (Contributory Negligence) Act 1945 apply to an action in occupiers' liability.

A question asked by many in occupation of dangerous sites is whether they can exclude liability by notice or warning. Section 2(1) of the 1957 Act provides that the occupier owes any visitor the common duty of care 'except insofar as he is free to and does extend, restrict, modify or exclude his duty to any visitor or visitors by agreement or otherwise'. In practice, there are limits to how far liability can be excluded; particularly as the Unfair Contract Terms Act 1977 (UCTA) limits the occupier's power of exclusion.

Exclusion by contract is relatively straightforward but is subject to the UCTA (see Chapter 3.1). Liability can also be excluded by a suitably worded notice, also subject to the UCTA. This is explained in law as conditional licence – the occupier allowing someone onto his or her land on the condition that the occupier is not liable for loss or damage. This is a common occurrence, for example, car parks and private parking areas often display such notices.

The power to exclude is wide. However, the notice must be sufficiently explicit in its terms. The question appears to be whether the occupier took reasonable steps to tell the visitor of the exclusion.[42] One exception which has a limiting effect is if the claimant did not have a choice to enter the premises. It has been held that in such cases the

[42] Clerk & Lindsell on *Torts*, 19th Edn, 12–47.

occupier cannot exclude liability. It has also been suggested that this principle should be rethought, given its potentially damaging effect on the ability to exclude liability on the part of the occupier.

5.9 Liability of occupier for independent contractors

Section 2(4)(b) of the 1957 Act provides that where damage is caused by faulty construction, maintenance or repair by an independent contractor employed by an occupier, the occupier is not liable if in all the circumstances he or she acted reasonably in entrusting the work to an independent contractor and had taken such steps (if any) as ought reasonably to have been taken in order to satisfy him or herself that the contractor was competent and that the work had been done properly.

6 DEFECTIVE PREMISES ACT 1972

A wide range of tortious duties are now imposed by statute. These range from the wide number of health and safety related duties which are often derived from EC law to duties on occupiers and builders. For the construction industry one of the most important sets of statutory duties can be found in the provisions of the Defective Premises Act 1972.

The Act applies to 'dwellings' by which is meant residential, rather than commercial properties.

Section 1 of the Act imposes a duty to build dwellings properly:

> '(1) A person taking on work for or in connection with the provision of a dwelling (whether the dwelling is provided by the erection or by conversion or enlargement of a building) owes a duty – if the dwelling is provided to the order of any person, to that person; and without prejudice to paragraph (a) above, to every person who acquires an interest (whether legal or equitable) in the dwelling; to see that the work which he takes on is done in a workmanlike or, as the case may be, professional manner, with proper materials and so that as regards that work the dwelling will be fit for habitation when completed'.

There is some doubt as to whether the final part of Section 1 (fitness for habitation) imposes a free-standing and separate duty from those relating to the work and the materials used. Certainly in the case of *Thompson* v. *Alexander & Partners* (1992) 59 BLR 81 it was thought that there was no separate duty and that the words simply explained or qualified the duty imposed earlier in the section.

The wide duty imposed by Section 1 applies to anyone who takes on the type of work described in the section and includes builders, subcontractors and even professionals such as architects and engineers. Section 1(4) extends the duty to developers and local authorities who organize the works. However, under Section 1(2) those working under the instructions of others will not be subject to the duty so long as they warn the person giving the instructions if the instructions themselves are defective.

The Act also applies to any failure to carry out remedial work as well as to carrying out such work badly (see *Andrews* v. *Schooling* [1991] 1 WLR 783, CA).

Any cause of action in respect of a breach of the duty imposed under Section 1 accrues when the building has been completed. However, if the person who has done the work returns to site after completion to do further work, then the cause of action accrues only once the further work has been completed. (Section 1(5) of the 1972 Act and Section 1.6 of this chapter).

7 TRESPASS

This section considers trespass to land. This is most easily defined as the unjustified interference with the possession of land. Trespass is distinct from negligence in that it is actionable *per se* without proof of damage.

7.1 Intention

While the interference with the possession of the land must be intentional, this is readily established as the intention that is required to be shown is simply that the trespasser intended to enter upon the land. It is not necessary to show that the trespasser intended to trespass or even knew that he or she was in fact trespassing. This has particular consequences for the construction industry where, for example, a crane operator may intend to swing the crane over adjoining land (and indeed may have no choice but to do so) but possess no intention to trespass on that land. Nevertheless the operator may be liable in trespass.

7.2 Possession

It is not necessary for the complainant to have some legal title to the land, possession of which has been interfered with. Unfortunately, there is as yet no coherent theory of possession in this area of the law and whether or not a complainant has a sufficient possessory interest to bring proceedings for trespass depends on the facts of the case. Physical presence or even control of the land will not be sufficient to found an action for possession. This might have particular consequences in the construction industry, where it will be the employer rather than the contractor who will be able to bring the action.

In the landlord and tenant context, it will often be the tenant rather than the landlord who will be best placed to bring proceedings for trespass to the demised property while the landlord will be unable to do so save if the trespass has caused damage to his or her reversionary interest. However, a person who is entitled to immediately possess land (otherwise known as having 'constructive possession') will be able, having taken possession, to sue for trespasses committed after the right to possess had accrued but before he or she was in physical possession of the land.

7.3 Interference

Interference with the right to possess may take place in a number of ways. For example, it is possible to trespass not only to the surface of the land but also to its subsoil, which may be owned by different entities. Thus, a construction project that involves tunnelling may cause a trespass to the owners of the subsoil while not trespassing on the surface. In contrast, digging holes vertically will trespass on both the surface and the subsoil.

A particularly problematic area in the construction industry is that with regard to trespass to airspace. It is now clear that while aircraft flying several hundred feet above a property will not be deemed to trespass, a crane swinging above property can be trespassing.[43]

It is also important to remember that trespass can be continuing, allowing several actions in respect of the same trespass to be brought. Thus, if bridge buttresses trespass on land and are not removed, actions in trespass can be brought for as long as the trespass continues (*Holmes* v. *Wilson* (1839) 10 A & E 50).

---

[43] See *Woollerton & Wilson Ltd* v. *Richard Costain Ltd* [1970] 1 WLR 411 and *Anchor Brewhouse Developments* v. *Berkley House (Docklands Developments)* (1987) 284 EG 625.

7.4 Defences

The most useful defence to an action for trespass is justification. The alleged trespasser may have the right to interfere with possession of the land by reason of permission (a licence) or by operation of law. For example, police and bailiffs are given the power to enter premises to carry out certain of their functions. However, if a person who is justified in interfering with possession of the land – whether by licence or law – acts without the conferred authority then he or she will be treated as a trespasser from the moment of entering onto the land.

An important statutory defence insofar as the construction industry is concerned is the Access to Neighbouring Land Act 1992. This allows a court to make an order granting access to land for the purpose of carrying out works that are reasonably necessary to preserve adjoining land. The works must be substantially more difficult to carry out without trespassing to justify the trespass. Further, the court will not make an order if to do so would cause unreasonable hardship or permit unreasonable interference with the enjoyment of the land. The works can include alteration, adjustment, improvement or demolition but these must be incidental to the work required for preservation. Thus, an order will not be granted so as to allow development.

7.5 Remedies

A complainant may seek to re-enter his or her land so long as no more than reasonable force is used.[44] Alternatively, the complainant may seek an order for recovery of the land so as to eject the trespasser. In addition, the complainant may recover mesne profits for the damage suffered while he or she has been out of the land. However, in the construction industry the most important remedies will often be an injunction and damages.

In practice, to avoid having an injunction made against them, contractors may be forced to offer large sums in damages to those whose land may be affected by building works. This will prevent the landowners obtaining an injunction because they will have been offered an alternative remedy for any trespass caused by the works. This appears to be the approach adopted in the case of tower cranes which swing over land adjoining the site (see *Woollerton & Wilson Ltd* v. *Richard Costain Ltd* [1970] 1 WLR 411). Thus, the works will be able to proceed but only at the cost of paying sums to the adjoining landowners. In practice, it will be a case of weighing the risk of injunctive proceedings and the consequent costs incurred by the delay in the works against paying sums in compensation to the adjoining landowners.

[44] It is outside the scope of this handbook to deal with trespass and squatters, where different considerations may apply.

General law

3.1 The law of contract

3.2 Construction health and safety

3.3 Insolvency in construction

3.4 Law of tort

3.5 Environmental issues

CHAPTER 3.5

Environmental issues

Kathryn Mylrea
CMS Cameron McKenna LLP

Peter Witherington
RSK Group plc

1 INTRODUCTION

This chapter will consider the framework of environmental regulation of the construction and demolition industry in the UK. It focuses on those areas which are of particular relevance to the construction industry so cannot be seen as a comprehensive guide to environmental regulation.

The quantity and complexity of environmental law continues to increase, as do public expectations about the environmental performance of all sectors of industry. Customer pressure has already delivered improvements in environmental performance in the sector and the setting of targets for further improvements. Like health and safety, much of environmental law is designed to be of universal application to commercial activity in the UK. However, it is fair to say that the construction industry may well be exposed to more aspects of environmental law than most. Laws now relate not only to compliance with environmental laws during the constructive period but also the environmental qualities of the buildings being constructed. In February 2007, the Environmental Agency stated that the UK construction industry faces commercial extinction if it does not come up with building designs that help people adapt to climate change.

The construction industry consistently ranks at or near the top of the tables of criminal prosecutions for failure to comply with environmental law making it a target for improvement. The issue of timber from sustainable sources was a high profile example of an issue that damaged the reputation of the industry. Industry and Government responded to the campaign and have taken steps to increase the use of timber from sustainable sources and recognition of forest certification standards.

2 SOURCES AND ENFORCEMENT OF ENVIRONMENTAL LAW

2.1 Sources of law

Legislation

Legislation is the principal source of environmental law in the UK. The main Acts of Parliament include a framework of broad principles and the rules needed to implement the principles set out in the acts are often provided in 'secondary' or 'derogated' legislation. This generally takes the form of:

- statutory instruments – generally referred to as 'regulations'
- guidance – which can be either statutory (i.e. a given Act requires regard to be had to it, such as guidance on contaminated land), or non-statutory
- by-laws – not frequently used but may be applicable (e.g. by-laws of the British Waterways Board related to canals).

Much of UK environmental law implements European environmental legislation. European environmental legislation is generally in the form of either a Directive or a Regulation. The difference between the two is that a regulation is binding on all member states as soon as it is issued and applies in that form while a directive needs to be implemented in member states through national legislation. Implementation of an EU Regulation may also involve national legislation to deal with details such as who is to act as the competent authority to enforce or administer the legislation. When implementing a directive, the member state must achieve the objectives set out in the directive but has some latitude about the means by which the objectives are achieved.

If a member state fails to implement or incorrectly implements European legislation then the remedy is generally action in the European Court of Justice against the

3.1 The law of contract
3.2 Construction health and safety
3.3 Insolvency in construction
3.4 Law of tort
3.5 Environmental issues

member state taken by the European Commission. There are some European directives which are of 'direct effect' and impose obligations on individuals within a member state rather than on the member state itself. The details of the 'direct effect' doctrine are beyond the scope of this chapter, but it is important to be aware of its existence particularly if working with utilities or other organizations which may be seen as an emanation of the state.

Case law

Case law has traditionally played an important role in environmental law in the UK. Civil actions dealing with nuisance, negligence and trespass have created a significant body of the UK case law considering environmental law issues.

There is also an increasing body of case law based on administrative law, in particular judicial review of decisions taken by regulators (e.g. challenging a decision on the basis that the decision maker did not follow the correct process when making it).

Most environmental legislation contains provision for an appeal to the relevant Secretary of State against refusal of authorizations and permits, and the grant of permits subject to conditions unacceptable to the holder. While each appeal needs to be determined on its merits, it can be relevant to review previous appeal decisions when considering launching an appeal. Time limits for commencing an appeal are set out in the legislation and need to be checked and strictly adhered to.

Most criminal prosecutions for breach of environmental laws take place in the Magistrates' Court. However, it should be borne in mind that most environmental provisions are 'triable' either way – in a Magistrates' Court or in the Crown Court. In a case where there has been major environmental damage, a fatality, or where the prosecuting authority considers the behaviour of the defendant to be so objectionable that a higher fine than that allowed in Magistrates' Court should be imposed, then the matter may be referred to the Crown Court. Appeals against criminal convictions are generally to the Court of Appeal (Criminal Division).

Cases in the European Court of Justice can also assist in interpretation of the law and what it obliges the UK regulators to do. Although not many cases actually make it to the European Court of Justice, understanding those decisions is necessary in order to understand issues such as those relating to the definition of waste or environmental impact assessment.

Environmental policy

Environmental law operates in a wider and continually developing policy context. Legislation tends to develop in order to respond to changed priorities in terms of environmental policy. Command papers and reports by bodies such as the Royal Commission on Environmental Pollution can be important indicators of environmental policy. Command papers are prepared by the Government and outline policies on matters of general interest to Parliament and to the public. Royal Commissions investigate for the Government and their reports aim to contain detailed, impartial and expert analysis of problems that Parliament does not have the time to consider fully.

An example of a policy development is the emphasis placed on the need to reduce construction and demolition waste. Provisions are contained in the Waste Strategy for England 2007 which sets out the Government's vision for sustainable waste management and proposes a target of halving the amount of this waste going to landfill by 2012 (possibly against 2005) as a result of waste reduction, re-use and recycling. (A target of this type will be the subject of consultation by the DTI 2007 as part of the Government's sustainable construction strategy). These measures may not need new legislation but the policy may mean that the existing legislation will be implemented more strictly or given greater priority. The work done by organizations such as WRAP (the Waste and Resources Action Programme) supports delivery of the policy to increase efficiency of the construction industries through better use of materials.

2.2 Environmental regulators

Environment Agency/Scottish Environmental Protection Agency

The agencies, which came into being in 1996, assumed the functions of various bodies that had previously been responsible for environmental regulation. They do not have a monopoly on regulation in the environmental field but the Environment Agency (EA) and Scottish Environmental Protection Agency (SEPA) do have a number of different functions.

In England and Wales, the EA's head office in Bristol is responsible for policies, standards, ensuring a consistent approach to environmental protection and financial control. The regional offices handle authorizations, licences, registration, regulation, monitoring and guidance, water management, pollution control and prevention, waste regulation and flood control. Some authorizations may be subject to a review by head office to ensure consistency of approval. The agencies also have inspectors who investigate alleged breaches of the environmental law regime and decide on prosecutions, subject to the advice of the EA lawyers.

The aim of the agencies is set out in the Environmental Protection Act 1990 and is to 'protect and enhance the environment taken as a whole so as to make . . . [a] . . . contribution towards obtaining the objective of sustainable development . . . subject to there being no deviation from the requirements of the Act and taking into account any likely costs as weighed against the possible benefits'.

Local authorities

For the construction industry, the local authority will often be as important a regulator as the EA. Local authorities have particular responsibility for the statutory nuisance provisions contained in the Environmental Protection Act 1990 as well as noise control under the Control of Pollution Act 1974. In England and Wales they also administer the air pollution control regime referred to as Local Authority Pollution Prevention and Control (LAAPC) or Local Authority Integrated Pollution Prevention and Control (LAIPPC).

Since April 2000, the regulation of contaminated land has rested with local authorities, although in cases of certain types (known as 'special sites'), contamination responsibility shifts to the Environment Agency. These responsibilities are in addition to the responsibilities for town and country planning and building regulation.

Water and sewerage companies

The Water Act 1989 established a new regulator for water pollution, the National Rivers Authority, and created new private water companies responsible for water and sewerage. The duties of the NRA passed to the EA in 1996 and the privatised sewerage undertakers are the licensing body for discharges to sewers through the grant of trade effluent consents or agreements to discharge. Appeals against the decisions of the water company go to the Director General of the Water Services (OFWAT) who is appointed under the Water Industry Act 1991 and whose main functions relate to the regulatory control of the water industry.

Health and Safety Executive (HSE)

One of the functions of the HSE is to enforce safety legislation and investigate accidents. The HSE also operates various licensing and approval schemes, for example, asbestos removal contractors. It is important to bear in mind that there can often be some overlap between environmental and health and safety duties and obligations (see Chapter 3.3).

Members of the public

Members of the public are generally entitled to bring private prosecutions for breaches of environmental legislation, although there can be some restrictions on this. Members of the public may also seek to become involved in enforcement of environmental law and policy through direct action including protest and sometimes trespass. Members of the public can write to the European Commission requesting investigation into Government decisions or legislation which they believe may not be in compliance with European law. Members of the public are encouraged to report environmental incidents e.g. the EA and many local authorities operate a fly-tipping hotline.

3 WASTE MANAGEMENT

3.1 Waste management and recycling

UK and European Community environmental legislation is increasing the complexity of laws relating to waste management. The cost of waste disposal, in particular landfill, has also increased significantly.

The basic legal rule is that to deposit, keep, treat or dispose of 'controlled waste', a waste management licence is mandatory unless the case falls within a licensing exemption. If the controlled waste is sufficiently hazardous to meet the definition of hazardous waste (formerly called special waste), then its handling and transport will attract additional procedural requirements and fees and usually means that waste management licensing exemptions are not available. Disposal costs for hazardous waste are also higher because of the limited range of sites which are now licensed to accept it since the implementation of the Landfill Directive. Disposing of waste can include burning it on site.

A waste management licence will only be granted to an individual meeting the definition of a 'fit and proper person'. Once a waste management licence is in existence it can only be surrendered when the EA is satisfied that the condition of the land in terms of the results of waste management activities is unlikely to cause pollution of the environment or harm to human health. This can be of real concern for those projects where the ongoing existence of a waste management licence will be seen as a commercial difficulty.

The construction industry will also be subject to the more general duty of care as regards waste, may be liable to pay landfill tax and may need to register as a waste carrier. Carriers are exempt from registration if they are carrying waste they have produced themselves, i.e. have not been contracted to carry someone else's waste, *unless* it is building or demolition waste.

Site waste management plans for the construction industry (SWMP) are likely to become a legal requirement for construction projects by April 2008 although some companies already prepare them on a voluntary basis. The stated aim of SWMPs is to reduce the amount of waste produced on construction sites and prevent fly-tipping. The proposal is for two levels of SWMP – standard, for projects costing between £250 000 and detailed, for projects costing more than £500 000. The SWMP must describe the amount and type of waste that will be produced on a construction site and how it will be reused, recycled or disposed of. It will also include a description of how the duty of care is being complied with. Enforcement will be by local authorities and it is proposed that the EA will have the power to prosecute for failure to make or keep a SWMP as well as failure to comply with or implement its terms. These offences will be triable either way. The possibility of a £300 fixed penalty notice for failing to produce the SWMP when requested to do so by an enforcing officer is also proposed. The financial threshold leaves the issue of how smaller projects handle waste open which is of concern and may well be addressed in the future.

What is waste? – Controlled waste and Hazardous Waste

Types of waste generally associated with construction activities include demolition, excavation, site and landscaping debris, contaminated soil and possibly equipment such as tanks or piping which has been removed. The legal definition of waste and 'controlled waste' can be confusing but, as a guiding principle, if someone is discarding or getting rid of something or intends to do so then you are probably dealing with waste. In situations where another party can re-use the material without having to treat or make any changes to it, then it may be possible to argue that the material is not waste, but this cannot be assumed to be the case (see below). The key concept in law is that something is being, or is intended to be discarded by its holder.

'Controlled waste' is defined in the Environmental Protection Act 1990 as 'household, industrial and commercial waste or any such waste'. The definition is expanded in the Controlled Waste Regulations 1992, SI 1992 No. 1056 as amended and provides that waste arising from works of construction or demolition, including waste arising from any preparatory works, is to be treated as industrial waste and is therefore controlled waste. 'Construction' includes not only the building of new structures, but also improvement, repair or alteration of existing buildings and structures. Waste arising from tunnelling or from any other excavation, waste removed from land on which it has previously been deposited and any soil with which such waste has been in contact, waste solvent and scrap metal (in many cases) are all treated as industrial waste and are therefore controlled waste. Some wastes that were outside the ambit of the Environmental Protection Act 1990, agricultural wastes and wastes from mines and quarries in particular are, since May 2006, treated as controlled wastes in the UK. The provisions of the EU Directive 2006/21/EC on the management of waste from the extractive industries need to be transposed by 1 May 2008 and will add additional requirements for minerals operators.

Interpretation of the definition of waste must be consistent with the European Court of Justice cases considering the point. The over-riding principle was set out in June 2000 in the ARCO Chemie Nederland Ltd etc case (joined cases C-418/97 and C-419/97) as being whether in fact something is waste must be determined in light of all the circumstances, regard being had to the aim of the directive and the need to ensure that its effectiveness is not undermined. This resulted in a very expansive and inclusive approach to defining waste.

In April 2002, the ECJ decision in Palin Granit Oy and Vehmassalon Kansanterveystön Kuntayhtymän Hallitus) dealt with leftover stone from quarrying which did not pose any real risk to human health or the environment. However, the fact that the holder of the stone had no particular plans to sell the leftover stone and stored it for an indefinite length of time meant that in that case, the leftover stone was waste.

In September 2003, in AvastaPolarit Chrome Oy (case C-114/01), the ECJ elaborated on leftover rock, holding that if the operator lawfully used the leftover rock on site for necessary works then it did not need to be categorised as waste.

However, later ECJ case law (Antonio Miselli, case C-457/02) confirmed the ECJ view that production or consumption residuals which can be or are reused in a cycle of consumption or production can still meet the definition of waste.

Difficult issues arise where something that is waste is treated – when does it cease being waste? A recent UK Court of Appeal case, *R (OSS Group Limited)* v. *Environment Agency (and others) and DEFRA*, considered whether waste lubricating and fuel oil collected from garages and then converted into 'marketable fuel oil' remained a waste once it was 'marketable fuel oil'. The Court of Appeal held that the 'fuel' did not have to be treated as waste – even though the original garages had intended to discard it. The Court focussed on whether the material needed to be treated as waste to provide the necessary legal protection and concluded, making a value judgment based on the policies contained in the Waste Framework Directive, that in this particular case, it did not.

These cases demonstrate that it may be possible to argue that a re-used or leftover material is not waste. These decisions take a long time to be finally resolved and the EA approach tends to be to treat anything discarded as waste.

Contaminated land can also be considered to be controlled waste, and European case law, in particular the *Paul Van de Walle, Daniel Laurent, Thierry Messch and Texaco Belgium SA (Case C-1/03, 7 Sept 2004)*, supports this proposition. The logic for this argument is that the contaminant, whatever it be, is waste since someone must intentionally or accidentally have discarded it. As the contaminant cannot sensibly be removed from the soil mass, consequently it must all be waste. However, legislation to implement proposed changes to the Waste Framework Directive is expected to clarify that a waste management licence is not needed for contaminated land which is not undergoing remediation.

The Hazardous Waste (England and Wales) Regulations 2005 and List of Wastes (England) Regulations 2005 set out the definition of hazardous waste. Hazardous waste was previously referred to as special waste. It is through these regulations that the UK implements the EC Directive on Hazardous Waste (91/689/EEC).

Determining if something is hazardous waste can be a complicated process which may require technical assistance. Hazardous Wastes are listed in the List of Wastes (England) Regulations 2005 and are marked with an asterix. Hazardous wastes display a specified hazardous property, for example being highly flammable, toxic, carcinogenic or eco-toxic. Of particular relevance to the construction industry is that contaminated soil being removed from a site can often be hazardous waste. Other hazardous wastes encountered on construction sites include asbestos, some treated timbers, adhesives, paints, cleaners, bitumen-based waterproofers, certain compounds of lead, electrical equipment and insulation.

Since April 2005, producers of hazardous waste have been required to notify their premises to the EA unless they fall within the exemptions set out in the Regulations. As a general rule, construction sites are not exempt from notification. The Regulations also changed the procedures for consignment notes including a consignment code based on a formula issued by the EA. They also include restrictions in mixing different categories of hazardous waste or mixing hazardous waste with non-hazardous waste. Notification lasts for twelve months and a small fee is payable. The Regulations prohibit any person, such as a waste carrier, from removing or transporting hazardous waste from premises that are either notified or exempt from the need to notify.

Failure to notify or comply with the other requirements of the Regulations constitutes a criminal offence and there is also provision in the Regulations for a fixed penalty notice for failure to comply with, *inter alia*, the notification provisions.

Re-using construction materials

It is usual practice on construction sites for excavated material to be stockpiled and reused as part of the development, e.g. for landscaping or land raising purposes. Quantities of this excavated material are often stored on site pending their use for these purposes. Whether or not a waste management licence is required for these activities must be considered on a case-by-case basis.

The legal argument for the stockpiled material not being waste is that the person who produced the material (i.e. the person who excavated it) did not intend, or was not required to discard it. In fact, the producer intended to produce the material for use in construction. This is then coupled with the fact that the material is put to a beneficial use without needing any special treatment or process. The EA does target 'sham re-cycling' so it is necessary to be able to show that 're-using' excavated materials as part of the development is not simply a convenient way to dispose of material that should be treated or disposed of in another way. It is critical if making this argument to be able to ensure that the quality of the excavated materials is appropriate for reuse and that a situation is not inadvertently created where a new hazard arises in the area where the material is used. The Waste Strategy for England 2007 includes a target for recycling of construction materials. The Department for Communities and Local Government (DCLG) Survey of Arisings and Use of Construction and Demolition Waste as Aggregate in England: 2005 estimates that 52% of the total construction and demolition waste produced in England in 2005 (estimated at 89.6 million tonnes) was recycled and this figure is set to improve.

The question of when something is or, particularly, is not waste will always be difficult where material is being re-used or recovered. Guidance on when something is *not* waste is still contained in Annex 2 of a joint circular from the DETR (11/94), Welsh Office (26/94) and Scottish Office (10/94) in Annex 2. Although some of the circulation has been superseded by European case law on waste, some provisions are still considered valuable by DEFRA and the EA. The circular introduces the concept of deciding whether or not a substance or object is still part of the 'normal commercial cycle or chain of utility' when determining if it has been discarded. If something can be used in its present form (albeit after repair) without going through a 'specialized recovery operation' then it is reasonable to consider that it is not waste. The example given in the guidance of a substance which is not waste is ash from power stations which is transferred for use as a raw material in the manufacture of building blocks. However, the same material, if it cannot be sold as a raw material and is consigned for disposal on a landfill site, will be waste.

In April 2006, the Environment Agency produced guidance that indicates that contaminated soils excavated for re-use on a site need not be classified as waste if they are suitable for the use to which they are intended, and there is certainty that the material will be put to that use. Further work is in progress by the Environment Agency and private sector stakeholders to develop protocols required to confirm that these two tests have been met.

Waste management licences – site licences and mobile plant licences

It is an offence under the Environmental Protection Act 1990 to deposit, treat, keep or dispose of controlled waste (or to knowingly cause or knowingly permit the same) without a waste management licence, or in breach of the terms of a licence. There are two types of waste management licence – a site licence authorising the deposit, recovery or disposal of controlled waste (including remediation of contaminated land) in or on land and a mobile plant licence authorising the recovery disposal of controlled waste using certain types of mobile plant. Recent changes to the licensing regime mean that a site licence can be either 'fixed' or 'bespoke'. Fixed licences cover specified activities and use a fixed set of conditions so they can usually be processed more quickly. Remediation of contaminated land and contaminated controlled wastes involving treatment requires a waste management licence. In order to address the problem, the EA has established an enforcement position whereby it will not generally prosecute if in-situ treatment of less than 1000 m^3 of contaminated land is required. For larger volumes, mobile plant licences rather than a full site licence can be obtained and the EA has a specific Application Form for a Mobile Treatment Licence for Contaminated Materials, Form WML1. (The terminology has recently changed and although the legislation still refers to mobile plant licences, the EA refer to mobile treatment licences (MTLs) in their guidance and application form). The advantage of this procedure is that it is the plant and not the site, which is licensed. The problems regarding a certificate of completion and surrendering a waste management licence are thereby largely avoided.

A bespoke licence is needed for other activities and would probably be appropriate if a site licence is needed as part of a construction project. There are exclusions and exemptions to the general rule about when a waste management licence is needed. Before relying on an exclusion or an exemption, the wording of the exemption should be checked carefully to ensure that all the specified criteria are, and continue to be, met. If the waste is 'hazardous' then an exemption does not apply unless that is specifically stated. Reliance on many of the exemptions depends on notification (i.e. registration) with the EA. Schedule 3 of the Waste Management Licensing Regulations 1994, sets out the possible exemptions. Possible exemptions relevant to the construction industry include:

(a) spreading of concrete, bricks, tiles and ceramics where the waste is specified for the purpose of reclamation, restoration or improvement of land which has been subject to industrial or other man-made development, and the use to which that land could be put would be improved by the spreading, is spread in accordance with any requirement in or under the Town and Country Planning Act 1990, is spread to a depth not exceeding 2 m and not more than 20 000 m^3 is spread per hectare (Exemption 9);
(b) manufacture of soil or soil substitutes from waste which arises from demolition, construction, tunnelling or other excavations – the manufacture must take place either on the site where the waste is produced or on the site where the manufactured product is to be applied and must not exceed 500 tonnes per day (Exemption 13);
(c) storage on site of waste which arises from demolition, construction, tunnelling or other excavation work or which consists of ash, slag, clinker, rock, wood, gypsum, bricks, blocks, roadstone or aggregate if the waste is to be used on that site and the total quantity does not exceed 20 000 tonnes (Exemption 13(4));
(d) crushing, grinding or other size reduction of waste bricks, tiles or concrete under authorization granted under Part 1 of the Environmental Protection Act 1990 (Exemption 24);
(e) baling, compacting, crushing, shredding or pulverizing waste at the place where it is produced (Exemption 27);
(f) temporary storage of waste pending its collection on the site where it is produced.

If no exemption is applicable and a party is depositing, treating, keeping or disposing of controlled waste then a waste management licence must be obtained. If a given material is not waste then there is no need for either an exemption or a licence. In practice, however, many people register an exemption because that may prove to be an easier course of action to enable schedules to be met rather than entering into a long and inconclusive discussion with the EA as to whether a particular material is or is not waste.

It should be noted however that there is a current review of the use of exemptions as part of a wider review of environmental permitting. The likelihood is that most of the exemptions that are currently available to the constructions industry will be dropped in favour of a 'light weight' environmental permit.

Application for a waste management licence should be a relatively straightforward process although it can be time consuming and may cause delay to a project if discussions are not initiated early enough with the EA. A minimum of four months after the application has been completed must be allowed for public consultation. A Working Plan will need to be included with the application which describes how the site or plant will be prepared, developed, operated or restored. The fee payable will depend upon what is being applied for.

In some projects, there may be no option but to apply for and obtain a waste management licence. However, it should be remembered that, once granted, a waste management licence can only be surrendered by the holder if the EA is satisfied that the condition of the land is such that environmental harm to human health is unlikely to be the result of its deposit. There may be concern that property which has been redeveloped but has a current waste management licence associated with it will have commercial disadvantages. Even surrendering a licence for inert waste disposal (e.g. from road building) can be difficult. The costs, including annual fees, of obtaining and maintaining a waste management licence will need to be factored into any budgets (see also Section 5 of this chapter). This makes a mobile treatment licence a much more attractive course of action where it is appropriate. The same sanctions for failure to have a waste management licence apply to failure to hold a mobile plant licence. A demolition company who showed the EA a false mobile plant licence were fined £45.00 in 2006.

Landfill directive

Implementation of the Landfill Directive (1999/31/EC) has resulted in there being far fewer landfill sites and the cost of landfill escalating. Certain specified wastes are not accepted in landfill – these include liquid wastes, explosive, corrosive, oxidizing or flammable wastes, used tyres (whole or shredded) and any other type of waste that does not meet the Waste Acceptance Criteria. Whilst inert demolition wastes will generally meet the Waste Acceptance Criteria, the cost of disposal of inert material to waste has increased significantly as a result of various changes to waste legislation.

Landfill tax

The Finance Act 1996 and the Landfill Tax Regulations 1996 (SI 1996 No. 1527) introduced a financial levy on all waste that is disposed of by landfill. All waste that is disposed of by way of landfill is liable to be taxed and operators of landfill sites are responsible for paying the tax. 2007 rates have been subject to a 'landfill tax escalator' of £3 per tonne since 2002 and are:

(a) inactive or inert wastes listed in the Landfill Tax (Qualifying Material) Order 1996, i.e. waste which does not give off methane or any other gas and does not have the potential to pollute groundwater – £2.00 per tonne increasing to £2.50 from 1 April 2008;
(b) active waste – £24.00 per tonne.

However, the Budget 2007 announced that landfill tax would increase more quickly and to a higher level than previously planned. An increase of £8 per year for active waste will apply from 1 April 2008 to at least 2010/2011.

Where a consignment of waste to landfill contains both active and inactive materials then the whole load is liable for tax at the standard rate of £24.00 per tonne. However, as long as it does not lead to any potential for pollution, it is possible to ignore the presence of an incidental amount of active waste in a mainly inactive load, and the lower rate of tax applies.

Unacceptable amounts of active waste in mixed loads would include a large piece of wood in a skip or lorry (e.g. a roof beam), rubble from the construction of a house containing mixed materials including paint tins, unused tar and leftover plaster and a skip containing mixed waste unless it is clearly all inactive waste.

There are some exemptions from the tax set out in the Finance Act 1996, the Landfill Tax (Contaminated Land) Order 1996 and the Landfill Tax (Site Restoration and Quarries) Order 1999. For waste landfilled temporarily with the intention of later removing it for recycling, incineration or re-use (other than at a landfill site), the landfill operator can claim a tax credit at the time the materials are moved, provided that prior arrangement has been made with Customs and Excise. Landfills may also have areas where waste designated for recycling, incineration or re-use (other than at a landfill site) within twelve months can be stored. These are referred to as 'tax free zones' and no landfill tax is payable provided the material is recycled or re-used within the specified time. Application for an exemption for disposal of contaminated land needs to be made to HM Customs and Excise at least thirty days *prior to* the proposed disposal.

The landfill tax can offer landfill operators an opportunity for cost effective spending on environmental objectives. A 90% tax credit, up to a ceiling of 6.6% of a licence holder's total annual landfill tax bill, was given to contributions to approved 'environmental bodies'. The Landfill Communities Fund is administered by ENTRUST on behalf of HM Revenue and Customs.

Currently the treasury are reviewing the landfill tax exemption for contaminated land and it is likely to be dropped to encourage more site based remediation technologies.

3.2 Duty of care as respects waste

Section 34 of the Environmental Protection Act 1990 creates a statutory duty of care applicable to all persons who produce, keep, carry or treat or dispose of controlled waste and to any person who is a broker or has control of controlled waste. The duty of care is essentially a requirement to take all reasonable steps in the circumstances to ensure that waste is handled lawfully and safely. In most cases, a contractor will be acting as a producer of waste. All waste producers must follow the duty of care, under which they must take all reasonable steps to ensure that:

(a) waste consigned to a disposal contractor or transporter is accompanied by a detailed, written description containing information necessary for the safe handling, treatment and disposal of the waste

(b) waste is consigned only to authorized persons, i.e. registered waste carriers, licensed waste contractors, local authority waste collectors or persons dealing with waste in ways that are exempt from licensing
(c) waste is securely contained to prevent it escaping to the environment both during storage and transit
(d) appropriate measures are taken to ensure that others involved in the handling and disposal of the waste do so in accordance with the law.

The Government published a Code of Practice in 1996 on the duty of care which provides guidance on how to comply with the duty of care. However, the Code does not meet every contingency and organizations should be aware that it is the failure to adhere to the duty of care, rather than to the Code of Practice, which is the offence. In December 2006, DEFRA advised that the Code of Practice is due to be updated and will be tailored to specific sectors. Site Waste Management Plans (SWMPs) are expected to require information on how the duty of care will be complied with.

The construction industry has considerable experience with the duty of care. [A construction company was convicted of a breach of the duty of care for failing to transfer an adequate description with ways to remove from one of its sites. The company described the waste as 'builders' waste' on the transfer note. At the bottom of the skip, covered with soil and rubble, were paint tins. The waste was transferred to a landfill which was not licensed to accept paint residues. The company unsuccessfully tried to argue that builders' waste could contain a wide range of materials. Similarly, a company was convicted for a breach of its duty of care in respect of a consignment described as 'general construction waste' which in fact contained asbestos pipe waste].

One particular complication of the duty of care for the construction industry is that the duty also applies to anyone acting as a broker who has control of the waste. Waste brokerage does not have to be described as such but will encompass anyone who has control of what happens to waste. Waste brokers must be registered and it is conceivable that a contractor could be acting as a waste broker if it were to make arrangements for and have control over where the waste is disposed of, even if it never handles the waste itself.

The duty of care is not an absolute one but does necessitate the taking of whatever steps are reasonable in the circumstances. In all cases this will involve all parties knowing who carries their waste, where it ends up and that the ultimate destination and all stops along the way are authorized to take that particular type and quantity of waste.

3.3 Penalties for breaches of Waste Management Law

Penalties for an offence under the waste licensing or duty of care provisions can be, in the Magistrates' Court, a maximum of £20 000 and/or imprisonment not exceeding six months. In the Crown Court there is the potential for an unlimited fine and up to two years (five years in the case of hazardous waste) imprisonment. The penalty for carrying on an exempt activity without registering is punishable in the magistrates' court by a fine not exceeding £10.

It will be a defence to a prosecution for failing to have a waste management licence or breaching it if:

(a) all reasonable precautions were taken and all due diligence exercised to avoid committing the offence;
(b) a party acted under instructions from an employer and did not know, and had no reason to suppose, that the relevant acts constituted an offence;

(c) it was an act done in an emergency in order to avoid damage to human health, provided that all reasonably practicable steps were taken to minimize pollution of the environment and harm to human health and the EA was informed promptly afterwards;

no licence is required because there was an applicable exemption and all conditions relating to it were met.

Powers in the Clean Neighbourhoods and Environment Act 2005 now allow local authorities to issue fixed penalty notices for £300 for failure to produce carrier registration documentation or waste transfer notes.

Fixed penalty notices issued by the EA are also provided for in the Hazardous Waste (England and Wales) Regulations 2005.

4 WATER POLLUTION

4.1 Summary

The construction industry continues to feature in water pollution prosecutions with discharge of silt-laden water appearing to be the most frequent offence. Another frequent offence involves the release of oil to controlled waters.

It is an offence to either cause or knowingly permit 'controlled waters' to be polluted by poisonous, noxious or polluting matter or the discharge of trade effluent, sewerage or any other polluting matter which might affect the quality of the water. Breach of a consent to discharge to controlled waters is also an offence. The law is contained in the Water Resources Act 1991 for England and Wales and the Control of Pollution Act 1974 for Scotland.

The legislation uses the term 'controlled waters'. The definition is very wide and it should be assumed that any water courses to controlled waters are being dealt with unless the EA has confirmed otherwise. In practice, the only type of water which may not be controlled water is a pond which does not discharge into a river or watercourse and does not have any hydraulic connection with groundwater. 'Poisonous, noxious or polluting matter' is interpreted very widely and even what may seem an innocuous material can be caught if it affects or could affect the quality of the controlled water.

4.1 Causing or knowingly permitting a discharge

It may not be obvious whether or not a party is causing or knowingly permitting a discharge. Contractors are often prosecuted for causing water pollution. In some cases the client may also be prosecuted on the basis that it did not adequately supervise the contractor.

In order to cause a discharge an active operation or chain of operations is carried on that gives rise to the pollution. The pollution need not be the intended result of the action. The leading case in this area is *Alphacell* v. *Woodward [1972] AC 824*. The House of Lords decision of *Empress Car Company (Abertillery) Ltd* v. *The National Rivers Authority [1999] 2 AC 22* decided that a company was liable for causing water pollution which was the direct result of an act of vandalism, for which the company was not responsible. The company had 'done something and therefore caused' but which was foreseeable.

Knowingly permitting requires both knowledge and the ability to stop the entry. The courts have less experience in dealing with the term 'knowingly permitting' but it does seem to need the ability to do something to stop the problem in order to permit. The extent of knowledge necessary can also be somewhat unclear. In one case, *Schulman Incorporated Ltd* v. *National Rivers Authority [1994] 158 JP 1101*, an engineer knew that polluting matter had entered the drains. He did not know that the matter which had entered the drains had discharged to a river. However, the court felt that he had knowingly permitted the entry to the river and the conviction was upheld.

It is a defence to a prosecution if the discharge was made in accordance with a consent granted by the EA. Although there is an additional defence that the entry was made or permitted in an emergency to avoid danger to life or health, the defence is only available if all reasonably practicable steps in the circumstances are taken for minimizing the extent of the entry and the EA is notified as soon as reasonably practicable up to the entry of the particulars of the discharge.

The Groundwater Regulations 1998 also make it an offence to cause or knowingly permit disposal or tipping (referred to as List 1 or List 2 substances) which might lead to an indirect discharge of that substance into groundwater unless there is an authorization granted under those Regulations.

4.3 Anti-pollution works notices

The Anti-Pollution Works Regulations 1999 provided the EA with a significant new enforcement option, however, it is one which is not frequently used. Anti-pollution works notices are a type of statutory notice which will require the person served to carry out specified works or actions to deal with or prevent pollution of controlled waters. The recipient of the works notice can be any person who caused or knowingly permitted poisonous, noxious or polluting matter or solid waste matter to be present at a place from which it is likely, in the opinion of the EA, to enter any controlled waters. A works notice can also be served on any person who caused or knowingly permitted the matter to be present in a place from which it might be released.

The clear advantage of an anti-pollution works notice for the EA is that it does not have to do the work itself or go through the process of recovering its costs from a person who is a causer or knowing permitter. It is an offence not to comply with an anti-pollution works notice. Anti-pollution works notices are rarely used.

4.4 Enforcement

Penalties for discharging poisonous, noxious or polluting matter to controlled waters or for breaching a discharge consent in the Magistrates Court can be up to £20 000 or imprisonment of up to three months (or both). On conviction in the Crown Court, an unlimited fine or a maximum term of imprisonment of two years (or both) may be imposed. Prohibition notices have recently been introduced to prohibit a person from making or continuing a discharge and specifying conditions to observe with respect to a discharge. Breach of a works notice or prohibition notice attracts the same penalties as an unlawful discharge.

4.5 Environment Agency clean-up

In addition to anti-pollution works notices, the legislation also allows the EA to carry out works and seek to recover its costs in so doing. The EA can also carry out a clean-up itself in circumstances where it can serve an anti-pollution works notice but chooses not to. It is then entitled to recover its *reasonable* costs from the person who caused or knowingly permitted the situation. The EA may seek to recover the costs of sampling and analysis using this power even in circumstances where it chooses not to prosecute.

4.6 Abstraction of water

The Water Resources Act 1991 requires those carrying out water abstraction or works to enable abstraction in England and Wales to have an abstraction licence granted by the EA. Abstraction licences must be applied for by the owner of the land. Licence conditions will govern the quantity which may be taken and possibly other matters such as when water may be taken and means of measurement. There is a right to abstract small quantities of water (not exceeding $5\,m^3$) if the abstraction is not a continuous operation. Consent may also be given for abstraction of quantities not exceeding $20\,m^3$, again provided that the abstraction does not form part of a continuous operation. Abstraction for fire fighting and for certain scientific experiments does not require a licence.

Abstraction licences must be processed within three months or are deemed to have been refused. If an abstraction licence is needed, then it is important to ensure that sufficient time is allowed to obtain it. Abstraction may well be restricted at certain times of the year. Abstraction licences now have a limited duration and abstraction charges apply.

4.7 Disposal to public sewers

If trade effluent is to be discharged to a public sewer then the consent of the relevant water company (in England and Wales) will be needed. Consents to discharge will contain conditions relating to the volume and quantity of the effluent, and trade effluent charges can depend on effluent quality. Consents to discharge certain particularly hazardous substances (set out in the Trade Effluents (Prescribed Processes and Substances) Regulations 1989 (SI 1989 No. 1156) must be obtained from the EA, although the consent is ultimately issued by the water company. If it is intended to put material into a public sewer during development, then a trade effluent consent will be needed. For existing premises there may already be a trade effluent consent in place, but the source of the permitted discharge will need to be checked.

5 CONTAMINATED LAND

Contaminated land is an area of particular relevance to the construction and development sectors. On 1 April 2000, new statutory provisions regarding clean-up and liability for contaminated land came into effect in England and Wales. Comparable provisions are also in effect in Scotland and Wales.

The EU Directive on Environmental Liability, 2004/35/EC, was adopted in April 2004 and requires implementation by April 2007. Although the UK is late implementing the Directive, it is not expected that Part 'A of the Environmental Protection Act 1990 will be fundamentally changed. There will need to be some adjustments but many of the requirements of the Directive are already achieved under Part 2A.

5.1 Summary

A number of existing Acts and Regulations, as well as common law, gave rise to legal remedies and obligations in respect of contamination of land. The new statutory regime, introduced by the Environment Act 1995 as Part 2A of the Environmental Protection Act 1990 and the Contaminated Land (England) Regulations 2000 (SI 2000 No. 227), was specifically designed to ensure the identification and ultimate remediation of contaminated land. Other legislation, in particular that dealing with pollution of controlled waters and waste management, is also relevant to dealing with contaminated land. Other considerations will be the land use planning system and building regulations, health and safety legislation, statutory and common law nuisance, and occupiers' liability legislation.

Legal risks associated with contaminated land include potential civil liability for damage caused by pollution migrating off-site, potential remediation costs pursuant to the service of a statutory notice (remediation costs can include investigation, cleanup and follow-up costs), or where remediation is done on a voluntary basis, potential criminal liability for breaches of legislation (especially in relation to water pollution) resulting from pollution migrating off-site, planning conditions or obligations associated with the redevelopment requiring investigation, restoration or aftercare and which act as a constraint on the scope of development or involve expenditure, or valuation issues regarding the value of the property.

Although it is not unlawful to own contaminated land, if the condition of the land is or begins to cause an unacceptable risk to human health or the environment, either on-site or off-site, then action will need to be taken. In practice, many landowners will take action voluntarily rather than wait for a legal requirement to be imposed on them.

Many construction projects will involve planned remediation of land in order to enable development to proceed. In other cases, it may be the construction personnel on site who discover heretofore unknown contamination which needs to be dealt with immediately. Those on site need to be aware of these possibilities and understand what steps to take in that event.

This chapter deals with environmental requirements, but it should be borne in mind that occupational health and safety risks due to exposure to contaminated land are extremely important; see Chapter 3.3.

5.2 What is 'Contaminated Land'?

As a general principle, land can be contaminated by having substances under, on or in it which may represent a direct, potential or indirect hazard to people or to the environment. The statutory definition of contaminated land is different and is contained in Part 2A of the Environmental Protection Act 1990. Not all land with contaminants present will meet this statutory definition. However, it should be noted that even if the land does not meet the statutory definition there may nonetheless be very good reasons for remediating contamination.

The definition of 'contaminated' land is land which appears to the local authority to be in such a condition, by reason of substances in, on or under it that either:

(a) significant harm is being caused or there is a significant possibility of such harm being caused ('harm-type' contaminated land), or
(b) pollution of controlled waters is being caused or is likely to be caused ('water pollution-type' contaminated land). (Although the word 'significant' has been inserted in this definition by the Water Act 2003, that change has not yet been brought into effect in England).

Under Part 2A of the Environmental Protection Act 1990 local authorities at district level are under a duty to inspect their areas from time to time for the purpose of identifying 'contaminated land'. In doing this they must have regard to the 'statutory guidance'. For England and Wales this guidance is contained in DEFRA Circular 01/2006 entitled 'Environmental Protection Act 1990; Part 2A, Contaminated Land' ('the guidance'). The circular includes guidance on what harm is to be regarded as 'significant', what degree of possibility of harm is to be regarded as 'significant' and whether pollution of controlled waters is being or is likely to be caused. The guidance incorporates the 'source pathway receptor' model of risk assessment – in relation to 'harm-type' contaminated land, there are tables showing which level of harm to which kinds of receptor will count as 'significant harm', and which risks of such damage occurring will count as a 'significant possibility' of such harm.

In some cases of 'contaminated land' the local authority will decide if the land should be designated as a 'special site'. That means that all enforcement responsibilities are taken over by the Environment Agency or the Scottish Environmental Protection Agency (as appropriate) from the local authority. The categories of 'special site' are set out in the Contaminated Land (England) Regulations 2000 and are intended to cover sites with particularly difficult contaminants and sites with significant water pollution issues. The fact that land has been designated as a special site will be entered on the public registers. The principles of liability are not changed by designation of the special site.

DEFRA and the Environment Agency have published a series of Soil Guideline Value (SGV) Reports which provide threshold values to assess if land meets the statutory definition of contamination. It should be noted however that there is currently much debate over these values and whether they do in fact match the requirements of the statutory test. In November 2006, DEFRA published as a consultation a document entitled 'The Way Forward'. DEFRA are currently considering the responses to the consultation and suggest there will be a proposal for change by the end of 2007.

Part 2A does not apply in certain circumstances. Of particular relevance to construction projects are the following:

- Part 2A does not apply to contamination of land in respect of which there is a current waste management licence, if that contamination was caused by the licensed activities or by breach of the licence conditions. Part 2A will apply to contamination on that land if it pre-dated or is otherwise unrelated to the licensed activities.
- Part 2A cannot be used where action may be taken under Section 59 of the Environmental Protection Act 1990 to deal with controlled water which has been unlawfully deposited (for example, fly-tipped) on land.
- Part 2A cannot be used so as to prevent or impede a consent to discharge to controlled waters pursuant to a discharge consent given under the Water Resources Act 1991 or, in Scotland, under the Control of Pollution Act 1974.

Part 2A now applies to radioactive contamination although this has only been the case since August 2006.

Where the enforcing authority decides that the contaminated land is in such a condition that there is imminent danger of serious harm or serious water pollution being caused then it can take immediate action and then seek to cover its costs. Personnel on site faced with a situation where the local authority or EA intends to take immediate action need to be aware of the appropriate response.

Since August 2006, most of the statutory nuisance provisions in Part III of the Environmental Protection Act 1990 do not apply to matters which consist of or are caused by land 'being in a contaminated state'. Statutory nuisance therefore no longer applies to sites which meet the definition of contaminated land but may no longer apply to some contamination situations which are less serious.

5.3 Who is responsible for remediation?

Primary responsibility for remediation of contamination rests with what the Guidance calls 'the Class A Liability Group': every person who caused or knowingly permitted the contaminating substances to be in, on or under the land. Class A liability can only make persons responsible for remedial action which is referable to substances which they caused or knowingly permitted to be present. While there are arguments that construction personnel are not persons who caused or knowingly permitted contamination on site, there could certainly be an argument that once contaminated soil has been moved within the site, the construction personnel are responsible for 'causing' that new situation. All persons who caused or knowingly permitted the presence of the relevant substances will be in Class A unless they specifically benefit from an exclusion test (see below).

If, after reasonable enquiry, no Class A person has been found, then for 'harm-type' contaminated land the current owners and occupiers are liable (the 'Class B Liability Group') even though by definition they have not caused or knowingly permitted the substances to be in, on or under the land. However, there is no Class B liability for 'water pollution-type' contaminated land.

In an appeal decision, *Circular Facilities (London) Ltd* v. *Sevenoaks District Council [2005] All ER (D) 126*, [2005] EWHC 865 (Admin) the Administrative Court considered an appeal from a decision of the Magistrates Court about whether Circular Facilities (London) Ltd ('CFL') should have been the recipient of a remediation notice served by the council.

The site, which had been used for residential purposes for approximately 20 years, was an infilled clay pit and in about 2002 the council discovered contamination sufficient to justify it being designated as contaminated land. CFL's role in the development of the site involved acquiring the site and developing it for housing. The issues in the case turned upon what information CFL had available to it that supported a finding that CFL was aware of the contamination at the time it redeveloped the property and allowed the contamination to remain underneath the houses. The District Judge was willing to infer knowledge of a technical report and this may be indicative of the reaction to an argument by a developer that they did not know and there was no reason why they should have known of the presence of contamination.

Class A persons

Where there are two or more persons in a liability group the enforcing authority must first apply the exclusion tests set out in Chapter B of the guidance which may exclude some members of the Class A group from liability provided that there is always at least one Class A person left, or, as the legislation says 'can be found'. There are six exclusion tests which the authority must apply sequentially to any Class A liability group.

Of most relevance to the construction industry is Test 1 ('excluded activities') which potentially transfers the liability of persons who could conceivably be described as having caused or knowingly permitted the presence of substances, but whose involvement is peripheral. This includes lenders, insurers, authorities who have granted permission for the polluting activity, consultants and other advisers and, in some cases, landlord and contractors. It also includes providing legal, financial, engineering, scientific or technical advice to (or design, contract management or works management services for) another person ('the Client') (whether or not that person can now be found) in relation to acts by reason which the client has been held liable under Part 2A, acts for the purpose of assessing the condition of the land (e.g. if it might be contaminated) or for the purpose of establishing what might be done to the land by way of remediation.

Test 2 ('payments made for remediation') excludes any liability group member who has paid another group member a sum to cover the cost of remediation or where the second group member has failed to remediate properly having been paid to do so.

Test 3 ('sold with information') transfers liability of those group members who have sold the land to another group member with adequate information about the contamination. Large businesses or public authorities buying from other group members since 1990 will normally be presumed to have known about the contamination if they were given an opportunity to carry out site investigations – it is irrelevant whether or not they actually did so. Where this test does apply so that the seller is excluded, the buyer inherits the seller's liability as well as keeping its own.

Tests 4, 5 and 6 ('changes to substances', 'escaped substances', and 'introduction of pathways or receptors') each apply where one or more group member has caused or knowingly permitted substances to be present, but it was the later conduct of another group member which created the problem which causes the land to qualify as 'contaminated land'. Test 6 will be of particular relevance in the redevelopment of land. The classic Test 6 scenario would be where several persons have caused or knowingly permitted contaminants to be present on land which, being a vacant brown-field site, does not present sufficient risk to qualify as 'contaminated land'. One of those persons then converts the land to residential use without adequately dealing with the contaminants. If the new use increases the risk posed by the contaminants sufficiently to render the land 'contaminated land' then Test 6 transfers liability of all Class A group members other than the person who converted the land to that use, assuming they can be found.

If Tests 1–6 leave more than one person in the Class A Liability Group then liability will be apportioned between them according to rules which are intended to equate to the respective contribution to the problem.

Class B persons

Exclusion in relation to the Class B Liability Group is much simpler. The basic principle is that every person in a Class B Liability Group (the current owners and occupiers of the land) is 'innocent' because otherwise they would be in Class A. The remediation can be expected to increase the capital value of the land, and its costs should therefore be borne in proportion to the group member's respective shares in that capital value. Accordingly, there is one exclusion test – the authority must identify licensees and rack rent tenants, who have no share in the capital value. If this leaves more than one group member, liability is apportioned between them according to their respective shares in the capital value of the land.

It should always be borne in mind that 'Remediation' covers not only actual clean-up, but also prior investigation to assess the condition of contaminated land and subsequent ongoing monitoring. The authority cannot use a remediation notice to require investigation to establish whether or not land is 'contaminated land'. It must already have satisfied itself that the land is 'contaminated land'. It can then use a remediation notice to require further characterization of the problem in order to determine which (if any) clean-up is reasonable for it to require by way of further notice.

5.4 Remediation notices

If the local authority has identified land as 'contaminated land' then it must notify the owner of land, any apparent occupier of the land and every person who appears to be an 'appropriate person' (i.e. a member of the relevant Class A or Class B Liability

Group). Before serving a remediation notice, the authority must reasonably endeavour to consult the person on whom the notice is to be served, the owner and any apparent occupier, concerning what is to be done by way of remediation. A three-month period must be allowed for such consultation before any remediation notice is served. Any construction project commencing during this consultation period should take into account the likelihood of some form of remediation being required. Where contamination is discovered during construction activities and notified to the local authority, it is conceivable that in the absence of a suitable voluntary proposal, a local authority could seek to serve a remediation notice during the construction phase.

Where the local authority is satisfied that appropriate measures are being or will be taken, then it should not serve a remediation notice. Often it will be the appropriate person who is carrying out or procuring the remediation but there is an option for an appropriate person to enter into a written agreement for the authority to carry out the remediation at the appropriate person's expense. When the authority is satisfied that there is nothing reasonable which can be done by way of remediation, it should not serve a notice. In considering what is reasonable, three factors are relevant – the likely cost involved, the seriousness of the harm or pollution in question, and the statutory guidance on remediation focusing on the concept of 'best practicable technique of remediation'. Only remediation actions which meet these tests should be required.

Where land has been identified as contaminated or designated as a special site, unless one of the restrictions referred to above on service of a remediation notice applies, the enforcing authority is under a duty to require remediation of contaminated land by serving a remediation notice.

A remediation notice can require a party to carry out works which it has no right to carry out (e.g. where the works are to be carried out on someone else's property) and any person (e.g. the landowner) whose consent is required for the works to be carried out must give the necessary consent, in return for statutory compensation if suitable compensation cannot be agreed.

There is a right of appeal to the Secretary of State against a remediation notice within a period of 21 days of service. An appeal automatically suspends the effect of a remediation notice until the appeal is determined or abandoned.

If a remediation notice is complied with, that will be the end of the matter. The person complying with it may give notice to the authority of the remediation measures carried out. That notice must be placed on the public register. However, in placing these facts on the register the authority does not represent that the remediation has been carried out, or has been carried out adequately.

If, without reasonable excuse, the remediation notice is not complied with, then the authority may prosecute under Section 78M for failure to comply.

Where the contaminated land in question is industrial, trade or business premises the maximum fine for non-compliance is £20 000 plus a daily fine of £2000 for each day in which the notice is not complied with. The only defence in relation to non-compliance (apart from 'reasonable excuse') is that the defendant is only liable for a proportion of the cost of the remediation required by the notice, and the only reason that the defendant has not complied with the notice is the refusal or inability of one or more of the other persons who are responsible for the rest of cost to bear their proportion of the cost.

There are provisions for action to be taken by the authority itself and for it to recover its costs. Cost recovery is qualified by the obligation to take into account two factors: the hardship which this would cause to the appropriate persons and the Chapter E statutory guidance on cost recovery. That guidance emphasizes that an authority should normally recover its reasonable costs in full, but draws attention to various cases where the authority should consider recovering none or only a proportion of its reasonable costs (such as where the appropriate person is a charity or registered social landlord, or where full cost recovery could lead to a company becoming insolvent). In relation to Class B appropriate persons, the guidance suggests that an authority should consider waiving some or all of its costs where such a person went into ownership or occupation without knowledge of the contamination, despite having taken all reasonable steps to discover the contamination before doing so.

5.5 Other remedies which may be applicable to contaminated land

There may be other persons or regulatory bodies who should be consulted before planning on commencing work on contaminated land. These include:

(a) the local planning authority – conditions on the planning permission may require approval of the remediation programme prior to commencement of development. If part of the site is dedicated to acceptable waste then planning permission may be required for the waste
(b) HM Customs and Excise – if seeking to dispose of contaminated soil to landfill and requiring an exemption certificate for payment of the landfill tax
(c) the Environment Agency and local authority – in practice if designing remedial measures then these bodies should usually be consulted to ensure that they are happy with what is being done. Although not a positive obligation, it does avoid the possibility of costly changes to the remedial method being required in future to accommodate their requirement
(d) the Environment Agency – removal of hazardous waste – if special waste is being removed from the site as part of the clean-up, procedural requirements governing its removal will need to complied with. Although this no longer requires pre-notification of the EA if the waste is being moved to a facility in England or Wales, pre-notification is still required if the waste is being moved to Scotland or Northern Ireland.
(e) Environmental Consultants who may have prepared a remediation plan based on site investigations. Questions can arise in relation to the plan.

5.6 Contaminated land and waste management licensing

Typically, when remediating contaminated land on site, contaminated soil is excavated, treated and then returned to its point of origin or placed elsewhere on site. The excavated material is considered to be controlled waste. Therefore, its keeping, treating or handling requires a waste management licence or the benefit of an exemption (see Section 3 of this chapter). The Environmental Protection Act 1990 makes provision for two types of waste management licence: site licences which authorize activities involving waste in or on specified land, and mobile plant licences which authorize activities involving the treatment or disposal of controlled waste by means of mobile plant. The types of licensable mobile plant are prescribed in regulations, but those in the construction industry should be aware that there is a statutory timeframe of four months for processing of either a waste management licence application or a mobile plant application. There have been delays in processing mobile plant licences although the Environment Agency is adopting a new structure to permitting and there will be four national permitting entries and mobile treatment plant licences will be processed in Nottingham.

Some sites will be designed with a waste management licensed area where contaminated soil which is not being removed from site can be contained. If this is intended, then the time needed to process a licence application should be noted. Surrender provisions on site licences are time consuming and difficult and may inhibit development. A permanent containment area will require a waste management licence to be in effect at all times. At the very least this will have cost and administration ramifications.

A useful discussion on guidance and the UK approach to safe development of housing on land affected by contamination has recently been published by the EA and NHBC. The report, entitled 'Guidance for the safe development of houses affected by contamination', takes into account the new statutory provisions on contaminated land described above and includes references to the statutory guidance. In addition to sections on risk assessment and evaluation and a section of remedial measures, there are a number of useful appendices. These deal with items such as key contaminants associated with industrial uses of land, key methodologies for risk estimation, background information on key contaminants, a summary of methods available for remedial treatment of contaminated land for housing developments and technology summaries for remediation of contaminated land.

5.7 Contaminated land and planning

Planning Policy Statement PPS 23 deals with contaminated land and links the evaluation of contaminated land under a planning permission into the process of risk assessment defined in Part 2A. It is a requirement that a developer must undertake any works necessary to ensure that after development, the site cannot be determined under Part 2A. If a Planning Authority does not consider that adequate information has been submitted in support or an application to show that the contamination risks can be properly evaluated, the guidance states they should refuse the application rather than granting a conditional approval.

6 AIR POLLUTION

Concerns in relation to air pollution and construction are widespread, especially pollution of the air by smoke and dust. There are a number of legislative controls over air emissions of which anyone operating on a construction site must be aware. These include provisions dealing with asbestos removal. Odour complaints may also arise from excavation, particularly in the case of remediation of contaminated land. Use of finishers and paints, especially those with a solvent base, also often lead to odour complaints. Prosecutions of members of the construction industry have followed burning materials on site.

6.1 Clean Air Act 1993

This Act restricts emissions of dark smoke from chimneys and industrial and trade premises. Causing or permitting emissions of dark smoke from the construction or demolition site can be a breach of the Clean Air Act 1993. Burning on site will almost inevitably generate dark smoke. There is an exemption for burning timber and other waste matter resulting from demolition or clearance of the site in connection with any building operation or work of engineering construction, but only if certain conditions are met. In practice, it will be extremely difficult to meet these conditions which include the proviso that there was no other reasonably safe practicable method of disposing of the matter. There is a defence to a charge that the emission was inadvertent and that the best practicable steps were used to prevent it.

Dark smoke is defined by reference to the British Standard Ringelmann chart. In relation to night-time emissions where it is not easy to prove that it was 'dark smoke' the authority will only need to prove that material was burned in circumstances where it would be likely to give rise to an emission of dark smoke. Local authorities and the Secretary of State can declare 'smoke control areas' within which smoke emissions are strictly controlled pursuant to this legislation.

6.2 Pollution prevention control

Part I of the Environmental Protection Act 1990 set out two pollution control regimes: integrated pollution control (IPC) which controlled release to air, water and land from specified industrial processes (regulated by the Environment Agency in England and Wales and the Scottish Environmental Protection Agency in Scotland) and local air pollution control (LAPC) which covered processes that release emissions into the air only (regulated by local authorities in England and Wales and the Scottish Environmental Protection Agency in Scotland).

The Pollution Prevention and Control Regulations (SI 2000 No. 1973) have now superseded Part I of the Environmental Protection Act 1990. This section discusses only the air pollution activities that continue to be regulated by the local authority – referred to as Part A(2) and B installations and is unlikely to be of direct relevance to the construction industry.

It is an offence to operate an installation or mobile plant which requires a PPC Permit without having a permit or otherwise than in compliance with it. Crushing, grinding or other size reduction of bricks, tiles or concrete, with machinery designed for that purpose, or screening these materials, is a Part B PPC process and will require a PPC permit. The permit must contain conditions to ensure that the installation or mobile plant is operated in such a way that:

(a) all the appropriate preventative measures are taken against pollution, in particular through application of the best available techniques;
(b) no significant pollution is caused.

BAT guidance continues to be contained in Process Guidance notes issued by the Secretary of State. For example, concrete crushing using mobile plant is dealt with by Note PG3/16 (04). It sets out what the Secretary of State considers to be BAT for the process. (The term BATNEEC was previously used. Although they are different, the PG Note regards the two concepts as having essentially the same effect and does not distinguish between them). It includes provisions dealing with matters such as use of water suppression to minimize dust emissions, prohibition of open storage except in certain circumstances and internal transport of materials. Authorizations for mobile plant will also normally include a requirement to notify the local authority in advance if it is proposed to relocate the plant.

On conviction in a magistrates' court (or in Scotland by the Sheriff) for operating without or in breach of a permit a maximum fine of £20 000 is available. On conviction in the Crown Court an unlimited fine or prison sentence not exceeding two years may be imposed.

6.3 Statutory nuisances

Part III of the Environmental Protection Act 1990 gives local authorities powers to deal with a wide range of statutory nuisances, including odour, fumes and dust emissions. This legislation has been in place in virtually the same form for more than a century and is something which local authorities are very familiar with. Statutory nuisance is potentially a very powerful remedy and is one which is frequently utilized by residents aggrieved by construction or demolition projects.

In the case of a statutory nuisance, the key concept is that the smoke, dust, steam, smell or other effluvia or any accumulation or deposits are 'prejudicial to health' or a 'nuisance'. (Note that noise can also be a statutory nuisance; see Section 7 of this chapter.)

If the local authority is satisfied that a statutory nuisance exists or is likely to occur, it is under a positive obligation to serve an abatement notice on the party responsible for the nuisance. Where that party cannot be found, the notice should be served on the owner or occupier of the premises. Identifying the appropriate party to receive the abatement notice may be a difficult question on a particular construction site, but there is a myriad of circumstances where the contractor could be a legitimate recipient.

Once an abatement notice has been served by the local authority (or if the magistrates' court has made an order regarding abatement), then failure to comply with the notice or order will be a breach of the Environmental Protection Act 1990. The abatement notice may require abatement of a nuisance, prohibit its recurrence or occurrence or require the carrying out of works and other steps to abate it.

There is a defence in relation to prosecution for breach of an abatement notice or court order for the categories of statutory nuisance relevant to air pollution. This is that the best practicable means were used to prevent or counteract the effects of a nuisance.

The abatement notice is served by the local authority on the party responsible for the nuisance. That party is the party to whose act, default or sufferance the nuisance is attributable. The notice does not now need to specify in detail how the nuisance is to be abated – that can be left to the recipient to sort out. A contractor in control of the site which creates a statutory nuisance by virtue of the construction activities taking place would clearly be a person responsible and an appropriate recipient for an abatement notice. However, where the nuisance has not yet occurred or the party responsible cannot be found, then the abatement notice should be served on the owner or occupier of the premises.

The Magistrates' Court can make an order requiring abatement of a statutory nuisance when a claim has been made by a private citizen. It can also impose a fine. Individuals who fail to persuade the local authority that a statutory nuisance exists or that enforcement action should be taken in relation to an abatement notice will often consider an application to the magistrates' court.

On conviction in the Magistrates' Court (or in Scotland by the Sheriff) for breaching an abatement notice a maximum fine of £20 000 is applicable, as is a daily fine of up to £500 for each day after conviction for which the nuisance continues.

7 NOISE

Noise can be particularly difficult to regulate because of the subjective element introduced by the differing reactions of people to the same levels of noise. Nonetheless, noise is reported to be the most frequent cause of complaint to local authorities and is an issue with which the construction industry has grappled for many years.

Noise from construction sites is regulated in England, Wales and Scotland by Sections 60 and 61 of the Control of Pollution Act 1974. Control of occupational noise and vibration which might affect employees is regulated by the Health and Safety at Work etc. Act 1974 and the Control of Noise at Work Regulations 2005 in England, Wales and Scotland (see Chapter [X] for discussion of this issue). Noise levels may also be prescribed in conditions in planning permissions for development and there may well be a condition prohibiting noise above a certain level at the site boundary. Noise is also a statutory nuisance for the purposes of Part III of the Environmental Protection Act 1990 and abatement notices can be served in relation to construction site noise.

7.1 Control of Pollution Act 1974, Sections 60 and 61

Section 60 of the Control of Pollution Act 1974 allows the local authority to serve a notice on a party carrying out work or otherwise responsible for it regarding the emission of noise from construction activities. The party responsible for the work could be a main contractor or subcontractor as well as the employer. The local authority notice may specify the plant or machinery, hours of work and noise levels. In serving the notice, the local authority is required to have regard to the need for ensuring that the best practicable means are utilized to minimize noise. 'Practicable' means reasonably practicable having regard to local conditions and circumstances, current state of technical knowledge and the financial implications. This test of best practicable means applies only so far as compatible with any duty imposed by law.

Further, in issuing a notice, the local authority should also have regard to the relevant provisions in any code of practice approved by the Secretary of State (see BS5228), before specifying any particular methods or plant or machinery, considering whether others would be substantially as affected in minimizing noise and acceptable to recipients, and the need to protect persons in the locality from the effects of noise. Some local authorities will have their own 'Code of Practice' regarding noise. The type of works for which a Section 60 consent can be issued are:

(a) the erection, construction, alteration, repair or maintenance of buildings, structures or roads
(b) breaking up, opening or boring under any road or adjacent land in connection with the construction, inspection, maintenance or removal of works
(c) demolition or dredging works, and
(d) any work of engineering construction.

It is a criminal offence, without reasonable excuse, to contravene a requirement of a Section 60 notice. It is a defence against statutory nuisance action brought by a local authority that the noise emitted was in accordance with a Section 60 consent.

Although this is a local authority initiative, if it is suspected that a notice will be received then it is often advisable to initiate consultations with the local authority to try to agree the contents. The timing implications of a notice being issued with which compliance is impossible are significant – the notice will need to be amended either by negotiation or by successfully appealing.

A contractor can avoid potential prosecution by applying to the local authority for a 'prior consent' governing work on the construction site, and adhering to the conditions set. These are referred to as Section 61 notices. The advantage of obtaining a consent is that the local authority should not, barring any unforeseen circumstances, serve a notice under Section 60 which could impose unexpected noise control requirements. If it does so, compliance with the consent will be a defence to proceedings for failure to comply with the notice.

Obtaining a consent is not, however, a defence to statutory nuisance proceedings, but it should be possible to establish a defence on the basis that the best practicable means were used to prevent or counteract the effects of the nuisance. The local authority must grant a consent if it is satisfied that the application contains sufficient information to enable it to assess the noise control requirements and that it would not serve a Section 60 notice if the works were carried out in accordance with the application. The local authority must have regard to the statutory codes of practice (BS 5228), whether the best practicable means are being used to minimize noise, and a need to protect any persons in the locality from the effects of noise. Some notices will include fixed noise levels rather than a general best practicable means approach. Care should be taken where this is the case. It is possible to appeal against a Section 60 notice within 21 days of its receipt. Grounds of appeal are limited and include the following facts:

- the service of the notice was not justified
- the notice contains a defect or irregularity
- the notice gives inadequate time for compliance
- the local authority acted unreasonably in refusing to accept alternative proposals
- the notice was served on the wrong person.

It is possible to appeal against the conditions on a Section 61 consent or against a refusal to grant a consent. The appeal is to the magistrates' court and must be made within 21 days after the expiry of 28 days from the date the local authority receives the application. However, the making of the appeal will not suspend the effect of the notice if the local authority has specified this. In practice, sufficient time to negotiate or, if necessary, appeal the consent is essential. It is a criminal offence to knowingly carry out works or permit works to be carried out in contravention of any conditions of a consent. If someone other than the person to whom the consent has been given carries out the works, it shall be duty of the applicant to take all reasonable steps to bring the consent to the notice of that other person.

Local authorities generally base the noise limits in consents or abatement orders on BS 5228: Noise control and construction on open sites. The standard consists of five parts:

- Part 1: Code of Practice for basic information and procedures for noise and vibration control
- Part 2: Guide to noise and vibration control legislation for construction and demolition including road construction and maintenance
- Part 3: Code of Practice for noise control applicable to surface coal extraction by open-cast methods
- Part 4: Code of Practice for noise and vibration control applicable to piling operations
- Part 5: Code of Practice applicable to surface minerals (excluding coal) extraction.

In addition to general requirements there are numerous regulations based on European Directive 84/532/EEC concerning the approximation of laws of member states relating to common provisions for construction of plant and equipment. Certain types of construction plant and equipment may not be marketed in Great Britain unless accompanied by a certificate issued by a body approved by the Secretary of State. The Construction Plant and Equipment (Harmonization of Noise Emissions Standards) Regulations 1985 (SI 1985 No. 1968) have been amended numerous times. It is the responsibility of the user of equipment to ensure that the plant or machinery is within the Regulations. Many plant hire agreements will address this point.

It is possible for an injunction, based on a private nuisance, to be granted by a court in the case of noise nuisance on the construction site and some councils are clear that they will take proceedings in the High Court where a serious nuisance occurs. The Court of Appeal decision in *City of London Corporation* v. *Bovis Construction Limited* [1992] confirmed that injunctions are available provided it can be shown that no other remedy will stop the nuisance.

8 ASBESTOS

Asbestos is a good example of a topic where an overlap exists between environmental and health and safety laws. The laws governing managing the risks associated with asbestos have been and will continue to be tightened up in the coming years.

There remains a considerable amount of asbestos in buildings, notwithstanding the fact that it is now unlawful to use it for these purposes. However, it remains the case that, provided that asbestos is in good condition, it does not need to be removed.

The Asbestos (Prohibitions) Regulations 1992 (SI 1992 No. 3067, as amended) prohibit the use of amphibole asbestos and products containing it, prohibit asbestos spraying and prohibit the supply and use of products containing chrysotile asbestos unless it was in use or installed in or formed part of any premises or plant before 24 November 1999. The HSE may grant an exemption, but only where it is satisfied that the health or safety of persons who are likely to be affected by the exemption will not be prejudiced in consequence of it.

The Asbestos (Licensing) Regulations 1983 (SI 1983 No. 1649, as amended) prohibit employers or self-employed persons from undertaking any work with asbestos insulation, asbestos coating or asbestos insulating board without holding a licence granted by the HSE. There are some exemptions available – for very short periods of exposure or where only monitoring or collecting of samples for identification is being carried out. It is possible to give 14 days' prior written notice of the work to the HSE and not need a licence where the work is undertaken at premises occupied by the employer of the persons carrying out the work.

The critical Control of Asbestos at Work Regulations 2006 (CAWR) impose duties on building owners and occupiers to identify where asbestos is present. A suitable and sufficient assessment must have been carried out (and kept under review), and employers must have a documented plan to manage asbestos risks.

9 NATURE CONSERVATION

The priority accorded to nature conservation issues has increased in recent years. The construction industry is particularly exposed to this heightened sensitivity and the changing legal requirements with which it must comply. Prosecution of members of the construction industry for disturbing wildlife habitats such as those used by crayfish and newts.

The law regulates the conservation of nature mainly by the protection of individual plants and animals and by general habitat protection through the designation of key sites. The principal sources of legislation in this area are the Wildlife and Countryside Act 1981 and the Conservation (Natural Habitats) Regulations 1994. The Countryside and Rights of Way Act 2000 extended rights of access to the countryside and the Natural Environment and Rural Communities Act 2006 amended nature conservation legislation (as well as amending the law relating to public rights of way) but the essential prohibitions on damaging or destroying protected species or their habitats remained with enhanced penalties – including increased fines and imprisonment for certain offences. Public authorities are also now under a duty to have regard, when exercising their functions, to the purpose of conserving biodiversity.

Probably the most important statutory designation for securing conservation interests is the Site of Special Scientific Interest (SSSI) provided for in the Wildlife and Countryside Act 1981. The previous conservation agencies (English Nature, the Countryside Council for Wales and Scottish Natural Heritage) have been reorganized and Natural England now advise on wildlife cases and are required to identify and notify SSSIs on the basis that their flora and fauna, and their geological, physiological or biological features. When notified of an SSSI designation on their site, owners and occupiers will be given a list of operations which Natural England considers are likely to damage the special interest on the site. Owners or occupiers will then be required to consult the Nature Conservation Agency before undertaking any of the listed operations. Currently, if the Nature Conservation Agency does not agree to the carrying out of the operations then it has powers to delay the activity for four months. Natural England has been able, since **[date]**, to prohibit operations likely to damage the special interest on the site. There will be a right of appeal against these decisions.

If working in an SSSI or adjacent to an SSSI it is important to be aware of any listed operations. It is also essential to be aware of whether or not there are any planning conditions regarding nature conservation. Planning Policy Statement 9 on Biodiversity and Geological Conservation and Circular 06/05 emphasize the national importance of SSSIs and other sites of biodiversity and conservation value and notes that the Government expects proper observance by local authorities of their obligations when authorizing developments likely to damage an SSSI and of protecting the special interest of such sites when considering development proposals.

Nature Conservation Orders (NCOs) made by the Secretary of State, pursuant to the Habitats Regulations, are similar to SSSIs but provide even greater protection for sites of national importance or where necessary to ensure the survival of any plant or animal or to comply with an international obligation. Where an NCO is made, a wider range of people than owners or occupiers may be prosecuted for carrying out damaging operations without consent and a wider range of sanctions is available. Natural England administers compliance with these orders.

Numerous nature conservation measures result from the implementation of European Directives, in particular the Wild Birds Directive (79/409/EEC) (as amended by Directive 97/39/EC) and the Habitats Directive 92/43/EEC. The Wild Birds Directive requires member states to designate special protection areas (SPAs) for the conservation of wild birds. The Habitats Directive provides for the creation of special areas of conservation (SACs) which will make up a network of European sites to be known as Natura 2000. International designations such as the Ramsar Convention (dealing with wetlands) or the UNESCO Man and Biosphere programme can also be a source of restrictions on the use of land.

10 ENVIRONMENTAL IMPACT ASSESSMENT

Environmental impact assessment is a procedure which is intended to ensure that the likely environmental effects of a proposed development are fully understood and taken into account before the development is allowed to go ahead. The environmental impact assessment will have been completed once the demolition or construction phase of a project starts. However, it is important to be aware of the provisions it

3.1 The law of contract
3.2 Construction health and safety
3.3 Insolvency in construction
3.4 Law of tort
3.5 Environmental issues

contained as operational or mitigation measures may well have been included in it. The UK regime on environmental impact assessment was introduced in order to comply with EC Directive 85/337/EEC on the assessment of the effects of certain public and private projects on the environment. This Directive was significantly revised in 1997 by Directive 97/1 1/EC. The main regulations implementing the revised Directive in the UK are the Town and Country Planning (Environmental Impact Assessment) (England and Wales) Regulations 1999 and the Environmental Impact Assessment (Scotland) Regulations 1999. There are specific Regulations for other types of development authorised other than through the planning permission process.

Development covered by the Regulations is divided into two categories. All development in Schedule 1 requires environmental impact assessment. Developments in Schedule 2 require environmental impact assessment only if they are likely to have significant effects on the environment by virtue of their nature, size or location. Schedule 2 development includes industrial estate development projects, urban development projects, including the construction of shopping centres and car parks, sports stadiums, leisure centres and multiplex cinemas, holiday villages and hotel complexes outside urban areas and associated developments, construction of local roads and installations for the disposal of waste. Developments listed in Schedule 2 of the Regulations will also require an environmental impact assessment where it is to be carried out in a 'sensitive area' or exceeds the relevant thresholds or meets the relevant criteria and is likely to have significant effects on the environment. 'Sensitive areas' include Sites of Special Scientific Interest, areas subject to Nature Conservation Orders, National Parks, Areas of Outstanding Natural Beauty, European sites and the Broads.

Where a development falls within Schedule 2, the local planning authority or the Secretary of State must make a formal decision on whether or not it requires environmental impact assessment. The decision will be based on 'screening criteria' set out in the Regulations. The characteristics of the development, its location and its potential impact will be considered. Environmental impact assessment may also be undertaken voluntarily by a developer even though the development does not fall under either of the Schedules in the Regulations.

If environmental impact assessment is required, the developer must prepare an environmental statement. The contents of the environmental statement are specified in the Regulations. The statement must include:

- a description of the development, including information on the site, design and size of the development
- a description of proposed measures to avoid, reduce or remedy significant adverse effects
- the data required to identify and assess the main likely effects of the development on the environment
- an outline of the main alternatives considered by the developer and the reasons for its choice
- a non-technical summary of the information provided.

Additional information should be included where it is reasonably required to assess the environmental effects of the development and where the applicant can reasonably be required to compile it. This would include:

- details of the physical characteristics of the development and land use require ments during construction and operational phases

- the nature and quantity of materials used, expected residues and emissions during operation of the development
- a description of the aspects of the environment likely to be significantly affected by the development, including population, fauna, flora, soil, water, air, climatic factors, architectural and archaeological heritage, and landscape
- a description of the likely significant effects of the development on the environment resulting from the existence of the development, the use of natural resources, the emission of pollutants, the creation of nuisances, and the elimination of waste
- a technical summary of the above information.

The type and amount of information required and the weight and emphasis attached to it will depend on the nature and location of the proposed development.

The local planning authority may request additional information after receiving an environmental statement if it considers it necessary to facilitate determination of the application. The planning authority will send copies of the environmental statement to the statutory consultation bodies and make it available to the public. Any representations received for the planning authority must be considered along with the environmental statement before granting or refusing planning consent.

Where environmental impact assessment is required, extra time and cost will be involved in obtaining planning permission. The time needed to prepare environmental statements can be considerable, particularly if the data relating to the environmental effects need to be obtained over various seasons. In addition, the local planning authority is granted extra time to consider the application.

11 ENVIRONMENTAL MANAGEMENT SYSTEMS

Environmental management systems are increasingly being adopted by many industries. The two best known schemes are:

- *ISO 14001* – written by the International Organization for Standardization, it has been adopted as a European standard by CEN. It is structured around five core principles: policy, planning, implementation and operation, checking and corrective action, and review. Emphasis is on compliance with relevant legislation, pollution prevention through avoidance, reduction and control and commitment to continual improvement of the system. Registration is by the company.
- *EM AS* – the Eco-Management and Audit Scheme is based on EEC Regulation EEC/1836/93. Registration is achieved by establishing environmental policies, programmes and management systems in relation to sites, systematically, objectively and periodically auditing their performances, and providing informa tion on environmental performance to the public in an environmental statement. Registration is by site and not by company.

A number of companies in the construction industry and building products industry gained accreditation under ISO 14001 although take up by the industry as a whole has been relatively limited. Due to the site-specific nature of EMAS, it has been less widely adopted by the construction industry although companies in the building products industry have registered various sites.

12 PUBLIC ACCESS TO INFORMATION

There is a great deal of information about companies' environmental performance available to the public, much of it via the Internet. The Environment Agency website, for example, contains a section entitled 'What's in your backyard?'. Entering a postal code highlights environmental features of the area, including the location of Pollution Inventory sites. The site also includes a copy of the EA's enforcement and prosecution policy as well as local and national news releases dealing, in particular, with successful prosecution and each year publishes a 'Spotlight on Business' listing by name and sector, those companies prosecuted by the EA in the previous year. The EA website is www.environment-agency.gov.uk.

Most environmental statutes contain provision for a public register of environmental information, it is prudent to assume that most environmental authorizations can be viewed by the public, as can any correspondence, including monitoring data, to do with those consents which is kept on the registers.

In addition to the statutory scheme of registers, the Environmental Information Regulations 2004 implement Directive 2003/4/EC on public access to information, came into effect on 1 January 2005. The Freedom of Information Act 2000 also came into force on 1 January 2005. There are some similarities between the two as well as some important differences – the EIR covers only environmental information whilst FOI covers all information held by public authorities and both impose a duty on public authority to comply with requests from the public for access to information. This includes information about the state of the environmental media or sites and activities or measures that adversely affect those media or sites (or are likely to) plus any administrative or other measures designed to protect them.

There are very limited exceptions to when environmental information must be disclosed and a positive presumption in favour of disclosure and a requirement that any non-disclosure be in the public interest. Environmental information must generally be made available within 20 days of the request and any refusal to provide information must be accompanied by reasons. Any person who is not satisfied with a public authority's handling of an information request can only challenge the decision by following the internal review procedure of the authority and an appeal can be made to the Information Commission if the internal review is unsatisfactory and the outcome of that appeal can be referred to the Information Tribunal.

There will often be a copying charge for provision of information. Some organizations, for example, the EA, will seek to charge for dealing with enquiries which are not based on the Environmental Information Regulations 1992, for example in connection with property transactions.

13 CLIMATE CHANGE AND ENERGY EFFICIENCY

The statistic that the energy used in constructing, occupying and operating buildings represents almost half of all greenhouse gas emissions in the UK is not entirely surprising. Whilst the construction sector has recognized and is managing the issue of climate change and energy efficiency of buildings; issues such as flood protection and drainage and building maintenance are also critical.

The Government's 2006 Energy Review indicated that improvements in energy efficiency (including efforts to reduce energy wasted because of poorly insulated buildings or poor control of heating, lighting, ventilation and appliances) represent potentially the most cost effective way of delivering the energy policy objectives. The 2007 Energy White Paper develops energy efficiency initiatives further.

A Climate Change Bill (currently the subject of consultation) proposes legally binding government targets for significant reduction of carbon dioxide. Further legislative charges in this area are inevitable and the construction industry will no doubt wish to participate in consultation and development of this new legislation.

The Energy Performance of Buildings Directive 2002/91/EC is implemented in England and Wales through Part L of the Building Regulations 2000 and will set maximum carbon dioxide emissions for whole buildings – both new buildings and renovation of existing buildings with a total surface area of over $1000\,m^2$. The Department of Communities and Local Government has also introduced a Code for Sustainable Homes applicable to all publicly funded housing developments.

Implementation of the Directive requires certification of energy performance of buildings and the inspection of boilers and air conditioning systems to be undertaken by independent, accredited or qualified experts. The UK is expected to have a shortfall, and availability of, a suitable assessor will be a practical issue. Energy Efficiency Certificates will also be contained within Home Information Packs.

PART 4

Construction disputes

Section editor: Mike O'Reilly
Adie O'Reilly LLP and Kingston University

CHAPTER 4.1

Administration of claims

Daniel Atkinson
Daniel Atkinson Limited

1 DISPUTE AVOIDANCE

1.1 Summary

Claims are essentially statements of entitlement, whereas a dispute often arises because of technical or legal uncertainty. Any consideration of the administration of claims in construction must include consideration of the procedures and approaches needed to prevent claims becoming disputes.

The choice of appropriate strategies and contract form is of course a vital step to avoiding disputes and this is examined below.

The conduct of the Parties and the A/E in dealing with claims is a significant factor in avoiding disputes. The English courts have been keen to promote various procedures to prevent litigation with the result that there is a considerable body of caselaw which provides useful guidance. This is also examined below.

In summary, the guidance from the courts and the pre-action protocols is that to avoid disputes the following approach should be adopted:

- The parties should each provide a clear summary of the relevant facts, the basis of each claim and the principal contractual terms and statutory provisions together with the nature of the relief claimed.
- Quantum claims should show a breakdown and extension of time claims the period claimed. The Parties should avoid overstated or exaggerated claims.
- The reasons given for rejection should be identified and the basis for rejection.
- The Parties should provide the names of any experts and the issues on which he will give evidence.
- The Parties should adopt a candid and open-handed approach in any discussions.
- Realistic offers of settlement should be made early in the process.

1.2 Choice of project strategy

Disputes can be reduced by rigorous analysis and management of risk and with the adoption of the appropriate organisational strategy for the project.

There are distinct advantages to an Employer in having one single contract for the whole project. The main contractor will be responsible for coordination of the various work packages and the Employer will be protected from claims for disruption between package contractors. On very large projects the finance and expertise required of a single contractor will mean that the Employer will need to deal with consortia of two or more contractors, each with their own expertise. It is usual for each of the consortia members to be severally liable for the defaults of the other members. The Employer will then be protected from coordination and disruption claims, he will not have to identify the particular member responsible for the default and indeed will have a choice of defendant in any dispute proceedings.

This single point organisational arrangement may not always be practical nor indeed desirable. So for instance enabling works may need to be let before the main works. Engineering considerations and financing arrangements may dictate several discrete contracts, with different contractors or consortia. The Employer may require to have more control of design of certain parts of the project, possibly the more specialist parts. It may be that the Employer will wish to be involved in the selection of the main equipment.

The division of the project into manageable packages creates a resultant risk of lack of coordination between different contractors, which may cause delays and disruption and give rise to disputes. This can be reduced by the appointment of a project manager and by clear identification of the interface responsibilities in each contract with well-defined procedures for the flow of information.

1.3 Choice of design strategy

Whatever organisational strategy is adopted, it will be necessary to decide the allocation of design responsibility.

Design as used here has a very wide meaning and includes the selection or specification of the quality of materials as well as the structural design of components and structures. Since the Employer will always define the project in some way by orientation, performance or function, there will always be some division of responsibility for design of the project.

In some projects, selection of the route or of certain materials by the Employer, may impose methods of construction on the Employer which may not be anticipated at tender stage. It is therefore not always apparent what is the design risk allocated to each contracting party. In the case of an equipment manufacture contract, extensive specification by the purchasing contractor may reduce the manufacturer's design liability to one of complying with the specification only, and not to supplying equipment which will perform at the required production rate.

The allocation of responsibility under a contract may not always be clear as shown by the decision of HH Judge Seymour QC in *Cooperative Insurance Society Limited* v. *Henry Boot Scotland Limited* [2002] EWHC 1270 (TCC). The form of contract was JCT 1980 Private With Quantities amended by the Contractor's Design Portion Supplement 1981 Edition revised July 1994. The preliminary issue was whether or not Henry Boot had any design obligation for the design of piled walls which formed part of the works and a concept prepared by Cooperative. Clause 2.1.2 provided that for the purpose of carrying out and completing the works Henry Boot was to complete the design for the Contractor's Design Portion including the selection of any specifications for any kinds and standards of the materials and goods and workmanship to be used in the construction of that Portion so far as not described or stated in the Employer's Requirements or Contractor's Proposals. Judge Seymour held that the obligation of Henry Boot under Clause 2.1.2 was to complete the design of the piled walls which involved developing the conceptual design of Cooperative into a completed design capable of being constructed. He held that the process of completing the design included examining the design at the point at which responsibility was taken over, assessing the assumptions upon which it was based and forming an opinion whether those assumptions were appropriate. When Henry Boot agreed to the obligation to complete a design begun by someone else, they agreed that the result, however much of the design work was done before the process of completion commenced, would be prepared with reasonable skill and care. The concept of completion of a design of necessity involved a need to understand the principles underlying the work done and to form a view as to its sufficiency. Insofar as the design remained incomplete at the date of the Contract, Henry Boot assumed a contractual obligation to complete it.

Accordingly, in order to avoid disputes, the contract needs to state clearly the responsibility for any aspects of the design, including concept designs as well as detailed design and the working up of conceptual designs and its construction or installation.

In performance related contracts, unless the operating conditions are clearly defined, this can give rise to many disputes. Design and construct contracts can however usefully be adopted where the method of construction dictates the design of the permanent works.

Where the contractor has responsibility for all the design as well as construction the contract is referred to as 'design and construct' or 'turnkey'. The term 'turnkey' is sometimes used to refer to projects with single point contracts, but the essential feature is the allocation of responsibility for design and construction with the contractor.

Design and construct contracts have many advantages for the Employer. First there is a single point responsibility for any defects either in materials or performance. The Employer does not need to ascertain whether the defect is due to design or due to workmanship. Secondly this type of contract lends itself to lump sum form of payment, or fixed payment at completion of identified stages. Provided the completion of the various stages is clearly identified then the administration of the contract is simpler than remeasure or unit price forms of contract.

1.4 Identification of legal systems risk

Disputes can arise from the misunderstanding of the legal environment itself. Common law legal systems such as English law have continued with the laisser-faire doctrine in construction, which is a freedom to decide whether and with whom to contract and to freely decide the allocation of risk and the payment mechanisms to be followed.

Normally in contracts governed by English law, the allocation of risk between the parties can therefore be found in the contract document itself. This is not the case in civil code systems which include German, French and Greek law.

In these systems, which in international contracts may be the stated law of the contract, many of the contentious issues which arise in English law are dealt with by specific legislation. There is no need to provide the detailed contracts seen in English law contracts.

Contractors more familiar with common law systems may therefore be misled by the brevity of contracts under civil code systems. In addition these systems operate to exclude allocation of certain substantial risks between the parties. Some systems operate a general principle of good faith against which contract terms are to be interpreted, common practice being taken into account. Contractors should therefore be familiar with the relevant provisions of the codes and their effect on the allocation of risk, when contracting under civil code legal systems.

1.5 Choice of performance strategy

A fundamental decision to be made in relation to each participant in the project is the allocation of risk defective function of specific elements of the project. The function of project elements can be defined at different levels. For instance, a requirement that an overhead crane should comply with a particular performance specification would transfer the risk of defective function to the manufacturer, but only in relation to the specification. The risk that the crane satisfying the specification would nonetheless not perform its overall function and achieve the required overall throughput, due to maintenance down-time for instance, would still reside with the specifier. This allocation of risk for function is best viewed therefore on a sliding scale. In the case of a labour-only contract for instance, the only risk function transferred to the supplier is to supply labour who can perform the skills specified. The specifier carries the risk that the specification is sufficient for his needs. In a turnkey project the risk allocation is essentially the same. The risk function transferred to the Contractor is to supply a plant which performs as specified. The specifier carries the risk that his specification is sufficient to allow him to fulfil supply obligations elsewhere. The description of the type of project is only a shorthand for the liabilities and risks allocated, but is not conclusive. It is the actual circumstances, the contract setting, which define the allocation of risk.

The risk of defective function is normally defined as 'design liability' and raises the familiar problem of fitness for purpose. It is, however, not always apparent what design risk is actually allocated to each party. The nature of construction projects, their attachment to land, means that design cannot be separated easily from method and manner of construction. For instance, the incremental construction of projects may normally result in locked-in-stresses that need to be allowed for in the design of the permanent works. The design of materials, concrete mixes or steel composition, will be an essential part of the design. All these factors can impose methods of construction on the Contractor that may not be anticipated by him at tender stage.

The crucial distinction in law appears to be between one who only designs, and another who designs and makes something. In the former case there will normally be no obligation that the result of the design will be fit for its purpose, but in the latter case an obligation as to reasonable fitness for purpose will normally be implied into the contact. This may change with particular circumstances and express terms of the contract and the particular legal system.

Good design involves examination of buildability and suitability, taking into account both the environment and the capability of potential Contractors/Designers. The division of design liability is not always apparent, and the extent to which statements in contract documents warranty the ease with which construction can be completed is not clear.

1.6 Choice of design and construct arrangement

Fixed price contacts are common in design and construct forms of contract. The major difficulty in the UK construction market has been the control of quality and performance of the contractor. This has manifest itself in the procedures for the client to monitor the design and the quality of the workmanship.

A distinction needs to be made between single point contracts and 'design and construct' or 'turnkey' contracts. A single point contract is one in which there is only one contract for the whole project. Where the Contractor has responsibility for all the design as well as construction the contract is referred to as 'design and construct' or 'turnkey'. Although the term 'turnkey' is sometimes used to refer to projects with single point contracts, the essential feature is the allocation of responsibility for design and construction to the Contractor.

The main advantages for the Employer of Design and Construct are, first that there is a single point responsibility for any defects either in materials or performance. The Employer does not need to ascertain whether the defect is due to design or due to workmanship. Secondly this type of contract lends itself to lump sum form of payment, or fixed payment at completion of identified stages. Provided the completion of the various stages is clearly identified then the administration of the contract is simpler than remeasure or unit price forms of contract.

The advantages for the Contractor are that he has more control over the whole project, and can adopt designs that suit his own resources and expertise. Design and Construct is the logical method of procurement for many types of project.

Although Design and Contract forms have many advantages for the Employer and Contractor, there are specific problems that frequently arise. These are:

- Uncertain definition of the contract due to lengthy pre-contract discussions/ negotiations.

- Ambiguity/discrepancy between Employer's Requirements and Contractor's Submission.
- Monitoring the adequacy of the design.
- Valuation of variations.
- Fair cashflow payments.
- Dealing with defects.

The selection of a turnkey contractor will preclude payment being made on a unit price or cost reimbursable basis. It will be very difficult for the Employer to ascertain accurately the unit cost of various elements of the work on account that the fact that the critical elements of cost may well be determined by matters of which he has no knowledge such as the contractor's specialist know-how and off-site manufacturing processes etc. If it is anticipated that the works will be varied, then it is essential for competitive pricing under both conventional and turnkey contracts that a breakdown of the contract price in terms of elements of work and key components is provided in order to assist in the valuation of the variations and, if necessary, interim payments.

As there is no bill of quantities in a turnkey contract, it is very difficult to allow for progress payments to be made monthly based on the quantity of work actually executed. There is less risk of dispute if payment is to be made in accordance with particular project milestones. For instance, it could be based on percentage completion of various elements of the work or, in the case of mechanical and electrical works, based upon completion of detailed design, manufacturing, equipment, arrival at site and installation of major equipment. Payments made on the basis of milestones have the advantage of being relatively easy for the Employer to administer and offer an incentive for the contractor to execute the works as efficiently and quickly as possible. When drafting a milestone payment schedule it is important to remember that the work is not complete when the plant has been installed therefore a sufficient percentage must be retained to cover the contractors commissioning and start up obligations. So as to avoid unnecessary disputes suitable mechanisms should be drafted into the contract to allow for the contractor to receive reimbursement in the event that he is unable to attain any particular milestone on account of any delay for which the Employer is responsible. In addition it must be remembered that the milestone payments are approximate and do not represent the true value of the work executed at the point of any milestone. Employers ought to be made aware that in the event of termination of the contractor's employment the amount paid out against milestones will almost certainly differ from the value cost of the work at that point.

1.7 Choice of contract strategy

Disputes can be reduced if a contract strategy is adopted which is appropriate to the works and the apportionment of risk between the parties. The contract strategy needs to take into account the nature of the risk events likely to arise and the ability of a party to deal with the consequences of the risk event. In recent years standard forms have been expanded to provide a family of forms for different contracting strategies. This allows a contract strategy to be implemented by selection of the appropriate contract form with little amendment.

Contract documents

Contract documents are tools for managing risks. They determine the consequence of particular events. A contract framework needs to bring certainty to the allocation of consequences of hazards. It is uncertainty which gives rise to many disputes.

Commercial considerations may lead to contacts in which there is inherent uncertainty: the design may not be fully developed and even in some cases the concept may not be fully defined. In such cases the flexibility of the contract forms is a significant benefit to the participants.

In such projects the choice of contract framework is vital. There are many standard civil engineering forms which are an example of such flexible forms. The detail design is carried out whilst the construction is being carried out, so that the quantities actually required are not known. In addition the uncertainties of the physical conditions of the site including the weather are matters which are dealt with flexibly in all forms of contract. It is important to identify the uncertainty before choosing the appropriate form.

It is not realistic in commercial projects to have a project fully defined at tender stage. This has led to different procurement methods such as construction management, or reimbursable or target cost contract arrangement.

Reimbursable forms are very flexible but have the potential of the contractor having little incentive to deploy his resources efficiently.

Apportionment of risk between the parties is achieved not only by clauses dealing directly with risk such as ground conditions, weather or force majeure, but also in the use of exclusion and limitation of liability clauses, by design liability clauses and by notice provisions which may act to transfer risk if they are properly followed.

Bills of Quantities

Contracts based on Bills of Quantities remains the traditional pattern for the larger type of contract particularly in the building and civil engineering industry. There are two types of arrangement. These are contracts based on firm quantities and contracts based on approximate quantities.

Contracts based on firm quantities are in essence lump sum contracts. The advantage of this arrangement is that all tenderers are pricing on the same basis and the quantities risk is transferred from the contractor to the Employer. The contractor is saved the cost of preparing his own quantities and any discrepancies in tender prices can easily be identified.

The other form of quantities contract is the Bill of Approximate Quantities such as the ICE 7th Edition and Option B of the NEC Form. Under this arrangement approximate quantities are prepared for tender documentation and the contract price is based upon the actual quantities of work executed which are remeasured during the course of construction. The advantage of this arrangement is that the works do not have to be fully designed prior to tenders being issued and that again the contractor is not assuming any of the quantities risk. In effect they permit the overlapping of design and construction. There is of course a danger that if the quantities are too approximate the actual quantities will be of little significance and the bill will become no more than a schedule of rates.

In all cases the bill of quantities should only be used as the basis for pricing the contract where there is a clear separation between design and construction.

Schedule of rates

As with the Bill of Approximate Quantities, the contractor under a schedule of rates contract is paid for the actual amount of work carried out at the rates contained in the schedule irrespective of the quantity, if any shown in the schedule. One problem with both types of arrangements is that if the final quantities differ markedly from those in the approximate bill or the schedule then the contractor may have an entitlement to a re-evaluation of the rate.

A variation of the Schedule of Rates contract is that of a schedule which is issued with the rates already inserted and contractors are then asked to tender on the basis of a plus or minus percentage addition to the actual rates. The use of such 'Schedule Contracts' as with 'Approximate Quantities Contracts' is that they allow the preparation of quantities from preliminary drawings at a very early stage. Whilst the quantities will not be accurate they should be sufficient to give the contractor a reasonable idea of the scope of work to be executed. In all cases the schedule should be prepared so that preliminary items are priced and identified separately and not included within the unit rates.

Cost reimbursable

In the traditional priced forms of contract or in the design and construct forms there is a high degree of definition of the project at contract award. This permits fairly clear allocations of risks between the parties. In such contracts it is normal to think of contractors carrying the risk in terms of time, cost, quality and liability. The risks carried by the employer are thought of as exceptions to this one-way allocation of risk, as for example:

- time – exceptional adverse weather, delays by the Employer
- cost – Employer variations
- quality – unforeseen ground conditions
- liability – liquidated damages, exclusion of consequential loss.

Little attempt is made in such traditional forms to encourage reduction of the Contract Price by the Contractor.

In essence, in cost reimbursement forms the contractor is paid the prime cost, that is the actual expenditure with an allowance for overheads and profits, normally on a percentage or formula basis. There is little incentive for the contractor to be efficient under such an arrangement and thc Employer has no assurance of the final cost. In addition such arrangements require detailed checking by the Employer's staff. On the other hand such arrangements are advantageous where there is a very short contract programme or where the importance of getting started on site as early as possible is regarded as more vital than obtaining the lowest initial capital cost. Other situations where the use of a cost plus contract would be appropriate are situations where the project cannot be defined in any detail prior to the start of the work and when the Employer wants to actively participate in the design of the project. When preparing cost plus contracts it is essential that a very detailed schedule of costs elements or schedule of rates is included within the contract documents.

Variants of the cost plus form of contract are the 'cost plus percentage fee' where the contractor seeks a percentage on top of his prime cost for overheads and profits, 'cost plus fixed fee' where the contractor seeks his prime cost and a fixed fee in respect of overheads and profits and 'target costs'. The latter arrangement differs from the former arrangement in that in the first instance the contractor is reimbursed on the basis of cost plus either a percentage or fixed fee. It is, however, further provided that if the final payment due on this basis differs from an estimate agreed between the parties by more than a certain margin either up or down then the contractor will receive a bonus or incur a penalty as the case may be. Accordingly there is a greater incentive for the contractor to economise than there is under the former two arrangements.

Cost reimbursable forms of contract involve a radical change in the cosy traditional division of risk. It creates shared risks, even more apparent in target cost forms of contract. This has a major effect on the relationship of the parties.

Cost reimbursable contracts place part if not the main proportion of the financial risk with the employer. This means that a contractor more used to the traditional forms of contract will have little incentive – other than repeat business from a large employer – to work efficiently and economically. Standard forms therefore contain express provisions for the contractor to do so.

The fundamental concern of the employer under a cost reimbursable form is to encourage the contractor to co-operate in forecasting the final or out-turn costs, so that joint action may be taken to prevent any cost over-run. Two approaches are possible

- to create a relationship which requires the contractor to notify the employer when he has reason to believe there will be a cost overrun; or
- to share the risk of cost between employer and contractor.

There is one additional factor which is instrumental in creating the co-operative relationship between contractor and employer. This is the adoption by employers of a value-engineering approach. The most significant change that cost reimbursable forms create is the change in the Employer's internal audit procedures to allow the adoption of value engineering concepts to solve on-site problems.

This involves a highly significant change in the Employer's management organisation and reporting procedures. So for instance a site engineer may find that compliance with the Specification will involve significant costs, but that a relaxation of the Specification will allow a change in method of working and cost savings. In the cost-reimbursable form, the site engineer can begin to ask the right questions from the stand point of benefit to the project. He will examine the change in the Specification in terms of:

- the maintenance costs;
- safety;
- the impact on the function of the project;
- the effect on the completion date of the project.

The direct cost saving is therefore weighed against the overall affects that it will have. Most importantly the Employer will have given his agent authority to make such judgments, and will be predisposed to approving such value judgments. This is particularly important in larger organisations, which are the type of organisation which use the cost reimbursable form.

The Employers attitude is therefore not one of ensuring that the project is built to a pre-conceived plan as in traditional forms, but he is pre-disposed to re-examining the plan during implementation using value engineering.

1.8 Claims and disputes

Claims are distinct from disputes. Claims are simply a statement of entitlement. A 'claim' is not the same thing as a cause of action by which the claim may be supported or the grounds on which it is based – a claim is an assertion of a right, Devlin J in *West Wake Price & Co* v. *Ching* [1956] 3 All ER 821. Disputes can be about a claim, but there is rather more to a dispute than simply a claim which is not accepted *Edmund Nuttall Limited* v. *R.G. Carter Limited* [2002] TCC. Claims are an integral part of construction contracts since they provide the flexibility required to deal with the uncertainties of construction and contract terms.

1.9 Contractual claims procedures

Appropriate claims procedures in contracts are an effective means of reducing the number of claims which become disputes. Many standard forms have claim procedures and some have general procedures applicable to all claims together with additional requirements for particular events.

Besides specifying that notices need to be given, which may or may not be condition precedent to entitlement, the claims procedures may circumscribe the type of evidence allowed to establish the measure of entitlement.

The FIDIC Red Book 4th Edition includes general provisions for claims which are similar to those in the ICE Remeasurement form 7th Edition. In addition to notice provisions in relation to particular events, Clause 53(1) requires the Contractor to give notice of his intention to make a claim for additional payment pursuant to any clause 'or otherwise' within 28 days after the happening of the event giving rise to the claim. Clause 53(2) requires that on the happening of such events that Contractor is required to keep such contemporary records as may reasonably be necessary to support any claim he may subsequently wish to make. These provisions are clearly intended to provide a disciplined approach to dealing with claims and to avoid prolonged disputes. Clause 53(4) is a default clause and comes into play if the contractor fails to comply with the other obligations of Clause 53. He can still make a claim but only for those sums considered verified by contemporary records.

In *HM Attorney General for the Falkland Islands* v. *Gordon Forbes Construction (Falklands) Limited* [2003] BLR 280 the Falkland Island Supreme Court held that the meaning of 'contemporaneous records' in the FIDIC 4th Edition depended on the facts surrounding the making of the record, but meant original or primary documents, or copies, produced or prepared at or about the time giving rise to the claim. It was held that it would be exceptional if any record would be considered contemporary if made more than a few weeks after the event it recorded. Subsequent witness statements could clarify the records, but where there were no contemporary records to support the claim, it would fail despite the witness statements. A part of a claim not so supported could succeed if supported by inferences properly drawn from contemporary records based on the balance of probabilities. This accords with common sense. A useful illustration was given by the Court involving a dispute whether labour was employed on the site on a certain date. It was considered acceptable to provide a timesheet or invoice showing hours worked or a statement from the contractor made at the time to say that they worked that week. A witness statement at a much later date would not be a record.

Contract programming

A trend in the construction industry shown by the Engineering Construction Contract is the adoption of rigid time-scales not only for submitting but for dealing with claims, referred to as compensation events in the Engineering Construction Contract.

The development of this trend is the publication in November 2001 of a consultation document by the Society of Construction Law entitled *Protocol for Determining Extensions of Time and Compensation for Delay and Disruption*. The central premise of the protocol is that disputes can be reduced by the introduction of a transparent and unified approach to the understanding of programmed works and identifying consequences of delay and disruption. The protocol strongly recommends the adoption of a critical path network programme in all but the simplest of projects with regular updates.

The protocol adopts a simplistic approach to the role of the programme and does not adequately relate the role of the programme to the various obligations under the contract. The role of programmes in the administration of contracts is set out below at Section 3.4.

Realistic claims

The attitude of the parties and the approach which they take to claims are important factors in reducing disputes. If the claims are prepared based on proper legal analysis with a reasonable attempt to present the facts honestly and to analyse the facts rigorously, then the parties are more likely to reach agreement on entitlement and avoid disputes.

Overstated claims in which the facts can easily be disputed or shown to be partial, not only increases the likelihood of disputes on that particular claim but also create doubt and mistrust and may prevent resolution of other claims.

In *Skanska UK Construction Limited* v. *Egger (Barony) Limited* [2005] EWHC 284 (TCC) HH Judge David Wilcox recorded that the costs of resolving the disputes amounted to approximately £9 million, but the amounts recovered were less than half the costs. Judge Wilcox observed that a failure to be open handed, or candid, exaggeration, unwillingness to treat and delay were matters that might render costs disproportionate to the achieved result. In this case there were faults on both sides. Eggar was under-resourced and failed to properly administer the contract. At certain times Skanska greatly exaggerated its claim, but Eggar was not so disadvantaged that it did not know the true nature and extent of the claim and its risk and could have made a well judged offer. On that basis Judge Wilcox ordered Eggar to pay costs up to no more than 55% of the total costs, even though Skanska was the net winner.

A dynamic for the early settlement of many disputes in litigation is the adoption of the statement of truth in the new Civil Procedure Rule (CPR) Part 22 and the expert statement in CPR Part 35 in the English Courts. The effect of the rule is to make a person making the statement on behalf of a party or as an expert guilty of contempt if a false statement is made without an honest belief in its truth. The provisions do not introduce new form of contempt but simply proved a summary mode of prosecuting a person for contempt in the case of false statement which had been verified by a statement of truth *Kabushiki Kaisha Sony Computer Entertainment* v. *Gaynor David Ball & Others* [2004] EWHC 1984 (Ch) and *Malgar Ltd* v. *R.E. Leach (Engineering) Ltd* [2000].

The adoption of similar statements by parties submitting claims before litigation or arbitration, with appropriate sanctions, would also reduce the incidence of disputes, although the sanctions available and the remedy is less clear.

1.10 Offers to settle

Disputes can be avoided if realistic attempts are made to settle claims. Parties may settle claims for a number of commercial reason. The settlement amount therefore may not always be based precisely on the measure of damages likely to be awarded by a court or arbitrator. It may instead take into account the cost of pursuing the claim and the need to complete the particular development with the necessary goodwill.

Since the cost of litigation and arbitration proceedings can be significant, offers to settle should be made at the appropriate time if such proceedings are likely. If it can be shown that the subsequent proceedings are a waste of time and could have been avoided if the offer had been accepted, then the party making the offer will be in a strong position to recover its costs in the proceedings.

In litigation in the English Courts the Civil Procedure Rules Part 36 requires payment of any offer into Court. It is now clear that the Courts encourage the avoidance of disputes by realistic and genuine offers to settle even if there is no payment in. If an offer is made which does not comply with Part 36 then the Court has a discretion whether or not to take into account the offer in the award of costs. In *Stokes Pension fund* v. *Western Power Distribution* [2005] BLR 497 the Court of Appeal held that an offer should normally be treated as having the same effect as a payment into Court if it was expressed in clear terms, if it was expressed to be open for acceptance for at least 21 days, if the offer was genuine and the party making the offer was clearly good for the money when the offer was made. On the last point Dyson LJ held that it would be difficult for a party to contend that the other party was not good for the money if it had not tested the genuineness of the offer by accepting conditional on payment.

In *EQ Projects Limited* v. *Javid Alavi* [2006] BLR 130 HH Peter Coulson QC held that even if the offer was silent on the period for acceptance it would be a valid Calderbank Offer if there was nothing to suggest that it would not be open for 21 days.

1.11 Pre-proceeding protocols

Pre-action protocols

The introduction of the Civil Procedure Rules in English Court proceedings has allowed judges to case manage the process of dispute resolution more effectively. There has been a shift of emphasis to early consideration of ADR and particularly mediation to resolve disputes. Pre-action protocols have been introduced in a number of areas of the law. In construction the protocol is the 'Pre-Action Protocol for Construction and Engineering Disputes' and applies to all construction and engineering disputes (including professional negligence claims against architects, engineers and quantity surveyors) – paragraph 1.1.

The adoption of the procedures in the pre-proceeding protocols reduces the incidence of disputes. The procedures are a useful guide to parties keen to avoid prolonged disputes. The approach of the Courts provides practical examples of how disputes and expensive dispute resolution can be avoided.

The purpose of the pre-action protocols for court proceedings is to ensure that the parties have identified the issues between them and have attempted negotiation or mediation to settle matters. One important purpose is to ensure that they have exchanged relevant factual and expert evidence. If the protocol is followed then the judge will have a better grasp of the case and be able to more efficiently manage the case. As important the Parties will also have a better understanding of their respective positions and the prospects of success.

The English Courts have shown a willingness not to award costs in the normal way if the winning party does not take the opportunity of alternative dispute resolution, where this is appropriate. The decisions demonstrate those aspects of pre-action procedures which the Courts consider are important to allow the possibility of early resolution of disputes.

In the building case of *Paul Thomas Construction Limited* v. *Damian Hyland and Jackie Power* [2000] TCC Judge Wilcox observed that Paul Thomas Construction had adopted a heavy-handed approach. It was very much at odds with the TCC ethos that ran through the CPR. Hyland and Power reminded Paul Thomas Construction of their duty in relation to the protocol practice direction. Judge Wilcox observed that it had no effect upon restraining the keenness and aggressive stance that was adopted by Paul Thomas Construction. Judge Wilcox held that Paul Thomas Construction had been uncooperative and were clearly in breach of the protocol practice direction. He held that it was wholly unnecessary to commence the litigation. It was wholly unreasonable. It was clear that there could have been and should have been explored alternative dispute resolution. That may include sensible discussions between the parties not necessarily involving a third party. There was in those terms some culpability in this case. He held that indemnity costs were warranted.

In *Susan Dunnett* v. *Railtrack plc* [2002] CA Susan Dunnett's appeal against the first instance decision was dismissed. Railtrack requested payment of its costs and in the usual course of events these would normally be awarded. When the judge at first instance had given his decision he had advised Susan Dunnett to explore the possibility of Alternative Dispute Resolution to 'get shot of this case as soon as possible'. Susan Dunnett had indicated she was willing to do so if Railtrack agreed. When Susan Dunnett referred the suggestion to Railtrack they turned it down flat. They were not even willing to consider it.

Lord Justice Brook observed that this was a case, at least before trial, when a real effort should have been made by way of alternative dispute resolution to see if the matter could be satisfactorily resolved by an experienced mediator, without the parties having to incur the heavy legal costs of contesting the matter at trial. Lord Justice Brooke made a significant statement on the nature of mediation and the role of Mediators. He stated that skilled mediators were now able to achieve results satisfactory to both parties in many cases which were quite beyond the power of lawyers and courts to achieve. Lord Justice Brooke emphasised the duty of lawyers in advising their clients of the overall objective. If they turn down out of hand the chance of alternative dispute resolution when suggested by the court they may have to face uncomfortable costs consequence. Lord Justice Brooke then gave judgment refusing to award costs to Railtrack. He held that in the particular circumstances of the case, given the refusal of Railtrack to contemplate alternative dispute resolution at a stage before the costs of the appeal started to flow, it was not appropriate to take into account the offers that were made. The appropriate order on the appeal was no order as to costs.

In *Halsey* v. *Milton Keynes General NHS Trust* [2004] EWCA Civ 576 the Court of Appeal listed the factors that could be relevant in deciding whether a party had acted unreasonably in refusing to agree to ADR. The factors included the nature of the dispute, the merits of the case, the extent to which other settlement methods had been attempted, whether the costs of ADR would be disproportionately high, whether any delay in setting up and attending the ADR would have been prejudicial and whether the ADR had a reasonable prospect of success. Where a successful party had refused to agree to ADR despite the court's encouragement, that was a factor that the Court would take into account when deciding whether his refusal was unreasonable.

In *Burchell* v. *Bullard* [2005] CA BLR 330 the Court of Appeal observed that *Halsey* had made plain not only the high rate of a successful outcome achieved by mediation but also its established importance as a track to a just result running parallel with that of the court system. It was also observed that paragraph 5.4 of the Pre-Action Protocol for Construction and Engineering Disputes expressly required the parties to consider at a pre-action meeting whether some form of ADR would be more suitable than litigation.

Pre-Action Protocol for Construction and Engineering Disputes

In *Daejan Investments Ltd* v. *Buxton Associates* [2004] BLR 223 although a letter before action had been sent, no claim letter under the Pre-Action Protocol for Construction and Engineering Disputes was issued and the Protocol was not followed. The claim letter was required under the Protocol to state the names of experts already appointed and identify the issues as to which evidence was to be directed. Daejan sought to amend its case as a result of an expert opinion on its claim for professional negligence. HH J Wilcox held that there had been prejudice to Buxton on loss of the opportunity to resolve their difficulties pre-litigation. The case had been started without any proper investigation and the amendment brought the Parties to the position that they would have reached if the Protocol had been followed. Accordingly he granted permission but on the basis that Daejan pay all Buxton's costs to that date and that Daejan be responsible for its own costs to that date.

In *McGlinn* v. *Waltham Contractors Limited* [2005] BLR 432 the Parties went through the steps prescribed by the Pre-Action Protocol for Construction and Engineering Disputes. This led to a mediation that was unsuccessful. As a result of the process the claims before the Court were different to those that existed at commencement of the Protocol procedure. HH Peter Coulson QC held that costs incurred at the Pre-Action Protocol stage could be recoverable as costs incidental to the proceedings, but not costs in dealing with issues that were dropped, since that would be to penalise a party for doing the very thing that the Protocol was designed to achieve.

In *Briggs Ltd* v. *Governors of Southfield School* [2005] (TCC) BLR 468 the Parties had complied with the Pre-Action Protocol for Construction and Engineering Disputes which had not yet reached the pre-action meeting stage. Briggs the contractor was faced with a £5m claim from the School for damages for asbestos contamination but considered that it did not have sufficient information on quantum to make an offer to settle and applied for pre-action disclosure of documents relating to quantum. HH Judge Coulson QC held that disclosure of those documents was desirable to assist settlement without proceedings and to save costs. He observed that costs incurred in wide pre-action disclosure would be extensive, but the disclosure of the quantum documents was different. Judge Coulson considered that during the months after the letter of claim, the School should have produced schedules identifying the full quantum claimed under each head of claim and demonstrating clearly how each headline figure had been made up. Accordingly pre-action disclosure of the quantum documents was granted.

Pre-adjudication protocols

The requirement of the Housing Grants, Construction and Regeneration Act 1996 that adjudication should be available at 'any time' which has been held to means exactly what it says, prevents the imposition of mandatory pre-adjudication protocols [*John Mowlem & Company plc* v. *Hydra-Tight Ltd* [2000] TCC, *R G Carter Ltd* v. *Edmund Nuttall Ltd* (2000) TCC and *Connex South Eastern Ltd* v. *M J Building Services Group plc* [2005] EWCA Civ 193].

Nonetheless voluntary pre-adjudication protocols should be considered, particularly on large and/or complex issues. It is doubtful that a pre-adjudication protocol should have the realistic objective of achieving settlement of all issues. The timescale for adjudication is so short, usually without any cost sanction (except for the adjudicator's fees), that the main purpose of such a protocol would be only to identify issues and evidence and allow a decision which is more likely to be accepted by the parties as finally determinative of the issues.

The judicial development of the definition of 'dispute' required to give an adjudicator threshold jurisdiction has been instrumental in encouraging the Parties to exchange views and facts which support their case, but it can be a rather blunt instrument for reducing disputes and far short of a pre-adjudication protocol.

A common practice has developed in the period before an adjudication in which the Parties exchange 'position statements' in the form of schedules in which each party states its position and response. This approach has been shown to greatly assist the Parties in identifying the differences between them and to identify the relevant documentary evidence relied upon. The resultant schedule greatly assists the adjudicator in the very short timescale of adjudication.

Although the pre-action protocols do not apply to adjudication, the approach of some form of ADR followed by a coercive process has clearly worked in avoiding disputes. It is suggested that a form of med-adjudication can work based on the same principles.

On first analysis, it may appear that the two approaches of Mediation and Adjudication cannot be combined in the appointment of one person as Med-Adjudicator. It is certainly the case that if a person appointed as an Adjudicator attempts to act also as Mediator using the traditional approach, that his decision may not be binding due to apparent lack of impartiality. This happened in *Glencot Development and Design Co Limited* v. *Ben Barrett & Son (Contractors) Limited* [2001]. In that case the adjudicator acted as mediator with the agreement of the parties during the adjudication. Eventually he issued his decision and the matter of his impartiality was heard before HH Judge Lloyd QC. There was no question of actual bias by the adjudicator. The issue was whether his actions were sufficient to give rise to apparent bias.

It was held that in adjudication whilst it is permissible to make enquiries and receive evidence and submissions from one party alone, there is a clear obligation on the adjudicator to give any absent party a complete and accurate account of what has taken place. In this case the adjudicator went to and fro between the parties. He was under no obligation to report what he heard or learnt. The private discussions could have conveyed material or impressions that subsequently influenced his decision. In the adjudication, the adjudicator was required to form a view about the credibility of one of the party's case. This was an area where unconscious or insidious bias may be present. It was held therefore that any fair-minded and informed observer would conclude that the adjudicator's participation in the lengthy discussions of the mediation process led to a real possibility of the adjudicator being biased. On that basis the adjudicator's decision was unenforceable for apparent bias.

The difficulties of combining mediation and adjudication can be avoided by an examination of the operation of mediation in construction. The traditional approach in Mediation is to meet the parties both together and separately. To encourage open dialogue the Mediator is required to keep confident from the other party anything disclosed in the separate meetings unless authorized by the party. This approach provides a psychological release from the need to maintain commercial positions, allows the legal position of the parties to be tested and exploration of possible solutions. Such confidentiality would undermine the need for justice and openness required of adjudication.

In most construction disputes there is seldom a need for extensive confidentiality. The issues in most cases relate to the valuation of parts of the work, the measure of extension of time and disagreements as to the facts and to interpretation of the terms of contracts. What is usually required of the Mediator is not to provide a psychological release, but to provide an environment in which the reality of the situation can be recognized. The professionals representing the parties usually conduct the fact-finding exercise with guidance from the Mediator. The Mediator does not give a view usually, but instead encourages critical valuation. This approach is similar to the inquisitorial approach adopted by an Adjudicator and leads to a natural combination of both methods.

Med-Adjudication commences with an agreement signed by the parties. The essence of any agreement is that at any time any party can refer issues to adjudication. The Med-Adjudicator follows the rules of natural justice as they apply to adjudication from the commencement of the process. He is master of the procedure subject to agreed requirements of the parties. The Med-Adjudicator meets with the parties together, but the essence of the procedure is that he meets with the professionals and key witnesses from each side together to discuss particular issues. Unlike a traditional Mediator, the Med-Adjudicator gives preliminary views to the parties on the basis of his meetings with the professionals and witnesses. If the parties settle then this is recorded in a written settlement agreement. If not settled within two weeks, the dispute proceeds to adjudication automatically. The preliminary views of the Med-Adjudicator are not binding on the parties nor on the Med-Adjudicator if the matter proceeds to Adjudication, but the views are recorded in any decision and either confirmed or distinguished in the decision.

A similar approach to that described above was adopted by HH Humphrey Lloyd QC acting as a judge (not adjudicator) in the *Floods of Queensferry Ltd* v. *Shand Construction Ltd* [1999] TCC BLR 319. He suggested to the parties an informal approach to the resolution of some typical issues, which he described then as experimental. The procedure involved the judge sitting down informally with the quantity surveyors (accompanied by junior counsel only to ensure that the interests of the parties were safeguarded) to discuss their respective positions directly with them. The judge then expressed his provisional views in writing, as a result of which the parties could take stock of his initial reactions and be better informed as to whether they wished to accept those views, although they were not obliged to do so. If they accepted the view then they could apply them to other comparable items in dispute. If not they could decide to have them decided in the ordinary way in the court proceedings. The procedure could be terminated at any time without any adverse reflection or comment by anybody. Judge Lloyd also reserved to himself the right to bring the procedure to an end if it was not likely to work or to achieve the objectives of being cost-effective. He also reserved the right to say that he needed more material or further submissions in open court. The parties agreed the procedure by a written agreement that bound the judge, since it was intended to serve their needs. The effect of the procedure was to reduce the issues that had to be decided in court.

It is suggested that the Med-Adjudication approach provides a rapid and cost effective means of dispute resolution for large and/or complex claims in keeping with the modern trend of reducing confrontation and encouraging dialogue.

Pre-arbitration protocols

If the contract is a construction contract as defined in the Housing Grants, Construction and Regeneration Act 1996 and the 1996 Act applies, then the process of statutory adjudication will meet the requirements of a pre-arbitration protocol. The adjudication will allow the Parties to identify the issues and will provide a reality check of each Party's position as well as the main evidence relied upon. Experience shows that the arbitration timetable can be considerably shortened where an intensive investigative adjudication has taken place.

Since statutory adjudication is not mandatory, a pre-action protocol could be in terms simply to require to complete an adjudication process before commencing arbitration on that dispute. It is likely that such a provision will be enforceable since it merely postpones the right to arbitration. Even if such a provision is not enforceable a party can commence an adjudication where the 1996 Act applies at 'any time' even during arbitration proceedings, and due to the different timescales have an adjudicator's decision before an arbitration award.

That approach has been adopted in the FIDIC Forms where adjudication is conducted not under the 1996 Act but by a Dispute Adjudication Board (DAB) appointed under the contract. Clause 20.4 provides that neither party is entitled to commence arbitration of a dispute until after a notice of dissatisfaction has been given in accordance with Clause 20.4. Such a notice, however, cannot be given until the DAB gives its decision or the period for giving a decision has passed. Under Clause 20.8 only in the situation where there is no DAB in place can a dispute be referred directly to arbitration.

A similar approach has been adopted under NEC3. Option W1 applies if the 1996 Act does not apply and Option W2 if it does. In both options Clause W1/2.4(1) provides that a party does not refer a dispute to the *tribunal* unless it has first been referred (W1) to the *Adjudicator* or decided (W2) by the *Adjudicator* in accordance with the contract and under Clause W1/2.4(2) that a notice of dissatisfaction has been given after the *Adjudicator's* decision.

The ICE form is less clear. In *JT Mackley* v. *Gosport* [2002] (TCC) BLR 367, the contract was the ICE 6th Edition but without changes to allow for adjudication. Accordingly, terms were implied into the contract by the provisions of the Construction Act, which gives the parties the right to adjudication at any time. Two disputes that arose between the parties were referred and decided in adjudication, while a third was referred to the engineer for his decision under Clause 66. One dispute was referred to arbitration, but the notice to refer did not identify whether it was dispute one, two or three. Judge Richard Seymour QC held that an engineer's decision was a condition precedent to the right to refer a dispute to arbitration, which was only available to challenge the decision of an adjudicator if the contract provided for arbitration and as the terms of the ICE 6th Edition required the engineer's decision first, Judge Seymour held that the notice to refer was invalid. This decision leaves open the prospect of disputes under the ICE 6th Edition having to be referred not only to an adjudicator but also to the engineer if the parties wish to determine the dispute. This difficulty has been avoided in the 7th Edition with adjudication into the Clause 66 procedure.

In the ICE 7th Edition Clause 66(3) provides that the Employer and the Contractor agree that there is no dispute unless and until the time for the Engineer to give his decision under Clause 66(2) has expired or is unacceptable and a Notice of Dispute has been issued. Clause 66(3) also provides for a dispute to arise when the adjudicator has given a decision under Clause 66(6) and effect is not given to his decision and in consequence a Notice of Dispute is issued. Clause 66(9)(a) provides that all disputes, apart from the failure to give effect to an adjudicator's decision, are to be finally determined by arbitration. Clause 66(9)(b) provides that where an adjudicator's decision has been given under Clause 66(6) then reference to arbitration must be within three months of the decision. Clause 66(6) provides that notice of adjudication can be given at any time. A reference to adjudication or an adjudicator's decision is not therefore required before commencing arbitration proceedings. The process of seeking an Engineer's decision is, however, a necessary pre-condition.

In the Scottish case of *The Construction Centre Group* v. *The Highland Council* [2002], Lord MacFadyen considered terms similar to Clause 66(4)(b) of the ICE 7th Edition. The clause provides that the parties shall give effect to an adjudicator's decision unless and until it is 'revised' pursuant to Clause 66, which provides for arbitration. Lord MacFadyen held that the same dispute, which was referred to the adjudicator for provisional determination, could be referred to arbitration but for final determination. There was a sense in which the arbitral decision would 'revise' the adjudicator's decision in that it may produce a different decision. However, the use of the word 'revised' in Clause 66(4) did not require the arbitrator to review the adjudicator's decision. But he had to approach the dispute resolution anew. So while the arbitrator had power to open up, review and revise decisions, he has no similar power over the adjudicator's decision. Lord MacFadyen stressed that enforcing an adjudicator's decision was enforcement of the contractual obligation that the parties would comply with the determination by that decision. By using that approach, the difficulties of the term 'revise' was avoided.

In *John Mowlem & Company plc* v. *Hydra-Tight Ltd* [2000] TCC, the standard form of contract was the Engineering Construction Contract 2nd Edition subcontract with the second option for adjudication. The contract had a similar term to Clause 66 of the ICE 7th Edition, that the parties agreed a dispute did not exist unless the right notice was issued. It was also agreed, and confirmed by Judge Toulmin, that the contract term redefining 'dispute' deprived the parties of a right to refer a dispute at any time to adjudication. The contract did not comply with the Act, so the Scheme for Construction Contracts applied, displacing the adjudication provisions. Allowing the parties to define a 'dispute', would allow the parties to contract out of the provisions of the 1996 Act, by making various notices condition precedent to the right to adjudication.

A pre-arbitration protocol in similar terms to a pre-action protocol might provide the same benefits as pre-action protocols, but would need to be agreed by the parties and would be without the sanctions of costs available for pre-action protocols. It is suggested that in general such a provision should not be included in a contract. In particular such a provision would introduce a further mandatory and unnecessary and probably costly step in the process of coercive dispute resolution, delaying the commencement of the arbitration process. Further, there would be significant difficulties in empowering the arbitrator with cost sanctions for failure to follow a pre-arbitration protocol.

2 LEGAL BASIS OF CLAIMS

A legal basis for compensation may arise as follows:

(a) under contract
(b) at common law for breach of contract
(c) at common law for breach of a duty arising in tort
(d) in restitution.

Claims for breach of a duty arising in tort are not examined in detail here, but should be considered.

Claims under the contract are claims for compensation for events for which specific provision is made within the conditions of contract. The claims at common law considered here are claims for damages for breach of contract. The two heads are entirely separate, although they may relate to the same event. If, for example, information is issued late there may be grounds for a claim under both heads. Of course, the claimant will not be able to recover twice for its loss. The measure of damages for breach will take into account the compensation received under the contract.

Some events which create an entitlement under the contract do not constitute a breach of contract; they are neutral events. The contract simply makes provision for compensation as a means of apportioning risk, there is no breach of a legal obligation. In some contracts this is the case with extensions of time for exceptional adverse weather conditions, for instance. Similarly, if a risk event of physical conditions or artificial obstructions causes the contractor to incur delay and extra cost, some contracts provide that the employer is liable for this risk. In neither case can it be said that the employer was in breach of an obligation with regard to the weather or physical conditions.

Therefore, in many situations there will be a choice, whether to pursue a claim under the contract and/or as an action for damages at common law. The use of the standard forms will not normally preclude the right to sue for damages for breach of contract at common law. In some cases a procedural failure, such as the lack of notice, may leave only a claim at common law if the procedure is a condition precedent to entitlement under the contract.

If the contract states that the contractual entitlement is an exhaustive remedy, then there will be no alternative remedy at common law since such suitably drafted clauses have been held to be enforceable. Lack of notice in that case will therefore exclude any contractual remedy for the particular event.

A claim in restitution is to be distinguished from a claim for contractual quantum meruit. The latter arises when the contract does not state the rate for the work carried out. It may also arise when the contract specifies that the valuation of a variation is to be at a reasonable rate, or such a term is implied by statute.

A claim in restitution will not succeed when there is an agreement between the parties which covers the situation. The following need to be established to succeed in a claim in restitution:

(i) no valid contact
(ii) a benefit has been conferred for work not paid as agreed
(iii) the benefit was not intended as a gift
(iv) the benefit has been accepted at the expense of the other party.

2.1 Claims under the contract

Presentation of a claim under the contract has the advantage that the procedure under the contract for compensation will in many cases be quicker and cheaper than coercive dispute resolution processes such as litigation or arbitration. A valid claim pursued under the contract has the following advantages:

(a) it will normally create a right to an interim payment
(b) it may create a right to an extension of time
(c) it may allow resolution of any resulting dispute or difference by statutory adjudication under the Housing Grants, Construction and Regeneration Act 1996 for agreements entered into after 1 May 1998.

2.2 Claims for breach of contract

Remedy of damages

The normal remedy for breach of contract is damages. Damages are intended to compensate the innocent party for the loss suffered as a result of the breach of contract. In order to establish an entitlement to substantial damages for breach of contract, the injured party must establish that:

(a) actual loss has been caused by the breach, and
(b) the type of loss is recognized as giving an entitlement to compensation, and
(c) the loss is not too remote, and
(d) quantification of damages to the required level of proof can be provided.

A breach of contract can be established even if there is no actual loss. In that case there will only be an entitlement to nominal damages.

In general, the claimant must prove its loss. This requires records to be kept during execution of the works so that loss can be established as a matter of fact.

A claim for damages is the means of putting the injured party back into the position in which it would have been but for the particular event complained of. Claims are not a means of turning a loss into a profit, or obtaining a windfall. The remedy for breach of contract is an award of damages. Damages at common law are intended to compensate the injured party for its loss, not to transfer to the injured party, if it has suffered no loss, the benefit which the wrongdoer had gained by its breach of contract.

Losses recoverable as damages is limited to those which are reasonably foreseeable.

Recoverable losses are those which may fairly and reasonably be considered as arising naturally according to the usual course of events from the breach of contract. Losses are also recoverable when they may reasonably be supposed to have been in the contemplation of both parties at the time they made the contract, as the probable result of breach of the contract.

Measure of damages

There are two possible measures of loss:

(i) loss of bargain
(ii) waste expenditure.

Loss of bargain

The normal measure for breach of contract is loss of bargain. This measure of damages is intended to place the injured party in the same situation, as far as money can accomplish this, as if the contract had been performed *Mertens* v. *Home Freeholds Co* (1921) CA. This principle arises from the nature of contracts. Contracts involve the making of bargains and create expectations on each side which are intended to be fulfilled by performance of the contract obligations. If, for instance, the contractor does not complete its part of the development, then the measure of damages in this case will be the cost of completing the project in a reasonable manner, less the contract price *Mertens* v. *Home Freeholds Co* (1921) CA. This measure of damages therefore protects the expectations of the parties arising from the contract. Allowance must be made for the expense which may have been saved by the contractor not having to complete its side of the bargain.

Cost of reinstatement

Where the breach of contract involves defective work, the normal measure of damages is the cost of reinstatement taken at the time when the defect was discovered *East Ham Corporation* v. *Bernard Sunley* (1966). The claimant will not necessarily lose its entitlement to damages if it waits for the outcome of the case before carrying out the remedial works, it all depends on the circumstances of the case *William Cory & Son Ltd* v. *Wingate Investment (London Colney) Ltd* (1980) 17 BLR 104 CA. An injured party will be entitled to the cost of making building works conform to contract unless that cost is significantly disproportionate to the benefit that is obtained from it *Roxley Electronics and Construction Ltd* v. *Forsyth* (1996).

The reasonableness of the pursuer's remedial works is not to be weighed in fine scales.

McLaren Murdoch & Hamilton Ltd v. *The Abercromby Motor Group Ltd* [2002] Court of Session Outer House.

Where the cost of reinstatement is out of proportion to the claimant's real loss then some other measure should be used. This is the case where there has been a modest effect on the utility of the works and where it would be reasonable to assess the loss on the basis of diminution in value *Birse Construction Ltd* v. *Eastern Telegraph Company Ltd* [2004] EWHC 2512 (TCC).

Loss of market value

In some cases the measure of damages for defective work may instead be the reduction in market value of the development. This will be the case when it is unreasonable for the defects to be put right, particularly where the value of remedial works is out of proportion to the value of the development and only affects the 'amenity value' of the development.

A loss of use claim in a building case is not a claim for the loss of use of the purchase price of the property, or for the loss of the consideration received for that purchase price.

The loss of use element of the claim for general damages has often been dealt with as part of an overall claim for inconvenience and distress and only recoverable by a natural person *Bella Casa Ltd* v. *Vinestone* [2005] EWHC 2807.

Wasted expenditure

In some circumstances the claimant may have difficulty in proving loss of profit. It may then elect to claim for wasted expenditure, that is expenditure rendered futile by the defendant's breach. This can include expenditure incurred before the contract was made *CCC Films (London)* v. *Impact Quadrant Films* (1985); *Anglia Television* v. *Reed* (1972). It cannot claim this reliance loss if it has made a bad bargain since the courts will not put a claimant in a better position than it would have been in if the contract had been performed. However, it is for the defendant in breach to show that the claimant made a bad bargain since it is the defendant who has made the matter an issue by the breach.

The two measures of damage, loss of bargain and wasted expenditure, are alternatives and mutually exclusive, at least so far as to prevent double recovery.

2.3 Claims in restitution

Quantum meruit

The expression quantum meruit means 'the amount he deserves' or 'what the job is worth'. A claim for Quantum Meruit is a claim for payment for work carried out where the price has not been quantified and is usually a claim for a reasonable sum.

A quantum meruit claim may be based in contract or in restitution, although the term 'quantum meruit' is frequently used to mean a claim in restitution only.

A claim for quantum meruit in contract is based on the agreement of the parties. It arises in two situations.

(i) In the first situation the contract is silent on the measure of remuneration for the services provided. In such a situation in construction, contract terms of payment of a reasonable remuneration will be implied by statute.
(ii) In the second situation the contract contains an express agreement to pay reasonable remuneration or similar terminology.

The above 'Contractual Quantum Meruit' claims are in fact simply claims in contract, so that the first issue is whether or not there is a contract which applies to the situation. If so, the main issue is then the measure of the reimbursement. In the second situation above the main issue will be the interpretation of a particular term of the contract.

Claims for quantum meruit in restitution seek to impose a right to payment by law arising from the circumstances of unjust enrichment by one party at the expense of another. The claim is occasionally referred to as a claim in quasi-contract. The issue in 'Restitutionary Quantum Meruit' is whether or not there is any entitlement at all in law. If so, then the second issue is how the reimbursement is to be measured.

The two types of claims are the extreme ends of a spectrum of circumstances – *Serck Controls Ltd* v. *Drake & Scull Engineering Ltd* [2000] (TCC) HH Judge Hicks QC.

The general principle is that a claim in restitution does not depend on an 'implied contract' theory and cannot be sustained if a contract already governs the situation – see Court of Appeal of New South Wales in *Trimis* v. *Mina* (2000) 2TCLR 346, *Mowlem plc* v. *Stena Line Ports Limited* [2004] EWHC 2206 (TCC) and *S & W Process Engineering Ltd* v. *Cauldron Foods Ltd* [2005] EWHC 153 (TCC).

Letters of intent and bare agreements

Many situations in which the claim for quantum meruit arises involve letters of intent or limited exchanges between parties each followed by rapid commencement of the works. The issue in those cases is whether or not there is a contract and if so the meaning of the terms of payment. The claim in restitution is usually presented as an alternative claim if indeed there is no contract.

To establish a contract not only requires agreement by the parties on all the terms they consider essential, but also sufficient certainty in their dealings to satisfy the requirement of completeness. An intention to create a legally binding relationship must also be present.

Letters of intent which state an intention to contract in the future frequently fail on both requirements since they are usually incomplete statements preparatory to a formal contract. In such cases a letter of intent is binding upon neither party *Turiff Construction Ltd* v. *Regalia Knitting Mills Ltd* (1971).

A contract may come into existence following a simple request to carry out work and may take one of two forms. It may be an ordinary executory contract. It may otherwise be an 'if' contract, i.e. a contract under which A requests B to carry out a certain performance and promises B that, if he does so, he will receive a certain performance in return *British Steel Corporation* v. *Cleveland Bridge & Engineering Co. Ltd* (1983). Terms may then be implied into that contract in accordance with normal principles.

In *Clarke & Sons* v. *ACT Construction* [2002] EWCA Civ 972 the judge at first instance held that there was no contract between the parties. He held that the parties' relationship was not a contractual one, with the consequence that the value of the work carried out by ACT could be recovered and paid for, but on the basis of a quantum meruit, a reasonable sum, a restitutionary basis in fact.

The Court of Appeal disagreed and held that the proper conclusion was that there was 'a contractual quantum meruit'. It was observed that in focusing on the essential ingredients for 'a building contract of some complexity' the judge may have lost sight of the fact that even if there was no entire contract, and especially if there is no 'formal' contract, there may still be an agreement to carry out work, the entire scope of which was not yet agreed, even if a price has not been agreed. It was held that provided there was an instruction to do work and an acceptance of that instruction, then there was a contract and the law would imply into it an obligation to pay a reasonable sum for that work. It was held that was the situation in the instant case. It was observed that reversing the judgement on this point did not significantly advance either case.

Simply carrying out work is not sufficient to create a contract, all the necessary ingredients of contract must be present *Mowlem plc* v. *PHI Group Limited* [2004].

For a contract to arise in the case of a letter of intent, the letter must contain all necessary terms. Further, it must be plain that the unilateral contract is to govern the main contract work in the event that no formal contract is concluded *Monk Building and Civil Engineering Ltd* v. *Norwich Union Life Assurance Society* (CA) (1993).

Although a letter of intent may not govern the main contract works, the letter may relate to part or preparatory works and in that case may create a contract for those limited works, if all the necessary ingredients of contract are present. In *Turiff Construction Ltd* v. *Regalia Knitting Mills Ltd* (1971) the employer's letter of intent was a legally binding agreement to reimburse the contractor his expenses for preliminary design work and feasibility studies for a main contract which was not in the event concluded.

In *ERDC Group Limited* v. *Brunel University* [2006] (TCC) HH Humphrey Lloyd QC considered five letters of intent issued over a period of time each increasing the total value of the work carried out.

In December 2001 ERDC submitted a tender for the works on new sports facilities for Brunel University which were to be carried out on the basis of the JCT Standard Form of Contract With Contractor's Design, 1998 Edition. Brunel decided to appoint ERDC but that the formal execution of contract documents would be deferred until after the grant of full planning permission. It was agreed that ERDC would progress with the design of the works under the terms of a letter of appointment issued on 6 February 2002. In all, three letters were issued and returned countersigned by ERDC. ERDC commenced on construction of the works on 27 May 2002. Two further letters were issued but not countersigned. Each letter offered a limited contract set by reference to value and covering a particular period. The authority under the last letter expired on 1 September 2002.

Lloyd J held that there was a clear intention to create legal relations and the letters and their acceptance by ERDC were contracts, possibly of the classic 'if' or 'conditional' variety. He held that both their background and their terms demonstrated that Brunel was not going to contract unconditionally for the whole of the works. Instead it decided to offer ERDC a familiar limited contract which would readily ensure that, when it was able to conclude the full contract that was contemplated, that contract would take effect retroactively with the minimum of difficulties.

Lloyd J held that the work done pursuant to the letter contracts prior to the expiry of the last contract on 1 September 2002 was to be treated and valued as if it had been carried out under the contract contemplated by the last letter. It was not to be valued on a quantum meruit basis. The valuation was to be made applying the relevant rates and prices. Where the 'contract' rates or prices were not be applicable, either party was free to contend for a different and more appropriate rate or price or valuation by reference to cost, if reasonable.

If work is carried out beyond the financial limit of the letter of intent, then there will only be an entitlement if the financial limit was not intended to prevent further payment. In *AC Controls Ltd* v. *British Broadcasting Corporation* [2002] EWHC 3132 (TCC) it was held that the spending cap was not intended to limit the amount that ACC could recover, but was intended to operate as a 'trigger' entitling the BBC to terminate the contract any time after the cap was reached. ACC was required to carry on working and was entitled to payment of a reasonable value for the work done.

Apart from the above particular circumstances, a contractor exceeding the financial limit will have great difficulty in establishing an entitlement to payment absent a clear instruction and acceptance that additional payment would be made *Mowlem plc* v. *Stena Line Ports Limited* [2004] EWHC 2206 (TCC).

Work outside the contract

In order to establish an entitlement to payment for work 'outside' the contract the necessary ingredients of either a collateral contract or restitution must be present. This may be difficult if the reason for the extra work not falling within the existing contract is the lack of a request for the work to be carried out or agreement to payment for the work.

In *Parkinson* v. *Commissioners of Works* (1949) 2 KB 632 the contractor agreed under a varied contract to carry out certain work to be ordered by the Commissioners on a cost plus profit basis subject to a limitation as to the total amount of profit. The Commissioners ordered work to a total value of £6 600 000 but it was held that on its true construction the varied contract only gave the Commissioners authority to order work to the value of £5 000 000. It was held that the work that had been executed by the contractors included more than was covered, on its true construction, by the variation deed, and that the cost of the uncovenanted addition had therefore to be paid for by a quantum meruit.

In *Costain Civil Engineering Ltd* v. *Zanen Dredging & Contracting Co* [1997] 85 BLR 77 the instructions purported to be given under the subcontract did not constitute authorized variations of the subcontract works because the instructions required work to be done outside the scope of the subcontractor's obligations under the subcontract. The subcontractor was therefore entitled to payment on a quantum meruit. In measuring a fair remuneration an allowance was to be made for profit and consideration had to be given to the relationship of the parties and the competitive edge that the subcontractor had by the significant advantage of having already mobilized his equipment.

In *S & W Process Engineering Ltd* v. *Cauldron Foods Ltd* [2005] EWHC 153 (TCC) HH Judge Peter Coulson QC considered that where there is a contract for specified work but the contractor does work outside the contract at the employer's request, the contractor may be entitled to be paid a reasonable sum for the work outside the contract: *Thorne* v. *London Corp* (1876) 1 Ap. Cas. 120 and *Parkinson and Co* v. *Commissioners of Works* [1949] 2 KB 632. He observed that this will always turn on what is meant in any particular instance by 'outside the Contract'. He held that S & W would have to demonstrate that, in some way, Cauldron freely accepted services in circumstances where they should have known that S & W would expect to be paid for them. He considered that might be difficult where the item of extra work in dispute was not clearly requested or instructed or authorised.

A claim for quantum meruit in restitution may arise in the following situations:

(i) Where the parties proceed on the mistaken basis that there is an enforceable contract, but there is no contract.
(ii) One party requests services from the other which are not governed by a contract.
(iii) Where the contract is frustrated.
(iv) Where before completion the contractor accepts a repudiation by the employer as terminating the contract. The contractor can elect to sue for damages for breach of contract or quantum meruit in restitution for the work performed.

In *Banque Financière de la Cité* v. *Parc (Battersea) Ltd* [1999] 1 AC 221 Lord Steyn identified four questions which arose in relation to any claim in restitution:

(i) Had the defendant benefited or been enriched?
(ii) Was the enrichment at the expense of the claimant?
(iii) Was the enrichment unjust?
(iv) Were there any defences?

If there has been a total failure of consideration in a contract, the injured part can then make a claim in restitution. So, for instance, if the subcontractor has not performed at all, the contractor can claim for the return of monies paid. If the subcontractor has been overpaid and has failed to complete, the contractor can recover the overpayment even if it has managed to have the work completed without, in fact, incurring any loss despite the overpayment.

Estoppel by convention can operate to prevent a claim to restitution of payment by mistake. If the money is spent in good faith, in reliance on the representation that there was an entitlement to it, then the order for repayment will create the detriment sufficient to found the estoppel.

Speculative work

If the parties enter upon a speculative venture then it will be difficult to succeed in a claim in restitution for reimbursement of the expense incurred if the venture fails, absent express agreement to payment. The reasons for the failure are highly relevant as is the nature of the risk that that was accepted.

In *Easat Antennas Ltd* v. *Racal Defence Electronics Ltd* [2000] (ChD) Racal succeeded in a bid in which Easat agreed to and carried out considerable work, but did not award Easat the subcontract.

HH Mr Justice Hart held that the work undertaken in order to obtain a contract does not give rise to a restitutionary remedy. The party providing the services is taken to have run the risk that the contract will not eventuate and he will not therefore be paid.

In this case there was no dispute that Racal had received a benefit as a result of the services. Justice Hart accepted that Easat only had an expectation of being rewarded for its work in the event of the bid succeeding and the conditions for placing the subcontract then being satisfied.

However, while Easat was prepared to take the risk that Racal's bid would fail, it was not prepared to run the risk that, if Racal's bid succeeded, as it did, that it would not be rewarded. It was held that that was the whole purpose and underlying assumption of the agreement. On that basis the claim by Easat was held to be a good one.

In *Countrywide Communications Ltd* v. *ICL Pathway Ltd* [2000] CLC 324 a consortium assembled to make a bid involved the members in considerable work. When the bid was successful the consortium excluded one of the members.

Mr Nicholas Strauss QC considered whether the excluded member had a claim in restitution. He held that appropriate weight was to be given to a number of considerations:

(i) Whether the services were of a kind which would normally be given free of charge.
(ii) The terms in which the request to perform the services was made may be important in establishing the extent of any risk (if any) which the plaintiffs may fairly be said to have taken that such service would in the end be uncompensated. It may be important whether the parties are simply negotiating, expressly or impliedly 'subject to contract', or whether one party has given some kind of assurance or indication that he will not withdraw, or that he will not withdraw except in certain circumstances.

(iii) The nature of the benefit which has resulted to the defendant and in particular whether such benefit is real (either 'realised' or 'realisable') or a fiction. There was more inclination to impose an obligation to pay for a real benefit, since otherwise the abortive negotiations would leave the defendant with a windfall and the plaintiff out of pocket. The performance of services requested may of itself amount to a benefit or enrichment.

(iv) The circumstances in which the anticipated contract does not materialise and in particular whether they can be said to involve 'fault' on the part of the defendant, or to be outside the scope of the risk undertaken by the plaintiff at the outset may be decisive.

Mr Nicholas Strauss QC held that justice required that Countrywide should be appropriately recompensed. Countrywide had accepted the risk that its services would not be accepted for submission with the bid or that the bid might fail or that negotiations might fail. It had not accepted the risk that it would be dismissed after the final bid had been submitted because Pathway changed personnel. The measure for repayment was time spent with associated costs.

In *Stephen Donald Architects Limited* v. *Christopher King* [2003] EWHC 1867 (TCC) the parties were friends and King did not have the means to pay fees for redevelopment of the property until completion of the project. HH Judge Seymour QC considered that the nature and extent of the risk assumed by the party claiming payment on a quantum meruit basis in relation to the abortive transaction was a material consideration in determining whether an enrichment has been unjust. There was nothing unjust about being visited with the consequences of a risk which one has consciously run. The Architects took on the risk that King might decide not to proceed, either for insufficient funds or on terms perceived by King to be unsatisfactory. That was the risk that eventuated.

Measure of contractual quantum meruit

In the situation where there is a contract, then the issue in a Contractual Quantum Meruit claim is either the measure of the 'reasonable sum' or the interpretation of similarly wide express terms. The issue is whether the measure is on the basis of cost or market price. There appears to be no hard and fast rule.

The assessment of a quantum meruit in the case of an unquantified price was usually based on actual cost which would include on- and off-site overheads provided that it was reasonable and was reasonably and not unnecessarily incurred, plus an appropriate addition for profit *ERDC Group Limited* v. *Brunel University* [2006] (TCC).

In *Clarke & Sons* v. *ACT Construction* [2002] EWCA Civ 972 the issue was the assessment of the reasonable remuneration. The judge at first instance decided that it was cost plus 15%. The judge found that it was 'slightly higher' than the bracket of 5–12% advanced by Clarke's expert but that that bracket was based on defined building contracts whereas dayworks were being charged for with higher uplifts in 1992/1994. He also took account of the higher percentages charged out and paid for pursuant to the earlier invoices.

The Court of Appeal held that there was no reason why the prices actually paid should not be factors to take into account in the instant case and stated that it should be very slow indeed to interfere with a judgment on such an issue made by an experienced judge in a specialist tribunal and upheld his finding that the uplift was 15%.

The express term for payment may yield a different result. Judge Bowsher QC in *Laserbore Ltd* v. *Morrison Biggs Wall Ltd* (1992) had to decide the meaning of the term 'Fair and reasonable payments for all works executed'. He considered that the costs plus basis was wrong in principle even though in some instances it may produce the right result. The appropriate approach was to adopt general market rates.

In *Robertson Group (Construction) Limited* v. *Amey-Miller (Edingburgh) Joint Venture)* [2005] CSIH89 the Inner House of the Court of Session considered the meaning of the phrase 'all direct costs and directly incurred losses shall be underwritten and reimbursed' in a letter of intent.

It was held that parties prospectively entering into a contract subject to JCT conditions could be expected to be familiar with the traditional loss and expense clause and the interpretation judicially placed on it. The phraseology used in the instant arrangement was different but similar. The adjective 'direct' qualified the word 'costs' and the phrase 'directly incurred' the word 'losses'. In the event (which occurred) of a formal contract not being entered into, Amey-Miller undertook that 'all direct costs and directly incurred losses' would be 'underwritten and reimbursed'. It was held that the first of the two verbs used ('underwritten') was, in its familiar sense of 'guaranteed', clearly wide enough to embrace elements beyond actual outlays. It was held that while the second verb ('reimbursed') might tend to suggest the making good of something expended, the phrase read as a whole did not have that restricted sense.

Measure in restitution

The practical issue is usually whether the measure of reimbursement is on the basis of cost incurred with contribution for profit and overheads, or whether it is to be based on market value. Where there is a contract with prices but which does not apply or an unconcluded contract with prices, this may be taken into account in considering the reimbursement. In some cases there will be little difference in the measure between cost and market value. It might be thought that a measure based on rates would always be higher than one based on costs. This may not always be the case where the rates are based on an unconcluded contract, since there are many commercial reasons for a contractor to bid low for a contract.

In the case of an express contract to do work at an unquantified price, the measure is the reasonable remuneration of the contractor. In the case of a benefit which it is unjust to retain the measure is the value to the employer normally the market value, namely the sum that would have been agreed including profit. In between there is a borderline, the position of which is debatable *Serck Controls Ltd* v. *Drake & Scull Engineering Ltd* (2000). The unconcluded contract may be good evidence of the appropriate measure.

In the measure of a fair remuneration and allowance for profit, consideration had to be given to the relationship of the parties and the competitive edge that the subcontractor had by the significant advantage of having already mobilized his equipment *Costain Civil Engineering Ltd* v. *Zanen Dredging & Contracting Co* [1997] 85 BLR 77.

The contractor's offer in the unconcluded contract should act as an upper limit to the measure of the quantum meruit, even though that might lead the contractor to sustain a loss see Mr Recorder Colin Reese QC in *Sanjay Lachhani* v. *Destination Canada (UK) Ltd* (1997).

In *ERDC Group Limited* v. *Brunel University* [2006] (TCC) the circumstances were unusual in that there was a move from contractual to a non-contractual basis. Lloyd J held that it was not right to switch from an assessment based on ERDC's rates to one based entirely on ERDC's costs. The move was not marked at the time.

Some allowance must be made for work which is defective or work carried out inefficiently. The issue then is the standard to be adopted to establish the defect or inefficiency and the duty owed by the contractor for performance (if any in the absence of a contract). Since restitution is not based on implied contract theory there is no scope for reducing the measure by something like a set-off or cross-claim equal to the costs of putting the work right, except perhaps where as a result of the contractor's performance there is no benefit or value – *Sanjay Lachhani* v. *Destination Canada (UK) Ltd* (1997), *Serck Controls Ltd* v. *Drake & Scull Engineering Ltd* (2000) 73 Con LR 100 and *ERDC Group Limited* v. *Brunel University* [2006] (TCC).

3 CLAIMS FOR EXTENSION OF TIME

3.1 Purpose of extension of time clauses

Delays frequently occur on construction projects and so standard forms make provision for extension of the time for completion in certain events. Such extension of time clauses are not intended to provide the contractor with a completion date to aim for, but are to protect the employer's right to levy or deduct liquidated damages for late completion by the contractor. If the employer causes delay, by its breach, and there is no provision for extension of time due to its breach, then the liquidated damages clause is unenforceable. The employer is then left only with an entitlement to claim such common law damages as it is able to prove. Extension of time clauses in standard forms are therefore drafted to compensate not only for specific risk events but also for breaches of contract by the employer. Extension of time clauses for selected standard forms in common use are described below.

ICE 6th and 7th Edition

Clause 44(1) of the ICE 6th Edition lists those matters which allow the engineer to grant extensions of time which, at clause 44(1)(e), includes all other special circumstances of any kind whatsoever. This may be argued to be wide enough to encompass breaches of contract by the employer.

Clause 44(1)(f) of the ICE 7th Edition is the equivalent of clause 44(1)(e) of the ICE 6th Edition. The new clause 44(1)(e) of the ICE 7th Edition makes the position clearer and allows the engineer to grant an extension of time for any delay, impediment, prevention or default by the employer. This is wide enough to include breach of contract by the employer.

FIDIC Forms

Clause 8.4 of the FIDIC Red, Yellow and Silver Book 1999 lists those matters which entitle the contractor (subject to notice) to an extension of the time for completion which, at clause 8.4(e), includes any delay, impediment or prevention caused by or attributable to the employer, its personnel or other contractors on the site. This is wide enough to include breach of contract by the employer.

ECC 2nd and 3rd Edition

Clause 60.1 lists those matters which are compensation events which, at clause 60.1(18), includes breaches of contract which are not one of the other compensation events.

MF/1 Rev 4

Clause 33(1) lists the matters which allow the Engineer to grant an extension of time and include any act or omission on the part of the Purchaser or Engineer.

IChemE Red Book 4th Edition

Clause 14.1 of the IChemE Red Book lists those matters for which the Project Manager may award an extension of time. Clause 14(1)(d) is widely drafted, referring to any breach of **Contract** by the **Purchaser**.

JCT 2005 (SBC/Q)

Clause 2.29 list the Relevant Events which may entitle the Contractor to an adjustment of the Completion Date.

Clause 2.29 is widely drafted to refer to 'impediment, prevention or default whether by act or omission', by the Employers participants in the project except to the extent cause or contributed to by a default of the Contractor.

CECA Blue Form of Subcontract

Clause 6(1) of the CECA Blue Form lists those matters which entitle the subcontractor to such extension of time as may be fair and reasonable and, at clause 6(1)(c), includes any breach of the subcontract by the contractor.

3.2 Parties' obligations as to time

Employer's duty to perform

The employer is required to complete its obligations specified in the contract, such as supplying information, giving possession, executing any work or providing any materials, at such times as to permit execution and completion of the works by the contractor at the times specified in the contract. If no such times are specified, the employer must carry out its obligations at reasonable times, having regard to the date of completion of construction, the provisions of any approved programme of work and the actual progress of the contractor.

These obligations of the employer do not require that it should comply with the provisions of the approved programme of work, but only that it should not hinder the contractor from carrying out its obligations to complete the works at the times specified in the contract. It is only if no time is specified that the approved programme is relevant, and then only in establishing what are reasonable times. This, therefore, is not an obligation to positively cooperate with a contractor to complete prior to the date provided for in the contract. The situation will, however, be different if the programme is incorporated in the contract as a contract document or if the express terms of the contract state otherwise.

Contractor's obligations as to time

The contractor's obligations as to time will depend upon the express terms of the contract and on the terms implied as a matter of business efficacy. In modern construction contracts there are usually three separate but inter-related express obligations. If the three obligations are not stated expressly then similar terms will not necessarily be implied into the contract.

The first obligation is usually that the contractor shall complete by a specified date or a specified period, and possibly with stage or sectional completion obligations.

In modern construction, the obligation to complete by a date is of little assistance to an employer or a contractor in a subcontract in the management of the project. In most cases the employer will wish action to be taken early to avoid late completion. This is the purpose of the second obligation in construction contracts. The second obligation is that the contractor shall progress the works regularly and diligently. In some subcontract forms the subcontractor's obligation to progress the subcontract works is stated in terms that progress must be in accordance with the progress of the main contract works.

The third obligation relates to the means by which the employer monitors progress and the implementation of corrective measures. The third obligation is that the contractor prepares and works to an accepted programme, updates the programme when actual progress differs from the programme and revises the programme to include corrective measures to mitigate the effects of delays.

Each of these obligations is examined below.

Obligation to complete the works

A construction contract will usually contain an express obligation to complete by a specified date or within a specified period. If a period is specified for completion then in order to fix the completion date, the commencement of the period must be clearly identified and established to avoid uncertainty. Some standard forms provide for the commencement date to be agreed after execution of the contract or, failing that, fixed by the architect/engineer. It should be clear whether or not periods of holiday or bank holidays are included, This is particularly relevant when extensions of time are granted. It should be clear what revised date has been fixed. Otherwise, confusion often arises on whether the extension of time is for calendar days or working days, particularly when the working week is less than seven days.

If no date or period is specified then a term will be implied by the Supply of Goods and Services Act 1982 that the contractor's obligation is to complete by a reasonable time. In a commercial contract the circumstances may require the implication of a term of completion by a fixed date to give business efficacy to the arrangement and to reflect the intention of the parties – see *Bruno Zornow (Builders) Ltd* v. *Beechcroft Developments Ltd* [1990] 51 BLR 16.

What constitutes a reasonable time is a question of fact. The principles to be applied are those in *Pantland Hick* v. *Raymond & Reid* [1893]. What constitutes a reasonable time has to be considered in relation to circumstances which existed at the time when the contract obligations are performed, but excluding circumstances which were under the control of the contractor. In *British Steel Corporation* v. *Cleveland Bridge Engineering Company Limited* [1981] 24 BLR 100 Lord Goff applied these principles by first considering what in ordinary circumstances was a reasonable time for performance and then considering to what extent the time for performance of the contractor was in fact extended by extraordinary circumstances outside its control. Whether a reasonable time has been taken to do the works cannot be decided in advance, but only after the work has been done.

Where time is at large because the specified date no longer applies following an act of prevention or breach by the employer, the original completion date is good evidence of what is a 'reasonable time in ordinary circumstances'.

In *Carr* v. *J. A. Berriman Pty Ltd* (1953) 27 ALJ 273 it was held that if the contractor's obligation to complete by a specified date is of the essence, then the employer is released from further obligation if the contractor is in breach. The employer can treat the contract as repudiated. The employer may instead elect not to exercise that right and continue to conduct himself or herself in accordance with the contract. Time will no longer be of the essence. The employer may, however, give notice requiring performance within a reasonable time, making time of the essence again.

In general, obligations in construction contracts to complete by a specified date are not regarded as of the essence, except when clear express wording is used. It is suggested that extension of time clauses and provisions for liquidated damages would, as a matter of interpretation, prevent the obligation to complete in time being of the essence.

Obligation to progress the works

If the contract includes an express obligation for the contractor to complete by a specified date or within a specified period, then a term will not be implied that the contractor is to proceed regularly and diligently with the works. In the absence of a contrary intention, the contractor has the right to plan, execute and progress the works as it considers, provided the contractor completes in accordance with the contract – *GLC* v. *Cleveland Bridge Engineering Company Limited* [1984] 34 BLR 50. The employer will be faced with severe evidential difficulties if it considers progress is too slow to ensure completion on time and wishes to take remedial action under the contract.

Many standard forms of contract include an express obligation for the contractor to proceed regularly and diligently with the works.

If the contractor does complete in time, but it can be shown that in breach of contract the contractor has not proceeded regularly and diligently, then the employer will have a remedy of substantial damages if a loss can be established. The term 'regularly and diligently' means to proceed continuously, industriously and efficiently with appropriate physical resources so as to progress the works steadily towards completion substantially in accordance with the contractual requirements as to time, sequence and quality of work – *West Faulkner Associates* v. *The London Borough of Newham* [1992] 71 BLR 6. If the contractor is well ahead with the works, the contractor is not allowed to slow down so that the work is completed on time, if it is under an obligation to proceed regularly and diligently – *Hounslow* v. *Twickenham Garden Developments* [1970] 7 BLR 89.

In *Ascon Contracting Limited* v. *Alfred McAlpine Construction Isle of Man Ltd* [1999], clause 11.1 required the subcontractor to carry out and complete the subcontract works reasonably in accordance with the progress of the main contract works. It was held, relying on *Pigott Foundations Ltd* v. *Shepherd Construction Ltd* [1993] 67 BLR 48, that the subcontractor was not required to comply with the detail of the main contractor's programme, either generally or in relation to the work of other specific subcontractors. The subcontractor was, however, to go somewhat beyond the negative duty not unreasonably to interfere with the actual carrying out of other works. The subcontractor will know the nature of the main contract works and the place of the subcontract works in them. The 'progress' referred to in the obligation was that expected and observed, although the obligation was only to proceed 'reasonably' in accordance with that progress. If the subcontractor was in breach of that obligation and caused follow-on trades to be delayed, then the contractor would be entitled to recover any loss so caused.

In *Serck Controls Ltd* v. *Drake & Scull Engineering Ltd* [2000] it was held that on the facts of the case the sum due to Serck was to be assessed by reference to what would be reasonable remuneration for executing the work of design and installation of a control system at a construction site. It was held that a firm working on a quantum meruit basis on a complex construction site could not wholly ignore the desirability of cooperation with others at work on the site. There was a duty at least not to unreasonably interfere with the carrying out of other works and more positively an obligation to be aware of the progress of other trades and, so far as consistent with the firm's own legitimate commercial interests, to cooperate in efficient working practices. It was held that there was no breach by Serck of the qualified duty of cooperation to disentitle Serck from having its work valued on the basis of the circumstances in which they were carried out.

In *Alfred McAlpine Capital Projects Limited* v. *Tilebox Limited* [2005] EWHC 281 (TCC) Mr Justice Jackson had to consider the meaning of the obligation to take reasonable steps to insure that completion was achieved by a specified date. It was held that the phrase 'take all reasonable steps' was regularly used in contractual documents to connote a low level obligation. It was the antithesis of a contractual provision requiring the promisor to achieve a particular result.

The obligation as to programme

If the contract requires the contractor to submit a programme in accordance with the requirements of the contract then the contractor's failure to do so will be a breach of contract. The contractor will then be liable for substantial damages if the employer can establish a loss. It is suggested that the employer will need to demonstrate:

- that the contractor was under an obligation to progress the works in accordance with the programme, and
- that the absence of the programme prevented the employer managing either the contract or other related work, so
- that as a result the employer suffered delay and/or loss which could have been avoided if the programme had been submitted.

In practice, establishing the necessary evidence is likely to be difficult. This is particularly so if the contractor has submitted a programme, but the extent of the breach is that the programme is not in accordance with the specified requirements.

If the requirement to submit a programme is considered an important obligation, then the contract may be drafted to make payment conditional on the submission of the programme. This is not usual in construction contracts, although the Engineering Construction Contract 2nd Edition makes such a provision at clause 50.3. The standard form has no related mechanism for the failure to comply with the obligation to revise the programme, which is equally important as the initial submission.

Some construction contracts require the contractor to carry out the works in accordance with the accepted programme, but there is no uniform approach. It is suggested, extending the principle in *GLC* v. *Cleveland Bridge Engineering Company Limited* [1984] 34 BLR 50 that a term will not be implied that a contractor is required to work to the accepted programme. Indeed, even standard forms that require a programme to be submitted appear to anticipate that the contractor has a discretion to modify its method of working or sequence of working and, therefore, not to follow the programme.

It is suggested that if the contractor is required to work to the programme, then the employer will be required to comply with it also to the extent necessary to allow the contractor to comply with that obligation. If the programme is an accurate indication of the progress that the contractor needs to make to fulfil its obligation to progress the works, then it is suggested that the employer is required to comply with the programme to the extent necessary to allow the contractor to comply with this further obligation.

The above obligations apart, the employer is not bound to comply with the accepted programme. In *Glenlion Construction Ltd* v. *The Guinness Trust* [1987] the contractor submitted a shortened programme. It was held that the contractor was entitled to complete earlier than the completion date since its obligation was to complete 'on or before' the Date of Completion. There was, however, no implied term requiring the employer to perform its obligations to allow the contractor to complete at the earlier date.

4.1 Administration of claims
4.2 Litigation
4.3 Arbitration
4.4 Adjudication
4.5 Alternative dispute resolution

The contract may refer to programme requirements either in less than clear terms or in conflict with the primary obligation to complete by a specified date. The exact obligations of the contractor and employer are then a matter of interpretation. Two decided cases show the approach taken by the courts.

In *J. F. Finnegan Ltd* v. *Sheffield City Council* [1988] 43 BLR 130 it was held that the reference to a shorter contract period in the Special Conditions in the Contract Bills did not contain an obligation to complete by an earlier completion date, applying the decision in *Glenlion*. It was held that the provisions applied to programming rather than time-related obligations. Accordingly, the prolongation costs were to be calculated from the end of the contract period.

In *DSND Subsea Ltd* v. *Petroleum Geo-Services ASA and PGS Offshore Technology AS* [2000] the previous programme of works had been overtaken by events and a revised programme was prepared. The parties executed a Memorandum of Understanding agreeing to the revised programme. The revised programme showed the dates and durations as being 'indicative'. It was held that the fact that the dates and durations were indicative did not mean that they were not intended to have contractual effect. It meant that the parties agreed that they would work in accordance with the revised programme to the best of their ability, but that the contractor would not be in breach of contract merely because the contractor failed to achieve the dates and durations. It was held that the revised programme was evidence of what the parties considered at the time of the Memorandum of Agreement to be expeditious and timely performance as required by the contract. The revised programme gave indicative dates and durations because the parties recognized that the situation was fraught with uncertainty due to weather affecting the sub-sea work and the uncertain availability of deep sea vessels.

Some construction contracts require the contractor to revise programmes either periodically or when progress does not follow the programme or both. There is no uniformity of approach and it is suggested that no term will usually be implied to that effect.

One consequence of the contractor not submitting or revising the programme is that the contractor's ability to prove an entitlement to extension of time may be reduced due to the absence of contemporary programming evidence. The accepted programme will be one of the main tools available to the A/E in understanding the construction logic and assessing delay. The A/E's assessment will be less accurate without the programme. It is suggested that since in many standard forms the A/E can take into account all circumstances and is required to make a fair assessment, the fact that no programme or revisions have been provided can properly be taken into account.

Obligation if the programme is a contract document

In most standard forms the programme that the contractor is required to submit is not stated to be a contract document. In that case the role of the programme may simply be an aid to the A/E monitoring the progress of the works.

If the programme is a contract document, then its role must be established by interpretation of the contract to ascertain the intention of the parties. Depending on the precedence of documents, the contract programme may define the obligations and responsibilities of the parties. Alternatively, the programme may only indicate the anticipated sequence of events which are considered acceptable progress of the works to achieve completion by the specified date. In some standard forms the programme is a contract document, but its use in defining the work is limited. In other forms the programme is not a contract document but is used to establish the entitlement to extension of time.

If the programme includes a method statement then that stated method may become the specified method of working and in that case may entitle the contractor to a variation if the specified method is required to be changed. The effect depends upon the standard form.

In *Yorkshire Water Authority* v. *Sir Alfred McAlpine and Son (Northern) Ltd* (1985) 32 BLR 114 under the ICE 5th Edition the contractor was required to submit a programme with its tender, expressly stated to be in addition to the requirement of clause 14 of the Conditions of Contract. The contractor duly submitted the programme and its method statement. The method statement followed the tender documents in providing for the construction of the works upstream. It was held that the method statement was not the programme submitted under clause 14 and that the incorporation of the method statement into the contract imposed on the contractors an obligation to follow it in so far as it was legally or physically possible to do so. The method statement therefore became the specified method of construction. If the change in method of construction was necessary for completion of the works because of impossibility within clause 13(1) then the contractor was entitled to a variation order under clause 51 and payment under clauses 51(2) and 52.

In *English Industrial Estates Corporation* v. *Kier Construction Ltd* [1991] 56 BLR 93 the contractor was required to submit with its tender a full and detailed programme indicating its proposed work sequence together with a brief description of the arrangements and methods of demolition and construction which it proposed to adopt. The method statement provided for suitable demolition materials to be crushed on site and unsuitable arisings to be removed from site. The engineer instructed all hard arisings to be crushed and the surplus stockpiled. It was held that this was a variation to contract removing from Kier an economic option.

In *Havant Borough Council* v. *South Coast Shipping Company Ltd* [1996] CILL 1146 the contractor was unable to follow the method statement due to a court injunction which restricted the hours of working. To overcome the problem, which involved excessive noise, the contractor worked a different system to that provided for in the method statement. The method statement was a contract document. The court held that the change in method constituted a variation.

Subcontractors and the main contract programme

Main contractors normally require flexibility from subcontractors so that they can manage subcontracts in the light of actual progress. It is, therefore, unusual for subcontractors to be entitled to follow the main contract programme.

In *Pigott Foundations Ltd* v. *Shepherd Construction Ltd* [1993] 67 BLR 48 it was held that where DOM/1 conditions apply a subcontractor is not required to comply with the main contractor's programme.

In *Ascon Contracting Ltd* v. *Alfred McAlpine Construction Isle of Man Ltd* [1999] clause 11.1 required the subcontractor to carry out and complete the subcontract works reasonably in accordance with the progress of the main contract works. It was held, relying on *Pigott Foundations Ltd* v. *Shepherd Construction Ltd* (1993), that the subcontractor was not required to comply with the detail of the main contractor's programme, either generally or in relation to the work of other specific subcontractors.

In *Kitson Sheet Metal Ltd* v. *Matthew Hall Mechanical and Electrical Engineers Ltd* [1989] 47 BLR 82 it was held that the parties must have recognized the likelihood of delays and of trades getting in each other's way and that the prospects of working to programme were small. Provided Matthew Hall did their best to make areas available for work they were not in breach of contract even if Kitsons were brought to a complete stop. Kitsons were therefore unable to recover the additional cost due to a substantial overrun on the contractor's programme.

A similar situation occurred in the case of *Martin Grant and Co. Ltd* v. *Sir Lindsay Parkinson and Co. Ltd* [1984]. Again, the court held that there was no entitlement for the subcontractor to claim extra due to delays to the main contract programme.

In *Scottish Power plc* v. *Kvaerner Ltd* [1998], it was held that the reference to the dates for completion of the work were a provisional indication of when the subcontracts might be carried out. In particular, clause F of the subcontract stated that the contractor did not give any guarantee of continuous working. Clause F was important in determining when the subcontract fixed the dates for commencement and completion of the subcontract works. Prima facie clause F contemplated that the subcontractor would start on site not on a contractually predetermined commencement date but when instructed by the main contractor. Clause F was clearly intended to give Kvaerner flexibility.

FIDIC 1999 Forms 1st Edition

Clause 8.2 of the FIDIC Red, Yellow and Silver Books 1999 requires the contractor to complete the whole of the works within the time for completion which is defined at clause 1.1.3.3 as the time stated in the Appendix to Tender with any extension under clause 8.4 calculated from the commencement date. The latter is defined at clause 1.1.3.2 as the date notified under clause 8.1. The express obligation is therefore to complete within a specified period. Clause 1.1.3.9 defines 'day' as a calendar day and 'year' as 365 days, but does not define 'week'. It is suggested that in the context of the other definitions that 'week' will mean seven calendar days unless expressly stated otherwise. It is suggested that periods should be defined in days not weeks and this is the approach adopted in the sample appendix attached to the Form.

Clause 8.1 of the FIDIC Red, Yellow and Silver Books 1999 requires the contractor to commence the execution of the works as soon as is reasonably practicable after the commencement date and then to proceed with due expedition and without delay. Clause 8.3 requires the contractor to proceed in accordance with the programme, subject to its other obligations under the contract. Clause 15.2(c)(i) of the Red and Yellow Forms and clause 15.2(c) of the Silver Form allow the employer to terminate the contract if the contractor fails to proceed with the works in accordance with clause 8, without reasonable excuse, and subject to notice.

ICE 7th Edition

Clause 43 provides that the whole of the works shall be substantially completed within the time stated in the appendix to the Form of Tender, or such extended time under clause 44 or 46(3). The contractor's obligation is therefore to complete within a specified period. There is no definition of 'days' or 'weeks'.

Clause 41(2) requires the contractor to start the works as soon as is reasonably practicable after the works commencement date (defined in clause 41(1) and then to proceed with due expedition and without delay in accordance with the contract. Clause 65(1) allows the employer to expel the contractor from site, if the engineer has certified in writing to the employer that despite previous warnings by the engineer in writing, in his or her opinion the contractor is failing to proceed with the works with due diligence.

ECC 2nd and 3rd Edition

Core clause 30.1 requires the contractor to do the work so that completion is on or before the Completion Date. ECC 2nd Edition; Clause 11.2(12) defines the Completion Date as the completion date unless later changed in accordance with the contract. Contract Data Part One defines the completion date if it is not to be stated by the Contractor in Contract Data Part Two. If Option L is adopted then completion dates for each Section are stated in Contract Data Part One. ECC 3rd Edition is in similar terms but Completion Date is defined in Clause 11.2(3) and the Option is X5 instead of Option L. The contractor's obligation is therefore to complete by a specified date.

Core clause 20.1 states that the contractor is to provide the works in accordance with the Works Information. Unless the Works Information specifies how the contractor is to progress the works, there is no express obligation to that effect. Control of the progress of the works is by revisions of the Accepted Programme which is required to show the order and timing of operations which the contractor plans to do and the revisions show actual progress and how the contractor plans to deal with any delays. There is no default listed under Core Clauses ECC 2nd 95.2 or 95.3 and ECC 3rd 91.2 and 91.3 which expressly refers to a failure to progress the works. Reason R11 only refers generally to the contractor's failure to comply with its obligations. The employer has the right to terminate for any reason.

ECC 3rd Edition has introduced the concept of Key Dates when work is required to meet a Condition. A Key Date is defined as the key dates in the Contract Data and Condition is the condition stated in the Contract Data. Clause 30.3 requires the Contractor to do the work so that the Condition stated for each Key Date is met by the Key Date and the obligation as to Programme is also amended to show this obligation.

The introduction in ECC 3rd Edition of the new mechanism tied to achieving a Condition allows the possibility of the Employer to control progress to meet his particular needs at each stage, particularly for follow-on works. The Conditions need to be specified accurately. There is no provision in the conditions of contract which limits the conditions to be specified. Under Clause 14.3 the Project Manager may give an instruction to change a Key Date and under Clause 60.1(4) the instruction is a compensation event.

ECC 2nd Clause 63.6 and ECC 3rd 63.7 provides that assessments of compensation events are based on the assumption that the contractor reacts competently and promptly to the compensation event.

MF/1 (Rev 4) 2000

The contractor's obligation as to time is to complete within a period with the commencement of the period defined by fulfilment of certain obligations. Clause 13.1 and clause 32.1 require the contractor to execute the works and carry out the tests on completion within the time for completion which is defined at clause 1.1.m as the period of time stated in the contract calculated from the later of three possibilities (a) to (c). Clause 1.1.m(a) is the date specified in the contract as the date for commencement. Clause 1.1.m(b) is the date of receipt of advance payment specified in the contract. Clause 1.1.m(c) is the date when requirements stated as condition precedent in the contract have been fulfilled. Clause 1.1.cc defines 'day' as calendar day. Clause 1.1.dd defines 'week' as any period of seven days. Clause 1.1.ee defines 'month' as calendar month.

Clause 13.1 requires the contractor to execute the works and carry out the tests on completion with due care and diligence. Clause 49.1 allows the purchaser to give the contractor 21 days notice of its intention to terminate the contract, enter the site and expel

4.1 Administration of claims
4.2 Litigation
4.3 Arbitration
4.4 Adjudication
4.5 Alternative dispute resolution

the contractor if, despite previous warnings in writing from the engineer, the contractor is failing to proceed with the works with due diligence.

Under clause 14.6 the engineer has power to notify the contractor if the engineer decides that the rate of progress of the works is too slow to meet the time for completion and that this is not due to a circumstance for which the contractor is entitled to an extension of time. The contractor is then required to take such steps as may be necessary and as the engineer might approve to remedy or mitigate the likely delay, including revision of the programme. The contractor is not entitled to additional payment for taking such steps.

IChemE Red Book – 4th Edition 2001

Clause 13.1 requires the **Contractor** to complete the construction of the **Plant** ready for carrying out the take-over procedures on or before or within the periods stated in Schedule 11 (Times of Completion). Clause 2.5 defines 'day' as calendar day. Under Clause 13.6 if the **Project Manager** decides that the rate of progress by the **Contractor** will prejudice his ability to complete in accordance with Clause 13.1, and this is due to a cause for which the **Contractor** is responsible, the **Project Manager** has power to give notice to that effect. The **Contractor** must then use his best endeavours to remedy the potential delay at his own cost.

Clause 43.2 gives the **Project Manager** power to issue a notice that the **Contractor** is in default by failing to proceed regularly and diligently with the **Works**. If the **Contractor** fails to commence and diligently pursue the rectification of such default within 14 days after receipt of the notice or at any time thereafter repeats the default, the **Purchaser** may forthwith terminate the employment of the Contractor under the **Contract**.

JCT 2005 (SBC/Q)

Clause 1.1 JCT 2005 defines the Date for Completion as the date stated in the Contract particulars for the Works or a Section. Article 1 of the Agreement provides for the Contractor to carry out and complete the Works in accordance with the Contract Documents. Clause 2.1 provides that the Contractor shall carry out and complete the Works in compliance with the Contract Documents. Clause 2.4 provides that the Contractor shall proceed with and complete the construction of the Works or Section on or before the relevant Completion Date.

Clause 2.4 requires the Contractor to proceed regularly and diligently with the construction of the Works or Section. Clause 2.28 provides for the Contractor to be granted extension of time for Relevant Events, but Clause 2.28.6.1 requires the Contractor to constantly use his best endeavours to prevent delay in the progress of the Works or any Section, however caused, and to prevent the completion of the Works or Section being delayed or further delayed beyond the relevant Completion Date. Clause 2.28.6.2 requires the Contractor in the event of delay to do all that may reasonably be required to the satisfaction of the Architect/CA to proceed with the Works or Section.

Under Clause 8.4.2, the Architect/CA may give notice to the Contractor specifying a default if the Contractor fails to proceed regularly and diligently with the Works or the design of the Contractor's Designed Portion. Under Clause 8.4.2 if the Contractor continues a specified default for 14 days from receipt of the notice under clause 8.4.1, the Employer may on, or within 10 days from the expiry of the 14 day period by a further notice terminate the Contractor's employment under the Contract. If the Employer's notice is not issued, then if the Contractor repeats a specified default then upon or within a reasonable time after such repetition, the Employer may give notice terminating the Contractor's employment.

Clause 1.5 defines the reckoning of periods of days for acts required to be done within a specified period of days or from a specified date which excludes public holidays, but otherwise there is no definition of days or weeks. Clause 1.7 specifies the requirements for effective service of notices.

JCT 1998 Forms

Clause 1.3 of the JCT 1998 Form defines the date for completion as the date stated in the Appendix. Under clause 23.1.1, the contractor is required to complete on or before the completion date. Clause 25 provides for the contractor to be granted extension of time for relevant events, but importantly clause 25.3.4.1 requires the contractor constantly to use its best endeavours to prevent delay in the progress of the works, however caused, and to prevent the completion of the works being delayed or further delayed beyond the completion date. Clause 1.8 defines the reckoning of periods of days for act are required to be done within a specified period of days, but otherwise there is no definition of days or weeks.

Under clause 23.1.1 the contractor is required to regularly and diligently proceed with the works. Clause 25.3.4.2 requires the contractor to do all that may be reasonably required to the satisfaction of the architect to proceed with the works. Clause 27.2.1.2 allows the architect to give notice of default if before the date of practical completion the contractor fails to proceed regularly and diligently with the works. If the contractor continues the default for 14 days from receipt of the notice, the employer may, within ten days after the expiry of 14 days, give notice determining the employment of the contractor. If the employer's notice is not issued, then if the contractor repeats the default then upon or within a reasonable time after such repetition, the employer may give notice determining the contractor's employment, taking effect on the date of receipt of the notice.

JCT 1998 with Contractor's Design

JCT 1998 with Contractor's Design is in similar terms to JCT 1998 and similar considerations apply, except that the employer administers the contract instead of the architect under JCT 1998.

JCT 1998 Prime Cost Contract

The JCT 1998 Prime Cost Contract is similar in structure to the JCT 1998 Form and similar considerations apply.

Under clause 2.1.1 the contractor is required to regularly and diligently proceed with the works and complete on or before the completion date. Clause 2.5 provides for the contractor to be granted extension of time for relevant events, but importantly clause 2.5.4 requires the contractor to use constantly its best endeavours to prevent delay in the progress of the works, however caused. Further, clause 2.5.4 requires the contractor to do all that may be reasonably required to the satisfaction of the architect to proceed with the works. Clause 2.5.5 requires the contractor to review the progress of the works whenever the architect considers it reasonably necessary, which review includes consideration of additional resources required to maintain progress for which the cost would be included in the prime cost.

Clause 7.2.1 allows the architect to give notice of default if before the date of practical completion the contractor fails to proceed regularly and diligently with the works. If the contractor continues the default for 14 days from receipt of the notice, the employer may within ten days after the expiry of 14 days give notice determining the employment of the contractor. If the employer's notice is not issued, then if the contractor repeats the default upon or within a reasonable time after such repetition, the employer may give notice determining the contractor's employment, taking effect on the date of receipt of the notice.

IFC 1998

The IFC 1998 is similar in structure to the JCT 1998 Form and similar considerations apply. Clause 2.1 requires the contractor to complete by the date for completion stated in the Appendix. Under clause 2.1, the contractor is required to regularly and diligently proceed with the works and complete on or before the completion date. Clause 2.3 provides for the contractor to be granted extension of time for specified events, but importantly the contractor is required constantly to use its best endeavours to prevent delay and to do all that may be reasonably required to the satisfaction of the architect to proceed with the works.

Clause 7.2.1 allows the architect to give notice of default if before the date of practical completion the contractor fails to proceed regularly and diligently with the works. If the contractor continues the default for 14 days from receipt of the notice, the employer may within ten days after the expiry of 14 days give notice determining the employment of the contractor. If the employer's notice is not issued, then if the contractor repeats the default upon or within a reasonable time after such repetition, the employer may give notice determining the contractor's employment, taking effect on the date of receipt of the notice.

JCT 1998 Minor Works

Clause 2.1 requires the contractor to complete the works by a specified date. Clause 1.1 requires the contractor to carry out and complete the works with due diligence. Clause 7.2.1 allows the architect to give notice of default if the contractor fails to proceed diligently with the works. If the contractor continues the default for seven days from receipt of the notice, the employer may give further notice determining the employment of the contractor.

CECA Blue Form 1998

Clause 6(1) requires the subcontractor to complete within the period for completion specified in the Third Schedule. The commencement of the period is not clear, whether it is the date of the contractor's instruction under clause 6(1) or the date the subcontractor enters the site and commences the execution of the subcontract works. It is suggested that the proper interpretation of clause 6(1) is that the commencement of the period is the agreed date of commencement or, if not agreed, the date of commencement if this is within ten days of the contractor's instruction, otherwise the date ten days from the contractor's instruction to commence.

Clause 6(1) requires the subcontractor to proceed with the subcontract works with due diligence and without delay except as expressly sanctioned or ordered by the contractor or as may be wholly beyond the control of the subcontractor. Clause 17(1)(b) allows the contractor, by written notice, to determine the subcontractor's employment if the subcontractor fails to proceed with due diligence after being required in writing to do so by the contractor.

Under clause 3(1) the subcontractor is deemed to have full knowledge of the main contract. Under clause 3(2) the subcontractor is required to carry out its obligations so as not to cause or contribute to any breach by the contractor of any of its obligations under the main contract.

DOM/1

Clause 11.1 of DOM/1 requires the subcontractor to complete the subcontract works in accordance with the details in Appendix Part 4 which provides for insertion of the notice period to commence work on site, the range of dates for the date of commencement and the period for carrying out and completing the subcontract works. The obligation is subject to receipt of notice to commence work on site in accordance with Appendix Part 4.

Clause 11.1 of DOM/1 requires the subcontractor to complete the subcontract works reasonably in accordance with the progress of the works. The subcontractor's entitlement to extension of time is subject to the proviso in clause 11.8 which requires the subcontractor to use its best endeavours to prevent delay in the progress of the subcontract works, however caused, and to prevent any such delay resulting in the completion of the subcontract works being delayed beyond the period for completion. The subcontractor is required to do all that may be reasonably required to the satisfaction of the architect and the contractor to proceed with the subcontract works.

Clause 29.2.1.2 allows the contractor to give notice of default if before the date of practical completion the subcontractor fails to proceed regularly and diligently with the subcontract works. If the contractor continues the default for ten days from receipt of the notice, the contractor may within ten days after the expiry of ten days give notice determining the employment of the subcontractor. If the contractor's notice is not issued, then if the subcontractor repeats the default then upon or within a reasonable time after such repetition, the contractor may give notice determining the contractor's employment, taking effect on the date of receipt of the notice.

3.3 Substantial completion

The use of the term 'completion'

The completion of an obligation by the contractor will usually mark the transfer of certain risks or the crystallization of certain rights. The term 'completion' may therefore have a number of different meanings in a contract, depending upon the obligation. For example, completion for the purposes of payment may differ from that defining the end of the construction stage, which in turn may differ from that defining the end of the defects correction period.

The term 'completion' may be used in different parts of a contract without identifying what state of completion is required. In terms of the whole works, completion may mean completion for the purpose of handover and commencement of the defects liability period. It may instead mean completion including the remedy of all defects and any outstanding work sufficient for the issue of a Final Certificate. The term 'completion' may also be used to determine the extent of the right to interim payment in cases of stage payments.

The meaning of 'completion' depends upon the proper interpretation of the contract and the related obligation.

If the contractor is required to 'complete' the works in accordance with the contract before being entitled to payment, then the contract is said to be an entire contract (*Sumpter* v. *Hedges* (1898)). The rule is strict so that if work is completed but not in accordance with the contract no payment is due (*Bolton* v. *Mahadeva* (1972)).

In *Close Invoice Finance Limited* v. *Belmont Bleaching and Dying Company* [2003] Eaton's right of action had been assigned to Close. Eaton had given a quotation for

4.1 Administration of claims
4.2 Litigation
4.3 Arbitration
4.4 Adjudication
4.5 Alternative dispute resolution

the delivery, installation and commissioning of a machine known as a Stetner that set fabrics to a certain width. The quotation was accepted and the contract terms agreed including timescale and payment terms. Three sums were to be paid. The second of £12 000 on completion of erection and the third of £9000 was payable once the Stetner had been commissioned and handed over. The issue was the whether or not the last two payments were due for payment.

Belmont argued that Eaton had contracted to perform entire obligations and were entitled to nothing until they completed a stage. Close argued that Eaton was entitled to be paid if they gave substantial performance of a stage.

HH Bowsher QC referred to *Hoenig* v. *Isaacs* [1952] 2 All ER 176 and held that Eaton was only entitled to be paid on completion of each stage. He held that Eaton had not completed either stage and therefore no payment was due other than for the supply of spare parts which was another issue.

Construction contracts involve the fixing and incorporation of the works on land, with the consequent transfer of ownership. The owner is therefore likely to receive substantial benefit even if the works are not entirely complete. The doctrine of substantial performance mitigates the harshness of the above rule and allows the contractor payment for work if substantially completed with an allowance for defects. It is a question of fact whether the contractor has substantially performed its obligations. The contractor cannot rely on the doctrine to seek payment for work carried out if it has abandoned the works. It applies where the work has been completed except for minor defects or minor outstanding works.

The requirements of 'completion' in relation to a time obligation are likely to be different than for the obligation for payment, particularly when the contract makes provision for the contractor to remedy defects and/or outstanding work in the defects liability or correction period. So, for instance, occupation by the employer may be good evidence of completion for payment purposes, particularly with the employer's exercise of the right of abatement of price. It will not necessarily be relevant evidence of completion of the time obligation.

The general meaning of 'completion' for the obligation to complete the construction or installation of the works is that the works should be free from known or patent defects and that any outstanding work is minor or *de minimus*, so that the use for the purpose intended is not affected or beneficial occupancy as intended is not prevented.

Standard forms of contract generally do not require complete performance by the date for completion of installation or construction, but allow a defects liability period for the correction of minor defects and defects which only become apparent later. Completion is normally identified by the date stated in a certificate by the A/E stating that completion has taken place. The date stated in the certificate will mark the end of the period for which the contractor is liable for liquidated damages, mark the change in responsibility to insure, require the release of retention and mark the commencement of the defects liability period.

In some standard forms 'completion' of the construction or installation stage is defined by achieving specified standards in tests. In other forms completion of construction is defined by the term 'substantial completion'. The ICE Form is such a form and provides for the contractor to apply for a Certificate of Substantial Completion together with an undertaking to carry out outstanding work in the defects liability period. It is suggested that the outstanding work may include the making good of defects identified before the issue of the certificate. In any event it is suggested that the ICE Form places an obligation on the contractor under clause 49(2) to correct defects 'of whatever nature' which is wide enough to cover defects known at the date of the certificate. This is to be contrasted with the term 'practical completion' used in JCT Forms. Clause 17.2 of JCT 1998 for instance relates to the making good of defects that appear within the defects liability period. There is no power for the architect to issue instructions for the remedy of defects that were known or patent at the date of the Certificate of Practical Completion. As a matter of interpretation therefore the architect is not required to issue a certificate if there are known or patent defects. The contractor's obligation of practical completion is therefore different to the obligation of substantial completion under the JCT and ICE Forms respectively.

Legal definition of completion

There have been a number of decisions attempting a legal definition of the terms 'practical completion' and 'substantial completion'.

In *J. Jarvis and Sons* v. *Westminster Corporation* (1978) 7 BLR 64 HL, Lord Justice Salmon defined practical completion as completion for the purpose of allowing the employers to take possession of the works and use them as intended. He held that practical completion did not mean completion down to the last detail, however trivial and unimportant. Lord Dilhorne's definition was that practical completion meant almost but not entirely finished.

In *H.W. Neville (Sunblest) Ltd* v. *William Press and Son Ltd* (1981) 20 BLR 78, it was held that practical completion did not mean that very minor *de minimus* work had to be carried out, but did mean that if there were any patent defects the architect should not give a certificate of practical completion.

In *Emson Eastern Ltd* v. *E.M.E. Developments Ltd* (1991) 55 BLR 114, Emson were the contractors and E.M.E. developers under the JCT 80 Form. Practical completion was certified but some time after Emson went into administrative receivership and their employment in compliance with clause 27.2 of the conditions of contract was automatically determined. The issue was whether Emson were entitled to further payment. The matter turned on whether completion under clause 27 meant the same as practical completion, or whether it meant that all snagging and remedial works has to be made good at the end of the defects period before the works could be said to be complete.

His Honour Judge John Newey QC, in arriving at a decision, took account of what happens on building sites. He considered he should keep in mind that building construction is not like the manufacture of goods in a factory. The size of the project, site conditions, use of many materials and employment of various types of operatives made it virtually impossible to achieve the same degree of perfection as can a manufacturer. His view was that it must be rare for a new building to have every screw and every brush of paint correct. Further, a building can seldom be built precisely as required by the drawings and specification. Judge Newey, in considering the meaning of practical completion, thought he stood somewhere between Lords Salmon and Dilhorne in the Jarvis case. He concluded that there was no difference in meaning between completion and practical completion. Completion, he considered, was like practical completion, something which occurs before defects and other faults have to be remedied. Were it otherwise, the deduction of liquidated damages under clause 24 would be unworkable, he considered. In view of this reasoning Judge Newey held that the contractor was entitled to be paid as practical completion had been achieved.

The Court of Appeal of Hong Kong in *Big Island Contracting (H.K.) Ltd* v. *Skink Ltd* (1990) 52 BLR 110 upheld the decision of the judge at first instance that in deciding practical completion account should be taken of the value of work outstanding and the importance of defects to the safety of the facility.

In *Voscroft (Contractors) Ltd* v. *Seeboard plc* (1996) 78 BLR 132, HH Judge Humphrey Lloyd QC was required to consider the operation of clauses 14.1 and 14.2 DOM/2 (in this respect the same as DOM/1) Form of Subcontract. Clause 14.1 required the subcontractor to give notice when it considered practical completion of the subcontract works had been achieved. The Form made provision for the parties to agree the date of practical completion, but in the event of disagreement practical completion was deemed to be the date of practical completion of the main contract works. There was, however, no provision for the situation which occurred of the subcontractor not giving notice. It was argued that in that situation practical completion was a question of fact to be decided by an arbitrator.

It was held that, from the other provisions of the contract, the presumed intention of the parties was that there should be some definition and certainty attached to practical completion. Without a firm or contractually ascertainable date the parties' obligations as set out in the insurance and indemnity provisions became uncertain in duration, the extension of time clauses became in part unworkable and there was no certainty as to when a part of retention might be paid. The point of defining terminal dates would be lost if the effect of the subcontractor failing to give notice was to make practical completion a question of fact and would deprive the definitions of practical value.

It was held that a subcontractor who failed to operate clause 14.1 could not achieve a result other than the one which would have been achieved had it given notice but not reached agreement. The subcontractor could not have the benefit of clause 14 in establishing a date for practical completion other than the deemed date. The date of practical completion was therefore the date of practical completion under the main contract.

The standard forms adopt different procedures for the identification of completion. Generally a certificate is issued.

FIDIC 1999 Forms 1st Edition

Completion is defined by tests and the completion of specified work. The contractor's obligation under clause 8.2 is to complete the whole of the works including the passing of the Tests on Completion and all work stated in the contract as being required for the works to be considered to be completed for the purposes of taking over under clause 10.1.

Clause 9.1 requires the contractor to carry out the Tests on Completion within 14 days of the date notified 21 days in advance. The contractor is required to issue a certified report of the results of the tests.

Clause 10.1 provides that the employer takes over the works when the tests have been successfully completed, the specified work has been completed and a Taking Over Certificate has been issued by the engineer or is deemed to have been issued.

Clause 11.9 provides that the contractor's obligations are not completed until the engineer (employer under the Silver Form) has issued the Performance Certificate. The engineer (employer under the Silver Form) is required to issue the Performance Certificate within 28 days after the latest of the expiry of the defects notification period, issue of all contractor's documents and the completion and testing of all the works including remedying defects.

ICE 7th Edition

Clause 48 provides that when the contractor considers that the whole of the works has been substantially completed and has satisfactorily passed any test that may be prescribed in the contract, it may give notice to that effect. The notice must be accompanied by an undertaking to finish any outstanding work in accordance with clause 49(1). This states that the undertaking may state a specified time (agreed with the engineer) for the outstanding work to be completed. If there is no agreement then the work must be completed as soon as practicable during the defects correction period.

Clause 48(2) allows the engineer to issue a Certificate of Substantial Completion stating the date when the works were substantially complete or give instructions specifying all the work which in the engineer's opinion is required to be done before the issue of such a certificate.

Clause 61(1) provides that at the end of the defects correction period and when all outstanding work referred to in clause 48 and all works of repair, etc. have been completed, the engineer issues to the employer a defects correction certificate stating the date on which the contractor completed its obligations to construct and complete the works to the engineer's satisfaction.

ECC 2nd and 3rd Edition

Clause 30.2 requires the *Project Manager* to decide the date of Completion and to certify completion within one week of Completion. Normally, the *Contractor* will request a certificate as soon as he considers he is entitled to it, but such a request is not essential. ECC 2nd Clause 11.2(13) and ECC 3rd Clause 11.2(2) defines the meaning of Completion as the date when the *Contractor* has done all the work which the Works Information states that he is to do by the Completion Date and corrected notified Defects which would have prevented the *Employer* using the Works. ECC 3rd Edition adds the term 'and others from doing their work'. The concept under the ECC form is that Completion is defined by the *Employer's* ability to use the Works. It is suggested that this is essentially 'substantial completion' or 'practical completion'. The Works Information may however expressly state that all Work is to be completed including making good of defects before completion. This would then be contrary to the notion of substantial completion, and require the Works to be free from defects.

There is no specific provision for the possibility of carrying out performance tests prior to or after take over and the issue of an Acceptance Certificate. If ECC 2nd Option S and ECC 3rd Option X17 (Low Performance Damages) is used then without such a specified Schedule of Tests it may be difficult to establish the level of Low Performance.

The *Employer* is required by ECC 2nd Clause 35.2 and ECC 3rd Clause 35.1 to take over the Works within two weeks after Completion. The *Employer* may state in the Contract Data that he does not wish to take over the Works before the Completion Date. It is not clear when the Employer in such a case is required to take over if the *Contractor* completes before the Completion Date. It is likely that this will be no later than the Completion Date if Completion is more than two weeks early.

ECC 2nd Ed Clause 43.2 and ECC 3rd Ed Clause 43.3 requires the *Supervisor* to issue the Defects Certificate at the later of the *defects date* and the end of the last *defects correction period.*

MF/1 (Rev 4) 2000

The MF/1 Form relating to mechanical/electrical plant has comprehensive provisions for completion, testing, taking over and performance tests.

Clauses 28.1 to 28.5 provide for tests on completion. Clause 1.1(v) defines tests on completion as the tests specified in the contract (or otherwise agreed by the purchaser and the contractor) which are to be made by the contractor upon completion of erection and/or installation before the works are taken over by the purchaser. Under clause 28.1 the contractor is entitled to make tests on completion within 31 days of giving notice that it will be ready.

Clauses 29.1 to 29.4 deal with taking over. Clause 29.2 provides that when the works have passed the tests on completion and are complete, except in minor respects that do not affect their use for the purpose for which they are intended, the engineer shall issue a Taking Over Certificate to the contractor and to the purchaser. The engineer shall in the Taking Over Certificate certify the date upon which the works passed the tests on completion and were so complete. Clause 29.2 also states that the purchaser shall be deemed to have taken over the works on the dates so certified. Clause 29.3 provides that from the date of taking over, as stated in the Taking Over Certificate, risk of loss or damage to the works to which the Taking Over Certificate relates shall pass to the purchaser.

The Taking Over Certificate requires both the passing of the tests on completion and completion. As defined in clause 29.2, completion is in effect substantial completion.

Clause 29.4 provides that the contractor shall rectify and complete to the reasonable satisfaction of the engineer within the time stated in the Taking Over Certificate any outstanding items of work or plant noted as requiring rectification or as incomplete. To be effective, clause 29.4 requires the engineer to list outstanding works on each Taking Over Certificate.

Clauses 35.1 to 35.8 deal with performance testing. Clause 35.1 states that where performance tests are included in the contract they are to be carried out as soon as is reasonably practicable and within a reasonable time after the works have been taken over by the purchaser. Clause 35.2 requires a performance test to be carried out by the purchaser or the engineer under the supervision of the contractor and in accordance with the procedures and under the operating conditions specified in the contract. They are also required to be in accordance with such other instructions as the contractor may give in the course of carrying out such tests.

IChemE Red Book 4th Edition 2001

Clause 13.1 of the Red Book places an obligation on the contractor to complete the construction of the plant ready for the carrying out of the take-over procedures on or before the date or dates or within the period specified in Schedule 11 (Times of Completion).

Clause 32 describes the procedure to be followed for establishing the completion of construction, in particular clauses 32.3 and 32.4, ready for the take-over tests and involves issue of a Construction Completion Report stating that the contractor has demonstrated that the plant was substantially complete and procedures to put the plant in operation can be safely carried out.

Clause 33 provides a taking-over procedure. Clause 33.2 states that as soon as the construction of any part of the plant has been demonstrated to be complete in accordance with the provision of sub-clause 32.3, the contractor is to notify the project manager and specify the time when the procedure specified in the Schedule of Take-Over Procedures is to be commenced. If the contract does not include a Schedule of Take-Over Procedures, Schedule 15, any take-over procedures required by the project manager are treated as a variation.

Under clause 33.7, as soon as the minor items noted by the project manager on the Construction Completion Report have been successfully completed, and when all the procedures specified in the Schedule of Take-Over Procedures have also been successfully completed, the project manager is required to issue to the contractor and copy to the purchaser a Taking-Over Certificate. This may include a list of minor items still to be completed by the contractor. It is to be noted that under clause 33.10 if by reason of any act or omission of the purchaser or the project manager or any other contractors employed by the purchaser, the contractor is prevented from carrying out the take-over test then a Taking-Over Certificate may be issued if the contractor is of that opinion and the project manager considers the action to be reasonable.

It is only on the issue of the Taking-Over Certificate that the purchaser can take over the plant. It is at this point that risk passes to the purchaser. This is reflected in the insurance provisions in clause 31. Clause 30.1 provides that the plant shall be under the direction and control of the contractor until the plant is taken over by the purchaser. Under clause 30.2 the contractor is liable for the cost and expense of making good loss or damage, however caused, that may occur to the plant before the plant is taken over. The defect liability period starts after the date of the Take-Over Certificate, clause 37.

Clause 38.1 provides that as soon as the defects liability period has expired and the contractor has made good all defects that have appeared in the plant in that period, the project manager issues the Final Certificate. Clause 38.4 states that the issue of the Final Certificate shall be conclusive evidence for all purposes and in any proceedings whatsoever between the purchaser and contractor that the contractor has completed the works and made good all defects in all respects in accordance with its obligations under the contract, subject to fraudulent misrepresentation or fraudulent concealment.

JCT 2005 (SBC/Q)

Clause 2.30.1 requires the Architect/CA to issue a Practical Completion Certificate when he is of the opinion that practical completion of the Works has been achieved and the Contractor has complied sufficiently with Clause 2.40 (As-built Drawings for the Contractor's Design Portion) and 3.25.3 (information for the preparation of the health and safety file). Clause 2.30.2 makes similar provisions in relation to a Section and Section Completion Certificate. Clause 2.30 provides that practical completion is deemed for all the purposes of the contract to have taken place on the day named in the Certificate. The term 'practical completion' is not defined.

The issue of the Practical Completion Certificate starts the Rectification Period for the Works or Section as stated in the Contract Particulars and marks the end of the period for deduction of any liquidated damages.

Clause 4.15.1 requires the Architect/CA to issue the Final Certificate not later than 2 months from the later of the end of the Rectification Period or the date of issue of the Certificate of Completion of Making Good Defects or the date on which the Architect makes the ascertainment of adjustment to the Contract Sum with the Quantity Surveyors statement under Clause 4.5.2. Clause 1.10 defines the extent to which the Final Certificate has effect as conclusive evidence in adjudication, arbitration or legal proceedings.

JCT 1998 Forms

JCT 1998 clause 17.1 requires the architect to issue a certificate when he or she is of the opinion that practical completion of the works has been achieved. Practical completion is deemed for all the purposes of the contract to have taken place on the day named in the certificate. Practical completion is not defined.

The issue of the Practical Completion Certificate starts the defects liability period and marks the end of the period for deduction of any liquidated damages.

Clause 30.8.1 requires the architect to issue the Final Certificate not later than two months from the later of the end of the defects liability period or the date of issue of the Certificate of Completion of Making Good Defects or the date on which the architect makes the ascertainment of final adjustment to the contract sum with the quantity surveyors' statement under clause 30.6.1.2. Clause 30.9 defines the extent to which the Final Certificate has effect as conclusive evidence in adjudication, arbitration or legal proceedings.

JCT 1998 with Contractor's Design

JCT 1998 with Contractor's Design clause 16.1 requires the employer to issue a statement when the works have reached practical completion to that effect. The written statement is not to be unreasonably delayed or withheld. Practical completion is deemed for all the purposes of the contract to have taken place on the day named in the statement. Practical completion is not defined.

The issue of the Practical Completion Certificate starts the defects liability period and marks the end of the period for deduction of any liquidated damages.

Clause 30.5.1 requires the contractor to issue a final account and final statement within three months of practical completion for agreement by the employer. Clause 30.5.5 provides that the final account or final statement become conclusive as to the balance between the parties except to the extent that the employer disputes anything in them before one month of the latest of the end of the defects liability period or the day named in the notice of completion of making good defects or the date of submission of the final account and the final statement. Clauses 30.5.6–8 define the issue of the employer's final account in the absence of the contractor's final account and final statement. Clause 30.8 defines the extent to which the final statement or the employer's final statement has effect as conclusive evidence in adjudication, arbitration or legal proceedings.

JCT 1998 Prime Cost Contract

JCT 1998 Prime Cost clause 2.8.1 requires the architect to issue a certificate when he or she is of the opinion that practical completion of the works has been achieved. Practical completion is deemed for all the purposes of the contract to have taken place on the day named in the certificate. Practical completion is not defined.

The issue of the Practical Completion Certificate starts the defects liability period and marks the end of the period for deduction of any liquidated damages.

Clause 4.12.1 requires the architect to issue the Final Certificate not later than two months from the later of the end of the defects liability period or the date of issue of the certificate of completion of making good defects or the date on which the architect makes the ascertainment of final Adjustment to the contract sum with the quantity surveyors' statement under clause 4.9.2. Clause 1.17 defines the extent to which the Final Certificate has effect as conclusive evidence in adjudication, arbitration or legal proceedings.

IFC 1998

IFC 1998 clause 12.9 requires the architect to issue a certificate when he or she is of the opinion that practical completion of the works has been achieved. Practical completion is deemed for all the purposes of the contract to have taken place on the day named in the certificate. Practical completion is not defined.

The issue of the Practical Completion Certificate starts the defects liability period and marks the end of the period for deduction of any liquidated damages.

Clause 4.6.1 requires the architect to issue the Final Certificate not later than 28 days from the later of the sending of the computations of the adjusted contract sum to the contractor or the date of issue of the Certificate stating that the contractor has discharged its obligations in relation to defects under clause 2.10. Clause 4.7.1 defines the extent to which the Final Certificate has effect as conclusive evidence in adjudication, arbitration or legal proceedings.

JCT Minor Works

JCT 1998 Minor Works clause 2.4 requires the architect to issue a certificate when he or she is of the opinion that practical completion of the works has been achieved.

The issue of the Practical Completion Certificate starts the defects liability period and marks the end of the period for deduction of any liquidated damages.

Clause 4.5.1.1 requires the architect to issue the Final Certificate within 28 days from the submission of documentation from the contractor provided that the architect has issued a certificate under clause 2.5 for the making good of defects.

CECA Blue Form 1998

Clause 13(1) requires the subcontractor to maintain the subcontract works in the condition required by the main contract (fair wear and tear excepted) to the satisfaction of the engineer and make good every defect and imperfection therein from whatever cause arising, from the completion of the subcontract works to substantial completion of the main works. Clause 13(2) provides that after completion of the main works, the subcontractor shall maintain the subcontract works and make good such defects and imperfections therein as the contractor is liable to make good under the main contract for a like period and otherwise upon the like terms as the contractor is liable to do under the main contract.

Clause 15(7) provides that the contractor shall not be liable to the subcontractor for any matter or thing arising out of or in connection with the subcontract or the carrying out of the subcontract works unless the subcontractor has made written claim to the contractor before the engineer issues the Defects Correction Certificate in respect of the main works.

DOM/1

Clause 14.1 DOM/1 provides for the subcontractor to notify the contractor in writing of the date in its opinion when the subcontract works were practically completed. If not dissented from in writing by the contractor within 14 days of receipt of the notice, then practical completion is deemed to have taken place on the date notified. If the contractor dissents then it is required to give reasons in the written notice. In such a case, under clause 14.2, practical completion is the date agreed, otherwise the date certified by the architect under clause 17.1 of the main contract.

Clause 21.9 defines the amount in the final payment which depends on whether the subcontract is for a lump sum or subject to re-measure. Clause 21.9 provides that the final payment is due not later than 7 days after the date of issue of the Final Certificate issued by the architect under clause 30.8 of the main contract conditions. Clause 21.10 defines the extent to which the Final Certificate has effect as conclusive evidence in adjudication, arbitration or legal proceedings.

4.1 Administration of claims
4.2 Litigation
4.3 Arbitration
4.4 Adjudication
4.5 Alternative dispute resolution

3.4 Programme of works

Many standard forms require the contractor to produce a programme. The programme only creates contractual obligations if it is a contract document or an essential part of the assessment of entitlements created under the contract.

The programme has two possible roles in the management of the contract, either a monitor role or a dynamic role. The monitor role allows the extent of compliance with the parties' obligations as to time to be assessed at particular stages. The dynamic role allows an analysis of progress to determine the corrective actions to be taken to comply with the particular obligation or to ascertain the right to compensation.

Overall there are five functions of a programme of which the first three are monitoring roles and two dynamic roles. It is necessary to identify the intended role of the programme in the contract, in order to decide the type of programme required by the contract. The five functions of the programme are shown below for the monitoring role and the dynamic role.

(a) Monitor role:
  (i) milestone programme
  (ii) progress programme
  (iii) prediction programme.
(b) Dynamic role:
  (iv) management programme
  (v) compensation programme.

Each succeeding programme function in the above list requires an additional 'dimension' from its predecessor in order to fulfil its role. The first, the milestone programme, is a single dimension comprising only a list of dates for activities. The most simple form is a single completion date for completion of the whole project. The second, the progress programme, includes not only dates but the durations of activities. The third, the prediction programme, requires logic links between the activities which introduces a project dimension. The fourth, the management programme, requires not only logic links but also a mathematical dimension, a predictive model, which allows the criticality of activities and float trends to be assessed to allow management decisions to be made. This usually requires a network analysis. The fifth, the compensation programme, introduces the complicated issues of the incidence of liability, causation and measurement of compensation, which is a legal dimension.

Monitor role – function 1: milestone programme

The first function of the programme is to identify the dates when actions, information and other interfaces are required to be carried out. This may include supply of information by the employer, the carrying out of work by the employer or statutory authorities or undertakers. The programme may also identify important milestones which are required to be achieved by the contractor to allow the employer to carry out other parts of the project.

In order to be effective there must be contract mechanisms to revise the dates for specified risk events. These are usually extension of time clauses. How the compensation is determined using programmes, if this is necessary, is examined in function 5 – the compensation programme.

If this first function is the only function of the programme, then it can be fulfilled in many cases by a simple schedule. It may be referred to as an Information Release

Schedule or Interface Coordination Schedule and need only list the information or activity, the date for performance and the responsibility for performance.

Monitor role – function 2: progress programme

The second possible function of the programme is to allow both parties to monitor the contractor's progress towards compliance with the obligation to complete the works by the specified date, or to complete sections of the work by the specified dates. To be of any value, the progress must be monitored before completion occurs, which requires the progress of each of the activities to be compared to a plan. That plan is the programme of works. The actual progress of activities can be compared with the planned progress.

There are significant limits to this method of monitoring. Some activities may take longer than planned, others less. Some risk events predicted in the model represented by the planned programme may not materialize or may not have the effect anticipated. The comparison of actual to planned progress will be a reasonable indication of progress, but only if the construction logic of the programme is actually adopted. Caution is required because a programme is only one model of how the work can be carried out. Actual progress may be different for a number of reasons, not least that risk events may or may not occur, performance may improve at a later stage in the duration of an activity or the method of working may be changed requiring greater initial preparation followed by rapid progress.

The bar chart is the type of programme which allows this type of monitoring. An example is shown below for the 'Equipment project' (Fig. 1).

The planned programme for each activity is shown as bars with estimated durations and start and finish dates. If the actual progress is plotted on the bar chart, then an indication of progress is shown. In the example given the activity 'procure supplier' is shown as starting late, of taking the duration planned and finishing late. The impact of a 'start later than planned' on other activities cannot be analysed since there are no

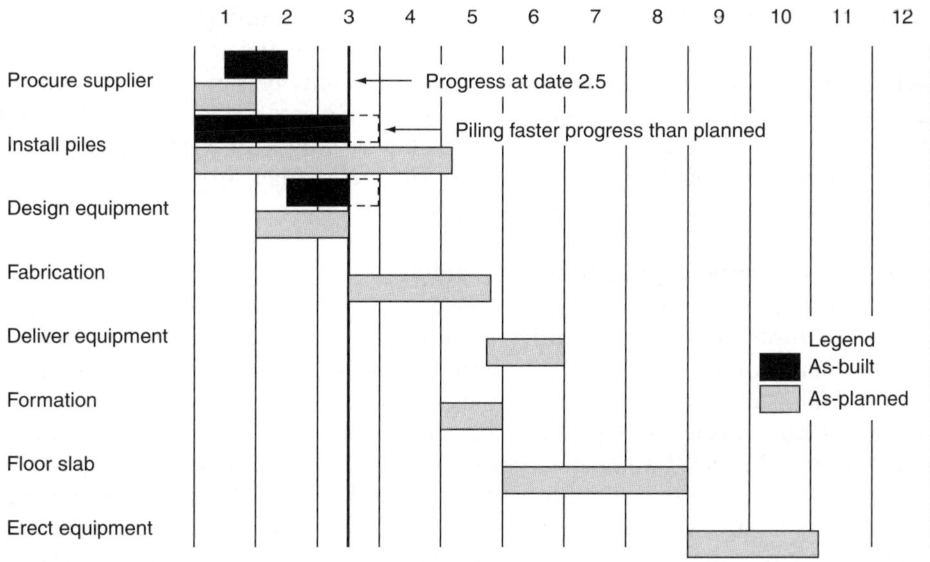

© Daniel Atkinson Limited

Figure 1. Equipment project bar chart – completion progress

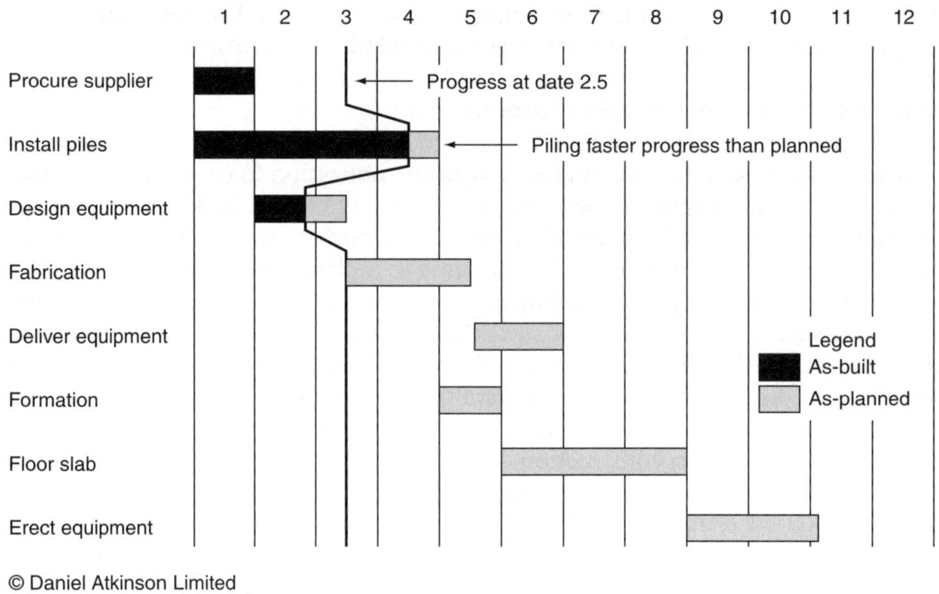

Figure 2. Equipment project bar chart – rate of progress

logic links between activities. The effect on completion also cannot be analysed logically and reliably. Information not shown on the programme needs to be used.

It is usual when monitoring progress by this method to do so against a 'timeline'. This is shown in the example above for the 'date 2.5'. This shows that the activity 'install piles' started on time, but a prediction of completion based on the planned duration will be incorrect as in this example piling progressed faster than planned. The 'timeline' method may not, therefore, provide accurate predictions of future progress.

One solution using the bar chart is to use a 'rate of progress timeline'. An example is shown in Fig. 2 for the 'Equipment project'. In this type of monitoring the timeline is adjusted at each activity on the planned programme to show the percentage completion of each activity. The line then shows whether or not the activity is on time to the planned programme and the approximate time remaining for each activity. The method has little analytical value for predictions of completion but is useful for identifying trends in progress if a series of timelines are compared. The method has little analytical value if actual progress differs substantially from the plan.

Monitor role – function 3: prediction programme

The third possible function of the programme is to provide a means of updating the prediction of future progress. In order to fulfil this function, the programme must model the time characteristics of the project. Inevitably, the programme must model the inter-relationship of activities through logic links.

The linked bar chart is the type of programme that will fulfil this role. An example is shown in Fig. 3 for the 'Equipment project'. If the linked programme is updated to include the actual and predicted effect of events and changes in duration and logic, then modern software will allow accurate predictions of future progress. In practice, in many situations and projects, particularly repetitive trade subcontracts or in logically linear works, such as tunnels or roads, the logic may be simple and will not require computer software except for presentation.

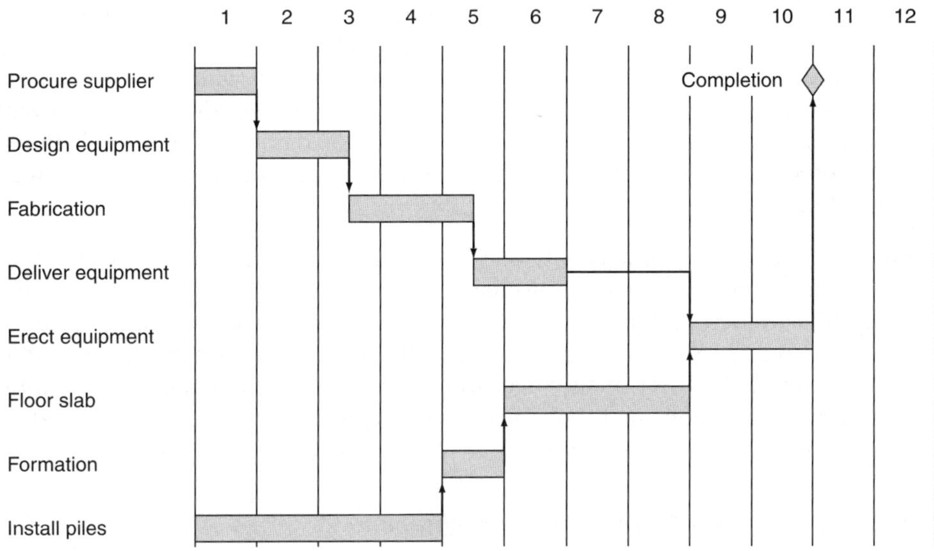

© Daniel Atkinson Limited

Figure 3. Equipment project – linked bar chart

If actual progress differs from planned, then the planned programme loses its effectiveness as a means of predicting future progress. If, however, the programme is revised to show actual progress of activities, revised to show changes in the construction logic and the incidence of actual events, then the revised programme will provide a more accurate means of monitoring progress. The management of information to provide accurate revisions to the programme requires considerable effort. The information is required on an interim basis during the execution of the activity.

The personnel managing day-to-day activities may not have an overall view of the project and may not recognize or report changes in the planned rate of progress or changes in the method of working. A systematic approach to recording and reporting is required which may involve some or all of the following.

- *Measurement of work* – a comparison of actual to estimated measure of work may provide an indication of the rate of progress as well as identifying changes. This method of monitoring is the minimum required to accurately record progress. In some contracts the method of payment will require an estimate of percentage completion of activities or stages, or a measure of bill items. This information can then usefully be used to measure progress.
- *Valuation of resource cost* – a comparison of the actual rate of expenditure of resource to the estimate may indicate that a change to the planned programme is required.
- *Productivity measurement* – a comparison of actual productivity to the estimated will identify the validity or otherwise of the assumptions made for the planned duration of activities. This information is usually readily available to those involved on a day-by-day basis, but very difficult to analyse later due, usually, to lack of records. A systematic approach to records, such as labour allocation sheets and/or ongoing histograms, is needed. Work sampling may be sufficient in many cases, particularly when warned by those involved on a day-to-day basis.

- *Management briefings* – regular team briefings in which progress in terms of start and finish dates, durations, productivities, method of working and inter-relationship of activities is examined will allow a 'project-wide' view to be developed. This type of review brings together the team knowledge of recent events, increases awareness and increases the accuracy of reporting. It is vital that the result of such analytical briefings are recorded and, if necessary, incorporated in revised programmes.

The initial planned programme is only one model of the way in which the works could proceed. It is important when recording changes to recognize that the initial plan may be incorrect, either underestimating or overestimating productivity or durations or the effects of risk events. Some changes to the planned progress are therefore not the result of external factors but of the inaccuracies inherent in the planned programme. Whenever one assumption in the planned programme is shown to be inaccurate by actual events, other similar assumptions may need to be revised.

Dynamic role – function 4: management programme

The fourth possible function of the programme is to provide a model for analysis and implementation of corrective action. The action may involve changes to the method of working or sequence of working either to improve efficiency or in response to delay events. The management programme allows representation of the corrective action, the analysis of the consequences of the actions on the timing and duration of activities, and revision of the model to update the prediction of how the works are required to progress to achieve the specified completion date.

To be effective, the management programme needs to be based on up-to-date progress, represent an accurate prediction of future events as well as accurately model the time characteristics of the project by logic links. The requirements in this respect are the same as described for the prediction programme. The additional mathematical dimension is required of a management programme to allow the criticality of activities and float trends to be assessed and allow management decisions to be made based on priorities. The aim is to identify the corrective actions that need to be taken at the time of analysis by realistically predicting the future effects of a selection of actions. A critical path network analysis will usually be required.

The critical path analysis for the 'Equipment project' is shown in Fig. 4. The supply contract for the equipment which involves the activities of 'procure supplier', 'design equipment', 'fabrication' and 'delivery of equipment' are shown as not being critical to the planned completion date for the project. These activities have 'float'. If any of the activities are delayed or the durations are longer than planned, then this will have no time effect on the planned completion, provided the overall delay and increased duration is less than the float. The site work, however, is critical, so any delay or increased duration in that case will delay planned completion. The management effort at the commencement of the project will therefore be concentrated on the site activities in order to meet the planned programme.

The critical path network analysis in Fig. 5 is an update of the initial programme for the 'Equipment project' but now incorporating an update of progress on the supply contract at a report date 2.5.

The procurement is shown as having been delayed initially from the planned start or, more strictly, the earliest date on which procurement could have started. There is no overall effect on the planned completion date since the initial delay is less than available

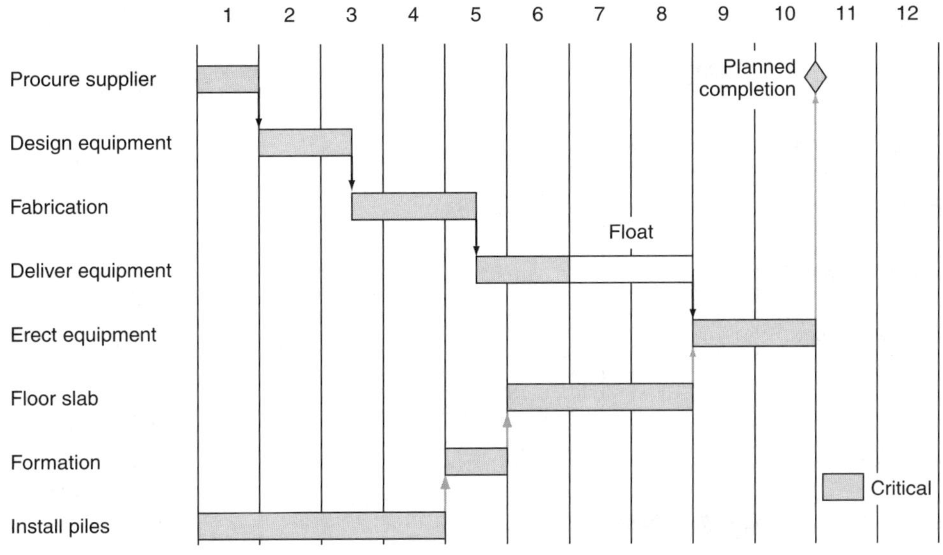

© Daniel Atkinson Limited

Figure 4. Equipment project – critical path planned

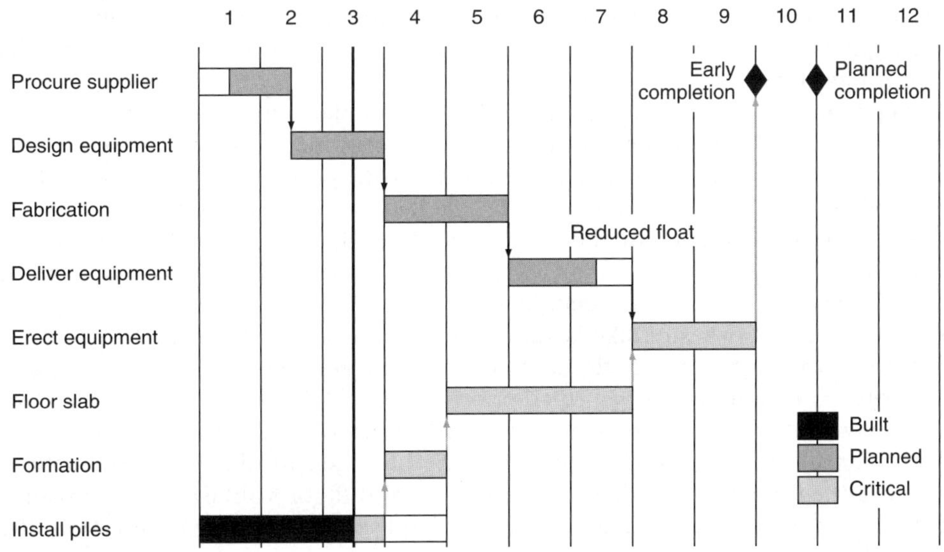

© Daniel Atkinson Limited

Figure 5. Equipment project – critical path interim analysis

float. All that has happened is that the contractor has used part of the available float. In practice, float is an essential requirement of a management programme. Management resources are limited, so giving priority to critical or near critical activities is only possible without affecting planned completion if lack of action on other activities can be accommodated by available float. In the 'Equipment project', the priority has been the site activities with the result that the placing of the order for the supply contract was delayed but well within the available float.

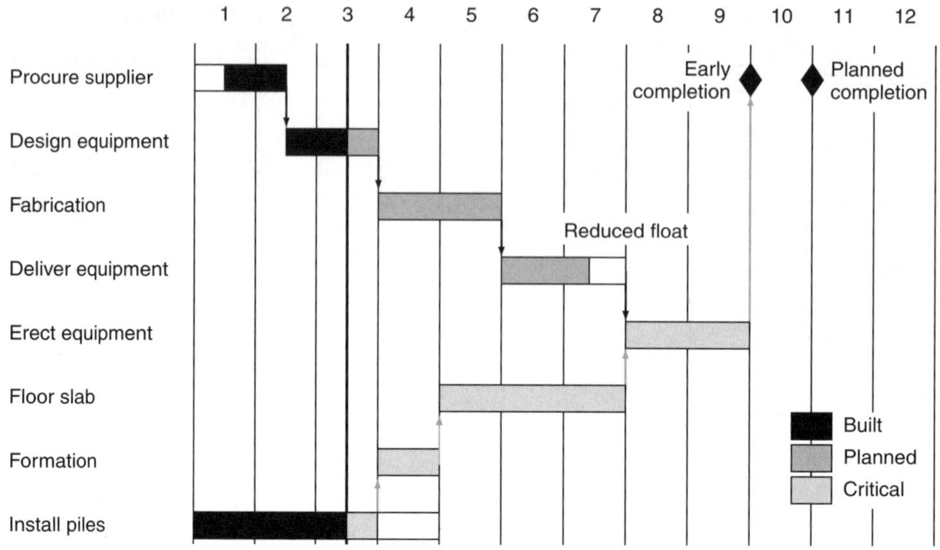

© Daniel Atkinson Limited

Figure 6. Equipment project – critical path interim analysis

The critical path network analysis in Fig. 6 is a further update of the programme for the 'Equipment project' but now incorporating an update of progress on the site work at the same report date 2.5.

The update shows that piling was in fact faster than planned. Since the installation of piles is an activity that is on the critical path, the effect of the shorter duration is to allow an earlier completion date than planned as shown on the programme. The 'benefit' to the project of the reduced duration depends on the incidence of the critical path following update of the programme. In this case, the effect of the shorter duration did not change the critical path but in many cases it will. The network analysis will allow this change in the critical path to be identified.

If the contractor wishes to take advantage of the possible earlier completion and the cost benefits, then in practice both the supply contract and the site works in the 'Equipment project' will need to be given equal priority at report date 2.5. Although the supply contract is shown as having some float, it is in fact 'nearly critical'.

The effect of the reduced duration of piling has been to allow the contractor to commence the follow-on activities of 'formation' and 'floor slab' earlier than planned if the contractor wishes to take advantage of the possible earlier completion. This may not be realistic if there is a construction restraint not shown on the programme, but assumed, which is not within the contractor's control. The assumption is that the design information will be available in sufficient time to allow the early start. If the information is to be provided by third parties, whether subcontracted consultants or the employer, the contractor may not be able to require or rely on supply of the information to suit its revised programme. This applies equally to the supply of the equipment under the supply contract. Even if the supplier of the equipment is late in delivery, there may be little the contractor can do in practice, except rely on compensation under the supply contract and the obligation to progress the supply. It is an important aspect of management programmes that they should identify the activities by others and that the contract obligations of others are measured by reference to actual progress and the updated main programme. This is difficult to achieve in practice without a consistent project approach to the use of the management programme on the project.

Dynamic role – function 5: compensation programme

The fifth possible function of the programme is as a compensation programme to establish a contractual entitlement and its measure, or to establish the circumstances necessary for the exercise of certain rights. The particular entitlement or right (the compensation) needs to be identified in order to ascertain the exact role of the programme and include:

- the contractor's entitlement to additional time for completion of the works as a whole or for sections of the works, in accordance with the rights stated in the contract
- the contractor's entitlement to additional payment for delay and/or disruption, in accordance with the rights stated in the contract and/or for breach of contract by the purchaser
- the contractor's entitlement to additional payment for instructed acceleration, in accordance with the rights stated in the contract and/or on the terms agreed
- the right of the purchaser to deduct liquidated damages for the contractor's failure to comply with the obligation to complete the works
- the right of the purchaser to instruct the contractor to accelerate due to the contractor's failure to comply with the obligation to progress the works, and
- the right of the purchaser to terminate the contractor's employment for the contractor's failure to comply with the obligation to progress the works.

Establishing the contractual entitlements and the rights requires the comparison of baseline and actual progress, as well as compliance with any contractual preconditions.

In the case of the obligation to complete by a specified date, this only requires the date of actual completion to be compared with the specified date to establish whether the obligation has been discharged. Even this conceptually most simple obligation requires interpretation of the meaning of 'completion' in the contract and evidence of when 'completion' actually occurred. If the date for completion is not specified in the contract, then evidence will be required to determine the reasonable time for completion, which will depend upon all the circumstances.

In the case of the obligation to progress the works, this requires the actual progress measured in terms of both time and resources to be compared to the standard of progress specified in the contract. This obligation is the most difficult to monitor and analyse. It requires the standard required to be determined by interpretation of the contract. Inevitably the obligation is specified in most general terms. A programme can provide evidence of necessary facts, either as evidence of fact or opinion, of both the reasonable standard of progress and the actual progress achieved for comparison as follows.

- The planned programme, whether prepared at tender, at commencement of the works or revised during construction provides evidence of the opinion of the contractor as to the productivity and the durations which were economically achievable in the circumstances known at the date of preparation of the programme.
- The revised programme provides a record of the actions taken by the contractor as a reaction to events or circumstances.
- If the planned programme has been accepted by the contract administrator, then depending on the terms of the contract, the planned programme may be evidence

of the opinion of the contract administrator that the planned durations and/or productivity were reasonable, or that the actions of the contractor shown by the revised programme were a reasonable reaction to events or circumstances.

The cogency of the evidence provided by the planned programme will depend upon the accuracy of the available information and the effort applied in producing the programme. Programmes produced at tender will reflect the usually limited time available to contractors to prepare their bid, the likelihood of being awarded the contract and the contractual status of the tender programme. In most projects, the most realistic programme is usually prepared some weeks after award of the contract, when subcontract packages are more clearly defined. By then inadequacies in the contractor's bid may have become apparent. Programmes may then include an element of optimism or programmemanship and not state realistically achievable productions or durations. For all these reasons the assumptions made in any planned programmes must be verified and tested as accurate.

The cogency of the evidence provided by revised programmes, and programmes showing actual progress, depends upon the accuracy of the record of dates and events and the providence of the evidence on which they are based. The programme should refer directly to the source of dates and durations. Programmes show clearly defined start and finishes of activities, but it is usually difficult in practice to define these two dates precisely. The finish date for the purpose of defining the end of tasks for that activity may not be the same date as the finish required to allow another activity to start. There may be different finish dates for the same activity for different logic links. To further complicate matters, in practice once an activity has reached a level of completion to allow other activities to commence, the activity may be left for some time before being finished. If records show the later date of finish and the programme uses logic links based on that date, the programme will be inaccurate and of little evidential value.

The planned programmes and the revisions will be evidence of the steps taken, or the failure to take sufficient steps, by the contractor to fulfil its obligations as to the programme. The specific obligations vary with the contract, but may include the requirement to revise and update programmes, to record actual progress and projected future progress, and to show the steps to be taken to overcome the delay caused by events.

The evidence provided by the programme of works is not sufficient in itself to justify compensation. It is necessary to establish:

- *the causative event* – there must be a liability to compensate for the event, either in contract or at law
- *causation* – there must be a causal connection between the compensation and the causative event of the type prescribed by the contract and/or at law
- *measure of compensation* – the compensation must follow the rules and principles of valuation prescribed by the contract and/or at law.

Establishing the incidence of liability for a causative event requires the event to be identified as a fact and the liability determined by interpretation of the contract terms and/or recognition of the operation of law. Many causative events which change the planned progress of the works, or change actual progress, can be identified without reference to the programme of works. Ordered variations, weather conditions, changed ground conditions or defects in either drawings, materials, plant or workmanship are some of the events which may be identified directly. Other causative events are identified from documents, such as notifications to contractors from subcontractors or suppliers. In some situations, however, the events are first identified by their effect on progress. The late supply of information or plant and the increased quantities of work are some events which may be first identified by comparison of actual progress to planned progress. In these cases, an accurate planned programme of works is essential for early identification. In some cases, the causative event identified may itself have been caused by a previous causative event. The delay and loss of productivity caused by winter working, for example, may have been caused by the delay into winter due to an earlier causative event. This chain of causation, the incidence of secondary causative events, will need to be established by a logic analysis of the inter-relationship of activities and events. In complex situations a network programme analysis of as-built progress and events will usually be required.

Whether or not the causative event has caused the type of loss which is required to be compensated is a matter of analysis of causation – of cause and effect – which is a mixed question of fact and law.

In the case of the right to deduct liquidated damages for the contractor's breach of the obligation to complete by a specified date, usually no complicated analysis of cause and effect is required. The contractor may, however, properly rely on the prevention principle to prevent a purchaser from taking advantage of its own breach, even in the absence of an extension of time. It is suggested that this is essentially an issue of causation. The right to liquidated damages may not arise unless the pre-conditions to that right are fulfilled and this will usually be notice provisions if at all.

In the case of compensation in the form of the right to an extension of time, the contract will usually prescribe causation, either in terms of the actual delay to the date for completion and/or the estimated future delay and/or the probable future delay. These provisions will therefore determine the method of analysis that is required. It is usual, in all but the most simple of cases, to carry out the analysis using a network analysis programme. The method of network analysis, whether impact analysis on the planned programme, window or snapshot analysis or collapse method using the as-built programme, will depend upon the prescription for causation in the extension of time clause. The accuracy of any analysis will depend upon the accuracy of the information on which it is based.

In the case of compensation in the form of payment for delay and/or disruption and/or acceleration, the compensation may be prescribed in terms of costs or rates and may state whether or not overhead and profit are to be part of the compensation. The prescription may determine the causation rules, whether evidence that actual loss has been caused is required. The role of the programme is usually to demonstrate the period in which the delay or disruption or acceleration occurred so that a separate analysis can be carried out of the change in resources in the period and hence the compensation.

Once it has been established that there is a right to compensation, then the same method used to establish causation may determine the measure of compensation. In the case of the right to extension of time, a network analysis will show not only the link between event and change in progress, but also the extent of the change. Problems of concurrency will usually be resolved by interpretation of the extension of time clause or principles of causation at law. The standard of proof for the measure of compensation for time may not be the same as the measure for time-related financial compensation, a matter of interpretation of the contract. Frequently, available evidence is not sufficient to establish the precise measure of compensation, even in the case of extension of time, but more so in the case of disruption and acceleration compensation. The contract itself may state the standard to be adopted by terms such as 'he . . . estimates is fair and reasonable' or '. . . the delay suffered fairly entitles the contractor to an extension of time' or '. . . such extension of the time for completion as may be reasonable'.

FIDIC 1999 1st Edition

As expected with a modern contract, the contractor's obligation under FIDIC Forms is tied into a programme and progress reports. It is suggested that the programme under the Red and Yellow Forms must include logic links to fulfil the specified function. This is not necessary under the Silver Form where there is no engineer and the employer has a less active role.

Clause 8.3 (Red and Yellow Forms) requires the contractor to submit a 'detailed time programme' to the engineer within 28 days of the notice of commencement. The term 'detailed time programme' is not defined, but clause 8.3 lists details which are to be included with any programme submitted. The Silver Form uses the term 'programme' and requires the programme to be submitted within 28 days after the commencement date. All the forms require the programme to include the order in which the contractor intends to carry out the works, anticipated timing of various stages of work and the sequence and timing of inspections and tests specified in the contract. Importantly, the programme is required to include a supporting report which gives a general description of the methods which the contractor intends to adopt, and the major stages, in the execution of the works. The report must also give details of resources. The term 'programme' is therefore not simply a list of activities and dates, nor just a bar chart, but includes the method statement and allocation of resources.

The description of the programme in clause 8.3 does not specify the form that the programme should take. Although there is an obligation to submit a method statement, there is no obligation to represent the method of working stated in the method statement on the programme in the form of logic links between activities, to show the construction logic. It is suggested, therefore, that the obligation under clause 8.3 can be satisfied by a programme in the form of a bar chart, together with the supporting report. It is suggested further, in order to fulfil the role of the programme prescribed by clauses 8.3, 8.6 and 4.21(h) and described below, that the Red and Yellow Forms require a prediction programme in the form of a linked bar chart.

The first role of the programme under the FIDIC Forms is to monitor the progress of the works by comparison of actual progress with the programme (refer to the article monitoring role of programme and, particularly, the progress programme). Clause 8.3 provides that unless the engineer (employer under the Silver Form) gives notice that a submitted programme does not comply with the contract, the contractor is required to proceed in accordance with the programme, subject to the contractor's other obligations under the contract. The employer is expressly entitled to rely on the programme when planning its activities. The contractor therefore has an express obligation to follow the programme, although this is stated to be subject to its other obligations.

The monitor role is expressly stated in clause 4.21. Clause 4.21(a) provides that monthly progress reports are required to include charts and detailed descriptions of progress. Clause 4.21(h) provides that monthly progress reports are required to compare actual and planned progress. The monthly progress report does not expressly refer to the programme, but it is suggested that planned progress is that shown on the clause 8.3 programme. There is no statement of the form that the comparison should take. It is suggested that, although not essential, a rate of progress timeline will satisfy this requirement.

It is suggested that the role of the programme in the Red Form, and to a lesser extent in the Yellow Form, is more than simply to allow the progress to be monitored. The programme is not a contract document but, nonetheless, defines (if not creates) the obligations and rights of the parties by the dates for performance stated in the programme. This may be demonstrated by examination of clause 1.9 (Red Form), which deals with the contractor's right to be provided with drawings and instructions. The same cannot be said of the Silver Form.

Clause 1.9 (Red) requires the contractor to give notice to the engineer whenever the works are likely to be delayed or disrupted if any necessary drawing or instruction is not issued to the contractor within a particular time, which shall be reasonable. It is suggested that if the programme submitted under clause 8.3 shows the date when instructions and drawings are required, and is sent to the address required by clause 1.3, that the programme will be sufficient to constitute notice for the purposes of clause 1.9.

Clause 1.9 (Red) provides compensation to the contractor if the engineer fails to issue the notified drawing or instruction within a time that is reasonable, and the contractor suffers delay and/or incurs cost as a result. It is suggested that one measure of a reasonable time (although not necessarily the only measure) will be the times stated in the programme issued under clause 8.3. It is suggested that the employer is under an obligation to provide, or have others provide, information and drawings in accordance with the programme and/or at such times as to allow the contractor to proceed in accordance with the programme. Unless the contract expressly states to the contrary, then a failure to do so will be a breach of contract.

A further example of the programme defining rights and obligations is clause 2.1 (Red and Yellow), which deals with the primary obligation of the employer to provide access. Clause 2.1 (Red and Yellow) requires the employer to give the contractor right of access to, and possession of, all parts of the site within the times stated in the Appendix to Tender. If no time is stated, then access and possession must be given to the contractor at such times as will enable the contractor to proceed in accordance with the programme submitted under clause 8.3. In that case, a failure to comply with the access requirements in the programme will be breach of contract by the employer under the Red and Yellow Forms.

Although not stated expressly, it is clear that the programme issued under clause 8.3 is intended to comply with the contract, so that specified access dates should be shown on the programme as prescribed by the contract. If the programme does not, and the engineer (employer under the Silver Form) does not notify within the 21 days required in clause 8.3, then there may be two conflicting obligations to provide access – one stated in the programme and the other prescribed in the contract. It is suggested that the prescribed obligation cannot be modified unilaterally by the contractor's issue of the programme under clause 8.3, because of the clear wording of clause 2.1 and the obligation to revise in clause 8.3. Clause 8.3 requires the contractor to submit a revised programme whenever the previous programme is inconsistent with the contractor's obligations, and this could include programme access dates inconsistent with the prescribed dates. Clause 8.3 also provides that at any time the engineer may give notice that the programme fails to comply with the contract and the contractor is required to issue a revised programme. This will also apply where programme access dates are inconsistent with the prescribed dates. It is suggested that a programme which does not show the correct prescribed access dates will need to be revised.

The programme under clause 8.3 is not only intended to allow progress to be monitored, not only defines some of the time obligations of the parties, but it also records the actual progress of the works. Clause 8.3 requires the contractor to submit a revised programme when the engineer gives notice that the programme is inconsistent with actual progress (and the contractor's stated intentions under the Red and Yellow Forms). Clause 8.3 independently requires the contractor to submit a revised programme whenever the previous programme is inconsistent with actual progress.

A further role of the programme is to provide a means of predicting the effect of identified events, and this role is shown in the requirements of clauses 8.3, 4.21(h) and 8.6. It is suggested that for the Red and Yellow Forms this role, as defined in the FIDIC Form, requires a prediction programme in the form of a linked bar chart, but not necessarily a management programme and a network programme, although desirable.

Clause 8.3 requires the contractor to promptly give notice to the engineer of specific probable future events or circumstances which may delay the execution of the work. Under the Red and Yellow Forms, the engineer may require the contractor to submit an estimate of the anticipated effect. In order to provide the estimate, it is suggested that a logical analysis will be required based on an up-to-date programme – a prediction programme. The engineer may also require a proposal for a variation under clause 13.3 under the Red and Yellow Forms. The contractor is required to state reasons why it cannot comply, or make a submission which includes a programme for the proposed work and the necessary modifications to the programme. It is suggested that any proposals for modification to the programme must be based on a logical analysis of the effects of the proposed work on the progress of the other work based on an up-to-date programme showing actual and predicted progress. This again will require a prediction programme. It is suggested that the role of the programme under the Silver Forms differs in this respect from the Red and Yellow Forms and that a prediction programme is not intended under the Silver Form.

Clause 4.21(h) provides that monthly progress reports are required to state details of any events or circumstances which may jeopardize completion in accordance with the contract and, crucially, the measures being (or to be) adopted to overcome delays. Although it is likely that a network programme will be used on many projects to demonstrate the measures to be taken to overcome delays, it is not a necessary requirement of clause 4.21(h).

Clause 8.6 gives the engineer (employer under the Silver Form) power to instruct the contractor to submit a revised programme with revised methods to expedite progress and complete within the time for completion. The power arises if the actual progress is too slow to complete within the time for completion, or if the progress has fallen or will fall behind the programme. The contractor is required to adopt the revised methods which are stated to include increases in the working hours and/or increase in resources and/or goods. The measure of progress against the clause 8.3 programme can, therefore, define the right of the employer to order acceleration and the obligation of the contractor to do so. Since each programme is required to include resources, the increase in resources can be monitored. The revised methods are at the contractor's cost and risk, and the contractor is liable for the employer's additional costs incurred in addition to any delay damages. There is no such power if the cause is one of the matters which entitles the contractor to an extension of time.

Under clause 15.2(c), the employer is entitled to terminate the contract and expel the contractor from the site, after notice, if the contractor without reasonable excuse fails to proceed with the works in accordance with clause 8. The obligations under clause 8 include the following:

- the obligation to proceed with due expedition and without delay (clause 8.1)
- the obligation to proceed in accordance with the programme (clause 8.3)
- the obligation to submit revisions to the programme on certain events (clause 8.3)
- the obligation to give notice of probable future events which may delay execution of the works (clause 8.3), and
- the obligation to accelerate if properly instructed (clause 8.6).

In practice, the measure of actual progress against the programme will be cogent evidence of a failure to proceed with due expedition. The failure of the contractor to proceed in accordance with the programme will be sufficient, without more, to terminate the contract, providing that this is 'without reasonable excuse'. The meaning of that term is not defined further, but an entitlement to an extension of time will clearly qualify. It is suggested that the 'failure to proceed' must be significant in terms of the overall contract or a particularly critical activity for the project, and not simply a failure to follow the timing of isolated activities on the programme.

The clause 8.3 programme is not the specified basis for evaluation of extension of time – it is not a compensation programme. The entitlement to compensation under clause 8.4 arises if completion 'is or will be delayed' by the particular cause. The extension of time may, therefore, be retrospective or prospective. In a retrospective analysis, the programme will only be cogent evidence if it accurately recorded actual progress. If the programme includes logic links, as suggested above, then it may form the basis for valuation of the entitlement in a prospective analysis, but, except in the simplest situations, a network programme will need to be prepared from the clause 8.3 programme.

Clause 20.1 requires the contractor to give notice of a claim for extension of time and to provide particulars of the claim, including the extension of time claimed. Any failure by the contractor to comply with the contract requirements in relation to the claim can be taken into account to the extent that it has prevented or prejudiced proper investigation of the claim. The engineer (employer under the Silver Form) is required to reach a 'fair determination' under clause 3.5 following consultation and failure to reach agreement.

There is a lack of consistency in the FIDIC Form in the use of the clause 8.3 programme. The contractor has the primary obligation to proceed in accordance with the programme and to update the programme and the employer has the right to terminate for failure to follow the programme. In view of this, it is not clear why the entitlement to extension of time should not be determined by analysis of the clause 8.3 programme. It is suggested that unless the programme clearly does not accurately predict future progress, it would not be a 'fair determination' to ignore the results of analysis of the entitlement to extension of time based on, or using, the clause 8.3 programme.

ICE 7th Edition

Clause 14 requires the contractor to submit both a programme and a method statement. These are two separate obligations which are not inter-related under ICE 7th Edition. Clause 14(1)(a) requires the contractor to submit a programme for acceptance showing the order in which it proposes to carry out the works, within 21 days of award of the contract, taking into account possession releases, access and specified order of construction prescribed in the contract. At the same time, under clause 14(1)(b), the contractor is required to submit a general description of the method of construction. The programme and the method statement are administered separately.

Clauses 14(2), (3) and (4) relate to the programme. Clause 14(2) allows the engineer to request further information to satisfy the engineer as to the programme's reasonableness, having regard to the contractor's obligations under the contract. It is intended, therefore, that one role of the programme is to be a measure of reasonable progress of the works. It is suggested that the comparison of actual progress to the programme will be evidence of the contractor's obligation to proceed with due expedition and without delay under clause 41(2). The programme is intended only to fulfil the role of a progress programme. A bar chart will be sufficient to fulfil the function identified in the ICE 7th Edition, since it will show the order of carrying out the works and allow actual progress to be monitored. Clause 14(4) requires the contractor to submit a revised programme showing such modifications to the original programme as may be necessary to ensure completion of the works within the time for completion, if it appears to the engineer at any time that actual progress does not conform with the accepted programme. This requirement emphasizes the monitor role of the programme, since the obligation to update ensures that the programme is an accurate statement of progress required to achieve completion within the time for completion.

The obligations as to the method statement are set out in clauses 13(2), 14(1)(b) and 14(6). Clause 14(1)(b) requires the contractor to submit a general description of the arrangements and methods of construction. Although required to be submitted at the same time as the programme, there is no express requirement that the programme should represent the method of working by showing logic links between activities showing the construction logic. Clause 13(2) provides that the mode manner and the speed of construction of the works are to be of a kind and conducted in a manner acceptable to the engineer. Clause 14(7) prohibits the contractor from changing the methods which have received the engineer's consent, except with further consent of the engineer which cannot be unreasonably withheld.

The obligation under clause 14(4) to revise the programme only arises if actual progress does not conform with the programme. Strictly, revision of the programme is not required if the future method of working has been changed under clause 14(7). In that case, the programme may no longer accurately represent the anticipated order of carrying out the works.

It is suggested that the programme is not intended to be a prediction programme.

The programme is not intended to be a compensation programme. The contractor's entitlement to extension of time under clauses such as clause 42(3) (possession), clause 7(4) (information), clause 13(3) (instructions) or clauses 44(2)(a), (3) or (5) is based on actual delay. Clause 44(2)(a) requires the engineer to consider all the circumstances known to the engineer at the time of making his or her assessment of the delay suffered by the contractor. Clause 44(3) requires the engineer to consider if the delay suffered fairly entitles the contractor to an extension of the time for substantial completion of the works.

The entitlement does not depend upon an analysis of the clause 14 programme, nor do the employer's obligations of possession and access (clause 42(2)) or supply of information (clause 7(1)) refer to the programme. Any entitlement is based on actual delay.

The employer's entitlement to terminate and to expel the contractor from site under clause 65(1)(j) is, subject to notice, for failure of the contractor to proceed with the works with due diligence. While the programme may be evidence of reasonable progress, failure to proceed in accordance with the programme of itself is not sufficient under clause 65(1)(j).

ECC 2nd and 3rd Edition

The accepted programme is an important tool in the management and administration of the contract under the ECC Form and there are extensive provisions for both the submission of programmes for acceptance and their revision.

Contract Data Part Two allows the contractor to identify the accepted programme with its tender and this becomes the accepted programme, by the definition in ECC 2nd Ed Clause 11.2(14) and 3rd Ed 11.2(1). There is no requirement for the programme so identified to comply with the provisions of clause 31.2 described below. The identified programme is the accepted programme simply by acceptance of the contractor's tender. Since 'contract' is not defined in the ECC standard form, the status of the identified programme is not expressly stated, but it is suggested that it is a contract document unless the agreement or the exchange of correspondence forming the contract states to the contrary.

There is no precedence for interpretation of contract documents, but it is suggested that the identified programme should be used to interpret the intention of the parties as any other contract document. If the identified programme states tasks to be carried out by the employer, or limits the work to be carried out by the contractor, then this will need to be taken into account in the interpretation of the contract.

The definition of compensation events at clauses 60.1(3) and (5) is in terms of the accepted programme, so that it is envisaged under the ECC Form that the contractor may define these obligations in the identified programme, and if the employer accepts the tender it is suggested that the employer will be taken to have accepted responsibility to carry out those obligations under the terms of the programme.

The term 'programme' in the ECC Form means more than simply a bar chart, but also includes a method statement as identified at clause 31.2. It is suggested, therefore, that the programme identified may include the contractor's method statement. If the identified method statement is changed or cannot be followed then this is a situation which has given rise to considerable case law under the ICE Form in which it has been decided that the contractor was entitled to compensation on the basis of the change being a variation (see the article *Programme as a Contract Document*). It is suggested that this would not be the result under the ECC Form.

ECC 2nd Clause 19.1 and 3rd Ed Clause 18.1 which deals with illegal or impossible requirements, refers to the works information and not to the accepted programme. It is suggested that the contractor will be entitled to compensation for a change to its method statement, only to the extent that the method statement is defined by the works information. In this context, the only relevant compensation event is clause 60.1(1), which is an instruction changing the works information. If the contractor's method statement cannot be followed then it is suggested that this is not a breach of contract by the employer, unless and to the extent that the employer may have warranted the accuracy of information on which the statement was based.

If the project manager instructs a change to the contractor's method statement identified in the Contract Data Part Two, then it is suggested that this will entitle the contractor to compensation. If the works information does not restrict or constrain the contractor from carrying out the work in accordance with its method statement, then the instruction will of necessity be a change to the works information giving compensation under clause 60.1(1). If the identified method statement is contrary to the works information, then the complicated issue is whether acceptance of the identified method statement was intended to be an agreement to a change to the works information. Since the identified method statement will be produced later than the works information, it is likely that the identified statement will be considered to more accurately reflect the intention of the parties.

If the contractor is not to submit a programme with its tender, then it is for the employer to state in Contract Data Part One the period in weeks from the contract date when the contractor is to submit the 'first programme'. Clause 2nd 11.2(14) and 3rd 11.1(2) defines the accepted programme as either the programme identified in the contract data or as the latest programme accepted by the project manager. Clause 11.2(14) and 11.1(2) expressly states that the latest programme accepted by the project manager supersedes previous accepted programmes.

The importance of the accepted programme is shown by the sanction at clause 50.3 which applies when no programme is identified in the contract data. The sanction under clause 50.3 is that one quarter of the price for work done to date is retained in assessments of the amount due until the contractor has submitted a 'first programme' to the project manager for acceptance showing the information which the contract requires. Clause 31.3 provides a list of reasons for the project manager not accepting a programme, which includes reasons in addition to the programme not showing the information which the contract requires. It is possible, therefore, for a programme not to be accepted so that there is no accepted programme, but the clause 50.3 sanction will not apply.

The ECC Form makes detailed provisions for programmes submitted for acceptance. Clause 31.2 provides that any submitted programme is required to show key specified dates as well as a method statement for each operation which includes resources, and the order and timing of operations the contractor plans to do and planned completion. Clause 31.2 lists the information that any submitted programme must include. The contractor is required to show on each programme provision for:

- float
- time risk allowances
- health and safety requirements, and
- the procedures set out in the contract.

The reference to 'float' and 'time risk allowances' suggests that the programme is intended to be a network programme, since both provisions require the project dimension which such a programme provides. The provisions for revision to the accepted programme confirm this interpretation since the programme is clearly intended to fulfil the role of a management programme, allowing analysis of the effects of events on future progress. So, for instance, clause 32.1 requires the revised programme to show:

- actual progress achieved and the effect on the timing of remaining work
- the effects of implemented compensation events and of notified early warning matters, and
- how the contractor plans to deal with any delays.

It is suggested that in order to show the effect of actual progress on the timing of the remaining work, the programme must include the logic inks necessary to allow a predictive analysis. The programme is intended to be more than simply a predictive model, since it must also show how the contractor intends to deal with any delays. This clearly shows an intention that the programme is required to be a management programme. In order to fulfil this function, the programme must be both realistic and an accurate representation of the contractor's plans. This is confirmed by clause 31.3, which lists reasons why a project manager may decide not to accept a programme. They include the project manager's subjective judgment that the programme:

- shows that the contractor's plans are not practicable
- does not represent the contractor's plans realistically.

There is no express statement that the contractor is required to follow the accepted programme or that the contractor is prohibited from changing the method of working without consent and it is suggested no such obligations will be implied. The provisions for revision to the programme under clause 32.2 will ensure that programmes are updated to reflect actual progress and changes in the contractor's plans. It is suggested that the intention is to allow the contractor flexibility in the planning of the work subject to express requirements in the works information.

If the employer does not provide information or carry out work in accordance with the accepted programme, then the contractor will be entitled to compensation, so that it would appear that the employer is under an obligation to follow the accepted programme.

So, for instance, clause 31.2 provides for the contractor to identify in the programme the dates when the contractor will need plant and materials and other things to be provided by the employer in order to Provide the Works in accordance with the programme. Under clause 60.1(3), the failure of the employer to provide something which the employer is to provide by the date for providing it required by the accepted programme is a compensation event. It is to be noted that ECC 2nd Edition Clause 60.1(2) refers to dates 'required by' and not 'shown on' the accepted programme, which contrasts with ECC 3rd Edition which uses the term 'shown'. It is suggested that the intention under ECC 2nd Edition is that a date shown on the programme is not sufficient on its own to establish an entitlement following default. Instead there must be some logical connection (which may include float) between the date derived from the programme and connected events. The 'required date' will be the latest date allowing for float derived from an analysis of the programme.

So, for instance, clause 31.2 provides for the contractor to show the order and timing of the work of the employer and others either as stated in the works information or as later agreed with them by the contractor. Under clause 60.1(5) the failure of the employer or others to work within the times shown on the accepted programme is a compensation event.

The obligation of the employer to follow the accepted programme is limited in the case of the obligation to give possession. The limitation operates to prevent the employer being required to give possession earlier than the dates given in the contract data. The dates on which the contractor may enter and take possession of the various parts of the site are stated in the contract data and are the ECC 2nd *possession dates* or ECC 3rd *access dates*. The obligation of the employer under clause 33.1 is to give possession of each part of the site to the contractor on or before the later of its *possession date* or *access date* and the date shown on the accepted programme. The employer cannot, therefore, be required to give early possession. Under clause 60.1(2), the failure of the employer to give possession/access of part of the site by the later of its possession date and the date required by the accepted programme is a compensation event.

The accepted programme is also used to establish the delay to the completion date and it is suggested is a compensation programme. Under clause 62.2, the contractor is required to submit a quotation for a compensation event, which includes an assessment of any delay to the completion date. Crucially, if the 'programme for remaining work' is affected by the compensation event then the contractor is required to include a revised programme in its quotation showing the effect. It is suggested that the clear intention is that analysis of delay is intended to be based on the accepted programme revised to take into account not only the delay but also time risk allowances for the consequences of the compensation event. Clause 63.5 states that the assessment of the effect of a compensation event includes time risk allowances for matters which have a significant chance of occurring and are at the contractor's risk under the contract. Clause 63.3 provides that a delay to the completion date is assessed as the length of time that, due to the compensation event, planned completion is later than planned completion as shown on the accepted programme. It is suggested that the terminology used in clause 63.3 confirms that the compensation for delay is based on the assessment in the revised programme.

The revised programme may need to be modified to take into account ECC 2nd clause 63.4 or ECC 3rd clause 63.5 when used as a compensation programme. The clause is the early warning sanction. If the project manager has notified that the contractor did not give an early warning, which an experienced contractor could have given, then the event is assessed as if the contractor had given an early warning.

The grounds for termination for default do not include failure to follow the accepted programme, but do provide for the contractor's hindrance of the employer. Clause 95.3 provides that the employer may terminate if the project manager has notified that the contractor has substantially hindered the employer and had not stopped defaulting within four weeks of notification.

MF/1Rev 4 2000

It is suggested that in order to fulfil the functions required under the MF/1 Rev 4 2000 Form, a progress programme in the form of a bar chart is all that is required, subject to express provisions in the special conditions. Absent of such provisions, it is suggested that it would not be reasonable for the engineer to require a programme other than a bar chart.

The term 'programme' is defined at clause 1.1p as the programme referred to in clause 14. Clause 14.1 requires the contractor to submit a programme within the time stated in the contract or, if no time is stated, within 30 days after the letter of acceptance. The programme is required to show the sequence and timing of the activities by which the contractor proposes to carry out works, anticipated resources, the respective times for submission by the contractor of drawings and operating and maintenance instructions, and the times by which the contractor requires the purchaser to provide information and access, to have completed any necessary work, obtained permits, etc. and provided site utilities. Clause 14.2 provides that the programme shall be in such form as specified in the special conditions or, if not specified, as may be reasonably required by the engineer.

The programme, therefore, is intended to be a detailed document, although its role appears only to be to allow progress to be monitored. The contractor's obligation to progress the work is stated in clauses 13.1 and 32.1 in terms of due diligence and completion within the time for completion and not in terms of progressing in accordance with the programme.

It is clear that the programme is required to be an accurate measure of actual progress since under clause 14.5 the engineer has the power to order the contractor to revise the programme if the engineer decides that progress does not match the programme. The contractor is then required to revise the programme to show the modifications necessary to ensure completion of the works within the time for completion. If the modifications are required for reasons for which the contractor is not responsible, the cost of producing the revised programme is added to the contract price. In addition, clause 14.4 requires that the contractor shall not make any material alteration to the approved programme without the engineer's consent. The power under clause 14.5 is limited and can only be exercised if actual progress does not match the programme, not if, for instance, the future method of working has changed. The role of the programme is clearly intended only to allow the monitoring of progress and not to fulfil the role of a prediction programme. It is suggested that a bar chart is sufficient to fulfil the required role subject to express terms to the contrary in the special conditions.

Clause 14.6 appears to give the engineer some power to manage progress. If the engineer decides that the rate of progress of the works is too slow to meet the time for completion, and not due to circumstances which entitle the contractor to an extension of time, then the engineer can give notice to that effect. Clause 14.6 requires the contractor, following receipt of notice, to take such steps as may be necessary and as the engineer may approve to remedy or mitigate the likely delay, including revision of the programme. The contractor is not entitled to any additional payment for taking such steps. The comparison of actual progress to the programme will be evidence of the contractor's fulfilment (or otherwise) of its obligation to proceed with diligence and the likelihood that the contractor will complete by the time for completion. The weight to be given to the programme will depend upon the accuracy of the programme in predicting future progress. Failure to follow the programme will not be sufficient cause for the engineer to exercise the power under clause 14.6.

The programme is not intended to be a compensation programme, since under clause 33.1 the entitlement is based on actual delay. Under clause 33.1 the extension of time granted is such as may be reasonable and under clause 33.3. The contractor is required to determine what steps can be taken to overcome or minimize the actual or anticipated delay in consultation with the engineer. There is no mention of the programme in clause 33.

The purchaser's right to terminate and expel the contractor from site under clause 49.1 is, subject to notice, for failure of the contractor to proceed with due diligence. While the programme may be evidence of reasonable progress, failure to proceed in accordance with the programme of itself is not sufficient under clause 49.1.

IChemE Red Book 4th Edition 2001

The term 'approved programme' is defined in clause 1 as the programme approved in accordance with clause 13.

Clause 13.3 requires the contractor within the time stated in Schedule 11 to prepare and submit to the project manager for approval a programme of work setting out in such manner as the project manager shall reasonably require the sequence in which, and dates by which, the contractor proposes to perform its obligations under the contract. The programme is also required to show the dates by which the contractor reasonably requires that the purchaser should provide any further documentation or information or take any action to permit the contractor to perform its obligations. Clause 13.4 requires the contractor to submit details of the personnel and other resources which the contractor proposes to use, if required by the project manager and in such a form as the project manager reasonably requires. The project manager is required to approve the programme if it complies with the specified dates and is 'otherwise reasonable'. The approved programme is therefore intended to demonstrate the progress that the project manager considers could reasonably be made by the contractor.

The contractor's obligations are stated in terms of the approved programme in addition to its obligations to complete by the specified dates or periods (clause 13.1) and to proceed regularly and diligently. Clause 13.3 requires the contractor to use its reasonable endeavours to perform the contractor's obligations in accordance with the approved programme. Clause 13.5 gives the project manager power to require the contractor either to take steps as may be practicable in order to achieve the approved programme or to revise the approved programme, if the contractor falls behind the approved programme or it becomes clear the contractor will fall behind. The approved programme is therefore required to be an accurate prediction of likely progress. The power of the project manager can only be used if the contractor falls behind the approved programme and not if, for instance, the progress is faster than programmed for some activities. Since the contractor is required to use reasonable endeavours to perform its obligations in accordance with the approved programme, this does not prevent the contractor adopting a different method of working if that is reasonable in the circumstances. In that case, there appears to be no power for the project manager to require the approved programme to be revised.

Clause 13.7 deals with the contractor's failure to revise the programme within a reasonable time or when the project manager does not approve the revised programme. In that case, the project manager may instruct reasonable revisions to the programme which the contractor is required to implement.

It is suggested that the primary obligations are to complete by the specified dates or periods and to proceed regularly and diligently and that the obligation to follow the approved programme is a secondary requirement to achieve the primary obligations. This interpretation can be seen in the operation of clause 13.3 described above and clause 13.6 and clause 43.2. Under clause 13.6, the project manager may give notice that he or she decides that the rate of progress is likely to prejudice the contractor's ability to complete in accordance with clause 13.1, which is the primary obligation of completion on time, if due to a cause for which the contractor is responsible. In that case, the contractor is required to use its best endeavours to remedy the potential delay at the contractor's own cost.

Clause 43.2 allows the purchaser to determine the employment of the contractor on notice and continuing default for any material breach of the contract as well as failing to proceed regularly and diligently. Since the submission and revision of the programme takes such prominence in the Form, it is suggested that, in some circumstances, particularly on complex sites, it could be argued that the contractor's failure would constitute a material breach.

The IChemE Red Book 4th Edition 2001 has a rather ambiguous approach to the use of the programme. The role of the programme is intended only to allow the monitoring of progress and not fulfil the role of a prediction programme. It is suggested that a bar chart is sufficient to fulfil the required role. The programme is not intended to be a compensation programme, since under clause 14.1 the entitlement is based on actual delay and indeed the resultant variation order is only given once the extent and consequence of any delay are known.

JCT 2005 (SBC/Q)

Clause 2.9.1.2 requires the Contractor to provide the Architect with two copies of his master programme for the execution of the Works. Within 14 days of the Architect's decision to grant an extension of time by fixing a later Completion Date under clause 2.28.1 the Contractor is required to issue two copies of any amendments and revisions to take into account the decision. Clause 2.9.1 makes clear that nothing contained in the Master Programme or its revision shall impose any obligation beyond those imposed by the Contract Documents.

There is no indication in the Form what is required of a 'Master Programme'. There is no provision for the Architect to approve or reject the Master Programme and it is not referred to in terms of monitoring progress nor in the assessment of extension of time. There is no express requirement for the Contractor to proceed in accordance with the Master Programme.

Clause 2.11 refers to an Information Release Schedule and requires the Architect to issue information stated in the Schedule at the times stated in the Schedule. Under clause 2.12 the Architect is required to issue other information, drawings and instructions to allow the Contractor to carry out and complete the Works in accordance with the Conditions. The failure of the Architect to comply with clause 2.11 and 2.12 is not an express Relevant Event, but Relevant Event 2.29.6 is in sufficient wide terms to deal with the Architect/CA default by omission under either clause 2.11 or 2.12.

JCT 1998 Forms

Clause 5.3.1.2 requires the contractor to provide the architect with two copies of its master programme for the execution of the works. Within 14 days of the architect's decision to grant an extension of time by fixing a later completion date the contractor is required to issue two copies of any amendments and revisions to take into account the decision. The provision is optional and may be deleted. Clause 5.3.2 makes clear that nothing contained in the master programme or its revision shall impose any obligation beyond those imposed by the contract documents.

There is no indication in the Form of what is required of a 'master programme'. It is suggested that at the least the master programme should show the commencement and finishing dates of major activities. There is no provision for the architect to approve or reject the master programme and it is not referred to in terms of monitoring progress nor in the assessment of extension of time. There is no requirement for the contractor to proceed in accordance with the master programme.

Clause 5.4.1 refers to an information release schedule and requires the architect to issue information stated in the schedule at the times stated in the schedule. Under clause 5.4.2 the architect is required to issue other information, drawings and instructions to allow the contractor to carry out and complete the works in accordance with the conditions. The failure of the architect to comply with clause 5.4.1 or 5.4.2 is a relevant event under clause 25.4.6 and may entitle the contractor to an extension of time and loss and expense under clause 26.2.1.

JCT 1998 with Contractor's Design

JCT 1998 with Contractor's Design makes no reference to a master programme or any programme. There is no reference to an information release schedule.

JCT 1998 Prime Cost Contract

The JCT 1998 Prime Cost Contract makes no reference to a master programme or any programme. There is no reference to an information release schedule.

Intermediate Form of Contract 1998

The IFC 1998 Contract makes no reference to a master programme or any programme. Clause 1.7.1 refers to an information release schedule and clause 2.4.7 lists failure to release information in accordance with the schedule as an event which may entitle the contractor to an extension of time.

JCT 1998 Minor Form

JCT 1998 Minor Works Contract makes no reference to a master programme or any programme. There is no reference to an information release schedule.

CECA Blue Form

Under clause 3(1) the subcontractor is deemed to have full knowledge of the main contract. Under clause 3(2) the subcontractor is required to carry out its obligations so as not to cause or contribute to any breach by the contractor of any of its obligations under the main contract. Clause 7(2) gives the contractor the like powers in relation to the subcontract works as the engineer has in relation to the main works under the main contract. There is no reference to programme in the Form, but the second schedule does allow further documents forming part of the subcontract to be listed.

DOM/1

Clause 11.1 of DOM/1 requires the subcontractor to complete the subcontract works in accordance with the details in Appendix Part 4 which provides for insertion of the notice period to commence work on site, the range of dates for the date of commencement and the period for carrying out and completing the subcontract works. Clause 11.1 of DOM/1 requires the subcontractor to complete the subcontract works reasonably in accordance with the progress of the works. There is no reference to a programme nor to an information schedule.

3.5 Notice

Many standard forms of contract require the contractor to give notice when delays occur to the progress of the works. Two issues arise in relation to these notices. The first issue is whether the failure to submit the required notice in accordance with the contract will exclude the contractor from its entitlement to an extension of time. In other words, whether the service of notice is a condition precedent to the right to an extension of time. This is a matter of interpretation of the particular clause.

For a notice clause to be a condition precedent, the clause must state the precise time within which the notice is to be served and must make plain by express language that unless the notice is served within the time, the party required to give notice will lose its right to extension of time under the contract. *Bremer Handelsgesellschaft Gmbh* v. *Vanden Avenne-Izegem* [1978] 2 LLR 109.

If notice is such a condition precedent, the second issue is what formalities must be complied with to constitute proper notice such as:

(a) what details need to be provided
(b) what form must the communication take
(c) how is the notice to be communicated
(d) where the notice is to be communicated.

The fact that the A/E is familiar with the project and in some cases has detailed knowledge of the progress of the work and of the contractor's planning, is a factor in considering whether the contractor has acted reasonably and with reasonable expedition in providing notice. In some situations, the briefest notification will suffice.

Standard forms of contract vary in their requirements for notice. The current trend in the industry is for notice to be a condition precedent to an entitlement to extension of time to allow for more effective management of the contract. This reflects a growing need for employers and contractors to plan the works and use extension of time clauses as management tools rather than simply to protect the employer's rights to liquidated damages. The nature of the notice provisions of selected standard forms in common use is given below.

ICE 6th and 7th Edition

Clause 44(1) of the ICE 6th and 7th Editions requires the contractor, within 28 days after the cause of delay has arisen or as soon thereafter as is reasonable, to deliver to the engineer full and detailed particulars in justification of any claim to an extension of time, in order that the claim may be investigated at the time. It is considered that the clause is not drafted as a condition precedent to an entitlement to an extension of time, particularly since clause 44(2)(b) allows the engineer to make an interim assessment in the absence of a claim. Further, clause 44(4) requires the engineer to make an assessment within 14 days of the date of completion whether or not the contractor has made a claim and clause 44(5) requires the engineer to make a final determination in the light of all the circumstances within 28 days (ICE 6th – 14 days) of the issue of the Certificate of Substantial Completion.

FIDIC Forms

Clause 8.4 of the FIDIC Red, Yellow and Silver Books 1999 entitles the contractor to an extension of the time for completion only if it has complied with clause 20.1. This requires the contractor to give notice to the engineer describing the event or circumstance as soon as practicable and not later than 28 days after the contractor becomes aware of the event or circumstance. Clause 20.1 expressly states that if the contractor fails to give notice within 28 days then the time for completion is not extended.

Engineering Construction Contract 2nd Edition

Clause 61.3 of the Engineering Construction Contract 2nd Edition requires the contractor to notify an event which has happened or which it expects to happen within ECC 2nd two weeks ECC 3rd eight weeks of becoming aware of the event. A compensation event cannot be notified after the defects date, which is the date fixed in the contract data in weeks after completion for defects identification and correction. The timescales for action by the contractor and project manager are strong indications that the notification is intended to be a condition precedent to entitlements under the contract. It is to be noted, that there is an express statements of loss of rights for failure to give notice only in ECC 3rd Edition.

MF/1 Rev 4

Clause 33.1 allows the engineer to grant an extension of time, from time to time, but only on the proviso that the contractor has given notice of its claim for an extension of time with full supporting details and that the notice has been given as soon as reasonably practicable. It could be argued that the clause is written in terms of notice being a condition precedent to an entitlement. There are, however, no such express words.

IChemE Red Book 4th Edition 2001

Clause 14.1 requires the contractor to give notice 'forthwith' if it is delayed in the performance of its obligation under the contract. The Project Manager is required to act as soon as the extent and consequence of the delay is known, and issue a variation extending the approved programme. The wording in clause 14.1 and the procedure adopted does not suggest that notice is a condition precedent to an entitlement and there is no such express provision.

JCT 2005 (SBC/Q)

JCT 2005 Clause 2.28.5.1 makes it clear that the Architect's duties with regard to extending the Completion Date after the date of practical completion are not dependent upon service of notice by the Contractor.

JCT 1998

JCT 1998 Clause 25.2.1.1 requires the contractor, if and when it becomes reasonably apparent that the progress of the works is delayed, to forthwith give written notice to the Architect. Clause 25.3.3.1 makes it clear that the Architect's duties with regard to extending the completion date are not dependent upon service of notice by the contractor.

CECA Blue Form of Subcontract

CECA Blue Form of Subcontract clause 6(2) stipulates that it is a condition precedent to the subcontractor's rights to an extension of time for a notice to be served within 14 days of a delay first occurring for which the subcontractor considers itself entitled to extra time.

3.6 Time at large

In commercial contracts the parties usually intend the works to be completed by an agreed date. In many contracts the date for completion will be stated as an express term. The term 'time at large' is not a legal term, but describes the situation where there is no identified date for completion, either by absence from the contract terms or arising from events and the operation of law. Time is said to be 'at large' because the time or date for completion is not fixed before carrying out the work, but determined after the work has been completed.

The term 'time at large' is usually used in construction contracts in the situation where liquidated damages are an issue. If time is 'at large' then it is argued liquidated damages cannot be applied, because there is no date fixed from which the liquidated damages can be calculated.

Time is made 'at large' in four situations:

(a) where no time or date is fixed by the terms of the contract by which performance must take place or be completed, and
(b) when the time for performance has been fixed under the contract, but has ceased to apply either by agreement or by an act of prevention (which includes instructed additional work) or breach of contract by the employer with no corresponding entitlement to extension of time, and
(c) where the employer has waived the obligation to complete by the specified time or date or where the employer, faced with a breach of contract by the contractor which would entitle the employer to terminate the employment of the contractor

and/or to bring to an end the primary obligations of the parties to perform, instead elects to continue with the performance of the contract, and
(d) where the employer has interfered in the certification process to prevent proper administration of the contract.

No time or date fixed in contract

If no date or period is fixed by the contract then the objective intention of the parties must be ascertained. In the case of a contract under the Supply of Goods and Services Act 1982, if the date is not fixed by a course of dealing between the parties, a term will be implied that the contractor's obligation is to complete within a reasonable time (section 14(1)).

In *J. and J. Fee Ltd* v. *The Express Lift Company Ltd* [1993] 34 ConLR 147 there had been correspondence between the parties on the date of commencement and completion. The last correspondence from Express Lift stated that it could see little possibility of improvement on the dates previously given, but suggested that the situation be monitored and, if it became possible, reviewed. It was held that as a matter of construction of its express terms Express Lift made a contractual offer of the completion date which it consistently offered before and that offer was accepted. The last letter was not written in plain 'take it or leave it' terms but held out the possibility of bettering the completion date. Nonetheless, there were dates for commencement and completion as a express term of the contract. HH Judge Peter Bowsher QC stated that if he was wrong on that issue, then there was a term implied that Express Lift would complete within a reasonable time. He gave a provisional view, without deciding, that based on the documents before him that it would be impossible for Express Lift to contend that a reasonable time for completion of the works would be any later than the date they had consistently put forward.

In *Bruno Zornow (Builders) Ltd* v. *Beechcroft Developments Ltd* [1990] 51 BLR 16, Bruno as contractor entered into a contract with Beechcroft as employer for preliminary works and later varied by a further agreement by letter. The effect of the letter was to include additional work and to agree a programme for the additional work. There was no express term of the agreement stating that the additional work would be carried out by any completion date. The issue therefore was whether any such provision could be implied. The contract contained a date for completion before variation, when it was, relatively, a much smaller contract. HH Judge John Davies QC considered whether time for completion was to be left at large subject only to the implication that the works should be finished within a reasonable time. The alternative was to presume as necessary for business efficacy that the parties must have intended that it should continue to have a fixed date for completion. It was held that in a lump sum contract involving a commercial development with an attendant risk of an indeterminate loss of profits claim it was commercially unrealistic to suppose that the parties did not mutually intend that it should contain a date for completion linked to the liquidated damages provision which it contained already. Both provisions were inter-related and both were material elements, so far as the contractor and employer were concerned in deciding whether to enter into the bargain at all, and if so, what price. It was held that it was necessary to imply into the contract a date for completion. It was held that the parties intended that the date for completion would be the period which both parties had in mind for the whole of the works when the first tier tender was submitted. It was that date, as modified by extensions of time granted by the architect, that was the relevant date for the application of liquidated damages.

Time or date ceases to apply

In many situations where the issue of 'time at large' arises, the parties are concerned with the application of liquidated damages and whether or not the contract makes provision for extension of time for acts of prevention by the employer. Relevant decided cases are:

- *Wells* v. *Army and Navy Co-operative Society Ltd* [1902]
- *Peak Construction (Liverpool) Ltd* v. *McKinney Foundations Ltd* [1976] 1 BLR 114
- *Percy Bilton Ltd* v. *Greater London Council* [1982] 20 BLR 1
- *Bramall & Ogden Ltd* v. *Sheffield City Council* [1985] 29 BLR 73
- *Rapid Building Group Ltd* v. *Ealing Family Housing Association* [1985] 29 BLR 5
- *Davy Offshore Ltd* v. *Emerald Field Contracting Ltd* [1992] 55 BLR 1
- *Inserco Ltd* v. *Honeywell Control Systems* [1996].

In *Davy Offshore Ltd* v. *Emerald Field Contracting Ltd* [1992] 55 BLR 1, Emerald employed Davy to carry out design and provide certain facilities including a semi-submersible drilling rig and a floating storage unit together with the provision of sub-sea work. The contract terms were extensive and complex and HH Judge Thayne Forbes QC was asked an extensive list of preliminary questions. It was held that, under the contract, time only became at large when the failure to complete on time was due to an act or omission by Emerald. For one of the issues it was common ground that time was at large which, it was held, meant that Davy was obliged to complete the work within a reasonable time making allowance for the period of delay attributable to Emerald's default.

In *Inserco Ltd* v. *Honeywell Control Systems* [1996], Inserco contracted to complete all work by 1 April 1991. Due to additional and revised work, and lack of proper access and information Inserco was prevented from completing by 1 April 1991. There was no provision in the contract for extending the completion date and time was held to be at large.

Waiver or election

Time may become at large if the original obligation to complete is waived. In *Charles Rickards Ltd* v. *Oppenheim* [1950], a Rolls Royce motor car was not built by the agreed delivery date, but new dates were agreed. Eventually, Oppenheim gave written notice to Rickards stating that unless he received the car by a firm date, four weeks away, he would not accept it. The car was not delivered within the time specified and was not completed until some months later when Oppenheim refused to accept it. The Court of Appeal held that he was justified in doing so. After waiving the initial stipulation as to time, Oppenheim was entitled to give reasonable notice making time of the essence again, and on the facts the notice was reasonable.

This principle applies to construction contracts. If, because of waiver, time becomes 'at large', the employer can give the contractor reasonable notice to complete within a fixed reasonable time, thus making time of the essence again, *Taylor* v. *Brown* [1839]. The employer will have lost the right to liquidated damages so that if the contractor fails to complete by the revised agreed date the employer will be left with the remedy of general damages. It is not clear whether the employer can make time of the essence, if it was not previously so.

Failure of contractual machinery

If the time or date for completion is effected by events which entitle the contractor to an extension of time, but the contractual machinery can no longer operate, then time is at large. The circumstances will be rare.

In *Bernhard's Rugby Landscapes Ltd* v. *Stockley Park Consortium (No. 2)* [1998], BRL was awarded the contract for the construction of a new golf course on a reclaimed landfill site under an amended ICE 5th Edition. One issue was whether the contractual machinery had broken down and, if so, the effect. It was held that a breakdown of the contractual machinery occurs when, without material default or interference by a party to the contract, the machinery is not followed by the person appointed to administer and operate it and, as a result, its purpose is not achieved, and is either no longer capable of being achieved or is not likely to be achieved. HH Judge Humphrey Lloyd stated that this could for most practical purposes be equated to interference by a contracting party in the process whereby the other is deprived of a right or benefit. Examples were the failure of an employer to re-appoint an administrator or certifier on the resignation of the previously appointed person or where that person fails or is unwilling to do his or her duty and the employer will not take steps to rectify the position. Reference was made to the decision in *Panamena Europea Navigacion* v. *Frederick Leyland Ltd* [1947]. It was held that non-compliance with the machinery by the administrator was not in itself sufficient: the effect must be that either or both of the parties to the contract do not in consequence of the breakdown truly know their position or cannot or are unlikely to know it. If the true position is or can be established by other contractual means then the breakdown is likely to be immaterial even when the result of the breakdown is that one party does not obtain the contractual right or benefit which would or might otherwise have been established by the machinery, provided that the true position can be restored by the operation of other contractual machinery.

Reasonable time

If time does become 'at large', the contractor's obligation is to complete within a reasonable time. What constitutes a reasonable time is a question of fact. The principles to be applied are those in *Pantland Hick* v. *Raymond & Reid* [1893]. What constitutes a reasonable time has to be considered in relation to circumstances which existed at the time when the contract obligations are performed, but excluding circumstances which were under the control of the contractor. In *British Steel Corporation* v. *Cleveland Bridge & Engineering Company* [1981] 24 BLR 100, Lord Goff applied these principles by first considering what in ordinary circumstances was a reasonable time for performance and then considering to what extent the time for performance of the contractor was in fact extended by extraordinary circumstances outside his control. Whether a reasonable time has been taken to do the works cannot be decided in advance, but only after the work has been done.

If time is at large because no time or date was fixed in the contract, then it is not clear whether the test of a reasonable time and the extent of control required is an objective or subjective test. It is suggested that since the obligation is an implied term, that the reasonable time must be determined from the objective intention of the parties. If the contractor has been specifically chosen then it will be a subjective test. If, as is likely to be more usual, the contractor has been selected in competitive tendering, then it will be an objective test of how a reasonably experienced contractor in the actual circumstances would have carried out the works.

If time is at large because the specified time or date no longer applies following an act of prevention or breach by the employer, the original completion date is good evidence of what is a 'reasonable time in ordinary circumstances'. The original completion date is not conclusive, it is suggested. Part of the ordinary circumstances will include the fact that a contractor would be expected to resource and plan the works in order to achieve the original completion date. The delay and disruption caused by the act of prevention or breach needs to be taken into account.

It is suggested that if time is at large by waiver or election that this does not mean, without more, that the employer has waived the right to damages for the breach of the obligation to complete.

In *Shawton Engineering Ltd* v. *DGP International Limited* [2005] EWCA Civ 1359 there were variations to the contract but there was no contractual mechanism for extending time on account of the variations. It was accepted that the effect in law of the variations was that DGP became obliged to complete their work within a reasonable time.

The Court of Appeal held that a reasonable time had to be judged at the time when the question arises in the light of all relevant circumstances. One of the circumstances was the original contract date, even if DGP had underestimated the work content. The nature of the variation was relevant.

The original completion dates, and, indeed, the original completion periods had ceased to be of any relevance because Shawton were not insisting on the stipulations as to time, nor were they insisting on any times or periods for completion. That overlaid to extinction any question of calculating time periods by reference to the original dates for completion and the work content of variations. In this case, a reasonable time for completion was literally at large.

3.7 Power of A/E to grant extensions of time

The Architect/Engineer cannot simply take a passive role in the examination of extension of time, without jeopardising the validity of his certificates *Holland Hannon Cubitts (Northern) Ltd* v. *Welsh Health Technical Services Organisation* (1981).

There are four issues to be considered in deciding on the time for exercise of the A/E power to grant extensions of time:

(a) The contract may contemplate the exercise of a power at once upon the occurrence of the event causing delay, for example for non-continuing causes of delay such as the ordering of extras.
(b) The contract may contemplate the power being exercised only when the full effect on progress is known such as continuing causes of delays such as strikes, withholding of the site etc.
(c) The contract may contemplate exercise of the power at any time before issue of the final certificate.
(d) The contractor's entitlement to receive an early indication on request of the A/E's decision on individual grounds of extension as they arise.

It is necessary to examine the precise provisions of the construction contract in order to determine whether or not there has been a breach of contract in relation to granting of extension of time. The fourth issue is clearly important to enable the contractor to decide whether or not to incur possible substantial acceleration expenditure and avoid the prospect of paying liquidated damages *Perini Corporation* v. *Commonwealth of Australia* [1969] 2. N.S.W.L.R. 530.

The contractors actions particularly in providing particulars to substantiate the delays claimed may give rise to issues of waiver and estoppel which would prevent the contractor claiming that the employer is in breach of contract in not ensuring that the A/E granted extensions of time at the appropriate time.

In *John Barker Construction Ltd* v. *London Portman Hotel Ltd* [1996] it was held that the Architect's exercise of his judgment in assessing a fair and reasonable extension of time must be fairly and rationally based. In this case the Architect's assessment was fundamentally flawed. For instance, he had not carried out a logical analysis in a methodical way of the impact of the relevant matters on the contractor's planned programme. Instead he had made an impressionistic, rather than a calculated assessment of the time consequences. Being a JCT Contract the Architect had not paid sufficient attention to the contents of the bills of quantities.

In *Amalgamated Building Contractors Ltd* v. *Waltham Holy Cross Urban District Council* (1952) it was held that where the cause of delay operated partially but not wholly, every day, until the works were completed, then the Architect could not decide the extension of time until completion. The parties intended that the Architect could grant an extension of time retrospectively. It was also held that if the contractor has overrun the contract time without legitimate excuse and during that period an event occurred causing further delay, then if it was a qualifying event the contractor is entitled to extension of time for that further delay, which operates retrospectively.

In *Temloc* v. *Errill* (1987) it was held that the 12 week period in the JCT80 Form for reviewing the extension of time after completion was directly and not mandatory.

In *Fernbrook Trading Co. Ltd* v. *Taggart* (1979), it was held that the contractor must be informed of the new completion date as soon as reasonably practicable. If the entitlement to extension of time was the order of extra work then in the normal course extensions should be given at the time of the order. It is suggested, however, that if the fact of additional work can only be ascertained by measure of the drawings and comparison with the original definition of the work, then the assessment of extension of time may not be possible at the time of issue of the drawings.

It was held that if the cause of delay lies beyond the Employer, and particularly where its duration is uncertain, then the grant of extension of time should be given a reasonable time after the factors which govern the assessment have been established. Where there are multiple causes of delay, there may be no alternative but to leave the final decision to just before the issue of the Final Certificate.

In *Perini Corporation* v. *Commonwealth of Australia* (1969) it was held that in the particular contract, there was an implied term which required extensions of time to be given within a reasonable time. The measurement of a reasonable time was a question of fact. The Architect/Engineer must have sufficient time as is necessary to enable him to investigate the facts which are relevant in making the decision. When the investigation is complete then the decision must be made.

There is no reason why the Architect/Engineer's failure to grant an extension of time within the specified time or a reasonable time as appropriate, should bring down the mechanism of liquidated damages. The remedy is to have the matter decided in arbitration or litigation, or adjudication if a construction contract. The extension of time provision is a means of apportionment of liability for delay and liquidated damages and not intended to give the contractor a date to aim for.

3.8 Omitted work

Whether the A/E is entitled to reduce the contract period or reissue an extension of time already granted but showing a shorter period when work has been omitted by a variation, depends on the terms of the contract. Terms of some standard forms in common use are described below.

ICE 6th and 7th Edition

Clause 44(2) of the ICE 6th and 7th Edition requires the engineer to make an assessment of the delay suffered by the contractor for specified events. This, logically, will take into account the effect of omission of part of the works as part of the circumstances required to be considered by the engineer in making an assessment, although this is not expressly stated. The powers of the engineer are defined in terms of either granting an extension of time or notifying the contractor that no extension of time is due, so there is no express power to reduce or extend the period for completion. The final determination under clause 44(5) states that it cannot result in a decrease to any extension of time already granted.

FIDIC Forms 1999 1st Edition

Clause 8.4 of the FIDIC Red, Yellow and Silver Books 1999 provides that the determination of each extension of time will include a review of previous determinations and may increase, but shall not decrease, the total extension of time.

ECC 2nd and 3rd Edition

Clause 62(2) of the Engineering Construction Contract requires the contractor to assess delays to the completion date when submitting its quotation. Under clause 63.3–63.6 the assessment is required to be the delay to the completion date based on the length of time that planned completion is later than planned completion shown on the accepted programme. Under clause 65.2 the assessment of compensation events is not revised if forecasts are shown later to be wrong. It is suggested that this scheme allows the effect of omissions to be taken into account in each assessment but does not allow the extensions of time already granted to be reduced.

MF/1 Rev 4

MF/1 clause 33.1 provides that the engineer will grant an extension of time if the contractor has been delayed in the completion of the works by stated events, whether the delay occurs before or after the time for completion. The assessment of actual delay to the works will logically take into account the effect of omission of part of the works, although this is not expressly stated. The powers of the engineer are defined in terms of granting an extension of time, so there is no power to reduce the period or extended period for completion.

IChemE Red Book 4th Edition 2001

Clause 14.1 provides for the **Contractor** to be granted a **Variation Order** involving an extension to the **Approved Programme** and the Times of Completion in Schedule 11, if the **Contractor** is delayed in the performance of his obligations under the contract by stated events. Again the powers of the **Project Manager** are defined in terms of granting an extension of time, so there is no power to reduce the period or extended period for completion.

JCT 2005 (SBC/Q)

Under JCT 2005 Clause 2.28 the power of the Architect is only to fix a later date as the Completion Date for the Works or Section.

After the first fixing of a later Completion Date clause 2.28.4 allows and after the date of practical completion clause 2.28.5.2 allows, the Architect/CA to fix a Completion Date earlier than previously fixed having regard to any Relevant Omissions for which instructions have been issued after the last occasion on which a new Completion date was fixed. In that case he is required under clause 2.28.3.2 to state in his decision the reduction in time that he has attributed to each Relevant Omission. A Relevant Omission includes under clause 2.26.3 the omission of any work or obligation through an instruction for a Variation under clause 3.14 (instructions requiring Variation). The exercise of the power under both clauses is limited by clause 2.28.6.3 so that no decision can fix a Completion Date earlier than the relevant Date for Completion.

It is suggested that in his deliberations on extension of time, the Architect/CA cannot reconsider and reduce the extension of time previously granted for Relevant Events, except for the effect of those instructions issued after his last fixing which involve omission of work or obligations. Accordingly he can only take into account omissions since he last fixed an extension of time.

JCT 1998 Form

Under JCT 1998 clause 25.3.1 the power of the Architect is only to fix a later date as the Completion Date. He is required to state the extent, if any, he has had regard to instructions which require as a Variation the omission of Work. The Architect/CA can therefore reduce the extension of time he is considering by the effect of omissions, but there is no power under clause 25.3.1 to fix an earlier date. He can only notify that it is not fair and reasonable to fix a later date having regard to the sufficiency of the notice.

Under JCT 1998 clauses 25.3.2 and clause 25.3.3.2 the Architect can fix a Completion Date earlier than previously fixed under clause 25 having regard to any instructions issued after the last occasion on which the Architect fixed a new Completion Date. This only allows the Architect to take into account those instructions after the previous fixing which require or sanction as a Variation the omission of any work or obligation. The Architect cannot reconsider and reduce the extension of time previously granted for Relevant Events, except for the effect of the later instructions which involve omission of work or obligations. Clause 25.3.6 stipulates that no decision under the two clauses can fix a Completion Date earlier than the Date for Completion stated in the Appendix.

CECA Blue Form

CECA Blue Form clause 6(2) is written in terms of the subcontractor having been delayed in the execution of the subcontract works, and in terms of extensions of time. Again, this suggests that omissions can be taken into account in assessing the actual causes of delay, but prevent the period for completion being reduced.

3.9 Acceleration

The problem of deciding when to accelerate

'Acceleration' is not a legal term. Its natural and common meaning is to 'bring about in an earlier point in time' (Webster's dictionary), which is a comparative measure. There must be some benchmark against which to measure the acceleration. In construction, the main issue is the date against which progress is measured. There are two situations relating to the overall works as opposed to discrete areas or sections of work.

The first acceleration situation arises if the contractor is required to complete earlier than the contract date fixed for completion. The main issue will be whether this requirement is a variation to the contract. In practice, the issue will turn on whether it can be established that an instruction was given in those terms. A complication is whether the failure of the A/E to properly grant an extension of time, or simply the timing of the ascertainment of the extension of time due, together with pressure from the employer or its agents for the contractor to complete by the then fixed date for completion, is effectively an instruction to accelerate. This is the issue of the 'constructive order' and of 'constructive acceleration' examined below.

The second acceleration situation arises if the contractor is likely to complete later than the contract date fixed for completion due to reasons which may not entitle him to an extension of time. If the contractor is in default then the issue is whether it is under an obligation to reduce or avoid the effects of the delay including taking acceleration measures. If it is not clear whether the contractor is entitled to an extension of time, in practice the contractor is left with the same choice whether or not to accelerate. This is the 'temporary default' problem, in which the contractor, until the extension of time is granted, is in default or likely to be in default and may decide that the most reasonable action in its commercial interests is to take acceleration measures rather than incur potential liquidated damages. There is also the related issue of the extent of the contractor's obligation to take measures to mitigate the consequences of a delay for which the contractor may be entitled to an extension of time and the effect this has on any entitlement to extension of time and whether it can recover the cost of such measures and this is examined below.

Acceleration measures

Acceleration may be achieved by a change in the deployment of resources. In some cases it may be achieved by simply changing the order or sequence for carrying out the work and may therefore not cause additional cost. More usually, acceleration is achieved by adopting longer working hours or additional days of working with the same resources. In many cases acceleration involves employing resources additional to those originally planned either for the same hours or days of working, or in additional shifts or days of working.

The possible acceleration measures are summarized below.

(a) Increased resources to reduce the time taken for critical activities. The increase in resource may at some level have the effect of reducing productivity and thereby increasing unit cost of construction. There will normally be an optimum level of resource for any one activity.
(b) Increased man hours is a means of increasing resource input, but will introduce inefficiency and both quality and health and safety issues.
(c) Incentives will motivate labour to increase productivity.
(d) Changed methods of working may open up additional workforces or workplaces as well as introducing economies in the use of plant and equipment.
(e) Re-sequencing work is a fundamental part of managing the progress of the work and is why float is always required on most of the activities on a project.

Effect of acceleration

When tendering and planning for the efficient completion of the works, contractors can optimize resources and progress. The interface between different resources can be properly managed so that a pattern develops which the workforce can follow with reduced planning, so increasing productivity.

Most standard forms of contract allow the contractor to complete the works before the completion date. It is not unusual for a contractor to decide once work commences to adopt a different approach than assumed at tender. The contractor may see advantages in completing early due to factors which only come to light once more detailed planning is undertaken. In other words, the contractor may decide to accelerate because it perceives a commercial advantage. This may create problems for the employer in supplying the relevant information or completing other works.

In *Glenlion Construction Ltd* v. *Guinness Trust* [1987] 39 BLR 89, Glenlion was contractor under JCT 63 for the construction of a residential development for Guinness in Bromley, Kent. The issue that arose was whether Glenlion was entitled to complete the works before the completion date. Glenlion had submitted a programme which showed early completion.

It was held that it was self-evident from clause 21 of JCT 63 that Glenlion was entitled to complete before the date of completion. This was so whether or not Glenlion produced a programme with an earlier date and whether or not it was required to produce a programme.

While Glenlion was entitled to complete before the contractual completion date it was held that the Guinness Trust was not required to actively co-operate to enable the earlier date to be achieved but was only required not to hinder completion.

It is suggested that the situation will, however, be different if the programme is incorporated in the contract as a contract document or if the entitlement under the contract is bound up with the programme. If the employer does not wish to take possession of the works early, then this needs to be dealt with by amendment of the contract terms so that the contractor can price accordingly.

If acceleration is adopted as a reaction to events which have caused delay, rather than a planned strategy for optimization of resources, then this will normally result in additional costs. The late or unplanned timing of acceleration measures will normally mean that the resources deployed are different to the resources planned, due to lack of availability. The available additional equipment may operate at less than full capacity, being overcapacity for the work intended but with the additional hire costs involved. The need to use material more quickly than planned may result in a reduced number of uses such as formwork, which will increase unit costs. The change in the sequence of working may result in an increased number of moves and/or distances for plant, such as cranage in piling. Additional resources and out of sequence working will place additional burden on the management to order materials and consumables, and increase the supervision required.

Acceleration will affect the pattern of work, and has an effect on efficiency, material delivery, equipment availability and therefore the cost of the work. In most situations acceleration will mean carrying out the work at a rate that is less than optimum in terms of cost. Acceleration in many situations will disrupt the works, affecting smooth trade interfaces and increasing interference between follow-on operations. In some cases it will mean unplanned access to working areas, reduced productivity and increase in defects as well as stoppages.

The additional payments for overtime or weekend working do not necessarily result in increased productivity. Indeed extended overtime and long hours will usually reduce efficiency. Additional shifts are not always productive. Evening or back shifts and night shifts are more likely to be less productive than day shifts, and may create more defects and less safe working. The out-of-hours working may increase the cost of delivery of materials, together with the additional cost of larger stockpile areas. New suppliers may need to be found for the increase in consumption, which may involve increase in unit costs.

4.1 Administration of claims
4.2 Litigation
4.3 Arbitration
4.4 Adjudication
4.5 Alternative dispute resolution

Obligation to accelerate

The employer's remedy for the contractor's breach of contract in failing to complete by the completion date will be damages, whether general damages or liquidated damages. Many standard forms require the contractor not only to complete by the completion date but also to proceed regularly and diligently. Many standard forms provide a power for acceleration to be ordered in the event of the contractor's default in progressing with due diligence, without additional payment. Many standard forms also provide a power for ordering the contractor to adopt acceleration measures if it is considered that progress is not in accordance with the programme, if due to the contractor's default. Such powers do not normally extend to agreeing to accelerate in the absence of the contractor's default, which requires a separate agreement. If such an agreement is entered into it is important to ensure that the terms relating to liquidated damages still operate.

In *John Barker Construction Ltd* v. *London Portman Hotel Ltd* [1996] 83 BLR 35, John Barker were building contractors carrying out refurbishment of works to the London Portman Hotel. The contract was the JCT 80 Form with quantities. The contract provided for completion of floors 9 to 11 on 16 July 1994, floors 5 to 8 by 29 July 1994 and floors 2 to 4 by 14 August 1994. Clause 24 provided that liquidated damages would be paid at £30 000 per week for each section of the contract which was not completed by the specified date. Delays occurred and it was apparent to all concerned that John Barker was entitled to extensions of time. After negotiations it was agreed that the work would be accelerated so that all the work would be completed by 14 August 1994 and John Barker would receive additional payment.

After the acceleration agreement there were further delays and further instructions from the architect. One of the issues which arose was the effect of the acceleration agreement on the sectional completion provisions of the contract in relation to liquidated damages.

John Barker argued that the effect of the acceleration agreement was to dispense with all the provisions of the sectional agreement supplement, including the provisions for liquidated damages. It was argued that the substitution of a single date was logically inconsistent with such provisions having continuing contractual force. This was not accepted. It was common ground that at the time of the acceleration agreement no one raised the question of abandoning the liquidated damages provisions. It was held that it was neither intended by the parties nor logically necessary that the liquidated damages would no longer apply. It was held that the provisions of the sectional completion supplement regarding liquidated damages were capable of continuing to have contractual force by merely substituting the new date of 26 August 1994 for completion of each section. The parties' intention did not go beyond that.

In *Ascon Contracting Limited* v. *Alfred McAlpine Construction Isle of Man Limited* [1999] there had been delays due to a number of causes and Ascon, the concrete subcontractor, claimed extension of time. It was held that, in considering the subcontractor's entitlement to extension of time, it could not be refused or reduced because of the possibility of future acceleration. That would impose an obligation on the subcontractor to incur expense in order to mitigate the consequences of the contractor's breaches of contract.

It would also deprive the subcontractors of the opportunity, knowing how much of the current delay had been allowed, of assessing whether it was necessary to consider incurring additional expense in accelerative measures in order to reduce its potential liability in damages for any disallowed balance, and if so to decide for itself how far it was in its own interests to incur that expense in the absence of instructions to do so as a variation. Accordingly Ascon was awarded an extension of time.

It was not in dispute that Ascon was also entitled to damages to the extent of any recoverable loss which could be established as caused by the period of delay, and a sum was awarded.

Ascon also claimed for loss caused by acceleration measures it had undertaken. HH Judge Hicks QC stated that acceleration had no precise technical meaning. Acceleration which was not required to meet a contractor's existing obligations was likely to be the result of an instruction from the employer for which the employer must pay. On the other hand, pressure from the employer to make good delay caused by the contractor's own default was unlikely to be so construed. There was no instruction in this case. Ascon was under pressure from McAlpine to accelerate the works to recover the time lost, but was insisting that it was not going to pay for acceleration. Ascon's claim on that basis did not therefore succeed.

Ascon claimed that it allocated additional resources, worked longer hours, worked seven days per week and purchased and supplied duplicate plant and equipment. Ascon claimed that these acceleration measures were taken in order to mitigate the delays caused.

It was held that there could not be both an extension to the full extent of the employer's culpable delay, with damages on that basis, and also damages in the form of expenses incurred by the way of mitigation, unless it was alleged and established that the attempt at mitigation, although reasonable, was wholly ineffective. Ascon had not put its case in that way. It contended that the work was indeed completed sooner than it would have been in the absence of the accelerative measures. The mitigation claim wholly failed at the outset and the acceleration claim also failed.

In *Motherwell Bridge Construction Limited* v. *Micafil Vakuumtecchnik* [2002] TCC 81 ConLR 44 the issue of acceleration was addressed in a long and complicated judgment by Judge Toulmin CMG QC.

Motherwell was a subcontractor to Micafil for the construction of an autoclave for the employer BICC under modified FIDIC Forms of contract. The autoclave was a large steel vessel used in the manufacture of high quality power cables. There were a large number of claims by Motherwell.

One of two claims was for acceleration costs for the work in relation to on site fabrication for hours worked by Motherwell's staff in excess of 46 hours for the period from 8 October 1998 to March 1999. Micafil raised the defence that a term of the contract provided that if unexpected delays and difficulties occurred, Motherwell was required to provide additional personnel at no extra cost at the request of Micafil in order to meet the required completion date. It was held that the delays and difficulties came within the definition of 'unexpected'. There was no dispute that Micafil constantly urged Motherwell to increase its resources to meet the requested completion date. Accordingly, Judge Seymour held that Motherwell could not succeed in recovering damages for this item.

The second acceleration claim is examined below.

Acceleration agreements

Some standard Forms make provision for the parties to agree to accelerate the works. Even without such clauses, it is always possible for the parties to agree to vary the contract to their mutual benefit. If the acceleration is necessary solely due to the contractor's default, it may be argued that the agreement to accelerate has no legal effect for lack of consideration, since the employer will simply obtain that which it is already contractually required to receive.

In *Lester Williams* v. *Roffey Brothers & Nicholls (Contractors) Ltd* [1989] 48 BLR 69 Roffey was the main contractor for the refurbishment of a block of flats known as Twynholm Mansions. Williams was a carpentry subcontractor providing labour for the roof and first and second fix to the flats with a total price of £20 000. The price was too low and a reasonable price should have been £23 783. This was further aggravated by Williams failing to supervise his men adequately, which reduced productivity. Williams therefore were experiencing financial difficulties.

In April 1989 Roffey agreed to pay Williams an additional £10 300 at the rate of £575 for each completed flat in order to have Williams continue with the works and complete on time. The carpentry work was on the critical path of Roffey's global operations so that failure by Williams to complete the work in accordance with the subcontract would lead to Roffey being liable for liquidated damages for delay under the main contract. The expected payments were not made by Roffey so that in May 1989 Williams ceased work. Roffey engaged other contractors to complete the work.

It was argued that the agreement to make additional payments was not legally binding on Roffey, since they had agreed to pay for work which Williams was already bound to carry out under the subcontract. There was no consideration.

There was some difficulty in finding consideration. It was held that in this case a benefit was derived from the agreement by each party and that was sufficient consideration for the promise to pay additional sums to be binding.

Although not referred to as such, it is suggested that the agreement was in the form of an acceleration agreement, the delay in this case having been caused by William's own default.

There may be considerable difficulties in evaluating the additional costs of acceleration and differentiating those costs from the costs of carrying out the works at the normal pace. Good records are vital, but it may be appropriate to simply take a broad approach.

In *Amec & Alfred McAlpine (Joint Venture)* v. *Cheshire County Council* [1999] BLR 303, Cheshire appointed the Joint Venture as contractor for construction of the Wilmslow and Handforth Bypass at Manchester under the ICE 5th Edition. By the end of 1994 there had been various delays for which the Joint Venture was not responsible. An acceleration agreement was entered into for which the Joint Venture was paid various sums for completing by 25 October 1995. Early in 1995 it became clear that there was likely to be another overrun and the Joint Venture was entitled to further extensions of time. An informal agreement was entered into in which the Joint Venture agreed to use its best endeavours to complete by 25 October 1995 and Cheshire would pay fair and reasonable recompense for the additional acceleration measures necessary. The date was achieved.

No specific method of valuation had been agreed and disputes arose as to the method of valuation, particularly because of delays for which Cheshire was not responsible and because of the difficulties of separating out the cost of work which the Joint Venture was already obliged to carry out under the original contract. A method of valuation was decided as a preliminary issue which was endorsed by the Court.

First, the Joint Venture's actual costs (X) were ascertained for the period of acceleration. The amount that the work carried out in the period of acceleration should have cost was evaluated (Y). The evaluation took into account all the events that had taken place before commencement of the acceleration period. The basic calculation of the acceleration costs was therefore $X - Y$. Further subtractions were made for factors and events for which the Joint Venture was liable (A). A further subtraction was the cost of variations ordered in the acceleration period (B) since these were included in X but not in Y. The *prima facie* entitlement was therefore $X - Y - (A + B)$ plus a reasonable amount for overheads and profit. This approach was adopted because of the difficulties of causation by analysis of particular items of work and of how time had been saved.

One issue before the Court was the adjustment to be made for payments received by the Joint Venture from their insurers for events during the acceleration period. The essential question was whether insurance payments should be taken into account in deciding a fair and reasonable remuneration. It was held that to allow a deduction would give Cheshire the full benefit of the insurance cover whereas it was primarily for the benefit of the Joint Venture and only incidentally Cheshire. Further, there would be no double recovery because the principles of indemnity which lie at the basis of insurance law would require the Joint Venture to be accountable to the insurers for the proceeds of amounts received from Cheshire of the relevant amounts.

Claims for acceleration

If the contract does not make completion by a particular date or time an obligation under the contract then the contractor will not be able to make a claim for the cost of acceleration measures. The only obligation will be to complete within a reasonable time which will involve optimization of the resources for greatest efficiency and productivity. In most standard forms the contractor has an obligation to complete by a particular date or within a specified period. Even with such an obligation, the contractor will have some difficulty in pursuing the additional costs of acceleration where the contract entitles him or her to an extension of time for the delays which have occurred. In the case where the extension of time provisions are not properly operated, the contractor may consider a constructive acceleration claim, but this is not without its difficulties.

If the contractor is ordered to accelerate in the mistaken belief that the delay is due to the contractor's default, whereas the delay was the responsibility of the employer under the contract, then the contractor may be entitled to the acceleration costs.

FIDIC 1999 1st Edition

Clause 3.1 of the Red and Yellow Forms provides that the engineer has no authority to amend the contract. There is no power therefore for the engineer to negotiate an acceleration agreement for the employer.

As expected with a modern contract, the contractor's obligation under FIDIC Forms is tied into a programme. Clause 8.1 of the Red, Yellow and Silver Forms requires the contractor to proceed with the works with due expedition and without delay. Clause 8.4 of the Red and clause 8.3 of the Yellow and Silver Forms requires the contractor to proceed in accordance with the programme, subject to its other obligations under the contract.

Clause 8.6 of the Red, Yellow and Silver Forms gives the engineer (employer under the Silver Form) power to instruct the contractor to submit a revised programme with revised methods to expedite progress and complete within the time for completion. The power arises if the actual progress is too slow to complete within the time for completion, or if the progress has fallen or will fall behind the programme. There is no such power if the cause is one of the matters which entitle the contractor to an extension of time. The contractor is required to adopt the revised methods which are stated to include increases in the working hours and/or increases in resources and/or goods. The revised methods are at the contractor's cost and risk and the contractor is liable for the employer's additional costs incurred in addition to any delay damages.

Clause 15.2(c)(i) of the Red and Yellow Forms and clause 15.2(c) of the Silver Form allows the employer to terminate the contract if the contractor fails to proceed with the works in accordance with clause 8, without reasonable excuse, and subject to notice.

ICE 7th Edition

Clause 2(1)(c) provides that the engineer has no authority to amend the contract or to relieve the contractor of any of its obligations under the contract, except as expressly stated in the contract. Clause 46(3) refers to acceleration agreements. The employer or the engineer may request the contractor to complete in less than the time or extended time for completion. If the contractor agrees, then special terms and conditions of payment are to be agreed before any acceleration measures are taken.

Clause 14(4) requires the contractor to submit a revised programme showing such modifications to the original programme as may be necessary to ensure completion of the works within the time for completion, if it appears to the engineer at any time that actual progress did not conform with the accepted programme.

Clause 46(1) gives the engineer power to notify the contractor that in his or her opinion the progress of the works is too slow to ensure substantial completion by the time for completion. On doing so, the contractor is required to take such steps as are necessary, and to which the engineer consents, to expedite progress so as to substantially complete the works by the time for completion. The power arises only if the reason for delay is not an event which entitles the contractor to an extension of time. The contractor is not entitled to any additional payment for taking the steps. Under clause 46(2) he may not unreasonably withhold permission to work on site at night or on Sundays if requested.

Clause 65(1) allows the employer to expel the contractor from site, if the engineer has certified in writing to the employer that despite previous warnings by the engineer in writing, in the engineer's opinion the contractor is failing to proceed with the works with due diligence.

ECC 2nd and 3rd Edition

Clause 30.1 requires the *Contractor* to do the work so that Completion is on or before the Completion Date.

Clause 32.2 requires the *Contractor* to issue revised programmes regularly and these are required to show actual progress achieved and the effect on the timing of the remaining work. The programme is also required to show how the *Contractor* plans to deal with any delays.

Clause 36.1 gives the *Project Manager* power to instruct the *Contractor* to submit a quotation for an acceleration to achieve completion before the Completion Date. The *Contractor* may submit a quotation which is required to comprise changes to the Prices and the Completion Date. Alternatively the Contractor may give reasons for not doing so. Clause 36.3 (Clause 36.4 Options E and F) provides that when the *Project Manager* accepts a quotation for acceleration, he changes the Completion Date (and Prices Options A to D) and he accepts the revised programme.

One of the secondary options is ECC 2nd Option Q and ECC 3rd Option X6 which provides for the *Contractor* to be paid a bonus for early completion at a specified rate from the date of Completion or take-over and the Completion Date.

Clause 60.1(9) provides that withholding of acceptance for a reason not stated in the contract is a compensation event, but expressly states that withholding acceptance of a quotation for acceleration is not a Compensation Event.

ECC 2nd clause 63.6 and ECC 3rd clause 63.7 provides that assessments of compensation events are based on the assumption that the Contractor reacts competently and promptly to the compensation event.

ECC 2nd clause 95.2 and ECC 3rd clause 91.2 provides that the Employer may terminate if the Project Manager has notified that the Contractor is in default by substantially failing to comply with his obligations and has not put right the default within four weeks of notification.

IChemE Red Book 4th Edition 2001

Clause 11.1 provides that the project manager has full authority to act on behalf of the purchaser in connection with the contract. An exception is clause 36.6; the project manager does not have power to issue a notice stating the purchaser's election to take over the plant, which the purchaser may do at any time.

Clause 13.1 requires the contractor to complete the construction of the plant within the periods stated in Schedule 11 (Times of Completion). The contractor is also required to use its reasonable endeavours to perform its obligations in accordance with the approved programme. Clause 13.4 gives the project manager power to require the contractor either to take steps as may be practicable in order to achieve the approved programme or to revise the approved programme. In addition, under clause 13.5 if the project manager decides that the rate of progress by the contractor will prejudice its ability to complete in accordance with clause 13.1, and this is due to a cause for which the contractor is responsible, the project manager has power to give notice to that effect. The contractor must then use its best endeavours to remedy the potential delay at the contractor's own cost. Such action does not affect the contractor's obligations under the contract (clause 13.8).

Clause 43.2 gives the project manager power to issue a notice that the contractor is in default by failing to proceed regularly and diligently with the works. If the contractor fails to commence and diligently pursue the rectification of such default within 14 days after receipt of the notice or at any time thereafter repeats the default, the purchaser may forthwith determine the employment of the contractor under the contract.

MF/1 (Rev 4) 2000

Clause 2.1 requires the engineer to carry out the duties specified in the contract. If the engineer is required to obtain prior specific approval of the purchaser before exercising his or her duties, by reason of the terms of appointment, then these are required to be set out in the special conditions.

Clause 13.1 requires the contractor to execute the works and carry out the tests on completion within the time for completion. Clause 14.1 requires the contractor to submit a programme for approval.

Under clause 14.5, the engineer has the power to order the contractor to revise the programme if the engineer decides that progress does not match the programme. The contractor is then required to revise the programme to show the modifications necessary to ensure completion of the works within the time for completion. If the modifications are required for reasons for which the contractor is not responsible, the cost of producing the revised programme is added to the contract price.

Under clause 14.6, the engineer has power to notify the contractor if the engineer decides that the rate of progress of the works is too slow to meet the time for completion and that this is not due to a circumstance for which the contractor is entitled to an extension of time. The contractor is then required to take such steps as may be necessary and as the engineer might approve to remedy or mitigate the likely delay, including revision of the programme. The contractor is not entitled to additional payment for taking such steps.

Clause 49.1 allows the purchaser to give the contractor 21 days' notice of its intention to terminate the contract, enter the site and expel the contractor, if despite previous warnings in writing from the engineer the contractor is failing to proceed with the works with due diligence.

JCT 2005 (SBC/Q)

Clause 3.10 requires the Contractor to comply forthwith will all instructions issued by the Architect/CA, but only in respect of matters which the Architect is expressly empowered by the Conditions to issue instructions. There are no express powers for the Architect/CA to instruct acceleration.

The Contractor's obligations may require him to take steps to arrange his resources to reduce delay but it is suggested that this falls short of an obligation to accelerate for the Contractor's obligations.

JCT 1998

The JCT 1998 Forms do not provide clear express provisions for the architect to require the contractor to accelerate in order to achieve the completion date. The contractor is required under clause 4.1.1 to comply forthwith will all instructions issued by the architect, but only in respect of matters on which the architect is expressly empowered by the conditions to issue instructions.

Under clause 23.1.1, the contractor is required to regularly and diligently proceed with the works and complete on or before the completion date. Clause 25 provides for the contractor to be granted extension of time for relevant events, but, importantly, clause 25.3.4.1 requires the contractor constantly to use its best endeavours to prevent delay in the progress of the works, however caused, and to prevent the completion of the works being delayed or further delayed beyond the completion date. Further, clause 25.3.4.2 requires the contractor to do all that may be reasonably required to the satisfaction of the architect to proceed with the works.

Clause 27.2.1.2 allows the architect to give notice of default if before the date of practical completion the contractor fails to proceed regularly and diligently with the works. If the contractor continues the default for 14 days from receipt of the notice, the employer may within 10 days after the expiry of 14 days give notice determining the employment of the contractor. If the employer's notice is not issued, then if the contractor repeats the default, then upon or within a reasonable time after such repetition, the employer may give notice determining the contractor's employment, taking effect on the date of receipt of the notice.

JCT 1998 with Contractor's Design

JCT 1998 with Contractor's Design is in similar terms to JCT 1998 and similar considerations apply, except that the employer administers the contract instead of the architect under JCT 1998.

JCT 1998 Prime Cost Contract

The JCT 1998 Prime Cost Contract is similar in structure to the JCT 1998 Form and similar considerations apply. There is no clear express provision for the architect to require the contractor to accelerate in order to achieve the completion date. The contractor is required under clause 3.3.2 to comply forthwith will all instructions issued by the architect, but subject to reasonable objection under clause 3.3.3 and subject to request for authority under clause 3.3.5.

Under clause 2.1.1, the contractor is required to regularly and diligently proceed with the works and complete on or before the completion date. Clause 2.5 provides for the contractor to be granted extension of time for relevant events, but, importantly, clause 2.5.4 requires the contractor constantly to use its best endeavours to prevent delay in the progress of the works, however caused. Further, clause 2.5.4 requires the contractor to do all that may be reasonably required to the satisfaction of the architect to proceed with the works.

Clause 7.2.1 allows the architect to give notice of default if before the date of practical completion the contractor fails to proceed regularly and diligently with the works. If the contractor continues the default for 14 days from receipt of the notice, the employer may within 10 days after the expiry of 14 days give notice determining the employment of the contractor. If the employer's notice is not issued, then if the contractor repeats the default then upon or within a reasonable time after such repetition, the employer may give notice determining the contractor's employment, taking effect on the date of receipt of the notice.

IFC 1998

The IFC 1998 is similar in structure to the JCT 1998 Form and similar considerations apply. There is no clear express provision for the architect to require the contractor to accelerate in order to achieve the completion date. Under clause 2.1, the contractor is required to regularly and diligently proceed with the works and complete on or before the completion date. Clause 2.3 provides for the contractor to be granted extension of time for specified events, but, importantly, the contractor is required constantly to use its best endeavours to prevent delay and to do all that may be reasonably required to the satisfaction of the architect to proceed with the works.

Clause 7.2.1 allows the architect to give notice of default if before the date of practical completion the contractor fails to proceed regularly and diligently with the works. If the contractor continues the default for 14 days from receipt of the notice, the employer may within 10 days after the expiry of 14 days give notice determining the employment of the contractor. If the employer's notice is not issued, then if the contractor repeats the default then upon or within a reasonable time after such repetition, the employer may give notice determining the contractor's employment, taking effect on the date of receipt of the notice.

JCT 1998 Minor Works

The contractor is required to forthwith carry out the instructions of the architect under clause 3.5. There is no clear express provision for the architect to require the contractor to accelerate in order to achieve the completion date. Clause 1.1 requires the contractor to carry out and complete the works with due diligence. Clause 7.2.1 allows the architect to give notice of default if the contractor fails to proceed diligently with the works. If the contractor continues the default for 7 days from receipt of the notice, the employer may give further notice determining the employment of the contractor.

4.1 Administration of claims
4.2 Litigation
4.3 Arbitration
4.4 Adjudication
4.5 Alternative dispute resolution

CECA Blue Form 1998

Clause 7(2) gives the contractor under the subcontract the same powers as the engineer under the main contract, which under the ICE 7th Edition will include the powers under clause 46 for acceleration. Clause 7(1) requires the subcontractor to comply with all instructions and decisions of the engineer which are notified and confirmed in writing by the contractor.

Clause 6(1) requires the subcontractor to proceed with the subcontract works with due diligence and without delay except as expressly sanctioned or ordered by the contractor or as may be wholly beyond the control of the subcontractor. The subcontractor is required to complete within the period for completion specified in the Third Schedule.

Clause 17(1)(b) allows the contractor by written notice to determine the subcontractor's employment if the subcontractor fails to proceed with due diligence after being required in writing to do so by the contractor.

DOM/1

Clause 11.1 requires the subcontractor to complete the subcontract works and reasonable in accordance with the progress of the works. The subcontractor's entitlement to extension of time is subject to the proviso in clause 11.8 which requires the subcontractor to use its best endeavours to prevent delay in the progress of the subcontract works, however caused, and to prevent any such delay resulting in the completion of the subcontract works being delayed beyond the period for completion. The subcontractor is required to do all that may be reasonably required to the satisfaction of the architect and the contractor to proceed with the subcontract works.

Clause 29.2.1.2 allows the contractor to give notice of default if before the date of practical completion the subcontractor fails to proceed regularly and diligently with the subcontract works. If the contractor continues the default for 10 days from receipt of the notice, the contractor may within 10 days after the expiry of 10 days give notice determining the employment of the subcontractor. If the contractor's notice is not issued, then if the subcontractor repeats the default then upon or within a reasonable time after such repetition, the contractor may give notice determining the contractor's employment, taking effect on the date of receipt of the notice.

3.10 Mitigation of delay

The issue of the contractor's right or obligation to reduce the effect of qualifying delays may arise in three ways.

(a) The contractor may be considered to have a right to choose how to deal with a qualifying delay and whether for instance to accelerate or not and to recovery on the basis of this right.
(b) The contractor may be considered to be entitled to extension of time and any associated loss only to the extent that it has mitigated the effect of the delays.
(c) The contractor may be under an obligation to progress the works including an express obligation to mitigate delays and the failure to do so prevents remedies of extension of time and associated losses and may make the contractor liable in damages.

These three possibilities are examined below. Since the issue of the contractor's right to choose is a positive aspect of mitigation it has been examined below with mitigation.

Mitigation of loss

The main remedy for breach of contract is damages. The measure of damages does not include losses caused by the injured party's failure to take reasonable steps to mitigate the loss. There are three rules relating to mitigation for breach of contract. First, an injured party cannot recover damages for a loss which could have been avoided by reasonable steps. The injured party is not required to do anything other than in the ordinary course of business. Second, if the injured party takes steps which it could not reasonably have been required to do, and avoids the potential loss it cannot recover the potential loss as damages. Thirdly, the injured party may recover its loss or expense in taking reasonable steps to mitigate the loss due to breach of contract. This is so even if the mitigation is unsuccessful and even increases the loss *British Westinghouse* v. *Underground Electric Railway* [1912].

Although the injured party must act with the other party's as well as its own interests in mind, it is only required to act reasonably and the standard of reasonableness is not high in view of the fact that the other party is the wrongdoer: *Dimond* v. *Lovell* [1999] approving the statement in McGregor on damages 16th Edition para 322.

In *White and Carter (Councils) Ltd* v. *McGregor* [1962] it was held that the rules of mitigation do not apply in the situation where the injured party has a legitimate interest in performing the contract rather than stopping and claiming damages. The injured party is not required in that case to discontinue performance even though the employer may no longer require him or her to continue.

Although commonly referred to as a 'duty to mitigate' the loss, it is not a duty but a principle adopted in the measure of loss: *The Soholt* [1983]. The onus of proving the failure to mitigate rests on the party alleging the failure: *Garmac Grain Co.* v. *Faire and Fairclough* [1968].

Mitigation of delay

The remedy of extension of time is a contractual remedy for acts of prevention and breach of contract by the employer and for events at the risk of the employer. It may therefore be thought that if the remedy of extension of time is based on causation, the principles referred to as the 'duty to mitigate' should apply. It is suggested that there are two situations to consider, first when the contractor responds positively and the second when the contractor takes no positive action.

In the first situation the contractor may react to the qualifying delay by making changes to its methods of working, or sequence of working, or even accelerate the work. The issue then is whether it is entitled to recover the loss incurred by this reaction and that depends on whether or not the contractor has a right to react as it did. This issue has been examined below. It is suggested that subject to the express terms of the contract, the contractor has no right to accelerate and is not entitled to recover additional costs incurred in acceleration measures to mitigate the effect of qualifying delays without an instruction from the employer. Since many contracts contain provisions for the grant of extensions of time and express terms for agreement of acceleration measures, the unilateral action by the contractor in giving priority to the fixed date for completion over the cost of working efficiently cannot bind the employer in those contracts. It is suggested that this interpretation can be expressed in terms of the reasonableness in mitigation. It is not reasonable when there are sufficient contractual remedies for the contractor to decide to accelerate the works. This interpretation must be examined in the context of express obligations to progress the works.

In the second situation the contractor may not react to the qualifying delay and the issue then is what minimum measures it is required to take in order to mitigate the effects of the qualifying delay and if it fails to take those measures whether this affects the extent of the contractor's entitlement to extension of time. It is suggested that the rules of mitigation do not generally apply to construction contracts in relation to time where there are extension of time provisions.

In *Ascon Contracting Limited* v. *Alfred McAlpine Construction Isle of Man Limited* [1999], HH Judge Hicks QC held that it was difficult to see how there could be any room for the doctrine of mitigation in relation to damage suffered by reason of the employer's culpable delay in the face of express contractual machinery for dealing with the situation of extension of time and reimbursement of loss and expense. This decision was made in relation a submission that the contractor should have incurred additional expenditure in accelerating the works to overcome the delay.

In *Motherwell Bridge Construction Limited* v. *Micafil Vakuumtecchnik* (2002) TCC 81 ConLR 44 the claim for acceleration costs of site works failed. There was a term of the contract that if unexpected delays and difficulties occurred, Motherwell was required to provide additional personnel at no extra cost at the request of Micafil in order to meet the required completion date.

Obligation to mitigate delay or to progress the works

It is suggested that although the rules of mitigation do not generally apply to construction contracts with extension of time provisions and provision for recovery of time-related losses, the contractor will have some obligation to progress the works which will involve an aspect of management of resources and planning of activities in the circumstances of actual events. Although a matter of interpretation of the terms of the contract, it is suggested that such an obligation will usually be intended by the parties to apply equally to events causing qualifying delays. The obligation to progress the works may, however, require the contractor to take some positive action, and a failure to do so may sound in damages measured by the liquidated damages for additional periods of over-run which could have been avoided but for the breach. Since the obligation to proceed 'regularly and diligently' means to proceed continuously, industriously and efficiently with appropriate physical resources so as to progress the works steadily towards completion, it is suggested this will include managing the effects of the delay.

It is suggested that, faced with delay, the contractor will not be able to claim extension of time for delays which could have been avoided by changing the planned sequences of working, unless the sequence is a specified sequence, so that the contractor could carry on with other work as best it could. It cannot be considered reasonable that a contractor should maintain a sequence of working, doing no further work and incurring delay when by changing the sequence it would be able to open up other areas of work and progress some of the works. It is suggested that the contractor is not required to take steps which would reduce productivity such as acceleration measures, and increase direct costs by procuring additional plant or materials. It will usually be required to properly manage the progress of the works, including terms as to proceeding regularly and diligently as examined above. The obligation will apply to the consequences of the delay.

In *DSND Subsea Ltd* v. *Petroleum Geo-Srevices ASA and PGS Offshore Technology AS* [2000] the contractor was under an obligation to carry out and complete the work involving deep-sea diving in an expeditious and timely manner. The sequence of the phases of work was specified in a programme incorporated in a Memorandum of

Agreement agreed by the parties as the way to deal with delays that had occurred. There were further delays. It was held that the obligation to progress the works in an expeditious and timely manner did not impose an obligation on the contractor to carry out the work in a different sequence and particularly to carry out deep-sea diving work before all other work specified to be carried out (the riser installations), had been completed. The contractor had carried out a significant amount of diving before the installation of the risers, but that was not something he was obliged to do. Since plant was on site it made sense for it to do some diving work as and when it was able to do so, but there was no obligation to do so.

It is suggested also that if the entitlement to extension of time is on the basis of what is fair and reasonable, that this must include consideration of the positive steps taken by the contractor to reduce the consequences of the delay, and the steps which could have been taken, without the expenditure of substantial sums.

It is because of these difficulties that many standard forms require the contractor to take steps to reduce the effects of delays, to mitigate the delay, but the extent of the obligation differs. Failure to comply with the obligation may reduce or even extinguish the contractor's entitlement to extension of time.

The most onerous obligation is that the contractor must use its best endeavours to reduce the delay. It is suggested that the obligation does not require the contractor to expend substantial sums to reduce the delay. In *Midland Land Reclamation Ltd* v. *Warren Energy Ltd* [1997] it was held that the best endeavours obligation was not the next best thing to an absolute obligation or guarantee. In *Terrell* v. *Mabie Todd and Co.* [1952] it was held that a best endeavours obligation only required a party to do what was commercially practicable and what it could reasonably do in the circumstances.

It is suggested that an express obligation to proceed regularly and diligently will include applying resources in such a way as to reduce the consequences of a qualifying delay, so that work is carried out efficiently. It is suggested that the reasonable steps to be taken by the contractor when faced with a qualifying delay is to provide the appropriate notices required by the contract together with the details required or requested by the A/E. It is also suggested that where a contractor takes reasonable steps to mitigate the effects of the delay and succeeds in reducing the effect of the delay, then its entitlement to extension of time is reduced accordingly. If the entitlement is based on actual delay evaluated retrospectively and if the contractor is entitled to recover losses due to the delay, then it is suggested that losses incurred in taking reasonable steps are part of the recoverable loss. If, on the other hand, the contractor is awarded an extension of time prospectively, there is then no reason to mitigate the delay, since it has been granted the compensation under the contract. Whether or not the contractor would be entitled in that case to recover its loss due to the delay depends upon the terms of the contract.

FIDIC 1999 Forms

Clause 8.1 of the FIDIC Red, Yellow and Silver Books 1999 requires the contractor to proceed with the works with due expedition and without delay. The determination of the extension of time is required under clause 3.5 to be a fair determination taking due regard of all relevant circumstances. It is suggested that this requires account to be taken of the steps which could reasonably have been taken by the contractor to mitigate the delay. In this regard, the contractor is also required, under clause 8.3, to promptly give notice of specific probable future events or circumstances which may delay execution of the works.

ICE 6th and 7th Edition

Clause 41(2) of the ICE 6th and 7th Edition requires the contractor to proceed with the works with due expedition and without delay in accordance with the contract. If part of the delay has been caused by the contractor's failure to comply with clause 41(2) then it is suggested the engineer can take that into account in his or her assessment.

ECC 2nd and 3rd Edition

ECC 2nd clause 63.6 and ECC 3rd clause 63.7 provides that any assessment for the revised completion date is to be based on the assumption that the contractor reacts competently and promptly to compensation events.

MF/1 Rev 4

Clause 33.3 MF/1 Rev 4 requires the contractor to consult with the engineer in order to determine the steps (if any) which can be taken to overcome or minimize the actual or anticipated delay.

IChemE Red Book 4th Edition 2001

Clause 14.3 IChemE Red Book requires both parties to the contract at all times to use all reasonable endeavours to minimize any delay in performance of their obligations under the contract, whatever may be the cause of such delay.

JCT 2005 (SBc/Q)

Clause 2.28.6.1 requires the Contractor to constantly use his best endeavours to prevent delay in the progress of the Works or any Section, however caused, and to prevent the completion of the Works or Section being delayed or further delayed beyond the relevant Completion Date.

JCT 1998

Clause 25.3.4 JCT 1998 requires the contractor to constantly use its best endeavours to prevent delay in the progress of the works.

3.11 Particulars

Many standard forms require the contractor to submit to the A/E particulars of the events complained of and the delays. Some standard forms require the A/E to ascertain the delay caused and the extension of time due, but in other forms the contractor is required to provide some analysis as part of the particulars submitted. Similarly, in coercive proceedings such as litigation or arbitration, the claimant is required to plead its case with particulars of the events and delays and, in a subsequent forum, to prove its case. It is suggested that in both processes a distinction needs to be made between the particularization required to be submitted to establish a right to have the claim considered, and the ascertainment or proof itself. Whether sufficient particulars have been submitted is solely a question of fact and degree.

The contractor must set out a proper particularized case of those events complained of, such as late information or instructions, which gave rise to the delay and the reasons why they did so. This does not mean that the contractor must at that stage put a period of delay against each event, unless the contract so requires, but some indication must be given as to those matters which caused substantial delay and why that should have been the case. The basic purpose of particularization and pleadings is to enable the A/E or other party to know what case is being made in sufficient detail to enable a proper answer or ascertainment to be made. The particulars must identify the events which give rise to the delay and which of these events were the fault of the employer.

It is suggested that proper particularization of an event causing delay requires at least:

(a) particulars of the event describing the factors necessary for the event to be a qualifying event either under the contract or as a breach of contract. So, for instance, if the complaint is that the specification was inadequate, the description and grounds of the inadequacy. If the complaint is that the information or instruction was late, then the particulars must identify when the information ought to have been given and when it was given
(b) demonstration of the link between the particular event and the particular trade or operation to show the nature of the work which was delayed and to show any ways in which the event caused or contributed to the delay
(c) the dates between which the delay occurred and whether such delay was continuous or intermittent.

3.12 Cause and effect

Causation is an issue of fact. A common-sense approach is required involving evidence from which it can be inferred that, more likely than not, the delay was caused by the event complained of, *BHP Billiton Petroleum Ltd* v. *Dalmine SpA* [2003] EWCA Civ 170.

The usual approach is to carry out a retrospective and dissectional reconstruction of events if appropriate day by day, and/or drawing by drawing, and/or information by information to show that the event complained of delayed or disrupted progress of the works. It will usually be necessary to examine events in addition to those complained of, if only to demonstrate that they could not have caused the delay.

The type of evidence and the extent of analysis required will depend on the particular circumstances, but will involve some or all of the following:

(a) a programme showing the planned construction process
(b) an as-built programme showing actual progress for the particular part of the work delayed
(c) documentary evidence of dates and progress such as diary extracts, progress reports, progress programmes, correspondence, photographs, video evidence, etc.
(d) network analysis normally showing construction logic links and identifying the delays
(e) evidence of witnesses and experts.

3.13 Concurrent delays

One particular problem in the analysis of cause and effect is the situation which arises when two events contribute to the same delay. So, for instance, the situation may be that the contractor has been delayed due to variations or late issue of information, both of which are the responsibility of the employer, but some if not all of the delay would have occurred in any event due to other factors, either neutral events or breach of contract which are the responsibility of the contractor.

Whether or not the contractor is entitled to an extension of time depends on the construction of the extension of time clause.

Several cases show the modern development of the interpretation of extension of time clauses under the JCT 80 Standard Form in which extensions of time may be due only for 'Relevant Events' defined by the form.

In the case of *Balfour Beatty Building Ltd* v. *Chestermount Properties Ltd* (1993) 62BLR12 the Architect issued a variation (a Relevant Event) after the construction of the office block should have been completed and during a period of contractor's culpable delay. Was it the 'gross' method – an extension of time up to the date when the contractor completed the varied work? Was it instead the 'net' method. It was held to be the 'net' method, as this was fair and reasonable as required by the contract, an extension of time representing the additional delay caused by the Relevant Event. The 'net' approach left open difficult questions of causation, particularly where the Relevant Event could have been avoided if the contractor had not been late in the first place.

In the case of *Henry Boot Construction (UK) Ltd* v. *Malmaiston Hotel (Manchester) Ltd* (1999) 70 ConLR 32 completion of construction of the hotel was late. Although the Architect had granted some extensions of time for Relevant, this did not account for all the delay. Malmaiston therefore deducted £250 000 in liquidated damages. The parties agreed that if two events caused delay to completion and only one was the responsibility of the Employer, then the contractor was nonetheless entitled to an extension of time. The issue was how should the Architect establish whether an event was the cause of delay. It was held as a matter of interpretation of JCT 80 that the Architect was permitted to consider the effect of all events to establish whether the Relevant Event caused any delay to completion, (i.e. that it was on the critical path), or whether another event actually caused the delay. This was the first time that the UK courts accepted the principle that the contractor is entitled to an extension of time in the situation of concurrent delays. Whether the principle applies to other forms of contract other than JCT 80 is yet to be decided.

In the case of *The Royal Brompton Hospital NHS Trust* v. *Watkins Gray International* (Dec 2000) the proper approach to the asessment of extensions of time for concurrent was considered. It was held that where a Relevant Event occurs during a period of contractor's culpable delay, which does not cause any further delay, then this is not a case of a concurrent event. No extension of time is due. On the other hand, where two events happen before either has caused delay and each would on its own have caused delay, then this is a real concurrency. If one of the events is a Relevant Event then the contractor is entitled to an extension of time. The decision confirmed and emphasised the need for proper analysis of the actual causes of delay. It was recognised that different methods may give different results. The case left open the development of methods of analysis.

In *Motherwell Bridge Construction Limited* v. *Micafil AG* [2002] HH Judge Toulmin QC examined concurrent delay and referred to and adopted the approach of Dyson J in *Henry Boot Construction (UK) Ltd* v. *Malmaison Hotel (Manchester) Ltd* [1999] which in turn adopted the approach in *Balfour Beatty Ltd* v. *Chestermount Properties* [1993] in relation to FIDIC conditions.

In some standard forms, the clause determines the matter of causation for concurrent causes of the same delay. Where it does not, the law on causation in contract is not clear. Until recently it was considered that the courts did not have inherent jurisdiction to apportion liability for truly concurrent causes, and so various theories have been adopted to establish liability.

The dominant cause approach avoids the issue of concurrency and is difficult to apply in delay situations. Nonethless this is an important part of the process of analysis. A close examination of *H Fairweather and Co Ltd* v. *London Borough of Wandsworth* (1987) 39 BLR 106, shows that the case is not authority against the dominant cause theory.

In *Great Eastern Hotel Company Ltd* v. *John Laing Construction Ltd* [2005] EWHC 181 (TCC) it was argued that if it was established that some breach or breaches caused delay to an identified critical path, of itself that cannot establish the necessary causal link citing in support *Galoo Limited* v. *Bright Grahame Murray* [1995] 1 All Eng 16 and the dicta of Glidewell LJ and *Quin* v. *Burch Brothers (Builders) Limited* [1968] 2 All Eng 283 and the Australian case *Alexander* v. *Cambridge Credit Corporation* [1987] 9 NSWLR.

HH David Wilcox observed that in the cited cases the courts were considering the consequences of breach and were careful to distinguish between the consequence of merely giving rise to the opportunity or occasion of loss as opposed to causing it.

HH David Wilcox held that if a breach of contract is one of the causes both co-operating and of equal efficiency in causing loss to the Claimant the party responsible for breach is liable to the Claimant for that loss.

He held that the contract breaker was liable as long as his breach was an 'effective cause' of his loss and referred to *Heskell* v. *Continental Express Limited* [1995] 1 All Eng 1033.

He held that the Court need not choose which cause was the more effective. He referred to the approach of Devlin J in *Heskell* which was adopted by Steyn J (as he then was) in *Banque Keyser SA* v. *Skandia* [1991] QB and accepted by the Court of Appeal.

In the important part of the judgment in relation to the issue of concurrent delay, Judge Wilcox emphasised the importance of the terms of the contract. He held that each claim or group of claims must be examined on their own facts and in the context of the specific contractual provisions such as variations which may give rise to a consideration of the comparative potency of causal events and to apportionment.

He held that in the absence of such provision the appropriate test was that if a party proved the breach and the proven breach materially contributed to the loss then it could recover the whole loss, even if there is another effective contributory cause provided that there is no double recovery. This approach caused no injustice, because the Defendant who pays is protected, because it was open to him to seek contribution from any other contract breaker.

He held that on the basis of the evidence that the dominant cause of Trade Contractor delay was in fact the delay to the project caused by Laing's proven breaches.

In the Scots case of *John Doyle Construction Ltd* v. *Laing Management Ltd* [2004] it was stated that in determining what is a significant cause, the 'dominant cause' approach is of relevance. If an event or events for which the employer is responsible can be described as the dominant cause of an item of loss, that will be sufficient to establish liability, notwithstanding the existence of other causes that are to some degree at least concurrent.

It was held that if an item of loss results from concurrent causes, and one of those causes can be identified as the proximate or dominant cause of the loss, it will be treated as the operative cause, an the person responsible for it will be responsible for the loss.

The dominant cause theory is to be distinguished from the situation where one event caused by one of the parties influences the actions of the other party. So, for example, if the contractor is aware that the works are to be delayed due to matters which are the responsibility of the employer, it may delay the delivery of certain materials or the commencement of part of the works as part of efficient planning of the works. A retrospective analysis may show superficially concurrent causes of delay, whereas one event has, in fact, set the circumstances for the second event.

It now appears that where a defect was caused equally by the default of the plaintiff and the defendant and where each default was insufficient to cause the defect in the absence of the other, then the court is entitled to ascertain and exercise the jurisdiction to apportion where required to do justice. This is an example of 'composite' or 'compound' causation.

In *W Lamb Ltd* v. *J Jarvis & Sons plc* (1998) ORB the plaintiff subcontractor installed pipework to a petrol filling station for the contractor defendant. The pipework leaked and was replaced. The matter to be decided as a preliminary issue was whether the failure was caused by the faulty workmanship on the pipework by the plaintiff or acts or omissions in the construction of the concrete supports by the defendant. It was found that failure was caused equally by the plaintiff and the defendant. The defaults were each insufficient to cause the leaks in the absence of the other. It was held that following *Tennant Radiant Heat Ltd* v. *Warrington Development Corporation* (1988) 1 EGLR 41 that the court was entitled to ascertain and exercise the jurisdiction to apportion where required to do justice.

If this jurisdiction applies to the situation where each event would have caused the same delay in the absence of the other event, then apportionment will assist in resolving the problem of concurrent causes. In the Scots case of *John Doyle Construction Ltd* v. *Laing Management Ltd* [2004] it was stated that if it cannot be said that events the employer's responsibility are the dominant cause of the loss, it may be possible to apportion the loss between the causes. The events for which the employer is responsible should be a material cause of the loss.

It was held that apportionment of loss between the different causes is possible where the causes of the loss are truly concurrent, in the sense that both operate together at the same time to produce a single consequence, e.g. late provision of information during a period bad weather might have prevented work for a part of the time. In such a case responsibility for the loss can be apportioned between the two causes, according to their relative significance.

3.14 Method of analysis

There are many methods of analysis to demonstrate entitlement to an extension of time. The choice of the appropriate analysis depends on the evidence available, the existing programme evidence, the particular circumstances and the terms of the extension of time clause. Whatever method is chosen, it should be sufficiently detailed to explain the situation convincingly but not so complex as to be difficult to understand.

In practice the method of analysis is a means of demonstrating causation and inevitably will be theoretical based on disputed facts and opinion. There are indeed only two methods, of which there are different variants and hybrids given different names (impact as-planned, as-planned v. as-built, as-built but-for, collapsed as-built, time impact method, window slice method).

The method of analysis using an as-built programme has the advantage that it creates an accurate record of actual progress if based on traceable evidence. In practice, it is necessary to focus the analysis on key areas of delay to avoid unnecessary expense. This makes the method iterative. It is not usually sufficient to simply compare the as-built programme to the planned programme without verifying the planned programme. It is necessary instead to prepare a construction logic which explains the sequence of events and the reasons for the actions taken and the delay caused.

The method of analysis using the time impact or snapshot approach requires the base programme initially adopted by the contractor to be updated for each event. The update requires the construction logic to be examined for any change with new activities created if necessary and the durations re-evaluated. This update may create a new critical path and an extended period. The updated programme is then updated for the next event and so on. If data is not available at the time of the delay then another method needs to be used. The advantage of this method is that it records the unfolding of events and places actions in context.

Whatever method is adopted, it is necessary that the expert preparing the programme understands the construction issues involved as well as the limitations of the particular programme software and the method. The expert must also be able to explain the analysis to allow the judge, arbitrator, adjudicator or A/E to understand.

4 LIQUIDATED DAMAGES

4.1 Agreed value of damages

Damages is one of the most important remedies for breach of contract in the construction industry, but requires two significant legal hurdles to be overcome before there can be recovery. First the injured party must prove he has incurred actual loss as a result of the breach. Secondly the loss must not fall foul of the legal rules as to remoteness; *Hadley* v. *Baxendale* (1854); *Victoria Laundry (Windsor) Ltd.* v. *Newman Industries Ltd* (1949).

These rules prevent recovery of losses which arise from special circumstances, unless the circumstances are known and there is an implied acceptance that the contract was directed to these special circumstances. In practice this means that the injured party is faced with expensive legal action if he is to obtain compensation.

Liquidated damages (LD) clauses in a contract avoid these legal hurdles. Just as the parties at the time of contracting can agree their obligations under the contract, so they can agree the amount of compensation to be paid if the particular obligation is not performed. There is no need to look for an implied agreement to compensate for losses due to special circumstances. The liquidated damages clause is an express agreement, so compensation is payable whether or not the special circumstances which make the loss likely are known. In other words the parties are not bound by the rules as to remoteness for the particular breach specified; *Robophone Facilities Ltd* v. *Blank* (1966) 3 All ER 128 CA. By this mechanism of LD clauses, disputes are either avoided altogether or if there is a dispute the cost involved in proving damages is avoided.

There is no reason in public policy why the parties should not enter into an arrangement under which each know where they stand in the event of a breach and can avoid the heavy costs of proving the actual damage *Robophone Facilities Limited* v. *Blank* [1966] 1 WLR 1428.

Particularly in building and engineering contracts it is to the parties advantage that they should be able to know with a reasonable degree of certainty the extent of their liability and the risk which they run as a result of entering into the contract. Liquidated damages provisions enable the Employer to know the extent to which he is protected in the event of the contractor failing to perform his obligations *Philips Hong Kong Ltd* v. *The Attorney General of Hong Kong* (1993).

A liquidated damages provision is commercially very attractive to both parties, since it allows the Contractor to know when he tenders precisely the level of his liability for the risk inherent in the particular obligation and hence may allow the contractor to reduce the level of his bid. The reduced bid which may result from the adoption of liquidated damages clauses benefits the purchaser, providing the extent of the risk which materialises is not greater than allowed for in the liquidated damages clause. If so, then the liquidated damages clause will have had the effect of passing part of the risk of the particular event from the contractor to the purchaser.

It cannot be assumed that the LD rate is the measure of the full loss likely to be suffered. The parties may may deliberately have agreed to limit the financial loss recoverable *Bath and North East Somerset District Council* v. *Mowlem plc* [2004] EWCA Civ 115.

The parties might even agree that liquidated damages as '£ nil' per week as decided in *Temloc* v. *Errill Properties Ltd* (1987) 39 BLR 30 (CA).

If a contractor wishes to pass to a subcontractor the risk under the main contract of paying liquidated damages as a result of the subcontractor's breach, he may choose to do so either by a subcontract liquidated damages clause or by giving the subcontractor notice of the provisions of the main contract. In the latter approach, the rules of remoteness above will require the Subcontractor to acknowledge that any breach by the Subcontractor which may result in breaches by the Contractor under the main contract and other contracts made in connection with the main works, and that the consequent damages, including liquidated damages payable, are within the contemplation of the parties.

4.2 Types of LD clauses

Conceptually an LD clause could apply to any type of breach of contract, either a single event or a continuing breach. If the clause does not relate to a breach of contract then it simply operates to allocate risk and/or determine the measure of payment *Exports Credits Guarantee Department* v. *Universal Oil Products Company* [1983] 23 BLR 106 HL.

Failure to complete by a specified date is the most common breach of contract for which LD clauses are used in the construction industry.

The damages are usually expressed in Standard Forms as an amount per day or per week of delay to completion to be paid by the Contractor to the Purchaser. In some commercial developments there may be a critical delay beyond which the damages change – such as a critical date for supply or the date for opening a development. In such cases a limit is usually stated for the overall amount of LDs or another rate is stated to apply after the critical date. It may be necessary in specific situations to stipulate a maximum delay beyond which the LD provision is no longer an adequate remedy and the contractor's performance is considered and agreed as no performance at all.

If sections of the works have different importance to the Purchaser, sectional completion dates should be stated with different LD rates together with a rate for the remainder of the works.

Standard Forms usually allow the Purchaser the flexibility to take over parts of the works. The entitlement to LDs should be modified in that case to reflect the reduced damages for any delay caused by the contractor, so that the right to LDs for the remainder of the works is not lost.

FIDIC 1999 Forms 1st Edition

Clause 8.7 Red, Yellow and Silver provides for delay damages for the Contractor's failure to comply with clause 8.2 which requires the Contractor to complete the whole of the Works and each Section within the Time for Completion for the Works or Section. There does not appear to be provision for stating delay damages for each Section.

The rate of delay damages is stated in the Appendix (Red and Yellow) or the Particular Conditions (Silver) as a rate per day of delay and there is provision for stating a maximum amount of delay damages. The Appendix (Red and Yellow) requires a percentage of the Accepted Contract Amount to be stated for both the delay damages and the limit. Clause 14.15(b) (Red and Yellow) provides that the payment of damages are to be made in the currencies and proportions stated in the Appendix to Tender, which states that the proportions are those in which the Contract Price is payable.

Clause 8.2 Red, Yellow and Silver expressly states that the delay damages are the only damages due from the Contractor for default under clause 8.2 except in the event of termination under clause 15.2.

The mechanism of liquidated damages is built into the form and the Appendix or Particular Conditions are therefore required to be completed and must not be left blank.

The Employer's right in relation to delay damages is subject to clause 2.5 (Red and Yellow) which specifies the notice of claim required to be provided by the Employer.

ICE 7th Edition

Clause 47(1) provides for liquidated damages where the whole of the Works is not divided into Sections. The clause requires a sum to be stated in the Appendix to the Form of Tender. The Employer has no discretion – liquidated damages are built into the ICE 7th form. Clause 47(4)(b) states that if no sum is stated in the Appendix or a sum of 'nil' is inserted then 'to that extent damages are not payable'. It is suggested on an interpretation of the Contract as a whole that this does not mean that the LD provisions do not apply but that the level of LDs is nil.

Clause 47(1) states that the sum stated represents the Employer‘s genuine pre-estimate of the damages likely to be suffered if the whole of the Works is delayed. This is required to be expressed as a sum per week or per day. The sum is required to be the genuine pre-estimate, not a lesser sum.

Clause 47(2) repeats the provisions in clause 47(1), but for sectional completion.

Clause 47(4)(a) provides that a limit may be stated in the Appendix, but if not then liquidated damages without limit shall apply.

ICE 7th Edition now makes clear that it is the Contractor's failure to achieve 'substantial completion' within the time prescribed which triggers the entitlement to liquidated damages and not failure to complete as it was under ICE 6th Edition.

Clause 47(5) entitles the Employer to deduct LD‘s or requires the Contractor to pay LD‘s when they become due and the amounts become due by virtue of clauses 47(1)(b) or 47(2)(b). The Employer is required to repay that proportion of LD‘s already deducted, which are no longer due following an extension of time or further extension of time. The clause also requires the Employer to pay interest at the rate in Clause 60(7). ICE 7th Edition now requires the interest to be compounded monthly.

Clause 47(6) provides for the effect of certain events which arise after liquidated damages become payable, that is when a contractor is in a period of culpable delay. The events are:

- the Engineer orders a variation under clause 51
- adverse physical conditions or artificial obstructions within the meaning of clause 12 are encountered
- any other situation outside the Contractor's control arises.

Clause 47(6)(b) provides that if the Engineer is of the opinion that these will result in further delay to that part of the Works, then the Employer's further entitlement to liquidated damages is suspended until the Engineer notifies that the further delay has come to an end. It is now clear in ICE 7th Edition that any liquidated damages already deducted or paid can be retained by the Employer, but subject to any subsequent or final review of the circumstances causing delay. It is suggested that it is intended that if an extension of time is granted for the events then the value of the liquidated damages due will be affected. The clause does not deal with the inter-relation between the suspension of liquidated damages and the extension of time provisions. The term 'any other situation outside the Contractor's control' is not one of the events listed in clause 44 entitling a contractor to an extension of time. It would appear therefore that the extension of time entitlement and the suspension of liquidated damages are separate and cumulative entitlements. It is not clear whether the liquidated damages are simply no longer operated or postponed until either notification by the Engineer under clause 47(6)(b) or final review of the circumstances causing delay.

NEC3

Option X7 provides for delay damages at the rate stated in the Contract Data from the Completion Date to the earlier of Completion or the date when the Employer takes over the works. The Contract Data Part One provided by the Employer specifies delay damages per day. Option X7 requires the Contractor to pay the delay damages. Clause 50.2 provides that the amount due (at each assessment date) is to be reduced by the amount to be paid by the Contractor.

Option X7 also provides that if the Completion Date is changed to a later date after delay damages have been paid, then the Employer repays the overpayment of damages with interest. The date of repayment is stated to be an assessment date. Clause 51.4 provides that interest is calculated on a daily basis at the interest rate and is compounded annually.

Option X7 also provides for adjustment of the delay damages if part of the works is taken over by the Employer before Completion, based on a proportion of the benefit to the Employer assessed by the Project Manager.

Option X5 provides for section of the works and Contract Data Part One allows the section to be described, the completion date for each section to be specified and the amount of delay damages for each section to be specified.

There appears to be no provision in NEC3 to limit the overall amount of delay damages. Option X18 specifies various limits on liability, but excluded matters which include delay damages.

JCT 2005 (SBC/Q)

Clause 2.32 allows the Employer to withhold or deduct liquidated damages or to require the Contractor to pay liquidated damages at the rate stated in the Contract Particulars. The Contract Particulars requires a rate and the period for the rate to be inserted.

The sixth recital (if not deleted) states that the division of the Works into Sections is shown in the Contract Bills and/or the Contract Drawings or in such other documents as are identified in the Contract Particulars. The Contract Particulars allows the Dates for Completion of Sections to be specified together with the rate of liquidated damages for each Section.

Clause 2.32.3 provides that if a later Completion Date is fixed or stated then the Employer pays or repays to the Contractor any amounts recovered, allowed or paid under clause 2.32 for the period up to that later Completion Date. There appears to be no provision for payment of interest, although clause 4.23 allows recovery of loss and expense. If the events which entitle a revised Completion Date are Relevant Matters under clause 4.24 then it could be argued that the loss of interest on the monies paid or withheld as liquidated damages are recoverable. The difficulty, however, is establishing causation.

Clause 2.33 allows the Employer early possession of parts of the Works with the consent of the Contractor and clause 2.37 provides for the rate of liquidated damages stated in the Contract Particulars to be reduced from the Relevant Date, by the same proportion as the value of the Relevant Part bears to the Contract Sum. The assumption therefore is that the measure of loss for delay of a part is proportional to the construction value of the part measured by the Contract Sum. This is unlikely to be correct unless the loss is related directly and only to the financing of the project.

There appears to be no provision in JCT 2005 to limit the overall amount of delay damages.

MF/1 (Rev 4)/2000

Clauses 32 and 33 deal with the Time for Completion, extension of time and delay and do not provide for sectional completion. There are Additional Special Conditions for use where the Contract is to provide sectional completion and damages for delay in completion of sections by replacing clauses 33.1, 33.2 and 34.1.

Clauses 34.1 and 34.2 deal with liquidated damages.

Clause 34.1 states that if the Contractor fails to complete the Works in accordance with the Contract within the Time for Completion, or if no time is fixed within a reasonable time, then the percentage stated in the Appendix of the Contract Value is to be deducted from the Contract Price or paid to the Purchaser by the Contractor.

The percentage only applies to those parts of the Works which cannot be put to use intended as a consequence of the failure to complete. This is an unusual provision. It is necessary because the LDs are expressed as a percentage, in this case a percentage of the Contract Value which is defined as the part of the Contract Price properly apportionable to the Plant or work in question. It is necessary therefore to both identify and value the part of the Works not put to the use intended before the amount of LDs can be determined.

The deduction/payment is stated to be for each week of delay and this is repeated in the Appendix.

It is unusual in any model form for the provision of completion to be within a reasonable time. It is normal that the time for completion to be fixed.

The Special Conditions clause 34.1 is in similar terms as the standard clause but with reference to sections as well as the Works.

Clause 34.1 provides that the amount of deduction/payment shall not exceed the maximum percentage stated in the Appendix. The deduction/payment is stated to be in full satisfaction of the Contractor's liability for the failure to complete, subject to clause 34.2. There are therefore two delay damages regimes in the Contract. The first is a liquidated damages regime which applies up to a limit, but if that is exceeded then clause 34.2 applies. It is suggested that on a proper interpretation of the Contract that the remedies under clause 34.1 and 34.2 are not mutually exclusive. The rights under clause 34.2 are additional to LDs under clause 34.1.

Clause 34.2 relates to prolonged delay and allows the Purchaser by notice to require the Contractor to complete and to fix a final Time for Completion where the Contractor has been so delayed as to incur the maximum amount provided under clause 34.1. Further the Purchaser may decide to terminate the Contract in respect of that part of the Works and recover from the Contractor any loss suffered by the Purchaser by reason of the said failure up to an amount not exceeding the sum stated in the Appendix, or if no sum is stated, that part of the Contract Price that is properly proportional to such part of the Works as cannot by reason of the Contractor's failure be put to the use intended.

The combination of liquidated damages and unliquidated damages for late completion is an unusual feature of MF/1. The approach does properly deal with the situation where the delay is so great that it is not commercially practical to estimate the loss using the LD mechanism.

IChemE Red Book 4th Edition

Clause 15.1 states that if the Contract provides for payment of liquidated damages for delay, then the Contractor is to pay or allow the Purchaser LD's at the rate prescribed in Schedule 9 for failure to complete the Works or any specified section or stage in Schedule 5.

Clause 15.1 provides that the Contractor has no liability to pay LD's in excess of the maximum (if any) stated in Schedule 9.

The IChemE Red Book is drafted so that the detail of the LD provisions is in Schedules 5 and 9. If LDs for delay do not apply then it is prudent to expressly so state in Schedule 9 or the Special Conditions. Schedule 5 is required to state the times and stages of completion and Schedule 9 should state the rates for LD's.

The main event in Schedule 5 for the purpose of clause 15 is likely to be completion of construction under clause 33. However, take over under clause 34 may be the event if full production is the more relevant benefit.

Failure to pay by a certain date is a breach of contract not usually associated with liquidated damages clauses, but such a clause could provide for payment of interest at an increased rate for the period of delay.

Mr Justice Jacob in the Court of Appeal in *Jeancharm Limited* v. *Barnet Football Club Limited* [2003] EWCA Civ 58 considered that one can have an increased rate of interest as a valid clause in some circumstances and referred to the decision of Colman J in *Lordvale Finance plc* v. *Bank of Zambia* [1996] QB 752. In that case there was an uplift of 1% for late payment of a debt. That was held to be a genuine pre-estimate on the basis that it indicated that the borrower was a risky borrower. Mr Justice Jacob observed that there was nothing in the decision which suggests that anything other than what Colman J called a 'modest increase' would do.

Failure to provide a plant which gives the required throughput is the breach of contract for which LD clauses are used in contracts for industrial and/or mechanical plant. A measurable performance target is required. It may be necessary to stipulate a minimum level of performance required. If performance falls below this level, the plant may be considered and agreed no longer to be a viable plant, the LD provision no longer an adequate remedy and the contractor's performance not to be performance at all.

In order to establish the threshold for levy of liquidated damages the required performance needs to be prescribed by measurable parameters. It is necessary to specify the duration of the tests, performance criteria and method of assessment by reference to standards together with tolerances. It may be necessary to specify correction factors if the operating conditions required for the tests cannot be created.

The specified performance may include plant throughput, energy or feedstock useage, quality of product and extent of waste or byproduct. These performance criteria may be inter-related, so that some criteria should be grouped if a realistic measure of the benefit to the Purchaser is to be measured.

FIDIC 1999 Forms 1st Edition

The FIDIC Forms Red, Yellow and Silver do not provide for performance related liquidated damages, but at clause 9.4(b) provides that if a Works or section fails to pass the Tests on Completion and if the failure deprives the Employer of substantially the whole benefit of the Works or Section, then the Employer can reject the Works or Section and terminate the Contract as a whole or in respect of the major part which cannot be put to intended use. The Employer is then entitled to recover all sums paid for the Works or such part plus financing costs, the costs of dismantling, clearing the Site and returning Plant and Materials to the Contractor, without prejudice to the Employer's other rights.

NEC3

Option X17 provides for low performance damages as stated in the Contract Data. The Contract Data Part One provided by the Employer specifies the amount of low performance damages for each specified performance level. Option X17 requires the Contractor to pay the low performance damages. Clause 50.2 provides that the amount due (at each assessment date) is to be reduced by the amount to be paid by the Contractor.

MF/1 (Rev 4)/2000

Clause 35.8(a) provides that if the Works or any Section fails to pass the Performance Tests within the period specified in the Special Conditions, or if no period is specified within a reasonable time, the Contractor pays or allows liquidated damages if they are specified in the Special Conditions for failure to achieve guaranteed performance. On payment/deduction the Purchaser accepts the Works.

The clause 35.8(a) provision only applies if the results are within the stipulated acceptance limits. If not then clause 35.8(b) applies instead. Clause 35.8(b) also applies if liquidated damages have not been specified for failure to achieve guaranteed performance. Clause 38.8(b) provides that the Purchaser can accept the Works with a reasonable reduction of the Contract Price.

The Purchaser has an alternative remedy under clause 35.8(d) if the failure to pass the Performance Tests is such as to deprive the Purchaser of substantially the whole benefit of the Works or Section. In that case the Purchaser is entitled to reject the Works or Section and proceed under clause 49 which relates to termination of the Contract for Contractor's default.

IChemE Red Book 4th Edition

Clause 35.10 provides that if the Plant does not pass any performance test within 90 days of the date of the relevant Take-Over Certificate, the Contractor pays liquidated damages to the Purchaser in accordance with Schedule 10.

If the results of any performance tests are outside any limits specified in Schedule 10, then instead of liquidated damages, the Purchaser may either accept the Plant with a reasonable reduction in the Contract Price or reject the Plant in accordance with clause 41.

Clause 35.2 states that the performance tests to be carried out are those specified in Schedule 7.

Schedules 7 and 10 are inter-related and need to be carefully drafted by the Purchaser. The threshold for performance needs to be easily established by reference to Schedule 7. The level of liquidated damages for ranges of low performance needs to be specified in Schedule 10, by reference to the tests in Schedule 7, and a limit specified beyond which the liquidated damages are no longer the contractual remedy for the breach of contract.

4.1 Administration of claims
4.2 Litigation
4.3 Arbitration
4.4 Adjudication
4.5 Alternative dispute resolution

4.3 Freedom of contract

The Courts will strive to give effect to the agreement of the parties to a contract and the agreed allocation of risk freely entered into *Jeancharm Limited* v. *Barnet Football Club Limited* [2003] EWCA Civ 58. This approach to the construction of the LD clauses creates the certainty required for commercial contracts.

The Courts have been careful not to strike down as a penalty a clause negotiated between willing parties who had similar bargaining strengths *Jeancharm Limited* v. *Barnet Football Club Limited* [2003] EWCA Civ 58.

The concept of a penalty clause was not confined to situations where one party had a dominant bargaining power over the other, otherwise, the concept would have little relevance in most commercial contracts. There was no broad discretionary approach to be applied *Jeancharm Limited* v. *Barnet Football Club Limited* [2003] EWCA Civ 58.

The fact that had two parties were well capable of protecting their respective commercial interests agreed the LD provision will usually suggest that the formula for calculating liquidated damages was unlikely to be oppressive *Philips* v. *The Attorney General of Hong Kong* [1993] 61 BLR 41.

The Courts are predisposed to uphold contractual terms which fix the level of damages for breach, even stronger in the case of commercial contracts freely entered into between parties of comparable bargaining power *Alfred McAlpine Capital Projects Limited* v. *Tilebox Limited* [2005] EWHC 281 (TCC).

There are very few construction cases where the relevant clause has been struck down as a penalty. In each case there was a very wide gulf between the level of damages likely to be suffered, and the level of damages stipulated in the contract.

4.4 Rules of penalty clauses

Although the rules on penalty clauses set out in *Jeancharm Limited* v. *Barnet Football Club Limited* [2003] EWCA Civ 58 are an anomalous feature of the law, there has been no abandonment of the rule that the clause must be a genuine pre-estimate of damage.

The test remained one of ascertaining whether the provision was a genuine pre-estimate of loss or was a penalty for non-performance of the contractual obligation. The first type of provision was essentially compensatory in nature. The second was there to deter the party in question from breaking the contract by providing for a punitive level of payment *Jeancharm Limited* v. *Barnet Football Club Limited* [2003] EWCA Civ 58.

So long as the sum payable in the event of non-compliance with the contract is not extravagant, having regard to the range of losses that it could reasonably be anticipated it would have to cover at the time that the contract was made, it can still be a genuine pre-estimate of the loss that would be suffered and so a perfectly valid liquidated damage provision *Philips* v. *The Attorney General of Hong Kong* [1993] 61 BLR 41.

There seem to be two strands in the authorities. In some cases judges consider whether there is an unconscionable or extravagant disproportion between the damages stipulated in the contract and the true amount of damages likely to be suffered. In other cases the courts consider whether the level of damages stipulated was reasonable. I accept, that these two strands can be reconciled. In my view, a preestimate of damages does not have to be right in order to be reasonable.

The test of genuine pre-estimate does not refer to the genuineness or honesty of the party or parties who made the pre-estimate. The test is primarily an objective one, even though the court has some regard to the thought processes of the parties at the time of contracting. There must be a substantial discrepancy between the level of damages stipulated in the contract and the level of damages which is likely to be suffered before it can be said that the agreed pre-estimate is unreasonable *Alfred McAlpine Capital Projects Limited* v. *Tilebox Limited* [2005] EWHC 281 (TCC).

A clause in a hire purchase agreement requiring the hirer to pay compensation for premature termination was a penalty since it provided a sliding scale which operated in the wrong direction. The less the depreciation of the vehicle, the greater was the compensation payable *Campbell Discount Co Ltd* v. *Bridge* [1962] AC 600 HL.

The amount stipulated as damages should be proportionate to the extent of the breaches. It is not unreasonable to take an overall figure for a failure to return all or a substantial part of the specified parts. Where the same sum was payable for failure to return even a few of some comparatively unimportant items, the sum was out of all proportion to any loss suffered and was a penalty *Ariston SRL* v. *Charly Records Limited* [1990] Court of Appeal.

An agreement that if payment was late interest was to be paid at 5% per week was a penalty clause.

The 5% per week figure amounted to an annual rate of about 260% percent which was an extraordinarily large amount to have to pay for the suggested administrative costs, even if the sums involved were relatively small. It was purely a matter of speculation, and the clause went wider than that and covered comparatively large debts too.

The provision of graduated sums increasing in proportion to the seriousness of the breach was characteristic of a liquidated damages clause which was commonplace in commercial contracts *North Sea Ventilation Limited* v. *Consafe Engineering (UK) Limited* [2004].

A liquidated damages clause is construed on the basis that the amount stipulated as damages should be proportionate to the breach. If there was a substantial discrepancy between the level of damages stipulated in the contract and the level of damages which is likely to be suffered the liquidated damages would be unreasonable.

It is a strong indication of a penalty if the clause provides for a single sum to be payable on a number of different breaches, which may give rise to widely different amounts of damage. This can give employers difficulties, particularly when an LD clause is drafted in anticipation of the several different ways that the plant may not fulfil its performance requirements. Many separate performance criteria may need to be met if the intended overall plant performance is to be achieved. In practice, providing easily ascertainable sums as liquidated damages means that different performance criteria need to be grouped together, in order to assess the likely loss in production and increased costs due to their cumulative effect.

The liquidated damages should not be out of all proportion to any part of the range of losses, particularly where the range is broad. Special provision will need to be made for such parts of the likely losses otherwise the LD clause may be held to be a penalty. This means that there should not be too great a difference between the greatest and the smallest possible losses.

The LDs are not unenforceable simply because it is difficult to pre-estimate the loss from a breach. In such cases the courts will not become involved in examining different scenarios to find a likely loss less than the liquidated damages. This would effectively defeat the purpose of LD clauses in providing the parties with a level of certainty and a mechanism for avoiding disputes. Even if the liquidated damages are greater than the loss it would still be a genuine pre-estimate of the loss if it was not so great in relation to the range of losses that it could reasonably be anticipated it would have to cover at the time the contract was made.

The employer is not required to demonstrate that it has suffered loss as a result of the breach. Liquidated damages are enforceable even if in the event there has been no loss. If the actual loss is greater than the sum stated in the LD clause and the LD clause is enforceable, the stated sum is exhaustive of the employer's entitlement to damages. It cannot elect to sue for damages in addition to the sum stated in the LD clause.

If the LD clause is a penalty, then the injured party must then prove its loss in the ordinary way. The law is not entirely clear on whether the stated sum will limit the amount recoverable as damages. It has been argued that the sole purpose of the courts using their power to strike down a penalty clause is to provide relief against oppression. If, having struck down the clause, the courts then allowed recovery of a sum greater than the stipulated penalty, this would be productive of an injustice.

The agreement on liquidated and ascertained damages was not an agreed price to permit a party to breach its contract and did not preclude the Court granting any other relief that may be appropriate such as injuncture.

It may be significant in that case that the level of LDs was less than the anticipated loss and to show that it would not be adequately compensated if it were left to a claim in damages *Bath and North East Somerset District Council* v. *Mowlem plc* [2004] EWCA Civ 115.

4.5 Liquidated damages expressed as a percentage

Liquidated damages expressed as a percentage of the contract sum would appear not to be a genuine covenanted pre-estimate of damage, since the value will depend on the contract value of the successful tenderer. If, however, the likely loss is calculated in terms of the cost of servicing the debt, funding the project, comprising the contract value, then in that case an appropriate percentage may be a genuine pre-estimate.

4.6 Onus of proof

The onus of showing that an LD clause is a penalty clause falls on the party who is sued upon the clause. If the contractor challenges the LD clause as being a penalty, then the contractor is required to prove that it is a penalty. In such a case, it is not for the employer to prove that the liquidated damages amount is a reasonable pre-estimate of loss *Robophone Facilities Ltd* v. *Blank* [1966] confirmed by the Court of Appeal in *Jeancham Ltd* v. *Barnet Football Club Ltd* [2003] EWCA Civ 58.

4.7 Loss of right to LD's

If a liquidated damages clause is unenforceable because it is construed as a penalty, then the Employer will have lost the right to liquidated damages.

In addition many contracts contain provisions which deal with failures by the Employer in order to keep alive the entitlement to liquidated damages. The basis for this approach is a rule of construction that there is a rebuttable presumption that a party would not be entitled to take advantage of its own wrong to the detriment of the other party *Alghussein Establishment* v. *Eton College* (1988) 1 WLR 587. Applying liquidated damages in a situation caused by the Employer or by a failure of the contractual machinery might be considered to conflict with this rule of construction and not intended by the parties.

If the Engineer or Project Manager does not operate the Extension of Time Clause provisions properly it is not clear whether the Courts will rule against the Employer receiving the benefit from the liquidated damages provisions as a result. It is suggested that the nature of the non-compliance with the time scale for granting an extension of time is important. It is also suggested that the provision for review of interim Extension of Time awards or application to an adjudicator and the availability of final determination by the Court or arbitration are highly relevant.

Under the JCT 80 contract JCT forms of contract include a procedure for levying liquidated damages which requires the issue of a non-completion certificate by the Architect and the issue of a written notice by the Employer.

The right of recovery of liquidated damages under clause 24 does not depend on whether the architect has given his certificate by the stipulated day. *Temloc Ltd* v. *Errill Properties Ltd* (1987) 39 BLR 34.

The Employer will lose the right to deduct liquidated damages if the condition precedent of the issue of an Architect's non-completion certificate had not been fulfilled including the re-issue in the case of revised dates for completion. *A. Bell and Son (Paddington) Ltd* v. *CBF Residential Care and Housing Association* (1989) 46 BLR 102.

Clause 24 and 25 provided a complete code for the payment or allowance by the Contractor to the Employer of LDs.

Where the Architect fixes a later Completion Date there was an obligation on the Employer to make a payment or repayment of the amounts recovered, allowed or repaid for the period up to the later Completion Date. The requirement in writing by the Employer is a condition precedent to any lawful deduction of LDs.

The requirement in writing required no more and no less than the Employer's intention with regard to LDs, whether he required payment or an allowance and whether in part or whole.

If an extension of time is granted after a notice of withholding of liquidated damages has been given but before the Final Date for payment, the notice of withholding is still valid under JCT 1998. There is an implied terms to repay the additional liquidated damages withheld in a reasonable time. Court of Appeal in *Reinwood Limited* v. *L. Brown & Sons Limited* [2007] EWCA Civ 601.

JCT 2005 (SBC/Q)

Clause 2.30.1 provides for the Architect/CA to issue a Practical Completion Certificate or in the case of Sections clause 2.30.2 provides for Section Completion Certificates.

Clause 2.31 provides for the Architect/CA to issue a Non-Completion Certificate in the event that the Contractor fails to complete the Works or a Section by the relevant Completion Date. If a new Completion Date is fixed after the issue of a Non-Completion Certificate, then clause 3.31 provides that the fixing cancels the Non-Completion Certificate and the Architect/CA is required where necessary to issue a further certificate. In such a case clause 2.32.3 provides that the Employer is required to pay or repay the amounts recovered, allowed or repaid for the period up to the later Completion Date.

Clause 2.32.2.1 prescribes that the Employer's notice must state that for the period between the Completion Date and the date of practical completion of the Works/Section the Employer requires the Contractor to pay liquidated damages at the rate stated in the Contract Particulars. Clause 2.32.2.1 allows that the Employer may state a lesser rate. If the notice is issued then the amount is stated to be recovered as a debt. Clause 2.32.2.2 provides an alternative that the notice may state that the Employer will withhold or deduct liquidated damages at the rate stated in the Contract Particulars from monies due to the Contractor. Clause 2.32.1 provides that either type of Employer's notice must be issued not later than five days before the final date for payment of the debt due under the Final Certificate.

Clause 2.32.1 specifies that before the Employer can issue the Employer's notice the Architect/CA must have issue a Non-Completion Certificate. In addition the Employer must have informed the Contractor in writing that he may require payment of or may withhold or deduct liquidated damages. The Employer's warning must be given before the date of the Final Certificate.

Clause 2.32.4 provides that if a Non-Completion Certificate is cancelled or a further Non-Completion Certificate is issued, then the Employers warning given under clause 2.32.1.2 remains satisfied. There is no express statement with regard to the Employer's notice.

It is suggested that the logic and arguments of the above decided cases in relation to the Architects/CA Non-Completion Certificate and the Employer's notice apply equally to JCT 2005. The provisions of clause 2.32.4 applies to the Employer's warning and not the Employer's notice.

4.8 Contractor's Failure to Apply for EOT

If the contractor loses the right to extension of time for the Employer's breach of contract, because he fails to provide effective notice, it has been argued that the Employer is not entitled to deduct liquidated damages for the delay caused by the breach. It is argued that the principle in Alghussein would to prevent the Employer benefiting from his own breach to the detriment of the contractor. This has been examined in two recent cases, one Australian and one Scottish.

It is suggested that the failure of the contractor to give notice condition precedent to an extension of time, will not prevent the Employer deducting LDs. The principle in Alghussein is a principle of construction of the contract. The presumption must be that a contractor will act to preserve his rights. His failure to do so will not prevent LDs being levied.

An extension of time notice provision in a JCT80 Contract did not impose any obligation on the contractor when he received an architect's instruction. It merely provided the contractor with an option to take certain action if he sought the protection of an extension of time in the circumstances in which the clause applied.

If the contractor failed to take action and the notice was condition precedent to an extension of time, the Employer was entitled to deduct liquidated damages for the contractor's failure to complete *City Inn Ltd* v. *Shepherd Construction Ltd* [2003] Inner House.

5 CLAIMS FOR SITE CONDITIONS

5.1 Changed ground conditions

It is not possible to investigate every existing physical condition which will affect construction. The normal approach of both designers and contractors is to prepare a reasonable model of the conditions based on the limited information and engineering experience. The model will be the basis of the design and estimates or the basis of prices and the programme. It is when the model is found to be inaccurate that disputes and differences arise. The interaction of information, analysis and methods of construction which affect the model, means that the nature of the risk event will not be immediately clear.

The above interaction makes it difficult to define a risk event in a contract clearly so that when it occurs the allocation of liability for the consequences can be readily determined. Although the principles for allocation of risk are clearly understood, in practice, when a risk event occurs, the liability for the consequences of the risk event depends on such a number of interrelated factors, that inevitably the allocation of liability will involve a legal process of proof of legal obligation or entitlement. Any risk allocation will therefore create a substantial legal risk – the risk of disputes or differences. The management of the risk must recognize and cater for this aspect of the risk.

5.2 The nature of the risk

The claims, differences or disputes which arise in construction contracts have their roots in the incomplete information about the nature of the ground properties and in the misunderstandings which only become apparent after work has commenced. Apart from natural phenomena such as floods, earthquakes and adverse weather conditions, disputes about 'changed conditions' arise from the choices and judgments made by the contracting parties. In short, when a 'changed condition' arises, it is not the condition which has changed but the parties' perception of it.

The apportionment of risk between the parties to the contract must be accomplished through the terms of the contract against the background of the law of the contract. The complexity of the risk of 'changed conditions' means that it is difficult to fully place the risk with one party. In addition, the consequences of a risk event once it materializes will be determined by the actions already taken by the parties such as the issue of information, the selection of the method of construction or the selection of the payment mechanism, as well as the reaction of the parties to the risk event.

The complexity of the interacting factors means that clear and unambiguous allocation of liability for the consequences of 'changed conditions' cannot easily be achieved by drafting of contract terms. The major practical risk from 'changed conditions' in construction contracts is therefore the protracted resolution of the differences and disputes which subsequently arise. It is, however, precisely in this area that well drafted contract procedures for rational and logical dispute resolution can reduce the consequences of the legal risk. The aim must be to provide a mechanism for rapidly providing certainty in the interpretation of the various terms of the contract and in rapidly providing a practical evaluation of the technical, time and financial consequences of 'changed conditions'.

This conclusion appears to fly in the face of industry views of disputes on 'changed conditions'. It is often said that disputes should not be an inherent part of construction contracts. The resort to dispute resolution procedures is seen as a failure of management. It is suggested that this is to misunderstand the nature of the risk of 'changed conditions'. The risk is not solely a technical risk but is predominantly a legal risk involving proof of legal obligation or entitlement and which accordingly requires a management approach which recognizes the legal nature of the risk.

5.3 Incomplete information – disclosure

The general principle, subject to the express terms of the contract, is that if a contractor has contracted to carry out the whole of the construction works, then it must satisfy itself as to the nature and condition of the site for the works. It cannot assume that the statements in the contract documents about the state of the site, or the extent of work involved are accurate. It cannot assume that the statements about the method of working are practical. The general principle is that the employer has not warranted the accuracy of the information or statements in the contract documents.

Information may be incomplete for a number of reasons. First, there may be insufficient site investigation. Experience shows that a proper site investigation is always an effective means of reducing the risk of 'changed conditions' since it provides the information necessary to create an accurate model of the conditions. Secondly, sufficient information may be available in the form of old maps, aerial photographs, previous site investigations and even public reports and articles. The incompleteness may arise from the failure of one or both parties to locate and take account of the information. Thirdly, even though information is available and has been obtained, the model of the condition may be incomplete because the interpretation of the information or analysis of the information is incorrect. Finally, despite the collation and analysis of the information, the limitations of the information and analysis techniques do not allow the accurate position of probable features to be established. This is the case where the possibility of the occurrence of a feature is recognized but cannot be predicted in any tangible and practicable form. These four types of incompleteness are defined only in relation to the particular operation to be carried out in or on the ground. The extent and the nature of the site investigation required will depend on the method of working or the type of ground treatment to be carried out.

In many construction projects, the employer will have relevant information about the site which will not otherwise be available to the contractor. The contractor may not be aware that such information is available. The question which arises is whether the employer is under a legal obligation to disclose this information.

There is no general duty of disclosure in English law in commercial transactions such as construction projects. The mere non-disclosure of information does not, of itself, create a cause of action. In order to succeed, the contractor has to establish either a breach of contract or negligent misrepresentation which induced the contract. An action in negligent misrepresentation will require the contractor to show that the employer assumed or accepted responsibility for assembling and transmitting full and accurate information. The contractor will need to show that it relied on the employer assembling and transmitting the information. The success of such an action will depend on the circumstances, including the language of the contract, the specification relating to the site, the respective positions of the parties and their respective knowledge.

In normal circumstances, a person in pre-contract negotiations will not be under a duty to assemble or present information relating to the subject matter of the contract. Instead he or she is entitled solely to look after his or her own interests and make the best deal possible.

Some forms of contract recognize that the employer may have information not available from other sources and by various provisions encourage the employer to make full disclosure. The ICE 6th and 7th Edition clause 11 is such a provision. The Engineering Construction Contract clause 60 is another such provision.

ICE 6th and 7th Edition clause 11 deals with the information in relation to the site and the ground conditions, which the contractor is taken to have allowed for in the tender. Since contractors have a limited period in which to prepare their bids, there is always the possibility that the information on which their bid is based does not identify particular risks which would affect either their design or the level of their bid. Clause 11 describes two distinct sources of information as:

- information obtained by or on behalf of the employer
- inspection by the contractor of the site and its surroundings.

ICE 6th Edition clause 11(1) provides that the employer is deemed to have made available to the contractor the information obtained before submission of the tender. Clause 11(3) provides that the contractor is deemed to have based its tender on the information made available. The intention appears to be to place a duty on the employer to make available all relevant information which it has obtained which is not otherwise readily available and for the contractor to be entitled to assume that the employer has done so.

ICE 7th Edition clause 11(1) clarifies the provisions of ICE 6th Edition, and provides that information obtained by or on behalf of the employer shall be taken into account, but only to the extent that it was made available to the contractor before the submission of its tender. Such information is limited to that arising from 'investigations undertaken relevant to the Works'. Clause 11(3), however, makes clear that the contractor is deemed to have based its tender on all information made available by the employer.

Clause 4.10 of the FIDIC Red and Yellow Books 1999, requires the employer to have made available to the contractor for its information, prior to the base date, all relevant data in its possession on sub-surface and hydrological conditions at the site, including environmental aspects. The base date is defined as 28 days prior to the latest date for submission of the tender. The employer is required similarly to make available to the contractor all such data which come into the employer's possession after the base date. The contractor is only responsible for interpreting the data. Under clause 4.11(b) the contractor is deemed to have based the accepted contract amount on such data, and in the case of the Yellow Book any further data relevant to the contractor's design. This effectively means that the employer warrants the accuracy of the information which it has provided.

The FIDIC Silver Book 1999 adopts a different approach. Under clause 4.10 the employer is required to have made available to the contractor all relevant data in the employer's possession on hydrological and sub-surface conditions at the site, including environmental aspects. The employer is required similarly to make available to the contractor all such data which come into the employer's possession after the base date. The contractor, however, is responsible for verifying as well as interpreting the data. There is therefore no warranty by the employer of the accuracy of the information, and there is indeed an express exclusion of responsibility for the accuracy, sufficiency or completeness of such data.

The Engineering Construction Contract 2nd Edition clause 60.2 recognizes the unique position of the employer and places emphasis on disclosure. Clause 60.2 provides that a contractor is assumed to have taken into account the following information:

- site information about the site which the employer has provided
- publicly available information referred to in the site information
- information available from a visual inspection of the site
- other information which an experienced contractor could reasonably be expected to have or to obtain.

The employer must, of course, ensure that its selection of information will not constitute misrepresentation, for example by only issuing one of a number of sub-soil surveys for the site. For the same reason, the employer should ensure that advice or opinion given by the specialists carrying out the surveys are excluded from the information issued. It cannot be pretended that this is an easy matter. If this is carried too far, it may create the very risk of underpricing which the issue of information is intended to avoid.

If the employer does supply information, then it may attempt to exclude the information from the contract and/or exclude liability for the accuracy of the information. Whether such a disclaimer is successful will depend on the terms of the disclaimer and the circumstances.

If the employer is to rely on a disclaimer for information supplied to the contractor then it will need to be carefully drafted.

Inevitably, the definition of the information which the contractor is required to have obtained for itself is in terms which are open to interpretation.

5.4 Contractual risk model

Many standard forms have a changed conditions clause. In the ICE 6th and 7th Edition this is clause 12, in FIDIC Forms clause 4.12 and in the Engineering Construction Contract 2nd Edition it is clause 60.1(12). The tests adopted to establish liability are different, however.

5.5 ICE foreseeability test

The objective foreseeability model is used in many of the ICE 6th and 7th clauses which give an entitlement to additional payment or extensions of time. The test is also adopted in ICE Clause 12 which deals with unforeseen physical conditions and artificial obstructions.

The clause 12(1) foreseeability test is not limited to supervening events, i.e. events arising after the contract was formed. It applies to existing physical conditions and artificial obstructions and applies to peculiar characteristics of the soil which causes it to behave in an unforeseeable manner under the stress which was applied to it.

5.6 FIDIC Forms

Clause 4.12 defines the allocation of risk for changed ground which, in the Red and Yellow Books 1999, follows the ICE forseeability test. The employer carries the risk of physical condition which could not have reasonably been foreseen by an experienced contractor by the date for submission of the tender. Physical conditions are defined as both natural physical conditions and man-made and other physical obstructions and pollutants. The definition excludes climatic conditions, but includes hydrological conditions.

The FIDIC Silver Book 1999 adopts a different approach. Under clause 4.10 the employer is required to have made available to the contractor all relevant data in the employer's possession on hydrological and sub-surface conditions at the site, including environmental aspects. The employer is required similarly to make available to the contractor all such data which come into the employer's possession after the base date. The contractor, however, is responsible for verifying as well as interpreting the data. There is therefore no warranty by the employer of the accuracy of the information, and there is indeed an express exclusion of responsibility for the accuracy, sufficiency or completeness of such data.

5.7 ECC probability test

The test in ECC clause 60.1(12) is a probability test. The contractor is entitled to be compensated if it encounters physical conditions which an experienced contractor would have judged at the formation of contract to have such a small chance of occurring that it would have been unreasonable for the contractor to have allowed for them. This is a different test to the ICE 6th and 7th Edition foreseeability test. In the ECC test, the possibility of the risk event has been foreseen but has been discounted as not having a reasonable probability of occurring. Again, opinion will be divided as to whether an experienced contractor should have priced the risk.

5.8 Effect of selected method of working

The contractor's selection of a particular method of working may bring about a risk event. When the risk event occurs the party which will bear liability for the consequences will inevitably be a difficult matter of interpretation.

ICE 6th and 7th Edition clause 8 makes the contractor responsible for the design of all temporary works, subject to express exceptions. The conditions do not mention the standard for the design of temporary works. However, clause 8 also states that the contractor shall take full responsibility for the adequacy, stability and safety of all site operations and methods of construction. Clause 8 does not apply to a case where the inadequacy or instability is brought about by the contractor having encountered physical conditions within clause 12.

It is important for an employer to take into account this aspect when examining methods of construction proposed at tender stage. If one particular method increases the likelihood of clause 12 claims, for instance by being more susceptible to variable characteristics of the site, then sensitivity analysis may be necessary to establish the most acceptable bid. It may be necessary to state that the contractor takes on the extra risk due to a particular method of working.

5.9 Pricing mechanism

Even without a changed condition clause the pricing mechanism may in effect transfer the risk to the employer of the as-built quantities being greater than those estimated at tender. Depending on the method of measurement, the employer may still carry the risk of changed conditions, for example with regard to:

- longer piles in the event of deeper suitable bearing strata
- increased volume of unsuitable material and imported fill.

5.10 Reaction to risk events

One additional factor which may determine liability for the consequences of a risk event is the reaction of the parties to the risk event. Many standard forms with changed condition clauses have requirements for the issue of notices of both the risk event and particulars of measures to overcome the consequences. This is the case under ICE 6th and 7th Edition clause 12. If the contractor fails to serve notice as soon as is reasonable, its entitlement to payment is limited to the extent that the engineer is prevented or prejudiced by the late notice in the engineer's investigation of the claim. In the ICE 4th Edition, clause 12 included a requirement for the contractor to give notice and provided that the cost of all work done prior to the giving of such notice was deemed to have been recovered in the rates and prices under the contract. In such a case, the risk of the effect of the encountered conditions only passes to the employer after the notice is given, and the risk remains with the contractor until it is able to comply with the requirements relating to notice.

6 FINANCIAL CLAIMS

6.1 Payment

If the parties have not agreed a price then the contractor will be entitled to a reasonable price for the work. Some contracts only provide for payment from the time the works or services are substantially complete. If they are not substantially complete there is no entitlement to any payment. Many building contracts are lump sum or entire contracts under which the contractor undertakes to complete the whole of the works for an agreed sum. However, even for these arrangements, the forms will provide a mechanism under which the contractor's entitlement is calculated in the event of non-completion. In general, standard forms of contract normally provide for two types of payment, namely periodic payments on account or interim payments and the payment of the final price.

Interim payment

There is no common-law right to interim payment unless the parties have agreed. Generally, a party is entitled to payment only when it has completed its part of the contract, fully in accordance with the contract.

In construction contracts this is seen as creating substantial cash flow problems for smaller contractors. The normal practice in the industry has been for contracts to specify interim payment mechanisms which depend in some way on a certification process. This therefore creates a contractual right to interim payments. It is not clear whether a term will be implied in a construction contract for interim payments in the absence of an express term but it is suggested that a term will not be implied. There is no authority on this issue but there is the dicta of Lord Diplock in *Gilbert-Ash (Northern) Limited* v. *Modern Engineering (Bristol) Limited* [1974] AC 689 which suggest to the contrary.

Section 109(1) of the Housing Grants, Construction and Regeneration Act 1996 gives a party to a relevant construction contract (as defined by the Act) a statutory right to interim payments by implying such a term in the absence of an express term. This is an entitlement to payment by instalments, stage payments or other periodic payments for any work under the contract. There is no such right under a construction contract for short duration contracts as defined in the Act.

Abatement

Employers do not normally wish to pay the full payment requested by the contractor if the work carried out is defective, or if the employer has claims against the contractor. To do so increases the employer's exposure to the consequences of the contractor's possible insolvency. Instead, the employer will wish to deduct the cost of remedial works and the value of the claims from the amount due to the contractor.

The employer has the right at common law to raise a defence of abatement against any action for payment in full by the contractor This right of abatement only applies to defects which are patent at the time payment is due. The amount by which the employer might rightfully reduce the amount due to the contractor is limited to the cost which the contractor would have incurred in remedying any defect. Where the defects are the responsibility of the contractor and it does not carry out the remedial work within a reasonable time, then the employer is entitled to abate the amount otherwise due to the contractor, by the amount it would cost the employer to remedy the defect. This additional liability arises from the contractor's further breach of contract in not remedying the defect.

During the defects liability period, defects may be discovered. Once the contractor has remedied those defects which have appeared during the defects liability period, the A/E under many standard forms is required to issue a final certificate. Some standard forms provide that such a certificate is conclusive of certain matters and particularly that there are no other patent defects and therefore prevents operation of the right to abate the price.

Set-off

If the paying party has claims against the other party, in addition to or instead of claims of abatement, it will normally wish to make a deduction from the sums otherwise due for payment. The deduction is known as set-off. For a deduction to amount to a valid set-off against the claim for payment, both the claim and set-off must arise out of and be inseparably connected with a single transaction. Where the parties have entered into two different contracts it is exceptional for one party to be allowed to use a claim arising under one contract as a set-off in response to a claim made against it on the other contract.

If the contract does not expressly state the right of set-off then the right to set-off is only for matters so closely connected to the demand for payment that it would be manifestly unjust to allow the enforcement of payment without taking set-off into account. There is a right of set-off unless expressly restricted or withdrawn by the terms of contract. Many standard form of subcontract include provisions which limited the main contractor's rights of set-off, by means of notice requirements. If these provisions are not complied with then there may be no right of set-off and it may then be easier to obtain summary judgment for the amounts due. Otherwise in practice it is difficult to obtain summary judgment for payment of amounts due when there is a claim of set-off.

Section 111(1) of the Housing Grants, Construction and Regeneration Act 1996 makes the giving of notice a condition precedent to a right to withhold payment beyond the final date for payment for construction contracts under the Act. Such rights may include the right of set-off and the right of abatement of price. Such a notice must specify the amount proposed to be withheld and the grounds for withholding payment, or if there is more than one ground, each ground and the amount attributable to it.

Retention

Many standard forms provide for the employer to retain a percentage of payments due until the contractor has completed the work. This percentage varies but is usually not more than 5% nor less than 3% of the sums due for payment prior to completion. Unless there are specific provisions in the contract which give the contractor a legally identifiable interest in retention money, then in the event of insolvency by the employer, the contractor joins the queue of unsecured creditors. The contractor should therefore seek terms in the contract that the retention is given the status of a trust fund. It is the duty of the trustee to keep the trust funds separate and, provided this is done, the fund cannot form part of the employer's assets in the event of insolvency. In that case, the contractor is entitled to an injunction ordering the employer to place the retention fund in a separate account. If the contractor acts too late to preserve the retention fund before the employer becomes insolvent, then it will be unable to recover ahead of a bank floating charge for instance.

Discount

Many standard forms of subcontract allow for discount, typically of 22%. This can represent the difference between profit and loss for contractors, and so it is not surprising that disputes arise. Different terminology is used to describe discounts such as 'cash' or 'preferential' or 'trade' or simply 'discount'. The key question in each case is whether the discount is entirely unconditional and therefore a reduction in the price or whether it is conditional, normally on prompt payment. In each case this will be a matter of interpretation of the contract. There is no presumption that the parties intend the discount to be dependent on prompt payment, and each contract is to be interpreted in the light of its own particular facts.

6.2 Certificates

Many standard forms of contract provide a certification system for payments. The amount stated in the certificate for payment by the employer depends upon the A/E's assessment based on his or her personal opinion. The parties have agreed that the

A/E will be the particular expert to carry out this function. The interim certificate states the amount due on account, but the actual determination of the contractor's entitlement is not made until the final certificate. Most standard forms make the issue of a certificate a condition precedent to the contractor's right to payment. Subject to express provisions, such interim payments are not usually binding on subsequent certificates, but allow the work to be revalued for each subsequent certificate as well as the final certificate.

Whether or not a certificate is condition precedent to the right to payment depends upon the proper construction of the contract, read as a whole *Henry Boot Construction Ltd* v. *Alstom Combined Cycles Ltd* [2005] EWCA Civ 814 CA.

In *Brodie* v. *Corporation of Cardiff* [1919] AC 337 the House of Lords held effectively that it was a condition precedent to the right of payment for extra works that an order was given, or ought to have been given and the finding of the arbitrator took the place of the order that should have been given.

In *Prestige* v. *Brettell* [1938] 4 All ER 346 the Court of Appeal applied *Brodie* and Greer LJ explicitly acknowledged that certificates were a condition precedent to payment, but the arbitrator and the court had power to dispense with the condition where a certificate ought to have been issued.

In *Henry Boot Construction Ltd* v. *Alstom Combined Cycles Ltd* [2005] EWCA Civ 814 CA the contract incorporated ICE 6th Edition It was held that certificates were a condition precedent to Boot's entitlement to payment under clause 60(2) and (4) and they were not merely evidence of the Engineer's opinion. The right to payment only arose when a certificate was issued, **or ought to have been issued**, and not earlier and not when the work was done (**although the doing of the work is itself a condition precedent to the right to a certificate**). From clause 60(2) a sum was payable forthwith upon the issue of an interim certificate.

The certificate had to be issued within 28 days of the delivery of the Contractor's statement which on the terms was at least 28 days after the end of the month to which the statement related or even later if the contractor took time to deliver the statement.

It was held that the absence of a certificate was not a bar to the right of payment since the decision of the Engineer in relation to the certification was not conclusive of the rights of the parties, unless they have clearly so provided.

If the Payment Certificate has not been issued due to wrongful interference by the Employer then the contractor may be entitled to payment even in the absence of the certificate *Panamena Europea Navigacon* v. *Frederick Leyland* [1974] HL.

The Employer may not interfere in the timing of the issue of any certificate, but is not in breach of contract if a particular certificate is not issued or is erroneous unless he is directly responsible for the failure. If and when it comes to the Employers notice that the Architect has failed to comply with his administrative obligations by, for example, failing to issue a certificate required by the contract, the Employer has an implied duty to instruct the Architect to perform that function in so far as it remains within the power of the Architect to perform it and the Employer is in breach the contract with the Contractor to the extent that he does not intervene to arrange for the correct or correcting step to be taken by the Architect. *B R Cantrell* v. *Wright & Fuller Ltd* [2003] EWHC 1545 TCC.

The Employer's duty to call the Architect to boot was part of the duty of cooperation since the contract was not commercially workable unless the certifier does what is required of him. *Penwith District Council* v. *VP Developments Ltd* [1999] EWHC 231.

The final certificate of payment certifies the total amount payable to the contractor under the contract. There is generally a special procedure set out in the general conditions which should be followed leading up to its issue. A contract may state that the final certificate of payment will be conclusive evidence that the works are in accordance with the contract, that the contractor has performed all its obligations under the contract, and of the value of the works. This means that neither the contractor nor the employer can allege that the work is incomplete or defective or that the true value of the work has not been reflected in the certificate once the certificate is issued. This would even apply to defects appearing after the issue of the certificate. The final certificate of payment will normally not be conclusive evidence if arbitration or other proceedings have been commenced, either before the issue of the certificate, or within a stipulated period of issue, in respect of the matters referred to arbitration. The final certificate of payment again will not normally be conclusive regarding any matter within it where that matter is affected by fraud or dishonesty.

In *Penwith District Council* v. *VP Developments Ltd* [1999] EWHC 231 (TCC), HH Judge Lloyd considered the final certificate provisions in the JCT 80 Form. He stated that the last act once the works are completed was the issue of the final certificate. It had a dual role, it ostensibly dealt only with the final accounting and arrive at the Adjusted Contract Sum and it is also deemed to express the Architect's satisfaction with the quality of the works and with apparent compliance with the contract. The intention was that with certain exceptions there should be finality on all matters and on all issues.

In *B R Cantrell* v. *Wright & Fuller Ltd* [2003] EWHC 1545 TCC, HH Judge Thornton again considered JCT 80. He held that when the Architect certified he was recording for the parties his professional, personal and objectively arrived at opinion that the fact situation recorded by the certificate was accurate at the time when the certificate was issued.

It is suggested that a Final Certificate must be assessed by examining the power of the certifier. The certificate is then only conclusive on matters which he has power to decide finally between the parties. This is unlikely to include latent defects, or the value of consequential loss. The certificate could, depending upon its terms, be conclusive as to patent defects having been remedied, or the valuation of the Contract Sum being final or conclusive as to the certifier having been satisfied.

In *Colbart Ltd* v. *Kumar* [1992] the issue was the Final Certificate under clause 4.7 of the JCT Intermediate Form. It was held to be conclusive not only on whether the quality of materials or the standard of workmanship was to the reasonable satisfaction of the Architect, but also on matters where the standard of the work was to the approval of the Architect.

In *Crown Estate Commissioners* v. *John Mowlem & Co Ltd* [1994] 70 BLR 1, CA the Final Certificate under clause 30.9.1.1 of the JCT 1980 was considered. It was held that the certificate was conclusive not only on materials and workmanship expressly stated to be for the opinion of the Architect for approval of quality and standard, but also of all materials and workmanship where approval was inherently for the opinion of the Architect.

In *Matthew Hall Ortech Limited* v. *Tarmac Roadstone Limited* [1997] the main issue was whether the Final Certificate prevented claims for defects which were latent at the time of the issue of the certificate. The contract incorporated that IChemE Red Book 1981 revision.

It was also held that there was commercial justification for the Contract to provide a defined cut-off point for liability.

The Final Certificate therefore meant that the contractor had a complete defence to a claim for breach of contract.

In *B R Cantrell* v. *Wright & Fuller Ltd* [2003] EWHC 1545 TCC, HH Judge Thornton again considered JCT 80. He held that the Final Certificate need not be issued on the standard template produced by the JCT for a Final Certificate, but it had to make clear that it was a Final Certificate and the certifying process must have been undertaken in the manner required by the contract, to have taken into account all matters required of the certifier by the contract and must be the opinion of the certifier and not the opinion of some other person and in a form that shows that the opinion is that of the Architect.

In *B R Cantrell* v. *Wright & Fuller Ltd* [2003] EWHC 1545 TCC, HH Judge Thornton held that the time for issue of the Final Certificate and for payment of the certified sum under Clause 30.8 was mandatory. The mandatory timescales could be relaxed so long as the steps which were linked to the issue of the final or other certificate were still to be taken before it was issued late and the power to postpone the issue of the Final Certificate was exercised reasonably and in accordance with any express or implied agreement of, or waiver by, the parties to relax the timetable for its issue.

Although the certifier has an implied power to issue certificates out of time, the power was limited by the requirement for the parties to be notified of the intended exercise and the parties should not be prejudiced by the exercise. The power must be used reasonably. The parties should be given advance notice of the intention to issue late and of the proposed contents of the certificate, the nature of which will depend on the circumstances.

To the extent that the adjudicator had decided a matter that was relevant to the final certificate, the architect was bound by the adjudicator's decision.

If new material had emerged since the date of the adjudicator's decision, the architect was entitled to take that into account in preparing the final certificate, or indeed any interim certificate, and to make any appropriate modification to the adjudicator's decision *Castle Inns (Sterling) Ltd* v. *Clark Contracts Ltd* [2005] CS OH178.

6.3 Variations

Work which needs to be carried out in order to fulfil existing obligations under the contract is not a variation to the contract. In a lump sum contract, works or materials which are necessary for completion of the contract do not constitute variations. This is so even if they are not described in the specification. If the contractor has contracted to achieve a particular result for a lump sum then, if it fails to do so, it will be liable in damages. This is so even if the contractor complies with the specification. If it uses additional material to achieve the result, the contractor cannot claim for that additional material. This is based on the contractor being obliged to achieve a particular result for a lump sum.

In the absence of express provisions in the contract, variation to the original contract requires the agreement of both parties. Without such a clause, the employer is under no obligation to pay for varied work carried out, unless it has previously consented. Conversely, without such a clause the contractor is not required to carry out work which constitutes a variation if ordered by the employer.

If there is a variation clause in the contract there will also normally be a variation payment clause. The practical question will therefore be whether the instructed work falls within the variation clause so that valuation is to follow the contract provisions or whether it falls outside the contract so that payment will have to be established by other principles. That is, whether the variation is within the contract scope of work.

If the additional or omitted work which has been ordered is of a character contemplated by the contract, it will fall within the conditions of the contract relating to the power to order variations. For instance, under the ICE 6th and 7th Edition the engineer has authority to order any variations to any part of the works that may in his or her opinion be necessary for the completion of the works and shall have power to order any variation that, for any other reason, shall in his or her opinion be desirable for the satisfactory completion and functioning of the works. The engineer's authority is therefore limited.

6.4 Omitted work

Many standard forms of contract include the omission of work in the definition of variations which can be ordered under the contract. Despite this, the employer does not have a right to omit work from the contract and give it to another party in the absence of express terms to that effect. This is a breach of contract *Carr* v. *Berriman Pty Ltd* (1953).

A contract for the execution of work confers on the contractor not only the duty to carry out the work but the corresponding right to be able to complete the work which it contracted to carry out. To take away or to vary the work is an intrusion into and an infringement of that right and is a breach of contract.

Reasonably clear words are needed in order to remove work from the contractor simply to have it done by somebody else, whether because the prospect of having it completed by the contractor will be more expensive for the employer than having it done by somebody else, although there can well be other reasons such as timing and confidence in the original contractor. The basic bargain struck between the employer and the contractor has to be honoured and an employer who finds that it has entered into what he might regard as a bad bargain is not allowed to escape from it by the use of the omissions clause so as to enable it then to try and get a better bargain by having the work done by somebody else at a lower cost once the contractor is out of the way. *Abbey Developments Limited* v. *PP Brickwork Limited* [2003] EWHC 1987 (TCC).

There was no power to issue omission instructions which would detract from or change the fundamental characteristic of the works. *Trustees of the Stratfield Saye Estate* v. *AHL Construction Limited* [2004] EWHC 3286 (TCC).

The main contractor has a right to do that work which is set out in the contract documents for him to do, and it cannot be taken away from him in order that it be done by a nominated subcontractor. Conversely, if work is set out to be done by a nominated subcontractor, the main contractor cannot be forced to do it instead; nor, for that matter, can he resist upon it himself (this was an important part of the ratio decidendi in the case *T.A. Bickerton & Son Ltd* v. *North West Metropolitan Regional Hospital Board* (1969) concerning the architect's obligation to nominate a new subcontractor under the JCT Form 63 Edition where the original nominee could not complete).

6.5 Measurement and valuation

Many standard forms of contract use bills of quantities to measure the value of the works. The bills are also used as a schedule of rates in order to value varied work and the effect of varied work on other work.

This dual function of the bills of quantities can give rise to considerable difficulty in the administration of the contract. The normal starting point is that the contractor is entitled to assume that the bill of quantities has been prepared in accordance with the specified method of measurement. Standard forms normally make provision for the A/E to value corrections where the bill does not accurately describe the work shown on the drawings and described in the specification. This is clause 55(4) of the ICE 7th Edition (clause 55(2) of ICE 6th Edition). The work itself is not a variation since all that has happened is that the works have not been fully or properly set out in the bill.

Two main methods for valuation of variations are found in standard forms – evaluations based on rates and evaluation based on loss. Where the first method applies, most such standard forms adopt the following approach:

(a) valuation on the basis of bill of quantity rates or schedules
(b) valuation on the basis of rates analogous to (a) above
(c) valuation on the basis of fair or reasonable prices – fair valuation
(d) valuation on the basis of dayworks.

Whether bill of quantity rates or rates analogous thereto are used as the basis of the valuation will depend largely on the timing of the variation order, the location of the work, the quantity of the work involved and the circumstances in which the work is executed. If it can be established that these factors preclude the valuation on the basis of bill rates, then the valuation will be based on fair or reasonable prices. A fair valuation generally means a valuation which does not give a contractor more than its actual costs reasonably and necessarily incurred plus similar allowances for overheads and profit. Fairness is an objective test which takes into account the position of both parties.

7 DELAY AND DISRUPTION – FINANCIAL CLAIMS

7.1 Causation

Tests for causation

When a failure occurs of either part or all of the works, it may be difficult to identify precisely the cause of that failure. It may be caused by a number of separate events, or by the unique combination of two or more events. This creates significant problems in deciding the liability for the failure. There are several possible tests to establish causation in fact and in law. English law prefers a simple approach.

In *BHP Billiton Petroleum* v. *Dalmine SpA* [2003] the Court of Appeal considered the issue of causation in relation to failure of a pipeline and observed that although it was a matter of common sense it could still be a difficult concept.

The cause of the loss was pipe failure solely where non-compliant pipe was in place. This was clearly an overwhelmingly important fact. The issue was whether the welding procedure as distinct from non-compliant pipe would have caused the loss of a hypothetical pipeline, even if that had been constructed solely out of compliant pipes. Dalmine argued that the onus of proving that but for the incorporation of non-compliant pipes the pipeline would not have failed in any event rested on BHP. This was the 'but for' test of causation.

The Court of Appeal rejected an approach that was unrealistically theoretical. The Court of Appeal held that the role of the 'but for' test was not to be exaggerated. The purpose of that test was to eliminate irrelevant causes.

The Court of Appeal restated the general rule that proof rests on 'him who affirms not him who denies'. If Dalmine wished to show that a hypothetical pipeline made up only of compliant pipe, given more time and the operation of the pipeline at the ultimate working pressure, would have failed in any event, then it had the burden of proving that on the balance of probabilities. For these purposes, a mere possibility of such a failure would not be enough. The burden of proving Dalmine's negative hypothetical case rested on Dalmine.

Global claims

The process of construction can be a complicated interaction of activities. Normally a party making a claim must show a connection between the event and each item of loss. If the overall loss has been caused by the interaction of a number of events, and it is impossible to trace the connection between each individual event and the individual loss, then a global claim is often made. The loss is attributed to the list of events, without a connection between each part of the loss and each event.

It is clear that a global claim for loss may be advanced in certain circumstances: *L. B. Merton* v. *Stanley Hugh Leach*, *Wharf Properties Ltd* v. *Eric Cumine Associates*, *John Holland Construction* v. *Kvaerner R. J. Brown* (1996) 82 BLR 83 and, recently, *John Doyle Construction Ltd* v. *Laing Management (Scotland) Ltd* (2002).

However advancing a claim for loss in global form is a risky approach.

- A global claim will fail if a material part of the cause of the loss was an event for which the other party was not liable and if the evidence disclosed no rational basis for the award of any lesser sum.
- If a lesser claim is to be made out, that must be done on the basis of evidence which was properly led within the scope of the existing case as represented.

7.2 Head office overheads

If a claim is made on the basis of loss for delay then one head of loss is head office overheads. This is a claim that there has been an under-recovery of overheads due to the reduced volume of work caused by the delay It is necessary to prove that loss has occurred and establish the reduction in contribution as a matter of fact.

This normally involves showing that adequate profit and fixed overheads could have been recovered in the prevailing market conditions if it had not been for the use of resources in the period of delay. It is usually necessary to show that the contractor's resources were limited or stretched until released from the delayed construction to such an extent that the contractor was unable to take on work elsewhere. However, it must be shown that there has been a reduction in volume of work overall. Variations may be a cause of the delay and the contribution of this additional work needs to be taken into account in measuring the supposed loss. If there is no reduction in overall turnover, so that the cost of the fixed overheads continues to be met from other sources, there will be no loss attributable to the delay.

Evidence has to be presented to prove that the contractor lost the opportunity of employing the workforce on another contract and that this alternative work would have funded the overheads during the period of delay.

Subject to such proof, the difficulties of evaluation allow a formula method to be adopted to ascertain the measure of the loss. One formula which has judicial approval is the Emden formula which is the ratio of the total overhead cost and profit of the contractor's organization to the total turnover as shown by the contractor's accounts for a fair annual average, multiplied by the contract sum and the period of delay in weeks, divided by the contract period.

The formula is used to solve the difficulties of establishing the measure of loss and not to avoid valuation if this should have been possible. So, for instance, contractors are expected to record managerial time spent on particular projects so that they can show evidence of the extent to which their trading routine was disturbed by the delay.

The evaluation of the loss of contribution needs to take into account the measure of contribution to overhead through the final account and recognition of the contribution from the project resources which have actually been deployed on other sites.

7.3 Finance charges

Finance charges are a measure of loss either as a result of the contractor having to borrow capital to make payments to progress the works or locking up capital in plant, labour and materials capital which it would have invested elsewhere. The loss is the interest which the contractor has to pay on the borrowed capital or the loss of interest on the capital which it is not able to invest.

The rate of interest premium for borrowed capital will depend upon the contractor's arrangement with the lender. The premium is added to the basic lending rate set by the lender which will vary over time. The rate of interest earned on the contractor's own capital will usually differ from the basic lending rate by a margin which will depend upon the amount deposited and the contractor's arrangement with the lender. The rest period for compound interest will vary, but interest is usually earned daily and capitalized either monthly or quarterly.

In *Amec Process and Energy Ltd* v. *Stork Engineers & Contractors BV* [2002] it was held that a claim for financing charges or interest on the amount awarded may be put forward on three alternative bases.

(a) Compound interest may be claimed as a contractual claim for financing charges for variations pursuant to the valuation provisions of the contract.
(b) Compound interest may be claimed as damages for breach of contract.
(c) Interest may be claimed on the basis of the discretionary power of the court or the arbitrator.

Contractual claim

The principles which apply to a contractual claim for financing charges are stated in the twin decisions of the Court of Appeal in *Minter* v. *WHTSO* [1981] 13 BLR 1 and *Rees & Kirby* v. *Swansea City Council* [1986] 30 BLR 1 restated in *Amec Process and Energy Ltd* v. *Stork Engineers & Contractors BV* [2002] as follows.

(a) Recovery, even for compound interest, is not intrinsically irrecoverable as being usurious or contrary to public policy.
(b) Whether such costs are recoverable as a contractual entitlement under the contract, is a matter for the parties and the terms of their contract.
(c) The expression 'direct loss and expense' under standard JCT Forms confers an entitlement for ascertainable loss caused by financing the expenditure for such parts of the period between the loss and expense arising and payment that are not directly excluded from an entitlement to payment by the terms of the contract. If the financing costs were not directly incurred as a result of the instructions of other causes which give rise to an obligation on the employer to pay but were incurred, instead, as a result of some other cause, these costs would not be recoverable as direct loss and expense.
(d) Interest reasonably paid on capital required to finance variations or work disrupted by the lack of necessary instructions was recoverable under 'direct loss and expense'.
(e) The cost of financing the necessary work for periods before any entitlement to payment arose under the contract would not ordinarily be recoverable.
(f) Any necessary notification procedures imposed on the contractor would need to be followed.

In order to succeed in a claim for financing costs it was necessary to show that:

(a) the contractor incurred the financing charges in question
(b) the basis of the relevant contractual evaluation was authorized by the terms of the contract
(c) compound interest was recoverable
(d) the relevant period was one for which the contractor may recover interest under the terms of the contract.

In *Amec Process and Energy Ltd* v. *Stork Engineers & Contractors BV* [2002], Stork had an obligation to agree or stipulate the basis of payment during the work. The contract allowed Stork to specify the basis of evaluation when instructing a variation. If an estimate was called for and not agreed then the basis of remuneration was reimbursable cost. Amec were required to give Stork access to its accounts and records. Stork had a contractual obligation to operate and give effect to the evaluation provisions of the contract such that the appropriate sum for variations would be determined, invoiced and paid within the timescales envisaged, being within one month from the execution of the work for invoicing and a 60-day further period for payment. In consequence, Amec became immediately entitled, once the variation work in question had been carried out, to payment on a reimbursable cost basis. The provisions of the contract were wide enough to embrace interest paid to enable the work to be financed. The costs arose because Stork varied the contractual arrangements for evaluating, invoicing and paying for these variations. Stork unilaterally decided not to reach agreement during the work or to issue stipulations or pay the sums being claimed. On that basis the claim succeeded.

ICE 6th Edition and MF/1 Edition 3 includes finance charges in the definition of the term 'costs'. The Engineering Construction Contract Schedule of Cost Components allows a cost component of finance charges in the evaluation of actual cost.

Damages for breach of contract
It is usually not possible to recover interest as damages where the relevant breach of contract has been non-payment of a debt. Interest may be awarded as the measure of damages for breach of contract under the second limb of *Hadley* v. *Baxendale* where such damages would also be recoverable under the first limb, *Wadsworth* v. *Lydall* [1991] CA, *La Pintada* [1985] HL and *President of India* v. *Lips Maritime Corp* [1988] HL restated in *Amec Process and Energy Ltd* v. *Stork Engineers & Contractors BV* [2002].

Discretionary interest by tribunal
The court has discretion to award simple interest under the Law Reform Act.

An arbitrator has discretion to award interest, whether simple or compound, under clause 49 of the Arbitration Act 1996.

It is suggested that an adjudicator does not have the discretion to award interest absent an express power.

7.4 Constructive acceleration claim
Uncertainty due to absence of extension of time
A 'constructive acceleration' claim is an attempt by the contractor to recover its expenditure incurred due to the uncertainty created by the A/E's failure to grant extensions of time. This has been accepted in the US courts but in English law there is little authority. The situation is characterized by the A/E's mistaken belief that no extension of time is due and the employer pressing the contractor to complete by the fixed date for completion.

The problem faced by the contractor is that in the absence of an extension of time it may be faced with the possibility of liquidation damages being levied against it. The contractor has a stark choice. It can continue to work as planned and (presumably) efficiently in the hope that it can prove that it is entitled to an extension of time and that this will be granted by the A/E. Alternatively, the contractor can accept that it is in default, at least temporarily, and take steps to mitigate the consequences of this temporary default by increasing resources and reorganizing the work.

This choice was recognized in *Ascon Contracting Limited* v. *Alfred McAlpine Construction Isle of Man Limited* [1999]. It was held that there was no obligation on the subcontractor to mitigate the consequences of the contractor's breaches of contract, since that would deprive the subcontractor of the opportunity, knowing how much of the current delay had been allowed, of assessing whether it was necessary to consider incurring additional expense in accelerative measures in order to reduce its potential liability in damages for any disallowed balance, and if so to decide for itself how far it was in its own interests to incur that expense in the absence of instructions to do so as a variation.

The decision in Ascon suggests that the choice of whether or not to accelerate is at the discretion of the contractor, but there is no obligation to do so. It is implicit in the decision that the contractor has a discretion in relation to its own culpable delay, but for delays for which the contractor is entitled to an extension of time it will not recover costs unless instructed to accelerate. The decision leaves open the issue whether there is any failure in the administration of the contract and particularly the extension of time provisions which would ever allow the contractor to recover acceleration costs in consequence.

The judgment to be made by the contractor is whether the additional costs of acceleration consequent on disruption are less than the liquidated damages which may be levied against it if it continues its normal sequence of working. The measure of acceleration costs is not always obvious so the choice is difficult. In addition, the contractor has to judge the real risk of levy of liquidated damages since it may eventually be granted an extension of time.

If the contractor is successful in accelerating the works then it may find that it has no or a reduced entitlement to an extension of time. The contractor will have succeeded in avoiding the levy of liquidated damages, but may find that this was not a risk in any event, because it had an entitlement to an extension of time.

In *Motherwell Bridge Construction Limited* v. *Micafil Vakuumtecchnik* (2002) TCC 81 ConLR 44 the issue of acceleration was addressed in a long and complicated judgment by Judge Toulmin CMG QC.

Motherwell was a subcontractor to Micafil for the construction of an autoclave for the employer BICC under modified FIDIC Forms of contract. The autoclave was a large steel vessel used in the manufacture of high quality power cables. There were a large number of claims by Motherwell.

One of two claims was for acceleration costs for the work in the shop for working night shift from 19 June 1998 to 11 September 1998 in order to keep the work to schedule as a result of additional substantial work due changes in design by Micafil.

Motherwell had requested an extension of time in its facsimile dated 11 May 1998, indicating that it was possible, at Micafil's expense, to work additional hours to reduce the over-run. In a facsimile dated 18 June 1998 Motherwell stated that it was considerably increasing its labour force and working night shift in an effort to meet the changes to the workscope. Motherwell recorded that it would record the costs associated with the work and sought recompense for acceleration of the programme.

At a meeting on 23 and 24 June 1998, Motherwell stated that if Micafil was not prepared to acknowledge that there was an expanded contract, either Motherwell had to be compensated for accelerating the contract or granted an extension of time. At this point Micafil offered an extension of time of 3–4 weeks. The meeting finished without resolution with an action for Motherwell to prepare a substantial case for additional costs for acceleration. In a facsimile dated 25 June 1998 Micafil complained that Motherwell had still not increased their personnel resources on site. On 7 July 1998, Motherwell set out its claims which included additional costs for acceleration, and stated that if this was not acceptable that they would require an extension of time.

Judge Toulmin held that the costs were incurred by Motherwell in an attempt to recover time lost in completing the work in circumstances where Motherwell were subject to significant penalties for delay if they failed to complete the work in time. The causes were the restrictions encountered on site and the very substantial increased scope of the work. He held that Motherwell was entitled to additional costs, the quantum of which had been agreed by the parties. Motherwell was held also to be entitled to recover sums which were paid to their employees for work carried out at premium rates in order to keep to the required timetable. It was held that it was entirely reasonable for Motherwell to require its employees to work in excess of the hours allowed in its tender on order to try to keep to the time schedule which had been imposed upon them and in respect of which they had not been given relief by Micafil to reflect the increase in work or the difficulties of working on site. Motherwell was also entitled to payment for the consequences of excessive overtime, which it was agreed resulted in a 10% loss of productivity equivalent to a delay in progress equivalent to 10% of the 'as planned' task duration.

The decision in Motherwell is a recognition of a constructive acceleration claim. It appears to be an important fact that Micafil complained that resources had not been increased and that it was accepted that Motherwell would prepare its acceleration claim. It is by no means clear from the judgment that Micafil insisted that Motherwell should keep work up to schedule, but it appears to have been sufficient that no extension of time was granted. Unfortunately, there is little in the way of legal analysis and it is suggested that the decision is very much on its own facts.

Nature of the problem

The difficulty faced by the contractor is that many standard forms of contract envisage several stages in the determination of extensions of time by the A/E. Many standard forms provide for the interim assessment of extensions of time followed by final review at some later stage. There would therefore appear to be a contractual remedy available to the contractor for the failure of the A/E to award the extension of time at the interim stage. In addition, there are remedies available in adjudication, arbitration and litigation. These remedies are of little help to the contractor at the time when it needs to make the decision whether or not to accelerate.

The essence of the problem is the exact nature of the 'temporary default', when the contractor may appear to be in breach of contract pending the final determination of extension of time. If the situation has been brought about by the employer's breach of contract in not ensuring that the contract is administered properly, then this may allow the contractor to recover acceleration costs. There are significant difficulties in this approach. First, it is difficult to establish grounds for such a breach and, secondly, even if such grounds can be established, acceleration measures are not so clearly the natural consequence of such a failure.

Employer's breach of contract

There are a number of cases which deal with the failure of the A/E to certify payment and the issue of whether this is can be a breach of contract by the employer.

In carrying out his or her role as a certifier, the A/E must act fairly, reasonably and impartially as between the employer and contractor, in exercising discretion and forming opinions. In *Hickman* v. *Roberts* [1913] the contractor was entitled to payment in the absence of a certificate because the architect had allowed himself to be influenced by the employer. In *Minster Trust Ltd* v. *Traps Tractors Ltd* [1954], Devlin J. held that there was an implied term that the parties would not do anything to prevent the certifier acting independently. *John Mowlem & Co. plc* v. *Eagle Star Insurance Co. Ltd* confirms that such a term will be implied into a contract if it is necessary having regard to the express terms of the contract. The fact that the A/E is employed by the employer does not in principle prevent him or her acting fairly between the parties. In *Panamena*, below, the certifying surveyor was the President of the employer company. This relationship was known to the contractor when the contract was made.

In *Panamena Europea Navigation Compania Limitada* v. *Frederick Leyland & Co. Ltd* [1947] the surveyor was required to certify the amount due to be paid under the contract. The issue of the certificate was a condition precedent to payment. It was found that the employer had hindered the proper execution of the certificate. It was held that, if the employer was aware that the certifier was failing to carry out his function properly, he was under a contractual duty to stop him and tell him what were his functions. The employer had failed to do so and it was held that the contractor was entitled to payment in the absence of a certificate. The decision was based on breach of a contractual duty implied as a term of the contract, and based on the principle that no person can take advantage of the non-fulfilment of a condition, if he or she has personally hindered the performance of it.

In *Lubenham* v. *South Pembrokeshire District Council* (1986) 33 BLR 46 the contract was a JCT Form. In contrast to *Panamena*, in this case the employer had not tried to influence its architect but had simply followed his advice. In addition, there was one fundamental difference between the JCT Form and the contract in *Panamena*. The JCT Form had a very wide arbitration clause which permitted arbitration upon interim certificates before practical completion. There was no arbitration clause at all in the *Panamena* contract. Because of the arbitration clause there was no need nor any scope for the implication of a term as in *Panamena*. If the contractor wished to challenge any interim certificate, there was a simple remedy which did not require the implication of a term. The contractor could request the appropriate adjustment in another certificate or, if this was refused, go to arbitration and have the certificate corrected. It followed therefore that the responsibility on the part of the employer was merely to pay the amount certified even though he clearly knew the amount to be wrong.

In *Reed* v. *Van der Vorm* 33 BLR 140 (1985) the distinction between final and interim certificates was seen to be important. The contract was cost-plus. There was no arbitration clause. The employer agreed to pay the amount certified on a monthly basis. The works were not revalued as a whole each time a certificate was issued so that they were not interim certificates in that sense. It was held that since there was a mechanism chosen for payment, it was not open to the courts to re-open payments made on other past certificates.

On the basis of the above case law, there is no contractual duty implied as a term of the contract that the employer should oversee or supervise the A/E's functions of certification of payment under the contract. If the contractor wishes to challenge any interim certificate, it can request the appropriate adjustment in another certificate or, if this is refused, go to arbitration or litigation and have the certificate corrected.

In addition to the above cases dealing with certificates of payment, there are also cases which deal with the A/E's failure to grant an extension of time and the affect that this has on the liquidated damages provisions. There is an important distinction between the above cases and claims for damages for constructive acceleration. In the former, the claim is simply for payment of the contract price and the central issue is the avoidance of the need for the A/E certificate. Alternatively, the claim uses the failure of the A/E to operate the extension of time provisions to resist the levy of liquidated damages. In contrast, in acceleration claims the damages are claimed in addition to the contract price.

In the Australian case of *Perini Corporation* v. *Commonwealth of Australia* (1969) 12 BLR 82, McFarlin J. agreed that *Panamena* was authority for the proposition that in the case of a wrongful, in the sense of an unauthorized, exercise of powers by the certifier with the knowledge of the employer, the contractor was entitled to disregard the provisions of the contract with respect to time and either sue for price or resist a claim for liquidated damages. McFarlin held further, however, that it did not follow, nor had it been decided that if the contractor has otherwise suffered damage it was not entitled to sue upon an implied term.

It was held in *Perini* that there was an implied term ('a positive implied term') in the contract that the employer would ensure that the A/E did his or her duty as a certifier. In *Perini* the equivalent of the A/E repeatedly refused to give a decision on a contractor's applications for an extension of time. The contractor accelerated in order to avoid liquidated damages being imposed and to meet the contractual completion date. McFarlane J. found in favour of the contractor but indicated clearly that this type of claim could only be sustained on the basis of some proven breach by the employer; the breach in this case being the refusal or failure of the certifier to give any consideration at all to the contractor's applications. The contract in this case contained an arbitration clause, and the fact that the contractor could have sought the resolution of the matter at an early stage did not appear to be significant, the issue does not seem to have been raised.

It would therefore appear that where it can be shown that the A/E has unreasonably or unnecessarily delayed the grant of extensions of time, there is little difficulty in establishing that this is a breach of contract by the employer. In cases which deal with the failure to grant an extension of time and the affect that this has on the liquidated damages provisions, it appears to be accepted that the said failure by the A/E is a breach of contract by the employer. It is suggested that a distinction needs to be made between an express refusal or continued failure to deal promptly with an extension of time application on the part of the A/E, and an honestly held view or assessment that no extension of time is due. The issue, however, is when can the A/E be considered to have unreasonably or unnecessarily delayed the grant of an extension of time.

7.5 Evaluation of disruption

The employer's breach of contract, such as late supply of information and late possessions, may disrupt the contractor's method of working. This may show itself as a loss of productivity with loss of motivation of the workforce due to the inability to offer incentive bonuses and the inability of management to plan properly due to the uncertainties caused by the breach.

The very fact of disruption may itself prevent the record keeping required to accurately evaluate the loss caused by disruption. A claim based simply on global overspend is unlikely to be sufficient to evaluate loss. Once liability and causation has been established, the courts will not allow the difficulties of proving exact measure of loss to prevent a contractor being compensated. So, the steps to establishing a claim for disruption are as follows.

(a) A breach of contract needs to be proved.
(b) A loss needs to be proved.
(c) The loss complained of needs to be proved to have been caused by the breach of contract – cause and effect.
(d) If some loss is shown as having occurred then several methods are available to quantify the loss:
  (i) a global claim may be sufficient but this will be unusual
  (ii) the adoption of norms will normally be sufficient based either on industry-specific norms, contractor-specific norms or site-specific norms
  (iii) assessments may be sufficient if reasonable.

If it is possible to compare the productivity of the workforce before the disruption occurred with the productivity during the disrupted period, then the courts are willing to accept this as the basis for quantifying the loss. This method requires clear labour records, so that the area which the labour resources are working on can be identified.

It may not be possible due to the nature of the disrupting matters and the complexity of the project to employ the comparison of norms approach. There may be difficulties in isolating the additional hours of labour and plant which result from each and every disrupting event. It may be appropriate then to base the measure of loss on the rate which the contractor would have charged if the disruptive conditions had been known in advance. The rate must be shown to be a reasonable estimate.

Where there are competing causes, apportionment is possible in cases of disruption according to the relative importance of the various causation events in producing the loss.

The contractor should be able to recover for part of his loss and expense, and the practical difficulties of carrying out the exercise should not prevent him from doing so *John Doyle Construction Ltd* v. *Laing Management Ltd* [2004].

8 MANAGEMENT OF CLAIMS

8.1 Strategy plan

The main purpose of a claim is to present sufficient information to another party, to persuade them that there is an entitlement to the remedy sought and, together with information and experience they already have to decide the measure of that entitlement. In construction, most claims will require legal argument to be presented, even if in some cases this is only a statement as to the clause of the contract. In addition, the claim will be a statement of relevant facts with an explanation of the technical consequences of the facts in terms of engineering, and/or time and/or cost. The extent of analysis and explanation and the level of proof will depend on the experience of the other party as well as the forum in which the claim is presented.

A claim does not necessarily create a dispute, but some consideration must be given to the possibility that the parties will not be able to agree. Many costs incurred in preparing claims and resolving any disputes can be avoided if a structured approach is taken. The first consideration is the forum in which resolution is to be achieved. The level of proof, and therefore the cost, rises in proportion to the unwillingness of the other party to settle the claim or dispute at the level expected. Management of a claim means quickly establishing realistic levels of expectation of both parties. Understanding the other side's position is the key to a structured approach to disputes. It is necessary to know the restraints on, and the attitude of, the other side. In all cases dialogue is vital.

If the preparation of the claim and resolution of any dispute is to be managed efficiently, then it is necessary to manage both the technical and legal investigation. These two aspects are interrelated, and the process is essentially iterative. Such an investigation benefits from the type of project management approach adopted on construction projects themselves, but the skills required are different. A flexible approach is required. Because of the diverse disciplines normally involved and the commitment of the participants to existing tasks, some form of strategy plan, however short, will be required.

In order to prepare such a plan it will first be necessary to carry out an initial analysis so that the strategy for the claim can be established. In some claims this may simply be a short meeting with the manager of the project. On larger or complicated claims it may involve three or four days of intensive meetings with the team members led by a legally qualified facilitator experienced in the management of claims.

The plan addresses the main problems which will jeopardize the success of the process, such as the availability of evidence, both in terms of witnesses and documents, and the effort required to analyse the facts. The plan should identify the members of the dispute team, including witnesses of fact, the experts and their disciplines and any legal experts required. The plan will normally include a programme identifying the key elements of the investigation, the input required from witnesses and any experts, and the cost of the preparation of the claim.

The plan, which in many claims will be in the form of a network programme, is the main tool for reporting progress and managing the resources required. Efficient claims management requires the benefit or value of further investigation in increasing the chances of success, to be weighed against the cost of that further investigation. This is a form of claim value engineering but, to be effective, it must be based on the following:

(a) the loss incurred
(b) the loss likely to have been incurred by the other party
(c) the direct cost profile of the likely forum of dispute resolution
(d) the indirect cost profile of the likely forum of dispute resolution
(e) the likely range of levels of award.

Decision tree models can be constructed to allow analysis by computer of the various possibilities. While the necessary technology is available, in complex claims such models do not easily allow decisions to be made without a considerable investment in the construction of the model.

8.2 Management of evidence

Efficient fact management requires all data to be easily traced so that at any stage the relevant fact supporting a statement can be retrieved. Various systems can be adopted depending on the extent of information.

A system commonly used is electronic data management. This involves creating electronic copies of documents usually indexed initially by document type, date and reference number. As the investigation progresses the index is expanded by subject references. Once the documents have been scanned and the initial indexing completed, CD-ROMs are created. Some proprietary systems include on the CD all the software necessary to run the database of electronic documents from the CD. This is a significant benefit when the investigation involves team members in different geographic locations, since they can access the full evidence on the CD without needing to access the originals. If the full benefit is to be obtained, the integrity of the system needs to be protected and appropriate procedures followed.

8.3 Management of delay and disruption analysis

The analysis of delay and disruption needs to be based on a factual analysis of events. Inevitably, the emphasis is on the engineering of the project. Management of the evidence of this element of the investigation can be by the use of two programme schedules, below.

Schedule of dates and evidence

Activity	Description	Start date	Document reference definition	Finish date	Document reference definition

Each activity shown as a bar on the as-built programme is described in the above schedule. This provides not only documentary evidence of each date used, but the definition assumed for 'start' and 'finish'. The data management system described above allows traceability of evidence.

Schedule of construction logic

Activity	Start restraint activities						Description
	Activity	Type	Activity	Type	Activity	Type	

The schedule of construction logic is a summary of the engineering operations which dictate the commencement of certain key activities, e.g. an explanation why an activity cannot start until the previous activity has finished; an explanation of the various construction restraints on the start of an activity; an explanation of the main operations which dictate the period of the activity. The details of the schedule are incorporated into the as-built programme as logical restraints.

8.4 Settlement

An essential aim in managing claims is to achieve early agreement to the entitlement at an optimum level. Part of the implementation of the plan is to identify at an early stage the likely acceptable settlement range. This will take into account the perceived strengths and weaknesses of the case, the perceptions of and the pressures on the other party and the costs involved in pursuing the dispute. The settlement range is likely to change as the case develops.

It is important in any settlement negotiations that the negotiator has the skills necessary to present a persuasive case. He or she must to be able to recognize and deal with new evidence which either weakens or strengthens the case, and therefore changes the settlement range. The negotiator needs to understand both the technical and legal aspects of the disputes.

The structured approach to resolution of disputes described above, allows advantage to be taken of settlement opportunities when they arise.

8.5 Relevance of third party settlement

A contractor may settle the claims of its subcontractors or suppliers for a number of commercial reasons. The employer may also settle with direct contractors on large commercial projects, for similar commercial reasons. The settlement amount therefore may not always be based precisely on the measure of damages likely to be awarded by a court or arbitrator. It may instead take into account the cost of pursuing the claim and the need to complete the particular development with the necessary goodwill. When the contractor seeks to recover its loss from the employer, or the employer to contra-charge the contractor, it may then be faced with the argument that the settlement is irrelevant or be put to the expense of proving the third party loss.

The third party settlement is not irrelevant if it can be shown to be a reasonable settlement in the circumstances; then it should be the measure of damages. The evidence that may be sufficient to establish reasonableness is proof that the settlement had been made under legal advice and that a vital matter had not been overlooked. If it can be shown that the damages would be somewhere around the figure of the third party settlement, then that will be the measure of damages. The question is not whether the other party had acted reasonably in settling the claim, but whether the settlement was a reasonable one, and, in considering it, the costs of litigation can be taken into account *Biggins and Co Ltd* v. *Permanite Ltd* (1950), (1951) 2 All ER 191 and *Oxford University Press* v. *John Stedman Design Group* (1990). In *John F. Hunt Demolition Limited* v. *ASME Engineering Limited* [2007] EWHC 1507 (TCC) Coulson J held that it is not necessary to prove that the claim settled would probably have succeeded. It is enough to establish that the claim had sufficient substance for the settlement of it to be regarded as reasonable. A claim will usually have to be so weak as to be obviously hopeless before it could be said that the settlement of the claim was unreasonable. Even though later investigation of the underlying facts demonstrates that there was no liability at all, the settlement of the claim may still be considered to be reasonable. If on the facts the amount paid was an unreasonable settlement then, prima facie, it was not recoverable.

The best action for a contractor or employer intending to settle a third party claim, is to seek an independent assessment or audit of both the legal basis of the claim and the measure of damages claimed.

9 PARTICULAR ADMINISTRATIVE CLAIM ISSUES

9.1 Access to the site

Access to the site in which the works are being constructed is necessary to allow transport and delivery of materials, plant and equipment, as well as to allow services and the workforce to reach the site. In order to be effective the access must be suitable for the type of transport required and must be available to the contractor at the appropriate time. Even if access is physically available, local permissions and customs clearances may be necessary to allow legal use of access.

The extent of any responsibility for providing the required access across adjacent property and buildings, obtaining the necessary permissions and the apportionment of risk for events that prevent the required access, will depend upon the terms of the contract. Even if a term implied that physical access is to be provided by one party, the term may not extend to requiring that party to take responsibility for the adequacy of the access for the transport of plant and equipment for the works. The responsibility may only be to provide the opportunity to enter the site, with no breach of contract if, for instance, access is prevented by strike pickets *LRE Engineering Services Ltd* v. *Otto Simon Carves Ltd* [1981] 24 BLR 131.

Standard forms

The standard forms generally expressly state the responsibilities for access to site, in terms that reflect the type of work envisaged and the expected use of the forms.

FIDIC Forms: The FIDIC Red, Orange and Yellow Forms 1999 place the main responsibility for access on the contractor and reflect the international and civil/mechanical type of works envisaged.

ICE 7th Edition: The ICE 7th Edition also places the main responsibility for access on the employer, subject to specific prescription in the contract, with particular emphasis on the apportionment of liability for use of UK public highways reflecting the civil engineering, UK-based type of works envisaged. The contractor is, however, required to satisfy himself that the access is suitable.

ECC 2nd Edition: The Engineering Construction Contract is said to be applicable to all types of construction contracts. Its main use has been in civil engineering works. The form places an unqualified obligation on the employer to provide access to site, but is silent on the responsibility for the condition or suitability of the access. The subcontract form is in similar terms and does not address common issues of attendance, for which see below.

IChemE Red Book: The IChemE Red Book 3rd Edition places the main responsibility for physical means of access on the purchaser, with responsibility for obtaining permissions on the contractor. The form reflects the processing type of works envisaged in which the contractor's main expertise is envisaged as designing and installing Plant.

MF/1 Form (Rev 4): The MF/I Form makes the purchaser responsible for providing suitable access to the site, subject to specified limitations. The purchaser is also responsible for obtaining import licences.

JCT 1998: The JCT 1998 Forms do not include express terms stating responsibility for access to the site, but the apportionment of responsibility and risk is to be found in the list of relevant events that entitle the contractor to extension of time and the list of matters that entitle payment of loss and expense. It appears that the employer is responsible for providing access to the site through adjacent areas providing it has possession and control of those adjacent areas. This will normally be the case if the works are building works, as envisaged by the JCT Form.

Subcontracts and attendance

Where work is subcontracted, the contractor will normally have possession of the overall site and access to the overall site will already be provided. The issue in subcontracts will then be the availability of suitable access within the overall site and particular access to a part of the site by special means. The particular access may require scaffolding or hoists or other means of physical access to the relevant part of the works during construction. The access may be provided through 'attendance' by the contractor on the subcontractor.

In the absence of express terms, it is likely that terms will be implied that the contractor will provide the subcontractor with reasonable access within the site to allow it to carry out its obligations in a reasonable manner without undue or unreasonable interference.

Since the contractor may have employed a number of contractors on the site, the subcontractor will be concerned to identify access or attendance that is exclusive to him, and if not exclusive the extent of interference likely from other contractors. The standard subcontract forms deal with access and attendance in different ways.

CECA Blue Form 1998: Under the CECA the contractor provides access to parts of the site but only from time to time and not exclusively, unless specified. Attendance is provided but the obligation to do so is heavily circumscribed.

DOM/1: The DOM/1 Form provisions for access are similar to the JCT 1998 Form. Clause 27 deals with attendance.

9.2 Possession of the site

A construction contract necessarily requires the owner to give the contractor such possession, occupation or use as is necessary to enable him to perform the contract (*The London Borough of Hounslow* v. *Twickenham Gardens Development* (1970) 78 BLR 89). In a new project a term would normally be implied into a construction contract (in the absence of an express term) that the site would be handed over within a reasonable time and, in most cases, with a sufficient uninterrupted possession to allow the contractor to carry out its obligations by the method of its choice: the Canadian case of *Penvidic Contracting Co. Ltd* v. *International Nickel Co. of Canada Ltd* [1975] 53 DLR 748. If a contract contains an 'entire agreement' clause, this will not prevent the implication of a right to possession without clear words (*Milburn Services Limited* v. *United Trading Group (UK) Limited* (1995) 52 ConLR 130.

The degree of possession or access provided by the employer will vary with the circumstances. Generally, more than the actual site on which the structure stands is required to erect the structure. The employer is normally required to give possession of sufficient portions of the site of the work to permit compliance with the contract: the Canadian Case of *The Queen in Rights of Canada* v. *Walter Cabbott Construction Ltd* (1975) 21 BLR 26.

A term will normally be implied that the employer will not interfere with the work. Generally, if it is necessary for one party to cooperate in order for the other to carry out the work, then a term will be implied (in the absence of express terms) requiring that party to do all that is necessary for it to do to complete the works (*London Borough of Merton* v. *Leach* (1988) 32 BLR 51). This may include obtaining building permits *Ellis-Don Ltd* v. *The Parking Authority of Toronto* (1978) 28 BLR 106.

The type and extent of use of the site will depend upon the nature of work and the stage of construction. A main contractor will usually have exclusive occupation and use the site and a subcontractor will not. At the end of the contract period, the contractor may require partial occupation to carry out performance tests. The meaning and extent of possession depends upon the express and implied terms of the contract. In subcontracts there may not be continuous working (*Kitson Sheet Metal Ltd* v. *Matthew Hall Mechanical and Electrical Engineers Ltd* (1989) 47 BLR 82) and the contractor's failure to obtain areas and access needed by the subcontractors will not be a breach of contract, provided that the contractor made sufficient effort to obtain them, although this will be unusual.

The meaning of 'possession' under clause 21(1) of JCT 63 has been held to confer on the contractor a licence to occupy the site up to the date of completion. On completion, that licence comes to an end, and there is then only a right to re-enter to such an extent as is necessary to remedy defects (*H.W. Nevill (Sunblest) Ltd* v. *William Press & Son Ltd* (1981) 20 BLR 83). It is suggested that this is the usual meaning in the construction industry.

The decision in *The London Borough of Hounslow* v. *Twickenham Gardens Development Ltd* (1970) 7 BLR 89 is authority for the implication of a term, in the absence of express terms, that a contractual licence granted by the employer is irrevocable. The decision is doubted however and unlikely to be followed today. In *Tara Civil Engineering Ltd* v. *Moorfield Developments Ltd* (1989) 46 BLR 74 the court refused to follow the decision in *Hounslow* and refused to look behind a certificate under the contract. In *Wiltshier Construction (South) Limited* v. *Parkers Developments Limited* the decision in *Tara* was distinguished since the contract administrator's notice of default was invalid, and an injunction was continued to prevent the employer issuing a notice of default determining the contractor's employment. In the New Zealand decision of *Mayfield Holdings Ltd* v. *Moona Reef Ltd* (1973) INZLR 309 the decision in *Hounslow* and the implications of an irrevocable licence was criticized comprehensively.

The decision of HH Judge Thornton QC in *Impresa Castelli SpA* v. *Cola Holdings Limited* (2002) TCC deals with the meaning of the terms 'access', 'partial possession' and 'use or occupation' in the context of JCT Forms of contract. Judge Thornton identified three relevant and separate types of possession and occupation which needed to be considered.

(a) The contractor, while carrying out the works, has exclusive possession of those works.
(b) Following partial possession, the employer takes back exclusive possession from the contractor for that part of the works.
(c) The contractor retains exclusive possession but allows the employer to use or occupy part or all of the site or the works. When this occurs, the exclusive possession of the contractor is modified by the presence of the employer to the extent and in the manner that that use or occupation has been agreed to by the contractor.

Judge Thornton provided a useful summary of the JCT provisions for possession, partial possession and occupation.

(a) The contractor is granted exclusive possession of the site and of the works and retains exclusive possession until practical completion occurs unless parts of the works are handed back to the employer and are taken into the employer's exclusive possession at an earlier stage.
(b) That can occur whether or not those parts of the works have been completed and, if this happens, the contractor's obligation to continue with the works in that portion ceases and is replaced by a defects liability obligation.
(c) It is the return of exclusive possession by the contractor to the employer which brings the working period of the contract to an end.
(d) Although the works and each part of them are in the exclusive possession of either the contractor or the employer, a lesser form of physical presence on or within the works that is defined as the use or occupation of the incomplete works by the employer is allowed, notwithstanding the exclusive possession of the works by the contractor.

(e) This presence by the employer has no effect on the contractor's exclusive possession of the works nor on the contractor's obligations and entitlements with regard to liquidated damages, retention, defects liability, insurance, reinstatement or the preparation of a final account. The employer is, in effect, a sub-licensee to the contractor who, otherwise, retains exclusive possession of the works.

Express terms of standard forms

The standard forms generally expressly state the extent of possession of the site, in terms that reflect the type of work envisaged and the expected use of the forms.

FIDIC Forms: The FIDIC Red, Orange and Yellow Forms 1998 place the responsibility for providing possession of the site on the employer and, as expected in a modern contract, the programme figures largely in deciding when possession is to be given. The extent of the site to be provided is defined very widely. The employer's obligations in obtaining necessary legal permissions for access are severely limited. The contractor's obligations include the safety of the site and require it to have extensive control of the site. The extent of possession is not exclusive to the contractor, but the right of access to other contractors is prescribed, otherwise interference will be a variation to the contract with consequent entitlements. There is an express right of access for the engineer to carry out their functions under the contract. After completion, the contractor has rights of access to remedy defects during the defects notification period, and access to the works, although circumscribed, to repeat failed tests after completion. The employer may terminate the contract at any time for its convenience.

ICE 7th Edition: The ICE 7th Edition requires the employer to provide immediate possession of all of the site subject to express provisions otherwise. The possession granted appears not to be exclusive to the contractor, although it has extensive control of the site and entitlement to compensation if there is undue interference. The division of responsibility for permissions makes the employer responsible for complying with acts etc. relating to the permanent works or the unavoidable result of constructing the works in accordance with the contract. By means of various indemnities the contractor is protected from third party liabilities which are the unavoidable result of constructing the works in accordance with the contract.

ECC 2nd Edition: The Engineering Construction Contract is said to be applicable to all types of construction contracts. Its main use has been in civil engineering works. The employer is required to provide the contractor possession and use of the site in accordance with the accepted programme, a central management document in this form. The possession is not exclusive to the contractor since it must be shared with others, but the failure of others to do work within the conditions in the works information is a compensation event. The working areas are implicitly defined as the areas that are necessary to provide the works.

IChemE Red Book: The IChemE Red Book requires the purchaser to give the contractor possession of the site such as to allow it to carry out its obligations under the contract. The contractor does not have exclusive possession but has control of the site and cannot withhold access to other contractors where access would impede its own performance of the contract. The employer may stop execution of the works at any time and have the contractor withdraw from site.

MF/1 (Rev 4): The provisions in the MF/1 Form reflect the type of work envisaged which is essentially manufacture of plant off-site and then delivery to site and installation, on what may in many cases be an operational site. The contractor is required to comply with the purchaser's safety regulations. The purchaser is required to obtain all permissions in relation to the works. The purchaser is required to permit the contractor access to repeat performance tests and even shut down any part of the works if necessary. The purchaser is liable for damage that is the inevitable result of constructing the works in accordance with the contract.

JCT 1998: The JCT 1998 Forms are intended to be used in building works. The employer is required to give the contractor possession and this appears to be exclusive possession, with a right of access to the architect so that they can carry out their function. JCT 1998 does not state the degree of interference allowed by others, but work by others is to be carried out only with the consent of the contractor unless specified in the contract. The apportionment of responsibility and risk is to be found in the list of relevant events that the contractor to extension of time and the list of matters that entitle payment of loss and expense.

Express terms of subcontracts

Where work is subcontracted, the contractor will normally have possession of the overall site and the subcontractor's work will need to be carried out under the contractor's site regulations. The issue in subcontracts will then be the extent of possession provided by the contractor. Normally, the subcontractor would be required to work with other contractors with no guarantee of continuous working, although this would depend upon the circumstances and the details of the subcontract.

CECA Blue Form 1998: The CECA Form limits the contractor's liability to the subcontractor to the employer's liability to the contractor. The contractor has full control of when the subcontractor has possession of the site.

DOM/1: DOM/1 is similar to the JCT 1998 Forms.

9.3 Acceleration

Acceleration in construction means carrying out an obligation in a shorter period than originally planned, and can affect design as well as construction activities. There are two types of acceleration. The first is the completion of the same work in a shorter time than planned. The second is completion of additional or delayed work by the same completion date as originally planned.

Most standard forms of contract allow the contractor to complete the works before the completion date (*Glenlion Construction Ltd* v. *Guinness Trust* (1987) 39 BLR 89).

Acceleration in many situations will disrupt the works, affecting smooth trade interfaces and increasing interference between follow-on operations. In some cases it will mean unplanned access to working areas, reduced productivity and increase in defects as well as stoppages.

Many standard forms provide a power for ordering the contractor to adopt acceleration measures if it is considered that progress is not in accordance with the programme, due to the contractor's default.

It is always possible for the parties to agree to accelerate the works for their mutual benefit, but it is important to ensure that the terms relating to liquidated damages still operate (*John Barker Construction Ltd* v. *London Portman Hotel Ltd* (1996) 83 BLR 35).

There may be considerable difficulties in evaluating the additional costs of acceleration and differentiating those costs from the costs of carrying out the works at the normal pace. Good records are vital, but it may be appropriate to simply take a broad approach (*AMEC & Alfred McAlpine (Joint Venture)* v. *Cheshire County Council* (1999) BLR 303).

Standard forms

The standard forms generally give the contract administrator power to require the contractor to revise the programme to reduce the effects of delays that are the contractor's default. Some forms also give the contract administrator power to order acceleration to achieve the completion date if the delay is due to the contractor's default. Only few forms allow the contract administrator to negotiate acceleration agreements. Generally, the contractor's obligations are to complete by the specified date and to proceed regularly and diligently. Breach of these obligations normally allows the employer to terminate the contractor's employment following notice and failure to remedy the default.

FIDIC 1998: Clause 3.1 of the Red and Yellow Forms provides that the engineer has no authority to amend the contract. There is no power therefore for the engineer to negotiate an acceleration agreement for the employer.

ICE 7th Edition: Clause 2(1)(c) provides that the engineer has no authority to amend the contract or to relieve the contractor of any obligations under the contract, except as expressly stated in the contract. Clause 46(3) refers to acceleration agreements. The employer or the engineer may request the contractor to complete in less than the time or extended time for completion. If the contractor agrees, then special terms and conditions of payment are to be agreed before any acceleration measures are taken.

ECC 2nd Edition: Clause 30.1 requires the contractor to do the work so that completion is on or before the completion date.

Clause 32.1 requires the contractor to issue revised programmes regularly and these are required to show actual progress achieved and the effect on the timing of the remaining work. The programme is also required to show how the contractor plans to deal with any delays.

Clause 36.1 gives the project manager power to instruct the contractor to submit a quotation for an acceleration to achieve completion before the completion date. The contractor may submit a quotation, which is required to comprise changes to the prices and the completion date. Alternatively, the contractor may give reasons for not doing so. Clause 36.3 (clause 36.4 options E and F) provides that when the project manager accepts a quotation for acceleration, the completion date is changed (and prices options A to D) and the revised programme accepted.

IChemE Red Book: Clause 11.1 provides that the project manager has full authority to act on behalf of the purchaser in connection with the contract.

Clause 41.2 gives the project manager power to issue a notice that the contractor is in default by failing to proceed regularly and diligently with the works. If the contractor fails to commence and diligently pursue the rectification of such default within 14 days after receipt of the notice, or at any time thereafter repeats the default, the purchaser may forthwith determine the employment of the contractor under the contract.

MF/1 (Rev 4): Clause 2.1 requires the engineer to carry out the duties specified in the contract. If the engineer is required to obtain prior specific approval of the purchaser before exercising his or her duties, by reason of the terms of appointment, then these are required to be set out in the special conditions.

Under clause 14.6 the engineer has power to notify the contractor if the engineer decides that the rate of progress of the works is too slow to meet the time for completion and that this is not due to a circumstance for which the contractor is entitled to an extension of time. The contractor is then required to take such steps as may be necessary and as the engineer might approve to remedy or mitigate the likely delay, including revision of the programme. The contractor is not entitled to additional payment for taking such steps.

Clause 49.1 allows the purchaser to give the contractor 21 days' notice of intention to terminate the contract, enter the site and expel the contractor, if despite previous warnings in writing from the engineer the contractor is failing to proceed with the works with due diligence.

JCT 1998: The JCT 1998 Forms do not provide clear express provisions for the architect to require the contractor to accelerate in order to achieve the completion date.

Clause 27.2.1.2 allows the architect to give notice of default if before the date of practical completion the contractor fails to proceed regularly and diligently with the works. If the contractor continues the default for 14 days from receipt of the notice, the Employer may within 10 days after the expiry of 14 days give notice determining the employment of the contractor. If the employer's notice is not issued, and if the contractor repeats the default then upon or within a reasonable time after such repetition the employer may give notice determining the contractor's employment, taking effect on the date of receipt of the notice.

CECA Blue Form 1998: Clause 7(2) gives the contractor under the subcontract the same powers as the engineer under the main contract, which under the ICE 7th Edition will include the powers under clause 46 for acceleration.

Clause 17(1)(b) allows the contractor by written notice to determine the subcontractor's employment if the subcontractor fails to proceed with due diligence after being required in writing to do so by the contractor.

DOM/1: clause 11.1 requires the subcontractor to complete the subcontract works in accordance with the progress of the works.

Clause 29.2.1.2 allows the contractor to give notice of default if, before the date of practical completion, the subcontractor fails to proceed regularly and diligently with the subcontract works. If the contractor continues the default for 10 days from receipt of the notice, the contractor may within 10 days, after the expiry of 10 days, give notice determining the employment of the subcontractor. If the contractor's notice is not issued, and if the subcontractor repeats the default then upon or within a reasonable time after such repetition, the contractor may give notice determining the contractor's employment, taking effect on the date of receipt of the notice.

9.4 Approvals and satisfaction

In many standard forms, the standard or value of work is decided by the opinion, satisfaction or approval of the employer or the architect/engineer and are not usually final or binding on the parties without express and clear provisions in the contract, and are usually simply intended to be administrative.

In some standard forms, a decision on a dispute may become final and binding by the operation of a time bar if steps are not taken to resolve the dispute by legal proceedings. Similarly, some standard forms make the final certificate conclusive in legal proceedings as evidence of the acceptability of the quality and standard of the work and to entitlements to extension of time under the contract, subject to objection and commencement of legal proceedings within a specified period.

In interpreting a contract, the starting point is the presumption that neither party intended to abandon any remedies for breach of contract arising by operation of law (*Gilbert Ash (Northern) Ltd* v. *Modern Engineering (Bristol) Ltd* (1974)).

There is nothing to prevent a party from requiring that work shall be done to its own satisfaction, even if through an agent (*Minster Trust Ltd* v. *Traps Tractors Ltd* (1954)).

If the work satisfies the architect/engineer, but is below the standard specified in the contract, then whether or not the contractor is liable for defective work will depend upon the interpretation of the contract as a whole. This depends on whether the obligation to satisfy the architect/engineer is interpreted as an overriding obligation or simply cumulative or complementary to the specified standards.

The modern approach is that there are two independent obligations (*National Coal Board* v. *Wm Neill & Son (St Helens) Ltd* (1984) 1 All ER 555). The contractor therefore would be in breach of contract if it failed to execute the work in accordance with the contract, even if the engineer expressed satisfaction, and even if the defect was obvious to the engineer. The satisfaction of the engineer was therefore a superadded protection for the benefit of the employer in addition to the contractor's primary obligation to complete the work according to specification.

Most standard forms provide that approval does not relieve the contractor from its responsibilities. If an A/E is involved in checking or approving drawings and designs, by doing so he or she may incur liability to the employer for any defective design. The extent of any such liability depends upon the facts and the terms of the contract between employer and A/E. There is a distinction between issuing a drawing for comment and issuing a drawing for approval (*J. Sainsbury plc* v. *Broadway Malyan* (1999) 61 ConLR 31). A consultant may find itself liable to the employer under the terms of the contract of appointment if it fails to take proper care in providing clarification of drawings and fails to pick up errors (*London Underground Ltd* v. *Kenchington Ford plc* (1998) QBD 63 ConLR 1).

Many standard forms of contract provide a certification system for payments – interim and final certificates. It is a matter of fact whether payment for work carried out is a statement of acceptance or approval. Most contract provisions for interim certification and payment are based on cumulative valuation of work done, and are only for payments on account. They are not binding nor conclusive of acceptance of the work (*Fairclough Building* v. *Rhuddlan Borough Council* (1985) 30 BLR 26).

Some standard forms of contract, notably JCT Forms, IChemE Forms and MF/1, include clauses that make conclusive the final certificate in relation to the fulfilment of specified obligations under the contract. The courts have upheld such clauses and given effect precisely to the terms of the clause. In all cases it is a matter of construction of the particular contract.

The conclusive effect of the final certificate is a complete defence for a contractor against any action for contribution and indemnity pursuant to the Civil Liability (Contribution) Act 1978 (*Oxford University Fixed Assets Limited* v. *Architects Design Partnership* (1999) TCC).

Standard forms

The modern trend is to rely on Quality Assurance Systems for checking of drawings and designs, and to adopt objective testing standards instead of the subjective opinion of a third party. Nonetheless, the A/E's approval is still adopted in some standard forms, particularly in the building industry. The device of the conclusive effect of the Final Certificate is used to achieve finality, particularly in processing and mechanical/electrical works, but less so in building works.

FIDIC 1998: The FIDIC Forms do not expressly state that the works should be carried out to the employer's (Silver Form) or engineer's (Red and Yellow Forms) satisfaction. As expected, there is a distinct difference in approach between the Red Form and the design and construct forms of Yellow and Silver. The latter rely on the main obligation that the works when completed shall be fit for their purpose because the works are designed by the contractor. The Red Form in which the employer is responsible for design, except where specified otherwise, requires the contractor to follow instructions and the contract procedures imply that consents and approvals will be given as the works proceed. Only the performance certificate is stated to constitute acceptance of the works. As expected in a modern contract, reliance is placed on the contractor's quality assurance system. The contractor is not relieved of its obligations by any approvals or consents.

ICE 7th Edition: The ICE 7th Edition assumes that the main part of design will be the responsibility of the employer. The role of the engineer in giving instructions and giving approval and consents is prominent. The contractor is not relieved of its obligations by any approvals or consents. The issue of the defects correction certificate is not intended to affect the obligations or rights of the parties.

ECC 2nd Edition: The ECC 2nd Edition makes the project manager central to the administration of the contract. The project manager is required to accept designs before they are implemented and subcontractors before they are appointed. The programmes are required to be accepted. The only limit on the power of the project manager is that withholding acceptance for a reason not stated in the contract is a compensation event.

IChemE Red Book: The IChemE Red Book requires the contractor to carry out work to the satisfaction of the project manager as well as in accordance with the contract. The Form is a design and construct form and requires the plant, when completed, to be suitable for the purpose intended as defined in the specification. Tests are prominent in the form. For this reason the IChemE Red Book brings finality for liability for latent defects. The final certificate is intended to be conclusive on the matter of latent defects.

MF/1(Rev 4): The MF/1 Form is intended to be for supply of electrical, electronic or mechanical plant. It would be expected, and this is the case, that the engineer's approval is decisive and final in terms of design as shown in the contractor's documents submitted for approval (Clauses 15 and 16). Otherwise, the engineer's approval does not relieve the contractor from its obligations under the contract. Similarly, no certificates are final approval except for the final certificate for payment under clause 39.12.

JCT 1998: The JCT Form is intended for use in building works and the architect's role is central. It is the nature of building works that many matters are not easily defined by reference to an objective standard. The architect's approval or satisfaction is therefore an important part of the management of building contracts. The final certificate is intended to be conclusive of such satisfaction, but only if expressly stated in the contract.

CECA Blue Form 1998: Clause 2(1) provides that the subcontractor shall execute, complete and maintain the subcontract works in accordance with the subcontract and to the reasonable satisfaction of the contractor and the engineer.

DOM/1: Clause 4.1.1 requires the subcontractor to carry out and complete the subcontract works in compliance with the subcontract documents and in conformity with all reasonable directions and requirements of the contractor.

Clause 4.1.2 and 4.1.3 requires that all materials and goods and workmanship where and to the extent approval of the quality standards or workmanship is a matter of opinion of the architect, such quality, standard and workmanship are to be to the reasonable satisfaction of the architect.

Clause 4.3.2.3 refers to a code of practice for the opening up for inspection or test to establish to the reasonable satisfaction of the contractor, the likelihood or extent of any further non-compliance. The code of practice provides criteria for the contractor to consider.

Clause 21.10 deals with the effect of the final payment. Unless adjudication, arbitration or other legal proceedings have been commenced before the final payment has been made, the final payment is conclusive evidence that where and to the extent that qualities of expressly stated to be for the approval of the architect, the particular quality or standard was to the reasonable satisfaction of the architect. The final payment is not conclusive evidence that the materials or goods or workmanship comply with any other requirements of the contract. The final payment is also conclusive evidence that effect has been given to the payment and valuation terms of the contract, and that extensions of time due have been given and that any reimbursement of loss and expense is in final settlement of all claims which the subcontractor has or may have. If adjudication, arbitration or other legal proceedings are commenced within 10 days of the final payment, then the final payment has the above conclusive effect, except in respect of all matters to which those proceedings relate.

CHAPTER 4.2

Litigation

Nigel Robson
Eversheds

1 INTRODUCTION

In civil proceedings other than appeal cases, the courts are divided into the High Court and county court. The High Court is further divided into three divisions, namely the Queen's Bench Division, the Chancery Division and the Family Division. The High Court generally handles disputes worth over £15 000 and/or those which involve complex issues. In construction cases, the courts most likely to deal with particular cases in the High Court are the Queen's Bench Division or the Chancery Division. The Queen's Bench Division has a further specialist court called the Technology and Construction Court (formerly known as the Official Referee's Court) which deals primarily with construction and technological claims. Civil trials in the High Court or county court are normally dealt with by a single judge. On 26 April 1999, new Civil Procedure Rules were introduced, which have radically transformed how disputes are handled and the procedures followed. Where previously there existed two sets of rules by which the High Court and county court operated respectively, there now exists a single set of rules called 'The Civil Procedure Rules' (the Rules). These can be accessed on the Department for Constitutional Affairs website at www.lcd.gov.uk/civil/procrules-fin/index.htm or the court service website at www.courtservice.gov.uk. There has also been something of a revolution in the funding of cases, following the introduction of the Conditional Fee Agreements Regulations 2000 and the possibility of taking out legal expenses insurance to cover the costs of litigation. These issues will be considered at the end of this chapter.

2 THE OVERRIDING OBJECTIVE

Part 1 of the Rules sets out their overriding objective. The overriding objective is to enable the courts to deal with cases justly – judges and the courts must further this objective by actively managing cases. Dealing with a case justly includes, so far as is practicable:

- ensuring that the parties are on an equal footing;
- saving expense;
- dealing with cases in ways which are proportionate in terms of the money involved, the importance of the case, the complexity of the issue and the financial position of each party;
- ensuring that the case is dealt with expeditiously and fairly;
- allotting to it an appropriate share of the court's resources while taking into account the need to allot resources to other cases.

Thus, for example, a case involving only a small amount of money will not be allowed the same amount of court time at trial as a more complicated one involving large sums of money and where the issues at stake are of great importance to the parties.

The parties to litigation and their lawyers are obliged to help the court to further the overriding objective of the court. This means that all decisions and actions should be taken with the overriding objective in mind.

It is important to appreciate that while the parties to litigation will have the opportunity to express their views on how the case should be managed, the final decision will be with the judge based on his or her interpretation of justice in the particular case.

3 PRE-ACTION

It is important to appreciate that because of the overriding objective, the courts, in their management of cases, will be paying particular attention to:

- adherence to time limits;
- reasonable conduct by the parties to the dispute (including any offers made to settle the matter) both prior to and during proceedings; and
- the costs of each stage of the dispute.

There are therefore a number of matters which require careful consideration before litigation is decided on as a method of resolving a dispute.

3.1 Analysis of case and formulation of case theory

In order to succeed cost-effectively in litigation, the Rules require a litigant to understand its case fully before the proceedings are commenced; in other words, what the dispute is about, what the litigant expects to achieve from the proceedings and how to establish this. It is important to assess the strengths and weaknesses of a case including evaluation of the evidence on each of the items which are claimed. From this evaluation it should be possible to formulate a 'case theory'. For example, D had a contractual duty to C under a contract dated 9/9/99 to do X, Y and Z, D was in breach of contract through breaches of X, Y and Z which occurred on dd/mm/yy, C has suffered loss and therefore C has a right to damages under clause A of the contract.

An initial strategy as to how the case could be conducted should then be formed. Once this has been done, preliminary calculations must be made as to the likely costs and time involved in each stage of bringing the matter to trial. Parties will be required to provide estimates of costs, at various stages, to the court. These will all assist in furthering the overriding objective, especially when it comes to justifying the costs of any action proposed and in anticipating any problems which the parties might encounter in keeping to timetables fixed by the court during the successive stages of the litigation. Deadlines must be strictly adhered to and so parties to litigation need to propose realistic timescales and be prepared to comply with them, whatever timetable the court decides.

The court can order a claim or defence to be struck out or give summary judgment (i.e. judgment without trial on a claim) if the claim or defence is found to have no real prospect of success and there is no other compelling reason why the matter should go to trial. The losing party is likely to have to bear the costs of the litigation. Therefore, it is important that a proper evaluation of the case and the evidence supporting it is carried out at the outset.

3.2 Pre-action offers to settle

The parties to a dispute should also consider whether to make an offer even before proceedings are started and will have to consider carefully any such offer made by the other party. Rule 36.10 provides that an offer made pre-action can have the same costs consequences as described below for 'Part 36 offers', provided that the offer complies with the criteria laid down in the Rules.

This may have the consequence of one party having to pay the entire costs of an action (and possibly additional interest at a penalty rate) if a pre-action Part 36 offer is rejected and later turns out to be more generous than the amount awarded at trial. Hence, this is another reason for careful preparation of a case analysis prior to commencing an action.

3.3 Conduct of the parties to the dispute

The court has the power to look at the parties' conduct before proceedings and any unreasonable behaviour or lack of cooperation may be penalized by adverse costs orders or other sanctions, including penalty interest.

Parties to litigation should be aware that all conduct, both before and after proceedings are issued, and particularly any offer to settle, is likely to have costs consequences. Reasonableness, in terms of the actions taken by the parties, is therefore important. Parties should be prepared for the court to examine their conduct in giving or refusing to give information for the purposes of enabling a settlement offer to be made or evaluated. Also, deadlines must be strictly adhered to and failure to do so will be penalized by the court. If the court considers any aspect of a party's conduct to be unreasonable, disproportionate or otherwise contrary to the overriding objective, the court has complete discretion on costs. So, even if a party is ultimately successful in its case, it may not necessarily be awarded all its costs if the court considers its conduct to have been worthy of criticism.

3.4 Pre-action protocol

Six types of case now involve pre-action protocols which set out actions to be complied with by the parties before litigation begins, e.g. the release of expert reports to an opponent.

A pre-action protocol for Construction and Engineering disputes came into force on 2 October 2000. A copy of the protocol can be found on the CPR website at www.lcd.gov.uk/civil/procrules–fin/contents/protocols/prot–ced.htm. It applies to all construction and engineering disputes, including professional negligence claims against architects, engineers and quantity surveyors. There are four specific exceptions to the pre-action protocol which are set out at paragraph 1.2. The protocol includes provisions for the exchange of information including strict timescales for compliance and a detailed list of the type of information which should be included. Once all information has been exchanged, the parties are also required to attend a pre-action meeting with the aim of agreeing the main issues, identifying the root cause of the disagreement, assessing whether a resolution can be reached without the need for litigation; or if litigation is inevitable, considering what steps should be taken to ensure that the claim will be conducted in accordance with the overriding objective.

As one of the aims of the Civil Procedure Rules is to encourage the parties to a dispute to reach settlement, the court will expect the parties to cooperate as far as practicable with each other. This means acting reasonably in exchanging information and documents, which may avoid the need to issue proceedings. The court also expects the parties to have considered alternative means of dispute resolution such as mediation. Even if the parties are unable to come to a settlement, the process is designed to help any proceedings which are issued to proceed more efficiently.

Parties that fail to comply with the protocol may well find themselves penalised in costs should litigation ensue. The only occasion in which the parties will be excused from complying is where limitation is about to expire so that proceedings need to be issued without delay.

4 COMMENCING PROCEEDINGS

Typical stages which a Technology and Construction Court case might follow are outlined below, but are briefly summarized in the flowchart at Fig. 1.

5 ISSUING A CLAIM

Once the pre-action considerations outlined above have been dealt with by the claimant, and if the dispute is still unresolved, the claimant should issue a claim. Part 60 and its

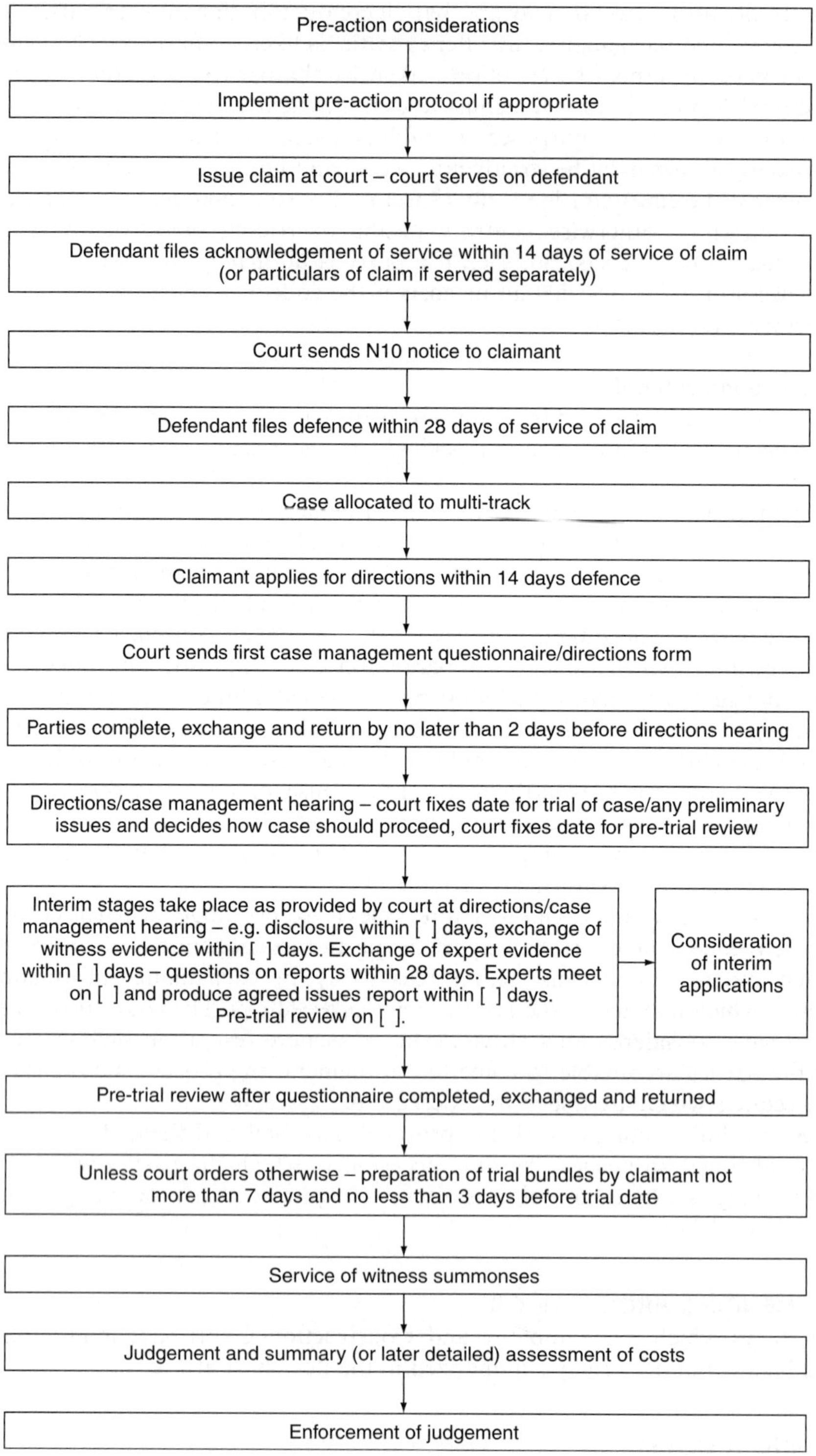
Pre-action considerations
Implement pre-action protocol if appropriate
Issue claim at court – court serves on defendant
Defendant files acknowledgement of service within 14 days of service of claim (or particulars of claim if served separately)
Court sends N10 notice to claimant
Defendant files defence within 28 days of service of claim
Case allocated to multi-track
Claimant applies for directions within 14 days defence
Court sends first case management questionnaire/directions form
Parties complete, exchange and return by no later than 2 days before directions hearing
Directions/case management hearing – court fixes date for trial of case/any preliminary issues and decides how case should proceed, court fixes date for pre-trial review
Interim stages take place as provided by court at directions/case management hearing – e.g. disclosure within [ ] days, exchange of witness evidence within [ ] days. Exchange of expert evidence within [ ] days – questions on reports within 28 days. Experts meet on [ ] and produce agreed issues report within [ ] days. Pre-trial review on [ ].
Consideration of interim applications
Pre-trial review after questionnaire completed, exchanged and returned
Unless court orders otherwise – preparation of trial bundles by claimant not more than 7 days and no less than 3 days before trial date
Service of witness summonses
Judgement and summary (or later detailed) assessment of costs
Enforcement of judgement

Figure 1. Flowchart illustrating the course of Technology and Construction Court proceedings

associated Practice Direction applies to Technology and Construction Court claims and should be consulted before issuing any claim. A claim is issued by way of a claim form which should be written in clear and simple English. To ensure that the case is allocated to the Technology and Construction Court it should be marked 'Technology and Construction Court' in the top right-hand corner. The contents of the claim form and any separate particulars of claim must be verified by a statement of truth. This is a signed statement by a representative of the claimant that he or she believes the facts stated in the claim to be true. It is essential for a claimant to check the claim very carefully, as any inaccurate or misleading statement may result in severe cost penalties or even contempt of court proceedings being brought against the claimant. In very serious cases, this can result in imprisonment. The claimant should also make sure that the person with the appropriate knowledge and seniority signs the statement of truth. In the case of a company, this means a director, secretary, chief executive, manager or other officer.

The choice between conducting the action in the High Court or county court is not as significant as it once was. Technology and Construction Court claims can be issued either in the county court or High Court, although only in certain county courts as specified in the Practice Direction to Part 60 (paragraph 3.4).

A court fee is payable to issue a claim. The amount will vary according to the monetary value of the claim.

Once the court has issued a claim, it has to be served on the defendant within four months, but normally this will be done by the court. The defendant must provide a full defence within fourteen days after the particulars of claim have been served or, alternatively, within twenty-eight days if an acknowledgement of service form is filed within fourteen days. This form will be served with the claim. The parties may agree a longer period for service of the defence, but only up to a maximum of a further 28 days. Thereafter, permission of the Court for any further extensions would be required. Either party may request from the other clarification of, or additional information in relation to, any matter in dispute. This may be by letter, if brief, or alternatively in a separate document. The procedure for this is governed by Part 18. Once a defence has been served and filed at court, the speed and manner in which the matter is then dealt with is controlled by the court using its case management powers. Severe costs penalties can result for parties not adhering to the timetable.

5.1 The track

Once the defence has been filed, the case will be allocated to a particular track. This will be one of the following:

- the small claims track (generally for claims less than £5000)
- the fast track (generally for claims of less than £15 000 or for larger value, straightforward claims)
- the multi-track (generally for claims of more than £15 000 or more complex cases).

There are different provisions regarding costs and timetabling dependent on the track to which the case is allocated.

The allocation of a case will involve the court making a decision to allocate the case to a particular track. However, the great majority of construction cases are likely to be dealt with in the multi-track, and all cases which are issued in the Technology and Construction Court will be allocated to the multi-track and will therefore proceed as detailed below.

6 DIRECTIONS/CASE MANAGEMENT CONFERENCE

The Court will fix a case management conference ('CMC') within 14 days of filing by the defendant of a defence or acknowledgement of service, whichever is the earlier.

When the court notifies the parties of the time and date of the hearing, it will also send them a case management information sheet and a case management directions form, which the parties must complete, exchange and return to the court no later than two days before the date of the CMC. If the parties wish to apply for a specific order at the CMC, they must also file the appropriate application notice and supporting evidence by the same date. If the parties fail to file the required documents, sanctions (including, in some cases, the striking out of a claim or defence) may be imposed by the court. To further the overriding objective, parties are encouraged to agree directions in advance, referring to the case management directions form. Of course, agreement by the parties is no guarantee that such directions will be ordered. This will be at the discretion of the court ultimately.

At the CMC, the court will usually fix a date for trial of the case and of any preliminary issues which it orders should be tried first. It will also give case management directions on how the case should proceed to trial and a date will also be fixed for a pre-trial review, at which the court will give the necessary directions as to how the trial is to be conducted.

7 IS SUMMARY JUDGMENT APPROPRIATE?

An important consideration, particularly in the early stages of a case, is whether to apply for summary judgment. The court may give judgment without trial, if it considers that the claimant has no real prospect of succeeding on the claim or that the defendant has no real prospect of successfully defending the claim and there is no other compelling reason why a trial should be held. Even with a good case, a party which is not well prepared and has not given proper particularization in the statements of case or has not obtained supporting evidence risks summary judgment against it.

As with any application, the parties should be prepared to give a detailed account of costs expended to date 24 hours in advance of the hearing, if it is a hearing of one day or less.

If a summary judgment application is unsuccessful, case management directions will be issued. The parties should therefore have at their disposal details of witness names and availability, expert evidence requirements, requirements for the disclosure of evidence, information as to whether other means of dispute resolution than litigation have been considered (and if not why not) and suitable timetable suggestions.

8 DISCLOSURE (FORMERLY CALLED DISCOVERY) – RULE 31

Disclosure is the process by which each party in a dispute discloses to the other the documents it has which are relevant to the case. A document is anything in which information is recorded and includes emails, disks, databases, tapes and hard disks of computers. Disclosure usually takes place once proceedings have commenced and statements of case have been served. However, pre-action disclosure may be ordered where the circumstances set out in Rule 31.16 are complied with (in particular, that such disclosure will ensure fair disposal of the anticipated proceedings, or will assist the dispute to be resolved without proceedings).

Before the Rules came into force, all documents which were relevant and in the possession, custody or power of a party had to be disclosed, i.e. revealed to the other side, irrespective of difficulty or cost. Under the Rules, the process is now a balancing act, making sure that everything is disclosed which should be but that the cost involved in the exercise is proportionate. Since the overriding objective applies to disclosure, the total cost involved may not be recoverable if the court considers that one side has spent a disproportionate effort on disclosure or if it considers that irrelevant information has been disclosed. It is nonetheless the responsibility of both parties to disclose to the other any documents which could assist or undermine their own or the other party's case. This is known as standard disclosure. Even where documents are confidential, this responsibility has to be fulfilled. Parties to a dispute must carry out what the court calls 'a reasonable search' for documents. This means that the court will not expect a party to search for a particular document within thousands of other documents unless that particular document is proportionally important. There is, therefore, a difficult balancing act between the significance of the documents, how easy they are to find and retrieve, how much finding and retrieving them will cost, how many documents there are and how complex the case is. The duty to disclose documents continues until proceedings are over.

A party can object to producing a document even if it is normally disclosable if it is privileged, that is, it has been created for the purpose of giving legal advice or it has been created in contemplation of litigation. In both these circumstances, public policy considerations demand that such documents are of such a private and confidential nature that other parties should not be allowed sight of them.

A party may also object to providing a document if it would be disproportionately costly to produce, particularly if it is not of any significant importance to the case. One example might be handwritten timesheets which have been globally archived in a storage facility where electronic records of the same documents have already been disclosed and there is no reason to think that the electronic time recording is not reliable.

Documents are disclosed by way of a list sent to the other party. The list must contain a statement ('the disclosure statement') signed by an appropriately senior person within an organization (e.g. a director) certifying that he or she understands the responsibility to disclose documents and that this responsibility has been complied with and confirming the extent of the search for documents. Documents can either be copied to the other side or alternatively inspected. A party inspecting a document must give the party disclosing it written notice of the wish to inspect it and the inspecting party must be allowed to inspect no more than seven days after receipt of the notice. A party, instead of physically inspecting documents, may request copies if it undertakes to pay the reasonable photocopying costs of the other party. The copies must be supplied no later than seven days after the date of receipt of the request for copies.

9 SPECIFIC DISCLOSURE AND INSPECTION

The court may at any time under Rule 31.12 make an order for a specific document or class of document to be disclosed, or for a search to be carried out so that a specific document or class of document can be disclosed.

The court can also make an order for specific inspection, in other words, an order that a party allows a particular document named in that order to be inspected, where the party disclosing it has previously sought to exclude it. The party inspecting the document also has a choice as to whether to inspect or have a copy of the document provided, which the disclosing party must do within seven days, if the party examining the document also undertakes to pay the reasonable photocopying costs.

10 IS IT APPROPRIATE TO MAKE AN OFFER OF SETTLEMENT?

The Rules are intended to create a culture in which disputes are managed and determined quickly and there are various mechanisms designed to encourage the parties to exchange information and behave reasonably and to promote settlement.

The most effective tool for promoting settlement is the Part 36 offer or payment. Part 36 offers or payments provide an opportunity for either a claimant or defendant to propose a settlement to the other. They obtain a special status which the offeree cannot sensibly ignore.

If a defendant makes a Part 36 offer or payment which is accepted by the claimant within 21 days, the action will be stayed on the terms of the settlement offer and the claimant will be entitled to be paid its assessed costs up to the date of acceptance. This exerts pressure on a claimant because, if it fails at trial to obtain a greater or more advantageous outcome than that offered under Part 36, it will have to pay the defendant's costs and its own from the latest date when the offer could have been accepted. These costs may be very substantial. The earlier a Part 36 offer or payment is made, the greater the pressure on the claimant. Generally speaking, a defendant's offer to settle a money claim must be made by way of a payment into court, once proceedings have been issued, if these sanctions are to apply although recent case law suggests that there may be limited circumstances in which a defendant's offer which complies with Part 36 (apart from making a payment into court) could still attract Part 36 consequences.

If a claimant makes a Part 36 offer, i.e. stating the terms on which it is prepared to settle the claim and the defendant rejects the offer, the cost consequences for the defendant could be even more severe if the outcome at trial is that the claimant obtains a more advantageous result than the offer. The defendant runs the risk of being ordered to pay interest on the award of up to 10% above base rate from the period following the latest date when it could have accepted the offer, together with costs on an indemnity basis and interest on those costs, again up to 10% above base rate. A defendant must therefore consider a claimant's Part 36 offer extremely carefully.

A Part 36 offer must comply with the strict requirements set out at r36.5 in order for the above consequences to apply. The recipient of a Part 36 offer can, within seven days of the offer being made, request the offeror to clarify its offer. Clarification must be provided within seven days of receipt of the request. If clarification is not forthcoming, the offeree can apply to the court for an order requiring the offeror to clarify the terms of an offer (this is called a clarification order). In that case, the application notice should state what clarification is required.

11 EVIDENCE

11.1 Witness evidence

The general rule is that any fact which needs to be proved by the evidence of witnesses must be proved at trial by oral evidence, or at any other hearing by evidence in writing. The court will order a party to serve on the other parties any witness statements of oral evidence which one party to the dispute intends to rely on in relation to any issue of fact to be decided at trial. The court will give directions as to the order in which witness statements are to be served and whether or not these are to be filed with the court as well as served on the other parties. A witness statement should be signed by the person making it and contain the evidence which that person would be allowed to give orally. As far as possible, a witness statement should be in the witness's own words and must always be verified by a statement of truth. Proceedings for contempt of court may be brought against a person if he or she makes or causes a false statement to be made in a document which is verified by a statement of truth and there is no honest belief in its truth.

It is important to consider, as early as possible, and preferably before an action is commenced, who should give evidence in the case if it comes to trial. One of the matters which the court will need to know in order to manage the case and allocate appropriate time to it is the number of witnesses to be called. This information should be available at the time of the first CMC. It is also vital to plan the content of witness statements, since these will usually be relied on as the evidence in chief given by the parties. Similarly, a party should carefully examine the other parties' witnesses statements and develop a line of questioning for cross-examination which is in accordance with their case theory, as the court may limit the extent to which cross-examination of witnesses takes place.

It should also be noted that, in view of the emphasis on proportionality in terms of costs, the parties to an action should ensure that witness statements are prepared as efficiently as possible to enable the costs of producing these to be recoverable. It is unlikely that, for example, the cost of producing many successive drafts of a witness statement will be recoverable.

11.2 Expert evidence

In construction disputes, as well as evidence about the facts of the dispute, expert evidence relating to specific areas of the case is invariably required. Experts have a duty to the court which overrides their duty to the parties who instruct them. The implications of this are that the court expects experts to be non-partisan. Indeed, the courts have heavily criticised the experts instructed in a number of recent cases for being 'hired guns' and for lacking the required degree of impartiality. Of course, experts may be concerned that to be totally impartial could lead to claims being made against them by their instructing party, In order to alleviate this fear, the courts have held that public interest requires that experts should be able to have frank discussions before trial, and their evidence at trial or in a report, if this is used at trial, should enjoy immunity from claims by the party who has appointed them. The court expects parties to cooperate in instructing a single joint expert, where this is appropriate. Where the parties cannot agree on an expert, the court may still direct that a joint expert is appointed. Therefore, an important consideration in the early stages of the case is which experts might be instructed jointly by the parties in dispute.

The Rules state that no party can call an expert witness or use an expert's report as evidence without permission from the court. In order to obtain such permission, the party must identify the field of expertise, e.g. welding, of the experts on whose evidence it intends to rely and, where practicable, the identities of the experts. The court has powers to limit the extent to which experts' fees and expenses should be recoverable from the other party. Late applications for permission to admit expert evidence have not generally been looked upon favourably by the courts – it is therefore very important to consider the expert evidence upon which a party would wish to rely at an early stage in the proceedings.

Expert evidence will usually, unless the court directs otherwise, be given in the form of a written report. At the end of the expert's report there must be a statement that the expert understands his or her duty to the court and has complied with that duty. The experts report must also include a statement of truth which complies with paragraph 2.4 of the Practice Direction to Part 35.

An expert must address the report to the court and, in doing so, must state the substance of all instructions received from the parties. Those instructions are not protected by privilege but will only have to be disclosed to the other party if the court is satisfied that there are reasonable grounds for believing that the expert's statement of the instructions which he or she has been given are inaccurate or incomplete. However, where parties are instructing a single joint expert, a copy of those instructions must be sent to the other parties and it is usual for the parties to agree the wording of the joint instructions in any event. The courts will prevent experts giving their evidence unless they comply with their duties under the Rules.

A party may put written questions to its opponent's expert on one occasion only within 28 days of service of the expert's report. These questions should, unless the court or the other party agrees otherwise, be for the sole purpose of clarifying the report. The answers given by the expert will be treated as part of the report.

Generally, the court will direct that experts have discussions on the technical issues in the proceedings and, if possible, reach agreement on them. The court may specify which issues the experts should discuss and direct that, following a discussion between them, they prepare a statement setting out the issues on which they agree and those on which they do not agree and a summary of their reasons for any lack of agreement.

11.3 Written submissions

In some cases, a court may deal with an interim application without a hearing, such as where the parties agree as to the terms of an Order which is sought, where the parties agree that the court should deal with the application without a hearing or where the court does not consider a hearing would be appropriate. Where the judge agrees that the application is suitable for consideration without a hearing, the court will inform the parties and may give directions as to the evidence which should be filed for the application. If necessary, as with any other interim applications, the parties must anticipate that the court may wish to review the conduct of a case as a whole and give any necessary case management directions. Therefore, they should be ready to assist the court in doing this and be able to answer any questions that the court may ask, including the costs incurred to date and the projected costs of taking the matter to trial.

12 HEARINGS – INTERIM APPLICATIONS

12.1 General considerations

During the interim stages of a matter before it goes to trial, the Rules provide that the parties to a dispute must consider, at each step, whether the costs of the steps proposed to be taken are proportionate to the benefits likely to be obtained. If the costs cannot be justified in this way, they will almost certainly be disallowed on any assessment. It is also possible that if an application is made to the court to obtain its permission to take any particular step and the court considers that the step is totally inappropriate, an indemnity costs order may be made against a party applying. Costs will usually be assessed summarily at the time of the interim hearing if it is a day or less in duration, or alternatively at the end of the case.

In general, interim hearings are public and the public will be admitted, if practicable. Interim hearings may in some instances be conducted by telephone or videoconference with the agreement of the court.

As mentioned above, the court has the power at any stage, including following an interim hearing, to exercise its case management powers and to give directions as to how the conduct of the matter should proceed.

12.2 Time/compliance applications

To obtain an extension to a period of time set by the court or by agreement, a party must have good reasons as to why it needs extra time, and this must be supported by evidence. It is therefore essential from the outset to consider the likely duration of each stage of the proceedings and to update such estimates before they become a problem. Where a party is in default of any time period, the court may impose costs sanctions, which will be assessed immediately. However, the Courts are increasingly adopting a pragmatic approach to applications for further time and are tending towards granting such requests where the interests of fairness and justice demand it. What is more, parties who refuse to grant extensions of time may themselves be penalised in costs even if they themselves are not in default of the time limits set.

12.3 Applying to amend statement of case

Once served, a statement of case can only be amended with the consent of all other parties to a dispute, or the permission of the court. Any amendment which is made to a statement of case should be accompanied by a verifying statement of truth. Costs will be awarded against the party amending and these will be assessed and payable summarily.

12.4 Security for costs

An application for security for costs can only be made by a party in the position of a defendant, i.e. a defendant or a claimant defending a counterclaim. An application is usually made if the defendant is confident that it can successfully defend the claim brought against it and obtain an order for costs in its favour but believes that the claimant might not be able to pay those costs. If the application is successful, the claimant will usually have to pay an appropriate sum of money into court to cover the estimated costs or provide other suitable security. If security is ordered and not given, then the claim will be struck out.

An application for security for costs can be made at any time during the course of the proceedings. There are six grounds for an application for security for costs against the claimant. These are as follows:

(a) the claimant is (i) resident out of the jurisdiction; but (ii) not resident in a Brussels contracting state or Lugano contracting state or a Regulation state, as defined in Section 1(3) of the Civil Jurisdiction and Judgments Act 1982; or
(b) the claimant, not being a representative claimant under Part 19, is a nominal claimant suing for the benefit of another party (e.g. a shell company) and there is no reason to believe that it will be able to pay the costs of the defendant if ordered to do so; or
(c) the claimant's address is not stated in the claim form or is otherwise incorrectly stated; or
(d) the claimant has changed its address during the course of the proceedings so as to avoid the consequences of any litigation; or
(e) the claimant has taken steps in relation to its assets that would make it difficult to enforce an order against it; or
(f) the claimant is a company (incorporated in the UK or overseas) and there is reason to believe that the company will be unable to pay the defendant's costs if ordered to do so.

If the court is satisfied that one of these grounds exists and the court thinks that it is just to do so, it will order that the claimant gives security for costs to an appropriate level.

An application for security for costs against a company, unlike most interim applications, may be heard in private.

In some cases, it may be more appropriate to make an application for summary judgment rather than an application for security for costs. If it can be shown that the claimant has no real prospect of succeeding on its claim and there is no other reason why the case or issue should be disposed of at trial, then the application should be for summary judgment.

In certain circumstances, a defendant may also make an application under the Rules for security for costs from someone other than the claimant (see rule 25.14).

12.5 Interim relief

Interim relief includes remedies such as an injunction to stop the other party from doing a particular act, or a declaration that a particular state of affairs exists at that time. Orders can also be made for interim payments, for property or assets to be preserved or detained, for a person to enter property or for information or evidence to be provided.

An application for an interim remedy may be made at any time, even before proceedings are started or after judgment has been given. The Rules provide that the court will only grant an interim remedy before proceedings if the matter is urgent or if it is otherwise desirable to do so in the interests of justice. One typical example would be where there is a dispute regarding the ownership of unfixed materials which need to be incorporated in the works. A court may also grant an interim remedy on an application made without notice to the other party, if it appears to the court that there are good reasons for not giving notice. One example of this might be a freezing injunction (formerly known as 'Mareva injunction') which is an injunction to freeze the assets of a party to a dispute. The order can be made without notice to the other party in cases where the transfer of assets to another country to avoid payment is feared or is a possibility.

An application for an interim remedy must be supported by evidence unless the court orders otherwise. An application for an interim remedy without giving notice to the other side must also state in support of the application why notice has not been given to the other side.

12.6 Interim payments

These are unusual in construction cases, since it is often more appropriate where elements of a claim can be readily proved for a claimant to apply for summary judgment in respect of those elements. The court will only make an order for interim payment if the defendant against whom the order is sought has admitted liability to pay damages or another sum of money to the other side, the claimant has obtained judgment against the defendant for damages to be assessed or for a sum of money to be assessed (not costs), or if the court is satisfied that if the claim went to trial the claimant would obtain judgment for a substantial amount of money (other than costs) against the other side. The court must not, in any case, order an interim payment of more than a reasonable proportion of the likely amount of the final judgment and, in determining the amount, the court will take into account any contributory negligence or relevant set-off or counterclaim.

13 PRE-TRIAL REVIEW

When a date has been fixed for the pre-trial review, the court will send the parties a pre-trial review questionnaire and a pre-trial review directions form which the parties should complete, exchange and return to the court by no later than two days before the date on which the pre-trial review takes place, failing which sanctions (including in some cases the striking out of a claim or defence) may be imposed by the court, or the court may hold a pre-trial review without the forms.

14 TRIALS

As already mentioned, virtually all construction cases are multi-track cases. As a part of the multi-track procedure for technology and construction cases, there is a pre-trial review and, if necessary, a further case management conference prior to trial. At pre-trial review the court will mainly be concerned that the case is ready for trial and with the way in which the trial will be conducted.

The claimant should file the trial bundle at court not more than seven days and not less than three days before the start of the trial.

The trial bundle should include a copy of the following documents:

(a) the claim form and all statements of case;
(b) a case summary and/or chronology (if appropriate);
(c) requests for further information and responses to the requests;
(d) all witness statements to be relied on as evidence;
(e) any summaries of witness evidence;
(f) any notice of intention to rely on hearsay evidence;
(g) any notice of intention to rely on evidence such as plans, photographs, etc., which are not contained in witness statements, affidavits or experts' reports;
(h) any experts' reports and responses;
(i) any order giving directions as to the conduct of the trial;
(j) any other necessary documents.

The originals should be available at trial and the trial bundle should be paginated continuously throughout and indexed.

The contents of the trial bundle should be agreed between the parties where possible.

If a witness will not attend court voluntarily, a witness summons can be issued and served on the witness compelling his or her attendance at court. When a witness is served with a witness summons, he or she must be offered a sum to cover travelling expenses to and from the court and compensation for loss of earnings.

The trial usually commences with opening speeches from both parties. Then both sides' principal evidence will be presented by their written witness statements. This evidence will then be subject to cross-examination and the witness can then be re-examined on points raised in the cross-examination. The court has the power to restrict the time during which a witness is examined or cross-examined as it has to control the presentation of evidence at trial. After all witness evidence has been presented, the parties deliver their closing speeches. The judge will then give judgment, either shortly afterwards or after some consideration. There may then follow an assessment of costs. There will always be a summary assessment of costs at the end of a fast-track trial but in multi-track cases, it is more likely that costs will be dealt with separately.

Judgments and oral hearings will normally be recorded.

15 JUDGMENTS

When the judge has made a decision, a judgment will be issued. Usually, the court will draw up a judgment, unless the court orders one of the parties to do so or when it is a consent order.

4.1 Administration of claims
4.2 Litigation
4.3 Arbitration
4.4 Adjudication
4.5 Alternative dispute resolution

Once the judgment has been drawn up, it will then be served by the court on each of the parties. A judgment or order takes effect from the date when it is given or made. Under the Judgments Act 1838 and section 74 of the County Courts Act 1984, interest on judgments runs from the date that the judgment is given unless otherwise stated by the court. The court has the power to order interest to run from before the date of the judgment.

16 TIME FOR COMPLYING WITH THE JUDGMENT OR ORDER

A party must comply with the judgment or order for the payment of an amount of money (including costs) within 14 days of the date of the judgment or order unless a different date is stated in the order or the court has stayed the judgment.

17 ENFORCEMENT AND COSTS

Generally speaking, in the case of payments of money to the other side, if the other side does not comply with a judgment of the court, any one of six methods may be used to enforce that judgment. These are as follows:

(a) writ of *fieri facias*;
(b) third party debt orders (previously known as garnishee proceedings);
(c) charging order;
(d) appointment of a receiver;
(e) writ of sequestration;
(f) order of committal.

All these procedures have been the subject of Lord Chancellor's Department consultation papers recently – reforms are likely in all and have already been introduced in relation to third party debt orders and charging orders.

17.1 Writs of *fieri facias*/third party debt orders

Writs of *fieri facias* are generally referred to as writs of execution. In order for a writ of execution to be issued by the court it has to be filed at court together with a *praecipe* (an accompanying document signed by or on behalf of the person entitled to execution) and the judgment on which the writ is to be issued. The writ of execution will then be sealed by the court. A writ of *fieri facias* then has to be lodged with the under sheriff of the county in which the court lies. The under sheriff sends the writ to an officer of the court (a sheriff or bailiff) for execution. Permission to issue a writ of execution is not usually needed except in certain specific cases, for example where six years have elapsed since the date of the judgment or, for example, where any change has taken place, such as the death of either the party entitled or liable to execution. In executing the writ, the sheriff or bailiff can seize as many of the debtor's goods as may be sufficient to pay off the debt and expenses (including the sheriff's or bailiff's expenses) contained in the judgment. The items seized are usually sold by public auction.

Third party debt orders are used if the judgment debtor itself is owed money by a third party. For example, if it can be shown that the judgment debtor has a bank account which is in credit, it is possible to obtain a third party debt order requiring the bank to pay the judgment creditor. Obtaining such an order involves two steps. First, an interim order is obtained by issuing a prescribed form application notice at the court which must include information set out in the Practice Direction to Part 72, including the last known address of the judgment debtor, details of the judgment and amount due, information relating to the third party and that the third party is indebted to the judgment debtor and is within the jurisdiction. The application is dealt with by a Judge without a hearing and any interim order made is then served on the third party and attaches to the money owed by the third party to the judgment debtor. If the third party objects to paying the judgment creditor he or she must attend court and show good reason why the payment should not be made. The judgment debtor may also attend the hearing to object to the final order being made. At the hearing, the judge will make a final order if satisfied that he should do so. If the debt is not paid to the judgment creditor, execution may then be issued against the third party.

17.2 Charging orders

If a charging order is made by the court, this is equivalent to a mortgage or legal charge over the property specified in the order. Charging orders can be made on land or on other securities. If a judgment remains unpaid, the judgment creditor can apply for an order for the sale of the charged property. The procedure for obtaining a charging order is similar to obtaining a third party debt order, i.e. the judgment creditor must show that the debtor has property which can be charged, and then an interim order will be made by the court. The order must be made final before it can be enforced. Both the interim order and the final order should be registered as soon as possible with the Land Registry if the order is made over land, to enable the charging order to be enforceable on sale of the land after discharge of prior mortgages or charges. There are also special rules relating to charging orders over securities and partnership property.

17.3 Appointment of a receiver

This is often a clumsy and expensive procedure, but one which can reach property which other methods cannot, e.g. legacies and incomes from a business which the debtor owns in partnership with others. The application is made to a district judge by summons.

17.4 Sequestration

This is a rare form of contempt proceedings. An application should be made to a judge for leave to issue a writ of sequestration appointing sequestrators and directing them to take possession of all the property of the relevant person until the contempt of court order is obeyed.

17.5 Order of committal

This is also a rare form of enforcement proceedings. It can be used where there has been a contempt of court, e.g. if an order or judgment of the court is deliberately and persistently flouted. An application can only be made with permission of the court. If an order is made, then the person against whom it is made will be committed to prison until such time as the contempt is purged and the order is lifted.

18 FUNDING ISSUES

18.1 Conditional Fee Agreements

The Conditional Fee Agreements Regulations 2000 now govern all issues in relation to Conditional Fee Agreements (CFAs). The Regulations set out certain procedures which must be complied with in order to create an enforceable CFA. It is now permissible for any party to litigation (whether that be an individual or a company) to enter into a CFA with their legal advisers in respect of almost any type of civil proceeding. In essence, the result of a CFA will be that if the client which has entered into the CFA with their legal adviser is ultimately unsuccessful in the litigation, that client will not be required to pay any of the legal adviser's costs in pursuing or defending that litigation. If the client were successful, they would obviously be responsible for their legal adviser's costs, but in the usual course of events, the losing party would be ordered to pay at least some of those costs. Due to the fact that the legal advisers are taking on a certain element of risk in entering into a CFA (on the basis that if the client loses they do not get paid) there is also what is called a 'success fee' included in the CFA. This must be expressed as a percentage of the basic legal costs incurred in the litigation and that percentage will generally be agreed between the client and the legal adviser, depending upon the intendent risk attached. However, that success fee does not have to be paid by the client, but once again, by the losing party.

There has recently been a considerable amount of litigation in relation to CFAs, principally with defendants (and their insurers) attempting to challenge the enforceability of CFAs and challenge the amount of the success fee claimed. Many cases have been heard by the courts in which defendants seek to claim that a CFA is unenforceable because certain aspects of the Regulations have not been complied with. Generally speaking, if there is a serious defect in the CFA, it could well be held to be unenforceable, generally leading to the result that the legal adviser does not get paid. However, a recent decision of the Court of Appeal has made it clear that mere technical breaches which are of no significance to the main thrust of the CFA will not be found to deem the CFA unenforceable. As for success fees, this is clearly a difficult area since each success fee will depend upon the facts and circumstances of the case involved. For construction related matters, this is likely to be the case. It should, however, be noted that defendants will often seek to challenge the success fee agreed.

18.2 Legal expenses insurance

Closely aligned to the subject of CFAs is that of legal expenses insurance. If a client is taking out a CFA, it is usual to also take out legal expenses insurance to protect themselves against having to pay the other side's costs if unsuccessful. Other risks can also be protected against by legal expenses insurance, for example, the risk that the client wins the case but that their opponent cannot pay the costs, or the risk that other unforeseen matters may arise which will cause additional expense to the litigation (for example, a Judge dying or becoming unwell during trial and being unable to continue).

Legal expenses insurance generally falls into one of two types – before the event, where an existing policy offers cover for possible legal problems which arise during the period of the policy, or after the event, where insurance is specifically bought to cover the cost of specific litigation after a dispute has arisen. At the start of any dispute, it is always vital to consider whether or not the parties already have insurance in place, and if not, whether or not they would like to take out insurance to cover their risks of the litigation. Legal expenses insurance can be taken out whether or not a CFA is also being entered into.

Legal expenses insurance can be obtained from a number of insurance companies, who are now becoming much more familiar with this concept. The costs of the premium will depend on a number of factors, such as the level of costs to be insured against, the complexity of the case, the likelihood of success, the amount of the excess prepared to be carried, and whether the policy covers both parties or only one party's costs. One important further point to note however is that if a party is successful in the legal proceedings, the insurance premium on an after the event policy can be reclaimed as part of the costs of the litigation. Of course, whether the whole of the premium will be recoverable is still questionable – this is a new area of law and matters such as this will be in the discretion of the costs Judge.

Construction disputes

4.1 Administration of claims

4.2 Litigation

4.3 Arbitration

4.4 Adjudication

4.5 Alternative dispute resolution

CHAPTER 4.3

Arbitration

Sir Vivian Ramsey QC
Keating Chambers

Julian Critchlow
Fenwick Elliott LLP

1 INTRODUCTION

Arbitration provides an alternative to the use of the court system as a method of resolving disputes. It depends on the consent of the parties. Therefore, before disputes can be referred to arbitration the parties to a dispute must make an agreement that it is to be resolved by arbitration. That agreement is usually contained in a clause of the contract between the relevant parties, for instance, the contractor and the employer or the employer and the engineer or between other participants in the construction process, for example, contractor and subcontractor. It is also possible, however, for the parties to agree that a dispute will be resolved by arbitration only when the dispute has actually arisen.

Arbitration has been referred to as litigation in the private sector. The arbitrator, like a judge, has to find the facts, apply the law and grant relief to one or both of the parties. The proceedings are usually less formal than court procedure but the arbitrator often follows a parallel procedure to that which applies in court. The arbitrator hears evidence, considers the arguments and evidence and then provides a written award which contains his or her decision on the matters to be determined.

1.1 The Arbitration Act 1996

Although arbitration arises out of the agreement of the parties, any arbitration based in England and Wales or in Northern Ireland is now subject to the provisions of the Arbitration Act 1996 (the 1996 Act). Scotland has a separate system. The 1996 Act provides a statutory framework for arbitration. It contains some mandatory provisions, some provisions which only apply if the parties have not agreed otherwise and some provisions which apply unless the parties expressly exclude them.

It contains provisions dealing with most aspects of procedure and practice in relation to the arbitration, together with provisions which regulate the relationship between the courts and the arbitration.

Prior to the 1996 Act, there was the Arbitration Act 1950 which still applies to arbitrations commenced prior to 31 January 1997. There are many changes in the 1996 Act and care should be taken in referring to any case decided under the provisions of the 1950 Act.

1.2 Arbitration procedure and rules

As the parties are free to agree many aspects of arbitral procedure, various institutions have introduced rules to be applied to arbitrations. Examples are the ICE Arbitration Procedure (1997), the Construction Industry Model Arbitration Rules (CIMAR), the JCT Arbitration Rules and, in the international context, the Uncitral Arbitration Rules, the International Chamber of Commerce (ICC) Rules and the London Court of International Arbitration (LCIA) Rules.

1.3 Advantages and disadvantages of arbitration

Why do parties choose arbitration in preference to court procedure? Very often the choice is made by the adoption of a standard form of contract which contains an arbitration clause, such as clause 66 of the ICE 7th Edition.

Traditionally, the advantages of arbitration have been said to be speed, cost and privacy. In practical terms there is often very little difference in the time taken to resolve a dispute by arbitration compared to the courts, especially in the light of the new Civil Procedure Rules for court proceedings. Equally, the arbitrator and the arbitration venue have to be paid for by the parties, while the judge and courts are made available out of public funds. This means that the overall costs of arbitration and court proceedings are, generally, not significantly different and it is not thought that this will change under the new Civil Procedure Rules. The advantage of privacy still remains. Many commercial organizations would prefer to have disputes resolved in private. The proceedings are protected, to a large extent, by confidentiality under English law: see *Hassneh Insurance* v. *Mew* [1993] 2 Lloyd's Rep. 243. The parties also see advantages in the fact that the arbitrator can be a construction professional or a lawyer with construction expertise. This may help to inspire confidence and assist in the resolution of issues related to construction practice.

The disadvantages of arbitration are that, unlike the court systems, the arbitrator may not be experienced in dealing with complex questions of law and procedure. In addition, there is an extent to which the arbitration procedure is dependent on the court, although this is much reduced under the 1996 Act. This is sometimes given as a reason for adopting the court system in the first place.

1.4 Domestic and international arbitration

Since construction disputes very often have an international element, either in the project being located abroad or one or both parties being foreign, many disputes are not domestic but have an international dimension. In such cases the Arbitration Act 1996 may not apply and questions arise as to the arbitration procedure, the arbitration venue and the law to be applied.

2 COMMENCING AN ARBITRATION

When a dispute arises between two parties to a contract containing an arbitration clause, the initial question is the method by which the arbitration is commenced.

2.1 The dispute

Before any arbitral process can commence it is necessary for there to be a dispute or difference. Under some arbitration rules there is a necessity to give a notice of dispute as a formal precursor to the commencement of arbitration.

In some cases there may be a doubt as to whether a dispute has arisen. While this may seem surprising, there are many cases in which, for instance, a contractor may have made a claim but there has been no formal response to or no rejection of the claim. In the ICE Arbitration Procedure Rule 2.1 provides, generally, that '*a dispute or difference is deemed to arise when a claim or assertion made by one party is rejected by the other party and that rejection is not accepted, or no response is received within a period of 28 days*'. That Rule still requires a rejection. In the absence of the rule, there is a dispute or difference when there is a claim and a rejection: see *Monmouthshire CC* v. *Costelloe & Kemple* (1965) 5 BLR 83.

2.2 Pre-arbitral procedures

Many arbitration clauses provide for a pre-arbitral process such as an engineer's decision or requirement for the dispute to be considered by a conciliator or mediator. In these cases, the wording of the clause needs to be scrutinized to see whether the process is a condition precedent to commencing arbitration or whether it provides an option, which may, if appropriate, be bypassed. In addition, many arbitration clauses in engineering standard forms of contract both make an engineer's decision a condition precedent to arbitration and also prescribe a limited time within which the arbitration must be commenced. If it is not commenced within that period, the decision of the engineer becomes final and binding. While there is an ability for the court to extend the time, the grounds under the 1996 Act are severely limited (Arbitration Act 1996, Section 12).

Before commencing an arbitration, it is necessary to confirm, therefore, that there is a dispute and that any mandatory pre-arbitral process has been complied with. The formalities for commencement of an arbitration depend first on the arbitration clause and any applicable arbitration rules. In the context of certain editions of the ICE Conditions of Contract and some subcontracts, the clause states that the arbitration 'may be' conducted in accordance with the ICE Arbitration Procedure. In addition, even where it says that it 'shall be' conducted in accordance with that Procedure, the version of the Procedure is, curiously, the version which applied at the date of the appointment of the arbitrator: see clause 66(11)(a) of the ICE 7th Edition. This emphasizes the need for care in considering whether rules do apply and, if so, which rules are the relevant ones.

In order to commence an arbitration under the ICE Arbitration Procedure it is necessary to give both a notice of dispute and a notice to refer.

2.3 Methods of commencing arbitration

If there is no express requirement within the arbitration clause or the applicable rules as to the method by which arbitration is to be commenced, then the provisions of Section 14 of the 1996 Act apply. That section requires a notice in writing and the contents of the notice depend on whether the arbitrator is named or designated in the arbitration agreement, is to be appointed by the parties or is to be appointed by a person other than one of the parties. While no particular form of notice is necessary, it is good practice to identify the dispute, identifying the relevant arbitration clause, set out the manner by which any pre-arbitral process has been complied with as well as dealing with the method by which the arbitrator is to be appointed. It is also advisable to date the notice and establish that the notice has been given by asking for acknowledgement or making delivering of the notice by a means which is recorded. While there is no objection to service by fax, it is generally preferable to ensure delivery of a hard copy.

2.4 Date of commencement of arbitration and the Limitation Acts

The date of the notice will, in the first place, be relevant to ensure that any time limits within the arbitration clause have been complied with. In addition, under Section 13 of the Arbitration Act 1996, the provision of the Limitation Acts apply to arbitral proceedings. This means that the arbitration must be commenced within a particular period (generally six years but with important exceptions) after the date on which a cause of action accrued. The provisions of Section 14 deal with the process by which arbitrations are commenced both for the purpose of any time limits provided in the arbitration clause and for the purpose of the Limitation Acts.

2.5 Method of appointment of arbitrator

The method of appointing the arbitrator depends on the terms of the arbitration clause and follows, in principle, one of the methods identified in Section 14 of the 1996 Act. Sometimes an individual is identified by name or is designated by an office. Often, however, domestic arbitration clauses require the parties to attempt to agree on a single arbitrator. There may be a default process in the absence of agreement, for example, nomination by the President of the ICE under the ICE 7th Edition. In arbitration clauses in international contracts there is often the need to commence arbitration by filing a document with an organization (for example, a request for arbitration with the

ICC in Paris) and to name an arbitrator. Frequently, in such cases there are three arbitrators. However, in domestic arbitration there is, generally, a sole arbitrator. Section 15 of the 1996 Act states that there is a sole arbitrator, if the parties have not made an agreement as to the number of arbitrators. If there are any problems in appointing an arbitrator, Sections 15 to 21 of the 1996 Act contain detailed provisions including any necessary involvement by the court to resolve the difficulty.

2.6 Conflicts of interest and terms and conditions

Once an arbitrator has been agreed between the parties, or as part of the process of agreeing on the arbitrator, there are two matters to be considered. First, it must be confirmed that the arbitrator has no conflicts of interest. Secondly, the terms and conditions, including fees, must be agreed between the parties and the arbitrator, unless the method of appointment (for instance by the ICC or LCIA) deals with this aspect.

When the arbitrator has been agreed and the questions of conflicts of interest and of terms and conditions have been dealt with, the arbitrator normally makes a formal acceptance of the appointment. When the arbitrator has accepted the appointment, there are only limited grounds on which an arbitrator's appointment can be revoked or an arbitrator can be removed (see Sections 23 and 24 of the 1996 Act). Equally, there are limits on the arbitrator's ability to resign (Section 25).

2.7 Procedure after appointment

The arbitrator then, generally, fixes a preliminary meeting at which directions are given for the conduct of the arbitration. Sometimes the directions can be agreed without the necessity of a meeting and under some rules, for instance, the ICC Rules, there may be a necessity for a formal signed terms of reference.

2.8 Representation in arbitration

While parties often choose to be represented by lawyers in arbitration proceedings, there is no requirement for that and anyone can represent a party to arbitral proceedings (see Section 36 of the Arbitration Act).

3 THE ARBITRATION PROCESS

3.1 General principles

The arbitrator will aim to lay down procedures suitable for the particular case, avoiding unnecessary delay or expense, so as to provide a fair means for resolving the dispute (Section 33(1)(b) of the 1996 Act). The arbitrator must act fairly, impartially and give each party the opportunity to put its case and deal with the opposing case (Section 33(1)(a)). The ability of the arbitrator to determine procedure is, however, subject to the parties' overriding entitlement to agree between themselves what the procedure should be. In a construction dispute involving significant sums, complex facts, and difficult legal issues, the appropriate procedure may not differ significantly from that of an equivalent case in the High Court. However, as in the High Court, the need to avoid unnecessary delay and expense requires the procedures to be proportionate to the importance of the case to the parties.

3.2 Defining the issues

At the first preliminary meeting the arbitrator will direct the manner in which the parties are to set out their cases and the time periods for doing so. The usual order is either for service of points of claim and defence or for statements of case and defence. Points of claim and defence set out the unadorned basis of the parties' cases, excluding matters of evidence and argument of legal points. Statements of case and defence, which seem to be becoming the preferred option, require the parties to set out their cases in greater detail, including the evidence and law relied on, and will generally be accompanied by copies of the most important documents that the parties wish the arbitrator to see. The claimant will usually be allowed to serve a reply to the defence. The arbitrator may also make provision for service of any counterclaim (provided that he or she has jurisdiction to do so within the terms of reference), defence to counterclaim and reply to defence to counterclaim.

If a party's case appears to be incomplete or ambiguous, the opposing party can request further information to enable it fully to understand the case it has to meet and, if the request is refused, the arbitrator may order the information to be produced.

3.3 Disclosure

The arbitral timetable will usually require the parties to list all those documents which are relevant to the dispute, i.e. which support or damage their own case or the case of the other party. Each party is then entitled to inspect the documents in the other party's list except where those documents are privileged. In broad terms, documents are regarded as privileged if they concern attempts between the parties to settle or have been generated in the course and for the purpose of conducting the dispute. Disclosure may not, however, be undertaken as an independent step in the process if the arbitrator has ordered the parties to serve the documents they wish to rely on with their statements of case. If a party considers that specific documents which are of relevance have been withheld, it can apply to the arbitrator for their disclosure.

4 PREPARATION OF FACTUAL EVIDENCE

4.1 Documents

In construction disputes, especially those concerning delay or disruption, the parties' cases are likely to depend on a significant body of documentary evidence. Categories of document may include: pre-contract correspondence, documentation containing or evidencing the contract (articles, conditions, drawings, specification, method statement (if any), programme (possibly)), correspondence referable to the construction phase, site meeting minutes, site diaries, plant and labour returns, internal memoranda, board meeting minutes, and company accounts. Documentary evidence is usually fundamental to success in arbitration and participants in construction contracts are well advised to ensure that meticulous records are maintained from the invitation to tender stage through to completion and beyond – however amicable the parties' relationship might be at project commencement.

4.2 Witnesses

The timetable for directions will generally provide for the parties to exchange statements of evidence of witnesses as to fact after disclosure is complete (although some arbitrators favour the exchange of expert evidence before witness statements). Statements should be comprehensive as they may be ordered to stand as evidence-in-chief, i.e. be intended to deal with all the positive aspects of the case of the party on whose behalf the witnesses are called. Indeed, where there is not to be an oral hearing they will be the sole source of witness evidence (although it is rare in construction arbitrations for an oral hearing to be dispensed with where witness evidence is seriously in dispute). Preparation of witness statements is a less technical process than formerly, now that first hand hearsay (i.e.

indirect) evidence is generally admissible (Civil Evidence Act 1995) and given that the arbitrator may, in any event, choose not to apply formal rules of evidence (Section 34(2)(f) of the 1996 Act).

4.3 Technical issues

The majority of construction arbitrations require the assistance of one or more technical experts who may give evidence as to liability, e.g. in respect of quality of workmanship or materials, or as to quantum. Traditionally, each party appoints its own experts and, having seen their statements and heard their cross-examination, the arbitrator decides which evidence he or she prefers. It is usual for the arbitrator to direct the opposing experts to meet before the hearing on a without prejudice basis (i.e. on terms that the deliberations are not discloseable to the arbitrator) to try to agree as many facts as possible and to narrow the differences in their opinions. Unless the parties agree otherwise, the arbitrator may appoint a technical assessor to provide assistance or may appoint an expert (possibly a legal adviser) to report both to the parties and to the arbitrator (Section 37 of the 1996 Act). The intention behind this provision is to avoid the duplication involved where each party appoints its own expert. However, use of the mechanism can sometimes cause problems. Thus, in practice, the parties may require their own experts to assist in evaluating their cases even before a reference is commenced, thereby reducing the cost advantages of a single expert. Furthermore, technical analysis can be stifled where an issue is susceptible to more than one technical viewpoint and the sole expert is not alive to all the possibilities.

4.4 Preparation for the hearing

In a reference of more than a moderate size, the arbitrator will generally order a pre-trial review to take place, usually some weeks (or even months) before the final hearing to ensure that all directions made up to that stage have been complied with and to finalize the details of pre-hearing preparation. Typical directions will include provision for the parties to prepare an agreed joint bundle of those documents they intend to rely on, sometimes together with a small core bundle of the documents they expect to refer to most frequently. The arbitrator will also require skeleton arguments to be submitted by the parties' representatives. The parties will need to ensure that all case reports and other references to legal authority are available for the use of the arbitrator at the hearing as they will not be readily to hand in the same way as in a courtroom. The arbitration room itself will also need to be reserved, usually at an agreed venue and with the claimant generally being responsible in the first instance for the cost of it (pending the final award on costs).

Each party's witnesses will need as much notice of the hearing as is realistic: if possible, the availability of the most important witnesses will be established before the date is fixed. Where a witness appears reluctantly it is prudent to apply to the court to obtain a witness summons requiring his or her attendance. Failure to attend when so summoned is a contempt of court.

Ensuring the availability of experts is also, of course, essential.

5 PRESENTATION OF THE CASE TO THE ARBITRATOR

5.1 Documents only or oral hearing

Depending on what has been ordered or agreed, the reference will proceed either on a documents only basis or with an oral hearing. Even in the latter case the arbitrator may, subject to any rules to which he or she is bound to the contrary, seek further clarification in writing or order a further meeting although, unlike an adjudicator under the Housing Grants, Construction and Regeneration Act 1996, the arbitrator may not communicate with one party privately to the exclusion of the other.

5.2 Oral hearings – the procedure

At an oral hearing the arbitrator is not generally constrained by any specific rules as to procedure other than the general obligations under the 1996 Act to act fairly and impartially and efficiently. It is, however, customary in the more complex sort of case to provide for the parties to commence with brief opening oral submissions followed by their leading of the substance of their cases, the claimant first and then respondent, and concluding with closing submissions. Frequently, the statements of witnesses and experts stand as evidence-in-chief and when they are called to give evidence it is usual, subject to any brief points of clarification, to move straight to their cross-examination. The arbitrator may direct that a party or witness is to be examined on oath or affirmation, which the arbitrator is empowered to administer (Section 38(5) of the 1996 Act).

Unless the parties agree otherwise, they may be represented both at the preliminary stages and at the hearing either by a lawyer or other person (Section 36 of the 1996 Act).

5.3 The involvement of the arbitrator

Traditionally, in the High Court, the judge allows the parties' representatives to present their cases largely uninterrupted, it being considered in the English tradition that 'an over-speaking judge is no well-tuned cymbal'. With the new Civil Procedure Rules that tradition is changing and judges are encouraged to play a more interventionist role. Arbitrators, on the other hand, have historically tended to exercise greater direct control over the process, as an interventionist approach is necessary for the full advantages of procedural flexibility to be realized. It is noteworthy that, at least in theory, the entitlement of an arbitrator to intervene is now actually less than that of a judge because the judge can override even the joint views of the parties, whereas the arbitrator cannot (see Section 1(b) of the 1996 Act). In practice, however, the arbitrator is likely to have considerable discretion and, at the hearing, may exercise it by, for example, limiting the time made available to the advocates to present their cases or to cross-examine. An extreme example of such limitations occurs in the 'chess clock' sort of arbitration where each party is allotted a certain period to use as it considers appropriate. This has the advantage of keeping hearings to a minimum but can cause difficulties if one party is too prodigal of his time in the early stages and finds itself unable to lead or challenge important evidence towards the end. The validity of the award may be imperilled where an arbitrator refuses to extend a party's time in such circumstances.

6 THE ARBITRATOR'S AWARD

6.1 Effect of the award

The publication of the final award by the arbitrator brings his or her jurisdiction to an end. Except where the parties agree otherwise, the award will be final and binding, i.e. conclusive of the party's rights in respect of the dispute, subject to the limited rights to challenge referred to below.

6.2 Contents of the award

The parties may agree the form of the award. Where (as is usual) they do not do so the award must (by Section 52 of the 1996 Act):

(a) be in writing and signed by the arbitrators or, where the decision is by a majority of a tribunal, by all those arbitrators who assent to it;
(b) contain reasons;
(c) state the seat of the arbitration, i.e. the place where the award was made or is deemed to have been made (e.g. England and Wales);
(d) state the date on which it was made.

The award must also deal with all the issues that were the subject matter of the dispute.

Irrespective of the above, and again subject to the contrary agreement of the parties, the arbitrator may either on his or her own initiative or on the application of one of the parties, correct the award to rectify minor errors or ambiguities or to make an additional award to deal with an element of the dispute omitted from the main award (such as in respect of costs or interest). Subject to the arbitrator's entitlement to withhold the award until payment of the arbitrator's fees, he or she must give notice to the parties of the award by serving them copies.

6.3 Awards of interest

Except where the parties agree otherwise, the arbitrator may award either simple or compound interest at such rates as he or she considers just on the principal sum contained in the award. The arbitrator may also award interest on any amount paid by a party before the award was made, but only up to the date it was paid.

6.4 Awards of costs

Again subject to the parties' agreement, the award of costs is at the arbitrator's discretion. In exercising that discretion, costs must be awarded to the successful party unless there are unusual circumstances that would make it inappropriate to do so. The arbitrator must also set out the basis on which the decision has been reached (Section 63 of the 1996 Act) and specify each item of recoverable costs. The award should usually grant the receiving party a reasonable sum in respect of all costs reasonably incurred. Where there is doubt as to whether an item of costs is reasonable, the paying party should usually be given the benefit of the doubt. However, there can be an exception where the paying party has been guilty of improper conduct in the course of the proceedings, in which case the arbitrator can decide to give the receiving party the benefit of the doubt as to whether costs are reasonable. This effectively replicates the indemnity basis for costs in the equivalent High Court situation. It should be noted that what amounts to improper conduct for these purposes is a matter of some debate. It should also be noted that costs include the reasonable and appropriate fees of the arbitrator.

6.5 Enforcement of the award

The 1996 Act (Section 66) provides that the award may, subject to the leave of the court, be enforced in the same way as a court judgment or order. Application to the court is on affidavit attesting that the award was regularly arrived at. If the opposing party contends that the award is defective, it can object to leave being granted and the court will decide whether or not the award is formally correct – i.e. that there is no serious irregularity and that the arbitrator had jurisdiction to make it. Leave will not be granted for error of law – such error must be dealt with by appeal (see below). Although not specified in the Act, proceedings can also be brought on the award as a breach of contract – it being an implied term of the parties' agreement to arbitrate that they will honour the final award.

If, once leave has been given to enforce the award, or a judgment has been given for failure to honour it, the defaulting party still fails to perform, all the usual enforcement processes of the court are available.

6.6 Challenges to the award

Awards may be challenged in the following ways.

(a) By application (pursuant to Section 67 of the 1996 Act) to set aside the award, or an application for a declaration that the award is of no effect, on the grounds that the arbitrator did not have jurisdiction to make it. This provision is most commonly invoked where there is a dispute as to whether there was ever a valid arbitration clause. The right to object may, however, be lost if a party has proceeded with the arbitration without lodging an objection at the time the issue could first have been raised.

(b) By application to set the award aside for serious irregularity. Again, the right may be lost if not made timeously. Circumstances where such an application may succeed are where one of the following irregularities has caused or will cause substantial injustice to the applicant, namely (by Section 68 of the 1996 Act):
   (i) failure by the arbitrator to comply with the general obligations of fairness and impartiality or failure to select appropriate proceedings;
   (ii) the arbitrator exceeding his or her powers (otherwise than by exceeding the substantive jurisdiction);
   (iii) failure by the arbitrator to conduct the proceedings in accordance with any agreement to the parties;
   (iv) failure by the arbitrator to deal with the issues put to him or her;
   (v) an arbitral or other institution or person given authority by the parties in respect of the award exceeding its powers;
   (vi) uncertainty or ambiguity as to the effect of the award;
   (vii) the award's being procured by fraud or in a way contrary to public policy;
   (viii) failure by the arbitrator to comply with the requirements as to the form of the award;
   (ix) any irregularity in the conduct of the proceedings or in the award which the arbitrator (or an arbitral or other empowered person) admits.

   Where serious irregularity is proved, the court can remit the award to the arbitrator for reconsideration, set the award aside, or declare it to be ineffective.

(c) By appeal on point of law (Section 69 of the 1996 Act). In order to seek leave, an applicant needs the agreement of the other party or the leave of the court, and the court will only grant such leave in restrictive circumstances. There are two tests for granting leave. Either the arbitrator's decision must be obviously wrong, or the point at issue must be of general public importance (e.g. because it relates to the interpretation of a standard form of contract) in which case the decision must be open to serious doubt. As such, the Act largely confirms the pre-1996 Act case law such as the *Nema* [1980] 2 Lloyd's Rep 83, 339, and the *Antaios* [1981] 2 Lloyd's Rep 284. Once leave to appeal has been granted, the court simply determines whether or not the award is legally correct – the applicant does not have to satisfy any higher legal test than does the respondent.

   After hearing the appeal, the court may confirm the award, vary it, remit it to the arbitrator for reconsideration, or set it aside.

An application to set aside for lack of jurisdiction, serious irregularity, or by way of appeal, may not be brought more than 28 days after the date of the award. Since the arbitrator is entitled to withhold the award from the parties until the arbitrator's fees have been paid (by Section 56 of the 1996 Act) a party who believes it may need to appeal must consider paying the arbitrator's unpaid fees in full or, if it forms the view that the fees are excessive, apply to the court. In such circumstances, the court may order the award to be delivered on payment of the disputed fees into court, or arrange to determine what the fees should be. It should be noted that the 28-day time limit does not apply where a person has played no part whatsoever in the arbitral proceedings and then seeks a declaration or injunction challenging enforcement of the award on the basis that the arbitrator did not have jurisdiction.

7 PARTICULAR POWERS OF ARBITRATORS

It was observed earlier that the arbitrator has certain general obligations of fairness and impartiality, and to lay down appropriate procedures (by Section 33 of the 1996 Act).

To assist the arbitrator in fulfilling those obligations the Act gives certain express powers. Perhaps the most important power (which is also an obligation) is that contained in Section 34(1) which provides that the arbitrator is to decide the procedure (except to the extent that the parties reach agreement). Subsection 34(2) states that procedural and evidential matters include where to hold the proceedings, the language to be used (often important in international references) whether and what written statements of claim and defence are to be used, what documents should be disclosed by the parties, what questions should be put to the parties, whether to apply strict rules of evidence (or, more correctly, whether to apply rules of evidence strictly), the extent to which the arbitrator should take the initiative in finding out the facts and the law, and what written and oral evidence or submissions should be admitted. These provisions are intended to give the arbitrator an extremely broad discretion as to procedure so as to provide the flexibility required for laying down the most effective and efficient procedures for the particular dispute. In particular, except where the parties have agreed to limit this discretion, the arbitrator need no longer fear an application for his or her removal, or impeachment of award, on the grounds that he or she has adopted an inquisitorial methodology. Thus, he may ask his or her own questions and pursue a line of enquiry instead of merely assessing passively the evidence presented by the parties.

In addition, the arbitrator has certain other specific powers, again intended to promote the efficient running of the reference. Some of the most important are as follows, each of them being subject, however, to the ability of the parties by agreement between themselves to divest the arbitrator of these powers.

7.1 Jurisdiction (Section 30 of the 1996 Act)

The arbitrator may decide whether he or she has jurisdiction to determine whether there is a valid arbitration agreement, whether the tribunal is properly constituted, and what issues are properly included although, as seen above, this decision may be challengeable by one or other party.

7.2 Security for costs (Section 38(3) of the 1996 Act)

The arbitrator may require a claimant (or counterclaimant) to give security to the respondent for the costs which the arbitrator can show the claimant will incur in conducting the defence. This power is usually operated where a claimant's finances are so lacking in substance that it is probable that they will be insufficient to enable it to reimburse the respondent's costs if the defence succeeds.

7.3 Directions as to property (Section 38(4) of the 1996 Act)

The arbitrator has various powers in respect of property concerned in the proceedings including ordering its preservation, inspection, or sampling.

7.4 Provisional relief (Section 39 of the 1996 Act)

This power differs from the others mentioned here in that it has to be conferred on the arbitrator by agreement of the parties (which is unlikely after a dispute has arisen as its exercise is only of obvious benefit to claimants). However, where he or she has the power, the arbitrator may make a provisional order of anything which the arbitrator may finally order in the award, such as payment of money or disposition of property. The arbitrator may then confirm, vary, or reverse the provisional order in the award. It seems that provisional orders are intended to be made only where it is highly likely that the relief given will be confirmed at the hearing. The rationale is to ensure that a party with a good case is not kept out of its entitlement until the end of a long reference. This mitigates the absence of an entitlement to give a summary decision, i.e. to reach a final decision by use of a truncated procedure, for example on affidavit evidence alone, where the defence appears to be insubstantial.

7.5 Party default (Section 41 of the 1996 Act)

The arbitrator needs to be able to imbue the process with some discipline where one or other party fails to comply with its obligations (which are expressed in Section 40(1) of the 1996 Act) to do everything required to enable the dispute to be dealt with efficiently and speedily. Accordingly, the arbitrator may dismiss a claim for a lengthy delay which prejudices the respondent or the possibility of a fair trial. Where a party fails to attend a hearing or make written submissions for a hearing the arbitrator may proceed to an award in their absence. Where a party defaults on any order, the arbitrator may make a peremptory order requiring compliance. If the default is continued, a range of options is available. If the failure is of a claimant to give security for costs, the arbitrator can dismiss the claim. In respect of other failures the arbitrator can prevent a party from relying on certain allegations or materials, draw adverse inferences, proceed to an award on the basis of such material as has already been submitted, or penalize the offending party in costs.

8 PARTICULAR PROBLEMS

8.1 Relationship with the courts

In general terms, the policy of the Arbitration Act 1996 was to provide the arbitrator and the parties with more authority in the arbitration process and to reduce the extent to which the courts would be involved in that process.

The courts are now involved in a more limited way. The range of involvement is as follows:

- to stay legal proceedings where there is a relevant arbitration clause: Section 9;
- to extend time for commencement of arbitration proceedings: Section 12;
- to appoint arbitrators in default: Section 18;

- to remove an arbitrator: Section 24;
- to determine a preliminary point of jurisdiction: Section 32;
- to enforce orders of the arbitrator: Section 42;
- to order the attendance of witnesses or the production of documents by non-parties: Section 43;
- to make orders, including granting injunctions in relation to or to aid an arbitration: Section 44;
- to determine a preliminary point of law: Section 45;
- to enforce an award: Section 66;
- to consider a challenge to an award on the basis of substantive jurisdiction: Section 67;
- to consider a challenge to an award on the ground of serious irregularity: Section 68;
- to consider an appeal on a point of law: Section 69.

In each case, the ability of the court to be involved is very limited. However, subject to complying with the individual requirements in relation to each type of application, the court provides a function in both assisting the arbitral process and ensuring that serious miscarriages do not occur in arbitration.

8.2 Court proceedings commenced by a party to an arbitration clause

One particular aspect of the interrelationship between the courts and arbitration is the position where one party to an arbitration clause ignores that provision and commences proceedings in court.

In such circumstances, if the opposing party makes no objection, the court can proceed to consider the merits of the dispute as it would in any other case. At one time, it was thought that the powers of the court might be limited but that is not generally so. This was on the basis that arbitration clauses in standard engineering and building forms of contract often have an express provision that the arbitrator may open up, review and revise a certificate or decision of the engineer or architect. It was argued that the courts did not have that power and the Court of Appeal accepted that argument (*Northern Regional Health Authority* v. *Crouch* [1984] QB 644). That decision was later overturned and therefore the courts can now review the merits of any certificate or decision by the engineer or architect (*Beaufort Developments* v. *Gilbert Ash* [1998] 2 WLR 860).

However, if one party does commence proceedings in breach of the arbitration clause, it is open for the opposing party, provided that it does not take a step in the court proceedings to answer the substantive claim, to apply to the court to stay those proceedings to enable a dispute to be referred to arbitration. Under Section 9 of the Arbitration Act 1996 the court must stay the proceedings unless it is satisfied that the arbitration agreement is null and void, inoperative or incapable of being performed. This is markedly different from the 1950 Act under which the court had a discretion whether or not to stay the proceedings.

9 THE INTERNATIONAL DIMENSION

The provisions of the Arbitration Act 1996 generally only apply to arbitrations where the 'seat of the arbitration' is in England and Wales or Northern Ireland. Some provisions do apply to other international arbitrations, for instance, the seeking of attendance of witnesses: see Section 2.

9.1 Seat of arbitration

The seat (or place) of arbitration is defined as the judicial seat of the arbitration. It is generally determined by the parties. If there is no agreement then Section 3 of the Arbitration Act makes provision for it to be determined having regard to the parties' agreement and all relevant circumstances.

The relevance of the seat of the arbitration is that any mandatory procedural law applicable at that place will apply to the arbitration; a challenge might be made in the courts at that location and the award may be made or deemed to be made at that place. While the arbitration will frequently take place at the seat of the arbitration, by agreement between the parties, including the provisions of any agreed rules, hearings and deliberations of the tribunal may take place elsewhere. If that happens without such agreement, difficult questions may arise as to the effect of the arbitration taking place at a venue other than the seat of the arbitration.

9.2 The proper law

A different question arises as to the law to be applied to the merits of the disputes by an arbitrator or arbitrators, wherever the seat or place of arbitration may be. To determine the proper law, it is first necessary to see whether there has been agreement by the parties, then to see if the parties have designated a procedure by which the proper law is to be determined, for instance by the choice of particular rules. In the absence of any such procedure, the arbitrator will then have to consider whether there is any mandatory provision of the law at the seat of arbitration. If not, then the arbitrator will have to decide which rules of conflict to apply in deciding what is the proper law. Often the test will be the law with which the contract has the closest connection.

For an arbitration with its seat in England and Wales or Northern Ireland, Section 46(3) of the 1996 Act provides that if there is no choice or agreement on the substantive law, the tribunal shall apply the law determined by the conflict of laws rules which it considers applicable.

9.3 International arbitration rules

While in the domestic situation the court system and arbitration run in parallel, in the international context the choice may not, in reality, be available for a number of reasons. If, for example, an English contractor is carrying out work overseas, the overseas client may not be prepared to have any disputes resolved in the English courts and the English contractor may not be prepared to have these disputes dealt with in the courts of the country of the overseas client. It is in that context that international arbitration provides a necessary method of resolving disputes.

It is more common in that context for the parties to elect to have the arbitration made subject to the rules of an institution which administers the arbitration. The most common rules are those of the International Chamber of Commerce (ICC) in Paris or the London Court of International Arbitration (LCIA) in London. In addition, rules have been made, known as the UNCITRAL Rules, which can involve the administration of the arbitration.

The details of those rules is beyond the scope of this text but in general terms they provide an administration of the arbitration process. They do not act as a court in deciding any case. Rather they administer the appointment of the arbitral tribunal which then acts as any other arbitrator, but with the assistance of the relevant arbitral institution. The award given by the arbitral tribunal is then enforceable, as any other arbitration award made at the relevant seat of arbitration.

Construction disputes

4.1 Administration of claims

4.2 Litigation

4.3 Arbitration

4.4 Adjudication

4.5 Alternative dispute resolution

CHAPTER 4.4

Adjudication

Ian Wright
Barrister & Mediator, Crown Office Chambers

Franco Mastrandrea
Northcrofts Management Services Limited

1 WHAT IS ADJUDICATION?

Adjudication is a summary process in which parties to a contract refer disputes to a neutral third party, the adjudicator, for a decision. Unless agreed otherwise, the adjudicator's decision is binding on the parties until the dispute is finally determined in legal proceedings, arbitration or by agreement. In the construction industry adjudication is used to obtain a speedy, impartial decision on disputes arising from a project.

Adjudication, as a binding form of dispute resolution in construction contracts in the United Kingdom, arises under contract or its availability is a creature of statute. It is compulsory in any contract within the meaning of a 'construction contract' (see Section 2.1 below). The contracting parties can determine the precise ambit and application of the adjudication to specific contracts by contractual provisions, provided that certain basic statutory requirements are satisfied in that contract. If they are not, the adjudication provisions of the Scheme for Construction Contracts Regulations ('the Scheme') provided for in Section 108(5) of the Housing Grants, Construction and Regeneration Act 1996 ('the HGCRA 1996') will apply.

Adjudication differs from ADR (see chapter 4.5 below) in that unlike those means of resolving disputes (including negotiation directly between the parties and the facilitative forms of ADR involving a third party intermediary such as mediation), the outcome is a decision by a third party which is **binding** on the parties.

In *Glencot Development and Design Co. Ltd* v. *Ben Barrett & Son (Contractors) Ltd* [2001] BLR 207, HHJ Humphrey Lloyd QC dealt with allegation of bias arising out of these different forms of dispute resolution. He concluded that an adjudicator who had earlier in the process acted as mediator might be perceived as biased when he later purported to act as adjudicator in the same dispute. The learned judge said:

> 'Whilst in an adjudication it is permissible to make enquiries and receive evidence and submissions from one party alone, there is a clear obligation on the Adjudicator to give any absent party a complete and accurate account of what has taken place. (The Adjudicator) went to and fro between the parties. We do not know what he heard or learned. He was under no obligation to report it, nor, given that the content was "without prejudice" and confidential, ought there to be an inquiry as to what happened... These are areas where unconscious or insidious bias may well be present'.

Adjudication also differs from litigation or arbitration in that, unless specifically agreed by the parties the adjudicator's decision does not **finally** resolve the dispute between them. This same distinction also exists between adjudication and expert valuation: see the first instance decision of Dyson J (as he then was) in *Bouygues (UK) Ltd* v. *Dahl-Jensen UK Ltd* [2000] BLR 49.

A decision in an adjudication does not establish a legal liability to pay: only a contractual obligation to do so. Failing agreement, liability is not established until the adjudication decision is enforced by a judgment of the Court. Thus, it has been held that an adjudication decision does not constitute liability for the purposes of the Third Parties (Rights Against Insurers) Act 1930: *Galliford (UK) Ltd Trading as Galliford Northern* v. *Markel Capital Ltd* (unreported, 12 May 2003, Behrens, J).

It seems that if there is an adjudicator's decision it may be necessary to comply with further contractual machinery before it may be referred to arbitration or legal proceedings are commenced for final resolution of the dispute. For example, there may be a contractual requirement that the complaints (and which are already the subject of a decision) identified by a contracting party should be considered by the Contract

Administrator before the matter might be made the subject of a final resolution process. It has in such circumstances been held that such machinery must be operated before arbitration might be invoked, even in the light of an existing adjudicator's decision: see *JT Mackley & Co. Ltd* v. *Gosport Marina Ltd* [2002] BLR 367, in which HHJ Seymour held that the requirement in the ICE 6th Edition first to refer disputes to the Engineer for a decision applied notwithstanding that the reference to arbitration for final resolution of the dispute involved challenging the decision of an adjudicator.

Adjudication is not new. A form of adjudication was available under the JCT family of contracts, the ICE forms and the FIDIC forms for a number of years. Adjudication under the JCT forms was first introduced into construction sub-contracts in the UK about 1976. Initially, its use was almost exclusively limited to financial disputes over set-off of monies otherwise due from a main contractor to a nominated sub-contractor under a sub-contract. A particular feature of the adjudication procedures was the referral of the dispute to a neutral third person, not the Contract Administrator, the Engineer or other certifier under the contract. Over time adjudication provisions have expanded and now cover not only disputes involving rights of set-off but almost every kind of dispute that may arise 'under' a contract (see Section 3.2 below) and, in some cases, also disputes arising 'in connection with' a contract (see Section 3.2 below). In the later case, the provision is probably sufficiently wide to cover virtually all disputes arising, except a dispute as to the existence of the contract itself.

Why was it thought necessary to introduce a statutory right to adjudication? It had been recognised for some time that the available means of resolving construction contract disputes, and in particular the time taken to resolve those disputes, was unsatisfactory. This, together with a number of free market 'abuses' and the unsatisfactory state of the common law, where many sub-contracts contained an arbitration clause which stated that an arbitration between a main contractor may not be commenced until the main contract works had been completed, was having a markedly detrimental effect on confidence and cash flow in the industry.

The promotion of this wider form of adjudication crystallized in the Latham Report ('Constructing the Team', Final Report, July, HMSO, 1994).

Parliament introduced a statutory right to adjudication under the HGCRA 1996, giving a party to a 'construction contract', within the meaning in Section 105 of the HGCRA 1996, the right to refer a dispute arising under that contract to adjudication. The intention was to provide a speedy and effective disputes resolution procedure resulting in an interim remedy. The need for prompt resolution of disputes over monies due was from a practical standpoint heightened by the decision in *Halki Shipping Corpn.* v. *Sopex Oils Ltd* [1998] 2 All ER 23, in which the Court of Appeal effectively closed the hitherto widely used summary Court procedure for claims where the existence of an arbitration clause in a contract prevented a sub-contractor from obtaining summary judgment in court for recovery of monies notwithstanding there was no arguable defence to the claim.

The HGCRA 1996 applies in England and Wales and came into force on 1 May 1998. Corresponding provisions apply to Scotland and Northern Ireland.

In *Comsite Projects Ltd* v. *Andritz AG* [2003] EWHC 958 (TCC) a provision in the sub-contract, which was for work carried out in the UK, that

> 'all disputes arising in interpretation or execution of the present contract ... will be settled amicably. If no agreement can be reached ... the jurisdiction in the event of a dispute will be in Austria, Graz. Austrian law will be applied ...'.

did not prevent the English Court from deciding whether (and in fact finding that) the HGCRA 1996 applied.

In *The Atlas Ceiling & Partition Co. Ltd* v. *Crowngate Estates (Cheltenham) Ltd* (2000) 18 Const LJ 49, HHJ Anthony Thornton QC held that a contract signed on 3 April 1998 was nevertheless entered into after 1 May 1998 because the parties lacked the necessary intention to create legal relations before that date. Accordingly, the contract was subject to the HGCRA 1996.

In *Christiani & Nielsen* v. *The Lowry Centre* (2005) Const LJ T7, HHJ Anthony Thornton QC held that the effect of an agreement or understanding that the HGCRA 1996 would not apply (in this case, that it should be back-dated to a date before 1 May, 1998) was to deny one of the parties its statutory right to adjudication.

In *Yarm Road Ltd* v. *Costain Ltd* (unreported, 30 July 2001, TCC), HHJ Richard Havery QC decided that a contract which was originally entered into in August 1995 and was novated in August 1998 was nevertheless a contract that was subject to adjudication.

The approach of the HGCRA 1996 is to require adjudication to be available to resolve construction contract disputes and to limit the freedom of the parties to determine the terms upon which that right may be exercised. A party has a right to give notice of an intention to refer a dispute to adjudication '*...at any time*' (see Section 108(2)(a) of the HGCRA 1996).

In *John Mowlem & Co. plc* v. *Hydra-Tight Ltd* (2001) Const LJ 358 it was held that although the parties had agreed to a contractual provision requiring the service of a notice of dissatisfaction prior to the commencement of adjudication, this was not in compliance with the statutory right to adjudication at any time. Clause 66 of ICE 7th Conditions has been amended to remove the ICE's traditional approach of requiring a decision of the Engineer before a dispute is said to arise (see chapter 4.5, Section 10.1 below).

In *RG Carter Ltd* v. *Edmund Nuttall Ltd* (unreported, 21 June 2000, TCC) HHJ Anthony Thornton QC held that a contractual provision purporting to require mediation before resort to adjudication did not comply with the statutory right to adjudication at any time and would not therefore be upheld.

In *Midland Expressway Ltd* v. *Carillion Construction Ltd (No. 1)* [2005] EWHC 2963 (TCC) it was held that '*equivalent project relief*' provisions in a sub-contract in connection with a PFI could not be used to prevent the bringing of an adjudication at a time of the sub-contractor's choosing.

It was held in *Connex South Eastern Ltd* v. *MJ Building Services Group plc* [2005] EWCA Civ 193, [2005] BLR 201, CA, that a party may be entitled to refer a dispute to adjudication even after the limitation period has expired. Dyson LJ observed:

> 'The phrase "at any time" means exactly what it says. It would have been possible to restrict the time within which an adjudication could be commenced, say, to a period by reference to the date when work was completed or the contract terminated. But this was not done'.

2 WHAT CONTRACTS MUST PROVIDE A STATUTORY RIGHT TO ADJUDICATION?

The statutory right to adjudication is set out in Section 108(1) of the HGCRA 1996, which provides that:

'A party to a construction contract has the right to refer a dispute arising under the contract for adjudication under a procedure complying with this section'.

2.1 What is a 'construction contract'?

The contract must be a '*construction contract*' as defined in Section 104 of the HGCRA 1996 Part II. Construction contracts are agreements with a person for the carrying out of or arranging for the carrying out of or the provision of labour for the carrying out of '*construction operations*'. Construction contracts include, among others, agreements to do architectural, design or surveying work, and advice on building and engineering, in relation to construction operations. It follows that the agreements appointing professionals to provide services as above are within the meaning of a construction contract.

In *Fence Gate Ltd* v. *James R Knowles Ltd* (unreported, 31 May 2001, HHJ Gilliland QC) it was held that the provision of factual evidence or assisting at arbitration was not a construction operation; such services were rather rendered in relation to litigation support work. By contrast, in *Diamond* v. *PJW Enterprises Ltd* [2002] Scotcs 340 it was held that a firm of surveyors appointed to act as contract administrator was performing services which were essentially '*surveying work . . . in relation to construction operations*' under a construction contract within Section 104(2) of the HGCRA 1996.

In *Pegram Shopfitters Ltd* v. *Tally Weijl (UK) Ltd* [2003] BLR 296, HHJ Anthony Thornton QC held at first instance that both parties accepted that there was a construction contract, although there was disagreement as to the relevant terms; the negotiations had consisted of a series of offers and counter-offers and the concluded contract was not comprehensively brought together. This meant that the contract failed to contain the terms in a manner and form that enabled the conditions which made them compliant to be readily ascertained without dispute. Accordingly the Scheme applied. This was rejected by the Court of Appeal ([2004] BLR 65), which found that there was a real, not fanciful, prospect of establishing that the Adjudicator had acted without jurisdiction, that the Scheme probably did not apply (holding that the finding that the Scheme applied because (as the judge below thought) there was a construction contract but the parties were not able clearly to identify its terms, was simply ducking the critical question) that if there was a written contract it provided for adjudication in accordance with its express terms, or (more likely) that there was no written construction contract within s.107 at all.

There must, of course, be a concluded contract (see chapter 3.1 above).

It was held in *Oakley and another* v. *Airclear Environmental Ltd and another* (unreported, 4 October 2001, Etherton J) that whilst the parties had intended to enter into a NAM/T form of contract, no such contract had ever been entered into; there was therefore no jurisdiction for the Adjudicator appointed by the RIBA. On the question of estoppel (by convention), the facts showed that there was a common assumption at the time of the application for the appointment of the Adjudicator that their contractual relations were governed by NAM/T and NAM/SC, including, in particular, their dispute resolution provisions. This estoppel could be resiled from, however, because there was no significant detriment (by way of significant expenditure having been incurred by the parties in the adjudication).

In *Gibson* v. *Imperial Homes* (unreported, 18 June 2002, HHJ John Toulmin CMG QC) the respondent had throughout disputed the jurisdiction of the adjudicator, alleging that no contract came into existence between the parties to the adjudication as the contract was entered into with the applicant as a limited company rather than with Mr Gibson. Further, even if a contract did exist with Mr Gibson, it was not concluded with Imperial Homes but with Chinadome Ltd, for which Imperial Homes was a non-trading holding company. The respondent also argued that Gibson had failed to demonstrate that there was a contract in writing for the purposes of s.107 of the HGCRA 1996. The Court held that a letter of 7 October 1999 evidenced an agreement in writing under s.107(4) of the HGCRA 1996 in that it was recorded by a third party, with the authority of the parties to an agreement. Nor did it matter whether Mr Gibson or the limited company was the applicant, as on a proper construction of Section 36C of the Companies Act 1985 either party could enforce the contract (invoking *Braymist* v. *Wise Finance Ltd* [2002] 2 All ER 333, CA); there was no real prospect of showing that Imperial Homes' agents had no ostensible authority to contract with Gibson nor of showing that the contract was made with Chinadome Ltd rather than with Imperial Homes.

In *Galliford Try Construction Ltd* v. *Michael Heal Associates Ltd* (2004) 99 Con LR 19, HHJ Richard Seymour QC refused to enforce an adjudicator's decision as it was based on an erroneous conclusion by the Adjudicator that there was a contract between the parties. Neither party had any intention, at the relevant date, of entering into a binding agreement. The Adjudicator therefore had no jurisdiction.

A contract which otherwise complies with the statutory requirements but which is made by an agent on behalf of his principal becomes a contract with the principal, in keeping with the general law: *Universal Music Operations Ltd* v. *Flairnote Ltd and others* (unreported, 24 August 2000, HHJ David Wilcox QC), in which it was held that a contract made by a Project Manager with express authority to do so was in law a contract made between the Contractor and the principal.

2.2 The agreement must involve 'construction operations'

Section 105 of the HGCRA 1996 describes what is, and is not, within the meaning of 'construction operations'. Notwithstanding the detailed descriptions in Section 105, a considerable body of case law has grown up on what falls within the meaning.

In *Nottingham Community Housing Association Ltd* v. *Powerminster Ltd* [2000] BLR 309, Dyson J (as he then was) held that an agreement for the annual servicing and the provision of responsive repairs to gas appliances within a number of properties owned by the claimant fell within Section 105(1)(a) of the HGCRA 1996 (which defines construction operations as the 'construction, alteration, repair, maintenance, extension, demolition or dismantling of buildings, or structures forming, or to form, part of the land, (whether permanent or not)'), as opposed to Section 105(1)(c) (which expressly refers to systems of heating but is restricted to works of *installation* of such systems).

In *Staveley Industries plc* v. *Odebrecht Oil & Gas Services Ltd* (unreported, 28 February 2001, TCC), HHJ Richard Havery QC held that a sub-contract for the design, engineering, procurement, supply, delivery to site, installation, testing and commissioning of instrumentation, fire and gas, electrical and telecommunications equipment within modules intended for an oil rig to be fixed to a sea-based platform in the Gulf of Mexico did not form part of the land, as required by Section 105(1)(c) of the HGCRA 1996 because it related to structures which were or were to be founded in the sea bed below the low water mark, which structures were intended to be excluded from the ambit of the Act.

In *Gibson Lea Retail Interiors Ltd* v. *MAKRO Self-Service Wholesalers Ltd* [2001] BLR 407, HHJ Richard Seymour QC held that shop-fitting did not amount to construction operations unless (which in the case they did not) the works consisted of the construction of 'structures forming, or to form, part of the land, (whether permanent

4.1 Administration of claims
4.2 Litigation
4.3 Arbitration
4.4 Adjudication
4.5 Alternative dispute resolution

or not)', as required by Section 105(1)(a) or 'installation in any building or structure of fittings forming part of the land' referenced at Section 105(1)(c).

In *Ruttle Plant Hire Ltd* v. *Secretary of State for the Environment, Food and Rural Affairs* [2004] EWHC 2152 (TCC) it was held that a contract for foot and mouth clean-up operations on farm premises was a construction contract as defined in Sections 105(d) and (e) of the HGCRA 1996. Furthermore, some works were carried out in relation to the provision of temporary or permanent offices, which were construction operations by virtue of Section 105(a) of the HGCRA 1996.

In *Palmers Ltd* v. *ABB Power Construction Ltd* [1999] BLR 426 an issue arose whether scaffolding under a sub-sub-subcontract associated with the erection of a heat recovery steam generator boiler and associated pipework (involving initial erection and thereafter regular modification to facilitate permanent works until final removal of that scaffolding) the commercial rates for which had been the subject of a Memorandum of Understanding was a 'construction operation'. It was held that the scaffolding fell within Section 105(1)(e) of the HGCRA 1996, as

> 'operations which form an integral part of, or are preparatory to, or are for rendering complete, such operations as are previously described in this subsection, including site clearance, earth-moving, excavation, tunnelling and boring, laying of foundations, erection, maintenance or dismantling of scaffolding, site restoration, landscaping and the provision of roadways and other access works'.

2.3 Operations that are not within the meaning 'construction operation'

Section 105(2) sets out those matters that are *not* construction operations within HGCRA 1996 Part II. The main categories of exempt operations are:

- drilling for or extraction of oil or natural gas (Section 105(2)(a));
- extraction of minerals (Section 105(2)(b));
- assembly, installation or demolition of plant or machinery or erection of steelwork for the purposes of supporting or providing access to plant or machinery where the primary activity is nuclear processing, power generation, water or effluent treatment, or the production, transmission, processing or bulk storage of chemicals, pharmaceuticals, oil, gas, steel or food and drink (Section 105(2)(c));
- the making, installation and repair of artistic works (Section 105(2)(e)).

In *Homer Burgess Ltd* v. *Chirex (Annan) Ltd* [2000] BLR 124, Lord MacFadyen held that an Adjudicator had misconstrued the provisions of Section 105(2)(c) of the HGCRA 1996 in relation to the word 'plant'. Although the pursuers had undertaken the erection of steelwork to support or provide access to such plant, the primary activity on the site which was the subject of the disputes before the adjudicator was the 'production transmission processing or bulk storage of pharmaceuticals'. Adjudication was not therefore required and the adjudicator had no jurisdiction to decide the bulk of the disputes.

In *ABB Power Construction Ltd* v. *Norwest Holst* (2001) 77 Con LR 20, HHJ Humphrey Lloyd QC held that a sub-contract for the insulation of boilers, ducting, silencers, pipework, drums and tanks in relation to the building of heat recovery steam generator boilers as a part of a project to extend an existing power station was exempt: the work was necessary to achieve the aims or purposes of a power generation plant, being an exempt operation under Section 105(2)(c) of the HGCRA 1996.

In *ABB Zantingh Ltd* v. *Zedal Building Services Ltd* [2001] BLR 66, HHJ Peter Bowsher QC held that the words 'a site where the primary activity is...' in Section

105(2)(c) of the HGCRA1996 had to be construed by reference to the whole site and that a generator surrounded by a security fence for the purposes of generating emergency power in the event of a Y2k problem commissioned by an organisation whose business was the printing of magazines, was not a 'site' where the primary activity was power generation so as to attract exemption. Adjudication was therefore appropriate.

In *Mitsui Babcock Energy Services Ltd* 2001 S.L.T. 1158, Lord Hardie held that the works which were the subject of the dispute were to further the primary activity of the processing of chemicals and oil on a petrochemical complex and were therefore not subject to adjudication by virtue of Section 105(2)(c) of the HGCRA 1996. Accordingly, the adjudicator had been right to decline jurisdiction.

In *Comsite Projects Ltd* v. *Andritz AG*, above, the defendant argued that a contract to install dryer plant and fit out a building to house that plant at a sewage sludge recycling centre was subsidiary to the primary activity on site which was effluent treatment and was therefore not caught by the HGCRA 1996. This was dismissed by the court: the dryer plant could work without the building services and a requirement that the services be installed lawfully to operate the plant was of itself, and in the absence of a physical connection between the works in issue and the plant, insufficient to bring it within the Section 105(2)(c) exception to the HGCRA 1996.

In *Conor Engineering Ltd* v. *Les Constructions Industrielle de la Mediterranee* [2004] BLR 212, the court held that determining what was the primary act*ivity* at a particular site was a question of fact and not necessarily determined by the primary *purpose* of that site. In this case the primary activity was the incineration of waste and not the generation of electricity, which was a mere spin-off. A subcontract for boiler works was therefore caught by the HGCRA 1996.

The manufacture and delivery, that is supply only, of certain items, including 'building or engineering components or equipment, materials plant or machinery or components for [mechanical and electrical services] systems' are not 'construction operations' unless the contract also provides for installation: Section 105(2)(d).

In *Baldwins Industrial Services plc* v. *Barr Ltd* [2003] BLR 176, HHJ Frances Kirkham had to decide whether an arrangement for the hire of an item of plant (a mobile crane) plus a driver was a construction contract. The learned judge decided that it did not fall within the exception set out at Section 105(2)(d) of the HGCRA 1996 in that it was not one for the mere delivery of plant to the site; it was for the supply of plant and labour for use in construction operations on a building site. Accordingly, it was a construction contract within the meaning of Section 104 of the HGCRA 1996.

2.4 'Contracts in writing'

The contract must be in writing within the meaning of Section 107 of the HGCRA 1996. This extends to agreements made in writing whether or not signed by the parties, agreements made by the exchange of written communications, agreements evidenced in writing and agreements made otherwise than in writing but by reference to terms which are in writing. Subsection 107(5) provides that an agreement otherwise than in writing may be constituted as an agreement in writing by an allegation in written submissions of its existence by one party not denied by the other in adjudication, arbitral or legal proceedings.

In *Grovedeck Ltd* v. *Capital Demolition Ltd* [2000] BLR 181, HHJ Peter Bowsher QC held that an adjudicator had no jurisdiction because the relevant contracts were not in writing and submissions by one party to an otherwise unauthorised adjudication did not give to the supposed adjudicator a jurisdiction which he did not have when he was appointed.

The Court of Appeal reviewed Section 107 of the HGCRA 1996 in *RJT Consulting Engineers Ltd* v. *DM Engineering (NI) Ltd* [2002] BLR 217 and by a majority concluded that it is not sufficient if the writing supports merely the existence of the agreement or its substance (being the parties to it, the nature of the work and the price). Unless conceded as part of the adjudication proceedings (see Subsection 107(5) of the HGCRA 1996), the writing must evidence the whole of the agreement not parts of it, including the *terms* of the oral agreement. Although the requirements for the relevant contract to be in writing should be interpreted purposively and the general purpose of Part II of the HGCRA 1996 was to facilitate and encourage the process of adjudication it was intended to be a swift and summary process (as was apparent from the time limits in Section 108(2)) and Parliament had decided that it was inappropriate for an adjudicator to have to deal with the disputes which often arise as to the terms of an oral contract. Whilst agreeing with the decision, the minority judgment of Auld LJ was that it was the *material* terms of the agreement which were to be recorded (although in this case they had not been). Leave to appeal this decision was refused by the House of Lords. See also *Carillion Construction Ltd* v. *Devonport Royal Dockyard Ltd* [2003] BLR 79 in which HHJ Peter Bowsher QC declined to enforce the decision of an adjudicator who found that an agreement had been reached by the parties varying the terms such that the contract would become cost reimbursable; any such agreement was not evidenced in writing within the meaning of Section 107(2)(c) of the HGCRA 1996 and the Adjudicator was accordingly acting without jurisdiction; *Thomas-Fredric's (Construction) Ltd* v. *Keith Wilson* [2004] BLR 23, CA; *Redworth Construction Ltd* v. *Brookdale Healthcare Ltd* [2006] EWHC 1994 (TCC), in which HHJ Richard Havery QC concluded that the date of possession, the contract period and the date for completion of the works were manifestly relevant to the claim before the adjudicator, which was for the recovery of sums withheld because the contract overran the agreed date for completion of the works. As those terms were not recorded in writing this was not a contract in writing within the meaning of Section 107 of the HGCRA 1996.

In *Trustees of the Stratfield Saye Estate* v. *AHL Construction Ltd* [2004] EWHC 3286, Jackson J held that it was not possible to regard the minority reasoning of Auld LJ in *RJT* as some kind of gloss upon or amplification of the reasoning of the majority; attractive though it was, it did not form part of the ratio of *RJT*. An agreement was therefore only evidenced in writing for the purposes of Section 107, subsections (2), (3) and (4), if *all* the express terms of that agreement were recorded in writing.

2.5 The status of the contracting parties

In *Total M & E Services Ltd* v. *ABB Building Technologies Ltd* (2003) 87 Con LR, HHJ David Wilcox QC held that the fact that a notice of adjudication had referenced a different party than the referral did not affect the Adjudicator's jurisdiction, as the parties had at all times been aware of the true identity of the contracting parties and no one had been misled.

In *Andrew Wallace Ltd* v. *Artisan Regeneration Ltd and another* [2006] EWHC 15 (TCC), Architects issued an enforcement notice against a developer based upon an Adjudicator's decision. The developer challenged the validity of the Adjudicator's decision based on the identity of the referring party in the adjudication. It contended that it contracted with an individual, not a limited company. HHJ Frances Kirkham found that the developer had throughout proceeded on the basis that it had contracted with the company. It paid substantial sums of money into the company's account. It was considered most unlikely that the developer would not have raised the question of the identity of the contracting party at an earlier stage had there been any real question on its part with respect to that matter.

In *Michael John Construction Ltd* v. *Golledge and others* [2006] EWHC 71 (TCC) the claimant sought recovery of monies arising out of two adjudication decisions. The employer was an unincorporated association of individuals, which at law had no separate legal identity or status. The question was who were the right individuals for the claimant to pursue in the adjudications and in the enforcement proceedings? The claimant secured the first adjudication decision against the fourth defendant, and the second against all four defendants. HHJ Peter Coulson QC held that the fourth defendant had signed the contract on behalf of the trustees. The first, second and third defendants were the principals on whose behalf the contract was made; their agent was the fourth defendant. The claimant could elect to sue either the first, second and third defendants as principals, or, alternatively, the fourth defendant, either personally or as agent.

Where the parties to a construction contract have agreed to adjudication by incorporating into their agreement a standard form of contract providing for adjudication, the adjudication provisions will be binding upon them: *Harvey Shopfitters Ltd* v. *ADI Ltd* [2004] 2 All ER 982, CA. Subject to the Unfair Contracts legislation this is so even in relation to consensual adjudication provisions involving a residential occupier: see *Bryen and Langley Ltd* v. *Boston* [2005] BLR 508 (CA). Cf. *Allen Wilson Shopfitters* v. *Buckingham* [2005] 102 Con LR 154.

2.6 Contracts to which the provisions of HGCRA 1996 Part II do not apply

By Section 106(1)(a) of the HGCRA 1996, Part II of that Act does not apply to a construction contract with a residential occupier. A construction contract with a residential occupier is defined in Section 106 as 'construction contract which principally relates to operations on a dwelling, which one of the parties to the contract occupies, or intends to occupy, as his residence'.

In *Samuel Thomas Construction* v. *J&B Developments* (unreported, 28 January 2000) the Court was asked to interpret the word 'principally' in Section 106. The judge held that conversion of two barns for dwellings, one for occupation by the owner and another for onward sale, nevertheless fell within the HCGRA 1996, and adjudication over those conversions was therefore appropriate.

Construction contracts with residential occupiers are excluded from the statutory adjudication regime. However, when drafting contracts on behalf of residential occupiers professionals need to be alert to the inclusion of adjudication provisions in the majority of standard form contracts, and decide whether the adjudication provisions are to be incorporated or not. A lack of care in using standard form contracts has meant that it is not unusual for contracts with residential occupiers to include for adjudication.

Where the residential occupier is ordinarily a consumer, the adjudication provisions will come within the purview of the Unfair Terms in Consumer Contracts Regulations 1999 (SI 1999 No. 2083), although whether or not the occupier has had the benefit of professional advice may be relevant. In *Picardi* v. *Cuniberti* [2003] BLR 487, (2003) Const LJ 350, HHJ Toulmin CMG QC commented that a provision for adjudication, which was to be included as a matter of contract, was to be treated as an unusual provision, which had to be brought to the specific attention of the lay party (in this

4.1 Administration of claims
4.2 Litigation
4.3 Arbitration
4.4 Adjudication
4.5 Alternative dispute resolution

case, the residential occupier) if it was to be validly incorporated. Further, the adjudication procedure could cause the consumer to incur irrecoverable expenditure in bringing or defending a claim and might hinder the consumer's right to take legal action, and also give the impression of unfairness unless properly explained, which created a significant imbalance in the parties' rights and obligations for the purposes of those regulations to the detriment of the consumer.

In *Lovell Projects Ltd* v. *Legg and Carver* [2003] BLR 452 it was held that the adjudication provisions (incorporated on the insistence of the occupier who had available advice both from solicitors and its nominated contract administrator) did not create a significant imbalance in the parties' rights and obligations for the purposes of those regulations; they applied equally to both parties and there was no breach of the requirements of good faith, as the adjudication terms were fully, clearly and legibly set out. See also *Westminster Building Co. Ltd* v. *Andrew Beckingham* [2004] BLR 265; *Allen Wilson Shopfitters* v. *Buckingham* (2005) 102 Con LR 154, concluding likewise.

In *Bryen & Langley Ltd* v. *Boston* above, the Court of Appeal held that building works for a dwelling house carried out under a contract with a residential occupier, to which the HGCRA 1996 did not apply, were nevertheless undertaken under a JCT Form of contract and therefore that the adjudicator had jurisdiction, because that Form had been incorporated into the contract by agreement of the parties.

Pursuant to Section 106(1)(b) of HGCRA 1996, a number of other types of contract were excluded from operation of Part II by the *Contracts (England and Wales) Exclusion Order 1998* ('the 1998 Exclusion Order'). The excluded contracts include certain agreements under statute, contracts entered into under private finance initiatives, finance agreements and development agreements.

Paragraph 6 of the 1998 Exclusion Order provides that a contract is excluded if it is a development agreement. A contract is a development agreement if it includes provision for the grant or disposal of a relevant interest in the land on which take place the principal construction operations to which the contract relates. In *Captiva Estates Ltd* v. *Rybarn Ltd (in administration)* [2005] EWHC 2744 (TCC), HHJ David Wilcox QC concluded that a contract which included provisions granting the defendant options for the grant of leases for each of seven flats was a contract giving the defendant an interest in land and therefore excluded; there could therefore be no compulsory adjudication.

3 THE EXISTENCE OF A DISPUTE

3.1 'Dispute'

There must be a dispute before it can be referred to adjudication. However, often a party will contend that no dispute exits in order to avoid the adjudication process. Therefore, it is important to be able to say when a 'dispute' has come into existence. In *AMEC Civil Engineering Limited* v. *Secretary of State for Transport* [2004] EWHC 2339 (TCC) the law was summarized (at para. 68 of the judgement) by Jackson J in seven propositions (see Chapter 4.5 Section 10.1 below). These propositions were viewed as 'broadly correct' in the Court of Appeal, see [2005] EWCA 291. The propositions included the views that the word 'dispute' should be given its natural meaning and that there are no hard-edged legal rules as to what is and is not a dispute. A dispute does not arise until it emerges that the claim is not admitted. Jackson J's propositions had also been approved earlier by the Court of Appeal in *Collins (Contractors) Ltd* v. *Baltic Quay Ocean Management (1994) Ltd* [2005] BLR 63 (CA). Although the decision in the

AMEC case was concerned with a dispute under an arbitration agreement in the ICE 6th Conditions, it represents the law relating to the existence of a dispute and is relevant to adjudication. Therefore the case law in adjudication proceedings below which pre-date the decision in the *AMEC* case should be read in the context of Jackson J's propositions.

Whether or not a dispute has arisen is a matter of fact, usually where a claim or assertion is rejected in clear language without the possibility of further discussion: *Griffin and Tomlinson* v. *Midas Homes Ltd* (2000) 78 Con LR 121, in which HHJ Humphrey Lloyd QC concluded that a general claim, unsupported by back-up and in relation to which no sufficient opportunity had been given to consider the same, did not amount to a dispute.

In *Sindall Ltd* v. *Solland and others* (2001) 80 Con LR 152, HHJ Humphrey Lloyd QC held that in order for there to be a dispute it must be clear that a point has emerged from the process of discussion or negotiation that had ended and that there was something which needed to be decided. This approach was endorsed by Forbes J in *Beck Peppiatt Ltd* v. *Norwest Holst Construction Ltd* [2003] BLR 316.

In *Monmouthshire County Council* v. *Costelloe and Kemple Ltd* (1965) 5 BLR 83, Lord Denning MR said in relation to a case under the ICE 4th Conditions:

> 'Was there any dispute or difference arising between the Contractor and the Engineer? It is accepted that, in order that a dispute or difference can arise under this contract, there must in the first place be a claim by the Contractor. Until that claim is rejected, you cannot say that there is a dispute or difference. There must be both a claim and a rejection of it in order to constitute a dispute or difference.'

The descriptions in *AMEC* as to when a dispute exists are less well-defined than the very clear definition given in *Monmouthshire County Council*; following *AMEC* it is likely to be more difficult in many circumstances to know the precise time at which a dispute has come into existence.

Construction disputes can be extremely complex. The data which surround them can involve large volumes of documents. Given the time constraints of the adjudication process, there is justifiable concern that one or other of the parties may be 'ambushed'. One effective way of reducing the impact of an ambush is to require that the details must already have been fully aired between the parties.

Does this put adjudications into a special category? HHJ Richard Seymour QC appears to have adopted such an approach in *Edmund Nuttall Ltd* v. *RG Carter Ltd* [2002] BLR 312, in which he held that for there to be a dispute there must have been opportunity for the protagonists each to consider the position adopted by the other and to formulate arguments of a reasoned kind; what constitutes a 'dispute' between the parties is not only a 'claim' which has been rejected, but the whole package of arguments advanced and facts relied upon by each side.

But the decision *in Edmund Nuttall* above appears to be too restrictive. In *Ellerine Bros. (Pty.) Ltd* v. *Klinger* [1982] 1 WLR 1375 the Court of Appeal held that a dispute exists for so long as any claim is not admitted as due and payable. Templeman LJ said:

> 'But the fact that the Plaintiffs make certain claims which, if disputed, would be referable to arbitration and the fact that the Defendant then does nothing (he does not admit the claim, he merely continues a policy of masterly inactivity) does not mean that there is no dispute. There is a dispute until the Defendant admits that a sum is due and payable...'

Also, in *Halki Shipping Corpn.* v. *Sopex Oils Ltd*, above, dispute was given a wide meaning. Swinton Thomas LJ said:

> 'There is a dispute once money is claimed, unless and until the Defendants admit that the sum is due and payable'.

The 'restricted view' of a dispute in *Edmund Nuttall* above was expressly not followed in *Cowlin Construction* v. *CFW Architects* (2003) BLR 241; *London & Amsterdam Properties Ltd* v. *Waterman Partnership* (2003) EWHC (TCC) 3059, (2003) 94 Con LR 154; *AWG Construction Services Ltd* v. *Rockingham Motor Speedway Ltd* (2004) EWHC 88 (TCC); and in *William Verry (Glazing Systems)* v. *Furlong Homes Ltd* [2005] EWHC 138 (TCC). These cases adopted the wider meaning of dispute based on the approach in *Halki* above.

'The Courts have stated that the word "dispute" is to be given its ordinary and natural meaning and that it "included any claim which the other party refused to admit or did not pay whether or not there was an answer in fact or in law" ', per HHJ Peter Coulson QC in *William Verry (Glazing Systems) Ltd* v. *Furlong Homes Ltd* above.

Taking account of the case law, it seems that in many cases a dispute may often be constituted both very simply and quickly, and may be achieved by challenge or even silence.

The broad, inclusive, definition of disputes, rather than the 'restricted view' has been adopted in many adjudication cases: see, for example, *Cowlin Construction Ltd* v. *CFW Architects* [2003] BLR 241 and *Orange EBS* v. *ABB Ltd* [2003] BLR 323. Cf. *Watkin Jones & Son* v. *Lidl UK GmbH* (unreported, Cardiff TCC, HH Moseley QC); *Lovell Projects Ltd* v. *Legg and Carver*, above.

The question of whether a dispute existed came before HHJ Richard Seymour QC again in *Dean & Dyball Construction Ltd* v. *Kenneth Grubb Associates* [2003] 100 Con LR 92. In that case he held that it was not necessary for each and every fact and each and every element of the claim to have been put forward for the other party to consider before it could be said that a dispute had crystallised. It was all a matter of fact and degree in each particular case. Whilst the learned judge did not seek to resile from anything he had said in his earlier decision in *Edmund Nuttall Ltd* v. *RG Carter Ltd* above, several commentators viewed his judgment as a tacit acknowledgment that the approach in his earlier judgment had been too narrow a definition of dispute.

In *London & Amsterdam Properties Ltd* v. *Waterman Partnership Ltd* [2005] BLR 179, an adjudication involving allegations of professional negligence, HHJ David Wilcox QC held that the reasoning in *Halki* above, as to what constitutes a dispute in arbitration proceedings, applies with equal effect in adjudication proceedings. A similar finding was made in *CIB Properties Ltd* v. *Birse Construction Ltd* [2005] BLR 173.

In *Carillion Construction Ltd* v. *Devonport Royal Dockyard Ltd* [2003] BLR 79, an application for payment had been made but not paid. The court held that these facts did not necessarily constitute a dispute; the respondent had merely sought further information and clarification, and neither party had denied the claim outright or ignored it.

In considering if and when a dispute has arisen, the courts have generally adopted a robust and common-sense approach in enforcement proceedings, rather than taking a legalistic or overly technical approach: see, for example, the decision of HHJ David Wilcox QC in *All in One Building & Refurbishments Ltd* v. *Makers UK Ltd* [2005] EWHC 2943 (TCC).

Difficulties often arise in knowing whether a new claim is being made or the 'claim' referred to adjudication is merely a development of an existing claim already set out in the notice of referral to adjudication. If it is properly a new claim, and therefore outside the scope of the dispute already referred, then unless the parties agree, the adjudication will not have jurisdiction to decide the new claim. The courts do not adopt an excessively legalistic view of what is a 'new' claim; if it is simply a fuller explanation for the claim originally made and which can properly be described as a refinement or enhancement of the claim that had been made at the time that the adjudication started it is not a new claim; see, for example *AWG Construction Services Ltd* v. *Rockingham Motor Speedway Ltd* above. If the notice of referral to adjudication is drafted sufficiently broadly, it will generally be easier to demonstrate that further matters, or even a further claim, are not a new claim: see, for example: *William Verry (Glazing Systems)* v. *Furlong Homes Ltd* above.

It should be noted that in *William Verry (Glazing Systems)* v. *Furlong Homes Ltd*, HHJ Peter Coulson QC observed that *AMEC* was mainly concerned with the issue as to when a failure to respond to a claim or claim document as opposed to an outright rejection of a claim can trigger a dispute that can be referred to adjudication.

In *Petition of British Waterways Board* (unreported, the Outer House, Court of Session, 5 July 2001, Lord McCluskey) it was alleged that there was no 'dispute' between the parties, given the express terms of the contract between them. This was challenged by the joint venture Contractor, arguing that there was a dispute within the meaning of Section 108 of the HGCRA 1996 and that any provision in the contract that purported to redefine a 'dispute' fell to be disregarded, in the light of Section 108(5). Lord McCluskey refused to bar the adjudication proceedings, holding that if the matter was not already in issue it could be put in issue without delay as the parties had had some months to investigate and consider their respective positions so that the extra cost of putting the relevant matters in an appropriate form before an adjudicator was likely to be limited.

It appears that a dispute may be contractually defined in such a way as to prevent adjudication before the contractual review procedure has been exhausted: see *R Durtnell & Sons Ltd* v. *Kaduna Ltd* [2003] BLR 225. In that case HHJ Richard Seymour held that until an application for an extension of time had been submitted to the architect and he had determined the extension or time for such determination had expired, it was not possible to know if there was any dispute in existence or not.

The HGCRA 1996 also extends to any 'difference' and it has been suggested that this is wider than 'dispute'. Support for this conclusion is available from decisions in related areas of law: see for example *F&G Sykes (Wessex) Ltd* v. *Fine Fare Ltd* [1967] 1 Lloyd's Rep. 53, CA, although in *CIB Properties Ltd* v. *Birse Construction Ltd* HHJ John Toulmin CMG QC doubted that the presence of the word 'difference' added anything of substance.

3.2 A dispute 'under the contract'

In Section 108(1) of HGCRA 1996, the dispute must arise 'under the contract'. These words have been considered in the context of arbitration. In *Ashville Investments Ltd* v. *Elmer Contractors Ltd* [1988] 2 Lloyd's Rep 73 the Court of Appeal decided that a claim for the rectification of a building contract on the grounds of mistake, and resolution of allegations of misrepresentation or negligent mis-statement could be brought within an arbitration agreement empowering the arbitrator to resolve any dispute or difference as to any matter or thing of whatsoever nature arising 'in connection with' the contract, although Balcombe LJ doubted whether these disputes could arise 'under the contract'. Bingham LJ (as he then was) agreed that the words 'in connection with' were wider than the words 'arising under the contract'. In *Fillite (Runcorn) Ltd* v. *Aqua-Lift* (1989) 45 BLR 27 (CA) it was held that jurisdiction over disputes 'arising under these heads of agreement' did not extend to issues which did not concern obligations created by or incorporated into the contract and excluded disputes under a collateral agreement, and resolution of allegations of negligent mis-statement or innocent misrepresentation.

It should be noted that certain contractual provisions for adjudication may be wider in scope than the statutory requirements, which limit the right to adjudication to matters 'under the contract'. For example, the dispute resolution provisions in clause 66B(1)(a) the ICE 7th Conditions, provide for the referral to adjudication of 'any matter in dispute arising under or in connection with the Contract or the carrying out of the Works'.

In *Shepherd Construction Ltd* v. *Mecright* [2000] BLR 489, HHJ Humphrey Lloyd QC decided that matters which preceded the making of a subcontract, such as questions as to whether a contract was entered into on a false basis or as a result of a misrepresentation or on the basis of promises which did not materialise, were not within the jurisdiction of an adjudicator.

This formulation does not, however, prevent the adjudicator from making decisions on financial remedies other than those falling within the express remedy-granting provisions created by the contract (such as clause 26 of JCT 2005 Private With Quantities form, which deals with loss and/or expense). The secondary obligations of a party in breach of contract (such as the obligation to pay monetary compensation) are a creature of that very contract: see *Photo Productions Ltd* v. *Securicor Transport Ltd* [1980] 1 All ER 556 (HL), per Lord Diplock:

> 'The contract, however, is just as much the source of secondary obligations as it is of primary obligations'.

An adjudicator can therefore award damages: see, for example, *Diamond* v. *PJW Enterprises Ltd* above, in which it was held that if a breach of contract was proved, the adjudicator had the power to award damages.

Rights consequent upon the exercise of a common law power to terminate further performance for repudiatory conduct are matters arising under the contract and likewise capable of adjudication: *Northern Developments (Cumbria) Ltd* v. *J&J Nichol* [2000] BLR 158 (although in that case they were beyond the adjudicator's jurisdiction, not having been made the subject of notice to withhold). In this regard, by analogy with arbitration (see, for example, *Heyman and another* v. *Darwins Ltd* [1942] AC 356, HL), adjudication survives termination. In *A&D Maintenance and Construction Ltd* v. *Pagehurst Construction Services Ltd* (1999) CILL 1518, HHJ David Wilcox QC said:

> 'Even if the contract had been terminated, the matters referred to the Adjudicator remain disputes under the contract. Where there is a contract to which the Act applies, as in this case, and there are disputes arising out of the contract to be adjudicated, the adjudication provisions clearly remain operative just as much as an arbitration clause would remain operative'.

To the extent that the decision in *Barr Ltd* v. *Law Mining Ltd* (2001) 80 Con LR 134, (the Outer House, Court of Session, 15 June 2001, Lord MacFadyen) is inconsistent with the view above on the effect of rescission consequent upon breach of contract it is, so far as English law is concerned, probably unsafe.

Where, however, the contract is void or voidable (and has been avoided), the adjudicator may have no jurisdiction: *Capital Structures plc* v. *Time & Tide Construction Ltd* [2006] EWHC 591 (TCC), in which HHJ David Wilcox QC, held that it there was an arguable (albeit shadowy) case that there had been economic duress, supported by lengthy documentary evidence adduced, which could be effective in providing evidence that the defendants were properly avoiding the settlement agreement (which itself provided for disputes to be resolved by adjudication) made in consequence of such duress. Summary judgment of the adjudicator's decision was therefore refused and leave to defend was given on terms that there be payment into court of the amount of the adjudicator's decision. See also *Shepherd Construction Ltd* v. *Mecright*, above, in which HHJ Humphrey Lloyd QC decided that if a settlement agreement had been secured under duress (as had been contended in the proceedings to enforce an adjudicator's decision) such an agreement would be voidable rather than void and, because it had not been avoided, could only be deprived of its effect once pronounced upon by an arbitrator or the court.

4 WHAT PROVISIONS MUST BE INCORPORATED INTO A CONSTRUCTION CONTRACT TO COMPLY WITH THE HGCRA 1996?

4.1 The minimum requirements imposed by HGCRA 1996

The HGCRA 1996 identifies requirements which must be incorporated into any construction contract if it is to comply with that Act. Section 108(5) provides that if these minimum requirements are not included, the Scheme will apply.

In *John Mowlem & Co. plc* v. *Hydra-Tight Ltd*, above, HHJ John Toulmin CMG QC held that where some parts only of a construction contract comply with the HGCRA 1996, they cannot be retained and the Act used in substitution for or to fill in those parts of the contract which are contrary to the Act; either a party complies in its own terms and conditions with the requirements of Sections 108(1) to (4) of the HGCRA 1996 or the provisions of the Scheme apply.

Section 108(2) provides that for a construction contract to comply with the HGCRA 1996 it shall:

(a) Enable a party to give notice at any time of his intention to refer a dispute to adjudication.
(b) Provide a timetable with the object of securing an appointment of the Adjudicator and referral of the dispute to him within seven days of such notice.
(c) Require the Adjudicator to reach a decision within 28 days of referral or such longer period as is agreed by the parties after the dispute has been referred.
(d) Allow the Adjudicator to extend the period of 28 days by up to 14 days, with the consent of the party by whom the dispute was referred.
(e) Impose a duty on the Adjudicator to act impartially.
(f) Enable the Adjudicator to take the initiative in ascertaining the facts and the law.

4.2 The right to give notice at any time of an intention to refer a dispute to adjudication

In *KNS Industrial Services (Birmingham) Ltd* v. *Sindall Ltd* [2000] 75 Con LR 71, HHJ Humphrey Lloyd, QC held that an adjudicator is appointed to decide a dispute and it is the notice of adjudication which determines his jurisdiction. Cf. *McAlpine PPS Pipeline Systems* v. *Transco* [2004] BLR 352; *Karl Construction (Scotland) Ltd* v. *Sweeney Civil Engineering (Scotland) Ltd* (2002) 85 Con LR 59 (the Inner House, Court of Session).

4.1 Administration of claims | 4.2 Litigation | 4.3 Arbitration | 4.4 Adjudication | 4.5 Alternative dispute resolution

4.1 Administration of claims
4.2 Litigation
4.3 Arbitration
4.4 Adjudication
4.5 Alternative dispute resolution

See also *LPL Electrical Services Ltd* v. *Kershaw Electrical Services Ltd* (unreported, 2 February 2001, TCC, HHJ Richard Havery QC), from which, however, it seems clear that the Courts will not allow the process to be subverted by narrow and formal points on the content of the notice of adjudication, although no doubt those drafting such notices will want to draw them as widely as the circumstances will allow in order to avoid jurisdictional challenges.

In *Griffin and Tomlinson* v. *Midas Homes Ltd* above, the notice was drafted by a solicitor and was to be treated therefore as having been carefully prepared. Nevertheless, the definition of the dispute was vague and uncertain and the Adjudicator's jurisdiction (and the ambit of enforcement) was therefore narrower than might otherwise have been intended by the Applicant. In *Jerome Engineering Ltd* v. *Lloyd Electrical Services Ltd* (unreported, 23 November 2001, TCC, HHJ Cockroft QC), it was held that although the notice did not specify the exact relief sought, an officious bystander would not have had any difficulty concluding that the dispute was about the withholding of money allegedly due.

In *Herschel Engineering Ltd* v. *Breen Property Ltd* [2000] BLR 272, Dyson J (as he then was) held that a dispute might be referred to adjudication even after litigation or arbitration had commenced. Cf. *Quality Street Properties (Trading) Ltd* v. *Elmwood (Glasgow) Ltd* (2002) CILL 1922.

In *John Mowlem & Co. plc* v. *Hydra Tight & Co. plc* above a subcontract incorporated the provisions of NEC (Option A) Y(U.K.)2 with amendments, which provided for service of a 'Notification of Dissatisfaction'. The expressed purpose of the provisions was to delay adjudication for four weeks to allow the parties an opportunity to meet and resolve their difference. The clause also provided that the parties had agreed that in the period above a dispute shall not have arisen and therefore there was no matter that could be referred to arbitration. HHJ Toulmin CMG QC adopted the parties' agreement that insofar as the sub-contract required a notice of dissatisfaction to be served before a dispute was deemed to have arisen, it contravened Section 108 of HGCRA 1996, which gives a party an unfettered right to given notice 'at any time' of its intention to refer a dispute to adjudication.

There is no time limit on when the notice of adjudication may be given, *Connex South Eastern Ltd* v. *MJ Building Services Group plc* [2005] BLR 201 (CA) and concurrent proceedings are not an abuse of process; see *Connex South Eastern Ltd* v. *MJ Building Services Group plc* (2004) 95 Con LR 43, not affected on this point by the Court of Appeal judgment above.

4.3 The timetable for securing an appointment of the Adjudicator and referral of the dispute

Given the wording of Section 108(2)(b), it is thought that a Referral made even after the seven days identified in this section will not be fatal, provided it is reasonably prompt in all the circumstances. This approach has now been endorsed in *The Mayor and Burgesses of the London Borough of Lambeth* v. *Floyd Slaski Partnership and Mastrandrea* (unreported, 2 November 2001, Forbes, J). See also *William Verry Ltd* v. *North West London Communal Mikvah* [2004] BLR 308, in which a distinction was drawn between the permissive language of this section and the more rigid language of Section 108(2)(c).

4.4 A decision within 28 days of the referral

The Scheme provides that an adjudicator is to reach his decision not later than 28 days after the date of the referral notice. The period may be extended to 42 days if the referring party consents, or such further period as may be agreed between the parties (Paragraph 19).

In *Simons Construction Ltd* v. *Aardvark Developments Ltd* [2004] BLR 117 it was held that the provisions of neither the HGCRA 1996 nor the Scheme prescribed any final date for an adjudicator to give his decision if the parties agreed an extension of time. An adjudicator's decision whenever given was binding on the parties but subject to certain stipulations. First, that the adjudication agreement, if any, had not been terminated for failure to produce a decision in time before the decision was given. Second, that a fresh notice of referral had not been given by one of the parties before the decision was made. By contrast, it has been held in Scotland in *Ritchie Brothers (PWC) Ltd* v. *David Philp Commercial Ltd* [2005] BLR 384 that the 28 days starts from the date that the Referral is dispatched, not when it first comes into the adjudicator's possession; the natural meaning of paragraph 19(1)(a) of the Scheme is simple and straightforward. It provides a clear time limit that leaves all parties knowing where they stand. It is mandatory.

In *Barnes & Elliott Ltd* v. *Taylor Woodrow Holdings Ltd. and another* [2004] BLR 111, whilst the decision was made within the time limit it was communicated late; nevertheless it was held that a delay of a day or two in communicating the decision was not fatal (subject to separate considerations where the party had agreed to a longer period). Cf. *M Rohde Construction* v. *Nicholas Markham-David* [2006] EWHC 814 (TCC).

In *Lafarge (Aggregates) Ltd* v. *Newham London Borough Council* [2005] EWHC 1337 (Comm.) it was held that a dated but unsigned decision sent by e-mail was effective from the time it was received in that form, and not when a hard, signed, copy of it was.

In *Stiell Ltd* v. *Riema Controls* (unreported, 23 June 2000, the Inner House, Court of Session) it was held that an adjudicator's decision does not require any further perfection before enforcement of it will be granted.

4.5 Taking the initiative in ascertaining the facts and the law

In relation to the power to take the initiative in ascertaining the facts and the law in *Costain Ltd* v. *Strathclyde Builders Ltd* 2004 S.L.T. 102, Lord Drummond Young held that adjudication was an adversarial, not an inquisitorial, process and that taking the initiative extended only to obtaining further evidence that was necessary to decide the dispute.

4.6 Adjudicator's decision is binding

Section 108(3) requires that the compliant contract shall provide for the decision of the adjudicator to be binding until the dispute is finally determined by legal proceedings, by arbitration (if the contract provides for arbitration or the parties otherwise agree to arbitration) or by agreement. This section also envisages that the parties may agree to treat the decision as finally determining the dispute.

The circumstances may be such as to render the adjudicator's decision final and binding: see, for example, *Castle Inns (Stirling) Ltd* v. *Clark Contracts Ltd* [2005] ScotCS CSOH 178.

4.7 The adjudicator's immunity

Section 108(4) requires that the compliant contract shall provide that the adjudicator is not liable for anything done or omitted in the discharge or purported discharge of his functions as adjudicator unless the act or omission is in bad faith, and that any employee or agent of the adjudicator is similarly protected from liability. The effect of this clause and the extent of the adjudicator's immunity is considered further in Section 22 below.

4.1 Administration of claims
4.2 Litigation
4.3 Arbitration
4.4 Adjudication
4.5 Alternative dispute resolution

4.8 Dates for payment

The proper value to be placed upon an interim payment was a common area of dispute prior to the introduction of the HGCRA 1996. One of the principal aims of the HGCRA 1996 was to ensure the prompt payment of sums due under the contract. Section 110 of the HGCRA 1996 provides:

> '(1) Every construction contract shall (a) provide an adequate mechanism for determining what payments become due under the contract, and when, and (b) provide for a final date for payment in relation to any sum which becomes due. The parties are free to agree how long the period is to be between the date on which a sum becomes due and the final date for payment.
>
> (2) Every construction contract shall provide for the giving of notice by a party not later than five days after the date on which a payment becomes due from him under the contract or would have become due if (a) the other party had carried out his obligations under the contract, and (b) no set-off or abatement was permitted by reference to any sum claimed to be due under one or more other contracts specifying the amount (if any) of the payment made or proposed to be made, and the basis on which the amount was calculated'.

Accordingly, a construction contract must contain a proper mechanism for determining what is due and the date for payment. If and to the extent that a contract does not contain provisions equivalent to those mentioned in Subsections 110(1) or (2), the relevant provisions of the Scheme apply (Section 110(3)). Lord Clarke held in *Hills Electrical and Mechanical plc* v. *Dawn Construction Ltd* [2003] ScotCS 107 that where the parties have failed to provide for one or other aspect required by the legislation to be agreed by the parties this does not substitute *all* of the Scheme provisions regarding payment, but rather imports into the parties' contract the appropriate provision from the Scheme to make up for their omission, or to replace their own inadequate term, with the Scheme's provision, as the case may be.

In *Maxi Construction Management Ltd* v. *Mortons Rolls Ltd* [2001] ScotCS 199 a Contractor alleged in connection with a contract let under the Scottish form of Building Contract with Contractor's Design (August 1998 including correction sheet dated 31 August 1998) that it was entitled to an interim payment based on its 'Application for Payment No. 10'. Lord MacFadyen held that the application did not constitute a 'claim by the payee' within the meaning of paragraph 12 of Part II of the Scheme, because it was an application for agreement of the pursuer's valuation in terms of paragraph 2.5.20 of the Employer's Requirements, and not a claim for payment at all. Further, it did not comply with the requirements of paragraph 12 in that it did not specify the basis on which it was calculated.

In *SL Timber Systems Ltd* v. *Carillion Construction Ltd* [2001] BLR 516, Lord MacFadyen concluded that there was nothing to prevent a Respondent in adjudication from maintaining that a sum alleged by the Applicant to be due (whether by way of earlier application or otherwise), was not due. The absence of such a Section 110(2) notice did not:

> '... in any way or to any extent, preclude dispute about the sum claimed'.

In *VHE Construction plc* v. *RBSTB Trust Co. Ltd* [2000] BLR 187, HHJ John Hicks QC reviewed the status of the decisions of two adjudicators. The second Adjudicator had gone further than a simple determination of what was due and decided that he was empowered to order:

'repayment of any sum in excess of that which ought properly to have been applied for even though in the meantime a greater sum may have accrued for payment by reason of lack of challenge to the amount applied for'.

The Court in the subsequent enforcement proceedings gave effect to both adjudicators' decisions, albeit in the context of further developments in the case since those decisions had been made (in particular, the issue of a notice by the Defendant advising the deduction of liquidated damages which the Court found did not comply with the contractual or statutory provisions and therefore had no effect).

In *Woods Hardwick Ltd* v. *Chiltern Air Conditioning Ltd* [2001] BLR 23, HHJ Anthony Thornton QC had observed, in contextualising an adjudicator's decision relating to a claim for architectural fees upon which he was asked to give summary judgment, that an abatement would not 'of course' be caught by Section 111 of the HGCRA 1996. An equivalent conclusion was reached in *KNS Industrial Services (Birmingham) Ltd* v. *Sindall Ltd* (2000) 75 Con LR 71, although HHJ Humphrey Lloyd QC there used language which some have read as conflating the provisions of Sections 110 and 111 as follows:

'The term withhold is... used in Section 111 to cover both the situation where in arriving at a valuation the Contractor had not taken account of a countervailing factor as well as the situation where there is to be reduction in or deduction from an amount that had been declared or thought to be due. In the former case the word "withhold" may not always be correct, for one cannot withhold what is not due'.

In *Whiteways Contractors (Sussex) Ltd* v. *Impresa Castelli Construction UK Ltd* (2000) 75 Con LR 92, HHJ Peter Bowsher QC appears to have conflated the sections in holding that it was necessary for a Section 111 notice to have been given in order to successfully challenge the sum claimed (the burden of proving the claim does not appear to have been a factor). If that is a proper interpretation of the decision, it has been said to go too far. Lord MacFadyen in *SL Timber Systems Ltd* v. *Carillion Construction Ltd*, above, was concerned as to the consequences of this approach:

'I am of the opinion that, if Judge Bowsher is to be understood to have meant that, without a Section 111 notice, there can be no dispute of any sort as to whether the sum claimed is properly due, His Honour to that extent took too broad a view of the effect of Section 111. In my opinion, the absence of a timeous notice of intention to withhold payment does not relieve the party making the claim of the ordinary burden of showing that he is entitled under the contract to receive the payment he claims. It remains incumbent on the Claimant to demonstrate, if the point is disputed, that the sum claimed is contractually due'.

The extremes were noted in *Rupert Morgan Building Services (LLC) Ltd* v. *David Jervis and Harriett Jervis* [2004] BLR 18, CA. The Court ordered payment to a Contractor of an Architect's interim certificate said by the Employer to have been invalidly high because it included sums for work were not done at all, or were duplications of items already paid or were charged as extras when they were within the original contract, or represent snagging for works already done and paid for in the absence of a Section 111 notice. The Court relied on the decision of Sheriff Taylor *Clark Contracts Ltd* v. *The Burrell Co. (Construction Management) Ltd* 2002 S.L.T. 103 which emphasised the transient nature of construction payment certificates (a feature missing from the *SL Timber Systems Ltd* v. *Carillion Construction Ltd*, above where there was no

Architect or system of certificates), errors in which can be corrected by means of subsequent certificates.

A contractual, as opposed to statutory, right of adjudication will be construed in the context of the terms of the contract and general principles of law such as the common law and equitable rights of set-off, as opposed to the HGCRA 1996 or the Scheme: *Parsons Plastics (Research and Development) Ltd* v. *Purac* [2002] BLR 334, CA. Cp., in the context of statutory adjudication provisions, *The Construction Centre Group Ltd* v. *The Highland Council* [2003] ScotCS 114.

4.1 Administration of claims
4.2 Litigation
4.3 Arbitration
4.4 Adjudication
4.5 Alternative dispute resolution

5 NOTICE OF INTENTION TO WITHOLD PAYMENT

The HGCRA 1996 sought to address disputes that arise over payments that have been withheld and a payment may not be withheld unless formal notice is given.

Section 111 of the HGCRA 1996 is linked to the mandatory requirements of Section 110 above and requires the service of a notice of intention to withhold payment if a party is intending to withhold all or part of any payment that is due. The notice must specify not only the amount which is proposed to withheld but the reason or reasons for such amount being withheld.

Section 111 provides:

> '(1) A party to a construction contract may not withhold payment after the final date for payment of a sum due under the contract unless he has given an effective notice of intention to withhold payment. The notice mentioned in Section 110(2) may suffice as a notice of intention to withhold payment if it complies with the requirements of this section.
>
> (2) To be effective such a notice must specify (a) the amount proposed to be withheld and the ground for withholding payment, or (b) if there is more than one ground, each ground and the amount attributable to it and must be given no later than the prescribed period before the final date for payment.
>
> (3) The parties are free to agree what that prescribed period is to be'.

One of the principal purposes of Section 111 is that any set-off is excluded in the absence of an effective notice to withhold payment: *VHE Construction plc* v. *RBSTB Trust Co. Ltd* above ('Section 111 now constitutes a comprehensive code governing the right to set off against payments contractually due', per HHJ John Hicks QC); *Re a Company (No. 1299 of 2001)* (unreported, 15 May 2001, David Donaldson QC); *Millers Specialist Joinery Co. Ltd* v. *Nobles Construction Co. Ltd* (unreported, 13 August 2001, HHJ Gilliland QC).

It has been held by Lord MacFadyen that Section 111 is not designed ordinarily to allow a notice to be served against an adjudicator's decision: *The Construction Centre Group Ltd* v. *The Highland Council* [2002] BLR 476.

In *Shimizu Europe Ltd* v. *LBJ Fabrications Ltd* [2003] BLR 381, HHJ Frances Kirkham held that a withholding notice issued against an invoice consequent upon an Adjudicator's decision was valid; here a bespoke payments provision prevented an amount becoming due for payment unless and until the specified conditions precedent had been satisfied, including the submission of a VAT invoice. The Contractor was held entitled to raise a set-off notice following upon the raising of a VAT invoice by the subcontractor in the sum found as due by an Adjudicator.

'It has been held that the absence of a Section 111 notice may undermine the operation of standard provisions on termination in the event of insolvency in common use in the building industry for many years. In *Melville Dundas Ltd* v. *George Wimpey Ltd and another* [2005] ScotCS CSIH 88 it was decided that the standard provisions for payment following valid termination for insolvency, which would otherwise have entitled the defenders to withhold payment of further sums until after completion of the works and the preparation of the account, could not validly be operated in the absence of a Section 111 notice. That was because it would affect the operation of the final date for payment established by the *interim payment* provisions, albeit that the provisions on termination are clearly expressed to suspend operation of those provisions in the event of termination for insolvency.'

Whatever may be the true answer to this problem where there is no adjudication decision the termination provisions are to be treated as subsidiary to an adjudicator's decision: see *Ferson Contractors Ltd* v. *Levolux AT Ltd* [2003] BLR 118 (CA). In that case an adjudicator decided that a Section 111 notice issued by a contractor failed to specify the ground for withholding against a subcontractor. Enforcement of that decision was resisted on the ground that the contractual provisions for termination had purportedly been operated by the contractor in consequence of the unjustified suspension of works by the subcontractor (for non-payment of sums subsequently found to be due by the adjudicator), rendering – according to the terms of the termination provisions – sums due or accruing as no longer due. This was rejected by the Court; the adjudicator's decision was to be given precedence over the termination provisions.

Where there is a contractual, non-compulsory adjudication (i.e. one that does not fall within the ambit of the HGCRA 1996), effect will be given to set-off provisions in the contract: see *Parsons Plastics (Research and Development) Ltd* v. *Purac*, above.

In *Strathmore Building Services Ltd* v. *Colin Scott Greig* [2000] ScotCS 133, Lord Hamilton held that a withholding notice under this section was required to be in writing and that whilst a communication sent earlier than the application could be referred to in the relevant notice, it could not act as a substitute for that notice.

In *Palmers Ltd* v. *ABB Power Construction Ltd* above, a sub-subcontractor had not paid a sub-sub-subcontractor because the sub-contractor for which it was erecting a boiler had intimated that liquidated damages would be set-off and the sub-sub-contractor felt that the sub-sub-subcontractor was responsible for a 180-day delay to completion of its work as a result of providing insufficient labour. It purported to rely upon two letters intimating non-payment as effective notices of intention to withhold. It was held that neither of those letters was sufficient in that they did not identify any amount that it was proposed to withhold. Since the final date for payment had passed and no effective notice could therefore be served, the sum due was payable without set-off.

Section 111(4) of the HGCRA 1996 provides:

> 'Where an effective notice to withhold is given, but on the matter being referred to adjudication it is decided that the whole or part of the amount should be paid, the decision shall be construed as requiring payment not later than (a) seven days from the date of the decision, or (b) the date which apart from the notice would have been the final date for payment'.

It was held in *VHE Construction plc* v. *RBSTB Trust Co. Ltd* above, that a notice referable to Section 111(4) must be served before the date of referral to adjudication and that the 'matter' referred to adjudication must include the effect of that notice and the validity of the grounds for withholding payment which it asserts. In *Northern Developments (Cumbria) Ltd* v. *J&J Nichol*, above, HHJ Peter Bowsher QC said:

'... it is clear from the general scheme of the Act that this is a temporary arrangement which does not prevent the presentation of other set-offs abatements or indeed counterclaims at a later date by litigation arbitration or adjudication. For the temporary striking of balances which are contemplated by the Act, there is to be no dispute about any matter not raised in a notice of intention to withhold payment. Accordingly, in my view, the Adjudicator had no jurisdiction to consider any matter not raised in the notice of intention to withhold payment in this case'.

But it seems to go too far to conclude that the absence of a notice is validation of the application for payment which forms the foundation for the adjudication as appears to have been suggested in *Re a Company (No. 1299 of 2001)*, above. In *SL Timber Systems Ltd* v. *Carillion Construction Ltd*, above, Lord MacFadyen was not prepared to accept that the failure to give a notice under Section 111 meant that the amount applied for became due, holding:

'In my opinion, the words "sum due under the contract" cannot be equiparated with the words "the sum claimed"'.

It has been held that there is nothing to convert an amount which otherwise becomes due in accordance with the HGCRA 1996 because of failure to operate its withholding provisions into an amount which is indisputably due for the purposes of Section 9 of the Arbitration Act 1996: *Collins (Contractors) Ltd* v. *Baltic Quay Ocean Management (1994) Ltd*, above.

6 THE STATUTORY RIGHT TO SUSPEND PERFORMANCE FOR NON-PAYMENT

Dispute that arises over the contractor's right to suspend work in circumstances where payments have not been made may be referred to an adjudicator for decision. A contract may expressly provide for specific rights in circumstances where amounts due under the contract are not paid. However there is no general right at common law to suspend work even if payment is wrongly withheld. In relation to contractor and amounts not paid under certificates see *Lubenham Fidelities* v. *South Pembrokeshire District Council* (1986) 33 BLR 39 (CA). Section 112 of HGCRA 1996 gives a party to a construction contract a statutory right to suspend performance of his obligations if a payment is not made by the final date for payment. The statutory right is incorporated into the contract as an implied term.

Section 112 of the HGCRA 1996 provides:

'(1) Where a sum due under a construction contract is not paid in full by the final date for payment and no effective notice to withhold payment has been given, the person to whom the sum is due has the right (without prejudice to any other right or remedy) to suspend performance of his obligations under the contract to the party by whom payment ought to have been made ("the party in default").

(2) The right may not be exercised without first giving to the party in default at least seven days' notice of intention to suspend performance, stating the ground or grounds on which it is intended to suspend performance.

(3) The right to suspend performance ceases when the party in default makes payment in full of the amount due.

(4) Any period during which performance is suspended in pursuance of the right conferred by this Section shall be disregarded in computing for the purposes

of any contractual time limit the time taken, by the party exercising the right or by a third party, to complete any work directly or indirectly affected by the exercise of the right.

Where the contractual time limit is set by reference to a date rather than a period, the date shall be adjusted accordingly.'

It is important that the final date for payment is clearly specified in the contract and in the matters referred to adjudication. In *Palmers Ltd* v. *ABB Power Construction Ltd* above, a sub-sub-subcontractor purported to give notice to suspend under Section 112(2). On the facts, it was not clear when the invoice to which the payment related had been submitted (final payment under the terms of the sub-sub-subcontract being required 60 days after the date of receipt of a relevant invoice). The judge declined to decide whether the sub-sub-subcontractor had complied with the statutory precondition in respect of notice.

7 THE 'SCHEME' FOR CONSTRUCTION CONTRACTS

SI 1998 No. 649 brought into force the Scheme for Construction Contracts (England and Wales) Regulations 1998 on 1 May 1998 ('the Scheme'). If the construction contract does not comply with Sections 108(1) to (4) of HGCRA 1996 (see above), the provisions of the Scheme apply (Section 108(5) of the HGCRA 1996). Features of the Scheme include the following:

(1) A notice of adjudication has to be given by the referring party to the other party setting out brief details of the dispute and relief sought (paragraph 1).
(2) A request (accompanied by a copy of the notice) must be made, either to a named adjudicator directly or the nominating body (paragraph 2).
(3) A proposed adjudicator is to indicate within 2 days of the request whether he will act (paragraphs 2 or 5).
(4) No one who is an employee of one of the parties is to act as adjudicator. Any adjudicator is to declare any interest, financial or otherwise, in any matter relating to the dispute (paragraph 4).

It has been held that an inability to act must be indicated to both parties before the step is taken by one of the parties inviting a substitute: *IDE Contracting Ltd* v. *RG Carter Cambridge Ltd* [2004] BLR 172. Cp. *Palmac Contracting Ltd* v. *Park Lane Estates Ltd* [2005] BLR 301 in which a *contractual* as opposed to a Scheme adjudication procedure did not preclude nomination before the notice of adjudication.

Where the contract specifies selection by an adjudicator nominating body, that body is given five days to propose someone from the date of the request (paragraph 5).

The referring party 'shall' refer the matter in dispute within seven days of the notice. A referral is to be accompanied by relevant extracts from the construction contract and such other documents as that party intends to rely upon (paragraph 7). Albeit expressed in apparently mandatory language it is not a condition precedent to the adjudicator's jurisdiction that the Referral be made within seven days; a failure to comply with it does not render an adjudicator's decision nevertheless to continue invalid. The sanction for failure to comply is a matter for the adjudicator who may take into account the parties' conduct and the extent of the overrun in deciding whether or not to continue. The adjudicator's decision to continue is reviewable if at all at the enforcement stage, at which point the court may decide that the continuance may have been sufficiently unjustified as to render it a matter of poor conduct on the part of the adjudicator or such conduct as to render it a matter beyond the adjudicator's jurisdiction: *The Mayor and Burgesses of the London Borough of Lambeth* v. *Floyd Slaski Partnership and Mastrandrea*, above. See also *William Verry Ltd* v. *North West London Communal Mikvah*, above.

Section 114(4) of the HGCRA 1996 provides that where the Scheme applies by reason of default in contractual provisions, the terms of the Scheme are to have effect as implied contractual terms: see *Griffin and Tomlinson* v. *Midas Homes Ltd*, above.

Paragraph 20(c) of the Scheme allows an Adjudicator:

> 'having regard to any term of the contract relating to the payment of interest [to] decide the circumstances in which, and the rates at which, and the periods for which simple or compound rates of interest shall be paid'.

Jackson J held in *Carillion Construction Ltd* v. *Devonport Royal Dockyard Ltd* [2005] BLR 310 that paragraph 20(c) envisaged a free-standing power to avoid interest even absent any contractual provision for interest; not only was a power to award interest the more natural interpretation of the words used in this paragraph of the Scheme but it made obvious commercial sense for an adjudicator to have such power. This did not find favour in the Court of Appeal. Chadwick LJ speaking for the Court in *Carillion Construction Ltd* v. *Devonport Royal Dockyard Ltd* [2006] BLR 15, said:

> 'It is necessary to have regard to the structure of paragraph 20 as a whole. There are three sentences: (1) The adjudicator *shall* decide the matters in dispute; (2) [In deciding those matters] he *may* take into account other matters (which are specified); (3) In particular [in deciding those matters] he *may* (a) open up, revise and review decisions already taken or certificates already given (unless the contract otherwise provides), (b) decide that any of the parties is liable to make payment and if so when and in what currency and (c) decide the circumstances in which (and the rates at which and the periods for which) interest is to be paid. Within that structure effect has to be given to the words "In particular" at the beginning of the third sentence. We can see no reason why those words should not bear their usual and natural meaning. What comes after them is intended to be a particularisation of what has gone before. What comes after elaborates and explains what has gone before; it does not add to what has gone before. So the adjudicator may decide questions as to interest if, but only if, (i) those questions are "matters in dispute" which have been properly referred to him or (ii) those are questions which the parties to the dispute have agreed should be within the scope of the adjudication or (iii) those are questions which the adjudicator considers to be "necessarily connected with the dispute". Questions which do not fall within one or other of those categories are not within the scope of paragraph 20(c) of the Scheme. There is no freestanding power to award interest'.

8 THE NATURE OF DISPUTES USUALLY ADJUDICATED

In practice, disputes over payment of amounts due are the most common types of disputes referred to adjudication. Allegations of a failure to comply with the statutory notice requirements have formed a substantial ground for many of the early referrals, particularly in relation to progress payments. See the case law above in relation to Sections 110 and 111 of the HGCRA 1996.

Disputes over matters involving the exercise of discretion by a person authorised under the construction contract to exercise such discretion are likely to pose greater problems for an adjudicator than decisions over payment or time for payment, but there is nothing in principle against review of such a decision by an adjudicator. In this connection paragraph 20(a) of the Scheme empowers the adjudicator to open up revise and review any decision taken or certificate given by any person referred to in the contract unless the contract states that the decision is final and conclusive.

Perhaps one of the most difficult areas on which an adjudicator may be asked to make a decision is a dispute which encroaches upon the operational or substantive expertise of someone directly involved in the project. Take, for example, a dispute in a design and build contract over whether a particular proposal from the contractor satisfies the Employer's Requirements or whether the employer is entitled to require the Contractor to remove the allegedly non-compliant work and substitute it with a satisfactory alternative. Not only does an issue couched in these terms potentially involve the adjudicator in choosing between design alternatives in circumstances where he is unlikely to be aware of the full ramifications and complexities of the design, but if his decision takes the form 'the works shall be constructed as follows...' such wording may result in the designer alleging that his responsibility for design thereafter is diluted or removed. The prudent adjudicator will seek to limit his decision to a statement that the work appears to comply with the contractual provisions, although it may be difficult to avoid a commitment in all cases.

Adjudication, as a summary process conducted in the short time frame required by statute, is not well-suited to a dispute which is complex, involving the evaluation of the activities of a number of parties over a long period of time or where the project is substantially complete. Professional appointments ordinarily also fall within the ambit of a 'construction contract' and employers have been prepared to refer complaints involving allegations of professional negligence against professionals to adjudication; see, for example, *London & Amsterdam Properties Ltd* v. *Waterman Partnership Ltd* [2004] BLR 179 and the comments of HHJ Wilcox on the appropriateness of the process in that case. Other cases involving professional include *RJT Consulting Engineers Ltd* v. *DM Engineering (NI) Ltd*, above and *Diamond* v. *PJW Enterprises Ltd*, above.

Particular difficulties arise in cases involving professional negligence. In litigation a finding of negligence requires evidence from an expert in the relevant discipline: see for example, *Sansom and another* v. *Metcalfe Hambleton & Co.* [1998] 26 EG 154 (CA). However, in adjudication it will ordinarily not be possible to obtain the necessary expert evidence within the time limits. In such circumstances the adjudicator will probably be limited to making informed enquiries of, or taking evidence from, the parties themselves (mindful of the weight that should be applied to such evidence); see, for example the decisions in *David Michael Lusty* v. *Finsbury Securities Ltd* (1991) 58 BLR 66 (CA) and *Field* v. *Leeds City Council* (Times, 18 January, 2000 CA). It is questionable whether a summary process such as adjudication conducted within strict short time limits, is an appropriate or fair process for the resolution, even on an interim basis, of matters involving allegations of professional negligence. However, it is permitted by statute and it seems likely that professionals will continue to face the risk of adjudication in cases where employers raise complaints of professional negligence.

The adjudicator's decision may directly affect the rights of a third party. Take the example of a decision under the JCT 98 Private With Quantities form made by an architect that a nominated subcontractor is in default following a request to that effect from the contractor (under clause 35.24.1) made with a view to seeking an instruction to determine the employment of that subcontractor and securing a replacement (clause 35.24.6). An adjudicator may in these circumstances feel that he needs to

4.1 Administration of claims
4.2 Litigation
4.3 Arbitration
4.4 Adjudication
4.5 Alternative dispute resolution

secure greater protection than is afforded to him by the statutory immunity (as to which, see Section 22 below).

A claimant may not commence adjudication proceedings against a respondent in administration without the permission of the court: *A Straume (UK) Ltd* v. *Bradlor Developments Ltd* [2000] BCC 333, applying Section 11(3)(d) of the Insolvency Act 1986, adjudication being 'other proceedings' for the purposes of that Section. *Canary Riverside Development (Private) Ltd* v. *Timtec International Ltd* (2000) 19 Const LJ 283 concerned an appeal against the Registrar's refusal to grant leave under Section 11(3)(d) of the Insolvency Act 1986 to adjudication proceedings by an Employer against a package contractor in administration. The reasoning of the Registrar appears to have been that the employer had already issued legal proceedings against the package contractor and that it would not be productive to have a non-binding adjudication procedure at the same time as legal proceedings. Mr DKR Oliver QC refused to upset the Registrar's order.

9 WHO MAY BE AN ADJUDICATOR?

An adjudicator must be a natural person acting in his personal capacity (see the Construction Contracts Exclusion Order, Schedule 1, Part 4). This does not, however, prevent his fees and charges being the subject of a corporate invoice or being administered by such an organisation: *Faithful and Gould Ltd* v. *Arcal Ltd and others* (unreported, 25 May 2001, TCC, HHJ Wood).

In particularly complex adjudications it may be necessary for the adjudicator to have some of the work carried out by assistants. Given the risk that the task may otherwise be considered non-delegable, it is always best to secure the parties' express agreement to this. In any event, the adjudicator should always set out those delegated tasks clearly and give clear guidance on the constraining principles to those charged with those tasks such as the view he takes of a particular contractual provision, so that he can be seen to have exercised matters of discretion and judgement personally.

10 THE ADJUDICATOR'S JURISDICTION

10.1 Jurisdiction: general

The case law has established that the court will take a robust aaproach in the enforcement of adjudicator's decisions. If an adjudicator did not have jurisdiction, the decision will not be enforced. A challenge to jurisdiction, if successful, is one of very few ways of resisting enforcement of the adjudicator's decision, and a considerable body of case law has grown up the matter of jurisdiction.

It seems that adjudication is to be treated as a contractual rather than a statutory procedure (albeit one clothed in contractual form): *Macob Civil Engineering Ltd* v. *Morrison Construction Ltd* [1999] BLR 93.

An Adjudicator who purports to make a decision he is not empowered to make is acting beyond his jurisdiction and his decision will not bind.

In *The Project Consultancy Group* v. *The Trustees of the Gray Trust* [1999] BLR 377 a decision made by an adjudicator in relation to professional fees due under a contract made before the HGCRA 1996 came into force was held not to be binding on the parties because of lack of jurisdiction. Dyson J (as he then was) held that:

> '. . . a decision purportedly made under (Section 108(3) of the HGCRA1996) in respect of a contract which is not a construction contract at all, or which is a construction

contract entered into before Part II came into force, is not a decision within the meaning of the sub-Section, and is, therefore, not binding on the parties'.

Whilst it might be thought that a decision made by applying the wrong contract terms merely constitutes an error in the decision and therefore within jurisdiction, it has been held that the error may be so fundamental as to transform the decision into one which is made in want of jurisdiction because it resulted from the wrong question being asked: *Joinery Plus Ltd (In Administration)* v. *Laing Ltd* [2003] BLR 184.

The parties may grant the adjudicator jurisdiction, even if there is no contract to which the HGCRA 1996 applies: see *Maymac Environmental Services Ltd* v. *Faraday Building Services Ltd* (2000) 75 Con LR 101, HHJ John Toulmin CMG QC. Cf. *Nordot Engineering Services Ltd* v. *Siemens plc* (unreported, 14 April 2001, HHJ Gilliland QC). This matter was further clarified in *Thomas-Fredric's (Construction) Ltd* v. *Keith Wilson* above, in which it was held that a party to adjudication who has submitted to the jurisdiction of the Adjudicator in the full sense of having agreed not only that the Adjudicator should determine the question of jurisdiction but also that he would be bound by that determination even if the Adjudicator should be wrong on that issue would then be bound by his decision.

It seems that the parties may by their conduct extend an adjudicator's jurisdiction. The most obvious example of this is likely to be participation without protest in proceedings which are beyond the adjudicator's actual remit. Where a party wishes to prevent that situation arising, it should object at the earliest opportunity (as was held to have happened in *The Project Consultancy Group* v. *The Trustees of the Gray Trust*, above).

It has been said that the question whether a failure by a contracting party to reserve its position on jurisdiction would amount to a submission to it is a highly fact sensitive question. To succeed on such a basis at trial, a claimant would have to show that such silence, when considered with all the other material facts, amounted to a clear submission to the jurisdiction: *Rhodia Chirex Ltd* v. *Laker Vent Engineering Ltd* (2003) 20 Const LJ 155, CA.

What practical steps can be taken during the life of the adjudication when there is a challenge to an adjudicator's jurisdiction? The parties and the adjudicator may take the initiative and case law has provided some guidance on the appropriate course of action.

In *Fastrack Contractors Ltd* v. *Morrison Construction Ltd and another* [2000] BLR 168, (2000) 75 Con LR 33, HHJ Anthony Thornton QC suggested that the party which seeks to challenge the adjudicator's jurisdiction might:

- agree to widen the jurisdiction of the adjudicator so as to refer the dispute as to jurisdiction to the same adjudicator;
- refer the dispute as to jurisdiction to a different adjudicator;
- seek a declaration from the Court whether the adjudicator had jurisdiction; or
- reserve its position, participate in the adjudication and then challenge any attempt to enforce the decision on jurisdictional grounds.

Cf. *Watson Building Services Ltd* v. *Graham Harrison and Miller (Preservation) Ltd* (unreported, the Outer House, Court of Session, 13 March 2001, Lady Paton).

In *Christiani* v. *The Lowry Centre* above, HHJ Anthony Thornton QC suggested that the adjudicator might proceed in one of three ways:

- he can ignore the challenge and proceed as if he had jurisdiction leaving it to the court to determine the question of jurisdiction if and when the decision is the subject of enforcement;

4.1 Administration of claims
4.2 Litigation
4.3 Arbitration
4.4 Adjudication
4.5 Alternative dispute resolution

- he can investigate the question of jurisdiction, decide on it, and if his decision is that he does have jurisdiction, proceed with the adjudication; or
- he can investigate the question of jurisdiction, decide on it, and if his decision is that he does not have jurisdiction, decline to act further.

The adjudicator may also agree that the Courts should resolve the matter of his jurisdiction. It seems that in this situation, the adjudicator may either suspend proceedings or continue until such time as he is ordered by the Court to desist.

ABB Zantingh Ltd v. *Zedal Building Services Ltd*, above, is an example of where the proceedings were adjourned.

It may be that the parties will agree, or can be persuaded to agree, to use an expedited form of arbitration, whether under an existing or an *ad hoc* arbitration agreement, to decide issues of jurisdiction. The Royal Institution of Chartered Surveyors operates such a scheme, with the objective of appointing an arbitrator and determining the jurisdictional challenge within 48 hours. The Court's reaction to this sort of approach can be seen in *Cygnet Healthcare plc* v. *Higgins City Ltd* (2000) 16 Const LJ 366, in which the underlying issue whether or not there was a contract (and therefore whether adjudication might at all be appropriate) had been made he subject of an *ad hoc* arbitration agreement. Notwithstanding this, the claimant started adjudication and the adjudicator delivered a decision. HHJ Anthony Thornton QC decided that the appropriate course was to adjourn the summary judgment application until the hoped-for speedy resolution of the question of the existence or otherwise of a contract by way of the *ad hoc* arbitration.

The party resisting jurisdiction may seek an injunction. A Court will not grant an injunction to restrain the adjudication from proceeding if there is a risk that to do so may be interfering with a valid adjudication. In such circumstances the balance of advantage favours allowing the adjudication process to continue: *Workplace Technologies plc* v. *E Squared Ltd and another* (unreported, 16 February 2000, TCC, HHJ David Wilcox QC). Cp. *Naylor* v. *Greenacres Curling Ltd* [2001] ScotCS 163, per Lord Bonomy.

By contrast, in a case where it was clear to the Court that the adjudication proceedings were not valid, an injunction was issued: *John Mowlem & Co. plc* v. *Hydra-Tight Ltd*, above. See also *Quality Street Properties (Trading) Ltd* v. *Elmwood (Glasgow) Ltd*, above.

The person who seeks the adjudication will ordinarily be liable for the fees of the adjudicator in relation to a decision which the adjudicator has no authority to make: *Griffin and Tomlinson* v. *Midas Homes Ltd*, above.

Examples of certain jurisdictional challenges are given below.

10.2 Where there is no contract

Adjudication under the statute requires the existence of a contract which complies with the HGCRA 1996. If there is no such contract, the Adjudicator has no jurisdiction under the HGCRA 1996.

Where there is doubt over the existence of a contract it is thought that the adjudicator should raise the matter with the parties at the earliest opportunity and seek to have the matter of his jurisdiction clarified.

But a dispute as to the *terms* of a contract is one that can be decided in adjudication: *Tim Butler Contractors Ltd* v. *Merewood Homes Ltd* (2000) 18 Const LJ 74 (HHJ Gilliland QC). Cf. *Watson Building Services Ltd* v. *Graham Harrison and Miller (Preservation) Ltd*, above, dealing with the question whether the terms of the standard form

Scottish Building Contract Contractors Designed Portion without Quantities (April 1998 revision) had been incorporated into a subcontract.

10.3 Where the contract is not a 'construction contract'

In *Lathom Construction Ltd* v. *Cross* (1999) CILL 1568 an adjudicator found that the parties had reached a compromise of their disputes and went on to make findings as to the operation of that compromise. He found that the defendants had failed to pay all the sums due under that compromise. These further findings were held by HHJ Mackay QC to be beyond his jurisdiction because the compromise was not a construction contract within the meaning of the HGCRA 1996.

In *Shepherd Construction Ltd* v. *Mecright*, above, HHJ Humphrey Lloyd QC held that the question whether a dispute had been compromised was not one that arose under the contract because it extinguished all disputes then extant. In any event, the compromise agreement replaced the original agreement, including the valuation and payment obligations under the original contract. (The parties were also admonished in that case not to mislead the Court by putting incomplete material before it verified as accurate by the signatory of a statement or, more importantly in the context of the particular adjudication, that a compromise agreement had been made.) Cf. *Quality Street Properties (Trading) Ltd* v. *Elmwood (Glasgow) Ltd*, above.

In *CPL Contracting Ltd* v. *Cadenza Residential* (2005) 21 Const LJ T1 it was held that the parties had by their conduct in fact compromised their dispute albeit that there was perhaps no express intention to do so. Looking at the matter objectively, there was simply no dispute between the parties.

A compromise based on an agreement not to adjudicate in return for the payment of an agreed sum is one made for good consideration and binds the parties, given that otherwise the parties would be involved in expenditure of time and money pursuing the adjudication: *Joseph Finney plc* v. *Vickers and Vickers* (unreported, 7 March 2001, TCC, HHJ David Wilcox QC).

A variation, which amends the terms of the underlying agreement between the parties, is not a compromise in this context, so that a dispute under that amended agreement is one arising under the contract and subject to adjudication: *Westminster Building Co. Ltd* v. *Andrew Beckingham*, above.

10.4 Where a decision on the matter in dispute has already been made

Once a decision is made at adjudication, it excludes a second adjudication in respect of the same issue.

By contrast, no issue estoppel arises on enforcement proceedings except to the extent that it is a necessary ingredient to those proceedings. Thus, in *Elanay Contracts Ltd* v. *The Vestry*, above, HHJ Richard Havery QC decided that the only issue which was necessary to those proceedings was simply and solely the fact that a decision had been made by the adjudicator. Cf. *Stiell Ltd* v. *Riema Controls*, above, in which it was argued, unsuccessfully, that the decision of the adjudicator rendered the unsuccessful part of the pursuer's claim contingent upon final determination by legal proceedings or agreement between the parties.

In *VHE Construction plc* v. *RBSTB Trust Co. Ltd*, above, the court held that the second adjudicator had no jurisdiction to set aside revise or vary the first adjudicator's decision. HHJ John Hicks QC observed that the second adjudicator had been

> 'conspicuously careful to avoid any form of words which might convey the contrary impression'.

The Scheme provides, at paragraph 9(2), that an adjudicator must resign where the dispute is the same or substantially the same as one which has previously been referred to adjudication and a decision has been taken in that adjudication.

In the context of the Scheme, it has been held that disputes over the value of an interim application for payment (albeit the last such application made soon after practical completion) and a dispute over the value of a final account where the contents of the final account were similar to the interim application, were nevertheless distinct disputes: *Sherwood & Casson Ltd* v. *MacKenzie Engineering Ltd* (unreported, 30 November 1999, TCC, HHJ Anthony Thornton QC). Cf. *Skanska Construction UK Ltd* v. *ERDC and another* [2002] ScotCS 307 in which Lady Paton held in relation to the effect of findings in an adjudication which took place relating to an application for interim payment No. 7 upon an adjudication over the final account that a different stage in the contract had been reached by the date of issue of the final account to which different considerations and perspectives might apply and considerably more information might be available. Once the valuation of a particular interim application has been the subject of adjudication, however, it cannot be adjudicated again: *Watkin Jones & Son* v. *Lidl UK GmbH* (2002) 85 Con LR 155 (HHJ Humphrey Lloyd QC).

In *Holt Insulation Ltd* v. *Colt International Ltd* (unreported, 2 February 2001, HHJ Mackay QC) two adjudications had been brought in relation to interim payment application No. 10 under an insulation subcontract. In the first adjudication the adjudicator had been asked to determine whether a sum certain was due. He decided that it was not. In the second, he was asked to determine what (if any) sum was due. He decided that there was a sum due (different from the sum certain asked for in the first adjudication). The court decided that the second adjudicator (the same person as in the first adjudication) did have jurisdiction, as the adjudications arose in relation to different matters under the relevant application for payment.

In *Emcor Drake & Scull* v. *Costain Skanska Joint Venture* [2004] EWHC 2439 HHJ Richard Havery QC held that a decision refusing an extension of time based on a failure to discharge the burden of proof was not the same as that purported to made in the second adjudication a year later granting an extension of time and payment, being based on wider matters. In *Quietfield Ltd* v. *Vascroft Contractors Ltd* [2006] EWHC 174 an adjudicator declined to grant an extension of time to the Contractor because it had provided neither evidence nor reasoned analysis to justify delay to the completion of the works. A second adjudication started by the employer was abandoned. A third adjudication before the same adjudicator was started by the employer. The contractor responded by asserting that it was entitled to an extension of time in respect of the entire period of delay. The grounds upon which the contractor now claimed an extension of time were a significant elaboration upon those set out in the material for the first adjudication. The adjudicator declined to consider the contractor's submissions on extension of time, holding that this matter had been determined in the first adjudication. Jackson J formulated the issue before him as: 'was the adjudicator correct in treating his own decision in the first adjudication as conclusive in relation to extension of time?' He decided that the adjudicator should have had regard to the revised (and significantly elaborated) delay claim. The responding party was not restricted to defences of which it had previously given notice and which had thereby generated the 'dispute' referable to adjudication. The employer's application for summary judgment was therefore dismissed.

10.5 Where the adjudicator fails to deal with or confine himself to the matters referred

The adjudicator is required to make a decision, provided it falls within his jurisdiction; failure to make a decision renders the process a nullity (and another adjudicator may decide the matter): *Ballast plc* v. *The Burrell Co. (Construction Management) Ltd*, 2001 S.L.T. 1039.

The adjudicator must take care to work within the limits of his remit.

10.6 Does an adjudicator have power to determine his own jurisdiction?

A much-debated question is whether an adjudicator can determine the ambit of his own jurisdiction.

It seems that an adjudicator has an inherent power, if not an obligation, as part of the adjudication process, to make enquiries into his jurisdiction and to come to a conclusion on that matter, so that he may determine his further conduct, see *Homer Burgess Ltd* v. *Chirex (Annan) Ltd*, above. See also *Fastrack Contractors Ltd* v. *Morrison Construction Ltd and another*, above.

But, an adjudicator may not ordinarily decide his own jurisdiction: *Smith* v. *Martin* [1925] 1 KB 745; *Palmers Ltd* v. *ABB Power Construction Ltd*, above (holding that a declaratory judgment by the Court on the question of jurisdiction is appropriate where jurisdiction is central to the dispute). It has been observed that it is a contradiction in terms to create a tribunal with limited jurisdiction and an unlimited power to determine such limit at its own will and pleasure: *R.* v. *Shoreditch Assessment Committee* [1910] 2 KB 859 (CA), per Farwell LJ. The position therefore is that whilst ordinarily an adjudicator cannot determine his own jurisdiction, he can make a decision which, if within his jurisdiction, will be valid. Accordingly, if his conclusion on the matter of jurisdiction is wrong the decision may be successfully resisted.

In *Sherwood & Casson Ltd* v. *MacKenzie Engineering Ltd*, above, the Court held that, notwithstanding the power given to the adjudicator under the Scheme to decide whether two disputes are substantially the same, that power was subject to challenge. The position was said to be the same even under institutional rules in circumstances where it could be said that no dispute remained in existence which was capable of being referred.

There is it seems nothing to prevent an adjudicator being expressly empowered to determine his own jurisdiction: *Nolan Davis Ltd* v. *Steven P Catton* (unreported, 22 February 2000, TCC, HHJ David Wilcox QC). In *Whiteways Contractors (Sussex) Ltd* v. *Impresa Castelli Construction UK Limited*, above, it was held that a letter written by the respondent's solicitors and the parties' written submissions made by solicitors on behalf of both parties constituted requests to the adjudicator to determine his own jurisdiction.

Certain of the institutional adjudication rules provide expressly for the adjudicator to be able to determine his own jurisdiction. In *Farebrother Building Services Ltd* v. *Frogmore Investments Ltd* (unreported, 20 April 2001, TCC, HHJ Gilliland QC) the adjudication was under version 1.3 of the TeCSA rules clause 12 of which provided that the Adjudicator 'may rule upon his own substantive jurisdiction and as to the scope of the adjudication'. See also ICE 7th Edition, clause 66B(4)(a).

The Courts have indicated that where there is a *bona fide* dispute as to jurisdiction which raises no substantial issues of fact, they will grant a declaratory ruling on the matter: see *Palmers Ltd* v. *ABB Power Construction Ltd*, above. Where the contract provides for disputes to be finally determined by arbitration, arbitrators are presumably similarly empowered under the provisions of Section 48(3) of the Arbitration Act 1996.

Whilst most jurisdictional challenges are likely to be against a claimed excess of jurisdiction, injustice can equally result from the adjudicator's denial of jurisdiction in circumstances where he should have accepted that jurisdiction. *Northern Developments (Cumbria) Ltd* v. *J&J Nichol*, above, recognised just such a possibility, although it was not relevant on the facts of that case. HHJ Peter Bowsher QC held that the adjudicator had decided that he had no jurisdiction to consider a repudiation claim because (wrongly) it was not a claim under the contract. In fact, the adjudicator (who had come to the right decision for the wrong reason) had no jurisdiction because the claim, which could only be taken into account if it had been referred to in a notice of intention to withhold payment, had not been the subject of such notice.

11 THE APPOINTMENT OF THE ADJUDICATOR

The parties may agree on the identity of the adjudicator. Either this may be at the time the contract is entered into or once the dispute has arisen.

In *John Mowlem & Co. plc* v. *Hydra-Tight Ltd*, above, HHJ John Toulmin CMG QC held that a provision specifying that the Contractor should select the adjudicator from barristers in a particular set of chambers was sufficiently clear and enforceable and that an appointment which purported to fall outside those requirements was invalid.

Alternatively, the contract may specify that a particular nominating body shall select an adjudicator. Nominating bodies include the ICE, RICS, RIBA, CIOB, TECBAR, TeCSA, and CIArb. The nominating body typically selects appointees from a list of accredited adjudicators kept (and in some cases such as the ICE, published) by the body. Some of these bodies typically make a charge to the Applicant to cover the cost of administering the selection and appointments service.

Another alternative is for the appointment to be made by an 'adjudicator nominating body' (see, for example, paragraph 2(1)(c) of the Scheme). These are bodies which hold themselves out publicly as bodies that will select an adjudicator when requested to do so by a referring party. Any one of these bodies is competent where the contract does not specify who the adjudicator or nominating body is to be: *David McLean Housing Contractors Ltd* v. *Swansea Housing Association Ltd* [2002] BLR 125.

Ordinarily the practice is that if a request is made to the nominating body, it will appoint an adjudicator and that once the appointment has been made, the adjudicator is left to get on with the adjudication without interference (or, usually, further involvement) by the nominating body. Thus, the nominating body would probably be unwilling (and unwise) to seek to resolve a dispute between the parties as to whether or not an appointment should be made: see *United Co-operatives Ltd* v. *Sun Alliance & London Assurance Co. Ltd* [1987] 1 EGLR 126.

12 FEES AND COSTS

An adjudicator proceeding *bona fide* is ordinarily entitled to his fees even where he decides (rightly or wrongly, having investigated the matter) that he does not have jurisdiction: *Prentice Island Ltd* v. *Castle Contracting Ltd* [2003] ScotSC 61.

It is normal for the adjudicator to set his fees by reference to a time charge. The charges can vary widely depending upon the qualifications and experience of the particular adjudicator, the complexity of the issues and location. In the absence of an agreement on fees, it is considered that the adjudicator will be entitled to a reasonable fee commensurate with the demands and complexities of the case and his own standing; where the Scheme applies this is clearly the case: see paragraph 25(1).

A challenge to an adjudicator's fees unsupported by expert evidence may well fail. It is not a proper approach to what constitutes a reasonable fee for an adjudicator to ask what the fees for a reasonably competent solicitor might have been. Furthermore, a court should be slow to substitute its own view of what constitutes reasonable hours: *Stubbs Rich Architects* v. *WH Tolly & Son Co. Ltd* (unreported, Bristol County Court, 8 August 2001, Mr Recorder Lane QC).

However, it is in the best interests of the parties and the adjudicator to avoid controversy over the adjudicator's fees by having a written agreement in place setting out the level of fees and any terms that attach to their payment.

It has been held that the allocation and apportionment of the adjudicator's fees is a matter for the adjudicator, not the Courts: see *Castle Inns (Stirling) Ltd* v. *Clark Contracts Ltd*, above.

Some adjudicators seek security for their fees. This is usually achieved by way of a deposit advanced by each party. This can lead to difficulty both practically and with perception over the adjudicator's independence and impartiality, especially where one of the parties lodges his contribution and the other does not. This situation is best avoided by returning the single deposit. Some adjudicators seek interim payments, usually in circumstances where the adjudication lasts longer than 28 days, but is thought unwarranted in the majority of cases, given the timescale under which adjudication operates.

Many of the standard forms of contract contain standard adjudication agreements, with the procedures usually identified by reference to the adjudication rules into which that form of contract is tied, for example the JCT and ICE forms. These rules will typically deal with the basis of the adjudicator's fees, the responsibility of each of the parties for those fees and the circumstances in which the adjudication agreement may be terminated and the consequences which arise on that termination.

Certain institutional adjudication rules expressly provide that each party shall bear its own costs.

Whether or not an adjudicator has power to award costs in the absence of an express provision for the same was first considered in *John Cothliff Ltd* v. *Allen Build (NW) Ltd* (1999) CILL 1530, in which HHJ Marshall Evans QC held that an adjudicator did have power to award costs either under an express term of the scheme or possibly under a separate implied term. The reasoning was probably not correct and the decision was not followed in *Northern Developments (Cumbria) Ltd* v. *J&J Nichol*, above, in which HHJ Peter Bowsher QC held that an adjudicator did not normally have jurisdiction to award costs. There was, however, nothing to prevent the parties expressly agreeing that the adjudicator should have power to order one party to an adjudication to pay the costs of the other party and that there was an implied agreement between the parties that the adjudicator should have jurisdiction to award costs of the adjudication by virtue of the facts that one party was represented by experienced solicitors the other party by experienced claims consultants, that both asked in writing for their costs and neither submitted to the adjudicator that he had no jurisdiction to award cost. The decision in *Northern Developments* above was considered wrong, at least in part, by May LJ in *John Roberts Architects Ltd* v. *Parkcare Homes (No. 2) Ltd* [2006] BLR 106 (CA); (see judgment at para. 12).

It was held in *Bridgeway Construction Ltd* v. *Tolent Construction Ltd* (2000) 18 CLD-09-22 by HHJ Mackay QC that a provision in a contract freely entered into that the applicant in the adjudication would be responsible for all the costs of the adjudication did not offend the HGCRA 1996. See also the similar decision in *Deko Scotland Ltd* v. *Edinburgh Royal Joint Venture and others* 2003 SLT 727.

In *John Roberts Architects Ltd* v. *Parkcare Homes (No. 2) Limited*, above, a construction contract for the provision of architectural services incorporated by reference an amended Construction Industry Council ('CIC') Model Adjudication Procedure, 3rd Edition for adjudication. Amended clause 29 of the procedure provided:

> 'The Adjudicator may in his discretion direct the payment of legal costs and expenses of one party by another as part of his decision. The Adjudicator may determine the amount of costs to be paid or may delegate the task to an independent costs draftsman'.

The amended clause 29 did not limit the adjudicator's power to direct the payment of legal costs to circumstances in which he made a substantive contested decision on the dispute referred to him; the more natural meaning of the clause in its context, and the commercially sensible meaning, was that the words 'as part of his decision' meant 'as part of what he may decide'.

In *Total M & E Services Ltd* v. *ABB Building Technologies Ltd*, above, the court held that the costs of adjudication could not be recovered as damages. To allow costs on that basis would be to subvert the Scheme.

13 THE ADJUDICATOR'S POWERS

Section 108(2)(f) of the HGCRA 1996 provides that an Adjudicator is empowered to take the initiative in ascertaining the facts and the law. Many institutional adjudication rules contain similar provisions. This is probably the most effective practical tool available to the adjudicator. It gives the adjudicator wide powers, including those allowing him to require the production of particular information, to interrogate the parties, to make site visits, to carry out tests and investigations, to secure specialist assistance, to research the law, etc.

Subject to the requirements for impartiality and considerations of natural justice, since the HGCRA 1996 does not expressly deal with the matter the practice and procedure to be adopted in the adjudication seems to be a matter entirely for the adjudicator. Contractual provisions may, of course, seek to deal with the matter of procedure in substantial detail (see, for example, Clause 41.A.5 of JCT 98 Private With Quantities form) and it seems that it must ultimately be a matter for the Adjudicator to decide whether to accept an appointment that requires a procedure that he finds unacceptable.

It is not clear whether an adjudicator may exercise a lien upon his decision; the cases, particularly *St Andrew's Bay Development* v. *HBG Management and another* (2003) CILL 2016, suggest otherwise. If he proposes to exercise a lien, it is a matter best raised by the Adjudicator with the parties at the outset and made the subject of express agreement. The ICE Adjudication Procedure, at Clause 6.6, deals with the matter expressly.

13.1 The Adjudicator's main powers under the Scheme

The adjudicator's main powers under the Scheme are as follows:

Paragraph 8

The adjudicator may, with the consent of the parties, adjudicate on more than one dispute under the same contract. Again with consent, he may adjudicate at the same time on related disputes on different contracts. This arguably places too much of a restriction on the powers of the Adjudicator, particularly where a number of similar disputes arise out of common contractual obligations, for example a series of 'term' contracts made between the same parties based upon one pricing document, and one party withholds its consent to consolidation. In these circumstances it makes sense for those disputes to be resolved by one Adjudicator (both from the point of view of economy and consistency) and for him to have the power to consolidate those disputes without the parties' consent.

In *Grovedeck Ltd* v. *Capital Demolition Ltd*, above, it was observed, *obiter*, that under Scheme adjudications Paragraph 8 of the Scheme prevented the adjudicator, without the consent of the other party from determining more than one dispute under the same contract or disputes under different contracts. There was, however, no reason why a compliant construction contract should not provide for the referral of either, without the consent of the other party. In *Barr Ltd* v. *Law Mining Ltd*, above, Lord MacFadyen decided that paragraph 8 of the Scheme permitted the adjudicator to adjudicate at the same time on more than one dispute under the same contract only with the consent of all parties to those disputes; albeit that on the facts the various matters were sufficiently connected for the Adjudicator not to err in concluding that he was dealing with one dispute. In *David McLean Housing Contractors Ltd* v. *Swansea Housing Association Ltd*, above, HHJ Humphrey Lloyd QC decided a common-sense approach was to be adopted and that a dispute over the payment due in respect of a particular application might properly extend to matters of valuation, extension of time, prolongation loss and/or expense, etc. Cf. *Shimizu Europe Ltd* v. *Automajor Ltd* [2002] BLR 113; *Chamberlain Carpentry & Joinery Ltd* v. *Alfred McAlpine Construction Ltd* (unreported, 25 March 2002, TCC, HHJ Richard Seymour QC); *Pring & St Hill* v. *CJ Hafner* (2004) 20 Const LJ 402, HHJ Humphrey Lloyd QC holding that a related dispute was one sharing some of the same facts or the same contractual provision.

In *Solland International* v. *Daraydan Holdings* (unreported, 15 February 2002, TCC, HHJ Richard Seymour QC) it was held that, without the agreement of both parties, a second dispute or counterclaim could not be incorporated into the adjudication.

Specific adjudication rules invoked into the construction contract may allow more than one dispute to be adjudicated at any one time. In *Balfour Kilpatrick* v. *Glauser International SA* (unreported, TCC), HHJ Gilliland QC held that Rule 11 of the TeCSA Rules which provides that the dispute concerned is the 'matters identified in the notice', does not confine the dispute to one and one only, thus generating a need for separate notices for each dispute.

Paragraph 13

The adjudicator may take the initiative in ascertaining the facts and the law in order to determine the dispute. He may decide upon the procedure to be followed in the adjudication, including requests for the supply of relevant documents or statements, determining the language of the adjudication and the provisions of translations, conducting meetings and interrogation of the parties or their representatives, making site visits and inspections, carrying out tests and experiments, obtaining assistance and advice, directing the timetable and other matters relating to conduct of the adjudication.

It seems from this provision that the adjudicator is free to conduct an entirely inquisitorial investigation or to use an adversarial process or to use a combination of the two, as best suits the circumstances of the case.

Paragraph 15
The adjudicator may proceed in the absence of one party or without a requested document or statement; he may draw appropriate inferences, and he may make his decision based on the information before him making such allowances for weight as may be appropriate given the timing of that information.

Paragraph 16
The adjudicator may restrict oral representation.

Paragraph 20
The adjudicator is required to decide the matters in dispute. He may take into account any other matters which the parties to the dispute agree should be within the scope of the adjudication or which are matters under the contract which he considers are necessarily connected with the dispute. Thus, in *Northern Developments (Cumbria) Ltd* v. *J&J Nichol*, above, the Court held that the Adjudicator would (had he otherwise had the relevant jurisdiction) have been entitled to take into account matters of allegations of defective work and delays as necessarily connected with applications for payment of outstanding monies.

Paragraph 20(a)
The adjudicator may open up, revise and review any decision taken or certificate given by any person referred to in the contract, unless that decision or certificate is declared by the contract to be final and conclusive, decide that any of the parties is liable to make a payment under the contract and when that payment is due and the final date for payment, and subject to the terms of the contract decide on the payment of interest.

In *Allied London and Scottish Properties plc* v. *Riverbrae Construction Ltd* [1999] BLR 346 the petitioner was concerned about the applicant's financial standing. It asked the Court to amend the adjudicator's decision that payment should be made within 14 days to one whereby the sums found by him to be due to the respondents should be placed in a joint deposit account pending the resolution of all claims between the parties. It seems that the adjudicator had decided that he did not have the power to order payment into such an account. The court refused to interfere with the adjudicator's decision, although it is thought that the adjudicator may have been unduly pessimistic about his perception of a limitation on his powers.

Certain institutional adjudication rules allow for payment to be made to a stakeholder. Mandatory payment to a stakeholder is probably contrary to the HGCRA 1996.

14 DUTIES OF THE ADJUDICATOR

The adjudicator's basic obligation is to render a decision: *Ballast plc* v. *The Burrell Co. (Construction Management) Ltd*, above. Without a decision he has failed in his fundamental task and his decision is a nullity.

The adjudicator's primary duties are to act impartially (Section 108(2)(e) of the HGCRA 1996) and to reach his decision within the statutory timescale (Sections 108(2)(c) and (d) of the HGCRA 1996).

There is no separate requirement that the adjudicator should be independent of the parties but the potential adjudicator should disclose any connection with a party so that any objection can be considered.

A difficulty, which may arise in practice, relates to appointment of the same adjudicator on different disputes between the same parties on the same project. Whilst there may be sound practical reasons for such an appointment, there may have been differences between the adjudicator and one of the parties on an earlier adjudication which affects the parties' perceptions of the adjudicator's likely conduct on the latter (such as a dispute over the adjudicator's fees). In such circumstances it is thought the adjudicator should carefully consider the matter before accepting the latter appointment.

It seems, too, that the requirements of natural justice are not as important a consideration in adjudication as they are in other (generally binding) forms of dispute resolution. In *Macob Civil Engineering Ltd* v. *Morrison Construction Ltd*, above, the defendants challenged the adjudicator's decision on the grounds that he had not given them an opportunity to make representations relating to:

- The question whether a mechanism for payment and final payment which was ambiguous was inadequate for the purposes of the HGCRA 1996; and
- A decision to invoke Section 42 of the Arbitration Act 1996.

These complaints were dismissed; Dyson J (as he then was) observed that it must be taken to be a recognised risk of the adjudication process that the tight timescales involved may generate some injustice.

Nevertheless, it seems clear that such considerations cannot be ignored. In *Discain Project Services Ltd* v. *Opecprime Development Ltd* [2001] BLR 285, HHJ Peter Bowsher QC declined to enforce an adjudicator's decision in circumstances where the adjudicator had conducted private communications with one of the parties but had not recorded the same to the other and given him an opportunity to comment. He stressed that an unsuccessful party must do more than merely assert a breach of the rules of natural justice to defeat the claim. Any breach must be substantial and relevant. In *Woods Hardwick Ltd* v. *Chiltern Air Conditioning Ltd*, above, HHJ Anthony Thornton QC refused to enforce an adjudicator's decision where the adjudicator had failed to make available to one of the parties information obtained from the other party and third parties and had secured legal advice without notifying of his intention so to do. Further, the adjudicator had submitted a witness statement to the enforcement proceedings in support of the one of the parties to the adjudication, which left the impression that he was not impartial. In *Balfour Beatty Construction* v. *London Borough of Lambeth* [2002] BLR 288 an adjudicator used a different methodology to that which either party had put forward and made his own independent analysis of the critical path. The adjudicator did not invite either party to comment on this approach before issuing his decision. HHJ Humphrey Lloyd QC refused to enforce the decision.

In *RSL (South West) Ltd* v. *Stansell* (unreported, 16 June 2003, TCC), HHJ Richard Seymour QC held that it was essential for an adjudicator to give the parties the opportunity to comment upon any material, from whatever source, including the knowledge or experience of the adjudicator himself to which the adjudicator is minded to attribute significance in reaching his decision. This decision is to be contrasted with *Try Construction Ltd* v. *Eton Town House Group* [2003] BLR 286 in which HHJ David Wilcox QC decided that the parties had agreed as a matter of fact that a time analyst employed by the adjudicator's firm could be employed to assist him and that such analyst could go beyond the strict confines of the parties' arguments in order to establish what events caused delays to the project. The learned judge there commented that the need to observe the rules of natural justice are not to be regarded as diluted for the purposes of the adjudication process, but that they must be adjudged in the light of such material matters as time restraints, the provisional nature of the decision and any concessions or agreements made by the parties as to the nature of the process in a particular case.

In *Costain Ltd* v. *Strathclyde Builders*, above, the court held that that the adjudicator must follow certain procedures in acting fairly. These included giving the parties an opportunity to comment, even in a tight timescale, telling the parties what the adjudicator's own views are so that they can comment, and the disclosure of any technical or legal advice.

Notwithstanding this, an adjudicator cannot be criticised for ignoring a possible order if the material to allow him to reach that decision is not properly put before him: *Allied London and Scottish Properties plc* v. *Riverbrae Construction Limited* above.

It has been said that a failure to comply with the requirements of natural justice does not allow the good parts of the decision to be severed from the bad; the whole is tainted and therefore unenforceable: *RSL (South West) Ltd* v. *Stansell* above.

In *Dean & Dyball Construction Ltd* v. *Kenneth Grubb Associates* above, the court held that it did not follow that an adjudicator should necessarily convene a hearing, or allow cross-examination in every case. If in all the circumstances the adjudication is considered to be intrinsically unfair, the decision will not be enforced: *Buxton Building Contractors Ltd* v. *Governors of Durand Primary School* [2004] BLR 374, in which it was held that the adjudicator had failed to consider or decide core issues that had been referred and also failed to take account of relevant material and information that had previously been placed before the adjudicator. In *AWG Construction Services Ltd* v. *Rockingham Motor Speedway* (2004) 20 Const LJ T107, HHJ John Toulmin CMG QC, held that the respondent had not been given a proper opportunity to respond to new material.

Jackson J sought to distil the essence of these (sometimes disparate and conflicting) principles in *Carillion Construction Ltd* v. *Devonport Royal Dockyard Ltd* [2005] BLR 310. He held that a court will not enforce a decision if the adjudicator has acted in serious breach of the rules of natural justice, but will otherwise do so. He recognised that it will often not be practicable for an adjudicator to put to the parties his provisional conclusions (which conclusions may very often represent some intermediate position for which neither party was contending) and that it will only be in exceptional cases that an adjudicator's failure to put his provisional conclusions to the parties will constitute such a serious breach of the rules of natural justice that the court will decline to enforce his decision.

In *Carillion Construction Ltd* v. *Devonport Royal Dockyard Ltd* [2006] BLR 15 (CA), Chadwick LJ indicated that the need to have the 'right' answer has been subordinated to the need to have an answer quickly. The Scheme was not enacted in order to provide definitive answers to complex questions; to seek to challenge the adjudicator's decision on the ground that he has exceeded his jurisdiction or breached the rules of natural justice (save in the plainest cases) is likely to lead to a substantial waste of time and expense. The Court of Appeal particularly doubted the correctness of the decision in *Buxton Building Contractors Ltd* v. *Governors of Durand Primary School* above. In a subsequent decision, *Kier Regional Ltd* v. *City & General (Holborn) Ltd* [2006] EWHC 848 (TCC), Jackson J applied these principles in refusing to reject an adjudicator's decision reached in disregard of two expert reports submitted by the responding party.

In *Ardmore Construction* v. *Taylor Woodrow Ltd* [2006] CSOH 3 the defence to an action to enforce an adjudicator's decision alleged breach of natural justice. A major difference was liability for and the value of a subcontractor's overtime claim. The adjudicator decided that the Contractor was liable to pay overtime because it had either given verbal instructions to the subcontractor to carry out the work, alternatively the contractor had acquiesced in the subcontractor carrying out the work in question.

The contractor alleged that at no time prior to the issuing of his decision was either alternative basis for the subcontractor being entitled to be paid the sums in question ever raised, or discussed, before the adjudicator, far less were these alternative bases of entitlement matters about which the contractor was given notice, all of which amounted to a breach of natural justice. Lord Clarke said, having regard to *Carillion Construction Ltd* v. *Devonport Royal Dockyard Ltd*, that he needed no persuasion that, on the whole, the courts should be generally resistant to invitations to pick over adjudicators' decisions and to analyse over closely, and critically, their procedures. Nevertheless, the case before him involved a clear and substantial breach of natural justice in relation to matters which were determinative of the Adjudicator's decision.

Under the Scheme the Adjudicator's duties include the following:

Paragraph 12

To act impartially and carry out his duties in accordance with any relevant provisions of the contract and reach his decision in accordance with the applicable law in relation to the contract and avoid unnecessary expense.

Glencot Development and Design Co. Ltd v. *Ben Barrett & Son (Contractors) Ltd*, above, is instructive. There an adjudicator acting under the Scheme, in a dispute over a payment, met with the parties to pursue questions of interest to him in the adjudication. The parties' representatives met at the venue and agreed the gross valuation of the works which were the subject of the dispute. They did not agree over matters of discount and certain other terms of payment. The adjudicator volunteered to mediate to seek to finalise the agreement and he shuttled between the parties over the next six hours. In the event, the parties did not agree. The adjudicator was subsequently invited by the respondent to withdraw from the adjudication it being suggested that his position as adjudicator had been compromised. The adjudicator, having taken counsel's advice, refused to withdraw. He stated that he did not believe that his impartiality had been compromised by his involvement in the settlement negotiations. HHJ Humphrey Lloyd QC considered the provisions of paragraph 12(a) of the Scheme and concluded that the test of bias was objective, not subjective and that earlier cases pointing to a subjective test could not be relied upon at the present day. It did not matter what the adjudicator thought or what he said in relation to his impartiality. There was a very real prospect that the respondent would be able to show that the adjudicator was no longer impartial and the adjudicator should have withdrawn. See also *Locabail* v. *Bayfield* [2000] QB 415; *Balfour Beatty Construction* v. *London Borough of Lambeth* [2002] BLR 288 and *RG Carter Ltd* v. *Edmund Nuttall Ltd* [2002] BLR 359.

The modern test for bias is set out in the speech of Lord Hope in *Porter* v. *Magill* [2002] 2 AC 357 (H.L), namely whether at the time when he gave his decision the fair-minded and informed observer, having considered the facts, would conclude that there was a real possibility that the (adjudicator) was biased. See also *Re Medicaments and Related Classes of Goods* (No. 2) [2001] 1 WLR 700 (CA), per Lord Phillips, applied in adjudication in *Amec Capital Projects Ltd* v. *Whitefriars City Estates Ltd* [2005] BLR 1 (CA) and *A&S Enterprises Ltd* v. *Kema Holdings Ltd* [2005] BLR 76. In *A&S Enterprises* above, HHJ Richard Seymour QC held that the adjudicator had been influenced in his conclusions on the merits of the case by the absence of a witness from the hearing of whom the adjudicator was critical (saying he 'chose not to attend') when there was no evidence to explain why the witness did not attend. All the adjudicator needed to say was that he had not heard from the witness. This criticism was held to demonstrate bias. The Court of Appeal has adopted a less censorious approach to the conduct of adjudicators and it is not clear whether the decision in *A&S Enterprises* would be upheld in Court of Appeal.

Placing of without prejudice or other privileged material before an adjudicator does not *per se* render it inappropriate to continue with the adjudication: *Specialist Ceiling Services Northern Ltd* v. *ZVI Construction (UK) Ltd* [2004] BLR 403.

Someone asked to act as arbitrator in relation to a dispute on which he has previously acted as adjudicator should, it is suggested, do so only with the express agreement of both parties. It may readily be suggested that the Adjudicator will be reluctant to move away from his own earlier views. See also the observations of HHJ Humphrey Lloyd, QC in *Pring & St Hill* v. *CJ Hafner*, above.

Paragraph 17
To consider any relevant information submitted and make available to the parties any information to be taken into account in reaching his decision.

Paragraph 18
Not to disclose information provided on a confidential basis.

Paragraph 19
To reach his decision not later than 28 days after the date of the referral notice or 42 days if the Referring Party so consents or such further period as may be agreed between the parties. The Adjudicator is required to deliver a copy of the decision as soon as possible after he has reached that decision. For these purposes making a decision and delivering it have been treated as equivalent: see *Bloor Construction (UK) Ltd* v. *Bowmer & Kirkland (London) Ltd* [2000] BLR 314 and *St Andrew's Bay Development* v. *HBG Management and another*, above, in which it was noted that the HGCRA 1996 is silent on the question of intimation or communication of a decision and it was concluded that a decision cannot be said to be made until it is intimated.

Paragraph 22
If requested by one of the parties to the dispute, the adjudicator is required to provide reasons for his decision. This provision lacks clarity. For example, when does the request to provide reasons have to be made? If there is no request before the date that he has made his decision, is the adjudicator bound to furnish reasons after he has made it? The adjudicator may have approached the adjudication on the basis that he would not furnish reasons and after having given his decision he may consider that as he has given a decision and delivered copies of it to the parties, his appointment has expired, and it is too late. Therefore, the requirement for decisions should be addressed at the outset and this may best be done by the adjudicator requiring the parties within a specified time shortly after the referral to state whether or not they will require reasons, and that in the absence of a such a request at that time that he will proceed on the assumption that no reasons will be required.

In contrast with the Scheme the JCT Adjudication provisions, by way of example, expressly state that the adjudicator shall not be obliged to give reasons for his decision. The decision required by Section 108(2)(c) of the HGCRA 1996 taken together with paragraph 22 of the Scheme contemplates a decision with reasons, if requested by a party. Therefore, it is by no means clear whether the JCT and other adjudication rules that state the adjudicator is not obliged to give reasons comply with the requirements of Section 108(2) of HGCRA 1996.

15 DUTIES OF THE PARTIES

Section 108(2)(f) of the HGCRA 1996 provides that the adjudicator shall be enabled to take the initiative in ascertaining the facts and the law.

In the absence of contractual provisions requiring the parties to co-operate in particular ways, it is thought that the matter can only be left to the common-sense of the adjudicator, who would seem to be entitled in those circumstances to draw adverse inferences where appropriate.

Under the Scheme the parties have the following particular duties:

Paragraph 14

The parties shall comply with any request or direction of the adjudicator in relation to the adjudication. Failure to comply without showing sufficient cause may lead to exercise of the adjudicator's powers under paragraph 15 (proceeding in the absence of one party).

Paragraph 18

Not to disclose information provided on a confidential basis.

16 ADJUDICATION UNDER CONTRACT

Provided they comply with the minimum requirements set out in Section 108 of the HGCRA 1996, the parties are free to specify in their contract the basis upon which the adjudication is to proceed.

It is advisable for the contract to deal expressly with areas of possible controversy that are not included in the requirements of a contractual framework that complies with the HGCRA 1996. By way of examples, the HGCRA 1996 says nothing about the following: The level of, or power to apportion, responsibility for the adjudicator's charges (Cp. the Scheme at paragraph 25).

Recovery of the parties' costs. This is also a deficiency in the Scheme, which was considered in *John Cothliff Ltd* v. *Allen Build (NW) Ltd* above, and *Northern Developments (Cumbria) Ltd* v. *J&J Nichol* above, with differing conclusions.

The furnishing of reasons for the Adjudicator's decision (the Scheme deals with the giving of reasons at paragraph 22 – see Section 14 above).

The Adjudicator's power to exercise a lien on his decision until he has been paid.

17 SPECIFIC PROVISIONS IN THE ICE (AND OTHER STANDARD FORM) CONTRACTS

The Institution of Civil Engineers published its Adjudication Procedure in 1997. Particular points to note are as follows:

> The scope of the matters that may be referred under clause 66B(1)(a) of the ICE 7th. Conditions is wider than adjudication under the Scheme. The clause provides a right to refer not only any matter arising 'under' the contract but also any matter 'in connection with' the contract (see above).

The adjudicator may rely on his own expert knowledge and experience (Clause 1.4). Similar provisions appear in other institutional adjudication rules. Whilst this provision seems to be directed at removing the difficulties arising from decisions in related areas of law such as *Fox* v. *PG Wellfair Ltd* [1981] 2 Lloyd's Rep 514, CA. (Cf. *Top Shop Estate*

Ltd v. *Danino* [1985] 1 EGLR 9; *Checkpoint Ltd* v. *Strathclyde Pension Fund* [2003] 14 EG 124]), it is submitted that the prudent adjudicator will nevertheless disclose his thinking and allow the parties an opportunity to comment, consistent with the position which obtains in the absence of an express provision such as clause 1.4: *RSL (South West) Ltd* v. *Stansell*, above.

The Adjudicator may be named in the contract or agreed between the parties. The ICE is named as the nominating body in default of agreement (Clause 3.3).

Standard terms and conditions apply to the appointment (Clause 3.4). These are annexed to the Procedure.

The adjudicator is to have 'complete discretion' in the conduct of the adjudication (Clause 5.5).

The adjudicator is empowered to obtain legal or technical advice after notifying the parties (Clause 5.6). Similar provisions appear in other institutional adjudication Rules.

There is provision for joinder if the parties agree (Clause 5.7).

The adjudicator is not required to give reasons (Clause 6.1).

The adjudicator may direct the payment of simple or compound interest (Clause 6.2).

The parties are to bear their own costs (Clause 6.5).

The parties are jointly and severally responsible for the adjudicator's fees, which may however be allocated between them by the adjudicator, failing which each party is responsible for half (Clause 6.5). Similar provisions appear in other institutional adjudication Rules.

The adjudicator may by notice at least seven day before his decision is due advise that he will exercise a lien on his decision (Clause 6.6).

The adjudicator may correct clerical errors, etc. within 14 days of notification of his decision (Clause 6.9).

The JCT 2005 forms have abandoned bespoke adjudication provisions and largely adopted the Scheme. Points particular to the 1998 Edition of the JCT contracts (for example the provisions at Clause 41A of JCT 98 Private With Quantities form) are that: Adjudication only applies to any dispute or difference arising 'under' the contract (Clause 41A.1).

No adjudicator may be agreed or nominated unless the adjudicator executes the JCT standard form of agreement for appointment of an adjudicator (Clause 41A.2.1). By contrast, failure by the parties to execute the agreement (or, indeed, to comply with the majority of the procedural requirements laid down in Clause 41A) will not invalidate the adjudicator's decision (Clause 41A.5.6).

The adjudicator is not obliged to give reasons for his decision (Clause 41A.5.4).

Article 7A provides that the enforcement of an adjudicator's decision does not need to be by arbitration, even if there is an arbitration agreement. Thus, the parties may take legal proceedings to secure compliance.

The Appendix entry deals with choice of the adjudicator nominating body.

18 WHAT IS THE POSITION IF ONLY THE REFERRING PARTY TAKES PART IN THE ADJUDICATION?

This matter is addressed by paragraph 15 of the Scheme. In particular, if the non-referring party does not comply with the adjudicator's directions, the adjudicator may continue the adjudication in the absence of that party.

It is thought that a compliant contractual adjudication would, in the absence of an express term, incorporate an implied term to like effect.

It is thought that an adjudicator who does proceed in the absence of one party should:

- Make it clear that he intends so to do;
- Subject to his obligation as to timetable, afford the recalcitrant party the opportunity at all times to be involved;
- Perhaps involve himself in a more rigorous enquiry into the facts and the law than otherwise;
- Seek specific information/comment/submissions in relation to what appear to the Adjudicator to be critical areas of relevance.

19 THE FORM AND CONTENT OF AN ADJUDICATOR'S DECISION

The form and content will vary but a suggested outline of the necessary content of the decision is set out below:

(a) By way of introduction, the background to the dispute.
(b) A short description of the key events in the adjudication.
(c) A statement of the issues to be decided. In the event of doubt, it may be sensible, particularly if the issues have gone through some refinements during the process to set out a formulation of the issues for the parties' agreement: see, by way of example, the second Adjudicator's approach in *VHE Construction plc* v. *RBSTB Trust Co. Ltd*, above. Whilst definition of the dispute may be circumscribed it may inevitably involve resolution of other matters which may not specifically have been raised into separate or discrete disputes: *Sindall Ltd* v. *Solland and others*, above.
(d) A recital of the relevant contract terms.
(e) A brief narrative drawing on the salient facts.
(f) A section setting out the formal decision stating the adjudicator's findings and directions, which should be clear and concise and should be easily referable to the matters referred for a decision.
(g) Obviously, if reasons are to be given these also need to be clearly set out. This may be done either as the narrative of the decision is unfolded in its various sections or, if more convenient and practicable, at the end. The need of adequacy in those reasons has been said to be circumscribed by the fact that adjudicator's decisions do not finally determine the rights of the parties, that even if they are given those reasons may be erroneous without undermining the temporarily binding effect of the decision, and that adjudicators are often not required to give reasons at all; only where reasons are absent or unintelligible and as a result the complainant had suffered substantial prejudice should the decision not be enforced: *Carillion Construction Ltd* v. *Devonport Royal Dockyard Ltd* [2005] BLR 310.
(h) The decision should be dated and signed.

20 TO WHAT EXTENT IS THE DECISION BINDING ON THE PARTIES?

Once there is a decision on the matters referred, it is binding until the dispute is finally resolved by arbitration or litigation. That final resolution will require reconsideration of the issues afresh and the earlier adjudication decision does not affect the burden of proof in later proceedings. Neither the court nor an arbitrator has any appellate jurisdiction over adjudicators: *City Inn Ltd* v. *Shepherd Construction Ltd* (unreported, the Outer House, Court of Session, 17 July 2001, Lord MacFadyen).

The distinction between a decision founded on an excess of jurisdiction, which will not be enforced, and one founded on an error of fact or law, which will be enforced, may not always be easy to maintain. It appears essentially to turn on whether the adjudicator answers the right question, albeit erroneously (an error), which will be enforced or answers the wrong question (resulting in a lack of jurisdiction), which will not be enforced: *Bouygues UK Ltd* v. *Dahl-Jensen UK Ltd* [2000] BLR 522 (CA). Cf. *C&B Scene Concept Design Ltd* v. *Isobars Ltd* [2002] BLR 93 (CA); *SL Timber Systems Ltd* v. *Carillion Construction Ltd*, above; *Diamond* v. *PJW Enterprises Ltd*, above; *Barr Ltd* v. *Law Mining Ltd*, above.

Ordinarily a decision whose validity is challenged on the grounds of error on the facts or the law or because of procedural error, will nevertheless be treated as a decision and will be enforced: *Macob Civil Engineering Ltd* v. *Morrison Construction Ltd*, above. If it were otherwise, it would substantially undermine the effectiveness of adjudication. Cf. *Ferson Contractors Ltd* v. *Levolux AT Ltd*, above. See also *Rentokil Ailsa Environmental Ltd* v. *Eastend Civil Engineering Ltd* (unreported, 31 March 1999, Sheriff Principal Cox upholding Sheriff Gilmour), holding that the arrestment process cannot in Scotland be used to subvert the adjudication process. Despite some earlier doubts in the Scottish cases there seems now to be acceptance that the English cases correctly summarise the legal conclusions; *Watson Building Services Ltd* v. *Graham Harrison and Miller (Preservation) Ltd*, above; *SL Timber Systems Ltd* v. *Carillion Construction Ltd*, above.

It does not follow that an adjudicator who has made a mistake as to what he was supposed to decide or as to the basis upon which he was being invited to decide a question inevitably goes to his jurisdiction and vitiates his determination: *Shimizu Europe Ltd* v. *Automajor Ltd*, above.

If the decision falls within the adjudicator's jurisdiction, it is binding even if the errors are of fundamental importance. In *Bouygues UK Ltd* v. *Dahl-Jensen UK Ltd*, CA, above, a mechanical services subcontractor claimed damages consequent upon an allegedly wrongful determination of its employment, met by a counterclaim from the main contractor. The adjudicator made a decision that was patently wrong in that the calculation of the amount awarded had not properly treated the matter of retention. The effect of his decision was that retention would be released to the subcontractor before it was due under the contract, a matter of common ground between the parties at the adjudication. Dyson J (as he then was) upheld the decision at first instance. The result was challenged in the Court of Appeal and, in the first decision on adjudication at that level, the court dismissed the appeal holding that an adjudicator's decision is to stand, even if there is an error in it.

Where, as was not the case in *Bouygues*, the adjudicator is willing to acknowledge a slip, he has an implied power under the HGCRA 1996 and the Scheme to correct an accidental error or omission in his decision: *Bloor Construction (UK) Ltd* v. *Bowmer & Kirkland (London) Ltd*, above; *Edmund Nuttall* v. *Sevenoaks District Council* (unreported, 14 April 2000, TCC, Dyson J as he then was), in which the adjudicator acknowledged that he had made an error in not taking into account a previous payment on account. In this context the Court of Appeal decision in *Markos* v. *Goodfellow and others* [2002] EWCA Civ 1542 is pertinent. It was there held that Civil Procedure Rules rule 40.12 ought to be used only to correct an accidental slip or omission in a judgment or order. That rule was limited to a genuine slip and was not designed to correct a substantive issue.

21 ENFORCEMENT OF THE ADJUDICATOR'S DECISION

The thrust of the HGCRA 1996 is that the losing party should give effect to the decision and, if still aggrieved, argue its case later in further proceedings directed at finally resolving the dispute. This is the effect of Section 108(3) which provides that:

> '... the decision of the Adjudicator is binding until the dispute is finally determined by legal proceedings, by arbitration ... or by agreement'.

In *Macob Civil Engineering Ltd* v. *Morrison Construction Ltd*, above, Dyson J (as he then was) said:

> 'The intention of Parliament in enacting the Act was plain. It was to introduce a speedy mechanism for settling disputes in construction contracts on a provisional interim basis, and requiring the decisions of adjudicators to be enforced pending the final determination of disputes by arbitration, litigation or agreement'.

The most usual route to enforcement for a parties' non-compliance with an adjudicator's decision is the issue of proceedings. Section 9 of the 2nd edition of the TCC Guide is titled 'Adjudication Business' and includes guidance on the procedures in the TCC for the enforcement of an adjudicator's decision. Enforcement proceedings normally seek a monetary judgment and therefore Civil Procedure Rules ('CPR') Part 7 proceedings are usually appropriate. However, if the enforcement proceedings raise a question which is unlikely to involve a substantial dispute of fact and no monetary judgment is sought, CPR Part 8 may be used. Often the claimant's application will seek an abridgment of time for the various procedural steps and an application for summary judgment under CPR Part 24: see, for example, *Macob Civil Engineering Ltd* v. *Morrison Construction Ltd*, above; *A&D Maintenance and Construction Ltd* v. *Pagehurst Construction Services Ltd*, above; *VHE Construction plc* v. *RBSTB Trust Co. Ltd*, above.

In the absence of special considerations it seems clear, then, that adjudicators' decisions are intended to be enforced summarily: *Allen Wilson Shopfitters* v. *Buckingham*, above.

In *Balfour Beatty Construction* v. *Serco Ltd* (unreported, 21 December 2004), Jackson J held that that as no definitive conclusion as to the total extension of time due had been reached by the Adjudicator, no specific entitlement to liquidated damages logically arose and summary judgment excluding liquidated damages was therefore appropriate.

Interserve Industrial Services Ltd v. *Cleveland Bridge UK Ltd* [2006] EWHC 741 (TCC) involved an application for summary judgment to enforce Adjudicator's decision No. 2. The question of principle was whether the defendant was entitled to withhold payment on the grounds that the Defendant was pursuing a further adjudication in which it reasonably expected to recover an equivalent sum. Jackson J considered Section 49(2) of the Supreme Court Act 1981, which provides that 'subject to the provisions of ... any other Act', Courts shall give effect to all equitable estates, titles, rights, reliefs, defences and counterclaims, and to all equitable duties and liabilities. The HGCRA 1996 was such an 'other Act', one of the purposes of which was to ensure that payments passed promptly down the line to contractors, subcontractors and suppliers, without the hold-ups which had become endemic in the construction industry by the 1990s. The losing party could not withhold payment on the ground of his anticipated recovery in a future adjudication based upon different issues. Cf. *Hillview Industrial Developments (UK) Ltd* v. *Botes Building Ltd* [2006] EWHC 1365 (TCC).

4.1 Administration of claims
4.2 Litigation
4.3 Arbitration
4.4 Adjudication
4.5 Alternative dispute resolution

In *Verry* v. *London Borough of Camden* (unreported, 20 March 2006) the defendant did not pay in accordance with an adjudicator's decision and the claimant, having brought proceedings, applied for summary judgment to enforce that decision. Before the adjudicator issued his decision, the defendant issued a final certificate. The defendant sought to avoid enforcement on the basis that the adjudicator's decision had been superseded by the final certificate and that it had a cross-claim for defects that was due to be determined by another adjudicator. Ramsey J found that the effect of Section 108 of the HGCRA 1996 was generally to exclude the right of set-off from an adjudicator's decision where that set-off arose out of other contractual terms, defences and cross-claims. It would defeat the intention of Parliament if payment of an adjudicator's award of an amount due under an interim certificate was to be subject to the issue of a subsequent and inconsistent certificate. Accordingly, summary judgment would be granted.

For an example of what appears to have been treated as exceptional circumstances see *William Verry Ltd* v. *North West London Communal Mikvah*, above, in which an adjudicator's decision contained a number of admitted errors and in the circumstances the court viewed it as fair to delay enforcement of judgment so that the defendant could attempt to have those points rectified by a separate action.

Summary judgment may be denied where it is clear that a set-off for mutual dealings in the event of insolvency is or is likely to become relevant. Thus, whilst the point was not directly argued by the parties, a stay of execution, having the same effect, was granted in *Bouygues UK Ltd* v. *Dahl-Jensen UK Ltd*, above. See also the comments of Dyson J (as he then was) in *Herschel Engineering Ltd* v. *Breen Property Ltd* [2000] BLR 272, who contemplated a possible stay in circumstances where the evidence clearly showed that the successful party would be unable to repay the amount which was the subject of the Adjudicator's decision. In *Rainford House Ltd (in administrative receivership)* v. *Cadogan Ltd* [2001] BLR 416 it was held that that vague fears or unsubstantiated rumours of insolvency will not merit much attention, but evidence that some third party has taken action which puts the continued financial viability of the claimant at hazard must be evaluated seriously (in that particular case the evidence raised a strong prima facie case that Rainford was insolvent, justifying a stay upon the summary judgment pending the trial of the counterclaim, or further order, such stay being conditional upon Cadogan paying the judgment sum into court by a stated date). In *Wimbledon Construction Co. 2000* v. *Derek Vago* [2005] BLR 374 a stay was refused because the defendant was unable satisfactorily to show that the claimant would probably be unable to repay the judgment sum. For further decisions exploring the relevant principles, see *Absolute Rentals* v. *Glencor Enterprises Ltd* (unreported, 16 January 2000, HHJ David Wilcox QC), *Herschell Engineering Ltd* v. *Breen Property Ltd* (unreported, 28 July 2000, HHJ Humphrey Lloyd QC), *Baldwins Industrial Services plc* v. *Barr Ltd*, above, *Total M & E Services Ltd* v. *ABB Building Technologies Ltd*, above, *AWG Construction Services Ltd* v. *Rockingham Motor Speedway*, above; *All In One Building Refurbishments Ltd* v. *Makers UK Ltd* [2005] EWHC 2943 (TCC); *Harlow & Milner Ltd* v. *Teasdale* [2006] EWHC 1708 (TCC), *Michael John Construction Ltd* v. *Golledge and others*, above.

It appears that these considerations which are appropriate in England do not act as constraints to enforcement under Scottish law. Thus, in *SL Timber Systems Ltd* v. *Carillion Construction Ltd*, above, Lord MacFadyen has described the English conclusions as turning on the:

> 'specialities of English procedure relating to the circumstances in which it is appropriate (a) to grant summary judgment and (b) to grant a stay of execution... There seems to me to be nothing in the legislative provisions to qualify the expressed intention that an adjudicator's provisional award should be enforced pending final resolution of the dispute, to the effect of making an exception in the case where the Claimant, although not in liquidation, can be shown to be insolvent. I am therefore not persuaded that the defenders' averments to the effect that the pursuers are insolvent constitute a relevant defence'.

In *George Parke* v. *The Fenton Gretton Partnership* (2000) CILL 1712 it was held that an adjudication decision could validly form the basis of a statutory demand although the existence of a cross-claim was a matter which could be considered under Rule 6.5(4) of the 1986 Insolvency Rules even if it would not have amounted to an acceptable defence in response to an application for summary judgment. By contrast, *Guardi Shoes Ltd* v. *Datum Contracts* (unreported, 28 October 2002, Ferris, J) shows that a winding up petition may be allowed if a sufficient opportunity to issue a Section 111 notice had existed but not been taken by the Respondent.

A decision will be enforced as it appears; it will not be dismembered and reconstructed: *KNS Industrial Services (Birmingham) Ltd* v. *Sindall Ltd*, above. See also *Farebrother Building Services Ltd* v. *Frogmore Investments Ltd*, above.

Where summary judgment is inappropriate, but the court is satisfied that some amount is certainly due, it may award an appropriate sum under the interim payments provisions of part 25 of the Civil Procedure Rules, provided that application for such relief has been made: see *Glencot Development and Design Co. Ltd* v. *Ben Barrett & Son (Contractors) Ltd*, above.

An alternative is laid down in the Scheme, which provides at paragraph 24 that Section 42 of the Arbitration Act 1996 is to apply. This approach is limited to those instances where the Adjudicator's decision contains a peremptory order: *Outwing Construction Ltd* v. *H Randell and Son Ltd* [1999] BLR 156.

A further possibility is for the party seeking enforcement to secure a mandatory injunction. Its use, however, is likely to be rare to enforce money obligations. In *Macob Civil Engineering Ltd* v. *Morrison Construction Ltd*, above, Dyson J (as he then was) said:

> 'I am in no doubt that the Court has jurisdiction to grant a mandatory injunction to enforce an Adjudicator's decision, but it would rarely be appropriate to grant injunctive relief to enforce an obligation on one contracting party to pay the other. Clearly, different considerations apply where the Adjudicator decides that a party should perform some other obligation e.g. return to site, provide access or inspection facilities, open up work or carry out specified work etc. Nor do I intend to cast any doubt on decisions where mandatory injunctions have been ordered requiring payment of money to a third party'.

In addition, the HGCRA 1996 provides that performance may be suspended if payment due is not made in full by the final date: Section 112 (see above).

22 THE ADJUDICATOR'S IMMUNITY

Section 108(4) of the HGCRA 1996 states that a compliant construction contract must contain a provision that:

> 'the Adjudicator is not liable for anything done or omitted in the discharge or permitted discharge of his functions as Adjudicator unless the act or omission is in bad faith, and that any employee or agent of the Adjudicator is similarly protected from liability'.

Where there is a non-compliant contract, the Scheme deals with this at paragraph 26, which repeats the words in Section 108(4) above.

The immunity under Section 108(4) is contractual and should be expressly incorporated into the adjudicator's appointment.

Section 108(4) provides only limited scope for a dissatisfied party to bring a claim against the adjudicator; in particular where there is bad faith on the part of adjudicator. However, unless the parties expressly give the adjudicator a wider form of immunity, the contractual immunity which is envisaged by Section 108(4) of the HGCRA falls short of an indemnity. For example, by virutue of Section 2(1) of the Unfair Contract Terms Act 1977 ('UCTA') a person cannot by reference to any contractual term exclude liability for death or personal injury resulting from negligence. Therefore if an adjudicator's negligent decision resulted in death or injury to one of the parties, the adjudicator would be liable. In relation to other loss or damage, liability may be excluded where the requirement of reasonableness is satisfied (Section 2(2) of UCTA). Also, the contractual immunity does not affect the rights of third parties who are not parties to the adjudication.

Therefore, in certain disputes the statutory provisions may not be entirely satisfactory, particularly where the adjudicator's decision may directly affect the performance or safety of the works or a third party. The adjudicator will therefore be prudent to ensure that appropriate insurance is in place to cover any liability that may result from his decision and as a consideration of his willingness to act, that the terms of appointment include a provision under which the parties to the contract indemnify him against liability to third parties, including negligent liability.

23 DOES THE HUMAN RIGHTS ACT 1998 APPLY TO ADJUDICATION?

Despite early suggestions in some quarters that the Human Rights Act 1998 ('HRA 1998') might have some significant relevance to or impact upon adjudication, case law has established that HRA 1998 does not apply in adjudication.

HHJ Richard Havery QC held in *Elanay Contracts Ltd* v. *The Vestry* [2001] BLR 33 that Article 6 of the European Convention on Human Rights does not apply to proceedings before an adjudicator because an adjudication decision does not finally determine the rights of the parties; nor are the proceedings carried out in public.

In *Austin Hall Building Ltd* v. *Buckland Securities Ltd* [2001] BLR 272, HHJ Peter Bowsher QC held that proceedings before an adjudicator are not legal proceedings but proceedings designed to avoid the need for legal proceedings. Further, an adjudicator is not a public authority for the purposes of the legislation.

Construction disputes

4.1 Administration of claims

4.2 Litigation

4.3 Arbitration

4.4 Adjudication

4.5 Alternative dispute resolution

CHAPTER 4.5

Alternative dispute resolution

Ian Wright
Barrister & Mediator, Crown Office Chambers

Franco Mastrandrea
Northcrofts Management Services Limited

1 INTRODUCTION

The principal forms of dispute resolution include:

- litigation;
- arbitration;
- a formal decision by the engineer or contract administrator;
- adjudication;
- negotiated settlements;
- mediation;
- conciliation;
- mini-trial;
- dispute resolution panels;
- early neutral evaluation;
- expert determination;
- mediation–arbitration;
- amicable settlement.

The resolution of disputes by litigation, arbitration and adjudication are considered in Chapters 4.2, 4.3 and 4.4.

Certain forms of contract provide for a decision by the engineer or the contract administrator to be binding on the parties, either finally or until opened up and revised in litigation or arbitration proceedings. This form of dispute resolution, referred to as 'the engineer's decision' is not considered further in this section (see Chapter 4.1 – Administration of Claims).

The term 'alternative dispute resolution' has no precise meaning. It is sometimes used in the sense of an alternative to litigation. However, perhaps a more accurate definition of a process which falls within the meaning of alternative dispute resolution is one in which the procedure and outcome are 'interest' based rather than 'rights' based, and throughout the process the parties remain in control of the proceedings.

Until recently, arbitration was also viewed as an alternative form of dispute resolution. However, although in arbitration the parties still retain considerable control over the proceedings, in the UK and elsewhere arbitration is generally no longer considered as being within the meaning of an alternative dispute resolution process. In the USA arbitration was traditionally the main ADR process, and is still considered as being within the processes referred to as ADR.

In this chapter, alternative dispute resolution is referred to by the commonly used acronym 'ADR'. However, the 'A' in ADR may often be used elsewhere to mean 'amicable' or 'assisted' rather than 'alternative'.

With the exception of the first four types of process, the forms of dispute resolution identified in the introductory list above all fall to be properly considered within the generic title of ADR.

In the USA, formal procedures for the use of various forms of ADR in commercial disputes came to prominence in the late 1970s, primarily because of the cost and delay caused by litigation. The use of formal ADR for resolving commercial disputes in the UK has grown since the late 1980s, also principally due to the costs of litigation and of arbitration and the delays in both forms of proceedings.

The reforms to the civil justice system of England and Wales which came into effect on 26 April 1999 with the introduction of the Civil Procedure Rules 1998 (the CPR) gave a new impetus to ADR.

One of the features introduced to civil litigation by the CPR is that, before the court allocates the case to a particular 'track', each party is required to complete an allocation questionnaire in which the first question is whether the parties wish the action to be stayed to allow an attempt at settlement. Under the CPR Part 26.4(1) the attempt at settlement may be by ADR or by 'other means'.

Neither the form of ADR to be attempted nor the other means are defined in the CPR. However, the expressed intention is that the parties to a dispute are expected to endeavour to reach a compromise, and the court is given power to impose cost sanctions to penalize a party that makes no attempt to settle.

Unless the contract provides otherwise, for example an arbitration clause which would entitle a party to a stay under Section 9 of the Arbitration Act 1996, it remains the right of any legal entity in the English jurisdiction to bring an action in the courts. Many ADR processes, for example mediation, are ordinarily voluntary, non-binding, and conducted on a without prejudice basis. At the time of the first edition of the handbook it was not certain whether or not the higher Courts or the European Court would uphold cost sanctions against a party who refused to endeavour to resolve a dispute under a procedure defined in an ADR clause that would otherwise not be enforceable in the Courts.

The authors referred to the case of *Capolingua* v. *Phylum Pty Limited* (1991) 5 WAR 137, in the Supreme Court of Western Australia, as a possible indication of the approach that the English Courts might adopt in the use of their powers on costs, if parties did not enter into an ADR process in good faith.

In *Capolingua*, Ipp J. had been prepared to make a finding that, where it can be shown that a party to a mediation has adopted an obstructive and uncooperative attitude, and but for such conduct the issues for trial would have been reduced, the court may take into account the unnecessary extension of the period of the trial in deciding on the award of costs.

Guidelines as to the approach that the English Courts should adopt were eventually given by the Court of Appeal some five years after the introduction of the CPR, in *Halsey* v. *Milton Keynes NHS Trust* [2004] EWCA Civ 576. See also *England and Wales High Court (Supreme Court Cost Office Decisions)* [2004] EWHC 90. The Court used two 'test' cases to found some general and significant *dicta* as to the extent to which ADR could be ordered in ongoing litigation and the consequences of failure by one party to comply with an order for ADR in terms of costs at the end of the case.

In *Halsey* the Court of Appeal held that European jurisprudence meant that the Court could not order ADR as this would be infringing the parties' rights, but nevertheless the courts should continue to adopt a 'robust' attitude to directing ADR (in the test cases, it was mediation), since there was evident advantage to its use. The Court ruled that a party who refused to go to mediation should not automatically be penalised in costs if otherwise successful in the litigation. The burden of showing that it was unreasonable for a successful party who had refused or failed to go to mediation to have all their costs lay firmly on the person making the allegation.

The Court of Appeal then set out factors that may be relevant to the Court's consideration of whether a party has unreasonably refused ADR, which include, but are not limited to, the following:

(1) the nature of the dispute;
(2) the merits of the case;
(3) the extent to which other settlement methods have been attempted;

(4) whether the costs of the ADR would be disproportionately high;
(5) whether any delay in setting up and attending the ADR would have been prejudicial; and
(6) whether the ADR had a reasonable prospect of success.

The court emphasised that the list above was not exhaustive and that in many cases no single factor would be decisive.

Although the CPR expressly refer to ADR and other means of dispute resolution, certain courts had already recognized the benefit of exploring alternative means to resolve disputes. It has been the practice of the Commercial Court for some time to require parties to explore the use of ADR (see the Commercial Court Guide). Also, since the late 1980s certain official referees (now judges of the Technology and Construction Court ('TCC')) have made orders requiring parties to explore means of settling cases using ADR, particularly in complex multi-party disputes. The use of ADR is now expressly recognised and encouraged in the second edition of the TCC Guide which came into effect on 3 October 2005.

The evidence in the seven years since the introduction of the CPR is that many potential commercial litigants are concerned that the CPR give the Court virtually unfettered powers in respect of case management and that these powers not only often prevent the parties agreeing many procedural matters but also give the judge powers to override the wishes of the parties. One effect of the CPR has been a significant reduction in the number of cases going through the civil court system to in the region of 35%, or even less, of the number before the introduction of the CPR. There is no doubt that the increase in the use of ADR, almost exclusively mediation, has played a part in this reduction.

In addition to the CPR, another factor that has lead to an increase in the use of ADR is the view of many clients that arbitration has become too legalistic, and that even under the Arbitration Act 1996 it remains a costly and lengthy method of resolving disputes. However, there is now evidence of growing dissatisfaction with mediation as a form of dispute resolution, particularly in certain large complex disputes, where the costs of preparation for a mediation, which will ordinarily not be recoverable, are often viewed as being disproportionate to the perceived, or actual, benefits of using the process, particularly at an early stage in the court proceedings.

Nonetheless, the situation now is that any party to litigation who does not wish to proceed to mediation, or any other form of ADR, must have careful regard to the guidelines in *Halsey* above, otherwise there is a risk of being penalised in costs even if eventually successful in the litigation.

2 NEGOTIATED SETTLEMENTS

Negotiated settlements may be regarded as the least formal method of ADR; and importantly, it is the process over which the parties can exercise greatest control.

When a dispute arises, most parties will initially seek to resolve it by negotiation. Unfortunately, negotiations often fail because the parties do not pay sufficient attention to providing a formal structure to the negotiating process, or (more usually) the negotiators do not possess the necessary negotiating skills to conduct negotiations in a manner that enhances the prospects of a settlement.

In addition to being the process over which the parties have greatest control, constructive negotiations undertaken in a structured way can offer many other advantages in that they will usually be conducted by persons who have direct knowledge of the subject-matter of the dispute, the parties are free to determine the form of the negotiations, and costs are minimized.

If negotiations can be conducted in a constructive manner to achieve a settlement, this may have an additional benefit of allowing the parties to preserve and build on their existing commercial relationship.

However, the fact that the negotiators have knowledge of the subject matter of the dispute and may also have been directly involved in the dispute, can also be a significant disadvantage in achieving a settlement. If early negotiations do not result in a compromise, the dispute may become personalized or positions may become entrenched, and this may prevent further effective communication with the consequence that the dispute is referred to persons at a higher level in the organizations (or lawyers) who have no direct knowledge of the matters giving rise to the dispute.

A decision must be made at an early stage as to whether all or any part of the negotiations are to be conducted on a 'without prejudice' basis. Negotiations conducted on such a basis offer the parties an opportunity to explore proposals for settlement without prejudicing either party's position.

At the conclusion of each stage of any negotiations it is beneficial to record any matters that have been agreed in the form of heads of agreement which each of the parties then signs.

The TCC Pre-Action Protocol recognises the importance of negotiations at an early stage in a dispute and requires a face-to-face meeting between the parties before commencing proceedings. The second edition of the TCC Guide (at par. 7.2.2) states '[a]t this meeting, there should be sufficient time to discuss and resolve the dispute'. The guide also states that because of this opportunity, the court will not necessarily grant a stay of proceedings for ADR at a later stage at the request of the parties. Unfortunately this meeting is often regarded as nothing more than a formality required to satisfy the Pre-Action Protocol, rather than an opportunity to resolve the dispute.

3 MEDIATION

There is often confusion as to what is meant by the term 'mediation', as there are a variety of fundamentally different processes which are referred to as 'mediation'. In addition, the terms 'mediation' and 'conciliation' are often used interchangeably. Therefore, if the term 'mediation' is being used in a specific context, it is important that the parties both understand and agree to the nature of the ADR process that the term is being used to describe.

Mediation may be given a broad definition as a dispute resolution process in which a third party (the mediator) intervenes in the dispute with the consent of the parties, facilitates communication between them, and assists each party to understand the strengths and weaknesses of the respective cases, with the objective that the parties will reach agreement.

Ordinarily, the mediation process is voluntary, non-binding, and held on a without prejudice basis, the intention being that this will encourage the parties to be open and frank, and more willing to move from their previously stated positions and explore potential areas of agreement. In contrast to adjudication or expert determination, which both impose a decision on the parties, mediation allows the parties to settle their dispute by agreement.

It is important to distinguish between the non-binding nature of the process itself, which is voluntary and non-binding, and any agreement that may be reached. If the parties reach an agreement, then in the absence of express provisions to the contrary, such agreement will be binding on the parties and will be enforceable in the courts: see *Thakrav* v. *Ciro Citterio Menswear plc* [2002] EWHC 1975.

3.1 Principal forms of mediation

It is the nature of the mediator's role in the mediation process that determines the two principal types of mediation: either facilitative or evaluative. However, it is important to recognize that even within each of these broad types there may be further differences in the procedures adopted and in the role of the mediator.

3.2 The facilitative approach

In a mediation where a facilitative approach is used, ordinarily the mediator does not express a view as to the merits of the parties' cases or attempt to impose a solution. The mediator explores the parties' positions (often acting as 'devil's advocate'), clarifies the issues between the parties, identifies the parties' interests, acts as a communicator between the parties, explores areas of common interest, and generally endeavours to provide a background which enhances the parties' will to settle, and against which the parties can identify and agree how a compromise can be reached.

In the UK the term 'mediation' is usually given a narrow meaning and is associated almost exclusively with the facilitative approach. In construction and other commercial disputes in the UK, mediation using the facilitative approach has almost become synonymous with the term ADR. This has come about, not because facilitative mediation is necessarily the appropriate form of ADR for every dispute (which often in practice it is not), but because certain commercial organisations have promoted mediation heavily using non-technical mediators (mainly lawyers). There has also been a general unwillingness to explore other, often more suitable, forms of ADR, for example conciliation and dispute review boards (see below), even on major projects.

3.3 The evaluative approach

Where an evaluative approach is adopted for the mediation, the mediator will endeavour to evaluate the strengths and weaknesses of each party's case, and express a view. The intention of this approach is that once the parties know the mediator's view they will review and possibly change their respective positions, and as a consequence progress the resolution of the dispute.

Although in the UK the form of 'mediation' is almost exclusively the facilitative approach, in many 'technical' disputes the evaluative approach may have significant benefits, especially where expert evidence would normally be determinative of the issues, and the mediator is competent and experienced in the field in which the dispute has arisen (see Section 4.1 below on the ICE's Conciliation Procedure (1999)).

3.4 The mediation process

Once the parties have agreed to mediate their dispute, a mediator is appointed. Some contracts may already identify a mediator or an appointing organization. A location (preferably neutral) is then arranged at which to hold the mediation.

Prior to the mediation, each party submits a brief statement of its case to the mediator. The parties may, or may not, wish to have legal representation. However, for the mediation to be effective each party must have a person present with authority to settle the case.

There is no set procedure for mediation, although most organizations involved in ADR and the appointment of mediators have formal guidelines or protocols or codes of practice.

The mediation process normally begins with an 'open' joint session at which all parties are present, and during which the mediator makes an opening statement explaining the process and setting out the ground rules for the mediation. After the mediator has answered any questions which the parties may have, each party is then given an opportunity to explain its case to the mediator in the presence of the other party. A party's explanation will usually include a summary of its contentions, reference to the documents on which it relies, and a brief description of the evidence. Ordinarily there are no formal rules of evidence in a mediation.

After the joint opening session, the parties retire to separate rooms and the mediator then engages in a form of 'shuttle diplomacy' by holding a series of private meetings (sometimes referred to as 'caucuses') with each party in turn, during which the mediator will discuss the issues raised by the dispute and explore the strengths and weaknesses of the parties' respective cases. These private meetings are confidential and, unless expressly agreed by a party, no information provided to the mediator by that party will be conveyed to the other party. The mediator will identify the key issues and explore any common ground which may assist the parties to reach a settlement. The mediator will often act as 'devil's advocate' in the private sessions. If necessary, the mediator will assist each of the parties to formulate outline proposals for settlement. If authorized by a party, he or she will put its proposals to the other party. However, it should be noted that although the mediator will often assist the parties to formulate proposals for settlement, he or she does not determine the final nature and form of such proposals; these are matters solely for the respective parties.

If deemed appropriate by the mediator, or requested by the parties, further joint sessions may take place.

There are common features of a facilitative mediation and an evaluative mediation, particularly in the early stages. However, in an evaluative mediation the mediator will express a view on the merits to the parties in a joint session. The stage at which the mediator expresses such a view will vary, and the appropriate time at which to express a view requires the exercise of careful judgment on the part of the mediator, if the parties do not accept the mediator's initial evaluation, the mediator will endeavour to establish a 'range' within which settlement may be possible, and formulate outline proposals for consideration by the parties.

In both types of mediation, if the parties reach agreement on a way to resolve the dispute, the mediator should summarize the nature of the agreement that has been reached at a joint closing session. The extent of the mediator's participation after an agreement has been reached will depend on the procedures agreed or the wishes of the parties. Opinions differ as to whether the mediator should, or should not, assist the parties to set down the agreement in writing. Depending on the procedure adopted, the mediator's involvement usually ends either after agreement has been reached or after the parties have been assisted to draw up the agreement.

3.5 The final agreement

It is essential to achieve certainty in respect of any agreement reached at the end of any ADR process involving 'negotiation'. For the avoidance of doubt, the parties should expressly agree in advance that any agreement reached at the conclusion of the (nonbinding) process is to be binding. After the conclusion of the mediation, the parties should draw up and sign a document setting out all the matters on which agreement has been reached.

If the parties conclude an agreement, such agreement will be binding on the parties and enforceable at law: see *Thakrav* v. *Ciro Citterio Menswear plc* above.

Contrary to some views, the mediator is not a party to, and should not sign, what is in effect the parties' agreement.

In complex disputes it may not be possible to set down the full terms of the agreement in writing immediately after the mediation. This may create difficulties for the parties' representatives in trying to set out an agreement with sufficient certainty. For example, if the parties' concluded agreement consists only of 'heads of agreement', and the parties require an enforceable agreement, it will be necessary to ensure that there is in law a concluded agreement, not merely an 'agreement to agree' which would not be enforceable (see Chapter 3.1, Law of Contract).

If court proceedings have commenced, the final agreement is often drawn up in the form of a 'Tomlin' order comprising the order to be made by the court with the parties' consent and a schedule incorporated into the order setting out the matters agreed which form the basis on which the proceedings will be stayed.

If the ADR has been concluded during arbitration proceedings, the agreement may be incorporated into a consent award. In such circumstances the parties should also include a provision in the consent award conferring power on the arbitrator to make the award as, strictly speaking, after conclusion of an agreement there is no dispute in existence, and the arbitrator will be *functus officio*.

An alternative method of achieving an enforceable agreement is for the parties to agree that the agreement reached shall be deemed to have the same effect as an award to which the Arbitration Act 1996 applies. If it became necessary, a party could then enforce the award in the courts under Section 66 of the Arbitration Act 1996.

In the context of an international dispute, having an agreement in the form of an arbitral award will allow it to be enforced in any state that is a signatory to the Convention on the Recognition and Enforcement of Foreign Arbitral Awards adopted by the United Nations Conference on International Arbitration on 10 June 1958, usually referred to as 'the New York Convention'.

If agreement is not reached in a mediation, the mediation ordinarily will end. However, in certain ADR processes which commence with a mediation, the parties agree that if agreement is not reached at the end of the mediation stage, the process can progress to the next stage. For example, the parties may wish to change a facilitative mediation to that of an evaluative mediation, or to arbitration proceedings (see mediation-arbitration below); or the parties may request the mediator to provide a written opinion as to how the dispute may be resolved (cf. the ICE Conciliation Procedure (1999) in Section 4.1 of this chapter).

4 CONCILIATION

In the preceding section on mediation, reference was made to the importance of ascertaining the nature of the process that is being described. Similar care must be taken with any process described as 'conciliation'. Not only are the terms 'mediation' and 'conciliation' used interchangeably, but there are also a variety of fundamentally different processes which are referred to as 'conciliation'.

The ADR processes referred to as 'conciliation' range from what should properly be called facilitative mediation, through evaluative mediation to adjudicative procedures for dispute resolution. Therefore, as in the case of mediation, it is important for the parties to understand, and agree, the nature of any ADR process that is being referred to as 'conciliation'.

In this text, conciliation is used in the sense of an ADR process that involves referring the dispute to a third party who facilitates settlement by (if necessary) expressing an opinion, but who is not acting in an adjudicative capacity. The process remains consensual, and either party remains free to accept or reject the opinion of the third party.

The conciliator's primary role is to assist in the negotiations between the parties with the aim of achieving a settlement. The conciliation process is conducted on a confidential and without prejudice basis, and at the initial stages there are superficial similarities between the third party's role as conciliator and the mediator's role in a facilitative mediation. However, certain of the formal procedures for conciliation are significantly different from facilitative mediation.

Formal procedural rules for conciliation often give wide powers to the conciliator that would not ordinarily be available to a mediator. For example, certain rules confer a power that allows the conciliator to act as arbitrator if agreement is not reached during the initial stages of the process, or the rules may place an obligation on the conciliator to give a recommendation on a solution to the dispute if the parties do not reach an agreement. In the context of engineering contracts, probably the most commonly used formal conciliation procedures are the ICE Conciliation Procedures, and, in international projects, the ICC Conciliation Procedures.

4.1 The ICE's Conciliation Procedure (1999)

The first edition of the Institution of Civil Engineers' Conciliation Procedure was published in 1988 and was intended for use with the ICE Conditions of Contact for Minor Works. The 1999 edition of the ICE's Conciliation Procedure is incorporated into the following ICE standard form contracts: the ICE Conditions of Contract 6th and 7th Editions (ICE 7th); the ICE Design and Construction Contract; the ICE Minor Works Contract 2nd Edition, and the ICE Conditions of Contract for Ground Investigation. The procedure is also incorporated into the standard form subcontracts published by the Civil Engineering Contractors Association that complement the main contract forms above.

The principal aim of the ICE Conciliation Procedure is to achieve settlement of a dispute by agreement, in order to avoid referring it to arbitration. The procedure may, of course, be adopted by agreement even in the absence of incorporation of any ICE Conditions.

Under clause 66A(2)(a) of the ICE 7th, the conciliation process may be commenced at any time by one party to the contract giving written notice to the other party requesting agreement that a dispute be referred to a conciliator. The conciliator may already be named in the contract. If not, the parties are required to agree a conciliator within 21 days of such notice. In default of agreement, the appointment is to be made by the President of the Institution Civil Engineers.

The conciliator's powers include, under rule 4.5 of the ICE Conciliation Procedure, powers to issue instructions that the conciliator considers appropriate, to make requests for the production of documents by any party, or require the attendance of persons whom the conciliator considers could assist in any way.

If an agreement is reached, and if requested by all the parties, the conciliator will assist the parties to set out the agreement in writing.

The ICE 7th provides, under clause 66B(2)(b), that any recommendation or proposal of the conciliator shall only be binding on both parties if incorporated into a written agreement which is signed by both parties.

Under rule 4.10 of the ICE Conciliation Procedure, if all the parties so request in writing, the conciliator may be appointed as an arbitrator, and in this role is given an express power limited to issuing a consent award. If a consent award is made, the settlement agreement becomes enforceable as an arbitral award.

The ICE Conciliation Procedure includes a provision that in certain circumstances the conciliator shall make a 'recommendation'. Under the procedure, the conciliator is obliged to make a recommendation if an agreement is not achieved, or if in the conciliator's opinion the parties are unlikely to settle, or if a party fails to comply with an instruction of the conciliator, or if a recommendation is requested by a party.

Rule 5.2 of the ICE Conciliation Procedure defines the nature and scope of the conciliator's recommendation which is to be his or her opinion as to the way in which the dispute referred for conciliation may be resolved. The scheme of the rules of the ICE Conciliation Procedure is such that the conciliator's opinion does not require to be based on any principles of contract, law or equity.

It is important to note that if a reference to conciliation is made following an engineer's decision under one of the earlier ICE forms of contract prior to the ICE 7th Edition incorporating amendment ICE/Clause-66 July 2004 (see Section 10.1 below), then the provisions of rule 5.2 of the ICE Conciliation Procedures are such that they permit the parties and the conciliator to consider options for resolving the dispute that would not have been available to the engineer. Although not expressly stated in the rules of the ICE Conciliation Procedure, the conciliator may, in effect, act in the capacity of an *amiable compositeur*. If the conciliator acts in this way, this may have a significant effect if the subject of the dispute is eventually referred to arbitration. For example, the arbitrator will be required to apply the contractual provisions and therefore may not be able to award the relief contained in the conciliator's recommendation.

The reference of a dispute to conciliation is now provided as merely part of the 'amicable dispute resolution' provisions in the ICE 7th Edition, and unlike the position under clause 66 in earlier forms of the ICE contract, is no longer a formal 'stage', within the normal meaning, in the dispute resolution procedures (see further under Section 10.1 below).

Rule 6.1 of the ICE Conciliation Procedure prohibits any party to the conciliation calling the conciliator as a witness in any subsequent adjudication, litigation or arbitration concerning the subject matter of the conciliation.

4.2 The ICC Rules of Conciliation

The preamble to the ICC Rules of Optional Conciliation (the ICC Rules) recognizes that settlement of international business disputes is desirable, and states that the object of the rules is to facilitate the amicable settlement of business disputes of an international character.

Under Article 2 of the ICC Rules, a party wishing to commence the conciliation process applies to the Secretariat of the Court of the ICC setting out 'succinctly' the purpose of the request and encloses the appropriate fee to open the file. The provisions of Article 3 require the Secretariat to inform the other party as soon as possible; and after being informed, the other party is given 15 days to inform the Secretariat whether or not it agrees to participate in the conciliation process.

4.1 Administration of claims
4.2 Litigation
4.3 Arbitration
4.4 Adjudication
4.5 Alternative dispute resolution

If the other party agrees to conciliation, the Secretary General of the Court appoints a single conciliator. Article 5 of the ICC Rules grants the conciliator wide powers to conduct the conciliation as he or she thinks fit, guided only by the principles of impartiality, equity and justice. The conciliator may request the parties to provide any further information which he or she deems necessary.

Article 6 of the ICC Rules provides expressly that the conciliation process is confidential.

Article 7 of the ICC Rules sets out three circumstances that will bring the conciliation process to an end:

(a) the parties sign an agreement;
(b) the conciliator produces a report that the conciliation has failed (reasons are not required);
(c) one of the parties gives notice to the conciliator that it no longer intends to participate in the process.

Article 7(a) of the ICC Rules provides that the parties are bound by the signed agreement which, except to the extent to which disclosure is necessary to carry it into effect, is confidential.

Under Article 8 of the ICC Rules, the conciliator is required to provide the Secretariat of the Court with the settlement agreement signed by the parties, or with a report that the conciliation failed, or a notice from a party that it no longer intends to participate.

Article 10 of the ICC Rules provides that unless the parties agree otherwise, the conciliator cannot act in any subsequent arbitration or judicial proceedings whether as arbitrator or a representative of a party. As in the rules of the ICE Conciliation Procedure above, no party may call the conciliator as a witness in any subsequent proceedings concerning the subject matter of the conciliation, except by agreement of the parties.

Under Article 11 of the ICC Rules, the parties agree that in any subsequent proceedings they will not seek to advance any view expressed by a party during the conciliation process, or any proposal put forward by the conciliator, or refer to any party's readiness to accept a settlement proposal suggested by the conciliator.

5 MINI-TRIAL

This process was first given formal recognition in the US in the late 1970s in commercial disputes. Although the process is generally referred to as a 'mini-trial', it is ordinarily intended to be a process involving a structured negotiation of a settlement, and is not a trial within the normal meaning of the word. The mini-trial process is also given other names including 'executive tribunal', 'supervised settlement' or 'modified settlement conference'.

The process begins with each party presenting its case to a tribunal consisting of a senior executive with authority to settle from each party, and often (but not always) a 'neutral', sometimes referred to as a 'neutral adviser'. The presentations of the respective cases may be made by the employees of the parties involved in the dispute, or other non-legal employees (generally not above middle management level), or the parties' legal representatives.

After the parties have presented their respective cases, the senior executives meet together privately and endeavour to negotiate a settlement. The role of the neutral varies. The neutral may act merely as chairperson, or may assist the executives on technical or legal matters, or may express a view on the likely outcome if the dispute were to proceed further to litigation or arbitration.

The mini-trial process is flexible, and the manner and scope of the presentation and the constitution of the panel may be tailored to match the nature of the dispute. The intention of the process is to have a short hearing to focus on the issues in dispute, followed by negotiation by senior management with a view to settling the dispute. At the hearing stage, this focus on the issues is likely to be lost, and the achievement of a settlement prejudiced, if the process is allowed to develop into a process akin to a full trial with the calling of witnesses of fact, experts, and full legal submissions.

Several organizations publish procedural rules for mini-trials. For example, the Chartered Institute of Arbitrators has provided guidelines for mini-trials since 1990 in its publication *The Chartered Institute of Arbitrators: guidelines for supervised settlement procedure*.

6 DISPUTE RESOLUTION PANELS

The use of dispute resolution panels, often referred to as dispute resolution (or review) boards (DRBs), has grown in the 1990s, particularly on large-scale and international projects. Funders of major projects, such as the World Bank, may often require contracts to provide for the setting up of a dispute resolution panel and for the resolution of disputes during the project by this process.

In this ADR process, disputes are submitted to a tribunal consisting of three (or sometimes five) experts for a decision. The experts are chosen from disciplines that are likely to be appropriate, taking into account the nature of the project. The experts may be all 'neutrals', and named in the contract documents. Alternatively, the panel may be appointed after the contract has been awarded but before any dispute has arisen, in which case the tribunal usually comprises one (or possibly more) representative from each party and a third 'neutral' member either agreed by the parties or appointed by a nominating body.

In complex projects there may be several panels with each panel constituted to deal with disputes arising in a particular discipline or even at a particular stage of the project. For example, in the early stages of construction of a power station disputes may arise over the civil works, requiring experts in the field of civil engineering, whereas in the later stages where the work involves the incorporation of mechanical or electrical plant, mechanical or electrical engineers may be more appropriate to sit on the panel. The total number of experts appointed to the panel often exceeds the number of persons who sit on the tribunal at any one time, to allow for non-availability of members from time to time.

Generally, a dispute resolution panel will be constituted at, or even before, the commencement of a project on the basis that the process is most effective if the panel members are provided with full details of the project at the time of their appointment, and are kept fully informed periodically of progress and other relevant matters during the course of construction. If a dispute arises, the panel members then have the background knowledge of the matters which have given rise to the dispute to assist them in making a decision.

The status of the decision or recommendation of a dispute resolution panel varies. In certain contracts the panel's decision may only be advisory or it may provide a nonbinding decision for acceptance by the parties. More usually, the panel will provide a decision that will be binding on the parties for a defined period, usually until revised in further proceedings. If the decision is to be binding on the parties, whether finally or until reviewed in subsequent proceedings, the contractual provisions may require the panel members to reach a unanimous view.

6.1 The Dispute Adjudication Board under The Fédération Internationale des Ingénieurs-Conseils (FIDIC) Conditions of Contract 4th Edition

In the traditional standard form engineering contracts, for example the Conditions of Contract published by the ICE and FIDIC respectively, the engineer was given authority to provide a decision in the event of a dispute arising between the employer and contractor. Indeed, previously under the provisions of certain standard form engineering contracts, a decision by the engineer was in effect a condition precedent to a dispute coming into existence, see for example *Monmouthshire County Council* v. *Costelloe & Kemple Limited* (1965) 5 BLR 83 (CA), a case which concern an Engineer's decision under the ICE 4th Edition.

However, this decision-making role of the engineer can affect the perception of his or her neutrality if either the employer or the contractor disagrees with the engineer's decision. The decision-making process by itself often leads to disputes. In order to avoid this potential difficulty for the engineer, one method adopted in certain contracts, particularly in the international context, is the incorporation of a clause requiring disputes to be referred to a dispute resolution board for a decision, not to the engineer.

The supplement dated 1996 to the FIDIC Conditions of Contract 4th Edition 1987 (FIDIC 4th), includes (optional) amendments to clause 67 which deal with the settlement of disputes. The amendments contain express provisions for incorporation into FIDIC 4th, if the contract is intended to have a dispute resolution panel as the decision-maker in place of the engineer.

Amended clause 67.1 of FIDIC 4th provides that if a dispute arises during the course of the works, a party must refer any disputes to a board, described as the Dispute Adjudication Board (DAB), for a decision. The number of members of the DAB is either one or three, and must be stated in the appendix to tender.

The supplement also contains guidance notes on the amendments of clause 67 of F1DIC 4th, and model terms of appointment and 'Procedural Rules' for DABs of one and three members respectively. However, there appears to be a lacuna in the supplement in that the amendments to clause 67 do not include any term expressly incorporating the Procedural Rules.

An oblique link to the Procedural Rules is contained in the provisions of amended clause 67.1(a) of FIDIC 4th. This clause expressly incorporates 'the model terms' (of appointment) referred to in clause 3(e), and the model terms refer in turn to the Procedural Rules but notably only in the context that a DAB member shall not give 'advice' to the parties or the engineer other than in accordance with the Procedural Rules. However, it is submitted that the DAB's powers under amended clause 67.2 mean that the ambit of the DAB's role extends far beyond the giving of 'advice'.

Under rule 5 of the Procedural Rules a DAB member is prohibited during a hearing from expressing an opinion on the merits of any argument advanced by the parties.

The DAB is obliged to give its decision in writing, and rule 6 requires the members of a DAB to endeavour to reach a unanimous decision. However, if the DAB members are unable to reach a unanimous decision, the decision shall be by a majority and in such circumstances the minority member may provide a report to the contractor, the employer and the engineer.

6.2 The Dispute Adjudication Board under FIDIC Conditions of Contract for Construction 1st Edition 1999

The FIDIC Conditions of Contract for Construction 1st Edition 1999 (FIDIC 99) incorporate provisions under clause 20.2 for adjudication of disputes by a DAB. FIDIC 99 also includes an appendix containing 'General Conditions of Dispute Adjudication Agreement' and an annexe setting out 'Procedural Rules' for the DAB.

Clause 20.4 of FIDIC 99 incorporates by reference the General Conditions of the Dispute Adjudication Agreement and any agreed amendments. The extent to which the Procedural Rules apply to the DAB in FIDIC 99 are not limited to 'advice' as in the supplement to the FIDIC 4th. Clause 4(e) of the General Conditions of the Dispute Adjudication Agreement states that members of the DAB are obliged to comply with the Procedural Rules and with clause 20.4 of FIDIC 99 which deals with obtaining a decision of the DAB.

Rule 9 is similar to rule 5 of the earlier Procedural Rules in relation to FIDIC 4th, and no member of the DAB may express an opinion during a hearing on the merits of any argument. Rule 9(b) contains similar provisions in respect of a unanimous decision, except that under FIDIC 99 the majority of members may require the minority member to prepare a written report to the contractor, the employer and the engineer.

7 EARLY NEUTRAL EVALUATION

This procedure is designed to provide the parties with an independent assessment of the dispute, or of particular issues giving rise to the dispute, by a 'neutral' who is usually a judge (or lawyer) or arbitrator, or expert in a discipline relevant to the nature of the dispute.

Each party presents its case to the neutral third party who provides a non-binding evaluation of the likely outcome if the matter were to proceed to court or arbitration.

The Commercial Court and the TCC both recognize the possible benefit of early neutral evaluation, and provide a formal facility within the jurisdiction of the Court for early neutral evaluation by a judge of the Commercial Court or the TCC, as the case may be. The process is ordinarily conducted on a without prejudice basis and is non-binding (see the *Commercial Court Guide: Section G2* and *TCC Guide Section 7.5*).

If a judge of the Commercial Court or TCC is of the view that early neutral evaluation is likely to assist in the resolution of the dispute, he may offer to provide the evaluation or arrange for another judge to provide it. If the parties agree to an early neutral evaluation of the case, the judge undertaking the evaluation will give directions as to the form of evaluation that he considers appropriate, and the preparatory steps which the parties are to take.

Unless the parties agree otherwise, the judge providing the early neutral evaluation will take no further part in the case either during the interlocutory stage or at trial.

In circumstances where an expert gives an evaluation concerning 'technical' matters, the process is often referred to as 'early expert determination'.

8 EXPERT DETERMINATION

Expert determination is used primarily in disputes of a 'technical' nature which require what is, in effect, an 'opinion' on a specific issue or issues. The parties agree that a third party, who is of a relevant discipline and is independent of both parties, should be appointed to give a decision on a specific issue or determine a particular dispute. The expert is required to use his or her own skills and expertise and to make the necessary enquiries or conduct their own investigations. The parties will usually have an opportunity to make submissions to the expert. The process ordinarily provides a fast and final solution to the matters in dispute and has been used successfully for many years in property disputes concerning valuations.

It is important to note that expert determination, unlike an arbitral award, may only be challenged in certain limited circumstances of fraud or collusion, or where the expert has departed from their instructions. Otherwise, the expert's determination will be final and binding on the parties. See, for example, *Dixons Group plc* v. *Jan Andrew Murray-Oboynski* (1998) 86 BLR 16.

In view of the limited grounds on which an expert's determination may be challenged, instructions to an expert must be drafted with particular care in order to set out the expert's duties and obligations fully and precisely, and to make it clear that the person instructed is intended to act in the capacity of an expert.

In the absence of the parties' agreement otherwise, the expert does not enjoy the immunity from suit of a judge or arbitrator, and may be the subject of an action by either party if he or she acts negligently.

9 MEDIATION–ARBITRATION

Mediation–arbitration (sometimes abbreviated to 'med–arb') is in effect a two-stage dispute resolution process that commences with mediation. If no agreement is reached, the role of the neutral third party changes from mediator to that of arbitrator, and the dispute resolution process continues as an arbitration or other form of adjudicative process in which the third party gives a decision.

One of the advantages given for mediation–arbitration is that at the first stage the parties have an opportunity to reach agreement by mediation but, if that fails, the mediator is familiar with the subject of the dispute, and therefore there is a saving in costs by then appointing the mediator as arbitrator.

However, the change in the role of the third party from mediator to that of arbitrator may give rise to difficulties. In the role of mediator, the third party would ordinarily be privy to information provided by the parties on a confidential basis. If a party is reluctant to disclose information at the mediation stage because it knows that the mediator may act in the subsequent stage as an arbitrator, this may inhibit the mediation process and prevent agreement being reached. In addition, if a party provides the mediator with information that is prejudicial to that party's case, the mediator is then required to act in an independent and impartial role as an arbitrator required to decide the proceedings judicially.

Although certain statutory provisions and procedural rules provide expressly for mediation–arbitration (see, for example, Section 27 of the Commercial Arbitration Act 1984 (New South Wales) and Article 10 of the ICC Rules), opinions vary as to whether mediation–arbitration is an appropriate form of ADR in any circumstances because of the change in the role of the person initially appointed as mediator.

In England and Wales, any mediation–arbitration process needs to satisfy the requirements of both the common law and the Arbitration Act 1996. In the USA, the process has been modified by appointing different people as the mediator and subsequent arbitrator, in order to avoid the difficulties that arise with using the same person. It is submitted that this modified approach negates most of the advantages that are normally advanced in support of the mediation–arbitration process.

10 'STAGED' DISPUTE RESOLUTION PROVISIONS

The growth in the scale and complexity of projects has resulted in many construction contracts containing 'staged' (or stepped) provisions for dispute resolution. The intention is generally to resolve the dispute speedily and at the earliest opportunity by having an appropriate procedure in place at each stage in order to settle the dispute at that stage without the need to raise the dispute to a higher level; the final stage being an adjudicative procedure which results in a final and binding decision but which is used only if the parties fail to settle the dispute at one of the earlier stages. By resolving the dispute at the earliest opportunity, ongoing 'grumbling' disputes are avoided, and if the process is successful the parties will also avoid subsequent lengthy and costly litigation or arbitration.

Traditionally, at an early stage in any staged dispute resolution provisions, the procedure seeks to avoid formal proceedings, for example by using negotiations or by an Engineer's decision. However, the statutory right to adjudication 'at any time' under Section 108(2)(a) of the Housing Grants, Construction and Regeneration Act 1996, and the need for contractual provisions which comply with the statutory provisions, has had a significant effect on the extent to which staged provisions could be enforced, if at all.

One casualty in the aftermath of the introduction of the HGCRA 1996 has been the staged dispute resolution provisions in the various editions of the ICE conditions. In 2004 the dispute resolution provisions in the ICE 7th Edition were necessarily amended to provide contractual procedures that were in line with the statutory requirements for a right adjudication at any time.

The amended dispute resolution procedures of the ICE 7th Edition and other innovative 'ad hoc' provisions for dispute avoidance or resolution are considered below.

10.1 The dispute resolution procedures in the ICE 7th Edition

Clause 66 of the ICE 7th Edition is entitled 'Avoidance and settlement of disputes'. The current clause 66 is the result of a significant amendment (reference ICE/Clause-66 July 2004) to clause 66 in the original ICE 7th Edition. The previous clause 66 has been deleted and replaced with new clauses 66, 66A, 66B, 66C and 66D.

Clause 66 states the intention that the procedures are intended to facilitate clear definition of disputes and early resolution. Traditionally, the ICE Conditions had staged procedures, where the starting point was an Engineer's decision. The amended provisions for dispute resolution in clauses 66, 66A and 66B of the ICE 7th Edition have been drafted in the light of the statutory provisions for adjudication in the HGCRA 1996 and recent case law. The amendments have necessarily abandon the previous 'step-by-step' approach the original ICE 7th Edition, and allow the parties to use the various procedures that are available in any order that they wish. The principal differences introduced into the ICE 7th Edition by the 2004 amendments are that the the dispute resolution provisions comply with the statutory requirements and do not require any reference back to the Engincer for a decision and a new dispute avoidance provision has been introduced.

The background to the amendment of clause 66 is important.

Often a party will contend that no dispute exists in order to resist either the adjudication or arbitration process. It is therefore important to know when, in law, a 'dispute' exists. The ICE 7th Edition, as in earlier editions of the ICE Conditions, seeks to define precisely the time at which a dispute will exist (or be deemed to exist) and to avoid the question which often arises as to whether or not there is a 'dispute'. See, for example, *Monmouthshire County Council* v. *Costelloe & Kemple Limited* above, in which the Court of Appeal considered the meaning of the words 'dispute or difference' under clause 66 of the ICE

Conditions of Contract 4th Edition, and held that a letter from the contractor to the engineer merely requesting comments on a claim was not a reference to the engineer, and a 'dispute or difference' only came into existence when the engineer formally rejected the claim.

The decision in *Monmouthshire County Council* v. *Costelloe & Kemple Limited* as to when a 'dispute' exists must, however, now be seen in the context of the statutory provisions for adjudication provided for in the Housing Grants, Construction and Regeneration Act 1996 (HGCRA 1996) and more recent case law concerning the ICE provision for dispute resolution in the ICE 6th Edition.

In respect of differences arising between the parties, the now superseded clause 66(2) of the original unamended version of the ICE 7th Edition sought at the first stage of dispute resolution, to avoid adversarial language, and referred not to 'disputes or differences' between the parties, but to 'matters of dissatisfaction' which might arise between the contractor and the engineer's representative or between the employer and the contractor. 'Matters of dissatisfaction' were to be referred to the Engineer who was required to notify the parties of his or her decision in writing within one month.

The matters which were stated as giving rise to 'dissatisfaction' included not only decisions, opinions, instructions, directions, certificates and valuations but also 'any other matter arising under or in connection with the Contract or the carrying out of the Works'.

However, the term 'matter of dissatisfaction', as used in the now superseded clause 66(2) of the unamended ICE 7th Edition was contrived. The intended purpose of the term was to prevent a 'dispute' arising until after the matter of dissatisfaction has been referred to the Engineer and a decision had been given. The intention of the ICE 7th Edition was (and in the amended version is) also that the contractual provisions for adjudication should apply, not the statutory provisions. In the first edition of this handbook the authors expressed the view that, although there was no decided case on the point, the purpose above might no longer be achieved because of the effect of the statutory provisions in Section 108 of HGCRA 1996, which give a party to a construction contract a right to give notice 'at any time' of its intention to refer a dispute to adjudication. Therefore, it followed that if any 'matter of dissatisfaction' fell within the meaning of 'dispute' (which in Section 108 of HGCRA 1996 also includes 'any difference'), then such a matter could be referred to adjudication without prior reference to the Engineer for a decision, thereby defeating the intended purpose of clause 66(2).

Although there was no decided case which considered the operation of the original clause 66(2), in *John Mowlem & Co. plc* v. *Hydra Tight & Co. plc* [2001] 17 CLJ 358 the court was required to consider a similar provision and the decision provides some guidance as to how the court was likely to view the operation of the now superseded clause 66(2). In *John Mowlem & Co. plc* v. *Hydra Tight & Co. plc* a sub-contract incorporated the provisions of NEC (Option A) Y(U.K.)2 with amendments, which provided for service of a 'Notification of Dissatisfaction', the expressed purpose of which was to delay adjudication for four weeks to allow the parties an opportunity to meet and resolve their difference. The clause also provided that the parties had agreed that in the period above a dispute shall not have arisen and therefore there was no matter that could be referred to arbitration.

Section 108(5) of the statutory Scheme provides that if contractual provisions for adjudication do not comply with Sections 108(1)–(4) inclusive, the adjudication provisions under the statutory Scheme shall apply to the contract. In the *John Mowlem & Co. plc* v. *Hydra Tight & Co. plc*, HHJ Toulmin CMG QC adopted the parties' agreement that insofar as the subcontract required a notice of dissatisfaction to be served before a dispute was deemed to have arisen, it contravened Section 108 of HGCRA 1996, which gives a party an unfettered right to given notice 'at any time' of its intention to refer a dispute to adjudication.

In the original ICE 7th Edition, the now superseded clauses 66(2) and 66(3) taken together, also sought to restrict the meaning of 'dispute' and, required one or more of the condition precedents set out in clause 66(3), all requiring an Engineer's decision, to be satisfied before there was a dispute. These provisions also did not comply with the statutory requirements.

Accordingly, notwithstanding the intention to have staged dispute resolution provisions in an endeavour to resolve disputes at the lowest possible stage, the now superseded clauses 66(2) and 66(3) in the ICE 7th Edition contravened the statutory provisions in Section 108 of the HGCRA 1996 and were unenforceable, at least in circumstances where a party wished to exercise its right to adjudication before there had been an Engineer's decision. However, a party has the option of whether to refer a dispute to adjudication or not. In circumstances where a party did not wish to refer a dispute to adjudication (rare in the current litigious climate), the referral of a 'matter of dissatisfaction' arguably remained the starting point for the contractual provisions for dispute resolution. In the event, the ICE decided to re-draft the dispute resolution provisions to comply fully with the statutory provisions.

The dispute resolution provisions in the amended clause 66 in the ICE 7th Edition are, in effect, no longer staged and include the following:

(1) 'advance warning' (clause 66(2);
(2) notice of a dispute (clause 66A(1));
(3) 'amicable dispute resolution' (clause 66A(2));
(4) adjudication (clause 66B);
(5) arbitration (clause 66C); and
(6) appointments (clause 66D).

Each of these clauses is considered further below.

Clause 66(2): 'advance warning'. Once a party become aware of 'any matter which if not resolved might become a dispute', it is required to give a warning in writing to the other party, with a copy to the Engineer. The parties are required to meet within seven days to try to resolve the matter. If the matter is not resolved 'within a reasonable period', the parties are required to define those parts of the matter that remain unresolved. Although expressed in mandatory language, the provision is, in effect, consensual.

Clause 66A: 'Notice of Dispute'. This clause sets out a mechanism for defining when a dispute comes into existence by the service of a 'Notice of Dispute' stating the nature of the 'dispute or difference'. The notice is intended to provide a clear starting point for any further action. Clause 66A(1) expressly provides that a party may not serve the notice unless and until any steps required by procedures available elsewhere in the contract have been taken. Clauses in the ICE 7th Edition that require particular steps to be taken include clause 12 (adverse physical conditions and artificial obstructions) and clause 44 (extension of time).

The question of when a dispute has come into existence continues to exercise the courts. In AMEC *Civil Engineering Limited* v. *Secretary of State for Transport* the Court of Appeal was principally concerned with the question of whether the Engineer was in breach of the rules of natural justice in giving his decision, in the absence of representations by one of the parties. However, the question of whether a dispute had arisen within the meaning in clause 66 of the ICE 6th Edition was also considered. The material facts in the *AMEC* case are summarised below.

The contract works were remedial works to the Thelwall Viaduct on the M6; including the replacement of an existing reinforced concrete deck and provision of new bridge roller bearings. The contractor was AMEC Civil Engineering Limited ('AMEC') and the Employer was the Secretary of State for Transport. The works had been certified as being substantially complete on 23 December 1996.

In June 2002 substantial structural defects were noticed. An initial investigation was undertaken and report was prepared which identified cracks and the failure of a bearing at one pier identified. On 29 July 2002 the Highways Agency (as agents of the Employer) informed AMEC of the problems with the roller bearing. Further investigations were undertaken and various meetings took place, which included a meeting held on 19 September 2002, at which AMEC stated that it did not accept responsibility for the defects. On 6 December 2002 the Highways Agency sent AMEC a formal letter of claim. On 10 December 2002 AMEC replied in non-committal terms saying it was not in a position to comment on liability. On 11 December 2002 the Highways Agency referred the 'dispute' to the Engineer, relying on its letter of 6 December 2002, saying that AMEC had not acknowledged responsibility. Significantly, no copy of the letter requesting the Engineer's decision was sent to AMEC. On 18 December 2002, the Engineer gave his decision under clause 66, including a short description of the defects then known to exist. On 19 December 2002, the Treasury Solicitor (on behalf of the Employer) sent a fax to AMEC, seeking confirmation that AMEC accepted the Engineer's decision, and saying that otherwise it would regard AMEC as dissatisfied with the decision. At end of the afternoon on 16 December 2002, the Treasury Solicitor served a notice of arbitration on AMEC, referring to the Highway Agency's letter of 6 December 2002. The limitation period arguably expired on 23 December 2002 (6 years from date on which substantial completion had been certified).

After the arbitrator had given his decision, AMEC appealed to the court on, among others, the ground that there had been no dispute which was capable of being referred to the arbitrator. Jackson J dismissed the appeal and AMEC appealed to the Court of Appeal, which also dismissed the appeal.

The Court of Appeal accepted, as 'broadly correct', seven propositions in the judgment of Jackson J at first instance as to the law on whether a dispute had arisen. The propositions may be summarised as follows:

(1) The word 'dispute' should be given its normal meaning. It does not have some special or unusual meaning conferred upon it by lawyers.
(2) Litigation has not generated any hard-edged legal rules as to what is or is not a dispute. The judicial decisions provide helpful guidance.
(3) The mere fact that one party notifies the other party of a claim does not automatically and immediately give rise to a dispute. A dispute does not arise unless and until it emerges that the claim is not admitted.
(4) The circumstances from which it may emerge that a claim is not admitted are 'Protean'; for example, express rejection; discussions from which objectively it is to be inferred that the claim is not admitted; the respondent may prevaricate, giving rise to the inference that it does not admit the claim; the respondent may simply remain silent for a period of time, giving rise to the same inference.
(5) The period of time for which a respondent may remain silent before a dispute is to be inferred depends upon the facts of the case and the contractual structure. If the

gist of the claim is well known and it is obviously controversial, a very short period of silence may suffice to give rise to this inference. If the claim is notified to an agent of the respondent, who has a legal duty to consider the claim independently and then give a considered response, a longer period of time may be required.

(6) If a claimant imposes a deadline for responding, that will not have the automatic effect of curtailing what would otherwise be a reasonable time for respond. However, a stated deadline and the reasons for its imposition may be relevant factors when the court comes to consider what constitutes a reasonable time for responding.

(7) If the claim is vague and ill-defined such that the respondent cannot sensibly respond, neither silence nor even an express non-admission is likely to give rise to a dispute for the purposes of arbitration or adjudication.

However, in the Court of Appeal, May LJ went further and was prepared to accept that in all the circumstances of the case, including the imminence of the end of the statutory limitation period, there was a dispute or difference capable of being referred to the Engineer under clause 66 at any time after the meeting held on 19 September 2002, when AMEC had indicated orally that it did not accept responsibility.

Following the decision in *AMEC* the narrow, but very clear, approach to defining a 'dispute' in the contractual dispute resolution procedure of the ICE Conditions as, for example, in the *Monmouthshire County Council* case above, has been eroded. In the majority of cases, there are often ongoing discussions in relation to matters that may subsequently lead to a full-blown dispute. However, if the wider approach at first instance and the Court of Appeal, in particular the comment of May LJ above that a mere oral rejection of responsibility may be sufficient to create a dispute, is widely adopted by the courts, in many projects it may be difficult for the parties to say with any precision whether a dispute has come into existence or not. It remains an open question as to whether the new procedure using a Notice of Dispute in clause 66A(1) will be enforced by the courts as defining the start of a dispute, or whether this will also fall outside the statutory provisions requiring an unfettered right to adjudication 'at any time'.

Clause 66A(2): 'amicable dispute resolution'. Once the Notice of Dispute has been served or if a party has identified a matter which if not resolved could become a dispute. Either party may at any time give notice in writing seeking agreement of the other party for a dispute described in the Notice of Dispute (or any matter that is a potential dispute) to be considered for resolution by negotiation, or by other means including conciliation or mediation. Clause 66A(2)(a) expressly provides for conciliation under the ICE Conciliation Procedure 1999 and for mediation under the ICE Construction Mediation Procedure 2002. If such means are used, any recommendation or proposal arising from the procedure is only binding if incorporated into a written agreement signed by both parties.

Clause 66B: adjudication. Under clause 66(B)(1)(a) of the ICE 7th Edition either party has a contractual right to refer a dispute to adjudication (see Chapter 4.4, Adjudication). The contractual provisions for adjudication in clause 66(B) seek to comply with the requirements for adjudication under HGCRA 1996 and the Scheme. Clause 66B: Adjudication. Adjudication is outside the scope of this section (see 4.4 above) but there are several matters to note in clause 66(B). The provision for adjudication recognises the right of either party to refer 'any matter in dispute arising under or in connection with the contract' to adjudication and that either party may 'at any time' give notice of its intention to refer the dispute to adjudication. The HGCRA

4.1 Administration of claims
4.2 Litigation
4.3 Arbitration
4.4 Adjudication
4.5 Alternative dispute resolution

1996 limits adjudication to disputes *under* the contract. Clause 66(B)(1)(a) widens the range of disputes to include disputes 'arising in connection with' the contract. Such disputes would probably include disputes about mistake, misrepresentation, negligent misstatement and rectification of the contract; see *Ashville Investments Ltd* v. *Elmer Construction Ltd* [1988] 2 All ER 577 (CA) for the interpretation of 'in connection with the contract' in the context of arbitration. The clause requires the adjudication to be conducted under *The Institution of Civil Engineers Adjudication Procedure (1997)*.

Clause 66B(3) of the ICE 7th Edition provides that the parties are bound by the decision of the adjudicator until the dispute is finally determined by legal proceeding or by arbitration or by agreement. If a dispute is referred for adjudication, under clause 66(B)(3) the decision of the adjudicator will be final and binding in any event unless a notice to refer to arbitration has been given within three months of the decision.

Clause 66C: arbitration. Clause 66C provides for disputes to be finally determined by reference to arbitration (see Chapter 4.3 above). Arbitration is outside the scope of this section. However, in the absence of staged procedures in the amended provisions in the ICE 7th Edition, in particular clause 66C, it should be noted that contrary to the procedures in carlier versions of the ICE Conditions, a Notice to Refer to arbitration need no longer await completion of any antecedent step, except (probably) the Notice of Dispute. In the absence of a Notice of Dispute there would, arguably, be no dispute. However, the requirement for such a notice to bring a dispute into existence may not be quite as clear as intended: see the comments of May LJ in *AMEC Civil Engineering Limited* v. *Secretary of State for Transport* [2005] EWCA 291 (CA) referred to above.

Clause 66D: appointments. The arbitrator, adjudicator, conciliator or mediator shall be a person appointed by agreement. Clause 66D(2) provides that if the parties fail to appoint an arbitrator, conciliator or mediator within 21 days of either party serving notice on the other to agree the appointment, the dispute or matter shall the referred to a person to be appointed on the application of either party to the President of the Institution of Civil Engineers. If the parties fail to aapoint an adjudicator pursuant to clause 66B(1)(b), the appointment is to be by application of either party to the Institution of Civil Engineers.

10.2 'Ad hoc' staged dispute resolution provisions

The contract for the Channel Tunnel project contained staged dispute resolution provisions under which any dispute was first to be referred to a panel of three independent experts who were required to give a unanimous decision within 90 days. The decision of the panel was binding on the parties unless and until revised in arbitration. If dissatisfied with the panel's decision, a party was to give notice of arbitration within 90 days, and any resulting arbitration was to be held in Brussels under the Rules of Conciliation and Arbitration of the International Chamber of Commerce (ICC).

The contracts used by the Hong Kong government on Chek Lap Kok airport contained a four-stage dispute resolution procedure. First, disputes were submitted to the engineer under the contract who had limited powers in respect of money claims and the award of extensions of time in respect of which decisions were made by a government representative. Where the engineer made a decision with which a party disagreed, that party had to serve a notice of dispute requiring a further formal decision of the engineer within 28 days. Where a dispute arose over a decision made by the government representative or the engineer's formal decision, the dispute proceeded to the second stage of mediation which was to be completed within 42 days. Only disputes relating to payment or extensions of time could be referred to the third stage, adjudication. The fourth and final stage in the scheme was arbitration which, except in certain limited circumstances, could only take place after substantial completion. The scheme for dispute resolution included the setting up of a panel of expert mediators and arbitrators at the outset.

An innovative approach to ADR, more correctly dispute avoidance, was adopted by the British Columbia Hydroelectric Company on its major projects in Canada. The company adopted a model process offered by some construction associations in Canada which involved 'refereeing' or 'partnering' under which a neutral party, experienced in ADR, made regular site visits for the purpose of resolving problems at an early stage before they escalated into full-blown disputes.

A more radical approach to dispute avoidance and ADR was introduced by the city of Boston in the USA on its Central Arterial Highway and Tunnel Project. This multi-billion dollar project involved the construction of a main highway and tunnel through the centre of the city and was extremely complex. After the award of the contract, and throughout the construction period, the employer's team, the designers, and the construction team attended educational seminars conducted by people experienced in dispute avoidance and resolution, in order to encourage 'partnering' between all the parties involved in the project. Claims that did arise during the course of the project were submitted in a detailed claim document to an 'authorized representative' identified in the contract, who was required to make a decision on the claim. If a dispute arose over a decision of the authorized representative, this was referred to a dispute resolution board which comprised two technical members who selected a chairman experienced in dispute resolution. If the parties agreed, a dispute could be referred for mediation at any time after it had been submitted to the dispute resolution board and before the board had given a decision. Although, the contract price escalated very substantially during the course of the works as a result of ground conditions and design changes and there was a significant delay in completion, the ADR process itself appears to have been successful, at least during the course of the works, in resolving or at least minimising the effect of disputes, which might have further delayed the project.

Ironically, at a time when the courts are requiring parties to endeavour to resolve disputes without resort to litigation, a consequence of the requirement for construction contracts in the UK to comply with the statutory provisions of HGCRA 1996 and the Scheme is that the majority of innovative procedures, such as those above, cannot be used effectively under contractual provisions at an early stage unless there is a willingness by both parties not to proceed to adjudication as the preferred first stage of the dispute resolution process. The dispute resolution provisions in all construction contracts are now dominated by adjudication because of the statutory requirement for a provision that provides a right to give notice 'at any time' of an intention to refer a dispute to adjudication and because of the 'quick-fix' nature of the adjudication process, often irrespective of its suitability or merits.

11 AMICABLE SETTLEMENT

The new clause 66A(2) in the ICE 7th Edition seeks to retain a consensual approach to dispute resolution by offering either conciliation or mediation (see Section 10.1 above).

FIDIC 4th and FIDIC 1999 both make provision for an undefined form of ADR referred to as 'amicable settlement', and seek to provide a 'cooling-off' period between the giving of notice of arbitration and the commencement of proceedings.

Clause 67.2 of the FIDIC 4th Edition and clause 20.5 of FIDIC 1999 both provide for the 'amicable settlement' of disputes. Under both forms, unless the parties agree

4.1 Administration of claims
4.2 Litigation
4.3 Arbitration
4.4 Adjudication
4.5 Alternative dispute resolution

otherwise, no arbitration may be commenced until at least 56 days from a notice of intention to commence arbitration under FIDIC 4th or from a notice of dissatisfaction under FIDIC 1999. However, neither clause contains any guidance as to the form of amicable settlement process to be adopted or how, and by whom, the process is to be commenced. In any contract to which the HGCRA 1996 applies, the provisions for 'amicable settlement' in the FIDIC forms may not achieve the intended purpose of using a 'low-key' dispute resolution process early in the dispute as the contract will, of course, be subject to the statutory requirement to allow a party to give notice at any time of an intention to refer a dispute to adjudication.

12 THE LEGAL EFFECT OF ADR CLAUSES – TO WHAT EXTENT ARE THEY ENFORCEABLE?

In the context of the enforcement of ADR clauses it is important to distinguish between ADR processes that result in a binding 'determination' or 'decision', for example expert determination and adjudication, and those processes which involve 'negotiations', for example mediation and mini-trials. The difficulties with the law in relation to agreements to negotiate generally do not arise in the ADR processes in the former category. The potential difficulties that arise with the enforcement of ADR provisions in relation to the processes in the latter category are considered further below.

Under English law, an agreement to negotiate is not enforceable at law. In *Courtney & Fairbairn* v. *Tolaini Brothers (Hotels) Limited* [1975] 1 WLR 297 the Court of Appeal rejected the argument that an agreement to enter into negotiations was enforceable.

> 'If the law does not recognise a contract to enter into a contract (when there is a fundamental term yet to be agreed) it seems to me it cannot recognize a contract to negotiate. The reason is because it is too uncertain to have any binding force...' per Lord Denning MR.

The courts do not readily relinquish jurisdiction, and clauses in contracts that purport to oust or limit the jurisdiction of the court are strictly construed. Any agreement that ousts the court's jurisdiction entirely is contrary to public policy and void (see *Scott* v. *Avery* [1856] 5 HLC 811 (HL)). However, the courts have been prepared to require a party to comply with procedures that are a condition precedent to the commencement of litigation or arbitration proceedings. In *Scott* v. *Avery* above, the House of Lords upheld an agreement under which the award of an arbitrator was a condition precedent to the right to bring an action on the contract. This type of clause is now known as a *Scott* v. *Avery* clause.

Therefore, although the general jurisdiction of the court cannot be ousted, the commencement of proceedings may, in certain circumstances, be validly delayed by incorporating into an agreement defined procedures that must be completed as a condition precedent to either party commencing either litigation of arbitration proceedings.

Under the Supreme Court Act 1981, the court has power to stay any action that it considers should not be allowed to continue. In addition, the CPR now expressly provide for a stay to allow the parties to proceed to ADR.

There is also high judicial support for the court not interfering in the dispute resolution procedures agreed by the parties given by the House of Lords in *Channel Tunnel Group Limited* v. *Balfour Beatty Construction Limited* (1993) 61 BLR 1 (HL):

> 'I would endorse the powerful warnings against encroachment on the parties' agreement to have their commercial differences decided by their chosen tribunals, and on

> the international policy exemplified in the English legislation that this consent should be honoured by the courts, given by Parker LJ in *Home and Overseas Insurance Co. Ltd* v. *Mentor Insurance Co. (UK) Ltd* [1990] 1 WLR 153, at pages 158 to 159 and Saville J. in *Hayter* v. *Nelson* [1990] 2 Lloyd's Rep. 265', per Lord Mustill, at page 26.

Although the *Channel Tunnel Group Limited* v. *Balfour Beatty Construction Limited* case above was principally concerned with dispute resolution first by an expert panel and then, if there was still dissatisfaction, by arbitration, the House of Lords also confirmed its willingness to enforce agreements to resolve disputes which were outside normal litigation or arbitration clauses, in this case in an international context.

ADR processes which involve 'negotiations' are generally similar to settlement negotiations in that the processes are consensual, non-binding and have the same objectives. Therefore a potential difficulty arises if one party to a contract refuses to comply with a contractual provision that requires disputes to be resolved by an ADR process which relies on negotiating a settlement. There is an obvious lack of certainty in a mere undertaking to negotiate a contract or settlement agreement, as there is in an agreement to merely strive to settle a dispute amicably, because the court would have insufficient objective criteria to decide whether one or both parties were in compliance or breach of such a provision.

There are, however, fundamental differences that may be said to distinguish ADR from merely direct negotiations between the parties. First, the parties submit the dispute to a process which is outside the parties' direct negotiations, and which involves a third party; for example the mediator or, in a mini-trial, a panel. Secondly, the process itself will be governed (to varying degrees) by the role and input from the third party and by the protocol adopted. In the first edition of the handbook, in the absence of directly relevant case law, the authors expressed the view that the court might be prepared to enforce an ADR process which involved 'negotiations' if the ADR procedure was defined with sufficient precision to allow the court to say whether a party had complied with it or not and the process set time limits in which agreement was to be achieved.

Cable & Wireless plc v. *IBM United Kingdom Limited* [2002] EWHC 2059 (Comm Ct), was the first case to provide clear guidance on the court's approach to the enforcement of ADR provisions which involved a 'consensual' process. The court reviewed the enforceability of bespoke 'escalating' dispute resolution provisions, which included ADR in the form of mediation. A dispute arose and *IBM* tried to proceed by way of mediation. *Cable & Wireless* refused, arguing that the ADR clause 'imposed no more than an agreement to negotiate... and an agreement to negotiate [was] not enforceable in English law.' Coleman J stated: '... parties who enter into an ADR agreement must be taken to appreciate that mediation as a tool for dispute resolution is not designed to achieve solutions which reflect the precise legal rights and obligations of the parties, but rather solutions which are commercially acceptable at the time of the mediation'. However, the judge then stated 'For the courts now to decline to enforce contractual references to ADR on the grounds of intrinsic uncertainty would be to fly in the face of public policy as expressed in the CPR and as reflected in the judgment of the Court of Appeal in *Dunnett* v. *Railtrack plc* [2002] EWCA 2002.'

In the *Cable & Wireless* case a factor which weighed heavily with the court in upholding the ADR provisions was the incorporation into the contract of ADR provisions that could be analysed as requiring not merely an attempt in good faith to achieve resolution of a

4.1 Administration of claims
4.2 Litigation
4.3 Arbitration
4.4 Adjudication
4.5 Alternative dispute resolution

dispute but also the participation of the parties in a particular procedure to be recommended by an established external organisation which provided dispute resolution services. The judge found that the parties' intended engagement of a recognised organisation to provide the mediator and their participation in the recommended procedure of that organisation, provided sufficient certainty for a court readily to ascertain whether the parties had complied with the dispute resolution provisions in the contract.

In *Halsey* v. *Milton Keynes NHS Trust* above, the court recognised that it could not positively order mediation against the wishes of a party unwilling to mediate but that it could make ADR 'orders' of the kind used for some time in the Commercial Court (in the form used in *Kinstreet* v. *Balmargo* CH 1994, 2999 and *Shirayama* v. *Danovo* [2003] EWHC 3006, where there were reluctant parties). The court affirmed the views expressed in *Dunnett* v. *Railtrack* above, and provided the following further guidance:

(1) All member of the legal profession who conduct litigation should now routinely consider with their clients whether their disputes are suitable for ADR.
(2) The court should not compel mediation although it could make orders encouraging parties to mediate. Where an order has been made, the test for refusing to proceed to mediation will be higher.

The situation concerning the enforceability of ADR clauses may be further strengthened in contracts which contain both an arbitration clause governed by the Arbitration Act 1996 and provisions for a 'staged' approach to dispute resolution.

Under Section 9(1) of the Arbitration Act 1996 the court has power to stay court proceedings commenced by a party to an arbitration agreement if the subject matter of the dispute is within the ambit of the arbitration agreement. Section 9(4) of the Arbitration Act 1996 provides for the granting of a mandatory stay other than in circumstances where the arbitration agreement is null and void, inoperative, or incapable of being performed.

However, in the context of enforceability of ADR clauses, Section 9(2) is important in that it extends the court's power to stay proceedings 'notwithstanding that the matter is to be referred to arbitration only after the exhaustion of the dispute resolution procedures'.

It is submitted that if there are staged dispute resolution provisions in a contract with, say, a 'negotiated' form of ADR followed by arbitration, then if the ADR process does not result in settlement, Section 9(2) of the Arbitration Act 1996 may entitle a party to the contract to stay not only arbitration proceedings but also any legal proceedings pending completion of the ADR process.

In summary, although the court has no power to order mediation against the wishes of a party, it can, however, adopt other means where there is an unreasonable refusal of a party to proceed to ADR. In particular, a recalcitrant party may be penalised in costs, even if successful at trial. The *Cable & Wireless* case above also shows that the court will, in appropriate circumstances, be willing to enforce an ADR clause although on the facts of the case, this is likely to be restricted to circumstances where the nature and form of the intended ADR process can be clearly identified from the contractual provisions.

It should, however, be noted that the discussion above on the enforceability of ADR clauses is concerned with the contractual position. In the case of adjudication the position will be different in that any contractual ADR provision that seeks to circumvent, or will even delay, adjudication will not be upheld, and where there has been a reference to adjudication, the court will not enforce an ADR clause and grant a stay to allow ADR: see *R G Carter Ltd* v. *Edmund Nuttall Ltd* (unreported, 21 June 2001).

13 ADVANTAGES AND DISADVANTAGES OF ADR

ADR can help in preventing disputes proceeding to trial or arbitration. However, without more, this may be a perceived rather than a real advantage, as prior to the introduction of the CPR over 90% of the disputes in which proceedings were commenced settled in any event and did not proceed to trial.

The primary benefits of ADR are the flexibility and speed of the process and the reduction in overall cost. Even in the most complex disputes, the majority of ADR processes may be completed in no more than one or two days, with a consequent saving in cost. In addition, the process may generally be set up as soon as the parties wish, subject to the availability of those who are required to attend.

The success rate for mediation is said to be in excess of 80%. Therefore the prospects of mediation achieving a settlement generally appear to be high. There is evidence that even cases that do not settle on the day of the mediation, will often settle a short time afterwards.

A process that achieves an early settlement benefits all parties. For example, in a delay and disruption claim, early settlement may assist the contractor's cash flow and provide the employer with better prospects for completion on time, and at the same time avoid 'grumbling' disputes throughout the project.

The litigation and arbitration processes in the UK are adversarial. In contrast, ADR is more likely to minimize confrontation, and prevent (or at least limit) further deterioration in the working relationship between the parties.

ADR can provide a more certain outcome which is reached by mutual agreement. In contrast, the outcome in litigation and arbitration is largely dependent on the tribunal's findings on evidence of fact and expert evidence, which may not come up to proof on the day. In addition, the parties can agree solutions to the dispute that would not be available in court or arbitration proceedings where the decision is determined by the strict legal position rather than the present, and future, interests of the parties.

In ADR processes involving 'structured negotiations', the parties are able to control the outcome of the settlement which enhances the prospect of maintaining the business or personal relationship.

Litigation takes place in the public forum of the courts. Although initially arbitration is a private process, the cloak of confidentiality is lost if an appeal is lodged and the matter moves to the courts. In any event, many construction arbitrations run for periods of weeks or months, rather than days, and the longer the period, the more likely it is that confidentiality will be lost.

In contrast, ADR is a private (and generally short) process, and confidentiality about the matters in dispute, or the dispute itself, may be maintained. Adverse publicity and damage to the reputation of the parties may be avoided.

In *re D (Minors)* (1993) TLR 12 February 1993, the Court of Appeal endorsed the confidential nature of mediation and held that, except in certain very limited circumstances (in that case a person causing severe harm to a child), admissions or conciliatory gestures made during a mediation are not admissible in subsequent court proceedings following an unsuccessful mediation.

However, ADR also has certain disadvantages, and there may be risks inherent in certain of the processes.

Parties to litigation and arbitration are required to adopt an 'open' approach which includes the disclosure of all relevant documents, and the exchange of witness statements and experts' reports, the intention being that no party should be taken by surprise by the other party. In the majority of ADR processes there will be no general disclosure of documents or evidence. This means that a party may not be aware of the existence of a document or evidence which would be adverse, or even fatal, to the other party's case, if the matter were to proceed to court or litigation.

Unless the contract provides a timetable, careful judgment may be needed as to the point at which ADR should be commenced. While disputes may be, and often are, resolved before a party has all the available information, in certain disputes it may not be appropriate to enter into ADR before sufficient information is available to both parties to allow them to formulate the terms of a settlement.

If a wholly equitable settlement is to be achieved in certain disputes, full disclosure of documents may be required. This may prevent the use of ADR at an early stage and limit the potential savings in costs.

Although ADR in the form of mediation is generally without prejudice and non-binding, a party may disclose information that the other party would not otherwise have obtained except for the mediation. If agreement is not reached, such information may be beneficial to the other party in assessing the merits of the respective cases if the dispute proceeds to trial.

ADR is an additional layer in the dispute resolution process. Although the costs of ADR are generally lower than the costs of litigation and arbitration for an equivalent dispute, in a complex case the costs of, say, a mediation are likely to be substantial. If the process is not successful, a large proportion of these substantial costs may be wasted and become an additional cost to those incurred in subsequent proceedings.

Certain ADR processes, for example mediation, are not controlled by the courts. If a mediator is guilty of misconduct, say by revealing information given in confidence by one party to the other party, and this only comes to light after a settlement has been reached, the aggrieved party cannot appeal to the court and may only have a remedy if it commences an action in negligence against the mediator.

14 SELECTING A MECHANISM FOR CONSTRUCTION DISPUTES

Certain contracts provide for a specific form of ADR, for example the conciliation procedure in the ICE 7th Edition. In addition, contracts may include provisions that a particular form of ADR is a condition precedent to proceeding to arbitration or litigation.

In the UK, facilitative mediation has become virtually synonymous with ADR. The primary reason for this is that the move to use ADR in recent years has been largely driven by the Courts and by lawyers who have no technical expertise and by certain organisations which provide mediators, the majority of whom are lawyers. It is submitted that if mediation is the appropriate form of ADR, evaluative mediation, with a competent person of the appropriate discipline as mediator may often be more suitable in the majority of construction disputes.

Although mediation is arguably the most flexible of the ADR processes, it is important not to be prescriptive as other forms of ADR may offer a more appropriate process and/or be more cost effective for resolving specific types of dispute. Selected examples of types of dispute and possible forms of ADR to be used are given below.

(a) Construing contractual provisions: the interpretation of contractual provisions may either be determinative of the dispute or may form part of a larger dispute. In either case a non-binding early expert evaluation by an independent lawyer is likely to assist the parties in assessing the merits of the respective cases. Alternatively, if the parties are prepared to be bound by an expert determination by a lawyer, such determination may dispose of the dispute. In particularly important cases involving the interpretation of a contract, early neutral evaluation by a judge of the Commercial Court or the Technology and Construction Court may be justified.

(b) Claims relating to loss and expense, extensions of time, and the valuation of variations: these types of dispute are normally the most protracted and complex. If the parties can agree to a final and binding decision, expert determination by an independent engineer or a quantity surveyor (as appropriate to the form of contract) may offer the most effective means of settling these types of dispute in terms of time and cost. However, conciliation or non-binding early expert determination by an independent engineer or quantity surveyor (as appropriate) are likely to be more acceptable alternatives to the parties.

(c) Defective construction work: expert determination or non-binding early expert evaluation by an independent architect or engineer, depending on the nature of the work.

(d) Disputes between an employer and contractor over defective services: expert determination or non-binding early expert evaluation by an independent mechanical or electrical engineer, as appropriate for the type of work.

(e) Disputes between a purchaser and a regular supplier over the performance of plant and equipment: although early expert evaluation may be appropriate, the mini-trial process would enable the dispute to be resolved by senior management who are familiar with technical matters and trade custom and practice, and who want to preserve the existing business relationship.

(f) Professional negligence: a non-binding early expert evaluation by an independent professional of the appropriate discipline will allow the parties to review the merits of their respective cases at an early stage.

A binding decision on the dispute by referring if for adjudication may also be preferable to a full ADR process such as mediation.

In any large construction project, consideration should be given to the inclusion in the contract of provisions for a 'staged' dispute resolution process. The number of stages and the form of dispute resolution to be used at each stage may be geared to the nature and complexity of the project.

There are certain types of dispute in which ADR may not be appropriate, including disputes in which:

- a party seeks an injunction or declaratory relief which is only available in court proceedings;
- the nature of the dispute is such that a party requires the court to establish a legal precedent, for example over the interpretation of a clause in a contract;
- a party is entitled to summary judgment under CPR Part 24;
- a local authority requires a decision based on contractual provisions to satisfy the district auditor; and
- a party to the dispute does not act in good faith.

15 LIMITATION PERIODS AND TIME LIMITS

It is essential for any claiming party considering ADR to be aware of any potential difficulties which may arise by the expiry of any relevant limitation period or contractual time limit.

The Limitation Act 1980 and the other legislation which defines limitation periods in which court proceedings or arbitration must be commenced are discussed in Section 2.4 of Chapter 4.3.

In addition to the statutory provisions, certain standard form contracts also contain specific dispute resolution mechanisms with which the parties are required to comply. For example, clause 66B(3) of the ICE 7th Edition requires any Notice to Refer to arbitration to be served not later than three months after an adjudicator's decision, otherwise the adjudicator's decision will become final and binding, and clause 28.7 of the JCT Major Project Construction Contract 2005 requires the contractor to refer any dispute over the final payment advice to adjudication or litigation within 28 days of the final payment advice being issued.

If limitation or contractual timetables are likely to be a problem, it is open to the parties to agree to the postponement of time running or to extend contractual time limits.

In relation to any action which arises in connection with the enforcement of the agreement concluded at the end of the ADR process, a party's cause of action accrues on the date of the other party's failure to fulfil its obligations under such agreement.

construction law HANDBOOK

Newsletter

For subscribers to the *Construction Law Handbook*

No. 42 November 2007

EDITORIAL

In this edition of the *Newsletter* we report a case *Gerald Martin Scott v. Belfast Education and Library Board* that considers the tender process. It has concluded that employers need to act fairly and in good faith. We also provide a further update on the issue of 'global claims'. This time we consider *Petromec Inc v. Petroleo Brasileiro SA Petrobras* which appears to be at odds with cases we have previously reported.

We have also chosen to look at a number of recent cases dealing with the procedural and legal difficulties that can arise with dispute resolution clauses. For example, the words 'shall in the first instance be submitted to adjudication' in respect of a dispute meant that court proceedings could not be commenced in *DGT Steel and Cladding v. Cubitt Building and Interiors*.

We conclude by reminding readers of the difficulty in challenging an arbitrator's award and by looking at two cases dealing with adjudication: *Ringway Infrastructure Services Ltd v. Vauxhall Motors* which has provided further clarification on when a dispute arises and *Treasure & Son v. Dawes* sought to open up the debate about oral variations.

The information contained in this *Newsletter* is not intended to be a comprehensive study, or to provide legal advice, and should not be relied upon or treated as a substitute for specific advice concerning individual situations.

Hamish Lal
Partner
Dundas & Wilson LLP
hamish.lal@dundas-wilson.com

TENDER DOCUMENTS

Chapter 1.3 Public Sector Projects

Do tender documents give rise to an implied contract between tenderers and the prospective employer, the terms of which, are that an employer must act fairly and in good faith? This question was addressed in *Gerald Martin Scott v. Belfast Education and Library Board*.

The Court held that such an implied term would be implied into the tendering process. Further that the concept of fairness applied to:

- the nature and application of the specified procedure;
- the assessment of the tenders according to the stated criteria;
- the evaluation of the tenders in a uniform manner and as intended by the tender documents.

A gloss on the above issue is whether the implied term requires the absence of any material ambiguity in the tender documents that would significantly affect the tender? The Court concluded that the answer was also yes. This latter aspect may lead to

Contents

thomas telford

further litigation in this area. Employers will need to ensure that there are no mistakes or undetected ambiguities in the tender documents that might lead tenderers tendering on an unequal basis.

GLOBAL CLAIMS

Chapter 3.1 The Law of Contract

In *Newsletter 41* we discussed *London Underground v. Citylink Telecommunications [2007] EWHC 1749*, which discussed the issue of global claims. *Petromec Inc v. Petroleo Brasileiro SA Petrobras [2007] EWHC 1589* is a case decided a few days earlier and presents a slightly harder view of global claims.

In Petromec the contractor sought to argue that it could claim additional cost arising out of changed work scope on the basis of a global total costs claim being the difference between actual costs and anticipated costs. By way of background, Petromec looked at the total cost incurred in constructing a rig to a higher specification less the cost it would have incurred in producing the rig to a lower specification. The Judge disagreed with this approach and held that Petromec must specify the instructions, the work required to comply with those instructions and the cost attributable to that work. The changes and causal nexus must be pleaded. Petromec could not contend that the work and the cost is reasonable and wait for any challenge to that. Further, that Petromec's approach was not what the law allowed, nor what the Rules of Court required for it to put and establish its case.

By one means or another, Petromec was required to, with sufficient particularity, plead the work done and the cost thereof by reference to the amended specification or the instructions given. On a practical level, Petromec tends to the view that a global or total cost evaluation of a claim will be, generally, disapproved by the court on the basis that it does not meet the 'basic' requirements of proof of cause and effect/entitlement. This places a higher burden than expressed in *London Underground.*

DISPUTE PROCEDURE TIPS

Chapter 4.1: Administration of Claims

Four recent cases have highlighted the procedural and legal difficulties that can arise with dispute resolution clauses.

In *Premium Nafta Products v. Fili Shipping Company [2007] UKHL 40* the House of Lords looked at arbitration clauses and the narrow distinctions which have in the past been drawn between disputes 'arising under' and 'arising out of' agreements. Lord Hoffman said that these distinctions reflected no credit on English commercial law, and the time had come to draw a line and make a fresh start. Such technical niceties will no longer be entertained. Any dispute arising out of the relationship entered into will be decided by the tribunal agreed upon. If you want to exclude certain disputes, for example, disputes about the validity of the contract itself, then you will have to explicitly say so.

The practical lesson is clear: if you do want to exclude a specific type of dispute from a specified form of resolution then you must clearly say so. The courts will not favour technical legal arguments when you attempt to "shut the stable door after the horse has bolted".

In the context of expert determination *Harper v. Interchange Group [2007] EWHC 1834 (Comm)* an agreement contained a clause referring a dispute to an independent accountant who "shall act as expert (not as arbitrator) and whose decision shall... be final and binding on the parties".

The agreed procedure was as follows: (i) Interchange must make payments to Mr Harper in accordance with the terms and the timetable set out in clause 3.3; (ii) at the same time as payment is made, Interchange must deliver to Mr Harper a statement of the gross margin and/or licence fees forming the basis of the payment made; (iii) Mr Harper has 28 days in which to agree the statement or to notify Interchange of the basis on which he objects to the statement (an 'objection'); (iv) if Mr Harper makes an 'objection', then the parties will endeavour to resolve it within 28 days; (v) if Interchange and Mr Harper are unable to agree the statement issued or settle the objection then the dispute will be referred to an independent chartered accountant; (vi) once the accountant is appointed he will act as an expert, not as an arbitrator. His decision shall be final and binding on the parties in the absence of manifest error.

Harper was prevented from claiming additional commission because he had failed to operate the contractual machinery and appoint an expert to determine his level of commission. On a practical level, it is clear that the parties should, if a procedure is stipulated for resolving a dispute, make it expressly clear whether use of that procedure is a precondition to entitlement and whether any further rights will be barred by a failure to operate the procedure.

Finally, in the context of adjudication, *DGT Steel and Cladding v. Cubitt Building and Interiors [2007] EWHC 1584* considered whether an adjudication clause directing that disputes "shall in the first instance, be submitted to adjudication" meant that court proceedings could not be commenced. The Court interpreted this as a binding agreement to adjudicate with the result that the court could stay or freeze court proceedings which had been commenced in breach of the agreement.

HHJ Coulson QC summarised the position as follows:

a) The court will not grant an injunction to prevent one party from commencing and pursuing adjudication proceedings, even if there is already court or arbitration proceedings in respect of the same dispute.
b) The court has an inherent jurisdiction to stay court proceedings issued in breach of an agreement to adjudicate.
c) If a binding adjudication agreement has been identified then the persuasive burden is on the party seeking to resist the stay to justify that stance.

In practical terms Parties should consider very carefully the implications of making a form of dispute resolution mandatory for example is it intended that adjudication be concluded before recourse to anything else.

APPEAL OF ARBITRATION AWARDS

Chapter 4.3: Arbitration

Penwith District Council v. VP Developments [2007] EWHC 2544 (TCC) provides a sharp reminder to readers about the finality of arbitral awards and the real difficulties in seeking to challenge an arbitrator's award. The Court, has in effect, issued a warning about appeals sought on law but really based on facts: Akenhead J said "Applications for leave to appeal on questions of law must not be dressed up as questions of law when they are, on proper analysis, criticisms of the arbitrator's findings of primary or secondary fact. It is not enough to say on an application for leave to appeal on a question of law that the arbitrator made findings of fact which no reasonable arbitrator could or should have made. It is not for the Court to substitute its own view of the facts for that of the arbitrator. Whilst one can understand the frustration of a party against whom an arbitrator has made a controversial finding of fact, that frustration does not justify an application to the Court for leave to appeal on a question of law."

The relevant facts of *Penwith* are straight forward. Penwith employed VP Developments Ltd ('VP'), to carry out planned maintenance works at the Alverton Estate, Penzance, Cornwall. There was an arbitration agreement in that contract. In March 1996 VP served a notice of arbitration. Essentially, VP's claims in the arbitration relate to sums due to them on their final account. The net sum claimed is just over £350,000. A further important issue arose between the parties, namely relating to whether or not VP was entitled to compound interest on any principal sums awarded to it. This formed the basis of the appeal. Penwith arguing that the arbitrator erred in law in holding that VP was entitled to compound interest.

The Judge disagreed holding that this was a question of fact, stating "The Court will not and should not treat what may arguably be an incorrect finding of fact as a question of law. One cannot and should not 'dress up' a question of law in the way in which Penwith has done on this application, namely a challenge based on a finding of fact which no reasonable or rational arbitrator allegedly should have come to". The Judge did however conclude that where the true basis of the appeal is 'factual' then if the arbitrator has acted perversely and in breach of natural justice then other redress may be possible.

HOW AND WHEN A 'DISPUTE' ARISES?

Chapter 4.4: Adjudication

Ringway Infrastructure Services v. Vauxhall Motors [2007] EWHC 2421 provides a recent reminder of how and when a dispute arises. The relevant facts are straight forward. An adjudicator was appointed pursuant to the terms of a construction contract between Vauxhall Motors Limited ('Vauxhall') and Ringway Infrastructure Services Limited ('Ringway'), whereby Vauxhall employed Ringway to construct a new vehicle distribution centre to carry out various associated works at Vauxhall's premises at North Road, Ellesmere Port, Cheshire. The adjudicator ordered Vauxhall to pay Ringway £1,303,704.95 plus VAT and interest together with the adjudicator's fees and expenses. Vauxhall sought declarations that the adjudicator's decision was void and unenforceable on the grounds that the adjudicator had no jurisdiction. A key argument being that the dispute referred to adjudication was not a dispute.

On the question of when a dispute arises the Judge held:

a) The existence of a dispute or difference may be inferred from what is said or not said by the party in receipt of what may be termed "a claim".
b) There does not have to be an express rejection of a 'claim' by the recipient. In so far as the case of *Monmouthshire County Council v. Costelloe and Kemple Ltd (1965) 5 BLR 83* suggests otherwise, the more recent cases of *Amec* and *Collins* suggest otherwise.
c) A 'claim' for the purpose of giving rise to a dispute or difference may not be a claim for money or for the payment of money. The variety, extent and scope of disputes are infinite. It may involve simply an assertion of a right by one party.
d) One needs to determine whether there is 'claim' and whether or not that claim is disputed from the surrounding facts, circumstances and evidence pertaining up to the moment that the dispute, subsequently referred to adjudication (or arbitration), has crystallised.

On the facts the Judge decided that the matter of an interim payment was a claim related to the final account entitlement and so within the adjudicator's jurisdiction. Readers may also be interested in the Judge's comments concerning challenges to adjudicators' decisions: "I do not read these decisions as saying that a party seeking to avoid enforcement of an adjudicator's decision starts with one hand tied behind its back or that there is some evidential or legal presumption against allowing the challenge which it is seeking to make. However, because most such challenges have failed to date and given the policy of the 1996 Act, judges should examine the evidence and argument particularly carefully before allowing the challenge. If a properly arguable case is advanced on a jurisdictional challenge, it must be properly and fully considered by the Court ... A less arguable case may attract a more rigorous costs or interest sanction than would otherwise be the case."

ORAL VARIATIONS

Treasure & Son v. Dawes [2007] EWHC 2420 addressed an interesting question concerning an oral variation of the written construction contract, which means that the adjudicator has no jurisdiction. The position is settled that for recourse to statutory adjudication the majority in *RJT Consulting Engineers v. DM Engineering (Northern Ireland) [2002] BLR 217*, (Ward and Robert Walker LJJ), decided that all terms (including immaterial terms) had to be in or evidenced in writing as required by Section 107 of the HGCRA 1996. But what if we have a contractual agreement to adjudicate and the parties have varied the terms of the agreement by oral agreements?

Akenhead J held that where there is a contractual agreement to adjudicate that adjudication process is not undermined, jurisdictionally or otherwise by the fact (if it be the case) that the terms of the original contract (containing the adjudication clause) were orally varied. There could only be such undermining if it was an express term of the contract itself to the effect that oral variations of the terms were not to be considered valid unless recorded or evidenced in writing. Essentially the parties will have agreed in a binding contract that disputes will be referable to adjudication. If there is some oral variation to the terms of that contract, that does not itself undermine the contractual enforceability of the adjudication process. If the original agreement is binding and whether or not the oral variation is binding, there still remains a binding adjudication agreement of which either or both parties may make use from time to time.

Comments or contributions for the *Newsletter* should be sent to:
The Editor, *Construction Law Handbook Newsletter*, Thomas Telford Publishing, 1 Heron Quay, London, E14 4JD; or e-mailed to: clh@thomastelford.com.
Subscriptions enquiries: please telephone Maria Davis on 020 7665 2460
or email: maria.davis@thomastelford.com

construction
law HANDBOOK

Newsletter

For subscribers to the *Construction Law Handbook*

No. 43 January 2008

EDITORIAL

In this edition of the *Newsletter* we report *Bodill & Sons (Contractors) Ltd v. Mattu* which gives very helpful judicial guidance on how retention monies ought be treated by the employer.

We have also chosen to look at *Hart Investments Ltd v. Terence Maurice Charles Fidler* which deals with the duty to warn. Here, it was held that an engineer employed by an owner in respect of permanent works who observes a state of temporary works which is dangerous and causing immediate peril to the permanent works, is obliged to take such steps as are open to him to obviate that danger. The steps included warning of an immediate danger to those works.

We continue the theme of 'warning' by reporting *Harris Calnan Construction Co. Ltd v. Ridgewood* which provides a warning about resisting enforcement; *Ledwood Mechanical Engineering Ltd v. Whessoe Oil & Gas* which warns about trying to set-off against an adjudicator's award; and *Cundall Johnson and Partners v. Whipps Cross University Hospital* which warns parties who fail to comply with the Pre-Action Protocol. We have also included *Mark Morrison v. Tile It All* which warns employers about the role of 'text messaging' when reporting absences from work. In short, employers of all tiers will need to be pragmatic.

The information contained in this *Newsletter* is not intended to be a comprehensive study, or to provide legal advice, and should not be relied upon or treated as a substitute for specific advice concerning individual situations. Finally, I wish all readers a very happy, enjoyable and prosperous New Year.

Hamish Lal
Partner
Dundas & Wilson LLP
hamish.lal@dundas-wilson.com

GUIDANCE ON RETENTION

Chapter 1.2: Financing the Project

The question of the status of retention monies crops up frequently. We now have some very helpful judicial guidance on how retention monies should be retained and treated by the employer. *Bodill & Sons (Contractors) Ltd v. Mattu [2007] EWHC 2950 (TCC)* is a rare case providing that guidance.

Bodill deals with the form of Building Contract, Private Edition, with Contractor's Design Portion Supplement, 1998 edition, Amendments 1 to 5. This, as readers will know, provides that retention monies are held on trust. Clause 30.5.1 of the contract conditions says this 'The employer's interest in the retention is fiduciary as trustee for the contractor and for any nominated subcontractor (but without obligation to invest).' Clause 30.5.1 also states:

"The employer shall, to the extent that the employer exercises his right under clause 30.4, if the contractor... so requests at the date of payment under each Interim Certificate place the retention

Contents

thomas telford

in a separate banking account (so designated as to identify the amount as the retention held by the employer on trust as provided in clause 30.5.1) and certify to the architect with a copy to the contractor that such amount has been so placed. The employer shall be entitled to the full beneficial interest in any interest accruing in the separate banking account and shall be under no duty to account for any such interest to the contractor or any subcontractor."

Here, there was no issue that the employer's interest was as a trustee but the case deals with how the above clause should operate. In particular, the learned Judge considered the reasonable time to establish the separate bank account and how it should be described. In terms of time to establish the account, the Judge said: 'Even the law of trust, let alone the law of contract, does not require instantaneous setting up of an account and transfer of money. One must take into account the commercial realities. It would seem clear that a reasonable period for the setting up of the account and the transfer of the money would be two to three weeks.'

Here, the account was named 'Harmail Singh Mattu, trading as Urban Suburban, re Bodill retention money account'. The Judge said this was not sufficiently clear such that it can be described as a designated trust account. The Judge said 'It seems to me that that does not make it anywhere near clear enough to the bank or anyone else that it is a trust account or that the sums in it are impressed with a trust' and required that 'the account should have been designated as a trust account.'

This latter point is especially important and is tied to the notice required if the employer seeks to remove monies from the designated account. In *Bodill* the Judge considered that three clear working days' written notice was acceptable.

CHANGE TO BUILDING REGULATIONS

Chapter 1.6: The Construction Contract

Building and Approved Inspectors (Amendment) Regulations 2007 - *SI 2007/3384* entered force on 2 January 2008. The regulations provide that those carrying out work to fixed building services must notify local authorities and approved inspectors that those services have been commissioned in line with building regulations. There are also changes to the time limits for having an inspection and exempt group who don't need specific work inspected. These regulations also clarifying energy efficiency measures for building works.

ENGINEERS' DUTY TO WARN

Chapter 2.4: The Engineer's Appointment

Hart Investments Ltd v. Terence Maurice Charles Fidler [2007] EWHC 1058 (TCC) provides a very sharp reminder to readers about the duty of a structural engineer to warn.

Here, Mr Fidler was employed to design deep basement excavation works. These works required a substantial degree of underpinning. As a result of a failure of any temporary support to the underpinning, part of the side and front facades of the buildings collapsed. The claimant claimed damages on the basis which included breach of duty of care on the part of Mr Fidler in that he failed to require the contractor to take precautions to support the underpinning when he saw that it was unsupported.

The learned Judge held that an engineer employed by an owner in respect of permanent works who observes a state of temporary works which is dangerous and causing immediate peril to the permanent works in respect of which he is employed, is obliged to take such steps as are open to him to obviate that danger. The steps included warning of an immediate danger to those works caused by an imperilling act by the contractor. The Judge added 'It seems to me that that follows, partly as a matter of common sense, but also because the engineer is, after all, instructed in relation to the permanent works as a whole. It would appear strange if he is under a duty to take such steps as he can to see that they survive for say, the next 25 years, or whatever the design life for the building is, but is not obliged to take any steps to warn of an immediate danger to those works caused by an imperilling act by the contractor.'

The legal analysis in this case builds on the duties of a solicitor to 'report back matters of concern' (discussed in *Credit Lynonnaise v. Russell Jones and Walker [2003] PNLR 17*) which in turn used the analogy of a dentist who, in course of treating a patient's tooth, notices that an adjacent one also requires treatment due to decay. The dentist must warn his patient accordingly.

USE OF 'TEXT MESSAGING'

Chapter 2.7: Employment Law

A highly topical issue in employment law is the use of mobile phone text messaging. In *Mark Morrison v. Tile It All (2007)* a salesman was found to have been unfairly dismissed after being dismissed for texting in sick.

The facts are as follows: Mark Morrison initially texted in to report that he was sick. This was on the day that his brother died. He followed this up by sending a further text to say he would not be back at work until after the funeral. When Mr Morrison failed to cope with his grief he texted in on a further five days and was then 'signed off' work for two weeks with depression. Before he returned to work Mr Morrison was summoned to a disciplinary meeting for failure to follow the company absence procedure. The company policy required employees to phone in sick rather than text.

Mr Morrison was subsequently dismissed. The Tribunal decided that the dismissal was unfair. The chairman described the company's complaint as 'petty' and in the chairman's view 'a modicum of common sense could have straightened the situation out'!

This case highlights the risks that the digital age poses for employers. Having a clear absence policy is essential if employers are to manage short term absence effectively. If use of text messaging is not acceptable then it would be advisable for employers to state this in the absence procedure. However, following this case it is clear that employers need to be pragmatic and in exceptional circumstances, the reasons for the absence should be taken into account when considering how the policy is enforced.

FAILURE TO COMPLY WITH PRE-ACTION PROTOCOL

Chapter 4.2: Litigation

Cundall Johnson and Partners v. Whipps Cross University Hospital NHS Trust [2007] EWHC 2178 (TCC) provides an important guidance on when the courts will restrain a party from proceeding in litigation where the Protocol of Construction and Engineering Disputes (the Protocol) has not been complied with. This is not a case dealing with the cost consequences of failing to comply with the protocol.

In this case the claimant, a firm of consulting engineers, commenced proceedings against the trust to recover amounts alleged to be outstanding. The claimant's solicitors had set out the claim in correspondence and the trust had requested further information. It was not in dispute that this request did not receive a proper response. Notwithstanding this the claimant commenced proceedings without complying with the Protocol and the defendant sought to stop the proceedings until the Protocol had been complied with. The defendant succeeded.

The Judge held that in this case (1) there was a real possibility of settlement if the parties went through the Protocol processes which would save costs and (2) the trust was entitled to adequate details of the case it had to meet before proceedings were commenced. The Judge decided that this was a case where he could exercise his discretion to grant a stay. This is a significant decision since it shows how a claimant can be stopped in its tracks.

The Judge was clear that there are exceptions where a claimant shall not be required to comply with the Protocol before commencing proceedings, namely where the proposed proceedings:

- are for the enforcement of the decision of an adjudicator to whom a dispute has been referred pursuant to section 108 of the Housing Grants Construction & Regeneration Act 1996 (the 1996 'Act');
- include a claim for interim injunctive relief;
- will be the subject of a claim for summary judgment pursuant to Part 24 of the Civil Procedure Rules; or
- relate to the same or substantially the same issues as have been the subject of recent adjudication under the 1996 Act, or some other formal alternative dispute resolution procedure.

There have been other cases (for example, *Charles Church Developments Ltd v. Stent Foundations Ltd [2007] EWHC 855*) where the Court has imposed cost sanctions against parties not following the Protocol. The overall analysis of the cases in this area tends to the view that a claimant fails to make any credible attempt to comply with the Protocol is at risk that either the proceedings will be stayed to enable compliance with the Protocol (unless the Court considers that this would serve no benefit) or of a costs sanction. The message is pretty clear: unless one of the exceptions is applicable a claimant is advised to follow the Pre-Action Protocol.

WARNING ABOUT RESISTING ENFORCEMENT

Chapter 4.4: Adjudication

Harris Calnan Construction Co. Ltd v. Ridgewood (Kensington) Ltd [2007] EWHC 2738 (TCC) provides another reminder that a party resisting adjudication enforcement proceedings in the absence of a substantive basis for challenge will be required to pay all of the other sides costs (on an indemnity basis). HHJ Coulson QC reinforced the points he had made previously in *Gray & Sons (Builders) Bedford Ltd v. The Essential Box Co [2006] EWHC 2520.*

In *Gray* the resisting party dropped opposition to the enforcement application a day before the Hearing. In *Harris Calnan* the Judge decided that the 'defences' were simply not credible and that the defending party should have paid the adjudicator's award months earlier. The Judge said "Although I have been carefully through the points raised by the defendant in the correspondence in order to satisfy myself that the adjudicator's decision was properly enforceable, it is plain from the earlier paragraphs of this Judgment that the defendant had no substantive basis for challenging the decision. This sum ought to have been paid months ago. This court will not encourage parties, who have no defence to a claim based on an adjudicator's decision, to use up valuable court time and the resources of the successful party in running unmeritorious points that are doomed to fail. For those reasons, therefore, it seems to me that it is appropriate to award indemnity costs..."

The practical lesson is clear: non-paying parties resisting enforcement proceedings need to assess whether there is a 'substantive defence' otherwise there is a real risk of indemnity costs being awarded against it.

SETTING OFF SUBSEQUENT SUMS AGAINST AWARD

Ledwood Mechanical Engineering Ltd v. Whessoe Oil & Gas Ltd [2007] EWHC 2743 (TCC) deals with the problem of set-off against an adjudicator's award. Here, the defendants engaged the claimant under a subcontract which provided for adjudication. The contract provided for a risk and reward calculation by reference to man hours, with the claimant benefiting from an 'under-spend' in man-hours, but becoming liable for overspends. A dispute was referred to adjudication, and the adjudicator found that the defendants had wrongfully withheld money on the claimant's interim payment application, (number 19), and he ordered interest to run on that sum until the date of payment. The effect of the decision was that the number of man hours expended was increased. Having received the adjudicator's award, the defendant revised its payment notice issued in response to interim payment application (number 22) by making a reduction in respect of risk and reward so that no sum remained owing to the claimant. The claimant applied for summary judgment to enforce the award.

The Court held that in general, a claiming party was entitled to a sum awarded by an adjudicator without taking into account subsequent events. The authority for setting off liquidated and ascertained damages for delay against an adjudicator's award did not give rise to a wider power to set off sums generally against such an award. In all the circumstances, the claimant was entitled to summary judgment on the adjudicator's award. The setting off of LADs was a limited exception to the enforcement of an adjudicator's award, which arose when LADs could be calculated by reference to a number of weeks delay found by the adjudicator and the rate agreed by the parties.

Comments or contributions for the *Newsletter* should be sent to:
The Editor, *Construction Law Handbook Newsletter*, Thomas Telford Publishing, 1 Heron Quay, London, E14 4JD; or e-mailed to: clh@thomastelford.com.
Subscriptions enquiries: please telephone Maria Davis on 020 7665 2460
or email: maria.davis@thomastelford.com

construction law HANDBOOK

Newsletter

For subscribers to the *Construction Law Handbook*

No. 44 March 2008

EDITORIAL

In this edition of the *Newsletter* we report the Site Waste Management Regulations expected to come into force on 6 April 2008.

We have also chosen to look at *Drake v. Harbour [2008]* which concerns the correct approach to causation and *Braes of Doune Wind Farm (Scotland) Limited v. Alfred McAlpine Business Services Limited,* which is a very rare case where a liquidated damages provision was held to be unenforceable. Whilst, restricted to the particular wording used, this case is likely to make contract drafters revisit bespoke liquidated damages clauses.

We conclude by looking at two very noteworthy cases dealing with adjudication. *Reinwood Limited v. L Brown & Sons Limited* is only the second adjudication case to reach the House of Lords and reinforces the point that withholding notices issued on time will not be disturbed if subsequent events ocurring before the due date alter the numbers. *Cantillon Ltd v. Urvasco Limited* is a significant case that provides excellent guidance on when the courts will conclude that an adjudicator's decision should not be enforced on the grounds of breach of natural justice.

The information contained in this *Newsletter* is not intended to be a comprehensive study, or to provide legal advice, and should not be relied upon or treated as a substitute for specific advice concerning individual situations.

Hamish Lal
Partner
Dundas & Wilson LLP
hamish.lal@dundas-wilson.com

CAUSATION

Chapter 2.6: Professional Indemnity Insurance

Drake v. Harbour [2008] EWCA Civ 25 concerns a claim against a construction professional where the Court of Appeal considered the correct approach to causation in a case where negligence has been established but the claimant cannot show exactly which, of a number of possible factors, caused his loss.

The court confirmed that a robust approach to causation must be taken. If the loss is of the kind which one would expect to flow from the negligence, then a court can infer that the defendant's negligence caused the claimant's loss. Of significant practical consequence for readers is the ruling that the onus is on the defendant to show that other possible causes were at least as likely as his negligence to have caused the loss. The case is also noteworthy because it reinforces that defendants cannot rely on bare denials and putting the claimant to proof to defend claims, consistent with the approach of the Civil Procedure Rules generally.

Contents

thomas telford

The facts are relatively simple. The defendant had been found to have been negligent by failing to check that the cable insulation was not unacceptably damaged. The defendant argued that other causes however were possible and the claimant had failed because he had not proved that the defendant's negligence caused the loss. The Court of Appeal (Longmore LJ) rejected this holding that "in a case where negligence has been found and the damage which has occurred is the sort of damage which one might expect to occur from the nature of the work which the defendants have been carrying out, a court should (as Chadwick LJ said in the slightly different context of *Roadrunner v Dean [2003] EWCA Civ 1816,* para 29) "... be prepared to take a reasonably robust approach to causation."

This decision and rational is likely to have much implications in the construction law arena, especially, in the context of concurrent delay claims.

SITE WASTE MANAGEMENT PLANS

Chapter 3.5: Environmental Issues

Following consultation, new Site Waste Management Regulations are expected to come into force on 6 April 2008 making Site Waste Management Plans (SWMP) compulsory for all construction projects in England costing over £300,000. The cost is assessed at the date of entering into the contract; and the regulations and greater detail is required for those contracts with an initial contract sum greater than £500,000.

A SWMP records the amount and type of waste produced on a construction site and how it will be reused, recycled or disposed. According to Defra the regulations aim to:

- increase the amount of construction waste that is recovered, re-used and recycled and improve materials resource efficiency;
- prevent illegal waste activity by requiring that waste is disposed of appropriately, in accordance with the waste duty of care provisions.

The regulations will not apply to projects planned before 6 April 2008 as long as the construction work begins before 1 July 2008. The government has also published draft non-statutory guidance. Consultation on the guidance is underway and comments are due by 20 March 2008. For more details on the regulations readers should visit *http://www.defra.gov.uk/environment/waste/topics/construction/index.htm*

The maximum penalty for non-compliance will now be £50,000 and it ought to be noted that the usual custodial penalties usually found in environment legislation, will not apply.

LIQUIDATED DAMAGES & ARBITRATION

Chapter 1.6: The Construction Contract

Chapter 4.3: Arbitration

Braes of Doune Wind Farm (Scotland) Limited v. Alfred McAlpine Business Services Limited is a very rare case where a liquidated damages provision was held to be unenforceable. As the learned Judge said, it is unusual for liquidated damages clauses freely agreed to by the parties to be regarded as unenforceable, a fact that makes this case noteworthy.

The case does not concern a full trial but is an application for leave to appeal an arbitration award. The award related to an Engineering Procurement and Construction Contract (EPC) between the claimant employer and the defendant contractor. The Contractor undertook to carry out works in connection with the provision of 36 wind turbine generators. There was an interface agreement between the employer, contractor and the specialist wind turbine generator. The employer sought to argue that the arbitrator who had held that the liquidated damages clause was unenforceable had got the law "obviously wrong" such that Section 69(3) of the Arbitration Act 1996 allowed an appeal on a point of law.

The liquidated damages clause allowed an extension of time to the extent that overall or critical delay was caused by the wind turbine generator but there was no provision to deal with defaults by the wind turbine generator that caused delay to the individual wind turbine. The Judge decided that this was therefore a penalty under English Law and so unenforceable.

The leave to appeal failed but interestingly the Judge held that whilst arbitrator's analysis was not the same as the Judge's this does not mean that the arbitrator had got the law "obviously wrong". The Judge commented "the test of obviousness is only passed if it is not obviously wrong after half an hours reading of the papers by the Judge considering leave".

WITHHOLDING NOTICES

Chapter 4.4: Adjudication

Reinwood Limited v. L Brown & Sons Limited [2008] UKHL 12A is the second case on adjudication to reach the House of Lords. A contract was made between the claimant employer, the defendant contractor, and the architect. It was in the JCT Standard Form of Building Contract 1998. That contract was designed to satisfy the requirements of the Housing Grants, Construction and Regeneration Act 1996, (the Act).

The contract was for the construction of 59 apartments. The completion date was 18 October 2004, and liquidated and ascertained damages (LADs) were agreed at £13,000 per week or part thereof. As is normal, clause 25 of the contract allowed the architect to give an extension of time on the application of the contractor. On 7 December 2005, the contractor made an application for an extension of time. On 14 December, the architect issued a certificate of non-completion under clause 24.1 of the agreement. On 11 January 2006, he issued interim certificate no. 29 showing a net amount payable of £187,988. Pursuant to clause 30.1.1.1, the final date for payment of that sum was 25 January.

Clause 30.1.1.4 provided that such a notice had to specify any amount proposed to be withheld and the ground or grounds for such withholding. On 17 January, the employer served two notices on the contractor. The first notice was stated to be under clause 24.2 and said that it was the employer's 'intention to deduct from monies due to you under Interim Certificates issued after 14 December 2005 [LADs] … for the period from 14 December 2005 up to the date of Practical Completion of the Works'. clause 24.2.1. stated that 'provided [(a)] the architect has issued a certificate under clause 24.1; and [(b)] the employer has informed the contractor in writing before the date of the Final Certificate that he may require payment of, or may withhold or deduct [LADs], then the employer may, not later than five days before the final date for payment of the debt due under the Final Certificate, either: 24.2.1.1 require in writing the contractor to pay to the employer [LADs] … or 24.2.1.2 give notice pursuant to Clause 30.1.1.4 … to the contractor that he will deduct from monies due to the contract [LADs] …' The second notice stated that the employer proposed to withhold £61,629 LADs from the sum due under certificate no. 29.

On 23 January, pursuant to the contractor's request, the architect granted an extension of time until 10 January. The following day, the contractor wrote to the employer stating that the effect of that extension was to reduce the LADs. Thereafter, the contractor claimed to be entitled to determine the contract on the basis, *inter alia*, of the alleged failure of the employer to pay the sum due under the interim certificate in full by the final date for payment, namely 25 January 2006. The employer was of the opinion that the notices which had been served, taken together, satisfied all the requirements of an effective notice within the meaning of s111(1) of the Act.

The question of whether the employer was in default because he had not paid the balance of the amount due to the contractor before the final date for payment under clause 30.1.1.4 came before the Court of Appeal. That court answered that question in the negative and holding that the employer was not in default as a valid clause 30.1.1.4 notice did not cease to be effective when a Certificate of Non-Completion was cancelled. The contractor appealed. The appeal was dismissed.

The effect of clause 24.2 of the JCT Standard Form was clear. Provided the two preconditions were satisfied, namely that the architect had issued a certificate under clause 24.1 and the employer had informed the contractor in writing before the date of the Final Certificate that he might require payment of, or might withhold or deduct, [LADs], clause 24.2.1.2 entitled the employer to give notice under clause 30.1.1.4. Although not spelt out it had to follow that, save perhaps in special circumstances, where the two preconditions were satisfied and the employer had served a withholding notice under clause 30.1.1.4, both parties should be entitled to proceed on the basis that payment would, and could properly, be made in accordance with that notice.

The House of Lords held that it followed that the employer was entitled to make the deduction from the sum due under the interim certificate that it made in respect of the LADs based on the December non-completion certificate. The issue of that certificate satisfied the first precondition, in clause 24.2.1[(a)], the service of the preliminary notice satisfied the second pre-condition, in clause 24.2.1[(b)] and the service of the withholding notice complied with clause 24.2.1.2. The fact that the preliminary notice was served later than the date identified in clause 30.1.1.3 and in s110(2) did not invalidate it, not least because there was no reference to such a date in clause 24.2.1[(b)].

Perhaps the clearest message coming from this case is that so long as a contract complies with the payment terms as set out in the Act then the Courts will not disturb those terms. The rational appears to be the eagerness of the courts to preserve certaintity. As Lord Walker stated "All these provisions are ... aimed at letting the parties know where they stand, in order to avoid unpleasant last-minute suprises and disputes. Parties cannot know where they stand if their obligations are liable to be changed at the last moment, with retrospective effect".

BREACHES OF NATURAL JUSTICE

Cantillon Ltd v. Urvasco Ltd [2008] EWHC 282 (TCC) provides a very useful guide on the latest thinking of the courts on when arguments about breaches of natural justice will succeed. In this case the defendant argued that the adjudicator failed to comply with the rules of natural justice since he had no jurisdiction to address and resolve any issue relating to a delay occurring and prolongation costs being incurred in a period other than a specific 13 week period identified by the claimants and secondly, that he failed to give to *Urvasco* any or any reasonable opportunity to make submissions and adduce evidence in relation to the amount of costs being incurred in the later period. Evidence was adduced that if the adjudicator had specifically given the parties more time or opportunity to address costs incurred during the later period, they would or could have put in further evidence and it might have made a difference of somewhere between about £17,000 and £60,000 lower than the amount allowed by the adjudicator for the 13 Weeks Claim.

As a general proposition the Judge said that the court should not take an "over-analytical approach to questions of jurisdiction and natural justice arising in adjudications under the HGCRA 1996." The Judge then concluded that the following principles were applicable in relation to breaches of natural justice in adjudication cases:

a) It must first be established that the adjudicator failed to apply the rules of natural justice.
b) Any breach of the rules must be more than peripheral; they must be material breaches.
c) Breaches of the rules will be material in cases where the adjudicator has failed to bring to the attention of the parties a point or issue which they ought to be given the opportunity to comment upon if it is one which is either decisive or of considerable potential importance to the outcome of the resolution of the dispute and is not peripheral or irrelevant.
d) Whether the issue is decisive or of considerable potential importance or is peripheral or irrelevant obviously involves a question of degree, which must be assessed by any judge in a case such as this.
e) It is only if the adjudicator goes off on a frolic of his own, that is wishing to decide a case upon a factual or legal basis which has not been argued or put forward by either side, without giving the parties an opportunity to comment or, where relevant put in further evidence, that the type of breach of the rules of natural justice with which the case of *Balfour Beatty Construction Company Ltd v. The Camden Borough of Lambeth* was concerned comes into play. It follows that, if either party has argued a particular point and the other party does not come back on the point, there is no breach of the rules of natural justice in relation thereto.

Comments or contributions for the *Newsletter* should be sent to:
The Editor, *Construction Law Handbook Newsletter*, Thomas Telford Publishing, 1 Heron Quay, London, E14 4JD; or e-mailed to: clh@thomastelford.com.
Subscriptions enquiries: please telephone Maria Davis on 020 7665 2460
or email: maria.davis@thomastelford.com

construction
law HANDBOOK

Newsletter

For subscribers to the *Construction Law Handbook*

No. 45 May 2008

EDITORIAL

In this edition of the *Newsletter* we report *Tyco Fire & Integrated Solutions (UK) Ltd v. Rolls-Royce Motor Cars Ltd* which deals with 'joint insured' issues. There had been a great deal of interest in the improvement of payment practices and we discuss how one solution 'Project Bank Accounts' would work in practice.

We have also chosen to look at *Ferryways NV v. Associated British Ports,* which concerns the 'indirect and consequential loss'. We conclude by looking at very noteworthy cases dealing with adjudication and mediation. *Earl of Malmesbury v. Strutt and Parker* reinforces the point that taking an unreasonable stance in a mediation will be visited by cost sanctions. *BSF Consulting Engineers Ltd v. Macdonald Crosbie* tells us that there is no room for implied terms if one is seeking to use statutory adjudication and *Aedas Architects v. Skanska Construction* explains what needs to go into withholding notices.

The information contained in this *Newsletter* is not intended to be a comprehensive study, or to provide legal advice, and should not be relied upon or treated as a substitute for specific advice concerning individual situations.

Hamish Lal
Partner
Dundas & Wilson LLP
hamish.lal@dundas-wilson.com

PROJECT BANK ACCOUNTS

Chapter 1.2: Financing The Project

The concept of Project Bank Accounts was considered by both *Egan* and *Latham* in reviews of construction procurement. The Office of Government Commerce in its *Guide to best 'Fair Payment' Practices* recommends as an option to improve payment processes, that employers consider paying subcontractors and suppliers directly by the use of Project Bank Accounts.

This would involve the employer giving a commitment to a payment period linked to a Project Bank Account; a bank account with trust status being set up and various authorisations regarding operation of the account being put in place; an interim payment certified being issued; money paid directly into the account by the employer; the employer and main contractor authorising direct payment from the account to the subcontractors.

So how might these work in practice? Amendment of the tender documents and contract conditions will be required. One concern is insolvency of

Contents

thomas telford

themain contractor, particularly where administration or liquidation is possible, where the direct payment to the subcontractor could constitute an 'attackable preference'. In liquidation, there is also the possibility that such a payment could constitute an unlawful contracting out of the rules on equal sharing. The consequence of that might be that the employer pays twice. Further, abatement and set off will have to be accommodated within the structure as otherwise the main contractor may be giving up certain rights.

JOINTLY INSURED PARTIES

Chapter 1.7: Construction Insurance

The recent Court of Appeal decision in *Tyco Fire & Integrated Solutions (UK) Ltd v. Rolls-Royce Motor Cars Ltd [2008] EWCA Civ 286 (02 April 2008)* provides a startling reminder that 'joint names' insurance *may* not mean exactly what is commonly understood by that term. The warning is primarily aimed at those drafting such insurance clauses such that drafters should expressly state exactly who the joint insured are.

Tyco (the contractor) was contracted to design and construct a fire protection system for Rolls-Royce (the employer). Under the bespoke building contract, the contractor was to indemnify the employer against damage arising from the contractor's negligence. During construction, water escaped from a supply pipe and damaged the existing structure. This is an important point since *Tyco's* works were not in issue in the case. The employer claimed damages and the contractor accepted (for the purposes of the proceedings) that it was negligent. However, the contractor resisted the employer's claim, arguing its liability was excluded because the contract required the employer to maintain joint names insurance against damage to the existing structure.

The critical clause in the contract on which *Tyco* relied is clause 13.5: "The Employer shall maintain, in the joint names of the Employer, the Construction Manager and others including, but not limited to, contractors, insurance of existing structures... against the risks covered by the Employer's insurance policy referred to in Schedule 2 (i.e. the Specified Perils) subject to the terms, conditions, exclusions and excesses (uninsured amounts) of the said policy."

Rolls-Royce had not in fact taken out any insurance in the joint names of *Tyco* and itself, but it was common ground that the issue between the parties had to be resolved just as if it had. *Tyco* said that one joint named insured cannot recover from another joint named insured in respect of the same loss.

The Court of Appeal rejected the contractor's argument on the basis that, properly read, the contract did not require the contractor to be named as a joint insured. This was because the court held that 'others' is not a natural way to refer, even inclusively, to the contractor under an individual package contract, and that the position is not improved by saying that 'others' includes 'contractors', a phrase which does not in terms embrace the 'contractor' such that "nothing in the definition section ... incline me to read 'others' or 'contractors'as including *Tyco*." The conclusions drawn from this important case are:

- It is not necessarily a rule of law that jointly insured parties cannot claim against each other in respect of insured risks.
- Whether claims between jointly insured parties are permitted depends on the "true construction of the underlying contract". Where the contract is silent, the court may imply a term into the contract preventing claims between the parties.
- Jointly insured parties can use an express term to permit claims between them.
- Express language should be used to ensure that two or more parties are indeed 'joint insured'.

INDIRECT OR CONSEQUENTIAL LOSS

Chapter 3.1: The Law of Contract

A question that often arises concerns the precise meaning of losses that are termed 'indirect or consequential'. *Ferryways NV v. Associated British Ports [2008] EWHC 225 (Comm)* is not a construction case but gives another useful court reminder of what such terms mean. This case considered the interpretation of a clause in a shipping contract which excluded a stevedores' liability for indirect or consequential loss 'including without limitation...the liabilities of the customer to any other party'. The chief officer of the claimant's vessel was killed by the negligence of an employee of subcontractors engaged by the defendant stevedores. The claimant sought to recover from the defendant sums which it had been obliged to pay to the chief officer's next of kin. The defendant relied upon the exclusion clause, arguing that the exclusion clause had defined 'indirect or consequential' losses as including 'the liabilities of the Customer to any other party'.

The Judge rejected this argument and held that it is well established that the term 'indirect and consequential' loss referred to loss which was not the direct and natural result of the breach of contract. In *Ferryways NV* the losses claimed were not indirect or consequential, and so the exclusion clause could not be relied upon by the stevedore. Further, the Judge commented that where an exclusion clause referred to 'indirect and consequential' loss, 'very clear words indeed' would be required to indicate an intention to exclude losses falling outside that established meaning. The words 'including without limitation' were not sufficiently clear to extend the exclusion of liability to the losses claimed. Rather, those words were intended to identify types of loss which might fall within the scope of the clause, but only if they were also indirect or consequential.

ADJUDICATION – CONTRACT IN WRITING CONTINUED

Chapter 4.4: Adjudication

BSF Consulting Engineers Ltd v. Macdonald Crosbie grapples with the 'contracts in writing' issue and is noteworthy since it addresses the question of whether implied terms can be used to say that all the terms are in writing so that statutory adjudication is permissible.

The claimant was a firm of civil and structural engineers which rendered services to the defendant contractor. A dispute arose as to the claimant's entitlement to be paid, and it referred the matter to adjudication. The adjudicator made an award in the claimant's favour, which the defendant failed to pay. The claimant brought proceedings enforcing the award and applied for summary judgment.

The defendant maintained that the scope of work to be carried by the claimant and the claimant's charges had not been agreed, and that there was, accordingly, no contract in writing for the purposes of section 107 of the Housing Grants Construction and Regeneration Act 1996 (the 'Act'). The defendant argued that the statutory scheme for adjudication could not be implied into the contract between the parties and thus that the adjudicator had no jurisdiction.

Interestingly, the claimant relied, on section 15 of the Supply of Goods and Services Act 1982 as implying a term that a reasonable charge would be paid for the services that it rendered and argued that, in those circumstances, the contract met the requirements of s107 of the 1996 Act. The court ruled:

- Whilst there might be circumstances in which a term might be implied under s15 of the 1982 Act as to the payment of a reasonable charge for services provided, those circumstances did not arise in cases such as the present where it was sought to rely on the statutory adjudication scheme being implied into the contract, rather than adjudication provisions in the contract itself.
- The statutory scheme could only be implied into contracts in writing within the meaning of s107 of the 1996 Act, and, in order to come within that provision, all express terms had to be recorded in writing.
- In the instant case, there was no written evidence as to any agreed scope of works or charges so as to render the contract compliant with s107 of the 1996 Act. Conflicts of evidence could only be resolved at a hearing. It followed that it was arguable that the adjudicator had no jurisdiction.

WITHHOLDING NOTICES

Aedas Architects v. Skanska Construction considered key questions relevant to anyone who may have to draft a Withholding Notice. The contractor subcontracted design elements for the renovation of schools to consultants. Some of the consultant's interim payment applications were met with Withholding Notices as the contractor sought to apply a large and ongoing fund of contract set -offs.

Section 111 of the 1996 Act says that to be effective a Withholding Notice must specify:

- the amount proposed to be withheld and the ground for withholding it; or
- if there is more than one ground, each ground and the amount attributable to it.

In this particular case, the contract between the consultants and the contractor was slightly differently worded and said that the notice must specify the amount proposed to be withheld, the ground or grounds and the deduction attributable to each ground.

Six Withholding Notices were sent referring to nine grounds. The amount to be retained greatly exceeded the sum claimed in any particular notice for payment or indeed all of them added together. Some of the Withholding Notices attributed part of this overall amount to particular grounds; some attributed only the whole figure to all of the grounds.

The consultants said that the Withholding Notices were not effective. They said that cases such as *Melville Dundas* had stressed the need for clarity when interim payments are to be withheld. It was not enough to simply set out (as many Withholding Notices do) a brief general indication of the grounds for withholding. They argued that the 'Act' required enough specification of the grounds such that it was immediately clear why the payment was to be withheld. In effect, they were arguing that there was no precise apportionment of the sum being withheld among the various grounds.

The contractor said that there was sufficient specification of the grounds and in each of the notices there was attribution. Where the total retention vastly exceeded any amount claimed, detailed attribution was neither necessary nor realistic.

The dispute came before the court as part of a procedural hearing on whether the contractor was bound to fail in its defence. The decision was therefore made in the context of whether there could be a legal defence to the arguments on whether there was sufficient detail and on attribution. The Judge rejected both of the consultant's arguments and held that the Withholding Notices were effective. In terms of attribution of on-going, global sums he said;

"The contract demands attribution to each ground. It does not ask for any apportionments and in my view it is a competent way to procedd by debiting all sums. The Statute speaking of 'each ground' says attribution to 'it' must take place. In my view that also is what the counter notice has done. All the grounds which can be calculated have so been and a global figure debited. That in my opinion is compliance."

FAILURE TO MEDIATE

Chapter 4.5: Alternative Dispute Resolution

Earl of Malmesbury v. Strutt and Parker [2008] EWHC 424 is an excellent case dealing with what happens when there is a failure to mediate. Here the Judge considered the relevance to costs of the fact that the claimant had adopted a wholly unreasonable stance in a mediation which it had attended. The relevant conduct was the fact that the claimant's best offer at the mediation had been unreasonably high, and had been based upon the claimant succeeding at a forthcoming damages hearing and at an appeal from a decision on issues of law relating to the proper measure of damages.

The claimant's stance was unrealistic and led to the Judge imposing a 20% reduction of the costs recoverable in relation to the hearing on damages. This case is noteworthy because it extends of the principle in *Halsey* to unreasonable conduct in the mediation. The substantive point is that a party who agreed to mediation, but who then caused the mediation to fail because of their unreasonable position was in the same position as a party who refused to mediate, and such conduct could and should be taken into account in the order for costs in accordance with previous cases on this topic.

However, please note that in this case the Judge was able to consider the relevant evidence of what went on at the mediation because both parties had waived any privilege over the 'Without Prejudice' material generated in and in connection with the mediation. The practical issue is that in the absence of such waiver, it may be very difficult to show any unreasonable conduct such as may give rise to a reduction in costs.

2012 OLYMPICS INDEPENDENT DISPUTE AVOIDANCE PANEL

An Independent Dispute Avoidance Panel (IDAP) has been set up to help avoid contractual disputes during the construction work to deliver the venues and infrastructure for the London 2012 Olympic and Paralympic Games. IDAP is made up of eleven construction professionals with experience in major projects. It will focus on finding pragmatic solutions to problems which may arise before they become disputes that could require lengthy resolution.

Any disputes that are not resolved through the IDAP may be dealt with by a dedicated Adjudication Panel. If either party challenges an adjudicator's decision, the final tribunal will be the Technology and Construction Court.

Comments or contributions for the *Newsletter* should be sent to:
The Editor, *Construction Law Handbook Newsletter*, Thomas Telford Publishing, 1 Heron Quay, London, E14 4JD; or e-mailed to: clh@thomastelford.com.
Subscriptions enquiries: please telephone Maria Davis on 020 7665 2460
or email: maria.davis@thomastelford.com

construction
law HANDBOOK

Newsletter

For subscribers to the *Construction Law Handbook*

No. 46 July 2008

EDITORIAL

In this edition of the *Newsletter* we report on the governments proposed reform of the Construction Act which will now allow oral contracts to be adjudicated. We have also chosen to look at *Alan Auld Associates Ltd v. Rick Pollard Associates* which looks at whether a party is in repudiatory breach by failing to make payments on time.

We conclude by looking at noteworthy cases and points dealing with mediation, expert determination and litigation. *Owen Pell Ltd v. Bindi (London) Ltd* reinforces the point that decisions of an expert are very difficult to challenge and *Galliford Try Construction Ltd v. Mott MacDonald Ltd* provides an excellent index into when negotiations are admissible.

The information contained in this *Newsletter* is not intended to be a comprehensive study, or to provide legal advice, and should not be relied upon or treated as a substitute for specific advice concerning individual situations.

Hamish Lal
Partner
Dundas & Wilson LLP
hamish.lal@dundas-wilson.com

REFORM OF THE CONSTRUCTION ACT

Chapter 1.6: The Construction Contract

Ten years after the Housing Grants, Construction and Regeneration Act 1996 (the so-called 'Construction Act') came into force the government's proposal for it's 'reform' have now been announced. Reform will be lead by the Community, Empowerment, Housing and Economic Regeneration Bill. But what will change?

Was 'reform' needed?

Two key issues appear to have driven the desire for change to the Construction Act. Firstly, the issue of whether project agreements and other agreements related to PFI should be included in the Construction Act or put another way whether design and build contracts in the PFI sector should be excluded?

The second (more high profile) concern was that about the 'rule' that only contracts in writing should be covered by the Construction Act. The cornerstone of the argument is that section 107 has 'wasted money, wasted adjudicator and court time' and has lead to 'jurisdictional attacks on adjudicators that has nothing to do with the merits of the referring party's case'. The high point in this issue concerns *RJT Consulting Engineers Ltd v. DM Engineering (Northern Ireland) Ltd [2002] EWCA Civ 270* where the Court of Appeal decided that *all* the terms of a construction contract had to be in writing in order for the Construction Act to apply. This meant that agreements which had some terms, even minor terms that had not been agreed, could not be referable to statutory adjudication.

What will change?

Reform is likely to follow the proposals discussed in *Improving Payment Practices in the Construction Industry – 2nd Consultation.*

Oral Contracts

The Construction Act will now apply to construction contracts which are agreed wholly in writing,

Contents

thomas telford

only partly in writing, entirely orally or varied by oral agreement. This is perhaps the most significant reform – both in legal and practical terms. This is likely to lead to a far greater number of 'contracts' being referred to adjudication. The view that 'disputes as to the terms, express and implied, of oral construction agreements are surprisingly common and are not readily susceptible of resolution by a summary procedure such as adjudication' (per HHJ Bowsher QC in *Grovedeck v. Capital Demolition Ltd [2000] EWHC 139*) will be tested.

Payments

Construction contracts often provide that decisions on interim or stage payments will be conclusive such that adjudicators have no jurisdiction to open up, revise or review the decision. The government want's to change this so that such agreements made by the parties as to conclusiveness of the amount of an interim or stage payment will only be effective if the agreement is made after the relevant adjudicator's decision is handed down (and not at the time of entry into the contract).

Reform will also cover payment notices ('section 110 notices') and withholding notices ('section 111 notices'). The former will now be always required even if there is no obligation to make a payment (e.g. because of an abatement). This new section 110 notice when issued will set the amount that is due subject to any subsequent withholding notice. As far as section 111 notices are concerned the changes require that they follow the format of the new section 110 notices but will now allow withholding in respect of any amount (i.e. including abatement) and not just withholding 'of a sum due' as the present Construction Act allows.

Adjudication costs

In some contracts the parties actually agree that the 'loser' will pay the costs of the adjudication or even that the referring party will pay (regardless of whether it wins or losses). Considered wisdom tells us that such clauses can operate as a practical disincentive to adjudicate or can even encourage one party to escalate costs. The proposal is that any agreement about who pays the costs of the adjudication will only be valid if made in writing after the adjudicator's appointment. Where such agreements are made (unless otherwise agreed) only reasonable costs will be recoverable and the parties will be jointly and severally liable for the adjudicator's costs and expenses. Importantly, the adjudicator's decision on costs will be generally final binding.

Pay-when-certified clauses

The government proposal is that pay-when-certified clauses in construction contracts will be banned and be ineffective.

In *Midland Expressway Ltd v. Carillion Construction Ltd & Ors (No. 2) [2005] EWHC 2963* Jackson J considered the following clause:

... the employer shall bear no risk or liabilities whatsoever arising from a department's change, and accordingly, the employer shall have no liability to make payment in connection with or arising from a department's change... and concluded that such pay-when-paid clauses were ineffective. There was some debate whether pay-when-certified clauses should be treated in the same way. The government has now said yes.

Suspending performance

Under the Construction Act contractors are allowed to suspend performance where there is non-payment by the employer. The problem is that the current regime 'involves suspension of all the contractor's obligations and does not make clear what compensation the contractor receives if and when performance is resumed.

The proposal is that the contractor does not need to suspend all his obligations so that a key obligation could be suspended. Another 'tweak' is that the suspending party will be compensated for reasonable losses caused by the suspension and that an extension of time will be provided for any delay caused by the suspension.

REPEATED DELAYED PAYMENT

Chapter 2.4: The Engineer's Appointment

Alan Auld Associates Ltd v. Rick Pollard Associates [2008] EWCA Civ 655 is an interesting case dealing with the increasingly common problem of late payment. The facts may not be that unusual but the question put to the court is noteworthy. The parties had a contract for professional engineering services and the claimant had failed to meet its payment obligations to Dr Pollard. In fact, none of his nineteen invoices, issued between 31 December 2004 and 30 April 2006, were paid on time. A schedule produced by Dr Pollard, that payment should have been made to him eight weeks after the date of his invoice, showed substantial and increasing periods of delay ranging between one and nine months with more than half of the invoices paid over four months late. By the end of May 2006 he was owed £21,000.

However, after 7 June, Dr Pollard continued to provide advice to the authority through another consultant, URS. This lead the claimant to start these proceedings, in which it claimed that Dr Pollard's defection to URS was in breach of implied terms of mutual trust, confidence and loyalty in the agreement between them. Dr Pollard's response was that the agreement with the claimant had been terminated on 7 June 2006 by his acceptance of the claimant's repudiatory breach of its terms by persistently paying late and with every prospect of continuing to do so in the future. The question for the court was: 'The repeated breaches of contract by the claimant constituted repudiatory breach of contract by the claimant, which [Dr Pollard] was entitled to accept on 7 June 2006.'

The Court of Appeal held that the judge was entitled to find that the claimant company had repudiated the agreement by repeatedly delaying payments of submitted invoices for advisory work and that the engineer was entitled to bring the agreement to an end. The court held that here the employment of the engineer was analogous to a contract of employment (an important distinction), when deciding whether one party no longer had the intention to be bound by an agreement, inferences could be drawn from past breaches and the likelihood of future breaches. The breaches were substantially persistent and cynical. No payments were made on time and the breaches occurred against a background of repeated complaints. In those circumstances the engineer was entitled to consider that he would be treated in the same way for the duration of the rest of the agreement.

It is likely that employers and engineers may look at this case very carefully and argue along similar lines. For example, an engineer who has suffered delayed payment may decide that it is better to argue repudiatory breach and seek to recover loss of profit.

WHEN ARE 'NEGOITATIONS' WITHOUT PREDJUDICE

Chapter 4.2: Litigation

The recent construction law case of *Galliford Try Construction Ltd v. Mott MacDonald Ltd [2008] (EWHC 603 TCC)* provides an excellent jurisprudential judicial analysis that addresses the above question. In *Galliford Try* the defendant sought an order that certain parts of a witness statement (a director of the claimant) be removed from the initial bundle on the basis that material in the witness statement and the associated exhibits related to without prejudice discussions. The claimant sought to rely on this witness evidence because according to the claimant Mr Wilson of the defendant had made an express admission not only as to the defendant's liability to the claimant, but also as to the costs of any extra work necessary. The material part of the claimant's witness evidence recalled that at the meeting on 10th November, Mr Wilson accepted that 'it looked as though I might be right' about the defendant's liability for the extra costs, and that Mr Wilson acknowledged that 'our significant costs would be honoured'.

Mr Justice Coulson summarised the legal position as follows:

a) The without prejudice rule excludes 'all negotiations genuinely aimed at settlement, whether oral or in writing'.
b) The privilege cannot apply unless there is a dispute which is genuinely the subject of settlement negotiations.
c) There is a distinction to be drawn between true negotiations and the mere assertion each side's case or the making of criticisms of the other side's case. The without prejudice rule does not apply to a communication which does not unequivocally indicate the maker's intention to negotiate.

Coulson's J comments are highly instructive. For example, a claim was in fact issued on 18 May and the claimant argued that all the discussions prior to this date were not and could not therefore be 'negotiations' capable of attracting privilege. The claimant asserted that the controversial parts of the statement were simply setting out the background prior to the presentation of the formal claim on 18 May and were merely setting out the 'rules of the game. The learned judge appears to have placed much emphasis on reasons why the claimants had then bothered to set out all the details prior to the date of issue of the claim.

The judge was not convinced how important admissions could have been made prior to the issue of the formal claim unless the parties were in the process of negotiating. Of the facts, the claimant pleaded that the above mentioned admission had been made in November, which promoted the learned judge to comment 'it seems to me that that is wholly contrary to the suggestion that was being discussed at the meeting was either irrelevant to the claims or that all that was happening was a statement or restatement of each side's case'.

MEDIATION COSTS

Chapter 4.5: Alternative Dispute Resolution

The Centre for Effective Dispute Resolution (CEDR) has now revised its model mediation agreement and procedure. The 10th edition allows parties to now agree that any court or tribunal may treat both the mediation fees and each party's legal costs as costs in the case in relation to any litigation or arbitration although parties can choose to opt out of this). However, the parties will still share mediator costs equally. The issue as to whether or not costs incurred in mediation, particularly one that has failed, can subsequently be recovered as costs between the parties, has been the subject of case comment in the past. The rules on mediation confidentiality have also been tightened. The fact that mediation takes place is not confidential, unless the parties choose otherwise.

Another structural change has been splitting the procedure from the agreement. The mediation agreement stipulates that mediations must follow the model procedure and contracts the mediator to abide by the CEDR Code of Conduct on ethical practice. Each party warrants that someone has authority to bind them to the mediation agreement and to any settlement terms.

EXPERT DETERMINATION

Owen Pell Ltd v. Bindi (London) Ltd (2008) QBD (TCC) is exceptionally noteworthy because it provides a strong reminder that an expert's determination is binding, even if he has made errors in his conclusions, where the parties had agreed to be bound and where he had answered the question asked and there was no evidence of bias. This case provides further support that unless the parties' agreement says otherwise the rules of natural justice do not apply. This had been decided in the earlier case of *Bernhard Schulte v. Nile Holdings [2004] Lloyds's Rep 352.*

In short, readers should note that expert determination is a creature of contract and that the expert's jurisdiction is entirely dependent on the contractual provisions and there are no statutory default rules of procedure and process. The rule appears to be that a party can only resist complying with an expert's decision if the expert has failed to act within his jurisdiction or has acted in actual bias or acted fraudulently. A mistake is not capable of making the decision invalid – this was decided in *Nikko Hotels (UK) Ltd v MEPC plc [1991] 2 EGLR 103* where the judge said 'If he [the expert] has answered the right question in the wrong way, his decision will be binding. If he has answered the wrong question, his decision will be a nullity'.

In *Owen Pell* the defendant employer argued that the expert decision should be void and unenforceable, or alternatively that it be set aside on the basis that the expert had breached an implied term in the agreement. The implied term relied upon was that the principles of natural justice were applicable. In particular the defendant argued that the expert was guilty of bias or partiality, both actual and perceived, and acted in breach of natural justice in a number of ways:

- He gave the impression of being dismissive of the Employer's complaints.
- He declined to consider a letter from an architectural technician engaged on the construction works on the ground that it was submitted out of time.
- He wrongly concluded that the parties had agreed a 'walk away situation' as at the date the contractor left the site.
- He reached other conclusions which contained gross and obvious errors and which were perverse.

The judge gave summary judgement and enforced the expert's decision. The judge held that the agreement between the parties did not disturb the established position in respect of expert determination and there was no need to imply the term contended for. Of major significance for readers is that the judge made it clear that the 'test' was to decide whether the decision which 'C' made was within his jurisdiction, that is, whether he decided the issues referred to him. If he did not, his decision was a nullity. If he did, his decision was binding, even if he made errors, unless there was fraud or actual bias. It was not open to the court to set aside or refuse to enforce the expert decision because of errors in the determination, whether gross, obvious or perverse.

In practical terms if parties want to increase the grounds for challenge of experts' decisions then they need to make express provision in the expert determination agreement. Increasing the position from actual bias to apparent bias may be a starting point. However, readers should be mindful that expert determination is supposed to be as final and binding as possible.

Comments or contributions for the *Newsletter* should be sent to:
The Editor, *Construction Law Handbook Newsletter*, Thomas Telford Publishing, 1 Heron Quay, London, E14 4JD; or e-mailed to: clh@thomastelford.com.
Subscriptions enquiries: please telephone Maria Davis on 020 7665 2460
or email: maria.davis@thomastelford.com

construction
law HANDBOOK

Newsletter

For subscribers to the *Construction Law Handbook*

No. 47 September 2008

EDITORIAL

In this edition of the *Newsletter* we take a detailed look at four cases. The cases deal with the mandatory nature of multi-tier dispute resolution clauses; letters of intent and procedural issues in adjudication. *Diamond Build Ltd v. Clapham Park Homes* provides a reminder on the 'dangers posed by letters of intent, which are not followed up promptly by the parties' whilst *Ardentia Ltd v. British Telecommunications PLC* highlights the judicial support that is given to contractual resolution provisions. We conclude by looking at noteworthy cases and points dealing with 'apparent bias' and breach of natural justice.

The information contained in this *Newsletter* is not intended to be a comprehensive study, or to provide legal advice, and should not be relied upon or treated as a substitute for specific advice concerning individual situations.

Hamish Lal
Partner
Dundas & Wilson LLP
hamish.lal@dundas-wilson.com

LETTERS OF INTENT

Chapter 1.6: The Construction Contract

Diamond Build Ltd v. Clapham Park Homes [2008] EWHC 1439 provides a reminder on the 'dangers posed by letters of intent which are not followed up promptly by the parties' processing the formal contract anticipated by them at the letter of intent stage'. In this case a letter of intent (LOI) was issued whilst the parties sought to agree and conclude a JCT contract.

Of particular importance is the fact that the LOI stated that "*Should it not be possible for us to execute a formal Contract with you in place of this letter, we undertake to reimburse your reasonable costs up to and including the date on which you are notified that the contract will not proceed provided that the supervising officer is satisfied that those costs are appropriate and that, in any event, total costs will not exceed the sum of £250,000*". The contract sum in the JCT was intended to be £2,489,302.

Work commenced on site but the JCT contract was not executed. *Clapham Homes* then decided to 'terminate' the relationship and did so by stating that no further work is to be carried out under the LOI but relied on the £250,000 as being the cap on their liability. *Diamond Build* disagreed and sought to argue that the LOI did not limit the employer's liability to the sum of £250,000 because variations had been issued in excess of that amount and because the contractor had been directed to place large subcontract orders. The fundamental issue was whether the terms of unsigned JCT contract (which *Diamond Build* argued had been acted upon as if it had been concluded) bound the parties or whether the LOI was the operative contractual

Contents

thomas telford

relationship.

The court, helpfully, explained that there can be "*letters of intent which do not give rise to a contract at all. There are others which do give rise to a simple contract in themselves and are applicable pending the execution of a formal contract. There are others which are a contract so far as they go, but not subject to the entering into of a formal contract*" and concluded that on the facts the LOI gave rise to a simple contract. This was because it provided for a commencement date, a completion date, an overall contract sum and an undertaking to pay the contractor's reasonable costs. Further, the contractor's argument that 'cap' produces an unfair position because it was foreseeable that the cap would be reached within a relatively short space of time was firmly rejected. This provides a pertinent warning to contractors especially since the court rejected a number of arguments:

a) It was always open to *Diamond Build* to commit itself to its subcontractors and suppliers in a similar way to that predicated by the LOI.
b) If the cap was being approached it would have been open to *Diamond Build* to approach the employer for an increase of the cap.
c) If the sole reason why the JCT contract was not being executed was the withholding of signing by the employer the insistence by it that *Diamond Build* proceed beyond the cap would lead to at the very least to an equitable claim for additional payment.
d) The LOI, and the cap, relate to the work which was the subject matter of the tender. If additional or different work was ordered by or on behalf of the employer to be done by *Diamond Build*, that would attract payment in addition to and above the cap on a *quantum meruit* basis; that could be by way of a mini or implied contract or in restitution. Similarly, any breach of express or implied terms of the LOI agreement would attract damages which would not be caught by or subject to the cap.

Clearly, letters of intent serve practical and commercial purposes and extreme care should be exercised when drafting and administering such letters, especially where there are caps on liability.

MULTI-TIER DISPUTE RESOLUTION

Chapter 4.2: Litigation

Detailed step-by-step dispute resolution procedures are becoming increasingly common but there are concerns about the extent to which one party can unilaterally decide to 'side-step' one of the procedures. This question was addressed in *Ardentia Ltd v. British Telecommunications PLC [2008] EWHC B12 (Ch)*.

In *Ardentia, BT* had been appointed the main contractor by the Department of Health for the provision of the so-called Data Spine in the NHS national programme for information technology. *BT* subcontracted to *Ardentia* the provision of certain secondary usage services involving the development of programmes making secondary use of anonymised data taken from patient records and the licensing of those programmes to *BT*. A dispute arose in respect of licence fees and *Ardentia* sought an injunction against *BT* who responded with an application for a stay under section 9 of the Arbitration Act 1996. The central question for the court was whether *Ardentia* had followed the dispute resolution procedure as set out in the contract?

The dispute resolution provisions were initiated by notice in writing followed shortly thereafter by a meeting between two nominated representatives. If there was disagreement at that level the dispute moved upward to management level, and if that failed to CEO level. Should that in turn fail, the contract provided that "*the parties shall consider mediation unless either (a)* BT *considers that the dispute is not suitable for mediation or (b) the contractor does not agree to mediation*". The contract also provided that " ... *the parties shall not institute court proceedings until the applicable procedures ... under paragraph 2, 3 to 4 (inclusive) ... have been exhausted, save that: 7.1.1* BT *may at any time before court proceedings are commenced serve a notice on the contractor requiring that the dispute be referred to arbitration ... 7.1.3 if the contractor intends to commence court proceedings it shall serve written notice on* BT *of its intention and* BT *shall have 15 (fifteen) business days following receipt of such notice to serve a notice in reply on the contractor requiring that the dispute should be referred to arbitration ...* " The court held that the above procedure imposed three restrictions on the instigation of court proceedings, namely:

a) the procedures up to and including consideration of mediation, and where applicable, the conclusion of the mediation process, must first have been exhausted;
b) *Ardentia* must have given 15 days notice of its intention to commence court proceedings;

c) the matter is to be referred to arbitration if *BT* serves an appropriate notice within the 15 days period.

Ardentia had not complied completely with the procedure but argued the dispute provisions did not apply in the case of an interim injunction. Indeed the contract stated: "*Nothing in this dispute resolution procedure shall prevent the parties from seeking from any court of competent jurisdiction an interim order restraining the other party from doing any act or compelling the other party to do any act...*".

However, the court decided that the above wording had to be read within the context of the overall multi-dispute resolution procedure such that interim relief should only be given to support the dispute resolution process and sit outside that process. This case highlights the judicial support that is given to contractual resolution provisions. If parties want flexibility in the method used then 'may' ought to be used rather than 'shall'.

APPARENT BIAS

Chapter 4.4: Adjudication

Makers UK Limited v. The Mayor and Burgesses of the London Borough of Camden [2008] EWHC 1836 raised the question of whether contact with an adjudicator prior to nomination by a nominating body is sufficient to resist enforcement on the grounds of apparent bias.

The facts are relatively straight forward. Issues arose between the parties over variations and delays. *Camden* apparently sought to resolve these issues by dismissing the independent contract administrator and appointing itself as contract administrator. Whilst *Camden* did appoint another independent firm relations between the parties became very strained. By a default notice *Camden* alleged that *Makers* was in default of their contractual obligation to proceed regularly and diligently with the works and by a determination notice *Camden* asserted that that *Makers* had "*continued the default for 14 days from receipt of the default notice*" and purported to determine *Makers*' employment under the contract. *Makers* disputed this determination and sought to argue that it was invalid. It asserted that camden had itself repudiated the contract.

The solicitor acting for *Makers* considered that the dispute was largely 'legal' and that an adjudicator with a legal background or qualification would be most appropriate to decide the dispute. The nominating body was expressed in the contract to be the Royal Institute of British Architects (RIBA). *Maker's* solicitor undertook an internet search for a RIBA panel member with legal qualifications. He ascertained that a Mr. Philip Harris of a solicitors' firm in the Midlands, Wright Hassall, was a member of the RIBA Panel of Adjudicators and then telephoned the office of Mr. Harris and left a message asking Mr. Harris to return his call.

The same day Mr. Harris telephoned *Maker's* solicitor whose contemporaneous telephone attendance note of the conversation reads: "*Philip Harris returned my call. He confirmed that he was available to act if asked on an adjudication between* Makers *and the London Borough of Camden that had legal issues arising. I said that it would be inappropriate, obviously, for me to give him more details at this time.*"

The note also records "*Time Engaged: 12 mins*".

The adjudicator made a decision that held that *Makers* had not repudiated the contract and that *Camden* should pay his fees. *Camden* refused to pay the fees and at the enforcement proceedings argued that the decision is unenforceable on the basis if apparent bias. In particular, *Camden* said that a term ought to be implied into the contract that 'neither party may seek to influence unilaterally the nominator's determination regarding the identity of an adjudicator, by making unilateral representations to the nominator concerning whom he should nominate or otherwise'.

The court repeated that the test for apparent bias is "*whether a fair-minded and informed observer, having considered all the circumstances which have a bearing on the suggestion that the decision-maker was biased, would conclude that there was a real possibility that he was biased*". However, the court concluded that on the facts there had been no reason for a finding of apparent bias. This was because:

- There was no obligation on *Makers* to liaise with *Camden* before applying to RIBA for the nomination of an adjudicator.
- It is wrong to describe *Makers* as 'selecting' Mr. Harris; ultimately, RIBA selected him.
- Whilst there is no positive encouragement for a party to contact a potential adjudicator to check his availability, there is no discouragement in the contract. Such contact if limited to checking availability or checking if there is any conflict

is in itself unexceptionable and can be a sensible and practical step to take.

- As to the telephone attendance note, there is nothing suspicious in the '*T*ime Engaged' being '12 minutes'. There were two telephone calls, the first being abortive. The second is not inconsistent with there being some time spent on the telephone discussing the limited matters as suggested in the attendance note itself.
- There was nothing reprehensible in *Maker's* solicitor not mentioning to RIBA or *Camden* that he had contacted for limited purposes the person whose name he was putting forward. *Makers* had no obligation to do so.

In practical terms this means that if parties wish to preclude contact with adjudicators prior to contacting nominating bodies then the implied term contended for by *Camden* should be an express term in of contract.

DELAY IN THE PROCEDURE

Chapter 4.4: Adjudication

CJP Builders Ltd v. William Verry Ltd [2008] EWHC (TCC) is a highly noteworthy case dealing with time limits in and during the adjudication process. Here the non-paying party sought to argue that the adjudicator had breached the rule of natural justice by disregarding the response which had been served some five to six hours late.

In short, *Verry* did not serve its response to the referral within the requisite seven day period apparently called for in the subcontract or within an extension of time permitted by *CJP*. *Verry* was some five to six hours late in serving the substantial part of its response and the adjudicator formed the view that he had no discretion to permit any extension of time and having told the parties of his views about this he informed them that he could have no regard to the contents of that response. He then produced his reasoned decision ordering *Verry* to pay the full amount outstanding on *CJP's* valuation 15 in the sum of £94,692.40 plus VAT plus interest plus the adjudicator's fees and expenses and the Royal Institute of Chartered Surveyors' nomination fee.

As summarized by the court, the adjudicator formed the view that he had no discretion to extend the seven day time for the response. He accepted that, if he had a discretion, he would have allowed the extension of time until the time on 14 May 2008 when the response was substantially served by email. The court decided that the adjudicator had in fact failed to apply the rule of natural justice that each party has a right to be heard and to have its evidence and arguments considered by the tribunal. The fact that the adjudicator acted honestly and in an open way does not mean however that there is no breach of the rules of natural justice. In particular and of fundamental importance the court held that despite the fact the contract made express provision for the response to be served no later than seven days after the date of the referral, the adjudicator did have discretion to consider an extension to that time.

This was because there was nothing that expressly barred the adjudicator from doing so. Further, the contract allowed the adjudicator to 'set his own procedure' which gives him an 'absolute discretion' in taking the initiative in ascertaining the facts and the law as he considers necessary. "*One would have expected that, if he can set his own procedure and has an absolute discretion, he can grant appropriate extensions of time*." Furthermore, clause 38A.2.5.1 is not written in prescriptive terms: it identifies that *Verry* (in this case) may send within seven days of the date of a referral a response. Whilst it is true that it is not stated elsewhere in clause 38A.2.5.1 that the responding party may serve its response at a time later than that seven day period, there is nothing which says it cannot if the adjudicator agrees.

Comments or contributions for the *Newsletter* should be sent to:
The Editor, *Construction Law Handbook Newsletter*, Thomas Telford Publishing, 1 Heron Quay, London, E14 4JD; or e-mailed to: clh@thomastelford.com.
Subscriptions enquiries: please telephone Maria Davis on 020 7665 2460
or email: maria.davis@thomastelford.com

Index

Note: chapter subjects are shown in **emboldened text**; Figures and Tables are indicated by *italic page numbers*, and footnotes by suffix 'n' (e.g. 588n1)